USA TODAY BASEBALL WEEKLY

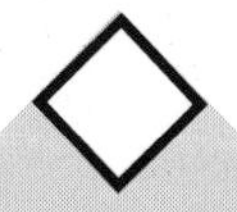

ALMANAC

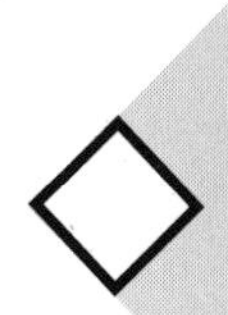

EDITED BY:
Editor / *Baseball Weekly*, Paul White
Managing Editor / Sports, *USA TODAY*, Gene Policinski
Assistant to Managing Editor / Sports, *USA TODAY*, Robert Barbrow

With contributions from the staffs of *Baseball Weekly*
and *USA TODAY* Sports

Managing Editor, Liz Barrett

A Balliett & Fitzgerald Book

New York

ISBN # 1-56282-919-X

FIRST EDITION
10 9 8 7 6 5 4 3 2 1

Acknowledgments

We are grateful, first of all, for the vision, support, skill and good humor of Carolyn Martin, Susan Bokern and Silvia Molina at Gannett New Business, without whom this book would not have been possible; also many thanks to the support staff at USA TODAY. We send kudos to everyone at Hyperion, especially publisher Bob Miller, Leslie Wells, Lesley Krauss and Linda Prather. We could never have completed this book without our own hard-working and talented production staff. We truly appreciate the efforts of designer Michael Harvey, technical consultants Stephen Johnson and John Jordan, and page artists Akos Toth and Jean Carbain; and especially associate editor Duncan Bock.

Major league statistics provided by Elias Sports Bureau.
Minor league statistics provided by Howe SportsData International.
Record book and historical statistics provided by Pete Palmer.
Disabled list information provided by Gary Gillette.

BASEBALL WEEKLY 1993

Contents

BASEBALL WEEKLY 1993

Leading Off

USA SNAPSHOTS®

A look at statistics that shape the sports world

Perennial base thieves

Montreal's Marquis Grissom is the National League's stolen-base leader for the second consecutive year. Most consecutive years leading the leagues:

American League	
Luis Aparicio 1956-64	9
Rickey Henderson 1980-86	7

National League	
Maury Wills 1960-65	6
Vince Coleman 1985-90	6

Source: USA TODAY research

By Sam Ward, USA TODAY

INSIDE:

1993 survival tips: How to keep the faith

There's no better way to watch a ballgame than to kick back on a beautiful summer day, hot dog in one hand and scorecard in the other. Keeping score is a must for total enjoyment of the game, no matter what method you use. And there's no better year for it than 1993—no matter where you go, you're likely to need a scorecard just to figure out who the players are. Between free agency, trades, and the expansion draft, there have been more reasons for offseason movement than ever before.

How do you root for a team anymore? Guys win a World Series and skip town—or are told they won't get a new contract—before they've had time to send their champagne-soaked uniforms to the dry cleaners. Players like George Brett and Robin Yount, who pile up 3,000 hits in one uniform, are looked upon as fossils because they have never changed teams.

Maybe Charlie Finley had the right idea: Make every player a free agent after every season—an open market, like a fantasy league. Let's face it, we like player movement. Our favorite offseason game is trade speculation. We love the rumors about who might be headed where. Even the big-money free agency game, though it rankles so many of us, has drama and suspense. The expansion draft provoked more speculation and excitement than anything baseball has done in years.

No matter what you think of players bouncing from city to city, it's a lot more fun than some other movement—teams heading to other cities or other divisions—that sours our enjoyment of such a wonderful game. The year of 1992 was as big for lawyers as it was for Toronto fans. They battled over the Giants' near-move, over National League realignment, over new rules for the amateur draft, and over who the heck is in charge. We lost our commissioner (like him or not), we wasted too much time focusing on the owners' games (we know we don't like that), and we wondered daily about a lockout (we don't even want to think about that).

Wait! Enough of that! Yes, it's all part of the past year and will be part of the year ahead. And yes, we sports writers are responsible to report the information. But this book, just like every edition of *Baseball Weekly*, is a celebration of what we love most—the game and its players, its statistics, its excitement, its grip on our souls.

That's why we speculate and anticipate all winter about player moves. We're merely trying to keep the fever alive until spring. And, thankfully, we have plenty to look forward to:

▸Every time we think of one of last year's court cases, we can blot out the memory with vivid recollections of the first glimpse of Baltimore's beautiful new ballpark.

▸Every time someone mentions the threat of a labor disagreement shutting down the game, we can dream of a future opening day for the new ballyards in Cleveland and Texas.

▸Every time we cringe at the price of the latest free-agent contract, we can think about the charm and simplicity of the minor league game.

▸And every time any part of life gets us down, we can search for a field, a parking lot, or even a mind's-eye picture of our childhood—any place where kids choose up sides by putting their hands one above the other on a bat, where a hit to right field is an out because each team has only five players, where there is no coach or umpire and parents are allowed only if they're willing to play catch or keep patiently tossing the ball no matter how many times you miss.

Keep turning these pages. Find your heroes of today, tomorrow, and yesterday. Drift off into daydreams of games past or fantasies future. But most of all, play ball!

—by Paul White

1993: A bustling free agent market

Free agent compensation: How the system works

When the Blue Jays made the deal that brought New York Mets' David Cone, then the NL strikeout leader, to Toronto for the stretch drive last year, Oakland GM Sandy Alderson said it totally changed the balance of power in the league—not only because Cone would surely help win the pennant, but because Toronto couldn't lose in the deal. If they didn't sign Cone as a free agent after the season, they'd get two draft picks in compensation.

Ironically, the compensation system was designed to prevent imbalances, but neither the owners nor the players association is satisfied with it.

Here's how it works: Teams that lose free agents are compensated according to the ranking of the player.

▸Players are divided into five categories (starting pitchers, relief pitchers, catchers, middle infielders/third basemen, and first basemen/outfielders/designated hitters), then are ranked in terms of their performance as it compared to other players at the same position during the past two seasons. The top 30 percent are ranked as "A" players, 31 to 50 percent "B," 51 to 60 percent "C," and the remainder are unranked.

▸Clubs that sign an "A" free agent lose their first-round draft pick the following June (unless they are among the 13 worst teams, in which case they lose their second-round pick). Clubs that lose an "A" agent get the draft pick the signing team lost, plus a "sandwich" pick (an extra selection between the first two rounds).

▸Clubs that lose a "B" player get the signing team's highest available regular pick (the first 13 picks are exempt).

▸Clubs that lose a "C" player get a pick between the first two rounds.

1993 AL free agents

▸**Baltimore (6):** Pat Clements, LHP; Storm Davis, RHP; Mike Flanagan, LHP; Craig Lefferts, LHP; Joe Orsulak, OF; Rick Sutcliffe, RHP.

▸**Boston (5):** Wade Boggs, 3B; Tom Brunansky, OF; Billy Hatcher, OF; Steve Lyons, OF; Herm Winningham, OF.

▸**California (5):** Bert Blyleven, RHP; Hubie Brooks, OF; Mike Fitzgerald, C; Rene Gonzales, 3B; Ken Oberkfell, 3B.

▸**Chicago (2):** Charlie Hough, RHP; Dale Sveum, SS.

▸**Cleveland (3):** Brook Jacoby, 3B; Junior Ortiz, C; Eric Plunk, RHP.

▸**Detroit (8):** Dave Bergman, 1B; Bill Gullickson, RHP; Eric King, RHP; Gary Pettis, OF; Frank Tanana, LHP; Walt Terrell, RHP; Alan Trammell, SS; Lou Whitaker, 2B.

▸**Kansas City (4):** Jim Eisenreich, OF; Mark Gubicza, RHP; Bob Melvin, C; Curtis Wilkerson, SS.

▸**Milwaukee (9):** Chris Bosio, RHP; Scott Fletcher, 2B; Jim Gantner, 2B; Paul Molitor, 1B; Jesse Orosco, LHP; Dan Plesac, LHP; Bruce Ruffin, LHP; Kevin Seitzer, 3B; Robin Yount, OF.

▸**Minnesota (6):** Randy Bush, OF; Chili Davis, OF; Greg Gagne, SS; Mike Pagliarulo, 3B; Kirby Puckett, OF; John Smiley, LHP.

▸**New York (7):** Jesse Barfield, OF; Tim Burke, RHP; Mel Hall, OF; Steve Howe, LHP; Pascual Perez, RHP; Scott Sanderson, RHP; Curt Young, LHP.

▸**Oakland (14):** Harold Baines, OF; Ron Darling, RHP; Kelly Downs, RHP; Rich Gossage, RHP; Rick Honeycutt, LHP; Mark McGwire, 1B; Mike Moore, RHP; Jamie Quirk, C; Randy Ready, 2B; Jeff Russell, RHP; Ruben Sierra, OF; Terry Steinbach, C; Dave Stewart, RHP; Willie Wilson, OF.

▸**Seattle (4):** Henry Cotto, OF; Mark Grant, RHP; Lance Parrish, C; Harold Reynolds, 2B.

Texas (5): Brian Downing, OF; Jose Guzman, RHP; Al Newman, 2B; Edwin Nunez, RHP; John Russell, C.

Toronto (12): Joe Carter, OF; David Cone, RHP; Mark Eichhorn, RHP; Alfredo Griffin, SS; Tom Henke, RHP; Jimmy Key, LHP; Manuel Lee, SS; Candy Maldonado, OF; Rance Mulliniks, 3B; Dave Stieb, RHP; Pat Tabler, OF; Dave Winfield, OF.

1993 NL free agents

Atlanta (4): Mike Bielecki, RHP; Alejandro Pena, RHP; Jeff Reardon, RHP; Lonnie Smith, OF.

Chicago (5): Andre Dawson, OF; Greg Maddux, RHP; Jeff D. Robinson, RHP; Luis Salazar, 3B; Dave Smith, RHP.

Cincinnati (6): Scott Bankhead, RHP; Glenn Braggs, OF; Darnell Coles, 3B; Dave Martinez, OF; Jeff Reed, C; Greg Swindell, LHP.

Houston (2): Pete Incaviglia, OF; Rob Murphy, LHP.

Los Angeles (8): Dave Anderson, SS; John Candelaria, LHP; Eric Davis, OF; Jay Howell, RHP; Roger McDowell, RHP; Bob Ojeda, LHP; Mike Scioscia, C; Mitch Webster, OF.

Montreal (3): Gary Carter, C; Bill Krueger, LHP; Spike Owen, SS.

New York (7): Kevin Bass, OF; Daryl Boston, OF; Lee Guetterman, LHP; Barry Jones, RHP; Dave Magadan, 1B; Willie Randolph, 2B; Dick Schofield, SS.

Philadelphia (5): Wally Backman, 2B; Ken Howell, RHP; Stan Javier, OF; Steve Lake, C; Dale Murphy, OF.

Pittsburgh (4): Barry Bonds, OF; Danny Cox, RHP; Doug Drabek, RHP; Gary Redus, 1B.

St. Louis (10): Frank DiPino, LHP; Andres Galarraga, 1B; Rich Gedman, C; Pedro Guerrero, OF; Bob McClure, LHP; Bryn Smith, RHP; Ozzie Smith, SS; Scott Terry, RHP; Milt Thompson, OF; Todd Worrell, RHP.

San Diego (4): Larry Andersen, RHP; Jim Deshaies, LHP; Randy Myers, LHP; Benito Santiago, C.

San Francisco (5): Mike Felder, OF; Scott Garrelts, RHP; Chris James, OF; Cory Snyder, OF; Jose Uribe, SS.

1993 team managers

Managers are not exactly part of the free agent market, but their jobs seem to come and go—with an alarming degree of unpredictability under some of baseball's more eccentric regimes. The reasons for their dismissal range from obvious to utterly perplexing, as do the criteria for hiring their replacements. When Cincinnati Reds' owner Marge Schott did not rehire Lou Piniella (after he won 90 games in '92), her selection process included lining candidates up for inspection by her St. Bernard. Only Tony Perez patted the pup and said, "Nice doggie." And only Tony Perez was hired. These are major league baseball's managers for 1993:

National League East
Chicago Cubs: Jim Lefebvre
Florida Marlins: Rene Lachemann
Montreal Expos: Felipe Alou
New York Mets: Jeff Torborg
Philadelphia Phillies: Jim Fregosi
Pittsburgh Pirates: Jim Leyland
St. Louis Cardinals: Joe Torre

National League West
Atlanta Braves: Bobby Cox
Colorado Rockies: Don Baylor
Cincinnati Reds: Tony Perez
Houston Astros: Art Howe
Los Angeles Dodgers: Tom Lasorda
San Diego Padres: Jim Riggleman
San Francisco Giants: Dusty Baker

American League East
Baltimore Orioles: John Oates
Boston Red Sox: Butch Hobson
Cleveland Indians: Mike Hargrove
Detroit Tigers: Sparky Anderson
Milwaukee Brewers: Phil Garner
New York Yankees: Buck Showalter
Toronto Blue Jays: Cito Gaston

American League West
California Angels: Buck Rodgers
Chicago White Sox: Gene Lamont
Kansas City Royals: Hal McRae
Minnesota Twins: Tom Kelly
Oakland Athletics: Tony LaRussa
Seattle Mariners: Lou Piniella
Texas Rangers: Kevin Kennedy

National League expansion draft

How the draft was done

The Florida Marlins and Colorado Rockies each selected 36 players from the National and American leagues.

Each NL and AL club was allowed to protect 15 players from being drafted. Some players had to be protected: Those with 10 years in the majors, including at least the last five with the same club (10-and-5 men); players with no-trade clauses; most players with three or more years in minor leagues.

There were three draft rounds. No club could lose more than one player per round. When the eighth AL team lost a player in the third round, the other six AL teams had their rosters frozen.

After each pick, an NL club could protect three more players and an AL team could protect four more.

Players drafted from AL

▸**Baltimore:** RHP Kip Yaughn, RHP Richie Lewis.

▸**Boston:** 2B Jody Reed, C Eric Wedge.

▸**California:** RHP Bryan Harvey, RHP Brett Merriman, OF Junior Felix.

▸**Chicago:** LHP Greg Hibbard, RHP Robert Person.

▸**Cleveland:** OF Darrell Whitmore, RHP Jack Armstrong, LHP Denis Boucher.

▸**Detroit:** LHP Scott Aldred, RHP Kevin Ritz.

▸**Kansas City:** 1B-OF Jeff Conine, RHP Andres Berumen, OF Kerwin Moore.

▸**Milwaukee:** RHP Darren Holmes, 3B Jim Tatum, LHP Jeff Tabaka.

▸**Minnesota:** C Jay Owens, RHP Tom Edens, RHP Curtis Leskanic.

▸**New York:** 3B Charlie Hayes, OF Carl Everett, C Brad Ausmus.

▸**Oakland:** C Eric Helfand, RHP Jim Corsi.

▸**Seattle:** OF Jesus Tavarez, RHP Calvin Jones.

▸**Texas:** OF-DH Kevin Reimer, RHP Scott Chiamparino, OF Monty Fariss.

▸**Toronto:** OF Nigel Wilson, RHP David Weathers, RHP Marcus Moore.

Players drafted from NL

▸**Atlanta:** RHP David Nied; SS Vinny Castilla; RHP Armando Reynoso.

▸**Chicago:** C Joe Girardi; RHP Ryan Hawblitzel; 3B Pedro Castellano.

▸**Cincinnati:** RHP Trevor Hoffman; IF Fred Benavides; RHP Mo Sanford.

▸**Houston:** RHP Willie Blair; LHP Butch Henry; RHP Ryan Bowen.

▸**Los Angeles:** 2B Eric Young; IF Roberto Mejia; RHP Jamie McAndrew.

▸**Montreal:** 2B Bret Barberie; RHP Doug Bochtler; C Bob Natal.

▸**New York:** RHP Jose Martinez; RHP John Johnstone, 3B Chris Donnels.

▸**Philadelphia:** RHP Andy Ashby; RHP Keith Shepherd; OF Braulio Castillo.

▸**Pittsburgh:** OF Alex Cole; SS Ramon Martinez; LHP Danny Jackson.

▸**St. Louis:** OF Chuck Carr; RHP Cris Carpenter; LHP Scott Baker.

▸**San Diego:** OF Jerald Clark; LHP Lance Painter; RHP Scott Fredrickson.

▸**San Francisco:** RHP Patrick Rapp; C Steve Decker; RHP Steve Reed.

Draft day trades

The Mariners traded Kevin Mitchell to the Reds for reliever Norm Charlton. The Cubs traded shortstop Alex Arias and third baseman Gary Scott to the Marlins for starter Greg Hibbard. The A's traded shortstop Walt Weiss to the Rockies to retrieve catcher Eric Helfand (and a player to be named later). The Rockies traded outfielder Kevin Reimer to the Brewers for Dante Bichette. The Dodgers traded pitcher Rudy Seanez to the Rockies for second baseman Jody Reed.

—by Rick Lawes

Rockies chose experience

The Colorado Rockies' goal was to select a team that could be competitive in 1993 and beyond. Seven hours after they picked right-handed pitcher David Nied as their No. 1 choice, team executives felt they had succeeded. Twelve of the Rockies' 13 first-round picks have major league experience.

GM Bob Gebhard stayed close to his strategy: Emphasize pitching. Starting with Nied, the Rockies drafted 20 pitchers—12 of them pitched in the major leagues last year.

They emerged with a potential starting rotation of Nied, left-handers Butch Henry and Scott Aldred, and right-handers Andy Ashby and Willie Blair. They also picked several minor league pitchers who figure into their long-range plans, and obtained right-hander Rudy Seanez (Los Angeles) for second baseman Jody Reed.

Right-hander Darren Holmes is expected to be the Rockies' closer. They also chose Steve Reed, who set the minor league saves record in '92, and Mo Sanford to go along with Seanez in the bullpen.

The Rockies also went for right-handed power hitters to take advantage of light air and a short left-field wall in Denver. They got a jump on that by signing first baseman Andres Galarraga (manager Don Baylor was his hitting coach in St. Louis this season). Then they picked third baseman Charlie Hayes, who was not protected by the Yankees. Jerald Clark is the probable left fielder, and Dante Bichette will start in right. All four are right-handed hitters.

Up the middle, the Rockies put an emphasis on speed and defense—and saw catcher Joe Girardi, shortstop Freddie Benavides, second baseman Eric Young, and center fielder Alex Cole as a solid answer.

—by Rob Rains

Marlins went for youth

The Marlins chased younger players than the Rockies, those whom GM Dave Dombrowski described as "ready to break in at the major-league level."

First pick Nigel Wilson, a promising outfielder from the Toronto Blue Jays' organization, might not be on April's roster, but he's expected to blossom into an All-Star. While Dombrowski concedes that the Rockies might be able to field a better team this spring, the Marlins might be ready to make a quantum leap in the standings a year or two from now. Besides Wilson, the Marlins landed such top-flight prospects as outfielder Carl Everett (22) first baseman Jeff Conine (25), and pitchers Trevor Hoffman (26) and Jose Martinez (21).

But the Marlins also dealt themselves a respectable major league roster for the '93 season. Manager Rene Lachemann, former third base coach for Oakland, especially liked the deal that brought shortstop Walt Weiss to Florida: "I like how he plays the game of baseball," Lachemann said. "He's a winning ballplayer." Weiss could be joined in the infield by third baseman Gary Scott, second baseman Bret Barberie and first baseman Jeff Conine.

Veteran pitchers were available, but the Marlins stayed with youth. Dombrowski calculated that he had more than 20 "quality arms with above-average fastballs."

Jack Armstrong, Scott Chiamparino, David Weathers, Pat Rapp, and Ryan Bowen are possibilities for the starting rotation. Closer Bryan Harvey. Jim Corsi, Cris Carpenter, and Trevor Hoffman provide depth in the bullpen.

Steve Decker and Bob Natal will share the catching duties. The outfield will be Chuck Carr (center), Junior Felix (right), and either Jeff Conine or Monty Farris (left).

—by Tim Wendel

1993 Florida Marlins (NL East) 

Surprise! The Marlins will be fielding a young and inexperienced team in 1993. But the ingredients are in place for a promising future.

A key player will be shortstop Walt Weiss, who anchored the infield of the Oakland A's that won AL West titles in 1988, '89, '90, and '92. His experience will be the perfect complement to double-play partner Bret Barberie, the promising former Expo who hit .353 in 1991.

At the infield corners, Jeff Conine and Gary Scott get chances to prove themselves. Conine was stuck behind Wally Joyner at first base in Kansas City, and highly-touted Scott buckled under the pressure in two chances at third base with the Cubs.

Former Angel Junior Felix (.259 last year) is the only outfielder with any significant experience. Signing Benito Santiago allows time for catcher Charles Johnson to develop.

Florida has a proven closer in former Angel Bryan Harvey, but many young arms are competing for spots in the starting rotation.

—by Gary Kicinski

1993 preliminary roster

▸**Pitchers:** Jack Armstrong, Andres Berumen, Ryan Bowen, Cris Carpenter, Hector Carrasco, Scott Chiamparino, Jim Corsi, Brian Griffiths, Bryan Harvey, Trevor Hoffman, John Johnstone, Richie Lewis, Jose Martinez, Jamie McAndrew, Mike Myers, Pat Rapp, Stan Spencer, Jeffery Tabaka, Dave Weathers, Kip Yaughn.

▸**Catchers:** Steve Decker, Bob Natal, Benito Santiago.

▸**Infielders:** Alex Arias, Bret Barberie, Jeff Conine, Orestes Destrade, Chris Donnels, Ramon Martinez, Gary Scott, Walt Weiss.

▸**Outfielders:** Chuck Carr, Carl Everett, Monty Fariss, Junior Felix, Kerwin Moore, Scott Pose, Jesus Tavarez, Darrell Whitmore, Nigel Wilson.

1992 minor league report

▸**Class A, New York-Penn League:** Erie finished 40-37, second in the Stedler Division. They lost to Geneva in two games for the league championship. Todd Pridy (1B) hit .310 and led the league with 14 HR and 61 RBI; Lou Lucca (3B) had 13 HR; Doug Pettit had 11 saves.

▸**Class A, Gulf Coast League:** The Marlins finished 33-27, second in the Central Division. Dan Robinson hit .335 (26 RBI). The club was fourth in the league in batting (.246) and drew a league-high 272 walks. Greg Weeder had seven wins; Tony Saunders led the club with seven saves.

Team directory

▸**Owner:** Wayne Huizenga

▸**General Manager:** David Dombrowski

▸**Ballpark:**
Joe Robbie Stadium
2269 N.W. 199th St., Miami, Fla.
305-779-7070
Capacity 48,000
Parking available, over 14,000 spaces on-site
Public transportation available
Wheelchair section, family section, alcohol-free section, ramps and elevators

▸**TV, radio broadcast stations:**
WBFS Channel 33, Sunshine cable network, WQAM 560 AM (English), WCMQ 1210 AM (Spanish)

▸**Spring Training:**
Cocoa Expo
Cocoa, Fla.
Capacity 6,500
407-253-4433

1993 Colorado Rockies (NL West)

Within hours of becoming the first pick in the expansion draft, David Nied made a prediction about his new club, the Rockies: "I see a team that is going to be very competitive. We're not going to fall off the face of the baseball earth." The Rockies felt they accomplished their goal—a competitive team—in the draft, especially with third baseman Charlie Hayes. They didn't think the Yankees would leave him available. Manager Don Baylor thinks Hayes can hit 25 homers in Denver's light air.

Baylor is also counting on first baseman Andres Galarraga, signed away from the Cardinals as a free agent. Galarraga missed much of 1992 with a broken wrist, but is a proven hitter who will be an instant force in the middle of the lineup.

The Rockies hope fresh starts will improve performances by catcher Joe Girardi and outfielder Jerald Clark, and they also like their young pitching arms: Scott Aldred, Butch Henry, Andy Ashby, and Willie Blair.

—by Rob Rains

1993 preliminary roster

▸**Pitchers:** Scott Aldred, Andy Ashby, Willie Blair, Doug Bochtler, Denis Boucher, Travis Buckley, Scott Fredrickson, Ryan Hawblitzel, Butch Henry, Darren Holmes, Calvin Jones, Curtis Leskanic, Brett Merriman, Marcus Moore, David Nied, Lance Painter, Steve Reed, Armando Reynoso, Kevin Ritz, Mo Sanford, Rudy Seanez, Keith Shepherd.

▸**Catchers:** Brad Ausmus, Joe Girardi, J. Owens, Eric Wedge.

▸**Infielders:** Freddie Benavides, Pedro Castellano, Vinny Castilla, Andres Galarraga, Charlie Hayes, Roberto Mejia, Jim Tatum, Eric Young.

▸**Outfielders:** Dante Bichette, Braulio Castillo, Jerald Clark, Alex Cole.

1992 minor league report

▸**Class A, Northwest League:** Bend finished 43-33, first in the South Division. They lost to Bellingham in two games for the league championship. RHP Mark Thompson was 8-4 with a 2.03 ERA and 102 SO in 102 IP to lead the league. RHP Roger Bailey was 5-2 (2.20 ERA, 81 SO/65 IP). RHP Jason Hutchins had 18 saves, which would have been a league record had he not been second in the league.

▸**Class A, Arizona League:** The Rockies were last in the league, 18-38 in a combined team with the Cubs. Maurice Gonzales hit .347; Greg Boyd shared the league lead with three HR. Chris Neier was 5-1 with a 2.24 ERA, and walked just eight in 56 IP.

Team directory

▸**Owner:** Jerry McMorris
▸**General Manager:** Bob Gebhard
▸**Ballpark:**
Mile High Stadium
2755 West 17th Ave., Denver, Colo.
303-292-0200
Capacity 76,100
Parking
Public transportation available
Wheelchair section, family section in all price ranges
▸**TV, radio broadcast stations:**
KWGN Channel 2, KOA 850 AM
▸**Spring Training:**
Hi Corbett Field
Tucson, Ariz.
Capacity 8,000
602-327-9467

Offseason news and announcements

Giants stay by the bay

National League owners voted 9-4 to reject owner Bob Lurie's attempt to move the Giants from San Francisco to St. Petersburg, Fla., opening the door for Lurie to sell to a group of San Francisco investors for $100 million, $15 million less than the Tampa Bay group's offer. Said Lurie: "I feel badly for Vincent Naimoli (head of the Tampa Bay group), but I congratulate Peter Magowan, the entire San Francisco investment group, and everyone throughout the Bay Area who worked so hard to keep the Giants in San Francisco."

—by Hal Bodley

Giants vote shakes antitrust

By keeping the Giants in San Francisco, baseball owners may have removed a pillar holding up protection of their treasured antitrust exemption. One of three separate lawsuits alleges the San Francisco group had an advantageous business relationship with owners, in violation of Florida antitrust laws. Baseball has had exemption from antitrust laws since 1922, when the U.S. Supreme Court ruled it was sport, not trade. But the exemption came under fire again when owners delayed action on the Giants and called for the commissioner to be a "CEO for the owners." Hearings on whether "baseball has abused its blanket exemption from federal antitrust laws," were set for Dec. 10 by the Senate.

"If baseball team owners are exploiting this extraordinary privilege in a way that hurts fans, the sport of baseball and the public interest, then Congress can take it away," warned Sen. Howard M. Metzenbaum.

—by Rick Lawes

1992 Gold Glove winners

▸**National League:** P, Greg Maddux, Cubs; C, Tom Pagnozzi, Cardinals; 1B, Mark Grace, Cubs; 2B, Jose Lind, Pirates; 3B, Terry Pendleton, Braves; SS, Ozzie Smith, Cardinals; OF, Barry Bonds, Pirates; OF, Andy Van Slyke, Pirates; OF, Larry Walker, Expos.

▸**American League:** P, Mark Langston, Angels; C, Ivan Rodriguez, Rangers; 1B, Don Mattingly, Yankees; 2B, Roberto Alomar, Blue Jays; 3B, Robin Ventura, White Sox; SS, Cal Ripken Jr., Orioles; OF, Ken Griffey Jr., Mariners; OF, Kirby Puckett, Twins; OF, Devon White, Blue Jays.

Winter meetings notes

Chaotic, costly, and ultimately somber, the winter meetings in Louisville, Ky., Dec. 7-9, reflected the uneasy state of baseball: Barry Bonds signed the biggest player contract in history—$43.75 million through 1998—with the San Francisco Giants, surprise winners over the Atlanta Braves and the New York Yankees in the Bonds sweepstakes. The 28-year-old outfielder—National League MVP in 1990 and 1992—will wear No. 25, once worn by his father, Bobby Bonds, who will also be his batting coach in San Francisco.

The press conference announcing the deal was a classic—Bonds had struck the deal with the group buying the Giants, but they weren't owners yet. Two more days of negotiations with then-owner Bob Lurie finalized the deal and protected Lurie from paying the contract if the team sale fell through.

The Bonds deal was just part of the player-signing frenzy at the winter meetings. Money was not an obstacle. In one day alone, clubs spent a record $125 million to sign free agents. Pennant winners Toronto and Atlanta remained the teams to beat.

Toronto re-signed Joe Carter, and added Dave Stewart and Paul Molitor, and the Braves signed NL Cy Young winner Greg Maddux. The Braves' starters—ERA leaders in the majors in 1992 (3.14)—now will be Maddux, Tom Glavine, Steve Avery, and John Smoltz.

The New York Yankees, after trading for Jim Abbott to anchor their pitching rotation, were shut out in pursuing free agents Bonds, Doug Drabek, David Cone, and Maddux--even though the team offered Maddux $6 million more than the Braves did.

The owners voted to reopen labor talks by a slim 15-13 margin. This raised the threat, but not the probability, of a lockout in 1993. The owners unanimously OK'd a rule change requiring 75 percent approval for a lockout, instead of a simple majority.

Richard Ravitch, the owners' negotiator, said the labor talks are needed to stop the salary escalation that pushed the average past $1 million last season.

"We want to move toward some change in the player compensation system," Ravitch said. "We are not seeking a confrontation."

Donald Fehr, head of the players association, said: "Let us hope history is not a guide this time." There have been seven work stoppages in 22 years: Owners locked out players in 1973, 1976, and 1990; players went on strike in 1972, 1980, 1981, and 1985.

Cincinnati Reds' general partner Marge Schott apologized for the use of racial slurs, which she termed "insensitive remarks."

"It was my mouth but not my heart speaking," she said. The Reds' organization has also been criticized for a lack of minorities in the front office. Schott could be fined or suspended by the ruling executive council. As the winter meetings concluded, NL president Bill White reportedly was negotiating a deal with Schott's lawyer that would have her agree to a penalty.

The Rev. Jesse Jackson spoke to a small delegation of owners and suggested that major league baseball may face a boycott unless it opens more top-level jobs to minorities.

"There are 28 presidents of clubs, zero blacks," Jackson said to a crowd at a local church. "General managers—28, zero black. Director of player personnel—zero. Chief of scouting—zero. Unless there's a plan to change that, when the stadium opens come opening day, the number going into that stadium must be zero.

"...They have until the spring to put forth a plan," Jackson continued. "Let's move from (Marge Schott's) language to (the Reds') behavior."

The meetings were interrupted by a tragedy, when Florida Marlins president and part-owner Carl Barger died Dec. 8 after suffering a heart attack. Barger, 62, who had previously been president of the Pittsburgh Pirates for six years, had talked his long-time golfing buddy, H. Wayne Huizenga, into buying the expansion team. He guided the Marlins from the summer of 1991 through the expansion draft, working 16-hour days to build the franchise from the ground up.

Milwaukee Brewers' owner Bud Selig, acting as commissioner pro tem, said a search committee would soon be appointed to find a new commissioner. An owners committee report on restructuring the commissioner's job—in the wake of Fay Vincent's forced resignation—was due by the end of the year and would be put to a vote by owners at a January meeting.

Selig said he expected a report shortly from an owners committee examining schedule formats, three-division play and a third tier of playoffs.

—by Tim McQuay

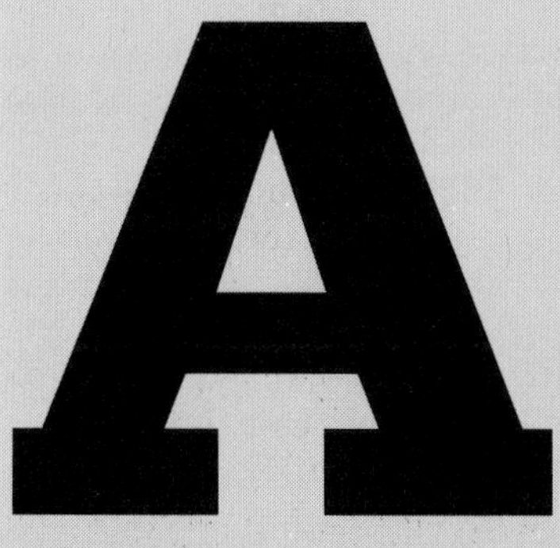

Around the League

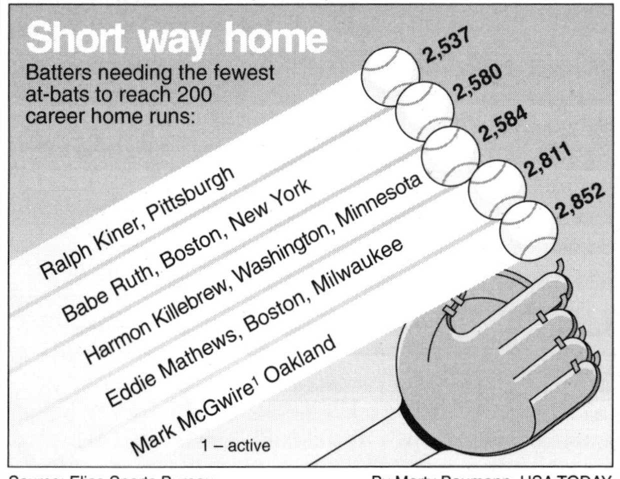

INSIDE:

- A season of turmoil: The commissioner resigns
- Labored relations
- 3,000 hits for Yount and Brett
- Big deals
- 1992 highlights
- League bests
- Milestones galore
- *... and more!*

Vincent struck out with owners

Following a "no-confidence" vote by Major League Baseball's team owners, Commissioner Fay Vincent resigned from his post Sept. 7, 1992.

Conflicts at a glance

▸**Expansion:** After the AL and NL could not agree on how to split the NL's $190 million in expansion fees, Vincent ruled that the AL would receive $42 million and supply players equally for the expansion draft.

▸**George Steinbrenner:** On July 30, 1990, Vincent signed an agreement with Steinbrenner under which the Yankees' principal owner resigned as managing general partner because of his dealings with gambler Howard Spira. Steinbrenner later caused the filing of three lawsuits, which were eventually withdrawn. Vincent said that Steinbrenner could resume an active role March 1, 1993.

▸**Steve Howe:** Vincent permanently banned Steve Howe after the Yankees' pitcher entered a no-contest plea in U.S. District Court to a misdemeanor charge of attempting to buy a gram of cocaine. Howe filed a grievance, and the players' association accused Vincent of pressuring team officials to change their testimony in the case. Vincent then issued a memorandum stating that team employees should feel free to testify as they wished. An arbitrator later reinstated Howe.

—Tim Wendel

Vincent's troubled term

▸**Sept. 1, 1989:** Named acting commissioner after A. Bartlett Giamatti's death.

▸**Sept. 13, 1989:** Unanimously chosen to be commissioner.

▸**Oct. 17, 1989:** Postponed World Series after earthquake struck San Francisco area.

▸**Oct. 27, 1989:** Resumed World Series and announced $1.3 million relief contribution; each club assessed $50,000.

▸**Feb. 1990:** Intervened in negotiations between players and owners.

▸**July 30, 1990:** Placed George Steinbrenner on permanent ineligible list for paying Howard Spira $40,000 for negative information about Dave Winfield.

▸**June 6, 1991:** Ordered National League to give American League $42 million of its $190 million expansion revenue.

▸**June 4, 1992:** Was asked to give up his powers to get involved in labor talks. Refused.

▸**June 8, 1992:** Suspended Yankees' relief pitcher Steve Howe for life for illegal use of cocaine, Howe's seventh offense.

▸**July 1, 1992:** Ordered Yankees' executives Gene Michael, Buck Showalter and Jack Lawn to explain their testimony in Howe's hearings.

▸**July 6, 1992:** Ordered National League realignment and was immediately taken to court by the Chicago Cubs, requesting a restraining order.

▸**July 24, 1992:** Ordered Steinbrenner reinstated March 1, 1993.

▸**July 23, 1992:** U.S. Court of Appeals issued preliminary injunction preventing Chicago Cubs moving from NL East to NL West.

▸**Aug. 4, 1992:** Proposed amendment to pending cable legislation that would affect superstations by eliminating duplicate telecasts when local teams are on TV.

▸**Aug. 17, 1992:** AL President Bobby Brown and NL President Bill White set meeting to consider powers and term of the commissioner.

▸**Aug. 20, 1992:** Vowed he would not resign.

▸**Sept. 3, 1992:** Owners took a no-confidence vote and asked for his immediate resignation.

▸**Sept. 7, 1992:** Resigned.

—by Hal Bodley

Vincent is gone, but the problems linger on

Fay Vincent's resignation eliminates owners' fears about his approach, but it doesn't do anything to solve the major problems facing the game.

▸**Labor negotiations:** The majority of owners believe they can't wait any longer to force a showdown with the players' association on rising salaries. The biggest issue for the owners is arbitration, which they consider to be a greater cause of rising salaries than free agency. Vincent believed that the owners are at fault, even though he acknowledged that clubs are losing money, and that something has to be done to stop the spiraling increases in salaries. "The main reasons clubs are losing money is because owners have made decisions and commitments that exceed their resources," Vincent told the *Washington Post*. He favored a salary cap and shared revenues.

▸**Television negotiations:** 1993 is the final year of the current television contracts with CBS and ESPN. Those revenues will almost certainly shrink greatly, and owners don't know how they are going to continue to pay escalating salaries. The key player in the television game is the Tribune Co., with broadcasting rights for the Cubs, White Sox, Dodgers, Angels, Yankees, Phillies, and Rockies. Vincent wanted the Tribune and other superstation companies to pay more money or to be more restricted in the number of games they could televise and where they could be shown.

▸**Commissioner's role:** The Major League Agreement clearly states that there can be no changes in the power and duties of the commissioner during his term in office. But now that Vincent is gone, White Sox owner Jerry Reinsdorf would like to make the commissioner more of a CEO for the owners, answering to them as if they were a board of directors.

—by Rob Rains

by Tim Dillon, *USA TODAY*

Commissioner Fay Vincent resigned under pressure.

From Landis to Vincent

▸**Judge Kenesaw Mountain Landis (1920-1944):** Died in office. Was brought in to clean up the game after the 1919 Black Sox scandal.

▸**A.B. Happy Chandler (1945-1951):** Alienated owners by supporting umpires' unionization and admitting blacks into the game. Served one seven-year term but stayed in office until a successor was found.

▸**Ford Frick (1951-1965):** Dodgers and Giants moved to the West Coast during his watch. Many contend that Dodgers' owner Walter O'Malley was the real force behind the throne.

▸**General William Eckert (1965-1968):** Another owners' man.

▸**Bowie Kuhn (1969-1984):** A lawyer. Sports economist Andrew Zimbalist claimed his policies were "imposed inconsistently and erratically."

▸**Peter Ueberroth (1984-1989):** Disciplined owners, but most of his work backfired with collusion, which left management with a $280 million settlement.

▸**A. Bartlett Giamatti (1989):** Served only five months before his death.

▸**Fay Vincent (1989-1992):** Appointed to serve the remainder of Giamatti's term.

Vincent's resignation letter

"As requested in the owners' resolution of Sept. 3, 1992, and in accordance with its terms, I tender my resignation as commissioner of baseball, effective immediately.

"On Aug. 20, I wrote each of the owners I would not resign the office of the commissioner of baseball. I stated that, in my judgment, to do so would do a great disservice to the office of the commissioner and to baseball itself. I strongly believe a baseball commissioner should serve a full term as contemplated by the Major League Agreement. Only then can difficult decisions be made impartially and without fear of political repercussions. Unfortunately, some want the commissioner to put aside the responsibility to act in the 'best interests of baseball'; some want the commissioner to represent only owners, and to do their bidding in all matters. I haven't done that, and I could not do so, because I accepted the position believing the commissioner has a higher duty and that sometimes decisions have to be made that are not in the interest of some owners.

"Unique power was granted to the commissioner of baseball for sound reasons—to maintain the integrity of the game and to temper owner decisions predicated solely on self-interest. The office should be maintained as a strong institution. My views on this have not changed. What has changed, however, is my opinion that it would be an even greater disservice to baseball if I were to precipitate a protracted fight over the office of the commissioner. After the vote at the meeting last week, I can no longer justify imposing on baseball, nor should baseball be required to endure, a bitter legal battle—even though I am confident that in the end I would win and thereby establish a judicial precedent that the term and powers of the commissioner cannot be diminished during the remaining months of my term. But what would that accomplish? What will the fight have been worth if, 14 months from now, prior to electing a new commissioner, the owners change the Major League Agreement to create a 'figurehead' commissioner? This is certainly the goal of some. And while it is bad for baseball, I cannot prevent that change.

"A fight based solely on principle does not justify the disruption when there is not greater support among ownership for my views. While I would receive personal gratification by demonstrating that the legal position set out in my Aug. 20 letter is correct, litigation does nothing to address the serious problems of baseball. I cannot govern as commissioner without the consent of owners to be governed. I do not believe that consent is now available to me. Simply put, I've concluded that resignation—not litigation—should be my final act as commissioner 'in the best interests of baseball.' I can only hope owners realize that a strong commissioner, a person of experience and stature in the community, is integral to baseball. I hope they learn this lesson before too much damage is done to the game, to the players, umpires and others who work in the game, and most importantly, to the fans.

"I am grateful to my friends, among the owners and around the country, for their warm and zealous support. I am especially grateful for all the messages of support from those in the game who care about me and who believe in what I have tried to accomplish. That support has meant a great deal to me—more than I can express. The game of baseball can, and will, survive far more difficult times than these.

"I bear no personal ill will towards any of the owners and I wish them well. At the same time, I remind all that ownership of a baseball team is more than ownership of an ordinary business. Owners have a duty to take into consideration that they own a part of America's national pastime—in trust. This trust sometimes requires putting self-interest second."

Sincerely, Francis T. Vincent, Jr.

Commentary: Owners are to blame

Owners can't be trusted

Baseball owners finally got their fondest wish: Fay Vincent's head on a platter. The sport—lock, stock, and lawyer fees—now rests totally in the owners' greedy little hands. The position of commissioner as we once knew it is now as dead as the Dodgers.

The owners want a new kind of commissioner. One who will grant their wishes. Dance to their music. Obey their commands. Stick to their party line. One who can be, in short, controlled. I nominate Kermit the Frog. Or Lambchop.

The owners, who have rarely been adept at controlling even themselves, now control the game—all of it. I do not begrudge their desire to run their own teams. But they don't own the game. They don't own its traditions or its past or its future or its present.

They don't own its soul—but they are bidding for it. They have never been the voice for the fans—but they have seized the office that tried to be.

Perhaps some of the owners do care enough about the game to occasionally go against what their accountants are telling them. Yet there is one plain truth in the aftermath of the owners' victory over Vincent: It's hard to trust them to run the game right.

Hard to trust them not to initiate devastating lockouts when labor negotiations don't go their way. Hard to trust them to put aside their own self-interests long enough to make the hard decisions that have to be made.

The owners' trophy from this triumphant power play is a skeptical public. Skeptical players. And a sport that appears to be in decline, even as it expands.

As for Vincent, he left as he came in. Gracious and eloquent. He made good judgments and bad, but he tried to speak for all of those who have a share of the game—from the millionaire in the on-deck circle to the 12-year-old in the bleachers. The same cannot be said for those who evicted him.

—by Mike Lopresti

The real issue is money

The owners' vote against Fay Vincent was like a manager's setup move with relievers. With Vincent out, the owners could call in the stopper and drop the real hammer later—locking out the players—without a nagging commissioner cluttering the scheme.

One of Vincent's biggest problems was that he knew how to read a map. Even with his thick eyeglasses, he could see that Atlanta was east of Chicago, and that the Braves and Cubs should switch National League divisions. But in the Chicago offices of the Tribune, common sense takes a back seat to television ratings. They believe that if you hold the map at just the right angle—and pretend really hard—Wrigley Field is practically a stop on the New Jersey Turnpike. So the Tribune Co., which would own the television rights of seven teams by 1993, reached for the remote. Zap. No more Vincent.

Much was made of Vincent riding roughshod on Yankees' officials during his investigation of Steve Howe. We're supposed to believe that the same owners who were locked in the Collusion I, II and III conspiracies are losing sleep about rights intrusions in the case of a seven-time drug offender? What really bothers them is losing money. Rising ticket prices and three-dollar hot dogs can't cover the cost of seven-figure contracts for .250 hitters, so owners lost money—and Fay Vincent lost his job.

—by Tom Weir

A look at baseball's labor relations

Labor history: Reserve clause to lockouts

▸**1897:** The reserve clause bound players to their teams. It remained in place until 1976.

▸**1920:** In the wake of the "Black Sox" scandal, Judge Kenesaw Mountain Landis was installed as baseball's first commissioner.

▸**1922:** The U.S. Supreme Court upheld a lower-court decision effectively giving baseball its antitrust exemption, calling it "sport, not trade."

▸**1948:** Danny Gardella, a returning war veteran who jumped to the Mexican League, sued baseball after being banned. The reserve clause was eventually struck down in circuit court.

▸**1953:** The U.S. Supreme Court essentially reaffirmed the reserve clause. Key to the decision: Congressional inaction during a number of hearings in 1951, which the court interpreted as upholding the antitrust exemption. During the hearings, a number of players supported the reserve clause.

▸**1954:** The Major League Baseball Players Association was formed. Its primary focus: improving the players' pension plan.

▸**1968:** The first bargaining agreement between the owners and the MLBPA established the commissioner as an arbiter in salary disputes.

▸**1970:** Curt Flood filed suit against major league baseball. After the '69 season, Flood was traded to the Phillies by the Cardinals. He wrote to commissioner Bowie Kuhn, asking for the deal to be nullified, citing his 12 years of service with St. Louis. ***Also:*** The second Basic Agreement was signed. Players gained the right to have grievances impartially arbitrated outside the commissioner's office.

▸**1972:** The first industry-wide players' strike took place, over funding for the players' pension fund. It lasted 13 days. ***Also:*** The U.S. Supreme Court upheld baseball's special monopoly by ruling against Flood's appeal. The opinion established the players' resolve to reform the contract structure through collective bargaining.

▸**1973:** The third Basic Agreement was signed. Though the players were seeking the end of the reserve clause (meaning free agency), they were left with what turned out to be a big prize: salary arbitration.

▸**1974:** Jim "Catfish" Hunter was made a free agent after an arbitrator ruled that the terms of his contract were violated by Oakland A's owner Charlie Finley. Hunter signed a multiyear deal with the Yankees. He was the only player in baseball with a multiyear deal.

▸**1975:** Dave McNally and Andy Messersmith were declared free agents. Each refused to sign contracts for the '75 season, and their teams (the Expos and Dodgers, respectively) exercised the standard renewal option. An arbitrator ruled they were no longer bound to those teams because they had played out their options.

▸**1976:** After losing appeals of the McNally and Messersmith decisions, and without a Basic Agreement in place, the owners locked out the players. Kuhn ordered spring training camps opened after 24 days. ***Also:*** Free agency was granted to players with six years of major league experience under the new Basic Agreement. In 1977, 281 players signed multiyear contracts.

▸**1981:** The players went on strike, after playing a season-and-a-half without a Basic Agreement.

▸**1985:** For the fourth time, the Basic Agreement expired, and players reported without a contract. This time, they went on strike for two days before a new deal was made. Major concessions: Arbitration eligibility was raised from two to three years, and additional draft picks were awarded to teams losing free agents.

▸**1985-86:** Thirty-three players declared free agency; 29 went back to their former teams without receiving bids. In February, the MLBPA filed its first collusion grievance.

▸**1986-87:** The average salary of free agents fell 16 percent. On Feb. 18, 1987, the second collusion grievance was filed.

▸**1988:** After the owners set up an information bank where they let each other know about bids to free agents, the MLBPA filed its third collusion grievance.

▸**1990:** Arbitrator George Nicolau found the owners guilty for the third time in collusion arguments, after they were found to have colluded in Sept. 1987 (Collusion I) and Jan. 1988 (Collusion II).

▸**1990:** The players were again locked out of the camps, this time for 32 days. The owners could not implement a salary cap nor their pay-for-performance scheme, but neither did they lower the service required to go to arbitration.

▸**1992:** The owners vote to reopen talks on their bargaining agreement that runs through Dec. 31, 1993.

The climb to a million

Year	Minimum	Mean
1910	N/A	$2,500
1929	N/A	$7,531
1946	N/A	$11,294
1967	N/A	$19,000
1970	$12,000	$29,303
1975	$16,000	$44,676
1980	$30,000	$143,756
1982	$33,500	$241,497
1984	$40,000	$329,408
1986	$60,000	$412,520
1988	$62,500	$438,729
1990	$100,000	$597,537
1991	$100,000	$851,492
1992	$109,000	$1,043,156

How other sports do it

Baseball could learn a thing or two from its rivals for the sporting dollar.

According to author Andrew Zimbalist (*Baseball and Billions,* BasicBooks, 1992), the average baseball team earned less than 37 percent of its revenue from shared league sources; in the National Football League, each of the 28 teams received more than 96 percent from shared sources. Zimbalist maintains that the NFL model makes the most sense, "if you're looking for the most competitive balance between unequal markets."

The National Basketball Association has less shared revenues, but it is bolstered by a salary cap and a popular commissioner, David Stern. While baseball owners gripe about shrinking revenues, Stern has expanded basketball into an international, billion-dollar industry.

The NBA's salary cap is computed as 53 percent of total league revenues for TV and gate monies (excluding concessions and parking). Teams can go over their cap to sign players already on their rosters.

Baseball owners proposed a 48 percent team salary cap in 1990, which Players Association director Don Fehr said the players would consider if they had veto power over "important structural decisions." Owners would have to provide a fair assessment of gate receipts, which seems unlikely in today's climate.

Those gate receipts are shared only in the least generous manner: In the American League, the visiting team gets only 20 percent, while in the National League, visitors pocket a paltry nine percent.

Teams in small markets suffer the most, perhaps, from lack of lucrative TV contracts. The TV packages vary from the Yankees' annual $50 million to the Mariners' $3 million. Of that, the NL shares maybe 20 percent, and the AL a mere 15 percent.

1992: A season of thrills and spills

▸**April 6:** Oriole Park at Camden Yards opened its gates. Rick Sutcliffe pitched a five-hit shutout, and Indian Paul Sorrento got the first hit. Bobby Bonilla hit two homers in his Mets' debut. It was one of his few highlights of the season.

▸**April 29:** The A's Mark McGwire hit his 10th home run of the season. He would be one of the comeback players of the year, finishing second to Juan Gonzalez's 43 homers with 42.

▸**May 21:** The Angels' team bus crashed on the New Jesery Turnpike, injuring 12, including manager Buck Rodgers, who was out for most of the year.

▸**May 30:** Mariners' rookie Dave Fleming pitched his first major league shutout. He won nine in a row.

▸**May 31:** Gary Carter caught his 2,000th career game.

▸**June 1:** The Blue Jays' Devon White became the 56th player in history to homer from both sides of the plate in the same game.

▸**June 8:** Cubs' pitcher Jim Bullinger hit a home run in his first major league at-bat.

▸**June 15:** Red Sox closer Jeff Reardon broke Rollie Fingers' all-time save record, with his 342nd.

▸**June 21:** The Dodgers lost their 10th consecutive game, the year's longest losing streak in the NL.

▸**July 14:** The Mariners' Ken Griffey Jr. was MVP as the AL defeated the NL 13-6 in the All-Star Game at San Diego. Griffey's father was rated the contest's best player in 1980.

▸**July 29:** The A's Dennis Eckersley set a major league record with his 33rd consecutive save. He finished the season with 51 saves and 36 in a row.

▸**August 16:** Tiger Cecil Fielder collected his 100th RBI of the season, on his way to becoming the first hitter to lead the major leagues in RBI three consecutive years since Babe Ruth in 1919-21.

▸**August 17:** Kevin Gross gave the Dodgers one highlight to their forgettable year by pitching the only no-hitter of the season.

▸**August 23:** The most-discussed road trip of the year—the Astros' 26-game, 28-day junket to eight NL cities—ended in Philadelphia. The trip was set up to accommodate the Republican convention in the Astrodome.

▸**August 25:** Houston rookie Andujar Cedeno became the only NL player to hit for the cycle in '92.

▸**August 31:** The A's dealt Jose Canseco to Texas for Ruben Sierra, Bobby Witt, Jeff Russell, and cash.

▸**September 7:** Commissioner Fay Vincent resigned.

▸**September 9:** Robin Yount became the 17th player in major league history to reach 3,000 career hits.

▸**September 11:** The Dodgers committed seven errors. Shortstop Jose Offerman made three, giving him 40 for the year, the first NL player to reach that milestone in 14 years.

▸**September 14:** Phillies' catcher Darren Daulton collected his 100th RBI, becoming the first NL catcher to reach triple figures in RBI since Gary Carter in 1985.

▸**September 18:** Pirate Barry Bonds hit his 30th homer of the season, the second season in his career he has reached 30 homers and 30 stolen bases.

▸**September 20:** Phillies' second baseman Mickey Morandini pulled off an unassisted triple play, first in the NL since 1927.

▸**September 23:** Cincinnati's Bip Roberts got his 10th consecutive hit, tying the NL record.

▸**September 24:** Dave Winfield (40) became the oldest player to get more than 100 RBI in a season.

▸**October 1:** George Brett got his 3,000th career hit.

by Robert Deutsch, *USA TODAY*

The A's Jose Canseco had "worn out his welcome" in Oakland and was traded to the Rangers.

When the going gets tough, the tough get traded

The Braves wanted to terminate their rivals' pennant hopes, so they called up the Red Sox and got themselves a terminator: Jeff Reardon, the all-time save leader, for two minor leaguers.

The Blue Jays were sick of being called "chokers," so they called New York and got one of the few Mets who didn't choke all year: David Cone, the reigning NL strikeout leader, for prospects Jeff Kent and Ryan Thompson.

The Athletics needed pitching—and were not in the mood to deal with clubhouse problems—after the Twins blocked their attempt to get Bruce Hurst from San Diego. So they sent a pinch-hitter to the plate and shipped Jose Canseco, one of the most feared home-run hitters in baseball, to the Rangers for Bobby Witt, Jeff Russell, and Ruben Sierra. (The A's voted Canseco a full postseason share.)

Reardon may have been pleased to go from a last-place team to the World Series, but both Cone and Canseco were both shocked to be suddenly traded. Canseco guessed he might have "worn out his welcome," and joked about the deal: "What did they get for me? Froot Loops and a burrito?"

Cone told the press he had no idea why the Mets thought they would have trouble signing him, and insisted that they had never even discussed contract issues with him. In postseason TV interviews, he called himself a "hired gun" for the Blue Jays.

Oakland general manager Sandy Alderson said that the Cone trade changed "the whole balance of power," even if Toronto couldn't sign Cone.

"The worst that can happen is that the Jays wind up with two draft picks," Alderson reasoned. They also wound up with a nice set of World Series rings.

How they fared

▸**David Cone:** He had a tough start in the American League, but finished the regular season with 4-3 record, a 2.55 ERA, and 47 strikeouts in 53 innings for the Blue Jays. In the ALCS, he was 1-1, with a 3.00 ERA and nine strikeouts in 12 innings. He had no decisions in the World Series, but he struck out eight in 10 1/3 innings and batted 2-for-4 with an RBI.

▸**Jeff Kent:** He hit .239 for the Mets—27 hits and 15 RBI in 37 games, including three home runs, a triple, and eight doubles. He also had three errors.

▸**Ryan Thompson:** He hit only .222 for the Mets, but had 24 hits in 30 games, with seven doubles, a triple, three home runs and 10 RBI. He stole two bases and got caught twice.

▸**Ruben Sierra:** He held his batting average steady at .278, with three home runs and 17 RBI in 101 at-bats for the A's. He was a shining star in the playoffs, in the field and at the plate. He hit .333 and drove in seven of the A's 24 runs.

▸**Bobby Witt:** He shaved some points off his ERA—from 4.46 to 4.29—and struck out 25, but was just 1-1 for the A's in the regular season. He had trouble in the ALCS: two earned runs in one inning, for a 18.00 ERA.

▸**Jeff Russell:** His ERA went down from 1.91 to 1.63, as he went 2-0 for the A's in the regular season, with two saves. He gave up two earned runs—walking four—in two innings in the ALCS for a 9.00 ERA, but he got one win.

▸**Jose Canseco:** His batting average dropped from .246 to .244, but he hit four home runs with 15 RBI for the Rangers.

▸**Jeff Reardon:** His ERA was 1.15, best on the Braves, after 4.25 in Boston. He added seven saves (30 total) and three wins to his record for the season. He won a game and saved a game in the NLCS, maintaining a 0.00 ERA. He didn't fare so well in the World Series: two earned runs in 1 1/3 innings, a loss, 13.50 ERA.

Robin Yount, George Brett hit 3,000

by Russell Beeker, *Baseball Weekly*

Milwaukee Brewer Robin Yount became the 17th player in major league history to get 3,000 career hits.

Yount prefers team wins to personal milestones

The night before he got his 3,000th hit, future Hall of Famer Robin Yount was thinking more about the Brewers' pennant chase than his own milestone: "I hope the hit drives in a run to help us win. I don't enjoy playing when we lose."

It was vintage Yount. It came from the heart. Ask Paul Molitor, Yount's teammate since 1978.

"Everyone talks about putting the team first, and that's easy to say," Molitor says. "But Robin Yount is one player who can say it with absolute honesty. If the team is playing well, Robin Yount doesn't need anything else." Yount was the first player to reach 3,000 hits since Rod Carew of the California Angels in 1985.

—by Mel Antonen

Brett didn't want to wait any longer for No. 3,000

One-for-40. That's what was in the back of George Brett's mind when, after career hit No. 2,999, he decided not to wait until the Royals went back to Kansas City to try for his historic 3,000th hit. The team got some angry phone calls from hometown fans who wanted to see No. 3,000, but Brett, who has played his entire career in Kansas City, didn't want to take a chance that a slump like his 1-for-40 stretch early in the season would leave him stranded at 2,999. So he stayed in the game and got four hits, including No. 3,000.

"If some people in Kansas City are upset, I don't think they're true fans," Brett said. "They don't know how hard it is to get a hit."

—by David Leon Moore

by Russell Beeker, *Baseball Weekly*

Kansas City's George Brett disappointed hometown fans when he got his 3,000th career hit on the road.

Players with 3,000 hits

Listed by total career hits (x-active):

Pete Rose, 4,256; Ty Cobb, 4,191; Hank Aaron, 3,771; Stan Musial, 3,630; Tris Speaker, 3,515; Honus Wagner, 3,430; Carl Yastrzemski, 3,419; Eddie Collins, 3,309; Willie Mays, 3,283; Nap Lajoie, 3,252; Paul Waner, 3,152; Cap Anson, 3,081; Rod Carew, 3,053; **x-Robin Yount, 3,025**; Lou Brock, 3,023; Al Kaline, 3,007; **x-George Brett, 3,005**; Roberto Clemente, 3,000.

Some players were long on fame, short on 3,000

Pete Rose is the only eligible player with more than 3,000 hits (4,256) not in the Hall of Fame. Here are some Hall of Fame players who didn't get 3,000 hits:

Rogers Hornsby, 2,930; Willie Keeler, 2,962; Mel Ott, 2,876; Babe Ruth, 2,873; Brooks Robinson, 2,848; George Sisler, 2,812; Lou Gehrig, 2,721; Ted Williams, 2,654; Jimmy Foxx, 2,646; Joe DiMaggio, 2,214.

All-time best: Reardon, Eckersley

Jeff Reardon passed Rollie Fingers

When Jeff Reardon moved ahead of Rollie Fingers and gained the all-time career save record (342), he used the occasion to salute Fingers: "Rollie Fingers was the best," Reardon said. "He's always going to be the best no matter what I do.

In the Red Sox's 1-0 victory against the Yankees at Fenway Park (June 15), Reardon, a native of Dalton, Mass., received a rousing ovation from the capacity crowd of 33,577. Teammates Roger Clemens and Tom Brunansky hoisted him onto their shoulders and carried him to the stands, where his wife, Phebe, was waiting to embrace him.

Reardon was traded to the Atlanta Braves later in the season. He pitched in the playoffs and the World Series.

—by Tom Pedulla, who writes for Gannett Suburban Newspapers

by Russell Beeker, *Baseball Weekly*

Jeff Reardon surpassed Rollie Fingers as the all-time career leader with his 342nd save.

by H. Darr Beiser, *USA TODAY*

Dennis Eckersley, 1992 AL Cy Young Award and MVP winner, may be the best closer in baseball history.

Dennis Eckersley: Most consecutive saves and four 40-save seasons

At 38 years old, Dennis Eckersley hasn't yet approached the all-time career saves record—he has saved 220 games in 246 chances over five-plus seasons—but he is well on his way to the Hall of Fame. He is now the only reliever ever to have four 40-plus save seasons, and has broken the consecutive-save mark with 36 in a row (the old mark was 32). He racked up 51 saves in 1992, second only to the 57 Bobby Thigpen had in 1990. In 1992, Eckersley had a hand in 60 percent of the A's victories, including seven wins of his own. The A's were 64-5 when he pitched. He was rewarded for his efforts with the American League Cy Young and Most Valuable Player awards.

Murray, Winfield: In the same club

by Robert Deutsch, *USA TODAY*

Eddie Murray got his 400th homer and 1,509th RBI, passing Mickey Mantle as the top switch-hit RBI man.

Eddie Murray: 400 HRs, most switch-hit RBIs

Eddie Murray made 1992 a banner year at the plate by hitting his 400th career home run and driving in his 1,509th run, passing Mickey Mantle as the all-time best switch-hitting RBI man. Murray and Mantle are the only switch-hitters in the 400 club.

Dave Winfield, the only other active player with 400 or more home runs, shares another record with Murray: They are the only 400-homer players never to have hit 40 in a season.

—by Ed Christine

Murray's homer history

Here are Eddie Murray's milestone homers, and the pitchers who allowed them.

▸**No. 1:** April 18, 1977, Pat Dobson, Cleveland.

▸**No. 100:** Aug. 19, 1980, Fred Martinez, California.

▸**No. 200:** April 20, 1984, Ron Davis, Minnesota.

▸**No. 300:** July 31, 1987, Dale Mohorcic, Texas.

▸**No. 400:** May 3, 1992, Marvin Freeman, Atlanta.

Dave Winfield: Getting better all the time

When Dave Winfield became the oldest player (40) to have 100 RBI in a season, he said: "To do it, you have to have a good team, a cause, and be healthy enough to play in a lot of games." His team was the Toronto Blue Jays and his cause was winning the whole thing.

"It wouldn't be as probable on a team that is out of the race," Winfield added. "This team has the energy and enthusiasm. We are working together on this." They worked together all the way to the world championship.

Winfield hit RBI No. 100 in his 2,700th career game. "Now, let me be like that battery and keep going and going and going," he said.

—by Mel Antonen

by H. Darr Beiser, *USA TODAY*

Dave Winfield was the oldest player to hit 100 RBI in a season. He has 1,500-plus RBI and 400-plus homers.

400-home run club

Hank Aaron, 755; Babe Ruth, 714; Willie Mays, 660; Frank Robinson, 586; Harmon Killebrew, 573; Reggie Jackson, 563; Mike Schmidt, 548; Mickey Mantle, 536; Jimmie Foxx, 534; Willie McCovey, 521; Ted Williams, 521; Ernie Banks, 512; Eddie Mathews, 512; Mel Ott, 511; Lou Gehrig, 493; Stan Musial, 475; Willie Stargell; 475; Carl Yastrzemski, 452; Dave Kingman, 442; **Dave Winfield, 432**; Billy Williams, 426; Darrell Evans, 414; **Eddie Murray, 414**; Duke Snider, 407;

The best of both leagues in 1992

AL Manager of the Year: Oakland's Tony LaRussa

Tony La Russa became the first manager to be named Manager of the Year three times when he got 25 of 28 first-place votes to win the AL title in 1992. (He also won in 1983 with the White Sox and 1988 with the A's). The A's went from bashers to survivors—putting 16 players on the disabled list 22 times and using 56 different outfield combinations—and still won their division by six games.

by Robert Deutsch, *USA TODAY*

Jim Leyland was named NL Manager of the Year.

by Robert Hanashiro, *USA TODAY*

Tony LaRussa was named AL Manager of the Year.

NL Manager of the Year: Pittsburgh's Jim Leyland

They said it couldn't be done, but Jim Leyland guided the Pittsburgh Pirates to their third consecutive NL East championship. Leyland received 20 of 24 first-place votes in the balloting for the award, 109 overall. Despite losing Bobby Bonilla and ace John Smiley before the season, the Pirates won 96 games and came within one victory of going to the World Series.

The voting

For the Baseball Writers Association of America's 1992 American League Manager of the Year, with name, team, and votes on a 5-3-1 point basis.

Manager, team	1	2	3	Total
Tony La Russa, Oak.	25	2	1	132
Phil Garner, Mil.	2	21	3	76
Johnny Oates, Bal.	0	4	15	27
Cito Gaston, Tor.	0	0	4	4
Mike Hargrove, Cle.	0	0	4	4

The voting

For the Baseball Writers Association of America's 1992 National League Manager of the Year, with name, team, and votes on a 5-3-1 point basis.

Manager, team	1	2	3	Total
Jim Leyland, Pit.	20	3	0	109
Felipe Alou, Mon.	3	15	5	65
Bobby Cox, Atl.	1	4	12	29
Art Howe, Hou.	0	1	6	9
Lou Piniella, Cin.	0	1	1	4

The best of the AL

▸**Most Valuable Player:** Dennis Eckersley, Oakland Athletics

▸**Cy Young Award:** Dennis Eckersley, Oakland Athletics

▸**Rookie of the Year:** Pat Listach, Milwaukee Brewers

The best of the NL

▸**Most Valuable Player:** Barry Bonds, Pittsburgh Pirates

▸**Cy Young winner:** Greg Maddux, Chicago Cubs

▸**Rookie of the Year:** Eric Karros, Los Angeles Dodgers

1992 baseball obituaries (partial listing)

Jean Yawkey

Jean Yawkey, majority owner of the Boston Red Sox, died Feb. 26. She was 83. Her husband, Thomas Yawkey, bought the team in 1933.

George Giles

George Giles, a former All-Star first baseman for the Negro Leagues' Kansas City Monarchs, died March 3. He was 82.

Larry Rosenthal

Larry Rosenthal, who played for the White Sox, Indians, Yankees, and Athletics, died March 4. He was 81.

Ralph Weigel

Ralph Weigel, former catcher for the Indians, White Sox and Senators, died April 15. He was 70.

Deron Johnson

Angels' batting instructor and former Phillies' slugger Deron Johnson died April 23. He was 53.

Bob Hazle

Bob "Hurricane" Hazle, who hit .403 for half of 1957 with the Milwaukee Braves, died April 25 at 61.

Harlond Clift

Harlond Clift, a former third baseman for the St. Louis Browns, died April 27. He was 79.

Joe Burke

The Kansas City Royals wore the initials "JRB" on their sleeves to honor former general manager Joe Burke, who died May 12. He was 68.

Carl Stotz

Carl Stotz, who started Little League baseball a half-century ago, died on June 4. He was 82.

Eddie Lopat

"Steady Eddie" Lopat, a key pitcher for the Yankees' team that won five consecutive World Series, died June 15. He was 73.

Jeffrey Hoffman

The Eastern League's Albany-Colonie Yankees wore number 38 on the back of their caps and initials on their sleeves to honor Jeffrey Hoffman, one of their pitchers, who died Aug. 29 at age 24.

Billy Herman

Hall of Fame second baseman Billy Herman died Sept. 5. He was 83. He played with the Cubs, Pirates, and Dodgers, and managed the Pirates and the Red Sox.

Aurelio Lopez

Aurelio Lopez, a key member of the bullpen that helped the Tigers win the World Series in 1984, died in a car accident Sept. 22 in Mexico. He was 44.

Bernice Gera

Bernice Gera, the first female umpire in baseball, died of cancer on Sept. 23. She was 61. She had called only one game, in the minor leagues.

Red Barber

Red Barber whose career as a baseball announcer spanned more than 60 years, died Oct. 22, at age 84. He called games for the Reds, Brooklyn Dodgers, and Yankees, and was inducted into the Hall of Fame in 1978.

Chuck Connors

Chuck Connors, former first baseman for the Brooklyn Dodgers and the Chicago Cubs, and star of *The Rifleman* television series, died Nov. 10. He was 71.

Stan Wasiak

Stan Wasiak, the winningest manager in minor league history, died Nov. 20 at 72. He managed 37 straight seasons (2,570-2,345).

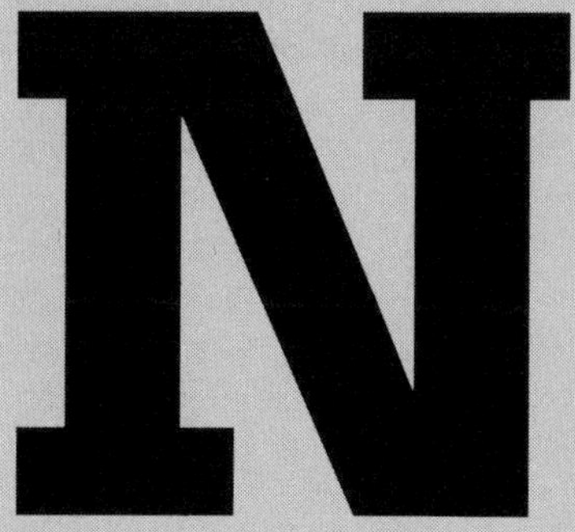

NL/AL Beat

USA SNAPSHOTS®

A look at statistics that shape the sports world

All-Star fixtures in the field

Major league baseball players who played in the most All-Star Games, by position:

Outfield: **Willie Mays** 22 games

Pitcher: **Jim Bunning, Don Drysdale, Juan Marichal, Tom Seaver** 8 games

Infield: **Brooks Robinson** 18 games

Catcher: **Yogi Berra** 14 games

Source: USA TODAY research

By Elys A. McLean, USA TODAY

INSIDE:

NL East 1992: Pirates' three-peat

National League Manager of the Year Jim Leyland admitted that in early spring he too held the majority opinion that the New York Mets were the favorite to win the NL East. The Pirates had lost Bobby Bonilla as a free agent to the Mets. They had traded pitcher John Smiley to the Twins. And they had released closer Bill Landrum.

Meanwhile, the Mets had signed Eddie Murray and Willie Randolph as free agents and had traded for two-time Cy Young-winner Bret Saberhagen. But the closest the Mets got to first place was on opening day. From there on, the season was a downhill dive. Saberhagen was out with a finger injury from May 15 until July 21, and Bonilla had a dismal year. The move of Howard Johnson to center field didn't work, Vince Coleman struggled with injuries and a sub-par performance for the second straight year, and the strong starting pitching never materialized. The Mets admitted it was over in early August, when they traded David Cone to Toronto for prospects Jeff Kent and Ryan Thompson.

The Pirates, on the other hand, began their march to a third consecutive title in April, pushing their way to the top with a nine-game winning streak. By June 3, they were on top to stay.

STANDINGS THROUGH JULY 12, 1992

Team	W	L	Pct	GB
Pittsburgh	49	39	.557	—
St. Louis	44	43	.506	4.5
Montreal	44	44	.500	5
New York	42	46	.477	7
Chicago	40	47	.460	8.5
Philadelphia	36	52	.409	13

Any hope the Cardinals had of getting back in the race ended in early August, when the Pirates swept consecutive four-game weekend series from them. That was part of an 11-game winning streak by the Pirates, whose last challenge came from the Expos.

Montreal had fired manager Tom Runnells on May 22 and replaced him with Felipe Alou. The change produced positive results. The young, inspired Expos managed to pull even with the Pirates for two days at the end of July, but could not bump them into second place. The Expos' last chance came in mid-September, in a two-game series in Pittsburgh. A sweep would have pulled Montreal within two games, but instead they split the two, leaving town four games out of first.

The Pirates clinched the division title on Sept. 27, beating the Mets 4-2. They finished the year with a 96-66 record, the only team in the majors to win 90 or more games each of the three years in the 1990s. Barry Bonds finished the year hitting .311 (34 HR, 103 RBI), and Andy Van Slyke, who had to adjust to a lighter bat due to a back injury, wound up with a .324 average, second in the league. Rookie knuckleballer Tim Wakefield gave the team an extra boost, winning eight of nine decisions after being recalled from Buffalo July 31.

The Cubs, under new manager Jim Lefebvre, were led by the 20-win season of Greg Maddux but didn't have the depth either on offense or their pitching staff to challenge the Pirates.

The Phillies enjoyed a big season from catcher Darren Daulton, who led the league with 109 RBI, and John Kruk, who led the league in hitting for much of the year—but they were mired in last place starting in June.

FINAL STANDINGS

Team	W	L	Pct	GB
x-Pittsburgh	96	66	.593	—
Montreal	87	75	.537	9
St. Louis	83	79	.512	13
Chicago	78	84	.481	18
New York	72	90	.444	24
Philadelphia	70	92	.432	26

—by Rob Rains

NL West 1992: Braves defied odds

Coming into 1992, no NL West team had repeated as division champion since 1978. The Braves thought they could break that streak, even though the Reds were odds-on favorites after trading in the offseason for pitchers Tim Belcher and Greg Swindell, and outfielders Bip Roberts and Dave Martinez. Early in the season, the Reds seemed to be on target. They built their lead to 4 1/2 games over the Braves on June 18, and were able to stay ahead until July 21.

STANDINGS THROUGH JULY 12, 1992

Team	W	L	Pct	GB
Cincinnati	51	35	.593	—
Atlanta	49	37	.570	2
San Diego	47	42	.528	5.5
San Francisco	43	44	.494	8.5
Houston	41	47	.466	11
Los Angeles	39	49	.443	13

The Braves got off to a slow start: They were in last place May 26, seven games behind the first-place Giants (and seven games under .500). Terry Pendleton said his team had to get their 1991-style fire back before 1992 became a lost season. Braves' starting pitchers then combined for a 37-6 record (May 27 to Aug. 10), giving them a four-game lead over the Reds. By Sept. 13, their were 10 1/2 games up, clinching on Sept. 29.

Tom Glavine was the best pitcher in the league in the first half (13-3 at the All-Star break). Pendleton drove in a career-high 105 runs during the season, hitting .311 with 21 homers.

The Reds, who were without several key players for much of the season due to injuries, lost their manager and general manager a week after the season ended. Manager Lou Piniella rejected a new offer, and GM Bob Quinn's contract was not renewed.

The Padres also changed managers, dumping Greg Riddoch on Sept. 23 and replacing him with Jim Riggleman, manager of their Triple A team (Las Vegas) the last two years. The Padres had the best offensive performer in the league, Gary Sheffield, acquired in spring training from Milwaukee. He flirted with becoming the first NL player to win the Triple Crown since 1937, but had to settle for just the batting title (.330, 33 HR, 100 RBI). Teammate Fred McGriff won the home run title (35).

Despite those standouts, Riddoch's team didn't have the pitching or overall offense to keep up with the Braves or Reds. They were barely able to hold off a challenge by the young Houston team for fourth place. The Astros finished with a .500 record and showed signs of being one of the up-and-coming teams in the division.

The problem for the Giants was uncertainty about where they would be playing in 1993. On Aug. 7, owner Bob Lurie announced he had reached an agreement to sell the team to a St. Petersburg, Fla., group that intended to move the Giants there. Then a local group countered with another offer, and the Giants played their final two months not knowing whether they'd ever play at Candlestick again. They limped home in fifth place.

The only reason the Giants didn't fall further was that their longtime rival, the Dodgers, had their worst season since moving to Los Angeles. They finished last for the first time since 1905, as injuries to Eric Davis and Darryl Strawberry wiped out any chance of being competitive. The only bright spot was Rookie-of-the-Year Eric Karros (first base), who hit 20 homers and drove in 88 runs.

FINAL STANDINGS

Team	W	L	Pct	GB
x-Atlanta	98	64	.605	—
Cincinnati	90	72	.556	8
San Diego	82	80	.506	16
Houston	81	81	.500	17
San Francisco	72	90	.444	26
Los Angeles	63	99	.389	35

—by Rob Rains

AL East 1992: Oh! Canada!

The American League East's three-team pennant race was a study in off-season moves. Heading into the season, Toronto was the best team on paper, but on grass and carpet they were second-best. Baltimore was coming off a 67-95 season—hardly a contender. Milwaukee was an aging team with a first-year manager.

Baltimore's first move toward contending in 1992 was actually made in June 1989 when the ground was broken for a new ballpark in Camden Yards. The Orioles were surrounded with a full house nearly every night; they fed off the enthusiasm for almost the entire season.

Phil "Scrap Iron" Garner took over the Brewers, promising a more exciting style of baseball—and he delivered, with help from AL Rookie of the Year shortstop Pat Listach.

Toronto general manager Pat Gillick filled his roster with that elusive quality known as "chemistry." Dave Winfield and Jack Morris brought maturity to a team that was still new to winning big.

STANDINGS THROUGH JULY 12

Team	W	L	Pct.	GB
Toronto	53	34	.609	—
Baltimore	49	38	.563	4
Milwaukee	45	41	.523	7.5
Boston	42	43	.494	10
New York	42	45	.483	11
Detroit	41	48	.461	13
Cleveland	36	52	.409	17.5

The Jays and Orioles tangled beak-to-beak with never more than five games separating them until Sept. 19. The Orioles rode the solid pitching of Sutcliffe (16 wins) and Mike Mussina (18-5, 2.54 ERA), who was a couple of bad starts from serious Cy Young consideration. They also got career years and acrobatic defense from outfielders Brady Anderson (.271, 21 HR, 80 RBI, 53 SB) and Mike Devereaux (.276, 24 HR, 107 RBI, 10 SB). Baltimore's main weakness: a punchless middle of the order with a disappointing Glenn Davis (13 HR, 48 RBI).

The job of catching the Blue Jays fell to Milwaukee. The Brewers led the league in stolen bases (256) and got solid efforts from Jaime Navarro (17-11, 3.33 ERA) and midseason call-up Cal Eldred (11-2, 1.79). Toronto took notice of the Milwaukee bats Aug. 28 at SkyDome when the Brewers set an AL record with 31 hits in a 22-2 win as they closed to within 4.5 games of the Jays. That was the last series between the two teams; the Brewers couldn't close the gap.

David Cone, acquired from the Mets for two prospects, made his first AL start the very next day. One of the game's best strikeout pitchers, Cone went 4-3 with a 2.55 ERA in seven starts, and the Blue Jays known for late-season swoons, went 21-9 in September and October.

Meanwhile, Detroit and New York had ignored their pitching deficiencies and fought losing battles all year.

Boston, with Roger Clemens' typical performance, had respectable starting pitching but its offense disappeared.

Cleveland had as heartening a 76-86 season as possible, with a host of young players improving almost daily. Carlos Baerga joined Rogers Hornsby as the only second basemen to hit .300 with 200 hits, 20 home runs and 100 RBI. Outfielder Kenny Lofton stole 66 bases, and Charles Nagy won four of his last five starts and finished with 17 wins—the most by an Indians right-hander since Bert Blyleven won 19 in 1984.

FINAL STANDINGS

Team	W	L	Pct.	GB
Toronto	96	66	.593	—
Milwaukee	92	70	.568	4
Baltimore	89	73	.549	7
Cleveland	76	86	.469	20
New York	76	86	.469	20
Detroit	75	87	.463	21
Boston	73	89	.451	23

—by John Hunt

AL West 1992: Oakland's comeback

The American League West was supposed to be one of the most competitive divisions in baseball in 1992.

It was, and it wasn't. After the Bret Saberhagen trade (for Gregg Jefferies, Kevin McReynolds and Keith Miller), Kansas City hoped to do well. But after starting 3-17, sixth place was a major accomplishment.

California boasted the best 1-2-3 starting pitchers in the division (Jim Abbott, Chuck Finley and Mark Langston) but none of them reached .500. The Angels finished in a fifth-place tie with the Royals.

Seattle had added slugger Kevin Mitchell to its arsenal, but its team ERA (4.55) was the second-worst in the majors. Seattle brought up the rear, 32 games out of first.

That left Chicago, Texas and Oakland in the race to overtake Minnesota—the defending world champions. Most observers picked Chicago, if any team could do it. Texas even got some votes. But the A's? Definitely not.

STANDINGS THROUGH JULY 12, 1992

Team	W	L	Pct	GB
Minnesota	53	34	.609	—
Oakland	51	36	.586	2
Texas	48	42	.533	6.5
Chicago	43	43	.500	9.5
Kansas City	37	50	.425	16
Seattle	36	53	.404	18
California	35	52	.402	18

Manager Tony La Russa was guiding a team that put 16 players on the disabled list and used 56 different outfield combinations. Dave Stewart, Rickey Henderson, Jose Canseco and Dave Henderson were among the regulars missing from the lineup. But Mark McGwire's return to form, Dennis Eckersley's dominance, and contributions from Mike Bordick and Lance Blankenship helped keep the A's in contention.

Minnesota's staff, led by newcomers John Smiley and Bill Krueger, was rounding into shape, and the hitting had been the majors' best for five years. Rick Aguilera's 26 saves were second only to Eckersley. But the Twins just couldn't shake the battered and bruised A's.

Meanwhile, the Rangers were struggling and the White Sox were floundering. Bobby Valentine was fired as Texas manager on July 9, replaced by Toby Harrah. Kevin Brown was off to a sensational season, winning 13 of his first 18. The offense was among the league's best. But the Rangers couldn't overcome their weak bullpen. They finished 19 games back.

Chicago's vaunted one-two punch turned out to be punchless. Steve Sax (brought over in a winter deal) and Tim Raines were well below .275 at midseason and had combined for only 39 steals. Worse yet, shortstop Ozzie Guillen was out for the year in April with a knee injury.

The race came down to the Twins and the A's. The Twins were 6 1/2 games out at the end of August. On Sept. 28, the A's took a day off, but the Twins lost to Chicago, and Oakland clinched the AL West for the fourth time in five years. La Russa was rewarded with the AL Manager of the Year for his efforts, piloting his team to a last-hurrah title. With 14 players who were free agents, the A's were certain to have a different look when the 1993 season opened.

FINAL STANDINGS

Team	W	L	Pct	GB
x-Oakland	96	66	.593	—
Minnesota	90	72	.556	6
Chicago	86	76	.531	10
Texas	77	85	.475	19
California	72	90	.444	24
Kansas City	72	90	.444	24
Seattle	64	98	.395	32

—by Deron Snyder

Top All-Star vote-getters: National League

Following are the final results of the 1992 All-Star balloting for the top five vote-getters at each position (top 15 for outfielders). A total of 6,622,808 votes were cast.

▸**CATCHER:** 1, Benito Santiago, San Diego, 1,323,419. 2, Darren Daulton, Philadelphia, 862,957. 3, Gary Carter, Montreal, 708,620. 4, Greg Olson, Atlanta, 502,265. 5, Mike Scioscia, Los Angeles, 474,415.

▸**FIRST BASE:** 1, Fred McGriff, San Diego, 1,262,985. 2, Will Clark, San Francisco, 1,246,822. 3, John Kruk, Philadelphia, 815,274. 4, Mark Grace, Chicago, 366,586. 5, Jeff Bagwell, Houston, 330,222.

▸**SECOND BASE:** 1, Ryne Sandberg, Chicago, 2,434,660. 2, Delino DeShields, Montreal, 479,655. 3, Craig Biggio, Houston, 363,841. 4, Kurt Stillwell, San Diego, 355,901. 5, Mark Lemke, Atlanta, 315,546.

▸**SHORTSTOP:** 1, Ozzie Smith, St. Louis, 1,275,282. 2, Tony Fernandez, San Diego, 1,140,280. 3, Barry Larkin, Cincinnati, 995,475. 4, Jay Bell, Pittsburgh, 437,208. 5, Spike Owen, Montreal, 313,253.

▸**THIRD BASE:** 1, Terry Pendleton, Atlanta, 1,222,688. 2, Gary Sheffield, San Diego, 1,155,630. 3, Chris Sabo, Cincinnati, 714,603. 4, Matt Williams, San Francisco, 520,565. 5, Steve Buechele, Pittsburgh, 457,242.

▸**OUTFIELD:** 1, Barry Bonds, Pittsburgh, 1,961,278. 2, Tony Gwynn, San Diego, 1,475,450. 3, Andy Van Slyke, Pittsburgh, 1,009,843. 4, Bobby Bonilla, New York, 935,755. 5, Darryl Strawberry, Los Angeles, 886,775. 6, David Justice, Atlanta, 799,989. 7, Ron Gant, Atlanta, 791,977. 8, Andre Dawson, Chicago, 680,343. 9, Len Dykstra, Philadelphia, 565,500. 10, Felix Jose, St. Louis, 471,295. 11, Brett Butler, Los Angeles, 391,277. 12, Larry Walker, Montreal, 390,911. 13, Marquis Grissom, Montreal, 377,741. 14, Willie McGee, San Francisco, 367,442. 15, Eric Davis, Los Angeles, 293,143.

1992 All-Star Game: NL can't flip losing trend

SAN DIEGO—The National League should have realized what was coming when Ozzie Smith performed his famous backflip running onto the field to start the All-Star Game—and CBS showed the nation a Pizza Hut commercial instead. The ensuing 13-6 loss to the AL marked the worst defeat the NL suffered since a 13-3 loss in 1983—when Smith made his first of 10 straight All-Star starts.

Tom Glavine was a junior in high school that year, and couldn't even remember whether he watched that game or not. The Braves' ace now hopes his memories of the 1992 game are as vague nine years from now. The AL pounced on Glavine for five runs in one-and-two-thirds innings.

The pounding at least helped erase some bad memories for Atlee Hammaker, who was the main victim of the AL's record-setting win in 1983. Hammaker, then with the Giants, was tagged for seven runs and six hits in two-thirds of an inning in that game, which was the record for most hits in an inning—until 1992.

The night would have been almost a total waste for the NL if not for a three-run homer in the eighth inning by the Giants' Will Clark, the first NL three-run homer since a ninth-inning blast by Johnny Callison of the Phillies won the 1964 game at Shea Stadium.

Clark's home run closed the AL lead from 13-1 to 13-4, and two unearned runs in the ninth off Dennis Eckersley helped produce a fitting end for the NL: Pitcher Norm Charlton (Cincinnati) went to bat with two outs and two runners on base because the NL was virtually out of players. Charlton swung at three pitches, fouling off one before fanning for the game's final out.

Charlton had come on to pitch the ninth, retiring the AL in order, after manager Bobby Cox called the bullpen and asked whether Lee Smith or Charlton wanted to pitch. Smith, who had pitched in two previous games—including the forgettable 1983 contest—offered Charlton the chance.

"It was just as good," said Smith, "because if I had had to come up to hit, I don't think I would have gotten the foul ball."

—by Rob Rains

Like father, like son: The Griffeys are an MVP family

SAN DIEGO—It hadn't been the best of seasons for Seattle's Ken Griffey Jr. But as he went 3-for-3 with a home run and was named MVP, his performance recalled the 1980 contest, when his father was named the All-Star MVP. In that game, Senior homered, while 11-year-old Junior was at home watching on TV.

Twelve years later, Junior's blast into the left-field stands was the exclamation point on the AL's 13-6 victory. In homering to the opposite field, Griffey amazed even his teammates.

"You look at the homer he hit and you shake your head," said Cal Ripken, last year's MVP. "We have some young superstars in this league, and he's right at the top."

The AL squad collected 19 hits—an All-Star Game record. Even Indians' pitcher Charles Nagy got into the act, picking up his first base hit since college.

"I thought I was done for the night," said Nagy, who pitched a hitless seventh inning. "Then they told me I had to bat because we were out of pinch-hitters. I thought, 'Oh, great. Let's not make this look too bad.' " Nagy borrowed Sandy Alomar's batting gloves and helmet, and strode to the plate. He swung and missed at the first pitch, but then got on with an infield single.

Roberto Alomar stole two bases in one inning for another All-Star record.

"If I'd known I'd already had a record," said the Blue Jays' second baseman, who stole second and third base in the second inning, "I would have stolen home plate too."

It was the AL's fifth straight win. Several AL veterans pointed to A's manager Tony La Russa, who had been at the helm 1989-91.

"Before him, this game was more of an exhibition," said Boston's Wade Boggs. "But beginning with La Russa and then now with Tom Kelly, we not only came to play, we came to win."

Griffey returned to the Pacific Northwest to try to turn around his team's misfortunes. Several months before, Griffey talked Kevin Mitchell out of quitting. "It was me and Harold Reynolds," Griffey said. "We told him, 'You go home and we're going to come over and bring you back.' People shouldn't quit on Kevin Mitchell yet." And they shouldn't have quit on the AL years ago in All-Star games.

—by Tim Wendel

Top All-Star vote-getters: American League

Following are the final results of the 1992 All-Star balloting for the top five vote-getters at each position (top 15 for outfielders). A total of 6,622,808 votes were cast.

▸**CATCHER:** 1, Sandy Alomar, Cleveland, 948,592. 2, Ivan Rodriguez, Texas, 647,849. 3, Carlton Fisk, Chicago, 602,136. 4, Chris Hoiles, Baltimore, 494,370. 5, Pat Borders, Toronto, 446,425.

▸**FIRST BASE:** 1, Mark McGwire, Oakland, 1,857,425. 2, Frank Thomas, Chicago, 661,903. 3, Cecil Fielder, Detroit, 541,787. 4, Rafael Palmeiro, Texas, 414,137. 5, Don Mattingly, New York, 390,435.

▸**SECOND BASE:** 1, Roberto Alomar, Toronto, 1,868,247. 2, Chuck Knoblauch, Minnesota, 752,822. 3, Steve Sax, Chicago, 521,597. 4, Julio Franco, Texas, 450,226. 5, Bill Ripken, Baltimore, 425,418.

▸**SHORTSTOP:** 1, Cal Ripken, Baltimore, 2,699,773. 2, Manny Lee, Toronto, 387,561. 3, Dickie Thon, Texas, 342,621. 4, Greg Gagne, Minnesota, 333,861. 5, Ozzie Guillen, Chicago, 243,491.

▸**THIRD BASE:** 1, Wade Boggs, Boston, 1,251,144. 2, Robin Ventura, Chicago, 714,872. 3, Carney Lansford, Oakland, 524,904. 4, Kelly Gruber, Toronto, 506,455. 5, Edgar Martinez, Seattle, 500,536.

▸**OUTFIELD:** 1, Kirby Puckett, Minnesota, 2,096,433. 2, Ken Griffey, Seattle, 2,071,407. 3, Jose Canseco, Oakland, 1,011,585. 4, Dave Winfield, Toronto, 926,113. 5, Joe Carter, Toronto, 885,242. 6, Rickey Henderson, Oakland, 809,470. 7, Ruben Sierra, Texas, 769,735. 8, Brady Anderson, Baltimore, 545,981. 9, Juan Gonzalez, Texas, 522,518. 10, Shane Mack, Minnesota, 442,070. 11, Devon White, Toronto, 373,517. 12, George Bell, Chicago, 338,328. 13, Tim Raines, Chicago, 288,677. 14, Kevin Mitchell, Seattle, 277,682. 15, Dave Henderson, Oakland, 273,893.

All-Star Game: AL box score

AMERICANS	4	1	1	0	0	4	0	3	0—13
NATIONALS	0	0	0	0	0	1	0	3	2— 6

AMERICAN LEAGUE

BATTER	ab	r	h	bi	lo	bb	so	avg
Alomar, 2b	3	1	1	0	0	0	0	.333
Baerga, 2b	1	1	1	1	0	0	0	1.000
Nagy, p	1	1	1	0	0	0	0	1.000
Mntgomry,p	0	0	0	0	0	0	0	—
Aguilera, p	1	0	0	0	0	0	1	.000
Eckersley,p	0	0	0	0	0	0	0	—
Boggs, 3b	3	1	1	0	1	0	1	.333
Ventura, 3b	2	1	2	1	0	0	0	1.000
Puckett, lf	3	1	1	0	1	0	1	.333
Clemens, p	0	0	0	0	0	0	0	—
Sierra, rf	2	2	1	2	0	0	0	.500
Carter, rf	3	1	2	1	0	0	0	.667
Fryman,ss	1	1	1	1	0	1	0	1.000
McGwire,1b	3	1	1	2	1	0	0	.333
Molitr,ph-1b	2	0	1	0	2	0	1	.500
Ripken, ss	3	0	1	1	0	0	0	.333
Mussina, p	0	0	0	0	0	0	0	—
Kelly, cf	2	0	1	2	0	0	1	.500
Griffey Jr, cf	3	2	3	2	0	0	0	1.000
Rodriguez, c	2	0	0	0	1	0	1	.000
Alomar Jr, c	3	0	1	0	0	0	0	.333
Langston, p	0	0	0	0	0	0	0	—
Knblch, ph-2b	1	0	0	0	0	1	0	.000
Brown, p	1	0	0	0	2	0	1	.000
McDowell, p	0	0	0	0	0	0	0	—
Martinez, ph	1	0	0	0	0	0	0	.000
Guzman, p	0	0	0	0	0	0	0	—
Anderson, lf	3	0	0	0	2	0	0	.000
TOTALS	**44**	**13**	**19**	**13**	**10**	**2**	**7**	

▸**BATTING—2B:** Baerga (1, off Tewksbury); Ventura (1, off Tewksbury); Kelly (1, off Jones); Griffey Jr (1, off Tewksbury). **HR:** Sierra (1, 6th inning off Tewksbury, 1 on, 2 out); Griffey Jr (1, 3rd inning off Maddux, 0 on, 1 out).

▸**BASERUNNING—SB:** Alomar 2 (2nd base off Glavine/Santiago; 3rd base off Glavine/Santiago). **Team LOB:** 6.

▸**FIELDING—E:** Molitor (1, groundball). **DP:** 1.

PITCHER	ip	h	r	er	bb	so	era
Brown W	1.0	0	0	0	0	1	0.00
McDowell	1.0	0	0	0	0	0	0.00
Guzman	1.0	2	0	0	1	2	0.00
Clemens	1.0	2	0	0	0	0	0.00
Mussina	1.0	0	0	0	0	0	0.00
Langston	1.0	2	1	1	0	1	9.00
Nagy	1.0	0	0	0	0	1	0.00
Montgmry	0.2	2	2	2	0	0	27.00
Aguilera	0.2	1	1	1	0	0	13.50
Eckersley	0.2	3	2	0	0	2	0.00
TOTAL	**9.0**	**12**	**6**	**4**	**1**	**7**	**4.00**

▸**Inherited runners/scored:** Aguilera 2/2.

Nervous newcomers take cues from veterans

When Cal Ripken made his first All-Star start nine years ago, he remembers trying to be invisible in an AL clubhouse that included Rod Carew, Reggie Jackson and George Brett.

"My perception at the time was that Brett had it all together," recalls Ripken. That year's classic was at wind-blown Candlestick Park in San Francisco, where anything hit in the air can be an adventure. As the AL team was taking the field, Brett, the starting third baseman, told Ripken, the starting shortstop, to take any and all popups.

"That threw me at first," said Ripken. "I realized that he was as insecure about playing there as I was. Then I felt like I belonged in a way."

This year's AL squad included 13 players in their first All-Star Game. The Tigers' Travis Fryman and the Twins' Chuck Knoblauch were the first ones in the AL clubhouse this time and, like Ripken almost a decade ago, they kept to themselves, watching the veterans.

"To me, it's great simply to be among these people," said Fryman, the youngest Tiger to hit 20 home runs and drive in 90 runs since Al Kaline in 1955. "I'll especially keep an eye on how Ripken and (Paul) Molitor do things."

As the Tigers' lone representative in this year's All-Star Game, Fryman couldn't forget that teammates Cecil Fielder and Mickey Tettleton had been left off this season's squad.

"They both deserved to be here," he said. "It's going to feel strange to take the field without them. But they both told me to go out and have fun."

Knoblauch said he would wait until after the All-Star break before trying to assess what he had seen and learned here.

"I'd think this has to be like playing in the World Series," he said. "It all sinks in after you've done it." About the only thing Knoblauch planned to do was to talk to NL starting shortstop Ozzie Smith, who had been his idol as a kid in Houston.

"To be playing in the same game that he is—that's where things get spooky for me," Knoblauch said.

Rangers' catcher Ivan Rodriguez wanted to shake hands with every player in the AL clubhouse.

"I'm going to see them all," he said. "I'm just going to have a good time here."

Cleveland's Charles Nagy stood nervously in front of his locker stall, wondering when it would be all right to get out the camera that teammate Brook

Jacoby suggested he bring to San Diego.

The White Sox' Jack McDowell, a returning All-Star, said he knew what Nagy and the others were going through: "Last year I just stood in the corner," he said. "I couldn't believe that I was there."

Nagy said he had "a thousand questions" to ask veteran pitchers Roger Clemens, Dennis Eckersley and Mark Langston. Nagy was the first AL pitcher to get a hit in an All-Star Game since 1962.

—by Tim Wendel

Birds of a feather bask in glory together

The Orioles' Brady Anderson arrived at the AL clubhouse and promptly began burrowing through the duffel bag of freebies given to every All-Star.

"This is the happiest day of my life," Anderson said. "Let's take a look at the goodies."

After a pile of T-shirts, sweatshirts and pants accumulated on the floor in front of his locker, he said, "I'm going to wear all of this out there for practice, even my after-game shower towel." Everybody got a souvenir bat, even the pitchers.

"What are you going to use that thing for?" Anderson asked his teammate, pitcher Mike Mussina.

"I don't know," Mussina replied.

"They should have given you guys broomsticks," Anderson said.

McGwire turned worries into home run barrage

Before winning the home run derby, and tying Cal Ripken's record in the process, Mark McGwire was complaining that he never did well in such contests.

"They used to really bother me—you're not sure about the pitchers, you're trying too hard," he said. "You're hitting a batting-practice fastball and that takes more muscle to get out of the park." After teammates Ripken, Ken Griffey Jr., and Joe Carter had staked the AL to an early lead with 15 homers, McGwire got rolling. It appeared he would break Ripken's mark of 12 set in 1991, but his last long fly died at the warning track.

—by Rob Rains and Tim Wendel

All-Star Game: NL box score

AMERICANS 4 1 1 0 0 4 0 3 0—13
NATIONALS 0 0 0 0 0 1 0 3 2 — 6

NATIONAL LEAGUE

BATTER	ab	r	h	bi	lo	bb	so	avg
O.Smith, ss	3	0	1	0	0	0	1	.333
Fernandz, ss	2	1	1	0	0	0	0	.500
Gwynn, rf	2	0	0	0	0	1	0	.000
Kruk, rf	2	1	2	0	0	0	0	1.000
Bonds, lf	3	1	1	0	3	0	0	.333
Roberts, lf	2	1	2	2	0	0	0	1.000
McGriff, 1b	3	0	2	1	0	0	0	.667
Martinez, p	0	0	0	0	0	0	0	—
Jones, p	0	0	0	0	0	0	0	—
Pagnozzi, ph	1	0	0	0	2	0	0	.000
Charlton, p	1	0	0	0	2	0	1	.000
Pendltn, 3b	2	0	1	0	0	0	0	.500
Tewksbry, p	0	0	0	0	0	0	0	—
Smoltz, p	0	0	0	0	0	0	0	—
Clark, ph-1b	2	1	1	3	1	0	1	.500
VanSlyke,cf	2	0	0	0	2	0	0	.000
Gant, ph-cf	2	0	0	0	1	0	0	.000
Sandberg, 2b	2	0	0	0	1	0	1	.000
Biggio, 2b	2	0	0	0	0	0	1	.000
Santiago, c	1	0	0	0	0	0	1	.000
Daulton, c	3	1	0	0	0	0	0	.000
Glavine, p	0	0	0	0	0	0	0	—
Maddux, p	0	0	0	0	0	0	0	—
Walker, ph	1	0	1	0	0	0	0	1.000
Cone, p	0	0	0	0	0	0	0	—
Sheffield, 3b	2	0	0	0	0	0	0	.000
Sharprsn, 3b	1	0	0	0	1	0	1	.000
TOTALS	**39**	**6**	**12**	**6**	**13**	**1**	**7**	

▸**BATTING—2B:** O.Smith (1, off Guzman); Bonds (1, off Langston). **HR:** Clark (1, 8th inning off Aguilera, 2 on, 2 out). **GIDP:** Van Slyke.

▸**BASERUNNING—Team LOB:** 7.

▸**FIELDING—E:** Kruk (1, 2-base line drive). **Outfield assist:** Gwynn 2 (Ripken at 2B; Fryman at 2B); Kruk (Rodriguez at 3B).

PITCHER	ip	h	r	er	bb	so	era
Glavine	1.2	9	5	5	0	2	27.00
Maddux	1.1	1	1	1	0	0	6.75
Cone	1.0	0	0	0	0	1	0.00
Tewksbury	1.2	4	4	4	1	0	21.60
Smoltz	0.1	1	0	0	0	0	0.00
Martinez	1.0	0	0	0	1	1	0.00
Jones	1.0	4	3	3	0	2	27.00
Charlton	1.0	0	0	0	0	1	0.00
TOTAL	**9.0**	**19**	**13**	**13**	**2**	**7**	**13.00**

▸**Inherited runners/scored:** Maddux 1/0; Smoltz 1/0.

▸**GAME DATA—T:** 2:55. **A:** 59,372.

▸**UMPIRES—HP:** Harvey. **1B:** Garcia. **2B:** Wendlestedt. **3B:** Kosc.

Past history: Overtime didn't pay for juniors

The last time the junior circuit won four games in a row was after World War II, when they reclaimed Ted Williams, Joe DiMaggio, and Bob Feller from the military. Their post-war run was broken in 1950, in the first extra-inning All-Star game. Eight overtime games have been played and the NL has won them all. Here are some highlights.

▸**1950:** The most traumatic overtime game—at least for Red Sox fans—cost Boston the pennant. Ted Williams broke his elbow crashing into the left field fence and didn't play again until mid-September.

▸**1961:** A record seven errors were committed in Candlestick Park's swirling winds and Stu Miller was actually blown off the mound.

▸**1966:** "Merciless sunshine" boosted the temperature to 105 degrees before Maury Wills ended the suffering in the bottom of the 10th.

▸**1967:** Tony Perez finally settled the 15-inning marathon with a home run that gave the NL a 2-1 victory. The 12 pitchers on both sides issued a record 30 strikeouts. AL hurlers didn't give up a single walk, and NL pitchers gave up just two.

▸**1970:** Pete Rose bowled over Ray Fosse (who had tried to block the plate) in the 12th, inflicting what was essentially a career-ending injury for Fosse.

Extra-inning All-Star games

▸**1950:** Nationals won 4-3 in 14
▸**1955:** Nationals won 6-5 in 12
▸**1961:** Nationals won 5-4 in 10
▸**1966:** Nationals won 2-1 in 10
▸**1967:** Nationals won 2-1 in 15
▸**1970:** Nationals won 5-4 in 12
▸**1972:** Nationals won 4-3 in 10
▸**1987:** Nationals won 2- 0 in 13

by H. Darr Beiser, *USA TODAY*

Ken Griffey Jr. followed his father's footsteps, homering and being named All-Star MVP.

All-Star Game: Between the lines at San Diego

▸**Four!:** The AL's four-run outburst in the first was the biggest All-Star inning since 1983.

▸**Brown and Blue:** Kevin Brown was the first All-Star starting pitcher with a color for a name since Vida Blue in 1978. When Blue started, the host Padres' primary color was brown. Now, it is blue.

▸**Numbers only:** New York's Roberto Kelly was the only AL player without a name on his uniform, playing in the Yankees' road jersey. Ryne Sandberg and Greg Maddux (in Cubs' home shirts) were the only nameless players in the NL.

▸**Junior juniors:** The junior circuit got three consecutive junior hits in the first inning: singles by Cal Ripken Jr., Ken Griffey Jr., and Sandy Alomar Jr.

▸**Top sticks in the NL:** Bip Roberts was 2-for-2 with two RBI and a run scored. Will Clark shook off a questionable called third strike and belted a three-run HR his next at-bat.

▸**Top gun in the NL:** David Cone (still a Met at the time) had no trouble with AL hitters in a 1-2-3 fourth inning.

▸**Quote of the day:** "I'd almost rather have gone out there and given up a 600-foot home run," Glavine said after a series of early soft hits doomed the NL.

—by Alvin A. Reid and John Hunt

American League leaders final 1992 statistics

Batting

BATTING AVERAGE	G	AB	R	H	AVG
E. Martinez, Sea	135	528	100	181	.343
Puckett, Minn	160	639	104	210	.329
Thomas, Chi	160	573	108	185	.323
Molitor, Mil	158	609	89	195	.320
Mack, Minn	156	600	101	189	.315
Baerga, Clev	161	657	92	205	.312
Alomar, Tor	152	571	105	177	.310
Griffey, Sea	142	565	83	174	.308
Harper, Minn	140	502	58	154	.307
Bordick, Oak	154	504	62	151	.300

HOME RUNS	
Gonzalez, Tex	43
McGwire, Oak	42
Fielder, Det	35
Belle, Clev	34
Carter, Tor	34
Deer, Det	32
Tettleton, Det	32
Griffey, Sea	27
3 tied	26

RUNS BATTED IN	
Fielder, Det	124
Carter, Tor	119
Thomas, Chi	115
Bell, Chi	112
Belle, Clev	112
Puckett, Minn	110
Gonzalez, Tex	109
Winfield, Tor	108
Devereaux, Balt	107
Baerga, Clev	105

STOLEN BASES	
Lofton, Clev	66
Listach, Mil	54
Anderson, Balt	53
Polonia, Cal	51
Alomar, Tor	49
R.Henderson, Oak	48
Raines, Chi	45
Curtis, Cal	43
Hamilton, Mil	41
Johnson, Chi	41

SLUGGING PERCENTAGE	
McGwire, Oak	.585
E. Martinez, Sea	.544
Thomas, Chi	.536
Griffey, Sea	.535
Gonzalez, Tex	.529
Carter, Tor	.498
Winfield, Tor	.491
Puckett, Minn	.490
Tartabull, NY	.489
Belle, Clev	.477

RUNS SCORED	
Phillips, Det	114
Thomas, Chi	108
Alomar, Tor	105
Knoblauch, Minn	104
Puckett, Minn	104
Raines, Chi	102
Mack, Minn	101
Anderson, Balt	100
E. Martinez, Sea	100
White, Tor	98

HITS	
Puckett, Minn	210
Baerga, Clev	205
Molitor, Mil	195
Mack, Minn	189
Thomas, Chi	185
Mattingly, NY	184
E. Martinez, Sea	181
Devereaux, Balt	180
Knoblauch, Minn	178
Alomar, Tor	177

BASES ON BALLS	
Tettleton, Det	122
Thomas, Chi	122
Phillips, Det	114
Milligan, Balt	106
Tartabull, NY	103
Anderson, Balt	98
R. Henderson, Oak	95
Ventura, Chi	93
McGwire, Oak	90
Knoblauch, Minn	88

DOUBLES	
E. Martinez, Sea	46
Thomas, Chi	46
Mattingly, NY	40
Yount, Mil	40
Griffey, Sea	39
Puckett, Minn	38
Ventura, Chi	38
4 tied	36

TRIPLES	
Johnson, Chi	12
Devereaux, Balt	11
Anderson, Balt	10
Raines, Chi	9
Alomar, Tor	8
Lofton, Clev	8
5 tied	7

ON-BASE PERCENTAGE	
Thomas, Chi	.439
Tartabull, NY	.409
Alomar, Tor	.405
E. Martinez, Sea	.404
Mack, Minn	.394
Molitor, Mil	.389
Phillips, Det	.387
Whitaker, Det	.386
Davis, Minn	.386
McGwire, Oak	.385

TOTAL BASES	
Puckett, Minn	313
Carter, Tor	310
Gonzalez, Tex	309
Thomas, Chi	307
Devereaux, Balt	303
Griffey, Sea	302
Baerga, Clev	299
E. Martinez, Sea	287
Winfield, Tor	286
Molitor, Mil	281

Pitching

EARNED RUN AVERAGE	
Clemens, Bos	2.41
Appier, KC	2.46
Mussina, Balt	2.54
Guzman, Tor	2.64
Abbott, Cal	2.77
Perez, NY	2.87
Nagy, Clev	2.96
McDowell, Chi	3.18
Wegman, Mil	3.20
Smiley, Minn	3.21

WON-LOST		
Morris, Tor	21	6
Brown, Tex	21	11
McDowell, Chi	20	10
Mussina, Balt	18	5
Clemens, Bos	18	11
Fleming, Sea	17	10
Nagy, Clev	17	10
Navarro, Mil	17	11
Moore, Oak	17	12
6 tied	16	

GAMES PITCHED	
Rogers, Tex	81
D. Ward, Tor	79
Olin, Clev	72
Lilliquist, Clev	71
Harris, Bos	70
Eckersley, Oak	69
Henry, Mil	68
Radinsky, Chi	68
Nelson, Sea	66
Parrett, Oak	66

SAVES	
Eckersley, Oak	51
Aguilera, Minn	41
Montgomery, KC	39
Olson, Balt	36
Henke, Tor	34
Farr, NY	30
Russell, Tex -Oak	30
Henry, Mil	29
Olin, Clev	29
Reardon, Bos	27

INNINGS PITCHED	
Brown, Tex	265.2
Wegman, Mil	261.2
McDowell, Chi	260.2
Nagy, Clev	252.0
Perez, NY	247.2
Clemens, Bos	246.2
Navarro, Mil	246.0
Mussina, Balt	241.0
Smiley, Minn	241.0
Morris, Tor	240.2

STRIKEOUTS	
Johnson, Sea	241
Perez, NY	218
Clemens, Bos	208
Guzman, Tex	179
McDowell, Chi	178
Langston, Cal	174
Brown, Tex	173
Nagy, Clev	169
Guzman, Tor	165
Smiley, Minn	163

COMPLETE GAMES	
McDowell, Chi	13
Brown, Tex	11
Clemens, Bos	11
Nagy, Clev	10
Perez, NY	10
Langston, Cal	8
Mussina, Balt	8
Abbott, Cal	7
Fleming, Sea	7
Wegman, Mil	7

SHUTOUTS	
Clemens, Bos	5
Fleming, Sea	4
Mussina, Balt	4
Darling, Oak	4
Erickson, Minn	3
Nagy, Clev	3
Navarro, Mil	3
11 tied	2

National League leaders final 1992 statistics

Batting

BATTING AVERAGE	G	AB	R	H	AVG
Sheffield, SD	146	557	87	184	.330
Van Slyke, Pitt	154	614	103	199	.324
Kruk, Phil	144	507	86	164	.323
Roberts, Cin	147	532	92	172	.323
Gwynn, SD	128	520	77	165	.317
Pendleton, Atl	160	640	98	199	.311
Bonds, Pitt	140	473	109	147	.311
Butler, LA	157	553	86	171	.309
Grace, Chi	158	603	72	185	.307
Larkin, Cin	140	533	76	162	.304

HOME RUNS	
McGriff, SD	35
Bonds, Pitt	34
Sheffield, SD	33
Daulton, Phil	27
Hollins, Phil	27
Sandberg, Chi	26
Walker, Mtl	23
Dawson, Chi	22
Justice, Atl	21
Pendleton, Atl	21

RUNS BATTED IN	
Daulton, Phil	109
Pendleton, Atl	105
McGriff, SD	104
Bonds, Pitt	103
Sheffield, SD	100
Bagwell, Hou	96
Hollins, Phil	93
Murray, NY	93
Walker, Mtl	93
Dawson, Chi	90

STOLEN BASES	
Grissom, Mtl	78
DeShields, Mtl	46
Finley, Hou	44
Roberts, Cin	44
O. Smith, StL	43
Lankford, StL	42
Butler, LA	41
Nixon, Atl	41
Bonds, Pitt	39
Biggio, Hou	38

SLUGGING PERCENTAGE	
Bonds, Pitt	.624
Sheffield, SD	.580
McGriff, SD	.556
Daulton, Phil	.524
Sandberg, Chi	.510
Walker, Mtl	.506
Van Slyke, Pitt	.505
Lankford, StL	.480
Clark, SF	.476
Pendleton, Atl	.473

RUNS SCORED	
Bonds, Pitt	109
Hollins, Phil	104
Van Slyke, Pitt	103
Sandberg, Chi	100
Grissom, Mtl	99
Pendleton, Atl	98
Biggio, Hou	96
Roberts, Cin	92

HITS	
Pendleton, Atl	199
Van Slyke, Pitt	199
Sandberg, Chi	186
Grace, Chi	185
Sheffield, SD	184
Grissom, Mtl	180
Finley, Hou	177
Lankford, StL	175
Roberts, Cin	172
2 tied	171

BASES ON BALLS	
Bonds, Pitt	127
McGriff, SD	96
Butler, LA	95
Biggio, Hou	94
Kruk, Phil	92
Daulton, Phil	88
Bagwell, Hou	84
Justice, Atl	79
O'Neill, Cin	77
Hollins, Phil	76

DOUBLES	
Van Slyke, Pitt	45
Clark, SF	40
Duncan, Phil	40
Lankford, StL	40
Grissom, Mtl	39
Pendleton, Atl	39
Grace, Chi	37
Murray, NY	37
Bell, Pitt	36
Bonds, Pitt	36

TRIPLES	
Sanders, Atl	14
Finley, Hou	13
Van Slyke, Pitt	12
Alicea, StL	11
Butler, LA	11
DeShields, Mtl	8
Morandini, Phil	8
Offerman, LA	8
Sandberg, Chi	8
A. Cole, Pitt	7

ON-BASE PERCENTAGE	
Bonds, Pitt	.456
Kruk, Phil	.423
Butler, LA	.413
McGriff, SD	.394
Roberts, Cin	.393
Sheffield, SD	.385
Daulton, Phil	.385
Clark, SF	.384
Van Slyke, Pitt	.381
Grace, Chi	.380

TOTAL BASES	
Sheffield, SD	323
Sandberg, Chi	312
Van Slyke, Pitt	310
Pendleton, Atl	303
Bonds, Pitt	295
McGriff, SD	295
Lankford, StL	287
Hollins, Phil	275
Grissom, Mtl	273
Walker, Mtl	267

Pitching

EARNED RUN AVERAGE	
Swift, SF	2.08
Tewksbury, StL	2.16
Maddux, Chi	2.18
Schilling, Phil	2.35
Martinez, Mtl	2.47
Morgan, Chi	2.55
Rijo, Cin	2.56
Hill, Mtl	2.68
Swindell, Cin	2.70
Fernandez, NY	2.73

WON-LOST		
Glavine, Atl	20	8
Maddux, Chi	20	11
Tewksbury, StL	16	5
Morgan, Chi	16	8
Hill, Mtl	16	9
Martinez, Mtl	16	11
5 tied	15	

GAMES PITCHED	
Boever, Hou	81
D. Jones, Hou	80
Hernandez, Hou	77
Perez, StL	77
Innis, NY	76
Carpenter, StL	73
McElroy, Chi	72
McClure, StL	71
3 tied	70

SAVES	
L. Smith, StL	43
Myers, SD	38
Wetteland, Mtl	37
D. Jones, Hou	36
Mit. Williams, Phil	29
Charlton, Cin	26
Dibble, Cin	25
Belinda, Pitt	18
Beck, SF	17
3 tied	15

INNINGS PITCHED	
Maddux, Chi	268.0
Drabek, Pitt	256.2
Smoltz, Atl	246.2
Morgan, Chi	240.0
Avery, Atl	233.2
Tewksbury, StL	233.0
Benes, SD	231.1
Mulholland, Phil	229.0
Belcher, Cin	227.2
2 tied	226.1

STRIKEOUTS	
Smoltz, Atl	215
Cone, NY	214
Maddux, Chi	199
Fernandez, NY	193
Drabek, Pitt	177
Rijo, Cin	171
Benes, SD	169
Harnisch, Hou	164
Ke. Gross, LA	158
Candiotti, LA	152

COMPLETE GAMES	
Mulholland, Phil	12
Drabek, Pitt	10
Schilling, Phil	10
Maddux, Chi	9
Smoltz, Atl	9
Cone, NY	7
Glavine, Atl	7
4 tied	6

SHUTOUTS	
Cone, NY	5
Glavine, Atl	5
Astacio, LA	4
Drabek, Pitt	4
Hurst, SD	4
Maddux, Chi	4
Schilling, Phil	4
5 tied	3

Postseason

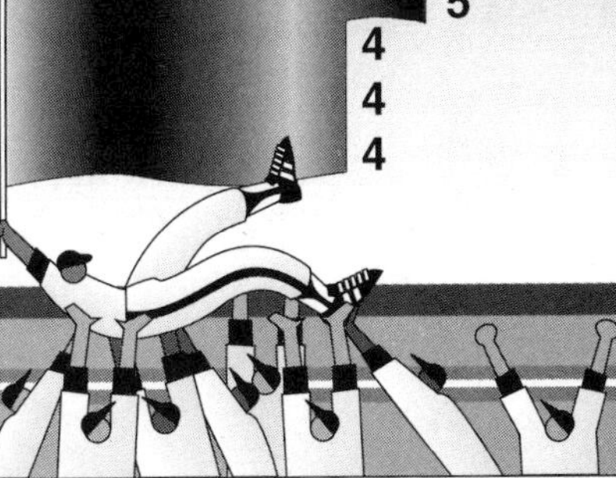

INSIDE:

- NLCS and ALCS game descriptions and composite box scores
- World Series: game-by-game wrap ups and box scores
- *... and more!*

American League Championship Series: Toronto 4, Oakland 2

by H. Darr Beiser, *USA TODAY*

Toronto second baseman Roberto Alomar was named the Most Valuable Player of the series.

Eckersley says Alomar is "the best in the game"

When Roberto Alomar was named ALCS MVP, Dennis Eckersley underlined the honor with a compliment of his own: "He might be the best in the game right now," Eckersley said.

Oakland's long relief led to series' longest game

Game 3 was one of the longest nine-inning games in ALCS history—three hours, 40 minutes—thanks in part to Tony La Russa's tinkering. He used six pitchers, something that has been done only three times in the last 15 years in an LCS game. The other two: Boston, 1990, against Oakland, and Oakland, 1988, against Boston.

Eight errors tied record

Toronto's eight team errors tied a League Championship Series record. Three other teams have reached the dubious mark: the Mets, 1988; the Angels, 1986; the Brewers, 1982. The Brewers and the Blue Jays went on to win the series despite their miscues.

ALCS Game 1: Oakland 4, Toronto 3

▸**Starting pitchers:** Oakland, Dave Stewart; Toronto, Jack Morris.

▸**Winning pitcher:** Jeff Russell, 1-0.

▸**Losing pitcher:** Morris, 0-1.

▸**Save:** Eckersley, 1.

▸**Highlights:** Harold Baines hit the game-winning homer in the ninth inning. All four A's runs came via homers (Mark McGwire and Terry Steinbach hit back-to-back home runs in the second). The Blue Jays added two: Pat Borders in the fifth and Dave Winfield in the sixth. Rickey Henderson was hitless, with a pair of walks. Dennis Eckersley pitched the last inning for the save.

▸**Stat:** The Blue Jays, who hadn't ever won a pennant, had 21 players with playoff experience; the A's, who had won six, had just 17.

▸**Quote:** Jack Morris—"I made three mistakes and the son-of-a-guns hit every one of them out of the park."

ALCS Game 2: Toronto 3, Oakland 1

▸**Starting pitchers:** Oakland, Mike Moore; Toronto, David Cone.

▸**Winning pitcher:** Cone, 1-0.

▸**Losing pitcher:** Moore, 0-1.

▸**Save:** Tom Henke, 1.

▸**Highlights:** Toronto tied the series with a strong performance from David Cone. The Jays jumped out in front in the fifth, when Kelly Gruber followed Candy Maldonado's base on balls with a home run. Cone baffled the A's through eight innings before he gave up a triple to Ruben Sierra in the ninth, then Tom Henke stepped in and got his first save of the series.

▸**Stat:** Oakland hit a meager .194 in the first two games.

▸**Quote:** Ruben Sierra—"We try to hit the ball, maybe try too hard."

ALCS Game 3: Toronto 7, Oakland 5

▸**Starting pitchers:** Toronto, Juan Guzman; Oakland, Ron Darling.
▸**Winning pitcher:** Guzman, 1-0.
▸**Losing pitcher:** Darling, 0-1.
▸**Save:** Henke, 2.
▸**Highlights:** Toronto pounded Oakland relievers to take a 2-1 series lead. The Jays picked up seven runs and 13 hits off four Oakland pitchers, with Candy Maldonado and Roberto Alomar hitting homers. Manny Lee hit a two-run triple off Kelly Downs in the top of the seventh inning, putting the Blue Jays up 5-2. Oakland scored twice in the bottom of the inning, and Tom Henke came in to get his second save of the series.
▸**Stat:** Ron Darling had pitched 19 consecutive scoreless innings against Toronto in 1992.
▸**Quote:** Mark McGwire after laying a hit on catcher Pat Borders—"I've never played football, but I've seen enough that I knew what to do."

ALCS Game 4: Toronto 7, Oakland 6

▸**Starting pitchers:** Toronto, Jack Morris; Oakland, Bob Welch.
▸**Winning pitcher:** Duane Ward, 1-0.
▸**Losing pitcher:** Kelly Downs, 0-1.
▸**Save:** Tom Henke, 3.
▸**Highlights:** The Blue Jays took a 3-1 series lead when Oakland's bullpen blew a 6-1 lead. Jeff Parrett relieved Bob Welch after Alomar doubled in the eighth inning. Alomar stole third, and Joe Carter singled him in. Dave Winfield singled Carter to third, and Eckersley came in. But he blew the save with five hits and two runs in 1 2/3 innings. Pat Borders' sacrifice fly drove in Derek Bell in the 11th for the win.
▸**Stat:** Duane Ward and Tom Henke threw 28 pitches—24 were strikes.
▸**Quote:** Dennis Eckersley—"They crushed me. They got me real bad."

ALCS Game 5: Oakland 6, Toronto 2

▸**Starting pitchers:** Toronto, David Cone; Oakland, Dave Stewart.
▸**Winning pitcher:** Stewart, 1-0.
▸**Losing pitcher:** Cone, 1-1.
▸**Highlights:** Oakland stayed alive with a stellar performance from Dave Stewart (6-0 in the ALCS). The A's pounded David Cone—six runs in the first five innings. Ruben Sierra hit a two-run homer, and Rickey Henderson flustered Cone into a bad throw that allowed him to get to third base. Then Jerry Browne (4-for-4, two RBI) singled in Henderson. Roberto Alomar increased his ALCS hitting streak to 10 games, and Dave Winfield hit his second homer of the series.
▸**Stat:** The Game 5 win tied Tony La Russa with Baltimore's Earl Weaver for the most wins in ALCS history.
▸**Quote:** Tony La Russa—"Stew had the eye of the tiger out there."

ALCS Game 6: Toronto 9, Oakland 2

▸**Starting pitchers:** Oakland, Mike Moore; Toronto, Juan Guzman.
▸**Winning pitcher:** Guzman, 2-0.
▸**Losing pitcher:** Moore, 0-2.
▸**Highlights:** Toronto wrapped up the series with Guzman's pitching and Alomar's bat. Guzman allowed only one earned run. Alomar went 3-for-5 with two stolen bases, and was named the series' MVP. Rickey Henderson's dropped fly ball in the first inning (allowing Devon White to reach base) proved costly when Joe Carter broke out of a series slump with a 405-foot homer.
▸**Stat:** Toronto's ALCS victory was the first for the AL East in six years.
▸**Quote:** Carney Lansford, who announced his retirement after the game—"I can't believe (Tom Henke) was wild enough to walk me. You've got to be wild to walk me, especially in my last at-bat."

ALCS composite box score

▸**Double plays:** Oakland 5, Toronto 7.

▸**Left on base:** Oakland 48, Toronto 45.

▸**Stolen bases:** Wilson 7, Alomar 5, Weiss 2, Carter 2, R. Henderson 2, Fox 2, Blankenship, Bordick, Sierra.

▸**Caught stealing:** White 4, Sierra 2, Maldonado.

▸**Sacrifices:** Baines, Browne, McGwire, Gruber.

▸**Sacrifice flies:** Sierra 2, Lee, Borders 2, White.

▸**Saves:** Eckersley, Henke 3.

▸**Pitching:** Cone pitched to 1 batter in the 9th (Game 2); Russell pitched to 1 batter in the 9th (Game 3); Welch pitched to 1 batter in the 8th (Game 4). Parrett pitched to 2 batters in the 8th (Game 4); Cone pitched to 4 batters in the 5th (Game 5).

▸**Intentional walks:** off Morris (McGwire), off Key (McGwire), off Moore (Winfield).

▸**Hit by pitch:** by Guzman (McGwire).

▸**Wild pitches:** Darling 2, Morris, Russell.

▸**Passed balls:** Borders 3.

▸**Umpires:** Denkinger, Young, Clark, Merrill, Brinkman, Coble.

▸**Official scorers:** Joe Sawchuk, John Hickey (*Hayward Review*, Calif.).

▸**Time:** Game 1, Toronto, 2:47; Game 2, Toronto, 2:58; Game 3, Oakland, 3:41; Game 4, Oakland, 4:25; Game 5, Oakland, 2:51; Game 6, Toronto, 3:15.

▸**Attendance:** Game 1 at Toronto, 51,039; Game 2 at Toronto, 51,114. Game 3 at Oakland, 46,911. Game 4 at Oakland, 47,732. Game 5 at Oakland, 44,955. Game 6 at Toronto, 51,335.

OAKLAND ATHLETICS BATTING

Player	G	AB	R	H	2B	3B	HR	RBI	SO	BB	Avg.	PO	A	E	Pct.
Baines dh	6	25	6	11	2	0	1	4	3	0	.440	0	0	0	—
Browne ph-cf-3b	4	10	3	4	0	0	0	2	0	2	.400	6	0	0	1.000
Sierra rf	6	24	4	8	2	1	1	7	1	2	.333	12	0	0	1.000
Steinbach c	6	24	1	7	0	0	1	5	7	2	.292	30	7	0	1.000
R.Henderson lf	6	23	5	6	0	0	0	1	4	4	.261	15	0	3	.833
Blnknship 2b-pr	5	13	2	3	0	0	0	0	4	3	.231	11	13	2	.923
Wilson cf	5	22	0	5	1	0	0	0	5	1	.227	16	0	0	1.000
Lansford 3b	4	18	0	3	0	0	0	1	1	1	.167	2	9	1	.917
Weiss ss	3	6	1	1	0	0	0	0	1	2	.167	5	6	0	1.000
McGwire 1b	6	20	1	3	0	0	1	3	4	5	.150	46	2	1	.980
Bordick ss-2b	6	19	1	1	0	0	0	0	2	1	.053	15	14	0	1.000
Fox pr-dh-lf	4	1	0	0	0	0	0	0	0	1	.000	1	0	0	1.000
Quirk ph	1	1	0	0	0	0	0	0	0	0	.000	0	0	0	—
Ready ph	1	1	0	0	0	0	0	0	1	0	.000	0	0	0	—
Corsi p	3	0	0	0	0	0	0	0	0	0	—	0	0	0	—
Darling p	1	0	0	0	0	0	0	0	0	0	—	1	0	0	1.000
Downs p	2	0	0	0	0	0	0	0	0	0	—	0	0	0	—
Eckersley p	3	0	0	0	0	0	0	0	0	0	—	0	0	0	—
Honeycutt p	2	0	0	0	0	0	0	0	0	0	—	0	0	0	—
Moore p	2	0	0	0	0	0	0	0	0	0	—	1	1	0	1.000
Parrett p	3	0	0	0	0	0	0	0	0	0	—	0	1	0	1.000
Russell p	3	0	0	0	0	0	0	0	0	0	—	0	0	0	—
Stewart p	2	0	0	0	0	0	0	0	0	0	—	1	1	0	1.000
Welch p	1	0	0	0	0	0	0	0	0	0	—	0	1	0	1.000
Witt p	1	0	0	0	0	0	0	0	0	0	—	0	0	0	—
Totals	**6**	**207**	**24**	**52**	**5**	**1**	**4**	**23**	**33**	**24**	**.251**	**162**	**55**	**7**	**.968**

TORONTO BLUE JAYS BATTING

Player	G	AB	R	H	2B	3B	HR	RBI	SO	BB	Avg.	PO	A	E	Pct.
Sprague ph	2	2	0	1	0	0	0	0	1	0	.500	0	0	0	—
Alomar 2b	6	26	4	11	1	0	2	4	1	2	.423	17	15	0	1.000
Olerud 1b	6	23	4	8	2	0	1	4	5	2	.348	50	1	0	1.000
White cf	6	23	2	8	2	0	0	2	6	5	.348	16	0	1	.923
Borders c	6	22	3	7	0	0	1	3	1	1	.318	37	3	1	.970
Lee ss	6	18	2	5	1	1	0	3	2	1	.278	12	15	3	.893
Maldonado lf	6	22	3	6	0	0	2	6	4	2	.273	10	1	0	1.000
Winfield dh	6	24	7	6	1	0	2	3	2	5	.250	0	0	0	—
Carter rf-1b	6	26	2	5	0	0	1	3	4	2	.192	16	1	1	.933
Gruber 3b	6	22	3	2	1	0	1	2	3	2	.091	5	16	1	.950
Griffin pr-ss	2	2	0	0	0	0	0	0	0	0	.000	0	3	0	1.000
Bell pr-rf	2	0	1	0	0	0	0	0	0	1	—	1	0	0	1.000
Cone p	2	0	0	0	0	0	0	0	0	0	—	0	1	1	.500
Eichhorn p	1	0	0	0	0	0	0	0	0	0	—	0	0	0	—
Guzman p	2	0	0	0	0	0	0	0	0	0	—	0	0	0	—
Henke p	3	0	0	0	0	0	0	0	0	0	—	0	0	0	—
Key p	1	0	0	0	0	0	0	0	0	0	—	0	0	0	—
Morris p	2	0	0	0	0	0	0	0	0	0	—	0	4	0	1.000
Stottlemyre p	1	0	0	0	0	0	0	0	0	0	—	0	0	0	—
Timlin p	2	0	0	0	0	0	0	0	0	0	—	0	0	0	—
Ward p	3	0	0	0	0	0	0	0	0	0	—	1	0	0	1.000
Totals	**6**	**210**	**31**	**59**	**8**	**1**	**10**	**30**	**29**	**23**	**.281**	**165**	**60**	**8**	**.966**

OAKLAND ATHLETICS PITCHING

Pitcher	G	CG	IP	H	R	BB	SO	HB	WP	W	L	Sv	Pct.	ER	ERA
Corsi	3	0	2	2	0	3	0	0	0	0	0	0	—	0	0.00
Honeycutt	2	0	2 0	0	0	1	0	0	0	0	0	0	—	0	0.00
Welch	1	0	7	7	2	1	7	0	0	0	0	0	—	2	2.57
Stewart	2	1	16.2	14	5	6	7	0	0	1	0	0	1.000	5	2.70
Darling	1	0	6	4	3	2	3	0	2	0	1	0	.000	2	3.00
Downs	2	0	2.1	3	3	1	0	0	0	0	1	0	.000	1	3.86
Eckersley	3	0	3	8	2	0	2	0	0	0	0	1	—	2	6.00
Moore	2	0	9.2	11	9	5	7	0	0	0	2	0	.000	8	7.45
Russell	3	0	2	2	2	4	0	0	1	1	0	0	1.000	2	9.00
Parrett	3	0	2.1	6	3	0	1	0	0	0	0	0	—	3	11.57
Witt	1	0	1	2	2	1	1	0	0	0	0	0	—	2	18.00
Totals	**6**	**1**	**54**	**59**	**31**	**23**	**29**	**0**	**3**	**2**	**4**	**1**	**.333**	**27**	**4.50**

TORONTO BLUE JAYS PITCHING

Pitcher	G	CG	IP	H	R	BB	SO	HB	WP	W	L	Sv	Pct.	ER	ERA
Henke	4	0	4.2	4	0	2	2	0	0	0	0	3	—	0	0.00
Key	1	0	3	2	0	2	1	0	0	0	0	0	—	0	0.00
Eichhorn	1	0	1	0	0	0	0	0	0	0	0	0	—	0	0.00
Guzman	2	0	13	12	3	5	11	1	0	2	0	0	1.000	3	2.08
Stottlemyre	1	0	3.2	3	1	0	1	0	0	0	0	0	—	1	2.46
Cone	2	0	12	11	7	5	9	0	0	1	1	0	.500	4	3.00
Morris	2	1	12.1	11	9	9	6	0	1	0	1	0	.000	9	6.57
Ward	3	0	4	5	3	1	2	0	0	1	0	0	1.000	3	6.75
Timlin	2	0	1.1	4	1	0	1	0	0	0	0	0	—	1	6.75
Totals	**6**	**1**	**55**	**52**	**24**	**24**	**33**	**1**	**1**	**4**	**2**	**3**	**.667**	**21**	**3.44**

National League Championship Series: Atlanta 4, Pittsburgh 3

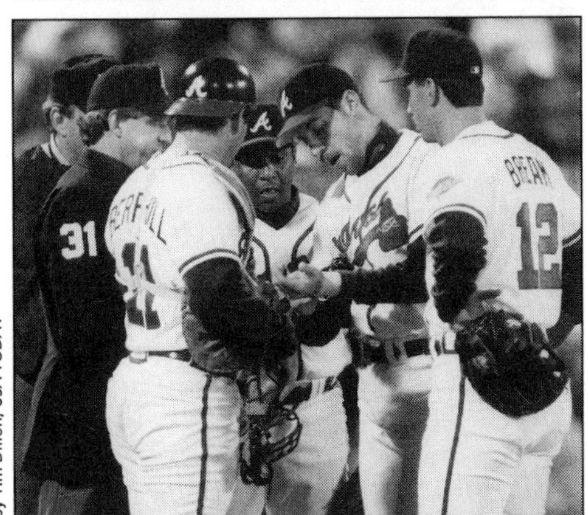

by Tim Dillon, *USA TODAY*

Pitcher John Smoltz was named NLCS MVP.

NLCS Game 1: Atlanta 5, Pittsburgh 1

▸**Starting pitchers:** Pittsburgh, Doug Drabek; Atlanta, John Smoltz.

▸**Winning pitcher:** Smoltz, 1-0.

▸**Losing pitcher:** Drabek, 0-1.

▸**Highlights:** Sid Bream scored on a Mark Lemke single, and the Braves never trailed again. Bream also hit a double in the fourth, driving in David Justice. Then he scored from third on a throwing error by Orlando Merced. Jeff Blauser hit a home run in the fifth inning. Pittsburgh's lone run was a homer from Jose Lind.

▸**Stat:** John Smoltz was 3-0 with a 1.43 ERA in five postseason starts.

▸**Quote:** John Smoltz—"Believe it or not, I think I've had better (stuff)."

NLCS Game 2: Atlanta 13, Pittsburgh 5

▸**Starting pitcher:** Pittsburgh, Danny Jackson; Atlanta, Steve Avery.

▸**Winning pitcher:** Avery, 1-0.

▸**Losing pitcher:** Jackson, 0-1.

▸**Highlights:** The Braves chased Pirate starter Danny Jackson after 1 2/3 innings. They scored four runs in the second inning and added four more in the fifth when Ron Gant smacked his first career grand slam. They put the game way out of reach in the seventh with five runs: Mike Stanton, a relief pitcher, doubled in Gant, Terry Pendleton doubled in Stanton and Otis Nixon, and Dave Justice singled in two more runs. Jose Lind was the Pirates' sole offense: a two-run triple.

▸**Stat:** Steve Avery's record string of scoreless LCS innings (22 1/3) dated back to 1991.

▸**Quote:** Jim Leyland—"We've got to score some runs, we've got to get out in front a little bit, and we've got to win a ballgame. It's that simple."

NLCS Game 3: Pittsburgh 3, Atlanta 2

▸**Starting pitchers:** Atlanta, Tom Glavine; Pittsburgh, Tim Wakefield.

▸**Winning pitcher:** Wakefield, 1-0.

▸**Losing pitcher:** Glavine, 0-1.

▸**Highlights:** Wakefield kept the Pirates alive with a five-hit, complete-game victory. Gary Redus was 3-for-3 with a double, a triple, and a run scored, and Don Slaught homered. Barry Bonds' slump continued; he went 0-for-3, lowering his 1992 NLCS average to .111. The Braves got home runs from Sid Bream and Ron Gant.

▸**Stat:** Jeff King's RBI double in the sixth put the Pirates ahead 2-1, the first time they had the lead in a postseason game since the fifth game of the 1991 playoffs.

▸**Quote:** Rookie knuckleballer Tim Wakefield—"God didn't bless me with a 95 mph fastball. I've got to get by with what I've got."

NLCS Game 4: Atlanta 6, Pittsburgh 4

▸**Starting pitcher:** Atlanta, John Smoltz; Pittsburgh, Doug Drabek.

▸**Winning pitcher:** Smoltz, 2-0.

▸**Losing pitcher:** Drabek, 0-2.

▸**Save:** Jeff Reardon, 1.

▸**Highlights:** Smoltz won his second matchup of the series with Drabek, and the Braves took a commanding 3-1 series lead. His fourth consecutive NLCS win tied Steve Carlton's record. Smoltz played a little offense as well, going 2-for-3 with an RBI, a run scored, and a stolen base. Drabek had another sub-par outing, lasting less than five innings for the second time in the series. Barry Bonds was 0-for-2 with a pair of walks and a pair of strikeouts, lowering his series average to .091. Jeff Reardon got his first save of the series.

▸**Stat:** Sixteen of 26 Braves' runs (in the first four games) were scored with two outs.

▸**Quote:** Bobby Cox—"When Otis (Nixon) gets on base, generally we win, period."

NLCS Game 5: Pittsburgh 7, Atlanta 1

▸**Starting pitchers:** Atlanta, Steve Avery; Pittsburgh, Bob Walk.

▸**Winning pitcher:** Walk, 1-0.

▸**Losing pitcher:** Avery, 1-1.

▸**Highlights:** The real Barry Bonds finally appeared, going 2-for-5 with an RBI, two runs scored, a stolen base, and a running catch worthy of any highlight film. Gary Redus added a pair of doubles. The Pirates hit four doubles in the first inning, and Steve Avery lasted only 1/3 of an inning. Bob Walk pitched the Pirates' second complete game of the series, a three-hitter. Atlanta's lone run came in the ninth inning; Jeff Blauser singled in Lonnie Smith, who had tripled to lead off the inning.

▸**Stat:** The Pirates' seven runs were the most they had scored in a playoff game since Game 3 in 1979. Their 13 hits were the most since Game 2 in 1971.

▸**Quote:** Bob Walk (35 years old)—"This was special to me because I know I'm kind of getting up there in years and I know I might not be in these kinds of situations much longer. I might never have a game like this again."

NLCS Game 6: Pittsburgh 13, Atlanta 4

▸**Starting pitchers:** Pittsburgh, Tim Wakefield; Atlanta, Tom Glavine.

▸**Winning pitcher:** Wakefield, 2-0.

▸**Losing pitcher:** Glavine, 0-2.

▸**Highlights:** The Pirates exploded for eight second-inning runs and tied the series, hoping to be the second team in playoff history to win after being down 3-1. Lloyd McClendon was hot: 3-for-3 with a home run, for a series average of .727. He and Barry Bonds each had two hits in the second, including a homer by Bonds. David Justice was the only Brave able to solve Wakefield's 55-mph knuckleball, hitting two home runs.

▸**Stat:** The Pirates scored 13 runs in the game—one more than they scored in the entire 1991 NLCS.

▸**Quote:** Tom Glavine—"I had mediocre stuff and good location. That's a bad combination."

NLCS Game 7: Atlanta 3, Pittsburgh 2

▸**Starting pitchers:** Pittsburgh, Doug Drabek; Atlanta, John Smoltz.

▸**Winning pitcher:** Reardon, 1-0.

▸**Losing pitcher:** Drabek, 0-3.

▸**Highlights:** Francisco Cabrera hit a ninth-inning, two-out, bases-loaded single, scoring David Justice and Sid Bream, and lifting the Braves past the stunned Pirates into the World Series. Doug Drabek had shut out the Braves for eight innings, but tired in the ninth and was replaced by reliever Stan Belinda, who pitched to Cabrera. John Smoltz, a two-game winner for the Braves, was named series MVP.

▸**Stat:** The 1987 St. Louis Cardinals were the last NL East team to make it to the World Series.

▸**Quote:** Pirate Andy Van Slyke on the Braves' ninth-inning rally—"They haven't invented a word yet to describe that."

PITTSBURGH PIRATES BATTING															
Player	G	AB	R	H	2B	3B	HR	RBI	SO	BB	Avg.	PO	A	E	Pct.
McClendon rf-ph	5	11	4	8	2	0	1	4	1	4	.727	10	0	0	1.000
Espy ph-rf-pr	4	3	0	2	0	0	0	0	1	0	.667	0	0	0	—
Varsho ph-rf	2	2	0	1	0	0	0	0	0	0	.500	0	0	0	—
Redus 1b-ph	5	16	4	7	4	1	0	3	3	2	.438	32	4	0	1.000
Slaught c-ph	5	12	5	4	1	0	1	5	3	6	.333	17	1	0	1.000
VanSlyke cf	7	29	1	8	3	1	0	4	5	1	.276	20	0	0	1.000
Bonds lf	7	23	5	6	1	0	1	2	4	6	.261	17	0	0	1.000
King 3b	7	29	4	7	4	0	0	2	1	0	.241	11	19	1	.968
Lind 2b	7	27	5	6	2	1	1	5	4	1	.222	15	23	2	.950
Cole rf-ph	4	10	2	2	0	0	0	1	2	3	.200	7	1	0	1.000
LaValliere c	3	10	1	2	0	0	0	0	3	0	.200	14	0	0	1.000
Bell ss	7	29	3	5	2	0	1	4	4	3	.172	6	8	1	.933
Merced 1b-ph	3	10	0	1	1	0	0	2	4	2	.100	27	2	1	.967
Drabek p	3	6	0	0	0	0	0	0	4	1	.000	0	0	0	—
Wakefield p	2	6	1	0	0	0	0	0	0	0	.000	3	2	0	1.000
Walk p	2	5	0	0	0	0	0	0	1	0	.000	1	2	0	1.000
Wehner ph	2	2	0	0	0	0	0	0	2	0	.000	0	0	0	—
Garcia 2b	1	1	0	0	0	0	0	0	0	0	.000	0	0	0	—
Belinda p	2	0	0	0	0	0	0	0	0	0	—	0	0	0	—
Cox p	2	0	0	0	0	0	0	0	0	0	—	0	0	0	—
Jackson p	1	0	0	0	0	0	0	0	0	0	—	0	0	0	—
Mason p	1	0	0	0	0	0	0	0	0	0	—	2	0	0	1.000
Neagle p	1	0	0	0	0	0	0	0	0	0	—	0	0	0	—
Patterson p	1	0	0	0	0	0	0	0	0	0	—	0	0	0	—
Tomlin p	2	0	0	0	0	0	0	0	0	0	—	0	1	0	1.000
Totals	**7**	**231**	**35**	**59**	**20**	**3**	**5**	**32**	**42**	**29**	**.255**	**182**	**63**	**5**	**.980**

ATLANTA BRAVES BATTING															
Player	G	AB	R	H	2B	3B	HR	RBI	SO	BB	Avg.	PO	A	E	Pct.
Stanton p	5	1	1	1	1	0	0	1	0	0	1.000	0	1	0	1.000
Treadway ph-2b	3	3	1	2	0	0	0	0	1	0	.667	0	0	0	—
Cabrera ph	2	2	0	1	0	0	0	2	0	0	.500	0	0	0	—
Lemke 2b-3b	7	21	2	7	1	0	0	2	3	5	.333	11	17	0	1.000
LSmith ph	4	6	1	2	0	1	0	1	0	0	.333	0	0	0	—
Nixon cf	7	28	5	8	2	0	0	2	4	4	.286	16	0	0	1.000
Smoltz p	3	7	1	2	0	0	0	1	2	0	.286	0	1	0	1.000
Justice rf	7	25	5	7	1	0	2	6	2	6	.280	19	3	0	1.000
Bream 1b	7	22	5	6	3	0	1	2	0	3	.273	53	4	0	1.000
Pendleton 3b	7	30	2	7	2	0	0	3	2	0	.233	4	19	0	1.000
Blauser ss	7	24	3	5	0	1	1	4	2	3	.208	7	15	2	.917
Hunter 1b-ph	3	5	1	1	0	0	0	0	1	0	.200	7	0	0	1.000
Gant lf	7	22	5	4	0	0	2	6	4	4	.182	16	0	0	1.000
Berryhill c	7	24	1	4	1	0	0	1	2	3	.167	43	5	0	1.000
Sanders ph-lf-cf	4	5	0	0	0	0	0	0	3	0	.000	1	0	0	1.000
Avery p	3	2	0	0	0	0	0	1	1	0	.000	0	0	0	—
Belliard pr-ss-2b	3	2	1	0	0	0	0	0	0	1	.000	2	3	0	1.000
Glavine p	2	2	0	0	0	0	0	0	0	0	.000	1	2	0	1.000
Leibrandt p	2	1	0	0	0	0	0	0	1	0	.000	0	1	0	1.000
Lopez c	1	1	0	0	0	0	0	0	0	0	.000	2	0	0	1.000
PSmith p	2	1	0	0	0	0	0	0	0	0	.000	0	1	0	1.000
Freeman p	3	0	0	0	0	0	0	0	0	0	—	0	2	0	1.000
Mercker p	2	0	0	0	0	0	0	0	0	0	—	0	0	0	—
Reardon p	3	0	0	0	0	0	0	0	0	0	—	0	0	0	—
Wohlers p	3	0	0	0	0	0	0	0	0	0	—	1	0	0	1.000
Totals	**7**	**234**	**34**	**57**	**11**	**2**	**6**	**32**	**28**	**29**	**.244**	**183**	**74**	**2**	**.992**

PITTSBURGH PIRATES PITCHING															
Pitcher	G	CG	IP	H	R	BB	SO	HB	WP	W	L	Sv	Pct.	ER	ERA
Mason	2	0	3.1	0	0	2	1	0	0	0	0	0	—	0	0.00
Belinda	2	0	1.2	2	0	0	2	0	0	0	0	0	—	0	0.00
Cox	2	0	1.1	1	0	1	1	0	0	0	0	0	—	0	0.00
Wakefield	2	2	18	14	6	5	7	0	1	2	0	0	1.000	6	3.00
Drabek	3	0	17	18	11	7	10	0	0	0	3	0	.000	7	3.71
Walk	2	1	11.2	6	5	7	6	0	0	1	0	0	1.000	5	3.86
Patterson	2	0	1.2	3	1	1	1	0	0	0	0	0	—	1	5.40
Tomlin	2	0	2.2	5	2	1	0	0	0	0	0	0	—	2	6.75
Jackson	1	0	1.2	4	4	2	0	0	0	0	1	0	.000	4	21.60
Neagle	2	0	1.2	4	5	3	0	0	0	0	0	0	—	5	27.00
Totals	**7**	**3**	**60.2**	**57**	**34**	**29**	**28**	**0**	**1**	**3**	**4**	**0**	**.429**	**30**	**4.45**

ATLANTA BRAVES PITCHING															
Pitcher	G	CG	IP	H	R	BB	SO	HB	WP	W	L	Sv	Pct.	ER	ERA
Stanton	5	0	4.1	2	1	2	5	0	0	0	0	0	—	0	0.00
Mercker	2	0	3	1	0	1	1	0	0	0	0	0	—	0	0.00
Reardon	3	0	3	0	0	2	3	0	1	1	0	1	1.000	0	0.00
Wohlers	3	0	3	2	0	1	2	0	0	0	0	0	—	0	0.00
Leibrandt	2	0	4.2	4	1	3	3	0	0	0	0	0	—	1	1.93
PSmith	2	0	3.2	2	1	3	3	0	0	0	0	0	—	1	2.45
Smoltz	3	0	20.1	14	7	10	19	0	1	2	0	0	1.000	6	2.66
Avery	3	0	8	13	8	2	3	0	1	1	1	0	.500	8	9.00
Glavine	2	0	7.1	13	11	3	2	2	0	0	2	0	.000	10	12.27
Freeman	3	0	3.2	8	6	2	1	0	0	0	0	0	—	6	14.73
Totals	**7**	**0**	**61**	**59**	**35**	**29**	**42**	**2**	**3**	**4**	**3**	**1**	**.571**	**32**	**4.72**

NLCS composite box score

▸**Double plays:** Pittsburgh 6, Atlanta 3.

▸**Left on base:** Pittsburgh 50, Atlanta 51.

▸**Stolen bases:** Nixon 3, Gant, Smoltz, Bonds.

▸**Caught stealing:** Merced, King.

▸**Sacrifices:** Wakefield 2, Gant, Blauser, Drabek.

▸**Sacrifice flies:** Avery, Van Slyke, McClendon, Merced, Gant.

▸**Pitching:** Patterson pitched to 3 batters in the 7th (Game 1). Stanton pitched to 1 batter in the 8th (Game 2). Glavine pitched to 8 batters in the 2nd (Game 6). P.Smith pitched to 1 batter in the 7th (Game 7). Drabek pitched to 3 batters in the 9th (Game 7).

▸**Intentional walks:** off Walk (Justice), off Neagle (Nixon), off Glavine (Slaught), off Drabek (Lemke), off Smoltz (Lind), off Smoltz (Bonds), off Stanton (McClendon).

▸**Wild pitches:** Smoltz, Avery, Wakefield, Reardon.

▸**Hit by pitch:** by Glavine (Bonds), by Glavine (Bell).

▸**Passed balls:** Slaught 2, Berryhill.

▸**Umpires:** McSherry, Marsh, Montague, Rippley, Darling, Davis.

▸**Official scorers:** Games 1, 2, 6, and 7—Mark Frederickson. Game 3—Bob Webb. Games 4 and 5—Bob Webb and Nick Peters.

▸**Time:** Game 1, Atlanta, 3:00. Game 2, Atlanta, 3:20. Game 3, Pittsburgh, 2:37. Game 4, Pittsburgh, 3:10. Game 5, Pittsburgh, 2:52. Game 6, Atlanta, 2:50. Game 7, Atlanta, 3:22.

▸**Attendance:** Game 1 at Atlanta, 51,971. Game 2 at Atlanta, 51,975. Game 3 at Pittsburgh, 56,610. Game 4 at Pittsburgh, 57,164. Game 5 at Pittsburgh, 52,929. Game 6 at Atlanta, 51,975. Game 7 at Atlanta, 51,975.

World Series Game 1 box

TORONTO —000100000—1
ATLANTA — 00000300x— 3

BATTING

Toronto	ab	r	h	bi	lo	bb	so	avg
White, cf	4	0	0	0	0	0	0	.000
Alomar, 2b	4	0	0	0	0	0	1	.000
Carter, 1b	4	1	1	1	0	0	0	.250
Winfield, rf	3	0	1	0	0	0	0	.333
Maldonado, lf	3	0	0	0	1	0	2	.000
Gruber, 3b	3	0	0	0	1	0	1	.000
Borders, c	3	0	2	0	0	0	0	.667
Lee, ss	3	0	0	0	3	0	0	.000
Morris, p	2	0	0	0	0	0	2	.000
Stottlemyre, p	0	0	0	0	0	0	0	—
Tabler, ph	1	0	0	0	0	0	0	.000
Wells, p	0	0	0	0	0	0	0	—
Totals	30	1	4	1	5	0	6	

▸**BATTING**—HR: Carter. GIDP: Lee.
▸**BASERUNNING**—Team LOB: 2.

Atlanta	ab	r	h	bi	lo	bb	so	avg
Nixon, cf	3	0	1	0	0	1	1	.333
Blauser, ss	4	0	0	0	3	0	2	.000
Belliard, ss	0	0	0	0	0	0	0	—
Pendleton, 3b	4	0	0	0	0	0	1	.000
Justice, rf	2	1	0	0	1	2	1	.000
Bream, 1b	3	0	1	0	0	1	0	.333
Gant, lf	3	1	0	0	2	1	2	.000
Berryhill, c	4	1	1	3	1	0	2	.250
Lemke, 2b	3	0	1	0	0	0	1	.333
Glavine, p	2	0	0	0	1	1	0	.000
Totals	28	3	4	3	8	6	10	

▸**BATTING**—HR: Berryhill.
▸**BASERUNNING**—SB: Nixon; Gant. Team LOB: 7.
▸**FIELDING**—DP: 1.

PITCHING

Toronto	ip	h	r	er	bb	so	era
Morris L,0-1	6	4	3	3	5	7	4.50
Stottlemyre	1	0	0	0	0	2	0.00
Wells	1	0	0	0	1	1	0.00
Atlanta	**ip**	**h**	**r**	**er**	**bb**	**so**	**era**
Glavine W,1-0	9	4	1	1	0	6	1.00

▸**PITCHING**—WP: Morris.

▸**UMPIRES**—HP: Crawford. 1B: Reilly. 2B: West. 3B: Morrison.

World Series Game 1: Atlanta 3, Toronto 1

▸**Key player:** When last seen, left-hander Tom Glavine had been ducking line drives as Pittsburgh routed him in Game 6 of the NLCS. Talk about a turnaround! Glavine used a rolling changeup to complement his fastball and resurrected curve. He yielded a home run to Joe Carter, then sat down the next 12 Jays in a row. "That's vintage Tom Glavine," said teammate John Smoltz.

▸**Key player, part II:** Damon Berryhill is never likely to clear .250, but he easily cleared 385, the sign on the right-field wall, when he mashed the game-winning, three-run homer.

▸**Key pitch:** The splitter is one of the fattest, most-inviting pitches in baseball when it hangs high in the strike zone. Jack Morris threw one with two on in the sixth to "Bye-Bye" Berryhill.

▸**Key inning:** The Blue Jays' seventh. They were suddenly down 3-1. Glavine went to a 3-1 count on three consecutive sluggers—Dave Winfield, Candy Maldonado, and Kelly Gruber—and fought back to retire all three.

▸**Key problem:** Morris couldn't throw strikes. He walked five Braves in innings four, five, and six.

—by Rod Beaton

Canadian baseball facts

▸**Draftees:** Twenty Canadians were selected in the 1992 draft.

▸**Minor figures:** The 1992 minor league season featured 62 Canadians.

▸**Major figures:** Canadians who appeared in the majors in 1992—Denis Boucher, Cleveland; Rheal Cormier, St. Louis; Rob Ducey, Toronto/California; Mike Gardiner, Boston; Vince Horsman, Oakland; Peter Hoy, Boston; Matt Maysey, Montreal; Kirk McCaskill, Chicago White Sox; Dave McKay (coach), Oakland; Paul Quantrill, Boston; Kevin Reimer, Texas; Matt Stairs, Montreal; Larry Walker, Montreal; Steve Wilson, Los Angeles.

▸**World Series:** Reggie Cleveland (Boston, 1975) was the last Canadian to play in the World Series. The last Canadian World Series winner was Ron Taylor, who pitched for the 1964 St. Louis Cardinals and the 1969 New York Mets. Dave McKay (coach, Oakland Athletics, 1990) was the last Canadian to participate in the World Series.

—Source: Major League Baseball Scouting Bureau.

World Series Game 2: Toronto 5, Atlanta 4

▸**Key play (and player):** Ed Sprague's pinch-hit, two-run home run in the ninth inning gave the Blue Jays the victory. This unlikely hero had 47 at-bats and one home run all year. Sprague turned around a Jeff Reardon serve.

▸**Key blunder:** Ninth inning. Reardon walked Derek Bell with one out, trying to close out a 4-3 victory. Walks are poison anytime, but walking a rookie in the ninth of a one-run World Series game is asking for trouble.

▸**Key at-bat:** Ninth inning. Terry Pendleton has a history of World Series heroics. He came up with two on and two out and the Braves an out from losing. He fouled out. They lost.

—*by Rod Beaton*

Canadians flipped over flopped flag

Canadians were up in arms after seeing their country's flag turned upside down during the singing of the national anthems at Game 2 of the World Series. A U.S. Marine color guard from Atlanta made the mistake, displaying the flag with the top of the red maple leaf pointed downward. It wasn't shown on U.S. television but was shown to millions of Canadian viewers. Switchboards lit up all over Canada, and Toronto newspapers were filled with reaction the following day.

Major League Baseball quickly issued an apology "to the people of Canada and to all baseball fans." Chief Warrant Officer Randy Gaddo, a Marine Corps spokesman, said, "It was certainly not intentional. And it will never happen again." But the flag flap wasn't the only mishap. Canadian singer Tom Cochrane left out some words and switched some lines in *O Canada!*, the national anthem.

There was an informal push among Toronto fans to show up at SkyDome with upside-down American flags. Many did. There was one rather obvious problem with that, though: Old Glory is the native flag of most Toronto players.

"I expected to see those USA flags upside-down," said Blue Jay Kelly Gruber. But he didn't like it. "We shouldn't lower ourselves to that," he stated.

—*by Chuck Johnson*

World Series Game 2 box

TORONTO — 0 0 0 0 2 0 0 1 2 — 5
ATLANTA — 0 1 0 1 2 0 0 0 0 — 4

BATTING

Toronto	ab	r	h	bi	lo	bb	so	avg
White, cf	5	0	1	1	1	0	1	.111
Alomar, 2b	4	1	1	0	2	1	0	.125
Carter, lf	3	0	1	0	1	1	1	.286
Winfield, rf	4	0	1	1	1	0	1	.286
Olerud, 1b	4	0	0	0	3	0	1	.000
Gruber, 3b	4	0	0	0	2	0	3	.000
Borders, c	3	1	1	0	0	1	0	.500
Lee, ss	3	1	1	0	1	0	1	.167
Bell, ph	0	1	0	0	0	1	0	—
Griffin, ss	0	0	0	0	0	0	0	—
Cone, p	2	0	2	1	0	0	0	1.000
Wells, p	0	0	0	0	0	0	0	—
Mldnado, ph	1	0	0	0	1	0	1	.000
Stottlemyre, p	0	0	0	0	0	0	0	—
D.Ward, p	0	0	0	0	0	0	0	—
Sprague, ph	1	1	1	2	0	0	0	1.000
Henke, p	0	0	0	0	0	0	0	—
Totals	**34**	**5**	**9**	**5**	**12**	**4**	**9**	

▸**BATTING**—2B: Alomar; Borders. HR: Sprague.
▸**BASERUNNING**—Team LOB: 6.
▸**FIELDING**—E: Borders; Lee. DP: 2.

Atlanta	ab	r	h	bi	lo	bb	so	avg
Nixon, cf	5	0	0	0	1	0	1	.125
Sanders, lf	3	1	1	0	0	2	0	.333
Pendleton, 3b	4	1	1	0	2	1	0	.125
Justice, rf	3	1	1	1	2	1	0	.200
Bream, 1b	1	1	0	0	1	1	0	.250
Hunter, ph-1b	1	0	0	1	0	0	0	.000
Blauser, ss	3	0	1	0	0	1	1	.143
Belliard, ss	0	0	0	0	0	0	0	—
Berryhill, c	3	0	0	0	4	1	2	.143
Lemke, 2b	4	0	1	1	2	0	0	.286
Smoltz, p	3	0	0	0	2	0	2	.000
Stanton, p	0	0	0	0	0	0	0	—
Reardon, p	0	0	0	0	0	0	0	—
L.Smith, ph	0	0	0	0	0	0	0	—
Gant, pr	0	0	0	0	0	0	0	.000
Totals	**30**	**4**	**5**	**3**	**14**	**7**	**6**	

▸**BATTING**—SF: Hunter. GIDP: Smoltz; Lemke.
▸**BASERUNNING**—SB: Sanders 2; Justice; Blauser; Gant. Team LOB: 8.
▸**FIELDING**—E: Bream. DP: 1.

PITCHING

Toronto	ip	h	r	er	bb	so	era
Cone	4.1	5	4	3	5	2	6.23
Wells	1.2	0	0	0	1	2	0.00
Stottlemyre	1	0	0	0	0	0	0.00
D.Ward W,1-0	1	0	0	0	0	2	0.00
Henke S,1	1	0	0	0	1	0	0.00
Atlanta	**ip**	**h**	**r**	**er**	**bb**	**so**	**era**
Smoltz	7.1	8	3	2	3	8	2.45
Stanton H,1	0.1	0	0	0	0	0	0.00
Reardn L,0-1	1.1	1	2	2	1	1	13.50

▸**PITCHING**—HBP: L.Smith by Henke. WP: Smoltz, 2; Cone.

▸**UMPIRES**—HP: Reilly. 1B: West. 2B: Morrison. 3B: Davidson.

World Series Game 3 box

ATLANTA — 0 0 0 0 0 1 0 1 0 — 2
TORONTO — 0 0 0 1 0 0 0 1 1 — 3

BATTING

Atlanta	ab	r	h	bi	lo	bb	so	avg
Nixon, cf	4	1	0	0	0	0	0	.083
Sanders, lf	4	1	3	0	1	0	0	.571
Pendleton, 3b	4	0	2	0	0	0	0	.250
Justice, rf	3	0	1	1	3	1	1	.250
L.Smith, dh	4	0	1	1	3	0	2	.250
Bream, 1b	4	0	2	0	2	0	0	.375
Hunter, pr-1b	0	0	0	0	0	0	0	.000
Blauser, ss	4	0	0	0	2	0	3	.091
Berryhill, c	4	0	0	0	1	0	3	.091
Lemke, 2b	3	0	0	0	1	0	0	.200
Totals	**34**	**2**	**9**	**2**	**13**	**1**	**9**	

▸**BATTING**—2B: Sanders.
▸**BASERUNNING**—SB: Nixon; Sanders. CS: Hunter. Team LOB: 6.
▸**FIELDING**—DP: 1.

Toronto	ab	r	h	bi	lo	bb	so	avg
White, cf	4	0	0	0	1	0	2	.077
Alomar, 2b	4	1	1	0	0	0	2	.167
Carter, rf	3	1	1	1	0	1	0	.300
Winfield, dh	3	0	1	0	0	0	1	.300
Olerud, 1b	3	0	0	0	1	0	2	.000
Sprague, ph	0	0	0	0	0	1	0	1.000
Maldonado, lf	4	0	1	1	1	0	1	.125
Gruber, 3b	2	1	1	1	0	1	0	.111
Borders, c	3	0	1	0	1	0	1	.444
Lee, ss	3	0	0	0	1	0	0	.111
Totals	**29**	**3**	**6**	**3**	**5**	**3**	**9**	

▸**BATTING**—HR: Carter; Gruber. S: Winfield. GIDP: Maldonado.
▸**BASERUNNING**—SB: Alomar; Gruber. Team LOB: 5.
▸**FIELDING**—E: Gruber. Outfield Assist: White; Maldonado. DP: 2.

PITCHING

Atlanta	ip	h	r	er	bb	so	era
Avery L, 0-1	8	5	3	3	1	9	3.38
Wohlers	0.1	0	0	0	1	0	0.00
Stanton	0	0	0	0	1	0	0.00
Reardon	0	1	0	0	0	0	13.50
Toronto	**ip**	**h**	**r**	**er**	**bb**	**so**	**era**
Guzman	8	8	2	1	1	7	1.12
D.Ward W, 2-0	1	1	0	0	0	2	0.00

▸**PITCHING**—Avery pitched to 1 batter in 9th; Stanton pitched to 1 batter in 9th. IBB: Carter by Wohlers; Sprague by Stanton; Justice by Guzman.

▸**UMPIRES**—HP: West. 1B: Morrison. 2B: Davidson. 3B: Shulock.

World Series Game 3: Toronto 3, Atlanta 2

▸**Key player:** Roberto Alomar. He set the winning ninth inning in motion with a lead-off single and a stolen base.

▸**Key play:** Fourth inning. Jays' center fielder Devon White made one of the greatest World Series catches ever, leaping up on the fence to deny David Justice an extra-base hit and probably two RBI. One Braves' baserunner, Terry Pendleton, passed the other, Deion Sanders. The Jays' were denied a triple play only after Sanders scrambled back to second, eluding a tag by Kelly Gruber that appeared to have been made.

▸**Key inning:** The ninth (again). Jays' catcher Pat Borders finally stopped a Braves' stolen-base attempt. The Jays answered with their own steal in the bottom half.

▸**Key blunders:** Fourth inning. The culprits were Pendleton and second-base umpire Bob Davidson. Pendleton passed Sanders and Davidson missed the tag (it hit Sanders' heel).

▸**Key ejection:** Braves' manager Bobby Cox got tossed by home plate umpire Joe West (National League) for complaining about a third strike on Jeff Blauser. The last World Series ejection was St. Louis pitcher Danny (no relation) Cox in Game 7, 1987. The last manager tossed was St. Louis' Whitey Herzog in Game 7, 1985.

▸**Key slump:** Kelly Gruber had a major-league-record postseason hitless streak of 0-for-23, but ended it with a game-tying, eighth-inning homer.

▸**Key gesture:** A U.S. Marine Corps Color Guard joined a Royal Canadian Mounted Police honor guard during the anthems of both countries. The Marines carried the Canadian flag and the Mounties carried the U.S. flag.

—by Rod Beaton

Carter played everywhere

Joe Carter became the first player in World Series history to start three consecutive games at three different positions: first base for Game 1, left field for Game 2, and right field for Game 3. He also hit a home run in Game 3, giving the Blue Jays at least one home run in each of their nine postseason games through Game 3 of the series—a record for consecutive postseason games with a home run.

World Series Game 4: Toronto 2, Atlanta 1

▸**Key player:** Toronto's Jimmy Key. His first World Series start was a gem. He racked up six strikeouts, walked no one, retired 16 in a row, and outdueled a Cy Young Award winner.

▸**Key play:** Braves' catcher Damon Berryhill tried to bunt with runners on the corners and no outs in the Braves' eighth. He popped out and a potentially big inning went on to be a one-run blip. Berryhill made the bunt decision on his own.

▸**Key pitch:** Key's hard sinker. He fired it too hard in the first inning and it flattened out. Then he calmed down, and the Braves flattened out.

▸**Key catch:** Toronto first baseman John Olerud leaned to his backhand behind the bag with two out and two on in the eighth. He retired Jeff Blauser on the sharp, critical play. "I don't know why he was standing two feet off the bag," said Braves' manager Bobby Cox.

▸**Key call:** Home-plate ump Dan Morrison, from the American League, expanded the plate several inches to call a third strike on Candy Maldonado with two on and two out in the Jays' sixth. It had not been a good Series for umpires.

▸**Key stratagem:** Jays' manager Cito Gaston had faith in his No. 4 starter, used him just long enough, got great relief, and had fresher Nos. 1-3 starters lined up, if he needed them

▸**Key pickoff:** Braves' center fielder Otis Nixon opened the game with a single, but got picked off. It helped Key survive a slightly rocky start because Blauser singled right after.

▸**Key stretch:** Key retired 16 consecutive Braves from one out in the first inning through two away in the sixth.

—by Rod Beaton

World Series Game 4 box

ATLANTA — 000000010—1
TORONTO — 00100010x—2

BATTING

Atlanta	ab	r	h	bi	lo	bb	so	avg
Nixon, cf	4	0	2	0	0	0	1	.188
Blauser, ss	4	0	1	0	3	0	1	.133
Pendleton, 3b	4	0	0	0	1	0	1	.188
L.Smith, dh	4	0	0	0	1	0	1	.125
Justice, rf	4	0	0	0	0	0	1	.167
Gant, lf	3	1	1	0	0	0	0	.167
Hunter, 1b	3	0	1	0	0	0	1	.250
Berryhill, c	3	0	0	0	2	0	1	.071
Lemke, 2b	3	0	0	1	0	0	1	.154
Totals	**32**	**1**	**5**	**1**	**7**	**0**	**8**	

▸**BATTING**—2B: Gant.
▸**BASERUNNING**—SB: Nixon; Blauser. Pickoff: Nixon. Team LOB: 4.
▸**FIELDING**—Outfield Assist: Gant. DP: 2.

Toronto	ab	r	h	bi	lo	bb	so	avg
White, cf	4	0	3	1	0	0	0	.235
Alomar, 2b	3	0	0	0	1	1	0	.133
Carter, rf	3	0	0	0	2	1	0	.231
Winfield, dh	3	0	0	0	2	1	0	.231
Olerud, 1b	3	0	2	0	0	0	1	.200
Maldonado, lf	3	0	0	0	4	0	1	.091
Gruber, 3b	2	1	0	0	2	1	0	.091
Borders, c	3	1	1	1	1	0	0	.417
Lee, ss	3	0	0	0	0	0	0	.083
Totals	**27**	**2**	**6**	**2**	**12**	**4**	**2**	

▸**BATTING**—2B: White. HR: Borders.
▸**BASERUNNING**—SB: Alomar. Team LOB: 5.

PITCHING

Atlanta	ip	h	r	er	bb	so	era
Glavine L,1-1	8	6	2	2	4	2	1.59
Toronto	**ip**	**h**	**r**	**er**	**bb**	**so**	**era**
Key W,1-0	7.2	5	1	1	0	6	1.17
D.Ward H,1	0.1	0	0	0	0	1	0.00
Henke S, 2	1	0	0	0	0	1	0.00

▸**PITCHING**—WP: D. Ward.

▸**UMPIRES**—HP: Morrison. 1B: Davidson. 2B: Shulock. 3B: Crawford.

SkyDome fast facts

▸**Date opened:** June 5, 1989.

▸**Playing surface:** Astroturf.

▸**Capacity:** 51,000, five levels including 161 Skyboxes on two levels.

▸**Highlights:** Retractable roof, Jumbotron scoreboard, a hotel with rooms overlooking the field, three restaurants, and a Hard Rock Cafe.

▸**Dimensions:** 328 feet down the lines, 375 in power alleys, and 400 to center field.

▸**Wall height:** 10 feet.

World Series Game 5 box

ATLANTA — 1 0 0 1 5 0 0 0 0 — 7
TORONTO — 0 1 0 1 0 0 0 0 0 — 2

BATTING

Atlanta	ab	r	h	bi	lo	bb	so	avg
Nixon, cf	5	2	3	0	1	0	0	.286
Sanders, lf	5	1	2	1	1	0	1	.500
Pendleton, 3b	5	1	2	1	4	0	1	.238
Justice, rf	3	2	1	1	1	1	1	.200
L.Smith, dh	4	1	1	4	1	0	1	.167
Bream, 1b	4	0	0	0	0	0	0	.250
Blauser, ss	4	0	1	0	0	0	1	.158
Belliard, ss	0	0	0	0	0	0	0	—
Berryhill, c	4	0	1	0	0	0	2	.111
Lemke, 2b	4	0	2	0	1	0	0	.235
Totals	**38**	**7**	**13**	**7**	**9**	**1**	**7**	

▸**BATTING**—2B: Nixon; Pendleton, 2. HR: Justice; L.Smith.
▸**BASERUNNING**—SB: Nixon, 2. CS: Blauser. Team LOB: 5.
▸**FIELDING**—DP: 1.

Toronto	ab	r	h	bi	lo	bb	so	avg
White, cf	4	0	0	0	3	0	2	.190
Alomar, 2b	3	0	0	0	1	1	0	.111
Carter, rf	4	0	1	0	1	0	1	.235
Winfield, dh	4	0	1	0	2	0	1	.235
Olerud, 1b	3	2	2	0	1	0	0	.308
Sprague,ph-1b	1	0	0	0	0	0	0	.500
Maldonado, lf	2	0	0	0	1	2	0	.077
Gruber, 3b	4	0	0	0	4	0	1	.067
Borders, c	4	0	2	2	0	0	0	.438
Lee, ss	3	0	0	0	2	1	0	.067
Totals	**32**	**2**	**6**	**2**	**15**	**4**	**5**	

▸**BATTING**—2B: Borders. GIDP: Alomar.
▸**BASERUNNING**—Team LOB: 7.
▸**FIELDING**—Outfield assist: Maldonado. DP: 1.

PITCHING

Atlanta	ip	h	r	er	bb	so	era
Smoltz W, 1-0	6	5	2	2	4	4	2.70
Stanton S, 1	3	1	0	0	0	1	0.00
Toronto	**ip**	**h**	**r**	**er**	**bb**	**so**	**era**
Morris L, 0-2	4.2	9	7	7	1	5	8.44
Wells	1.1	1	0	0	0	0	0.00
Timlin	1	0	0	0	0	0	0.00
Eichhorn	1	0	0	0	0	1	0.00
Stottlemyre	1	3	0	0	0	1	0.00

▸**PITCHING**—Smoltz pitched to 1 batter in 7th. IBB: Justice by Morris.

▸**UMPIRES**—HP: Davidson. 1B: Shulock. 2B: Crawford. 3B: Reilly.

World Series Game 5: Atlanta 7, Toronto 2

▸**Key player:** Lonnie Smith. The Braves' DH took aim at the right field (opposite-field) fence. His first two tries were routine flies. The third was anything but routine, a fifth-inning grand slam that buried the Blue Jays and returned the Series to Atlanta. It was the first grand slam by a World Series DH.

▸**Key pitcher:** John Smoltz again gave the Braves the big start in a big game. His control was off, but his stuff was prime and his grit helped.

▸**Key pitch:** Jack Morris got a ball up and over the outside half of the plate to Smith, who had been going the opposite way. Smith found a serve high enough to drive all the way for his grand slam homer.

▸**Key inning:** Atlanta's five-run fifth, naturally. All four hits and all five runs came after Morris retired the first two batters. Morris was clearly struggling, but manager Cito Gaston stayed with him; Morris has a man-melting glare for anyone who considers removing him from the mound.

▸**Key call:** Third-base umpire Mike Reilly (American League) called Devon White out for a third-strike swing on a fourth-inning appeal. The Jays stranded two and squandered a chance to break ahead instead of playing catch-up all night. That became too daunting a task an inning later.

—by Rod Beaton

Atlanta-Fulton County Stadium fast facts

▸**Date opened:** April 12, 1966.

▸**Playing surface:** Grass.

▸**Capacity:** 52,013.

▸**Dimensions:** 330 feet down the lines, 385 feet in the power alleys, and 402 feet to center field.

▸**Wall height:** 10 feet.

▸**Highlights:** Jane Fonda. Watching her sleep on husband Ted Turner's shoulder in the middle of a decisive game pales only by comparison to watching her pray for victory when she wakes up. And don't forget the tomahawk chop. You hate it or you love it, but either way it gives you something to argue about when you're standing in line for a hot dog.

▸**Average October temperature:** A mild 62 degrees (Fahrenheit).

World Series Game 6: Toronto 4, Atlanta 3

▸**Key player:** Atlanta's Otis Nixon. His two-out single in the ninth inning evoked and provoked. It evoked memories of Francisco Cabrera's ninth-inning, game-winning hit in Game 7 of the playoffs. It provoked a harried, hurried throw home from Toronto left fielder Candy Maldonado that was almost errant enough to let the winning run cross right there. Then Nixon tried for a two-out bunt single to tie the game in the Braves' valiant 11th-inning rally. It failed.

▸**Key player II:** Candy Maldonado. His play was good, bad, and ugly. Good: fourth-inning home run. Bad: misjudgment on a ninth-inning liner by Cabrera. He barely recovered. If he hadn't, the Jays would have lost right there. Ugly: his throw toward home, next hitter. Without a screen, it would've been some fan's souvenir.

▸**Key play:** Jays' reliever Mike Timlin scrambled off the mound quickly on Nixon's drag bunt. Timlin was fresh from the bullpen, but ready. He was too late for a tag, but made a poised throw over Nixon's left shoulder.

▸**Key inning:** The Braves' ninth. The Braves believed in miracles and nearly came up with one to match their Game 7 playoff shocker. As it is, they rallied for the run they needed to tie the game.

▸**Key stat:** When Jays' closer Tom Henke relinquished a 2-1 lead in the ninth, the Toronto bullpen's World Series scoreless streak ended at 15 1/3 innings. The Jays' pen blew a save for the first time since July 24.

—by Rod Beaton

World Series Game 6 box

TORONTO — 1 0 0 1 0 0 0 0 0 0 2 — 4
ATLANTA — 0 0 1 0 0 0 0 0 1 0 1 — 3

BATTING

Toronto	ab	r	h	bi	lo	bb	so	avg
White, cf	5	2	2	0	0	0	1	.231
Alomar, 2b	6	1	3	0	0	0	0	.208
Carter, 1b	5	0	2	1	3	0	0	.273
Winfield, rf	5	0	1	2	4	1	0	.227
Maldonado, lf	6	1	2	1	2	0	0	.158
Gruber, 3b	4	0	1	0	2	0	0	.105
Borders, c	4	0	2	0	1	1	0	.450
Lee, ss	4	0	1	0	4	0	1	.105
Tabler, ph	1	0	0	0	1	0	0	.000
Griffin, ss	0	0	0	0	0	0	0	—
Cone, p	2	0	0	0	2	1	0	.500
Stottlemyre, p	0	0	0	0	0	0	0	—
Wells, p	0	0	0	0	0	0	0	—
Bell, ph	1	0	0	0	2	0	0	.000
D.Ward, p	0	0	0	0	0	0	0	—
Henke, p	0	0	0	0	0	0	0	—
Key, p	1	0	0	0	0	0	0	.000
Timlin, p	0	0	0	0	0	0	0	—
Totals	**44**	**4**	**14**	**4**	**21**	**3**	**2**	

▸**BATTING**—2B: Carter, 2; Winfield; Borders. HR: Maldonado. S: Gruber. SF: Carter. GIDP: Cone.

▸**BASERUNNING**—SB: White; Alomar. Team LOB: 13.

▸**FIELDING**—E: Griffin.

Atlanta	ab	r	h	bi	lo	bb	so	avg
Nixon, cf	6	0	2	1	2	0	0	.296
Sanders, lf	3	1	2	0	0	0	0	.533
Gant, ph-lf	2	0	0	0	2	0	0	.125
Pendleton, 3b	4	0	1	1	2	0	2	.240
Justice, rf	4	0	0	0	1	1	1	.158
Bream, 1b	3	0	0	0	1	2	0	.200
Blauser, ss	5	2	3	0	1	0	1	.250
Berryhill, c	4	0	0	0	1	0	1	.091
Smoltz, pr	0	0	0	0	0	0	0	.000
Lemke, 2b	2	0	0	0	2	1	1	.211
L.Smith, ph	0	0	0	0	0	1	0	.167
Belliard, 2b	0	0	0	0	0	0	0	—
Avery, p	1	0	0	0	2	0	1	.000
P.Smith, p	1	0	0	0	1	0	1	.000
Treadway, ph	1	0	0	0	0	0	0	.000
Stanton, p	0	0	0	0	0	0	0	—
Wohlers, p	0	0	0	0	0	0	0	—
Cabrera, ph	1	0	0	0	2	0	0	.000
Leibrandt, p	0	0	0	0	0	0	0	—
Hunter, ph	1	0	0	1	0	0	0	.200
Totals	**38**	**3**	**8**	**3**	**17**	**5**	**8**	

▸**BATTING**—2B: Sanders. S: Belliard; Berryhill. SF: Pendleton.

▸**BASERUNNING**—SB: Sanders, 2. CS: Nixon. Team LOB: 10.

▸**FIELDING**—E: Justice. Outfield assist: Sanders. DP: 1.

PITCHING

Toronto	ip	h	r	er	bb	so	era
Cone	6	4	1	1	3	6	3.48
Stottlemyre H,1	.02	1	0	0	0	1	0.00
Wells H,1	0.1	0	0	0	0	0	0.00
D.Ward H,2	1	0	0	0	1	1	0.00
Henke BS,1	1.1	2	1	1	1	0	2.70
Key W,2-0	1.1	1	1	0	0	0	1.00
Timlin S,1	0.1	0	0	0	0	0	0.00
Atlanta	**ip**	**h**	**r**	**er**	**bb**	**so**	**era**
Avery	4	6	2	2	2	2	3.75
P.Smith	3	3	0	0	0	0	0.00
Stanton	1.2	2	0	0	1	0	0.00
Wohlers	0.1	0	0	0	0	0	0.00
Leibrandt L,0-1	2	3	2	2	0	0	9.00

▸**PITCHING**—IBB: Borders. HBP: White.

▸**UMPIRES**—HP: Shulock. 1B: Crawford. 2B: Reilly. 3B: West.

1992: Tied or broken records

▸**Most stolen bases, six-game series:** 5, Otis Nixon and Deion Sanders, 1992.

▸**Most stolen bases, team, six-game series:** 14, Atlanta Braves, 1992.

▸**Most consecutive scoreless innings, bullpen, one series:** 15 1/3, Toronto Blue Jays, 1992.

▸**Most saves, team, six-game series:** 3, Toronto Blue Jays, 1992; tied with Philadelphia, 1980.

▸**Most games won by relief pitcher, team, six-game series:** 2, Duane Ward, 1992; and five others.

▸**Most saves, six-game series:** 2, Tom Henke, 1992; tied with Tug McGraw and Rich Gossage.

Borders was MVP, but he gave the credit to the rest of the Blue Jays

by Robert Deutsch, *USA TODAY*

Catcher Pat Borders, World Series MVP, hit .450 and caught every inning of every game.

"I can't believe they really gave it to me," said Toronto Blue Jays' catcher Pat Borders, 1992 World Series Most Valuable Player. "I never thought I'd make it to the majors, much less win the World Series. Winning the MVP goes way beyond anything I thought I'd ever accomplish."

Borders etched his name alongside Bucky Dent, Gene Tenace, and other improbable Series MVPs by hitting .450 (9-for-20) with a home run and three RBI. He also caught every inning of every game.

Borders has a 14-game postseason hitting streak dating to Game 4 of the 1991 ALCS, longest ever by a catcher.

After committing an error in Game 2, he put in extra practice and was flawless the rest of the way.

"We have a lot of power pitchers," Borders said, "and sometimes their pitches aren't the easiest to handle. (But) I would never compromise their stuff just to make it easier to throw a runner out."

Borders viewed the MVP as a team award: "When you talk about the MVP, Devon White saved the game in Toronto and did some incredible hitting. Roberto Alomar had some great plays, and Joe Carter had a few home runs. It's a shame they had to give it to one person because so many deserve it."

But none more than Borders.

—by Chuck Johnson

World Series MVPs 1955-1991

1955: Johnny Podres, Brooklyn (NL)
1956: Don Larsen, New York (AL)
1957: Lew Burdette, Milwaukee (NL)
1958: Bob Turley, New York (AL)
1959: Larry Sherry, Los Angeles (NL)
1960: Bobby Richardson, New York (AL)
1961: Whitey Ford, New York (AL)
1962: Ralph Terry, New York (AL)
1963: Sandy Koufax, Los Angeles (NL)
1964: Bob Gibson, St. Louis (NL)
1965: Sandy Koufax, Los Angeles (NL)
1966: Frank Robinson, Baltimore (AL)
1967: Bob Gibson, St. Louis (NL)
1968: Mickey Lolich, Detroit (AL)
1969: Donn Clendenon, New York (NL)
1970: Brooks Robinson, Baltimore (AL)
1971: Roberto Clemente, Pittsburgh (NL)
1972: Gene Tenace, Oakland (AL)
1973: Reggie Jackson, Oakland (AL)
1974: Rollie Fingers, Oakland (AL)
1975: Pete Rose, Cincinnati (NL)
1976: Johnny Bench, Cincinnati (NL)
1977: Reggie Jackson, New York (AL)
1978: Bucky Dent, New York (AL)
1979: Willie Stargell, Pittsburgh (NL)
1980: Mike Schmidt, Philadelphia (NL)
1981: Ron Cey, Pedro Guerrero and Steve Yeager, Los Angeles (NL)
1982: Darrell Porter, St. Louis (NL)
1983: Rick Dempsey, Baltimore (AL)
1984: Alan Trammell, Detroit (AL)
1985: Bret Saberhagen, Kansas City (AL)
1986: Ray Knight, New York (NL)
1987: Frank Viola, Minnesota (AL)
1988: Orel Hershiser, Los Angeles (NL)
1989: Dave Stewart, Oakland (AL)
1990: Jose Rijo, Cincinnati (NL)
1991: Jack Morris, Minnesota (AL)

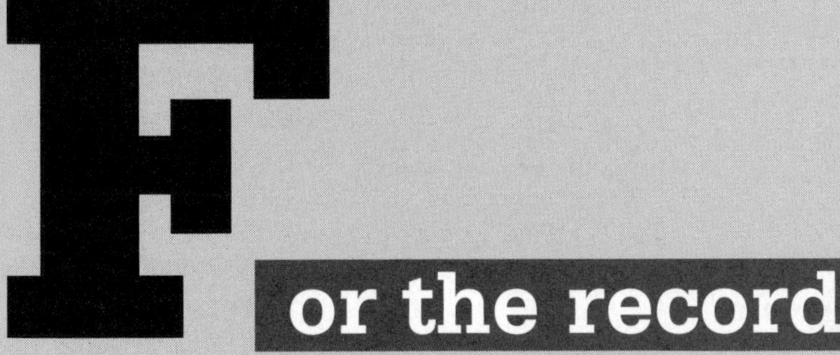

For the record

INSIDE:

- All-time single-season, league and club records
- Active player and individual records
- Top fielding marks
- Perfect game box scores

USA SNAPSHOTS®

A look at statistics that shape the sports world

Leading the league in batting

Ted Williams was the last player to hit .400 for the season in the majors — .406 in 1941. Highest and lowest league-leading season averages since then:

Highest

George Brett, Kansas City 1980	.390
Rod Carew, Minnesota 1977	.388

Lowest

Carl Yastrzemski, Boston 1968	.301
Snuffy Stirnweiss, N.Y. Yankees 1945	.309

Source: USA TODAY research

By Elys A. McLean, USA TODAY

Active player records

Games played: Most, career, active players

2729 Robin Yount, 1974-1992
2707 Dave Winfield, 1973-1992
2562 George Brett, 1973-1992
2474 Carlton Fisk, 1969-1992
2444 Eddie Murray, 1977-1992
2344 Brian Downing, 1973-1992
2310 Andre Dawson, 1976-1992
2296 Gary Carter, 1974-1992
2208 Ozzie Smith, 1978-1992
2202 Willie Randolph, 1975-1992

At-bats: Most, career, active players

10554 Robin Yount, 1974-1992
10047 Dave Winfield, 1973-1992
9789 George Brett, 1973-1992
9124 Eddie Murray, 1977-1992
8890 Andre Dawson, 1976-1992
8703 Carlton Fisk, 1969-1992
8087 Ozzie Smith, 1978-1992
8018 Willie Randolph, 1975-1992
7971 Gary Carter, 1974-1992
7918 Dale Murphy, 1976-1992

Runs: Most, career, active players

1570 Robin Yount, 1974-1992
1551 Dave Winfield, 1973-1992
1514 George Brett, 1973-1992
1472 Rickey Henderson, 1979-1992
1343 Eddie Murray, 1977-1992
1275 Paul Molitor, 1978-1992
1274 Carlton Fisk, 1969-1992
1259 Andre Dawson, 1976-1992
1239 Willie Randolph, 1975-1992
1211 Lou Whitaker, 1977-1992

Hits: Most, career, active players

3025 Robin Yount, 1974-1992
3005 George Brett, 1973-1992
2866 Dave Winfield, 1973-1992
2646 Eddie Murray, 1977-1992
2504 Andre Dawson, 1976-1992
2346 Carlton Fisk, 1969-1992
2281 Paul Molitor, 1978-1992
2210 Willie Randolph, 1975-1992
2145 Willie Wilson, 1976-1992
2108 Ozzie Smith, 1978-1992

Total bases: Most, career, active players

4821 Dave Winfield, 1973-1992
4801 George Brett, 1973-1992
4558 Robin Yount, 1974-1992
4414 Eddie Murray, 1977-1992
4333 Andre Dawson, 1976-1992
3986 Carlton Fisk, 1969-1992
3726 Dale Murphy, 1976-1992
3497 Gary Carter, 1974-1992
3340 Brian Downing, 1973-1992
3338 Paul Molitor, 1978-1992

2B: Most, career, active players

634 George Brett, 1973-1992
558 Robin Yount, 1974-1992
493 Dave Winfield, 1973-1992
462 Eddie Murray, 1977-1992
444 Andre Dawson, 1976-1992
422 Wade Boggs, 1982-1992
421 Carlton Fisk, 1969-1992
405 Paul Molitor, 1978-1992
371 Gary Carter, 1974-1992
369 Cal Ripken, 1981-1992

3B: Most, career, active players

142 Willie Wilson, 1976-1992
134 George Brett, 1973-1992
123 Robin Yount, 1974-1992
99 Brett Butler, 1981-1992
96 Tim Raines, 1979-1992
94 Andre Dawson, 1976-1992
86 Paul Molitor, 1978-1992
85 Juan Samuel, 1983-1992
83 Willie McGee, 1982-1992
83 Dave Winfield, 1973-1992

HR: Most, career, active players

432 Dave Winfield, 1973-1992
414 Eddie Murray, 1977-1992
399 Andre Dawson, 1976-1992
398 Dale Murphy, 1976-1992
375 Carlton Fisk, 1969-1992
340 Jack Clark, 1975-1992
324 Gary Carter, 1974-1992
316 Lance Parrish, 1977-1992
298 George Brett, 1973-1992
285 Darryl Strawberry, 1983-1992

RBI: Most, career, active players

1710 Dave Winfield, 1973-1992
1562 Eddie Murray, 1977-1992
1520 George Brett, 1973-1992
1425 Andre Dawson, 1976-1992
1355 Robin Yount, 1974-1992
1326 Carlton Fisk, 1969-1992
1259 Dale Murphy, 1976-1992
1225 Gary Carter, 1974-1992
1180 Jack Clark, 1975-1992
1073 Brian Downing, 1973-1992

SB: Most, career, active players

1042 Rickey Henderson, 1979-1992
730 Tim Raines, 1979-1992
660 Willie Wilson, 1976-1992
610 Vince Coleman, 1985-1992
542 Ozzie Smith, 1978-1992
437 Brett Butler, 1981-1992
437 Steve Sax, 1981-1992
412 Paul Molitor, 1978-1992
360 Lonnie Smith, 1978-1992
354 Gary Pettis, 1982-1992

BB: Most, career, active players

1286 Rickey Henderson, 1979-1992
1262 Jack Clark, 1975-1992
1243 Willie Randolph, 1975-1992
1197 Brian Downing, 1973-1992
1147 Eddie Murray, 1977-1992
1126 Dave Winfield, 1973-1992
1057 George Brett, 1973-1992
1047 Lou Whitaker, 1977-1992
1004 Wade Boggs, 1982-1992
981 Dale Murphy, 1976-1992

HBP: Most, career, active players

142 Carlton Fisk, 1969-1992
129 Brian Downing, 1973-1992
86 Lonnie Smith, 1978-1992
85 Andre Dawson, 1976-1992
68 Gary Carter, 1974-1992
64 Carney Lansford, 1978-1992
64 Tim Wallach, 1980-1992
60 Joe Carter, 1983-1992
60 Juan Samuel, 1983-1992
59 Willie Wilson, 1976-1992

GIDP: Most, career, active players

292 Dave Winfield, 1973-1992
230 Eddie Murray, 1977-1992
219 Willie Randolph, 1975-1992
215 George Brett, 1973-1992
206 Cal Ripken, 1981-1992
205 Robin Yount, 1974-1992
204 Carlton Fisk, 1969-1992
204 Dale Murphy, 1976-1992
198 Brian Downing, 1973-1992
196 Tony Pena, 1980-1992

BA: Highest, career, active players

.338 Wade Boggs, 1982-1992
.327 Tony Gwynn, 1982-1992
.321 Kirby Puckett, 1984-1992
.311 Don Mattingly, 1982-1992
.311 Edgar Martinez, 1987-1992
.307 George Brett, 1973-1992
.306 Mike Greenwell, 1985-1992
.303 Paul Molitor, 1978-1992
.301 Will Clark, 1986-1992
.301 Ken Griffey, 1989-1992

Slug avg: Highest, career, active players

.528 Fred McGriff, 1986-1992
.512 Darryl Strawberry, 1983-1992
.511 Danny Tartabull, 1984-1992
.511 Jose Canseco, 1985-1992
.509 Cecil Fielder, 1985-1992
.507 Will Clark, 1986-1992
.506 Kevin Mitchell, 1984-1992
.503 Barry Bonds, 1986-1992
.503 Mark McGwire, 1986-1992
.494 Ken Griffey, 1989-1992

Extra-base hits: Most, career, active players

1066 George Brett, 1973-1992
1008 Dave Winfield, 1973-1992
937 Andre Dawson, 1976-1992
924 Robin Yount, 1974-1992
908 Eddie Murray, 1977-1992
843 Carlton Fisk, 1969-1992
786 Dale Murphy, 1976-1992
726 Gary Carter, 1974-1992
711 Jack Clark, 1975-1992
676 Cal Ripken, 1981-1992

Pitchers

Games: Most, career, active players

927 Rich Gossage, 1972-1992
811 Jeff Reardon, 1979-1992
803 Charlie Hough, 1970-1992
794 Nolan Ryan, 1966-1992
787 Lee Smith, 1980-1992
740 Dennis Eckersley, 1975-1992
692 Bert Blyleven, 1970-1992
684 Bob McClure, 1975-1992
657 Jesse Orosco, 1979-1992
639 Dennis Lamp, 1977-1992

Complete games: Most, career, active players

242 Bert Blyleven, 1970-1992
222 Nolan Ryan, 1966-1992
170 Jack Morris, 1977-1992
143 Frank Tanana, 1973-1992
108 Dennis Martinez, 1976-1992
106 Charlie Hough, 1970-1992
103 Dave Stieb, 1979-1992
101 Mike Flanagan, 1975-1992
100 Dennis Eckersley, 1975-1992
89 Roger Clemens, 1984-1992

Shutouts: Most, career, active players

61 Nolan Ryan, 1966-1992
60 Bert Blyleven, 1970-1992
34 Roger Clemens, 1984-1992
34 Frank Tanana, 1973-1992
30 Dave Stieb, 1979-1992
28 Bob Welch, 1978-1992
27 Jack Morris, 1977-1992
23 Orel Hershiser, 1983-1992
23 Bruce Hurst, 1980-1992
23 Dennis Martinez, 1976-1992

Wins: Most, career, active players

319 Nolan Ryan, 1966-1992
287 Bert Blyleven, 1970-1992
237 Jack Morris, 1977-1992
233 Frank Tanana, 1973-1992
202 Charlie Hough, 1970-1992
199 Bob Welch, 1978-1992
193 Dennis Martinez, 1976-1992
181 Dennis Eckersley, 1975-1992
177 John Candelaria, 1975-1992
174 Dave Stieb, 1979-1992

Losses: Most, career, active players

287 Nolan Ryan, 1966-1992
250 Bert Blyleven, 1970-1992
219 Frank Tanana, 1973-1992
191 Charlie Hough, 1970-1992
168 Jack Morris, 1977-1992
156 Dennis Martinez, 1976-1992
145 Dennis Eckersley, 1975-1992
143 Floyd Bannister, 1977-1992
143 Mike Flanagan, 1975-1992
142 Mike Moore, 1982-1992

HR allowed: Most, career, active players

430 Bert Blyleven, 1970-1992
420 Frank Tanana, 1973-1992
357 Jack Morris, 1977-1992
346 Charlie Hough, 1970-1992
316 Nolan Ryan, 1966-1992
307 Dennis Eckersley, 1975-1992
291 Floyd Bannister, 1977-1992
286 Dennis Martinez, 1976-1992
271 Frank Viola, 1982-1992
251 Mike Flanagan, 1975-1992

BB: Most, career, active players

2755 Nolan Ryan, 1966-1992
1542 Charlie Hough, 1970-1992
1322 Bert Blyleven, 1970-1992
1258 Jack Morris, 1977-1992
1200 Frank Tanana, 1973-1992
1003 Dave Stieb, 1979-1992
975 Rick Sutcliffe, 1976-1992
942 Mark Langston, 1984-1992
935 Bob Welch, 1978-1992
926 Dennis Martinez, 1976-1992

K: Most, career, active players

5668 Nolan Ryan, 1966-1992
3701 Bert Blyleven, 1970-1992
2657 Frank Tanana, 1973-1992
2275 Jack Morris, 1977-1992
2171 Charlie Hough, 1970-1992
2118 Dennis Eckersley, 1975-1992
1873 Roger Clemens, 1984-1992
1862 Bob Welch, 1978-1992
1805 Mark Langston, 1984-1992
1723 Floyd Bannister, 1977-1992

Wild pitches: Most, career, active players

274 Nolan Ryan, 1966-1992
179 Jack Morris, 1977-1992
159 Charlie Hough, 1970-1992
114 Bert Blyleven, 1970-1992
112 Frank Tanana, 1973-1992
108 Mike Moore, 1982-1992
101 Dave Stewart, 1978-1992
95 Rick Sutcliffe, 1976-1992
84 Floyd Bannister, 1977-1992
84 Mike Flanagan, 1975-1992

Win pct: Highest, career, active players

.683 Dwight Gooden, 1984-1992
.679 Roger Clemens, 1984-1992
.654 Mike Henneman, 1987-1992
.622 David Cone, 1986-1992
.607 Bob Welch, 1978-1992
.602 Jack McDowell, 1987-1992
.598 John Smiley, 1986-1992
.598 John Candelaria, 1975-1992
.589 Jimmy Key, 1984-1992
.586 Orel Hershiser, 1983-1992

ERA: Lowest, career, active players

2.67 Dave Smith, 1980-1992
2.80 Roger Clemens, 1984-1992
2.84 Jesse Orosco, 1979-1992
2.86 Lee Smith, 1980-1992
2.87 Orel Hershiser, 1983-1992
2.93 Rich Gossage, 1972-1992
2.95 Alejandro Pena, 1981-1992
2.99 Dwight Gooden, 1984-1992
3.05 Jeff Reardon, 1979-1992
3.10 David Cone, 1986-1992

Innings: Most, career, active players

5319.2 Nolan Ryan, 1966-1992
4970.0 Bert Blyleven, 1970-1992
3985.2 Frank Tanana, 1973-1992
3530.0 Jack Morris, 1977-1992
3483.1 Charlie Hough, 1970-1992
3159.1 Dennis Martinez, 1976-1992
2971.1 Dennis Eckersley, 1975-1992
2856.2 Bob Welch, 1978-1992
2822.2 Dave Stieb, 1979-1992
2770.0 Mike Flanagan, 1975-1992

American League single-season records

(ACTIVE PLAYERS in caps)

At-bats: Most, season, AL

705 WILLIE WILSON, KC-1980
692 Bobby Richardson, NY-1962
691 KIRBY PUCKETT, Min-1985
689 Sandy Alomar, Cal-1971
687 TONY FERNANDEZ, Tor-1986
686 Horace Clarke, NY-1970
680 KIRBY PUCKETT, Min-1986
679 Harvey Kuenn, Det-1953
679 Bobby Richardson, NY-1964
677 DON MATTINGLY, NY-1986
677 Jim Rice, Bos-1978

Runs: Most, season, AL

177 Babe Ruth, NY-1921
167 Lou Gehrig, NY-1936
163 Lou Gehrig, NY-1931
163 Babe Ruth, NY-1928
158 Babe Ruth, NY-1920
158 Babe Ruth, NY-1927
152 Al Simmons, Phi-1930
151 Joe DiMaggio, NY-1937
151 Jimmie Foxx, Phi-1932
151 Babe Ruth, NY-1923

Hits: Most, season, AL

257 George Sisler, StL-1920
253 Al Simmons, Phi-1925
248 Ty Cobb, Det-1911
246 George Sisler, StL-1922
241 Heinie Manush, StL-1928
240 WADE BOGGS, Bos-1985
239 Rod Carew, Min-1977
238 DON MATTINGLY, NY-1986
237 Harry Heilmann, Det-1921
236 Jack Tobin, StL-1921

Total bases: Most, season, AL

457 Babe Ruth, NY-1921
447 Lou Gehrig, NY-1927
438 Jimmie Foxx, Phi-1932
419 Lou Gehrig, NY-1930
418 Joe DiMaggio, NY-1937
417 Babe Ruth, NY-1927
410 Lou Gehrig, NY-1931
409 Lou Gehrig, NY-1934
406 Jim Rice, Bos-1978
405 Hal Trosky, Cle-1936

2B: Most, season, AL

67 Earl Webb, Bos-1931
64 George Burns, Cle-1926
63 Hank Greenberg, Det-1934
60 Charlie Gehringer, Det-1936
59 Tris Speaker, Cle-1923
56 George Kell, Det-1950
55 Gee Walker, Det-1936
54 Hal McRae, KC-1977
53 DON MATTINGLY, NY-1986
53 Al Simmons, Phi-1926
53 Tris Speaker, Bos-1912

3B: Most, season, AL

26 Sam Crawford, Det-1914
26 Joe Jackson, Cle-1912
25 Sam Crawford, Det-1903
24 Ty Cobb, Det-1911
24 Ty Cobb, Det-1917
23 Ty Cobb, Det-1912
23 Earle Combs, NY-1927
23 Sam Crawford, Det-1913
23 Dale Mitchell, Cle-1949
22 Bill Bradley, Cle-1903
22 Earle Combs, NY-1930
22 Birdie Cree, NY-1911
22 Elmer Flick, Cle-1906
22 Tris Speaker, Bos-1913
22 Snuffy Stirnweiss, NY-1945

HR: Most, season, AL

61 Roger Maris, NY-1961
60 Babe Ruth, NY-1927
59 Babe Ruth, NY-1921
58 Jimmie Foxx, Phi-1932
58 Hank Greenberg, Det-1938
54 Mickey Mantle, NY-1961
54 Babe Ruth, NY-1920
54 Babe Ruth, NY-1928
52 Mickey Mantle, NY-1956
51 CECIL FIELDER, Det-1990

RBI: Most, season, AL

184 Lou Gehrig, NY-1931
183 Hank Greenberg, Det-1937
175 Jimmie Foxx, Bos-1938
175 Lou Gehrig, NY-1927
174 Lou Gehrig, NY-1930
171 Babe Ruth, NY-1921
170 Hank Greenberg, Det-1935
169 Jimmie Foxx, Phi-1932
167 Joe DiMaggio, NY-1937
165 Lou Gehrig, NY-1934
165 Al Simmons, Phi-1930

SB: Most, season, AL

130 RICKEY HENDERSON, Oak-1982
108 RICKEY HENDERSON, Oak-1983
100 RICKEY HENDERSON, Oak-1980
96 Ty Cobb, Det-1915
93 RICKEY HENDERSON, NY-1988
88 Clyde Milan, Was-1912
87 RICKEY HENDERSON, NY-1986
83 Ty Cobb, Det-1911
83 WILLIE WILSON, KC-1979
81 Eddie Collins, Phi-1910

BB: Most, season, AL

170 Babe Ruth, NY-1923
162 Ted Williams, Bos-1947
162 Ted Williams, Bos-1949
156 Ted Williams, Bos-1946
151 Eddie Yost, Was-1956
149 Eddie Joost, Phi-1949
148 Babe Ruth, NY-1920
146 Mickey Mantle, NY-1957
145 Harmon Killebrew, Min-1969
145 Ted Williams, Bos-1941
145 Ted Williams, Bos-1942

K: Most, season, AL

186 ROB DEER, Mil-1987
185 PETE INCAVIGLIA, Tex-1986
182 CECIL FIELDER, Det-1990
179 ROB DEER, Mil-1986
175 JOSE CANSECO, Oak-1986
175 ROB DEER, Det-1991
175 Dave Nicholson, Chi-1963
175 Gorman Thomas, Mil-1979
172 Bo Jackson, KC-1989
172 Jim Presley, Sea-1986

GIDP: Most, season, AL

36 Jim Rice, Bos-1984
35 Jim Rice, Bos-1985
32 Jackie Jensen, Bos-1954
32 CAL RIPKEN, Bal-1985
31 Tony Armas, Bos-1983
31 Bobby Doerr, Bos-1949
31 Jim Rice, Bos-1983
30 Billy Hitchcock, Phi-1950
30 DAVE WINFIELD, NY-1983
30 Carl Yastrzemski, Bos-1964

BA: Highest, season, AL

.426 Nap Lajoie, Phi-1901
.420 George Sisler, StL-1922
.420 Ty Cobb, Det-1911
.409 Ty Cobb, Det-1912
.408 Joe Jackson, Cle-1911
.407 George Sisler, StL-1920
.406 Ted Williams, Bos-1941
.403 Harry Heilmann, Det-1923
.401 Ty Cobb, Det-1922
.398 Harry Heilmann, Det-1927

Slug avg: Highest, season, AL

.847 Babe Ruth, NY-1920
.846 Babe Ruth, NY-1921
.772 Babe Ruth, NY-1927
.765 Lou Gehrig, NY-1927
.764 Babe Ruth, NY-1923
.749 Jimmie Foxx, Phi-1932
.739 Babe Ruth, NY-1924
.737 Babe Ruth, NY-1926
.735 Ted Williams, Bos-1941
.732 Babe Ruth, NY-1930

Extra-base hits: Most, season, AL

119 Babe Ruth, NY-1921
117 Lou Gehrig, NY-1927
103 Hank Greenberg, Det-1937
100 Jimmie Foxx, Phi-1932
100 Lou Gehrig, NY-1930
99 Hank Greenberg, Det-1940
99 Babe Ruth, NY-1920
99 Babe Ruth, NY-1923
98 Hank Greenberg, Det-1935
97 Babe Ruth, NY-1927

Pitchers

Games: Most, season, AL

90 Mike Marshall, Min-1979
89 MARK EICHHORN, Tor-1987
88 Wilbur Wood, Chi-1968
85 MITCH WILLIAMS, Tex-1987
84 Dan Quisenberry, KC-1985
83 Ken Sanders, Mil-1971
82 Eddie Fisher, Chi-1965
81 KENNY ROGERS, Tex-1992
81 DUANE WARD, Tor-1991
81 John Wyatt, KC-1964

Complete games: Most, season, AL

48 Jack Chesbro, NY-1904
42 George Mullin, Det-1904
42 Ed Walsh, Chi-1908
41 Cy Young, Bos-1902
40 Cy Young, Bos-1904
39 Bill Dinneen, Bos-1902
39 Joe McGinnity, Bal-1901
39 Rube Waddell, Phi-1904
38 Walter Johnson, Was-1910
38 Jack Powell, NY-1904
38 Cy Young, Bos-1901

Saves: Most, season, AL

57 BOBBY THIGPEN, Chi-1990
51 DENNIS ECKERSLEY, Oak-1992
48 DENNIS ECKERSLEY, Oak-1990
46 BRYAN HARVEY, Cal-1991
46 DAVE RIGHETTI, NY-1986
45 DENNIS ECKERSLEY, Oak-1988
45 Dan Quisenberry, KC-1983
44 Dan Quisenberry, KC-1984
43 DENNIS ECKERSLEY, Oak-1991
43 DOUG JONES, Cle-1990

Shutouts: Most, season, AL

13 Jack Coombs, Phi-1910
11 Dean Chance, LA-1964
11 Walter Johnson, Was-1913
11 Ed Walsh, Chi-1908
10 Bob Feller, Cle-1946
10 Bob Lemon, Cle-1948
10 Jim Palmer, Bal-1975
10 Ed Walsh, Chi-1906
10 Joe Wood, Bos-1912
10 Cy Young, Bos-1904

Wins: Most, season, AL

41 Jack Chesbro, NY-1904
40 Ed Walsh, Chi-1908
36 Walter Johnson, Was-1913
34 Joe Wood, Bos-1912
33 Walter Johnson, Was-1912
33 Cy Young, Bos-1901
32 Cy Young, Bos-1902
31 Jim Bagby, Cle-1920
31 Jack Coombs, Phi-1910
31 Lefty Grove, Phi-1931
31 Denny McLain, Det-1968

Losses: Most, season, AL

26 Pete Dowling, Mil-Cle-1901
26 Bob Groom, Was-1909
26 Happy Townsend, Was-1904
25 Patsy Flaherty, Chi-1903
25 Fred Glade, StL-1905
25 Walter Johnson, Was-1909
25 Scott Perry, Phi-1920
25 Red Ruffing, Bos-1928
24 Joe Bush, Phi-1916
24 Pat Caraway, Chi-1931
24 Sam Gray, StL-1931
24 Tom Hughes, NY-Was-1904

HR allowed: Most, season, AL

50 BERT BLYLEVEN, Min-1986
46 BERT BLYLEVEN, Min-1987
43 Pedro Ramos, Was-1957
42 Denny McLain, Det-1966
40 Fergie Jenkins, Tex-1979
40 JACK MORRIS, Det-1986
40 Orlando Pena, KC-1964
40 Ralph Terry, NY-1962
39 Catfish Hunter, Oak-1973
39 JACK MORRIS, Det-1987
39 Jim Perry, Min-1971
39 Pedro Ramos, Min-1961

BB: Most, season, AL

208 Bob Feller, Cle-1938
204 NOLAN RYAN, Cal-1977
202 NOLAN RYAN, Cal-1974
194 Bob Feller, Cle-1941
192 Bobo Newsom, StL-1938
183 NOLAN RYAN, Cal-1976
181 Bob Turley, Bal-1954
179 Tommy Byrne, NY-1949
177 Bob Turley, NY-1955
171 Bump Hadley, Chi-StL-1932

K: Most, season, AL

383 NOLAN RYAN, Cal-1973
367 NOLAN RYAN, Cal-1974
349 Rube Waddell, Phi-1904
348 Bob Feller, Cle-1946
341 NOLAN RYAN, Cal-1977
329 NOLAN RYAN, Cal-1972
327 NOLAN RYAN, Cal-1976
325 Sam McDowell, Cle-1965
313 Walter Johnson, Was-1910
308 Mickey Lolich, Det-1971

Win pct: Highest, season, AL

.938 Johnny Allen, Cle-1937
.893 Ron Guidry, NY-1978
.886 Lefty Grove, Phi-1931
.872 Joe Wood, Bos-1912
.862 Whitey Ford, NY-1961
.862 Bill Donovan, Det-1907
.857 ROGER CLEMENS, Bos-1986
.850 Chief Bender, Phi-1914
.849 Lefty Grove, Phi-1930
.842 Ralph Terry, NY-1961
.842 Schoolboy Rowe, Det-1940
.842 Sandy Consuegra, Chi-1954

ERA: Lowest, season, AL

0.96 Dutch Leonard, Bos-1914
1.14 Walter Johnson, Was-1913
1.16 Addie Joss, Cle-1908
1.26 Cy Young, Bos-1908
1.27 Ed Walsh, Chi-1910
1.27 Walter Johnson, Was-1918
1.30 Jack Coombs, Phi-1910
1.35 Walter Johnson, Was-1910
1.39 Walter Johnson, Was-1912
1.39 Harry Krause, Phi-1909

Innings: Most, season, AL

464.0 Ed Walsh, Chi-1908
454.2 Jack Chesbro, NY-1904
422.1 Ed Walsh, Chi-1907
393.0 Ed Walsh, Chi-1912
390.1 Jack Powell, NY-1904
384.2 Cy Young, Bos-1902
383.0 Rube Waddell, Phi-1904
382.1 George Mullin, Det-1904
382.0 Joe McGinnity, Bal-1901
380.0 Cy Young, Bos-1904

American League club records

Highest Batting Average season, AL

.316 Detroit, 1921
.313 St.Louis, 1922
.309 New York, 1930
.308 St.Louis, 1920
.308 Cleveland, 1921

Lowest Batting Average season, AL

.211 Chicago, 1910
.214 New York, 1968
.217 Texas, 1972
.218 St.Louis, 1910
.221 Chicago, 1909

Highest Slugging Percentage season, AL

.489 New York, 1927
.488 New York, 1930
.483 New York, 1936
.465 Boston, 1977
.464 New York, 1921

Most Runs season, AL

1067 New York, 1931
1065 New York, 1936
1062 New York, 1930
1027 Boston, 1950
1002 New York, 1932

Most Homers season, AL

240 New York, 1961
225 Minnesota, 1963
225 Detroit, 1987
221 Minnesota, 1964
216 Milwaukee, 1982

Most Stolen Bases season, AL

341 Oakland, 1976
288 New York, 1910
287 Washington, 1913
280 Chicago, 1901
280 Detroit, 1909

Most Grounded into Double Plays season, AL

174 Boston, 1990
171 Boston, 1982
171 Boston, 1983
170 Philadelphia, 1950
169 Boston, 1949
169 Boston, 1951
169 Boston, 1989

Highest Fielding Average season, AL

.986 Minnesota, 1988
.986 Baltimore, 1989
.986 Oakland, 1990
.986 Toronto, 1990
.986 Milwaukee, 1992

Most Errors season, AL

410 Detroit, 1901
401 Baltimore, 1901
393 Milwaukee, 1901
385 St.Louis, 1910
382 New York, 1912

Fewest Errors season, AL

84 Minnesota, 1988
86 Toronto, 1990
87 Oakland, 1990
87 Baltimore, 1989
89 Milwaukee, 1992

Most Double Plays season, AL

217 Philadelphia, 1949
214 New York, 1956
208 Philadelphia, 1950
207 Boston, 1949
206 Boston, 1980
206 Toronto, 1980

Lowest Earned Run Average season, AL

1.78 Philadelphia, 1910
1.93 Philadelphia, 1909
1.99 Chicago, 1905
2.02 Cleveland, 1908
2.03 Chicago, 1910

Most Shutouts season, AL

32 Chicago, 1906
28 Los Angeles, 1964
27 Cleveland, 1906
27 Philadelphia, 1907
27 Philadelphia, 1909

Most Homers Allowed season, AL

226 Baltimore, 1987
220 Kansas City, 1964
219 Cleveland, 1987
212 California, 1987
210 Minnesota, 1987

Fewest Homers Allowed season, AL

6 Boston, 1913
7 St.Louis, 1908
8 Philadelphia, 1910
8 Chicago, 1909
8 Detroit, 1907
8 Cleveland, 1907

Most Walks Allowed season, AL

827 Philadelphia, 1915
812 New York, 1949
801 St.Louis, 1951
779 Washington, 1949
770 Cleveland, 1971

National League single-season records

(ACTIVE PLAYERS in caps)

At-bats: Most, season, NL

701 JUAN SAMUEL, Phi-1984
699 Dave Cash, Phi-1975
698 Matty Alou, Pit-1969
696 Woody Jensen, Pit-1936
695 Omar Moreno, Pit-1979
695 Maury Wills, LA-1962
689 Lou Brock, StL-1967
687 Dave Cash, Phi-1974
681 Jo-Jo Moore, NY-1935
681 Lloyd Waner, Pit-1931

Runs: Most, season, NL

192 Billy Hamilton, Phi-1894
166 Billy Hamilton, Phi-1895
165 Willie Keeler, Bal-1894
165 Joe Kelley, Bal-1894
162 Willie Keeler, Bal-1895
160 Jesse Burkett, Cle-1896
160 Hugh Duffy, Bos-1894
159 Hughie Jennings, Bal-1895
158 Chuck Klein, Phi-1930
158 Bobby Lowe, Bos-1894

Hits: Most, season, NL

254 Lefty O'Doul, Phi-1929
254 Bill Terry, NY-1930
250 Rogers Hornsby, StL-1922
250 Chuck Klein, Phi-1930
241 Babe Herman, Bro-1930
240 Jesse Burkett, Cle-1896
239 Willie Keeler, Bal-1897
238 Ed Delahanty, Phi-1899
237 Hugh Duffy, Bos-1894
237 Joe Medwick, StL-1937
237 Paul Waner, Pit-1927

Total bases: Most, season, NL

450 Rogers Hornsby, StL-1922
445 Chuck Klein, Phi-1930
429 Stan Musial, StL-1948
423 Hack Wilson, Chi-1930
420 Chuck Klein, Phi-1932
416 Babe Herman, Bro-1930
409 Rogers Hornsby, Chi-1929
406 Joe Medwick, StL-1937
405 Chuck Klein, Phi-1929
400 Hank Aaron, Mil-1959

2B: Most, season, NL

64 Joe Medwick, StL-1936
62 Paul Waner, Pit-1932
59 Chuck Klein, Phi-1930
57 Billy Herman, Chi-1935
57 Billy Herman, Chi-1936
56 Joe Medwick, StL-1937
55 Ed Delahanty, Phi-1899
53 Stan Musial, StL-1953
53 Paul Waner, Pit-1936
52 Johnny Frederick, Bro-1929
52 Enos Slaughter, StL-1939

3B: Most, season, NL

36 Chief Wilson, Pit-1912
31 Heinie Reitz, Bal-1894
29 Perry Werden, StL-1893
28 Harry Davis, Pit-1897
27 George Davis, NY-1893
27 Jimmy Williams, Pit-1899
26 Kiki Cuyler, Pit-1925
26 John Reilly, Cin-1890
26 George Treadway, Bro-1894
25 Roger Connor, NY-StL-1894
25 Larry Doyle, NY-1911
25 Buck Freeman, Was-1899
25 Tom Long, StL-1915

HR: Most, season, NL

56 Hack Wilson, Chi-1930
54 Ralph Kiner, Pit-1949
52 George Foster, Cin-1977
52 Willie Mays, SF-1965
51 Ralph Kiner, Pit-1947
51 Willie Mays, NY-1955
51 Johnny Mize, NY-1947
49 ANDRE DAWSON, Chi-1987
49 Ted Kluszewski, Cin-1954
49 Willie Mays, SF-1962

RBI: Most, season, NL

190 Hack Wilson, Chi-1930
170 Chuck Klein, Phi-1930
166 Sam Thompson, Det-1887
165 Sam Thompson, Phi-1895
159 Hack Wilson, Chi-1929
154 Joe Medwick, StL-1937
153 Tommy Davis, LA-1962
152 Rogers Hornsby, StL-1922
151 Mel Ott, NY-1929
149 George Foster, Cin-1977
149 Rogers Hornsby, Chi-1929

SB: Most, season, NL
118 Lou Brock, StL-1974
111 Billy Hamilton, Phi-1891
111 John Ward, NY-1887
110 VINCE COLEMAN, StL-1985
109 VINCE COLEMAN, StL-1987
107 VINCE COLEMAN, StL-1986
104 Maury Wills, LA-1962
102 Jim Fogarty, Phi-1887
102 Billy Hamilton, Phi-1890
99 Jim Fogarty, Phi-1889

BB: Most, season, NL
148 Eddie Stanky, Bro-1945
148 Jim Wynn, Hou-1969
147 Jimmy Sheckard, Chi-1911
144 Eddie Stanky, NY-1950
137 Ralph Kiner, Pit-1951
137 Willie McCovey, SF-1970
137 Eddie Stanky, Bro-1946
136 JACK CLARK, StL-1987
136 Jack Crooks, StL-1892
132 JACK CLARK, SD-1989
132 Joe Morgan, Cin-1975

K: Most, season, NL
189 Bobby Bonds, SF-1970
187 Bobby Bonds, SF-1969
180 Mike Schmidt, Phi-1975
169 ANDRES GALARRAGA, Mon-1990
168 JUAN SAMUEL, Phi-1984
163 Donn Clendenon, Pit-1968
162 JUAN SAMUEL, Phi-1987
161 Dick Allen, Phi-1968
158 ANDRES GALARRAGA, Mon-1989
156 Tommie Agee, NY-1970
156 Dave Kingman, NY-1982

GIDP: Most, season, NL
30 Ernie Lombardi, Cin-1938
29 Ted Simmons, StL-1973
28 Sid Gordon, Bos-1951
27 John Bateman, Mon-1971
27 Carl Furillo, Bro-1956
27 Ron Santo, Chi-1973
27 Ken Singleton, Mon-1973
26 Sid Gordon, NY-1943
26 Cleon Jones, NY-1970
26 Billy Jurges, NY-1939
26 Ernie Lombardi, Cin-1933
26 Willie Montanez, Phi-SF-1975
26 Willie Montanez, SF-Atl-1976
26 Dave Parker, Cin-1985
26 Joe Torre, Mil-1964

BA: Highest, season, NL
.440 Hugh Duffy, Bos-1894
.424 Willie Keeler, Bal-1897
.424 Rogers Hornsby, StL-1924
.410 Ed Delahanty, Phi-1899
.410 Jesse Burkett, Cle-1896
.409 Jesse Burkett, Cle-1895
.407 Ed Delahanty, Phi-1894
.404 Billy Hamilton, Phi-1894
.404 Ed Delahanty, Phi-1895
.403 Rogers Hornsby, StL-1925

Slug avg: Highest, season, NL
.756 Rogers Hornsby, StL-1925
.723 Hack Wilson, Chi-1930
.722 Rogers Hornsby, StL-1922
.702 Stan Musial, StL-1948
.696 Rogers Hornsby, StL-1924
.694 Hugh Duffy, Bos-1894
.687 Chuck Klein, Phi-1930
.679 Rogers Hornsby, Chi-1929
.678 Babe Herman, Bro-1930
.669 Hank Aaron, Atl-1971

Extra-base hits: Most, season, NL
107 Chuck Klein, Phi-1930
103 Chuck Klein, Phi-1932
103 Stan Musial, StL-1948
102 Rogers Hornsby, StL-1922
97 Joe Medwick, StL-1937
97 Hack Wilson, Chi-1930
95 Joe Medwick, StL-1936
94 Babe Herman, Bro-1930
94 Rogers Hornsby, Chi-1929
94 Chuck Klein, Phi-1929

Pitchers

Games: Most, season, NL
94 Kent Tekulve, Pit-1979
92 Mike Marshall, Mon-1973
91 Kent Tekulve, Pit-1978
90 Wayne Granger, Cin-1969
90 Kent Tekulve, Phi-1987
87 ROB MURPHY, Cin-1987
85 Kent Tekulve, Pit-1982
85 Frank Williams, Cin-1987
84 Ted Abernathy, Chi-1965
84 Enrique Romo, Pit-1979
84 Dick Tidrow, Chi-1980

Complete games: Most, season, NL
75 Will White, Cin-1879
73 Charley Radbourn, Pro-1884
72 Jim Galvin, Buf-1883
72 Jim McCormick, Cle-1880
71 Jim Galvin, Buf-1884
68 John Clarkson, Chi-1885
68 John Clarkson, Bos-1889
67 Bill Hutchison, Chi-1892
66 Jim Devlin, Lou-1876
66 Charley Radbourn, Pro-1883

Saves: Most, season, NL
47 LEE SMITH, StL-1991
45 Bruce Sutter, StL-1984
44 MARK DAVIS, SD-1989
43 LEE SMITH, StL-1992
41 JEFF REARDON, Mon-1985
40 Steve Bedrosian, Phi-1987
39 JOHN FRANCO, Cin-1988
38 RANDY MYERS, SD-1992
37 Clay Carroll, Cin-1972
37 Rollie Fingers, SD-1978
37 Bruce Sutter, Chi-1979
37 JOHN WETTELAND, Mon-1992

Shutouts: Most, season, NL
16 Pete Alexander, Phi-1916
16 George Bradley, StL-1876
13 Bob Gibson, StL-1968
12 Pete Alexander, Phi-1915
12 Jim Galvin, Buf-1884
11 Tommy Bond, Bos-1879
11 Sandy Koufax, LA-1963
11 Christy Mathewson, NY-1908
11 Charley Radbourn, Pro-1884
10 John Clarkson, Chi-1885
10 Mort Cooper, StL-1942
10 Carl Hubbell, NY-1933
10 Juan Marichal, SF-1965
10 John Tudor, StL-1985

Wins: Most, season, NL
59 Charley Radbourn, Pro-1884
53 John Clarkson, Chi-1885
49 John Clarkson, Bos-1889
48 Charlie Buffinton, Bos-1884
48 Charley Radbourn, Pro-1883
47 Al Spalding, Chi-1876
47 John Ward, Pro-1879
46 Jim Galvin, Buf-1883
46 Jim Galvin, Buf-1884
45 George Bradley, StL-1876
45 Jim McCormick, Cle-1880

Losses: Most, season, NL
48 John Coleman, Phi-1883
42 Will White, Cin-1880
40 George Bradley, Tro-1879
40 Jim McCormick, Cle-1879
37 George Cobb, Bal-1892
36 Bill Hutchison, Chi-1892
36 Stump Weidman, KC-1886
35 Jim Devlin, Lou-1876
35 Red Donahue, StL-1897
35 Jim Galvin, Buf-1880

HR allowed: Most, season, NL
46 Robin Roberts, Phi-1956
41 Phil Niekro, Atl-1979
41 Robin Roberts, Phi-1955
40 Phil Niekro, Atl-1970
40 Robin Roberts, Phi-1957
39 Murry Dickson, StL-1948
38 Lew Burdette, Mil-1959
38 Warren Hacker, Chi-1955
38 Don Sutton, LA-1970
36 TOM BROWNING, Cin-1988
36 Larry Jansen, NY-1949
36 Art Mahaffey, Phi-1962
36 Ed Whitson, SD-1987

BB: Most, season, NL
289 Amos Rusie, NY-1890
267 Amos Rusie, NY-1892
262 Amos Rusie, NY-1891
227 Mark Baldwin, Pit-1891
218 Amos Rusie, NY-1893
213 Cy Seymour, NY-1898
203 John Clarkson, Bos-1889
200 Amos Rusie, NY-1894
199 Bill Hutchison, Chi-1890
194 Mark Baldwin, Pit-1892

K: Most, season, NL

441 Charley Radbourn, Pro-1884
417 Charlie Buffinton, Bos-1884
382 Sandy Koufax, LA-1965
369 Jim Galvin, Buf-1884
345 Mickey Welch, NY-1884
345 Jim Whitney, Bos-1883
341 Amos Rusie, NY-1890
337 Amos Rusie, NY-1891
335 Tim Keefe, NY-1888
323 Lady Baldwin, Det-1886

Win pct: Highest, season, NL

.880 Preacher Roe, Bro-1951
.875 Fred Goldsmith, Chi-1880
.870 DAVID CONE, NY-1988
.864 OREL HERSHISER, LA-1985
.857 DWIGHT GOODEN, NY-1985
.842 Emil Yde, Pit-1924
.842 Tom Hughes, Bos-1916
.838 Bill Hoffer, Bal-1895
.833 King Cole, Chi-1910
.833 Sandy Koufax, LA-1963
.833 Hoyt Wilhelm, NY-1952

ERA: Lowest, season, NL

1.04 Mordecai Brown, Chi-1906
1.12 Bob Gibson, StL-1968
1.14 Christy Mathewson, NY-1909
1.15 Jack Pfiester, Chi-1907
1.17 Carl Lundgren, Chi-1907
1.22 Pete Alexander, Phi-1915
1.23 George Bradley, StL-1876
1.28 Christy Mathewson, NY-1905
1.31 Mordecai Brown, Chi-1909
1.33 Jack Taylor, Chi-1902

Innings: Most, season, NL

680.0 Will White, Cin-1879
678.2 Charley Radbourn, Pro-1884
657.2 Jim McCormick, Cle-1880
656.1 Jim Galvin, Buf-1883
636.1 Jim Galvin, Buf-1884
632.1 Charley Radbourn, Pro-1883
627.0 Bill Hutchison, Chi-1892
623.0 John Clarkson, Chi-1885
622.0 Jim Devlin, Lou-1876
620.0 John Clarkson, Bos-1889

National League club records

Highest Batting Average season, NL

.349 Philadelphia, 1894
.343 Baltimore, 1894
.337 Chicago, 1876
.331 Boston, 1894
.330 Philadelphia, 1895

Lowest Batting Average season, NL

.208 Washington, 1888
.208 DET, 1884
.210 Washington, 1886
.213 Brooklyn, 1908
.219 New York, 1963

Highest Slugging Percentage season, NL

.484 Boston, 1894
.483 Baltimore, 1894
.481 Chicago, 1930
.476 Philadelphia, 1894
.474 Brooklyn, 1953

Most Runs season, NL

1220 Boston, 1894
1171 Baltimore, 1894
1143 Philadelphia, 1894
1068 Philadelphia, 1895
1041 Chicago, 1894

Most Homers season, NL

221 New York, 1947
221 Cincinnati, 1956
209 Chicago, 1987
208 Brooklyn, 1953
207 Atlanta, 1966

Most Stolen Bases season, NL

441 Baltimore, 1896
415 New York, 1887
409 Brooklyn, 1892
401 Baltimore, 1897
382 Chicago, 1887

Most Grounded into Double Plays season, NL

166 St.Louis, 1958
157 Chicago, 1938
154 Atlanta, 1985
153 New York, 1939
151 Brooklyn, 1952

Highest Fielding Average season, NL

.985 St.Louis, 1992
.984 Cincinnati, 1975
.984 Cincinnati, 1977
.984 Cincinnati, 1992
.984 Pittsburgh, 1992

Most Errors season, NL

639 Philadelphia, 1883
607 Pittsburgh, 1890
595 Chicago, 1884
584 Baltimore, 1892
565 New York, 1892

Fewest Errors season, NL

94 St.Louis, 1992
95 Cincinnati, 1977
96 Cincinnati, 1992
100 Cincinnati, 1958
101 Pittsburgh, 1992

Most Double Plays season, NL

215 Pittsburgh, 1966
198 Los Angeles, 1958
197 Atlanta, 1985
195 Pittsburgh, 1963
195 Pittsburgh, 1970

Lowest Earned Run Average season, NL

1.22 St.Louis, 1876
1.61 Providence, 1884
1.64 Providence, 1880
1.67 Hartford, 1876
1.69 Louisville, 1876

Most Shutouts season, NL

32 Chicago, 1907
32 Chicago, 1909
30 Chicago, 1906
30 St.Louis, 1968
29 Chicago, 1908

Most Homers Allowed season, NL

192 New York, 1962
185 St.Louis, 1955
185 Atlanta, 1970
184 Chicago, 1966
179 Cincinnati, 1953
179 Cincinnati, 1957

Fewest Homers Allowed season, NL

5 Cincinnati, 1909
6 Chicago, 1909
8 Philadelphia, 1908
11 Chicago, 1907
12 Pittsburgh, 1909
12 Pittsburgh, 1907
12 Chicago, 1906
12 Pittsburgh, 1905

Most Walks Allowed season, NL

716 Montreal, 1970
715 San Diego, 1974
702 Montreal, 1969
701 St.Louis, 1911
701 Atlanta, 1977

Career records

Games played: Most, career, all-time

3562 Pete Rose, 1963-1986
3308 Carl Yastrzemski, 1961-1983
3298 Hank Aaron, 1954-1976
3035 Ty Cobb, 1905-1928
3026 Stan Musial, 1941-1963
2992 Willie Mays, 1951-1973
2951 Rusty Staub, 1963-1985
2896 Brooks Robinson, 1955-1977
2834 Al Kaline, 1953-1974
2826 Eddie Collins, 1906-1930
2820 Reggie Jackson, 1967-1987
2808 Frank Robinson, 1956-1976
2792 Honus Wagner, 1897-1917
2789 Tris Speaker, 1907-1928
2777 Tony Perez, 1964-1986
2730 Mel Ott, 1926-1947
2729 ROBIN YOUNT, 1974-1992
2707 DAVE WINFIELD, 1973-1992
2700 Graig Nettles, 1967-1988
2687 Darrell Evans, 1969-1989

At-bats: Most, career, all-time

14053 Pete Rose, 1963-1986
12364 Hank Aaron, 1954-1976
11988 Carl Yastrzemski, 1961-1983
11434 Ty Cobb, 1905-1928
10972 Stan Musial, 1941-1963
10881 Willie Mays, 1951-1973
10654 Brooks Robinson, 1955-1977
10554 ROBIN YOUNT, 1974-1992
10430 Honus Wagner, 1897-1917
10332 Lou Brock, 1961-1979
10274 Cap Anson, 1871-1897
10230 Luis Aparicio, 1956-1973
10195 Tris Speaker, 1907-1928
10116 Al Kaline, 1953-1974
10078 Rabbit Maranville, 1912-1935
10047 DAVE WINFIELD, 1973-1992
10006 Frank Robinson, 1956-1976
9949 Eddie Collins, 1906-1930
9864 Reggie Jackson, 1967-1987
9789 GEORGE BRETT, 1973-1992

Runs: Most, career, all-time

2246 Ty Cobb, 1905-1928
2174 Hank Aaron, 1954-1976
2174 Babe Ruth, 1914-1935
2165 Pete Rose, 1963-1986
2062 Willie Mays, 1951-1973
1996 Cap Anson, 1871-1897
1949 Stan Musial, 1941-1963
1888 Lou Gehrig, 1923-1939
1882 Tris Speaker, 1907-1928
1859 Mel Ott, 1926-1947
1829 Frank Robinson, 1956-1976
1821 Eddie Collins, 1906-1930
1816 Carl Yastrzemski, 1961-1983
1798 Ted Williams, 1939-1960
1774 Charlie Gehringer, 1924-1942
1751 Jimmie Foxx, 1925-1945
1736 Honus Wagner, 1897-1917
1732 Jim O'Rourke, 1872-1904
1720 Jesse Burkett, 1890-1905
1719 Willie Keeler, 1892-1910

Hits: Most, career, all-time

4256 Pete Rose, 1963-1986
4189 Ty Cobb, 1905-1928
3771 Hank Aaron, 1954-1976
3630 Stan Musial, 1941-1963
3514 Tris Speaker, 1907-1928
3419 Carl Yastrzemski, 1961-1983
3415 Cap Anson, 1871-1897
3415 Honus Wagner, 1897-1917
3312 Eddie Collins, 1906-1930
3283 Willie Mays, 1951-1973
3242 Nap Lajoie, 1896-1916
3152 Paul Waner, 1926-1945
3053 Rod Carew, 1967-1985
3025 ROBIN YOUNT, 1974-1992
3023 Lou Brock, 1961-1979
3007 Al Kaline, 1953-1974
3005 GEORGE BRETT, 1973-1992
3000 Roberto Clemente, 1955-1972
2987 Sam Rice, 1915-1934
2961 Sam Crawford, 1899-1917

Total bases: Most, career, all-time

6856 Hank Aaron, 1954-1976
6134 Stan Musial, 1941-1963
6066 Willie Mays, 1951-1973
5854 Ty Cobb, 1905-1928
5793 Babe Ruth, 1914-1935
5752 Pete Rose, 1963-1986
5539 Carl Yastrzemski, 1961-1983
5373 Frank Robinson, 1956-1976
5101 Tris Speaker, 1907-1928
5060 Lou Gehrig, 1923-1939
5041 Mel Ott, 1926-1947
4956 Jimmie Foxx, 1925-1945
4884 Ted Williams, 1939-1960
4862 Honus Wagner, 1897-1917
4852 Al Kaline, 1953-1974
4834 Reggie Jackson, 1967-1987
4821 DAVE WINFIELD, 1973-1992
4801 GEORGE BRETT, 1973-1992
4712 Rogers Hornsby, 1915-1937
4706 Ernie Banks, 1953-1971

2B: Most, career, all-time

792 Tris Speaker, 1907-1928
746 Pete Rose, 1963-1986
725 Stan Musial, 1941-1963
724 Ty Cobb, 1905-1928
657 Nap Lajoie, 1896-1916
646 Carl Yastrzemski, 1961-1983
640 Honus Wagner, 1897-1917
634 GEORGE BRETT, 1973-1992
624 Hank Aaron, 1954-1976
605 Paul Waner, 1926-1945
582 Cap Anson, 1871-1897
574 Charlie Gehringer, 1924-1942
558 ROBIN YOUNT, 1974-1992
542 Harry Heilmann, 1914-1932
541 Rogers Hornsby, 1915-1937
540 Joe Medwick, 1932-1948
539 Al Simmons, 1924-1944
534 Lou Gehrig, 1923-1939
529 Al Oliver, 1968-1985
528 Frank Robinson, 1956-1976

3B: Most, career, all-time

309 Sam Crawford, 1899-1917
295 Ty Cobb, 1905-1928
252 Honus Wagner, 1897-1917
243 Jake Beckley, 1888-1907
233 Roger Connor, 1880-1897
222 Tris Speaker, 1907-1928
220 Fred Clarke, 1894-1915
205 Dan Brouthers, 1879-1904
194 Joe Kelley, 1891-1908
191 Paul Waner, 1926-1945
188 Bid McPhee, 1882-1899
186 Eddie Collins, 1906-1930
185 Ed Delahanty, 1888-1903
184 Sam Rice, 1915-1934
182 Jesse Burkett, 1890-1905
182 Edd Roush, 1913-1931
181 Ed Konetchy, 1907-1921
178 Buck Ewing, 1880-1897
177 Rabbit Maranville, 1912-1935
177 Stan Musial, 1941-1963

HR: Most, career, all-time

755 Hank Aaron, 1954-1976
714 Babe Ruth, 1914-1935
660 Willie Mays, 1951-1973
586 Frank Robinson, 1956-1976
573 Harmon Killebrew, 1954-1975
563 Reggie Jackson, 1967-1987
548 Mike Schmidt, 1972-1989
536 Mickey Mantle, 1951-1968
534 Jimmie Foxx, 1925-1945
521 Willie McCovey, 1959-1980
521 Ted Williams, 1939-1960
512 Ernie Banks, 1953-1971
512 Eddie Mathews, 1952-1968
511 Mel Ott, 1926-1947
493 Lou Gehrig, 1923-1939
475 Stan Musial, 1941-1963
475 Willie Stargell, 1962-1982
452 Carl Yastrzemski, 1961-1983
442 Dave Kingman, 1971-1986
432 DAVE WINFIELD, 1973-1992

RBI: Most, career, all-time

2297 Hank Aaron, 1954-1976
2213 Babe Ruth, 1914-1935
1995 Lou Gehrig, 1923-1939
1981 Cap Anson, 1871-1897
1951 Stan Musial, 1941-1963
1937 Ty Cobb, 1905-1928
1922 Jimmie Foxx, 1925-1945
1903 Willie Mays, 1951-1973
1860 Mel Ott, 1926-1947
1844 Carl Yastrzemski, 1961-1983
1839 Ted Williams, 1939-1960
1827 Al Simmons, 1924-1944
1812 Frank Robinson, 1956-1976
1732 Honus Wagner, 1897-1917
1710 DAVE WINFIELD, 1973-1992
1702 Reggie Jackson, 1967-1987
1652 Tony Perez, 1964-1986
1636 Ernie Banks, 1953-1971
1609 Goose Goslin, 1921-1938
1599 Nap Lajoie, 1896-1916

SB: Most, career, all-time

1042 RICKEY HENDERSON, 1979-1992
938 Lou Brock, 1961-1979
912 Billy Hamilton, 1888-1901
891 Ty Cobb, 1905-1928
744 Eddie Collins, 1906-1930
739 Arlie Latham, 1880-1909
738 Max Carey, 1910-1929
730 TIM RAINES, 1979-1992
722 Honus Wagner, 1897-1917
689 Joe Morgan, 1963-1984
660 WILLIE WILSON, 1976-1992
657 Tom Brown, 1882-1898
649 Bert Campaneris, 1964-1983
616 George Davis, 1890-1909
610 VINCE COLEMAN, 1985-1992
594 Dummy Hoy, 1888-1902
586 Maury Wills, 1959-1972
583 George Vanhaltren, 1887-1903
574 Hugh Duffy, 1888-1906
568 Bid McPhee, 1882-1899

BB: Most, career, all-time

2056 Babe Ruth, 1914-1935
2019 Ted Williams, 1939-1960
1865 Joe Morgan, 1963-1984
1845 Carl Yastrzemski, 1961-1983
1733 Mickey Mantle, 1951-1968
1708 Mel Ott, 1926-1947
1614 Eddie Yost, 1944-1962
1605 Darrell Evans, 1969-1989
1599 Stan Musial, 1941-1963
1566 Pete Rose, 1963-1986
1559 Harmon Killebrew, 1954-1975
1508 Lou Gehrig, 1923-1939
1507 Mike Schmidt, 1972-1989
1499 Eddie Collins, 1906-1930
1464 Willie Mays, 1951-1973
1452 Jimmie Foxx, 1925-1945
1444 Eddie Mathews, 1952-1968
1420 Frank Robinson, 1956-1976
1402 Hank Aaron, 1954-1976
1391 Dwight Evans, 1972-1991

HBP: Most, career, all-time

286 Hughie Jennings, 1891-1918
272 Tommy Tucker, 1887-1899
267 Don Baylor, 1970-1988
243 Ron Hunt, 1963-1974
214 Dan McGann, 1896-1908
198 Frank Robinson, 1956-1976
192 Minnie Minoso, 1949-1980
178 Jake Beckley, 1888-1907
173 Curt Welch, 1884-1893
156 Fred Clarke, 1894-1915
151 Chet Lemon, 1975-1990
142 CARLTON FISK, 1969-1992
142 Nellie Fox, 1947-1965
141 Kid Elberfeld, 1898-1914
141 Art Fletcher, 1909-1922
135 Frank Chance, 1898-1914
134 Nap Lajoie, 1896-1916
132 Steve Brodie, 1890-1902
132 John McGraw, 1891-1906
131 Dummy Hoy, 1888-1902

K: Most, career, all-time

2597 Reggie Jackson, 1967-1987
1936 Willie Stargell, 1962-1982
1883 Mike Schmidt, 1972-1989
1867 Tony Perez, 1964-1986
1816 Dave Kingman, 1971-1986
1757 Bobby Bonds, 1968-1981
1733 DALE MURPHY, 1976-1992
1730 Lou Brock, 1961-1979
1710 Mickey Mantle, 1951-1968
1699 Harmon Killebrew, 1954-1975
1697 Dwight Evans, 1972-1991
1570 Lee May, 1965-1982
1556 Dick Allen, 1963-1977
1550 Willie McCovey, 1959-1980
1537 Dave Parker, 1973-1991
1532 Frank Robinson, 1956-1976
1526 Willie Mays, 1951-1973
1513 Rick Monday, 1966-1984
1503 DAVE WINFIELD, 1973-1992
1495 Greg Luzinski, 1970-1984

GIDP: Most, career, all-time

328 Hank Aaron, 1954-1976
323 Carl Yastrzemski, 1961-1983
315 Jim Rice, 1974-1989
297 Brooks Robinson, 1955-1977
297 Rusty Staub, 1963-1985
292 DAVE WINFIELD, 1973-1992
287 Ted Simmons, 1968-1988
284 Joe Torre, 1960-1977
277 George Scott, 1966-1979
275 Roberto Clemente, 1955-1972
271 Al Kaline, 1953-1974
270 Frank Robinson, 1956-1976
268 Tony Perez, 1964-1986
266 Dave Concepcion, 1970-1988
261 Ernie Lombardi, 1931-1947
256 Ron Santo, 1960-1974
255 Buddy Bell, 1972-1989
254 Al Oliver, 1968-1985
251 Steve Garvey, 1969-1987
251 Willie Mays, 1951-1973

BA: Highest, career, all-time

.366 Ty Cobb, 1905-1928
.359 Rogers Hornsby, 1915-1937
.356 Joe Jackson, 1908-1920
.346 Ed Delahanty, 1888-1903
.345 Tris Speaker, 1907-1928
.344 Ted Williams, 1939-1960
.344 Billy Hamilton, 1888-1901
.342 Dan Brouthers, 1879-1904
.342 Babe Ruth, 1914-1935
.342 Harry Heilmann, 1914-1932
.342 Pete Browning, 1882-1894
.341 Willie Keeler, 1892-1910
.341 Bill Terry, 1923-1936
.340 George Sisler, 1915-1930
.340 Lou Gehrig, 1923-1939
.338 Jesse Burkett, 1890-1905
.338 Nap Lajoie, 1896-1916
.338 WADE BOGGS, 1982-1992
.336 Riggs Stephenson, 1921-1934
.334 Al Simmons, 1924-1944

Slug avg: Highest, career, all-time

.690 Babe Ruth, 1914-1935
.634 Ted Williams, 1939-1960
.632 Lou Gehrig, 1923-1939
.609 Jimmie Foxx, 1925-1945
.605 Hank Greenberg, 1930-1947
.579 Joe DiMaggio, 1936-1951
.577 Rogers Hornsby, 1915-1937
.562 Johnny Mize, 1936-1953
.559 Stan Musial, 1941-1963
.558 Willie Mays, 1951-1973
.557 Mickey Mantle, 1951-1968
.554 Hank Aaron, 1954-1976
.548 Ralph Kiner, 1946-1955
.545 Hack Wilson, 1923-1934
.543 Chuck Klein, 1928-1944
.540 Duke Snider, 1947-1964
.537 Frank Robinson, 1956-1976
.535 Al Simmons, 1924-1944
.534 Dick Allen, 1963-1977
.534 Earl Averill, 1929-1941

Extra-base hits: Most, career, all-time

1477 Hank Aaron, 1954-1976
1377 Stan Musial, 1941-1963
1356 Babe Ruth, 1914-1935
1323 Willie Mays, 1951-1973
1190 Lou Gehrig, 1923-1939
1186 Frank Robinson, 1956-1976
1157 Carl Yastrzemski, 1961-1983
1136 Ty Cobb, 1905-1928
1131 Tris Speaker, 1907-1928
1117 Jimmie Foxx, 1925-1945
1117 Ted Williams, 1939-1960
1075 Reggie Jackson, 1967-1987
1071 Mel Ott, 1926-1947
1066 GEORGE BRETT, 1973-1992
1041 Pete Rose, 1963-1986
1015 Mike Schmidt, 1972-1989
1011 Rogers Hornsby, 1915-1937
1009 Ernie Banks, 1953-1971
1008 DAVE WINFIELD, 1973-1992
995 Al Simmons, 1924-1944

Pitchers

Games: Most, career, all-time

1070 Hoyt Wilhelm, 1952-1972
1050 Kent Tekulve, 1974-1989
987 Lindy McDaniel, 1955-1975
944 Rollie Fingers, 1968-1985
931 Gene Garber, 1969-1988
927 RICH GOSSAGE, 1972-1992
906 Cy Young, 1890-1911
899 Sparky Lyle, 1967-1982
898 Jim Kaat, 1959-1983
874 Don McMahon, 1957-1974
864 Phil Niekro, 1964-1987
848 Roy Face, 1953-1969
824 Tug McGraw, 1965-1984
811 JEFF REARDON, 1979-1992
803 CHARLIE HOUGH, 1970-1992
802 Walter Johnson, 1907-1927
794 NOLAN RYAN, 1966-1992
787 LEE SMITH, 1980-1992
777 Gaylord Perry, 1962-1983
774 Don Sutton, 1966-1988

Complete games: Most, career, all-time

749 Cy Young, 1890-1911
646 Jim Galvin, 1875-1892
554 Tim Keefe, 1880-1893
531 Walter Johnson, 1907-1927
531 Kid Nichols, 1890-1906
525 Bobby Mathews, 1871-1887
525 Mickey Welch, 1880-1892
489 Charley Radbourn, 1880-1891
485 John Clarkson, 1882-1894
468 Tony Mullane, 1881-1894
466 Jim McCormick, 1878-1887
448 Gus Weyhing, 1887-1901
437 Pete Alexander, 1911-1930
434 Christy Mathewson, 1900-1916
422 Jack Powell, 1897-1912
410 Eddie Plank, 1901-1917
394 Will White, 1877-1886
392 Amos Rusie, 1889-1901
388 Vic Willis, 1898-1910
386 Tommy Bond, 1874-1884

Saves: Most, career, all-time

357 JEFF REARDON, 1979-1992
355 LEE SMITH, 1980-1992
341 Rollie Fingers, 1968-1985
308 RICH GOSSAGE, 1972-1992
300 Bruce Sutter, 1976-1988
251 DAVE RIGHETTI, 1979-1992
244 Dan Quisenberry, 1979-1990
239 DENNIS ECKERSLEY, 1975-1992
238 Sparky Lyle, 1967-1982
227 Hoyt Wilhelm, 1952-1972
226 JOHN FRANCO, 1984-1992
220 TOM HENKE, 1982-1992
218 Gene Garber, 1969-1988
216 DAVE SMITH, 1980-1992
200 BOBBY THIGPEN, 1986-1992
193 Roy Face, 1953-1969
188 Mike Marshall, 1967-1981
184 Steve Bedrosian, 1981-1991
184 Kent Tekulve, 1974-1989
180 Tug McGraw, 1965-1984
179 Ron Perranoski, 1961-1973
172 Lindy McDaniel, 1955-1975
164 DOUG JONES, 1982-1992
154 Stu Miller, 1952-1968
153 JAY HOWELL, 1980-1992

Shutouts: Most, career, all-time

110 Walter Johnson, 1907-1927
90 Pete Alexander, 1911-1930
79 Christy Mathewson, 1900-1916
76 Cy Young, 1890-1911
69 Eddie Plank, 1901-1917
63 Warren Spahn, 1942-1965
61 NOLAN RYAN, 1966-1992
61 Tom Seaver, 1967-1986
60 BERT BLYLEVEN, 1970-1992
58 Don Sutton, 1966-1988
57 Jim Galvin, 1875-1892
57 Ed Walsh, 1904-1917
56 Bob Gibson, 1959-1975
55 Mordecai Brown, 1903-1916
55 Steve Carlton, 1965-1988
53 Jim Palmer, 1965-1984
53 Gaylord Perry, 1962-1983
52 Juan Marichal, 1960-1975
50 Rube Waddell, 1897-1910
50 Vic Willis, 1898-1910

Wins: Most, career, all-time

511 Cy Young, 1890-1911
417 Walter Johnson, 1907-1927
373 Pete Alexander, 1911-1930
373 Christy Mathewson, 1900-1916
364 Jim Galvin, 1875-1892
363 Warren Spahn, 1942-1965
361 Kid Nichols, 1890-1906
342 Tim Keefe, 1880-1893
329 Steve Carlton, 1965-1988
328 John Clarkson, 1882-1894
326 Eddie Plank, 1901-1917
324 Don Sutton, 1966-1988
319 NOLAN RYAN, 1966-1992
318 Phil Niekro, 1964-1987
314 Gaylord Perry, 1962-1983
311 Tom Seaver, 1967-1986

Wins (Cont'd)

309 Charley Radbourn, 1880-1891
307 Mickey Welch, 1880-1892
300 Lefty Grove, 1925-1941
300 Early Wynn, 1939-1963

Losses: Most, career, all-time

316 Cy Young, 1890-1911
310 Jim Galvin, 1875-1892
287 NOLAN RYAN, 1966-1992
279 Walter Johnson, 1907-1927
274 Phil Niekro, 1964-1987
265 Gaylord Perry, 1962-1983
256 Don Sutton, 1966-1988
254 Jack Powell, 1897-1912
251 Eppa Rixey, 1912-1933
250 BERT BLYLEVEN, 1970-1992
248 Bobby Mathews, 1871-1887
245 Robin Roberts, 1948-1966
245 Warren Spahn, 1942-1965
244 Steve Carlton, 1965-1988
244 Early Wynn, 1939-1963
237 Jim Kaat, 1959-1983
232 Gus Weyhing, 1887-1901
231 Tommy John, 1963-1989
230 Bob Friend, 1951-1966
230 Ted Lyons, 1923-1946

HR allowed: Most, career, all-time

505 Robin Roberts, 1948-1966
484 Fergie Jenkins, 1965-1983
482 Phil Niekro, 1964-1987
472 Don Sutton, 1966-1988
434 Warren Spahn, 1942-1965
430 BERT BLYLEVEN, 1970-1992
420 FRANK TANANA, 1973-1992
414 Steve Carlton, 1965-1988
399 Gaylord Perry, 1962-1983
395 Jim Kaat, 1959-1983
380 Tom Seaver, 1967-1986
374 Catfish Hunter, 1965-1979
372 Jim Bunning, 1955-1971
357 JACK MORRIS, 1977-1992
347 Mickey Lolich, 1963-1979
346 CHARLIE HOUGH, 1970-1992
346 Luis Tiant, 1964-1982
338 Early Wynn, 1939-1963
324 Doyle Alexander, 1971-1989
320 Juan Marichal, 1960-1975

BB: Most career, all-time

2755 NOLAN RYAN, 1966-1992
1833 Steve Carlton, 1965-1988
1809 Phil Niekro, 1964-1987
1775 Early Wynn, 1939-1963
1764 Bob Feller, 1936-1956
1732 Bobo Newsom, 1929-1953
1704 Amos Rusie, 1889-1901
1566 Gus Weyhing, 1887-1901
1542 CHARLIE HOUGH, 1970-1992
1541 Red Ruffing, 1924-1947
1442 Bump Hadley, 1926-1941
1434 Warren Spahn, 1942-1965
1431 Earl Whitehill, 1923-1939
1408 Tony Mullane, 1881-1894
1396 Sam Jones, 1914-1935

BB (Cont'd)

1390 Tom Seaver, 1967-1986
1379 Gaylord Perry, 1962-1983
1371 Mike Torrez, 1967-1984
1363 Walter Johnson, 1907-1927
1343 Don Sutton, 1966-1988

K: Most, career, all-time

5668 NOLAN RYAN, 1966-1992
4136 Steve Carlton, 1965-1988
3701 BERT BLYLEVEN, 1970-1992
3640 Tom Seaver, 1967-1986
3574 Don Sutton, 1966-1988
3534 Gaylord Perry, 1962-1983
3509 Walter Johnson, 1907-1927
3342 Phil Niekro, 1964-1987
3192 Fergie Jenkins, 1965-1983
3117 Bob Gibson, 1959-1975
2855 Jim Bunning, 1955-1971
2832 Mickey Lolich, 1963-1979
2800 Cy Young, 1890-1911
2657 FRANK TANANA, 1973-1992
2583 Warren Spahn, 1942-1965
2581 Bob Feller, 1936-1956
2556 Jerry Koosman, 1967-1985
2545 Tim Keefe, 1880-1893
2502 Christy Mathewson, 1900-1916
2486 Don Drysdale, 1956-1969

Wild pitches: Most, career, all-time

343 Tony Mullane, 1881-1894
274 NOLAN RYAN, 1966-1992
274 Mickey Welch, 1880-1892
240 Tim Keefe, 1880-1893
240 Gus Weyhing, 1887-1901
226 Phil Niekro, 1964-1987
221 Mark Baldwin, 1887-1893
221 Will White, 1877-1886
220 Jim Galvin, 1875-1892
214 Charley Radbourn, 1880-1891
214 Jim Whitney, 1881-1890
206 Adonis Terry, 1884-1897
203 Matt Kilroy, 1886-1898
187 Tommy John, 1963-1989
185 Bobby Mathews, 1871-1887
183 Steve Carlton, 1965-1988
182 John Clarkson, 1882-1894
179 JACK MORRIS, 1977-1992
179 Toad Ramsey, 1885-1890
178 Hardie Henderson, 1883-1888

Win pct: Highest, career, all-time

.796 Al Spalding, 1871-1878
.717 Spud Chandler, 1937-1947
.690 Dave Foutz, 1884-1896
.690 Whitey Ford, 1950-1967
.688 Bob Caruthers, 1884-1893
.686 Don Gullett, 1970-1978
.683 DWIGHT GOODEN, 1984-1992
.680 Lefty Grove, 1925-1941
.679 ROGER CLEMENS, 1984-1992
.671 Joe Wood, 1908-1922
.667 Vic Raschi, 1946-1955
.665 Larry Corcoran, 1880-1887
.665 Christy Mathewson, 1900-1916
.660 Sam Leever, 1898-1910

Winning pct. (Cont'd)

.657 Sal Maglie, 1945-1958
.656 Dick McBride, 1871-1876
.655 Sandy Koufax, 1955-1966
.654 Johnny Allen, 1932-1944
.651 Ron Guidry, 1975-1988
.650 Lefty Gomez, 1930-1943

ERA: Lowest, career, all-time

1.82 Ed Walsh, 1904-1917
1.89 Addie Joss, 1902-1910
2.06 Mordecai Brown, 1903-1916
2.10 Al Spalding, 1871-1878
2.10 John Ward, 1878-1894
2.13 Christy Mathewson, 1900-1916
2.16 Rube Waddell, 1897-1910
2.16 Walter Johnson, 1907-1927
2.23 Orval Overall, 1905-1913
2.28 Will White, 1877-1886
2.28 Ed Reulbach, 1905-1917
2.30 Jim Scott, 1909-1917
2.31 Tommy Bond, 1874-1884
2.35 Eddie Plank, 1901-1917
2.35 Larry Corcoran, 1880-1887
2.38 George McQuillan, 1907-1918
2.38 Eddie Cicotte, 1905-1920
2.38 Ed Killian, 1903-1910
2.39 Doc White, 1901-1913
2.42 George Bradley, 1875-1888

Innings: Most, career, all-time

7355.1 Cy Young, 1890-1911
6003.1 Jim Galvin, 1875-1892
5923.2 Walter Johnson, 1907-1927
5404.1 Phil Niekro, 1964-1987
5350.1 Gaylord Perry, 1962-1983
5319.2 NOLAN RYAN, 1966-1992
5282.1 Don Sutton, 1966-1988
5243.2 Warren Spahn, 1942-1965
5217.1 Steve Carlton, 1965-1988
5189.1 Pete Alexander, 1911-1930
5056.1 Kid Nichols, 1890-1906
5047.1 Tim Keefe, 1880-1893
4970.0 BERT BLYLEVEN, 1970-1992
4956.1 Bobby Mathews, 1871-1887
4802.0 Mickey Welch, 1880-1892
4782.2 Tom Seaver, 1967-1986
4780.2 Christy Mathewson, 1900-1916
4710.1 Tommy John, 1963-1989
4688.2 Robin Roberts, 1948-1966
4564.0 Early Wynn, 1939-1963

General club records

Highest percentage for league champion

.832 St. Louis, UA-1884
.798 Chicago, NL-1880
.788 Chicago, NL-1876
.777 Chicago, NL-1885
.763 Chicago, NL-1906

Lowest percentage for league champion

.509 New York, NL-1973
.525 Minnesota, AL-1987
.551 New York, AL-1981
.556 Philadelphia, NL-1983
.556 Oakland, AL-1974

Most Wins

116 Chicago, NL-1906
111 Cleveland, AL-1954
110 Pittsburgh, NL-1909
110 New York, NL-1927
109 New York, NL-1961
109 Baltimore, AL-1969

Fewest Wins

36 Philadelphia, AL-1916
38 Washington, AL-1904
38 Boston, NL-1935
40 New York, NL-1962
42 Washington, AL-1909
42 Philadelphia, NL-1942
42 Pittsburgh, NL-1952

Most league championships

33 New York, AL
21 Brooklyn-Los Angeles, NL
19 New York-San Francisco, NL
16 Chicago, NL
15 St. Louis, NL
15 Philadelphia-Oakland, AL

Individual fielding records

Most Gold Gloves, Pitcher

16 Jim Kaat
9 Bob Gibson
8 Bobby Shantz
5 Phil Niekro
5 Ron Guidry
4 Jim Palmer
4 MARK LANGSTON
3 Harvey Haddix
3 GREG MADDUX
2 Andy Messersmith
2 Mike Norris
2 Rick Reuschel

Most Gold Gloves, Catcher

10 Johnny Bench
7 Bob Boone
6 Jim Sundberg
5 Bill Freehan
4 Del Crandall
4 TONY PENA
3 Sherm Lollar
3 Earl Battey
3 Thurman Munson
3 GARY CARTER
3 LANCE PARRISH
3 BENITO SANTIAGO

Most Gold Gloves, First base

11 Keith Hernandez
8 George Scott
7 Vic Power
7 Bill White
7 DON MATTINGLY
6 Wes Parker
4 Steve Garvey
3 Gil Hodges
3 Joe Pepitone
3 EDDIE MURRAY

Most Gold Gloves, Second base

9 RYNE SANDBERG
8 Bill Mazeroski
8 Frank White
5 Bobby Richardson
5 Joe Morgan
4 Bobby Grich
3 Nellie Fox
3 Bobby Knoop
3 Davey Johnson
3 Manny Trillo
3 LOU WHITAKER
3 HAROLD REYNOLDS

Most Gold Gloves, Third base

16 Brooks Robinson
10 Mike Schmidt
6 Buddy Bell
5 Ken Boyer
5 Ron Santo
5 Doug Rader
4 GARY GAETTI
3 Frank Malzone
3 TIM WALLACH
3 TERRY PENDLETON

Most Gold Gloves, Shortstop

13 OZZIE SMITH
9 Luis Aparicio
8 Mark Belanger
5 Dave Concepcion
4 ALAN TRAMMELL
4 TONY FERNANDEZ
3 Roy McMillan
2 Maury Wills
2 Zoilo Versalles
2 Gene Alley
2 Don Kessinger
2 Larry Bowa
2 CAL RIPKEN

Most Gold Gloves, Outfield

12 Roberto Clemente
12 Willie Mays
10 Al Kaline
8 Paul Blair
8 Garry Maddox
8 Dwight Evans
8 ANDRE DAWSON
7 Curt Flood
7 Carl Yastrzemski
7 DAVE WINFIELD

Fielding Average, Pitcher (92 chances accepted)

1.000 Kid Nichols, Bos/N-1896
1.000 Frank Owen, Chi/A-1904
1.000 Mordecai Brown, Chi/N-1908
1.000 Pete Alexander, Phi/N-1913
1.000 Walter Johnson, Was/A-1913
1.000 Eppa Rixey, Phi/N-1917
1.000 Walter Johnson, Was/A-1917
1.000 Hal Schumacher, NY/N-1935
1.000 Larry Jackson, Chi/N-1964
1.000 Randy Jones, SD/N-1976
1.000 GREG MADDUX, Chi/N-1990

Fielding Average, Catcher

1.000 Spud Davis, Phi/N-1939
1.000 Buddy Rosar, Phi/A-1946
1.000 Lou Berberet, Was/A-1957
1.000 Pete Daley, Bos/A-1957
1.000 Yogi Berra, NY/A-1958
1.000 RICK CERONE, Bos/A-1988
.999 TOM PAGNOZZI, StL/N-1992
.999 Joe Azcue, Cle/A-1967
.999 Wes Westrum, NY/N-1950
.998 Thurman Munson, NY/A-1971

Fielding Average, First Base

1.000 Steve Garvey, SD/N-1984
.999 Stuffy McInnis, Bos/A-1921
.999 Frank McCormick, Phi/N-1946
.999 Steve Garvey, LA/N-1981
.999 Jim Spencer, Cal-Tex/A-1973
.999 Wes Parker, LA/N-1968
.999 EDDIE MURRAY, Bal/A-1981
.999 HAL MORRIS, Cin/N-1992
.998 Jim Spencer, Chi/A-1976
.998 Jim Spencer, NY-Oak/A-1981

Fielding Average, Second Base

.997 Bobby Grich, Cal/A-1985
.996 JOSE OQUENDO, StL/N-1990
.995 RYNE SANDBERG, Chi/N-1991
.995 Rob Wilfong, Min/A-1980
.995 Bobby Grich, Bal/A-1973
.994 Frank White, KC/A-1988
.994 JOSE OQUENDO, StL/N-1989
.994 Jerry Adair, Bal/A-1964
.994 RYNE SANDBERG, Chi/N-1986
.994 Tim Cullen, Was/A-1970

Fielding Average, Shortstop

.996 CAL RIPKEN, Bal/A-1990
.992 TONY FERNANDEZ, Tor/A-1989
.991 Larry Bowa, Phi/N-1979
.990 Ed Brinkman, Det/A-1972
.990 CAL RIPKEN, Bal/A-1989
.989 SPIKE OWEN, Mon/N-1990
.989 OMAR VIZQUEL, Sea/A-1992
.989 TONY FERNANDEZ, Tor/A-1990
.988 DICK SCHOFIELD, NY/N-1992
.987 OZZIE SMITH, StL/N-1991

Fielding Average, Third Base

.991 STEVE BUECHELE, Tex/A-1991 (counting Pit/N in 1991, Buechele's average was .983)
.989 Don Money, Mil/A-1974
.988 Hank Majeski, Phi/A-1947
.987 Aurelio Rodriguez, Det/A-1978
.984 Willie Kamm, Cle/A-1933
.983 George Kell, Phi-Det/A-1946
.983 Heinie Groh, NY/N-1924
.983 CARNEY LANSFORD, Cal/A-1979
.982 George Kell, Det/A-1950
.982 Pinky Whitney, Phi/N-1937

Fielding Average, Outfield

1.000 Danny Litwhiler, Phi/N-1942
1.000 Willard Marshall, Bos/N-1951
1.000 Tony Gonzalez, Phi/N-1962
1.000 Don Demeter, Phi/N-1963
1.000 Rocky Colavito, Cle/A-1965
1.000 Curt Flood, StL/N-1966
1.000 Johnny Callison, Phi/N-1968
1.000 Mickey Stanley, Det/A-1968
1.000 Ken Harrelson, Bos/A-1968
1.000 Ken Berry, Chi/A-1969
1.000 Mickey Stanley, Det/A-1970
1.000 Roy White, NY/A-1971
1.000 Al Kaline, Det/A-1971
1.000 Ken Berry, Cal/A-1972
1.000 Carl Yastrzemski, Bos/A-1977
1.000 Terry Puhl, Hou/N-1979
1.000 Gary Roenicke, Bal/A-1980
1.000 Ken Landreaux, LA/N-1981
1.000 Terry Puhl, Hou/N-1981
1.000 Ken Singleton, Bal/A-1981
1.000 BRIAN DOWNING, Cal/A-1982
1.000 John Lowenstein, Bal/A-1982
1.000 BRIAN DOWNING, Cal/A-1984
1.000 BRETT BUTLER, LA/N-1991
1.000 DARRYL HAMILTON, Mil/A-1992

Fielding Average, Pitcher, active players (60 chances accepted)

1.000 Greg Maddux, Chi/N-1990
1.000 Bert Blyleven, Min-Tex/A-1976
1.000 Bob Welch, LA/N-1987
1.000 Tom Glavine, Atl/N-1991
1.000 Jimmy Key, Tor/A-1986

Fielding Average, Catcher, active players

1.000 Rick Cerone, Bos/A-1988
.999 Tom Pagnozzi, StL/N-1992
.998 Mike LaValliere, Pit/N-1991
.998 Rick Cerone, NY/A-1987
.998 Greg Olson, Atl/N-1992
.998 Chris Hoiles, Bal/A-1991
.998 Damon Berryhill, Atl/N-1992
.998 Rick Dempsey, Bal/A-1981

Fielding Average, First Base, active players

.999 Eddie Murray, Bal/A-1981
.999 Hal Morris, Cin/N-1992
.998 Dave Magadan, NY/N-1990
.998 Mark Grace, Chi/N-1992
.997 Wally Joyner, Cal/A-1989
.997 Kent Hrbek, Min/A-1990
.997 Pete O'Brien, Sea/A-1991
.997 Will Clark, SF/N-1991
.997 Eddie Murray, Bal/A-1982
.997 Don Mattingly, NY/A-1992
.997 Mark McGwire, Oak/A-1991
.997 Eddie Murray, Bal/A-1978

Fielding Average, Second Base, active players

.996 Jose Oquendo, StL/N-1990
.995 Ryne Sandberg, Chi/N-1991
.994 Jose Oquendo, StL/N-1989
.994 Ryne Sandberg, Chi/N-1986
.994 Lou Whitaker, Det/A-1991

Fielding Average, Shortstop, active players

.996 Cal Ripken, Bal/A-1990
.992 Tony Fernandez, Tor/A-1989
.990 Cal Ripken, Bal/A-1989
.989 Spike Owen, Mon/N-1990
.989 Omar Vizquel, Sea/A-1992
.989 Tony Fernandez, Tor/A-1990

Fielding Average, Third Base, active players

.991 Steve Buechele, Tex/A-1991 (counting Pit/N in 1991, Buechele's average was .983)
.983 Carney Lansford, Cal/A-1979
.980 Carney Lansford, Oak/A-1987
.979 Carney Lansford, Oak/A-1988
.979 Ken Oberkfell, Atl/N-1987

Fielding Average, Outfield, active players

1.000 Brian Downing, Cal/A-1982
1.000 Brian Downing, Cal/A-1984
1.000 Brett Butler, LA/N-1991
1.000 Darryl Hamilton, Mil/A-1992
.998 Brett Butler, Cle/A-1985
.998 Devon White, Tor/A-1991
.998 Gerald Young, Hou/N-1989

Assists, Pitcher

227 Ed Walsh, Chi/A-1907
223 Will White, Cin/A-1882
190 Ed Walsh, Chi/A-1908
178 Harry Howell, StL/A-1905
177 Tony Mullane, Lou/A-1882
174 John Clarkson, Chi/N-1885
172 John Clarkson, Bos/N-1889
166 Jack Chesbro, NY/A-1904
163 George Mullin, Det/A-1904
160 Ed Walsh, Chi/A-1911

Assists, Catcher

238 Bill Rariden, New/F-1915
215 Bill Rariden, Ind/F-1914
214 Pat Moran, Bos/N-1903
212 Oscar Stanage, Det/A-1911
212 Art Wilson, Chi/F-1914
210 Gabby Street, Was/A-1909
204 Frank Snyder, StL/N-1915
203 George Gibson, Pit/N-1910
202 Bill Bergen, Bro/N-1909
202 Claude Berry, Pit/F-1914

Assists, First Base

184 Bill Buckner, Bos/A-1985
180 MARK GRACE, Chi/N-1990
167 MARK GRACE, Chi/N-1991
166 SID BREAM, Pit/N-1986
161 Bill Buckner, Chi/N-1983
159 Bill Buckner, Chi/N-1982
157 Bill Buckner, Bos/A-1986
155 Mickey Vernon, Cle/A-1949
152 Fred Tenney, Bos/N-1905
152 EDDIE MURRAY, Bal/A-1985

Assists, Second Base

641 Frankie Frisch, StL/N-1927
588 Hughie Critz, Cin/N-1926
582 Rogers Hornsby, NY/N-1927
572 Ski Melillo, StL/A-1930
571 RYNE SANDBERG, Chi/N-1983
568 Rabbit Maranville, Pit/N-1924
562 Frank Parkinson, Phi/N-1922
559 Tony Cuccinello, Bos/N-1936
557 Johnny Hodapp, Cle/A-1930
555 Lou Bierbauer, Pit/N-1892

Assists, Shortstop

621 OZZIE SMITH, SD/N-1980
601 Glenn Wright, Pit/N-1924
598 Dave Bancroft, Phi-NY/N-1920
597 Tommy Thevenow, StL/N-1926
595 Ivan DeJesus, Chi/N-1977
583 CAL RIPKEN, Bal/A-1984
581 Whitey Wietelmann, Bos/N-1943
579 Dave Bancroft, NY/N-1922
574 Rabbit Maranville, Bos/N-1914
573 Don Kessinger, Chi/N-1968

Assists, Third Base

412 Graig Nettles, Cle/A-1971
410 Graig Nettles, NY/A-1973
410 Brooks Robinson, Bal/A-1974
405 Harlond Clift, StL/A-1937
405 Brooks Robinson, Bal/A-1967
404 Mike Schmidt, Phi/N-1974
399 Doug DeCinces, Cal/A-1982
396 Clete Boyer, NY/A-1962
396 Mike Schmidt, Phi/N-1977
396 Buddy Bell, Tex/A-1982

Assists, Outfield

50 Orator Shaffer, Chi/N-1879
48 Hugh Nicol, StL/A-1884
45 Hardy Richardson, Buf/N-1881
44 Tommy McCarthy, StL/A-1888
44 Chuck Klein, Phi/N-1930

Assists, Outfield (Cont'd)

43 Charlie Duffee, StL/A-1889
43 Jimmy Bannon, Bos/N-1894
42 Jim Fogarty, Phi/N-1889
41 Orator Shaffer, Buf/N-1883
41 Jim Lillie, Buf/N-1884

Assists, Pitcher, active players

64 Greg Maddux, Chi/N-1992
60 Orel Hershiser, LA/N-1988
59 Dennis Martinez, Bal/A-1979
58 Dave Stieb, Tor/A-1980
56 Dwight Gooden, NY/N-1988

Assists, Catcher, active players

108 Gary Carter, Mon/N-1980
107 Gary Carter, Mon/N-1983
104 Gary Carter, Mon/N-1982
101 Gary Carter, Mon/N-1977
100 Tony Pena, Pit/N-1985
100 Benito Santiago, SD/N-1991

Assists, First Base, active players

180 Mark Grace, Chi/N-1990
167 Mark Grace, Chi/N-1991
166 Sid Bream, Pit/N-1986
152 Eddie Murray, Bal/A-1985
146 Pete O'Brien, Tex/A-1987

Assists, Second Base, active players

571 Ryne Sandberg, Chi/N-1983
550 Ryne Sandberg, Chi/N-1984
539 Ryne Sandberg, Chi/N-1992
522 Ryne Sandberg, Chi/N-1988
515 Ryne Sandberg, Chi/N-1991

Assists, Shortstop, active players

621 Ozzie Smith, SD/N-1980
583 Cal Ripken, Bal/A-1984
570 Ozzie Guillen, Chi/A-1988
555 Ozzie Smith, SD/N-1979
549 Ozzie Smith, StL/N-1985

Assists, Third Base, active players

392 Terry Pendleton, StL/N-1989
383 Tim Wallach, Mon/N-1985
373 George Brett, KC/A-1979
372 Robin Ventura, Chi/A-1992
371 Terry Pendleton, StL/N-1986

Assists, Outfield, active players

22 Jesse Barfield, Tor/A-1985
22 Joe Orsulak, Bal/A-1991
21 Tim Raines, Mon/N-1983
20 Dave Winfield, SD/N-1980
20 Jesse Barfield, Tor/A-1986
20 Jesse Barfield, Tor-NY/A-1989

Individual records

Most consecutive games played, lifetime

2130 Lou Gehrig, 1925-1939
1735 CAL RIPKEN, 1982-1992
1307 Everett Scott, 1916-1925
1207 Steve Garvey, 1975-1983
1117 Billy Williams, 1963-1970
1103 Joe Sewell, 1922-1930
895 Stan Musial, 1951-1957
829 Eddie Yost, 1949-1955
822 Gus Suhr, 1931-1937
798 Nellie Fox, 1955-1960

Most consecutive games played, lifetime, active players

1735 Cal Ripken, 1982-1992
162 Jeff Bagwell, 1992
162 Craig Biggio, 1992
162 Steve Finley, 1992

Most consecutive games batted safely, season

56 Joe DiMaggio, NY/AL-1941
44 Willie Keeler, Bal/NL-1897
44 Pete Rose, Cin/NL-1978
42 Bill Dahlen, Chi/NL-1894
41 George Sisler, StL/AL-1922
40 Ty Cobb, Det/AL-1911
39 PAUL MOLITOR, Mil/AL-1987
37 Tommy Holmes, Bos/NL-1945
36 Billy Hamilton, Phi/NL-1894
35 Fred Clarke, Lou/NL-1895
35 Ty Cobb, Det/AL-1917
34 George Sisler, StL/AL-1925
34 George McQuinn, StL/AL-1938
34 Dom DiMaggio, Bos/AL-1949
34 BENITO SANTIAGO, SD/NL-1987
33 Hal Chase, NY/AL-1907
33 George Davis, NY/NL-1893
33 Rogers Hornsby, StL/NL-1922
33 Heinie Manush, Was/AL-1933
31 Ed Delahanty, Phi/NL-1899
31 Nap Lajoie, Cle/AL-1906
31 Sam Rice, Was/AL-1924
31 Willie Davis, LA/NL-1969
31 Rico Carty, Atl/NL-1970
31 Ken Landreaux, Min/AL-1980
30 Elmer Smith, Cin/NL-1898
30 Tris Speaker, Bos/AL-1912
30 Bing Miller, Phi/AL-1929
30 Goose Goslin, Det/AL-1934
30 Stan Musial, StL/NL-1950
30 Ron LeFlore, Det/AL-1976
30 GEORGE BRETT, KC/AL-1980
30 JEROME WALTON, Chi/NL-1989

Most consecutive games batted safely, season, active players

39 Paul Molitor, Mil/AL-1987
34 Benito Santiago, SD/NL-1987
30 George Brett, KC/AL-1980
30 Jerome Walton, Chi/NL-1989
28 Wade Boggs, Bos/AL-1985
26 Jack Clark, SF/AL-1978
25 Tony Gwynn, SD/NL-1983
25 Steve Sax, LA/NL-1986
25 Wade Boggs, Bos/AL-1987
25 Brian Harper, Min/AL-1990
25 Lance Johnson, Chi/AL-1992

Most pinch hits, lifetime

150 Manny Mota, 1962-1982
145 Smoky Burgess, 1949-1967
143 Greg Gross, 1973-1989
123 Jose Morales, 1973-1984
116 Jerry Lynch, 1954-1966
114 Red Lucas, 1923-1938
113 Steve Braun, 1971-1985
108 Terry Crowley, 1969-1983
108 DENNY WALLING, 1975-1992
107 Gates Brown, 1963-1975
103 Mike Lum, 1967-1981
102 Jim Dwyer, 1973-1990
100 Rusty Staub, 1963-1985
95 Larry Biittner, 1970-1983
95 Vic Davalillo, 1963-1980
94 Jerry Hairston, 1973-1989
93 Dave Philley, 1941-1962
93 Joel Youngblood, 1976-1989
92 Jay Johnstone, 1966-1985
90 Ed Kranepool, 1962-1979
90 Elmer Valo, 1940-1961

Most pinch hits, lifetime, active players

108 Denny Walling, 1975-1992
71 Dave Bergman, 1975-1992
70 Randy Bush, 1982-1992
59 Rance Mulliniks, 1977-1992
56 Milt Thompson, 1984-1992
56 Herm Winningham, 1984-1992
52 Jamie Quirk, 1975-1992
49 Kevin Bass, 1982-1992
49 Gary Varsho, 1988-1992
48 Gerald Perry, 1983-1992

Most pinch-hit home runs, lifetime

20 Cliff Johnson, 1972-1986
18 Jerry Lynch, 1954-1966
16 Gates Brown, 1963-1975
16 Smoky Burgess, 1949-1967
16 Willie McCovey, 1959-1980
14 George Crowe, 1952-1961
12 Joe Adcock, 1950-1966
12 Bob Cerv, 1951-1962
12 Jose Morales, 1973-1984
12 Graig Nettles, 1967-1988
11 Jeff Burroughs, 1970-1985
11 Jay Johnstone, 1966-1985
11 Fred Whitfield, 1962-1970
11 Cy Williams, 1912-1930
10 Jim Dwyer, 1973-1990
10 Mike Lum, 1967-1981

Most pinch-hit HR (Cont'd)

10 Ken McMullen, 1962-1977
10 Don Mincher, 1960-1972
10 Wally Post, 1949-1964
10 Champ Summers, 1974-1984
10 Jerry Turner, 1974-1983
10 Gus Zernial, 1949-1959

Most pinch-hit home runs, lifetime, active players

9 Candy Maldonado, 1981-1992
8 Mark Carreon, 1987-1992
6 Jesse Barfield, 1981-1992
6 Randy Bush, 1982-1992
6 Tommy Gregg, 1987-1992
6 Lloyd McClendon, 1987-1992
6 Tim Teufel, 1983-1992
6 Denny Walling, 1975-1992
5 Daryl Boston, 1984-1992
5 Sam Horn, 1987-1992
5 Ernie Riles, 1985-1992

Most consecutive scoreless innings, season

59 OREL HERSHISER, LA/NL - August 30 to September 28, 1988 (end of season)
58 Don Drysdale, LA/NL - May 14 to June 8, 1968
55.2 Walter Johnson, Was/AL - April 10 to May 14, 1913
53 Jack Coombs, Phi/AL - September 5 to 25, 1910
47 Bob Gibson, StL/NL - June 2 to 26, 1968
45.1 Carl Hubbell, NY/NL - July 13 to August 1, 1933 (allowed a run charged to starter in a relief appearance on July 19, after 12 scoreless innings, had a 33 inning string afterwards)
45 Cy Young, Bos/AL - April 25 to May 17, 1904
45 Doc White, Chi/AL - September 12 to 30, 1904
45 Sal Maglie, NY/NL - August 16 to September 13, 1950
44 Ed Reulbach, Chi/NL - September 17 to October 3, 1908 (end of season) (added 6 more innings on April 17, 1909 for a total of 50 over 2 years)
43.2 Rube Waddell, Phi/AL - August 22 to September 5, 1905
42 George "Rube" Foster, Bos/AL - May 1 to 26, 1914
41 Jack Chesbro, Pit/NL - June 26 to July 16, 1902
41 Grover Cleveland Alexander, Phi/NL - September 7 to 24, 1911
41 Art Nehf, Bos/NL - September 13 to October 4, 1917
41 Luis Tiant, Cle/AL - April 28 to May 17, 1968
40 Walter Johnson, Was/AL - May 7 to 26, 1918
40 Gaylord Perry, SF/NL - August 28 to September 10, 1967
40 Luis Tiant, Bos/AL - August 19 to September 8, 1972
39.2 Mordecai Brown, Chi/NL - June 8 to July 8, 1908
39.2 Billy Pierce, Chi/AL - August 3 to 19, 1953
39 Ed Walsh, Chi/AL - August 10 to 22, 1906
39 Christy Mathewson, NY/NL - May 3 to 21, 1901
39 Don Newcombe, Bro/NL - July 25 to August 11, 1956
39 Ray Culp, Bos/AL - September 7 to 25, 1968
39 Gaylord Perry, SF/NL - September 1 to 23, 1970
38.1 Bill Lee, Chi/NL - September 5 to 26, 1938
38 Jim Galvin, Buf/NL - August 2 to 8, 1884
38 John Clarkson, Chi/NL - May 18 to 27, 1885
38 Jim Bagby, Cle/AL - June 30 to July 16, 1917
38 Ray Herbert, Chi/AL - May 1 to 14, 1963
37 George Bradley, StL/NL - July 8 to 18, 1876
37 Cy Young, Bos/AL - June 13 to July 1, 1903
37 Walter Johnson, Was/AL - June 27 to July 13, 1913
37 Ed Walsh, Chi/AL - July 31 to August 14, 1910
37 Joel Horlen, Chi/AL - May 11 to 29, 1968
37 Mike Torrez, Oak/AL - August 29 to September 15, 1976
36 Ed Morris, Pit/NL - September 5 to 17, 1888
36 Hal Brown, Bal/AL - July 7 to August 8, 1961 (allowed 4 runs on July 17 in a rained out game)
36 Jim McGlothlin, Cal/AL - May 22 to June 11, 1967
36 CHARLIE HOUGH, Tex/AL - August 23 to September 14, 1983
(GREGG OLSON, Bal/AL had a streak of 41 scoreless innings over two seasons from August 4, 1989 to May 4, 1990, 26 in 1989 and 15 in 1990)

Most strikeouts, game

21 Tom Cheney, Was/AL - September 12, 1962 (16 innings)
20 ROGER CLEMENS, Bos/AL - April 29, 1986
19 Charlie Sweeney, Pro/NL - June 7, 1884
19 Hugh (One Arm) Daily, Chi/UA - July 7, 1884
19 Luis Tiant, Cle/AL - July 3, 1968 (10 innings)
19 Steve Carlton, StL/NL - September 15, 1969
19 Tom Seaver, NY/NL - April 22, 1970
19 NOLAN RYAN, Cal/AL - June 14, 1974 (12 innings)
19 NOLAN RYAN, Cal/AL - August 12, 1974
19 NOLAN RYAN, Cal/AL - August 20, 1974 (11 innings)
19 NOLAN RYAN, Cal/AL - June 8, 1977 (10 innings)
19 DAVID CONE, NY/NL - October 6, 1991
18 Jim Whitney, Bos/NL - June 14, 1884 (15 innings)
18 Dupee Shaw, Bos/UA - July 19, 1884
18 Henry Porter, Mil/UA - October 3, 1884
18 Jack Coombs, Phi/AL - September 1, 1906 (24 innings)
18 Bob Feller, Cle/AL - October 2, 1938 (1st g)
18 Warren Spahn, Bos/NL - June 14, 1952 (15 innings)
18 Sandy Koufax, LA/NL - August 31, 1959
18 Sandy Koufax, LA/NL - April 24, 1962
18 Jim Maloney, Cin/NL - June 14, 1965 (11 innings)
18 Chris Short, Phi/NL - October 2, 1965 (15 innings in an 18 inning game)
18 Don Wilson, Hou/NL - July 14, 1968
18 NOLAN RYAN, Cal/AL - September 10, 1976
18 Ron Guidry, NY/AL - June 17, 1978
18 BILL GULLICKSON, Mon/NL - September 10, 1980
18 RAMON MARTINEZ, LA/NL - June 4, 1990
18 RANDY JOHNSON, Sea/AL - September 27, 1992

Most bases on balls, game

16 Bill George, NY/NL - May 30, 1887 (1st game)
16 George Van Haltren, Chi/NL - June 27, 1887
16 Henry Gruber, Cle/PL - April 19, 1890
16 Bruno Haas, Phi/AL - June 23, 1915
16 Tommy Byrne, NY/AL - August 22, 1951 (13 innings)
15 Carroll Brown, Phi/AL - July 12, 1913
14 Ed Crane, Was/NL - September 1, 1886
14 Charlie Hickman, Bos/NL - August 16, 1899 (2nd game)
14 Henry Mathewson, NY/NL - October 5, 1906
14 Skipper Friday, Was/AL - June 17, 1923
13 Bill George, NY/NL - May 17, 1887
13 John Kirby, Ind/NL - June 9, 1887
13 Cy Seymour, NY/NL - May 24, 1899 (10 innings)
13 Mal Eason, Bos/NL - September 3, 1902
13 Pete Schneider, Cin/NL - July 6, 1918
13 George Turbeville, Phi/AL - August 24, 1935 (15 innings)
13 Tommy Byrne, NY/AL - June 8, 1949
13 Dick Weik, Was/AL - September 1, 1949
13 Bud Podbielan, Cin/NL - May 18, 1953 (11 innings)

No-hit games, nine or more innings (number to left is career total if greater than 1)

Joe Borden, Phi vs Chi NA, 4-0; July 28, 1875.
George Bradley, StL vs Har NL, 2-0; July 15, 1876.
Lee Richmond, Wor vs Cle NL, 1-0; June 12, 1880 (perfect game).
Monte Ward, Pro vs Buf NL, 5-0; June 17, 1880. (perfect game).
Larry Corcoran, Chi vs Bos NL, 6-0; August 19, 1880.
Jim Galvin, Buf at Wor NL, 1-0; August 20, 1880.
Tony Mullane, Lou at Cin AA, 2-0; September 11, 1882.
Guy Hecker, Lou at Pit AA, 3-1; September 19, 1882.
2 Larry Corcoran, Chi vs Wor NL, 5-0; September 20, 1882.
Charley Radbourn, Pro at Cle NL, 8-0; July 25, 1883.
Hugh (One Arm) Daily, Cle at Phi NL; 1-0; September 13, 1883.
Al Atkisson, Phi vs Pit AA, 10-1; May 24, 1884.
Ed Morris, Col at Pit AA, 5-0; May 29, 1884.
Frank Mountain, Col at Was AA, 12-0; June 5, 1884.
3 Larry Corcoran, Chi vs Pro NL, 6-0; June 27, 1884.
2 Jim Galvin, Buf at Det NL, 18-0; August 4, 1884.
Dick Burns, Cin at KC UA, 3-1; August 26, 1884.
Ed Cushman, Mil vs Was UA, 5-0; September 28, 1884.
Sam Kimber, Bro vs Tol AA, 0-0; October 4, 1884 (ten innings, darkness).
John Clarkson, Chi at Pro NL, 4-0; July 27, 1885.
Charlie Ferguson, Phi vs Pro NL, 1-0; August 29, 1885.
2 Al Atkisson, Phi vs NY AA, 3-2; May 1, 1886.
Adonis Terry, Bro vs StL AA, 1-0; July 24, 1886.
Matt Kilroy, Bal at Pit AA, 6-0; October 6, 1886.
2 Adonis Terry, Bro vs Lou AA, 4-0; May 27, 1888.
Henry Porter, KC at Bal AA, 4-0; June 6, 1888.
Ed Seward, Phi vs Cin AA, 12-2; July 26, 1888.
Gus Weyhing, Phi vs KC AA, 4-0; July 31, 1888.
Silver King, Chi vs Bro PL, 0-1; June 21, 1890, (8 innings, lost the game; bottom of 9th not played).
Cannonball Titcomb, Roch vs Syr AA, 7-0; September 15, 1890.
Tom Lovett, Bro vs NY NL, 4-0; June 22, 1891.
Amos Rusie, NY vs Bro NL, 6-0; July 31, 1891.
Ted Breitenstein, StL vs Lou AA, 8-0; October 4, 1891 (1st game, first start in the major leagues).
Jack Stivetts, Bos vs Bro NL, 11-0; August 6, 1892.
Ben Sanders, Lou vs Bal NL, 6-2; August 22, 1892.
Bumpus Jones, Cin vs Pit NL, 7-1; October 15, 1892 (first game in the major leagues).
Bill Hawke, Bal vs Was NL, 5-0; August 16, 1893.
Cy Young, Cle vs Cin NL, 6-0; September 18, 1897 (1st game).
2 Ted Breitenstein, Cin vs Pit NL, 11-0; April 22, 1898.
Jim Hughes, Bal vs Bos NL, 8-0; April 22, 1898.
Red Donahue, Phi vs Bos NL, 5-0; July 8, 1898.
Walter Thornton, Chi vs Bro NL, 2-0; August 21, 1898 (2nd game).
Deacon Phillippe, Lou vs NY NL, 7-0; May 25, 1899.
Noodles Hahn, Cin vs Phi NL, 4-0; July 12, 1900.
Earl Moore, Cle vs Chi AL, 2-4; May 9, 1901 (lost on two hits in the tenth).

No-hit games (Cont'd)

Christy Mathewson, NY at StL NL, 5-0; July 15, 1901.

Nixey Callahan, Chi vs Det AL, 3-0; September 20, 1902 (1st game).

Chick Fraser, Phi at Chi NL; 10-0; September 18, 1903 (2nd game).

2 Cy Young, Bos vs Phi AL, 3-0; May 5, 1904 (perfect game).

Bob Wicker, Chi at NY NL, 1-0; June 11, 1904 (won in 12 innings after allowing one hit in the tenth).

Jesse Tannehill, Bos at Chi AL, 6-0; August 17, 1904.

2 Christy Mathewson, NY at Chi NL, 1-0; June 13, 1905.

Weldon Henley, Phi at StL AL, 6-0; July 22, 1905 (1st game).

Frank Smith, Chi at Det AL, 15-0; September 6, 1905 (2nd game).

Bill Dinneen, Bos vs Chi AL, 2-0; September 27, 1905 (1st game).

Johnny Lush, Phi at Bro NL, 6-0; May 1, 1906.

Mal Eason, Bro at StL NL, 2-0; July 20, 1906.

Harry McIntyre, Bro vs Pit NL, 0-1; August 1, 1906 (lost on 4 hits in 13 innings after allowing the first hit in the 11th).

Frank (Jeff) Pfeffer, Bos vs Cin NL, 6-0; May 8, 1907.

Nick Maddox, Pit vs Bro NL, 2-1; September 20, 1907.

3 Cy Young, Bos at NY AL, 8-0; June 30, 1908.

Hooks Wiltse, NY vs Phi NL, 1-0; July 4, 1908 (1st game, ten innings).

Nap Rucker, Bro vs Bos NL, 6-0; September 5, 1908 (2nd game).

Dusty Rhoades, Cle vs Bos AL, 2-1; September 18, 1908.

2 Frank Smith, Chi vs Phi AL, 1-0; September 20, 1908.

Addie Joss, Cle vs Chi AL, 1-0; October 2, 1908 (perfect game).

Red Ames, NY vs Bro NL. 0-3; April 15, 1909 (lost on 7 hits in 13 innings after allowing the first hit in the tenth).

2 Addie Joss, Cle vs Chi AL, 1-0; April 20, 1910.

Chief Bender, Phi vs Cle AL, 4-0; May 12, 1910.

Tom L. Hughes, NY vs Cle AL, 0-5; August 30, 1910 (2nd game) (lost on 7 hits in 11 innings after allowing the first hit in the tenth)

Joe Wood, Bos vs StL AL, 5-0; July 29, 1911 (1st game).

Ed Walsh, Chi vs Bos AL, 5-0; August 27, 1911.

George Mullin, Det vs StL AL, 7-0; July 4, 1912 (2nd game).

Earl Hamilton, StL at Det AL, 5-1; August 30, 1912.

Jeff Tesreau, NY at Phi NL, 3-0; September 6, 1912 (1st game).

Jim Scott, Chi at Was AL, 0-1; May 14, 1914 (lost on 2 hits in the tenth).

Joe Benz, Chi vs Cle AL, 6-1; May 31, 1914.

George Davis, Bos vs Phi NL, 7-0; September 9, 1914 (2nd game).

Ed Lafitte, Bro vs KC FL, 6-2; September 19, 1914.

Rube Marquard, NY vs Bro NL, 2-0; April 15, 1915.

Frank Allen, Pit vs StL FL, 2-0; April 24, 1915.

Claude Hendrix, Chi vs Pit FL, 10-0; May 15, 1915.

Alex Main, KC vs Buf FL, 5-0; August 16, 1915.

Jimmy Lavender, Chi at NY NL, 2-0; August 31, 1915 (1st game).

Dave Davenport, StL vs Chi FL, 3-0; September 7, 1915.

2 Tom L. Hughes, Bos vs Pit NL, 2-0; June 16, 1916.

Rube Foster, Bos vs NY AL, 2-0; June 21, 1916.

Joe Bush, Phi vs Cle AL, 5-0; August 26, 1916.

Hubert (Dutch) Leonard, Bos vs StL AL, 4-0; August 30, 1916.

Eddie Cicotte, Chi at StL AL, 11-0; April 14, 1917.

George Mogridge, NY at Bos AL, 2-1; April 24, 1917.

Fred Toney, Cin at Chi NL, 1-0; May 2, 1917 (ten innings).

Hippo Vaughn, Chi vs Cin NL, 0-1; May 2, 1917. (lost on two hits in the 10th, Toney pitched a no-hitter in this game).

Ernie Koob, StL vs Chi AL, 1-0; May 5, 1917.

Bob Groom, StL vs Chi AL, 3-0; May 6, 1917 (2nd game).

Ernie Shore, Bos vs Was AL, 4-0; June 23, 1917 (1st game, perfect game). (Shore relieved Babe Ruth in the first inning after Ruth was thrown out of the game.The runner was caught stealing and Shore retired the remaining 26 batters in order)

2 Hubert (Dutch) Leonard, Bos at Det AL, 5-0; June 3, 1918.

Hod Eller, Cin vs StL NL, 6-0; May 11, 1919.

Ray Caldwell, Cle at NY AL, 3-0; September 10, 1919 (1st game).

Walter Johnson, Was at Bos AL, 1-0; July 1, 1920.

Charlie Robertson, Chi at Det AL, 2-0; April 30, 1922 (perfect game).

Jesse Barnes, NY vs Phi NL, 6-0; May 7, 1922.

Sam Jones, NY at Phi AL, 2-0; September 4, 1923.

Howard Ehmke, Bos at Phi AL, 4-0; September 7, 1923.

Jesse Haines, StL vs Bos NL, 5-0; July 17, 1924.

Dazzy Vance, Bro vs Phi NL, 10-1; September 13, 1925 (1st game).

Ted Lyons, Chi at Bos AL, 6-0; August 21, 1926.

Carl Hubbell, NY vs Pit NL, 11-0; May 8, 1929.

Wes Ferrell, Cle vs StL AL, 9-0; April 29, 1931.

Bobby Burke, Was vs Bos AL, 5-0; August 8, 1931.

Bobo Newsom, StL vs Bos AL, 1-2; September 18, 1934 (lost on 1 hit in the tenth).

Paul Dean, StL at Bro NL, 3-0; September 21, 1934 (2nd game).

Vern Kennedy, Chi vs Cle AL, 5-0; August 31, 1935.

Bill Dietrich, Chi vs StL AL, 8-0; June 1, 1937.

Johnny Vander Meer, Cin vs Bos NL, 3-0; June 11, 1938

2 Johnny Vander Meer, Cin at Bro NL, 6-0; June 15, 1938 (next start after June 11)

Monte Pearson, NY vs Cle AL, 13-0; August 27, 1938 (2nd game).

Bob Feller, Cle at Chi AL, 1-0; April 16, 1940 (opening day).

Tex Carleton, Bro at Cin NL, 3-0; April 30, 1940.

Lon Warneke, StL at Cin NL, 2-0; August 30, 1941.

Jim Tobin, Bos vs Bro NL, 2-0; April 27, 1944.

Clyde Shoun, Cin vs Bos NL, 1-0; May 15, 1944.

Dick Fowler, Phi vs StL AL, 1-0; September 9, 1945 (2nd game).

Ed Head, Bro vs Bos NL, 5-0; April 23, 1946.

2 Bob Feller, Cle at NY AL, 1-0; April 30, 1946.

Ewell Blackwell, Cin vs Bos NL, 6-0; June 18, 1947.

Don Black, Cle vs Phi AL, 3-0; July 10, 1947 (1st game).

Bill McCahan, Phi vs Was AL, 3-0; September 3, 1947.

Bob Lemon, Cle at Det AL, 2-0; June 30, 1948.

Rex Barney, Bro at NY NL, 2-0; September 9, 1948.

Vern Bickford, Bos vs Bro NL, 7-0; August 11, 1950.

Cliff Chambers, Pit at Bos NL, 3-0; May 6, 1951 (2nd game).

3 Bob Feller, Cle vs Det AL, 2-1; July 1, 1951 (1st game).

Allie Reynolds, NY at Cle AL, 1-0; July 12, 1951.

No-hit Games (Cont'd)

2 Allie Reynolds, NY vs Bos AL, 8-0; September 28, 1951 (1st game).
Virgil Trucks, Det vs Was AL, 1-0; May 15, 1952.
Carl Erskine, Bro vs Chi NL, 5-0; June 19, 1952.
2 Virgil Trucks, Det at NY AL, 1-0; August 25, 1952.
Bobo Holloman, StL vs Phi AL, 6-0; May 6, 1953 (first start in the major leagues).
Jim Wilson, Mil vs Phi NL, 2-0; June 12, 1954.
Sam Jones, Chi vs Pit NL, 4-0; May 12, 1955.
2 Carl Erskine, Bro vs NY NL, 3-0; May 12, 1956. Johnny Klippstein (7 innings), Hershell Freeman (1 inning) and Joe Black (3 innings), Cin at Mil NL, 1-2; May 26, 1956 (lost on 3 hits in 11 innings after allowing the first hit in the tenth)
Mel Parnell, Bos vs Chi AL, 4-0; July 14, 1956.
Sal Maglie, Bro vs Phi NL, 5-0; September 25, 1956.
Don Larsen, NY AL vs Bro NL, 2-0; October 8, 1956 (World Series, perfect game).
Bob Keegan, Chi vs Was AL, 6-0; August 20, 1957 (2nd game).
Jim Bunning, Det at Bos AL, 3-0; July 20, 1958 (1st game).
Hoyt Wilhelm, Bal vs NY AL, 1-0; September 20, 1958
Harvey Haddix, Pit at Mil NL, 0-1; May 26, 1959 (lost on 1 hit in 13 innings after pitching 12 perfect innings).
Don Cardwell, Chi vs StL NL, 4-0; May 15, 1960 (2nd game).
Lew Burdette, Mil vs Phi NL, 1-0; August 18, 1960.
Warren Spahn, Mil vs Phi NL, 4-0; September 16, 1960.
2 Warren Spahn, Mil vs SF NL, 1-0; April 28, 1961.
Bo Belinsky, LA vs Bal AL, 2-0; May 5, 1962.
Earl Wilson, Bos vs LA AL, 2-0; June 26, 1962.
Sandy Koufax, LA vs NY NL, 5-0; June 30, 1962.
Bill Monbouquette, Bos at Chi AL, 1-0; August 1, 1962.
Jack Kralick, Min vs KC AL, 1-0; August 26, 1962.
2 Sandy Koufax, LA vs SF NL, 8-0; May 11, 1963.
Don Nottebart, Hou vs Phi NL, 4-1; May 17, 1963.
Juan Marichal, SF vs Hou NL, 1-0; June 15, 1963.
Ken T. Johnson, Hou vs Cin NL, 0-1; April 23, 1964 (lost the game).
3 Sandy Koufax, LA at Phi NL, 3-0; June 4, 1964.
2 Jim Bunning, Phi at NY NL, 6-0; June 21, 1964 (1st game, perfect game).
Jim Maloney, Cin vs NY NL, 0-1; June 14, 1965 (lost on 2 hits in 11 innings after pitching 10 hitless innings).
2 Jim Maloney, Cin at Chi NL, 1-0; August 19, 1965 (1st game, 10 innings).
4 Sandy Koufax, LA vs Chi NL, 1-0; September 9, 1965 (perfect game).
Dave Morehead, Bos vs Cle AL, 2-0; September 16, 1965.
Sonny Siebert, Cle vs Was AL, 2-0; June 10, 1966.
Steve D. Barber (8 2/3 innings) and Stu Miller (1/3 inning), Bal vs Det AL, 1-2; April 30, 1967 (1st game, lost the game)
Don Wilson, Hou vs Atl NL, 2-0; June 18, 1967.
Dean Chance, Min at Cle AL, 2-1; August 25, 1967 (2nd game).
Joe Horlen, Chi vs Det AL, 6-0; September 10, 1967 (1st game).
Tom Phoebus, Bal vs Bos AL, 6-0; April 27, 1968.
Catfish Hunter, Oak vs Min AL, 4-0; May 8, 1968 (perfect game).
George Culver, Cin at Phi NL, 6-1; July 29, 1968 (2nd game).
Gaylord Perry, SF vs StL NL, 1-0; September 17, 1968.
Ray Washburn, StL at SF NL, 2-0; September 18, 1968.
Bill Stoneman, Mon at Phi NL, 7-0; April 17, 1969.
3 Jim Maloney, Cin vs Hou NL, 10-0; April 30, 1969.
2 Don Wilson, Hou at Cin NL, 4-0; May 1, 1969.
Jim Palmer, Bal vs Oak AL, 8-0; August 13, 1969.
Ken Holtzman, Chi vs Atl NL, 3-0; August 19, 1969.
Bob Moose, Pit at NY NL, 4-0; September 20, 1969.
Dock Ellis, Pit at SD NL, 2-0; June 12, 1970 (1st game).
Clyde Wright, Cal vs Oak AL, 4-0; July 3, 1970.
Bill Singer, LA vs Phi NL, 5-0; July 20, 1970.
Vida Blue, Oak vs Min AL, 6-0; September 21, 1970.
2 Ken Holtzman, Chi at Cin NL, 1-0; June 3, 1971.
Rick Wise, Phi at Cin NL, 4-0; June 23, 1971.
Bob Gibson, StL at Pit NL, 11-0; August 14, 1971.
Burt Hooton, Chi vs Phi NL, 4-0; April 16, 1972.
Milt Pappas, Chi vs SD NL, 8-0; September 2, 1972.
2 Bill Stoneman, Mon vs NY NL, 7-0; October 2, 1972 (1st game).
Steve Busby, KC at Det AL, 3-0; April 16, 1973.
NOLAN RYAN, Cal at KC AL, 3-0; May 15, 1973.
2 NOLAN RYAN, Cal at Det AL, 6-0; July 15, 1973.
Jim Bibby, Tex at Oak AL, 6-0; July 20, 1973.
Phil Niekro, Atl vs SD NL, 9-0; August 5, 1973.
2 Steve Busby, KC at Mil AL, 2-0; June 19, 1974.
Dick Bosman, Cle vs Oak AL, 4-0; July 19, 1974.
3 NOLAN RYAN, Cal vs Min AL, 4-0; September 28, 1974.
4 NOLAN RYAN, Cal vs Bal AL, 1-0; June 1, 1975.
Ed Halicki, SF vs NY NL, 6-0; August 24, 1975 (2nd game).
Vida Blue (5 innings), Glenn Abbott (1 inning), Paul Lindblad (1 inning) and Rollie Fingers (2 innings), Oak vs Cal AL, 5-0; September 28, 1975.
Larry Dierker, Hou vs Mon NL, 6-0; July 9, 1976.
Blue Moon Odom (5 innings) and Francisco Barrios (4 innings), Chi at Oak AL, 2-1; July 28, 1976.
JOHN CANDELARIA, Pit vs LA NL, 2-0; August 9, 1976.
John Montefusco, SF at Atl NL, 9-0; September 29, 1976.
Jim Colborn, KC vs Tex AL, 6-0; May 14, 1977.
DENNIS ECKERSLEY, Cle vs Cal AL, 1-0; May 30, 1977.
BERT BLYLEVEN, Tex at Cal AL, 6-0; September 22, 1977.
Bob Forsch, StL vs Phi NL, 5-0; April 16, 1978.
Tom Seaver, Cin vs StL NL, 4-0; June 16, 1978.
Ken Forsch, Hou vs AtL NL, 6-0; April 7, 1979.
Jerry Reuss, LA at SF NL, 8-0; June 27, 1980.
Charlie Lea, Mon vs SF NL, 4-0; May 10, 1981 (2nd game).
Len Barker, Cle vs Tor AL, 3-0; May 15, 1981 (perfect game).
5 NOLAN RYAN, Hou vs LA NL, 5-0; September 26, 1981.
DAVE RIGHETTI, NY vs Bos AL, 4-0; July 4, 1983.
2 Bob Forsch, StL vs Mon NL, 3-0; September 26, 1983.
Mike Warren, Oak vs Chi AL, 3-0; September 29, 1983.

No-hit Games (Cont'd)

JACK MORRIS, Det at Chi AL, 4-0; April 7, 1984.

Mike Witt, Cal at Tex AL, 1-0; September 30, 1984 (perfect game).

Joe Cowley, Chi at Cal AL, 7-1; September 19, 1986.

Mike Scott, Hou vs SF NL, 2-0; September 25, 1986.

Juan Nieves, Mil at Bal AL, 7-0; April 15, 1987.

TOM BROWNING, Cin vs LA NL, 1-0; September 16, 1988 (perfect game).

MARK LANGSTON (7 innings) and Mike Witt (2 innings), Cal vs Sea AL, 1-0; April 11, 1990.

RANDY JOHNSON, Sea vs Det AL, 2-0; June 2, 1990.

6 NOLAN RYAN, Tex at Oak AL, 5-0; June 11, 1990.

DAVE STEWART, Oak at Tor AL, 5-0; June 29, 1990.

Fernando Valenzuela, LA vs StL NL, 6-0; June 29, 1990.

Andy Hawkins, NY at Chi AL, 0-4; July 1, 1990 (8 innings, lost the game; bottom of 9th not played).

TERRY MULHOLLAND, Phi vs SF NL, 6-0; August 15, 1990.

DAVE STIEB, Tor at Det AL, 3-0; September 2, 1990.

7 NOLAN RYAN, Tex vs Tor AL, 3-0; May 1, 1991.

TOMMY GREENE, Phi at Mon NL, 2-0; May 23, 1991.

BOB MILACKI (6 innings), MIKE FLANAGAN (1 inning), MARK WILLIAMSON (1 inning), and GREGG OLSON (1 inning), Bal at Oak AL, 2-0; July 13, 1991.

MARK GARDNER, Mon at LA NL, 0-1; July 26, 1991 (9 innings, lost on 2 hits in 10th, relieved by Jeff Fassero, who allowed 1 more hit).

DENNIS MARTINEZ, Mon at LA NL, 2-0; July 28, 1991 (perfect game).

WILSON ALVAREZ, Chi at Bal AL, 7-0; August 11, 1991.

BRET SABERHAGEN, KC vs Chi AL, 7-0; August 26, 1991.

KENT MERCKER (6 innings), Mark Wohlers (2 innings) and ALEJANDRO PENA (1 inning), Atl at SD NL, 1-0; September 11, 1991.

MATT YOUNG, Bos at Cle AL, 1-2; April 12, 1992 (1st game) (8 innings, lost the game, bottom of 9th not played).

KEVIN GROSS, LA vs SF NL, 2-0; August 17, 1992.

No-hit games, less than 9 innings

Larry McKeon, six innings, rain, Ind at Cin AA, 0-0; May 6, 1884.

Charlie Gagus, eight innings, darkness, Was vs Wil UA, 12-1; August 21, 1884.

Charlie Getzien, six innings, rain, Det vs Phi NL, 1-0; October 1, 1884.

Charlie Sweeney (2 innings) and Henry Boyle (3 innings), five innings, rain, StL vs StP UA, 0-1; October 5,1884.

Dupee Shaw, five innings, agreement, Pro at Buf NL, 4-0; October 7, 1885 (1st game).

George Van Haltren, six innings, rain, Chi vs Pit NL, 1-0, June 21,1888.

Ed Crane, seven innings, darkness, NY vs Was NL, 3-0; September 27, 1888.

Matt Kilroy, seven innings, darkness, Bal vs StL AA, 0-0; July 29, 1889 (2nd game).

George Nicol, seven innings, darkness, StL vs Phi AA, 21-2; September 23, 1890.

Hank Gastright, eight innings, darkness, Col vs Tol AA, 6-0; October 12, 1890.

Jack Stivetts, five innings, called so Boston could catch train to Cleveland for Temple Cub playoffs, Bos at Was NL, 6-0; October 15, 1892 (2nd game).

Elton Chamberlain, seven innings, darkness, Cin vs Bos NL, 6-0; September 23, 1893 (2nd game).

Ed Stein, six innings, rain, Bro vs Chi NL, 6-0; June 2, 1894.

Red Ames, five innings, darkness, NY at StL NL, 5-0; September 14, 1903 (2nd game, first game in the major leagues).

Rube Waddell, five innings, rain, Phi vs StL AL, 2-0; August 15, 1905.

Jake Weimer, seven innings, agreement, Cin vs Bro NL, 1-0; August 24, 1906 (2nd game).

Jimmy Dygert (3 innings) and Rube Waddell (2 innings), five innings, rain, Phi vs Chi AL, 4-3; August 29, 1906. (Waddell allowed hit and two runs in 6th, but rain caused game to revert to 5 innings).

Stoney McGlynn, seven innings, agreement, StL at Bro NL, 1-1; September 24, 1906 (2nd game).

Lefty Leifield, six innings, darkness, Pit at Phi NL, 8-0; September 26, 1906 (2nd game).

Ed Walsh, five innings, rain, Chi vs NY AL, 8-1; May 26, 1907.

Ed Karger, seven perfect innings, agreement, StL vs Bos NL, 4-0; August 11, 1907 (2nd game).

Howie Camnitz, five innings, agreement, Pit at NY NL, 1-0; August 23, 1907 (2nd game).

Rube Vickers, five perfect innings, darkness, Phi at Was AL, 4-0; October 5, 1907 (2nd game).

Johnny Lush, six innings, rain, StL at Bro NL, 2-0; August 6, 1908.

King Cole, seven innings, called so Chicago could catch train, Chi at StL NL, 4-0; July 31, 1910 (2nd game).

Jay Cashion, six innings, called so Cleveland could catch train, Was vs Cle AL, 2-0; August 20, 1912 (2nd game).

Walter Johnson, seven innings, rain, Was vs StL AL, 2-0; August 25, 1924.

Fred Frankhouse, seven and two-thirds innings, rain, Bro vs Cin NL, 5-0; August 27, 1937.

John Whitehead, six innings, rain, StL vs Det AL, 4-0; August 5, 1940 (2nd game).

Jim Tobin, five innings, darkness, Bos vs Phi NL, 7-0; June 22, 1944 (2nd game).

Mike McCormick, five innings, rain, SF at Phi NL, 3-0; June 12, 1959. (allowed hit in 6th, but rain caused game to revert to 5 innings)

Sam Jones, seven innings, rain, SF at StL NL, 4-0; September 26, 1959.

Dean Chance, five perfect innings, rain, Min vs Bos AL, 2-0; August 6, 1967.

David Palmer, five perfect innings, rain, Mon at StL NL, 4-0; April 21, 1984 (2nd game).

Pascual Perez, five innings, rain, Mon at Phi NL, 1-0; September 24, 1988.

Melido Perez, six innings, rain, Chi at NY AL, 8-0; July 12, 1990.

Perfect game box scores

Lee Richmond, Wor vs Cle NL, 1-0; June 12, 1880

CLEVELAND	ab	r	h	po	a	e
Dunlap,2b	3	0	0	4	2	2
Hankinson,3b	3	0	0	0	0	0
Kennedy,c	3	0	0	9	1	0
Phillips,lb	3	0	0	7	0	0
Shaffer,rf	3	0	0	2	0	0
McCormick,p	3	0	0	0	10	0
Gilligan,cf	3	0	0	1	0	0
Glasscock,ss	3	0	0	0	2	0
Hanlon,lf	3	0	0	1	0	0
Team	27	0	0	24	15	2

WORCESTER	ab	r	h	po	a	e
Wood,lf	4	0	0	0	0	0
Richmond,p	3	0	1	0	6	0
Knight,rf	3	0	0	1	1	0
Irwin,ss	3	0	2	2	3	0
Bennett,c	2	0	0	8	0	0
Whitney,3b	3	0	0	1	2	0
Sullivan,lb	3	0	0	14	0	0
Corey,cf	3	0	0	1	0	0
Creamer,2b	3	0	0	0	4	0
Team	27	1	3	27	16	0

Cleveland	000	000	000	–0
Worcester	000	010	00x	–1

Runs batted in - none
Double play - Glasscock, Dunlap and Phillips

	ip	h	r	er	bb	so
McCormick (L)	8	3	1	0	1	7
Richmond (W)	9	0	0	0	0	5

Time - 1:27
Umpire - Bradley
Attendance - 700

John Montgomery Ward, Pro vs Buf NL, 5-0; June 17, 1880 (A.M.)

PROVIDENCE	ab	r	h	po	a	e
Hines,cf	5	0	2	2	0	0
Start,lb	5	1	1	14	0	0
Dorgan,rf	5	0	2	0	0	0
Gross,c	5	0	0	5	1	0
Farrell,2b	4	3	3	0	2	0
Ward,p	4	0	1	2	6	0
Peters,ss	4	0	1	0	6	0
York,lf	4	0	2	3	0	0
Bradley,3b	4	1	1	1	4	0
Team	40	5	13	27	19	0

BUFFALO	ab	r	h	po	a	e
Crowley,rf-c	3	0	0	4	0	2
Richardson,3b	3	0	0	0	1	0
Rowe,c-rf	3	0	0	3	1	0
Walker,lf	3	0	0	3	0	1
Hornung,2b	3	0	0	2	3	0
Mack,ss	3	0	0	3	3	1
Esterbrook,lb	3	0	0	10	0	0
Poorman,cf	3	0	0	2	0	1
Galvin,p	3	0	0	0	5	0
Team	27	0	0	27	13	5

Providence	010	100	111	–5
Buffalo	000	000	000	–0

Double - Farrell

Triples - Start, York, Bradley
Runs batted in - Ward, Hines, Dorgan
Passed ball - Crowley

	ip	h	r	er	bb	so
Ward (W)	9	0	0	0	0	6
Galvin (L)	9	13	5	3	0	2

Wild pitches - Galvin 2
Time - 1:40
Umpire - Daniels
Attendance - 2000

Cy Young, Bos vs Phi AL, 3-0; May 5, 1904

PHILADELPHIA	ab	r	h	po	a	e
Hartsel,lf	1	0	0	0	0	0
Hoffman,lf	2	0	0	2	1	0
Pickering,cf	3	0	0	1	0	0
Davis,lb	3	0	0	5	0	1
L.Cross,3b	3	0	0	4	1	0
Seybold,rf	3	0	0	2	0	0
Murphy,2b	3	0	0	1	2	0
M.Cross,ss	3	0	0	2	3	0
Schreck,c	3	0	0	7	0	0
Waddell,p	3	0	0	0	1	0
Team	27	0	0	24	8	1

BOSTON	ab	r	h	po	a	e
Dougherty,lf	4	0	1	1	0	0
Collins,3b	4	0	2	2	0	0
Stahl,cf	4	1	1	3	0	0
Freeman,rf	4	0	1	2	0	0
Parent,ss	4	0	2	1	4	0
LaChance,lb	3	0	1	9	0	0
Ferris,2b	3	1	1	0	3	0
Criger,c	3	1	1	9	0	0
Young,p	3	0	0	0	2	0
Team	32	3	10	27	9	0

Philadelphia	000	000	000	–0
Boston	000	001	20x	–3

Doubles - Collins, Criger
Triples - Stahl, Freeman, Ferris
Runs batted in - Freeman, Criger
Sacrifice - LaChance
Double plays - Hoffman and Schreck; L.Cross and Davis

	ip	h	r	er	bb	so
Waddell (L)	8	10	3	2	0	6
Young (W)	9	0	0	0	0	8

Time - 1:30
Umpire - Dwyer
Attendance - 10,267

Addie Joss, Cle vs Chi AL, 1-0; October 2, 1908

CHICAGO	ab	r	h	po	a	e
Hahn,rf	3	0	0	1	0	0
Jones,cf	3	0	0	0	0	0
Isbell,lb	3	0	0	6	1	1
Dougherty,lf	3	0	0	0	0	0
Davis,2b	3	0	0	1	0	0
Parent,ss	3	0	0	0	3	0
Schreck,c	2	0	0	13	1	0
Shaw,c	0	0	0	2	0	0
White,ph	1	0	0	0	0	0

Tannehill,3b	2	0	0	0	0	0
Donohue,ph	1	0	0	0	0	0
Walsh,p	2	0	0	1	3	0
Anderson,ph	1	0	0	0	0	0
Team	27	0	0	24	8	1

CLEVELAND	ab	r	h	po	a	e
Good,rf	4	0	0	1	0	0
Bradley,3b	4	0	0	0	1	0
Hinchman,lf	3	0	0	3	0	0
Lajoie,2b	3	0	1	2	8	0
Stovall,lb	3	0	0	16	0	0
Clarke,c	3	0	0	4	1	0
Birmingham,cf	4	1	2	0	0	0
Perring,ss	2	0	1	1	1	0
Joss,p	3	0	0	0	5	0
Team	29	1	4	27	16	0

Chicago	000	000	000	–0
Cleveland	001	000	00x	–1

Runs batted in - none
Stolen bases - Birmingham 2

	ip	h	r	er	bb	so
Walsh (L)	8	4	1	0	1	15
Joss (W)	9	0	0	0	0	3

Wild pitch - Walsh
Time - 1:40
Umpires - Connolly and O'Loughlin
Attendance - 10,598

Ernie Shore, Bos vs Was AL, 4-0; June 23, 1917 (1st game)

WASHINGTON	ab	r	h	po	a	e
Morgan,2b	2	0	0	4	2	0
Foster,3b	3	0	0	1	3	2
Leonard,3b	0	0	0	0	1	0
Milan,cf	3	0	0	1	0	0
Rice,rf	3	0	0	3	0	1
Gharrity,lb	0	0	0	0	0	0
Judge,lb	3	0	0	11	1	0
Jamieson,lf	3	0	0	0	0	0
Shanks,ss	3	0	0	1	2	0
Henry,c	3	0	0	1	0	0
Ayers,p	2	0	0	2	8	0
Menosky,ph	1	0	0	0	0	0
Team	26	0	0	24	17	3

BOSTON	ab	r	h	po	a	e
Hooper,rf	4	0	1	0	0	0
Barry,2b	4	0	0	2	1	0
Hoblitzel,lb	4	0	0	12	2	0
Gardner,3b	4	1	1	2	1	0
Lewis,lf	4	0	3	2	0	0
Walker,cf	3	1	1	4	0	0
Scott,ss	3	0	0	1	5	0
Thomas,c	0	0	0	0	0	0
Agnew,c	3	1	3	2	1	0
Ruth,p	0	0	0	0	0	0
Shore,p	2	1	0	2	6	0
Team	31	4	9	27	16	0

Washington	000	000	000	–0
Boston	010	000	30x	–4

Doubles - Walker, Agnew
Runs batted in - Agnew 2, Hooper 2
Sacrifices - Walker, Shore, Scott
Caught stealing - Morgan
Double plays - Ayers, Foster and Judge; Ayers and Judge

	ip	h	r	er	bb	so
Ayers (L)	8	9	4	2	0	0
Ruth	0	0	0	0	1	0
Shore (W)	9	0	0	0	0	2

Time 1:40
Umpires - Owens, McCormick and Dinneen
Attendance - 16,158

Charlie Robertson, Chi at Det AL, 2-0; April 30, 1922

CHICAGO	ab	r	h	po	a	e
Mulligan,ss	4	0	1	0	0	0
McClellan,3b	3	0	1	1	3	0
Collins,2b	3	0	1	4	3	0
Hooper,rf	3	1	0	3	0	0
Mostil,lf	4	1	1	3	0	0
Strunk,cf	3	0	0	0	0	0
Sheely,lb	4	0	2	9	0	0
Schalk,c	4	0	1	7	1	0
Robertson,p	4	0	0	0	1	0
Team	32	2	7	27	8	0

DETROIT	ab	r	h	po	a	e
Blue,lb	3	0	0	11	3	1
Cutshaw,2b	3	0	0	2	3	0
Cobb,cf	3	0	0	1	0	0
Veach,lf	3	0	0	2	0	0
Heilmann,rf	3	0	0	1	0	0
Jones,3b	3	0	0	1	5	0
Rigney,ss	2	0	0	2	1	0
Clark,ph	1	0	0	0	0	0
Manion,c	3	0	0	7	1	0
Pillette,p	2	0	0	0	3	0
Bassler,ph	1	0	0	0	0	0
Team	27	0	0	27	16	1

Chicago	020	000	000	–2
Detroit	000	000	000	–0

Doubles - Mulligan, Sheely
Runs batted in - Sheely 2
Sacrifices - McClellan, Collins, Strunk

	ip	h	r	er	bb	so
Robertson (W)	9	0	0	0	0	6
Pillette (L)	9	7	2	2	2	5

Time - 1:55
Umpires - Nallin and Evans
Attendance - 25,000

Don Larsen, NY AL vs Bro NL, 2-0; October 8, 1956 (World Series)

BROOKLYN	ab	r	h	po	a	e
Gilliam,2b	3	0	0	2	0	0
Reese,ss	3	0	0	4	2	0
Snider,cf	3	0	0	1	0	0
Robinson,2b	3	0	0	2	4	0
Hodges,lb	3	0	0	5	1	0
Amoros,lf	3	0	0	3	0	0
Furillo,rf	3	0	0	0	0	0
Campanella,c	3	0	0	7	2	0
Maglie,p	2	0	0	0	1	0
Mitchell,ph	1	0	0	0	0	0
Team	27	0	0	24	10	0

NEW YORK	ab	r	h	po	a	e
Bauer,rf	4	0	1	4	0	0
Collins,lb	4	0	1	7	0	0
Mantle,cf	3	1	1	4	0	0

Berra,c	3	0	0	7	0	0
Slaughter,lf	2	0	0	1	0	0
Martin,2b	3	0	1	3	4	0
McDougald,ss	2	0	0	0	2	0
Carey,3b	3	1	1	1	1	0
Larsen,p	2	0	0	0	1	0
Team	26	2	5	27	8	0

Brooklyn	000	000	000	–0
New York	000	101	00x	–2

Home run - Mantle
Runs batted in - Mantle, Bauer
Sacrifice - Larsen
Double plays - Reese and Hodges; Hodges, Campanella, Robinson, Campanella and Robinson

	ip	h	r	er	bb	so
Maglie (L)	8	5	2	2	2	5
Larsen (W)	9	0	0	0	0	7

Time - 2:06
Umpires - Pinelli, Soar, Boggess, Napp, Gorman, Runge
Attendance - 64,519

Harvey Haddix, Pit at Mil NL, 0-1; May 26, 1959 (12 perfect innings, lost on one-hit in the 13th inning)

PITTSBURGH	ab	r	h	po	a	e
Schofield,ss	6	0	3	2	4	0
Virdon,cf	6	0	1	8	0	0
Burgess,c	5	0	0	8	0	0
Nelson,lb	5	0	2	14	0	0
Skinner,lf	5	0	1	4	0	0
Mazeroski,2b	5	0	1	1	1	0
Hoak,3b	5	0	2	0	6	1
Mejias,rf	3	0	1	1	0	0
Stuart,ph	1	0	0	0	0	0
Christopher,rf	1	0	0	0	0	0
Haddix,p	5	0	1	0	2	0
Team	47	0	12	38	13	1

MILWAUKEE	ab	r	h	po	a	e
O'Brien,2b	3	0	0	2	5	0
Rice,ph	1	0	0	0	0	0
Mantilla,2b	1	1	0	1	2	0
Mathews,3b	4	0	0	2	3	0
Aaron,rf	4	0	0	1	0	0
Adcock,lb	5	0	1	17	3	0
Covington,lf	4	0	0	4	0	0
Crandall,c	4	0	0	3	5	0
Pafko,cf	4	0	0	6	0	0
Logan,ss	4	0	0	3	5	0
Burdette,p	4	0	0	1	3	0
Team	38	1	1	39	22	0

Pittsburgh	000	000	000	000	0–0
Milwaukee	000	000	000	000	1–1

Double - Adcock
Run batted in - Adcock
Sacrifice - Mathews
Double plays - Adcock, Logan and Adcock; Mathews, O'Brien and Adcock; Adcock and Logan

	ip	h	r	er	bb	so
Haddix (L)	12 2/3	1	1	0	1	8
Burdette (W)	13	12	0	0	0	2

Time - 2:54
Umpires - Smith, Dascoli, Secory and Dixon
Attendance - 19,194

Jim Bunning, Phi at NY NL, 6-0; June 21, 1964

PHILADELPHIA	ab	r	h	po	a	e
Briggs,cf	4	1	0	2	0	0
Herrnstein,lb	4	0	0	7	0	0
Callison,rf	4	1	2	1	0	0
Allen,3b	3	0	1	0	2	0
Covington,lf	2	0	0	1	0	0
Wine,pr-ss	1	1	0	2	1	0
T.Taylor,2b	3	2	1	0	3	0
Rojas,ss-lf	3	0	1	3	0	0
Triandos,c	4	1	2	11	1	0
Bunning,p	4	0	1	0	0	0
Team	32	6	8	27	7	0

NEW YORK	ab	r	h	po	a	e
Hickman,cf	3	0	0	2	0	0
Hunt,2b	3	0	0	3	2	0
Kranepool,lb	3	0	0	8	1	0
Christopher,rf	3	0	0	4	0	0
Gonder,c	3	0	0	6	2	0
R.Taylor,lf	3	0	0	1	0	0
C.Smith,ss	3	0	0	2	1	0
Samuel,3b	2	0	0	0	1	0
Altman,ph	1	0	0	0	0	0
Stallard,p	1	0	0	0	2	0
Wakefield,p	0	0	0	0	0	0
Kanehl,ph	1	0	0	0	0	0
Sturdivant,p	0	0	0	1	0	0
Stephenson,ph	1	0	0	0	0	0
Team	27	0	0	27	9	0

Philadelphia	110	004	000	– 6
New York	000	000	000	– 0

Doubles - Triandos, Bunning
Home run - Callison
Runs batted in - Callison, Allen, Triandos 2, Bunning 2
Sacrifices - Hernstein, Rojas

	ip	h	r	er	bb	so
Bunning (W)	9	0	0	0	0	10
Stallard (L)	5 2/3	7	6	6	4	3
Wakefield	1/3	0	0	0	0	0
Sturdivant	3	1	0	0	0	3

Wild pitch - Stallard
Time - 2:19
Umpires - Sudol, Pryor, Secory and Burkhart
Attendance - 32,026

Sandy Koufax, LA vs Chi NL, 1-0; September 9, 1965

CHICAGO	ab	r	h	po	a	e
Young,cf	3	0	0	5	0	0
Beckert,2b	3	0	0	1	1	0
Williams,rf	3	0	0	0	0	0
Santo,3b	3	0	0	1	2	0
Banks,lb	3	0	0	13	0	0
Browne,lf	3	0	0	1	0	0
Krug,c	3	0	0	3	0	1
Kessinger,ss	2	0	0	0	2	0
Amalfitano,ph	1	0	0	0	0	0
Hendley,p	2	0	0	0	5	0
Kuenn,ph	1	0	0	0	0	0
Team	27	0	0	24	10	1

LOS ANGELES	ab	r	h	po	a	e
Wills,ss	3	0	0	0	2	0
Gilliam,3b	3	0	0	0	1	0
W.Davis,cf	3	0	0	2	0	0
Johnson,lf	2	1	1	2	0	0
Fairly,rf	2	0	0	3	0	0
Lefebvre,2b	3	0	0	1	0	0
Tracewski,2b	0	0	0	0	0	0
Parker,lb	3	0	0	4	0	0
Torborg,c	3	0	0	15	0	0
Koufax,p	2	0	0	0	0	0
Team	24	1	1	27	3	0

Chicago	000	000	000	–0
Los Angeles	000	010	00x	–1

Double - Johnson
Runs batted in - none
Sacrifice - Fairly
Stolen base - Johnson

	ip	h	r	er	bb	so
Hendley (L)	8	1	1	0	1	3
Koufax (W)	9	0	0	0	0	14

Time - 1:43
Umpires - Vargo, Pelekoudas, Jackowski and Pryor
Attendance - 29,139

Jim "Catfish" Hunter, Oak vs Min AL, 4-0; May 8, 1968

MINNESOTA	ab	r	h	po	a	e
Tovar,3b	3	0	0	1	2	0
Carew,2b	3	0	0	4	1	0
Killebrew,lb	3	0	0	5	0	0
Oliva,rf	3	0	0	3	0	0
Uhlaender,cf	3	0	0	2	0	0
Allison,lf	3	0	0	0	0	0
Hernandez,ss	2	0	0	2	4	0
Roseboro,ph	1	0	0	0	0	0
Look,c	3	0	0	7	2	0
Boswell,p	2	0	0	0	1	1
Perranoski,p	0	0	0	0	0	0
Reese,ph	1	0	0	0	0	0
Team	27	0	0	24	10	1

OAKLAND	ab	r	h	po	a	e
Campaneris,ss	4	0	2	1	3	0
Jackson,rf	4	0	0	3	0	0
Bando,3b	3	0	1	0	2	0
Webster,lb	4	1	2	7	0	0
Donaldson,2b	3	0	0	1	2	0
Pagliaroni,c	3	1	0	11	0	0
Monday,cf	3	2	2	2	0	0
Rudi,lf	3	0	0	2	0	0
Robinson,ph	0	0	0	0	0	0
Cater,ph	0	0	0	0	0	0
Hershberger,lf	0	0	0	0	0	0
Hunter,p	4	0	3	0	0	0
Team	31	4	10	27	7	0

Minnesota	000	000	000 - 0
Oakland	000	000	13x - 4

Doubles - Hunter, Monday
Runs batted in - Hunter 3, Cater
Stolen base - Campaneris
Double plays - Boswell, Hernandez and Killebrew; Hernandez, Carew and Killebrew

	ip	h	r	er	bb	so
Boswell (L)	7 2/3	9	4	4	4	6
Perranoski	1/3	1	0	0	1	0
Hunter (W)	9	0	0	0	0	11

Hit by pitch - by Boswell (Donaldson)
Wild pitches - Boswell 2
Time - 2:28
Umpires - Napp, Salerno, Haller and Neudecker
Attendance - 6,298

Len Barker, Cle vs Tor AL, 3-0; May 15, 1981

TORONTO	ab	r	h	po	a	e
Griffin,ss	3	0	0	1	1	1
Moseby,rf	3	0	0	4	0	0
Bell,lf	3	0	0	2	0	0
Mayberry,lb	3	0	0	4	1	1
Upshaw,dh	3	0	0	0	0	0
Garcia,2b	3	0	0	3	2	1
Bosetti,cf	3	0	0	3	0	0
Ainge,3b	2	0	0	1	0	0
Woods,ph	1	0	0	0	0	0
B.Martinez,c	2	0	0	5	1	0
Whitt,ph	1	0	0	0	0	0
Leal,p	0	0	0	1	1	0
Team	27	0	0	24	6	3

CLEVELAND	ab	r	h	po	a	e
Manning,cf	4	1	1	4	0	0
Orta,rf	4	1	3	0	0	0
Hargrove,lb	4	1	1	9	0	0
Thornton,dh	3	0	0	0	0	0
Hassey,c	4	0	1	11	0	0
Harrah,3b	4	0	1	2	0	0
Charbonneau,lf	3	0	0	1	0	0
Kuiper,2b	3	0	0	0	4	0
Veryzer,ss	3	0	0	0	3	0
Barker,p	0	0	0	0	0	0
Team	32	3	7	27	7	0

Toronto	000	000	000 - 0
Cleveland	200	000	01x - 3

Home run - Orta
Runs batted in - Thornton, Hassey, Orta
Sacrifice - Thornton

	ip	h	r	er	bb	so
Leal (L)	8	7	3	1	0	5
Barker (W)	9	0	0	0	0	11

Time - 2:09
Umpires - Garcia, Kosc, Denkinger and McKean
Attendance - 7,290

Mike Witt, Cal at Tex AL, 1-0; September 30, 1984

(last game of the season)

CALIFORNIA	ab	r	h	po	a	e
Wilfong,2b	4	0	0	0	8	0
Sconiers,lb	3	0	0	10	1	0
Grich,lb	0	0	0	2	0	0
Lynn,cf-rf	4	0	2	1	0	0
DeCinces,3b	4	1	2	0	1	0
Downing,lf	4	0	0	1	0	0
Thomas,lf	0	0	0	0	0	0
Re.Jackson,dh	4	0	0	0	0	0
M.Brown,rf	3	0	3	2	0	0
Pettis,cf	0	0	0	0	0	0
Boone,c	3	0	0	10	0	0
Schofield,ss	2	0	0	0	3	0
Witt,p	0	0	0	1	0	0
Team	31	1	7	27	13	0

TEXAS	ab	r	h	po	a	e
Rivers,dh	3	0	0	0	0	0
Tolleson,2b	3	0	0	4	5	0
Ward,lf	3	0	0	0	0	0
Parrish,3b	3	0	0	0	3	0
O'Brien,lb	3	0	0	13	0	0
G.Wright,cf	3	0	0	3	0	0
Dunbar,rf	3	0	0	1	0	0
Scott,c	2	0	0	4	3	0
B.Jones,ph	1	0	0	0	0	0
Wilkerson,ss	2	0	0	2	4	0
Foley,ph	1	0	0	0	0	0
Hough,p	0	0	0	0	2	0
Team	27	0	0	27	17	0

California	000	000	100 - 1
Texas	000	000	000 - 0

Double - Brown
Triple - Brown
Run batted in - Jackson
Double plays - Parrish, Tolleson and O'Brien; Tolleson, Wilkerson and O'Brien
Passed ball - Scott

	ip	h	r	er	bb	so
Witt (W)	9	0	0	0	0	10
Hough (L)	9	7	1	0	3	3

Wild pitch - Hough
Time - 1:49
Umpires - Kosc, Hendry, Coble and Evans
Attendance - 8,375

Tom Browning, Cin vs LA NL, 1-0; September 16, 1988

LOS ANGELES	ab	r	h	po	a	e
Griffin,ss	3	0	0	0	4	0
Hatcher,lb	3	0	0	10	0	0
Gibson,lf	3	0	0	1	0	0
Gonzalez,lf	0	0	0	0	0	0
Marshall,rf	3	0	0	2	0	0
Shelby,cf	3	0	0	2	0	0
Hamilton,3b	3	0	0	0	1	1
Dempsey,c	3	0	0	7	0	0
Sax,2b	3	0	0	2	2	0
Belcher,p	2	0	0	0	2	0
Woodson,ph	1	0	0	0	0	0
Team	27	0	0	24	9	0

CINCINNATI	ab	r	h	po	a	e
Larkin,ss	3	1	1	0	4	0
Sabo,3b	3	0	1	0	3	0
Daniels,lf	3	0	0	3	0	0
Davis,cf	2	0	0	1	0	0
O'Neill,rf	3	0	0	4	0	0
Esasky,lb	3	0	0	10	1	0
Reed,c	3	0	0	7	0	0
Oester,2b	3	0	1	1	1	0
Browning,p	3	0	0	1	0	0
Team	26	1	3	27	9	0

Los Angeles	000	000	000 - 0
Cincinnati	000	001	00x - 1

Double - Larkin
Run batted in - none

	ip	h	r	er	bb	so
Belcher (L)	8	3	1	0	1	7
Browning (W)	9	0	0	0	0	7

Time - 1:51
Umpires - Quick, Hirschbeck, Kibler and Gregg
Attendance - 16,591

Dennis Martinez, Mon at LA NL, 2-0; July 28, 1991

MONTREAL	ab	r	h	po	a	e
DeShields,2b	3	0	1	0	9	0
Grissom,cf	4	0	0	2	0	0
Da.Martinez,rf	4	1	0	0	0	0
Calderon,lf	3	0	0	2	0	0
Wallach,3b	4	0	0	1	1	0
Walker,lb	4	1	1	17	0	0
Hassey,c	3	0	1	5	0	0
Owen,ss	3	0	0	0	2	0
De.Martinez,p	3	0	1	0	2	0
Team	31	2	4	27	14	0

LOS ANGELES	ab	r	h	po	a	e
Butler,cf	3	0	0	1	0	0
Samuel,2b	3	0	0	1	3	0
Murray,lb	3	0	0	8	2	0
Strawberry,rf	3	0	0	4	0	0
Daniels,lf	3	0	0	3	0	0
Harris,3b	3	0	0	0	0	0
Scioscia,c	3	0	0	5	1	0
Griffin,ss	2	0	0	4	4	2
Javier,ph	1	0	0	0	0	0
Morgan,p	2	0	0	1	2	0
Gwynn,ph	1	0	0	0	0	0
Team	27	0	0	26	12	2

Montreal	000	000	200 - 2
Los Angeles	000	000	000 - 0

Triple - Walker
Run batted in - Walker
Caught stealing - Hassey

	ip	h	r	er	bb	so
De.Martinez (W)	9	0	0	0	0	5
Morgan (L)	9	4	2	0	1	5

Wild pitch - Morgan
Time - 2:14
Umpires - Poncino, Froemming, DeMuth and Bonin
Attendance - 45,560

Major League Report

NL East

NL West

AL East

AL West

Pittsburgh Pirates

by Robert Deutsch, *USA TODAY*

MVP Barry Bonds hit .311, led the NL in runs (109), walks (127), slugging (.624), and OBA (.456).

1992 Pirates: Third time wasn't charm

In manager Jim Leyland's viewpoint, there is only one team that has a great season—the team that wins the World Series. If that is the case, his Pirates didn't have a great season in 1992—they had their third straight very good season. They won the NL East crown for the third straight year, the first team to three-peat in the division since the 1976-78 Phillies. But for the third straight year they were defeated in the playoffs, this time in an excruciating 3-2 loss to the Braves in game seven when they were just one strike away from winning.

To even get that far was an upset in the opinion of most observers. Bobby Bonilla, left-hander John Smiley, and team save leader Bill Landrum were gone. But they still had a pretty good collection of talent, led by All-Star outfielders Barry Bonds and Andy Van Slyke. Bonds hit .311 (34 HR, 103 RBI, 39 steals), reaching the 30-30 club for the second time in his career. Van Slyke adjusted his batting style by using a lighter bat to compensate for a back injury and finished with a .324 average, second in the league. Second baseman Jose Lind won his first Gold Glove.

Leyland maneuvered his platoon players—first basemen Gary Redus and Orlando Merced, and catchers Mike LaValliere and Don Slaught—into solid contributors, and got the best out of his reserve players. They finished 96-66, making them the only team to win at least 90 games in each of the first three years of the 1990s. Leyland's reward was his second NL Manager of the Year award.

He won by juggling a pitching staff that saw 18 pitchers win at least one game. The leader was again Doug Drabek (15-11). Randy Tomlin (14 wins) and Bob Walk (10) joined Drabek in double figures, but the new story was rookie knuckleballer Tim Wakefield, recalled July 31: He won eight of nine decisions. When he made his career debut, the Pirates were tied for first with the Expos, but his 3-2, complete-game victory over St. Louis put the Pirates on top to stay.

The bullpen was another juggling act for Leyland; seven pitchers saved at least one game, led by Stan Belinda's total of 18.

Second-half trades provided two key players: Danny Jackson (for Steve Buechele) from the Cubs and Alex Cole from Cleveland. The Buechele trade opened a spot for Jeff King, who hit 14 homers (65 RBI,) third best on the club.

"I'm very proud of what we did," Leyland said. "We did win 96 games. We'll look back on it and think this was a pretty good year for the Pittsburgh Pirates. We just fell one win short."

—by Rob Rains

1993 Pirates: Preview

Life after Barry Bonds may be more complicated than the Pirates imagined. Everybody figured he was a goner; it's pitching that most concerned them. They lost Danny Jackson to the Marlins in the expansion draft (he was subsequently traded to Philadelphia), and Doug Drabek as a free agent (to the Astros). And no one knows how Zane Smith will bounce back from shoulder surgery. He only pitched 10.1 innings after the All-Star break last season. That leaves a possible rotation of Tim Wakefield, Randy Tomlin, Bob Walk, and either Denny Neagle, Steve Cooke, or Paul Wagner.

The good news is Andy Van Slyke, Jeff King and the return of Jim Leyland, whose new contract extends through 1996. Still, the Pirates will have to scrap and claw to win a fourth consecutive division title.

—by Bill Koenig

1992 Pirates: Between the lines

▶**April 22:** So who needs Bobby Bonilla? Not Doug Drabek, who led the Pirates to their ninth straight win.

▶**April 29:** Zane Smith pitched a four-hit shutout with zero walks.

▶**May 2:** Just another workday for Barry Bonds: 2-for-4 with a three-run homer, a double and four RBI.

▶**May 5:** Andy Van Slyke—on a 26-for-52 tear—doubled and hit his first homer of the season.

▶**May 6:** The Pirates and Braves hooked up for the first time in 1992; the Pirates won 4-3 (16 innings.)

▶**May 7:** The Braves snapped the Pirates' eight-game home winning streak, to split the two-game series.

▶**May 23:** Doug Drabek's winless streak reached six games.

▶**May 29:** Van Slyke was 3-for-5, batting .500 (26-for-52) in his last 12 home games. He raised his average by 253 points (to .360) since April 17.

▶**May 31:** The Pirates finished out of first place at the end of a month for the first time since April 1990.

▶**June 2:** Pitcher Victor Cole was recalled from Triple-A Buffalo. He is the only major leaguer born in the former Soviet Union.

▶**June 4:** Bonds welcomed Bonilla back to Three Rivers Stadium, then homered, doubled, and scored three times to ruin the homecoming.

▶**June 15:** Jeff King became the fifth player to be caught stealing twice in an inning. As King tried to elude a rundown on a pickoff, Phillies' pitcher Terry Mulholland was called for interference. Although King was safe, he was charged with being caught stealing. He was then thrown out trying to steal third.

▶**June 22:** Randy Tomlin became the second 10-game winner in the NL. Tomlin was 5-0 with a 1.40 ERA in June after going 1-3 with a 7.33 ERA in May. Bob Walk worked a perfect ninth inning—his first save since 1990.

▶**June 27:** Reliever Stan Belinda was 1-0 with five saves and a 0.00 ERA in his last nine games.

▶**July 1:** Zane Smith won for the first time in 10 starts.

▶**July 6:** Smith pitched his second consecutive 1-0 game. A mere 15,358 fans were on hand, one day after manager Jim Leyland called the lack of fan support in Pittsburgh "a disgrace."

▶**July 12:** The current NL division leaders ended their season matchup as the Pirates beat the Reds 7-6.

▶**July 28:** Van Slyke took over as the majors' leading hitter—for awhile. He singled in his first at-bat to raise his average to .348 and supplant Phillie John Kruk (.347), who was playing later that evening. Kruk was back in first after Van Slyke made outs in his next three appearances, but he fell back into second (.343) by going 0-for-4 himself.

▶**July 31:** Rookie knuckleballer Tim Wakefield had a successful major league debut, beating the Cardinals. He was the fourth Pirates' rookie pitcher to debut that week. ***Quote of the day:*** Doug Drabek, who charted pitches for Wakefield—"It was real easy. Of his first 99 pitches, 80 were knuckleballs."

▶**August 2:** The Pirates completed a four-game sweep of the Cardinals. ***Quote of the day:*** Don Slaught—"This team is like a good pitcher. When a pitcher gets in a jam, the one who can make a pitch to get out of it is going to be a winner."

▶**August 4:** Slaught stole his second base in three years (15th of his 10-year career) and scored the winning run in the 6-2 win over the Mets.

▶**August 5** ***Quote of the day:*** Jim Leyland on the art of overseeing Tim Wakefield—"You never know when to take him out. He had me worried. That kid's going to have me looking like Telly Savalas before too long."

▶**August 6** ***Quote of the day:*** Denny Neagle, who got his second save despite a massive home run by Cardinal Felix Jose—"That one's still flying. I think we might run into it on our flight to New York."

▸**August 14:** Zane Smith lasted only 17 pitches against the Braves.

▸**August 18:** Stan Belinda's scoreless ninth inning improved his ERA at Three Rivers Stadium to 0.76.

▸**August 19:** Danny Cox got his first save in seven years in the majors.

▸**August 20:** Lloyd McClendon hit his first home run since April 19.

▸**August 21:** After riding his elusive knuckleball to a 3-0 record and a 1.32 ERA, Tim Wakefield finally proved human, giving up eight hits and six runs in six innings.

▸**August 22:** The Pirates' offense finally came through for Doug Drabek. Drabek had a 1.98 ERA in his last five starts, but his record in that span was only 1-2. He had either lost or received a no-decision in seven games in which he allowed two runs or less.

▸**August 26:** In the first matchup of NL knuckleballers in 10 years, Wakefield outdueled veteran Dodger Tom Candiotti to lead the Pirates to a shutout. The last time knuckleballers faced each other in the NL was 1982, when the Niekro brothers, Joe and Phil, squared off.

▸**September 6:** Bonds hit a three-run homer, walked twice, and stole his 32nd base. Sid Bream also hit a homer (23 RBI in his last 24 starts).

▸**September 14:** The Pirates' lead in the NL East stretched to four games, thanks to their 34th one-run win of the year. Jay Bell extended his hitting streak to 19 games, longest in the NL.

▸**September 19 *Milestone:*** Barry Bonds hit his 30th home run of the year, becoming the fifth player in history to have two 30-homer, 30-steal seasons. The others are Willie Mays, Howard Johnson, Ron Gant, and Barry's father, Bobby Bonds.

▸**September 21:** Rookie Steve Cooke pitched seven innings of three-hit shutout relief. The Pirates' lead grew to seven over Montreal.

▸**September 27:** Clinch! The Pirates clinched the NL East title with a 4-2 win over the Mets.

▸**October 4:** Barry Bonds led the league in runs (109), walks (127), slugging (.624), and on-base percentage (.456); he was second in homers (34), fourth in RBI (103), fifth in total bases (295), and seventh in batting (.311). Andy Van Slyke led the NL in doubles (45), and came in second in batting (.324) and hits (199); he was third in triples (12), runs (103), and total bases (310), and seventh in slugging (.505). On the mound, Doug Drabek was second in complete games (10) and innings (256 2/3), and fifth in strikeouts (177).

—by Jeanie Chung, John Hunt, Deron Snyder, and Lisa Winston.

Team directory

▸**Owner:** Pittsburgh Baseball Associates

▸**General Manager:** Ted Simmons

▸**Ballpark:**
Three Rivers Stadium
600 Stadium Circle, Pittsburgh, Pa.
412-323-5000
Capacity 58,729
Pay parking lot; $4
Public transportation available
Family and wheelchair sections, ramps, guest relations

▸**Team publications:**
Yearbook, Scorecard, Official Record and Info Guide

▸**TV, radio broadcast stations:**
KDKA 1020 AM, KDKA Channel 2, TCI Cable

▸**Camps and/or clinics:**
Camp Bradenton, 412-323-5000

▸**Spring Training:**
McKechnie Field
Bradenton, Fla.
Capacity 6,200
813-748-4610

PITTSBURGH PIRATES 1992 final stats

Batting	AVG	SLG	OB	G	AB	R	H	TB	2B	3B	HR	RBI	BB	SO	SB	CS	E
Young	.571	.571	.667	10	7	2	4	4	0	0	0	4	2	0	1	0	1
Slaught	.345	.482	.384	87	255	26	88	123	17	3	4	37	17	23	2	2	5
VanSlyke	.324	.505	.381	154	614	103	199	310	45	12	14	89	58	99	12	3	5
Bonds	.311	.624	.456	140	473	109	147	295	36	5	34	103	127	69	39	8	3
A.Cole	.278	.361	.335	64	205	33	57	74	3	7	0	10	18	46	7	4	1
Bell	.264	.383	.326	159	632	87	167	242	36	6	9	55	55	103	7	5	22
Espy	.258	.340	.310	112	194	21	50	66	7	3	1	20	15	40	6	3	4
LaValliere	.256	.328	.350	95	293	22	75	96	13	1	2	29	44	21	0	3	3
Redus	.256	.381	.321	76	176	26	45	67	7	3	3	12	17	25	11	4	1
McClendon	.253	.353	.350	84	190	26	48	67	8	1	3	20	28	24	1	3	3
Merced	.247	.385	.332	134	405	50	100	156	28	5	6	60	52	63	5	4	5
Lind	.235	.269	.275	135	468	38	110	126	14	1	0	39	26	29	3	1	6
King	.231	.371	.272	130	480	56	111	178	21	2	14	65	27	56	4	6	12
Pennyfeather	.222	.222	.222	15	9	2	2	2	0	0	0	0	0	0	0	0	0
Varsho	.222	.370	.266	103	162	22	36	60	6	3	4	22	10	32	5	2	1
Clark	.212	.394	.325	23	33	3	7	13	0	0	2	7	6	8	0	0	0
Garcia	.205	.231	.195	22	39	4	8	9	1	0	0	4	0	9	0	0	2
Gibson	.196	.304	.237	16	56	6	11	17	0	0	2	5	3	12	3	1	0
Wehner	.179	.228	.252	55	123	11	22	28	6	0	0	4	12	22	3	0	4
Martin	.167	.333	.154	12	12	1	2	4	0	1	0	2	0	5	0	0	0
Prince	.091	.136	.192	27	44	1	4	6	2	0	0	5	6	9	1	1	2

Pitching	W-L	ERA	G	GS	CG	GF	Sho	SV	IP	H	R	ER	HR	BB	SO
Wagner	2-0	0.69	6	1	0	1	0	0	13	9	1	1	0	5	5
Wakefield	8-1	2.15	13	13	4	0	1	0	92	76	26	22	3	35	51
Miller	1-0	2.38	6	0	0	1	0	0	11.1	11	3	3	0	1	5
Drabek	15-11	2.77	34	34	10	0	4	0	256.2	218	84	79	17	54	177
Patterson	6-3	2.92	60	0	0	26	0	9	64.2	59	22	21	7	23	43
Smith	8-8	3.06	23	22	4	0	3	0	141	138	56	48	8	19	56
Belinda	6-4	3.15	59	0	0	42	0	18	71.1	58	26	25	8	29	57
Walk	10-6	3.20	36	19	1	7	0	2	135	132	54	48	10	43	60
Tomlin	14-9	3.41	35	33	1	0	1	0	208.2	226	85	79	11	42	90
Cooke	2-0	3.52	11	0	0	8	0	1	23	22	9	9	2	4	10
Jackson	8-13	3.84	34	34	0	0	0	0	201.1	211	99	86	6	77	97
Mason	5-7	4.09	65	0	0	26	0	8	88	80	41	40	11	33	56
Palacios	3-2	4.25	20	8	0	4	0	0	53	56	25	25	1	27	33
Gleaton	1-0	4.26	23	0	0	6	0	0	31.2	34	16	15	4	19	18
Robinson	3-1	4.46	8	7	0	0	0	0	36.1	33	18	18	2	15	14
Neagle	4-6	4.48	55	6	0	8	0	2	86.1	81	46	43	9	43	77
Minor	0-0	4.50	1	0	0	0	0	0	2	3	2	1	0	0	0
Cox	5-3	4.60	25	7	0	8	0	3	62.2	66	37	32	5	27	48
Lamp	1-1	5.14	21	0	0	2	0	0	28	33	16	16	3	9	15
V.Cole	0-2	5.48	8	4	0	2	0	0	23	23	14	14	1	14	12
Batista	0-0	9.00	1	0	0	1	0	0	2	4	2	2	1	3	1

1993 preliminary roster

PITCHERS (19)
Stan Belinda
Victor Cole
Steve Cooke
Mariano DelosSantos
John Hope
Joel Johnston
Blas Minor
Dennis Moeller
Denny Neagle
Alejandro Pena
Rich Robertson
Rosario Rodriguez
Brian Shouse
Zane Smith
Randy Tomlin
Paul Wagner
Tim Wakefield
Bob Walk
Mike Zimmerman

CATCHERS (3)
Mike Lavalliere
Tom Prince
Don Slaught

INFIELDERS (10)
Jay Bell
Mike Bell
Carlos Garcia
Jeff King
Orlando Merced
Jeff Richardson
Jose Sandoval
Ben Shelton
John Wehner
Kevin Young

OUTFIELDERS (7)
Scott Bullett
Dave Clark
Al Martin
Lloyd McClendon
William Pennyfeather
Keith Thomas
Andy Van Slyke

Games played by position

Player	G	C	1B	2B	3B	SS	OF
BELL,JA	159	0	0	0	0	159	0
BONDS,B	140	0	0	0	0	0	139
CLARK,D	23	0	0	0	0	0	8
COLE,A	64	0	0	0	0	0	53
ESPY,C	112	0	0	0	0	0	82
GARCIA,C	22	0	0	14	0	8	0
GIBSON,K	16	0	0	0	0	0	13
KING,J	130	0	32	32	73	6	1
LAVALLIERE,M	95	92	0	0	1	0	0
LIND,J	135	0	0	134	0	0	0
MARTIN,A	12	0	0	0	0	0	7
MCCLENDON,L	84	0	18	0	0	0	60
MERCED,O	134	0	114	0	0	0	17
PENNYFEATHER,W	15	0	0	0	0	0	10
PRINCE,T	27	19	0	0	1	0	0
REDUS,G	76	0	36	0	0	0	15
SLAUGHT,D	87	79	0	0	0	0	0
VAN SLYKE,A	154	0	0	0	0	0	154
VARSHO,G	103	0	0	0	0	0	44
WEHNER,J	55	0	13	5	34	0	0
YOUNG,K	10	0	1	0	7	0	0

Sick call: 1992 DL report

Player	Days on the DL
Bonds, Barry	19
Miller, Paul*	48
Palacios, Vicente	108
Redus, Gary*	33
Slaught, Don	17
Smith, Zane*	62
Walk, Bob*	38

** On Disabled List twice during 1992 season (not counting transfers from one DL to another).*

Minor league report

Class AAA-Buffalo finished 87-57, 1st in the American Association Eastern Division. The team lost to Oklahoma City in four games for the league championship. 3B Kevin Young hit .314 with 8 HR and 65 RBI. OF Al Martin hit .305 with 20 HR and 59 RBI. SS Carlos Garcia hit .303 with 13 HR and 70 RBI. C Brian Dorsett had 21 HR and 102 RBI. **Class AA:** Carolina finished 52-92, last in both halves of the Southern League Eastern Division. LHP Rich Robertson was 6-7 with a 3.03 ERA. RHP Paul Wagner was 13-8 with a 3.06 ERA. **Class A:** Salem finished 64-76, 3rd in the Carolina League Northern Division in the 1st half and last in the 2nd half. OF Midre Cummings hit .305 with 14 HR and 75 RBI. SS Ramon Martinez hit .289 with 35 SB. OF Robert Bailey had 44 SB. OF Marty Neff had 23 HR and 70 RBI. Augusta finished 67-74, 3rd in the 1st half of the Sally League Southern Division and 4th in the 2nd half. OF Tony Womack had 50 SB. Jeff Conger had 36 SB. RHP Dave Doorneweerd was 9-13 with a 3.04 ERA and 152 K in 148 IP. Welland finished 31-46, last in the New York-Penn League Stedler Division. The club finished last in the league in batting at .215. Pirates finished 23-37, last in the Gulf Coast League Western Division. The club finished third in the league in batting at .246, but last in pitching at 4.34.

Tops in the organization

BATTING LEADERS	Club	Avg.	G	AB	R	H	HR	RBI
Kevin Young	Buf	.314	137	490	91	154	8	65
Al Martin	Buf	.305	125	420	85	128	20	59
Midre Cummings	Sal	.305	113	420	55	128	14	75
Carlos Garcia	Buf	.303	113	426	73	129	13	70
Greg Tubbs	Buf	.293	110	430	69	126	7	42

HOME RUNS			WINS		
Marty Neff	Sal	23	John Hope	Sal	11
Brian Dorsett	Buf	21	Victor Cole	Buf	11
Keith Thomas	Car	20	Esteban Loaiza	Aug	10
Al Martin	Buf	20	Tim Wakefield	Buf	10
Eddie Zambrano	Buf	16	Several players tied		9

RBI			SAVES		
Brian Dorsett	Buf	102	Blas Minor	Buf	18
Eddie Zambrano	Buf	79	Joe Ausanio	Buf	15
Midre Cummings	Sal	75	David Tellers	Sal	12
Marty Neff	Sal	74	Mariano Delossantos	Aug	12
Carlos Garcia	Buf	70	Several players tied		10

STOLEN BASES			STRIKEOUTS		
Tony Womack	Aug	50	Dave Doorneweerd	Aug	152
Robert Bailey	Sal	44	Richard Robertson	Car	134
Keith Thomas	Car	39	Esteban Loaiza	Aug	123
Jeff Conger	Aug	36	Paul Wagner	Buf	120
Ramon Martinez	Sal	35	Rick White	Car	115

PITCHING LEADERS	Club	W-L	ERA	IP	H	BB	SO
Dave Doorneweerd	Aug	9-13	3.04	148	129	58	152
Tim Wakefield	Buf	10-3	3.06	135	122	51	71
Victor Cole	Buf	11-6	3.11	116	102	61	69
Richard Robertson	Car	9-7	3.12	162	156	51	134
John Hope	Sal	11-8	3.47	176	169	46	106

Pittsburgh (1887-1992)

Runs: Most, career, all-time

1521 Honus Wagner, 1900-1917
1493 Paul Waner, 1926-1940
1416 Roberto Clemente, 1955-1972
1414 Max Carey, 1910-1926
1195 Willie Stargell, 1962-1982

Hits: Most, career, all-time

3000 Roberto Clemente, 1955-1972
2967 Honus Wagner, 1900-1917
2868 Paul Waner, 1926-1940
2416 Max Carey, 1910-1926
2416 Pie Traynor, 1920-1937

2B: Most, career, all-time

558 Paul Waner, 1926-1940
551 Honus Wagner, 1900-1917
440 Roberto Clemente, 1955-1972
423 Willie Stargell, 1962-1982
375 Max Carey, 1910-1926

3B: Most, career, all-time

232 Honus Wagner, 1900-1917
187 Paul Waner, 1926-1940
166 Roberto Clemente, 1955-1972
164 Pie Traynor, 1920-1937
156 Fred Clarke, 1900-1915

HR: Most, career, all-time

475 Willie Stargell, 1962-1982
301 Ralph Kiner, 1946-1953
240 Roberto Clemente, 1955-1972
176 BARRY BONDS, 1986-1992
166 Dave Parker, 1973-1983

RBI: Most, career, all-time

1540 Willie Stargell, 1962-1982
1475 Honus Wagner, 1900-1917
1305 Roberto Clemente, 1955-1972
1273 Pie Traynor, 1920-1937
1177 Paul Waner, 1926-1940

SB: Most, career, all-time

688 Max Carey, 1910-1926
639 Honus Wagner, 1900-1917
412 Omar Moreno, 1975-1982
312 Patsy Donovan, 1892-1899
271 Tommy Leach, 1900-1918

BB: Most, career, all-time

937 Willie Stargell, 1962-1982
918 Max Carey, 1910-1926
909 Paul Waner, 1926-1940
877 Honus Wagner, 1900-1917
795 Ralph Kiner, 1946-1953

BA: Highest, career, all-time

.340 Paul Waner, 1926-1940
.336 Kiki Cuyler, 1921-1927
.328 Honus Wagner, 1900-1917
.327 Matty Alou, 1966-1970
.324 Arky Vaughan, 1932-1941
.324 Elmer Smith, 1892-1901

Slug avg: Highest, career, all-time

.567 Ralph Kiner, 1946-1953
.529 Willie Stargell, 1962-1982
.513 Kiki Cuyler, 1921-1927
.512 Dick Stuart, 1958-1962
.503 BARRY BONDS, 1986-1992

Games started: Most, career, all-time

477 Bob Friend, 1951-1965
371 Wilbur Cooper, 1912-1924
364 Vern Law, 1950-1967
354 Babe Adams, 1907-1926
299 Sam Leever, 1898-1910

Saves: Most, career, all-time

188 Roy Face, 1953-1968
158 Kent Tekulve, 1974-1985
133 Dave Giusti, 1970-1976
59 Al McBean, 1961-1970
56 BILL LANDRUM, 1989-1991

Shutouts: Most, career, all-time

44 Babe Adams, 1907-1926
39 Sam Leever, 1898-1910
35 Bob Friend, 1951-1965
33 Wilbur Cooper, 1912-1924
29 Lefty Leifield, 1905-1912

Wins: Most, career, all-time

202 Wilbur Cooper, 1912-1924
194 Babe Adams, 1907-1926
194 Sam Leever, 1898-1910
191 Bob Friend, 1951-1965
168 Deacon Phillippe, 1900-1911

K: Most, career, all-time

1682 Bob Friend, 1951-1965
1652 Bob Veale, 1962-1972
1191 Wilbur Cooper, 1912-1924
1142 JOHN CANDELARIA, 1975-1985
1092 Vern Law, 1950-1967

Win pct: Highest, career, all-time

.683 Nick Maddox, 1907-1910
.667 Jesse Tannehill, 1897-1902
.660 Sam Leever, 1898-1910
.659 Vic Willis, 1906-1909
.656 Emil Yde, 1924-1927

ERA: Lowest, career, all-time

2.08 Vic Willis, 1906-1909
2.38 Lefty Leifield, 1905-1912
2.47 Sam Leever, 1898-1910
2.50 Deacon Phillippe, 1900-1911
2.60 Bob Harmon, 1914-1918

Runs: Most, season

148 Jake Stenzel, 1894
145 Patsy Donovan, 1894
144 Kiki Cuyler, 1925
142 Paul Waner, 1928
140 Max Carey, 1922

Hits: Most, season

237 Paul Waner, 1927
234 Lloyd Waner, 1929
231 Matty Alou, 1969
223 Lloyd Waner, 1927
223 Paul Waner, 1928

2B: Most, season

62 Paul Waner, 1932
53 Paul Waner, 1936
50 Paul Waner, 1928
47 Adam Comorosky, 1930
45 Dave Parker, 1979
45 ANDY VAN SLYKE, 1992
45 Honus Wagner, 1900

3B: Most, season

36 Chief Wilson, 1912
28 Harry Davis, 1897
27 Jimmy Williams, 1899
26 Kiki Cuyler, 1925
23 Adam Comorosky, 1930
23 Elmer Smith, 1893

HR: Most, season

54 Ralph Kiner, 1949
51 Ralph Kiner, 1947
48 Willie Stargell, 1971
47 Ralph Kiner, 1950
44 Willie Stargell, 1973

RBI: Most, season

131 Paul Waner, 1927
127 Ralph Kiner, 1947
127 Ralph Kiner, 1949
126 Honus Wagner, 1901
125 Willie Stargell, 1971

SB: Most, season

96	Omar Moreno, 1980
77	Omar Moreno, 1979
71	Omar Moreno, 1978
71	Billy Sunday, 1888
70	Frank Taveras, 1977

BB: Most, season

137	Ralph Kiner, 1951
127	BARRY BONDS, 1992
122	Ralph Kiner, 1950
119	Elbie Fletcher, 1940
118	Elbie Fletcher, 1941
118	Arky Vaughan, 1936

BA: Highest, season

.385	Arky Vaughan, 1935
.381	Honus Wagner, 1900
.380	Paul Waner, 1927
.374	Jake Stenzel, 1895
.373	Paul Waner, 1936

Slug avg: Highest, season

.658	Ralph Kiner, 1949
.646	Willie Stargell, 1973
.639	Ralph Kiner, 1947
.628	Willie Stargell, 1971
.627	Ralph Kiner, 1951

Games started: Most, season

55	Ed Morris, 1888
53	Mark Baldwin, 1892
50	Mark Baldwin, 1891
50	Jim Galvin, 1888
50	Pink Hawley, 1895
50	Frank Killen, 1896
42	Bob Friend, 1956 (12)

Saves: Most, season

34	JIM GOTT, 1988
31	Kent Tekulve, 1978
31	Kent Tekulve, 1979
30	Dave Giusti, 1971
28	Roy Face, 1962

Shutouts: Most, season

8	Babe Adams, 1920
8	Jack Chesbro, 1902
8	Lefty Leifield, 1906
8	Al Mamaux, 1915
7	Steve Blass, 1968
7	Wilbur Cooper, 1917
7	Sam Leever, 1903
7	Bob Veale, 1965
7	Vic Willis, 1908

Wins: Most, season

36	Frank Killen, 1893
31	Pink Hawley, 1895
30	Frank Killen, 1896
29	Ed Morris, 1888
28	Jack Chesbro, 1902
28	Jim Galvin, 1887

K: Most, season

276	Bob Veale, 1965
250	Bob Veale, 1964
229	Bob Veale, 1966
213	Bob Veale, 1969
199	Larry McWilliams, 1983

Win pct: Highest, season

.842	Emil Yde, 1924
.824	Jack Chesbro, 1902
.806	Howie Camnitz, 1909
.800	JOHN CANDELARIA, 1977
.800	Ed Doheny, 1902
.800	Sam Leever, 1905

ERA: Lowest, season

1.56	Howie Camnitz, 1908
1.62	Howie Camnitz, 1909
1.66	Sam Leever, 1907
1.73	Vic Willis, 1906
1.87	Lefty Leifield, 1906

Most pinch-hit homers, season

3	Ham Hyatt, 1913
3	Al Rubeling, 1944
3	Bob Skinner, 1956
3	Dick Stuart, 1959
3	Gene Freese, 1964
3	Jose Pagan, 1969
3	Willie Stargell, 1982

Most pinch-hit, homers, career

7	Willie Stargell 1962-1982

Most consecutive games, batting safely

27	Jimmy Williams, 1899
26	Danny O'Connell, 1953

Most consecutive scoreless innings

41	Jack Chesbro, 1902
36	Ed Morris, 1888

No hit games

Nick Maddox, Pit vs Bro NL, 2-1; September 20, 1907.

Cliff Chambers, Pit at Bos NL, 3-0; May 6, 1951 (2nd game).

Harvey Haddix, Pit at Mil NL, 0-1; May 26, 1959 (lost on 1 hit in 13 innings after pitching 12 perfect innings).

Bob Moose, Pit at NY NL, 4-0; September 20, 1969.

Dock Ellis, Pit at SD NL, 2-0; June 12, 1970 (1st game).

John Candelaria, Pit vs LA NL, 2-0; August 9, 1976.

Lefty Leifield, six innings, darkness, Pit at Phi NL, 8-0; September 26, 1906 (2nd game).

Howie Camnitz, five innings, agreement, Pit at NY NL, 1-0; August 23, 1907 (2nd game).

ACTIVE PLAYERS in caps.

Montreal Expos

by Robert Deutsch, *USA TODAY.*

Marquis Grissom led the league in stolen bases with 78, was fifth in doubles (39), and sixth in hits (180).

1992 Expos: Changes paid off

Things looked bleak for Les Expos coming into spring training. They had finished last in the NL East in 1991, playing the final month of the season on the road after a beam collapsed at Olympic Stadium, and had lost several key front office executives, including GM Dave Dombrowski. There had also been a change in club ownership.

They made a few off-season trades, but prognosticators predicted another bargain-basement finish: First baseman Andres Galarraga went to St. Louis for unheralded right-hander Ken Hill; outfielder Dave Martinez, reliever Scott Ruskin, and infield prospect Willie Greene went to the Reds for reliever John Wetteland. Nothing major—except for the fact that Hill went 16-9 (2.68 ERA) and Wetteland collected 37 saves.

But before the Expos had the last laugh, they had to go through some flops. Manager Tom Runnells wasn't a big hit at his first spring training. He greeted the players on opening day wearing army fatigues; the pressure-cooker atmosphere he created had the players grumbling and playing poorly. Some of his moves, such as shifting Tim Wallach from third to first to make room for rookie Bret Barberie, didn't go over any better, and he was fired May 22. Bench coach Felipe Alou thus became the first Dominican manager in the majors. He was a popular choice with players and fans alike. His relaxed attitude and confidence in young players was a marked difference from Runnells.

It was a family affair for Alou, yet he could hardly be accused of nepotism: Son Moises (.292, 9 HR, 56 RBI, 16 steals in 341 at-bats) finished second in rookie of the year voting, and nephew Mel Rojas was the bullpen's top setup man (7-1 , 10 saves, 1.43 ERA).

The Expos were 44-44 at the All-Star break, but with Alou's continued guidance, they played aggressively and were within 2 1/2 games of Pittsburgh in September.

Perhaps most energized by Alou was second baseman Delino DeShields. He had trouble with Runnells and struggled through the first month, but by the All-Star break, he was hitting .304 with 33 stolen bases. He finished with 56 RBI, a new high for an Expos' second baseman.

Outfielders Marquis Grissom and Larry Walker developed into major stars who would likely be even bigger names if they played south of the border. Grissom, one of the most well-rounded offensive players in the league, had a league-high 78 stolen bases. Walker batted .301 (23 HR, 93 RBI). Catcher Gary Carter doubled home the game-winning run in his final career at-bat in the final home game of the season.

The Expos finished second, Alou earned a contract extension and the team earned a reputation as the NL East's team to beat in 1993.

—by Lisa Winston

1993 Expos: Preview

With its exciting young lineup a year older—and a tremendous crop of talent on the farm—the Expos appear poised to not only challenge for the NL East title, but perhaps to be favored to win.

The outfield is one of the best, with budding superstars Moises Alou, Marquis Grissom and Larry Walker. The middle infield has outstanding potential as well; rookie Wil Cordero will take over at shortstop to join second baseman Delino DeShields.

The biggest questions are at the corners and behind the plate. First baseman Greg Colbrunn and rookie catcher Tim Laker are unproven. Veteran third baseman Tim Wallach had his worst season ever in '92.

On the mound, the Expos are loaded with talent. Ken Hill and Dennis Martinez had great seasons, while closer John Wetteland notched 37 saves.

—by Lisa Winston

1992 Expos: Between the lines

▸**April 22:** Dennis Martinez made only one bad pitch, which turned into a Kirk Gibson homer to start the game. Martinez, who gave up two hits in eight innings to Doug Drabek's five in nine, could have easily been the winner had he gotten more support.

▸**April 29:** Larry Walker hit his first two homers and a double.

▸**April 30:** Walker hit his third home run as Montreal knocked San Diego out of first place in the NL West. Delino DeShields, only 3-for-9 in stolen bases prior to the game, swiped two off Padre catcher Benito Santiago.

▸**May 5:** The Expos, 9-2 in day games, finally won under the lights, making their night games record 1-12 (.077).

▸**May 13:** Mark Gardner gave up one run and struck out 11 in 7 2/3 innings.

▸**May 16:** Dennis Martinez, who led the NL with a 2.39 ERA in 1991, surrendered no earned runs in picking up his third win and lowering his ERA to 1.82 for 1992.

▸**May 17 *Milestone:*** Tim Wallach collected his 1,598th hit, tying Tim Raines as the Expos' all-time leader in hits.

▸**May 31 *Milestone:*** Expo Gary Carter caught his 2,000th game. Only Bob Boone and Carlton Fisk have caught as many.

▸**June 7:** Larry Walker had missed the last six games because of a hamstring injury. He returned to his cleanup spot and went 2-for-3 with a solo home run.

▸**June 8:** Ken Hill barely missed a no-hitter when Mets pitcher Anthony Young hit a grounder to deep shortstop that Tom Foley couldn't field cleanly.

▸**June 18:** Chris Nabholz had a lucky charm—his mother, Maggie Nabholz. The Expos' young left-hander improved to 5-5 on the season, 3-0 when his mother was in attendance. His lifetime record with Mom in the stands: 8-0.

▸**June 24:** Pitcher Ken Hill hit his first career homer.

▸**June 26:** Since Opening Day 1989, when the Expos scored four or more runs, Dennis Martinez was 37-3 with 20 no-decisions.

▸**June 27:** Closer John Wetteland couldn't get anybody out as his ERA soared to a Randy-Myers-like 5.12.

▸**June 28:** Larry Walker homered twice. Moises Alou doubled, homered and had four RBI. Brian Barnes threw 8 1/3 scoreless innings.

▸**July 27:** Ken Hill improved his record to a career-high 12-4 with a 6-4 victory over the Cardinals, who traded him to St. Louis (in 1991) for first baseman Andres Galarraga. The win brought the Expos within a game of the NL East-leading Pirates. It was the closest the Expos had been after the All-Star break since Aug. 7, 1989.

▸**July 31:** Manager Felipe Alou benched his son Moises, admitting that he had called the younger Alou into his office and "got on his butt a bit." Manager Alou thought his son wasn't swinging the bat as well as he should.

▸**August 3 *Milestone:*** Tim Wallach, told by Felipe Alou that he might be benched, responded by going 3-for-3 and hitting his 200th career home run. Montreal fans who had booed the slumping Wallach gave him a standing ovation.

▸**August 9:** Gary Carter hit his 26th home run at Philadelphia, the most by a visiting player there.

▸**August 11:** Marquis Grissom stole a pair of bases and teammate Delino DeShields stole one as well. Grissom and DeShields were 1-2 in the league, and had combined for 99 stolen bases. Only six major league teams had more.

▸**August 12:** The Expos completed a three-game sweep at Chicago with a 3-1 victory. Gary Carter provided most of the offense with a two-run homer. Chris Nabholz pitched 8 2/3 shutout innings, yielding three hits and striking out five.

▸**August 20:** Montreal scored three in the ninth to beat Atlanta 3-2 and stay four games back in the NL East. Tim

Wallach's double off Alejandro Pena tied the game to ruin a strong outing from Braves' starter Steve Avery.

▸**August 25:** Chris Nabholz and Mel Rojas combined on the shutout as the Expos blanked Atlanta 6-0.

▸**August 26:** Expos' shortstop Spike Owen led his team in its title chase, as Montreal nipped the Braves 5-4. And yes, his given name is really Spike.

▸**August 30:** Ken Hill pitched a four-hitter for his third shutout this season.

▸**September 4:** Larry Walker had two hits, giving him 17 in his last 36 at-bats (.472) over nine games.

▸**September 12:** Montreal beat the Mets 4-1, denying Pittsburgh a chance to expand its lead. Since the All-Star break, Montreal was 35-19 and had won 22 of its last 34 games.

▸**September 15:** Ken Hill stifled the Phillies on three hits over eight innings as the Expos stayed alive in the NL East race with a 3-0 win.

▸**September 16:** Marquis Grissom singled, tripled, homered and stole two bases in the Expos' 3-2 victory at Pittsburgh. He also threw out Jay Bell at home plate.

▸**September 19:** The Expos bounced back from a disappointing split with Pittsburgh to hammer the Mets 10-4.

▸**September 23:** After Moises Alou's 14th-inning grand slam, the Expos still believed the NL East title was within reach. Alou's shot off Roger Mason gave Montreal a 5-1 win against Pittsburgh as it closed to within six games. ***Quote of the day:*** Manager Felipe Alou—"There's always a chance as long as you're not eliminated. But I believe the message is more a thank you note to fans of Montreal that we might be better next year."

▸**September 25:** Montreal remained mathematically alive as Larry Walker ended an 0-for-15 slump with a 10th-inning home run to beat Chicago 4-3.

▸**September 27:** The Expos' hopes were dashed when Pittsburgh beat the Mets to clinch the NL East title.

▸**October 4:** The Expos finished second in the NL East, nine games out. Larry Walker finished sixth in the league in slugging (.506), seventh in home runs (23), and ninth in RBI (93). Marquis Grissom led the majors in stolen bases (78), was fifth in the NL in doubles (39) and sixth in hits (180). Delino DeShields was a distant second in the NL with 46 steals.

—by Jeanie Chung, John Hunt, Deron Snyder, and Lisa Winston.

Team directory

▸**Owner:** Montreal Baseball Club Inc., Claude R. Brochu (president and general partner)

▸**General Manager:** Dan Duquette (vice president), Bill Stoneman (v.p., baseball operations)

▸**Ballpark:**
Olympic Stadium
4549 Avenue Pierre-de-Coubertin, Montreal, Que., Canada
514-253-3434
Capacity 43,739
Parking for 4,000 cars; $7
Public transportation available
Wheelchair sections, ramps, extensive food concessions, outfield bleachers

▸**Team publications:**
Yearbook, Expos Magazine
P.O. Box 500, Station M, Montreal, Que., Canada H1V 3P2

▸**TV, radio broadcast stations:**
CIQC 600 AM, C-TV, TSN (English); CKAC 730 AM, FRC-TV, RDS (French)

▸**Spring Training:**
Municipal Stadium
West Palm Beach, Fla.
Capacity 7,500
407-684-6801

MONTREAL EXPOS 1992 final stats

Batting	AVG	SLG	OB	G	AB	R	H	TB	2B	3B	HR	RBI	BB	SO	SB	CS	E
Berry	.333	.404	.345	24	57	5	19	23	1	0	1	4	1	11	2	1	4
Cordero	.302	.397	.353	45	126	17	38	50	4	1	2	8	9	31	0	0	8
Walker	.301	.506	.353	143	528	85	159	267	31	4	23	93	41	97	18	6	2
T.Haney	.300	.400	.300	7	10	0	3	4	1	0	0	1	0	0	0	0	0
Deshields	.292	.398	.359	135	530	82	155	211	19	8	7	56	54	108	46	15	15
Alou	.282	.455	.328	115	341	53	96	155	28	2	9	56	25	46	16	2	4
Grissom	.276	.418	.322	159	653	99	180	273	39	6	14	66	42	81	78	13	7
Cerone	.270	.381	.313	33	63	10	17	24	4	0	1	7	3	5	1	2	0
Owen	.269	.381	.348	122	386	52	104	147	16	3	7	40	50	30	9	4	9
Colbrunn	.268	.351	.294	52	168	12	45	59	8	0	2	18	6	34	3	2	3
Calderon	.265	.424	.323	48	170	19	45	72	14	2	3	24	14	22	1	2	1
Fletcher	.243	.333	.289	83	222	13	54	74	10	2	2	26	14	28	0	2	2
Cianfrocco	.241	.358	.276	86	232	25	56	83	5	2	6	30	11	66	3	0	8
Vanderwal	.239	.352	.316	105	213	21	51	75	8	2	4	20	24	36	3	0	2
Barberie	.232	.281	.354	111	285	26	66	80	11	0	1	24	47	62	9	5	13
Willard	.229	.375	.260	47	48	2	11	18	1	0	2	8	2	10	0	0	1
Wallach	.223	.331	.296	150	537	53	120	178	29	1	9	59	50	90	2	2	15
Carter	.218	.340	.299	95	285	24	62	97	18	1	5	29	33	37	0	4	6
Laker	.217	.283	.250	28	46	8	10	13	3	0	0	4	2	14	1	1	1
Foley	.174	.217	.230	72	115	7	20	25	3	1	0	5	8	21	3	0	5
Reed	.173	.383	.239	42	81	10	14	31	2	0	5	10	6	23	0	0	0
Stairs	.167	.233	.316	13	30	2	5	7	2	0	0	5	7	7	0	0	1
Lyons	.148	.222	.179	27	27	2	4	6	0	1	0	2	1	7	1	2	0
Bullock	.000	.000	.000	8	5	0	0	0	0	0	0	0	0	1	0	0	0
Goff	.000	.000	.000	3	3	0	0	0	0	0	0	0	0	3	0	0	0
Natal	.000	.000	.143	5	6	0	0	0	0	0	0	0	1	1	0	0	1

Pitching	W-L	ERA	G	GS	CG	GF	Sho	SV	IP	H	R	ER	HR	BB	SO
Rojas	7-1	1.43	68	0	0	26	0	10	100.2	71	17	16	2	34	70
Risley	1-0	1.80	1	1	0	0	0	0	5	4	1	1	0	1	2
Bottenfield	1-2	2.23	10	4	0	2	0	1	32.1	26	9	8	1	11	14
Valdez	0-2	2.41	27	0	0	9	0	0	37.1	25	12	10	2	12	32
Martinez	16-11	2.47	32	32	6	0	0	0	226.1	172	75	62	12	60	147
Hill	16-9	2.68	33	33	3	0	3	0	218	187	76	65	13	75	150
Fassero	8-7	2.84	70	0	0	22	0	1	85.2	81	35	27	1	34	63
Wetteland	4-4	2.92	67	0	0	58	0	37	83.1	64	27	27	6	36	99
Barnes	6-6	2.97	21	17	0	2	0	0	100	77	34	33	9	46	65
Sampen	1-4	3.13	44	1	0	10	0	0	63.1	62	22	22	4	29	23
Nabholz	11-12	3.32	32	32	1	0	1	0	195	176	80	72	11	74	130
Maysey	0-0	3.86	2	0	0	1	0	0	2.1	4	1	1	1	0	1
Young	0-0	3.98	13	0	0	6	0	0	20.1	18	9	9	0	9	11
Heredia	2-3	4.23	20	5	0	4	0	0	44.2	44	23	21	4	20	22
Gardner	12-10	4.36	33	30	0	1	0	0	179.2	179	91	87	15	60	132
C.Haney	2-3	5.45	9	6	1	2	1	0	38	40	25	23	6	10	27
Hurst	1-1	5.51	3	3	0	0	0	0	16.1	18	10	10	1	7	4
Krueger	0-2	6.75	9	2	0	3	0	0	17.1	23	13	13	0	7	13
Landrum	1-1	7.20	18	0	0	6	0	0	20	27	16	16	3	9	7
Service	0-0	14.14	5	0	0	0	0	0	7	15	11	11	1	5	11
Simons	0-0	23.63	7	0	0	2	0	0	5.1	15	14	14	3	2	6

1993 preliminary roster

PITCHERS (22)
Joe Ausanio
Ivan Arteaga
Brian Barnes
Miguel Batista
Kent Bottenfield
Reid Cornelius
Joey Eischen
Jeff Fassero
Mike Gardiner
Gil Heredia
Ken Hill
Jonathan Hurst
Dennis Martinez
Mike Mathile
Chris Nabholz
Len Picota
Bill Risley
Mel Rojas
Mike Thomas
Sergio Valdez
John Wetteland
Pete Young

CATCHERS (5)
Rob Fitzpatrick
Darrin Fletcher
Tim Laker
Raul Santana
Tim Spehr

INFIELDERS (8)
Sean Berry
Frank Bolick
Archi Cianfrocco
Greg Colbrunn
Wil Cordero
Delino DeShields
Mike Lansing
Tim Wallach

OUTFIELDERS (5)
Moises Alou
Marquis Grissom
Matt Stairs
John VanderWal
Larry Walker

Games played by position

Player	G	C	1B	2B	3B	SS	OF
ALOU,M	115	0	0	0	0	0	100
BARBERIE,B	111	0	0	26	63	1	0
BERRY,S	24	0	0	0	20	0	0
BULLOCK,E	8	0	0	0	0	0	0
CALDERON,I	48	0	0	0	0	0	46
CARTER,G	95	85	5	0	0	0	0
CERONE,R	33	28	0	0	0	0	0
CIANFROCCO,A	86	0	56	0	19	0	5
COLBRUNN,G	52	0	47	0	0	0	0
CORDERO,W	45	0	0	9	0	35	0
DESHIELDS,D	135	0	0	134	0	0	0
FLETCHER,D	83	69	0	0	0	0	0
FOLEY,T	72	0	12	13	4	33	1
GOFF,J	3	0	0	0	0	0	0
GRISSOM,M	159	0	0	0	0	0	157
HANEY,T	7	0	0	5	0	0	0
LAKER,T	28	28	0	0	0	0	0
LYONS,S	27	0	1	2	0	0	14
NATAL,B	5	4	0	0	0	0	0
OWEN,S	122	0	0	0	0	116	0
REED,D	42	0	0	0	0	0	29
STAIRS,M	13	0	0	0	0	0	10
VANDERWAL,J	105	0	7	0	0	0	57
WALKER,L	143	0	0	0	0	0	139
WALLACH,T	150	0	71	0	85	0	0
WILLARD,J	47	1	5	0	0	0	0

Sick call: 1992 DL report

Player	Days on the DL
Alou, Moises	20
Barberie, Bret	16
Calderon, Ivan**	119
Colbrunn, Greg	16
Fletcher, Darrin	34
Landrum, Bill	61
Owen, Spike	15
Reed, Darren	36
Reyes, Gil	28

*** On Disabled List three times during 1992 season.*

Minor league report

Class AAA — Indianapolis finished 83-61, 2nd in the American Association Eastern Division. LHP Doug Simons was 11-4 with a 3.08 ERA. RHP Kent Bottenfield was 12-8 with a 3.43. RHP David Wainhouse had 21 saves. C Bob Natal hit .301 with 12 HRs and 50 RBI. **Class AA:** Harrisburg finished 78-59, 3rd in the Eastern League. The team lost to Binghamton in the 1st round of the playoffs. 1B Derrick White had 81 RBI. SS Mike Lansing had 45 SB. RHP Mike Mathile was 12-5 with a 2.86 ERA. RHP Len Picota led the league with 26 saves, tying the league record. **Class A:** West Palm Beach finished 76-61, 1st in the 1st half of the Florida State League and 2nd in the 2nd half. The team lost to Lakeland in the 1st round of the playoffs. OF Rondell White hit .316 with 42 SB. 1B Randy Wilstead hit .285 with 8 HR and 71 RBI. RHP Tavo Alvarez won the league ERA crown, going 13-4 with a 1.49. LHP Joey Eischen K'd 167. Rockford finished 66-70, 4th in both halves of the Midwest League Northern Division. OF Tyrone Woods hit .291 with 12 HR and 47 RBI. SS Mike Hardge had 44 SB. LHP Kirk Rueter was 11-9 with a 2.58 ERA. LHP Gabe White led the league with 176 K and won 14 games. Albany (Ga.) finished 72-70, 5th in the 1st half of the Sally League Southern Division and 2nd in the 2nd half. OF Cliff Floyd hit .304 with 16 HR and a league-leading 97 RBI. He hit for the cycle twice. 3B Shane Andrews led the league with 25 HR and had 87 RBI. OF Antonio Grissom, younger brother of Expos star Marquis, had 61 SB. LHP Rick Dehart was 9-6 with a 2.46 ERA and 133 K in 117 IP. Jamestown finished 34-43, 4th in the New York-Penn League Stedler Division. LHP Dave Eggert K'd 23 in 15 IP without allowing an ER. He had 5 saves. Expos finished 35-24, 1st in the Gulf Coast League Eastern Division. The team lost to the Royals in three games for the league championship. 2B Jose Vidro hit .330 with 4 HR and 31 RBI. IF Isreal Alcantra had 37 RBI. LHP Jeff Hostetler was 6-2 with an 0.98 ERA. RHP Fernando Dasilva led the league in wins at 10-1 with a 1.33 ERA and allowed 59 hits in 95 IP. He K'd 86 to lead the league as well.

Tops in the organization

BATTING LEADERS	Club	Avg.	G	AB	R	H	HR	RBI
Rondell White	HRb	.314	132	539	102	169	6	48
Bob Natal	Ind	.302	96	344	50	104	12	50
Cliff Floyd	WPb	.302	135	520	83	157	16	98
Tyrone Woods	HRb	.288	120	434	61	125	13	54
Randy Wilstead	WPb	.285	129	449	56	128	8	71

HOME RUNS		
Shane Andrews	Aby	25
Cliff Floyd	WPb	16
Tim Laker	HRb	15
Jerry Goff	Ind	14
Several players tied		13

WINS		
Tavo Alvarez	HRb	17
Gabe White	Rkf	14
Rod Pedraza	Aby	13
Mike Mathile	HRb	12
Kent Bottenfield	Ind	12

RBI		
Cliff Floyd	WPb	98
Shane Andrews	Aby	87
Derrick White	HRb	81
Randy Wilstead	WPb	71
Tim Laker	HRb	68

SAVES		
Len Picota	HRb	26
David Wainhouse	Ind	21
Heath Haynes	HRb	15
Mark Larosa	WPb	12
Al Kermode	Aby	12

STOLEN BASES		
Antonio Grissom	Aby	61
Rondell White	HRb	48
Mike Hardge	WPb	46
Mike Lansing	HRb	45
Claudio Ozoria	Aby	39

STRIKE OUTS		
Gabe White	Rkf	176
Joey Eischen	WPb	167
Kirk Rueter	Rkf	153
Joe Norris	Rkf	143
Rick Dehart	Aby	133

PITCHING LEADERS	Club	W-L	ERA	IP	H	BB	SO
Tavo Alvarez	HRb	17-5	1.84	186	172	33	125
Rafael Diaz	WPb	8-4	2.26	124	91	27	79
Steve Long	WPb	9-7	2.44	151	121	42	67
Rick Dehart	Aby	9-6	2.46	117	91	40	133
Kirk Rueter	Rkf	11-9	2.58	174	150	36	153

Montreal (1969-1992)

Runs: Most, career, all-time

934 TIM RAINES, 1979-1990
828 ANDRE DAWSON, 1976-1986
737 TIM WALLACH, 1980-1992
707 GARY CARTER, 1974-1992
446 Warren Cromartie, 1974-1983

Hits: Most, career, all-time

1694 TIM WALLACH, 1980-1992
1598 TIM RAINES, 1979-1990
1575 ANDRE DAWSON, 1976-1986
1427 GARY CARTER, 1974-1992
1063 Warren Cromartie, 1974-1983

2B: Most, career, all-time

360 TIM WALLACH, 1980-1992
295 ANDRE DAWSON, 1976-1986
274 GARY CARTER, 1974-1992
273 TIM RAINES, 1979-1990
222 Warren Cromartie, 1974-1983

3B: Most, career, all-time

81 TIM RAINES, 1979-1990
67 ANDRE DAWSON, 1976-1986
31 TIM WALLACH, 1980-1992
30 Warren Cromartie, 1974-1983
25 MITCH WEBSTER, 1985-1988

HR: Most, career, all-time

225 ANDRE DAWSON, 1976-1986
220 GARY CARTER, 1974-1992
204 TIM WALLACH, 1980-1992
118 Bob Bailey, 1969-1975
106 ANDRES GALARRAGA, 1985-1991

RBI: Most, career, all-time

905 TIM WALLACH, 1980-1992
838 ANDRE DAWSON, 1976-1986
823 GARY CARTER, 1974-1992
552 TIM RAINES, 1979-1990
466 Bob Bailey, 1969-1975

SB: Most, career, all-time

634 TIM RAINES, 1979-1990
253 ANDRE DAWSON, 1976-1986
177 MARQUIS GRISSOM, 1989-1992
144 DELINO DeSHIELDS, 1990-1992
139 Rodney Scott, 1976-1982

BB: Most, career, all-time

775 TIM RAINES, 1979-1990
582 GARY CARTER, 1974-1992
514 TIM WALLACH, 1980-1992
502 Bob Bailey, 1969-1975
370 Ron Fairly, 1969-1974

BA: Highest, career, all-time

.301 TIM RAINES, 1979-1990
.294 Rusty Staub, 1969-1979
.288 Ellis Valentine, 1975-1981
.280 Warren Cromartie, 1974-1983
.280 ANDRE DAWSON, 1976-1986

Slug avg: Highest, career, all-time

.497 Rusty Staub, 1969-1979
.476 ANDRE DAWSON, 1976-1986
.476 Ellis Valentine, 1975-1981
.454 GARY CARTER, 1974-1992
.441 HUBIE BROOKS, 1985-1989

Games started: Most, career, all-time

393 Steve Rogers, 1973-1985
199 DENNIS MARTINEZ, 1986-1992
193 BRYN SMITH, 1981-1989
192 Steve Renko, 1969-1976
170 BILL GULLICKSON, 1979-1985

Saves: Most, career, all-time

152 JEFF REARDON, 1981-1986
101 TIM BURKE, 1985-1991
75 Mike Marshall, 1970-1973
52 Woodie Fryman, 1975-1983
37 JOHN WETTELAND, 1992-1992

Shutouts: Most, career, all-time

37 Steve Rogers, 1973-1985
15 Bill Stoneman, 1969-1973
13 DENNIS MARTINEZ, 1986-1992
8 Woodie Fryman, 1975-1983
8 Charlie Lea, 1980-1987
8 SCOTT SANDERSON, 1978-1983
8 BRYN SMITH, 1981-1989

Wins: Most, career, all-time

158 Steve Rogers, 1973-1985
85 DENNIS MARTINEZ, 1986-1992
81 BRYN SMITH, 1981-1989
72 BILL GULLICKSON, 1979-1985
68 Steve Renko, 1969-1976

K: Most, career, all-time

1621 Steve Rogers, 1973-1985
838 BRYN SMITH, 1981-1989
835 DENNIS MARTINEZ, 1986-1992
831 Bill Stoneman, 1969-1973
810 Steve Renko, 1969-1976

Win pct: Highest, career, all-time

.623 TIM BURKE, 1985-1991
.574 DENNIS MARTINEZ, 1986-1992
.573 Charlie Lea, 1980-1987
.556 Mike Torrez, 1971-1974
.544 SCOTT SANDERSON, 1978-1983

ERA: Lowest, career, all-time

2.93 DENNIS MARTINEZ, 1986-1992
3.17 Steve Rogers, 1973-1985
3.28 BRYN SMITH, 1981-1989
3.32 Charlie Lea, 1980-1987
3.33 SCOTT SANDERSON, 1978-1983

Runs: Most, season

133 TIM RAINES, 1983
123 TIM RAINES, 1987
115 TIM RAINES, 1985
107 ANDRE DAWSON, 1982
106 TIM RAINES, 1984

Hits: Most, season

204 Al Oliver, 1982
194 TIM RAINES, 1986
192 TIM RAINES, 1984
189 ANDRE DAWSON, 1983
188 Dave Cash, 1977

2B: Most, season

46 Warren Cromartie, 1979
43 Al Oliver, 1982
42 Dave Cash, 1977
42 ANDRES GALARRAGA, 1988
42 TIM WALLACH, 1987
42 TIM WALLACH, 1989

3B: Most, season

13 TIM RAINES, 1985
13 Rodney Scott, 1980
13 MITCH WEBSTER, 1986
12 ANDRE DAWSON, 1979
11 Ron LeFlore, 1980

HR: Most, season

32 ANDRE DAWSON, 1983
31 GARY CARTER, 1977
30 Larry Parrish, 1979
30 Rusty Staub, 1970
29 GARY CARTER, 1980
29 GARY CARTER, 1982
29 ANDRES GALARRAGA, 1988
29 Rusty Staub, 1969

RBI: Most, season

123	TIM WALLACH, 1987
113	ANDRE DAWSON, 1983
109	Al Oliver, 1982
106	GARY CARTER, 1984
103	Ken Singleton, 1973

SB: Most, season

97	Ron LeFlore, 1980
90	TIM RAINES, 1983
78	MARQUIS GRISSOM, 1992
78	TIM RAINES, 1982
76	MARQUIS GRISSOM, 1991

BB: Most, season

123	Ken Singleton, 1973
112	Rusty Staub, 1970
110	Rusty Staub, 1969
100	Bob Bailey, 1974
97	Bob Bailey, 1971
97	TIM RAINES, 1983

BA: Highest, season

.334	TIM RAINES, 1986
.331	Al Oliver, 1982
.330	TIM RAINES, 1987
.320	TIM RAINES, 1985
.311	Rusty Staub, 1971

Slug avg: Highest, season

.553	ANDRE DAWSON, 1981
.551	Larry Parrish, 1979
.540	ANDRES GALARRAGA, 1988
.539	ANDRE DAWSON, 1983
.526	Rusty Staub, 1969
.526	TIM RAINES, 1987

Games started: Most, season

40	Steve Rogers, 1977
39	Bill Stoneman, 1971
38	Steve Rogers, 1974
37	Carl Morton, 1970
37	Steve Renko, 1971
37	Steve Rogers, 1979
37	Steve Rogers, 1980

Saves: Most, season

41	JEFF REARDON, 1985
37	JOHN WETTELAND, 1992
35	JEFF REARDON, 1986
31	Mike Marshall, 1973
28	TIM BURKE, 1989

Shutouts: Most, season

5	DENNIS MARTINEZ, 1991
5	Steve Rogers, 1979
5	Steve Rogers, 1983
5	Bill Stoneman, 1969
4	MARK LANGSTON, 1989
4	Charlie Lea, 1983
4	Carl Morton, 1970
4	Steve Rogers, 1976
4	Steve Rogers, 1977
4	Steve Rogers, 1980
4	Steve Rogers, 1982
4	Bill Stoneman, 1972

Wins: Most, season

20	Ross Grimsley, 1978
19	Steve Rogers, 1982
18	Carl Morton, 1970
18	BRYN SMITH, 1985
17	BILL GULLICKSON, 1983
17	Steve Rogers, 1977
17	Steve Rogers, 1983
17	Bill Stoneman, 1971

K: Most, season

251	Bill Stoneman, 1971
206	Steve Rogers, 1977
202	Floyd Youmans, 1986
185	Bill Stoneman, 1969
179	Steve Rogers, 1982

Win pct: Highest, season

.783	BRYN SMITH, 1985
.704	Steve Rogers, 1982
.696	DENNIS MARTINEZ, 1989
.652	Mike Torrez, 1974
.645	Ross Grimsley, 1978

ERA: Lowest, season

2.39	DENNIS MARTINEZ, 1991
2.39	MARK LANGSTON, 1989
2.40	Steve Rogers, 1982
2.44	Pascual Perez, 1988
2.47	DENNIS MARTINEZ, 1992

Most pinch-hit homers, season

4	Hal Breeden, 1973

Most pinch-hit, homers, career

5	Jose Morales. 1973-1977

Most consecutive games, batting safely

19	Warren Cromartie, 1979
19	Andre Dawson, 1980

Most consecutive scoreless innings

32	Woodie Fryman, 1975

No hit games

Bill Stoneman, Mon at Phi NL, 7-0; April 17, 1969.

Bill Stoneman, Mon vs NY NL, 7-0; October 2, 1972 (1st game).

Charlie Lea, Mon vs SF NL, 4-0; May 10, 1981 (2nd game).

Mark Gardner, Mon at LA NL, 0-1; July 26, 1991 (9 innings, lost on 2 hits in 10th, relieved by Jeff Fassero, who allowed 1 more hit).

Dennis Martinez, Mon at LA NL, 2-0; July 28, 1991 (perfect game).

David Palmer, five perfect innings, rain, Mon at StL NL, 4-0; April 21, 1984 (2nd game).

Pascual Perez, five innings, rain, Mon at Phi NL, 1-0; September 24, 1988.

ACTIVE PLAYERS in caps.

St. Louis Cardinals

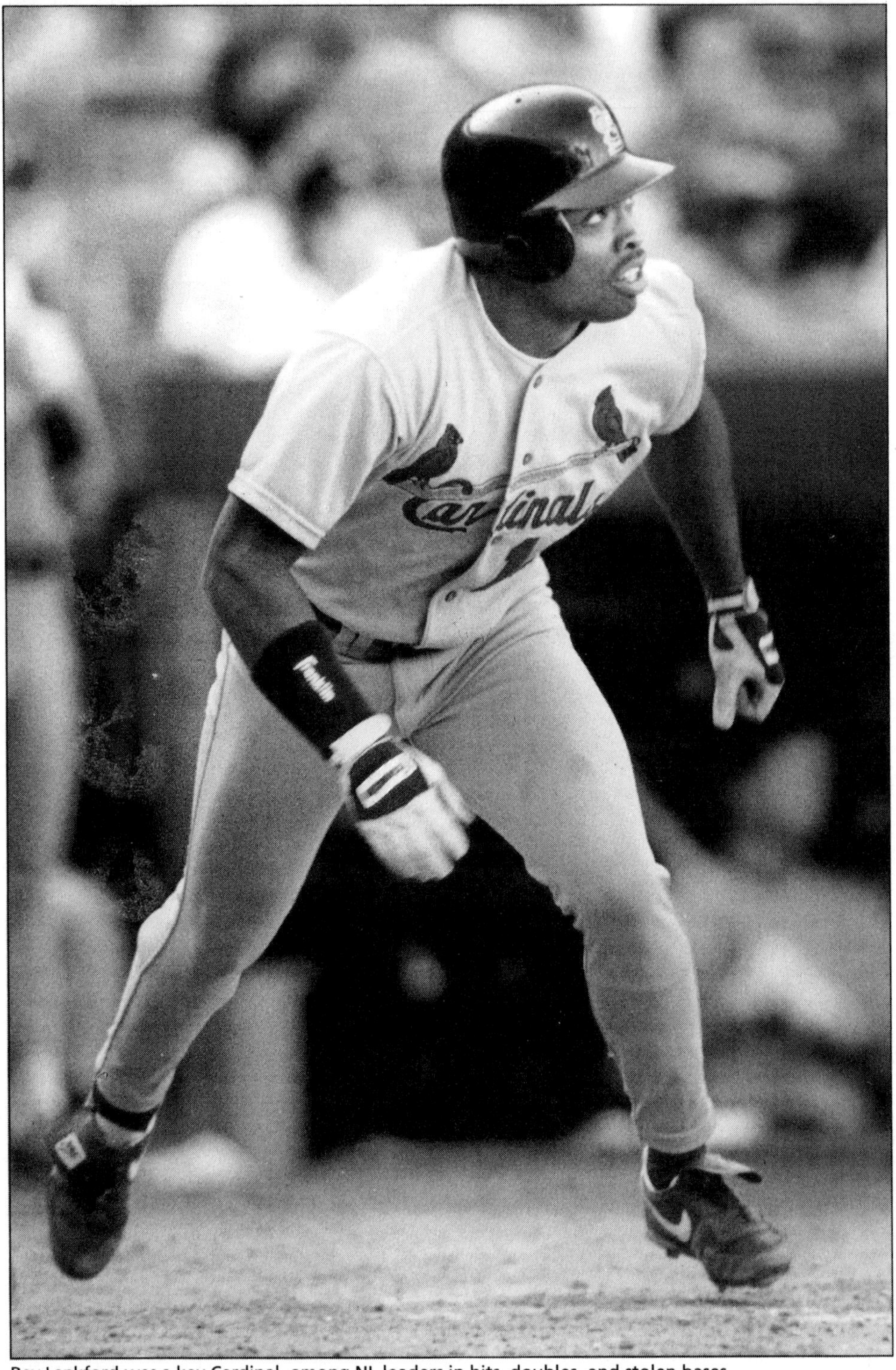

by Robert Deutsch, *USA TODAY*

Ray Lankford was a key Cardinal, among NL leaders in hits, doubles, and stolen bases.

1992 Cardinals: Who's on first?

The Cardinals spent 10 days in first place in 1992, which convinced manager Joe Torre that his team was good enough to get there. The fact that they couldn't stay there also convinced Torre that there will have to be some changes made. The Cardinals' biggest problem came in head-to-head competition against Pittsburgh—a woeful 3-15 record, including eight straight losses that killed any chance St. Louis had of getting back in the race.

The visit to first place in late May and early June ended when they fell into a 2-10 slump, punctuated by the problems that plagued the team all season: the inability to get a hit with runners in scoring position and the lack of consistent starting pitching.

Andres Galarraga, who had been a large part of the pre-season plan since he was acquired from Montreal for pitcher Ken Hill, was optimistic about returning to his form of a few years ago—until he broke his wrist on the third day of the season. One of 15 Cardinals who spent time on the DL, he was sidelined until the end of May, and ineffective for the rest of the year.

Todd Zeile (.257, seven HR, 48 RBI) was also expected to be a top performer, but he struggled with an early-season illness and was eventually sent back to Triple-A Louisville.

The brightest spot for the Cardinals' offense was center fielder Ray Lankford, the first St. Louis player to hit 20 homers and steal 20 bases in a season since Hall of Famer Lou Brock in 1967. He hit .293 with 20 homers, 86 RBI, and 42 stolen bases. He led the team in 13 offensive categories.

Ozzie Smith and Felix Jose led the team in batting average (tied at .295), and Smith—at age 37—won his 13th consecutive Gold Glove and led the team in stolen bases (43).

Bob Tewksbury (16-5) led the pitching staff, and made the All-Star team for the first time. His 2.16 ERA was second in the NL. Rookie Donovan Osborne was 11-9, and Rheal Cormier was 10-10. Reliever Lee Smith captured the NL Rolaids title for the second straight season. He led the league with 43 saves. Starter Joe Magrane and reliever Todd Worrell each returned after at least a year recovering from surgery. Magrane went 1-2 in five starts. Worrell, primarily a setup man for Smith, was 5-3 with three saves and a 2.11 ERA. Worrell's second save was the 128th of his career, making him the team's all-time career saves leader.

—by Rob Rains

1993 Cardinals: Preview

A famous Abbott and Costello question may hold the key to the Cardinals' 1993 season: *Who's on First?*

Andres Galarraga was a big disappointment and left as a free agent after the season. Rod Brewer, who went from prospect to suspect and back to prospect again, was the early favorite to win the starting position. The Cards were also thinking about experimenting with Ozzie Canseco, normally an outfielder. He represents the team's best hope for additional power.

Abbott and Costello's shortstop was I Don't Give a Damn; Joe Torre doesn't have to worry because he knows Ozzie Smith will be there for at least another year after a free agency scare.

New hitting coach Chris Chambliss' main target for 1993 will be a return to form for third baseman Todd Zeile. The team also has to hope for the continued improvement of outfielders Ray Lankford and Felix Jose.

The Cardinals' strength may be its starting pitching, led by Bob Tewksbury. Several youngsters will have a chance to crack the starting rotation, including right-hander Rene Arocha and left-hander Allen Watson.

—by Rob Rains

1992 Cardinals: Between the lines

▸**April 27:** Lee Smith got his fifth save as St. Louis took an 872-870 lead in its all-time series with L.A.

▸**May 2:** Donovan Osborne pitched eight-plus scoreless innings, striking out three and walking one.

▸**May 3:** Bob Tewksbury pitched a six-hitter, yielding just one run, walking none and striking out four.

▸**May 6:** Felix Jose, activated from the DL April 29, hit .419 (13-for-31) with seven RBI in his first seven games; his 11th inning homer won the game. Ray Lankford was 3-for-6 with a homer.

▸**May 10:** One good comeback deserves another: The Cardinals rallied for the second consecutive night, defeating the Braves, 6-5. Less than 24 hours after overcoming a 9-0 deficit, St. Louis fought its way back after trailing 5-2 in the seventh. Tom Pagnozzi's two-run single with two outs in the ninth was the winning blow.

▸**May 11:** Luis Alicea, with five RBI in 56 at-bats entering the game, doubled that total vs. the Braves.

▸**May 17:** Felix Jose had a grand slam among his career-high five RBI. Jose had hit in 16 of 17 games since coming off the disabled list, batting .414 with 20 RBI and four homers.

▸**May 23:** The Cardinals took over first place when Pagnozzi homered with one out in the ninth for a 4-3 victory against Houston. St. Louis moved a half-game ahead of the Pirates, who had been in first place since April 13.

▸**May 26 *Milestone:*** Ozzie Smith became the 15th active player (159th overall) to reach 2,000 hits.

▸**June 2:** St. Louis baserunners, who led the league with 75 stolen bases, were caught stealing twice and picked off twice.

▸**June 13:** Ray Lankford's two-run homer in the third inning helped the Cardinals to a 4-1 victory, only their fourth win in their last 16 games.

▸**June 14 *Milestone:*** Ozzie Smith broke Roy McMillan's NL mark, taking part in his 1,305th career double play in the sixth inning. He had tied the record in the second.

▸**June 18:** Omar Olivares pitched seven shutout innings, allowing just two hits.

▸**June 19:** Mike Perez had an 18-inning scoreless streak before giving up the game-winning run—the longest by a Cardinal reliever since Lee Smith had 21 consecutive in 1990.

▸**June 23:** Ray Lankford doubled, homered and had three RBI in the Cardinals' 6-4 loss to the Pirates.

▸**June 24:** Bob Tewksbury won his second game in five days, pitching on three days rest. Tewksbury pitched a total of 14 1/3 innings in the five days, yielding 15 hits but just one run.

▸**June 28:** St. Louis defeated New York 3-2 in 11 innings on Gerald Perry's two-out, bases-loaded single off John Franco. Each of the three games in the weekend series was decided by one run; the Cards took two.

▸**August 2:** St. Louis fell victim to a four-game sweep by the Pirates, who rallied for two runs in the ninth. The Cardinals wasted seven shutout innings from Rheal Cormier.

▸**August 3:** The Cardinals won just three of their last 11 games—all Tewksbury starts. Tewksbury gave up four hits and, of course, no walks in beating Philadelphia 2-1. He matched his season high of 11 wins in 1991 and had walked just 14 batters all season.

▸**August 11:** Tom Pagnozzi drove in the winning run with two outs in the ninth for a 7-6 victory over the Phillies. The Cards trailed 6-2 after the fifth, but rallied for three runs in the sixth and another in the eighth.

▸**August 14:** Rheal Cormier—born in Moncton, Canada—lost to Montreal for the third time in 1992.

▸**August 16 *Milestone:*** Lee Smith pitched a perfect ninth to pass Hall of Famer Rollie Fingers into second place on the all-time saves list in the Cardinals' 5-2 win against Montreal. It was Smith's 342nd save, 10 behind leader Jeff Reardon.

▶**August 20:** Tewksbury didn't walk a batter for his fourth consecutive start, giving him a 33-inning walkless streak. In fact, none of the four pitchers (Tewksbury, Lee Smith, Butch Henry and Xavier Hernandez) gave up a walk in the game with Houston.

▶**August 21:** St. Louis slowed the surging Braves with a 5-2 win in 10 innings at Atlanta. Second baseman Luis Alicea started a game-saving double play in the ninth.

▶**August 28:** Andres Galarraga's sacrifice fly in the first inning stood up for Mark Clark as the Cardinals edged Los Angeles 1-0. Clark scattered three hits over seven shutout innings, combining with two relievers for the win.

▶**September 11:** Lee Smith, the NL leader in saves with 38, had converted his last 14 save opportunities. Ozzie Smith had gone 11-for-19 in his last four games to raise his batting average to .301.

▶**September 13:** Ray Lankford made his one hit count, a fifth-inning grand slam. ***Milestone:*** Bob Tewksbury had walked just 17 batters in 213 innings pitched, placing him fourth on the all-time list for fewest walks per nine innings in a single season. The top five: 1. Babe Adams, 1920, .62; 2. Christy Mathewson, 1914, .62; 3. Cy Young, 1904, .69; 4. Bob Tewksbury, 1992, .72; 5. Red Lucas, 1933, .74.

▶**September 22:** St. Louis beat Pittsburgh for the first time in 14 tries. ***Quote of the day:*** Manager Joe Torre, who watched his troops lose 15 of 18 games against the Pirates this season—"We've been their punching bag. Maybe they haven't always knocked us out, but it's always been a unanimous decision."

▶**October 4:** The Cardinals won their final game of the year, and finished third in the NL East. In the end, they won 83 and lost 79, and were 13 games behind the first-place Pirates. Shining performances during the year, however, put Cardinals among the league's leaders in eight different categories. Ray Lankford was fourth in the NL in doubles (40), sixth in steals (42), and eighth in hits (175). Luis Alicea was fourth in triples (11). Ozzie Smith was sixth in steals (43). On the mound, Lee Smith led the NL in saves (43), Bob Tewksbury was second in ERA (2.16), and Cris Carpenter was sixth in games (73).

—by Jeanie Chung, John Hunt, Deron Snyder, and Lisa Winston.

Team directory

▶**Owner:** August A. Busch III

▶**General Manager:** Dal Maxvill

▶**Ballpark:**
Busch Stadium
250 Stadium Plaza, St. Louis, Mo.
314-421-3060
Capacity 56,627
Parking for over 7,000 cars; $4
Public transportation
Wheelchair section, ramps

▶**Team publications:**
Yearbook, Media Guide, The Cardinals Magazine
314-421-3060

▶**TV, radio broadcast stations:**
KMOX 1120 AM, KPLR Channel 11

▶**Spring Training:**
Al Lang Stadium
St. Petersburg, Fla.
Capacity 7,227
314-421-3060

St. LOUIS CARDINALS 1992 final stats

Batting	AVG	SLG	OB	G	AB	R	H	TB	2B	3B	HR	RBI	BB	SO	SB	CS	E
Royer	.323	.581	.333	13	31	6	10	18	2	0	2	9	1	4	0	0	3
Wilson	.311	.368	.368	61	106	6	33	39	6	0	0	13	10	18	1	2	3
Woodson	.307	.404	.331	31	114	9	35	46	8	0	1	22	3	10	0	0	3
Pena	.305	.478	.386	62	203	31	62	97	12	1	7	31	24	37	13	8	5
Gilkey	.302	.427	.364	131	384	56	116	164	19	4	7	43	39	52	18	12	5
Brewer	.301	.359	.354	29	103	11	31	37	6	0	0	10	8	12	0	1	0
O.Smith	.295	.342	.367	132	518	73	153	177	20	2	0	31	59	34	43	9	10
Jose	.295	.432	.347	131	509	62	150	220	22	3	14	75	40	100	28	12	6
Thompson	.293	.404	.350	109	208	31	61	84	9	1	4	17	16	39	18	6	2
Lankford	.293	.480	.371	153	598	87	175	287	40	6	20	86	72	147	42	24	2
Canseco	.276	.448	.417	9	29	7	8	13	5	0	0	3	7	4	0	0	1
Zeile	.257	.364	.352	126	439	51	113	160	18	4	7	48	68	70	7	10	13
Oquendo	.257	.400	.350	14	35	3	9	14	3	1	0	3	5	3	0	0	1
Pagnozzi	.249	.359	.290	139	485	33	121	174	26	3	7	44	28	64	2	5	1
Alicea	.245	.385	.320	85	265	26	65	102	9	11	2	32	27	40	2	5	7
Hudler	.245	.378	.265	61	98	17	24	37	4	0	3	5	2	23	2	6	3
Galarraga	.243	.391	.282	95	325	38	79	127	14	2	10	39	11	69	5	4	8
Perry	.238	.315	.311	87	143	13	34	45	8	0	1	18	15	23	3	6	3
Guerrero	.219	.295	.270	43	146	10	32	43	6	1	1	16	11	25	2	2	4
Gedman	.219	.286	.291	41	105	5	23	30	4	0	1	8	11	22	0	0	3
Carr	.219	.266	.315	22	64	8	14	17	3	0	0	3	9	6	10	2	0
Jordan	.207	.373	.250	55	193	17	40	72	9	4	5	22	10	48	7	2	1
Jones	.200	.228	.256	67	145	9	29	33	4	0	0	3	11	29	5	2	4
Figueroa	.182	.273	.250	12	11	1	2	3	1	0	0	4	1	2	0	0	1

Pitching	W-L	ERA	G	GS	CG	GF	Sho	SV	IP	H	R	ER	HR	BB	SO
DiPino	0-0	1.64	9	0	0	3	0	0	11	9	2	2	0	3	8
Perez	9-3	1.84	77	0	0	22	0	0	93	70	23	19	4	32	46
Worrell	5-3	2.11	67	0	0	14	0	3	64	45	15	15	4	25	64
Tewksbury	16-5	2.16	33	32	5	1	0	0	233	217	63	56	15	20	91
Carpenter	5-4	2.97	73	0	0	21	0	1	88	69	29	29	10	27	46
L.Smith	4-9	3.12	70	0	0	55	0	43	75	62	28	26	4	26	60
McClure	2-2	3.17	71	0	0	16	0	0	54	52	21	19	6	25	24
Cormier	10-10	3.68	31	30	3	1	0	0	186	194	83	76	15	33	117
Osborne	11-9	3.77	34	29	0	2	0	0	179	193	91	75	14	38	104
Olivares	9-9	3.84	32	30	1	1	0	0	197	189	84	84	20	63	124
Magrane	1-2	4.02	5	5	0	0	0	0	31.1	34	15	14	2	15	20
Clark	3-10	4.45	20	20	1	0	1	0	113.1	117	59	56	12	36	44
B.Smith	4-2	4.64	13	1	0	3	0	0	21.1	20	11	11	3	5	9
Agosto	2-4	6.25	22	0	0	10	0	0	31.2	39	24	22	2	9	13

1993 preliminary roster

PITCHERS (13)
Mark Clark
Fidel Compres
Rheal Cormier
Steve Dixon
Bryan Eversgerd
Joe Magrane
Mike Milchin
Omar Olivares
Donovan Osborne
Mike Perez
Lee Smith
Bob Tewksbury
Tom Urbani

CATCHERS (5)
Paul Ellis
Ed Fulton
Tom Pagnozzi
Marc Ronan
Hector Villanueva

INFIELDERS (14)
Luis Alicea
Juan Andujar
Rod Brewer
Tripp Cromer
Bien Figueroa
Tim Jones
Jose Oquendo
Geronimo Pena
Gerald Perry
Stan Royer
Ozzie Smith
Craig Wilson
Tracy Woodson
Todd Zeile

OUTFIELDERS (8)
Ozzie Canseco
Paul Coleman
Bernard Gilkey
Rex Hudler
Brian Jordan
Felix Jose
Ray Lankford
Lonnie Maclin

Games played by position

Player	G	C	1B	2B	3B	SS	OF
ALICEA,L	85	0	0	75	0	4	0
BREWER,R	29	0	27	0	0	0	4
CANSECO,O	9	0	0	0	0	0	8
CARR,C	22	0	0	0	0	0	19
FIGUEROA,B	12	0	0	3	0	9	0
GALARRAGA,A	95	0	90	0	0	0	0
GEDMAN,R	41	40	0	0	0	0	0
GILKEY,B	131	0	0	0	0	0	111
GUERRERO,P	43	0	28	0	0	0	10
HUDLER,R	61	0	8	16	0	0	12
JONES,TI	67	0	0	28	2	34	1
JORDAN,B	55	0	0	0	0	0	53
JOSE,F	131	0	0	0	0	0	127
LANKFORD,R	153	0	0	0	0	0	153
OQUENDO,J	14	0	0	9	0	5	0
PAGNOZZI,T	139	138	0	0	0	0	0
PENA,G	62	0	0	57	0	0	0
PERRY,G	87	0	29	0	0	0	0
ROYER,S	13	0	4	0	5	0	0
SMITH,O	132	0	0	0	0	132	0
THOMPSON,M	109	0	0	0	0	0	45
WILSON,C	61	0	0	11	18	0	3
WOODSON,T	31	0	3	0	26	0	0
ZEILE,T	126	0	0	0	124	0	0

Sick call: 1992 DL report

Player	Days on the DL
Alicea, Luis	51
Dipino, Frank*	131
Galarraga, Andres	44
Guerrero, Pedro*	121
Hudler, Rex	53
Jones, Tim	33
Jordan, Brian	30
Jose, Felix	23
Magrane, Joe*	148
Olivares, Omar	17
Oquendo, Jose**	131
Pena, Geronimo*	100
Smith, Bryn	145
Smith, Ozzie	15
Terry, Scott	182

** On Disabled List twice during 1992 season (not counting transfers from one DL to another).*

*** On Disabled List three times during 1992 season.*

Minor league report

Class AAA — Louisville finished 73-30, 3rd in the American Association Eastern Division. OF Chuck Carr hit .308 and led the league in SB with 53. OF Ozzie Canseco had 22 HR. 1B Rod Brewer had 86 RBI. LHP Jeff Ballard was 12-8 with a 2.52 ERA. RHP Rene Arocha was 12-7 with a 2.70 ERA. RHP Mark Grater led the league in saves with 24. **Class AA:** Arkansas finished 59-73, last in the Texas League Eastern Division in the 1st half and 3rd in the 2nd half. RHP Kevin Meier was 11-6 with a 2.58 ERA. RHP Dennis Wiseman was 9-12 with a 2.90 ERA. RHP Paul Anderson was 4-11 but had a 3.37 ERA.RHP Fidel Compres won the league save title with 28. The club finished 1st in the league in pitching at 2.91. **Class A:** St. Petersburg finished 57-76, 5th in both halves of the Florida State League West Division. OF Anthony Lewis had 15 HR. LHP Scott Baker was 10-9 with a 1.96 ERA. RHP John Kelly set a league record and moved into fourth on the all-time single-season saves list with 38. Springfield finished 84-56, 3rd in the 1st half of the Midwest League Southern Division and 2nd in the 2nd half. 3B Dmitri Young hit .310 with 14 HR and 72 RBI. 2B Darryl Deak hda 16 HR and 79 RBI. RHP Mike Badorek had 17 wins. RHP Gerald Santos led the league with 35 saves. Savannah finished 62-78, 2nd in the 1st half of the Sally League Southern Division and last in the 2nd half. SS Aaron Holbert had 62 SB. OF Rick Mediavilla had 46 SB. RHP John Frascatore had 23 saves. RHP Jason Hisey led the league with 182 K. Hamilton finished 56-20, 1st in the New York-Penn League Stedler Division. The team lost to Erie in the 1st round of the playoffs. 2B Brad Owens hit .304 with 4 HR and 24 RBI. RHP T.J. Mathews was 10-1 with a 2.18 ERA and 89 K in 87 IP. LHP David Oehrlein shared the league lead with Mathews in wins and led the league in K with 99. RHP Jamie Cochran set a league record with 24 saves. Johnson City finished 33-32, 2nd in the Appalachian League South Division. OF Basil Shabazz led the league with 41 SB. C Aldo Pecorilli hit .325 with 6 HR and 41 RBI. RHP Eric Miller shared the league lead in saves with 13. Cardinals finished 28-28, 6th in the Arizona League. SS Brian Rupp won the league batting crown at .385 and led the league in RBI with 40. OF Joe McEwing hit .335 with 23 SB. RHP Travis Burley had 9 saves. RHP Ray Davis was 5-4 with a 2.49 ERA and 74 K in 76 IP.

Tops in the organization

BATTING LEADERS	Club	Avg.	G	AB	R	H	HR	RBI
Allen Battle	Stp	.311	127	457	83	142	5	39
Dmitri Young	Spr	.310	135	493	74	153	14	72
Dan Cholowsky	Stp	.307	128	433	63	133	9	51
Chuck Carr	Lou	.297	124	488	85	145	4	34
Tracy Woodson	Lou	.296	109	412	62	122	12	59

HOME RUNS			WINS		
Ozzie Canseco	Lou	22	Mike Badorek	Spr	17
Rod Brewer	Lou	18	Scott Simmons	Spr	15
Darrel Deak	Spr	16	Allen Watson	Lou	14
Anthony Lewis	Stp	15	Jason Hisey	Sav	13
Dmitri Young	Spr	14	Several players tied		12

RBI			SAVES		
Rod Brewer	Lou	86	John Kelly	Stp	38
Darrel Deak	Spr	79	Gerald Santos	Spr	35
Stan Royer	Lou	77	Fidel Compres	Ark	28
Dmitri Young	Spr	72	Mark Grater	Lou	24
Jonas Hamlin	Sav	71	John Frascatore	Sav	23

STOLEN BASES			STRIKEOUT		
Aaron Holbert	Sav	62	Allen Watson	Lou	182
Chuck Carr	Lou	61	Jason Hisey	Sav	182
Dan Cholowsky	Stp	48	Brian Barber	Stp	158
Rick Mediavilla	Sav	47	Rene Arocha	Lou	128
Mateo Ozuna	Sav	44	Frank Speek	Spr	126

PITCHING LEADERS	Club	W-L	ERA	IP	H	BB	SO
Scott Baker	Stp	10-9	1.96	152	123	54	125
Allen Watson	Lou	14-9	2.00	198	166	46	182
Jeff Ballard	Lou	12-8	2.52	161	164	34	76
Kevin Meier	Ark	11-6	2.58	171	156	37	107
Rene Arocha	Lou	12-7	2.70	167	145	65	128

St. Louis (1892-1992)

Runs: Most, career, all-time

1949	Stan Musial, 1941-1963
1427	Lou Brock, 1964-1979
1089	Rogers Hornsby, 1915-1933
1071	Enos Slaughter, 1938-1953
1025	Red Schoendienst, 1945-1963

Hits: Most, career, all-time

3630	Stan Musial, 1941-1963
2713	Lou Brock, 1964-1979
2110	Rogers Hornsby, 1915-1933
2064	Enos Slaughter, 1938-1953
1980	Red Schoendienst, 1945-1963

2B: Most, career, all-time

725	Stan Musial, 1941-1963
434	Lou Brock, 1964-1979
377	Joe Medwick, 1932-1948
367	Rogers Hornsby, 1915-1933
366	Enos Slaughter, 1938-1953

3B: Most, career, all-time

177	Stan Musial, 1941-1963
143	Rogers Hornsby, 1915-1933
135	Enos Slaughter, 1938-1953
121	Lou Brock, 1964-1979
119	Jim Bottomley, 1922-1932

HR: Most, career, all-time

475	Stan Musial, 1941-1963
255	Ken Boyer, 1955-1965
193	Rogers Hornsby, 1915-1933
181	Jim Bottomley, 1922-1932
172	Ted Simmons, 1968-1980

RBI: Most, career, all-time

1951	Stan Musial, 1941-1963
1148	Enos Slaughter, 1938-1953
1105	Jim Bottomley, 1922-1932
1072	Rogers Hornsby, 1915-1933
1001	Ken Boyer, 1955-1965

SB: Most, career, all-time

888	Lou Brock, 1964-1979
549	VINCE COLEMAN, 1985-1990
395	OZZIE SMITH, 1982-1992
274	WILLIE McGEE, 1982-1990
203	Jack Smith, 1915-1926

BB: Most, career, all-time

1599	Stan Musial, 1941-1963
838	Enos Slaughter, 1938-1953
753	OZZIE SMITH, 1982-1992
681	Lou Brock, 1964-1979
660	Rogers Hornsby, 1915-1933

BA: Highest, career, all-time

.359	Rogers Hornsby, 1915-1933
.336	Johnny Mize, 1936-1941
.335	Joe Medwick, 1932-1948
.331	Stan Musial, 1941-1963
.326	Chick Hafey, 1924-1931

Slug avg: Highest, career, all-time

.600	Johnny Mize, 1936-1941
.568	Rogers Hornsby, 1915-1933
.568	Chick Hafey, 1924-1931
.559	Stan Musial, 1941-1963
.545	Joe Medwick, 1932-1948

Games started: Most, career, all-time

482	Bob Gibson, 1959-1975
401	Bob Forsch, 1974-1988
388	Jesse Haines, 1920-1937
319	Bill Doak, 1913-1929
243	Bill Sherdel, 1918-1932

Saves: Most, career, all-time

129	TODD WORRELL, 1985-1992
127	Bruce Sutter, 1981-1984
117	LEE SMITH, 1990-1992
64	Lindy McDaniel, 1955-1962
60	Al Brazle, 1943-1954
60	Joe Hoerner, 1966-1969

Shutouts: Most, career, all-time

56	Bob Gibson, 1959-1975
30	Bill Doak, 1913-1929
28	Mort Cooper, 1938-1945
25	Harry Brecheen, 1940-1952
24	Jesse Haines, 1920-1937

Wins: Most, career, all-time

251	Bob Gibson, 1959-1975
210	Jesse Haines, 1920-1937
163	Bob Forsch, 1974-1988
153	Bill Sherdel, 1918-1932
144	Bill Doak, 1913-1929

K: Most, career, all-time

3117	Bob Gibson, 1959-1975
1095	Dizzy Dean, 1930-1937
1079	Bob Forsch, 1974-1988
979	Jesse Haines, 1920-1937
951	Steve Carlton, 1965-1971

Win pct: Highest, career, all-time

.718	Ted Wilks, 1944-1951
.705	John Tudor, 1985-1990
.677	Mort Cooper, 1938-1945
.667	Al Hrabosky, 1970-1977
.641	Dizzy Dean, 1930-1937

ERA: Lowest, career, all-time

2.52	John Tudor, 1985-1990
2.67	Slim Sallee, 1908-1916
2.67	Jack Taylor, 1904-1906
2.74	Johnny Lush, 1907-1910
2.74	Red Ames, 1915-1919

Runs: Most, season

142	Jesse Burkett, 1901
141	Rogers Hornsby, 1922
135	Stan Musial, 1948
133	Rogers Hornsby, 1925
132	Joe Medwick, 1935

Hits: Most, season

250	Rogers Hornsby, 1922
237	Joe Medwick, 1937
235	Rogers Hornsby, 1921
230	Stan Musial, 1948
230	Joe Torre, 1971

2B: Most, season

64	Joe Medwick, 1936
56	Joe Medwick, 1937
53	Stan Musial, 1953
52	Enos Slaughter, 1939
51	Stan Musial, 1944

3B: Most, season

29	Perry Werden, 1893
25	Tom Long, 1915
20	Jim Bottomley, 1928
20	Duff Cooley, 1895
20	Rogers Hornsby, 1920
20	Stan Musial, 1943
20	Stan Musial, 1946

HR: Most, season

43	Johnny Mize, 1940
42	Rogers Hornsby, 1922
39	Rogers Hornsby, 1925
39	Stan Musial, 1948
36	Stan Musial, 1949

RBI: Most, season

154	Joe Medwick, 1937
152	Rogers Hornsby, 1922
143	Rogers Hornsby, 1925
138	Joe Medwick, 1936
137	Jim Bottomley, 1929
137	Johnny Mize, 1940
137	Joe Torre, 1971

ACTIVE PLAYERS in caps.

SB: Most, season

118 Lou Brock, 1974
110 VINCE COLEMAN, 1985
109 VINCE COLEMAN, 1987
107 VINCE COLEMAN, 1986
81 VINCE COLEMAN, 1988

BB: Most, season

136 JACK CLARK, 1987
136 Jack Crooks, 1892
121 Jack Crooks, 1893
116 Miller Huggins, 1910
107 Stan Musial, 1949

BA: Highest, season

.424 Rogers Hornsby, 1924
.403 Rogers Hornsby, 1925
.401 Rogers Hornsby, 1922
.397 Rogers Hornsby, 1921
.396 Jesse Burkett, 1899

Slug avg: Highest, season

.756 Rogers Hornsby, 1925
.722 Rogers Hornsby, 1922
.702 Stan Musial, 1948
.696 Rogers Hornsby, 1924
.652 Chick Hafey, 1930

Games started: Most, season

50 Ted Breitenstein, 1894
50 Ted Breitenstein, 1895
47 Jack Taylor, 1898
45 Kid Gleason, 1892
45 Kid Gleason, 1893
41 Bob Harmon, 1911 (11)

Saves: Most, season

47 LEE SMITH, 1991
45 Bruce Sutter, 1984
43 LEE SMITH, 1992
36 Bruce Sutter, 1982
36 TODD WORRELL, 1986

Shutouts: Most, season

13 Bob Gibson, 1968
10 Mort Cooper, 1942
10 John Tudor, 1985
7 Harry Brecheen, 1948
7 Mort Cooper, 1944
7 Dizzy Dean, 1934
7 Bill Doak, 1914

Wins: Most, season

30 Dizzy Dean, 1934
28 Dizzy Dean, 1935
27 Ted Breitenstein, 1894
26 Cy Young, 1899
24 Dizzy Dean, 1936
24 Jesse Haines, 1927

K: Most, season

274 Bob Gibson, 1970
270 Bob Gibson, 1965
269 Bob Gibson, 1969
268 Bob Gibson, 1968
245 Bob Gibson, 1964

Win pct: Highest, season

.811 Dizzy Dean, 1934
.810 Ted Wilks, 1944
.789 Harry Brecheen, 1945
.778 Johnny Beazley, 1942
.767 Bob Gibson, 1970

ERA: Lowest, season

1.12 Bob Gibson, 1968
1.72 Bill Doak, 1914
1.78 Mort Cooper, 1942
1.90 Max Lanier, 1943
1.93 John Tudor, 1985

Most pinch-hit homers, season

4 George Crowe, 1959
4 George Crowe, 1960
4 Carl Sawatski, 1961

Most pinch-hit, homers, career

8 George Crowe, 1959-1961

Most consecutive games, batting safely

33 Rogers Hornsby, 1922
30 Stan Musial, 1950

Most consecutive scoreless innings

47 Bob Gibson, 1968
37 George Bradley, 1876

No hit games

George Bradley, StL vs Har NL, 2-0; July 15, 1876.
Jesse Haines, StL vs Bos NL, 5-0; July 17, 1924.
Paul Dean, StL at Bro NL, 3-0; September 21, 1934 (2nd game).
Lon Warneke, StL at Cin NL, 2-0; August 30, 1941.
Ray Washburn, StL at SF NL, 2-0; September 18, 1968.
Bob Gibson, StL at Pit NL, 11-0; August 14, 1971.
Bob Forsch, StL vs Phi NL, 5-0; April 16, 1978.
Bob Forsch, StL vs Mon NL, 3-0; September 26, 1983.
Stoney McGlynn, seven innings, agreement, StL at Bro NL, 1-1; September 24, 1906 (2nd game).
Ed Karger, seven perfect innings, agreement, StL vs Bos NL, 4-0; August 11, 1907 (2nd game).
Johnny Lush, six innings, rain, StL at Bro NL, 2-0; August 6, 1908.

Chicago Cubs

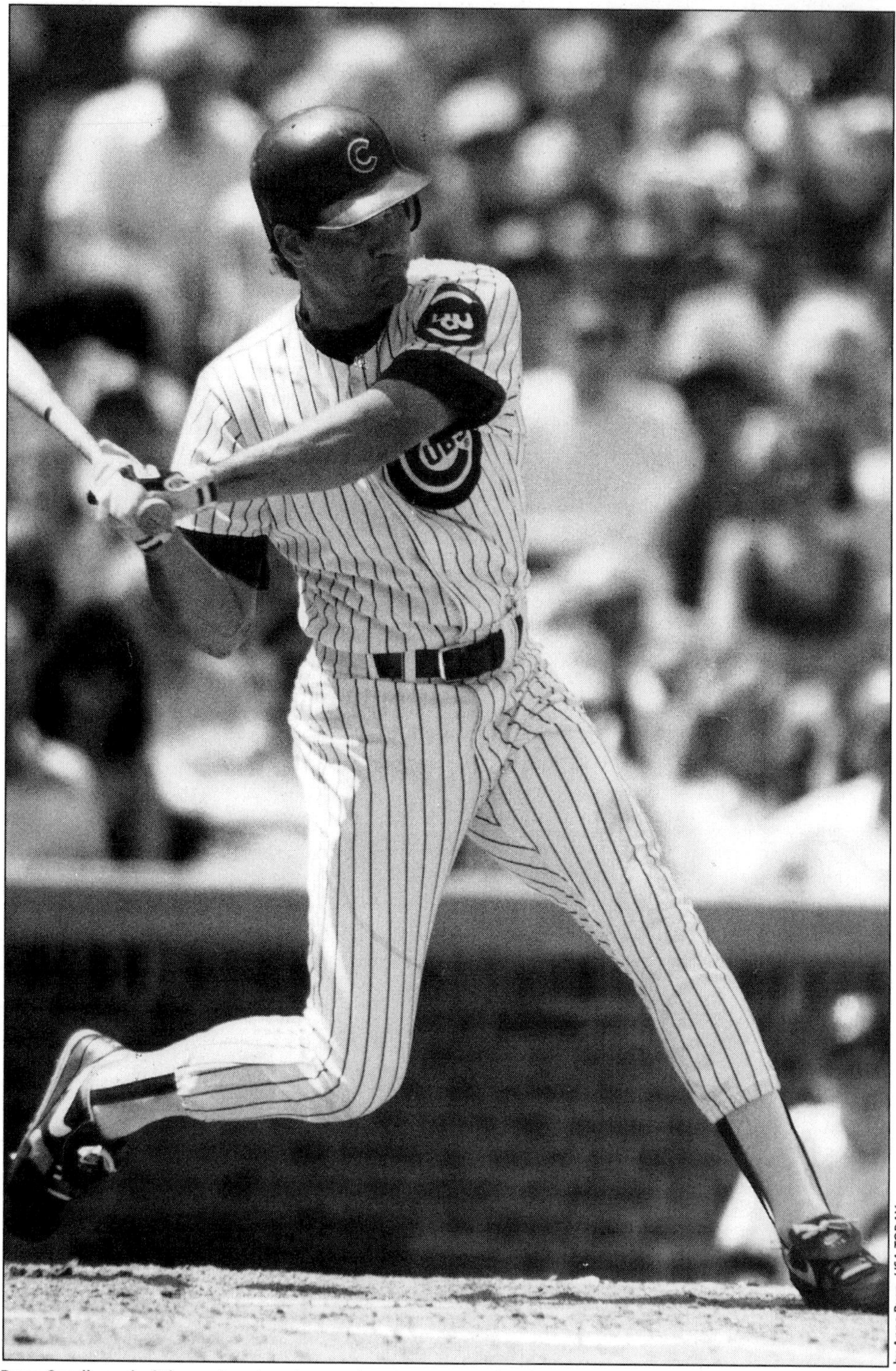

by Anne Ryan, *USA TODAY*

Ryne Sandberg led the majors in salary and was among NL leaders in five offensive categories as well.

1992 Cubs: Bitten by the injury bug

The Cubs had a great season—not on the field, but in the front office. Its victories included thwarting Fay Vincent's attempt to move the team to the NL West; Vincent's ouster (the Tribune Co. bristled at losing rights to televise games on superstations, and next year will televise games for seven teams); signing Ryne Sandberg to a long-term deal; signing pitcher Mike Morgan to a healthy contract, then watching him go out and prove he was worth it; and unloading Danny Jackson for Steve Buechele, who hit .261 with the Cubs (Jackson was benched during the NL playoffs).

But front office success didn't filter down to the field. The injury factor again climbed over Wrigley Field's ivy-covered walls. Shortstop Shawon Dunston was lost in April for most of the season. Jose Vizcaino filled in, got some big base hits, and played spectacular defense, but a hand injury put him on the DL for an extended stay. Then Rey Sanchez took over, raising his average 50 points in 10 days following Vizcaino's injury, but his back gave out and he went on the DL too. Outfielder Sammy Sosa went on the DL early in the year, then another injury ended his campaign on Aug.6. Right-hander Mike Harkey was supposed to fit in the starting rotation after a year-long rehab from a shoulder injury, but he tore up his knee turning cartwheels for fans, and that was it for Harkey. First year manager Jim Lefebvre said his pitching staff—especially the bullpen—never recovered from that blow. Chuck McElroy started out sizzling, then faded after his arm wore out; Shawn Boskie, back from an injury, was shelled by opponents during the final weeks; and Paul Assenmacher slumped in the stretch. The Cubs slipped from Sept. 1 contention to a fourth-place finish.

Hitting wasn't the Cubs' problem; run production was. They tied for fourth in the NL (.254), but they were seventh in home runs. The kicker was their on-base/slugging percentage (.671), ninth in the league.

How did the Cubs hang in the race for so long? Right fielder Andre Dawson hit .277 with 22 HRs and 90 RBI, and Ryne Sandberg turned in his usual steady numbers: .304, 26 HR, 87 RBI, and 17 steals. First baseman Mark Grace got his first Gold Glove and led the team in hitting (.307). Greg Maddux won 20 games, the NL Cy Young award, and a Gold Glove.

—by Alvin Reid

1993 Cubs: Preview

The Cubs found a decent closer, Randy Myers, a must if they are to reach the top of the NL East. They also need Rick Wilkins to emerge at catcher after losing Joe Girardi (to the Rockies) and putting Hector Villanueva on waivers.

Other expansion losses: Gary Scott and shortstop Alex Arias were traded to the Marlins for pitcher Greg Hibbard; pitching prospect Ryan Hawblitzel and infielder Pedro Castellano went to the Rockies.

Andre Dawson was run out of town with no obvious replacement in sight and Greg Maddux left on his own, creating two large holes. With Grace and Sandberg, the Cubs still can hang on as long as their pitching does. There's no replacement for Maddux, although signing Jose Guzman at least provides another dependable starter. Mike Harkey can't be counted on until he proves his knee is healthy. Hibbard brings a 10-7 record with him, but also a 4.40 ERA.

The Cubs' '93 fortunes also rest at the top of the lineup. If Sosa's health holds up, the Cubs will have a decent leadoff man, but if he goes down, so will offensive output. Doug Dascenzo hit just .255 and the Cubs' younger players were not up to the leadoff responsibility either.

—by Alvin Reid

1992 Cubs: Between the lines

▸**April 22:** Andre Dawson and Ryne Sandberg combined for two homers and six RBI in the Cubs' 9-5 win against the Phillies.

▸**May 1:** The Cubs' 4-0 shutout loss to the Reds was their fourth consecutive scoreless game, tying a major league record. The 36 consecutive scoreless innings wasn't a major league record, though—that mark (48) is shared by the 1906 Philadelphia Athletics and the 1968 Cubs.

▸**May 2:** The Cubs drought came to an end as they poured it on for a 10-2 victory over the Reds. But Chicago didn't necessarily work hard for the win—seven runs were unearned, including all six in the ninth inning. Andre Dawson accounted for the rest with a three-run homer.

▸**May 5:** The Cubs rallied twice for a 4-3 victory in 10 innings, breaking a five-game losing streak against Atlanta.

▸**May 6:** Ryne Sandberg hit a pair of two-run homers.

▸**May 7:** Mike Morgan went the distance, yielding two runs on seven hits.

▸**May 16:** The Cubs were 2-18 when they scored four runs or fewer—and, of course, had no wins at all when they scored zero, like they did in this game against San Francisco.

▸**May 20:** Danny Jackson fell to 0-6 as the Cubs lost against Los Angeles, 5-3. His ERA, an improvement over 1991's 6.75, rose to 5.14. It's not entirely his fault, though: The Cubs have provided him with only 22 runs in his nine starts.

▸**May 23:** Doug Strange hit his second career homer (the other came Sept. 4, 1989 with Detroit), and Mark Grace extended his hitting streak to eight games with an RBI double for Chicago.

▸**May 26:** Danny Jackson took a no-decision, extending his winless streak to 19 starts.

▸**May 31:** Danny Jackson was 14 days away from the one-year anniversary of his last victory. His record: 0-10 with 10 no decisions in his last 20 starts.

▸**June 14:** Two wins in two decisions usually isn't anything to brag about, but Chicago's Danny Jackson will take it. Jackson won for the second time this year, after 20 consecutive winless starts. The Cubs swept their first series of the season.

▸**June 19:** Cubs' rookie Derrick May entertained his wife, mom, dad and some 50 other relatives and friends with two homers and five RBI against the Phillies. May is from Newark, Del., about 45 miles from Philadelphia.

▸**June 25:** The Cubs snapped a three-game losing streak—all losses in New York—with a 9-2 victory against the Mets.

▸**June 26:** Mike Morgan pushed his ERA below 3.00 while combining with Paul Assenmacher and Jim Bullinger to shut out the Phillies.

▸**June 28 *Quote of the day:*** Jim Lefebvre, who was greeted with boos when he replaced Cubs' starter Frank Castillo after 8 2/3 innings of four-hit ball—"I don't care if it wasn't a popular move—the result was," Lefebvre said, after Paul Assenmacher retired John Kruk. "I wanted (Castillo) to finish as much as anyone else, but I can't let emotions control my decisions. Kruk had hit one into the next county the last time up."

▸**June 29:** The Cubs' 5-2 victory over the Mets snapped a 12-game, five-year losing streak against Dwight Gooden (24-4 vs. Chicago).

▸**July 4:** Andre Dawson ended the Cubs' string of 46 scoreless innings against Braves' pitching at Atlanta Fulton County Stadium with a bloop single in the eighth inning. The Braves won, anyway, running their record to 6-1 against Chicago.

▸**July 8:** The writing was on the wall when Rick Wilkins caught Greg Maddux's last two starts. The slumping Hector Villaneuva—Maddux's personal catcher—was optioned to Triple-A Iowa.

▸**July 22:** Greg Maddux threw his fifth complete game of the season, leading the Cubs to back-to-back shutouts.

▸**July 24:** The Cubs had permitted only three stolen bases in 24 games.

▸**July 27:** Greg Maddux struck out 10 Pirates. In his last seven starts, he was 6-1 with a 1.24 ERA. ***Quote of the day:*** Doug Drabek, after Cub Sammy Sosa hit a home run on the first pitch of the game—"I didn't even get a chance to see what kind of stuff I had."

▸**July 29:** Sammy Sosa continued bashing the Bucs, hitting a two-run homer in the 11th for a 6-4 victory against Pittsburgh. Sosa had seven hits, two homers and five RBI in the Cubs' three-game sweep.

▸**August 16:** Greg Maddux won his 15th game, making it five years in a row with at least 15. He's only the second Cubs' pitcher to do that in the last 50 years. Hall of Famer Ferguson Jenkins was the other.

▸**August 25:** Mike Harkey officially made it into the box score but didn't throw a pitch in the Cubs' 7-4 loss to the Padres, as he strained a groin muscle warming up and was replaced by Jeff D. Robinson.

▸**August 29:** Andre Dawson had a home run and a pair of doubles as the Cubs beat San Francisco 7-2.

▸**August 30:** Jim Bullinger nearly pitched a no-hitter in his third major league start, stymying the Giants through seven innings before Kirt Manwaring's homer.

▸**September 2:** Mike Morgan improved to 2-0 against the Dodgers—his old team—for his fourth consecutive win. His 14th victory matched the career high he set last season with L.A.

▸**September 11:** Greg Maddux struck out nine Cardinals and was 4-0 with a 1.69 ERA in four starts against St. Louis.

▸**September 17:** Mike Morgan earned his first shutout this year, a career-best two-hitter.

▸**September 21:** Greg Maddux was making a Cy Young push. His 19 wins, 2.24 ERA and .205 opponents' batting average were all second in the league. ***Milestone:*** Chicago's Andre Dawson became the 69th player in ML history to reach 2,500 hits.

▸**September 30:** Greg Maddux became the NL's second 20-game winner, beating the Pirates 6-0.

▸**October 4:** The Cubs finished fourth in the NL East. Ryne Sandberg was second in the league in total bases (312), third in hits (186), fourth in runs (100), fifth in slugging (.510), and sixth in home runs (26). Mark Grace was ninth in batting (.307). Andre Dawson was tenth in RBI (90). Greg Maddux tops in innings pitched (268), second in wins (20-11), and third in both ERA (2.18) and strikeouts (199).

—by Jeanie Chung, John Hunt, Deron Snyder, and Lisa Winston.

Team directory

▸**Owner:** Tribune Company

▸**General Manager:** Larry Himes

▸**Ballpark:** Wrigley Field
Clark and Addison Streets, Chicago, Ill.
312-404-2827
Capacity 38,710
Parking for 900; $10 (private lots available)
Public transportation available
Family and wheelchair sections, ramps

▸**Team publications:**
Yearbook, Vineline, Scorecard Magazine
800-248-WINS

▸**TV, radio broadcast stations:**
WGN 720 AM, WGN Channel 9

▸**Spring Training:**
HoHoKam Park
Mesa, Ariz.
Capacity 8,963

CHICAGO CUBS 1992 final stats

Batting	AVG	SLG	OB	G	AB	R	H	TB	2B	3B	HR	RBI	BB	SO	SB	CS	E
Dunston	.315	.384	.342	18	73	8	23	28	3	1	0	2	3	13	2	3	1
Grace	.307	.430	.380	158	603	72	185	259	37	5	9	79	72	36	6	1	4
Sandberg	.304	.510	.371	158	612	100	186	312	32	8	26	87	68	73	17	6	8
Arias	.293	.354	.375	32	99	14	29	35	6	0	0	7	11	13	0	0	4
Dawson	.277	.456	.316	143	542	60	150	247	27	2	22	90	30	70	6	2	2
Dw.Smith	.276	.392	.318	109	217	28	60	85	10	3	3	24	13	40	9	8	2
May	.274	.373	.306	124	351	33	96	131	11	0	8	45	14	40	5	3	5
Wilkins	.270	.414	.344	83	244	20	66	101	9	1	8	22	28	53	0	2	3
Girardi	.270	.300	.320	91	270	19	73	81	3	1	1	12	19	38	0	2	4
Buechele	.261	.372	.334	145	524	52	137	195	23	4	9	64	52	105	1	3	17
Sosa	.260	.393	.317	67	262	41	68	103	7	2	8	25	19	63	15	7	6
Dascenzo	.255	.311	.304	139	376	37	96	117	13	4	0	20	27	32	6	8	5
Sanchez	.251	.341	.285	74	255	24	64	87	14	3	1	19	10	17	2	1	9
Daniels	.241	.377	.315	83	212	21	51	80	11	0	6	25	22	54	0	2	2
Vizcaino	.225	.298	.260	86	285	25	64	85	10	4	1	17	14	35	3	0	9
Salazar	.208	.310	.237	98	255	20	53	79	7	2	5	25	11	34	1	1	6
Strange	.160	.202	.240	52	94	7	15	19	1	0	1	5	10	15	1	0	6
Scott	.156	.240	.198	36	96	8	15	23	2	0	2	11	5	14	0	1	5
Villanueva	.152	.259	.228	51	112	9	17	29	6	0	2	13	11	24	0	0	4
Kunkel	.138	.207	.138	20	29	0	4	6	2	0	0	1	0	8	0	0	1
Walton	.127	.164	.273	30	55	7	7	9	0	1	0	1	9	13	1	2	2
Ramsey	.120	.120	.120	18	25	0	3	3	0	0	0	2	0	6	0	0	0
Pedre	.000	.000	.000	4	4	0	0	0	0	0	0	0	0	1	0	0	0

Pitching	W-L	ERA	G	GS	CG	GF	Sho	SV	IP	H	R	ER	HR	BB	SO
Harkey	4-0	1.89	7	7	0	0	0	0	38	34	13	8	4	15	21
Maddux	20-11	2.18	35	35	9	0	4	0	268	201	68	65	7	70	199
Da.Smith	0-0	2.51	11	0	0	4	0	0	14.1	15	4	4	0	4	3
Morgan	16-8	2.55	34	34	6	0	1	0	240	203	80	68	14	79	123
Scanlan	3-6	2.89	69	0	0	41	0	14	87.1	76	32	28	4	30	42
Robinson	4-3	3.00	49	5	0	12	0	1	78	76	29	26	5	40	46
Castillo	10-11	3.46	33	33	0	0	0	0	205.1	179	91	79	19	63	135
McElroy	4-7	3.55	72	0	0	30	0	6	83.2	73	40	33	5	51	83
Patterson	2-3	3.89	32	1	0	4	0	0	41.2	41	25	18	7	27	23
Assenmacher	4-4	4.10	70	0	0	23	0	8	68	72	32	31	6	26	67
Bullinger	2-8	4.66	39	9	1	15	0	7	85	72	49	44	9	54	36
Boskie	5-11	5.01	23	18	0	2	0	0	91.2	96	55	51	14	36	39
Slocumb	0-3	6.50	30	0	0	11	0	1	36	52	27	26	3	21	27
Hartsock	0-0	6.75	4	0	0	0	0	0	9.1	15	7	7	2	4	6
Rasmussen	0-0	10.80	3	1	0	1	0	0	5	7	6	6	2	2	0
Hollins	0-0	13.50	4	0	0	3	0	0	4.2	8	7	7	1	5	0

1993 preliminary roster

PITCHERS (19)
Paul Assenmacher
Shawn Boskie
Jim Bullinger
Frank Castillo
Lance Dickson
Jose Guzman
Mike Harkey
Greg Hibbard
Jessie Hollins
Chuck McElroy
Mike Morgan
Randy Myers
Ken Patterson
Dan Plesac
Bob Scanlan
Heathcliff Slocumb
Dave Stevens
Dave Swartzbaugh
Turk Wendell

CATCHERS (4)
George Pedre
Steve Lake
Matt Walbeck
Rick Wilkins

INFIELDERS (8)
Steve Buechele
Shawon Dunston
Mark Grace
Rey Sanchez
Ryne Sandberg
Doug Strange
Jose Vierra
Jose Vizcaino

OUTFIELDERS (8)
Doug Dascenzo
Phil Dauphin
Candy Maldonado
Derrick May
Fernando Ramsey
Kevin Roberson
Dwight Smith
Sammy Sosa
Jerome Walton

Games played by position

Player	G	C	1B	2B	3B	SS	OF
ARIAS,A	32	0	0	0	0	30	0
BUECHELE,S	145	0	0	2	143	0	0
DANIELS,K	83	0	8	0	0	0	49
DASCENZO,D	139	0	0	0	0	0	122
DAWSON,A	143	0	0	0	0	0	139
DUNSTON,S	18	0	0	0	0	18	0
GIRARDI,J	91	86	0	0	0	0	0
GRACE,M	158	0	157	0	0	0	0
KUNKEL,J	20	0	0	3	0	6	3
MAY,D	124	0	0	0	0	0	108
PEDRE,J	4	4	0	0	0	0	0
RAMSEY,F	18	0	0	0	0	0	15
SALAZAR,L	98	0	5	0	40	12	34
SANCHEZ,R	74	0	0	4	0	68	0
SANDBERG,R	158	0	0	157	0	0	0
SCOTT,G	36	0	0	0	30	2	0
SMITH,DW	109	0	0	0	0	0	63
SOSA,S	67	0	0	0	0	0	67
STRANGE,D	52	0	0	12	33	0	0
VILLANUEVA,H	51	28	6	0	0	0	0
VIZCAINO,J	86	0	0	5	29	50	0
WALTON,J	30	0	0	0	0	0	24
WILKINS,R	83	73	0	0	0	0	0

Sick call: 1992 DL report

Player	Days on the DL
Assenmacher, Paul	16
Boskie, Shawn	36
Dunston, Shawon	153
Harkey, Mike*	134
Patterson, Ken	42
Rasmussen, Dennis	19
Sanchez, Rey	15
Smith, Dave	118
Sosa, Sammy*	84
Vizcaino, Jose*	37
Walton, Jerome	18

** On Disabled List twice during 1992 season (not counting transfers from one DL to another).*

Minor league report

Class AAA — Iowa finished 51-92, last in the American Association Western Division. OF Fernando Ramsey had 39 SB. RHP Jim Bullinger had 14 saves. OF Scott Bryant had 19 HR. **Class AA:** Charlotte finished 70-73, 3rd in the 1st half of the Southern League Eastern Division and 2nd in the 2nd half. C Matt Walbeck hit .301 with 7 HR and 42 RBI. OF Chris Ebright had 77 RBI. RHP Steve Trachsel was 13-8 with a 3.06 ERA. RHP Jessie Hollins had 25 saves. **Class A:** Winston-Salem finished 66-73, last in the Carolina League Southern Division in the 1st half and 2nd in the 2nd half. OF Corey Kapano won the league batting crown at .318 with 14 HR and 65 RBI. 1B Andy Hartung had 23 HR and led the league in RBI with 94. RHP Aaron Taylor had 20 saves. OF Doug Glanville had 32 SB. Peoria finished 62-74, 5th in the 1st half of the Midwest League Southern Division and 4th in the 2nd half. OF Ed Larregui hit .287 with 5 HR and 71 RBI. OF Joey Terilli hit .286 with 55 RBI. RHP Ken Krahenbuhl was 7-9 with a 3.45 ERA. Geneva finished 41-34, 1st in the New York-Penn League Pinckney Division. The team beat Erie in two games for the league championship. 2B Chad Tredaway hit .300 with 5 HR and 31 RBI. OF Robin Jennings hit .298 with 7 HR and 47 RBI. RHP Hector Trinidad was 8-6 with a 2.40 ERA. RHP Chuck Daniel was 5-5 with a 2.51 ERA. Huntington finished 28-34, 4th in the Appalachian League North Division. SS Tim Stutheit won the league batting title at .338. RHP Yogi Pacheco was 5-4 with a 2.00 ERA and 84 K in 90 IP. RHP Jay Hassel was 4-1 with a 2.39 ERA and 92 K in 75 IP. RHP Amaury Talemaco won the K title with 93. Cubs finished 18-38 in a combined team with the Rockies, last in the Arizona League. The team was last in pitching with a 5.42 ERA and next to last in batting at .243.

Tops in the organization

BATTING LEADERS	Club	Avg.	G	AB	R	H	HR	RBI
Corey Kapano	Iwa	.318	98	330	65	105	14	66
Matt Walbeck	Chr	.301	105	385	48	116	7	42
Ed Larregui	Peo	.287	129	478	62	137	5	71
Joey Terilli	Peo	.286	113	370	71	106	3	55
Andy Hartung	Chr	.279	134	505	77	141	24	97

HOME RUNS	Club	
Andy Hartung	Chr	24
Ozzie Timmons	Wns	21
Scott Bryant	Iwa	19
Jose Vierra	Wns	18
Chris Ebright	Chr	17

RBI	Club	
Andy Hartung	Chr	97
Paul Torres	Wns	78
Chris Ebright	Chr	77
Ed Larregui	Peo	71
Ozzie Timmons	Wns	69

STOLEN BASES	Club	
Fernando Ramsey	Iwa	39
Doug Glanville	Wns	32
Phil Dauphin	Chr	17
Joey Terilli	Peo	15
Ed Larregui	Peo	15

WINS	Club	
Steve Trachsel	Chr	13
Ryan Hawblitzel	Chr	12
Several players tied		10

SAVES	Club	
Jessie Hollins	Chr	25
Aaron Taylor	Wns	20
Jim Bullinger	Iwa	14
Mike Tidwell	Chr	13
Heath Slocumb	Iwa	7

STRIKEOUTS	Club	
Steve Trachsel	Chr	135
Tim Delgado	Wns	121
Ryan Hawblitzel	Chr	119
Ken Krahenbuhl	Peo	111
Dave Swartzbaugh	Chr	111

PITCHING LEADERS	Club	W-L	ERA	IP	H	BB	SO
Steve Trachsel	Chr	13-8	3.06	191	180	35	135
Scott Weiss	Wns	8-7	3.43	129	125	52	105
Ken Krahenbuhl	Peo	7-9	3.45	141	140	51	111
Tim Delgado	Wns	8-10	3.50	157	157	42	121
Brian Kenny	Wns	10-9	3.64	136	124	34	94

Chicago (1876-1992)

Runs: Most, career, all-time

1719 Cap Anson, 1876-1897
1409 Jimmy Ryan, 1885-1900
1306 Billy Williams, 1959-1974
1305 Ernie Banks, 1953-1971
1239 Stan Hack, 1932-1947

Hits: Most, career, all-time

2995 Cap Anson, 1876-1897
2583 Ernie Banks, 1953-1971
2510 Billy Williams, 1959-1974
2193 Stan Hack, 1932-1947
2171 Ron Santo, 1960-1973

2B: Most, career, all-time

528 Cap Anson, 1876-1897
407 Ernie Banks, 1953-1971
402 Billy Williams, 1959-1974
391 Gabby Hartnett, 1922-1940
363 Stan Hack, 1932-1947

3B: Most, career, all-time

142 Jimmy Ryan, 1885-1900
124 Cap Anson, 1876-1897
117 Frank Schulte, 1904-1916
106 Bill Dahlen, 1891-1898
99 Phil Cavarretta, 1934-1953

HR: Most, career, all-time

512 Ernie Banks, 1953-1971
392 Billy Williams, 1959-1974
337 Ron Santo, 1960-1973
231 Gabby Hartnett, 1922-1940
231 RYNE SANDBERG, 1982-1992

RBI: Most, career, all-time

1879 Cap Anson, 1876-1897
1636 Ernie Banks, 1953-1971
1353 Billy Williams, 1959-1974
1290 Ron Santo, 1960-1973
1153 Gabby Hartnett, 1922-1940

SB: Most, career, all-time

400 Frank Chance, 1898-1912
399 Bill Lange, 1893-1899
369 Jimmy Ryan, 1885-1900
314 RYNE SANDBERG, 1982-1992
304 Joe Tinker, 1902-1916

BB: Most, career, all-time

1092 Stan Hack, 1932-1947
1071 Ron Santo, 1960-1973
952 Cap Anson, 1876-1897
911 Billy Williams, 1959-1974
794 Phil Cavarretta, 1934-1953

BA: Highest, career, all-time

.336 Riggs Stephenson, 1926-1934
.330 Bill Lange, 1893-1899
.329 Cap Anson, 1876-1897
.325 Kiki Cuyler, 1928-1935
.323 Bill Everett, 1895-1900

Slug avg: Highest, career, all-time

.590 Hack Wilson, 1926-1931
.512 Hank Sauer, 1949-1955
.507 ANDRE DAWSON, 1987-1992
.503 Billy Williams, 1959-1974
.500 Ernie Banks, 1953-1971

Games started: Most, career, all-time

347 Fergie Jenkins, 1966-1983
343 Rick Reuschel, 1972-1984
340 Bill Hutchison, 1889-1895
339 Charlie Root, 1926-1941
296 Bill Lee, 1934-1947

Saves: Most, career, all-time

180 LEE SMITH, 1980-1987
133 Bruce Sutter, 1976-1980
63 Don Elston, 1953-1964
60 Phil Regan, 1968-1972
52 MITCH WILLIAMS, 1989-1990

Shutouts: Most, career, all-time

48 Mordecai Brown, 1904-1916
35 Hippo Vaughn, 1913-1921
31 Ed Reulbach, 1905-1913
29 Fergie Jenkins, 1966-1983
28 Orval Overall, 1906-1913

Wins: Most, career, all-time

201 Charlie Root, 1926-1941
188 Mordecai Brown, 1904-1916
182 Bill Hutchison, 1889-1895
175 Larry Corcoran, 1880-1885
167 Fergie Jenkins, 1966-1983

K: Most, career, all-time

2038 Fergie Jenkins, 1966-1983
1432 Charlie Root, 1926-1941
1367 Rick Reuschel, 1972-1984
1226 Bill Hutchison, 1889-1895
1138 Hippo Vaughn, 1913-1921

Win pct: Highest, career, all-time

.800 Al Spalding, 1876-1878
.773 Jim McCormick, 1885-1886
.706 John Clarkson, 1884-1887
.686 Mordecai Brown, 1904-1916
.677 Ed Reulbach, 1905-1913

ERA: Lowest, career, all-time

1.80 Mordecai Brown, 1904-1916
1.85 Jack Pfiester, 1906-1911
1.91 Orval Overall, 1906-1913
2.14 Jake Weimer, 1903-1905
2.24 Ed Reulbach, 1905-1913

Runs: Most, season

156 Rogers Hornsby, 1929
155 Kiki Cuyler, 1930
155 King Kelly, 1886
152 Woody English, 1930
150 George Gore, 1886

Hits: Most, season

229 Rogers Hornsby, 1929
228 Kiki Cuyler, 1930
227 Billy Herman, 1935
214 Woody English, 1930
212 Frank Demaree, 1936

2B: Most, season

57 Billy Herman, 1935
57 Billy Herman, 1936
50 Kiki Cuyler, 1930
49 Riggs Stephenson, 1932
47 Rogers Hornsby, 1929

3B: Most, season

21 Vic Saier, 1913
21 Frank Schulte, 1911
19 Bill Dahlen, 1892
19 Bill Dahlen, 1896
19 RYNE SANDBERG, 1984

HR: Most, season

56 Hack Wilson, 1930
49 ANDRE DAWSON, 1987
48 Dave Kingman, 1979
47 Ernie Banks, 1958
45 Ernie Banks, 1959

RBI: Most, season

190 Hack Wilson, 1930
159 Hack Wilson, 1929
149 Rogers Hornsby, 1929
147 Cap Anson, 1886
143 Ernie Banks, 1959

SB: Most, season

84 Bill Lange, 1896
76 Walt Wilmot, 1890
74 Walt Wilmot, 1894
73 Bill Lange, 1897
67 Frank Chance, 1903
67 Bill Lange, 1895

BB: Most, season

147 Jimmy Sheckard, 1911
122 Jimmy Sheckard, 1912
116 Richie Ashburn, 1960
113 Cap Anson, 1890
108 Johnny Evers, 1910

BA: Highest, season

.389 Bill Lange, 1895
.388 King Kelly, 1886
.380 Rogers Hornsby, 1929
.372 Heinie Zimmerman, 1912
.371 Cap Anson, 1886

Slug avg: Highest, season

.723 Hack Wilson, 1930
.679 Rogers Hornsby, 1929
.630 Gabby Hartnett, 1930
.618 Hack Wilson, 1929
.614 Ernie Banks, 1958

Games started: Most, season

71 Bill Hutchison, 1892
70 John Clarkson, 1885
66 Bill Hutchison, 1890
60 Larry Corcoran, 1880
60 Al Spalding, 1876
42 Fergie Jenkins, 1969 (18)

Saves: Most, season

37 Bruce Sutter, 1979
36 LEE SMITH, 1987
36 MITCH WILLIAMS, 1989
33 LEE SMITH, 1984
33 LEE SMITH, 1985

Shutouts: Most, season

10 John Clarkson, 1885
9 Pete Alexander, 1919
9 Mordecai Brown, 1906
9 Mordecai Brown, 1908
9 Bill Lee, 1938
9 Orval Overall, 1909

Wins: Most, season

53 John Clarkson, 1885
47 Al Spalding, 1876
44 Bill Hutchison, 1891
43 Larry Corcoran, 1880
42 Bill Hutchison, 1890
29 Mordecai Brown, 1908 (14)

K: Most, season

316 Bill Hutchison, 1892
313 John Clarkson, 1886
308 John Clarkson, 1885
289 Bill Hutchison, 1890
274 Fergie Jenkins, 1970

Win pct: Highest, season

.875 Fred Goldsmith, 1880
.833 King Cole, 1910
.833 Jim McCormick, 1885
.826 Ed Reulbach, 1906
.813 Mordecai Brown, 1906

ERA: Lowest, season

1.04 Mordecai Brown, 1906
1.15 Jack Pfiester, 1907
1.17 Carl Lundgren, 1907
1.31 Mordecai Brown, 1909
1.33 Jack Taylor, 1902

Most pinch-hit homers, season

3 Willie Smith, 1969
3 Thad Bosley, 1985

Most pinch-hit, homers, career

6 Thad Bosley, 1983-1986

Most consecutive games, batting safely

42 Bill Dahlen, 1894
30 Jerome Walton, 1989

Most consecutive scoreless innings

50 Ed Reulbach, 1908-09
39 Mordecai Brown, 1908
38 Bill Lee, 1938
38 John Clarkson, 1885

No hit games

Larry Corcoran, Chi vs Bos NL, 6-0; August 19, 1880.
Larry Corcoran, Chi vs Wor NL, 5-0; September 20, 1882.
Larry Corcoran, Chi vs Pro NL, 6-0; June 27, 1884.
John Clarkson, Chi at Pro NL, 4-0; July 27, 1885.
Walter Thornton, Chi vs Bro NL, 2-0; August 21, 1898 (2nd game).
Bob Wicker, Chi at NY NL, 1-0; June 11, 1904 (won in 12 innings after allowing one hit in the tenth).
Jimmy Lavender, Chi at NY NL, 2-0; August 31, 1915 (1st game).
Hippo Vaughn, Chi vs Cin NL, 0-1; May 2, 1917. (lost on two hits in the 10th, Toney pitched a no-hitter in this game).
Sam Jones, Chi vs Pit NL, 4-0; May 12, 1955.
Don Cardwell, Chi vs StL NL, 4-0; May 15, 1960 (2nd game).
Ken Holtzman, Chi vs Atl NL, 3-0; August 19, 1969.
Ken Holtzman, Chi at Cin NL, 1-0; June 3, 1971.
Burt Hooton, Chi vs Phi NL, 4-0; April 16, 1972.
Milt Pappas, Chi vs SD NL, 8-0; September 2, 1972.
George Van Haltren, six innings, rain, Chi vs Pit NL, 1-0, June 21, 1888.
King Cole, seven innings, called so Chicago could catch train, Chi at StL NL, 4-0; July 31, 1910 (2nd game).

ACTIVE PLAYERS in caps.

New York Mets

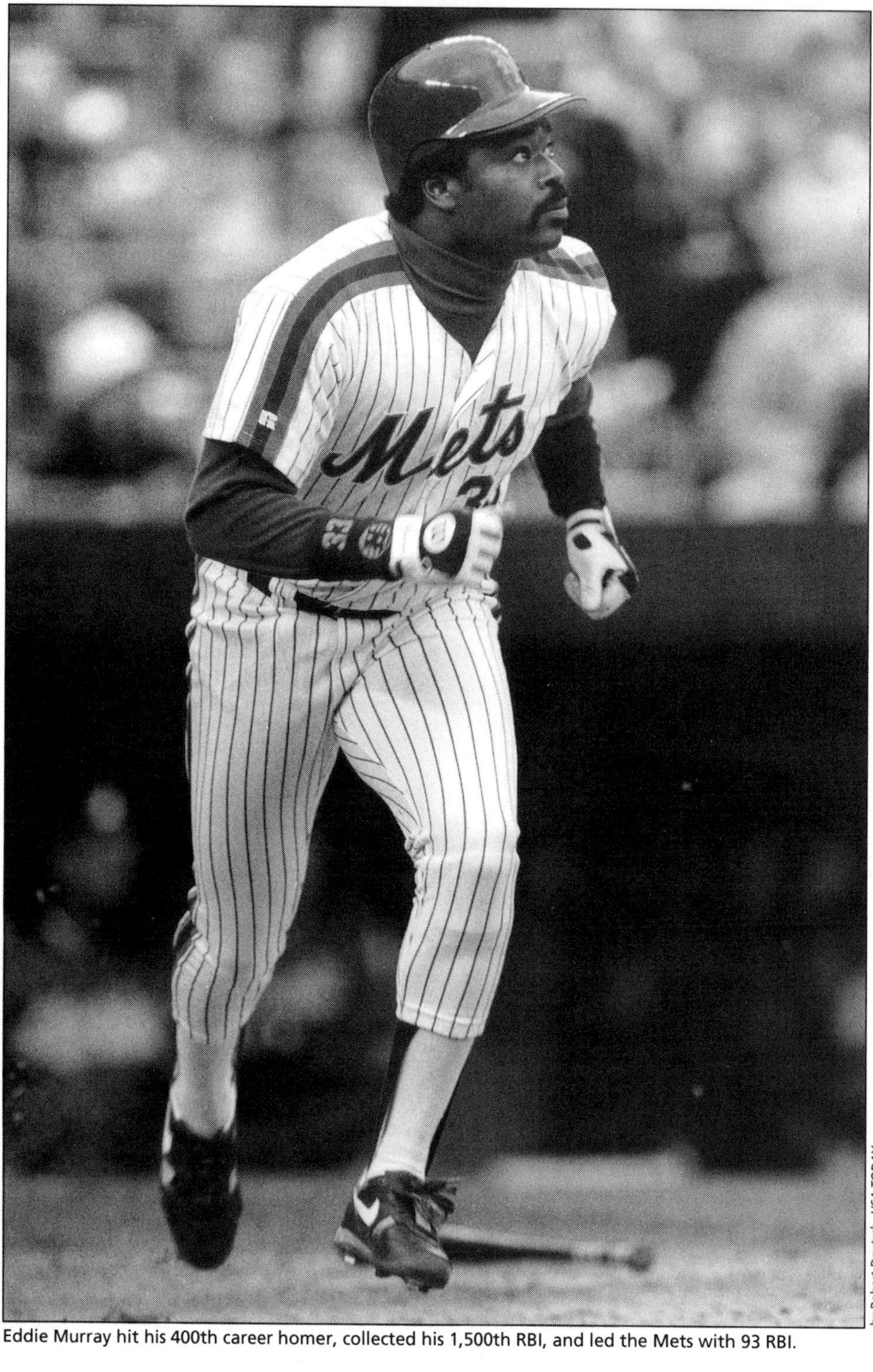

by Robert Deutsch, *USA TODAY*

Eddie Murray hit his 400th career homer, collected his 1,500th RBI, and led the Mets with 93 RBI.

1992 Mets: Big bucks, puny results

Money can't buy happiness. Just ask the Mets. They invested a league-high $44 million in salaries and reaped a league-worst .235 team batting average along with a 3.52 ERA (10th in the NL). The result was a 72-90, fifth-place finish that made the Mets an NL laughingstock.

The pieces seemed to be falling in place as the season started. Bobby Bonilla was signed to a multi-million-dollar contract, free agents Willie Randolph and Eddie Murray were in the lineup, and Bret Saberhagen came in a trade that ridded the Mets of Kevin McReynolds and Gregg Jefferies, both fan scapegoats. The steady Howard Johnson was returning and together with Vince Coleman would make the Mets' outfield a combination of raw power and speed. Dick Schofield would plug the hole at shortstop. Dwight Gooden was healthy; with Sid Fernandez and Anthony Young too, the pitching staff would be dominant.

When Bonilla tagged two homers on Opening Day, money was talkin' and the Mets looked to be walkin' to contention.

But things began to fall apart the very next day. Vince Coleman pulled a hamstring for the first of several stays on the DL. His performance and his attitude sagged, bottoming out in a shoving match with manager Jeff Torborg. Bonilla fizzled immediately—a month went by before he hit another home run. He was bad on the road and worse at home; Mets' fans booed him at Shea and a broken rib put him out for much of the latter part of the season. His own season ended in mid-September when he opted for arthroscopic surgery on his shoulder. He finished with 19 HR and 70 RBI in 128 games. Howard Johnson never came around at the plate (seven HR, 43 RBI), was a disaster in the field, and was also injured much of the season.

Bret Saberhagen had a finger injury that flared in mid-May; two trips to the DL left him searching for his lost season. He went 3-5 with a 3.50 ERA in just 17 games. Ten Mets underwent surgery during the season, including Dave Magadan and John Franco.

The TV ads promised that Torborg would bring "hardball" back to Shea Stadium—a spirited game of baserunning and power hitting. Instead, fans saw listless, boring baseball, incredibly stupid baserunning, and equally inept defense. Empty seats often outnumbered fans as the nightmare season dragged on.

There were exceptions: Eddie Murray had a solid season (16 HR, 93 RBI) and hit home run No. 400. Dwight Gooden pitched 206 innings. Pete Schourek pitched 136 innings, second to Sid Fernandez.

The Mets waved goodbye to 1992 on Aug. 31 when ace David Cone was dealt to Toronto for third baseman Jeff Kent and outfielder Ryan Thompson.

—by Alvin Reid

1993 Mets: Preview

For the Mets to contend in 1993, David Cone's arm has to be replaced and good health must return to Shea. Howard Johnson must rebound and lend offensive pop to Bonilla's efforts. Look for that duo in the outfield, but expect a new face in left field.

Wally Whitehurst and prospect D.J. Dozier were sent west to obtain shortstop Tony Fernandez. Fernandez was solid at shortstop but slumped in San Diego. Rookie catcher Todd Hundley didn't offer much offense in '92 but he was a steady catcher and showed he belongs in the big leagues.

As for Torborg, he has to settle his players down with a tougher stand on antics like Coleman's—and he can't be caught up in clubhouse squabbles.

Al Harazin also didn't rule out more free agents, but it certainly was not a success tonic in 1992.

—by Alvin Reid

1992 Mets: Between the lines

▶**April 22:** Eddie Murray hit his first home run as a Met—399th career.

▶**April 29:** Bret Saberhagen got his first NL victory.

▶**May 1:** Among the favorites to represent the NL in the World Series, the Mets and the Braves combined for 23 hits and 15 runs, with the Mets winning 8-7.

▶**May 3** ***Milestones:*** Eddie Murray became the 24th player to hit 400 career home runs and Howard Johnson became the 16th player with 200 steals and 200 homers.

▶**May 16:** The Mets were shut out for the second time in three days. Bobby Bonilla (3-for-30) earned the nickname "Bobby Boo" from fans.

▶**May 18:** Mets' pitchers led the majors in strikeouts with 291.

▶**May 19:** David Cone pitched a shutout and Bonilla cracked his homerless streak of 161 plate appearances.

▶**May 23:** Bonilla had four hits, including a three-run homer and three RBI. Cone tossed his fourth shutout. John Franco got his eighth save and still hadn't given up a run. ***Milestone:*** Eddie Murray got his 1,500th career RBI.

▶**May 29:** Willie Randolph's two-out, run-scoring double in the ninth inning gave the Mets their first run in four home games.

▶**May 30:** The Mets exploded for another run, giving them two over a 45-inning span. David Cone extended his scoreless streak to a career-best 20 innings before surrendering the tying run.

▶**June 1:** Bonilla went 3-for-3 with a career-high six RBI on a breakout night for the reeling Mets, who beat San Francisco 14-1.

▶**June 6:** After being booed unmercifully and struck with a golf ball in right field at Veterans Stadium, Bonilla went 4-for-4 with a double, homer and four RBI. ***Milestone:*** Eddie Murray became the all-time leader in RBI by a switch-hitter (1,510) and passed Mickey Mantle into 32nd place overall.

▶**June 7** ***Quote of the day:*** Dave Magadan, on a fielding error that turned an inning-ending double play into a Pirates' rally—"I was going to catch the ball, touch the bag and throw to first. I forgot Part A of the plan."

▶**June 8:** The Mets were shut out for the ninth time.

▶**June 10:** The Mets tied a club record by committing six errors in a single game.

▶**June 16:** David Cone recorded his league-leading sixth complete game.

▶**June 18:** Things got so bad that the clubhouse was shut down after the game for a players-only meeting.

▶**June 19:** Howard Johnson—batting .228—was benched. ***Milestone:*** Willie Randolph played in his 2,126th career game at second base, moving him into sixth place on the all-time list.

▶**June 24:** The Mets won their fourth consecutive game, matching their season high.

▶**June 26** ***Milestone:*** Vince Coleman became the 11th major leaguer to reach 600 career steals. He set a team record (four stolen bases) before injuring his left hamstring.

▶**July 1:** Lee Guetterman got his first NL victory and Anthony Young got his first major league save.

▶**July 17:** David Cone's 13-strikeout, complete-game shutout was the 19th shutout the Mets had been involved in—throwing eight and being blanked 11 times.

▶**July 22** ***Quote of the day:*** David Cone, after the Mets won four of five games, on their shot at the division title—"It's there for the taking. It might as well be us."

▶**July 25:** Shut out again—for the 12th time.

▶**July 26:**... And again (13).

▶**July 27:**... And yet again (14).

▶**August 2:** David Cone won his eighth consecutive decision. But, of course, there was bad news: Two-thirds of New York's starting outfield and the heart of the batting order—Bobby Bonilla and Howard Johnson—went on the 15-day DL.

▸**August 16:** More bad luck: After dropping one game to the Phillies, the series-ending doubleheader was postponed (rain), so the Mets were—technically—swept by the Phils.

▸**August 19:** Dwight Gooden, who was 14-1 lifetime against the Dodgers, lost to Orel Hershiser, who was 0-12 against the Mets.

▸**August 20:** Chico Walker led the Mets to an 11-4 rout of the Dodgers. During the Mets' power surge, they hit their first back-to-back homers of the year (Bonilla and Mackey Sasser). It was their first two-triple game (Dick Schofield and Walker) of the year and their first four-homer game in two years (Eddie Murray, Bonilla, Sasser and Bill Pecota).

▸**August 27:** The Mets traded David Cone to Toronto for third baseman Jeff Kent and minor-league outfielder Ryan Thompson. Cone was positioned to be the first pitcher since Johnny Vander Meer (1941-43) to get the NL strikeout title three years in a row.

▸**August 28:** Jeff Kent paid quick dividends: He was 2-for-5 with three RBI in the nightcap of a 4-3, 12-1 doubleheader sweep of the Reds.

▸**September 4** ***Milestone:*** Eddie Murray got his 78th RBI, the 16th year in a row he had driven in at least 75 runs. That tied Al Simmons' major league mark for most consecutive 75-plus RBI seasons to start a career. Only Hank Aaron has that many in more consecutive seasons (19).

▸**September 13:** Dwight Gooden got his ninth RBI, to lead all major league pitchers. He raised his average to .290, also tops among pitchers.

▸**September 16:** The Mets were mathematically eliminated from the pennant race.

▸**September 26:** Why not? For the first time in club history, the Mets sent a non-pitcher (Bill Pecota) to the mound. After all, it was the eighth inning, there was nobody left in the bullpen, and the game was well on its way to a final score of 19-2 in Pittsburgh's favor. ***Quote of the day:*** Pirate Andy Van Slyke—"It's not very often you face a middle infielder with a good sinker."

▸**October 4:** The Mets didn't finish last—they wound up two games out of the cellar. The only Met among the top five in any NL category was the one they traded away: David Cone. He led the league in shutouts with five and was eclipsed for the lead in strikeouts by just one K, and only on Brave John Smoltz's final start of the season. Eddie Murray finished eighth in the league with 93 RBI.

—by Jeanie Chung, John Hunt, Deron Snyder, and Lisa Winston.

Team directory

▸**Owner:** Fred Wilpon and Nelson Doubleday

▸**General Manager:** Al Harazin

▸**Ballpark:**
William A. Shea Municipal Stadium
126th Street and Roosevelt Avenue, Flushing, N.Y.
718-507-TIXX
Capacity 55,601
Parking for 6,000 cars; $4.50
Public transportation available
Family and wheelchair sections, ramps

▸**Team publications:**
Inside Pitch, Yearbook, Scorecard, Press Guide
919-688-0218

▸**TV, radio broadcast stations:**
WFAN 660 AM, WWOR Channel 9, Sportschannel

▸**Camps and/or clinics:**
Ulti-Met Week, 407-788-2222

▸**Spring Training:**
St. Lucie County Stadium
Port St. Lucie, Fla.
Capacity 7,000
407-871-2115

NEW YORK METS 1992 final stats

Batting	AVG	SLG	OB	G	AB	R	H	TB	2B	3B	HR	RBI	BB	SO	SB	CS	E
McCray	1.000	1.000	1.000	18	1	3	1	1	0	0	0	1	0	0	2	0	0
Springer	.400	.600	.400	4	5	0	2	3	1	0	0	0	0	1	0	0	0
Walker	.289	.391	.351	126	253	26	73	99	12	1	4	38	27	50	15	1	8
Magadan	.283	.346	.390	99	321	33	91	111	9	1	3	28	56	44	1	0	11
Coleman	.275	.358	.355	71	229	37	63	82	11	1	2	21	27	41	24	9	1
McKnight	.271	.400	.287	31	85	10	23	34	3	1	2	13	2	8	0	1	3
Bass	.269	.418	.308	135	402	40	108	168	23	5	9	39	23	70	14	9	3
Murray	.261	.423	.336	156	551	64	144	233	37	2	16	93	66	74	4	2	12
Randolph	.252	.318	.352	90	286	29	72	91	11	1	2	15	40	34	1	3	8
Boston	.249	.426	.338	130	289	37	72	123	14	2	11	35	38	60	12	6	1
Bonilla	.249	.432	.348	128	438	62	109	189	23	0	19	70	66	73	4	3	4
Sasser	.241	.326	.248	92	141	7	34	46	6	0	2	18	3	10	0	0	1
Gallagher	.240	.331	.307	98	175	20	42	58	11	1	1	21	19	16	4	5	2
Kent	.239	.407	.289	37	113	16	27	46	8	1	3	15	7	29	0	2	3
Pecota	.227	.297	.293	117	269	28	61	80	13	0	2	26	25	40	9	3	12
Johnson	.223	.337	.329	100	350	48	78	118	19	0	7	43	55	79	22	5	4
Elster	.222	.222	.222	6	18	0	4	4	0	0	0	0	0	2	0	0	0
Thompson	.222	.389	.274	30	108	15	24	42	7	1	3	10	8	24	2	2	1
O'Brien	.212	.327	.289	68	156	15	33	51	12	0	2	13	16	18	0	1	7
Hundley	.209	.316	.256	123	358	32	75	113	17	0	7	32	19	76	3	0	3
Schofield	.205	.286	.309	142	420	52	86	120	18	2	4	36	60	82	11	4	7
Dozier	.191	.234	.264	25	47	4	9	11	2	0	0	2	4	19	4	0	1
Howell	.187	.200	.218	31	75	9	14	15	1	0	0	1	2	15	4	2	0
Donnels	.174	.207	.275	45	121	8	21	25	4	0	0	6	17	25	1	0	5
Baez	.154	.154	.154	6	13	0	2	2	0	0	0	0	0	0	0	0	2
Noboa	.149	.149	.212	46	47	7	7	7	0	0	0	3	3	8	0	0	3

Pitching	W-L	ERA	G	GS	CG	GF	Sho	SV	IP	H	R	ER	HR	BB	SO
Franco	6-2	1.64	31	0	0	30	0	15	33	24	6	6	1	11	20
Filer	0-1	2.05	9	1	0	1	0	0	22	18	8	5	2	6	9
Fernandez	14-11	2.73	32	32	5	0	2	0	214.2	162	67	65	12	67	193
Innis	6-9	2.86	76	0	0	28	0	1	88	85	32	28	4	36	39
Cone	13-7	2.88	27	27	7	0	5	0	196.2	162	75	63	12	82	214
Saberhagen	3-5	3.50	17	15	1	0	1	0	97.2	84	39	38	6	27	81
Whitehurst	3-9	3.62	44	11	0	7	0	0	97	99	45	39	4	33	70
Schourek	6-8	3.64	22	21	0	0	0	0	136	137	60	55	9	44	60
Gooden	10-13	3.67	31	31	3	0	0	0	206	197	93	84	11	70	145
Young	2-14	4.17	52	13	1	26	0	15	121	134	66	56	8	31	64
Dewey	1-0	4.32	20	0	0	6	0	0	33.1	37	16	16	2	10	24
Gibson	0-1	5.23	43	1	0	12	0	0	62	70	37	36	7	25	49
Hillman	2-2	5.33	11	8	0	2	0	0	52.1	67	31	31	9	10	16
Jones	7-6	5.68	61	0	0	17	0	1	69.2	85	46	44	3	35	30
Burke	1-2	5.74	15	0	0	9	0	0	15.2	26	15	10	1	3	7
Guetterman	3-4	5.82	43	0	0	15	0	2	43.1	57	28	28	5	14	15
Birkbeck	0-1	9.00	1	1	0	0	0	0	7	12	7	7	3	1	2
Pecota	0-0	9.00	1	0	0	1	0	0	1	1	1	1	1	0	0
Vitko	0-1	13.50	3	1	0	1	0	0	4.2	12	11	7	1	1	6

1993 preliminary roster

PITCHERS (17)
Juan Castillo
Mark Dewey
Mike Draper
Sid Fernandez
John Franco
Paul Gibson
Dwight Gooden
Eric Hillman
Jeff Innis
Roger Mason
Steve Rosenberg
Bret Saberhagen
Pete Schourek
Frank Tanana
Dave Telgheder
Joe Vitko
Anthony Young

CATCHERS (4)
Brook Fordyce
Todd Hundley
Charlie O'Brien
Mackey Sasser

INFIELDERS (11)
Kevin Baez
Tim Bogar
Kevin Elster
Tony Fernandez
Butch Huskey
Jeff Kent
Aaron Ledesma
Jeff McKnight
Eddie Murray
Tito Navarro
Bill Pecota

OUTFIELDERS (8)
Bobby Bonilla
Jeromy Burnitz
Vince Coleman
Dave Gallagher
Howard Johnson
Darren Reed
Ryan Thompson
Chico Walker

Games played by position

Player	G	C	1B	2B	3B	SS	OF
BAEZ,K	6	0	0	0	0	5	0
BASS,K	135	0	0	0	0	0	111
BONILLA,B	128	0	6	0	0	0	121
BOSTON,D	130	0	0	0	0	0	95
COLEMAN,V	71	0	0	0	0	0	61
DONNELS,C	45	0	0	12	29	0	0
DOZIER,D	25	0	0	0	0	0	17
ELSTER,K	6	0	0	0	0	5	0
GALLAGHER,D	98	0	0	0	0	0	76
HOWELL,P	31	0	0	0	0	0	28
HUNDLEY,T	123	121	0	0	0	0	0
JOHNSON,H	100	0	0	0	0	0	98
KENT,J	37	0	0	34	1	1	0
MAGADAN,D	99	0	2	0	93	0	0
MCCRAY,R	18	0	0	0	0	0	13
MCKNIGHT,J	31	0	9	14	3	3	1
MURRAY,E	156	0	154	0	0	0	0
NOBOA,J	46	0	0	16	3	2	0
O'BRIEN,C	68	64	0	0	0	0	0
PECOTA,B	117	0	1	38	48	39	0
RANDOLPH,W	90	0	0	79	0	0	0
SASSER,M	92	27	12	0	0	0	9
SCHOFIELD,D	142	0	0	0	0	141	0
SPRINGER,S	4	0	0	1	1	0	0
THOMPSON,R	30	0	0	0	0	0	29
WALKER,C	126	0	0	18	38	0	21

Sick call: 1992 DL report

Player	Days on the DL
Baez, Kevin	17
Bonilla, Bobby	16
Coleman, Vince**	77
Elster, Kevin	175
Franco, John*	73
Gallagher, Dave	44
Gibson, Paul	33
Gooden, Dwight	21
Johnson, Howard	64
Magadan, Dave	57
Pecota, Bill	15
Randolph, Willie	50
Rosenberg, Steve	182
Saberhagen, Bret*	99

** On Disabled List twice during 1992 season (not counting transfers from one DL to another).*

*** On Disabled List three times during 1992 season.*

Minor league report

Class AAA — Tidewater finished 56-86, last in the International League West Division. IF Jeff McKnight hit .307 with 4 HR and 43 RBI. OF Jeromy Burnitz had 30 SBs. RHP David Telgheder threw a no-hitter the first week of the season. IF Steve Springer hit .290 with 16 HR and 70 RBI. **Class AA:** Binghamton finished 79-59, 2nd in the Eastern League. The team beat Canton-Akron in five games for the league championship. OF Rob Katzaroff hit .282. 3B Tim Howard had 77 RBI. RHP Bobby Jones was the league's Pitcher of the Year, winning the ERA title at 12-4 with a 1.88. LHP Todd Douma was 8-8 with a 2.82 ERA. **Class A:** Port St. Lucie finished 74-62, 2nd in the 1st half of the Florida State League East Division and 1st in the 2nd half. The team lost to Osceola in the 1st round of the playoffs. 2B Fernando Vina hit .295 with 36 SB. 3B Butch Huskey had 18 HR and 75 RBI. RHP Jose Martinez was 6-5 with a 2.05 ERA. He walked just 11 while picking up 114 K in 123 IP. RHP Mike Freitas had 24 saves. Columbia finished 79-59, 2nd in both halves of the South Atlantic League Northern Division. 2B Quilvio Veras led the league in batting at .319 and in SB with 66. OF Ricky Otero hit .300 with 8 HR and 60 RBI. OF Randy Curtis hit .295 with 33 SB. 1B Omar Garcia had 70 RBI and 35 SBs. Pittsfield finished 37-37, 2nd in the New York-Penn League McNamara Division. IF Edgar Alfonzo won the league batting title at .356 with 44 RBI. RHP Jim Popoff had a 19-strikeout game. Kingsport finished 27-35, 4th in the Appalachian League South Division. OF Don White hit .303 with 4 HR and 27 RBI. OF Eric Harris had 11 HR and 45 RBI. RHP Chris Berg had 10 saves. Mets finished at 29-30, 3rd in the Gulf Coast League Eastern Division. OF Randy Warner had 38 RBI. LHP Rafael Roque had 8 saves.

Tops in the organization

BATTING LEADERS	Club	Avg.	G	AB	R	H	HR	RBI
Quilvio Veras	Clb	.319	117	414	97	132	2	40
Jeff McKnight	Tdw	.307	102	352	43	108	4	43
Ricky Otero	Slu	.306	136	504	77	154	8	79
Randy Curtis	Clb	.295	102	353	53	104	1	56
Steve Springer	Tdw	.290	117	427	57	124	16	70

HOME RUNS		
Butch Huskey	Slu	18
Alan Zinter	Bng	16
Steve Springer	Tdw	16
Mitch Lyden	Tdw	14
Chris Butterfield	Bng	14

RBI		
Ricky Otero	Slu	79
Tim Howard	Bng	77
Butch Huskey	Slu	75
Omar Garcia	Clb	70
Steve Springer	Tdw	70

STOLEN BASES		
Quilvio Veras	Clb	66
Ricky Otero	Slu	48
Fernando Vina	Slu	36
Omar Garcia	Clb	35
Randy Curtis	Clb	33

WINS		
Brad Schorr	Clb	12
Joe Vitko	Bng	12
Bobby Jones	Bng	12
Several players tied		11

SAVES		
Mike Freitas	Slu	24
Julian Vasquez	Tdw	23
Steve Thomas	Clb	12
Greg Langbehn	Bng	9
Mark Dewey	Tdw	9

STRIKEOUTS		
Jose Martinez	Bng	153
Bobby Jones	Bng	144
Tom Wegmann	Bng	133
Ottis Smith	Slu	133
John Johnstone	Bng	121

PITCHING LEADERS	Club	W-L	ERA	IP	H	BB	SO
Bobby Jones	Bng	12-4	1.88	158	118	43	144
Jose Martinez	Bng	11-7	1.94	181	154	24	153
Jason Jacome	Slu	10-8	2.26	167	138	45	115
Juan Castillo	Slu	11-8	2.58	154	135	27	80
Ottis Smith	Slu	10-11	3.08	161	138	58	133

New York (1962-1992)

Runs: Most, career, all-time

662 DARRYL STRAWBERRY, 1983-1990
595 HOWARD JOHNSON, 1985-1992
592 Mookie Wilson, 1980-1989
563 Cleon Jones, 1963-1975
536 Ed Kranepool, 1962-1979

Hits: Most, career, all-time

1418 Ed Kranepool, 1962-1979
1188 Cleon Jones, 1963-1975
1112 Mookie Wilson, 1980-1989
1029 Bud Harrelson, 1965-1977
1025 DARRYL STRAWBERRY, 1983-1990

2B: Most, career, all-time

225 Ed Kranepool, 1962-1979
206 HOWARD JOHNSON, 1985-1992
187 DARRYL STRAWBERRY, 1983-1990
182 Cleon Jones, 1963-1975
170 Mookie Wilson, 1980-1989

3B: Most, career, all-time

62 Mookie Wilson, 1980-1989
45 Bud Harrelson, 1965-1977
33 Cleon Jones, 1963-1975
31 Steve Henderson, 1977-1980
30 DARRYL STRAWBERRY, 1983-1990

HR: Most, career, all-time

252 DARRYL STRAWBERRY, 1983-1990
185 HOWARD JOHNSON, 1985-1992
154 Dave Kingman, 1975-1983
118 Ed Kranepool, 1962-1979
118 KEVIN McREYNOLDS, 1987-1991

RBI: Most, career, all-time

733 DARRYL STRAWBERRY, 1983-1990
614 Ed Kranepool, 1962-1979
603 HOWARD JOHNSON, 1985-1992
521 Cleon Jones, 1963-1975
468 Keith Hernandez, 1983-1989

SB: Most, career, all-time

281 Mookie Wilson, 1980-1989
196 HOWARD JOHNSON, 1985-1992
191 DARRYL STRAWBERRY, 1983-1990
152 Lee Mazzilli, 1976-1989
116 LENNY DYKSTRA, 1985-1989

BB: Most, career, all-time

580 DARRYL STRAWBERRY, 1983-1990
573 Bud Harrelson, 1965-1977
513 HOWARD JOHNSON, 1985-1992
482 Wayne Garrett, 1969-1976
471 Keith Hernandez, 1983-1989

BA: Highest, career, all-time

.297 Keith Hernandez, 1983-1989
.292 DAVE MAGADAN, 1986-1992
.283 WALLY BACKMAN, 1980-1988
.281 Cleon Jones, 1963-1975
.278 LENNY DYKSTRA, 1985-1989

Slug avg: Highest, career, all-time

.520 DARRYL STRAWBERRY, 1983-1990
.465 HOWARD JOHNSON, 1985-1992
.463 KEVIN McREYNOLDS, 1987-1991
.453 Dave Kingman, 1975-1983
.429 Keith Hernandez, 1983-1989

Games started: Most, career, all-time

395 Tom Seaver, 1967-1983
346 Jerry Koosman, 1967-1978
267 DWIGHT GOODEN, 1984-1992
241 RON DARLING, 1983-1991
232 SID FERNANDEZ, 1984-1992

Saves: Most, career, all-time

107 JESSE OROSCO, 1979-1987
86 Tug McGraw, 1965-1974
84 ROGER McDOWELL, 1985-1989
78 JOHN FRANCO, 1990-1992
69 Neil Allen, 1979-1983

Shutouts: Most, career, all-time

44 Tom Seaver, 1967-1983
26 Jerry Koosman, 1967-1978
26 Jon Matlack, 1971-1977
21 DWIGHT GOODEN, 1984-1992
15 DAVID CONE, 1987-1992

Wins: Most, career, all-time

198 Tom Seaver, 1967-1983
142 DWIGHT GOODEN, 1984-1992
140 Jerry Koosman, 1967-1978
99 RON DARLING, 1983-1991
93 SID FERNANDEZ, 1984-1992

K: Most, career, all-time

2541 Tom Seaver, 1967-1983
1799 Jerry Koosman, 1967-1978
1686 DWIGHT GOODEN, 1984-1992
1368 SID FERNANDEZ, 1984-1992
1159 DAVID CONE, 1987-1992

Win pct: Highest, career, all-time

.683 DWIGHT GOODEN, 1984-1992
.625 DAVID CONE, 1987-1992
.615 Tom Seaver, 1967-1983
.586 RON DARLING, 1983-1991
.564 SID FERNANDEZ, 1984-1992

ERA: Lowest, career, all-time

2.57 Tom Seaver, 1967-1983
2.99 DWIGHT GOODEN, 1984-1992
3.03 Jon Matlack, 1971-1977
3.08 DAVID CONE, 1987-1992
3.09 Jerry Koosman, 1967-1978

Runs: Most, season

108 HOWARD JOHNSON, 1991
108 DARRYL STRAWBERRY, 1987
107 Tommie Agee, 1970
104 HOWARD JOHNSON, 1989
101 DARRYL STRAWBERRY, 1988

Hits: Most, season

191 Felix Millan, 1975
185 Felix Millan, 1973
183 Keith Hernandez, 1985
182 Tommie Agee, 1970
181 Lee Mazzilli, 1979

2B: Most, season

41 HOWARD JOHNSON, 1989
40 GREGG JEFFERIES, 1990
37 LENNY DYKSTRA, 1987
37 HOWARD JOHNSON, 1990
37 Felix Millan, 1975
37 EDDIE MURRAY, 1992
37 Joel Youngblood, 1979

3B: Most, season

10 Mookie Wilson, 1984
9 Steve Henderson, 1978
9 Charlie Neal, 1962
9 Frank Taveras, 1979
9 Mookie Wilson, 1982

HR: Most, season

39	DARRYL STRAWBERRY, 1987
39	DARRYL STRAWBERRY, 1988
38	HOWARD JOHNSON, 1991
37	Dave Kingman, 1976
37	Dave Kingman, 1982
37	DARRYL STRAWBERRY, 1990

RBI: Most, season

117	HOWARD JOHNSON, 1991
108	DARRYL STRAWBERRY, 1990
105	GARY CARTER, 1986
105	Rusty Staub, 1975
104	DARRYL STRAWBERRY, 1987

SB: Most, season

58	Mookie Wilson, 1982
54	Mookie Wilson, 1983
46	Mookie Wilson, 1984
42	Frank Taveras, 1979
41	HOWARD JOHNSON, 1989
41	Lee Mazzilli, 1980

BB: Most, season

97	Keith Hernandez, 1984
97	DARRYL STRAWBERRY, 1987
95	Bud Harrelson, 1970
94	Keith Hernandez, 1986
93	Lee Mazzilli, 1979

BA: Highest, season

.340	Cleon Jones, 1969
.328	DAVE MAGADAN, 1990
.319	Cleon Jones, 1971
.311	Keith Hernandez, 1984
.310	Keith Hernandez, 1986

Slug avg: Highest, season

.583	DARRYL STRAWBERRY, 1987
.559	HOWARD JOHNSON, 1989
.545	DARRYL STRAWBERRY, 1988
.535	HOWARD JOHNSON, 1991
.518	DARRYL STRAWBERRY, 1990

Games started: Most, season

36	Jack Fisher, 1965
36	Tom Seaver, 1970
36	Tom Seaver, 1973
36	Tom Seaver, 1975
35	RON DARLING, 1985
35	Gary Gentry, 1969
35	DWIGHT GOODEN, 1985
35	Jerry Koosman, 1973
35	Jerry Koosman, 1974
35	Jon Matlack, 1976
35	Tom Seaver, 1968
35	Tom Seaver, 1969
35	Tom Seaver, 1971
35	Tom Seaver, 1972
35	Craig Swan, 1979
35	FRANK VIOLA, 1990
35	FRANK VIOLA, 1991

Saves: Most, season

33	JOHN FRANCO, 1990
31	JESSE OROSCO, 1984
30	JOHN FRANCO, 1991
27	Tug McGraw, 1972
26	RANDY MYERS, 1988

Shutouts: Most, season

8	DWIGHT GOODEN, 1985
7	Jerry Koosman, 1968
7	Jon Matlack, 1974
6	Jerry Koosman, 1969
6	Jon Matlack, 1976

Wins: Most, season

25	Tom Seaver, 1969
24	DWIGHT GOODEN, 1985
22	Tom Seaver, 1975
21	Jerry Koosman, 1976
21	Tom Seaver, 1972

K: Most, season

289	Tom Seaver, 1971
283	Tom Seaver, 1970
276	DWIGHT GOODEN, 1984
268	DWIGHT GOODEN, 1985
251	Tom Seaver, 1973

Win pct: Highest, season

.870	DAVID CONE, 1988
.857	DWIGHT GOODEN, 1985
.783	BOB OJEDA, 1986
.781	Tom Seaver, 1969
.739	DWIGHT GOODEN, 1986

ERA: Lowest, season

1.53	DWIGHT GOODEN, 1985
1.76	Tom Seaver, 1971
2.08	Tom Seaver, 1973
2.08	Jerry Koosman, 1968
2.20	Tom Seaver, 1968

Most pinch-hit homers, season

4	Danny Heep, 1983
4	Mark Carreon, 1989

Most pinch-hit, homers, career

8	Mark Carreon, 1987-1991

Most consecutive games, batting safely

24	Hubie Brooks, 1984
23	Cleon Jones, 1970
23	Mike Vail, 1975

Most consecutive scoreless innings

31	Jerry Koosman, 1973

No hit games

None

ACTIVE PLAYERS in caps.

Philadelphia Phillies

by Eileen Blass, *USA TODAY*

John Kruk led the team with a .323 average (third in the NL) and .423 on-base percentage (second in the NL).

1992 Phillies: Back to the basement

Curt Schilling came into the dugout after giving up four runs to the Cardinals in his first three innings and, according to manager Jim Fregosi, challenged his team: "Let's score some runs, because they're not getting any more." The Cardinals didn't score again. But did the Phils win?

"No," said Fregosi. "This isn't Disneyland. This is the real world."

The real world was a harsh place for the Phillies in 1992. Their pitching staff owned a 4.13 ERA—no other NL team was over 4.00—and they finished last in the division for the third time in five years.

Like most last-place teams, injuries pervaded the Phillies. At the start of the season, the outfield—Wes Chamberlain, Lenny Dykstra, and Dale Murphy—brimmed with potential. By season's end the trio had played about a season between them. Only Murphy saw the end of the season in Philly, and he was activated Sept. 30.

Darren Daulton, 30, did prove to be a reliable foundation for the team; he turned in the best offensive performance of all catchers in the league (.270, 27 HR, 109 RBI). No other NL catcher contributed more than 57 RBI or 10 homers. His 32 doubles also led all NL catchers, and his .534 slugging percentage was fourth in the NL. He threw out 35.8 percent of prospective basestealers. His season was probably the finest at the position since Gary Carter in 1985.

The Phillies found another surprise in Dave Hollins. After an up-and-down two years, he established himself at third base. He tied Daulton with 27 home runs, added 93 RBI and scored 102 runs. If not for Gary Sheffield's phenomenal season, Hollins would have had the best offensive numbers of all NL third basemen. He did lead his position with 76 walks.

The old reliables on the Phillies roster also produced—when they played. Lenny Dykstra batted .301 (39 RBI) in 85 games, but a broken bone in his hand ended his season. John Kruk roared through the NL with a .323 average, leading the league most of the season. But he was sidelined with tendinitis in the last two weeks and Sheffield won the NL batting title.

Dale Murphy proved to be a non-factor, with just 62 at-bats. Going into '92, he needed four homers to reach 400. He still needs two more.

The Phillies' middle infield was a jumble. Second baseman Mickey Morandini, who completed the NL's first unassisted triple play in 65 years, was in and out as a starter, and Juan Bell settled in at shortstop, the sixth player to try the position. The team used 15 different double-play combinations.

Schilling proved to be the ace of the pitching staff (14-11, 2.35 ERA). Terry Mulholland went 13-11 (3.81 ERA), Ben Rivera was 7-4, and Mitch Williams had 28 saves. But Kyle Abbott was 1-14 (5.13 ERA). There was one happy ending, though: After four years without a win in the major leagues, Greg Mathews won two in the last week of the season.

—by Tom Sakell

1993 Phils: Preview

Things have to get better. General manager Lee Thomas thinks the liftoff has begun. They solidified their starting pitching by obtaining veteran left-hander Danny Jackson from the Marlins for minor league pitchers Matt Whisenant and Joel Adamson. Jackson (81-92 career) joins a promising rotation: lefty Terry Mulholland and righties Tommy Greene, Ben Rivera, and Curt Schilling. The Phils' offense is built around Darren Daulton, Dave Hollins, and John Kruk, on the mend from shoulder surgery. Hopefully Lenny Dykstra can stay healthy and play a full season.

—by Bill Koenig

1992 Phillies: Between the lines

▸**April 27:** Mariano Duncan extended his NL-best hitting streak to 14 games.

▸**May 2:** The hard luck award went to pitcher Kyle Abbott, whose record dropped to 0-5, worst in the NL. The Phillies scored less than three runs per nine innings when he pitched. ***Quote of the day:*** Abbott, asked if he was discouraged—"Nah. . .we're being paid too much to let it worry me."

▸**May 3:** Duncan hit his first triple and his first homer of the season.

▸**May 5:** Terry Mulholland went the distance for his first victory of the season. ***Quote of the day:*** Mulholland—"I felt like I could throw it through a brick wall."

▸**May 10:** Mulholland pitched his second consecutive complete game victory. The Phillies' Mother's Day Tribute saluted Wes Chamberlain's mom, Bettie. It wasn't much of a tribute, though—her son didn't even play, and after the game he was shipped to the minors.

▸**May 11:** John Kruk hit his first two home runs of the year.

▸**May 15:** Mulholland pitched the Phillies' first shutout of the season. It was just the third complete game for the Phils, all three by Mulholland.

▸**May 20:** ***Quote of the day***: Curt Schilling, traded from Houston in the offseason, on being motivated by a newspaper clip that said he reported to camp overweight and refused to play winter ball—"I had the article from the day it was written but I didn't read it (then) . . . I wanted to use it for incentive."

▸**May 26:** Don Robinson made his first appearance since April 21, allowing just one hit in six shutout innings. Manager Jim Fregosi saw the rotund veteran tiring and relieved him after the sixth. ***Quote of the day:*** Robinson—"With me, it's 85 pitches or two hours, whichever comes first."

▸**May 30:** John Kruk's average fell below .375 for the first time in 1992.

▸**June 19:** Mickey Morandini had stolen nine consecutive bases without getting caught, and had made just one error in his last 58 games.

▸**June 23:** Curt Schilling pitched a six-hit shutout. ***Quote of the day:*** John Kruk (strained groin) sat out his fifth straight game. He felt able to play but manager Jim Fregosi disagreed—"He's been a pain in the butt, but I just show him my pen. It's the only one in town. If I don't write his name in the lineup, he can't play."

▸**June 24:** Kruk played for the first time in six games, and stole his first base in four attempts.

▸**June 27** ***Quote of the day:*** Fregosi, on the change he's seen in Wes Chamberlain, who went 11 for 34 since returning from the minors June 18—"Sometimes when you send a young kid (to the minors), he comes back with a different attitude. I heard Wes say himself, 'I don't want to give them a reason to ever send me out again.' "

▸**June 30:** Fregosi gave the ball to 22-year-old Mike Williams, the 13th starter and eighth rookie pitcher to take the mound for the Phillies this season. The eight rookies' combined record was 3-20.

▸**July 24:** Daulton continued to lap the rest of the NL catching crop, with his 16th home run and 67th RBI.

▸**July 28:** Daulton hit a first-inning grand slam. Meanwhile, Pirate Andy Van Slyke had taken over as the major leagues' leading hitter—for awhile—singling in his first at-bat to raise his average to .348 and supplant John Kruk (.347). But Kruk was back in first after Van Slyke made outs in his next three appearances to fall to .345. Later that night, though, Kruk fell back into second place (.343) by going 0-for-4.

▸**August 9** ***Quote of the day:*** Kruk, after finding out that he would be playing left field despite his attempts to get rid of his outfielder's glove—"It's like a boomerang. I keep throwing it away and it keeps coming back . . . It must be made in Australia."

▸**August 11:** Juan Bell became the sixth shortstop used by the Phillies in 1992.

▸**August 15:** Kyle Abbott, no longer a starter, responded to his first bullpen assignment with 2 1/3 strong innings. ***Quote of the day:*** Abbott—"It really does feel like a new lease on life coming out of the bullpen. There's not as much pressure. I know I came in with the bases loaded tonight, but it still didn't feel like as much pressure."

▸**August 19:** Triple crown watch: Daulton regained the NL RBI lead with 85, one more than San Diego's Gary Sheffield. The home run was Daulton's 22nd, the most by an NL catcher since Gary Carter hit 24 as a Met in 1986. ***Quote of the day:*** Daulton—"The first thing I do in the morning is wake up and go down and get the newspaper. Larry Bowa also lets me know everything Sheffield does. Whether it's true or not, he lets me know about Sheffield."

▸**August 28:** Mulholland needed just 98 pitches to record his league-best ninth complete game.

▸**September 2 *Milestone:*** Mulholland recorded his 14th pickoff, the most by any pitcher in the three years the record has been kept.

▸**September 12 *Quote of the day:*** Fregosi, trying to explain the enigmatic Jose DeLeon in his Phillies' debut—"I thought DeLeon threw the ball well. He got a little tired in the seventh, and after that, there must have been a full moon someplace."

▸**September 14 *Quote of the day:*** Daulton, on getting his 100th RBI—"We've had champagne on ice for a couple of days. It feels good to finally get to 100. Now that I've made it, I want to win the RBI title."

▸**October 4:** The Phillies finished in the cellar (70-92, 26 games out), but Darren Daulton sat out the last game and took the NL RBI title (109). He was also fourth in the league in homers (27) and slugging (.524), and sixth in walks (88). John Kruk ended up third in batting (.323), second in on-base percentage (.423), and fifth in walks (92). David Hollins was second in runs (104), tied with Daulton in homers (27), and seventh in RBI (93). On the mound, Terry Mulholland led the NL in complete games (12). Curt Schilling was third in complete games (10) and fourth in ERA (2.35). Mitch Williams was fifth in saves (29).

—by Jeanie Chung, John Hunt, Deron Snyder, and Lisa Winston.

Team directory

▸**Owner:** Bill Giles

▸**General Manager:** Lee Thomas

▸**Ballpark:**
Veterans Stadium
Broad Street & Pattison Avenue,
Philadelphia, Pa.
215-463-1000
Capacity 62,382
Parking for 10,000 cars; $4
Public transportation available
Wheelchair section and ramps, TDD ticket information for hearing impaired (215-463-2998)

▸**Team publications:**
Media Guide, Yearbook, Scorebook

▸**TV, radio broadcast stations:**
WOGL 1210 AM, WPHL Channel 17

▸**Spring Training:**
Jack Russell Memorial Stadium
Clearwater, Fla.
Capacity 7,350
813-442-8496

PHILADELPHIA PHILLIES 1992 final stats

Batting	AVG	SLG	OB	G	AB	R	H	TB	2B	3B	HR	RBI	BB	SO	SB	CS	E
Kruk	.323	.458	.423	144	507	86	164	232	30	4	10	70	92	88	3	5	8
Jordan	.304	.417	.313	94	276	33	84	115	19	0	4	34	5	44	3	0	2
Dykstra	.301	.406	.375	85	345	53	104	140	18	0	6	39	40	32	30	5	3
Pratt	.283	.435	.340	16	46	6	13	20	1	0	2	10	4	12	0	0	2
Backman	.271	.292	.352	42	48	6	13	14	1	0	0	6	6	9	1	0	1
Daulton	.270	.524	.385	145	485	80	131	254	32	5	27	109	88	103	11	2	11
Hollins	.270	.469	.369	156	586	104	158	275	28	4	27	93	76	110	9	6	18
Duncan	.267	.389	.292	142	574	71	153	223	40	3	8	50	17	108	23	3	16
Morandini	.265	.344	.305	127	422	47	112	145	8	8	3	30	25	64	8	3	6
Chamberlain	.258	.422	.285	76	275	26	71	116	18	0	9	41	10	55	4	0	4
Lindeman	.256	.359	.310	29	39	6	10	14	1	0	1	6	3	11	0	0	0
Javier	.249	.314	.327	130	334	42	83	105	17	1	1	29	37	54	18	3	3
Lake	.245	.340	.255	20	53	3	13	18	2	0	1	2	1	8	0	0	2
Peguero	.222	.222	.417	14	9	3	2	2	0	0	0	0	3	3	0	0	0
Amaro	.219	.348	.303	126	374	43	82	130	15	6	7	34	37	54	11	5	2
Batiste	.206	.257	.224	44	136	9	28	35	4	0	1	10	4	18	0	0	13
Millette	.205	.205	.271	33	78	5	16	16	0	0	0	2	5	10	1	0	3
Bell	.204	.259	.292	46	147	12	30	38	3	1	1	8	18	29	5	0	6
Grotewold	.200	.369	.307	72	65	7	13	24	2	0	3	5	9	16	0	0	0
Marsh	.200	.304	.215	42	125	7	25	38	3	2	2	16	2	23	0	1	2
Castillo	.197	.342	.238	28	76	12	15	26	3	1	2	7	4	15	1	0	2
Sveum	.178	.252	.261	54	135	13	24	34	4	0	2	16	16	39	0	0	8
Murphy	.161	.274	.175	18	62	5	10	17	1	0	2	7	1	13	0	0	1
Scarsone	.154	.154	.214	7	13	1	2	2	0	0	0	0	1	6	0	0	0

Pitching	W-L	ERA	G	GS	CG	GF	Sho	SV	IP	H	R	ER	HR	BB	SO
Schilling	14-11	2.35	42	26	10	10	4	2	226.1	165	67	59	11	59	147
Ritchie	2-1	3.00	40	0	0	13	0	1	39	44	17	13	3	17	19
Rivera	7-4	3.07	28	14	4	7	1	0	117.1	99	40	40	9	45	77
Ayrault	2-2	3.12	30	0	0	7	0	0	43.1	32	16	15	0	17	27
Shepherd	1-1	3.27	12	0	0	6	0	2	22	19	10	8	0	6	10
Hartley	7-6	3.44	46	0	0	15	0	0	55	54	23	21	5	23	53
Mit.Williams	5-8	3.78	66	0	0	56	0	29	81	69	39	34	4	64	74
Mulholland	13-11	3.81	32	32	12	0	2	0	229	227	101	97	14	46	125
Brink	0-4	4.14	8	7	0	0	0	0	41.1	53	27	19	2	13	16
DeLeon	2-8	4.37	32	18	0	3	0	0	117.1	111	63	57	7	48	79
Brantley	2-6	4.60	28	9	0	6	0	0	76.1	71	45	39	6	58	32
Abbott	1-14	5.13	31	19	0	0	0	0	133.1	147	80	76	20	45	88
Mathews	2-3	5.16	14	7	0	1	0	0	52.1	54	31	30	7	24	27
Greene	3-3	5.32	13	12	0	0	0	0	64.1	75	39	38	5	34	39
Mik.Williams	1-1	5.34	5	5	1	0	0	0	28.2	29	20	17	3	7	5
Searcy	0-0	6.10	10	0	0	3	0	0	10.1	13	9	7	0	8	5
Robinson	1-4	6.18	8	8	0	0	0	0	43.2	49	32	30	6	4	17
Ashby	1-3	7.54	10	8	0	0	0	0	37	42	31	31	6	21	24
Combs	1-1	7.71	4	4	0	0	0	0	18.2	20	16	16	0	12	11
Baller	0-0	8.18	8	0	0	4	0	0	11	10	10	10	5	10	9
Chapin	0-0	9.00	1	0	0	0	0	0	2	2	2	2	1	0	1
Weston	0-1	12.27	1	1	0	0	0	0	3.2	7	5	5	1	1	0

1993 preliminary roster

PITCHERS (19)
Kyle Abbott
Bob Ayrault
Toby Borland
Cliff Brantley
Brad Brink
Pat Combs
Jose DeJesus
Jose DeLeon
Mike Farmer
Paul Fletcher
Tommy Greene
Terry Mulholland
Steve Parris
Wally Ritchie
Ben Rivera
Curt Schilling
David West
Mike Williams
Mitch Williams

CATCHERS (3)
Darren Daulton
Doug Lindsey
Todd Pratt

INFIELDERS (8)
Kim Batiste
Juan Bell
Mariano Duncan
Dave Hollins
Ricky Jordan
John Kruk
Ron Lockett
Mickey Morandini

OUTFIELDERS (9)
Ruben Amaro
Wes Chamberlain
Lenny Dykstra
Pete Incaviglia
Jeff Jackson
Tony Longmire
Tom Nuneviller
Milt Thompson
Cary Williams

Games played by position

Player	G	C	1B	2B	3B	SS	OF
AMARO,R	126	0	0	0	0	0	113
BACKMAN,W	42	0	0	10	2	0	0
BATISTE,K	44	0	0	0	0	41	0
BELL,JU	46	0	0	0	0	46	0
CASTILLO,B	28	0	0	0	0	0	24
CHAMBERLAIN,W	76	0	0	0	0	0	73
DAULTON,D	145	141	0	0	0	0	0
DUNCAN,M	142	0	0	52	4	42	65
DYKSTRA,L	85	0	0	0	0	0	85
GROTEWOLD,J	72	2	1	0	0	0	2
HOLLINS,D	156	0	1	0	156	0	0
JAVIER,S	130	0	0	0	0	0	101
JORDAN,R	94	0	54	0	0	0	11
KRUK,J	144	0	121	0	0	0	35
LAKE,S	20	17	0	0	0	0	0
LINDEMAN,J	29	0	0	0	0	0	9
MARSH,T	42	0	0	0	0	0	35
MILLETTE,J	33	0	0	1	3	26	0
MORANDINI,M	127	0	0	124	0	3	0
MURPHY,D	18	0	0	0	0	0	16
PEGUERO,J	14	0	0	0	0	0	14
PRATT,T	16	11	0	0	0	0	0
SCARSONE,S	7	0	0	3	0	0	0
SVEUM,D	54	0	4	0	5	34	0

Sick call: 1992 DL report

Player	Days on the DL
Ashby, Andy	106
Backman, Wally	61
Chamberlain, Wes	47
DeJesus, Jose	182
Dykstra, Lenny**	83
Greene, Tommy	111
Hartley, Mike	37
Howell, Ken	182
Jordan, Ricky	35
Lake, Steve	45
Lindeman, Jim*	95
Longmire, Tony	182
Marsh, Tom	31
Murphy, Dale*	156
Rivera, Ben	21
Robinson, Don	15
Sveum, Dale	15

** On Disabled List twice during 1992 season (not counting transfers from one DL to another).*

*** On Disabled List three times during 1992 season.*

Minor league report

Class AAA — Scranton/Wilkes-Barre finished 84-58, 1st in the International League East Division. The team lost to Columbus in five games for the league championship. 3B Rick Schu hit .310 with 10 HR and 49 RBI. RHP Mickey Weston was 10-6 with a 3.16 ERA. RHP Jay Baller had 22 saves. RHP Mike Williams was 10-1. **Class AA:** Reading finished 61-77, 6th in the Eastern League. LHP Paul Fletcher was 9-4 with a 2.83 ERA and 103 K in 127 IP. C/OF Steve Bieser hit .281. OF Mickey Hyde hit .277. SS Kevin Stocker had 32 SBs. **Class A:** Clearwater finished 75-59, 2nd in both halves of the Florida State League West Division. The team lost to Lakeland in the 2nd round of the playoffs. 1B Troy Rusk had 13 HR and 70 RBI. RHP Mark Randall had 16 saves. RHP Brad Hassinger was 10-2 with a 2.05 ERA. Spartanburg finished 70-68, last in the 1st half of the Sally League Northern Division and 1st in the 2nd half. The team lost to Charleston (W.Va.) in the 1st round of the playoffs. RHP Ricky Bottalico was 5-10 with a 2.41 ERA. RHP Ron Blazier was 14-7 with a 2.65 and shared the league lead in wins. RHP Dom Desantis was 6-9 with a 2.71 ERA. RHP Matt Whisenant had 151 K. Batavia finished 36-34, 2nd in the New York-Penn League Pinckney Division. OF Shawn Wills had 32 SB Martinsville finished 22-43, last in the Appalachian League North Division. 2B David Fisher hit .303 with 3 HR and 42 RBI. OF William Carmona hit 10 HR.

Tops in the organization

BATTING LEADERS	Club	Avg.	G	AB	R	H	HR	RBI
Rick Schu	Swb	.310	111	400	56	124	10	49
Steve Bieser	Rea	.281	106	342	53	96	0	18
Mickey Hyde	Rea	.277	119	375	44	104	2	48
Mike Lieberthal	Swb	.275	102	353	34	97	2	41
Jeff Bigler	Spt	.269	125	438	50	118	5	53

HOME RUNS		
Pat Brady	Swb	17
Todd Pratt	Swb	13
Troy Rusk	Clw	13
Braulio Castillo	Swb	13
Several players tied		12

RBI		
Pat Brady	Swb	84
Troy Rusk	Clw	70
Gene Schall	Clw	60
Sean Ryan	Rea	57
Sam Taylor	Rea	55

STOLEN BASES		
Kevin Stocker	Rea	32
Jerome Edwards	Spt	29
Stan Evans	Spt	22
Bruce Dostal	Swb	19
Corey Thomas	Clw	16

WINS		
Ron Blazier	Spt	14
Paul Fletcher	Swb	12
Matt Whisenant	Spt	11
Several players tied		10

SAVES		
Jeff Patterson	Swb	28
Jay Baller	Swb	22
Mark Randall	Clw	16
Ricky Bottalico	Spt	13
Matt Stevens	Rea	12

STRIKEOUTS		
Matt Whisenant	Spt	151
Ron Blazier	Spt	149
Paul Fletcher	Swb	129
Craig Holman	Spt	129
Ricky Bottalico	Spt	118

PITCHING LEADERS	Club	W-L	ERA	IP	H	BB	SO
Brad Hassinger	Clw	10-2	2.05	110	101	21	63
Ricky Bottalico	Spt	5-10	2.41	120	94	56	118
Ron Blazier	Spt	14-7	2.65	160	141	32	149
Dom Desantis	Spt	6-9	2.71	133	123	29	100
Paul Fletcher	Swb	12-4	2.83	150	120	49	129

Philadelphia (1883-1992)

Runs: Most, career, all-time

1506	Mike Schmidt, 1972-1989
1367	Ed Delahanty, 1888-1901
1114	Richie Ashburn, 1948-1959
963	Chuck Klein, 1928-1944
924	Sam Thompson, 1889-1898

Hits: Most, career, all-time

2234	Mike Schmidt, 1972-1989
2217	Richie Ashburn, 1948-1959
2213	Ed Delahanty, 1888-1901
1812	Del Ennis, 1946-1956
1798	Larry Bowa, 1970-1981

2B: Most, career, all-time

442	Ed Delahanty, 1888-1901
408	Mike Schmidt, 1972-1989
337	Sherry Magee, 1904-1914
336	Chuck Klein, 1928-1944
310	Del Ennis, 1946-1956

3B: Most, career, all-time

157	Ed Delahanty, 1888-1901
127	Sherry Magee, 1904-1914
106	Sam Thompson, 1889-1898
97	Richie Ashburn, 1948-1959
84	Johnny Callison, 1960-1969

HR: Most, career, all-time

548	Mike Schmidt, 1972-1989
259	Del Ennis, 1946-1956
243	Chuck Klein, 1928-1944
223	Greg Luzinski, 1970-1980
217	Cy Williams, 1918-1930

RBI: Most, career, all-time

1595	Mike Schmidt, 1972-1989
1286	Ed Delahanty, 1888-1901
1124	Del Ennis, 1946-1956
983	Chuck Klein, 1928-1944
957	Sam Thompson, 1889-1898

SB: Most, career, all-time

508	Billy Hamilton, 1890-1895
411	Ed Delahanty, 1888-1901
387	Sherry Magee, 1904-1914
289	Jim Fogarty, 1884-1889
288	Larry Bowa, 1970-1981

BB: Most, career, all-time

1507	Mike Schmidt, 1972-1989
946	Richie Ashburn, 1948-1959
946	Roy Thomas, 1899-1911
693	Willie Jones, 1947-1959
643	Ed Delahanty, 1888-1901

BA: Highest, career, all-time

.361	Billy Hamilton, 1890-1895
.348	Ed Delahanty, 1888-1901
.338	Elmer Flick, 1898-1901
.333	Sam Thompson, 1889-1898
.326	Chuck Klein, 1928-1944

Slug avg: Highest, career, all-time

.553	Chuck Klein, 1928-1944
.530	Dick Allen, 1963-1976
.527	Mike Schmidt, 1972-1989
.510	Dolph Camilli, 1934-1937
.508	Ed Delahanty, 1888-1901

Games started: Most, career, all-time

499	Steve Carlton, 1972-1986
472	Robin Roberts, 1948-1961
301	Chris Short, 1959-1972
279	Pete Alexander, 1911-1930
262	Curt Simmons, 1947-1960

Saves: Most, career, all-time

103	Steve Bedrosian, 1986-1989
94	Tug McGraw, 1975-1984
90	Ron Reed, 1976-1983
65	Turk Farrell, 1956-1969
59	Jack Baldschun, 1961-1965
59	MITCH WILLIAMS, 1991-1992

Shutouts: Most, career, all-time

61	Pete Alexander, 1911-1930
39	Steve Carlton, 1972-1986
35	Robin Roberts, 1948-1961
24	Chris Short, 1959-1972
23	Jim Bunning, 1964-1971

Wins: Most, career, all-time

241	Steve Carlton, 1972-1986
234	Robin Roberts, 1948-1961
190	Pete Alexander, 1911-1930
132	Chris Short, 1959-1972
115	Curt Simmons, 1947-1960

K: Most, career, all-time

3031	Steve Carlton, 1972-1986
1871	Robin Roberts, 1948-1961
1585	Chris Short, 1959-1972
1409	Pete Alexander, 1911-1930
1197	Jim Bunning, 1964-1971

Win pct: Highest, career, all-time

.676	Pete Alexander, 1911-1930
.642	Tom Seaton, 1912-1913
.607	Charlie Ferguson, 1884-1887
.606	Charlie Buffinton, 1887-1889
.603	Red Donahue, 1898-1901

ERA: Lowest, career, all-time

1.79	George McQuillan, 1907-1916
2.18	Pete Alexander, 1911-1930
2.48	Tully Sparks, 1897-1910
2.61	Frank Corridon, 1904-1909
2.63	Earl Moore, 1908-1913

Runs: Most, season

192	Billy Hamilton, 1894
166	Billy Hamilton, 1895
158	Chuck Klein, 1930
152	Chuck Klein, 1932
152	Lefty O'Doul, 1929

Hits: Most, season

254	Lefty O'Doul, 1929
250	Chuck Klein, 1930
238	Ed Delahanty, 1899
226	Chuck Klein, 1932
223	Chuck Klein, 1933

2B: Most, season

59	Chuck Klein, 1930
55	Ed Delahanty, 1899
50	Chuck Klein, 1932
49	Ed Delahanty, 1895
48	Dick Bartell, 1932

3B: Most, season

23	Nap Lajoie, 1897
21	Ed Delahanty, 1892
21	Sam Thompson, 1895
19	JUAN SAMUEL, 1984
19	George Wood, 1887

HR: Most, season

48	Mike Schmidt, 1980
45	Mike Schmidt, 1979
43	Chuck Klein, 1929
41	Cy Williams, 1923
40	Dick Allen, 1966
40	Chuck Klein, 1930
40	Mike Schmidt, 1983

RBI: Most, season

170	Chuck Klein, 1930
165	Sam Thompson, 1895
146	Ed Delahanty, 1893
145	Chuck Klein, 1929
143	Don Hurst, 1932

SB: Most, season

111	Billy Hamilton, 1891
102	Jim Fogarty, 1887
102	Billy Hamilton, 1890
99	Jim Fogarty, 1889
98	Billy Hamilton, 1894
72	JUAN SAMUEL, 1984 (7)

BB: Most, season

128	Mike Schmidt, 1983
126	Billy Hamilton, 1894
125	Richie Ashburn, 1954
121	VON HAYES, 1987
120	Mike Schmidt, 1979

BA: Highest, season

.410	Ed Delahanty, 1899
.407	Ed Delahanty, 1894
.404	Billy Hamilton, 1894
.404	Ed Delahanty, 1895
.398	Lefty O'Doul, 1929

Slug avg: Highest, season

.687	Chuck Klein, 1930
.657	Chuck Klein, 1929
.654	Sam Thompson, 1895
.646	Chuck Klein, 1932
.644	Mike Schmidt, 1981

Games started: Most, season

61	John Coleman, 1883
55	Kid Gleason, 1890
50	Ed Daily, 1885
49	Gus Weyhing, 1892
47	Charlie Ferguson, 1884
45	Pete Alexander, 1916 (8)

Saves: Most, season

40	Steve Bedrosian, 1987
30	MITCH WILLIAMS, 1991
29	Steve Bedrosian, 1986
29	Al Holland, 1984
29	MITCH WILLIAMS, 1992

Shutouts: Most, season

16	Pete Alexander, 1916
12	Pete Alexander, 1915
9	Pete Alexander, 1913
8	Pete Alexander, 1917
8	Steve Carlton, 1972
8	Ben Sanders, 1888

Wins: Most, season

38	Kid Gleason, 1890
33	Pete Alexander, 1916
32	Gus Weyhing, 1892
31	Pete Alexander, 1915
30	Pete Alexander, 1917
30	Charlie Ferguson, 1886

K: Most, season

310	Steve Carlton, 1972
286	Steve Carlton, 1980
286	Steve Carlton, 1982
275	Steve Carlton, 1983
268	Jim Bunning, 1965

Win pct: Highest, season

.800	Robin Roberts, 1952
.769	Charlie Ferguson, 1886
.760	Larry Christenson, 1977
.760	John Denny, 1983
.756	Pete Alexander, 1915

ERA: Lowest, season

1.22	Pete Alexander, 1915
1.53	George McQuillan, 1908
1.55	Pete Alexander, 1916
1.83	Lew Richie, 1908
1.83	Pete Alexander, 1917

Most pinch-hit homers, season

5	Gene Freese, 1959
4	Rip Repulski, 1958
4	Del Unser, 1979

Most pinch-hit, homers, career

9	Cy Williams, 1918-1930

Most consecutive games, batting safely

36	Billy Hamilton, 1894
31	Ed Delahanty, 1899
26	Chuck Klein, 1930 (2 streaks)

Most consecutive scoreless innings

41	Grover Cleveland Alexander, 1911

No hit games

Joe Borden, Phi vs Chi NA, 4-0; July 28, 1875.
Charlie Ferguson, Phi vs Pro NL, 1-0; August 29, 1885.
Red Donahue, Phi vs Bos NL, 5-0; July 8, 1898.
Chick Fraser, Phi at Chi NL; 10-0; September 18, 1903 (2nd game).
Johnny Lush, Phi at Bro NL, 6-0; May 1, 1906.
Jim Bunning, Phi at NY NL, 6-0; June 21, 1964 (1st game, perfect game).
Rick Wise, Phi at Cin NL, 4-0; June 23, 1971.
Terry Mulholland, Phi vs SF NL, 6-0; August 15, 1990.
Tommy Greene, Phi at Mon NL, 2-0; May 23, 1991.

ACTIVE PLAYERS in caps.

Atlanta Braves

by Robert Deutsch, *USA TODAY*

Terry Pendleton was second in the NL in RBI (105) and was among the best in four other offensive categories.

1992 Braves: Another great year

The Braves came to spring training in 1992 with the goal of winning one more game than they won in 1991—the one that would have given them the world championship.

They overcame predictions that the Reds were the team to beat in the NL West and, after spending one day in last place (May 26), they went on a roll that led them to their second straight division title. Their starting pitchers went 37-6 between May 27 and Aug. 10, and the Braves went from seven games under .500 (seven games out of first) to 24 games above .500—four games ahead of Cincinnati.

Included in that stretch was an NL-best 13-game winning streak, saved on the last day by Otis Nixon, who reached over the wall to rob a game-winning home run from the Pirates' Andy Van Slyke.

The Braves' lead never dropped to less than 3 1/2 games the rest of the season. A late-August trade for a relief pitcher again proved beneficial; the Braves dealt two prospects to Boston for all-time saves leader Jeff Reardon. He was 3-0 with three saves in 14 appearances, and the Braves became the first team to win consecutive NL West titles since the Dodgers in 1977-78. Tom Glavine was the first Braves' pitcher with consecutive 20-win seasons since Warren Spahn (1956-61). He was especially effective in the first half of the year, posting a 13-3 record that earned him the NL starting role in the All-Star Game for the second straight season.

John Smoltz finished the year with a 15-12 record and led the NL with 215 strikeouts. The Braves' staff combined for a league-best 3.14 ERA, and the best record in franchise history: 98-64.

Fans came to Fulton County Stadium in record numbers: 3,077,400, best in the NL and third highest in the majors. There was plenty to cheer about. In addition to Glavine, Smoltz, and Steve Avery, they saw another terrific season from Terry Pendleton. He topped his 1991 MVP numbers by hitting .311 with 21 homers and a career-best 105 RBI. He just missed the 200-hit mark on the season's final day, finishing at 199 to tie Andy Van Slyke for the NL lead. Dave Justice tied Pendleton for the team home run lead, and Ron Gant remained one of the most dangerous hitters in the league. Deion Sanders led the league with 14 triples, the first player ever to do so with less than 100 games played in a complete season.

The Braves followed their regular-season success with a dramatic playoff victory against the Pirates. They were one strike away from losing the final game when they rallied for a 3-2 victory that made Francisco Cabrera, who got the game-winning hit, a name to remember. It was the first time in history that a team had come from behind in the ninth inning to win the deciding game of a postseason series. The momentum didn't carry over into the World Series, however; they again lost to the AL champions, this time the Toronto Blue Jays in six games.

—by Rob Rains

1993 Braves: Preview

The Braves' pitching depth was evident when they lost starter David Nied in the expansion draft, then admitted they weren't sure he could've won a spot on their team in 1993.

Starting pitching figures to be the team's strength again with Cy Young winner Greg Maddux added to Glavine, Avery, Smoltz, and Peter Smith to create baseball's best rotation. The bullpen may finally be developing as well, anchored by Mark Wohlers and Mike Stanton, improving youngsters.

The offensive lineup should also be as good in 1993. The only question is at catcher, but if Greg Olson is slow to come back from last August's knee surgery, Damon Berryhill and rookie Javier Lopez will be capable fill-ins.

—by Rob Rains

1992 Braves: Between the lines

▸**May 1:** Among the favorites to represent the NL in the World Series, the Braves and the Mets combined for 23 hits and 15 runs, with the Mets winning 8-7.

▸**May 6:** The defending NL division champions hooked up for the first time in 1992; Pittsburgh had suffered three consecutive shutouts at home against Atlanta, and was blanked for seven more innings before beating the Braves 4-3 in 16 innings.

▸**May 18** ***Quote of the day:*** Slumping Dave Justice, after being pelted with peanuts at his home stadium—"It was amazing. It is no fun playing at home. Especially for me. The same people who cheered last year are booing us."

▸**May 23:** John Smoltz set a Braves' record and tied the franchise mark with 15 strikeouts. He fanned every player in Montreal's starting lineup.

▸**May 30:** Deion Sanders raised his average to .336 while nearly outhitting the entire Mets' team. (New York had six hits). Sanders also stole three bases, giving him five in two days.

▸**June 1:** Tom Glavine won his 10th career game vs. the Phillies, having lost only one. Meanwhile, reliever Mark Wohlers earned his first save; he had retired all seven batters he faced since his recall May 28.

▸**June 19:** Damon Berryhill drove in the winning run in a 3-2 victory that moved the Braves 3 1/2 games from the NL West lead.

▸**June 23:** Tom Glavine became the major leagues' first 11-game winner, tossing his fourth shutout and lowering his ERA to 2.68.

▸**June 24:** John Smoltz won for the fifth time in six decisions. Otis Nixon hit his first homer since Aug. 14, 1990. In Atlanta's last 24 games—which included 21 wins—starters were 16-1 with a 1.78 ERA.

▸**June 28:** Cincinnati put the finishing touches on Atlanta with a 6-5 victory to sweep the three-game series.

▸**July 8:** When Alejandro Pena entered the game against his former team with the bases loaded and no outs, the Mets' Howard Johnson—defending NL home run and RBI champion—popped out, and Willie Randolph grounded into a game-ending double play, for Pena's first save since April 28. ***Quote of the day:*** Pena—"I was just trying to get the ball over (against Johnson). He popped it up; I say, 'Thanks a lot.' "

▸**July 12:** Jeff Blauser connected for three homers, including the winning three-run shot in the 10th. He was 8-for-49 (.163) in the previous 23 games.

▸**July 22:** John Smoltz extended his scoreless streak to 27 innings.

▸**July 25:** The Braves won their 13th consecutive game to tie the club record set at the start of 1982. The 1-0 victory over Pittsburgh came on just one hit (Dave Justice's second-inning homer).

▸**July 26:** The Pirates won 5-4, ending the Braves' 13-game winning streak.

▸**July 27:** John Smoltz gave up a run, stopping his scoreless streak at 27 1/3 innings, but teammate Kent Mercker took over, pitching two scoreless innings to stretch his own scoreless streak to 25 innings.

▸**August 4:** Terry Pendleton's two-out, two-run homer secured a 7-5 victory over the Reds, extending Atlanta's NL West lead to 1 1/2 games.

▸**August 5:** The Braves beat the Reds again, 5-1, widening their lead in the NL West to 2 1/2 games.

▸**August 14:** The matchup of division leaders was a mismatch from the start. Atlanta jumped on Pirates' starter Zane Smith for four first-inning runs in the 15-0 romp. Smith lasted only 17 pitches, and another Smith, Atlanta's Lonnie, drove in six of the Braves' runs, on five hits. The Braves accumulated an NL season-high 22 hits. Included in Lonnie

Smith's career night was his first grand slam in six years.

▸**August 22** ***Quote of the day:*** Fifth starter Pete Smith, on winning games for the Braves (something he was expected to do years ago)—"Being part of that 'Young Gun' thing, it has been a tough two years. I don't have the speed to blow the ball by anyone anymore. I have developed my offspeed stuff, and learned how to pitch. Maybe it was in the cards for me to struggle before I matured."

▸**August 25:** The Expos shut out the Braves to snap Tom Glavine's club-record winning streak at 13 games.

▸**August 29** ***Milestone:*** Charlie Leibrandt recorded his 1,000th career strikeout. Leibrandt wanted to save the ball, and rolled it toward the Braves' dugout to be tucked away for safekeeping—but he neglected to call time out, and Ricky Jordan advanced to second base on the error.

▸**September 6:** Brian Hunter, who was only 1-for-15 as a pinch-hitter, capped a four-run ninth with a two-run pinch homer as Atlanta beat Philadelphia 6-5.

▸**September 10:** Deion Sanders was a late arrival at the ballpark, due to his earlier practice with the Atlanta Falcons. He still arrived in plenty of time to score the winning run for the Braves after entering the game as a pinch-runner in the ninth.

▸**September 11:** Pete Smith remained perfect with a 7-0 win at Houston, lowering his ERA to 2.12.

▸**September 16:** The Braves won at Cincinnati for the first time in eight tries. Magic number: eight.

▸**September 24:** Tom Glavine made his first start in 15 games, looked a little rusty, but said he felt fine after nursing a sore rib cage and weakened shoulder.

▸**September 26:** The Braves beat the Padres 2-1. Magic number: three.

▸**September 29:** Clinch! The Braves clinched the NL West title with a 6-0 win over the Giants.

▸**October 2:** John Smoltz struck out three for a season total of 215, overtaking David Cone for the 1992 NL strikeout title. Other NL leaders: Tom Glavine, victories (20-8) and shutouts (tied with David Cone, 5); Terry Pendleton, hits (199); Deion Sanders, triples (14). Pendleton was also fifth in batting (.311), 10th in home runs (21), sixth in doubles (39), second in RBI (105), and fourth in total bases (303). Otis Nixon was eighth in stolen bases (41), and David Justice was tied with Pendleton in home runs (21).

—by Jeanie Chung, John Hunt, Deron Snyder, and Lisa Winston.

Team directory

▸**Owner:** Ted Turner

▸**General Manager:** John Schuerholz

▸**Ballpark:**
Atlanta-Fulton County Stadium
521 Capitol Ave., SW, Atlanta, Ga.
404-522-7630
Capacity 52,007
Parking for 6,500 cars; $5
Public transportation available by bus
Family and wheelchair sections, non-alcohol section

▸**Team publications:**
Fan Magazine
404-522-7630

▸**TV, radio broadcast stations:**
WGST 640 AM, WTBS Channel 17

▸**Camps and/or clinics:**
Braves Fantasy Camp (ages 30+), February, 800-8-BRAVES

▸**Spring Training:**
Municipal Stadium
West Palm Beach, Fla.
Capacity 7,200
407-683-6100

ATLANTA BRAVES 1992 final stats

Batting	AVG	SLG	OB	G	AB	R	H	TB	2B	3B	HR	RBI	BB	SO	SB	CS	E
Lopez	.375	.500	.375	9	16	3	6	8	2	0	0	2	0	1	0	0	0
Pendleton	.311	.473	.345	160	640	98	199	303	39	1	21	105	37	67	5	2	19
Sanders	.304	.495	.346	97	303	54	92	150	6	14	8	28	18	52	26	9	3
Cabrera	.300	.900	.364	12	10	2	3	9	0	0	2	3	1	1	0	0	0
Nixon	.294	.346	.348	120	456	79	134	158	14	2	2	22	39	54	41	18	3
Gregg	.263	.421	.300	18	19	1	5	8	0	0	1	1	1	7	1	0	0
Blauser	.262	.458	.354	123	343	61	90	157	19	3	14	46	46	82	5	5	14
Bream	.261	.414	.340	125	372	30	97	154	25	1	10	61	46	51	6	0	10
Gant	.259	.415	.321	153	544	74	141	226	22	6	17	80	45	101	32	10	4
Justice	.256	.446	.359	144	484	78	124	216	19	5	21	72	79	85	2	4	8
Castilla	.250	.313	.333	9	16	1	4	5	1	0	0	1	1	4	0	0	1
L.Smith	.247	.437	.324	84	158	23	39	69	8	2	6	33	17	37	4	0	3
Hunter	.239	.487	.292	102	238	34	57	116	13	2	14	41	21	50	1	2	4
Olson	.238	.328	.316	95	302	27	72	99	14	2	3	27	34	31	2	1	1
Berryhill	.228	.384	.268	101	307	21	70	118	16	1	10	43	17	67	0	2	1
Lemke	.227	.304	.307	155	427	38	97	130	7	4	6	26	50	39	0	3	9
Treadway	.222	.286	.274	61	126	5	28	36	6	1	0	5	9	16	1	2	1
Belliard	.211	.239	.255	144	285	20	60	68	6	1	0	14	14	43	0	1	14
Nieves	.211	.263	.286	12	19	0	4	5	1	0	0	1	2	7	0	0	3
Klesko	.000	.000	.067	13	14	0	0	0	0	0	0	1	0	5	0	0	0

Pitching	W-L	ERA	G	GS	CG	GF	Sho	SV	IP	H	R	ER	HR	BB	SO
Reardon	3-0	1.15	14	0	0	11	0	3	15.2	14	2	2	0	2	7
Nied	3-0	1.17	6	2	0	0	0	0	23	10	3	3	0	5	19
P.Smith	7-0	2.05	12	11	2	0	1	0	79	63	19	18	3	28	43
Wohlers	1-2	2.55	32	0	0	16	0	4	35.1	28	11	10	0	14	17
Bielecki	2-4	2.57	19	14	1	0	1	0	80.2	77	27	23	2	27	62
Glavine	20-8	2.76	33	33	7	0	5	0	225	197	81	69	6	70	129
Smoltz	15-12	2.85	35	35	9	0	3	0	246.2	206	90	78	17	80	215
Avery	11-11	3.20	35	35	2	0	2	0	233.2	216	95	83	14	71	129
Freeman	7-5	3.22	58	0	0	15	0	3	64.1	61	26	23	7	29	41
Leibrandt	15-7	3.36	32	31	5	0	2	0	193	191	78	72	9	42	104
Mercker	3-2	3.42	53	0	0	18	0	6	68.1	51	27	26	4	35	49
Pena	1-6	4.07	41	0	0	31	0	15	42	40	19	19	7	13	34
Stanton	5-4	4.10	65	0	0	23	0	8	63.2	59	32	29	6	20	44
Reynoso	1-0	4.70	3	1	0	1	0	1	7.2	11	4	4	2	2	2
Berenguer	3-1	5.13	28	0	0	8	0	1	33.1	35	22	19	7	16	19
St.Claire	0-0	5.87	10	0	0	1	0	0	15.1	17	11	10	1	8	7
Borbon	0-1	6.75	2	0	0	2	0	0	1.1	2	1	1	0	1	1
Davis	1-0	7.02	14	0	0	7	0	0	16.2	22	13	13	3	13	1

1993 preliminary roster

PITCHERS (17)
Steve Avery
Brian Bark
Pedro Borbon
Dennis Burlingame
Mark Davis
Donnie Elliott
Marvin Freeman
Tom Glavine
Shawn Holman
Greg Maddux
Kent Mercker
Matt Murray
Mike Potts
Pete Smith
John Smoltz
Mike Stanton
Mark Wohlers

CATCHERS (5)
Damon Berryhill
Francisco Cabrera
Tyler Houston
Javy Lopez
Greg Olson

INFIELDERS (10)
Rafael Belliard
Jeff Blauser
Sid Bream
Ramon Caraballo
Brian Hunter
Ryan Klesko
Mark Lemke
Jose Oliva
Terry Pendleton
Hector Roa

INFIELDERS (8)
Ron Gant
Troy Hughes
Dave Justice
Keith Mitchell
Melvin Nieves
Otis Nixon
Deion Sanders
Tony Tarasco

Games played by position

Player	G	C	1B	2B	3B	SS	OF
BELLIARD,R	144	0	0	1	0	139	0
BERRYHILL,D	101	84	0	0	0	0	0
BLAUSER,J	123	0	0	21	1	106	0
BREAM,S	125	0	120	0	0	0	0
CABRERA,F	12	1	0	0	0	0	0
CASTILLA,V	9	0	0	0	4	4	0
GANT,R	153	0	0	0	0	0	147
GREGG,T	18	0	0	0	0	0	9
HUNTER,B	102	0	92	0	0	0	6
JUSTICE,D	144	0	0	0	0	0	140
KLESKO,R	13	0	5	0	0	0	0
LEMKE,M	155	0	0	145	13	0	0
LOPEZ,J	9	9	0	0	0	0	0
NIEVES,M	12	0	0	0	0	0	6
NIXON,O	120	0	0	0	0	0	111
OLSON,GR	95	94	0	0	0	0	0
PENDLETON,T	160	0	0	0	158	0	0
SANDERS,D	97	0	0	0	0	0	75
SMITH,L	84	0	0	0	0	0	35
TREADWAY,J	61	0	0	45	1	0	0

Sick call: 1992 DL report

Player	Days on the DL
Bielecki, Mike	68
Esasky, Nick	85
Freeman, Marvin	15
Gregg, Tommy	106
Justice, David	15
Olson, Greg	16
Pena, Alejandro*	33
Treadway, Jeff	81

** On Disabled List twice during 1992 season (not counting transfers from one DL to another).*

Minor league report

Class AAA — Richmond finished 73-71, 2nd in the International League West Division. The team lost to Columbus in the 1st round of the playoffs. IF Jeff Manto hit .291 with 13 HR and 68 RBI. RHP Armando Reynoso was 12-9 with a 2.66 ERA. RHP David Nied led the league in wins at 14-9 with a 2.84 ERA. He K'd 159 in 168 IP, also the league leader. RHP Billy Taylor had 12 saves. **Class AA:** Greenville finished 100-43, 1st in both halves of the Southern League Eastern Division. The team beat Chattanooga in five games for the league championship. C Javy Lopez hit .321 with 16 HR and 60 RBI. OF Tony Tarasco hit .286 with 15 HR, 54 RBI and 33 SB. OF Mike Kelly had 25 HR. RHP Nate Minchey was 13-6 with a 2.30 ERA. **Class A:** Durham finished 70-70, 2nd in the Carolina League Southern Division in the 1st half and 3rd in the 2nd half. OF Lee Heath led the league in SB with 50. 3B Tim Gillis had 21 HR and 84 RBI. OF Brian Kowitz hit .301 with 7 HR and 64 RBI. Macon finished 58-81, 6th in the 1st half of the Sally League Southern Division and 5th in the 2nd half. RHP Jerry Koller was 10-5 with a 2.37 ERA. OF Vince Moore had 25 SB. RHP Dirk Blair had 8 saves. RHP Chris Seelbach had 144 K. Pulaski finished 23-38, last in the Appalachian League South Division. C Rob Newman hit .306 with 6 HR and 31 RBI. OF Mark Chambers had 31 SB. RHP Mike D'Andrea was 8-1 with a 2.74 ERA and 79 K in 62 IP. He allowed just 39 hits. Idaho Falls finished 27-49, last in the Pioneer League South Division. RHP Chris Brock was 6-4 with a 2.31 ERA and 72 K in 78 IP. The club was last in pitching at 5.65 but hit .274. Braves finished 22-37, last in the Gulf Coast League Eastern Division. LHP Darrell May was 4-3 with a 1.36 ERA and 61 K in 53 IP. The club finished last in hitting at .205 but compiled a 2.85 staff ERA.

Tops in the organization

BATTING LEADERS	Club	Avg.	G	AB	R	H	HR	RBI
Javy Lopez	Grv	.321	115	442	64	142	16	60
Chipper Jones	Grv	.311	137	530	86	165	13	73
Brian Kowitz	Grv	.299	126	438	62	131	7	70
Jeff Manto	Rmd	.291	127	450	65	131	13	68
Melvin Nieves	Grv	.287	131	456	79	131	26	108

HOME RUNS			WINS		
Melvin Nieves	Grv	26	Mike Hostetler	Grv	15
Mike Kelly	Grv	25	David Nied	Rmd	14
Tim Gillis	Grv	21	Nate Minchey	Grv	13
Brad Ripplemeyer	Dur	19	Armando Reynoso	Rmd	12
Ryan Klesko	Rmd	17	Kevin Coffman	Rmd	12

RBI			SAVES		
Melvin Nieves	Grv	108	Don Strange	Grv	18
Tim Gillis	Grv	87	David Williams	Dur	15
Chipper Jones	Grv	73	Billy Taylor	Rmd	12
Mike Kelly	Grv	71	Mark Wohlers	Rmd	9
Brian Kowitz	Grv	70	Dirk Blair	Mac	8

STOLEN BASES			STRIKEOUTS		
Lee Heath	Grv	51	David Nied	Rmd	159
Tony Tarasco	Grv	33	Mike Hostetler	Grv	145
Kevin O'Connor	Dur	31	Chris Seelbach	Mac	144
Ramon Caraballo	Rmd	29	Greg McMichael	Rmd	139
Vince Moore	Mac	25	John Wilder	Mac	128

PITCHING LEADERS	Club	W-L	ERA	IP	H	BB	SO
Nate Minchey	Grv	13-6	2.30	172	137	40	115
Jerry Koller	Mac	10-5	2.37	133	104	31	114
Armando Reynoso	Rmd	12-9	2.66	169	156	52	108
David Nied	Rmd	14-9	2.84	168	144	44	159
Kevin Coffman	Rmd	12-5	2.85	129	89	86	111

Atlanta (1966-1992), incl. Boston (1876-1952) and Milwaukee (1953-1965)

Runs: Most, career, all-time

2107 Hank Aaron, 1954-1974
1452 Eddie Mathews, 1952-1966
1291 Herman Long, 1890-1902
1134 Fred Tenney, 1894-1911
1103 DALE MURPHY, 1976-1990

Hits: Most, career, all-time

3600 Hank Aaron, 1954-1974
2201 Eddie Mathews, 1952-1966
1994 Fred Tenney, 1894-1911
1901 DALE MURPHY, 1976-1990
1900 Herman Long, 1890-1902

2B: Most, career, all-time

600 Hank Aaron, 1954-1974
338 Eddie Mathews, 1952-1966
306 DALE MURPHY, 1976-1990
295 Herman Long, 1890-1902
291 Tommy Holmes, 1942-1951

3B: Most, career, all-time

103 Rabbit Maranville, 1912-1935
96 Hank Aaron, 1954-1974
90 Herman Long, 1890-1902
80 John Morrill, 1876-1888
79 Bill Bruton, 1953-1960

HR: Most, career, all-time

733 Hank Aaron, 1954-1974
493 Eddie Mathews, 1952-1966
371 DALE MURPHY, 1976-1990
239 Joe Adcock, 1953-1962
215 Bob Horner, 1978-1986

RBI: Most, career, all-time

2202 Hank Aaron, 1954-1974
1388 Eddie Mathews, 1952-1966
1143 DALE MURPHY, 1976-1990
964 Herman Long, 1890-1902
927 Hugh Duffy, 1892-1900

SB: Most, career, all-time

431 Herman Long, 1890-1902
331 Hugh Duffy, 1892-1900
274 Billy Hamilton, 1896-1901
260 Bobby Lowe, 1890-1901
260 Fred Tenney, 1894-1911
240 Hank Aaron, 1954-1974 (6)

BB: Most, career, all-time

1376 Eddie Mathews, 1952-1966
1297 Hank Aaron, 1954-1974
912 DALE MURPHY, 1976-1990
750 Fred Tenney, 1894-1911
598 Billy Nash, 1885-1895

BA: Highest, career, all-time

.338 Billy Hamilton, 1896-1901
.332 Hugh Duffy, 1892-1900
.327 Chick Stahl, 1897-1900
.317 Rico Carty, 1963-1972
.317 Ralph Garr, 1968-1975

Slug avg: Highest, career, all-time

.567 Hank Aaron, 1954-1974
.533 Wally Berger, 1930-1937
.517 Eddie Mathews, 1952-1966
.511 Joe Adcock, 1953-1962
.508 Bob Horner, 1978-1986

Games started: Most, career, all-time

635 Warren Spahn, 1942-1964
595 Phil Niekro, 1964-1987
501 Kid Nichols, 1890-1901
330 Lew Burdette, 1951-1963
302 Vic Willis, 1898-1905

Saves: Most, career, all-time

141 Gene Garber, 1978-1987
78 Cecil Upshaw, 1966-1973
57 Rick Camp, 1976-1985
50 Don McMahon, 1957-1962
41 Steve Bedrosian, 1981-1985

Shutouts: Most, career, all-time

63 Warren Spahn, 1942-1964
44 Kid Nichols, 1890-1901
43 Phil Niekro, 1964-1987
30 Lew Burdette, 1951-1963
29 Tommy Bond, 1877-1881

Wins: Most, career, all-time

356 Warren Spahn, 1942-1964
329 Kid Nichols, 1890-1901
268 Phil Niekro, 1964-1987
179 Lew Burdette, 1951-1963
151 Vic Willis, 1898-1905

K: Most, career, all-time

2912 Phil Niekro, 1964-1987
2493 Warren Spahn, 1942-1964
1667 Kid Nichols, 1890-1901
1161 Vic Willis, 1898-1905
1157 Jim Whitney, 1881-1885

Win pct: Highest, career, all-time

.679 Fred Klobedanz, 1896-1902
.655 Harry Staley, 1891-1894
.645 John Clarkson, 1888-1892
.643 Kid Nichols, 1890-1901
.631 Tommy Bond, 1877-1881
.581 Tony Cloninger, 1961-1968 (12)

ERA: Lowest, career, all-time

2.21 Tommy Bond, 1877-1881
2.49 Jim Whitney, 1881-1885
2.52 Art Nehf, 1915-1919
2.62 Dick Rudolph, 1913-1927
2.74 Pat Ragan, 1915-1919
3.20 Phil Niekro, 1964-1987 (16)

Runs: Most, season

160 Hugh Duffy, 1894
158 Bobby Lowe, 1894
152 Billy Hamilton, 1896
152 Billy Hamilton, 1897
149 Herman Long, 1893
131 DALE MURPHY, 1983 (9)

Hits: Most, season

237 Hugh Duffy, 1894
224 Tommy Holmes, 1945
223 Hank Aaron, 1959
219 Ralph Garr, 1971
218 Felipe Alou, 1966

2B: Most, season

51 Hugh Duffy, 1894
47 Tommy Holmes, 1945
46 Hank Aaron, 1959
44 Wally Berger, 1931
44 Lee Maye, 1964
39 TERRY PENDLETON, 1992 (12)

3B: Most, season

20 Dick Johnston, 1887
20 Harry Stovey, 1891
19 Chick Stahl, 1899
18 Dick Johnston, 1888
18 Ray Powell, 1921
17 Ralph Garr, 1974 (6)

HR: Most, season

47 Hank Aaron, 1971
47 Eddie Mathews, 1953
46 Eddie Mathews, 1959
45 Hank Aaron, 1962
44 Hank Aaron, 1957
44 Hank Aaron, 1963
44 Hank Aaron, 1966
44 Hank Aaron, 1969
44 DALE MURPHY, 1987

RBI: Most, season

145 Hugh Duffy, 1894
135 Eddie Mathews, 1953
132 Hank Aaron, 1957
132 Jimmy Collins, 1897
130 Hank Aaron, 1963
130 Wally Berger, 1935
127 Hank Aaron, 1966 (9)

SB: Most, season

84 King Kelly, 1887
83 Billy Hamilton, 1896
72 OTIS NIXON, 1991
68 King Kelly, 1889
66 Billy Hamilton, 1897

BB: Most, season

131 Bob Elliott, 1948
127 Jim Wynn, 1976
126 Darrell Evans, 1974
124 Darrell Evans, 1973
124 Eddie Mathews, 1963

BA: Highest, season

.440 Hugh Duffy, 1894
.387 Rogers Hornsby, 1928
.373 Dan Brouthers, 1889
.369 Billy Hamilton, 1898
.366 Rico Carty, 1970

Slug avg: Highest, season

.694 Hugh Duffy, 1894
.669 Hank Aaron, 1971
.636 Hank Aaron, 1959
.632 Rogers Hornsby, 1928
.627 Eddie Mathews, 1953

Games started: Most, season

72 John Clarkson, 1889
67 Charlie Buffinton, 1884
64 Tommy Bond, 1879
63 Jim Whitney, 1881
59 Tommy Bond, 1878
44 Phil Niekro, 1979 (22)

Saves: Most, season

30 Gene Garber, 1982
27 Cecil Upshaw, 1969
25 Gene Garber, 1979
24 Gene Garber, 1986
23 Bruce Sutter, 1985

Shutouts: Most, season

11 Tommy Bond, 1879
9 Tommy Bond, 1878
8 Charlie Buffinton, 1884
8 John Clarkson, 1889
7 Kid Nichols, 1890
7 Togie Pittinger, 1902
7 Warren Spahn, 1947
7 Warren Spahn, 1951
7 Warren Spahn, 1963
7 Irv Young, 1905
6 Phil Niekro, 1974 (11)

Wins: Most, season

49 John Clarkson, 1889
48 Charlie Buffinton, 1884
43 Tommy Bond, 1879
40 Tommy Bond, 1877
40 Tommy Bond, 1878
24 Tony Cloninger, 1965 (*)

K: Most, season

417 Charlie Buffinton, 1884
345 Jim Whitney, 1883
284 John Clarkson, 1889
270 Jim Whitney, 1884
262 Phil Niekro, 1977

Win pct: Highest, season

.842 Tom Hughes, 1916
.810 Phil Niekro, 1982
.788 Fred Klobedanz, 1897
.788 Bill James, 1914
.783 Jack Manning, 1876

ERA: Lowest, season

1.87 Phil Niekro, 1967
1.90 Bill James, 1914
1.96 Tommy Bond, 1879
2.02 Lefty Tyler, 1916
2.06 Tommy Bond, 1878

Most pinch-hit homers, season

5 Butch Nieman, Bos-1945
4 Tommy Gregg, 1990

Most pinch-hit, homers, career

7 Joe Adcock, Mil-1953-1962
6 Tommy Gregg, 1988-1992

Most consecutive games, batting safely

37 Tommy Holmes, Bos-1945
31 Rico Carty, 1970

Most consecutive scoreless innings

41 Art Nehf, Bos-1917

No hit games

Jack Stivetts, Bos vs Bro NL, 11-0; August 6, 1892.

Frank (Jeff) Pfeffer, Bos vs Cin NL, 6-0; May 8, 1907.

George Davis, Bos vs Phi NL, 7-0; September 9, 1914 (2nd game).

Tom L. Hughes, Bos vs Pit NL, 2-0; June 16, 1916.

Jim Tobin, Bos vs Bro NL, 2-0; April 27, 1944.

Vern Bickford, Bos vs Bro NL, 7-0; August 11, 1950.

Jim Wilson, Mil vs Phi NL, 2-0; June 12, 1954.

Lew Burdette, Mil vs Phi NL, 1-0; August 18, 1960.

Warren Spahn, Mil vs Phi NL, 4-0; September 16, 1960.

Warren Spahn, Mil vs SF NL, 1-0; April 28, 1961.

Phil Niekro, Atl vs SD NL, 9-0; August 5, 1973.

Kent Mercker (6 innings), Mark Wohlers (2 innings) and Alejandro Pena (1 inning), Atl at SD NL, 1-0; September 11, 1991.

Jack Stivetts, five innings, called so Boston could catch train to Cleveland for Temple Cub play-offs, Bos at Was NL, 6-0; October 15, 1892 (2nd game).

Jim Tobin, five innings, darkness, Bos vs Phi NL, 7-0; June 22, 1944 (2nd game).

ACTIVE PLAYERS in caps.

Leader from the franchise's current location is included. If not in the top five, leader's rank is listed in parenthesis; asterisk (*) indicates player is not in top 25.

Cincinnati Reds

by Russell Beeker, *Baseball Weekly*

Shortstop Barry Larkin hit .304 (10th in the NL) and led the Reds in RBI (78) and total bases (242).

1992 Reds: The big machine slowed down

The Reds' biggest news of the '92 season took place after it was over. Manager Lou Piniella, who guided the team to a World Series title in 1990, was not rehired; general manager Bob Quinn was shown the door as well. Owner Marge Schott wasn't happy about spending $36 million to finish second.

Hopes had been high due to Quinn's preseason acquisitions: Tim Belcher and Greg Swindell were to boost the starting staff, and Dave Martinez and Bip Roberts would add outfield depth. The Reds were in first place at the All-Star break, but injuries and the Braves' hot streak ended the race in early September. Belcher was the only uninjured starter. Jose Rijo had a sore elbow, Swindell cracked a rib, and Tom Browning missed half of the season with a torn knee.

The offense was likewise crippled. Chris Sabo was bothered all season by an ankle injury; his home run count dropped from 26 to 12. Barry Larkin had a sprained knee, but posted a career high 78 RBI anyway. Hal Morris visited the DL twice and hit less than .300 (.271) for the first time in his career. Roberts filled the void, playing left, center, second, and third. He also tied the NL record with 10 consecutive hits and hit .323, fourth in the league.

The Reds' power dropped dramatically. They led the league in homers in '91, but were eighth in '92. Paul O'Neill was counted on to fill Eric Davis' cleanup spot, but he hit just .246, falling from 28 HR and 91 RBI to 14 HR and 66 RBI. (The Reds traded him to the Yankees for Roberto Kelly in November.)

Also on the Reds' '92 DL: outfielders Glenn Braggs, Billy Hatcher, and Reggie Sanders; infielder Darnell Coles; catcher Jeff Reed; and reliever Rob Dibble.

Off-field incidents always seem to be part of the Reds' circus: Roberts complained that he wasn't being rested enough; Dibble complained that he wasn't being used enough; Dibble and Piniella got into a clubhouse fight; and Belcher created a stir by saying that canine mascot Schottzie 02 was interfering with pre-game workouts by running around on the field. Schott made it clear that Schottzie 02 would remain a part of the club. Every new managerial candidate was asked how he felt about the dog. First base coach Tony Perez—nicknamed "Doggie"—said he told her, "We'll have to figure out how we can get the dog on the field and not interfere with the players."

Perez, who has never managed even a minor league game, is now the Reds' manager.

—by Gary Kicinski

1993 Reds: Preview

The 1993 Big Red Machine has a new driver, some new wheels and a more powerful engine. New manager Tony Perez should have plenty of offense at his disposal, thanks to offseason acquisitions by new general manager Jim Bowden. The Reds have five players capable of 20 or more stolen bases (Chris Sabo, Bip Roberts, Barry Larkin, Reggie Sanders, and Roberto Kelly) and four capable of 20 or more homers (Kelly, Larkin, Sabo, and Kevin Mitchell). Hal Morris is a threat for the batting title.

They may need extra runs; their pitching staff has four dependable starters—Jose Rijo, Tim Belcher, John Smiley and Tom Browning—and Rob Dibble is an effective closer, but beyond that, the Reds are counting on some untested young arms.

The bench has more experience. The Reds tried to save money there, and if their regulars encounter a spate of injuries similar to 1992, they'll have veterans like Cecil Espy and Gary Varsho as replacements.

—by Gary Kicinski

1992 Reds: Between the lines

▸**April 21:** Reliever Norm Charlton hit Darryl Strawberry with a pitch as an earthquake shook Dodger Stadium. ***Quote of the day:*** Charlton—"I didn't feel a thing. I just thought it was the people booing me."

▸**May 2:** The Reds had committed just 11 errors—a .987 fielding percentage, best in the NL—entering the game. Then they proceeded to commit four in one day.

▸**May 3:** Jose Rijo—fresh off the disabled list—made his first start since April 17 and pitched 4 2/3 pain-free innings.

▸**May 7:** Rob Dibble's recovery from tendinitis seemed complete. He struck out five of the seven Mets he faced.

▸**May 10:** Tim Belcher ended a personal three-game losing streak and pitched his first complete game of the season.

▸**May 15:** Tom Browning continued his slump, giving up five runs in three-plus innings.

▸**May 16:** Belcher helped himself with his first home run in four years. ***Quote of the day:*** Belcher—"It's kind of mystifying to me how I can pitch so effortlessly and dominating, then five days later look like I've got one eye and one arm tied behind my back."

▸**May 17:** Chris Sabo (3-for-4) doubled twice, while Greg Swindell struck out nine in 7 1/3 innings.

▸**May 19:** Bill Doran's ninth-inning grand slam powered the Reds to a 7-4 win against host Montreal.

▸**May 23:** Hal Morris was 3-for-4 with two doubles, a triple and four RBI. Since coming off the DL May 16, Morris was 12 for 29 (.414). ***Quote of the day:*** Jose Rijo, after winning for the first time in nine starts—"I'm not sure who was president the last time I won. I forget, it's been so long. It might have been Nixon or Kennedy."

▸**June 3:** Barry Larkin and Chris Sabo led off the fourth inning with back-to-back homers as the Reds rallied from a four-run deficit, in an 8-7 victory against the Cardinals.

▸**June 13:** Tim Belcher went 2-for-3 with an RBI and a run scored, helping himself in an 11-1 win against his former team, Los Angeles.

▸**June 15** ***Quote of the day:*** Chris Sabo, after tangling with the Giants' Darren Lewis and emptying both dugouts—"There was no problem there. It was just two guys getting excited. That's baseball."

▸**June 17:** Pitcher Chris Hammond hit a towering, 405-foot two-run shot for his first major league home run.

▸**June 18:** The frontrunners in the NL West, scheduled to play each other seven times in the next 11 days, played 10 innings as the Reds won 7-5 in Atlanta.

▸**June 23:** Eight Reds' players took extra batting practice—and it showed. After scoring only five runs in their previous four games, they cranked out 12 hits and eight runs in the first five innings.

▸**June 24:** Houston's Pete Harnisch and coach Ed Ott, and the Reds' Glenn Braggs and Rob Dibble, were ejected after a bench-clearing incident in the fifth. Harnisch yielded a three-run dinger to Hal Morris, and threw the next pitch behind Reggie Sanders' head. ***Quote of the day:*** Houston manager Art Howe—"There would have been no fight if Braggs and Dibble hadn't charged out there. Dibble came out full bore. The guy's a maniac."

▸**June 28:** The Reds put the finishing touches on Atlanta with a 6-5 victory to sweep the series. In all three games, Cincinnati jumped out to a lead in the first inning, outscoring Atlanta 10-0.

▸**July 3:** The Reds got a season-high seven doubles among their 13 hits off Pirates Randy Tomlin and reliever Jerry Don Gleaton. Barry Larkin had three two-baggers, Reggie Sanders had two, and Joe Oliver and Dave Martinez had one each.

▸**July 4** ***Quote of the day:*** Home plate umpire Doug Harvey on Greg Swindell's stuff in Cincinnati's 5-2 win against Pittsburgh—"What a pleasure it is to work a game when the catcher sets up and the pitcher hits it every time."

▸**July 12:** The NL division leaders concluded their regular-season matchup, with Pittsburgh capturing a 7-6 comeback victory in 10 innings at Cincinnati.

▸**July 26:** Darnell Coles went 5-for-6, making him 9-for-10 in his last two games.

▸**July 29:** Surprise! Jeff Branson popped out in a pinch-hit appearance. The rookie infielder was the majors' best pinch-hitter (minimum 15 at-bats), batting .444 (8-for-18).

▸**August 3:** Chris Hammond (6-6) broke a personal four-game losing streak, shutting out the Astros 4-0 with help from Rob Dibble and Scott Ruskin. Dibble had pitched 9 1/3 innings of shutout relief with 18 strikeouts in his last seven games.

▸**August 5:** Bip Roberts crashed headlong into the wall chasing a David Justice triple that gave the Braves a 2-0 lead. The Braves went on to win 5-1, widening their lead in the NL West to 2 1/2 games over the Reds. Roberts suffered a mild concussion and neck sprain.

▸**August 12:** First, Joe Oliver's wife Kim delivered. Hours later, the Cincinnati catcher delivered, too, blasting a three-run homer in the fifth inning to snap a scoreless game.

▸**August 15:** Cincinnati's much-needed 5-4 win against San Diego snapped its two-game losing streak and halted its slide in the West. Coming in, the Reds had lost seven of 10 and trailed first-place Atlanta by 5 1/2 games.

▸**August 22:** Even Greg Swindell couldn't stop the Reds' slide toward oblivion. They wasted another strong performance by their ace in a 3-1 loss to Montreal.

▸**August 30:** Tim Belcher retired 23 consecutive batters, but manager Lou Piniella went to Rob Dibble in the ninth. Dibble walked two batters, then gave up a three-run homer to Bobby Bonilla. ***Quote of the day:*** Belcher, in defense of Piniella—"Absolutely the right move. Whether it's 30 (batters) in a row or two in a row, who cares. We have guys in the bullpen of good caliber."

▸**September 17:** Lou Piniella and Rob Dibble had a postgame fight in the clubhouse. No one was hurt in the 30-second scuffle.

▸**October 4:** The Reds finished second in the NL West at .556, eight games out. Bip Roberts was fifth in the NL in on-base percentage (.393); Jose Rijo was seventh in ERA (2.56) and sixth in strikeouts (171); Norm Charlton was fifth in saves (26) and Rob Dibble was sixth (25).

—by Jeanie Chung, John Hunt, Deron Snyder, and Lisa Winston.

Team directory

▸**Owner:** Marge Schott and a limited partnership

▸**General Manager:** James G. Bowden

▸**Ballpark:**
Riverfront Stadium
Pete Rose Way, Cincinnati, Ohio
513-421-7337, 800-829-5353
Capacity 52,952
Parking for 5,022 cars; $3.50-$5
Wheelchair locations, ramps

▸**Team publications:**
Media Guide, Yearbook/Program
513-651-7200

▸**TV, radio broadcast stations:**
WLW 700 AM, WLWT Channel 5, Sportschannel

▸**Spring Training:**
Plant City Stadium
Plant City, Fla.
Capacity 6,700
813-752-1878

CINCINNATI REDS 1992 final stats

Batting	AVG	SLG	OB	G	AB	R	H	TB	2B	3B	HR	RBI	BB	SO	SB	CS	E
Bradley	.400	.400	.500	5	5	1	2	2	0	0	0	1	1	0	0	0	0
Wilson	.360	.400	.429	12	25	2	9	10	1	0	0	3	3	8	0	0	0
Green	.333	.417	.333	8	12	3	4	5	1	0	0	0	0	2	0	0	0
Roberts	.323	.432	.393	147	532	92	172	230	34	6	4	45	62	54	44	16	7
Coles	.312	.482	.322	55	141	16	44	68	11	2	3	18	3	15	1	0	0
Larkin	.304	.454	.377	140	533	76	162	242	32	6	12	78	63	58	15	4	11
Branson	.296	.374	.322	72	115	12	34	43	7	1	0	15	5	16	0	1	7
Hatcher	.287	.383	.314	43	94	10	27	36	3	0	2	10	5	11	0	2	1
Hernandez	.275	.353	.275	34	51	6	14	18	4	0	0	4	0	10	3	1	1
Morris	.271	.385	.347	115	395	41	107	152	21	3	6	53	45	53	6	6	1
Sanders	.270	.462	.356	116	385	62	104	178	26	6	12	36	48	98	16	7	6
Oliver	.270	.388	.316	143	485	42	131	188	25	1	10	57	35	75	2	3	8
Greene	.269	.430	.337	29	93	10	25	40	5	2	2	13	10	23	0	2	3
Berroa	.267	.333	.389	13	15	2	4	5	1	0	0	0	2	1	0	1	0
Martinez	.254	.354	.323	135	393	47	100	139	20	5	3	31	42	54	12	8	6
O'Neill	.246	.373	.346	148	496	59	122	185	19	1	14	66	77	85	6	3	1
Sabo	.244	.422	.302	96	344	42	84	145	19	3	12	43	30	54	4	5	9
Braggs	.237	.410	.330	92	266	40	63	109	16	3	8	38	36	48	3	1	6
Doran	.235	.349	.342	132	387	48	91	135	16	2	8	47	64	40	7	4	5
Benavides	.231	.318	.277	74	173	14	40	55	10	1	1	17	10	34	0	1	6
Costo	.222	.278	.310	12	36	3	8	10	2	0	0	2	5	6	0	0	0
Afenir	.176	.324	.282	16	34	3	6	11	1	2	0	4	5	12	0	0	0
Wrona	.174	.174	.174	11	23	0	4	4	0	0	0	0	0	3	0	0	2
Reed	.160	.160	.192	15	25	2	4	4	0	0	0	2	1	4	0	0	0
Brumfield	.133	.133	.212	24	30	6	4	4	0	0	0	2	2	4	6	0	0

Pitching	W-L	ERA	G	GS	CG	GF	Sho	SV	IP	H	R	ER	HR	BB	SO
Menendez	1-0	1.93	3	0	0	1	0	0	4.2	1	1	1	1	0	5
Rijo	15-10	2.56	33	33	2	0	0	0	211	185	67	60	15	44	171
Pugh	4-2	2.58	7	7	0	0	0	0	45.1	47	15	13	2	13	18
Swindell	12-8	2.70	31	30	5	0	3	0	213.2	210	72	64	14	41	138
Foster	1-1	2.88	31	1	0	7	0	2	50	52	16	16	4	13	34
Bankhead	10-4	2.93	54	0	0	10	0	1	70.2	57	26	23	4	29	53
Charlton	4-2	2.99	64	0	0	46	0	26	81.1	79	39	27	7	26	90
Dibble	3-5	3.07	63	0	0	49	0	25	70.1	48	26	24	3	31	110
Hill	0-0	3.15	14	0	0	5	0	1	20	15	9	7	1	5	10
Henry	3-3	3.33	60	0	0	11	0	0	83.2	59	31	31	4	44	72
Belcher	15-14	3.91	35	34	2	1	1	0	227.2	201	104	99	17	80	149
Hammond	7-10	4.21	28	26	0	1	0	0	147.1	149	75	69	13	55	79
Ayala	2-1	4.34	5	5	0	0	0	0	29	33	15	14	1	13	23
Brown	0-1	4.50	2	2	0	0	0	0	8	10	5	4	2	5	5
Ruskin	4-3	5.03	57	0	0	19	0	0	53.2	56	31	30	6	20	43
Browning	6-5	5.07	16	16	0	0	0	0	87	108	49	49	6	28	33
Bolton	3-3	5.24	16	8	0	3	0	0	46.1	52	28	27	9	23	27

1993 preliminary roster

PITCHERS (19)
Bobby Ayala
Tim Belcher
Tom Browning
Greg Cadaret
Rob Dibble
Mike Ferry
Steve Foster
Chris Hammond
Dwayne Henry
Milton Hill
Larry Luebbers
Ross Powell
Tim Pugh
Jose Rijo
Scott Robinson
Scott Ruskin
Scott Service
John Smiley
Jerry Spradlin

CATCHERS (3)
Darron Cox
Joe Oliver
Dan Wilson

INFIELDERS (8)
Jeff Branson
Tim Costo
Bill Doran
Willie Greene
Tommy Gregg
Barry Larkin
Hal Morris
Chris Sabo

OUTFIELDERS (10)
Jacob Brumfield
Willie Canate
Cecil Espy
Keith Gordon
Cesar Hernandez
Roberto Kelly
Kevin Mitchell
Bip Roberts
Reggie Sanders
Gary Varsho

Games played by position

Player	G	C	1B	2B	3B	SS	OF
AFENIR,M	16	15	0	0	0	0	0
BENAVIDES,F	74	0	0	37	1	34	0
BERROA,G	13	0	0	0	0	0	3
BRADLEY,S	5	2	0	0	0	0	0
BRAGGS,G	92	0	0	0	0	0	79
BRANSON,J	72	0	0	33	8	1	0
BRUMFIELD,J	24	0	0	0	0	0	16
COLES,D	55	0	20	0	23	0	5
COSTO,T	12	0	12	0	0	0	0
DORAN,B	132	0	25	104	0	0	0
GREEN,G	8	0	0	0	1	6	0
GREENE,W	29	0	0	0	25	0	0
HATCHER,B	43	0	0	0	0	0	23
HERNANDEZ,CE	34	0	0	0	0	0	18
LARKIN,B	140	0	0	0	0	140	0
MARTINEZ,D	135	0	21	0	0	0	111
MORRIS,H	115	0	109	0	0	0	0
OLIVER,J	143	141	1	0	0	0	0
O'NEILL,P	148	0	0	0	0	0	143
REED,JS	15	6	0	0	0	0	0
ROBERTS,B	147	0	0	42	36	0	79
SABO,C	96	0	0	0	93	0	0
SANDERS,R	116	0	0	0	0	0	110
WILSON,D	12	9	0	0	0	0	0
WRONA,R	11	10	1	0	0	0	0

Sick call: 1992 DL report

Player	Days on the DL
Braggs, Glenn	15
Browning, Tom	95
Coles, Darnell	40
Dibble, Rob	10
Hatcher, Billy	17
Larkin, Barry	19
Morris, Hal*	57
Reed, Jeff	127
Rijo, Jose	15
Sabo, Chris	15
Sanders, Reggie*	32
Swindell, Greg	15

** On Disabled List twice during 1992 season (not counting transfers from one DL to another).*

Minor league report

Class AAA — Nashville finished 67-77, last in the American Association Eastern Division. OF Geronimo Berroa hit .328 with 22 HR and 88 RBI. 1B Russ Morman hit .310 with 14 HR and 63 RBI. OF Nick Capra had 31 SB. OF Jacob Brumfield had 22 SB. RHPs Keith Brown and Tim Pugh shared the league lead in wins with 12. RHP Milt Hill had 18 saves. **Class AA:** Chattanooga finished 90-53, 1st in both halves of the Southern League Western Division. The team lost to Greenville in five games for the league championship. 3B Willie Greene had 15 HR after his callup mid-season from Cedar Rapids. 1B Tim Costo led the league with 28 HR. OF Scott Pose led the league in batting at .342. RHP Mike Anderson was 13-7 with a 2.52 ERA. RHP Jerry Spradlin set a league record with 34 saves. LHP Bobby Ayala had 154 K. RHP John Roper threw a no-hitter down the stretch. **Class A:** Cedar Rapids finished 82-56, 1st in the 1st half of the Midwest League Southern Division and 3rd in the 2nd half. The team beat Beloit in five games for the league championship. OF Steve Gibralter was named league MVP, hitting .306 with 19 HR and 99 RBI. He led the league in HR and RBI. 1B Joe Deberry hit 15 HR. SS Brian Koelling had 47 SB. RHP Mike Ferry was 13-4 with a 2.71 ERA. RHP Chris Hook was 14-8 with a 2.72 ERA. Charleston (W.Va.) finished 77-64, 1st in the 1st half of the Sally League Northern Division and last in the 2nd half. The team lost to Myrtle Beach in 3 games for the league championship. 3B Bobby Perna hit .301 with 11 HR and 71 RBI, setting a franchise record for hits with 150. RHP John Courtright was 10-6 with a 2.50 ERA. RHP Carl Stewart had 167 K. Billings finished 53-23, 1st in the Pioneer League North Division. The team beat Salt Lake in two games for the league championship. 2B Dee Jenkins hit .336. OF Micah Franklin hit .332 with 11 HR and 60 RBI. He shared the league lead in RBI. RHP Jason Kummerfeldt, who is from Billings, was 8-0 with a 2.38 ERA. RHP Jason Angel also had 8 wins. RHP Bo Loftin set a league record for saves with 16. He was a catcher until this year. Princeton finished 34-31, 3rd in the Appalachian League North Division. SS Dan Frye hit .325 and led the league in HR with 15 and RBI with 59. RHP Curt Lyons was 5-3 with a 2.77 ERA. RHP Jim Nix shared the league lead with 13 saves.

Tops in the organization

BATTING LEADERS	Club	Avg.	G	AB	R	H	HR	RBI
Scott Pose	Cng	.342	136	526	87	180	2	45
Geronimo Berroa	Nvl	.328	112	461	73	151	22	88
Russ Morman	Nvl	.310	101	384	53	119	14	63
Steve Gibralter	Cdr	.306	137	529	92	162	19	99
Bobby Perna	Cng	.303	132	509	76	154	11	72

HOME RUNS			WINS		
Tim Costo	Cng	28	Scott Robinson	Cng	15
Willie Greene	Cng	27	Chris Hook	Cdr	14
Geronimo Berroa	Nvl	22	Larry Luebbers	Cng	13
Steve Gibralter	Cdr	19	Mike Anderson	Cng	13
Jamie Dismuke	Cwv	17	Mike Ferry	Cdr	13

RBI			SAVES		
Willie Greene	Cng	106	Jerry Spradlin	Cng	34
Steve Gibralter	Cdr	99	Milt Hill	Nvl	18
Geronimo Berroa	Nvl	88	John Hrusovsky	Cdr	16
Bobby Perna	Cng	72	Rusty Kilgo	Cng	11
Several players tied		71	Several players tied		8

STOLEN BASES			STRIKEOUTS		
Brian Koelling	Cdr	47	Carl Stewart	Cwv	167
Motorboat Jones	Cwv	37	Mo Sanford	Nvl	157
Nick Capra	Nvl	31	Bobby Ayala	Cng	154
Bernie Jenkins	Cdr	28	Mike Anderson	Cng	149
Eliezer Quinones	Cwv	25	John Courtright	Cwv	147

PITCHING LEADERS	Club	W-L	ERA	IP	H	BB	SO
Larry Luebbers	Cng	13-5	2.44	170	157	67	112
John Courtright	Cwv	10-5	2.50	173	147	55	147
Mike Anderson	Cng	13-7	2.52	172	154	61	149
Ross Powell	Nvl	8-9	2.57	151	132	60	140
Scott Robinson	Cng	15-4	2.67	182	155	51	131

Cincinnati (1890-1992)

Runs: Most, career, all-time

1741 Pete Rose, 1963-1986
1091 Johnny Bench, 1967-1983
1043 Frank Robinson, 1956-1965
993 Dave Concepcion, 1970-1988
978 Vada Pinson, 1958-1968

Hits: Most, career, all-time

3358 Pete Rose, 1963-1986
2326 Dave Concepcion, 1970-1988
2048 Johnny Bench, 1967-1983
1934 Tony Perez, 1964-1986
1881 Vada Pinson, 1958-1968

2B: Most, career, all-time

601 Pete Rose, 1963-1986
389 Dave Concepcion, 1970-1988
381 Johnny Bench, 1967-1983
342 Vada Pinson, 1958-1968
339 Tony Perez, 1964-1986

3B: Most, career, all-time

152 Edd Roush, 1916-1931
115 Pete Rose, 1963-1986
112 Bid McPhee, 1890-1899
96 Vada Pinson, 1958-1968
94 Curt Walker, 1924-1930

HR: Most, career, all-time

389 Johnny Bench, 1967-1983
324 Frank Robinson, 1956-1965
287 Tony Perez, 1964-1986
251 Ted Kluszewski, 1947-1957
244 George Foster, 1971-1981

RBI: Most, career, all-time

1376 Johnny Bench, 1967-1983
1192 Tony Perez, 1964-1986
1036 Pete Rose, 1963-1986
1009 Frank Robinson, 1956-1965
950 Dave Concepcion, 1970-1988

SB: Most, career, all-time

406 Joe Morgan, 1972-1979
337 Arlie Latham, 1890-1895
321 Dave Concepcion, 1970-1988
319 Bob Bescher, 1908-1913
316 Bid McPhee, 1890-1899

BB: Most, career, all-time

1210 Pete Rose, 1963-1986
891 Johnny Bench, 1967-1983
881 Joe Morgan, 1972-1979
736 Dave Concepcion, 1970-1988
698 Frank Robinson, 1956-1965

BA: Highest, career, all-time

.332 Cy Seymour, 1902-1906
.331 Edd Roush, 1916-1931
.325 Jake Beckley, 1897-1903
.314 Bubbles Hargrave, 1921-1928
.311 Rube Bressler, 1917-1927

Slug avg: Highest, career, all-time

.554 Frank Robinson, 1956-1965
.514 George Foster, 1971-1981
.512 Ted Kluszewski, 1947-1957
.509 ERIC DAVIS, 1984-1991
.498 Wally Post, 1949-1963

Games started: Most, career, all-time

356 Eppa Rixey, 1921-1933
322 Paul Derringer, 1933-1942
319 Dolf Luque, 1918-1929
296 Bucky Walters, 1938-1948
278 Johnny Vander Meer, 1937-1949

Saves: Most, career, all-time

148 JOHN FRANCO, 1984-1989
119 Clay Carroll, 1968-1975
88 Tom Hume, 1977-1987
76 Pedro Borbon, 1970-1979
73 Wayne Granger, 1969-1971

Shutouts: Most, career, all-time

32 Bucky Walters, 1938-1948
30 Jim Maloney, 1960-1970
29 Johnny Vander Meer, 1937-1949
25 Ken Raffensberger, 1947-1954
24 Paul Derringer, 1933-1942
24 Noodles Hahn, 1899-1905
24 Dolf Luque, 1918-1929

Wins: Most, career, all-time

179 Eppa Rixey, 1921-1933
161 Paul Derringer, 1933-1942
160 Bucky Walters, 1938-1948
154 Dolf Luque, 1918-1929
134 Jim Maloney, 1960-1970

K: Most, career, all-time

1592 Jim Maloney, 1960-1970
1449 Mario Soto, 1977-1988
1289 Joe Nuxhall, 1944-1966
1251 Johnny Vander Meer, 1937-1949
1062 Paul Derringer, 1933-1942

Win pct: Highest, career, all-time

.674 Don Gullett, 1970-1976
.653 Pedro Borbon, 1970-1979
.627 JOSE RIJO, 1988-1992
.623 Jim Maloney, 1960-1970
.623 Clay Carroll, 1968-1975

ERA: Lowest, career, all-time

2.18 Fred Toney, 1915-1918
2.37 Bob Ewing, 1902-1909
2.52 Noodles Hahn, 1899-1905
2.58 JOSE RIJO, 1988-1992
2.62 Hod Eller, 1917-1921

Runs: Most, season

134 Frank Robinson, 1962
131 Vada Pinson, 1959
130 Pete Rose, 1976
129 Arlie Latham, 1894
126 Tommy Harper, 1965

Hits: Most, season

230 Pete Rose, 1973
219 Cy Seymour, 1905
218 Pete Rose, 1969
215 Pete Rose, 1976
210 Pete Rose, 1968
210 Pete Rose, 1975

2B: Most, season

51 Frank Robinson, 1962
51 Pete Rose, 1978
47 Vada Pinson, 1959
47 Pete Rose, 1975
45 George Kelly, 1929
45 Pete Rose, 1974

3B: Most, season

26 John Reilly, 1890
22 Sam Crawford, 1902
22 Jake Daubert, 1922
22 Bid McPhee, 1890
22 Mike Mitchell, 1911

HR: Most, season

52 George Foster, 1977
49 Ted Kluszewski, 1954
47 Ted Kluszewski, 1955
45 Johnny Bench, 1970
40 Johnny Bench, 1972
40 George Foster, 1978
40 Ted Kluszewski, 1953
40 Tony Perez, 1970
40 Wally Post, 1955

RBI: Most, season

149 George Foster, 1977
148 Johnny Bench, 1970
141 Ted Kluszewski, 1954
136 Frank Robinson, 1962
130 Deron Johnson, 1965

SB: Most, season

87 Arlie Latham, 1891
80 Bob Bescher, 1911
80 ERIC DAVIS, 1986
79 Dave Collins, 1980
76 Dusty Miller, 1896

BB: Most, season

132 Joe Morgan, 1975
120 Joe Morgan, 1974
117 Joe Morgan, 1977
115 Joe Morgan, 1972
114 Joe Morgan, 1976

BA: Highest, season

.377 Cy Seymour, 1905
.372 Bug Holliday, 1894
.351 Edd Roush, 1923
.351 Mike Donlin, 1903
.348 Edd Roush, 1924

Slug avg: Highest, season

.642 Ted Kluszewski, 1954
.631 George Foster, 1977
.624 Frank Robinson, 1962
.611 Frank Robinson, 1961
.595 Frank Robinson, 1960

Games started: Most, season

49 Elton Chamberlain, 1892
47 Tony Mullane, 1891
45 Billy Rhines, 1890
43 Billy Rhines, 1891
42 Noodles Hahn, 1901
42 Pete Schneider, 1917
42 Fred Toney, 1917

Saves: Most, season

39 JOHN FRANCO, 1988
37 Clay Carroll, 1972
35 Wayne Granger, 1970
32 JOHN FRANCO, 1987
32 JOHN FRANCO, 1989

Shutouts: Most, season

7 Jack Billingham, 1973
7 Hod Eller, 1919
7 Fred Toney, 1917
6 Ewell Blackwell, 1947
6 Noodles Hahn, 1902
6 Jack Harper, 1904
6 DANNY JACKSON, 1988
6 Dolf Luque, 1923
6 Jim Maloney, 1963
6 Ken Raffensberger, 1952
6 Billy Rhines, 1890
6 Fred Toney, 1915
6 Johnny Vander Meer, 1941
6 Bucky Walters, 1944
6 Jake Weimer, 1906

Wins: Most, season

28 Billy Rhines, 1890
27 Pink Hawley, 1898
27 Dolf Luque, 1923
27 Bucky Walters, 1939
25 Paul Derringer, 1939
25 Eppa Rixey, 1922

K: Most, season

274 Mario Soto, 1982
265 Jim Maloney, 1963
244 Jim Maloney, 1965
242 Mario Soto, 1983
239 Noodles Hahn, 1901

Win pct: Highest, season

.826 Elmer Riddle, 1941
.821 Bob Purkey, 1962
.783 TOM BROWNING, 1988
.781 Paul Derringer, 1939
.771 Dolf Luque, 1923

ERA: Lowest, season

1.58 Fred Toney, 1915
1.73 Bob Ewing, 1907
1.77 Noodles Hahn, 1902
1.82 Dutch Ruether, 1919
1.86 Andy Coakley, 1908

Most pinch-hit homers, season

5 Jerry Lynch, 1961
4 Bob Thurman, 1957

Most pinch-hit, homers, career

13 Jerry Lynch, 1957-1963

Most consecutive games, batting safely

44 Pete Rose, 1978
30 Elmer Smith, 1898

Most consecutive scoreless innings

N/A

No hit games

Bumpus Jones, Cin vs Pit NL, 7-1; October 15, 1892 (first game in the major leagues).

Ted Breitenstein, Cin vs Pit NL, 11-0; April 22, 1898.

Noodles Hahn, Cin vs Phi NL, 4-0; July 12, 1900.

Fred Toney, Cin at Chi NL, 1-0; May 2, 1917 (ten innings).

Hod Eller, Cin vs StL NL, 6-0; May 11, 1919.

Johnny Vander Meer, Cin vs Bos NL, 3-0; June 11, 1938.

Johnny Vander Meer, Cin at Bro NL, 6-0; June 15, 1938 (next start after June 11).

Clyde Shoun, Cin vs Bos NL, 1-0; May 15, 1944.

Ewell Blackwell, Cin vs Bos NL, 6-0; June 18, 1947.

Johnny Klippstein (7 innings), Hershell Freeman (1 inning), and Joe Black (3 innings), Cin at Mil NL, 1-2; May 26, 1956 (lost on 3 hits in 11 innings after allowing the first hit in the tenth).

Jim Maloney, Cin vs NY NL, 0-1; June 14, 1965 (lost on 2 hits in 11 innings after pitching 10 hitless innings).

Jim Maloney, Cin at Chi NL, 1-0; August 19, 1965 (1st game, 10 innings).

George Culver, Cin at Phi NL, 6-1; July 29, 1968 (2nd game).

Jim Maloney, Cin vs Hou NL, 10-0; April 30, 1969.

Tom Seaver, Cin vs StL NL, 4-0; June 16, 1978.

Tom Browning, Cin vs LA NL, 1-0; September 16, 1988 (perfect game).

Elton Chamberlain, seven innings, darkness, Cin vs Bos NL, 6-0; September 23, 1893 (2nd game).

Jake Weimer, seven innings, agreement, Cin vs Bro NL, 1-0; August 24, 1906 (2nd game).

ACTIVE PLAYERS in caps.

San Diego Padres

by Russell Beeker, *Baseball Weekly*

Gary Sheffield flirted with the triple crown: tops in batting (.330), third in homers (33), fourth in RBI (100).

1992 Padres: Big bats weren't enough

Get ready for the Four Tops! The '92 Padres were energized by the first four hitters in their batting order: shortstop Tony Fernandez, outfielder Tony Gwynn, third baseman Gary Sheffield, and first baseman Fred McGriff. Nicknamed after the R&B singing group, they each sported .300-plus batting averages two weeks before the All-Star break.

Sheffield's was the most intriguing story. The nephew of Mets pitcher Dwight Gooden, he had languished in Milwaukee for three seasons and was traded to San Diego 10 days before the season opened. His career highs had been .294, 10 HR and 67 RBI, but as a Padre, he flirted with the Triple Crown all season, falling short by just two homers and nine RBI. He finished with a league-leading .330 batting average, 33 homers and 100 RBI.

But the Padres were more than a one-man gang. McGriff led the league with 35 home runs and was third in RBI (104). Gwynn, a four-time NL batting champ, settled into his customary position, hitting .317 (his 10th consecutive season at .300 or better). But there was a down side; Gwynn finished the season on the bench for the third straight year with a bad knee. (He had arthroscopic surgery on Oct. 5.) Fernandez faded in the second half, finishing at .275. But he was steady defensively; his .983 fielding was third among NL shortstops. But the Padres traded him—and his $2.3 million salary—to the Mets on Oct. 26.

Catcher Benito Santiago—who had been with the Padres his entire seven-year career—made what was likely his last season in San Diego a forgettable one. Santiago, who filed for free agency at the end of the season, was sidelined for six weeks with a broken finger. He finished at .251 with 10 homers and 42 RBI.

Darrin Jackson (17 homers, 70 RBI) and Jerald Clark (12 and 58) added to the offensive punch, but despite the high-powered attack, the Padres (82-80) could muster no better than third place. Manager Greg Riddoch was fired the day the Padres were eliminated from the race (Sept. 23); Jim Riggleman took over for the last 12 games. The Padres' league standing at the time of the firing—third in hitting, ninth in pitching—indicated one problem Riddoch faced. The lack of quality starters was a sore spot. Bruce Hurst (14-9, 3.85 ERA) was the subject of trade talks all season; Craig Lefferts was sent to the Baltimore Orioles for a pair of minor-leaguers minutes before the Aug. 31 deadline. Andy Benes (13-14, 3.35 ERA) may have proved that his first three seasons are his par (31-25, 3.32). Greg Harris (4-8, 4.12 ERA) was on the DL nearly half the season.

On a positive note, relief ace Randy Myers had a career-high 38 saves, second in the NL, and rookie starter Frank Seminara , who made his debut in June, was 9-4 with a 3.68 ERA.

—by Deron Snyder

1993 Padres: Preview

If the Padres finished third with Tony Fernandez, Benito Santiago, and Bruce Hurst, imagine how they'd do without them.

The front office vowed to slash the payroll from $28 million to $22 million, and since it takes $19 million just to pay Hurst, McGriff, Gwynn, Kurt Stillwell, Greg Harris, Andy Benes, and Sheffield, the incentive to dump some of those players is obvious. Benes put it in perspective: "I think they're going to do the best they can to compete," but breaking up that nucleus would be a "nightmare."

Low-cost Darrell Sherman probably will graduate from the minor leagues to battle Phil Plantier for the job of replacing Jerald Clark, lost to the Rockies in the expansion draft.

—by Tim McQuay

1992 Padres: Between the lines

▸**April 22:** Tony Fernandez singled and doubled to run his hitting streak to eight games. The hits helped the Padres drub the struggling Atlanta Braves 9-4.

▸**April 29:** Greg Harris went the distance, yielding just two runs and nine hits, with five strikeouts. Gary Sheffield went 3-for-5 with a pair of doubles.

▸**April 30:** Expo Delino DeShields, just 3-for-9 in stolen bases entering the game, swiped two off Padre catcher Benito Santiago.

▸**May 13:** Tony Gwynn was 3-for-5 with a double, homer and two RBI, as Bruce Hurst pitched a six-hit shutout.

▸**May 18:** San Diego pulled into a first-place tie in the NL West on Bruce Hurst's one-hitter, a 3-0 win against the Mets. The only hit off Bruce Hurst was an infield single by Chico Walker in the sixth.

▸**May 20:** The "first four" of Tony Fernandez (.335), Tony Gwynn (.369), Gary Sheffield (.336) and Fred McGriff (.320) was down to three, with the hardly missed Gwynn out with a broken finger.

▸**May 26:** The major leagues' longest hitting streak thus far in 1992 (18 games) ended, as Gary Sheffield grounded out four times and flied out once.

▸**May 29:** San Diego had a team batting average of .311 (205-for-659) over the last 19 games.

▸**June 2:** Pitcher Frank Seminara debuted in the Cubs' 3-2 11-inning victory. Seminara pitched a two-hit shutout for 6 1/3 innings before he was hit by a line drive and forced to leave.

▸**June 3:** Bruce Hurst turned in his third complete game in five starts. He had a 1.93 ERA over that 42-inning-span.

▸**June 10:** Tony Gwynn struck out for the first time in 137 at-bats since April 28.

▸**June 18:** Gary Sheffield hit two homers, including his first career grand slam. Giants' pitcher Trevor Wilson responded by plunking Fred McGriff on the first pitch after Sheffield's slam. The ensuing brawl included a rare occurrence in most bench-clearing incidents: Players actually threw real punches. During the melee, McGriff suffered strained muscles in his left rib cage and Sheffield a strained left shoulder. Wilson had an assortment of cuts and bruises on his face.

▸**June 21:** Pitcher Greg Harris, fresh from three weeks on the disabled list, suffered a fractured middle finger on his right hand when he was struck by a pitch in the third inning and was put right back on the disabled list.

▸**June 22:** Tony Gwynn, coming off a 4-for-31 tailspin on a 10-game road trip, hit a solo home run in the first inning.

▸**June 23:** Gary Sheffield doubled, homered and had three RBI.

▸**June 25:** Bruce Hurst recorded a season high 11 strikeouts. His career best is 14.

▸**June 30:** Gary Sheffield—sprained thumb and all—delivered a pinch-hit RBI single for a 2-1 victory at Los Angeles.

▸**July 6:** The Cardinals-Padres game was delayed for four minutes when a skunk wandered onto the field. The skunk came into the Cardinals' bullpen in the right-field corner, then sauntered into right field. It headed into center field, then followed the warning track into left field. While the St. Louis outfielders and a group of groundskeepers kept clear, the skunk walked into a garbage can laid onto its side by a groundskeeper.

▸**July 26:** Bruce Hurst shut out the Mets for the third time in 1992.

▸**August 3:** Fred McGriff hit two home runs, both off former brawl mate Trevor Wilson.

▸**August 9:** Gary Sheffield left the game with a concussion after an eighth-inning collision on the basepaths.

He was second in the league in hits, homers, and RBI.

▸**August 22:** Gary Sheffield wasn't leading the league in home runs, so he hit two of them to tie teammate Fred McGriff with 27.

▸**August 26:** Craig Lefferts allowed six hits over seven scoreless innings to lead the Padres to a 3-0 blanking of the Cubs.

▸**August 28:** Gary Sheffield and Fred McGriff had back-to-back homers and Darrin Jackson and Jerald Clark chipped in with three RBI each as the Padres beat Pittsburgh 11-6.

▸**August 29:** Closer Randy Myers had his sixth blown save of the season in a 3-2 loss to the Pirates. It was the fifth time he'd blown a potential win for Greg Harris. He also cost Harris yet another win earlier in the season, when the lead was too big to qualify as a blown save.

▸**September 2:** Fred McGriff was spoiling teammate Gary Sheffield's shot at the triple crown, but admitted that he was enjoying it. McGriff's 32nd homer put him three ahead of Sheffield, who led the league in hitting and RBI. ***Quote of the day:*** McGriff—"I wish him all the luck, but I've got to do what I've got to do."

▸**September 4:** Darrin Jackson and Tim Teufel hit 14th-inning home runs off Shawn Boskie to give the Padres a 7-5 win against Chicago.

▸**September 23:** Jim Riggleman lost his managerial debut as his Padres fell to Houston 7-6. Riggleman's first move was to replace Bruce Hurst, who gave up six runs in 3 1/3 innings.

▸**September 25:** Greg Harris, slowed by two stays on the disabled list this season, got his first victory since May 31 as San Diego beat the Braves 1-0. Randy Myers tied Rollie Fingers (1978) for second on San Diego's single-season saves list with 37. Mark Davis, now with the Braves, set the club record with 44 in 1989.

▸**October 4:** The Padres won their last game of the season—(beating the Braves 4-3)—and finished third in the NL West. Gary Sheffield won the NL batting title (.330) and was tops in total bases (323); he also came in second in slugging (.580), third in home runs (33), fifth in RBI (100), and fifth in hits (184). Teammate Fred McGriff was tops in home runs (35), second in walks (96), third in RBI (104), third in slugging (.556), fourth in on-base percentage (.394), and fifth in total bases (295). Tony Gwynn was fifth in batting (.317), Randy Myers was second in saves (38), and Andy Benes was seventh in strikeouts (169.)

—by Jeanie Chung, John Hunt, Deron Snyder, and Lisa Winston.

Team directory

▸**Owner:** San Diego Padres Baseball Partnership

▸**General Manager:** Joe McIlvaine

▸**Ballpark:**
San Diego Jack Murphy Stadium
9449 Friars Rd., San Diego, Calif.
619-283-4494
Capacity 59,254
Parking for 18,751 cars; $4
Public transportation available
Wheelchair sections, ramps, pre-registration for telephone paging, ATM machines

▸**Team publications:**
Padre Magazine
619-283-4494

▸**TV, radio broadcast stations:**
KFMB 760 AM, XEXX AM, KUSI Channel 51, Cox Cable

▸**Spring Training:**
Desert Sun Stadium
Yuma, Ariz.
Capacity 7,000
602-726-6040

SAN DIEGO PADRES 1992 final stats

Batting	AVG	SLG	OB	G	AB	R	H	TB	2B	3B	HR	RBI	BB	SO	SB	CS	E
Faries	.455	.545	.500	10	11	3	5	6	1	0	0	1	1	2	0	0	0
Howard	.333	.333	.333	5	3	1	1	1	0	0	0	0	0	0	0	0	0
Sheffield	.330	.580	.385	146	557	87	184	323	34	3	33	100	48	40	5	6	16
Gwynn	.317	.415	.371	128	520	77	165	216	27	3	6	41	46	16	3	6	5
Velasquez	.304	.435	.333	15	23	1	7	10	0	0	1	5	1	7	0	0	1
McGriff	.286	.556	.394	152	531	79	152	295	30	4	35	104	96	108	8	6	12
Fernandez	.275	.359	.337	155	622	84	171	223	32	4	4	37	56	62	20	20	11
Walters	.251	.391	.295	57	179	14	45	70	11	1	4	22	10	28	1	0	3
Santiago	.251	.383	.287	106	386	37	97	148	21	0	10	42	21	52	2	5	12
Vatcher	.250	.313	.368	13	16	1	4	5	1	0	0	2	3	6	0	0	0
Jackson	.249	.392	.283	155	587	72	146	230	23	5	17	70	26	106	14	3	2
Shipley	.248	.305	.262	52	105	7	26	32	6	0	0	7	2	21	1	1	1
Clark	.242	.383	.278	146	496	45	120	190	22	6	12	58	22	97	3	0	3
Lampkin	.235	.235	.458	9	17	3	4	4	0	0	0	0	6	1	2	0	0
Stillwell	.227	.298	.274	114	379	35	86	113	15	3	2	24	26	58	4	1	16
Teufel	.224	.337	.312	101	246	23	55	83	10	0	6	25	31	45	2	1	7
Pettis	.200	.233	.250	30	30	0	6	7	1	0	0	0	2	11	1	0	1
Ward	.197	.293	.274	81	147	12	29	43	5	0	3	12	14	38	2	3	4
Azocar	.190	.226	.230	99	168	15	32	38	6	0	0	8	9	12	1	0	4
Stephenson	.155	.211	.259	53	71	5	11	15	2	1	0	8	10	11	0	0	1
Bilardello	.121	.152	.216	17	33	2	4	5	1	0	0	1	4	8	0	0	0
Gardner	.105	.105	.150	15	19	0	2	2	0	0	0	0	1	8	0	0	0

Pitching	W-L	ERA	G	GS	CG	GF	Sho	SV	IP	H	R	ER	HR	BB	SO
Maddux	2-2	2.37	50	1	0	14	0	5	79.2	71	25	21	2	24	60
Rodriguez	6-3	2.37	61	1	0	15	0	0	91	77	28	24	4	29	64
Clements	2-1	2.66	27	0	0	7	0	0	23.2	25	9	7	0	12	11
Melendez	6-7	2.92	56	3	0	18	0	0	89.1	82	32	29	9	20	82
Ge.Harris	0-2	2.95	14	1	0	2	0	0	21.1	15	8	7	0	9	19
Deshaies	4-7	3.28	15	15	0	0	0	0	96	92	40	35	6	33	46
Andersen	1-1	3.34	34	0	0	13	0	2	35	26	14	13	2	8	35
Benes	13-14	3.35	34	34	2	0	2	0	231.1	230	90	86	14	61	169
Seminara	9-4	3.68	19	18	0	0	0	0	100.1	98	46	41	5	46	61
Lefferts	13-9	3.69	27	27	0	0	0	0	163.1	180	76	67	16	35	81
Hurst	14-9	3.85	32	32	6	0	4	0	217.1	223	96	93	22	51	131
Gr.Harris	4-8	4.12	20	20	1	0	0	0	118	113	62	54	13	35	66
Hernandez	1-4	4.17	26	0	0	11	0	1	36.2	39	17	17	4	11	25
Myers	3-6	4.29	66	0	0	57	0	38	79.2	84	38	38	7	34	66
Scott	4-1	5.26	34	0	0	16	0	0	37.2	39	24	22	4	21	30
Eiland	0-2	5.67	7	7	0	0	0	0	27	33	21	17	1	5	10
Brocail	0-0	6.43	3	3	0	0	0	0	14	17	10	10	2	5	15

1993 preliminary roster

PITCHERS (17)
Andy Benes
Doug Brocail
Terry Bross
Gene Harris
Greg Harris
Jeremy Hernandez
Bruce Hurst
Mike Maddux
Jim Pena
Rich Rodriguez
Scott Sanders
Erik Schullstrom
Tim Scott
Frank Seminara
Kerry Taylor
Wally Whitehurst
Tim Worrell

CATCHERS (3)
Brian Johnson
Tom Lampkin
Dan Walters

INFIELDERS (11)
Jay Gainer
Jeff Gardner
Ricky Gutierrez
Ray Holbert
Luis Lopez
Fred McGriff
Gary Sheffield
Craig Shipley
Kurt Stillwell
Tim Teufel
Guillermo Velasquez

OUTFIELDERS (8)
D.J. Dozier
Tony Gwynn
Darrin Jackson
Steve Pegues
Phil Plantier
Darrell Sherman
Dave Staton
Jim Vatcher

Games played by position

Player	G	C	1B	2B	3B	SS	OF
AZOCAR,O	99	0	0	0	0	0	37
BILARDELLO,D	17	14	0	0	0	0	0
CLARK,JE	146	0	11	0	0	0	134
FARIES,P	10	0	0	4	2	1	0
FERNANDEZ,T	155	0	0	0	0	154	0
GARDNER,J	15	0	0	11	0	0	0
GWYNN,T	128	0	0	0	0	0	127
HOWARD,T	5	0	0	0	0	0	0
JACKSON,DJ	155	0	0	0	0	0	153
LAMPKIN,T	9	7	0	0	0	0	1
MCGRIFF,F	152	0	151	0	0	0	0
PETTIS,G	30	0	0	0	0	0	14
SANTIAGO,B	106	103	0	0	0	0	0
SHEFFIELD,G	146	0	0	0	144	0	0
SHIPLEY,C	52	0	0	11	8	23	0
STEPHENSON,P	53	0	7	0	0	0	15
STILLWELL,K	114	0	0	111	0	0	0
TEUFEL,T	101	0	5	52	26	0	0
VATCHER,J	13	0	0	0	0	0	13
VELASQUEZ,G	15	0	3	0	0	0	2
WALTERS,D	57	55	0	0	0	0	0
WARD,K	81	0	0	0	0	0	51

Sick call: 1992 DL report

Player	Days on the DL
Andersen, Larry**	63
Bilardello, Dann	57
Eiland, Dave*	145
Harris, Greg*	81
Maddux, Mike	20
Santiago, Benito	41
Stillwell, Kurt	15
Whitson, Ed	182

** On Disabled List twice during 1992 season (not counting transfers from one DL to another).*

*** On Disabled List three times during 1992 season.*

Minor league report

Class AAA — Las Vegas finished 74-70, 1st in the 1st half of the Pacific Coast League Southern Division and 3rd in the 2nd half. The team lost to Colorado Springs in the 1st round of the playoffs. 2B Jeff Gardner hit .335 with 51 RBI. OF Dave Staton had 19 HR. 1B Guillermo Velasquez hit .309 with 99 RBI. RHP Tim Scott had 15 saves. RHP Tim Worrell threw a no-hitter. OF Darrell Sherman hit .307 with 9 HR and 47 RBI. He had 52 SB between Las Vegas and Wichita. **Class AA:** Wichita finished 70-66, 1st in the 1st half of the Texas League Western Division and last in the 2nd half. The team beat Shreveport in four games for the league championship. 1B Jay Gainer had 23 HR. OFs J.D. Noland and Vince Harris had 40 and 38 SB respectively. LHP Pedro Martinez was 11-7 with a 2.99 ERA. RHP Mark Ettles had 22 saves. LHP Lance Painter had 137 K. **Class A:** High Desert finished 71-65, 4th in the California League Southern Division in the 1st half and 2nd in the 2nd half. 2B Billy Hall won the batting title at .356 and the SB crown with 49. OF Ray McDavid had 24 HR, 94 RBI and 43 SB. OF Tookie Spann had 19 HR and 103 RBI. RHP Jose Lebron was 10-5 with a 3.30 ERA. RHP Rafael Chaves set a league record wtih 34 saves. Waterloo finished 59-78, 6th in the 1st half of the Midwest League Southern Division and 5th in the 2nd half. SS Jason Hardtke hit .304 with 8 HR and 47 RBI. RHP Bruce Bensching had 18 saves. Charleston (S.C.) finished 55-85, last in the 1st half of the Sally League Southern Division and 6th in the 2nd half. The club finished last in batting at .227 and last in pitching at 4.35. Spokane finished 32-44, last in the Northwest League North Division. OF Bill Robbs hit .305 with 2 HR and 28 RBI. C Mel Rosario had 10 HR. SS Sean Drinkwater had 41 RBI. RHP Ken Grzelaczyk was 5-5 with a 2.02 ERA and 86 K in 76 IP. RHP Jared Baker was 6-3 with a 2.82 ERA. RHP Todd Schmitt had 14 saves. Padres finished 20-36, 7th in the Arizona League. The club hit .219 as a team and had a 4.45 ERA. OF Earl Johnson had 19 SB.

Tops in the organization

BATTING LEADERS	Club	Avg.	G	AB	R	H	HR	RBI
Billy Hall	Hds	.356	119	495	92	176	2	39
Jeff Gardner	Lvg	.335	120	439	82	147	1	51
Guillermo Velasquez	Lvg	.309	136	512	68	158	7	99
Darrell Sherman	Lvg	.307	135	489	108	150	9	47
Tom Lampkin	Lvg	.306	108	340	45	104	3	48

HOME RUNS		
Ray McDavid	Hds	24
Jay Gainer	Wch	23
Dave Staton	Lvg	19
Tookie Spann	Hds	19
Several players tied		15

WINS		
Tim Worrell	Lvg	12
Luis Galindez	Hds	11
Mark Knudson	Lvg	11
Pedro Martinez	Wch	11
Several players tied		10

RBI		
Tookie Spann	Hds	103
Guillermo Velasquez	Lvg	99
Ray McDavid	Hds	94
Steve Gill	Hds	83
Dave Staton	Lvg	76

SAVES		
Rafael Chaves	Hds	34
Mark Ettles	Wch	22
Bruce Bensching	Hds	18
Tim Scott	Lvg	15
Cole Hyson	Hds	14

STOLEN BASES		
Darrell Sherman	Lvg	52
Billy Hall	Hds	49
Ray McDavid	Hds	43
J.D. Noland	Wch	40
Darius Gash	Wch	39

STRIKEOUTS		
Robbie Beckett	Wlo	147
Scott Sanders	Lvg	146
Pedro Martinez	Wch	142
Tim Worrell	Lvg	141
Cam Cairncross	Wlo	138

PITCHING LEADERS	Club	W-L	ERA	IP	H	BB	SO
Joey Hamilton	Wch	9-5	2.97	118	116	33	104
Pedro Martinez	Wch	11-7	2.99	168	153	52	142
Jose Lebron	Hds	10-5	3.30	145	133	53	79
Tim Worrell	Lvg	12-8	3.33	189	176	51	141
Craig Hanson	CSc	2-10	3.43	118	115	49	75

San Diego (1969-1992)

Runs: Most, career, all-time

842 TONY GWYNN, 1982-1992
599 DAVE WINFIELD, 1973-1980
484 Gene Richards, 1977-1983
442 Nate Colbert, 1969-1974
430 Garry Templeton, 1982-1991

Hits: Most, career, all-time

1864 TONY GWYNN, 1982-1992
1135 Garry Templeton, 1982-1991
1134 DAVE WINFIELD, 1973-1980
994 Gene Richards, 1977-1983
817 Terry Kennedy, 1981-1986

2B: Most, career, all-time

275 TONY GWYNN, 1982-1992
195 Garry Templeton, 1982-1991
179 DAVE WINFIELD, 1973-1980
158 Terry Kennedy, 1981-1986
130 Nate Colbert, 1969-1974

3B: Most, career, all-time

75 TONY GWYNN, 1982-1992
63 Gene Richards, 1977-1983
39 DAVE WINFIELD, 1973-1980
36 Garry Templeton, 1982-1991
29 Cito Gaston, 1969-1974

HR: Most, career, all-time

163 Nate Colbert, 1969-1974
154 DAVE WINFIELD, 1973-1980
85 BENITO SANTIAGO, 1986-1992
82 Carmelo Martinez, 1984-1989
77 Cito Gaston, 1969-1974

RBI: Most, career, all-time

626 DAVE WINFIELD, 1973-1980
591 TONY GWYNN, 1982-1992
481 Nate Colbert, 1969-1974
427 Garry Templeton, 1982-1991
424 Terry Kennedy, 1981-1986

SB: Most, career, all-time

249 TONY GWYNN, 1982-1992
242 Gene Richards, 1977-1983
171 Alan Wiggins, 1981-1985
147 OZZIE SMITH, 1978-1981
133 DAVE WINFIELD, 1973-1980

BB: Most, career, all-time

506 TONY GWYNN, 1982-1992
463 DAVE WINFIELD, 1973-1980
423 Gene Tenace, 1977-1980
350 Nate Colbert, 1969-1974
338 Gene Richards, 1977-1983

BA: Highest, career, all-time

.327 TONY GWYNN, 1982-1992
.291 Gene Richards, 1977-1983
.286 Johnny Grubb, 1972-1976
.284 DAVE WINFIELD, 1973-1980
.275 Steve Garvey, 1983-1987

Slug avg: Highest, career, all-time

.468 Nate Colbert, 1969-1974
.464 DAVE WINFIELD, 1973-1980
.433 TONY GWYNN, 1982-1992
.422 Gene Tenace, 1977-1980
.409 Steve Garvey, 1983-1987

Games started: Most, career, all-time

253 Randy Jones, 1973-1980
230 Eric Show, 1981-1990
208 Ed Whitson, 1983-1991
172 Andy Hawkins, 1982-1988
170 Clay Kirby, 1969-1973

Saves: Most, career, all-time

108 Rollie Fingers, 1977-1980
83 RICH GOSSAGE, 1984-1987
74 MARK DAVIS, 1987-1989
64 CRAIG LEFFERTS, 1984-1992
49 Gary Lucas, 1980-1983

Shutouts: Most, career, all-time

18 Randy Jones, 1973-1980
11 Steve Arlin, 1969-1974
11 Eric Show, 1981-1990
10 BRUCE HURST, 1989-1992
7 Andy Hawkins, 1982-1988
7 Clay Kirby, 1969-1973

Wins: Most, career, all-time

100 Eric Show, 1981-1990
92 Randy Jones, 1973-1980
77 Ed Whitson, 1983-1991
60 Andy Hawkins, 1982-1988
55 BRUCE HURST, 1989-1992

K: Most, career, all-time

951 Eric Show, 1981-1990
802 Clay Kirby, 1969-1973
767 Ed Whitson, 1983-1991
677 Randy Jones, 1973-1980
613 BRUCE HURST, 1989-1992

Win pct: Highest, career, all-time

.598 BRUCE HURST, 1989-1992
.535 Eric Show, 1981-1990
.530 ANDY BENES, 1989-1992
.517 Ed Whitson, 1983-1991
.515 Dave Dravecky, 1982-1987

ERA: Lowest, career, all-time

3.12 Dave Dravecky, 1982-1987
3.22 BRUCE HURST, 1989-1992
3.30 Randy Jones, 1973-1980
3.59 Eric Show, 1981-1990
3.69 Ed Whitson, 1983-1991

Runs: Most, season

119 TONY GWYNN, 1987
107 TONY GWYNN, 1986
106 Alan Wiggins, 1984
104 BIP ROBERTS, 1990
104 DAVE WINFIELD, 1977

Hits: Most, season

218 TONY GWYNN, 1987
213 TONY GWYNN, 1984
211 TONY GWYNN, 1986
203 TONY GWYNN, 1989
197 TONY GWYNN, 1985

2B: Most, season

42 Terry Kennedy, 1982
36 Johnny Grubb, 1975
36 TONY GWYNN, 1987
36 BIP ROBERTS, 1990
34 Ollie Brown, 1970
34 Steve Garvey, 1985
34 Ruppert Jones, 1981
34 GARY SHEFFIELD, 1992

3B: Most, season

13 TONY GWYNN, 1987
12 Gene Richards, 1978
12 Gene Richards, 1981
11 Bill Almon, 1977
11 TONY GWYNN, 1991
11 Gene Richards, 1977

HR: Most, season

38 Nate Colbert, 1970
38 Nate Colbert, 1972
35 FRED McGRIFF, 1992
34 DAVE WINFIELD, 1979
33 GARY SHEFFIELD, 1992

RBI: Most, season

118 DAVE WINFIELD, 1979
115 JOE CARTER, 1990
111 Nate Colbert, 1972
106 FRED McGRIFF, 1991
104 FRED McGRIFF, 1992

SB: Most, season

70	Alan Wiggins, 1984
66	Alan Wiggins, 1983
61	Gene Richards, 1980
57	OZZIE SMITH, 1980
56	TONY GWYNN, 1987
56	Gene Richards, 1977

BB: Most, season

132	JACK CLARK, 1989
125	Gene Tenace, 1977
105	FRED McGRIFF, 1991
105	Gene Tenace, 1979
104	JACK CLARK, 1990

BA: Highest, season

.370	TONY GWYNN, 1987
.352	TONY GWYNN, 1984
.336	TONY GWYNN, 1989
.330	GARY SHEFFIELD, 1992
.329	TONY GWYNN, 1986

Slug avg: Highest, season

.580	GARY SHEFFIELD, 1992
.558	DAVE WINFIELD, 1979
.556	FRED McGRIFF, 1992
.543	Cito Gaston, 1970
.511	TONY GWYNN, 1987

Games started: Most, season

40	Randy Jones, 1976
39	Randy Jones, 1979
37	Steve Arlin, 1972
37	Gaylord Perry, 1978
36	Randy Jones, 1975
36	Randy Jones, 1978
36	Clay Kirby, 1971

Saves: Most, season

44	MARK DAVIS, 1989
38	RANDY MYERS, 1992
37	Rollie Fingers, 1978
35	Rollie Fingers, 1977
28	MARK DAVIS, 1988

Shutouts: Most, season

6	Randy Jones, 1975
6	Fred Norman, 1972
5	Randy Jones, 1976
4	Steve Arlin, 1971
4	BRUCE HURST, 1990
4	BRUCE HURST, 1992

Wins: Most, season

22	Randy Jones, 1976
21	Gaylord Perry, 1978
20	Randy Jones, 1975
18	Andy Hawkins, 1985
16	La Marr Hoyt, 1985
16	Tim Lollar, 1982
16	Eric Show, 1988
16	Ed Whitson, 1989

K: Most, season

231	Clay Kirby, 1971
185	Pat Dobson, 1970
179	BRUCE HURST, 1989
175	Clay Kirby, 1972
169	ANDY BENES, 1992

Win pct: Highest, season

.778	Gaylord Perry, 1978
.692	Andy Hawkins, 1985
.667	La Marr Hoyt, 1985
.652	BRUCE HURST, 1991
.640	Tim Lollar, 1982

ERA: Lowest, season

2.10	Dave Roberts, 1971
2.24	Randy Jones, 1975
2.60	Ed Whitson, 1990
2.66	Ed Whitson, 1989
2.69	BRUCE HURST, 1989

Most pinch-hit homers, season

5	Jerry Turner, 1978

Most pinch-hit, homers, career

9	Jerry Turner, 1974-1983

Most consecutive games, batting safely

34	Benito Santiago, 1987
25	Tony Gwynn, 1983

Most consecutive scoreless innings

30	Randy Jones, 1980

No hit games

None

ACTIVE PLAYERS in caps.

Houston Astros

Jeff Bagwell led the Astros with 96 RBI (sixth in the NL), 34 doubles, and 260 total bases.

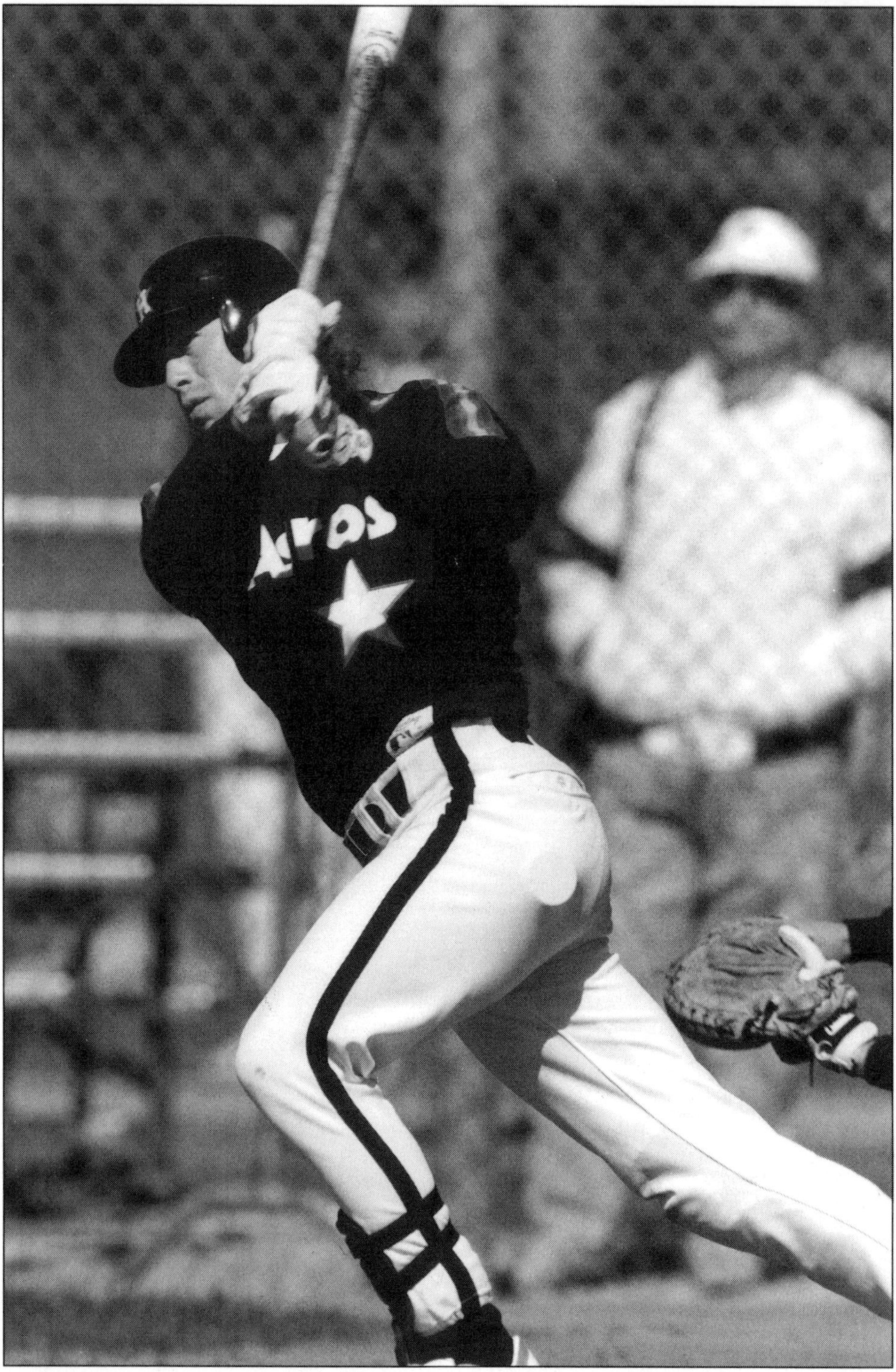

by Robert Deutsch, *USA TODAY*

1992 Astros: A surprisingly good year

The Astros entered 1992 in the second year of a massive rebuilding program. Having slashed payroll only a year earlier, the prospect of emerging as a serious contender for '93 looked far from promising. But the Astros' late-season push to finish the year at the .500 mark showed manager Art Howe that the plan was working.

From Aug. 11 to Sept 11, the Astros went 19-9, their best stretch since 1990 and the top mark in the NL. From Aug. 11 until the end of the season, they were 33-17. Most encouraging was a much-publicized 26-game road trip (necessitated by the Republican convention) that they survived with a respectable 12-14 record.

"Going into the season, I thought if we could get to 75 wins, we'd reach our goal," said manager Art Howe. "I honestly didn't believe we could get to .500, not when I looked at the schedule with the long road trip in August."

Craig Biggio moved from catcher to second base, and made the All-Star team in his first season at the new position. He played in every spring training game and all 162 regular-season games. Right fielder Eric Anthony emerged as the player the Astros had long envisioned. Although he hit only .239, he had 9 homers and 80 RBI. But the most unlikely performance was turned in by 35-year-old closer Doug Jones, who had fallen out of favor in Cleveland in 1991 and was signed by the Astros as a free agent. Jones threw 111.2 innings in relief, leading the team in wins (11) and compiling a club-record 36 saves. Said Howe: "Having him this season meant I didn't have to reach for the Maalox after the game."

The nucleus of the Astros offense enjoyed a second-straight strong campaign. First baseman Jeff Bagwell (18 HR, 96 RBI), center fielder Steve Finley (.292, 55 RBI, 44 steals), and Biggio (.277, 39 RBI, 38 steals) proved that the Astros' rebuilding program was taking off. Third baseman Ken Caminiti had a career year (.294, 13 HR, 62 RBI).

Other players were not as productive. Shortstop Andujar Cedeno hit just .173, spent two months in the minors, and finished the year with more strikeouts (71) than total bases (67). The Astros thought so much of catcher Eddie Taubensee that they surrendered Kenny Lofton to Cleveland in the off-season. But Taubensee failed to nail down the full-time catcher's job and also spent time in the minors. The pre-season Curt Schilling trade was also regrettable: He went 14-11 (2.35 ERA) as the Phillies' ace, while Jimmy Jones paced the Astros at 10-6 (4.07 ERA). After he won a 13-inning game on the next-to-last day of the season, Jones said, "There's probably not a guy in here who wants the season to end. Not when we're playing so well and things are coming together. I just wish this was May instead of October."

—by Pete Williams

1993 Astros: Preview

The Astros' '92 record was 16 games better than '91. Another 16-game increase, and the Astros will contend for the NL West pennant. But to see that kind of improvement for a second straight season, their pitching must improve. New owner Drayton McLane gave the Astros a much-needed financial boost, allowing them to sign free-agent Texans Doug Drabek and Greg Swindell. Add better years from Pete Harnisch and Mark Portugal, and another big season from closer Doug Jones, and the pressure is off their developing youngsters.

Craig Biggio and Eric Anthony also need to show their '92 seasons weren't anomalies. And the Astros are hoping young shortstop Andujar Cedeno and catcher Eddie Taubensee improve with the bat.

—by Rick Lawes

1992 Astros: Between the lines

▸**April 22:** No one expected the Houston Astros to take that "worst to first" thing quite so seriously—especially in April. Houston took sole possession of the top spot in the National League West after a 3-1, 12-inning win against San Francisco. All-Star Pete Harnisch, who was 3-0 lifetime against the Giants, gave up no runs in 6 1/3 innings, but also got only one in support. Chris Jones homered in the 12th with Eric Yelding aboard for the Houston win.

▸**April 29:** Darryl Kile went eight innings, yielding one run on five hits and striking out 11 batters.

▸**April 30:** Rafael Ramirez—who had just three home runs in 707 at-bats over three years, hit a game-tying eighth-inning homer off Sid Fernandez. ***Quote of the day:*** Ramirez—"I didn't hit it good."

▸**May 3:** The surprising Astros limited the Pirates to just four hits, and won 1-0 on Steve Finley's eighth-inning home run. Butch Henry pitched seven scoreless innings for Houston.

▸**May 10:** The Astros stopped a nine-game road losing streak with a 6-4 victory in 10 innings at Pittsburgh, handing the Pirates just their third loss in 15 home games. Jeff Bagwell hit a game-tying pinch-hit homer in the eighth inning and a go-ahead solo shot in the 10th.

▸**May 23:** Benny Distefano was 4-for-4 with two RBI.

▸**June 3:** Doug Jones struck out two of the three batters he faced, recording his 13th save in 16 chances.

▸**June 13:** Astros' reliever Doug Jones worked an inning and a third, retiring all four batters on strikeouts in earning his 15th save.

▸**June 14:** Pete Incaviglia produced almost as much in one game—two homers and a career-high seven RBI—as he had in his previous 50 games (two homers and 15 RBI).

▸**June 16:** Pitcher Brian Williams and catcher Scooter Tucker, called up the previous weekend, had impressive outings. Williams pitched six shutout innings for his first major league victory. Tucker had his first major league hits (3-for-3, two RBI), and was 1-for-2 in throwing out base-stealers.

▸**June 17:** The Astros entered play with an NL-low of 36 errors, but they committed two in the second inning and added another in the sixth, leading to five unearned runs.

▸**June 21:** Butch Henry won for the first time since May 25. Pete Incaviglia helped out—he went 3-for-4 with a two-run homer.

▸**June 24:** Houston's Pete Harnisch and coach Ed Ott, and Cincinnati's Glenn Braggs and Rob Dibble, were ejected after a bench-clearing incident in the fifth. The free-for-all held up play for eight minutes. Harnisch yielded a three-run dinger to Hal Morris, and threw the next pitch behind Reggie Sanders' head. ***Quote of the day:*** Manager Art Howe—"There would have been no fight if Braggs and Dibble hadn't charged out there. Dibble came out full bore. The guy's a maniac."

▸**July 1:** Scott Servais successfully blocked the plate against the Reds' hard-charging Tom Browning. Both players were left sprawled on the ground after Servais tagged out the Cincinnati pitcher, and both players left the game with knee injuries: Browning immediately, Servais two innings later.

▸**July 27:** Eric Anthony's 11th-inning grand slam opened Houston's longest road trip in club history. The Astros' 26-game trek was scheduled to allow the Republicans to play their games in the Astrodome.

▸**August 5:** Steve Finley stole his 29th base of the year.

▸**August 9:** Craig Biggio homered on the first pitch of the game.

▸**August 25:** Two big returns—the Astros from their marathon 26-game road trip along with Andujar Cedeno from the minor leagues—met with mixed success. Cedeno became the first Astro to hit for the cycle since Bob Watson in 1977, but the finally-home team lost the game to visiting St. Louis, 5-3, in 13 innings.

▸**August 26:** Another long day for the Astros: Luis Gonzalez was 3-for-5 with a two-run homer and Eddie Taubensee singled in the game-winner in the 10th as the Astros beat St. Louis 6-5 in 10 innings.

▸**August 28:** Pete Harnisch fanned a season-best 10 batters, including five in a row at one point, to beat Montreal 8-1. Harnisch, who was traded to the Astros from Baltimore for oft-injured slugger Glenn Davis, was aided by co-tradee Steve Finley, who was 4-for-5 with three RBI. (The third player the Orioles gave up for Davis was pitcher Curt Schilling, who became one of Philadelphia's aces.)

▸**September 2:** Pete Incaviglia put Philadelphia's Terry Mulholland into the loss column, two innings after putting him into the record book. Incaviglia was the victim when Mulholland recorded his 14th pickoff, the most by any pitcher in the three years the record has been kept. But Incaviglia hit a check-swing double in the eighth to drive in the winning run for the Astros.

▸**September 15:** Jeff Bagwell's three-run homer in the 11th inning gave the Astros a 9-6 win against San Francisco, and capped the first five-hit game for a Houston player since Billy Hatcher did it in 1988.

▸**October 4:** The Astros finished the season with the only three National Leaguers who played in all 162 games: Craig Biggio, Steve Finley, and Jeff Bagwell. The three earned other league honors as well. Craig Biggio was fourth in the NL with 94 walks; Steve Finley was second in the NL with 13 triples, third in the NL with 44 stolen bases, and seventh in the NL with 177 hits; and Jeff Bagwell was sixth in the NL with 96 RBI. The Astros finished fourth in the NL West with a final record of exactly .500: 81 wins and 81 losses.

—by Jeanie Chung, John Hunt, Deron Snyder, and Lisa Winston.

Team directory

▸**Owner:** Drayton McLane Jr.
▸**General Manager:** Bill Wood
▸**Ballpark:**
Houston Astrodome
8400 Kirby Dr., Houston, Texas
713-799-9500
Capacity 54,816
Parking for 26,000 cars; $4
Public transportation by bus
Wheelchair section and ramps
▸**Team publications:**
Astros Magazine, Astros Media Guide, Liftoff
713-799-9600
▸**TV, radio broadcast stations:**
KPRC 950 AM, KTXH Channel 20, Home Sports Entertainment Cable
▸**Camps and/or clinics:**
Astros Youth Clinics, during the season, 713-799-9500
▸**Spring Training:**
Osceola County Stadium
Kissimmee, Fla.
Capacity 5,130
407-933-5400

HOUSTON ASTROS 1992 final stats

Batting	AVG	SLG	OB	G	AB	R	H	TB	2B	3B	HR	RBI	BB	SO	SB	CS	E
Walling	.333	.333	.333	3	3	1	1	1	0	0	0	0	0	0	0	0	0
Caminiti	.294	.441	.350	135	506	68	149	223	31	2	13	62	44	68	10	4	11
Finley	.292	.407	.355	162	607	84	177	247	29	13	5	55	58	63	44	9	3
Biggio	.277	.369	.378	162	613	96	170	226	32	3	6	39	94	95	38	15	12
Bagwell	.273	.444	.368	162	586	87	160	260	34	6	18	96	84	97	10	6	7
Incaviglia	.266	.430	.319	113	349	31	93	150	22	1	11	44	25	99	2	2	6
Riles	.262	.328	.281	39	61	5	16	20	1	0	1	4	2	11	1	0	1
Ramirez	.250	.301	.283	73	176	17	44	53	6	0	1	13	7	24	0	0	7
Simms	.250	.417	.333	15	24	1	6	10	1	0	1	3	2	9	0	0	0
Yelding	.250	.250	.250	9	8	1	2	2	0	0	0	0	0	3	0	0	0
Gonzalez	.243	.385	.289	122	387	40	94	149	19	3	10	55	24	52	7	7	2
Servais	.239	.283	.294	77	205	12	49	58	9	0	0	15	11	25	0	0	2
Anthony	.239	.407	.298	137	440	45	105	179	15	1	19	80	38	98	5	4	5
Distefano	.233	.300	.303	52	60	4	14	18	0	2	0	7	5	14	0	0	0
Taubensee	.222	.323	.299	104	297	23	66	96	15	0	5	28	31	78	2	1	5
Candaele	.213	.266	.269	135	320	19	68	85	12	1	1	18	24	36	7	1	11
Guerrero	.200	.288	.261	79	125	8	25	36	4	2	1	14	10	32	1	0	2
C.Jones	.190	.302	.271	54	63	7	12	19	2	1	1	4	7	21	3	0	2
Young	.184	.224	.279	74	76	14	14	17	1	1	0	4	10	11	6	2	2
Cedeno	.173	.277	.232	71	220	15	38	61	13	2	2	13	14	71	2	0	11
Tucker	.120	.140	.200	20	50	5	6	7	1	0	0	3	3	13	1	1	2
Rhodes	.000	.000	.000	5	4	0	0	0	0	0	0	0	0	2	0	0	0

Pitching	W-L	ERA	G	GS	CG	GF	Sho	SV	IP	H	R	ER	HR	BB	SO
D.Jones	11-8	1.85	80	0	0	70	0	36	111.2	96	29	23	5	17	93
Hernandez	9-1	2.11	77	0	0	25	0	7	111	81	31	26	5	42	96
Boever	3-6	2.51	81	0	0	26	0	2	111.1	103	38	31	3	45	67
Portugal	6-3	2.66	18	16	1	0	1	0	101.1	76	32	30	7	41	62
Harnisch	9-10	3.70	34	34	0	0	0	0	206.2	182	92	85	18	64	164
Williams	7-6	3.92	16	16	0	0	0	0	96.1	92	44	42	10	42	54
Kile	5-10	3.95	22	22	2	0	0	0	125.1	124	61	55	8	63	90
Blair	5-7	4.00	29	8	0	1	0	0	78.2	74	47	35	5	25	48
Henry	6-9	4.02	28	28	2	0	1	0	165.2	185	81	74	16	41	96
Murphy	3-1	4.04	59	0	0	6	0	0	55.2	56	28	25	2	21	42
J.Jones	10-6	4.07	25	23	0	1	0	0	139.1	135	64	63	13	39	69
Osuna	6-3	4.23	66	0	0	17	0	0	61.2	52	29	29	8	38	37
Scheid	0-1	6.00	7	1	0	3	0	0	12	14	8	8	2	6	8
Reynolds	1-3	7.11	8	5	0	0	0	0	25.1	42	22	20	2	6	10
Mallicoat	0-0	7.23	23	0	0	6	0	0	23.2	26	19	19	2	19	20
Bowen	0-7	10.96	11	9	0	2	0	0	33.2	48	43	41	8	30	22

1993 preliminary roster

PITCHERS (19)
Joe Boever
Doug Drabek
Tom Edens
Jason Grimsley
Pete Harnisch
Xavier Hernandez
Bobby Hurta
Doug Jones
Jimmy Jones
Todd Jones
Jeff Juden
Darryl Kile
Rob Mallicoat
Al Osuna
Mark Portugal
Shane Reynolds
Rich Scheid
Greg Swindell
Brian Williams

CATCHERS (4)
Tony Eusebio
Scott Servais
Eddie Taubensee
Scooter Tucker

INFIELDERS (7)
Jeff Bagwell
Craig Biggio
Ken Caminiti
Casey Candaele
Andujar Cedeno
Juan Guerrero
Orlando Miller

OUTFIELDERS (9)
Willie Ansley
Eric Anthony
Steve Finley
Luis Gonzalez
Chris Hatcher
Brian Hunter
Gary Mota
Karl Rhodes
Mike Simms

Games played by position

Player	G	C	1B	2B	3B	SS	OF
ANTHONY,E	137	0	0	0	0	0	115
BAGWELL,J	162	0	159	0	0	0	0
BIGGIO,C	162	0	0	161	0	0	0
CAMINITI,K	135	0	0	0	129	0	0
CANDAELE,C	135	0	0	9	29	65	21
CEDENO,A	71	0	0	0	0	70	0
DISTEFANO,B	52	0	6	0	0	0	12
FINLEY,S	162	0	0	0	0	0	160
GONZALEZ,L	122	0	0	0	0	0	111
GUERRERO,J	79	0	0	2	12	19	3
INCAVIGLIA,P	113	0	0	0	0	0	98
JONES,JI	54	0	0	0	0	0	43
RAMIREZ,R	73	0	0	0	1	57	0
RHODES,K	5	0	0	0	0	0	1
RILES,E	39	0	4	2	5	6	0
SERVAIS,S	77	73	0	0	0	0	0
SIMMS,M	15	0	1	0	0	0	9
TAUBENSEE,E	104	103	0	0	0	0	0
TUCKER,E	20	19	0	0	0	0	0
WALLING,D	3	0	0	0	0	0	0
YELDING,E	9	0	0	0	0	2	2
YOUNG,G	74	0	0	0	0	0	57

Sick call: 1992 DL report

Player	Days on the DL
Caminiti, Ken	22
Gonzalez, Luis	15
Jones, Jimmy	36
Murphy, Rob	19
Portugal, Mark*	96
Ramirez, Rafael	23
Walling, Denny	177
Young, Gerald	80

** On Disabled List twice during 1992 season (not counting transfers from one DL to another).*

Minor league report

Class AAA — Tucson finished 70-74, 3rd in the 1st half of the Pacific Coast League Southern Division and 2nd in the 2nd half. 2B Trent Hubbard had 34 SB. RHP Shane Reynolds was 9-8 with a 3.68 ERA. RHP Mike Capel had 18 saves. RHP Jeff Juden had 120 K **Class AA:** Jackson finished 61-74, 3rd in the Texas League Eastern Division in the 1st half and last in the 2nd half. C Tony Eusebio hit .307 with 5 HR and 44 RBI. C Scott Makarewicz hit .287 with 7 HR and 39 RBI. RHP Dean Hartgreaves was 9-6 with a 2.76 ERA. RHP Todd Jones had 25 saves. **Class A:** Osceola finished 72-62, 1st in the 1st half of the Florida State League Central Division and 3rd in the 2nd half. The team lost to Baseball City in the 2nd round of the playoffs. OF Brian Hunter hit .299 with 62 RBI and 39 SB. 2B James Mouton led the league with 50 SB. OF Chris Hatcher had 17 HR. LHP Chris Hill led the league with 16 wins. RHP James Dougherty set a franchise record with 31 saves. Burlington finished 47-89, last in both halves of the Midwest League Southern Division. OF Buck McNabb had 56 SB. RHP Jim Waring was 11-7 with a 2.21 ERA and walked 19 in 122 IP. OF Jermaine Swinton had 13 HR. Asheville finished 74-66, 4th in both halves of the Sally League Northern Division. OF Gary Mota had 24 HR and 90 RBI. OF Jimmy White hit .296 with 61 RBI. LHP Alvin Morman had 15 saves. Auburn finished 32-41, 3rd in the New York-Penn League Pinckney Division. 2B Donovan Mitchell hit .291 with 1 HR and 18 RBI. He shared the league lead with 44 runs. The club was last in pitching at 4.40. Astros finished 27-33, 3rd in the Gulf Coast League Central Division. OF Richard Hidalgo hit .310 with 27 RBI. RHP Victor Valdez was 5-2 with a 1.28 ERA. He walked just 8 in 63 IP.

Tops in the organization

BATTING LEADERS	Club	Avg.	G	AB	R	H	HR	RBI
Trent Hubbard	Tcn	.310	115	420	69	130	2	33
Gary Cooper	Tcn	.300	127	464	66	139	9	73
Brian Hunter	Osc	.299	131	489	62	146	1	62
Jimmy White	Ash	.296	126	453	51	134	3	61
Roberto Petagine	Jck	.294	107	378	60	111	11	61

HOME RUNS		
Gary Mota	Ash	24
Eddie Ramos	Ash	17
Chris Hatcher	Osc	17
Jermaine Swinton	Bur	13
Lance Madsen	Jck	13

WINS		
Chris Hill	Osc	16
Chris White	Ash	13
Jim Waring	Ash	12
Donne Wall	Tcn	12
Tom Anderson	Ash	11

RBI		
Gary Mota	Ash	90
Mike Simms	Tcn	75
Gary Cooper	Tcn	73
Chris Hatcher	Osc	68
Dennis Colon	Bur	63

SAVES		
James Dougherty	Osc	31
Todd Jones	Tcn	25
Mike Capel	Tcn	18
Alvin Morman	Ash	15
Matt Turner	Tcn	14

STOLEN BASES		
Buck McNabb	Bur	56
James Mouton	Osc	51
Brian Hunter	Osc	39
Trent Hubbard	Tcn	34
Several players tied		27

STRIKEOUTS		
Donne Wall	Tcn	131
Chris Hill	Osc	126
Jim Waring	Ash	124
Jeff Juden	Tcn	120
Chuck Smith	Ash	117

PITCHING LEADERS	Club	W-L	ERA	IP	H	BB	SO
Jim Waring	Ash	12-8	1.96	142	111	23	124
Jim Lewis	Jck	8-6	2.50	151	118	64	108
Doug Ketchen	Osc	8-3	2.79	116	121	28	72
Chris Hill	Osc	16-7	2.93	160	154	58	126
Donne Wall	Tcn	12-7	3.20	163	162	35	131

Houston (1962-1992)

Runs: Most, career, all-time

890 Cesar Cedeno, 1970-1981
871 Jose Cruz, 1975-1987
829 Jim Wynn, 1963-1973
676 Terry Puhl, 1977-1990
640 Bob Watson, 1966-1979

Hits: Most, career, all-time

1937 Jose Cruz, 1975-1987
1659 Cesar Cedeno, 1970-1981
1448 Bob Watson, 1966-1979
1357 Terry Puhl, 1977-1990
1291 Jim Wynn, 1963-1973

2B: Most, career, all-time

343 Cesar Cedeno, 1970-1981
335 Jose Cruz, 1975-1987
241 Bob Watson, 1966-1979
228 Jim Wynn, 1963-1973
226 Terry Puhl, 1977-1990

3B: Most, career, all-time

80 Jose Cruz, 1975-1987
63 Joe Morgan, 1963-1980
62 Roger Metzger, 1971-1978
56 Terry Puhl, 1977-1990
55 Cesar Cedeno, 1970-1981
55 Craig Reynolds, 1979-1989

HR: Most, career, all-time

223 Jim Wynn, 1963-1973
166 GLENN DAVIS, 1984-1990
163 Cesar Cedeno, 1970-1981
139 Bob Watson, 1966-1979
138 Jose Cruz, 1975-1987

RBI: Most, career, all-time

942 Jose Cruz, 1975-1987
782 Bob Watson, 1966-1979
778 Cesar Cedeno, 1970-1981
719 Jim Wynn, 1963-1973
600 Doug Rader, 1967-1975

SB: Most, career, all-time

487 Cesar Cedeno, 1970-1981
288 Jose Cruz, 1975-1987
219 Joe Morgan, 1963-1980
217 Terry Puhl, 1977-1990
191 Enos Cabell, 1975-1985
191 BILL DORAN, 1982-1990

BB: Most, career, all-time

847 Jim Wynn, 1963-1973
730 Jose Cruz, 1975-1987
678 Joe Morgan, 1963-1980
585 BILL DORAN, 1982-1990
534 Cesar Cedeno, 1970-1981

BA: Highest, career, all-time

.297 Bob Watson, 1966-1979
.292 Jose Cruz, 1975-1987
.289 Cesar Cedeno, 1970-1981
.282 Jesus Alou, 1969-1979
.281 Enos Cabell, 1975-1985

Slug avg: Highest, career, all-time

.483 GLENN DAVIS, 1984-1990
.454 Cesar Cedeno, 1970-1981
.445 Jim Wynn, 1963-1973
.444 Bob Watson, 1966-1979
.429 Jose Cruz, 1975-1987

Games started: Most, career, all-time

320 Larry Dierker, 1964-1976
301 Joe Niekro, 1975-1985
282 NOLAN RYAN, 1980-1988
267 Bob Knepper, 1981-1989
259 Mike Scott, 1983-1991

Saves: Most, career, all-time

199 DAVE SMITH, 1980-1990
76 Fred Gladding, 1968-1973
72 Joe Sambito, 1976-1984
50 Ken Forsch, 1970-1980
43 FRANK DiPINO, 1982-1986

Shutouts: Most, career, all-time

25 Larry Dierker, 1964-1976
21 Joe Niekro, 1975-1985
21 Mike Scott, 1983-1991
20 Don Wilson, 1966-1974
19 J.R. Richard, 1971-1980

Wins: Most, career, all-time

144 Joe Niekro, 1975-1985
137 Larry Dierker, 1964-1976
110 Mike Scott, 1983-1991
107 J.R. Richard, 1971-1980
106 NOLAN RYAN, 1980-1988

K: Most, career, all-time

1866 NOLAN RYAN, 1980-1988
1493 J.R. Richard, 1971-1980
1487 Larry Dierker, 1964-1976
1318 Mike Scott, 1983-1991
1283 Don Wilson, 1966-1974

Win pct: Highest, career, all-time

.609 Jim Ray, 1965-1973
.601 J.R. Richard, 1971-1980
.576 Mike Scott, 1983-1991
.571 DANNY DARWIN, 1986-1990
.554 Joe Niekro, 1975-1985

ERA: Lowest, career, all-time

2.53 DAVE SMITH, 1980-1990
3.13 NOLAN RYAN, 1980-1988
3.15 Don Wilson, 1966-1974
3.15 J.R. Richard, 1971-1980
3.18 Ken Forsch, 1970-1980

Runs: Most, season

117 Jim Wynn, 1972
113 Jim Wynn, 1969
103 Cesar Cedeno, 1972
102 Joe Morgan, 1970
102 Jim Wynn, 1967

Hits: Most, season

195 Enos Cabell, 1978
189 Jose Cruz, 1983
187 Jose Cruz, 1984
185 Jose Cruz, 1980
185 Greg Gross, 1974

2B: Most, season

44 Rusty Staub, 1967
40 Cesar Cedeno, 1971
39 Cesar Cedeno, 1972
38 Bob Watson, 1977
37 Rusty Staub, 1968

3B: Most, season

14 Roger Metzger, 1973
13 Jose Cruz, 1984
13 STEVE FINLEY, 1992
12 Joe Morgan, 1965
11 BILL DORAN, 1984
11 Roger Metzger, 1971
11 Joe Morgan, 1967
11 Joe Morgan, 1971
11 Craig Reynolds, 1984

HR: Most, season

37 Jim Wynn, 1967
34 GLENN DAVIS, 1989
33 Jim Wynn, 1969
31 GLENN DAVIS, 1986
30 GLENN DAVIS, 1988

RBI: Most, season

110 Bob Watson, 1977
107 Jim Wynn, 1967
105 Lee May, 1973
102 Cesar Cedeno, 1974
102 Bob Watson, 1976

ACTIVE PLAYERS in caps.

SB: Most, season

65	GERALD YOUNG, 1988
64	ERIC YELDING, 1990
61	Cesar Cedeno, 1977
58	Cesar Cedeno, 1976
57	Cesar Cedeno, 1974

BB: Most, season

148	Jim Wynn, 1969
110	Joe Morgan, 1969
106	Jim Wynn, 1970
103	Jim Wynn, 1972
102	Joe Morgan, 1970

BA: Highest, season

.333	Rusty Staub, 1967
.324	Bob Watson, 1975
.320	Cesar Cedeno, 1972
.320	Cesar Cedeno, 1973
.318	Jose Cruz, 1983

Slug avg: Highest, season

.537	Cesar Cedeno, 1973
.537	Cesar Cedeno, 1972
.507	Jim Wynn, 1969
.498	Bob Watson, 1977
.495	Jim Wynn, 1967

Games started: Most, season

40	Jerry Reuss, 1973
39	J.R. Richard, 1976
38	Bob Knepper, 1986
38	Joe Niekro, 1979
38	Joe Niekro, 1983
38	Joe Niekro, 1984
38	J.R. Richard, 1979

Saves: Most, season

36	DOUG JONES, 1992
33	DAVE SMITH, 1986
29	Fred Gladding, 1969
27	DAVE SMITH, 1985
27	DAVE SMITH, 1988

Shutouts: Most, season

6	Dave Roberts, 1973
5	Larry Dierker, 1972
5	Bob Knepper, 1981
5	Bob Knepper, 1986
5	Joe Niekro, 1979
5	Joe Niekro, 1982
5	Mike Scott, 1986
5	Mike Scott, 1988

Wins: Most, season

21	Joe Niekro, 1979
20	Larry Dierker, 1969
20	Joe Niekro, 1980
20	J.R. Richard, 1976
20	Mike Scott, 1989

K: Most, season

313	J.R. Richard, 1979
306	Mike Scott, 1986
303	J.R. Richard, 1978
270	NOLAN RYAN, 1987
245	NOLAN RYAN, 1982

Win pct: Highest, season

.692	Mike Scott, 1985
.667	Mike Scott, 1989
.656	Joe Niekro, 1979
.652	Larry Dierker, 1972
.643	Mike Scott, 1986

ERA: Lowest, season

2.18	Bob Knepper, 1981
2.21	DANNY DARWIN, 1990
2.22	Mike Cuellar, 1966
2.22	Mike Scott, 1986
2.33	Larry Dierker, 1969

Most pinch-hit homers, season

5	Cliff Johnson, 1974

Most pinch-hit, homers, career

8	Cliff Johnson, 1972-1977

Most consecutive games, batting safely

23	Art Howe, 1981
22	Cesar Cedeno, 1977

Most consecutive scoreless innings

31	J. R. Richard, 1980

No hit games

Don Nottebart, Hou vs Phi NL, 4-1; May 17, 1963.

Ken T. Johnson, Hou vs Cin NL, 0-1; April 23, 1964 (lost the game).

Don Wilson, Hou vs Atl NL, 2-0; June 18, 1967.

Don Wilson, Hou at Cin NL, 4-0; May 1, 1969.

Larry Dierker, Hou vs Mon NL, 6-0; July 9, 1976.

Ken Forsch, Hou vs AtL NL, 6-0; April 7, 1979.

Nolan Ryan, Hou vs LA NL, 5-0; September 26, 1981.

Mike Scott, Hou vs SF NL, 2-0; September 25, 1986.

San Francisco Giants

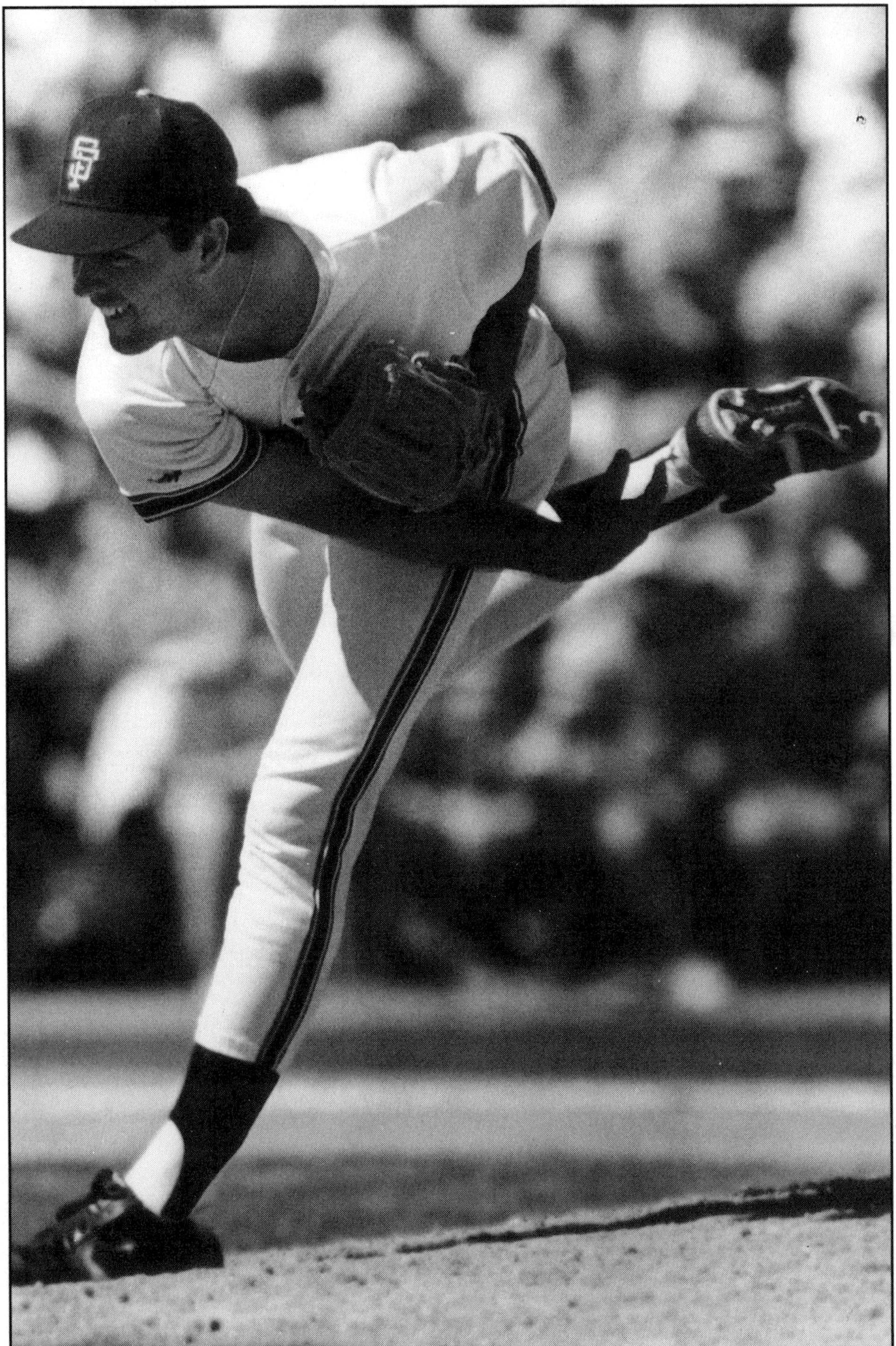

by Robert Hanashiro, *USA TODAY*

Starter John Burkett led the Giants in wins (13), strikeouts (107), and innings pitched (189.2).

1992 Giants: The sale kept them in a fog

The Giants received a three-minute standing ovation when they took the field for their final home game on Sept. 27—not that they did anything to deserve it. They finished fifth in the NL West with a 72-90 record, 26 games behind Atlanta. But the fans had come to beg them to stay. They got their wish two months later when NL owners voted 9-4 to reject the sale of the Giants to a group of investors in St. Petersburg, Fla.

A cloud of uncertainty had loomed over the Giants since owner Bob Lurie announced the sale Aug. 7. The players seemed to be in a fog while the negotiations dragged on. They were in first place June 1, but they stumbled to a 45-67 finish. The swoon began the day after voters in nearby San Jose defeated a stadium referendum—the Giants' fourth Bay Area rejection.

Then-GM Al Rosen blasted the team publicly: "I'm embarrassed because I put the team together. I'm embarrassed because I have to watch it."

On the field, there were a few highlights. Right-hander Bill Swift (10-4), who came from Seattle in the Kevin Mitchell trade, won the league ERA title. His 2.08 mark was the lowest in the NL since 1985. He got off to a 6-0 start with three complete games, but missed six weeks (shoulder problems).

Right-hander John Burkett was 13-9, but lefty Bud Black dipped to 10-12; no other pitcher won more than eight games. Scott Garrelts missed the season following elbow surgery.

Reliever Dave Righetti was tried as a starter, but he went back to the bullpen after four unsuccessful starts. Right-hander Rod Beck emerged as a dependable closer with 17 saves and a 1.76 ERA. Right-hander Jeff Brantley went 3-0 (0.44 ERA) in four starts in September.

The team hit just .244 with 105 homers, and scored only 574 runs—the third-lowest total since they moved to California in 1958. Will Clark hit a team-best .300, but finished with 16 homers and 73 RBI, his lowest totals since his rookie year. Third baseman Matt Williams battled injuries and hit just .227, but did hit 20 homers and 66 RBI. Backup Cory Snyder had 14 homers and 57 RBI in 124 games. Outfielder Willie McGee hit .297.

—by Bill Koenig

1993 Giants: Preview

After the Giants found out where they would play in '93, the question of who would be there became the focus of attention. One of the first casualties was manager Roger Craig but almost as quickly Barry Bonds was in town. The ink wasn't even wet yet on the sale of the team before it had a new superstar, new general manager, and new manager. And after a 90-loss season, it's obvious the Giants still need help in a number of places; the most pressing is pitching. Bill Swift's unusual muscle injury makes his ability to throw on a regular basis uncertain. He missed six weeks in '92. John Burkett was steady (13-9, 3.84 ERA), and Bud Black will probably fill another spot, but he faltered at the end of the season with a staggering 9.00 ERA the last month.

Craig said the Giants would be rebuilding for at least two years if a free agent pitcher was not signed. With new ownership, that isn't likely.

Royce Clayton has to prove that he's the Giants' future at shortstop or he might get shipped out in a trade, and streaky outfielder Willie McGee will probably be with his fifth organization next year after going unprotected but escaping the expansion draft.

The Giants lost pitcher Pat Rapp and catcher Steve Decker to the Marlins, and pitcher Steve Reed to the Rockies.

—by Alvin Reid

1992 Giants: Between the lines

▸**May 7:** Bill Swift became the league's first six-game winner, and lowered his league-leading ERA to 1.29 with his second shutout. He cruised the distance in two hours and four minutes. ***Quote of the day:*** Manager Roger Craig—"He pitched so fast, our plane isn't here yet."

▸**May 12:** Swift kept his perfect (6-0) record intact—but it came via a no-decision rather than a win. ***Quote of the day:*** Will Clark, on unruly fans at Veterans Stadium—"They were all over me all night . . . They talked about my mother, my sister. Hey, anyone who would boo Mike Schmidt, something has to be wrong."

▸**May 20:** Matt Williams was on one of his trademark hot streaks: .354 (17-for-48) in his last 14 games, with five home runs and 12 RBI.

▸**June 4:** Earlier in the day, San Jose voters had told the Giants to stay in San Francisco (by rejecting a plan to build a new stadium in San Jose). To add insult to injury, Giants' pitchers took a 12-6 beating from the Astros at Candlestick—with just 8,850 Giants' faithful in attendance. ***Quote of the day:*** Roger Craig, after a black cat got loose on the field and scurried into the Giants' dugout—"The cat had better control than my pitchers."

▸**June 6:** Cory Snyder had a career high in RBI, with seven, stroking a single, a pair of doubles and a two-run homer. He raised his average to .300 and was 12-for-19 with five extra-base hits and 10 RBI in his last five games.

▸**June 7:** Kirt Manwaring connected for his second career homer, the first since Sept. 19, 1988 (539 at-bats).

▸**June 14:** Pitcher Dave Burba collected his first major league hit.

▸**June 16:** Non-roster invitee Cory Snyder (RBI double and two solo homers) was paying big dividends as the Giants' cleanup hitter. He hit .454 (25-for-55) in the last 14 games, and was second on the team in homers (7) and RBI (28). ***Quote of the day:*** Snyder—"I'm not out to prove anybody wrong. I just want to play baseball."

▸**June 18:** Basebrawl: The fourth-inning fight between the Giants and the Padres—precipitated by Trevor Wilson plunking Fred McGriff on the first pitch after Gary Sheffield's grand slam—included a rare occurrence in most bench-clearing incidents: Players actually threw real punches. McGriff suffered strained muscles in his left rib cage and Sheffield a strained left shoulder. Wilson had an assortment of cuts and bruises on his face.

▸**June 25:** San Francisco was shut out for the third consecutive game, having scored just one run in the last 43 innings. ***Quote of the day:*** Batting coach Dusty Baker—"I think everyone's trying too hard to hit five-and six-run homers."

▸**June 26:** Cory Snyder, perhaps the biggest bright spot for the Giants in 1992, saved his team from a black mark in the record book. With Craig Lefferts pitching a no-hitter in the seventh, it appeared San Francisco would be shut out for the fourth game in a row—which would tie a major league record. Snyder homered, a 434-foot shot to the second deck, putting the Giants on the board, but they still dropped their fourth game in a row.

▸**June 29:** The game was a rainout, the 23rd in Candlestick Park's history and the first since Sept. 16, 1989, when the Giants-Padres game was postponed. The last time a Giants' home game in June was rained out was June 9, 1972 (vs. Chicago).

▸**July 1** ***Milestone:*** Bud Black earned his 100th career victory.

▸**July 2:** Will Clark stole his seventh and eighth bases of the year. His career best for steals in a season was nine, in 1988.

▸**July 12:** Montreal hit 19 ground-ball outs against Billy Swift—including four double plays—the Giants' outfield didn't record a single out.

▸**July 17:** Swift (7-2) and Bud Black (8-2) were fourth and fifth in the NL in winning percentage. The rest of the Giants' staff had a 29-41 record.

▸**July 24:** The Giants lost, 8-4, at Veterans Stadium—their 21st loss of 26 games away from Candlestick.

▸**July 25:** Willie McGee singled, doubled and homered to drive in as many runs (three) in the 6-2 victory over Philadelphia as he had in his previous 46 games.

▸**July 27:** Bud Black was 7-0 with a 1.29 ERA in nine Candlestick starts—the best home ERA in the National League.

▸**July 31:** Craig Colbert lined a bases-loaded single to cap a two-run ninth-inning rally, giving the Giants a 4-3 victory over the Braves to boot them out of first place.

▸**August 4:** John Burkett gave up a homer to Padre Gary Sheffield that was calculated at 468 feet. Nearly everyone on both teams disputed the distance, claiming it was a gross exaggeration. ***Quote of the day:*** Burkett—"If you ask me, I'd rather give up a home run that goes out of the entire stadium than give up one that scrapes the back of the fence."

▸**August 7:** Sold! The Giants announced that the team had been sold to Tampa Bay investors—reportedly for $110 million—and would move to St. Petersburg for the 1993 season pending approval of the sale and the move. San Francisco mayor Frank Jordan vowed not to let the Giants move without a fight.

▸**August 8:** The last 4,000 tickets for what could be the Giants' final Fan Appreciation Day at Candlestick Park were sold within a few hours. It was the Giants' first sellout since Game Four of the 1989 World Series.

▸**August 9:** Tommy Lasorda denied a report that he was prepared to end his 43-year association with the Dodgers to become the St. Petersburg Giants' manager in 1993.

▸**August 12:** During a pitching change at Candlestick, five youths snuck onto the field and paraded with a sign from foul line to foul line: "PLEASE DON'T GO." Will Clark was upset about the lack of response from the stadium's security force. ***Quote of the day:*** Clark—"I was just hoping they wouldn't come near me. I'd have punched one of them."

▸**August 16 *Quote of the day:*** Robby Thompson, trying on his new Tampa Bay Giants' cap—"You build for the future, wherever that might be."

▸**October 4:** The Giants finished fifth in the NL West. Billy Swift had the best ERA in the league (2.08) and Will Clark was second in the NL with 40 doubles.

—by Jeanie Chung, John Hunt, Deron Snyder, and Lisa Winston.

Team directory

▸**Owner:** Peter Magowan

▸**General Manager:** Bob Quinn

▸**Ballpark:**
Candlestick Park
Jamestown Avenue and Harney Way,
San Francisco, Calif.
415-467-8000
Capacity 62,000
Parking for 30,400 cars; $4-$5
Public transportation available
Family and wheelchair sections,
ramps, battery charger plug-ins for
wheelchairs, designated handicapped
pick-up and drop-off sights

▸**Team publications:**
Giants Magazine
415-468-3700, ext. 478

▸**TV, radio broadcast stations:**
KNBR 680 AM, KTVU Channel 2,
KLOK 1170 AM (Spanish),
SportsChannel

▸**Camps and/or clinics:**
Rob Andrews Baseball, June and July,
510-935-3505

▸**Spring Training:**
Scottsdale Stadium
Scottsdale, Ariz.
Capacity 7,500 (plus 2,500 on outfield
grass)
800-944-SFGIANTS

SAN FRANCISCO GIANTS 1992 final stats

Batting	AVG	SLG	OB	G	AB	R	H	TB	2B	3B	HR	RBI	BB	SO	SB	CS	E
Clark	.300	.476	.384	144	513	69	154	244	40	1	16	73	73	82	12	7	10
McGee	.297	.354	.339	138	474	56	141	168	20	2	1	36	29	88	13	4	6
Felder	.286	.382	.330	145	322	44	92	123	13	3	4	23	21	29	14	4	1
Snyder	.269	.444	.311	124	390	48	105	173	22	2	14	57	23	96	4	4	6
Thompson	.260	.415	.333	128	443	54	115	184	25	1	14	49	43	75	5	9	15
Hosey	.250	.321	.241	21	56	6	14	18	1	0	1	6	0	15	1	1	1
Manwaring	.244	.335	.311	109	349	24	85	117	10	5	4	26	29	42	2	1	4
James	.242	.375	.285	111	248	25	60	93	10	4	5	32	14	45	2	3	3
Uribe	.241	.346	.299	66	162	24	39	56	9	1	2	13	14	25	2	2	7
Leonard	.234	.383	.331	55	128	13	30	49	7	0	4	16	16	31	0	1	1
Lewis	.231	.272	.295	100	320	38	74	87	8	1	1	18	29	46	28	8	0
Colbert	.230	.325	.277	49	126	10	29	41	5	2	1	16	9	22	1	0	1
Litton	.229	.350	.285	68	140	9	32	49	5	0	4	15	11	33	0	1	4
Williams	.227	.384	.286	146	529	58	120	203	13	5	20	66	39	109	7	7	23
Clayton	.224	.308	.281	98	321	31	72	99	7	4	4	24	26	63	8	4	11
McNamara	.216	.270	.275	30	74	6	16	20	1	0	1	9	6	25	0	0	1
Wood	.207	.293	.292	24	58	5	12	17	2	0	1	3	6	15	0	0	1
Patterson	.184	.214	.229	32	103	10	19	22	1	1	0	4	5	24	5	1	4
Benjamin	.173	.267	.215	40	75	4	13	20	2	1	1	3	4	15	1	0	1
Decker	.163	.186	.280	15	43	3	7	8	1	0	0	1	6	7	0	0	0
Bailey	.154	.192	.241	13	26	0	4	5	1	0	0	1	3	7	0	0	0

Pitching	W-L	ERA	G	GS	CG	GF	Sho	SV	IP	H	R	ER	HR	BB	SO
Beck	3-3	1.76	65	0	0	42	0	17	92	62	20	18	4	15	87
Swift	10-4	2.08	30	22	3	2	2	1	164.2	144	41	38	6	43	77
Reed	1-0	2.30	18	0	0	2	0	0	15.2	13	5	4	2	3	11
Brantley	7-7	2.95	56	4	0	32	0	7	91.2	67	32	30	8	45	86
Hickerson	5-3	3.09	61	1	0	8	0	0	87.1	74	31	30	7	21	68
Downs	1-2	3.47	19	7	0	5	0	0	62.1	65	27	24	4	24	33
Pena	1-1	3.48	25	2	0	4	0	0	44	49	19	17	4	20	32
Oliveras	0-3	3.63	16	7	0	3	0	0	44.2	41	19	18	11	10	17
Jackson	6-6	3.73	67	0	0	24	0	2	82	76	35	34	7	33	80
Burkett	13-9	3.84	32	32	3	0	1	0	189.2	194	96	81	13	45	107
Black	10-12	3.97	28	28	2	0	1	0	177	178	88	78	23	59	82
Wilson	8-14	4.21	26	26	1	0	1	0	154	152	82	72	18	64	88
Rogers	0-2	4.24	6	6	0	0	0	0	34	37	17	16	4	13	26
Carter	1-5	4.64	6	6	0	0	0	0	33	34	17	17	6	18	21
Burba	2-7	4.97	23	11	0	4	0	0	70.2	80	43	39	4	31	47
Righetti	2-7	5.06	54	4	0	23	0	3	78.1	79	47	44	4	36	47
Rapp	0-2	7.20	3	2	0	1	0	0	10	8	8	8	0	6	3

1993 preliminary roster

PITCHERS (17)
Johnny Ard
Rod Beck
Bud Black
Jeff Brantley
Dave Burba
John Burkett
Dan Carlson
Larry Carter
Chris Hancock
Bryan Hickerson
Rick Huisman
Mike Jackson
Kevin McGehee
Dave Righetti
Kevin Rogers
Billy Swift
Trevor Wilson

CATCHERS (4)
Craig Colbert
Eric Christopherson
Kirt Manwaring
Jim McNamara

INFIELDERS (9)
Mike Benjamin
Will Clark
Royce Clayton
Paul Faries
Greg Litton
John Patterson
Andres Santana
Robby Thompson
Matt Williams

OUTFIELDERS (7)
Barry Bonds
Steve Hosey
Mark Leonard
Darren Lewis
Willie McGee
Dave Martinez
Ted Wood

Games played by position

Player	G	C	1B	2B	3B	SS	OF
BAILEY,M	13	7	0	0	0	0	0
BENJAMIN,M	40	0	0	0	2	33	0
CLARK,W	144	0	141	0	0	0	0
CLAYTON,R	98	0	0	0	1	94	0
COLBERT,C	49	35	0	2	9	0	0
DECKER,S	15	15	0	0	0	0	0
FELDER,M	145	0	0	3	0	0	105
HOSEY,S	21	0	0	0	0	0	18
JAMES,C	111	0	0	0	0	0	62
LEONARD,M	55	0	0	0	0	0	37
LEWIS,D	100	0	0	0	0	0	94
LITTON,G	68	0	8	31	10	3	1
MANWARING,K	109	108	0	0	0	0	0
MCGEE,W	138	0	0	0	0	0	119
MCNAMARA,J	30	30	0	0	0	0	0
PATTERSON,J	32	0	0	22	0	0	5
SNYDER,C	124	0	27	4	14	3	70
THOMPSON,RO	128	0	0	120	0	0	0
URIBE,J	66	0	0	0	0	62	0
WILLIAMS,MA	146	0	0	0	144	0	0
WOOD,T	24	0	0	0	0	0	16

Sick call: 1992 DL report

Player	Days on the DL
Bailey, Mark*	31
Bass, Kevin	13
Benjamin, Mike	60
Black, Bud	31
Colbert, Craig	15
Garrelts, Scott	182
James, Chris	17
Leonard, Mark	57
Manwaring, Kirt	15
Oliveras, Francisco	17
Patterson, John	16
Santana, Andres	182
Swift, Billy*	43
Thompson, Robby	23
Uribe, Jose	17
Wilson, Trevor	12
Wood, Ted	23

** On Disabled List twice during 1992 season (not counting transfers from one DL to another).*

Minor league report

Class AAA — Phoenix finished 66-78, 4th in the 1st half of the Pacific Coast League Southern Division and last in the 2nd half. RHP Steve Reed had 20 saves, to go with 23 at Shreveport for the new single-season minor-league record. RHP Pat Rapp was 7-8 with a 3.05 ERA. RHP Larry Carter had 11 wins and 126 K. OF Ted Wood hit .304 with 7 HR and 63 RBI. **Class AA:** Shreveport finished 77-59, 1st in the 1st half of the Texas League Eastern Division and 2nd in the 2nd half. The team lost to Wichita in four games for the league championship. 1B/3B Adell Davenport had 19 HR and led the league with 88 RBI. He hit .286. OF Pete Weber hit .288. RHP Kevin McGehee was 9-7 with a 2.96 ERA. RHP Dan Carlson was 15-9 with a 3.19 ERA, leading the league in wins. RHP Salomon Torres had 151 K. **Class A:** San Jose finished 78-58, 4th in the California League Northern Division in the 1st half and 2nd in the 2nd half. LHP Joe Rosselli was named the league's Pitcher of the Year, going 11-4 with a 2.41 ERA. RHP Dan Flanagan had 16 saves. Clinton finished 59-79, 4th in the 1st half of the Midwest League Southern Division and 6th in the 2nd half. LHP Jeff Locklear was 8-5 wit a 2.35 ERA. OF Andre Keene had 14 HR, 70 RBI and 28 SB. OF Dax Jones hit over .300 for the club. Everett finished 35-41, 3rd in the Northwest League North Division. OF Papo Ramos hit .306 with 2 HR and 34 RBI. SS Chad Fonville had 36 SB. LHP Jeff Myers was 5-5 with a 3.19 ERA and 90 K in 93 IP. The club was last in pitching at 4.61 but third in hitting at .259. Giants finished 32-24, tied for 2nd in the Arizona League. IF Bolivar Rivera hit .315 with 25 RBI and led the league in SB with 30. Mark Pooschke and C Hiram Ramirez shared the league lead in HR with 3. LHP Aaron Fultz was 3-2 with a 2.13 ERA and 72 K in 68 IP. RHP Jeff Martin shared the league lead in wins with 7. RHP Marcial Gomez had 7 saves. The club led the league in pitching at 2.87.

Tops in the organization

BATTING LEADERS	Club	Avg.	G	AB	R	H	HR	RBI
Joel Chimelis	Phx	.313	124	464	73	145	10	55
Ted Wood	Phx	.304	110	418	70	127	7	63
John Patterson	Phx	.301	94	362	52	109	2	37
Dax Jones	Shr	.299	98	361	55	108	2	49
Pete Weber	Shr	.288	118	417	64	120	3	33

HOME RUNS			WINS		
Brent Cookson	Sjo	20	Dan Carlson	Shr	15
Adell Davenport	Shr	19	Carl Hanselman	Shr	14
Andre Keene	Cln	14	Joe Rosselli	Sjo	11
Dan Lewis	Shr	13	Kevin Rogers	Phx	11
Clay Bellinger	Shr	13	Larry Carter	Phx	11

RBI			SAVES		
Adell Davenport	Shr	88	Steve Reed	Phx	43
Steve Decker	Phx	74	Jim Myers	Shr	28
Matt Davis	Phx	71	Ken Grundt	Sjo	19
Andre Keene	Cln	70	Dan Flanagan	Sjo	16
Barry Miller	Sjo	70	Gary Sharko	Shr	8

STOLEN BASES			STRIKEOUTS		
Adell Davenport	Shr	88	Kevin Rogers	Phx	172
Steve Decker	Phx	74	Dan Carlson	Shr	157
Matt Davis	Phx	71	Salomon Torres	Shr	151
Andre Keene	Cln	70	Rick Huisman	Phx	144
Barry Miller	Sjo	70	Kevin McGehee	Shr	140

PITCHING LEADERS	Club	W-L	ERA	IP	H	BB	SO
Jeff Locklear	Cln	8-5	2.35	126	117	42	69
Rick Huisman	Phx	10-6	2.37	159	124	55	144
Joe Rosselli	Sjo	11-4	2.41	150	145	46	111
Carl Hanselman	Shr	14-9	2.51	186	175	49	104
Kevin McGehee	Shr	9-7	2.96	158	146	42	140

San Francisco (1958-1992), incl. New York (1883-1957)

Runs: Most, career, all-time

2011 Willie Mays, 1951-1972
1859 Mel Ott, 1926-1947
1313 Mike Tiernan, 1887-1899
1120 Bill Terry, 1923-1936
1113 Willie McCovey, 1959-1980

Hits: Most, career, all-time

3187 Willie Mays, 1951-1972
2876 Mel Ott, 1926-1947
2193 Bill Terry, 1923-1936
1974 Willie McCovey, 1959-1980
1834 Mike Tiernan, 1887-1899

2B: Most, career, all-time

504 Willie Mays, 1951-1972
488 Mel Ott, 1926-1947
373 Bill Terry, 1923-1936
308 Willie McCovey, 1959-1980
291 Travis Jackson, 1922-1936

3B: Most, career, all-time

162 Mike Tiernan, 1887-1899
139 Willie Mays, 1951-1972
131 Roger Connor, 1883-1894
117 Larry Doyle, 1907-1920
112 Bill Terry, 1923-1936

HR: Most, career, all-time

646 Willie Mays, 1951-1972
511 Mel Ott, 1926-1947
469 Willie McCovey, 1959-1980
226 Orlando Cepeda, 1958-1966
189 Bobby Thomson, 1946-1957

RBI: Most, career, all-time

1860 Mel Ott, 1926-1947
1859 Willie Mays, 1951-1972
1388 Willie McCovey, 1959-1980
1078 Bill Terry, 1923-1936
929 Travis Jackson, 1922-1936

SB: Most, career, all-time

428 Mike Tiernan, 1887-1899
354 George Davis, 1893-1903
336 Willie Mays, 1951-1972
334 George Burns, 1911-1921
332 John Ward, 1883-1894

BB: Most, career, all-time

1708 Mel Ott, 1926-1947
1394 Willie Mays, 1951-1972
1168 Willie McCovey, 1959-1980
747 Mike Tiernan, 1887-1899
631 George Burns, 1911-1921

BA: Highest, career, all-time

.341 Bill Terry, 1923-1936
.332 George Davis, 1893-1903
.322 Ross Youngs, 1917-1926
.322 Frankie Frisch, 1919-1926
.321 George Vanhaltren, 1894-1903
.308 Orlando Cepeda, 1958-1966 (12)

Slug avg: Highest, career, all-time

.564 Willie Mays, 1951-1972
.549 Johnny Mize, 1942-1949
.536 KEVIN MITCHELL, 1987-1991
.535 Orlando Cepeda, 1958-1966
.533 Mel Ott, 1926-1947

Games started: Most, career, all-time

550 Christy Mathewson, 1900-1916
446 Juan Marichal, 1960-1973
431 Carl Hubbell, 1928-1943
412 Mickey Welch, 1883-1892
403 Amos Rusie, 1890-1898

Saves: Most, career, all-time

127 Gary Lavelle, 1974-1984
125 Greg Minton, 1975-1987
83 Randy Moffitt, 1972-1981
78 Frank Linzy, 1963-1970
58 Marv Grissom, 1946-1958

Shutouts: Most, career, all-time

79 Christy Mathewson, 1900-1916
52 Juan Marichal, 1960-1973
36 Carl Hubbell, 1928-1943
29 Amos Rusie, 1890-1898
28 Mickey Welch, 1883-1892

Wins: Most, career, all-time

372 Christy Mathewson, 1900-1916
253 Carl Hubbell, 1928-1943
238 Juan Marichal, 1960-1973
238 Mickey Welch, 1883-1892
233 Amos Rusie, 1890-1898

K: Most, career, all-time

2499 Christy Mathewson, 1900-1916
2281 Juan Marichal, 1960-1973
1819 Amos Rusie, 1890-1898
1677 Carl Hubbell, 1928-1943
1606 Gaylord Perry, 1962-1971

Win pct: Highest, career, all-time

.693 Sal Maglie, 1945-1955
.680 Tim Keefe, 1885-1891
.664 Christy Mathewson, 1900-1916
.656 Jesse Barnes, 1918-1923
.651 Doc Crandall, 1908-1913
.630 Juan Marichal, 1960-1973 (11)

ERA: Lowest, career, all-time

2.12 Christy Mathewson, 1900-1916
2.38 Joe McGinnity, 1902-1908
2.43 Jeff Tesreau, 1912-1918
2.45 Red Ames, 1903-1913
2.48 Hooks Wiltse, 1904-1914
2.82 Gary Lavelle, 1974-1984 (12)

Runs: Most, season

147 Mike Tiernan, 1889
139 Bill Terry, 1930
138 Mel Ott, 1929
137 Johnny Mize, 1947
136 George Vanhaltren, 1896
134 Bobby Bonds, 1970 (6)

Hits: Most, season

254 Bill Terry, 1930
231 Freddy Lindstrom, 1928
231 Freddy Lindstrom, 1930
226 Bill Terry, 1929
225 Bill Terry, 1932
208 Willie Mays, 1958 (13)

2B: Most, season

46 JACK CLARK, 1978
43 Willie Mays, 1959
43 Bill Terry, 1931
42 George Kelly, 1921
42 Bill Terry, 1932

3B: Most, season

27 George Davis, 1893
25 Larry Doyle, 1911
22 Roger Connor, 1887
21 Mike Tiernan, 1890
21 Mike Tiernan, 1895
21 George Vanhaltren, 1896
12 Willie Mays, 1960 (*)

HR: Most, season

52 Willie Mays, 1965
51 Willie Mays, 1955
51 Johnny Mize, 1947
49 Willie Mays, 1962
47 Willie Mays, 1964
47 KEVIN MITCHELL, 1989

RBI: Most, season

151 Mel Ott, 1929
142 Orlando Cepeda, 1961
141 Willie Mays, 1962
138 Johnny Mize, 1947
136 George Davis, 1897
136 George Kelly, 1924

SB: Most, season

111 John Ward, 1887
65 George Davis, 1897
62 George Burns, 1914
62 John Ward, 1889
61 Josh Devore, 1911
58 Billy North, 1979 (7)

BB: Most, season

144 Eddie Stanky, 1950
137 Willie McCovey, 1970
127 Eddie Stanky, 1951
121 Willie McCovey, 1969
118 Mel Ott, 1938

BA: Highest, season

.401 Bill Terry, 1930
.379 Freddy Lindstrom, 1930
.372 Bill Terry, 1929
.371 Roger Connor, 1885
.369 Mike Tiernan, 1896
.347 Willie Mays, 1958 (22)

Slug avg: Highest, season

.667 Willie Mays, 1954
.659 Willie Mays, 1955
.656 Willie McCovey, 1969
.645 Willie Mays, 1965
.635 KEVIN MITCHELL, 1989

Games started: Most, season

65 Mickey Welch, 1884
64 Tim Keefe, 1886
63 Amos Rusie, 1890
61 Amos Rusie, 1892
59 Mickey Welch, 1886
41 Gaylord Perry, 1970 (*)

Saves: Most, season

30 Greg Minton, 1982
24 DAVE RIGHETTI, 1991
22 Greg Minton, 1983
21 Frank Linzy, 1965
21 Greg Minton, 1981

Shutouts: Most, season

11 Christy Mathewson, 1908
10 Carl Hubbell, 1933
10 Juan Marichal, 1965
9 Joe McGinnity, 1904
8 Tim Keefe, 1888
8 Juan Marichal, 1969
8 Christy Mathewson, 1902
8 Christy Mathewson, 1905
8 Christy Mathewson, 1907
8 Christy Mathewson, 1909
8 Jeff Tesreau, 1914
8 Jeff Tesreau, 1915

Wins: Most, season

44 Mickey Welch, 1885
42 Tim Keefe, 1886
39 Mickey Welch, 1884
37 Christy Mathewson, 1908
36 Amos Rusie, 1894
26 Juan Marichal, 1968 (25)

K: Most, season

345 Mickey Welch, 1884
341 Amos Rusie, 1890
337 Amos Rusie, 1891
335 Tim Keefe, 1888
297 Tim Keefe, 1886
248 Juan Marichal, 1963 (11)

Win pct: Highest, season

.833 Hoyt Wilhelm, 1952
.818 Sal Maglie, 1950
.814 Joe McGinnity, 1904
.813 Carl Hubbell, 1936
.810 Doc Crandall, 1910
.806 Juan Marichal, 1966 (7)

ERA: Lowest, season

1.14 Christy Mathewson, 1909
1.28 Christy Mathewson, 1905
1.43 Christy Mathewson, 1908
1.44 Fred Anderson, 1917
1.57 Tim Keefe, 1885
1.99 Bobby Bolin, 1968 (16)

Most pinch-hit homers, season

4 Ernie Lombardi, NY-1946
4 Bill Taylor, NY-1955
4 Mike Ivie, 1978
4 Candy Maldonado, 1986
4 Ernie Riles, 1990

Most pinch-hit, homers, career

13 Willie McCovey, 1959-1980

Most consecutive games, batting safely

33 George Davis, NY-1893
26 Jack Clark, 1978

Most consecutive scoreless innings

45 Carl Hubbell, NY-1933
45 Sal Maglie, NY-1950
40 Gaylord Perry, 1967
39 Christy Mathewson, NY-1901
39 Gaylord Perry, 1970

No hit games

Amos Rusie, NY vs Bro NL, 6-0; July 31, 1891.

Christy Mathewson, NY at StL NL, 5-0; July 15, 1901.

Christy Mathewson, NY at Chi NL, 1-0; June 13, 1905.

Hooks Wiltse, NY vs Phi NL, 1-0; July 4, 1908 (1st game, ten innings).

Red Ames, NY vs Bro NL. 0-3; April 15, 1909 (lost on 7 hits in 13 innings after allowing the first hit in the tenth).

Jeff Tesreau, NY at Phi NL, 3-0; September 6, 1912 (1st game).

Rube Marquard, NY vs Bro NL, 2-0; April 15, 1915.

Jesse Barnes, NY vs Phi NL, 6-0; May 7, 1922.

Carl Hubbell, NY vs Pit NL, 11-0; May 8, 1929.

Juan Marichal, SF vs Hou NL, 1-0; June 15, 1963.

Gaylord Perry, SF vs StL NL, 1-0; September 17, 1968.

Ed Halicki, SF vs NY NL, 6-0; August 24, 1975 (2nd game).

John Montefusco, SF at Atl NL, 9-0; September 29, 1976.

Ed Crane, seven innings, darkness, NY vs Was NL, 3-0; September 27, 1888.

Red Ames, five innings, darkness, NY at StL NL, 5-0; September 14, 1903 (2nd game, first game in the major leagues).

Mike McCormick, five innings, rain, SF at Phi NL, 3-0; June 12, 1959 (allowed hit in 6th, but rain caused game to revert to 5 innings).

Sam Jones, seven innings, rain, SF at StL NL, 4-0; September 26, 1959.

ACTIVE PLAYERS in caps.

Leader from the franchise's current location is included. If not in the top five, leader's rank is listed in parenthesis; asterisk (*) indicates player is not in top 25.

Los Angeles Dodgers

by Robert Hanashiro, *USA TODAY*

NL Rookie of the Year Eric Karros brightened the Dodgers' dim season, leading the club in HR (20) and RBI (88).

1992 Dodgers: Worst record in 87 years

There was definitely a bright spot to the Dodgers' 1992 season: It ended.

The "Dodger Blues" had plenty to be sad about: They bumbled their way to a 63-99 record, worst in the majors, and finished in last place for the first time since 1905, 35 games behind NL West champion Atlanta.

They were hardly favored to win the division, but there was no reason to think that they would fall so far from the club that battled its way to second place in 1991, just one game behind. No reason until spring training, when the shambles that was once a team made itself apparent.

Even the offseason acquisitions of Tom Candiotti and Eric Davis left the team with more questions than answers. The infield was defensively weak and the bullpen was even worse. Closer Jay Howell and relief prospect Rudy Seanez were both on the DL; the pen finished with a league-low 29 saves.

Ironically it turned out that the outfield—the team's greatest strength, on paper—was its greatest disappointment. When the immensely talented Davis came over from the Reds, it was believed that his reunion with high school pal Darryl Strawberry would help him finally realize his potential in a season free of injuries and controversy. Instead, injuries to both stars limited the duo to just 30 games in the same lineup and a combined total of just 10 homers, 57 RBI, four stolen bases, and a sub-.235 average.

The Dodgers led the majors in errors with 174. Shortstop Jose Offerman led the way with 42 of his own, the first NL player to top the 40-error mark in 14 years.

Lack of offense was also a key factor. They were last in the league in runs, doubles, and homers, and 10th in hits.

Miraculously, the Dodgers didn't fall into the morass until a few months into the season. They were at .500 on June 1, just two-and-a-half games out of first. Three weeks later they were 12 games out and sinking fast. They were swept in series by the Reds, the Braves, and the Astros. On June 21 they lost their 10th consecutive game, longest losing streak in the NL, and they remained in last place for the rest of the season.

Things weren't all bad, however.

Journeyman starter Kevin Gross became the only pitcher in the majors to hurl a no-hitter in 1992; rookie right-hander Pedro Astacio made his major-league debut—a three-hit shutout with 10 strikeouts—and was 5-5 with a 1.98 ERA in 11 starts, with four shutouts; and first baseman Eric Karros was the team's first Rookie of the Year since 1982.

—by Lisa Winston

1993 Dodgers: Preview

It's hard to say that the names in the Dodgers' 1993 lineup will be new; no one but Eric Karros, Jose Offerman, and Brett Butler held down a job with enough regularity in '92 to be missed.

One new face will be former Red Sox' second baseman Jody Reed, acquired from the Marlins for Rudy Seanez. Reed, an excellent defensive second baseman who had an off year with the bat, should provide some stability to an error-prone middle infield.

Power-hitting rookie Mike Piazza should take free agent Mike Scioscia's place behind the plate.

Hopefully Ramon Martinez will return to form after an early end to his '92 season with elbow trouble. And a pair of Pedros—Martinez's younger brother and Astacio—show promise. They addressed one priority, adding closer Todd Worrell.

—by Lisa Winston

1992 Dodgers: Between the lines

▸**April 21:** Cincinnati reliever Norm Charlton hit Darryl Strawberry with a pitch as an earthquake shook Dodger Stadium. ***Quote of the day:*** Charlton—"I didn't feel a thing. I just thought it was the people booing me."

▸**April 29:** As the Dodgers were losing to the Phillies, 7-3, civil unrest broke out over the Rodney King verdict.

▸**May 11** ***Quote of the day:*** Tom Lasorda on his team's ninth loss in 10 games—"I know one thing, it's driving me out of my mind."

▸**May 12:** Kevin Gross had a career high in strikeouts, recording the 12th shutout of his career as L.A. beat Montreal 2-0.

▸**May 17:** Dodger starters had not allowed a home run in 86 1/3 innings—since April 25—until Ramon Martinez gave up a leadoff dinger to Met Chico Walker.

▸**May 20:** Reliever Roger McDowell was 2-0 with an 0.00 ERA and three saves at home, and 1-3 with a 5.73 ERA and two saves on the road.

▸**May 22** ***Quote of the day:*** Darryl Strawberry on his back injury—"It's really the first time in my career I've ever been afraid." Also on the Dodgers' ever-expanding sick call: Eric Davis (already playing with a herniated disk in his neck), who was reinjured making a diving catch. Prognosis: at least three weeks.

▸**May 23:** With Strawberry and Davis on the DL, Lasorda played three first basemen: Kal Daniels in left, Todd Benzinger in right and rookie Eric Karros at first.

▸**May 26:** Dave Hansen and Dave Anderson hit back-to-back homers, the first consecutive homers by L.A. since July 27, 1991. (Anderson averaged less than two home runs per season during his nine-year career.)

▸**May 29:** Ramon Martinez shut out the Cubs on three hits, 1-0, in a performance Lasorda said was his best in the last year-and-a-half.

▸**May 30:** The Dodgers kept their ERA at 2.55 for the last 13 games—lowering their overall mark to a league-best 3.25. ***Quote of the day:*** Roger McDowell on why other teams seem to take his Dodgers lightly—"Other teams figure, 'They don't have anybody who can hurt us.' It's the Big Bangless Theory."

▸**May 31:** Dave Anderson hit his second home run in six days—just his 18th career homer in 10 seasons. ***Quote of the day:*** Anderson—"I don't think I've ever hit two in a week. I don't think I've ever hit two in a month."

▸**June 3** ***Quote of the day:*** Anderson, on his home run "tear," after connecting on his third in eight games (one shy of his career high)—"There's no way to explain it. Pretty soon people will be checking my bat."

▸**June 4** ***Milestone:*** Tommy Lasorda won his 1300th game as manager of the Dodgers, a 7-4 victory over Cincinnati. Lasorda, in his 16th season, was 1,300-1,125 (.536), the second highest victory total among active managers, trailing only Detroit's Sparky Anderson (1,944).

▸**June 14** ***Quote of the day:*** Ex-Red Kal Daniels, who struck out four times and was booed loudly by the Riverfront Stadium crowd, responded by lifting his hands and asking for more—"They want me to put my head between my tail and cry like a whipped puppy, but I'm not going to do it."

▸**June 25:** Fresh off a dismal 1-10 road trip, the Dodgers kicked off a 22-game homestand, longest in club history.

▸**June 26** ***Milestone:*** Brett Butler scored the 1,000th run of his career on a wild pitch by Houston's Xavier Hernandez.

▸**July 1:** Orel Hershiser gave up 13 hits for the first time (the most previously was 12).

▸**July 2:** The Dodgers, with the fewest runs scored in the majors, exploded for eight runs in the fifth in a 9-4 win against Philadelphia. It was the biggest inning for Los Angeles since Sept. 14, 1990, at San Francisco.

▸**July 3:** Called up as a temporary fix for the doubleheader-playing Dodgers, Pedro Astacio became the first rookie Dodgers' starter to win his debut since Shawn Hillegas beat the Braves on Aug. 9, 1987. He was also the first Dodgers' rookie to pitch a shutout since Mike Hartley beat the Braves on Sept. 6, 1990.

▸**July 4:** Eric Davis hit his first homer as a Dodger at Dodger Stadium, ending a homerless string of 121 at-bats.

▸**July 8:** The nightcap of the Dodgers-Expos doubleheader concluded three straight doubleheaders. Net result: three wins for the Dodgers, three for the Expos.

▸**July 12:** After the 18-day, 22-game homestand, the Dodgers welcomed the All-Star break. ***Quote of the day:*** Eric Karros, who played in all but three innings—"I will be in my bed for the next three days, and I will not be moving out of it."

▸**July 25** ***Quote of the day:*** Pitcher Bob Ojeda—"People are looking at us like we're a carcass, saying, 'What can we pick off? What can we get?' I mean, it's fairly obvious that we might not win it."

▸**July 29:** Eric Karros hit his third homer in four days. His 15 homers (so far) were the most by a Dodgers' rookie since Greg Brock hit 20 in 1983. ***Quote of the day:*** Karros, who was just trying to avoid hitting into a double play—"That would have given Tommy (Lasorda) a heart attack. He told me if I did that, I'd better go open a car wash in San Diego."

▸**August 13:** The Dodgers boosted their major-league leading total to 121 errors in 114 games.

▸**August 17** ***No-hitter:*** Kevin Gross pitched the majors' first (and only) no-hitter of 1992. Gross hadn't had a winning season since 1985 with the Phillies.

▸**September 4:** Todd Benzinger hit a ninth-inning grand slam, but the Pirates came back with three in the bottom of the inning to win 6-5.

▸**September 8:** Brett Butler stole home against the Braves' Charlie Leibrandt. It was the Dodgers' first steal of home since Jose Gonzalez did it Aug. 26, 1990.

▸**October 4:** The Dodgers finished their dismal season in last place, 35 games out. It was the first time since 1905 that the Dodgers finished last.

—by Jeanie Chung, John Hunt, Deron Snyder, and Lisa Winston.

Team directory

▸**Owner:** Peter O'Malley

▸**General Manager:** Fred Claire

▸**Ballpark:**
Dodger Stadium
1000 Elysian Park Ave., Los Angeles, Calif.
213-224-1400
Capacity 56,000
Parking for 16,000 cars; $4
Wheelchair section and ramps

▸**Team publications:**
Dodger Magazine, Media Guide
800-762-1770

▸**TV, radio broadcast stations:**
KABC 790 AM, KWKW 1330 AM (Spanish), KTTV Channel 11, KTLA Channel 5

▸**Camps and/or clinics:**
Twenty clinics per year, 213-224-1435

▸**Spring Training:**
Holman Stadium
Dodgertown
Vero Beach, Fla.
Capacity 6,500
407-569-4900

LOS ANGELES DODGERS 1992 final stats

Batting	AVG	SLG	OB	G	AB	R	H	TB	2B	3B	HR	RBI	BB	SO	SB	CS	E
Butler	.309	.391	.413	157	553	86	171	216	14	11	3	39	95	67	41	21	2
Sharperson	.300	.394	.387	128	317	48	95	125	21	0	3	36	47	33	2	2	13
Anderson	.286	.440	.311	51	84	10	24	37	4	0	3	8	4	11	0	4	4
Harris	.271	.303	.318	135	347	28	94	105	11	0	0	30	24	24	19	7	27
Webster	.267	.420	.334	135	262	33	70	110	12	5	6	35	27	49	11	5	3
Samuel	.262	.303	.303	47	122	7	32	37	3	1	0	15	7	22	2	2	5
Offerman	.260	.333	.331	149	534	67	139	178	20	8	1	30	57	98	23	16	42
Hernandez	.260	.335	.316	69	173	11	45	58	4	0	3	17	11	21	0	1	7
Young	.258	.288	.300	49	132	9	34	38	1	0	1	11	8	9	6	1	9
Karros	.257	.426	.304	149	545	63	140	232	30	1	20	88	37	103	2	4	9
Benzinger	.239	.348	.272	121	293	24	70	102	16	2	4	31	15	54	2	4	1
Strawberry	.237	.385	.322	43	156	20	37	60	8	0	5	25	19	34	3	1	1
Goodwin	.233	.274	.291	57	73	15	17	20	1	1	0	3	6	10	7	3	0
Piazza	.232	.319	.284	21	69	5	16	22	3	0	1	7	4	12	0	0	1
Davis	.228	.322	.325	76	267	21	61	86	8	1	5	32	36	71	19	1	5
Scioscia	.221	.282	.286	117	348	19	77	98	6	3	3	24	32	31	3	2	9
Ashley	.221	.337	.260	29	95	6	21	32	5	0	2	6	5	34	0	0	6
Rodriguez	.219	.329	.258	53	146	11	32	48	7	0	3	14	8	30	0	0	3
Hansen	.214	.299	.286	132	341	30	73	102	11	0	6	22	34	49	0	2	8
Bournigal	.150	.200	.227	10	20	1	3	4	1	0	0	0	1	2	0	0	1

Pitching	W-L	ERA	G	GS	CG	GF	Sho	SV	IP	H	R	ER	HR	BB	SO
Howell	1-3	1.54	41	0	0	26	0	4	46.2	41	9	8	2	18	36
Astacio	5-5	1.98	11	11	4	0	4	0	82	80	23	18	1	20	43
P.Martinez	0-1	2.25	2	1	0	1	0	0	8	6	2	2	0	1	8
Gott	3-3	2.45	68	0	0	28	0	6	88	72	27	24	4	41	75
Candelaria	2-5	2.84	50	0	0	11	0	5	25.1	20	9	8	1	13	23
Candiotti	11-15	3.00	32	30	6	1	2	0	203.2	177	78	68	13	63	152
Ke.Gross	8-13	3.17	34	30	4	0	3	0	204.2	182	82	72	11	77	158
Ojeda	6-9	3.63	29	29	2	0	1	0	166.1	169	80	67	8	81	94
Hershiser	10-15	3.67	33	33	1	0	0	0	210.2	209	101	86	15	69	130
R.Martinez	8-11	4.00	25	25	1	0	1	0	150.2	141	82	67	11	69	101
McDowell	6-10	4.09	65	0	0	39	0	14	83.2	103	46	38	3	42	50
Ki.Gross	1-1	4.18	16	1	0	7	0	0	23.2	32	14	11	1	10	14
Wilson	2-5	4.19	60	0	0	18	0	0	66.2	74	37	31	6	29	54
Crews	0-3	5.19	49	2	0	13	0	0	78	95	46	45	6	20	43

1993 preliminary roster

PITCHERS (18)
Pedro Astacio
Albert Bustillos
Tom Candiotti
Dera Clark
Jim Daspit
Javier Delahoya
Jim Gott
Kevin Gross
Kip Gross
Greg Hansell
Orel Hershiser
Mike James
Pedro Martinez
Ramon Martinez
Roger McDowell
Chris Nichting
Steve Wilson
Todd Worrell

CATCHERS (3)
Carlos Hernandez
Mike Piazza
Don Wakamatsu

INFIELDERS (10)
Todd Benzinger
Rafael Bournigal
Mike Busch
Dave Hansen
Lenny Harris
Eric Karros
Jose Offerman
Eddie Pye
Jody Reed
Mike Sharperson

OUTFIELDERS (9)
Billy Ashley
Brett Butler
Eric Davis
Tom Goodwin
Raul Mondesi
Henry Rodriguez
Cory Snyder
Darryl Strawberry
Mitch Webster

Games played by position

Player	G	C	1B	2B	3B	SS	OF
ANDERSON,D	51	0	0	0	26	7	0
ASHLEY,B	29	0	0	0	0	0	27
BENZINGER,T	121	0	42	0	0	0	51
BOURNIGAL,R	10	0	0	0	0	9	0
BUTLER,B	157	0	0	0	0	0	155
DAVIS,E	76	0	0	0	0	0	74
GOODWIN,T	57	0	0	0	0	0	45
HANSEN,D	132	0	0	0	108	0	0
HARRIS,L	135	0	0	81	33	10	15
HERNANDEZ,C	69	63	0	0	0	0	0
KARROS,E	149	0	143	0	0	0	0
OFFERMAN,J	149	0	0	0	0	149	0
PIAZZA,M	21	16	0	0	0	0	0
RODRIGUEZ,H	53	0	1	0	0	0	48
SAMUEL,J	47	0	0	38	0	0	1
SCIOSCIA,M	117	108	0	0	0	0	0
SHARPERSON,M	128	0	0	63	60	2	0
STRAWBERRY,D	43	0	0	0	0	0	42
WEBSTER,M	135	0	0	0	0	0	90
YOUNG,E	49	0	0	43	0	0	0

Sick call: 1992 DL report

Player	Days on the DL
Anderson, Dave*	31
Candiotti, Tom	15
Daniels, Kal	20
Davis, Eric*	50
Howell, Jay	42
Samuel, Juan	44
Seanez, Rudy	182
Strawberry, Darryl*	95

** On Disabled List twice during 1992 season (not counting transfers from one DL to another).*

Minor league report

Class AAA — Albuquerque finished 65-78, last in the 1st half of the Pacific Coast League Southern Division and 4th in the 2nd half. C Mike Piazza hit .341 with 11 HRs and 74 RBI. 2B Eric Young hit .337 with 28 SB. SS Rafael Bournigal hit .324. RHP Pedro Martinez was 7-6 with a 3.81 ERA and K'd 124 in 125 IP. RHP Zak Shinall had 13 wins, all in relief. **Class AA:** San Antonio finished 62-74, last in the 1st half of the Texas League Western Division and 2nd in the 2nd half. OF Billy Ashley led the league with 24 HR. 1B Mike Busch had 18 HR, while 1B John Deutsch had 17. RHP Mike Mimbs had 10 wins. RHP Todd Williams had 22 saves. **Class A:** Bakersfield finished 68-68, 2nd in the California League Southern Division in the 1st half and 4th in the 2nd half. RHP Jose Parra was 7-8 with a 3.59 ERA. RHP Rick Gorecki K'd 115. LHP Mike Brady had 9 saves. OF Todd Hollandsworth had 27 SB. Vero Beach finished 53-82, last in both halves of the Florida State League East Division. OF Vernon Spearman had 27 SB before his mid-season promotion to San Antonio. LHP Ben Vanryn had 10 wins. Yakima finished 36-40, 2nd in the Northwest League North Division. SS Sandy Martinez won the league batting crown at .333 to go with 33 RBI. OF Matt Filson hit .303 with 6 HR and 34 RBI. C Chris Abbe hit .302 with 9 HR and 37 RBI. OF Alton Pinkney had 27 SB. Great Falls finished 38-35, 2nd in the Pioneer League North Division. OF Roger Cedeno hit .318 and led the league with 40 SB. LHP Chad Zerbe was 8-3 with a 2.14 ERA. RHP David Pyc had 9 saves. Dodgers finished 32-27, 2nd in the Gulf Coast League Eastern Division. RHP Jason Bobb had 67 K. The club was third in pitching at 2.71.

Tops in the organization

BATTING LEADERS	Club	Avg.	G	AB	R	H	HR	RBI
Mike Piazza	Abq	.350	125	472	72	165	23	89
Eric Young	Abq	.337	94	350	61	118	3	49
Tony Barron	Abq	.326	106	383	58	125	13	55
Rafael Bournigal	Abq	.324	122	395	47	128	0	34
Murph Proctor	San	.310	135	496	70	154	7	79

HOME RUNS			WINS		
Billy Ashley	San	26	Zak Shinall	Abq	13
Mike Piazza	Abq	23	Rick Gorecki	Bak	11
Mike Busch	San	18	Mike Walkden	Bak	11
John Deutsch	San	17	Ben Vanryn	Vrb	10
Several players tied		14	Mike Mimbs	San	10

RBI			SAVES		
Mike Piazza	Abq	89	Todd Williams	San	22
Murph Proctor	San	79	Lance McCullers	Abq	12
Jerry Brooks	Abq	78	Chris Sinacori	Vrb	10
Billy Ashley	San	76	Mike Brady	Bak	9
Henry Rodriguez	Abq	72	Kip Gross	Abq	8

STOLEN BASES			STRIKEOUTS		
Vernon Spearman	San	51	Pedro Martinez	Abq	124
Eric Young	Abq	28	Javier Delahoya	San	116
Tom Goodwin	Abq	27	Rick Gorecki	Bak	115
Todd Hollandsworth	Bak	27	Jose Parra	San	114
Ira Smith	San	26	Several players tied		109

PITCHING LEADERS	Club	W-L	ERA	IP	H	BB	SO
Ben Vanryn	Vrb	10-7	3.20	138	125	54	108
Jim Daspit	Vrb	6-12	3.44	149	135	57	109
Pedro Martinez	Abq	7-6	3.81	125	104	57	124
Jose Parra	San	9-8	3.82	158	173	54	114
Greg Hansell	San	7-9	3.86	161	164	68	104

Los Angeles (1958-1992), incl. Brooklyn (1890-1957)

Runs: Most, career, all-time

1338 Pee Wee Reese, 1940-1958
1255 Zack Wheat, 1909-1926
1199 Duke Snider, 1947-1962
1163 Jim Gilliam, 1953-1966
1088 Gil Hodges, 1943-1961

Hits: Most, career, all-time

2804 Zack Wheat, 1909-1926
2170 Pee Wee Reese, 1940-1958
2091 Willie Davis, 1960-1973
1995 Duke Snider, 1947-1962
1968 Steve Garvey, 1969-1982

2B: Most, career, all-time

464 Zack Wheat, 1909-1926
343 Duke Snider, 1947-1962
333 Steve Garvey, 1969-1982
330 Pee Wee Reese, 1940-1958
324 Carl Furillo, 1946-1960

3B: Most, career, all-time

171 Zack Wheat, 1909-1926
110 Willie Davis, 1960-1973
97 Hy Myers, 1909-1922
87 Jake Daubert, 1910-1918
82 John Hummel, 1905-1915
82 Duke Snider, 1947-1962

HR: Most, career, all-time

389 Duke Snider, 1947-1962
361 Gil Hodges, 1943-1961
242 Roy Campanella, 1948-1957
228 Ron Cey, 1971-1982
211 Steve Garvey, 1969-1982

RBI: Most, career, all-time

1271 Duke Snider, 1947-1962
1254 Gil Hodges, 1943-1961
1210 Zack Wheat, 1909-1926
1058 Carl Furillo, 1946-1960
992 Steve Garvey, 1969-1982

SB: Most, career, all-time

490 Maury Wills, 1959-1972
418 Davey Lopes, 1972-1981
335 Willie Davis, 1960-1973
298 Tom Daly, 1890-1901
290 STEVE SAX, 1981-1988

BB: Most, career, all-time

1210 Pee Wee Reese, 1940-1958
1036 Jim Gilliam, 1953-1966
925 Gil Hodges, 1943-1961
893 Duke Snider, 1947-1962
765 Ron Cey, 1971-1982

BA: Highest, career, all-time

.352 Willie Keeler, 1893-1902
.339 Babe Herman, 1926-1945
.337 Jack Fournier, 1923-1926
.317 Zack Wheat, 1909-1926
.315 Babe Phelps, 1935-1941
.315 Manny Mota, 1969-1982 (6)

Slug avg: Highest, career, all-time

.557 Babe Herman, 1926-1945
.553 Duke Snider, 1947-1962
.552 Jack Fournier, 1923-1926
.528 Reggie Smith, 1976-1981
.512 PEDRO GUERRERO, 1978-1988

Games started: Most, career, all-time

533 Don Sutton, 1966-1988
465 Don Drysdale, 1956-1969
335 Claude Osteen, 1965-1973
332 Brickyard Kennedy, 1892-1901
326 Dazzy Vance, 1922-1935

Saves: Most, career, all-time

125 Jim Brewer, 1964-1975
101 Ron Perranoski, 1961-1972
85 JAY HOWELL, 1988-1992
83 Clem Labine, 1950-1960
64 Tom Niedenfuer, 1981-1987

Shutouts: Most, career, all-time

52 Don Sutton, 1966-1988
49 Don Drysdale, 1956-1969
40 Sandy Koufax, 1955-1966
38 Nap Rucker, 1907-1916
34 Claude Osteen, 1965-1973

Wins: Most, career, all-time

233 Don Sutton, 1966-1988
209 Don Drysdale, 1956-1969
190 Dazzy Vance, 1922-1935
177 Brickyard Kennedy, 1892-1901
165 Sandy Koufax, 1955-1966

K: Most, career, all-time

2696 Don Sutton, 1966-1988
2486 Don Drysdale, 1956-1969
2396 Sandy Koufax, 1955-1966
1918 Dazzy Vance, 1922-1935
1759 Fernando Valenzuela, 1980-1990

Win pct: Highest, career, all-time

.715 Preacher Roe, 1948-1954
.674 Tommy John, 1972-1978
.674 Jim Hughes, 1899-1902
.658 Billy Loes, 1950-1956
.655 Sandy Koufax, 1955-1966

ERA: Lowest, career, all-time

2.31 Jeff Pfeffer, 1913-1921
2.42 Nap Rucker, 1907-1916
2.56 Ron Perranoski, 1961-1972
2.58 Rube Marquard, 1915-1920
2.62 Jim Brewer, 1964-1975

Runs: Most, season

148 Hub Collins, 1890
143 Babe Herman, 1930
140 Mike Griffin, 1895
140 Willie Keeler, 1899
136 Mike Griffin, 1897
130 Maury Wills, 1962 (10)

Hits: Most, season

241 Babe Herman, 1930
230 Tommy Davis, 1962
221 Zack Wheat, 1925
219 Lefty O'Doul, 1932
217 Babe Herman, 1929

2B: Most, season

52 Johnny Frederick, 1929
48 Babe Herman, 1930
47 Wes Parker, 1970
44 Johnny Frederick, 1930
43 Augie Galan, 1944
43 Babe Herman, 1931
43 STEVE SAX, 1986

3B: Most, season

26 George Treadway, 1894
22 Hy Myers, 1920
20 Dan Brouthers, 1892
20 Tommy Corcoran, 1894
19 Jimmy Sheckard, 1901
16 Willie Davis, 1970 (12)

HR: Most, season

43 Duke Snider, 1956
42 Gil Hodges, 1954
42 Duke Snider, 1953
42 Duke Snider, 1955
41 Roy Campanella, 1953
33 Steve Garvey, 1977 (11)

RBI: Most, season

153 Tommy Davis, 1962
142 Roy Campanella, 1953
136 Duke Snider, 1955
130 Jack Fournier, 1925
130 Babe Herman, 1930
130 Gil Hodges, 1954
130 Duke Snider, 1954

SB: Most, season

104 Maury Wills, 1962
94 Maury Wills, 1965
88 John Ward, 1892
85 Hub Collins, 1890
77 Davey Lopes, 1975

BB: Most, season

148 Eddie Stanky, 1945
137 Eddie Stanky, 1946
119 Dolph Camilli, 1938
116 Pee Wee Reese, 1949
114 Augie Galan, 1945
110 Jim Wynn, 1975 (6)

BA: Highest, season

.393 Babe Herman, 1930
.381 Babe Herman, 1929
.379 Willie Keeler, 1899
.375 Zack Wheat, 1924
.368 Lefty O'Doul, 1932
.346 Tommy Davis, 1962 (16)

Slug avg: Highest, season

.678 Babe Herman, 1930
.647 Duke Snider, 1954
.628 Duke Snider, 1955
.627 Duke Snider, 1953
.612 Babe Herman, 1929
.577 PEDRO GUERRERO, 1985 (14)

Games started: Most, season

44 George Haddock, 1892
44 Brickyard Kennedy, 1893
44 Adonis Terry, 1890
43 Tom Lovett, 1891
42 Don Drysdale, 1963
42 Don Drysdale, 1965
42 Ed Stein, 1892

Saves: Most, season

28 JAY HOWELL, 1989
24 Jim Brewer, 1970
24 Jim Hughes, 1954
22 Jim Brewer, 1971
22 CHARLIE HOUGH, 1977

Shutouts: Most, season

11 Sandy Koufax, 1963
9 Don Sutton, 1972
8 TIM BELCHER, 1989
8 Don Drysdale, 1968
8 OREL HERSHISER, 1988
8 Sandy Koufax, 1965
8 Fernando Valenzuela, 1981

Wins: Most, season

30 Tom Lovett, 1890
29 George Haddock, 1892
28 Jim Hughes, 1899
28 Joe McGinnity, 1900
28 Dazzy Vance, 1924
27 Sandy Koufax, 1966 (6)

K: Most, season

382 Sandy Koufax, 1965
317 Sandy Koufax, 1966
306 Sandy Koufax, 1963
269 Sandy Koufax, 1961
262 Dazzy Vance, 1924

Win pct: Highest, season

.880 Preacher Roe, 1951
.864 OREL HERSHISER, 1985
.833 Sandy Koufax, 1963
.824 Jim Hughes, 1899
.824 Dazzy Vance, 1924

ERA: Lowest, season

1.58 Rube Marquard, 1916
1.68 Ned Garvin, 1904
1.73 Sandy Koufax, 1966
1.74 Sandy Koufax, 1964
1.87 Kaiser Wilhelm, 1908

Most pinch-hit homers, season

6 Johnny Frederick, 1932
5 Lee Lacy, 1978

Most pinch-hit, homers, career

8 Johnny Frederick, 1929-1934
8 Lee Lacy, 1972-78

Most consecutive games, batting safely

31 Willie Davis, 1969
29 Zach Wheat, 1916

Most consecutive scoreless innings

59 Orel Hershiser, 1988
58 Don Drysdale, 1968
39 Don Newcombe, 1956

No hit games

Tom Lovett, Bro vs NY NL, 4-0; June 22, 1891.
Mal Eason, Bro at StL NL, 2-0; July 20, 1906.
Harry McIntyre, Bro vs Pit NL, 0-1; August 1, 1906 (lost on 4 hits in 13 innings after allowing the first hit in the 11th).
Nap Rucker, Bro vs Bos NL, 6-0; September 5, 1908 (2nd game).
Dazzy Vance, Bro vs Phi NL, 10-1; September 13, 1925 (1st game).
Tex Carleton, Bro at Cin NL, 3-0; April 30, 1940.
Ed Head, Bro vs Bos NL, 5-0; April 23, 1946.
Rex Barney, Bro at NY NL, 2-0; September 9, 1948.
Carl Erskine, Bro vs Chi NL, 5-0; June 19, 1952.
Carl Erskine, Bro vs NY NL, 3-0; May 12, 1956.
Sal Maglie, Bro vs Phi NL, 5-0; September 25, 1956.
Sandy Koufax, LA vs NY NL, 5-0; June 30, 1962.
Sandy Koufax, LA vs SF NL, 8-0; May 11, 1963.
Sandy Koufax, LA at Phi NL, 3-0; June 4, 1964.
Sandy Koufax, LA vs Chi NL, 1-0; September 9, 1965 (perfect game).
Bill Singer, LA vs Phi NL, 5-0; July 20, 1970.
Jerry Reuss, LA at SF NL, 8-0; June 27, 1980.
Fernando Valenzuela, LA vs StL NL, 6-0; June 29, 1990.
Kevin Gross, LA vs SF NL, 2-0; August 17, 1992.
Ed Stein, six innings, rain, Bro vs Chi NL, 6-0; June 2, 1894.
Fred Frankhouse, seven and two-thirds innings, rain, Bro vs Cin NL, 5-0; August 27, 1937.

ACTIVE PLAYERS in caps.

Leader from the franchise's current location is included. If not in the top five, leader's rank is listed in parenthesis; asterisk (*) indicates player is not in top 25.

Toronto Blue Jays

by H. Darr Beiser, *USA TODAY*

ALCS-MVP Roberto Alomar led the Jays with 105 runs (third in the AL), 49 steals (fifth), and eight triples.

1992 Blue Jays: They finally won it all

The Toronto Blue Jays buried their past while an entire nation cheered. Gone forever is the choke label.

The string of disappointments—1985, 1987, 1989, and 1991—hung around the neck of one of the most successful expansion franchises ever. Since 1983, the Jays were 906-711 in regular-season play, the best record in baseball. Veterans Dave Winfield and Jack Morris, free-agent acquisitions, were credited with pulling the '92 team to the final rung on the ladder.

After the California Angels gave up on him, Winfield staged a great comeback, hitting 26 home runs and driving in 108—the second highest total on the team. Morris won 21 games. And with the Blue Jays' staff often injured and ineffective, the 1991 World Series MVP held the rotation together for long stretches during the season.

Toronto's bullpen was one of the best in baseball. Closer Tom Henke, with the Blue Jays since 1985, enjoyed his third straight season with at least 32 saves. Setup man Duane Ward added a dozen saves and seven victories. Coming down the stretch, the Jays added insurance in the form of a trade for the Mets' ace, David Cone.

On the right side of the infield, the Blue Jays have two superstars in the making. Second baseman Roberto Alomar may be the best at his position in either league. Besides speed and stellar defense, Alomar has the potential to hit 15 home runs a season. His two-run HR off Dennis Eckersley helped Toronto derail Oakland in the playoffs. At first base, John Olerud made great strides in the second half of the season. Another good glove man, he's slowly making Blue Jays' fans forget they once had the choice of Cecil Fielder or Fred McGriff at that position.

Center fielder Devon White may not be a prototypical leadoff hitter—he hit just .248 in '92—but nobody roams the outfield better. His dramatic catch to save Game Three of the World Series for the Blue Jays was compared with Willie Mays' classic 1954 grab. And outfielder Candy Maldonado was on his way out in the spring, but when rookie Derek Bell was injured, Maldonado came on to hit .272 with 20 home runs.

The Blue Jays set a major league record for attendance with their 68th sellout in their season finale. They drew more than four million fans in '92—the third consecutive season the franchise has surpassed that mark.

—by Tim Wendel

1993 Blue Jays: Preview

The Jays, who have won more games than any other team in the last decade, are in the catbird seat. They had two worries going into the offseason: the expansion draft and the dozen players who became free agents. The expansion hurdle was cleared easily with the loss of three prospects, including Nigel Wilson, to the Marlins. The possibility of losing those free agents would cripple any other team, but between the Blue Jays' money and their mainstays, it probably left them a better team.

They kept top free agent Joe Carter, whose 119 RBI marked the sixth time in seven seasons he had 100-plus RBI, and whom general manager Pat Gillick made a priority No. 1.

Gillick kept right on going, adding veteran leaders Dave Stewart and Paul Molitor.

Besides, they still have Jack Morris, Duane Ward, and Todd Stottlemyre on the mound. Roberto Alomar and John Olerud will be there, as will Devon White. There are plenty of reasons for another four million spectators to cheer on the defending champions.

—by Margaret McCahill

1992 Blue Jays: Between the lines

▸**April 30:** Roberto Alomar had a 10-game hitting streak going.

▸**May 3:** Dave Stieb picked up his first win since May 11, 1991. He had been sidelined for nearly a year with back trouble. ***Milestone:*** Dave Winfield hit his 411th homer, leading all active major leaguers.

▸**May 7:** The Blue Jays scored five runs in the ninth inning—four on Dave Winfield's 10th career grand slam.

▸**May 9:** Winfield, who leads all active players in home runs and RBI, extended his hitting streak to 17 games, a career-best and five games short of the Toronto record held by George Bell.

▸**May 10:** Juan Guzman ran his record to 5-0 with a complete-game four-hitter and the Blue Jays regained their spot atop the AL East. Guzman was 15-1 in 16 career decisions.

▸**May 13:** Roberto Alomar continued his torrid spring with a 3-for-4 night, raising his season average to .370.

▸**May 20:** Pat Borders singled home the winning run in the 10th inning and rookie Derek Bell added his first major-league homer as the Blue Jays rallied to beat Minnesota and end their five-game losing streak.

▸**May 27:** Alfredo Griffin's eighth-inning RBI single snapped an 0-for-15 string since Opening Day.

▸**May 31 *Milestone:*** Dave Winfield hit his 415th career homer, to move past Darrell Evans into 21st place on the all-time list.

▸**June 1 *Milestone:*** Devon White became the 56th player in baseball history to homer from both sides of the plate in one game—including an inside-the-park shot. The last player to accomplish the feat was Roberto Alomar in May 1991.

▸**June 9:** Candy Maldonado's 451-foot homer was only the fifth ball to reach the center field bleachers since Yankee Stadium was renovated in 1976. It was also the game-winner.

▸**June 10:** Joe Carter homered, tripled and doubled to pace the Blue Jays to their third straight win, sweeping the Yankees. ***Quote of the day:*** Yankee pitcher Scott Sanderson, after allowing six runs in 1 2/3 innings—"I'm sure we made a impression on them. It wasn't the impression you want to make."

▸**June 11:** Jack Morris threw his first shutout since Game Seven of the 1991 World Series (when he was a Twin).

▸**June 17:** Manuel Lee was batting .545 (12-for-22) with two outs and runners in scoring position for the Blue Jays. He had just a single error so far in 1992.

▸**June 26:** Juan Guzman won his 10th of the season and improved to 20-4 in his career, shutting down the Indians on two hits over eight innings in a 6-1 Blue Jays' victory.

▸**July 3:** Dave Stieb allowed one hit in two scoreless innings in his first relief appearance since 1988. In the seventh inning of the same game, every Toronto starter hit safely, setting a club record with nine consecutive hits.

▸**July 4 *Milestone:*** Tom Henke recorded his 200th career save with a scoreless inning to close out the Blue Jays win. He was the 13th major-leaguer to hit that plateau.

▸**August 6:** Five home runs were among 26 hits in the Blue Jays' 15-11 victory at Detroit. Joe Carter, Dave Winfield, and Jeff Kent homered for the Jays.

▸**August 10:** Joe Carter, Candy Maldonado, and Dave Winfield each hit two-run homers to power Toronto past Baltimore, 9-4, in the first of a crucial series between the AL East rivals. The Jays finished the day three games up. ***Milestones:*** Dave Winfield hit his 487th career double, moving him into 36th place on the all-time list (one behind Mel Ott); his 995th extra-base hit tied him for 20th place on the all-time list with Al Simmons.

▸**August 13:** Toronto earned a split of a four-game series with second-place Baltimore on Joe Carter's homer and Roberto Alomar's RBI double.

▸**August 18:** Dave Winfield's bases-loaded double highlighted a five-run first inning as the Blue Jays routed Milwaukee 12-1 to increase their lead in the AL East to four games over Baltimore.

▸**August 20:** It was a rough night at the office for Blue Jays' starter David Wells, whose ERA skyrocketed from 4.46 to 5.37 with a 16-3 loss to Milwaukee.

▸**August 26:** Todd Stottlemyre took a no-hitter into the eighth inning and wound up with a one-hit shutout as the Blue Jays routed the White Sox to maintain a two-game lead over the Orioles in the AL East.

▸**August 29:** David Cone was mediocre in his Blue Jays debut, a 7-2 loss against Milwaukee. His American League ERA started out at 9.45.

▸**August 30:** The Blue Jays welcomed ace Juan Guzman back from the DL, as he turned in four innings of two-hit shutout ball in a 5-3 win against Milwaukee.

▸**September 4:** The Blue Jays set a league record with 10 hits in a row in the second inning of a 16-5 win against Minnesota.

▸**September 5:** Joe Carter collected his 100th RBI of the season as the Blue Jays beat Minnesota 7-3. He had driven in 100 or more runs in six of the last seven seasons.

▸**September 9:** David Cone limited the Royals to five hits over 8 1/3 scoreless innings as the Blue Jays beat Kansas City 1-0 to boost their AL East lead to 3 1/2 games.

▸**September 19:** Toronto's pennant-drive acquisition of Cone continued to pay off as he took a shutout through seven innings in a 1-0 blanking of Texas. The Blue Jays maintained a five-game lead in the AL East.

▸**September 24 *Milestone:*** Dave Winfield, 40, became the oldest player in major league history to hit the 100-RBI plateau in a season.

▸**September 27:** Jack Morris became the Blue Jays' first 20-game winner.

▸**October 2:** The Blue Jays squandered a 6-1 lead but managed to hang on for an 8-7 win over the Tigers, to clinch a tie in the AL East.

▸**October 3:** The Blue Jays clinched the AL East title, beating Detroit 3-1.

▸**October 4:** The Jays finished with a four-game cushion. Joe Carter was second in the AL in RBI (119) and total bases (310), and fifth in home runs (34). Roberto Alomar was third in runs (105), steals (49), and on-base percentage (.405). He came in fifth in triples (8) and seventh in batting (.310). Jack Morris led the league in victories (21-6), Tom Henke was fifth in saves (34), and Duane Ward was second in appearances (79). Dave Winfield was in the top ten in RBI, slugging percentage, and total bases.

—by Jeanie Chung, John Hunt, Deron Snyder, and Lisa Winston.

Team directory

▸**Owner:** Labatt's Breweries and the Canadian Imperial Bank of Commerce

▸**General Manager:** Pat Gillick

▸**Ballpark:**
Skydome
Toronto, Ontario
416-341-1000
Capacity 51,000
Public transportation available
Family and wheelchair sections, non-alcohol sections, ramps, Playland

▸**Team publications:**
Scorebook Magazine (Buzz Communications), 416-961-5141

▸**TV, radio broadcast stations:**
TSN and Baton Broadcasting, FAN 1430 Toronto

▸**Spring Training:**
Dunedin Stadium at Grant Field
311 Douglas Ave.
Dunedin, Fla.
Capacity 6,218
813-733-9302

TORONTO BLUE JAYS 1992 final stats

Batting	AVG	SLG	OB	G	AB	R	H	TB	2B	3B	HR	RBI	BB	SO	SB	CS	E
Martinez	.625	1.000	.625	7	8	2	5	8	0	0	1	3	0	1	0	0	0
Mulliniks	.500	.500	.667	3	2	1	1	1	0	0	0	0	1	0	0	0	0
T.Ward	.345	.552	.424	18	29	7	10	16	3	0	1	3	4	4	0	1	0
Alomar	.310	.427	.405	152	571	105	177	244	27	8	8	76	87	52	49	9	5
Winfield	.290	.491	.377	156	583	92	169	286	33	3	26	108	82	89	2	3	0
Zosky	.286	.571	.250	8	7	1	2	4	0	1	0	1	0	2	0	0	1
Olerud	.284	.450	.375	138	458	68	130	206	28	0	16	66	70	61	1	0	7
Maldonado	.272	.462	.357	137	489	64	133	226	25	4	20	66	59	112	2	2	6
Carter	.264	.498	.309	158	622	97	164	310	30	7	34	119	36	109	12	5	9
Knorr	.263	.421	.300	8	19	1	5	8	0	0	1	2	1	5	0	0	0
Lee	.263	.316	.343	128	396	49	104	125	10	1	3	39	50	73	6	2	7
Tabler	.252	.289	.306	49	135	11	34	39	5	0	0	16	11	14	0	0	0
White	.248	.390	.303	153	641	98	159	250	26	7	17	60	47	133	37	4	7
Bell	.242	.354	.324	61	161	23	39	57	6	3	2	15	15	34	7	2	0
Borders	.242	.385	.290	138	480	47	116	185	26	2	13	53	33	75	1	1	8
Kent	.240	.443	.324	65	192	36	46	85	13	1	8	35	20	47	2	1	11
Sprague	.234	.340	.280	22	47	6	11	16	2	0	1	7	3	7	0	0	1
Griffin	.233	.280	.273	63	150	21	35	42	7	0	0	10	9	19	3	1	7
Gruber	.229	.352	.275	120	446	42	102	157	16	3	11	43	26	72	7	7	17
Quinlan	.067	.133	.176	13	15	2	1	2	1	0	0	2	2	9	0	0	1
Maksudian	.000	.000	.000	3	3	0	0	0	0	0	0	0	0	0	0	0	0

Pitching	W-L	ERA	G	GS	CG	GF	Sho	SV	IP	H	R	ER	HR	BB	SO
D.Ward	7-4	1.95	79	0	0	35	0	12	101.1	76	27	22	5	39	103
Henke	3-2	2.26	57	0	0	50	0	34	55.2	40	19	14	5	22	46
Cone	4-3	2.55	8	7	0	0	0	0	53	39	16	15	3	29	47
Guzman	16-5	2.64	28	28	1	0	0	0	180.2	135	56	53	6	72	165
Eichhorn	4-4	3.08	65	0	0	26	0	2	87.2	86	34	30	3	25	61
Key	13-13	3.53	33	33	4	0	2	0	216.2	205	88	85	24	59	117
Morris	21-6	4.04	34	34	6	0	1	0	240.2	222	114	108	18	80	132
Timlin	0-2	4.12	26	0	0	14	0	1	43.2	45	23	20	0	20	35
MacDonald	1-0	4.37	27	0	0	9	0	0	47.1	50	24	23	4	16	26
Stottlemyre	12-11	4.50	28	27	6	0	2	0	174	175	99	87	20	63	98
Stieb	4-6	5.04	21	14	1	3	0	0	96.1	98	58	54	9	43	45
Hentgen	5-2	5.36	28	2	0	10	0	0	50.1	49	30	30	7	32	39
Wells	7-9	5.40	41	14	0	14	0	2	120	138	84	72	16	36	62
Weathers	0-0	8.10	2	0	0	0	0	0	3.1	5	3	3	1	2	3
Linton	1-3	8.63	8	3	0	2	0	0	24	31	23	23	5	17	16
Leiter	0-0	9.00	1	0	0	0	0	0	1	1	1	1	0	2	0
Trlicek	0-0	10.80	2	0	0	0	0	0	1.2	2	2	2	0	2	1

1993 preliminary roster

PITCHERS (18)
Scott Brow
Huck Flener
Juan Guzman
Pat Hentgen
Al Leiter
Doug Linton
Bob MacDonald
Paul Menhart
Jack Morris
Aaron Small
Rick Steed
Dave Stewart
Todd Stottlemyre
Billy Taylor
Mike Timlin
Rick Trlicek
Duane Ward
David Wells

CATCHERS (5)
Pat Borders
Carlos Delgado
Randy Knorr
Greg O'Halloran
Ed Sprague

INFIELDERS (8)
Roberto Alomar
Darnell Coles
Domingo Martinez
Paul Molitor
John Olerud
Tom Quinlan
Luis Sojo
Eddie Zosky

OUTFIELDERS (7)
Derek Bell
Brent Bowers
Joe Carter
Juan De La Rosa
Robert Perez
Turner Ward
Devon White

Games played by position

Player	G	C	1B	2B	3B	SS	OF	DH
ALOMAR,R	152	0	0	150	0	0	0	1
BELL,D	61	0	0	0	0	0	56	1
BORDERS,P	138	137	0	0	0	0	0	0
CARTER,J	158	0	4	0	0	0	129	24
GRIFFIN,A	63	0	0	16	0	48	0	0
GRUBER,K	120	0	0	0	120	0	0	0
KENT,J	65	0	3	17	49	0	0	0
KNORR,R	8	8	0	0	0	0	0	0
LEE,M	128	0	0	0	0	128	0	0
MAKSUDIAN,M	3	0	1	0	0	0	0	0
MALDONADO,C	137	0	0	0	0	0	132	4
MARTINEZ,DO	7	0	7	0	0	0	0	0
MULLINIKS,R	3	0	0	0	0	0	0	2
OLERUD,J	138	0	133	0	0	0	0	1
QUINLAN,T	13	0	0	0	13	0	0	0
SPRAGUE,E	22	15	4	0	1	0	0	2
TABLER,P	49	0	34	0	1	0	8	2
WARD,T	18	0	0	0	0	0	12	0
WHITE,D	153	0	0	0	0	0	152	1
WINFIELD,D	156	0	0	0	0	0	26	130
ZOSKY,E	8	0	0	0	0	8	0	0

Sick call: 1992 DL report

Player	Days on the DL
Bell, Derek	29
Dayley, Ken	182
Gruber, Kelly	25
Guzman, Juan	25
Hentgen, Pat	47
Knorr, Randy	41
Mulliniks, Rance	148
Stieb, Dave*	73
Stottlemyre, Todd	23
Timlin, Mike	67

** On Disabled List twice during 1992 season (not counting transfers from one DL to another).*

Minor league report

Class AAA — Syracuse finished 60-83, last in the International League East Division. OF Ryan Thompson led the team in hitting at .282 with 14 HR and 46 RBI. 1B Domingo Martinez had 21 HR. RHP Doug Linton K'd 126. **Class AA:** Knoxville finished 56-88, last in both halves of the Southern League Western Division. OF Juan Delarosa hit .329 with 12 HR and 53 RBI. OF Nigel Wilson had 26 HR and 69 RBI. RHP Mark Ohlms had 18 saves. **Class A:** Dunedin finished 78-59, 4th in the 1st half of the Florida State League West Division and 1st in the 2nd half. The team lost to Clearwater in the 1st round of the playoffs. C Carlos Delgado was named league MVP, hitting .324 with 30 HR and 100 RBI. OF Rob Butler won the batting title at .358. 3B Howard Battle had 17 HR and 85 RBI. Myrtle Beach finished 71-65, 4th in the 1st half of the Sally League Southern Division and 1st in the 2nd half. The team beat Charleston (W.Va.) in three games for the league championship. LHP Travis Baptist won the league ERA title with an 11-2 record and 1.44 mark. RHP Gregg Martin won the save title with 27. IF Joe Lis hit .300 with 13 HR and 79 RBI. St. Catherine finished 33-42, 5th in the New York-Penn League Stedler Division. RHP Tim Crabtree won the league ERA title at 1.57 with a 6-3 record. OF Lonell Roberts had 33 SB. Medicine Hat finished 23-52, last in the Pioneer League Northern Division. OF Jose Herrera had 32 SB. RHP Alonso Beltran was 4-5 with a 3.14 ERA. Blue Jays finished 35-24, 1st in the Gulf Coast League Western Division. The team lost to the Expos in the 1st round of the playoffs. IF Diomedes Vasquez hit .311 while IF Tilson Brito hit .307 with 3 HR and 36 RBI. OF Shannon Stewart led the league with 31 SB. LHP Tim Adkins was 6-2 with a 1.72 ERA. RHP Bart Rich led the league in saves with 16.

Tops in the organization

BATTING LEADERS	Club	Avg.	G	AB	R	H	HR	RBI
Rob Butler	Dun	.358	92	391	67	140	4	41
Juan Delarosa	Knx	.329	136	508	68	167	12	53
Carlos Delgado	Dun	.324	133	485	83	157	30	100
Joe Lis	Myr	.300	125	434	70	130	13	79
Chris Stynes	Myr	.284	127	489	67	139	7	46

HOME RUNS		
Carlos Delgado	Dun	30
Nigel Wilson	Knx	26
Domingo Martinez	Syr	21
Howard Battle	Dun	17
Several players tied		16

RBI		
Carlos Delgado	Dun	100
Howard Battle	Dun	85
Joe Lis	Myr	79
Butch Davis	Syr	74
Nigel Wilson	Knx	69

STOLEN BASES		
Carlos Delgado	Dun	100
Howard Battle	Dun	85
Joe Lis	Myr	79
Butch Davis	Syr	74
Nigel Wilson	Knx	69

WINS		
Scott Brow	Dun	14
Doug Linton	Syr	12
Chris Kotes	Myr	12
Several players tied		11

SAVES		
Gregg Martin	Myr	27
Mark Ohlms	Knx	18
Ricardo Jordan	Dun	15
Graeme Lloyd	Knx	14
Several players tied		10

STRIKEOUTS		
Paul Spoljaric	Myr	161
Dennis Gray	Myr	141
Jesse Cross	Knx	129
Doug Linton	Syr	126
Giovanni Carrara	My	116

PITCHING LEADERS	Club	W-L	ERA	IP	H	BB	SO
Travis Baptist	Myr	11-2	1.44	119	80	23	98
Huck Flener	Dun	7-3	2.24	112	70	50	93
Scott Brow	Dun	14-2	2.43	171	143	44	107
Paul Spoljaric	Myr	10-8	2.82	163	111	58	161
Woody Williams	Syr	6-8	3.13	121	115	41	81

Toronto (1977-1992)

Runs: Most, career, all-time

768 Lloyd Moseby, 1980-1989
641 GEORGE BELL, 1981-1990
538 Willie Upshaw, 1978-1987
530 JESSE BARFIELD, 1981-1989
510 TONY FERNANDEZ, 1983-1990

Hits: Most, career, all-time

1319 Lloyd Moseby, 1980-1989
1294 GEORGE BELL, 1981-1990
1142 TONY FERNANDEZ, 1983-1990
1028 Damaso Garcia, 1980-1986
982 Willie Upshaw, 1978-1987

2B: Most, career, all-time

242 Lloyd Moseby, 1980-1989
237 GEORGE BELL, 1981-1990
204 RANCE MULLINIKS, 1982-1992
192 TONY FERNANDEZ, 1983-1990
177 Willie Upshaw, 1978-1987

3B: Most, career, all-time

61 TONY FERNANDEZ, 1983-1990
60 Lloyd Moseby, 1980-1989
50 ALFREDO GRIFFIN, 1979-1992
42 Willie Upshaw, 1978-1987
32 GEORGE BELL, 1981-1990

HR: Most, career, all-time

202 GEORGE BELL, 1981-1990
179 JESSE BARFIELD, 1981-1989
149 Lloyd Moseby, 1980-1989
131 Ernie Whitt, 1977-1989
125 FRED McGRIFF, 1986-1990

RBI: Most, career, all-time

740 GEORGE BELL, 1981-1990
651 Lloyd Moseby, 1980-1989
527 JESSE BARFIELD, 1981-1989
518 Ernie Whitt, 1977-1989
478 Willie Upshaw, 1978-1987

SB: Most, career, all-time

255 Lloyd Moseby, 1980-1989
194 Damaso Garcia, 1980-1986
138 TONY FERNANDEZ, 1983-1990
102 ROBERTO ALOMAR, 1991-1992
80 KELLY GRUBER, 1984-1992

BB: Most, career, all-time

547 Lloyd Moseby, 1980-1989
416 RANCE MULLINIKS, 1982-1992
403 Ernie Whitt, 1977-1989
390 Willie Upshaw, 1978-1987
352 FRED McGRIFF, 1986-1990

BA: Highest, career, all-time

.289 TONY FERNANDEZ, 1983-1990
.288 Damaso Garcia, 1980-1986
.286 GEORGE BELL, 1981-1990
.280 RANCE MULLINIKS, 1982-1992
.278 FRED McGRIFF, 1986-1990

Slug avg: Highest, career, all-time

.530 FRED McGRIFF, 1986-1990
.486 GEORGE BELL, 1981-1990
.483 JESSE BARFIELD, 1981-1989
.461 Otto Velez, 1977-1982
.450 John Mayberry, 1978-1982

Games started: Most, career, all-time

405 DAVE STIEB, 1979-1992
345 Jim Clancy, 1977-1988
250 JIMMY KEY, 1984-1992
151 Luis Leal, 1980-1985
128 TODD STOTTLEMYRE, 1988-1992

Saves: Most, career, all-time

217 TOM HENKE, 1985-1992
76 DUANE WARD, 1986-1992
31 Joey McLaughlin, 1980-1984
30 Roy Lee Jackson, 1981-1984
16 Bill Caudill, 1985-1986

Shutouts: Most, career, all-time

30 DAVE STIEB, 1979-1992
11 Jim Clancy, 1977-1988
10 JIMMY KEY, 1984-1992
4 Jesse Jefferson, 1977-1980
3 Doyle Alexander, 1983-1986
3 Luis Leal, 1980-1985
3 Dave Lemanczyk, 1977-1980

Wins: Most, career, all-time

174 DAVE STIEB, 1979-1992
128 Jim Clancy, 1977-1988
116 JIMMY KEY, 1984-1992
51 Luis Leal, 1980-1985
51 TODD STOTTLEMYRE, 1988-1992

K: Most, career, all-time

1631 DAVE STIEB, 1979-1992
1237 Jim Clancy, 1977-1988
944 JIMMY KEY, 1984-1992
644 TOM HENKE, 1985-1992
571 DUANE WARD, 1986-1992

Win pct: Highest, career, all-time

.639 Doyle Alexander, 1983-1986
.589 JIMMY KEY, 1984-1992
.569 DAVE STIEB, 1979-1992
.560 DAVID WELLS, 1987-1992
.554 John Cerutti, 1985-1990

ERA: Lowest, career, all-time

3.39 DAVE STIEB, 1979-1992
3.42 JIMMY KEY, 1984-1992
3.56 Doyle Alexander, 1983-1986
3.87 John Cerutti, 1985-1990
4.10 Jim Clancy, 1977-1988

Runs: Most, season

111 GEORGE BELL, 1987
110 DEVON WHITE, 1991
107 JESSE BARFIELD, 1986
106 Lloyd Moseby, 1987
105 ROBERTO ALOMAR, 1992

Hits: Most, season

213 TONY FERNANDEZ, 1986
198 GEORGE BELL, 1986
188 ROBERTO ALOMAR, 1991
188 GEORGE BELL, 1987
186 TONY FERNANDEZ, 1987
186 TONY FERNANDEZ, 1988

2B: Most, season

42 JOE CARTER, 1991
41 ROBERTO ALOMAR, 1991
41 GEORGE BELL, 1989
41 TONY FERNANDEZ, 1988
40 DEVON WHITE, 1991

3B: Most, season

17 TONY FERNANDEZ, 1990
15 Dave Collins, 1984
15 ALFREDO GRIFFIN, 1980
15 Lloyd Moseby, 1984
11 ROBERTO ALOMAR, 1991

HR: Most, season

47 GEORGE BELL, 1987
40 JESSE BARFIELD, 1986
36 FRED McGRIFF, 1989
35 FRED McGRIFF, 1990
34 JOE CARTER, 1992
34 FRED McGRIFF, 1988

RBI: Most, season

134 GEORGE BELL, 1987
119 JOE CARTER, 1992
118 KELLY GRUBER, 1990
108 JESSE BARFIELD, 1986
108 GEORGE BELL, 1986
108 JOE CARTER, 1991
108 DAVE WINFIELD, 1992

SB: Most, season

60 Dave Collins, 1984
54 Damaso Garcia, 1982
53 ROBERTO ALOMAR, 1991
49 ROBERTO ALOMAR, 1992
46 Damaso Garcia, 1984

BB: Most, season

119 FRED McGRIFF, 1989
94 FRED McGRIFF, 1990
87 ROBERTO ALOMAR, 1992
82 DAVE WINFIELD, 1992
79 FRED McGRIFF, 1988

BA: Highest, season

.322 TONY FERNANDEZ, 1987
.315 Lloyd Moseby, 1983
.311 Bob Bailor, 1977
.310 TONY FERNANDEZ, 1986
.310 ROBERTO ALOMAR, 1992

Slug avg: Highest, season

.605 GEORGE BELL, 1987
.559 JESSE BARFIELD, 1986
.552 FRED McGRIFF, 1988
.536 JESSE BARFIELD, 1985
.532 GEORGE BELL, 1986

Games started: Most, season

40 Jim Clancy, 1982
38 Luis Leal, 1982
38 DAVE STIEB, 1982
37 Jim Clancy, 1987
36 Doyle Alexander, 1985
36 Jim Clancy, 1984
36 JIMMY KEY, 1987
36 DAVE STIEB, 1983
36 DAVE STIEB, 1985

Saves: Most, season

34 TOM HENKE, 1987
34 TOM HENKE, 1992
32 TOM HENKE, 1990
27 TOM HENKE, 1986
25 TOM HENKE, 1988

Shutouts: Most, season

5 DAVE STIEB, 1982
4 DAVE STIEB, 1980
4 DAVE STIEB, 1983
4 DAVE STIEB, 1988
3 Jim Clancy, 1982
3 Jim Clancy, 1986

Wins: Most, season

21 JACK MORRIS, 1992
18 DAVE STIEB, 1990
17 Doyle Alexander, 1984
17 Doyle Alexander, 1985
17 JIMMY KEY, 1987
17 DAVE STIEB, 1982
17 DAVE STIEB, 1983
17 DAVE STIEB, 1989

K: Most, season

198 DAVE STIEB, 1984
187 DAVE STIEB, 1983
180 Jim Clancy, 1987
167 DAVE STIEB, 1985
166 MARK EICHHORN, 1986

Win pct: Highest, season

.778 JACK MORRIS, 1992
.762 JUAN GUZMAN, 1992
.750 DAVE STIEB, 1990
.739 Doyle Alexander, 1984
.680 JIMMY KEY, 1987
.680 DAVE STIEB, 1989

ERA: Lowest, season

2.48 DAVE STIEB, 1985
2.64 JUAN GUZMAN, 1992
2.76 JIMMY KEY, 1987
2.83 DAVE STIEB, 1984
2.93 DAVE STIEB, 1990

Most pinch-hit homers, season

2 Al Woods, 1977
2 Otto Velez, 1979
2 Rico Carty, 1979
2 Ernie Whitt, 1982
2 Jeff Burroughs, 1985

Most pinch-hit, homers, career

4 Ernie Whitt, 1977-1989
4 Jesse Barfield, 1981-1989

Most consecutive games, batting safely

22 George Bell, 1989
21 Damaso Garcia, 1983
21 Lloyd Moseby, 1983

Most consecutive scoreless innings

31 Dave Stieb, 1988

No hit games

Dave Stieb, Tor at Det AL, 3-0; September 2, 1990.

ACTIVE PLAYERS in caps.

Milwaukee Brewers

by Russell Beeker, *Baseball Weekly*

AL Rookie of the Year Pat Listach was second in the AL with 54 stolen bases and led the Brewers in runs.

1992 Brewers: Last-minute contenders

Led by Phil "Scrap Iron" Garner's aggressive baseball philosophy and rookie Pat Listach's young legs, the Brewers ran circles around the rest of the league and almost ran Toronto out of first place. They led the majors in stolen bases (256), becoming the only AL East team to ever steal so much as 200 bases in a season. Listach stole a club-record 54 of those, hit .290, and was named AL Rookie of the Year.

But in the end, time ran out on the Brewers. They won 22 of 29 games down the stretch—giving Toronto a serious chase—but lost the final two in Oakland. The 92-70 season was their best in 10 years.

The high point of the pennant drive came Oct. 2 when the Brewers tied the game against Dennis Eckersley in the top of the ninth, saved it with a diving catch by Robin Yount in the bottom, and won in the 11th. It brought the Brewers within two games with two days left, but the race ended the next day when the Blue Jays beat Detroit in Toronto.

If Listach was the catalyst for the Brewers' exciting season, Paul Molitor was the main cog. Playing 158 games and staying healthy for the second year in a row, Molitor put up MVP-type numbers: .320 average, 12 home runs, 89 RBI and 31 stolen bases—one of 11 Brewers with double-digit steals.

Left fielder Greg Vaughn, coming off a monster 1991 season, slipped a bit to .228 but still managed to knock in 78 runs with the help of 23 homers. Dante Bichette (.287) and Darryl Hamilton (.298) were also productive and very strong defensively. Robin Yount had 147 hits, one of which was the 3,000th in his career. He drove in 77 runs as well; the emotional boost from his historic hit carried throughout the pennant drive.

The Brewers were among the top scoring teams in the league despite hitting only 82 home runs, second-worst in the AL. Franklin Stubbs was a disappointment, again, and was benched.

Defensively they were very solid, committing the fewest errors in the league (89). Kevin Seitzer played a reliable third base, making only 12 errors. Scott Fletcher batted .275 and teamed with Listach for a reliable double-play combination.

Led by rookie Cal Eldred, 11-2 with a 1.79 ERA, Chris Bosio (16-6, 3.62) and Jaime Navarro (17-11, 3.33), the Brewers had the best team ERA in the league at 3.43. Bosio and Eldred each had club-record 10-game winning streaks during the season. Middle reliever Mike Fetters, acquired in a trade with California, posted a 5-1 record, with a 1.87 ERA while allowing only 38 hits in 62 2/3 innings, and Doug Henry was slightly erratic but still saved 29 games. Bill Wegman had a less than glittering 13-14 record but had a 3.20 ERA and gave the Brewers 261 2/3 innings.

Manager Garner summed up the season: "You're never satisfied with finishing second, but we made Toronto win it...we never folded."

—by John Hunt

1993 Brewers: Preview

The Brewers are legitimate contenders in '93—if they can continue to avoid major injuries. The loss of Paul Molitor hurts but they kept golden oldie Robin Yount. And 1992 Rookie of the Year Pat Listach, pitcher Cal Eldred, catcher Dave Nilsson and slugger John Jaha are young players who have been worked into the flow. B.J. Surhoff may be moved to first or third base, and outfielder Alex Diaz could get a long look in spring training. Adding Kevin Reimer gives the team some pop and takes some pressure off the need to manufacture runs. They look to Greg Vaughn for more consistent power.

—by John Hunt

1992 Brewers: Between the lines

▸**April 22:** Game cancelled due to cold weather.

▸**April 23:** A smashing success: Right fielder Dante Bichette made a sensational over-the-shoulder catch while running full stride. He looked up immediately after catching the ball, and crashed head-first into the wall—which, fortunately, is padded.

▸**May 4:** Franklin Stubbs struck out twice as the Brewers managed just one hit against White Sox hurler Alex Fernandez. ***Quote of the day:*** Stubbs—"I heard he had some control problems. This is a heck of a night not to have control problems."

▸**May 13 *Quote of the day:*** Bill Wegman, who lowered his ERA while taking a 1-0 complete-game loss against Chicago (he made the error)—"If this doesn't change, I'll be 3-30 with a 1.30 ERA."

▸**May 18:** New catcher, same result: Dave Nilsson, just called up by the Brewers, knocked in three runs as Milwaukee won 9-1 in Detroit, their 13th win in the last 15 games at Tiger Stadium.

▸**May 19:** Frank Tanana, John Doherty and Mike Henneman combined on a three-hit shutout, blanking Milwaukee 3-0. It marked the first time in their last 15 games at Tiger Stadium that the Brewers had scored fewer than five runs, dating to August 1989.

▸**May 22:** Greg Vaughn, who had struck out three times and hit into a double play earlier, homered in the 14th inning to give the Brewers a 10-9 win against the Yankees.

▸**May 29:** Rookie shortstop Pat Listach sprained his left ankle and had to leave the game. Listach, who was hitting .316, had a hit as well as his 17th stolen base.

▸**June 8 *Milestone:*** Robin Yount moved into 21st place on the all-time list with 2,931 career hits, passing Jake Beckley and Rogers Hornsby.

▸**June 14:** Paul Molitor and Dave Nilsson had four hits each in the Brewers' club-record 22-hit attack against the Mariners and rookie Dave Fleming, spoiling Fleming's bid for his 10th consecutive win.

▸**June 18:** Bill Wegman pitched the first three-hitter of his career.

▸**June 19 *Milestone:*** Robin Yount had two doubles and a single to move to 20th place on the all-time hit list with 2,944. He passed Frank Robinson.

▸**June 28:** Dante Bichette was 4-for-5 with a homer, three RBI and three runs in the Brewers' 9-3 pasting of the Red Sox.

▸**July 25:** Ex-White Soxer Scott Fletcher hit a three-run homer in the bottom of the ninth, driving in all of the runs in the Milwaukee's 3-0 victory over Chicago. Chris Bosio tossed the shutout for the Brewers.

▸**August 2 *Quote of the day:*** Manager Phil Garner said it was too soon to count the slumping Brewers out—"We're resilient," he said. "The nails are not in the coffin and they better not give us up for dead."

▸**August 11:** The Brewers' baserunners were getting that Tingley feeling, as Angels' catcher Ron Tingley threw out four attempted thieves.

▸**August 14:** Jim Gantner hit only his third homer since 1987, in the 13th inning, to boost the Brewers to an 8-7 win against the Red Sox in the first game of a doubleheader.

▸**August 20:** It was a rough night at the office for Blue Jays' starter David Wells, whose ERA skyrocketed from 4.46 to 5.37 with a 16-3 loss to Milwaukee.

▸**August 24:** Countdown: Robin Yount got career hit No. 2,984, a two-run single in the eighth inning that skipped past Yankees right fielder Dion James and broke a 5-5 tie.

▸**August 28:** The Brewers collected an AL-record 31 hits and set a team record for runs as they slammed Toronto 22-2. Of all those hits and runs, though, only one was a homer—hit in the first inning by Paul Molitor—and 26 were singles.

▶**September 9** ***Milestone:*** Robin Yount became the 17th player in major league history to collect 3,000 hits.

▶**September 12:** First baseman John Jaha set a club record with four stolen bases in his team's win against the Orioles.

▶**September 18:** Kevin Seitzer was 2-for-3 with four RBI and Greg Vaughn was 2-for-3 with a home run and three RBI as Milwaukee beat Baltimore 12-4.

▶**September 19:** The Brewers knocked off the Orioles 4-1 to climb past Baltimore into second place in the AL East, marking the first time in 143 days that the O's were not in the top two.

▶**September 24:** Chris Bosio set a club record with his 10th consecutive win and led the Brewers to their second shutout in a row, 4-0 against California. John Jaha stole his 10th base of the season for the Brewers, the 11th player on the team to reach double digits. That ties a major league mark set by Philadelphia in 1908.

▶**September 25:** When Dan Plesac allowed a run in the eighth inning of the Brewers' 4-1 win against Oakland, it snapped a string of 27 shutout innings by the Milwaukee pitching staff.

▶**September 29:** The Brewers won their seventh in a row (7-4 over Seattle) to keep alive in the AL East race.

▶**September 30:** The Mariners snapped the Brewers' seven-game winning streak, but the Blue Jays lost as well (1-0, Boston), so the Brew Crew was still alive as the Jays' magic number shrank to two.

▶**October 1:** The Brewers just wouldn't give up. They beat Seattle 7-2 to stay alive in the AL East (Toronto had the day off).

▶**October 2:** The Brewers stayed alive—barely—as Dennis Eckersley blew just his second save of the season, eventually allowing Milwaukee to beat Oakland 3-2 in 11 innings.

▶**October 3:** The Brewers lost a 10-3 game to the A's, as the Blue Jays beat Detroit and clinched the AL East title for Canada.

▶**October 4:** The Brew Crew lost their final game to Oakland, finishing second in the AL East, four games out. Rookie Pat Listach was second in the AL in stolen bases (54). Paul Molitor was third in hits (195) and fourth in batting (.320). Robin Yount was fourth in doubles (40).

—by Jeanie Chung, John Hunt, Deron Snyder, and Lisa Winston.

Team directory

▶**Owner:** Allan H. (Bud) Selig

▶**General Manager:** Sal Bando

▶**Ballpark:**
Milwaukee County Stadium
201 South 46th St., Milwaukee, Wis.
414-933-4114
Capacity 53,192
Pay parking lot; $4
Public transportation available
Family and wheelchair sections, ramps, Designated Driver Program including free taxi transportation for single ticket holders participating in the DDP

▶**Team publications:**
Lead Off (program/scorecard)

▶**TV, radio broadcast stations:**
WTMJ 620 AM, WCGV-TV 24

▶**Camps and/or clinics:**
Gatorade Youth Camp, during the season, 414-933-4114
Fantasy Camp, January, 414-933-4114

▶**Spring Training:**
Compadre Stadium
Chandler, Ariz.
Capacity 5,000
602-895-1200

MILWAUKEE BREWERS 1992 final stats

Batting	AVG	SLG	OB	G	AB	R	H	TB	2B	3B	HR	RBI	BB	SO	SB	CS	E
Molitor	.320	.461	.389	158	609	89	195	281	36	7	12	89	73	66	31	6	2
Allanson	.320	.360	.346	9	25	6	8	9	1	0	0	0	1	2	3	1	2
Spiers	.313	.438	.353	12	16	2	5	7	2	0	0	2	1	4	1	1	0
Hamilton	.298	.400	.356	128	470	67	140	188	19	7	5	62	45	42	41	14	0
Listach	.290	.349	.352	149	579	93	168	202	19	6	1	47	55	124	54	18	24
Bichette	.287	.406	.318	112	387	37	111	157	27	2	5	41	16	74	18	7	2
Fletcher	.275	.360	.335	123	386	53	106	139	18	3	3	51	30	33	17	10	9
Seitzer	.270	.367	.337	148	540	74	146	198	35	1	5	71	57	44	13	11	12
Yount	.264	.390	.325	150	557	71	147	217	40	3	8	77	53	81	15	6	2
Surhoff	.252	.321	.314	139	480	63	121	154	19	1	4	62	46	41	14	8	6
Gantner	.246	.313	.278	101	256	22	63	80	12	1	1	18	12	17	6	2	3
Nilsson	.232	.354	.304	51	164	15	38	58	8	0	4	25	17	18	2	2	2
Stubbs	.229	.368	.297	92	288	37	66	106	11	1	9	42	27	68	11	8	8
Vaughn	.228	.409	.313	141	501	77	114	205	18	2	23	78	60	123	15	15	3
Jaha	.226	.308	.291	47	133	17	30	41	3	1	2	10	12	30	10	0	0
Suero	.188	.250	.316	18	16	4	3	4	1	0	0	0	2	1	1	1	1
McIntosh	.182	.221	.229	35	77	7	14	17	3	0	0	6	3	9	1	3	1
Tatum	.125	.125	.222	5	8	0	1	1	0	0	0	0	1	2	0	0	0
Diaz	.111	.111	.111	22	9	5	1	1	0	0	0	1	0	0	3	2	0
Valentin	.000	.000	.000	4	3	1	0	0	0	0	0	1	0	0	0	0	1

Pitching	W-L	ERA	G	GS	CG	GF	Sho	SV	IP	H	R	ER	HR	BB	SO
Eldred	11-2	1.79	14	14	2	0	1	0	100.1	76	21	20	4	23	62
Austin	5-2	1.85	47	0	0	12	0	0	58.1	38	13	12	2	32	30
Fetters	5-1	1.87	50	0	0	11	0	2	62.2	38	15	13	3	24	43
Holmes	4-4	2.55	41	0	0	25	0	6	42.1	35	12	12	1	11	31
Plesac	5-4	2.96	44	4	0	13	0	1	79	64	28	26	5	35	54
Wegman	13-14	3.20	35	35	7	0	0	0	261.2	251	104	93	28	55	127
Orosco	3-1	3.23	59	0	0	14	0	1	39	33	15	14	5	13	40
Navarro	17-11	3.33	34	34	5	0	3	0	246	224	98	91	14	64	100
Bosio	16-6	3.62	33	33	4	0	2	0	231.1	223	100	93	21	44	120
Henry	1-4	4.02	68	0	0	56	0	29	65	64	34	29	6	24	52
Heaton	3-1	4.07	32	0	0	9	0	0	42	43	21	19	5	23	31
Bones	9-10	4.57	31	28	0	0	0	0	163.1	169	90	83	27	48	65
Robinson	1-4	5.86	8	8	0	0	0	0	35.1	51	26	23	3	14	12
Ruffin	1-6	6.67	25	6	1	6	0	0	58	66	43	43	7	41	45

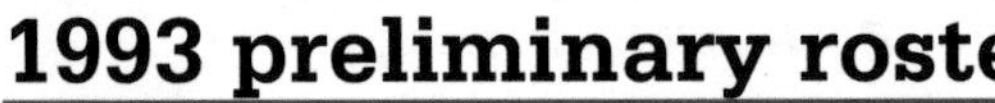

1993 preliminary roster

PITCHERS (22)
Jim Austin
Ricky Bones
Marshall Boze
Archie Corbin
Cal Eldred
Mike Fetters
Francisco Gamez
Chris George
Otis Green
Doug Henry
Ted Higuera
Mike Ignasiak
Mark Kiefer
Graeme Lloyd
Angel Miranda
Jaime Navarro
Rafael Novoa
Jesse Orosco
Ron Robinson
Larry Stanford
Bill Wegman
Rob Wishnevski

CATCHERS (4)
Joe Kmak
Tim McIntosh
Dave Nilsson
B.J. Surhoff

INFIELDERS (6)
John Jaha
Pat Listach
Bill Spiers
Franklin Stubbs
William Suero
Jose Valentin

OUTFIELDERS (7)
Alex Diaz
Darryl Hamilton
Matt Mieske
Troy O'Leary
Kevin Reimer
Greg Vaughn
Robin Yount

Games played by position

Player	G	C	1B	2B	3B	SS	OF	DH
ALLANSON,A	9	9	0	0	0	0	0	0
BICHETTE,D	112	0	0	0	0	0	101	4
DIAZ,A	22	0	0	0	0	0	11	2
FLETCHER,S	123	0	0	106	1	22	0	0
GANTNER,J	101	0	2	68	31	0	0	2
HAMILTON,D	128	0	0	0	0	0	124	0
JAHA,J	47	0	38	0	0	0	1	8
LISTACH,P	149	0	0	1	0	148	1	0
MCINTOSH,T	35	14	7	0	0	0	10	3
MOLITOR,P	158	0	48	0	0	0	0	108
NILSSON,D	51	46	3	0	0	0	0	2
SEITZER,K	148	0	1	2	146	0	0	0
SPIERS,B	12	0	0	4	1	5	0	1
STUBBS,F	92	0	68	0	0	0	1	16
SUERO,W	18	0	0	15	0	1	0	2
SURHOFF,B	139	109	17	0	3	0	7	9
TATUM,J	5	0	0	0	5	0	0	0
VALENTIN,JO	4	0	0	1	0	1	0	0
VAUGHN,G	141	0	0	0	0	0	131	7
YOUNT,R	150	0	0	0	0	0	139	11

Sick call: 1992 DL report

Player	Days on the DL
Allanson, Andy	43
Fetters, Mike	16
Gantner, Jim	15
Hamilton, Darryl	18
Higuera, Ted	182
McIntosh, Tim	15
Nilsson, Dave	18
Robinson, Ron*	114
Spiers, Billy	149

** On Disabled List twice during 1992 season (not counting transfers from one DL to another).*

Minor league report

Class AAA — Denver finished 73-71, 2nd in the American Association Western Division. 3B Jim Tatum won the batting title at .329, to go with 19 HR and 101 RBI. IF/OF Alex Diaz had 42 SB. RHP Mark Kiefer led the league in K with 145. **Class AA:** El Paso finished 73-63, 2nd in the 1st half of the Texas League Western Division and 1st in the 2nd half. The team lost to Wichita in the 1st round of the playoffs. OF Troy O'Leary won the batting title at .334 and had 79 RBI and 28 SB. IF Edgar Caceras hit .312. OF Tony Diggs had 31 SB. **Class A:** Stockton finished 83-53, winning both halves of the California League Northern Division. The team beat Visalia in four games for the league championship. OF Rob Lukachyk had 44 SB. LHP Brian Hancock was 14-4 with a 2.92 ERA, leading the league in wins. RHP Charlie Rogers had 17 saves. Beloit finished 77-58, 2nd in the 1st half of the Midwest League Northern Division and 1st in the 2nd half. The team lost to Cedar Rapids in five games for the league championship. 3B Jeff Cirillo hit .304 with 9 HR and 71 RBI. 1B Andy Fairman batted .291 with 7 HRs and 72 RBI. RHP Pat Fetty had 27 saves. Helena finished 49-26, 2nd in the Northwest League. C Brian Hostetler hit .318 with 8 HR and 59 RBI. SS Tim Unroe had 15 HR and 56 RBI. LHP Scott Karl won the ERA title with 1.46 at 7-0. Brewers finished 31-25, 4th in the Arizona League. OF Vince Zarate hit .308 with 31 RBI. 3B Jason Imperial shared the HR crown with 3. OF Ruben Cephas had 20 SB. RHP Frankie Rodriguez won the ERA title with 1.10, while RHP Richard Werner was 5-1 with a 2.56. RHP Kirk Demyan's 11 saves led the league.

Tops in the organization

BATTING LEADERS	Club	Avg.	G	AB	R	H	HR	RBI
Troy O'Leary	ElP	.334	135	506	92	169	5	79
Jim Tatum	Den	.329	130	492	74	162	19	101
Edgar Caceres	ElP	.312	114	378	50	118	2	52
John Byington	ElP	.306	130	468	60	143	4	64
Jeff Cirillo	Blt	.299	133	471	67	141	9	76

HOME RUNS:		
Matt Mieske	Den	19
Jim Tatum	Den	19
John Jaha	Den	18
Rob Lukachyk	Stk	15
Several players tied		13

WINS		
Brian Hancock	Stk	15
Mike Farrell	ElP	15
Marshall Boze	Blt	13
Tom McGraw	ElP	12
Brian McKeon	Blt	12

RBI		
Jim Tatum	Den	101
Rob Lukachyk	Stk	81
Troy O'Leary	ElP	79
Matt Mieske	Den	77
Jeff Cirillo	Blt	76

SAVES		
Pat Fetty	Blt	27
Charlie Rogers	Stk	17
Kurt Archer	Stk	15
Rob Wishnevski	Den	12
Several players tied		10

STOLEN BASES		
Rob Lukachyk	Stk	44
Alex Diaz	Den	42
Mike Carter	ElP	41
Duane Singleton	Stk	38
Mike Basse	Stk	36

STRIKEOUTS		
Mark Kiefer	Den	145
Tyrone Hill	Blt	133
Mike Farrell	ElP	133
Marshall Boze	Blt	126
Rafael Novoa	ElP	124

PITCHING LEADERS	Club	W-L	ERA	IP	H	BB	SO
Mike Farrell	ElP	15-10	2.49	199	177	46	133
Tom McGraw	ElP	12-4	2.70	167	172	57	123
Marshall Boze	Blt	13-7	2.83	146	117	82	126
Brian Hancock	Stk	15-4	2.93	166	145	87	92
Cal Eldred	Den	10-6	3.00	141	122	42	99

Milwaukee (1970-1992), includes Seattle (1969)

Runs: Most, career, all-time

1570 ROBIN YOUNT, 1974-1992
1275 PAUL MOLITOR, 1978-1992
821 Cecil Cooper, 1977-1987
726 JIM GANTNER, 1976-1992
596 Don Money, 1973-1983

Hits: Most, career, all-time

3025 ROBIN YOUNT, 1974-1992
2281 PAUL MOLITOR, 1978-1992
1815 Cecil Cooper, 1977-1987
1696 JIM GANTNER, 1976-1992
1168 Don Money, 1973-1983

2B: Most, career, all-time

558 ROBIN YOUNT, 1974-1992
405 PAUL MOLITOR, 1978-1992
345 Cecil Cooper, 1977-1987
262 JIM GANTNER, 1976-1992
215 Don Money, 1973-1983

3B: Most, career, all-time

123 ROBIN YOUNT, 1974-1992
86 PAUL MOLITOR, 1978-1992
42 Charlie Moore, 1973-1986
38 JIM GANTNER, 1976-1992
33 Cecil Cooper, 1977-1987

HR: Most, career, all-time

243 ROBIN YOUNT, 1974-1992
208 Gorman Thomas, 1973-1986
201 Cecil Cooper, 1977-1987
176 Ben Oglivie, 1978-1986
160 PAUL MOLITOR, 1978-1992

RBI: Most, career, all-time

1355 ROBIN YOUNT, 1974-1992
944 Cecil Cooper, 1977-1987
790 PAUL MOLITOR, 1978-1992
685 Ben Oglivie, 1978-1986
605 Gorman Thomas, 1973-1986

SB: Most, career, all-time

412 PAUL MOLITOR, 1978-1992
262 ROBIN YOUNT, 1974-1992
137 JIM GANTNER, 1976-1992
136 Tommy Harper, 1969-1971
108 MIKE FELDER, 1985-1990

BB: Most, career, all-time

922 ROBIN YOUNT, 1974-1992
755 PAUL MOLITOR, 1978-1992
501 Gorman Thomas, 1973-1986
440 Don Money, 1973-1983
432 Ben Oglivie, 1978-1986

BA: Highest, career, all-time

.303 PAUL MOLITOR, 1978-1992
.302 Cecil Cooper, 1977-1987
.287 ROBIN YOUNT, 1974-1992
.283 George Scott, 1972-1976
.277 Ben Oglivie, 1978-1986

Slug avg: Highest, career, all-time

.470 Cecil Cooper, 1977-1987
.461 Gorman Thomas, 1973-1986
.461 Ben Oglivie, 1978-1986
.456 George Scott, 1972-1976
.452 Sixto Lezcano, 1974-1980

Games started: Most, career, all-time

268 Jim Slaton, 1971-1983
231 Moose Haas, 1976-1985
217 Mike Caldwell, 1977-1984
185 Teddy Higuera, 1985-1991
175 BILL WEGMAN, 1985-1992

Saves: Most, career, all-time

133 DAN PLESAC, 1986-1992
97 Rollie Fingers, 1981-1985
61 Ken Sanders, 1970-1972
44 Bill Castro, 1974-1980
44 DOUG HENRY, 1991-1992

Shutouts: Most, career, all-time

19 Jim Slaton, 1971-1983
18 Mike Caldwell, 1977-1984
12 Teddy Higuera, 1985-1991
10 Bill Travers, 1974-1980
8 CHRIS BOSIO, 1986-1992
8 Moose Haas, 1976-1985

Wins: Most, career, all-time

117 Jim Slaton, 1971-1983
102 Mike Caldwell, 1977-1984
92 Teddy Higuera, 1985-1991
91 Moose Haas, 1976-1985
67 CHRIS BOSIO, 1986-1992

K: Most, career, all-time

1019 Teddy Higuera, 1985-1991
929 Jim Slaton, 1971-1983
800 Moose Haas, 1976-1985
749 CHRIS BOSIO, 1986-1992
540 Mike Caldwell, 1977-1984

Win pct: Highest, career, all-time

.622 Teddy Higuera, 1985-1991
.606 Pete Vuckovich, 1981-1986
.560 Mike Caldwell, 1977-1984
.553 JAIME NAVARRO, 1989-1992
.535 Moose Haas, 1976-1985

ERA: Lowest, career, all-time

3.37 Teddy Higuera, 1985-1991
3.65 Jim Colborn, 1972-1976
3.72 Lary Sorensen, 1977-1980
3.74 Mike Caldwell, 1977-1984
3.76 CHRIS BOSIO, 1986-1992

Runs: Most, season

136 PAUL MOLITOR, 1982
133 PAUL MOLITOR, 1991
129 ROBIN YOUNT, 1982
121 ROBIN YOUNT, 1980
115 PAUL MOLITOR, 1988

Hits: Most, season

219 Cecil Cooper, 1980
216 PAUL MOLITOR, 1991
210 ROBIN YOUNT, 1982
205 Cecil Cooper, 1982
203 Cecil Cooper, 1983

2B: Most, season

49 ROBIN YOUNT, 1980
46 ROBIN YOUNT, 1982
44 Cecil Cooper, 1979
42 ROBIN YOUNT, 1983
41 PAUL MOLITOR, 1987

3B: Most, season

16 PAUL MOLITOR, 1979
13 PAUL MOLITOR, 1991
12 ROBIN YOUNT, 1982
11 ROBIN YOUNT, 1988
10 ROBIN YOUNT, 1980
10 ROBIN YOUNT, 1983

HR: Most, season

45 Gorman Thomas, 1979
41 Ben Oglivie, 1980
39 Gorman Thomas, 1982
38 Gorman Thomas, 1980
36 George Scott, 1975

RBI: Most, season

126 Cecil Cooper, 1983
123 Gorman Thomas, 1979
122 Cecil Cooper, 1980
121 Cecil Cooper, 1982
118 Ben Oglivie, 1980

SB: Most, season

73 Tommy Harper, 1969
54 PAT LISTACH, 1992
45 PAUL MOLITOR, 1987
41 DARRYL HAMILTON, 1992
41 PAUL MOLITOR, 1982
41 PAUL MOLITOR, 1983
41 PAUL MOLITOR, 1988

BB: Most, season

98 Gorman Thomas, 1979
95 Tommy Harper, 1969
89 Darrell Porter, 1975
87 John Briggs, 1973
86 ROB DEER, 1987

BA: Highest, season

.353 PAUL MOLITOR, 1987
.352 Cecil Cooper, 1980
.331 ROBIN YOUNT, 1982
.327 WILLIE RANDOLPH, 1991
.325 PAUL MOLITOR, 1991

Slug avg: Highest, season

.578 ROBIN YOUNT, 1982
.573 Sixto Lezcano, 1979
.566 PAUL MOLITOR, 1987
.563 Ben Oglivie, 1980
.539 Cecil Cooper, 1980
.539 Gorman Thomas, 1979

Games started: Most, season

38 Jim Slaton, 1973
38 Jim Slaton, 1976
36 Jim Colborn, 1973
36 Marty Pattin, 1971
36 Lary Sorensen, 1978

Saves: Most, season

33 DAN PLESAC, 1989
31 Ken Sanders, 1971
30 DAN PLESAC, 1988
29 Rollie Fingers, 1982
29 DOUG HENRY, 1992

Shutouts: Most, season

6 Mike Caldwell, 1978
5 Marty Pattin, 1971
4 Mike Caldwell, 1979
4 Jim Colborn, 1973
4 Teddy Higuera, 1986
4 Bill Parsons, 1971

Wins: Most, season

22 Mike Caldwell, 1978
20 Jim Colborn, 1973
20 Teddy Higuera, 1986
18 Teddy Higuera, 1987
18 Lary Sorensen, 1978
18 Pete Vuckovich, 1982

K: Most, season

240 Teddy Higuera, 1987
207 Teddy Higuera, 1986
192 Teddy Higuera, 1988
173 CHRIS BOSIO, 1989
169 Marty Pattin, 1971

Win pct: Highest, season

.750 Pete Vuckovich, 1982
.727 Mike Caldwell, 1979
.727 CHRIS BOSIO, 1992
.710 Mike Caldwell, 1978
.682 BILL WEGMAN, 1991

ERA: Lowest, season

2.36 Mike Caldwell, 1978
2.45 Teddy Higuera, 1988
2.79 Teddy Higuera, 1986
2.81 Bill Travers, 1976
2.83 Jim Lonborg, 1972

Most pinch-hit homers, season

2 Max Alvis, 1970
2 Andy Kosco, 1971
2 Bob Hansen, 1974
2 Bobby Darwin, 1975
2 Ken McMullen, 1977

Most pinch-hit, homers, career

2 Mike Hegan, Sea-1969, 1970-1977
2 Max Alvis, 1970
2 Andy Kosco, 1971
2 Bob Hansen, 1974-1976
2 Bobby Darwin, 1975-1976
2 Ken McMullen, 1977

Most consecutive games, batting safely

39 Paul Molitor, 1987
24 Dave May, 1973

Most consecutive scoreless innings

32 Ted Higuera, 1987

No hit games

Juan Nieves, Mil at Bal AL, 7-0; April 15, 1987.

ACTIVE PLAYERS in caps.

Leader from the franchise's current location is included. If not in the top five, leader's rank is listed in parenthesis; asterisk (*) indicates player is not in top 25.

Baltimore Orioles

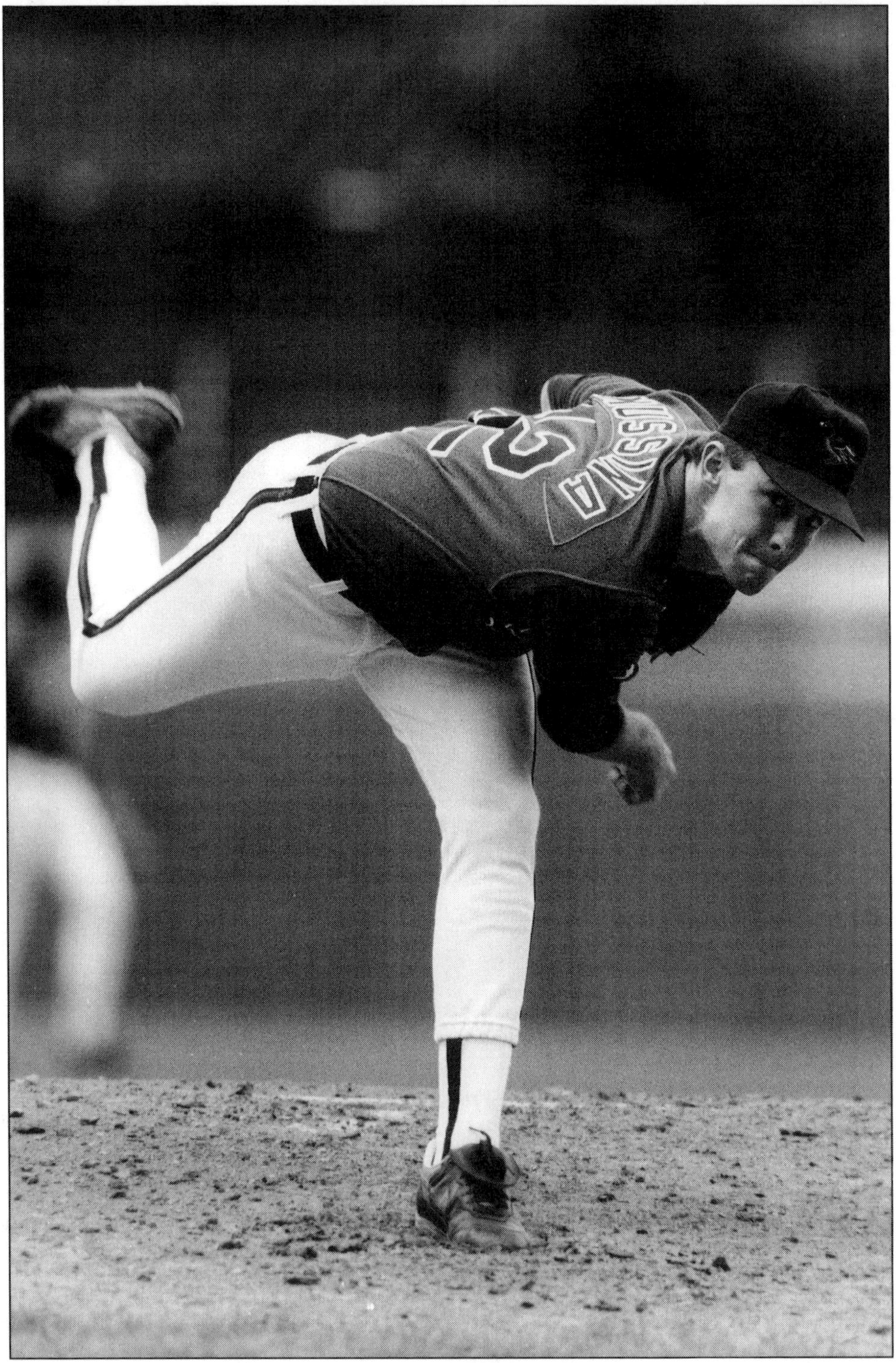

by Porter Binks, *USA TODAY*

Mike Mussina was third in the AL in wins (18-5) and ERA (2.54); he led the O's with four shutouts.

1992 Orioles: In need of the real Ripken

The Orioles were the comeback kids of 1992, capturing 89 games just a season after a dismal 67-win campaign. Their new ballpark—Oriole Park at Camden Yards—was heaped with praise by fans and players alike. Yet there was a sense of frustration: If Cal Ripken Jr. could've found his stroke, or if Glenn Davis could've stayed healthy, the Orioles might have won the AL East crown. As it was, they were in first or second place for 143 days until Sept. 19.

Unlike the Cinderella team of '89, this team looked like a bona fide contender, with a backbone of young players like Brady Anderson, Mike Devereaux, Mike Mussina, Chris Hoiles, and Leo Gomez. Anderson paid back manager Johnny Oates who stood by him when others looked at his career .219 batting average and thought Japan would be a good next stop. At leadoff, he became the first player in AL history to reach 20 homers, 50 stolen bases, and 75 RBI in the same season. Devereaux became the team's MVP, leading the club with 107 RBI and stellar defense in center field. Mussina (18-5, 2.54 ERA) developed into a Cy Young candidate in only his second full season. Hoiles had a torrid spring and wound up hitting .274 with 20 home runs, only the second Orioles' catcher ever to hit that many homers. Gomez quietly chipped in with .265 and 17 home runs and solid defense at third.

Pitching was the key to the Orioles' pennant bid: Warhorse veteran Rick Sutcliffe, Ben McDonald, and Mussina all pitched 200-plus innings. Four of their starting pitchers had at least 10 wins (compared to one pitcher in '91) and a league-leading 16 shutouts. Sutcliffe, a free agent pickup, was credited with infusing the staff with a new determination. And there was a late-season bonus: rookie left-hander Arthur Rhodes proved to be a quality starter, finishing 7-5 with a 3.63 ERA.

The Orioles got off to a hot start and were 15 games above .500 on June 12. They were in first place as late as June 19, but due to inconsistent pitching over the next month and half (23-24), they fell 4 1/2 games off the pace. They closed in on Toronto again in early August, but the Jays emerged from a crucial series with a split, and the O's stayed behind. They pulled within a half-game on Sept. 5, but then an offensive drought contributed to 12 losses in the next 18 games.

Two big guns were especially absent during long stretches of the year: Ripken had the worst offensive season of his career (.251 with 14 home runs and 72 RBI, both career lows), and Davis, hobbled by injuries, appeared in only 106 games.

Oates, who calmly managed the team through all the slumps, came in third in voting for manager of the year. His perspective on '92: "At some point this year, every person who wore a uniform for us had something to do with our success on the field."

—by Tim McQuay

1993 Orioles: Preview

The Baltimore Orioles leaped to contention in 1992, but they may be jogging in place in '93. After signing Cal Ripken Jr. to a megabucks contract, the O's seemed out of the market for any big-time additions. No big stick was destined to shore up their greatest hole—lack of consistent hitting and power from the No. 3 and 4 spots. They can hope for a revival from Ripken, but that's exactly what it is—hope.

The Orioles have a core of good young players, but they will be hard pressed to win more games—or even improve on their third place finish—without some added pop.

—by Tim McQuay

1992 Orioles: Between the lines

▸**April 22:** Rick Sutcliffe's arm seemed to be holding up just fine, thanks. He picked up his third win, after pitching two complete-game shutouts for the other two.

▸**April 23:** Mike Mussina pitched an 8-1 victory against Kansas City. It was the 11th time in 15 major league starts that he gave up fewer than three runs.

▸**April 27:** For the first time in 1992, Chris Hoiles failed to reach base via a hit or walk. He had been the only AL player to reach base in every game.

▸**April 29:** Brady Anderson had five triples and 13 extra-base hits in April.

▸**May 1:** Mike Devereaux slugged a grand slam and a solo homer. His six RBI were a career high.

▸**May 2:** Anderson continued his hot play, with a three-run homer and a double. ***Quote of the day:*** Manager Johnny Oates—"I was going to give Brady the day off tomorrow, but now I think I'll do that when he doesn't play as well as he did tonight." Meanwhile, Rick Sutcliffe's streak of consecutive scoreless innings ended at 23.

▸**May 3:** The O's beat Seattle and remained in first place in the AL East. ***Milestone:*** Gregg Olson became the youngest player in history (25) to record 100 saves. ***Quote of the day:*** Randy Milligan on fan reaction at Camden Yards—"It's louder than the last month of '89 when we were in a pennant race."

▸**May 6:** Anderson blasted a two-run homer and added his 10th stolen base of the season. ***Milestone:*** Cal Ripken Jr. played in his 1,600th consecutive game. His closest competition was Cub first baseman Mark Grace, who had a 199-game streak going.

▸**May 7:** The O's improved to 12-2 at their new park, for baseball's best winning percentage at home.

▸**May 9:** The O's notched their 20th win of 1992, the earliest a Baltimore team hit that plateau since 1970.

▸**May 26:** Glenn Davis, who had just one homer in 44 at-bats in his limited time off the DL, pounded a pair of two-run homers. Anderson had three hits and three RBI.

▸**May 30:** Gregg Olson notched his club-record 106th career save. The old record was held by Tippy Martinez.

▸**June 5:** Cal Ripken's eighth-inning single scored Anderson for the game's only run as the O's moved percentage points ahead of the Blue Jays atop the AL East. Rick Sutcliffe tossed eight shutout innings for his eighth win of the year.

▸**June 7:** The O's beat the Jays and again inched back into first place. The two teams were separated by one game or less for 38 straight days.

▸**June 8:** Bob Milacki beat the Red Sox for the first time in seven career starts against them.

▸**June 12:** Mike Mussina recorded his first major league shutout.

▸**June 15:** Rick Sutcliffe became the fourth pitcher to try—and fail—to win his 10th game.

▸**June 19:** Mike Devereaux made up for what could have been a costly outfield error with a big night at the plate, unloading his second grand slam of the season.

▸**June 21:** The O's lost catcher Chris Hoiles for 4-6 weeks with a fractured right wrist, injured when he was hit by a pitch from the Yankees' Tim Leary.

▸**June 22:** Gregg Olson, who hadn't allowed a hit in his last seven appearances, snapped a string of 19 straight saves, dating back to the first weekend of the season. The game at Camden Yards drew 45,156 spectators, giving the Orioles their 12th consecutive sellout and their 20th full house of 1992.

▸**June 23:** Cal Ripken hit a pair of homers and drove in four runs to extend his hitting streak to 11 games.

▸**June 26:** Mike Devereaux, who already had a pair of grand slams in 1992, broke a 4-4 tie with a two-run, bases-loaded single in a 6-5 win against the Royals. Devereaux was 7-for-11 with 16 RBI in bases-loaded situations.

▸**June 28:** Cal Ripken's single extended his second hitting streak of the season to 16 games.

▸**July 9:** Top pitching prospect Arthur Rhodes recorded his first major league win, also the first by a Orioles' lefty starter since July 1991.

▸**July 25:** Sutcliffe failed for his fifth straight time to get win No. 150.

▸**July 29:** Rhodes followed up his first major league complete game with his first major league shutout.

▸**August 11:** Alan Mills won his first decision as a starter, tossing five shutout innings as the O's blanked the Blue Jays to move back within two games of the lead in the AL East.

▸**August 12:** Mike Devereaux came to bat twice with the bases loaded and delivered a single and a double in the Orioles' 11-4 rout of the Blue Jays.

▸**August 24:** Jim Abbott didn't get caught up in the celebration of Cal Ripken's new contract. Abbott shut down the O's, leaving them three games behind Toronto and extending Ripken's on-field misery. The $30.5 million shortstop went 0-for-4, failed to hit a home run for the 56th game in a row, grounded into a double play and booted a ball for an error.

▸**August 25:** Rick Sutcliffe led the O's back to two games behind the Blue Jays.

▸**August 29:** Randy Milligan was 4-for-5 with a pair of doubles to help pull Baltimore to within 1 1/2 games of tumbling Toronto.

▸**August 30:** Sutcliffe shut down the Mariners for 8 2/3 innings; Mike Devereaux flied into a triple play, marking the second time this season the O's have hit into such a trick.

▸**September 5:** The Orioles ran their winning streak to seven in a row.

▸**September 9:** Brady Anderson stole his 50th base of the season.

▸**September 16:** Mussina threw a four-hit shutout. The O's were within three games of the Jays.

▸**October 4:** The Orioles finished third, seven games out. Devereaux was second in the AL in triples (11), fifth in total bases (303), eighth in hits (180), and ninth in RBI (107). Anderson was third in steals (53) and triples (10), and sixth in walks (98). Milligan was fourth in walks (106). On the mound, Mike Mussina was third in ERA (2.54) and shutouts (4) and fourth in wins (18-5). Gregg Olson was fourth in saves (36.)

—by Jeanie Chung, John Hunt, Deron Snyder, and Lisa Winston.

Team directory

▸**Owner:** Eli S. Jacobs

▸**General Manager:** Roland Hemond

▸**Ballpark:**
Oriole Park at Camden Yards
Baltimore, Md.
410-685-9800
Capacity over 48,041
Pay parking for 5,000 cars
Public transportation available
Family and wheelchair sections, ramps, elevators, sound amplification devices for the hearing impaired, special menu selection board for the speaking impaired

▸**Team publications:**
Orioles Gazette, The House of Magic, Program/Scorecard
410-685-9800

▸**TV, radio broadcast stations:**
WBAL 1090 AM, WMAR Channel 2, Home Team Sports Cable

▸**Camps and/or clinics:**
Fantasy Camp (ages 30+), February, 1-800-950-BIRD
Cal Ripken Sr. Baseball Camp (ages 8-18), Mount St. Mary's, Emmitsburg, Md., late June and early July, 301-447-5296
Elrod Hendricks Camp, McDonough School, McDonough, Md., July, 410-685-9800
Summer clinics, the Orioles region, during the season, 410-685-9800

▸**Spring Training:**
Al Lang Stadium
St. Petersburg, Florida
Capacity 7,600
813-822-3384

BALTIMORE ORIOLES 1992 final stats

Batting	AVG	SLG	OB	G	AB	R	H	TB	2B	3B	HR	RBI	BB	SO	SB	CS	E
Orsulak	.289	.381	.342	117	391	45	113	149	18	3	4	39	28	34	5	4	4
Hulett	.289	.408	.340	57	142	11	41	58	7	2	2	21	10	31	0	1	7
G.Davis	.276	.422	.338	106	398	46	110	168	15	2	13	48	37	65	1	0	0
Devereaux	.276	.464	.321	156	653	76	180	303	29	11	24	107	44	94	10	8	5
Hoiles	.274	.506	.384	96	310	49	85	157	10	1	20	40	55	60	0	2	3
Anderson	.271	.449	.373	159	623	100	169	280	28	10	21	80	98	98	53	16	8
Martinez	.268	.404	.366	83	198	26	53	80	10	1	5	25	31	47	0	1	3
Gomez	.265	.425	.356	137	468	62	124	199	24	0	17	64	63	78	2	3	18
C.Ripken	.251	.366	.323	162	637	73	160	233	29	1	14	72	64	50	4	3	12
McLemore	.246	.294	.308	101	228	40	56	67	7	2	0	27	21	26	11	5	7
Milligan	.240	.361	.383	137	462	71	111	167	21	1	11	53	106	81	0	1	7
Tackett	.240	.380	.307	66	179	21	43	68	8	1	5	24	17	28	0	0	1
Parent	.235	.441	.316	17	34	4	8	15	1	0	2	4	3	7	0	0	1
Horn	.235	.401	.324	63	162	13	38	65	10	1	5	19	21	60	0	0	0
Segui	.233	.296	.306	115	189	21	44	56	9	0	1	17	20	23	1	0	1
B.Ripken	.230	.312	.275	111	330	35	76	103	15	0	4	36	18	26	2	3	4
Alexander	.200	.200	.200	4	5	1	1	1	0	0	0	0	0	3	0	0	0
Scarsone	.176	.176	.222	11	17	2	3	3	0	0	0	0	1	6	0	0	2
Mercedes	.140	.180	.267	23	50	7	7	9	2	0	0	4	8	9	0	1	2
Dempsey	.111	.111	.273	8	9	2	1	1	0	0	0	0	2	1	0	0	0
Shields	_	_	_	2	0	0	0	0	0	0	0	0	0	0	0	0	0
Voigt	_	_	_	1	0	0	0	0	0	0	0	0	0	0	0	0	0

Pitching	W-L	ERA	G	GS	CG	GF	Sho	SV	IP	H	R	ER	HR	BB	SO
Poole	0-0	0.00	6	0	0	1	0	0	3.1	3	3	0	0	1	3
Williamson	0-0	0.96	12	0	0	5	0	1	18.2	16	3	2	1	10	14
Olson	1-5	2.05	60	0	0	56	0	36	61.1	46	14	14	3	24	58
Frohwirth	4-3	2.46	65	0	0	23	0	4	106	97	33	29	4	41	58
Mussina	18-5	2.54	32	32	8	0	4	0	241	212	70	68	16	48	130
Mills	10-4	2.61	35	3	0	12	0	2	103.1	78	33	30	5	54	60
Clements	2-0	3.28	23	0	0	4	0	0	24.2	23	10	9	0	11	9
S.Davis	7-3	3.43	48	2	0	24	0	4	89.1	79	35	34	5	36	53
Rhodes	7-5	3.63	15	15	2	0	1	0	94.1	87	39	38	6	38	77
Lefferts	1-3	4.09	5	5	1	0	0	0	33	34	19	15	3	6	23
McDonald	13-13	4.24	35	35	4	0	2	0	227	213	113	107	32	74	158
Sutcliffe	16-15	4.47	36	36	5	0	2	0	237.1	251	123	118	20	74	109
Milacki	6-8	5.84	23	20	0	1	0	1	115.2	140	78	75	16	44	51
Flanagan	0-0	8.05	42	0	0	15	0	0	34.2	50	34	31	3	23	17
Lewis	1-1	10.80	2	2	0	0	0	0	6.2	13	8	8	1	7	4

1993 preliminary roster

PITCHERS (15)
Todd Frohwirth
Ben McDonald
Bob Milacki
Alan Mills
Mike Mussina
John O'Donoghue
Gregg Olson
Mike Oquist
Brad Pennington
Jim Poole
Arthur Rhodes
Rick Sutcliffe
Anthony Telford
Jeff Williams
Mark Williamson

CATCHERS (4)
Cesar Devarez
Chris Hoiles
Mark Parent
Jeff Tackett

INFIELDERS (15)
Manny Alexander
Paul Carey
Glenn Davis
Leo Gomez
Sam Horn
Tim Hulett
Doug Jennings
T.R. Lewis
Mark McLemore
Randy Milligan
Sherman Obando
Bill Ripken
Cal Ripken
Steve Scarsone
David Segui

OUTFIELDERS (6)
Brady Anderson
Damon Buford
Mike Devereaux
Chito Martinez
Luis Mercedes
Jack Voigt

Games played by position

Player	G	C	1B	2B	3B	SS	OF	DH
ALEXANDER,M	4	0	0	0	0	3	0	0
ANDERSON,B	159	0	0	0	0	0	158	0
DAVIS,G	106	0	2	0	0	0	0	103
DEMPSEY,R	8	8	0	0	0	0	0	0
DEVEREAUX,M	156	0	0	0	0	0	155	0
GOMEZ,L	137	0	0	0	137	0	0	0
HOILES,C	96	95	0	0	0	0	0	1
HORN,S	63	0	0	0	0	0	0	46
HULETT,T	57	0	0	10	27	5	0	13
MARTINEZ,C	83	0	0	0	0	0	52	4
MCLEMORE,M	101	0	0	70	0	0	0	17
MERCEDES,L	23	0	0	0	0	0	16	7
MILLIGAN,R	137	0	129	0	0	0	0	6
ORSULAK,J	117	0	0	0	0	0	110	1
PARENT,M	17	16	0	0	0	0	0	0
RIPKEN,C	162	0	0	0	0	162	0	0
RIPKEN,B	111	0	0	108	0	0	0	2
SCARSONE,S	11	0	0	5	2	1	0	0
SEGUI,D	115	0	95	0	0	0	18	0
SHIELDS,T	2	0	0	0	0	0	0	0
TACKETT,J	66	64	0	0	1	0	0	0
VOIGT,J	1	0	0	0	0	0	0	0

Sick call: 1992 DL report

Player	Days on the DL
Davis, Storm	15
Davis, Glenn	28
Hoiles, Chris	57
Hulett, Tim	16
Orsulak, Joe	16
Poole, Jim	78
Williamson, Mark	141

Minor league report

Class AAA — Rochester finished 70-74, 3rd in the International League East Division. OF Luis Mercedes was 2nd in the league in batting at .313 and 3rd in SB with 35. 3B Tommy Shields hit .302 with 10 HR and 59 RBI. RHP Richie Lewis was 10-9 with a 3.28 ERA and 154 K in 159 IP. **Class AA:** Hagerstown finished 59-80, 7th in the Eastern League. OF Mark Smith hit .288 with 62 RBI. SS Manny Alexander had 43 SB. LHP John O'Donoghue had a 2.24 ERA, allowing 77 hits in 112 IP. **Class A:** Frederick finished 69-71, 2nd in the 1st half of the Carolina League Northern Division and 3rd in the 2nd half. OF Stanton Cameron set franchise records with 29 HR and and 92 RBI. OF Jim Wawruck hit .309. RHP Allen Plaster was 9-12 with a 2.87 ERA. Kane County finished 61-76, 6th in the 1st half of the Midwest League Northern Division and 5th in the 2nd half. OF Alex Ochoa hit .295 with 59 RBI. OF Curtis Goodwin had 51 SBs. RHP Bobby Chouinard won the ERA title at 2.08 despite a 10-14 record. He walked just 38 in 182 IP. Bluefield finished 37-25, 1st in the Appalachian League Northern Division. The team beat Elizabethton in three games for the league championship. OF Duane Thomas had 11 HR. OF Roy Hodge had 43 RBI. The club led the league in batting at .272. Orioles finished 29-29, 5th in the Gulf Coast League Western Division. RHPs Scott Conner and Hut Smith both ranked among the tops in the league in ERA. Conner was 4-5 with a 1.93 ERA, while Smith was 4-3 with a 1.95.

Tops in the organization

BATTING LEADERS	Club	Avg.	G	AB	R	H	HR	RBI
Luis Mercedes	Roc	.313	103	409	62	128	3	29
Jim Wawruck	Fre	.309	102	350	61	108	8	46
T.R. Lewis	Fre	.305	129	446	84	136	9	76
Tommy Shields	Roc	.302	121	431	58	130	10	59
Alex Ochoa	Knc	.295	133	499	65	147	1	59

HOME RUNS		
Stanton Cameron	Fre	29
Mark Parent	Roc	17
Jack Voigt	Roc	16
Several players tied		14

WINS		
Rick Krivda	Fre	17
Anthony Telford	Roc	12
John O'Donoghue	Roc	12
Mark Smith	Knc	11
Terry Farrar	Fre	11

RBI		
Stanton Cameron	Fre	92
Melvin Wearing	Roc	91
T.R. Lewis	Fre	76
Doug Jennings	Roc	76
Mark Parent	Roc	69

SAVES		
Chris Lemp	Knc	26
Dave Paveloff	Fre	16
Brad Pennington	Roc	14
Jim Poole	Roc	10
Joe Borowski	Fre	10

STOLEN BASES		
Damon Buford	Roc	64
Curtis Goodwin	Knc	51
Manny Alexander	Roc	45
Luis Mercedes	Roc	35
Several players tied		31

STRIKEOUTS		
Rick Krivda	Fre	188
Richie Lewis	Roc	154
Jimmy Haynes	Knc	141
John O'Donoghue	Roc	133
Anthony Telford	Roc	129

PITCHING LEADERS	Club	W-L	ERA	IP	H	BB	SO
Bobby Chouinard	Knc	10-14	2.08	182	152	38	112
Rick Forney	Knc	3-6	2.48	123	114	26	104
Jimmy Haynes	Knc	7-11	2.56	144	131	45	141
John O'Donoghue	Roc	12-8	2.62	182	137	59	133
Allen Plaster	Fre	9-12	2.87	150	113	75	128

Baltimore (1954-1992), incl. St. Louis (1902-1953)

Runs: Most, career, all-time

1232 Brooks Robinson, 1955-1977
1091 George Sisler, 1915-1927
1048 EDDIE MURRAY, 1977-1988
1043 CAL RIPKEN, 1981-1992
1013 Harlond Clift, 1934-1943

Hits: Most, career, all-time

2848 Brooks Robinson, 1955-1977
2295 George Sisler, 1915-1927
2021 EDDIE MURRAY, 1977-1988
1922 CAL RIPKEN, 1981-1992
1574 Boog Powell, 1961-1974

2B: Most, career, all-time

482 Brooks Robinson, 1955-1977
369 CAL RIPKEN, 1981-1992
351 EDDIE MURRAY, 1977-1988
343 George Sisler, 1915-1927
294 Harlond Clift, 1934-1943

3B: Most, career, all-time

145 George Sisler, 1915-1927
88 Baby Doll Jacobson, 1915-1926
72 Del Pratt, 1912-1917
72 Jack Tobin, 1916-1925
70 Ken Williams, 1918-1927
68 Brooks Robinson, 1955-1977 (6)

HR: Most, career, all-time

333 EDDIE MURRAY, 1977-1988
303 Boog Powell, 1961-1974
273 CAL RIPKEN, 1981-1992
268 Brooks Robinson, 1955-1977
185 Ken Williams, 1918-1927

RBI: Most, career, all-time

1357 Brooks Robinson, 1955-1977
1190 EDDIE MURRAY, 1977-1988
1063 Boog Powell, 1961-1974
1014 CAL RIPKEN, 1981-1992
959 George Sisler, 1915-1927

SB: Most, career, all-time

351 George Sisler, 1915-1927
252 Al Bumbry, 1972-1984
247 Burt Shotton, 1909-1917
192 Jimmy Austin, 1911-1929
174 Del Pratt, 1912-1917

BB: Most, career, all-time

986 Harlond Clift, 1934-1943
889 Boog Powell, 1961-1974
886 Ken Singleton, 1975-1984
860 Brooks Robinson, 1955-1977
857 EDDIE MURRAY, 1977-1988

BA: Highest, career, all-time

.344 George Sisler, 1915-1927
.326 Ken Williams, 1918-1927
.318 Jack Tobin, 1916-1925
.317 Baby Doll Jacobson, 1915-1926
.309 Bob Dillinger, 1946-1949
.301 Bob Boyd, 1956-1960 (8)

Slug avg: Highest, career, all-time

.558 Ken Williams, 1918-1927
.543 Frank Robinson, 1966-1971
.512 Jim Gentile, 1960-1963
.500 EDDIE MURRAY, 1977-1988
.486 Bob Nieman, 1951-1959

Games started: Most, career, all-time

521 Jim Palmer, 1965-1984
384 Dave McNally, 1962-1974
328 MIKE FLANAGAN, 1975-1992
309 Scott McGregor, 1976-1988
283 Mike Cuellar, 1969-1976

Saves: Most, career, all-time

131 GREGG OLSON, 1988-1992
105 Tippy Martinez, 1976-1986
100 Stu Miller, 1963-1967
74 Eddie Watt, 1966-1973
58 Dick Hall, 1961-1971

Shutouts: Most, career, all-time

53 Jim Palmer, 1965-1984
33 Dave McNally, 1962-1974
30 Mike Cuellar, 1969-1976
27 Jack Powell, 1902-1912
26 Milt Pappas, 1957-1965

Wins: Most, career, all-time

268 Jim Palmer, 1965-1984
181 Dave McNally, 1962-1974
143 Mike Cuellar, 1969-1976
141 MIKE FLANAGAN, 1975-1992
138 Scott McGregor, 1976-1988

K: Most, career, all-time

2212 Jim Palmer, 1965-1984
1476 Dave McNally, 1962-1974
1297 MIKE FLANAGAN, 1975-1992
1011 Mike Cuellar, 1969-1976
944 Milt Pappas, 1957-1965

Win pct: Highest, career, all-time

.638 Jim Palmer, 1965-1984
.620 Wally Bunker, 1963-1968
.619 Dick Hall, 1961-1971
.619 Mike Cuellar, 1969-1976
.616 Dave McNally, 1962-1974

ERA: Lowest, career, all-time

2.06 Harry Howell, 1904-1910
2.52 Fred Glade, 1904-1907
2.62 Barney Pelty, 1903-1912
2.63 Jack Powell, 1902-1912
2.67 Carl Weilman, 1912-1920
2.86 Jim Palmer, 1965-1984 (6)

Runs: Most, season

145 Harlond Clift, 1936
137 George Sisler, 1920
134 George Sisler, 1922
132 Jack Tobin, 1921
128 Ken Williams, 1922
122 Frank Robinson, 1966 (7)

Hits: Most, season

257 George Sisler, 1920
246 George Sisler, 1922
241 Heinie Manush, 1928
236 Jack Tobin, 1921
224 George Sisler, 1925
211 CAL RIPKEN, 1983 (10)

2B: Most, season

51 Beau Bell, 1937
49 George Sisler, 1920
47 Heinie Manush, 1928
47 CAL RIPKEN, 1983
47 Joe Vosmik, 1937

3B: Most, season

20 Heinie Manush, 1928
20 George Stone, 1906
18 George Sisler, 1920
18 George Sisler, 1921
18 George Sisler, 1922
18 Jack Tobin, 1921
12 Paul Blair, 1967 (24)

HR: Most, season

49 Frank Robinson, 1966
46 Jim Gentile, 1961
39 Boog Powell, 1964
39 Ken Williams, 1922
37 Boog Powell, 1969

RBI: Most, season

155 Ken Williams, 1922
141 Jim Gentile, 1961
134 Moose Solters, 1936
124 EDDIE MURRAY, 1985
123 Beau Bell, 1936

SB: Most, season

57 Luis Aparicio, 1964
53 BRADY ANDERSON, 1992
51 George Sisler, 1922
46 Armando Marsans, 1916
45 George Sisler, 1918

BB: Most, season

126 Lu Blue, 1929
121 Roy Cullenbine, 1941
118 Harlond Clift, 1938
118 Burt Shotton, 1915
118 Ken Singleton, 1975

BA: Highest, season

.420 George Sisler, 1922
.407 George Sisler, 1920
.378 Heinie Manush, 1928
.371 George Sisler, 1921
.358 George Stone, 1906
.328 Ken Singleton, 1977 (*)

Slug avg: Highest, season

.646 Jim Gentile, 1961
.637 Frank Robinson, 1966
.632 George Sisler, 1920
.627 Ken Williams, 1922
.623 Ken Williams, 1923

Games started: Most, season

40 Mike Cuellar, 1970
40 MIKE FLANAGAN, 1978
40 Dave McNally, 1969
40 Dave McNally, 1970
40 Bobo Newsom, 1938
40 Jim Palmer, 1976

Saves: Most, season

37 GREGG OLSON, 1990
36 GREGG OLSON, 1992
34 Don Aase, 1986
31 GREGG OLSON, 1991
27 Stu Miller, 1963
27 GREGG OLSON, 1989

Shutouts: Most, season

10 Jim Palmer, 1975
8 Steve Barber, 1961
7 Milt Pappas, 1964
6 Fred Glade, 1904
6 Harry Howell, 1906
6 Dave McNally, 1972
6 Jim Palmer, 1969
6 Jim Palmer, 1973
6 Jim Palmer, 1976
6 Jim Palmer, 1978

Wins: Most, season

27 Urban Shocker, 1921
25 Steve Stone, 1980
24 Mike Cuellar, 1970
24 Dave McNally, 1970
24 Urban Shocker, 1922

K: Most, season

232 Rube Waddell, 1908
226 Bobo Newsom, 1938
202 Dave McNally, 1968
199 Jim Palmer, 1970
198 Harry Howell, 1905

Win pct: Highest, season

.808 General Crowder, 1928
.808 Dave McNally, 1971
.800 Jim Palmer, 1969
.792 Wally Bunker, 1964
.783 MIKE MUSSINA, 1992

ERA: Lowest, season

1.59 Barney Pelty, 1906
1.77 Jack Powell, 1906
1.89 Harry Howell, 1908
1.89 Rube Waddell, 1908
1.93 Harry Howell, 1907
1.95 Dave McNally, 1968 (7)

Most pinch-hit homers, season

3 Whitey Herzog, 1962
3 Sam Bowens, 1967
3 Pat Kelly, 1979
3 Jim Dwyer, 1986
3 Sam Horn, 1991

Most pinch-hit, homers, career

9 Jim Dwyer, 1980-1988

Most consecutive games, batting safely

41 George Sisler, StL-1922
34 George Sisler, StL-1925
34 George McQuinn, StL-1938
22 Eddie Murray, 1982
22 Doug DeCinces, 1978-1979

Most consecutive scoreless innings

41 Gregg Olson, 1989-1990
36 Hal Brown, 1961

No hit games

Earl Hamilton, StL at Det AL, 5-1; August 30, 1912.
Ernie Koob, StL vs Chi AL, 1-0; May 5, 1917.
Bob Groom, StL vs Chi AL, 3-0; May 6, 1917 (2nd game).
Bobo Newsom, StL vs Bos AL, 1-2; September 18, 1934 (lost on 1 hit in the tenth).
Bobo Holloman, StL vs Phi AL, 6-0; May 6, 1953 (first start in the major leagues).
Hoyt Wilhelm, Bal vs NY AL, 1-0; September 20, 1958
Steve D. Barber (8 2/3 innings) and Stu Miller (1/3 inning) Bal vs Det AL, 1-2; April 30, 1967 (1st game, lost the game)
Tom Phoebus, Bal vs Bos AL, 6-0; April 27, 1968.
Jim Palmer, Bal vs Oak AL, 8-0; August 13, 1969.
Bob Milacki (6 innings), Mike Flanagan (1 inning), Mark Williamson, (1 inning) and Gregg Olson (1 inning), Bal at Oak AL, 2-0; July 13, 1991.
John Whitehead, six innings, rain, StL vs Det AL, 4-0; August 5, 1940 (2nd game).

ACTIVE PLAYERS in caps.

Leader from the franchise's current location is included. If not in the top five, leader's rank is listed in parenthesis; asterisk (*) indicates player is not in top 25.

Cleveland Indians

by Nell Seiler, *USA TODAY*

Albert Belle led the Indians with 34 homers (fourth in the AL) and 112 RBI (fifth in the AL).

1992 Indians: A startling finish

After 1991, there was nowhere to go but up. So the Indians looked down—to the farm—for talent. Coming out of spring training, they were the youngest team in the AL, with an average age of 26.4. If they had been secretly harboring a fantasy of contention, however, it was shattered when two key prospects—Reggie Jefferson and Jim Thome—were injured in spring training and started '92 on the DL.

The home opener was the longest game in Cleveland history—19 innings in six hours and 30 minutes. In the first game of a doubleheader the next day, the Indians were no-hit by Boston's Matt Young, yet scored two runs on three walks and an error for a 2-1 win. Then in the nightcap, Roger Clemens shut them down on two hits. It was the fewest hits—two—a team had ever collected in a doubleheader.

The Indians struggled through April and most of May to an abysmal 14-30, a pace which would have had them finish at 52-110 had it continued. But things turned around suddenly—and permanently—in Oakland, of all places. The Indians swept the A's in a three-game set May 25-27 and were 62-56 from then on. Their 76-86 record (19 games better than '91) gave them a fourth-place tie with the Yankees.

All-Star Carlos Baerga joined Hall of Famer Rogers Hornsby as the only second basemen to hit .300, collect 200 hits, 20 homers and 100 RBI in a season. He hit .312 with 20 homers, 105 RBI and 10 stolen bases.

Rookie Kenny Lofton finished second in the Rookie of the Year voting to Milwaukee's Pat Listach, but he may have an even brighter future. He was not caught stealing by an opposing catcher until May 31; he shattered the old AL rookie record for steals (50) with 66 and was the first Indian to steal home in 11 years. Albert Belle, moved from DH to left field in late May, set career highs with 34 homers and 112 RBI.

On the mound, the news wasn't as bright, but Charles Nagy earned a spot on the All-Star team and vied for Cy Young honors through the first half of the season. He struggled at points in the second half, but finished 17-10 (2.96 ERA), and emerged as an anchor to the rotation. Scott Scudder and Jack Armstrong, acquired in the Greg Swindell trade, were ineffective.

The team's youth also showed in some negative ways, however: They committed 141 errors, second worst in the league. Other disappointments included injuries that plagued All-Star catcher Sandy Alomar Jr., and the slow development of shortstop Mark Lewis. Lewis lost his job to journeyman Felix Fermin and was later found to have developed an ulcer.

—by Lisa Winston

1993 Indians: Preview

The Indians stockpiled a lot of young talent and began to learn winning ways in '92, but it was the way they did it that deserves notice—recovering from a bleak start to a 62-56 finish. Young stars abound: second baseman Carlos Baerga, Kenny Lofton, Albert Belle, and Charles Nagy. Reggie Jefferson and Jim Thome are also ready to emerge.

Progress in '93 depends on filling some of the holes: Finding a reliable rotation behind Nagy and getting games from oft-injured catcher Sandy Alomar Jr. (89 games in '92). The team has some trade possibilities in outfielders Glenallen Hill and Mark Whiten.

It is more likely that the young Indians are on track to become contenders in '94—just in time for their new stadium.

—by Tim McQuay

1992 Indians: Between the lines

▶**April 23:** It would've been a low-scoring football game, but the Indians' 13-8 loss to the Blue Jays was a slugfest that delighted offense-minded baseball fans. The teams combined for 29 hits, including four homers and two doubles. Six of Toronto's 13 RBI came with two outs. Cleveland starter Dave Otto and reliever Eric Bell each lasted less than two innings.

▶**April 26 *Milestone:*** Rookie Kenny Lofton became the first Indian to steal home in 11 years when he pulled it off against Milwaukee in the second game of the doubleheader.

▶**May 1:** Lofton recorded his league-leading 10th stolen base. He had been caught only once in 11 attempts.

▶**May 3:** Alex Cole—who had yet to steal a base in 12 games—tied his own Cleveland record by swiping five, including third twice. His four hits also tied his own career high.

▶**May 7:** Lofton was 3-for-4 with three RBI and his first major league homer. The Indians defeated the Rangers 8-7, overcoming the infield's apparent conspiracy to throw the game. The Indians committed four errors—one at first, second, third, and shortstop.

▶**May 19:** "Hard-Hittin" Mark Whiten lived up to his nickname with a seventh-inning grand slam.

▶**May 22:** Lofton stole three more bases to increase his total to 21. The AL rookie record for an entire season was 50, held by John Cangelosi.

▶**May 23:** The Indians used seven pitchers in their 5-4 win over the Mariners. Wearing out the mound were starter Denis Boucher, Rod Nichols, Kevin Wickander, Eric Plunk, Ted Power, Derek Lilliquist—who blew the save but got the win—and finally Steve Olin, who notched the save and snapped the Indians' six-game losing streak.

▶**May 26:** Dave Otto, just activated from the disabled list, tossed six innings of four-hit shutout ball against the A's, striking out five.

▶**May 27:** Paul Sorrento homered twice and Albert Belle added his fifth home run in as many games as the Indians completed their first series sweep against Oakland since 1986 with a 4-2 win.

▶**May 29:** Albert Belle hit two homers for the second time in a week, pacing the Indians' 14-2 win against California. Kenny Lofton was 3-for-6 with his 23rd stolen base of the year.

▶**May 31:** Lofton was thrown out by Angels' catcher Lance Parrish trying to steal second, the first time this season—in 25 attempts—he was caught by a catcher.

▶**June 9:** Glenallen Hill hit a pair of homers to lead the Indians to a 6-1 win against Detroit.

▶**June 10:** Hill turned in his second straight two-homer game, clouting his second of the night in the 11th inning to give the Indians a 4-2 win against the Tigers.

▶**June 12:** Ace Charles Nagy continued to mow down the opposition, needing just 90 pitches to shut out the Yankees. It was his fourth straight win and fifth complete game.

▶**June 17:** Nagy won his fifth in a row, tossing his sixth complete game. Carlos Baerga, who extended his hitting streak to 10 games, scored the winning run on a wild pitch by Oriole Mike Mussina.

▶**June 18:** Albert Belle hit his 15th homer of the season.

▶**June 28:** Paul Sorrento hit a pinch-hit two-run homer to rally the Indians to a 7-6 win against the Blue Jays.

▶**July 4:** Cleveland beat Oakland for the sixth straight time. It was the second of back-to-back 8-1 games.

▶**July 19:** Baerga, hitting .460 in his last 23 games, was 4-for-5 with a homer and three RBI.

▶**July 26:** Baerga's two-out homer in the bottom of the 13th gave the Indians a 2-1 win over Kansas City. Jose Mesa, who was traded from Baltimore, allowed just one run in eight innings to lower his ERA to 1.73 in his three starts as an Indian.

▸**July 29:** Lofton stole his 35th base and was 3-for-3 with a pair of RBI.

▸**August 1** ***Quote of the day:*** Manager Mike Hargrove on seeing Tiger Cecil Fielder step to the plate with the bases loaded and two outs in the seventh—"I considered walking him. I only signed a one-year extension." Fielder emptied the bases with a grand slam.

▸**August 19:** Nagy went the distance for his ninth complete game as the Indians once again trounced the Twins, 5-1.

▸**August 22:** In his first start in more than a month since being relegated to the Indians' bullpen, Jack Armstrong took a no-hitter into the sixth before tiring. Four pitchers combined for shutout relief in the 6-1 win against Texas. Cleveland moved into fourth place in the AL East.

▸**August 30:** Carlos Martinez had the first multi-homer game of his career, hitting a pair in the Indians' 7-5 loss to the A's.

▸**September 4:** Martinez doubled, tripled and homered in the Indians' 7-0 rout of the Mariners.

▸**September 5:** Albert Belle was 3-for-5 with three RBI in Cleveland's 5-4 win against the Mariners.

▸**September 15:** Lofton swiped a pair of bases to raise his AL-leading total to 56.

▸**September 24:** Lofton stole his 62nd base of the year, breaking the Cleveland single-season record of 61 set in 1980 by Miguel Dilone.

▸**September 25:** Carlos Baerga homered twice, reaching the 100-RBI plateau to join teammate Albert Belle as the first Cleveland teammates to reach the century mark since Larry Doby and Al Rosen in 1954.

▸**October 2** ***Milestone:*** Baerga became the first second baseman in AL history to hit .300 with 200 hits, 20 homers, and 100 RBI.

▸**October 4:** The Indians hosted the largest final-game crowd at Cleveland Stadium in 44 years: 30,187 fans. It was quite a comeback season for the Tribe; after a miserable start, they played better than .500 ball to hang onto fourth place in the AL East. Their rookie sensation, Kenny Lofton, led the American League in stolen bases with 66—18 more than all-time leader Rickey Henderson. Baerga was second in the AL in hits (205), fifth in batting (.312), and tenth in RBI (105). Albert Belle was fourth in homers (34) and fifth in RBI (112). Charles Nagy fourth in complete games (10) and innings pitched (252), and seventh in ERA (2.96). Relievers Steve Olin (72) and Derek Lilliquist (71) were third and fourth in appearances.

—by Jeanie Chung, John Hunt, Deron Snyder, and Lisa Winston.

Team directory

▸**Owner:** Richard E. Jacobs

▸**General Manager:** John Hart

▸**Ballpark:**
Cleveland Stadium
Boudreau Boulevard, Cleveland, Ohio
216-861-1200
Capacity 74,483
Parking for 4,000 vehicles; $4
Public transportation available
Family and wheelchair sections, ramps, Customer Service Center, and Designated Driver Program

▸**Team publications:**
Game Face Magazine
216-861-1200

▸**TV, radio broadcast stations:**
WKNR 1220 AM, WUAB Channel 43, SportsChannel Ohio

▸**Camps and/or clinics:**
Cleveland Indians Baseball Heaven (fantasy camp), January, 800-75-TRIBE

▸**Spring Training:**
Chain O' Lakes Park
Winter Haven, Fla.
Capacity 4,520
813-293-3900

CLEVELAND INDIANS 1992 final stats

Batting	AVG	SLG	OB	G	AB	R	H	TB	2B	3B	HR	RBI	BB	SO	SB	CS	E
Jefferson	.337	.483	.352	24	89	8	30	43	6	2	1	6	1	17	0	0	1
Baerga	.312	.455	.354	161	657	92	205	299	32	1	20	105	35	76	10	2	19
Lofton	.285	.365	.362	148	576	96	164	210	15	8	5	42	68	54	66	12	8
Levis	.279	.442	.279	28	43	2	12	19	4	0	1	3	0	5	0	0	1
Howard	.277	.346	.308	117	358	36	99	124	15	2	2	32	17	60	15	8	2
Fermin	.270	.321	.326	79	215	27	58	69	7	2	0	13	18	10	0	0	8
Sorrento	.269	.443	.341	140	458	52	123	203	24	1	18	60	51	89	0	3	8
Lewis	.264	.351	.308	122	413	44	109	145	21	0	5	30	25	69	4	5	26
Martinez	.263	.377	.283	69	228	23	60	86	9	1	5	35	7	21	1	2	4
Jacoby	.261	.326	.324	120	291	30	76	95	7	0	4	36	28	54	0	3	10
Belle	.260	.477	.320	153	585	81	152	279	23	1	34	112	52	128	8	2	3
Whiten	.254	.360	.347	148	508	73	129	183	19	4	9	43	72	102	16	12	7
Alomar	.251	.324	.293	89	299	22	75	97	16	0	2	26	13	32	3	3	2
Ortiz	.250	.279	.296	86	244	20	61	68	7	0	0	24	12	23	1	3	5
Hill	.241	.436	.287	102	369	38	89	161	16	1	18	49	20	73	9	6	6
Cole	.206	.216	.284	41	97	11	20	21	1	0	0	5	10	21	9	2	1
Thome	.205	.299	.275	40	117	8	24	35	3	1	2	12	10	34	2	0	11
Kirby	.167	.389	.286	21	18	9	3	7	1	0	1	1	3	2	0	3	0
Worthington	.167	.167	.231	9	24	0	4	4	0	0	0	2	2	4	0	1	4
Perezchica	.100	.150	.182	18	20	2	2	3	1	0	0	1	2	6	0	0	2
Hernandez	.000	.000	.000	3	4	0	0	0	0	0	0	0	0	2	0	0	1
Rohde	.000	.000	.222	5	7	0	0	0	0	0	0	0	2	3	0	0	1

Pitching	W-L	ERA	G	GS	CG	GF	Sho	SV	IP	H	R	ER	HR	BB	SO
Lilliquist	5-3	1.75	71	0	0	22	0	6	61.2	39	13	12	5	18	47
Olin	8-5	2.34	72	0	0	62	0	29	88.1	80	25	23	8	27	47
Power	3-3	2.54	64	0	0	16	0	6	99.1	88	33	28	7	35	51
Nagy	17-10	2.96	33	33	10	0	3	0	252	245	91	83	11	57	169
Christopher	0-0	3.00	10	0	0	4	0	0	18	17	8	6	2	10	13
Wickander	2-0	3.07	44	0	0	10	0	1	41	39	14	14	1	28	38
Plunk	9-6	3.64	58	0	0	20	0	4	71.2	61	31	29	5	38	50
Cook	5-7	3.82	32	25	1	1	0	0	158	156	79	67	29	50	96
Nichols	4-3	4.53	30	9	0	5	0	0	105.1	114	58	53	13	31	56
Mesa	7-12	4.59	28	27	1	1	1	0	160.2	169	86	82	14	70	62
Armstrong	6-15	4.64	35	23	1	5	0	0	166.2	176	100	86	23	67	114
Mlicki	0-2	4.98	4	4	0	0	0	0	21.2	23	14	12	3	16	16
Scudder	6-10	5.28	23	22	0	0	0	0	109	134	80	64	10	55	66
Boucher	2-2	6.37	8	7	0	0	0	0	41	48	29	29	9	20	17
Embree	0-2	7.00	4	4	0	0	0	0	18	19	14	14	3	8	12
Otto	5-9	7.06	18	16	0	0	0	0	80.1	110	64	63	12	33	32
Bell	0-2	7.63	7	1	0	2	0	0	15.1	22	13	13	1	9	10
Shaw	0-1	8.22	2	1	0	1	0	0	7.2	7	7	7	2	4	3
Mutis	0-2	9.53	3	2	0	0	0	0	11.1	24	14	12	4	6	8
Arnsberg	0-0	11.81	8	0	0	1	0	0	10.2	13	14	14	6	11	5

1993 preliminary roster

PITCHERS (20)
Shawn Bryant
Mike Christopher
Dennis Cook
Jerry Dipoto
Alan Embree
Tommy Kramer
Derek Lilliquist
Jose Mesa
Dave Mlicki
Jeff Mutis
Charles Nagy
Rod Nichols
Bob Ojeda
Steve Olin
Eric Plunk
Ted Power
Scott Scudder
Zak Shinall
Bill Wertz
Kevin Wickander

CATCHERS (3)
Sandy Alomar
Jesse Levis
Joel Skinner

INFIELDERS (9)
Carlos Baerga
Alvaro Espinoza
Felix Fermin
Jose Hernandez
Reggie Jefferson
Mark Lewis
Carlos Martinez
Paul Sorrento
Jim Thome

OUTFIELDERS (8)
Albert Belle
Glenallen Hill
Thomas Howard
Wayne Kirby
Kenny Lofton
Ken Ramos
Tracy Sanders
Mark Whiten

Games played by position

Player	G	C	1B	2B	3B	SS	OF	DH
ALOMAR,S	89	88	0	0	0	0	0	1
BAERGA,C	161	0	0	160	0	0	0	1
BELLE,A	153	0	0	0	0	0	52	100
COLE,A	41	0	0	0	0	0	24	4
FERMIN,F	79	0	2	7	17	55	0	0
HERNANDEZ,J	3	0	0	0	0	3	0	0
HILL,G	102	0	0	0	0	0	59	34
HOWARD,T	117	0	0	0	0	0	97	2
JACOBY,B	120	0	10	0	111	0	0	0
JEFFERSON,R	24	0	15	0	0	0	0	7
KIRBY,W	21	0	0	0	0	0	2	4
LEVIS,J	28	21	0	0	0	0	0	1
LEWIS,M	122	0	0	0	1	121	0	0
LOFTON,K	148	0	0	0	0	0	143	0
MARTINEZ,CA	69	0	37	0	28	0	0	4
ORTIZ,J	86	86	0	0	0	0	0	0
PEREZCHICA,T	18	0	0	4	9	4	0	1
ROHDE,D	5	0	0	0	5	0	0	0
SORRENTO,P	140	0	121	0	0	0	0	11
THOME,X	40	0	0	0	40	0	0	0
WHITEN,M	148	0	0	0	0	0	144	2
WORTHINGTON,C	9	0	0	0	9	0	0	0

Sick call: 1992 DL report

Player	Days on the DL
Alomar, Sandy	16
Egloff, Bruce	182
Hill, Glenallen	29
Jefferson, Reggie	89
Martinez, Carlos	53
Otto, Dave	16
Power, Ted	15
Scudder, Scott	49
Skinner, Joel	182
Thome, Jim*	68

**On Disabled List twice during 1992 season (not counting transfers from one DL to another).*

Minor league report

Class AAA — Colorado Springs finished 84-57, 2nd in the 1st half of the Pacific Coast League Southern Division and 1st in the 2nd half. The team beat Vancouver for the league championship. OF Wayne Kirby hit .345 with 11 HR, 74 RBI and 51 SB. 1B Mike Aldrete hit .322 with 84 RBI. RHP Mike Christopher had 26 saves. **Class AA:** Canton-Akron finished 80-58, 1st in the Eastern League. The team lost to Binghamton in five games for the league championship. OF Ken Ramos won the batting crown at .339. OF Tracy Sanders had 21 HR and 88 RBI. RHP Paul Byrd led the league in wins with 14. **Class A:** Kinston finished 65-71, 3rd in the 1st half of the Carolina League and last in the 2nd half. OF Omar Ramirez hit .299 with 13 HR and 49 RBI. RHP Chad Ogea had 13 wins before a mid-season promotion to Canton. RHP Greg McCarthy was shut down mid-season with arm trouble, but not before recording 12 saves without allowing a run. Columbus (Ga.) finished 77-62, 1st in the 1st half of the Sally League Southern Division and 3rd in the 2nd half. The team lost to Myrtle Beach in the 1st round of the playoffs. OF Willie Canate hit .318 with 63 RBI. OF Antonio Mitchell hit .295 with 23 HR and 83 RBI. RHP Ian Doyle had 26 saves. Watertown finished 37-39, last in the New York-Penn League McNamara Division. 1B Dave duPlessis hit .291 with 7 HR and 30 RBI. 3B Jamie Taylor hit .289. OF Pat Bryant had 33 SB. Burlington (N.C.) finished 35-31, 2nd in the Appalachian League North Division. OF Derek Hacopian hit .324 with 9 HR and 43 RBI. OF Damian Jackson had 29 SB. LHP Mike Matthews was 7-0 and won the league ERA title at 1.01.

Tops in the organization

BATTING LEADERS	Club	Avg.	G	AB	R	H	HR	RBI
Wayne Kirby	CSp	.345	123	470	101	162	11	74
Ken Ramos	Can	.339	125	442	94	150	5	42
Mike Aldrete	CSp	.322	128	463	69	149	8	84
William Canate	Clm	.316	133	528	110	167	5	63
Daren Epley	Can	.312	109	381	53	119	2	72

HOME RUNS		
Antonio Mitchell	Clm	23
Tracy Sanders	Can	21
George Canale	CSp	20
Rod McCall	Clm	20
Herbert Perry	Kin	19

WINS		
Chad Ogea	Can	19
Alan Embree	Can	17
Paul Byrd	Can	14
Albie Lopez	Kin	12
Several players tied		11

RBI		
Tracy Sanders	Can	88
Mike Aldrete	CSp	84
Antonio Mitchell	Clm	83
George Canale	CSp	80
Rod McCall	Clm	80

SAVES		
Mike Christopher	CSp	26
Ian Doyle	Clm	26
Mike Soper	Can	20
Mike Gardella	Can	12
Greg McCarthy	Kin	12

STOLEN BASES		
Wayne Kirby	CSp	51
Nolan Lane	Clm	27
William Canate	Clm	25
John Cotton	Kin	23
Miguel Flores	Can	22

STRIKEOUTS		
Alan Embree	Can	171
Chad Ogea	Can	163
Albie Lopez	Kin	161
Dave Mlicki	Can	146
Apolino Garcia	Kin	139

PITCHING LEADERS	Club	W-L	ERA	IP	H	BB	SO
Alan Embree	Can	17-7	2.85	180	150	60	171
Carlos Crawford	Clm	10-11	2.92	188	167	85	127
Kevin Logsdon	Clm	6-5	2.94	113	104	48	86
Paul Byrd	Can	14-6	3.01	152	124	74	118
Albie Lopez	Kin	12-4	3.13	161	136	59	161

Cleveland (1901-1992)

Runs: Most, career, all-time

1154	Earl Averill, 1929-1939
1079	Tris Speaker, 1916-1926
942	Charlie Jamieson, 1919-1932
865	Nap Lajoie, 1902-1914
857	Joe Sewell, 1920-1930

Hits: Most, career, all-time

2046	Nap Lajoie, 1902-1914
1965	Tris Speaker, 1916-1926
1903	Earl Averill, 1929-1939
1800	Joe Sewell, 1920-1930
1753	Charlie Jamieson, 1919-1932

2B: Most, career, all-time

486	Tris Speaker, 1916-1926
424	Nap Lajoie, 1902-1914
377	Earl Averill, 1929-1939
375	Joe Sewell, 1920-1930
367	Lou Boudreau, 1938-1950

3B: Most, career, all-time

121	Earl Averill, 1929-1939
108	Tris Speaker, 1916-1926
106	Elmer Flick, 1902-1910
89	Joe Jackson, 1910-1915
83	Jeff Heath, 1936-1945

HR: Most, career, all-time

226	Earl Averill, 1929-1939
216	Hal Trosky, 1933-1941
215	Larry Doby, 1947-1958
214	Andy Thornton, 1977-1987
192	Al Rosen, 1947-1956

RBI: Most, career, all-time

1084	Earl Averill, 1929-1939
919	Nap Lajoie, 1902-1914
911	Hal Trosky, 1933-1941
884	Tris Speaker, 1916-1926
869	Joe Sewell, 1920-1930

SB: Most, career, all-time

254	Terry Turner, 1904-1918
240	Nap Lajoie, 1902-1914
233	Ray Chapman, 1912-1920
207	Elmer Flick, 1902-1910
165	Harry Bay, 1902-1908

BB: Most, career, all-time

857	Tris Speaker, 1916-1926
766	Lou Boudreau, 1938-1950
725	Earl Averill, 1929-1939
712	Jack Graney, 1908-1922
703	Larry Doby, 1947-1958

BA: Highest, career, all-time

.375	Joe Jackson, 1910-1915
.354	Tris Speaker, 1916-1926
.339	Nap Lajoie, 1902-1914
.327	George Burns, 1920-1928
.323	Ed Morgan, 1928-1933

Slug avg: Highest, career, all-time

.551	Hal Trosky, 1933-1941
.542	Joe Jackson, 1910-1915
.542	Earl Averill, 1929-1939
.520	Tris Speaker, 1916-1926
.506	Jeff Heath, 1936-1945

Games started: Most, career, all-time

484	Bob Feller, 1936-1956
433	Mel Harder, 1928-1947
350	Bob Lemon, 1941-1958
320	Willis Hudlin, 1926-1940
305	Stan Coveleski, 1916-1924

Saves: Most, career, all-time

128	DOUG JONES, 1986-1991
53	Ray Narleski, 1954-1958
48	STEVE OLIN, 1989-1992
46	Jim Kern, 1974-1986
46	Sid Monge, 1977-1981

Shutouts: Most, career, all-time

45	Addie Joss, 1902-1910
44	Bob Feller, 1936-1956
31	Stan Coveleski, 1916-1924
31	Bob Lemon, 1941-1958
27	Mike Garcia, 1948-1959

Wins: Most, career, all-time

266	Bob Feller, 1936-1956
223	Mel Harder, 1928-1947
207	Bob Lemon, 1941-1958
172	Stan Coveleski, 1916-1924
164	Early Wynn, 1949-1963

K: Most, career, all-time

2581	Bob Feller, 1936-1956
2159	Sam McDowell, 1961-1971
1277	Bob Lemon, 1941-1958
1277	Early Wynn, 1949-1963
1160	Mel Harder, 1928-1947

Win pct: Highest, career, all-time

.667	Vean Gregg, 1911-1914
.663	Johnny Allen, 1936-1940
.630	Cal McLish, 1956-1959
.623	Addie Joss, 1902-1910
.622	Wes Ferrell, 1927-1933

ERA: Lowest, career, all-time

1.89	Addie Joss, 1902-1910
2.31	Vean Gregg, 1911-1914
2.39	Bob Rhoads, 1903-1909
2.45	Bill Bernhard, 1902-1907
2.50	Otto Hess, 1902-1908

Runs: Most, season

140	Earl Averill, 1931
137	Tris Speaker, 1920
136	Earl Averill, 1936
133	Tris Speaker, 1923
130	Charlie Jamieson, 1923

Hits: Most, season

233	Joe Jackson, 1911
232	Earl Averill, 1936
227	Nap Lajoie, 1910
226	Joe Jackson, 1912
225	Johnny Hodapp, 1930

2B: Most, season

64	George Burns, 1926
59	Tris Speaker, 1923
52	Tris Speaker, 1921
52	Tris Speaker, 1926
51	George Burns, 1927
51	Johnny Hodapp, 1930
51	Nap Lajoie, 1910

3B: Most, season

26	Joe Jackson, 1912
23	Dale Mitchell, 1949
22	Bill Bradley, 1903
22	Elmer Flick, 1906
20	Jeff Heath, 1941
20	Joe Vosmik, 1935

HR: Most, season

43	Al Rosen, 1953
42	Rocky Colavito, 1959
42	Hal Trosky, 1936
41	Rocky Colavito, 1958
37	Al Rosen, 1950

RBI: Most, season

162	Hal Trosky, 1936
145	Al Rosen, 1953
143	Earl Averill, 1931
142	Hal Trosky, 1934
136	Ed Morgan, 1930

SB: Most, season

66	KENNY LOFTON, 1992
61	Miguel Dilone, 1980
52	BRETT BUTLER, 1984
52	Ray Chapman, 1917
51	Braggo Roth, 1917

BB: Most, season

111	Mike Hargrove, 1980
109	Andy Thornton, 1982
106	Les Fleming, 1942
105	Jack Graney, 1919
102	Jack Graney, 1916

BA: Highest, season

.408	Joe Jackson, 1911
.395	Joe Jackson, 1912
.389	Tris Speaker, 1925
.388	Tris Speaker, 1920
.386	Tris Speaker, 1916

Slug avg: Highest, season

.644	Hal Trosky, 1936
.627	Earl Averill, 1936
.620	Rocky Colavito, 1958
.613	Al Rosen, 1953
.610	Tris Speaker, 1923

Games started: Most, season

44	George Uhle, 1923
42	Bob Feller, 1946
41	Gaylord Perry, 1973
40	Stan Coveleski, 1921
40	Bob Feller, 1941
40	Gaylord Perry, 1972
40	Dick Tidrow, 1973
40	George Uhle, 1922

Saves: Most, season

43	DOUG JONES, 1990
37	DOUG JONES, 1988
32	DOUG JONES, 1989
29	STEVE OLIN, 1992
23	Ernie Camacho, 1984

Shutouts: Most, season

10	Bob Feller, 1946
10	Bob Lemon, 1948
9	Stan Coveleski, 1917
9	Addie Joss, 1906
9	Addie Joss, 1908
9	Luis Tiant, 1968

Wins: Most, season

31	Jim Bagby, 1920
27	Bob Feller, 1940
27	Addie Joss, 1907
27	George Uhle, 1926
26	Bob Feller, 1946
26	George Uhle, 1923

K: Most, season

348	Bob Feller, 1946
325	Sam McDowell, 1965
304	Sam McDowell, 1970
283	Sam McDowell, 1968
279	Sam McDowell, 1969

Win pct: Highest, season

.938	Johnny Allen, 1937
.773	Bill Bernhard, 1902
.767	Vean Gregg, 1911
.767	Bob Lemon, 1954
.741	Gene Bearden, 1948

ERA: Lowest, season

1.16	Addie Joss, 1908
1.59	Addie Joss, 1904
1.60	Luis Tiant, 1968
1.71	Addie Joss, 1909
1.72	Addie Joss, 1906

Most pinch-hit homers, season

3	Gene Green, 1962
3	Fred Whitfield, 1965
3	Ted Ulaender, 1970
3	Ron Kittle, 1987

Most pinch-hit, homers, career

8	Fred Whitfield, 1963-1967

Most consecutive games, batting safely

31	Nap Lajoie, 1906
29	Bill Bradley, 1902

Most consecutive scoreless innings

41	Luis Tiant, 1968
38	Jim Bagby, 1917

No hit games

Earl Moore, Cle vs Chi AL, 2-4; May 9, 1901 (lost on two hits in the tenth).

Dusty Rhoades, Cle vs Bos AL, 2-1; September 18, 1908.

Addie Joss, Cle vs Chi AL, 1-0; October 2, 1908 (perfect game).

Addie Joss, Cle vs Chi AL, 1-0; April 20, 1910.

Ray Caldwell, Cle at NY AL, 3-0; September 10, 1919 (1st game).

Wes Ferrell, Cle vs StL AL, 9-0; April 29, 1931.

Bob Feller, Cle at Chi AL, 1-0; April 16, 1940 (opening day).

Bob Feller, Cle at NY AL, 1-0; April 30, 1946.

Don Black, Cle vs Phi AL, 3-0; July 10, 1947 (1st game).

Bob Lemon, Cle at Det AL, 2-0; June 30, 1948.

Bob Feller, Cle vs Det AL, 2-1; July 1, 1951 (1st game).

Sonny Siebert, Cle vs Was AL, 2-0; June 10, 1966.

Dick Bosman, Cle vs Oak AL, 4-0; July 19, 1974.

Dennis Eckersley, Cle vs Cal AL, 1-0; May 30, 1977.

Len Barker, Cle vs Tor AL, 3-0; May 15, 1981 (perfect game).

ACTIVE PLAYERS in caps.

New York Yankees

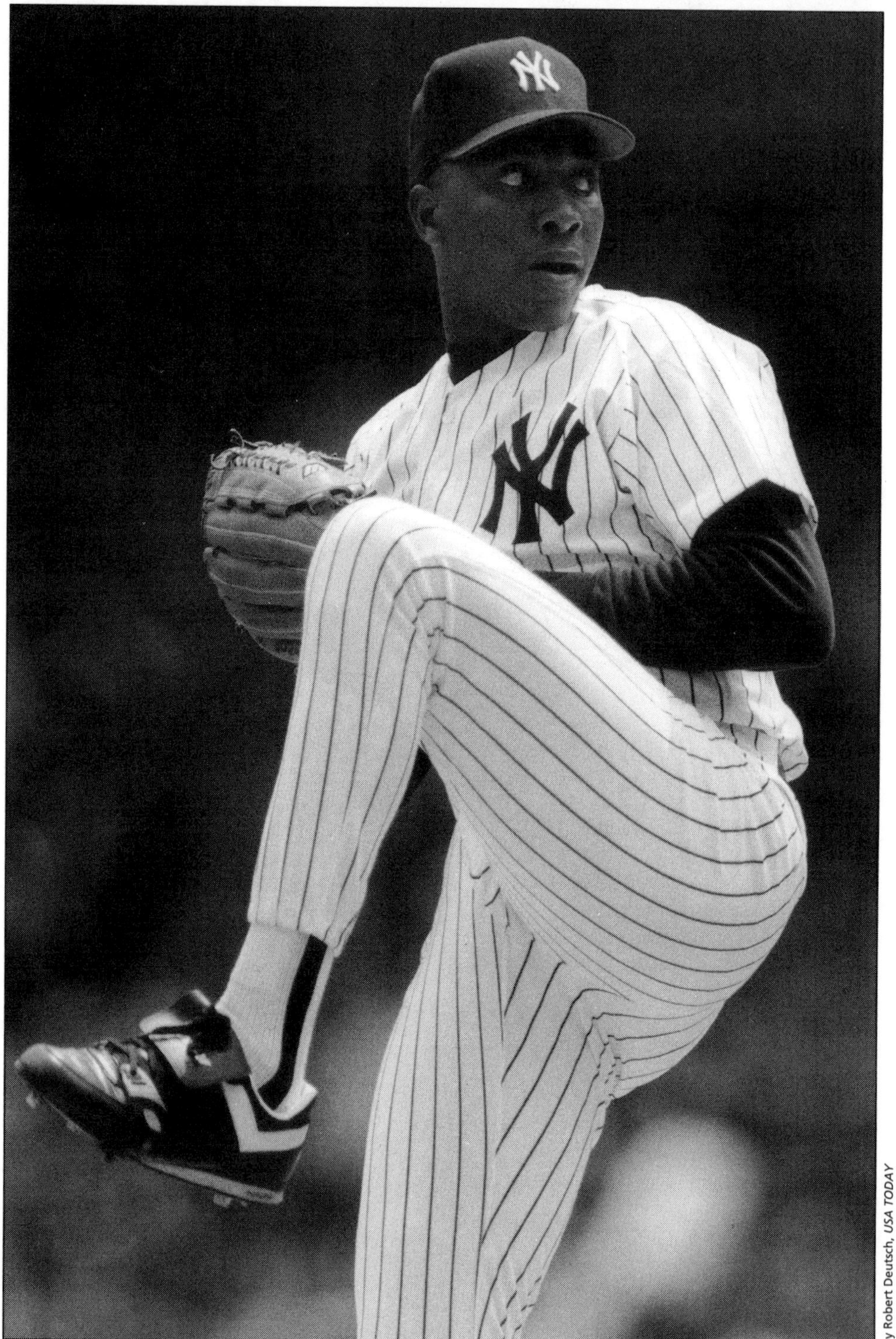

by Robert Deutsch, *USA TODAY*

Melido Perez pitched 10 complete games (fifth in the AL) with 218 strikeouts (second) and a 2.87 ERA (sixth).

1992 Yankees: A year of hot prospects

When the Yankees won their first six games in 1992, ankles were broken in record numbers as people rushed to jump on the bandwagon. Could the Bronx Bombers be as good as they seemed? No. But they weren't as bad either. Exciting rookies and other new faces brought new life to Yankee Stadium. Manager Buck Showalter took over the team and one of his first moves was to bring up Andy Stankiewicz when free agent Mike Gallego went on the DL April 7. Stankiewicz became an immediate fan favorite with his hustling play.

Another pleasant surprise was third baseman Charlie Hayes, acquired in the offseason from Philadelphia. He turned out to be the steadiest Yankee at the hot corner since Graig Nettles, ranking among the top third basemen in the league. But he was lost in the expansion draft.

Free agent Danny Tartabull lived up to his $25.5 million deal when he was healthy, but he missed 29 of the first 102 games, then went on the DL for a few more weeks. He led the club with 25 homers, and had 85 RBI—including a nine-RBI game.

Don Mattingly returned to form after battling chronic back trouble, hitting .288 with a team-high 86 RBI. Utilityman Randy Velarde hit .272 and played in six spots—shortstop, third base, second base and all three outfield positions.

Melido Perez came over from the White Sox with two pitching prospects for Steve Sax, and was the ace of the Yankees' staff. Despite his 13-16 record, he posted a 2.87 ERA and was among AL strikeouts leaders all season. He pitched 10 complete games.

The pitching staff was decimated early, though, by drug-related suspensions. Melido's older brother Pascual was suspended for a year and bullpen ace Steve Howe was banned for life (later overturned).

By early August, the Yankees began dipping into their farm system and bringing up highly-touted youngsters in droves. Bob Wickman and Sam Militello both had quick success. Militello fired seven innings of one-hit shutout ball in his debut. He finished with a 3.45 ERA. Wickman went 6-1 despite a 4.00-plus ERA. Outfielders Bernie and Gerald Williams (no relation) were recalled and will probably remain in the lineup.

The Yanks finished 76-86, tied for fourth with Cleveland.

—by Lisa Winston

1993 Yankees: Preview

He's back. George Steinbrenner has officially returned to the helm as of March 1993 but nobody seemed to want to join him. Barry Bonds, Doug Drabek and Greg Maddux couldn't be bought and sold on New York but the trade with the Angels for Jim Abbott provided one more great arm that, combined with the signing of free agent, journeyman Jimmy Key, plus Melido Perez and terrific prospects such as Sam Militello and Bob Wickman, may give the Yankees one of the top starting staffs in the league.

The outfield is strong, with young Bernie and Gerald Williams, and the experience of Danny Tartabull and Paul O'Neill (acquired from the Reds for Roberto Kelly).

The infield is a bigger question, however. Although the Yankees signed Wade Boggs to a three-year deal, he hit nearly 80 points below his career average last year, and has had back problems; second baseman Pat Kelly struggled with the bat, and Randy Velarde wasn't in one position long enough to emerge as a starter anywhere.

—by Lisa Winston

1992 Yankees: Between the lines

▸**April 26:** Steve Howe proved that his 1991-92 offseason problems didn't affect his performance. He picked up his third win over Baltimore, keeping his ERA at a perfect 0.00.

▸**April 27:** Roberto Kelly hit his first home run of the year. ***Milestone:*** Don Mattingly got his 1,589th hit, scooting past Phil Rizzuto into 11th place on the all-time Yankee hit list.

▸**May 1:** Melido Perez won his second of eight career decisions against the Twins.

▸**May 4:** Third baseman Charlie Hayes played his 25th consecutive errorless game. The longest streak at that position in 1991 was 11 games.

▸**May 10:** The Yankees' losing streak extended to six games, but not before reliever Steve Farr nailed Oakland's Jerry Browne on the backside in retaliation for a Yankee getting hit by a pitch earlier in the game. Farr was ejected. ***Quote of the day:*** Farr—"If we're going to get our lunch handed to us on the field, we don't want to get on the plane with bruises, too."

▸**May 13:** Matt Nokes hit his fifth career grand slam and his 100th career home run,

▸**May 17 *Quote of the day:*** Farr, after a brawl between the Yankees and the A's that included both teams' managers—"Their team has a lot of big egos, starting with their manager. It makes it sweeter when we stomp them by a touchdown and a field goal."

▸**May 24:** Stop the presses, the Yankees actually played a nine-inning game! It snapped a string of four extra-inning games for New York, one short of the major league record set in 1908 by Detroit.

▸**May 26 *Quote of the day:*** Steve Howe, after saving the Yankees' first win at the Metrodome since July 22, 1990—"I've always said (playing at the Metrodome) is like playing on a pool table. Anything can happen."

▸**May 30 *Milestone:*** Scott Sanderson became the ninth pitcher to defeat all 26 major league teams. The others: Nolan Ryan, Tommy John, Don Sutton, Mike Torrez, Rick Wise, Gaylord Perry, Doyle Alexander, and Rich "Goose" Gossage.

▸**June 9:** Candy Maldonado's 451-foot homer for Toronto was only the fifth ball to reach the center field bleachers since 1976. (It was also the game-winner.)

▸**June 10 *Quote of the day:*** Sanderson, after allowing six runs in 1 2/3 innings in the Blue Jays' 10-3 win—"I'm sure we made a impression on them. It wasn't the impression you want to make."

▸**June 24:** Commissioner Fay Vincent permanently banned Steve Howe from baseball after Howe entered a no-contest plea in U.S. District Court to a misdemeanor charge of attempting to buy a gram of cocaine. (The ban was overturned after Vincent was ousted.)

▸**June 26:** Vincent sent a memorandum to teams, stating that employees should feel free to testify as they wished in the grievance filed by Howe against the commissioner.

▸**June 29:** Led by ex-Mets making their homecoming, the Royals defeated the Yankees 7-3. Keith Miller, Gregg Jefferies and Kevin McReynolds returned to New York for the first time since they were traded.

▸**June 30:** Sanderson threw a complete-game shutout of the Royals.

▸**July 7:** Mike Gallego's right wrist was fractured when hit by a pitch, sidelining him for up to six weeks.

▸**July 10:** A large contingent of fans from nearby Mahopac, N.Y., flocked to Yankee Stadium to see local hero Dave Fleming (Seattle) pitch against the Yankees. He stifled the hosts on five hits in eight innings.

▸**July 20:** Shawn Hillegas pitched his first complete game in 45 major league starts. He had not won as a starter since Sept. 16, 1989.

▸**July 21:** Melido Perez allowed just one earned run on four hits (striking out seven) in a 5-1 win over Oakland.

▸**August 1:** Perez struck out nine, moving ahead of Clemens for the AL lead (141). The last Yankee to lead in strikeouts was Al Downing in 1964.

▸**August 8:** In his major league debut, Sam Militello shut out the Red Sox for seven innings in the 6-0 win.

▸**August 11:** Perez threw his seventh complete game of the season—four more than the entire Yankees' staff had in all of 1991—and also took over the AL lead in strikeouts.

▸**August 15:** Militello won his second game in as many starts, and discovered what New York media attention is all about. ***Quote of the day:*** Militello—"It's something I'm going to have to live with, but two good games don't make a pitcher—just like two bad games don't."

▸**August 18:** Mel Hall made a diving catch of a two-out line drive by Carney Lansford with bases loaded in the eighth to preserve the lead. ***Quote of the day:*** Oakland catcher Jamie Quirk, who was on deck when Hall made his game-saving catch—"It was going to be a great play or an inside-the-park home run."

▸**August 19:** Randy Velarde drove in a career-high four runs, and the Yankees collected season highs with 18 hits and 14 runs.

▸**August 22:** Perez strained his side warming up for the ninth inning and had to leave the game, costing him his shot at his first shutout since 1990.

▸**August 26:** Danny Tartabull's second grand slam of the season gave the Yankees a win against the Brewers, and their first sweep of Milwaukee since 1988. It was his ninth career grand slam. ***Quote of the day:*** Tartabull—"It feels great to beat a team that is contending in the division, but slams give you the grandest feeling of them all."

▸**August 27:** Perez finally got his first shutout of the season, pushing his scoreless-innings streak to 17 and again moving him ahead of Clemens in the strikeout race.

▸**September 7:** Perez pitched nine innings, giving up two unearned runs to lower his ERA to 0.79 in his last four starts. The game marked Mattingly's 10th anniversary in the big leagues.

▸**September 8:** Tartabull had career highs with five hits and nine RBI.

▸**October 2:** Bob Wickman allowed just one run over six innings to improve to 6-1 as the Yankees beat the Red Sox 6-3. It was the best start for a Yankee rookie in more than 40 years.

▸**October 4:** The Yanks finished fourth in the AL East. Don Mattingly was third in the league in doubles (40) and sixth in hits (184). Danny Tartabull was second in on-base percentage (.409) and fifth in walks (103). Melido Perez was second in strikeouts (218), fifth in ERA (2.87), complete games (10), and innings pitched (247 2/3).

—by Jeannie Chung, John Hunt, Deron Snyder, and Lisa Winston.

Team directory

▸**Owner:** George Steinbrenner, Joseph Molloy

▸**General Manager:** Gene Michael

▸**Ballpark:**
Yankee Stadium
East 161st Street and River Avenue, Bronx, New York
212-293-4300
Capacity 57,545
Parking (independently owned); $5
Public transportation available
Family and wheelchair sections, ramps, Senior Citizen Discount ($1 tickets day of game), group discounts, monument park behind right field with plaques honoring famous Yankees

▸**Team publications:**
Yankees Magazine, Media Guide, Scorecard, Yearbook
212-293-4300

▸**TV, radio broadcast stations:**
WABC 770 AM, WPIX Channel 11, MSG Network

▸**Camps and/or clinics:**
TBA

▸**Spring Training:**
Fort Lauderdale Stadium
Fort Lauderdale, Florida
Capacity 8,340
305-776-1921

NEW YORK YANKEES 1992 final stats

Batting	AVG	SLG	OB	G	AB	R	H	TB	2B	3B	HR	RBI	BB	SO	SB	CS	E
Meulens	.600	1.200	.667	2	5	1	3	6	0	0	1	1	1	0	0	0	0
Silvestri	.308	.615	.308	7	13	3	4	8	0	2	0	1	0	3	0	0	2
G.Williams	.296	.704	.296	15	27	7	8	19	2	0	3	6	0	3	2	0	2
Mattingly	.288	.416	.327	157	640	89	184	266	40	0	14	86	39	43	3	0	4
B.Williams	.280	.406	.354	62	261	39	73	106	14	2	5	26	29	36	7	6	1
Hall	.280	.429	.310	152	583	67	163	250	36	3	15	81	29	53	4	2	3
R.Kelly	.272	.384	.322	152	580	81	158	223	31	2	10	66	41	96	28	5	7
Velarde	.272	.386	.333	121	412	57	112	159	24	1	7	46	38	78	7	2	15
Stankiewicz	.268	.348	.338	116	400	52	107	139	22	2	2	25	38	42	9	5	12
Tartabull	.266	.489	.409	123	421	72	112	206	19	0	25	85	103	115	2	2	3
James	.262	.379	.359	67	145	24	38	55	8	0	3	17	22	15	1	0	0
Hayes	.257	.409	.297	142	509	52	131	208	19	2	18	66	28	100	3	5	13
Leyritz	.257	.444	.341	63	144	17	37	64	6	0	7	26	14	22	0	1	1
Gallego	.254	.358	.343	53	173	24	44	62	7	1	3	14	20	22	0	1	6
Stanley	.249	.428	.372	68	173	24	43	74	7	0	8	27	33	45	0	0	6
Maas	.248	.406	.305	98	286	35	71	116	12	0	11	35	25	63	3	1	2
P.Kelly	.226	.374	.301	106	318	38	72	119	22	2	7	27	25	72	8	5	11
Nokes	.224	.424	.293	121	384	42	86	163	9	1	22	59	37	62	0	1	4
Snow	.143	.214	.368	7	14	1	2	3	1	0	0	2	5	5	0	0	0
Barfield	.137	.221	.210	30	95	8	13	21	2	0	2	7	9	27	1	1	2
Humphreys	.100	.100	.100	4	10	0	1	1	0	0	0	0	0	1	0	0	0

Pitching	W-L	ERA	G	GS	CG	GF	Sho	SV	IP	H	R	ER	HR	BB	SO
Farr	2-2	1.56	50	0	0	42	0	30	52	34	10	9	2	19	37
Howe	3-0	2.45	20	0	0	10	0	6	22	9	7	6	1	3	12
Perez	13-16	2.87	33	33	10	0	1	0	247.2	212	94	79	16	93	218
Burke	2-2	3.25	23	0	0	10	0	0	27.2	26	14	10	2	15	8
Monteleone	7-3	3.30	47	0	0	15	0	0	92.2	82	35	34	7	27	62
Militello	3-3	3.45	9	9	0	0	0	0	60	43	24	23	6	32	42
Habyan	5-6	3.84	56	0	0	20	0	7	72.2	84	32	31	6	21	44
Young	4-2	3.99	23	7	0	5	0	0	67.2	80	35	30	2	17	20
Wickman	6-1	4.11	8	8	0	0	0	0	50.1	51	25	23	2	20	21
Cadaret	4-8	4.25	46	11	1	9	1	1	103.2	104	53	49	12	74	73
Kamieniecki	6-14	4.36	28	28	4	0	0	0	188	193	100	91	13	74	88
Nielsen	1-0	4.58	20	0	0	12	0	0	19.2	17	10	10	1	18	12
Sanderson	12-11	4.93	33	33	2	0	1	0	193.1	220	116	106	28	64	104
Springer	0-0	6.19	14	0	0	5	0	0	16	18	11	11	0	10	12
Johnson	2-3	6.66	13	8	0	3	0	0	52.2	71	44	39	4	23	14
Hitchcock	0-2	8.31	3	3	0	0	0	0	13	23	12	12	2	6	6
Guetterman	1-1	9.53	15	0	0	7	0	0	22.2	35	24	24	5	13	5

1993 preliminary roster

PITCHERS (19)
Jim Abbott
Andy Cook
Steve Farr
John Habyan
Sterling Hitchcock
Steve Howe
Mark Hutton
Domingo Jean
Jeff Johnson
Scott Kamieniecki
Jimmy Key
Ed Martel
Sam Militello
Rich Monteleone
Bobby Munoz
Melido Perez
Mariano Rivera
Bob Wickman
Mike Witt

CATCHERS (3)
Jim Leyritz
Matt Nokes
Mike Stanley

INFIELDERS (12)
Wade Boggs
Russell Davis
Robert Eenhoorn
Mike Gallego
Pat Kelly
Kevin Maas
Don Mattingly
Hensley Meulens
Spike Owen
Dave Silvestri
Andy Stankiewicz
Randy Velarde

OUTFIELDERS (6)
Mike Humphreys
Dion James
Paul O'Neill
Danny Tartabull
Bernie Williams
Gerald Williams

Games played by position

Player	G	C	1B	2B	3B	SS	OF	DH
BARFIELD,JE	30	0	0	0	0	0	30	0
GALLEGO,M	53	0	0	40	0	14	0	0
HALL,M	152	0	0	0	0	0	136	11
HAYES,C	142	0	4	0	139	0	0	0
HUMPHREYS,M	4	0	0	0	0	0	2	1
JAMES,D	67	0	0	0	0	0	46	5
KELLY,P	106	0	0	101	0	0	0	1
KELLY,R	152	0	0	0	0	0	146	0
LEYRITZ,J	63	18	2	1	2	0	2	31
MAAS,K	98	0	22	0	0	0	0	62
MATTINGLY,D	157	0	143	0	0	0	0	15
MEULENS,H	2	0	0	0	2	0	0	0
NOKES,M	121	111	0	0	0	0	0	0
SILVESTRI,D	7	0	0	0	0	6	0	0
SNOW,JT	7	0	6	0	0	0	0	1
STANKIEWICZ,A	116	0	0	34	0	81	0	1
STANLEY,M	68	55	4	0	0	0	0	6
TARTABULL,D	123	0	0	0	0	0	69	53
VELARDE,R	121	0	0	3	26	75	23	0
WILLIAMS,B	62	0	0	0	0	0	62	0
WILLIAMS,G	15	0	0	0	0	0	12	0

Sick call: 1992 DL report

Player	Days on the DL
Barfield, Jesse*	133
Burke, Tim	31
Farr, Steve	18
Gallego, Mike*	113
Kamieniecki, Scott	23
Kelly, Pat	16
Ramos, John	90
Stanford, Larry	59
Stankiewicz, Andy	15
Tartabull, Danny*	35
Witt, Mike	182
Young, Curt	27

** On Disabled List twice during 1992 season (not counting transfers from one DL to another).*

Minor league report

Class AAA — Columbus finished 95-49, 1st in the International League West Division. The team beat Scranton/Wilkes-Barre in five games for the league championship. 1B J.T. Snow won the league batting crown at .313, and was the league's MVP and Rookie of the Year. RHP Sam Militello was Pitcher of the Year, going 12-2 with a 2.29 ERA and 152 K in 141 IP. 3B Hensley Meulens led the league in HR with 26 and RBI with 100. RHP Mike Draper set a Triple-A record with 37 saves. **Class AA:** Albany-Colonie finished 71-68, 4th in the Eastern League. The team lost to Canton-Akron in the 1st round of the playoffs. 1B Don Sparks hit .311 with 14 HR and 72 RBI. 3B Russ Davis hit .285 with 22 HR and 71 RBI. LHP Sterling Hitchcock had a 2.58 ERA and led the league in K with 156. **Class A:** Prince William finished 69-71, last in the 1st half of the Carolina League Northern Division and 2nd in the 2nd half. 2B Kevin Jordan hit .311 with 8 HR, 63 RBI and a franchise-record 8 triples. RHP Bruce Prybylinski was 12-10 with a 3.01 ERA and walked just 27 in 165 IP. RHP Rich Polak had 22 saves. Fort Lauderdale finished 59-76, 3rd in the both halves of the Florida State League East Division. LHP Brien Taylor was 6-8 with a 2.57 ERA and led the league in K with 187 in 161 IP, while RHP Domingo Jean K'd 172. OF Jovino Carvajal had 40 SB. Greensboro finished 74-67, 3rd in the 1st half of the Sally League Northern Division and 6th in the 2nd half. OF Lew Hill hit .310 with 15 HR and 52 RBI. 1B Tate Seefried had 20 HR and 90 RBI. LHP Andy Pettitte was 10-4 with a 2.20 ERA. Oneonta finished 37-38, 3rd in the New York-Penn League McNamara Division. OF Nick Delvecchio had 12 HR. RHP Jeff Antolick was 4-2 with a 2.13 ERA. RHP Mike Dejean had 16 saves. Yankees finished 31-28, 2nd in the Gulf Coast League Western Division. OF Ruben Rivera had 21 SB. RHP Jeff Cindrich led the league in ERA at 8-3 with a 0.80. He K'd 85 in 68 IP. RHP Marty Janzen had 7 wins and 73 K.

Tops in the organization

BATTING LEADERS	Club	Avg.	G	AB	R	H	HR	RBI
J.T. Snow	Col	.313	135	492	81	154	15	78
Lew Hill	Gbo	.313	98	374	75	117	15	52
Don Sparks	Alb	.311	134	505	64	157	14	72
Kevin Jordan	Prw	.311	112	438	67	136	8	63
Bernie Williams	Col	.306	95	363	68	111	8	50

HOME RUNS		
Hensley Meulens	Col	26
Russ Davis	Alb	22
Tate Seefried	Gbo	20
Torey Lovullo	Col	19
Sherman Obando	Alb	17

RBI		
Hensley Meulens	Col	100
Tate Seefried	Gbo	90
Torey Lovullo	Col	89
Gerald Williams	Col	86
J.T. Snow	Col	78

STOLEN BASES		
Richard Barnwell	Alb	42
Jovino Carvajal	Ftl	40
Mike Humphreys	Col	37
Gerald Williams	Col	36
Andy Fox	Prw	28

WINS		
Keith Garagozzo	Gbo	14
Mark Hutton	Col	13
Several players tied		12

SAVES		
Mike Draper	Col	37
Rich Polak	Prw	22
Doug Gogolewski	Alb	18
Ben Short	Prw	16
Jerry Nielsen	Col	12

STRIKEOUTS		
Brien Taylor	Ftl	187
Domingo Jean	Alb	178
Sterling Hitchcock	Alb	156
Sam Militello	Col	152
Keith Garagozzo	Gbo	137

PITCHING LEADERS	Club	W-L	ERA	IP	H	BB	SO
Andy Pettitte	Gbo	10-4	2.20	168	141	55	130
Sam Militello	Col	12-2	2.29	141	105	46	152
Brien Taylor	Ftl	6-8	2.57	161	121	66	187
Sterling Hitchcock	Alb	6-9	2.58	147	116	42	156
Domingo Jean	Alb	6-11	2.60	163	121	52	178

New York (1903-1992)

Runs: Most, career, all-time

1959 Babe Ruth, 1920-1934
1888 Lou Gehrig, 1923-1939
1677 Mickey Mantle, 1951-1968
1390 Joe DiMaggio, 1936-1951
1186 Earle Combs, 1924-1935

Hits: Most, career, all-time

2721 Lou Gehrig, 1923-1939
2518 Babe Ruth, 1920-1934
2415 Mickey Mantle, 1951-1968
2214 Joe DiMaggio, 1936-1951
2148 Yogi Berra, 1946-1963

2B: Most, career, all-time

534 Lou Gehrig, 1923-1939
424 Babe Ruth, 1920-1934
389 Joe DiMaggio, 1936-1951
363 DON MATTINGLY, 1982-1992
344 Mickey Mantle, 1951-1968

3B: Most, career, all-time

163 Lou Gehrig, 1923-1939
154 Earle Combs, 1924-1935
131 Joe DiMaggio, 1936-1951
121 Wally Pipp, 1915-1925
115 Tony Lazzeri, 1926-1937

HR: Most, career, all-time

659 Babe Ruth, 1920-1934
536 Mickey Mantle, 1951-1968
493 Lou Gehrig, 1923-1939
361 Joe DiMaggio, 1936-1951
358 Yogi Berra, 1946-1963

RBI: Most, career, all-time

1995 Lou Gehrig, 1923-1939
1971 Babe Ruth, 1920-1934
1537 Joe DiMaggio, 1936-1951
1509 Mickey Mantle, 1951-1968
1430 Yogi Berra, 1946-1963

SB: Most, career, all-time

326 RICKEY HENDERSON, 1985-1989
251 WILLIE RANDOLPH, 1976-1988
248 Hal Chase, 1905-1913
233 Roy White, 1965-1979
184 Ben Chapman, 1930-1936
184 Wid Conroy, 1903-1908

BB: Most, career, all-time

1847 Babe Ruth, 1920-1934
1733 Mickey Mantle, 1951-1968
1508 Lou Gehrig, 1923-1939
1005 WILLIE RANDOLPH, 1976-1988
934 Roy White, 1965-1979

BA: Highest, career, all-time

.349 Babe Ruth, 1920-1934
.340 Lou Gehrig, 1923-1939
.325 Earle Combs, 1924-1935
.325 Joe DiMaggio, 1936-1951
.313 Bill Dickey, 1928-1946

Slug avg: Highest, career, all-time

.711 Babe Ruth, 1920-1934
.632 Lou Gehrig, 1923-1939
.579 Joe DiMaggio, 1936-1951
.557 Mickey Mantle, 1951-1968
.526 Reggie Jackson, 1977-1981

Games started: Most, career, all-time

438 Whitey Ford, 1950-1967
391 Red Ruffing, 1930-1946
356 Mel Stottlemyre, 1964-1974
323 Ron Guidry, 1975-1988
319 Lefty Gomez, 1930-1942

Saves: Most, career, all-time

224 DAVE RIGHETTI, 1979-1990
151 RICH GOSSAGE, 1978-1989
141 Sparky Lyle, 1972-1978
104 Johnny Murphy, 1932-1946
76 Joe Page, 1944-1950

Shutouts: Most, career, all-time

45 Whitey Ford, 1950-1967
40 Red Ruffing, 1930-1946
40 Mel Stottlemyre, 1964-1974
28 Lefty Gomez, 1930-1942
27 Allie Reynolds, 1947-1954

Wins: Most, career, all-time

236 Whitey Ford, 1950-1967
231 Red Ruffing, 1930-1946
189 Lefty Gomez, 1930-1942
170 Ron Guidry, 1975-1988
168 Bob Shawkey, 1915-1927

K: Most, career, all-time

1956 Whitey Ford, 1950-1967
1778 Ron Guidry, 1975-1988
1526 Red Ruffing, 1930-1946
1468 Lefty Gomez, 1930-1942
1257 Mel Stottlemyre, 1964-1974

Win pct: Highest, career, all-time

.725 Johnny Allen, 1932-1935
.717 Spud Chandler, 1937-1947
.706 Vic Raschi, 1946-1953
.700 Monte Pearson, 1936-1940
.690 Whitey Ford, 1950-1967

ERA: Lowest, career, all-time

2.54 Russ Ford, 1909-1913
2.58 Jack Chesbro, 1903-1909
2.72 Al Orth, 1904-1909
2.73 Tiny Bonham, 1940-1946
2.73 George Mogridge, 1915-1920

Runs: Most, season

177 Babe Ruth, 1921
167 Lou Gehrig, 1936
163 Lou Gehrig, 1931
163 Babe Ruth, 1928
158 Babe Ruth, 1920
158 Babe Ruth, 1927

Hits: Most, season

238 DON MATTINGLY, 1986
231 Earle Combs, 1927
220 Lou Gehrig, 1930
218 Lou Gehrig, 1927
215 Joe DiMaggio, 1937

2B: Most, season

53 DON MATTINGLY, 1986
52 Lou Gehrig, 1927
48 DON MATTINGLY, 1985
47 Lou Gehrig, 1926
47 Lou Gehrig, 1928
47 Bob Meusel, 1927

3B: Most, season

23 Earle Combs, 1927
22 Earle Combs, 1930
22 Birdie Cree, 1911
22 Snuffy Stirnweiss, 1945
21 Earle Combs, 1928

HR: Most, season

61 Roger Maris, 1961
60 Babe Ruth, 1927
59 Babe Ruth, 1921
54 Mickey Mantle, 1961
54 Babe Ruth, 1920
54 Babe Ruth, 1928

RBI: Most, season

184 Lou Gehrig, 1931
175 Lou Gehrig, 1927
174 Lou Gehrig, 1930
171 Babe Ruth, 1921
167 Joe DiMaggio, 1937

SB: Most, season

93 RICKEY HENDERSON, 1988
87 RICKEY HENDERSON, 1986
80 RICKEY HENDERSON, 1985
74 Fritz Maisel, 1914
61 Ben Chapman, 1931

BB: Most, season

170 Babe Ruth, 1923
148 Babe Ruth, 1920
146 Mickey Mantle, 1957
144 Babe Ruth, 1921
144 Babe Ruth, 1926

BA: Highest, season

.393 Babe Ruth, 1923
.381 Joe DiMaggio, 1939
.379 Lou Gehrig, 1930
.378 Babe Ruth, 1924
.378 Babe Ruth, 1921

Slug avg: Highest, season

.847 Babe Ruth, 1920
.846 Babe Ruth, 1921
.772 Babe Ruth, 1927
.765 Lou Gehrig, 1927
.764 Babe Ruth, 1923

Games started: Most, season

51 Jack Chesbro, 1904
45 Jack Powell, 1904
42 Jack Chesbro, 1906
39 Pat Dobson, 1974
39 Whitey Ford, 1961
39 Catfish Hunter, 1975
39 Al Orth, 1906
39 Mel Stottlemyre, 1969
39 Ralph Terry, 1962

Saves: Most, season

46 DAVE RIGHETTI, 1986
36 DAVE RIGHETTI, 1990
35 Sparky Lyle, 1972
33 RICH GOSSAGE, 1980
31 DAVE RIGHETTI, 1984
31 DAVE RIGHETTI, 1987

Shutouts: Most, season

9 Ron Guidry, 1978
8 Whitey Ford, 1964
8 Russ Ford, 1910
7 Whitey Ford, 1958
7 Catfish Hunter, 1975
7 Allie Reynolds, 1951
7 Mel Stottlemyre, 1971
7 Mel Stottlemyre, 1972

Wins: Most, season

41 Jack Chesbro, 1904
27 Carl Mays, 1921
27 Al Orth, 1906
26 Joe Bush, 1922
26 Russ Ford, 1910
26 Lefty Gomez, 1934
26 Carl Mays, 1920

K: Most, season

248 Ron Guidry, 1978
239 Jack Chesbro, 1904
218 MELIDO PEREZ, 1992
217 Al Downing, 1964
210 Bob Turley, 1955

Win pct: Highest, season

.893 Ron Guidry, 1978
.862 Whitey Ford, 1961
.842 Ralph Terry, 1961
.839 Lefty Gomez, 1934
.833 Spud Chandler, 1943

ERA: Lowest, season

1.64 Spud Chandler, 1943
1.65 Russ Ford, 1910
1.74 Ron Guidry, 1978
1.82 Jack Chesbro, 1904
1.83 Hippo Vaughn, 1910

Most pinch-hit homers, season

4 Johnny Blanchard, 1961

Most pinch-hit, homers, career

9 Yogi Berra, 1946-1963

Most consecutive games, batting safely

56 Joe DiMaggio, 1941
33 Hal Chase, 1907

Most consecutive scoreless innings

N/A

No hit games

Tom L. Hughes, NY vs Cle AL, 0-5; August 30, 1910 (2nd game) (lost on 7 hits in 11 innings after allowing the first hit in the tenth)
George Mogridge, NY at Bos AL, 2-1; April 24, 1917.
Sam Jones, NY at Phi AL, 2-0; September 4, 1923.
Monte Pearson, NY vs Cle AL, 13-0; August 27, 1938 (2nd game).
Allie Reynolds, NY at Cle AL, 1-0; July 12, 1951.
Allie Reynolds, NY vs Bos AL, 8-0; September 28, 1951 (1st game).
Don Larsen, NY AL vs Bro NL, 2-0; October 8, 1956 (World Series, perfect game).
Dave Righetti, NY vs Bos AL, 4-0; July 4, 1983.
Andy Hawkins, NY at Chi AL, 0-4; July 1, 1990 (8 innings, lost the game; bottom of 9th not played).

ACTIVE PLAYERS in caps.

Detroit Tigers

by H. Darr Beiser, *USA TODAY*

Another great year for Cecil Fielder: tops in the AL with 124 RBI, and third in the home-run race with 35.

1992 Tigers: Best bats, worst arms

For the pitching-starved Tigers, the 1992 season was more of the same—more runs and more losses. They led the majors in runs (791) and home runs (182), but their starters gave up 5.08 runs a game and served up 115 home runs, worst in baseball on both counts. Those numbers added up to a 75-87 record and a sixth-place finish.

They dropped their first six games of the season and never really recovered. Shortly after the All-Star break, they appeared to right themselves with a four-game winning streak that catapulted them up to fourth place (three games under .500), but a six-game skid in late July erased all hopes of another Sparky Anderson championship. Finally, Cecil Fielder's two home runs against Cleveland July 31 ended the losing streak.

Fielder had 35 homers and drove in 124 runs. He became the first player to lead the major leagues in RBI three consecutive seasons since Babe Ruth. Rob Deer (32 HR), Mickey Tettleton (32), Travis Fryman (20), and Lou Whitaker (19) also contributed to Detroit's cushion in the homer race.

When the Tigers didn't go deep, they couldn't manufacture runs. In 24 of their defeats, the Tigers were held to one run or were shut out. In 51 of their losses, they scored three runs or fewer. And it's hard to win close ballgames with a 4.60 team ERA.

The absence of speed (main stolen base threat Milt Cuyler managed only eight steals in about half of the season) and contact hitting (league-high 1,055 strikeouts) made the team one-dimensional. They were the fourth team in major league history to lead the league in runs and still be outscored.

Injuries limited shortstop Alan Trammell and rightfielder Deer to 29 and 110 games, respectively. Trammell's injury forced Fryman to move from third base; he became arguably the league's best shortstop. His replacement at third, Scott Livingstone, was solid (.282) but not nearly as productive (four homers, 46 RBI).

Among Detroit's mound of problems: Bill Gullickson fizzled in the second half, losing nine of his last 14 decisions with a 7.79 ERA in his last six starts; Eric King (4-6, 5.22) and Les Lancaster (3-4, 6.33) were free agent signees gone sour; Scott Aldred was taken by the Colorado Rockies in the expansion draft. If there was a bright spot on the staff, it was rookie John Doherty, who moved from the bullpen and earned a spot in the '93 rotation. Doherty was 7-4 with a 3.88 ERA and three saves. David Haas (26), another right-hander, was also very effective. Reliever Mike Henneman had only 24 saves, but then again, with the staff struggling as it did, he had only 28 chances.

—by John Hunt

1993 Tigers: Preview

It will be nearly impossible to transform an all-power, no-speed, and no-pitching team into a balanced contender in one season.

The Tigers retain baseball's best RBI man in Cecil Fielder (132, 133 and 124 the last three years), baseball's best-kept secret in shortstop Travis Fryman (led all major league shortstops in homers and RBI), and baseball's best power-hitting catcher in Mickey Tettleton (63 homers in the last two years). But they need to find ways to manufacture runs. Only one player, Tony Phillips, reached double figures in stolen bases in 1992.

And they must resolve their obvious pitching problems. Keeping Bill Gullickson and signing Mike Moore were major steps in the right direction. New owner Mike Ilitch must loosen the purse strings if the Tigers are to contend—Detroit's payroll was only $27.8 million on Opening Day 1992.

—by Gary Kicinski

1992 Tigers: Between the lines

▸**April 22:** Tiger hitters blasted four homers, leading the majors with 25.

▸**April 30:** The Tigers finished April 1-9 at Tiger Stadium. Their team ERA grew to 5.72.

▸**May 22:** Rob Deer hit a pair of home runs to raise his season total to 13, and Cecil Fielder added his eighth of the year, as both went 2-for-4 with three RBI.

▸**May 26:** Veteran Bill Gullickson threw just 84 pitches, 55 of them for strikes, to record his third complete game of the season in an 8-1 win against Kansas City. It was the sixth win in a row for Gullickson, who just two years earlier was working the mound in Japan.

▸**May 31:** Detroit was 8-24 at the Metrodome since May 1987, and was swept there over Memorial weekend. ***Quote of the day:*** Tigers' reliever Mike Henneman—"Myself, I don't like domes, they're clammy, and I don't like artificial turf. But the Twins sure make themselves comfortable."

▸**June 1 *Milestone:*** Lou Whitaker played his 2,000th career game at second base for Detroit. ***Quote of the day:*** Mickey Tettleton, on the Tigers' five-game losing streak—"There's no explaining this stupid game. All we can do is come back tomorrow and try again. The sun has been coming up for two million years, I guess it will come up again."

▸**June 6 *Milestone:*** Whitaker, who had three hits on the day, collected his 2,000th career hit.

▸**June 11:** Rob Deer hit a 480-foot homer that almost cleared the Tiger Stadium roof in left. He would have been the fourth player to do that (joining Harmon Killebrew, Frank Howard and Cecil Fielder), but the ball hit just below the roof's peak, bounced and rolled back.

▸**June 19:** Rob Deer was 2-for-6 with four RBI, thanks to a pair of homers to raise his season total to 21, as the Tigers beat the White Sox 8-3.

▸**June 22 *Quote of the day:*** Sparky Anderson had no worries with Kevin Ritz on the mound against the powerless Red Sox, who hadn't scored more than five runs in their last 18 games—"I don't know if it was the most comfortable he's been on the mound, but it was the most comfortable I've been with him on the mound."

▸**June 23 *Quote of the day:*** Red Sox pitcher Matt Young, on the grand slam he surrendered to Cecil Fielder—"A shot of almost biblical proportions."

▸**June 28 *Quote of the day:*** Third baseman Scott Livingstone, who lives in Texas in the off-season, on being happy just to make contact against opposing pitcher Nolan Ryan—"He's a wonder. I was happy to hit the ball, but I'm not going to say much about that. He might end up being our governor, and I don't want him to raise my taxes."

▸**July 1:** The Tigers dropped two games in a row to the Red Sox to stall their attack on fifth place in the AL East; Sparky Anderson didn't think it was going to have a major effect on the pennant race. ***Quote of the day:*** Anderson—"This would have been a four-game swing for a team like Baltimore, but it's not any kind of swing for a team like us. When you're 10 1/2 out, you're not swinging from anything but a pole."

▸**July 3:** The Tigers pulled off their first triple play since 1980.

▸**July 5 *Quote of the day:*** Sparky Anderson on Seattle starter Rich DeLucia, who did not retire any of the six Detroit batters he faced—"I saw him on TV last week when he was pitching a good game against Oakland, I think it was. I wondered if this was the same guy."

▸**July 7 *Quote of the day:*** Scott Livingstone, whose defensive gem in the third inning contributed to the Tigers' win against Oakland, on what he thought after he made the play—"I thought, 'What time is *SportsCenter* on?' "

▸**July 12:** Despite hitting .378 in 19 games, the Tigers' Phil Clark was sent down for Rob Deer, off the DL.

▸**July 18:** Deer pounded a pair of homers, but had to leave the game in the ninth when he sprained an ankle trying to steal second base.

▸**July 21:** Built for comfort, not for speed: The Tigers beat Seattle 6-2, despite the fact that Frank Tanana was clocked as slow as 49 mph, while Randy Johnson—who struck out a career-high 13 in just six innings—was clocked as fast as 98 mph.

▸**August 2:** Cecil Fielder homered for the fourth time in three days.

▸**August 8 *Milestone:*** Lou Whitaker hit his 200th career homer while playing second base, giving him 2,000-plus hits, 2,000-plus games and 200 homers. The only other second baseman to have reached those marks is Hall of Famer Joe Morgan.

▸**August 16:** Cecil Fielder collected his 100th RBI, blasting his 27th homer. He was the first Tiger since Hank Greenberg (1940) to drive in 100 runs for three seasons in a row.

▸**August 24 *Quote of the day:*** Sparky Anderson, warning new owner Mike Ilitch not to expect the Tigers' 6-2 win to happen every day—"His first day in control and he's already got a win. He's going to think this game is easy."

▸**August 29:** Lou Whitaker hit his second career grand slam. The other one came in 1984.

▸**September 10:** Rookie David Haas tossed a four-hit shutout, with no walks and two strikeouts. Rob Deer hit his 28th home run and Cecil Fielder hit his 31st. But more noteworthy was teammate Scott Livingstone, who made his first of the season a three-run shot. ***Quote of the day:*** Livingstone, after his first homer in 306 at-bats—"What I need now is a triple. That would complete my cycle—for the season."

▸**September 18:** Lou Whitaker tied a career high with five RBI. It was the fifth time in his career he'd reached that plateau.

▸**September 23:** Rob Deer and Mickey Tettleton both homered, the 30th of the season for both. The feat marked the first time in team history three Detroit teammates had 30 homers in the same season—Cecil Fielder already had 32.

▸**September 25 *Milestone:*** Sparky Anderson collected his 1,131st victory to tie Hughie Jennings as all-time winningest Detroit skipper.

▸**October 4:** Rookie Phil Clark finished the season with a .407 average, the first major leaguer in 10 years to hit over .400 with more than 50 at-bats.

—by Jeanie Chung, John Hunt, Deron Snyder, and Lisa Winston.

Team directory

▸**Owner:** Michael Ilitch

▸**General Manager:** Jerry Walker

▸**Ballpark:**

Tiger Stadium
2121 Trumbull Avenue, Detroit, Mich.
313-962-4000
Capacity 52,416
Pay parking lot (independently owned)
Public transportation available
Wheelchair section, ramps, Group Sales department

▸**Team publications:**

Tiger Yearbook, Scorebook/Program

▸**TV, radio broadcast stations:**

WJR 760AM, WDIV Channel 4, PASS Cable

▸**Camps and/or clinics:**

Jim Price's Sports Fantasy, 313-353-5643

▸**Spring Training:**

Marchant Stadium
Lakeland, Fla.
Capacity 7,027
813-499-8229

DETROIT TIGERS 1992 final stats

Batting	AVG	SLG	OB	G	AB	R	H	TB	2B	3B	HR	RBI	BB	SO	SB	CS	E
Clark	.407	.537	.467	23	54	3	22	29	4	0	1	5	6	9	1	0	2
Livingstone	.282	.376	.319	117	354	43	100	133	21	0	4	46	21	36	1	3	10
Whitaker	.278	.461	.386	130	453	77	126	209	26	0	19	71	81	46	6	4	9
Phillips	.276	.388	.387	159	606	114	167	235	32	3	10	64	114	93	12	10	11
Trammell	.275	.392	.370	29	102	11	28	40	7	1	1	11	15	4	2	2	3
Barnes	.273	.388	.318	95	165	27	45	64	8	1	3	25	10	18	3	1	11
Fryman	.266	.416	.316	161	659	87	175	274	31	4	20	96	45	144	8	4	22
Gladden	.254	.357	.304	113	417	57	106	149	20	1	7	42	30	64	4	2	3
Kreuter	.253	.332	.321	67	190	22	48	63	9	0	2	16	20	38	0	1	5
Deer	.247	.547	.337	110	393	66	97	215	20	1	32	64	51	131	4	2	4
Fielder	.244	.458	.325	155	594	80	145	272	22	0	35	124	73	151	0	0	10
Cuyler	.241	.316	.275	89	291	39	70	92	11	1	3	28	10	62	8	5	4
Tettleton	.238	.469	.379	157	525	82	125	246	25	0	32	83	122	137	0	6	2
Carreon	.232	.360	.278	101	336	34	78	121	11	1	10	41	22	57	3	1	4
Bergman	.232	.265	.305	87	181	17	42	48	3	0	1	10	20	19	1	0	5
Rowland	.214	.214	.353	6	14	2	3	3	0	0	0	0	3	3	0	0	0
Pettis	.202	.302	.338	48	129	27	26	39	4	3	1	12	27	34	13	4	1
Brogna	.192	.346	.276	9	26	3	5	9	1	0	1	3	3	5	0	0	1
Hare	.115	.154	.172	15	26	0	3	4	1	0	0	5	2	4	0	0	0

Pitching	W-L	ERA	G	GS	CG	GF	Sho	SV	IP	H	R	ER	HR	BB	SO
Kiely	4-2	2.13	39	0	0	20	0	0	55	44	14	13	2	28	18
Munoz	1-2	3.00	65	0	0	15	0	2	48	44	16	16	3	25	23
Doherty	7-4	3.88	47	11	0	9	0	3	116	131	61	50	4	25	37
Haas	5-3	3.94	12	11	1	1	1	0	61.2	68	30	27	8	16	29
Henneman	2-6	3.96	60	0	0	53	0	24	77.1	75	36	34	6	20	58
Leiter	8-5	4.18	35	14	1	7	0	0	112	116	57	52	9	43	75
Gullickson	14-13	4.34	34	34	4	0	1	0	221.2	228	109	107	35	50	64
Tanana	13-11	4.39	32	31	3	0	0	0	186.2	188	102	91	22	90	91
Knudsen	2-3	4.58	48	1	0	14	0	5	70.2	70	39	36	9	41	51
Terrell	7-10	5.20	36	14	1	7	0	0	136.2	163	86	79	14	48	61
King	4-6	5.22	17	14	0	2	0	1	79.1	90	47	46	12	28	45
Ritz	2-5	5.60	23	11	0	4	0	0	80.1	88	52	50	4	44	57
Groom	0-5	5.82	12	7	0	3	0	1	38.2	48	28	25	4	22	15
Lancaster	3-4	6.33	41	1	0	17	0	0	86.2	101	66	61	11	51	35
Aldred	3-8	6.78	16	13	0	0	0	0	65	80	51	49	12	33	34

1993 preliminary roster

PITCHERS (18)
Tom Bolton
Steve Cummings
John DeSilva
John Doherty
Dan Gakeler
Greg Gohr
Frank Gonzales
Bill Gullickson
Buddy Groom
David Haas
John Hudek
Mike Henneman
John Kiely
Kurt Knudsen
Mark Leiter
Mike Lumley
Mike Moore
Mike Munoz

CATCHERS (3)
Chad Kreuter
Rich Rowland
Mickey Tettleton

INFIELDERS (9)
Skeeter Barnes
Rico Brogna
Ivan Cruz
Cecil Fielder
Travis Fryman
Scott Livingstone
Tony Phillips
Alan Trammell
Lou Whitaker

OUTFIELDERS (9)
Danny Bautista
Mark Carreon
Phil Clark
Milt Cuyler
Rob Deer
Dan Gladden
Shawn Hare
Jody Hurst
Riccardo Ingram

Games played by position

Player	G	C	1B	2B	3B	SS	OF	DH
BARNES,BR	95	0	17	7	39	0	15	7
BERGMAN,D	87	0	55	0	0	0	1	12
BROGNA,R	9	0	8	0	0	0	0	2
CARREON,M	101	0	0	0	0	0	83	13
CLARK,P	23	0	0	0	0	0	13	7
CUYLER,M	89	0	0	0	0	0	89	0
DEER,R	110	0	0	0	0	0	106	2
FIELDER,C	155	0	114	0	0	0	0	43
FRYMAN,T	161	0	0	0	26	137	0	0
GLADDEN,D	113	0	0	0	0	0	108	2
HARE,S	15	0	4	0	0	0	9	0
KREUTER,C	67	62	0	0	0	0	0	1
LIVINGSTONE,S	117	0	0	0	112	0	0	0
PETTIS,G	48	0	0	0	0	0	46	0
PHILLIPS,T	159	0	0	57	20	1	69	34
ROWLAND,R	6	3	1	0	1	0	0	2
TETTLETON,M	157	113	3	0	0	0	2	40
TRAMMELL,A	29	0	0	0	0	27	0	1
WHITAKER,L	130	0	0	119	0	0	0	10

Sick call: 1992 DL report

Player	Days on the DL
Carreon, Mark	18
Cuyler, Milt	71
Deer, Rob*	45
Doherty, John	19
Gakeler, Dan	182
Gladden, Dan	31
Hare, Shawn	63
King, Eric	79
Leiter, Mark	31
Ritz, Kevin	62
Trammell, Alan	142

** On Disabled List twice during 1992 season (not counting transfers from one DL to another).*

Minor league report

Class AAA — Toledo finished 64-80, 3rd in the International League West Division. OF Steve Carter hit .300 with 9 HR and 58 RBI. C Rich Rowland had 25 HR and 82 RBI. IF Greg Smith had 24 SB. **Class AA:** London finished 67-70, 5th in the Eastern League. 1B Greg Sparks led the league in HR with 25. 1B/DH Ivan Cruz won the RBI title with 104. OF Lou Frazier ran away with the SB crown at 58. **Class A:** Lakeland finished 70-62, 3rd in the 1st half of the Florida State League Central Division and 1st in the 2nd half. The team beat Baseball City in three games for the league championship. 1B Mike Rendina had 69 RBI. RHP Jason Pfaff was 7-7 with a 2.14 ERA, walking just 33 in 134 IP. RHP Jose Lima had 143 K. Fayetteville finished 74-67, 5th in the 1st half of the Sally League Northern Division and 3rd in the 2nd half. RHP Tom Schwarber had 24 saves. OF Justin Mashore had 31 SB. LHP Rich Kelley was 13-5 with a 2.82 ERA. Niagara Falls finished 39-39, 3rd in the New York-Penn League Stedler Division. OF Keith Kimsey hit 12 HR and drove in 46. 2B Shannon Penn had 31 SB. LHP Sean Whiteside was 8-4 with a 2.45 ERA and K'd 72 in 70 IP. Bristol finished 33-35, 3rd in the Appalachian League South Division. OF Roberto Rojas had 32 SB. RHP Blas Cedeno was 8-2 with a 2.01 ERA, sharing the league lead in wins. LHP Paul Magrini K'd 84.

Tops in the organization

BATTING LEADERS	Club	Avg.	G	AB	R	H	HR	RBI
Bob Reimink	Tol	.300	137	470	64	141	3	48
Steve Carter	Tol	.300	130	470	56	141	9	58
Evan Pratte	Fay	.284	131	465	73	132	3	43
Tyrone Kingwood	Lon	.284	108	377	57	107	7	47
Ivan Cruz	Lon	.275	134	524	71	144	14	104

HOME RUNS:		
Greg Sparks	Tol	27
Rich Rowland	Tol	25
Jody Hurst	Lon	14
Ivan Cruz	Lon	14
Several players tied		12

WINS		
Ben Blomdahl	Lak	15
Rich Kelley	Fay	13
Jim Henry	Lon	11
Felipe Lira	Lak	11
Several players tied		10

RBI		
Ivan Cruz	Lon	104
Rich Rowland	Tol	82
Greg Sparks	Tol	77
Brian Dubose	Fay	75
Several players tied		69

SAVES		
Ben Blomdahl	Lak	15
Rich Kelley	Fay	13
Jim Henry	Lon	11
Felipe Lira	Lak	11
Several players tied		10

STOLEN BASES		
Lou Frazier	Lon	58
Justin Mashore	Fay	31
Rudy Pemberton	Lak	25
Greg Smith	Tol	24
Tyrone Kingwood	Lon	22

STRIKEOUTS		
Jose Lima	Lak	137
Sean Bergman	Lon	126
Brian Edmondson	Fay	125
Rich Kelley	Fay	117
David Haas	Tol	112

PITCHING LEADERS	Club	W-L	ERA	IP	H	BB	SO
Jason Pfaff	Lak	7-7	2.14	134	112	33	79
Rich Kelley	Fay	13-5	2.82	163	140	63	117
Jamie Moyer	Tol	10-8	2.86	139	128	37	80
Dennis Walsh	Fay	8-5	3.11	122	98	41	101
Jim Henry	Lon	11-8	3.14	146	130	65	95

Detroit (1901-1992)

Runs: Most, career, all-time

2088	Ty Cobb, 1905-1926
1774	Charlie Gehringer, 1924-1942
1622	Al Kaline, 1953-1974
1242	Donie Bush, 1908-1921
1211	LOU WHITAKER, 1977-1992

Hits: Most, career, all-time

3900	Ty Cobb, 1905-1926
3007	Al Kaline, 1953-1974
2839	Charlie Gehringer, 1924-1942
2499	Harry Heilmann, 1914-1929
2466	Sam Crawford, 1903-1917

2B: Most, career, all-time

665	Ty Cobb, 1905-1926
574	Charlie Gehringer, 1924-1942
498	Al Kaline, 1953-1974
497	Harry Heilmann, 1914-1929
402	Sam Crawford, 1903-1917

3B: Most, career, all-time

284	Ty Cobb, 1905-1926
249	Sam Crawford, 1903-1917
146	Charlie Gehringer, 1924-1942
145	Harry Heilmann, 1914-1929
136	Bobby Veach, 1912-1923

HR: Most, career, all-time

399	Al Kaline, 1953-1974
373	Norm Cash, 1960-1974
306	Hank Greenberg, 1930-1946
262	Willie Horton, 1963-1977
239	Rudy York, 1934-1945

RBI: Most, career, all-time

1804	Ty Cobb, 1905-1926
1583	Al Kaline, 1953-1974
1442	Harry Heilmann, 1914-1929
1427	Charlie Gehringer, 1924-1942
1264	Sam Crawford, 1903-1917

SB: Most, career, all-time

864	Ty Cobb, 1905-1926
400	Donie Bush, 1908-1921
317	Sam Crawford, 1903-1917
294	Ron LeFlore, 1974-1979
212	ALAN TRAMMELL, 1977-1992

BB: Most, career, all-time

1277	Al Kaline, 1953-1974
1186	Charlie Gehringer, 1924-1942
1148	Ty Cobb, 1905-1926
1125	Donie Bush, 1908-1921
1047	LOU WHITAKER, 1977-1992

BA: Highest, career, all-time

.368	Ty Cobb, 1905-1926
.342	Harry Heilmann, 1914-1929
.337	Bob Fothergill, 1922-1930
.325	George Kell, 1946-1952
.321	Heinie Manush, 1923-1927

Slug avg: Highest, career, all-time

.616	Hank Greenberg, 1930-1946
.518	Harry Heilmann, 1914-1929
.516	Ty Cobb, 1905-1926
.503	Rudy York, 1934-1945
.501	Rocky Colavito, 1960-1963

Games started: Most, career, all-time

459	Mickey Lolich, 1963-1975
408	JACK MORRIS, 1977-1990
395	George Mullin, 1902-1913
388	Hooks Dauss, 1912-1926
373	Hal Newhouser, 1939-1953

Saves: Most, career, all-time

125	John Hiller, 1965-1980
120	Willie Hernandez, 1984-1989
104	MIKE HENNEMAN, 1987-1992
85	Aurelio Lopez, 1979-1985
55	Terry Fox, 1961-1966

Shutouts: Most, career, all-time

39	Mickey Lolich, 1963-1975
34	George Mullin, 1902-1913
33	Tommy Bridges, 1930-1946
33	Hal Newhouser, 1939-1953
29	Bill Donovan, 1903-1918

Wins: Most, career, all-time

222	Hooks Dauss, 1912-1926
209	George Mullin, 1902-1913
207	Mickey Lolich, 1963-1975
200	Hal Newhouser, 1939-1953
198	JACK MORRIS, 1977-1990

K: Most, career, all-time

2679	Mickey Lolich, 1963-1975
1980	JACK MORRIS, 1977-1990
1770	Hal Newhouser, 1939-1953
1674	Tommy Bridges, 1930-1946
1406	Jim Bunning, 1955-1963

Win pct: Highest, career, all-time

.654	MIKE HENNEMAN, 1987-1992
.654	Denny McLain, 1963-1970
.639	Aurelio Lopez, 1979-1985
.629	Schoolboy Rowe, 1933-1942
.616	Harry Coveleski, 1914-1918

ERA: Lowest, career, all-time

2.34	Harry Coveleski, 1914-1918
2.38	Ed Killian, 1904-1910
2.42	Ed Summers, 1908-1912
2.49	Bill Donovan, 1903-1918
2.61	Ed Siever, 1901-1908

Runs: Most, season

147	Ty Cobb, 1911
144	Ty Cobb, 1915
144	Charlie Gehringer, 1930
144	Charlie Gehringer, 1936
144	Hank Greenberg, 1938

Hits: Most, season

248	Ty Cobb, 1911
237	Harry Heilmann, 1921
227	Charlie Gehringer, 1936
226	Ty Cobb, 1912
225	Ty Cobb, 1917
225	Harry Heilmann, 1925

2B: Most, season

63	Hank Greenberg, 1934
60	Charlie Gehringer, 1936
56	George Kell, 1950
55	Gee Walker, 1936
50	Charlie Gehringer, 1934
50	Hank Greenberg, 1940
50	Harry Heilmann, 1927

3B: Most, season

26	Sam Crawford, 1914
25	Sam Crawford, 1903
24	Ty Cobb, 1911
24	Ty Cobb, 1917
23	Ty Cobb, 1912
23	Sam Crawford, 1913

HR: Most, season

58	Hank Greenberg, 1938
51	CECIL FIELDER, 1990
45	Rocky Colavito, 1961
44	CECIL FIELDER, 1991
44	Hank Greenberg, 1946

RBI: Most, season

183	Hank Greenberg, 1937
170	Hank Greenberg, 1935
150	Hank Greenberg, 1940
146	Hank Greenberg, 1938
140	Rocky Colavito, 1961

SB: Most, season

96	Ty Cobb, 1915
83	Ty Cobb, 1911
78	Ron LeFlore, 1979
76	Ty Cobb, 1909
68	Ty Cobb, 1916
68	Ron LeFlore, 1978

BB: Most, season

137	Roy Cullenbine, 1947
135	Eddie Yost, 1959
125	Eddie Yost, 1960
124	Norm Cash, 1961
122	MICKEY TETTLETON, 1992

BA: Highest, season

.420	Ty Cobb, 1911
.409	Ty Cobb, 1912
.403	Harry Heilmann, 1923
.401	Ty Cobb, 1922
.398	Harry Heilmann, 1927

Slug avg: Highest, season

.683	Hank Greenberg, 1938
.670	Hank Greenberg, 1940
.668	Hank Greenberg, 1937
.662	Norm Cash, 1961
.632	Harry Heilmann, 1923

Games started: Most, season

45	Mickey Lolich, 1971
44	George Mullin, 1904
42	Mickey Lolich, 1973
42	George Mullin, 1907
41	Joe Coleman, 1974
41	Mickey Lolich, 1972
41	Mickey Lolich, 1974
41	Denny McLain, 1968
41	Denny McLain, 1969
41	George Mullin, 1905

Saves: Most, season

38	John Hiller, 1973
32	Willie Hernandez, 1984
31	Willie Hernandez, 1985
27	Tom Timmermann, 1970
24	MIKE HENNEMAN, 1992
24	Willie Hernandez, 1986

Shutouts: Most, season

9	Denny McLain, 1969
8	Ed Killian, 1905
8	Hal Newhouser, 1945
7	Billy Hoeft, 1955
7	George Mullin, 1904
7	Dizzy Trout, 1944

Wins: Most, season

31	Denny McLain, 1968
29	George Mullin, 1909
29	Hal Newhouser, 1944
27	Dizzy Trout, 1944
26	Hal Newhouser, 1946

K: Most, season

308	Mickey Lolich, 1971
280	Denny McLain, 1968
275	Hal Newhouser, 1946
271	Mickey Lolich, 1969
250	Mickey Lolich, 1972

Win pct: Highest, season

.862	Bill Donovan, 1907
.842	Schoolboy Rowe, 1940
.838	Denny McLain, 1968
.808	Bobo Newsom, 1940
.784	George Mullin, 1909

ERA: Lowest, season

1.64	Ed Summers, 1908
1.71	Ed Killian, 1909
1.78	Ed Killian, 1907
1.81	Hal Newhouser, 1945
1.91	Ed Siever, 1902

Most pinch-hit homers, season

3	Gus Zernial, 1958
3	Norm Cash, 1960
3	Vic Wertz, 1962
3	Gates Brown, 1968
3	Ben Oglivie, 1976
3	John Grubb, 1984
3	Larry Herndon, 1986

Most pinch-hit, homers, career

16	Gates Brown, 1963-1975

Most consecutive games, batting safely

40	Ty Cobb, 1911
35	Ty Cobb, 1917
30	Goose Goslin-1934
30	Ron LeFlore, 1976

Most consecutive scoreless innings

N/A

No hit games

George Mullin, Det vs StL AL, 7-0; July 4, 1912 (2nd game).

Virgil Trucks, Det vs Was AL, 1-0; May 15, 1952.

Virgil Trucks, Det at NY AL, 1-0; August 25, 1952.

Jim Bunning, Det at Bos AL, 3-0; July 20, 1958 (1st game).

Jack Morris, Det at Chi AL, 4-0; April 7, 1984.

ACTIVE PLAYERS in caps.

Boston Red Sox

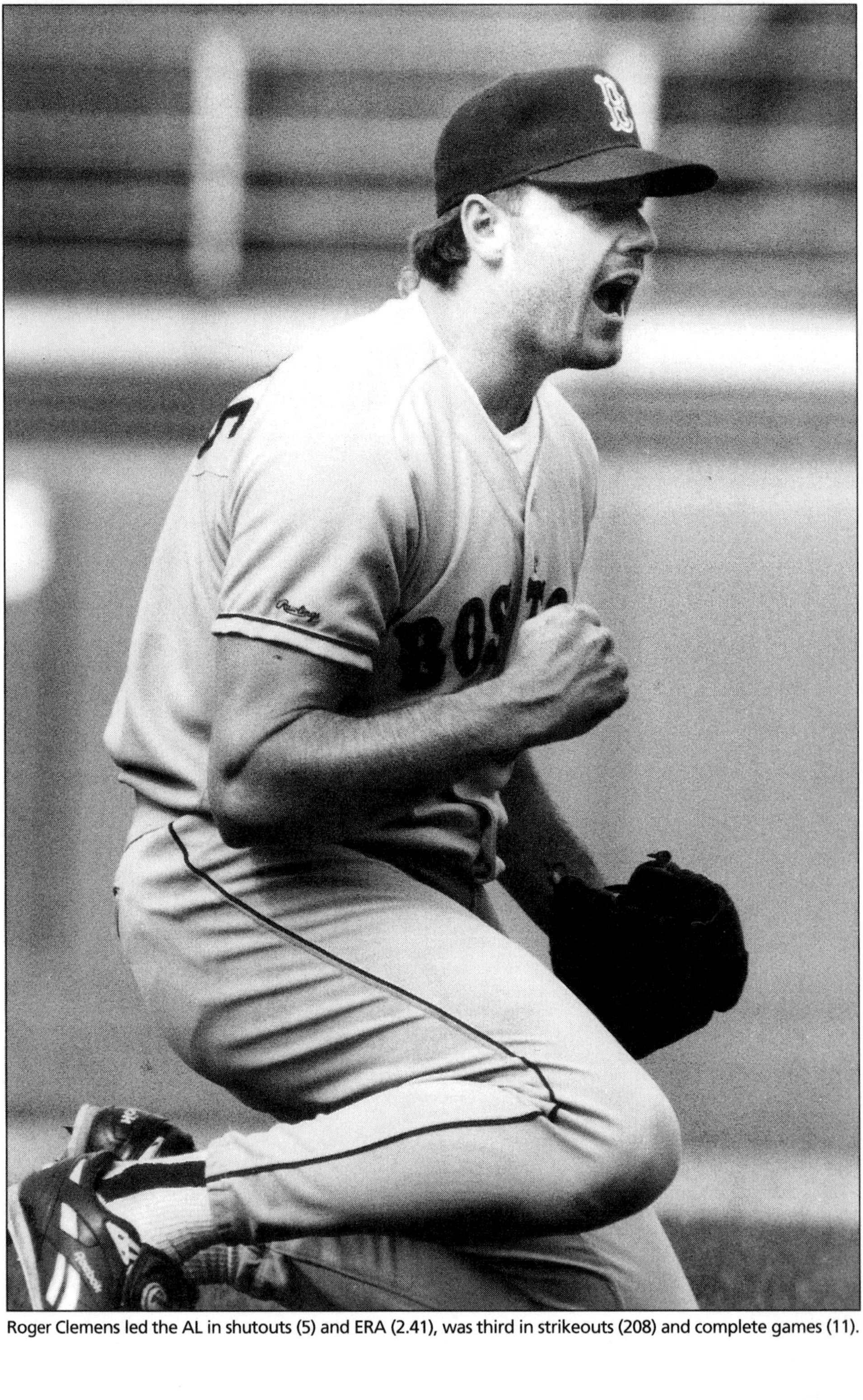

by Russell Beeker, *Baseball Weekly*

Roger Clemens led the AL in shutouts (5) and ERA (2.41), was third in strikeouts (208) and complete games (11).

1992 Red Sox: The gods stole their bats

Red Sox fans no longer held their breath waiting for the hammer to fall on pennant hopes. The gods delivered the blow in spring training—they bestowed pitching, but stole the bats. The only mystery was whether the team would stay at .500. It didn't, finishing 73-89, last in the AL East for the first time in 60 years.

Only Roger Clemens did his usual outstanding job. But even a lone ace can draw a full house at Fenway: The fans kept coming, 2.5 million of them. The owners took out full-page ads in Boston newspapers to thank the town and offer an implicit apology.

"The 1992 season has been as much a disappointment for the entire Red Sox organization as it has been for our many great fans," said the open letter. "We thank you for your wonderful support and we promise to redouble our efforts to put a winning team on the field in 1993."

The season began on a sad note: Owner Jean Yawkey died Feb. 26, ending the family's 60-year association with the team. With trademark binoculars and scorecard in hand, she had been a devout fan and steadfast occupant of her rooftop box.

Butch Hobson had trouble adjusting to big-league life his rookie year at the helm of a team that couldn't hit, field, or run straight: Boston's team batting average was .246, and errors totaled 139—both were second-worst in the league. While most teams succeeded in two out of three steal attempts, the Sox managed only a pathetic 44 stolen bases and were caught 48 times.

Yet pitching was sterling. Starting pitchers had a 3.65 ERA, best in the league. Clemens had the league-best ERA for the third consecutive year and won 18 games. Jeff Reardon became the all-time saves leader (342) June 15, but was traded in time to go to the World Series with the Braves.

Otherwise, the news was all bad. Veterans suffered from injuries and slumps. Carlos Quintana was badly injured in a car accident just before spring training; reliever Jeff Gray, suffered dizziness and weakness in his right side, the aftermath of a 1991 stroke. Neither rejoined the team. Mike Greenwell underwent elbow and knee surgery July 2, and Ellis Burks didn't play after June 24 (back problems). Big-bucks DH Jack Clark never found his bang, batting .210 with five homers and 33 RBI. Wade Boggs put on glasses, popped in contacts, and shaved his mustache to try to snap his slump. He had a 2-for-3 day, but it was just a flicker. He and Jody Reed combined to finish more than 100 points below their career averages.

The top hitter was Tom Brunansky, whose .266 average was the lowest by a Boston team leader in 31 years. His 15 homers led the club—the lowest figure to do so since 1974. His 74 RBI were the fewest by a club leader in 39 years.

Yet the owners remained patient—they extended Hobson's contract.

—by Margaret McCahill

1993 Red Sox: Preview

Boston spent $42 million on salaries, third-highest payroll in the American League, just to finish last. Reardon, Tom Brunansky and Wade Boggs are gone. Fear not, the money will be spent on Andre Dawson, Ivan Calderon, Scott Fletcher and Scott Bankhead. But the team's future lies with its kids. Vaughn showed Mo signs of life at the end of '92, as did Bob Zupcic, Scott Cooper, and John Valentin. Ken Ryan and Paul Quantrill could be a promising bullpen. If these youngsters get to play out from under the shadow of overpriced egos, they might develop into a team that acts as if its members are all on the same side.

—by Margaret McCahill

1992 Red Sox: Between the lines

▸**April 23:** Designated hitter Tom Brunansky found himself in the sixth spot, as the designated bunter. ***Quote of the day:*** Brunansky—"I've never bunted twice in a game. Not even in Little League."

▸**April 29:** Frank Viola and Jeff Reardon gave up just one run to the White Sox for a 6-1 victory.

▸**May 2:** Jack Clark was 3-for-4 with a double and three RBI.

▸**May 4:** Ellis Burks' home run—his first since Aug. 12, 1991—ended Boston's string of 99 homerless innings.

▸**May 9:** Clemens pitched his 31st career shutout, a three-hit 5-0 blanking of Kansas City. His ground ball-to-fly ball ratio was a nifty 16-3.

▸**May 10:** Jack Clark, who was batting under .200, hit a pair of homers, including a three-run shot in the third that fell a few feet short of becoming the first ball to actually leave Royals Stadium.

▸**May 16:** Frank Viola threw seven shutout innings to complete Boston's second straight shutout of California.

▸**May 17 *Milestone:*** Wade Boggs collected his 2,000th career hit.

▸**May 18:** Red Sox pitchers had gone 50 innings without allowing a home run before Seattle's Pete O'Brien took Jeff Reardon deep in the ninth inning.

▸**May 20:** Ellis Burks added the firepower in a 6-4 Boston win against Seattle, hitting a tie-breaking grand slam in the eighth inning. It was his sixth career grand slam.

▸**May 26:** Clemens continued his mastery against the Angels, beating them for the seventh straight time. He struck out eight, to increase his league-leading total in that department to 74, while lowering his league-best ERA to 1.65.

▸**June 6:** Clemens won his sixth straight decision. His nine wins led the league, and his 1.56 ERA was also the league's best.

▸**June 7:** Joe Hesketh and Danny Darwin combined for a shutout. It was the first time in nine games that Boston won without Clemens on the mound.

▸**June 11:** Clemens got rocked for four runs (including three homers) in 7 1/3 innings. ***Quote of the day:*** Opposing pitcher Jack Morris (Toronto)—"It just proves that (Clemens) is human after all. There's no denying he's one of the great pitchers in the game today—probably the best. But he's been beaten before and he'll be beaten again."

▸**June 13:** Milestone watch: Jeff Reardon struck out Candy Maldonado to notch career save number 341, tying Hall of Famer Rollie Fingers for the all-time save mark.

▸**June 14:** Wade Boggs (back problems) DH'd, with Ellis Burks (back problems) and Mike Greenwell (elbow injury) on the bench, as manager Butch Hobson wrote in his 47th different lineup in 58 games.

▸**June 15 *Milestone:*** Jeff Reardon became the all-time save leader, passing Rollie Fingers. ***Quote of the day:*** Hobson on the ramifications had he not brought Jeff Reardon in for his historic save—"They'd have hung me if I didn't bring him in there, it was set up just right. I couldn't have written it any better."

▸**June 28:** The Red Sox got blown out, 9-3, by the Brewers, but there was some good news: Since being recalled from Pawtucket to replace Greenwell, Mo Vaughn had maintained a five-game hitting streak.

▸**June 30 *Quote of the day:*** Detroit reliever Mike Henneman, after Bob Zupcic (who had hit only one home run in his entire pro career) hit a grand slam that gave the Red Sox an 8-5 win—"It doesn't take much analysis. He hit it; they beat me. Simple as that. This game can humble you in an instant. It took me only 12 minutes to get my butt kicked."

▸**July 1:** Wade Boggs shaved his trademark mustache after batting practice, and proceeded to snap an 0-for-18 skid with a 2-for-3 day, including a triple. He also drew a walk.

▸**July 2:** Clemens, averaging eight innings and seven strikeouts, gave up five earned runs to the White Sox in just five innings—with no strikeouts.

▸**July 10:** A new habit? Bob Zupcic hit another grand slam to rally the Red Sox from a five-run deficit in the eighth.

▸**July 18:** Clemens snapped his string of six straight no-decisions with a two-hit shutout of the Twins.

▸**July 25:** Danny Darwin lost his no-hitter, his shutout, then the game in the sixth inning when he loaded the bases full of Twins and reliever Paul Quantrill let them all score.

▸**July 27:** Tom Brunansky hit his sixth home run of the month, a first-inning grand slam. He had driven in as many runs in July (23) as in the rest of the season combined, bringing his season total to 46.

▸**August 13:** Clemens improved to 18-2 against Cleveland.

▸**August 18:** Clemens' complete-game 8-0 blanking of California was his 34th career shutout.

▸**August 22:** Boston came in with the lowest team batting average in the league and collected 14 hits, their season high, to beat Seattle 10-8.

▸**August 25:** Jeff Reardon converted his 27th save in 35 chances.

▸**August 26:** Frank Viola went the distance in the Red Sox's 2-1 10-inning win against Oakland.

▸**August 30:** Boston traded Reardon to the Atlanta Braves for pitcher Nate Minchey and outfielder Sean Ross.

▸**September 7:** Clemens faced his idol, Nolan Ryan, in great form. He had seven consecutive strikeouts and didn't allow a fair ball to be hit from the end of the fourth inning until the eighth. (He came within one of the AL consecutive strikeout record of eight, held by himself, Nolan Ryan and Ron Davis.)

▸**September 30:** Frank Viola took a no-hitter into the ninth inning before Toronto's Devon White spoiled it with a clean single to center field. Viola settled for a one-hit shutout (1-0); it was his first shutout since 1991 and the furthest he'd ever taken a no-hitter.

▸**October 4:** The Red Sox finished in the cellar. As usual, however, Roger Clemens was a major bright spot: He led the AL in ERA (2.41) and shutouts (5), was third in strikeouts (208) and complete games (11), and—despite the team's weak bats—won 18 games to finish fifth in the league in victories.

—by Jeanie Chung, John Hunt, Deron Snyder, and Lisa Winston.

Team directory

▸**Owner:** JRY Corporation and Haywood Sullivan

▸**General Manager:** Lou Gorman

▸**Ballpark:**
Fenway Park
4 Yawkey Way, Boston, Mass.
617-267-8661
Capacity 33,925
Public transportation available
Family, wheelchair, and vision-impaired sections, ramps, sound amplification and TDD ticket information for hearing impaired

▸**Team publications:**
Media Guide, Official Scorebook, Yearbook
617-267-9440

▸**TV, radio broadcast stations:**
WRKO 680 AM, WSBK Channel 38, New England Sports Network Cable TV

▸**Spring Training:**
City of Palms Park
Ft. Myers, Fla.
Capacity TBA
617-267-8661

BOSTON RED SOX 1992 final stats

Batting	AVG	SLG	OB	G	AB	R	H	TB	2B	3B	HR	RBI	BB	SO	SB	CS	E
Cooper	.276	.383	.346	123	337	34	93	129	21	0	5	33	37	33	1	1	9
Valentin	.276	.427	.351	58	185	21	51	79	13	0	5	25	20	17	1	0	10
Zupcic	.276	.352	.322	124	392	46	108	138	19	1	3	43	25	60	2	2	6
Brunansky	.266	.445	.354	138	458	47	122	204	31	3	15	74	66	96	2	5	6
Boggs	.259	.358	.353	143	514	62	133	184	22	4	7	50	74	31	1	3	15
Burks	.255	.417	.327	66	235	35	60	98	8	3	8	30	25	48	5	2	2
Lyons	.250	.321	.300	21	28	3	7	9	0	1	0	2	2	1	0	1	0
Wedge	.250	.500	.370	27	68	11	17	34	2	0	5	11	13	18	0	0	0
Reed	.247	.316	.321	143	550	64	136	174	27	1	3	40	62	44	7	8	14
Plantier	.246	.361	.332	108	349	46	86	126	19	0	7	30	44	83	2	3	4
Pena	.241	.305	.284	133	410	39	99	125	21	1	1	38	24	61	3	2	6
Hatcher	.238	.311	.283	75	315	37	75	98	16	2	1	23	17	41	4	6	5
Winningham	.235	.291	.266	105	234	27	55	68	8	1	1	14	10	53	6	5	3
Vaughn	.234	.400	.326	113	355	42	83	142	16	2	13	57	47	67	3	3	15
Greenwell	.233	.278	.307	49	180	16	42	50	2	0	2	18	18	19	2	3	0
Naehring	.231	.323	.308	72	186	12	43	60	8	0	3	14	18	31	0	0	3
Rivera	.215	.260	.287	102	288	17	62	75	11	1	0	29	26	56	4	3	14
Clark	.210	.311	.350	81	257	32	54	80	11	0	5	33	56	87	1	1	1
Flaherty	.197	.227	.229	35	66	3	13	15	2	0	0	2	3	7	0	0	2
Marzano	.080	.160	.132	19	50	4	4	8	2	1	0	1	2	12	0	0	3
Barrett	.000	.000	.400	4	3	1	0	0	0	0	0	0	2	0	0	0	0
Brumley	.000	.000	.000	2	1	0	0	0	0	0	0	0	0	0	0	0	0

Pitching	W-L	ERA	G	GS	CG	GF	Sho	SV	IP	H	R	ER	HR	BB	SO
Quantrill	2-3	2.19	27	0	0	10	0	1	49.1	55	18	12	1	15	24
Clemens	18-11	2.41	32	32	11	0	5	0	246.2	203	80	66	11	62	208
Fossas	1-2	2.43	60	0	0	17	0	2	29.2	31	9	8	1	14	19
Harris	4-9	2.51	70	2	1	22	0	4	107.2	82	38	30	6	60	73
Bolton	1-2	3.41	21	1	0	6	0	0	29	34	11	11	0	14	23
Viola	13-12	3.44	35	35	6	0	1	0	238	214	99	91	13	89	121
Darwin	9-9	3.96	51	15	2	21	0	3	161.1	159	76	71	11	53	124
Dopson	7-11	4.08	25	25	0	0	0	0	141.1	159	78	64	17	38	55
Reardon	2-2	4.25	46	0	0	39	0	27	42.1	53	20	20	6	7	32
Hesketh	8-9	4.36	30	25	1	1	0	1	148.2	162	84	72	15	58	104
Young	0-4	4.58	28	8	1	4	0	0	70.2	69	42	36	7	42	57
Gardiner	4-10	4.75	28	18	0	3	0	0	130.2	126	78	69	12	58	79
Taylor	1-1	4.91	4	1	0	1	0	0	14.2	13	8	8	4	4	7
Irvine	3-4	6.11	21	0	0	8	0	0	28	31	20	19	1	14	10
Ryan	0-0	6.43	7	0	0	6	0	1	7	4	5	5	2	5	5
Hoy	0-0	7.36	5	0	0	2	0	0	3.2	8	3	3	0	2	2

1993 preliminary roster

PITCHERS (18)
Scott Bankhead
Roger Clemens
Brian Conroy
Danny Darwin
John Dopson
Tony Fossas
Jeff Gray
Greg A. Harris
Joe Hesketh
Daryl Irvine
Derek Livernois
Jose Melendez
Nate Minchey
Paul Quantrill
Ken Ryan
Scott Taylor
Frank Viola
Matt Young

CATCHERS (3)
John Flaherty
John Marzano
Tony Pena

INFIELDERS (10)
James Byrd
Jack Clark
Scott Cooper
Scott Fletcher
Cheo Garcia
Tim Naehring
Carlos Quintana
Luis Rivera
John Valentin
Mo Vaughn

OUTFIELDERS (9)
Greg Blosser
Ellis Burks
Ivan Calderon
Andre Dawson
Mike Greenwell
Billy Hatcher
Jeff McNeely
Sean Ross
Bob Zupcic

Games played by position

Player	G	C	1B	2B	3B	SS	OF	DH
BARRETT,T	4	0	0	2	0	0	0	0
BOGGS,W	143	0	0	0	117	0	0	21
BRUMLEY,M	2	0	0	0	0	0	0	0
BRUNANSKY,T	138	0	28	0	0	0	92	17
BURKS,E	66	0	0	0	0	0	63	1
CLARK,JA	81	0	13	0	0	0	0	64
COOPER,S	123	0	62	1	47	1	0	2
FLAHERTY,J	35	34	0	0	0	0	0	0
GREENWELL,M	49	0	0	0	0	0	41	6
HATCHER,B	75	0	0	0	0	0	75	0
LYONS,S	21	0	8	1	0	0	5	2
MARZANO,J	19	18	0	0	0	0	0	1
NAEHRING,T	72	0	0	23	10	30	1	4
PENA,T	133	132	0	0	0	0	0	0
PLANTIER,P	108	0	0	0	0	0	76	23
REED,JO	143	0	0	142	0	0	0	1
RIVERA,L	102	0	0	1	1	93	1	2
VALENTIN,J	58	0	0	0	0	58	0	0
VAUGHN,M	113	0	85	0	0	0	0	20
WEDGE,E	27	5	0	0	0	0	0	20
WINNINGHAM,H	105	0	0	0	0	0	67	6
ZUPCIC,B	124	0	0	0	0	0	114	5

Sick call: 1992 DL report

Player	Days on the DL
Burks, Ellis	102
Dopson, John	41
Gray, Jeff	182
Greenwell, Mike*	120
Marzano, John	111
Naehring, Tim	40
Quintana, Carlos	182
Young, Matt	16

** On Disabled List twice during 1992 season (not counting transfers from one DL to another).*

Minor league report

Class AAA — Pawtucket finished 71-72, 2nd in the International League East Division. The team lost to Scranton/Wilkes-Barre in the 1st round of the playoffs. 1B Mike Twardoski led the club in batting at .290 with 13 HR and 49 RBI. RHP Larry Shikles was 13-8 with a 3.56 ERA. RHP Daryl Irvine had 18 saves. **Class AA:** New Britain finished 58-82, last in the Eastern League. OF Greg Blosser set a franchise record with 22 HR. RHP Ken Ryan set a franchise record with 22 saves. RHP Gar Finnvold K'd 135. **Class A:** Lynchburg finished 77-58, winning both halves of the Carolina League Northern Division. The team lost in five games to Peninsula for the league championship. IF John Malzone hit .306. RHP Joe Caruso won the league ERA title with a 1.98 mark in relief. He K'd 132 in 118 IP, allowing just 68 hits. RHP Cory Bailey won the save title with 23. Winter Haven finished 51-86, last in the Florida State League Central Division in both halves. 1B Les Wallin had 18 doubles, 11 HR and 55 RBI. LHP Joe Ciccarella had 12 saves. OF Derek Vinyard had 15 SB. RHP Joel Bennett had 154 K. Elmira finished 31-44, last in the New York-Penn League Pinckney Division. OF Jose Malave was the league's Rookie of the Year, hitting .325 with 12 HR and 46 RBI. RHP Gettys Glaze K'd 88. RHP Bret Donovan was 5-4 with a 2.21 ERA. He K'd 82 in 85 IP, allowing just 52 hits. Red Sox finished 18-41, last in the Gulf Coast League Central Division. The pitching staff issued a league-high 253 walks and allowed a league-high 544 hits.

Tops in the organization

BATTING LEADERS	Club	Avg.	G	AB	R	H	HR	RBI
John Malzone	Lyn	.306	117	386	49	118	4	52
Mike Twardoski	Paw	.290	121	389	55	113	13	49
Luis Ortiz	Lyn	.290	94	355	43	103	10	61
Paul Rappoli	Lyn	.267	111	344	47	92	6	42
Jason Friedman	Lyn	.267	135	495	68	132	14	68

HOME RUNS:			WINS		
Greg Blosser	Paw	22	Aaron Sele	Nbr	15
Boo Moore	Lyn	19	Derek Livernois	Paw	14
John Shelby	Paw	17	Larry Shikles	Paw	13
Jason Friedman	Lyn	14	Tim Vanegmond	Lyn	12
Mike Twardoski	Paw	13	Frank Rodriguez	Lyn	12

RBI			SAVES		
Greg Blosser	Paw	71	Ken Ryan	Paw	29
Jason Friedman	Lyn	68	Cory Bailey	Lyn	23
John Shelby	Paw	64	Daryl Irvine	Paw	18
Luis Ortiz	Lyn	61	Joe Caruso	Lyn	15
Jim Crowley	Lyn	59	Joe Ciccarella	Whv	12

STOLEN BASES			STRIKEOUTS		
Wayne Housie	Paw	20	Joel Bennett	Whv	154
Jim Morrison	Lyn	17	Aaron Sele	Nbr	141
Willie Tatum	Nbr	16	Tim Vanegmond	Lyn	140
Derek Vinyard	Whv	15	Gar Finnvold	Nbr	135
Mike Brumley	Paw	14	Joe Caruso	Lyn	132

PITCHING LEADERS	Club	W-L	ERA	IP	H	BB	SO
Joe Caruso	Lyn	6-4	1.98	118	68	40	132
Ed Riley	Nbr	10-8	2.55	127	115	39	67
Frank Rodriguez	Lyn	12-7	3.09	149	125	65	129
Bob Henkel	Whv	5-7	3.32	117	110	37	102
Tim Vanegmond	Lyn	12-4	3.42	174	161	52	140

Boston (1901-1992)

Runs: Most, career, all-time

1816 Carl Yastrzemski, 1961-1983
1798 Ted Williams, 1939-1960
1435 Dwight Evans, 1972-1990
1249 Jim Rice, 1974-1989
1094 Bobby Doerr, 1937-1951

Hits: Most, career, all-time

3419 Carl Yastrzemski, 1961-1983
2654 Ted Williams, 1939-1960
2452 Jim Rice, 1974-1989
2373 Dwight Evans, 1972-1990
2098 WADE BOGGS, 1982-1992

2B: Most, career, all-time

646 Carl Yastrzemski, 1961-1983
525 Ted Williams, 1939-1960
474 Dwight Evans, 1972-1990
422 WADE BOGGS, 1982-1992
381 Bobby Doerr, 1937-1951

3B: Most, career, all-time

130 Harry Hooper, 1909-1920
106 Tris Speaker, 1907-1915
90 Buck Freeman, 1901-1907
89 Bobby Doerr, 1937-1951
87 Larry Gardner, 1908-1917

HR: Most, career, all-time

521 Ted Williams, 1939-1960
452 Carl Yastrzemski, 1961-1983
382 Jim Rice, 1974-1989
379 Dwight Evans, 1972-1990
223 Bobby Doerr, 1937-1951

RBI: Most, career, all-time

1844 Carl Yastrzemski, 1961-1983
1839 Ted Williams, 1939-1960
1451 Jim Rice, 1974-1989
1346 Dwight Evans, 1972-1990
1247 Bobby Doerr, 1937-1951

SB: Most, career, all-time

300 Harry Hooper, 1909-1920
267 Tris Speaker, 1907-1915
168 Carl Yastrzemski, 1961-1983
141 Heinie Wagner, 1906-1918
134 Larry Gardner, 1908-1917

BB: Most, career, all-time

2019 Ted Williams, 1939-1960
1845 Carl Yastrzemski, 1961-1983
1337 Dwight Evans, 1972-1990
1004 WADE BOGGS, 1982-1992
826 Harry Hooper, 1909-1920

BA: Highest, career, all-time

.344 Ted Williams, 1939-1960
.338 WADE BOGGS, 1982-1992
.337 Tris Speaker, 1907-1915
.320 Pete Runnels, 1958-1962
.320 Jimmie Foxx, 1936-1942

Slug avg: Highest, career, all-time

.634 Ted Williams, 1939-1960
.605 Jimmie Foxx, 1936-1942
.520 Fred Lynn, 1974-1980
.502 Jim Rice, 1974-1989
.492 Vern Stephens, 1948-1952

Games started: Most, career, all-time

297 Cy Young, 1901-1908
272 ROGER CLEMENS, 1984-1992
238 Luis Tiant, 1971-1978
232 Mel Parnell, 1947-1956
228 Bill Monbouquette, 1958-1965

Saves: Most, career, all-time

132 Bob Stanley, 1977-1989
104 Dick Radatz, 1962-1966
91 Ellis Kinder, 1948-1955
88 JEFF REARDON, 1990-1992
69 Sparky Lyle, 1967-1971

Shutouts: Most, career, all-time

38 Cy Young, 1901-1908
34 ROGER CLEMENS, 1984-1992
28 Joe Wood, 1908-1915
26 Luis Tiant, 1971-1978
25 Dutch Leonard, 1913-1918

Wins: Most, career, all-time

192 Cy Young, 1901-1908
152 ROGER CLEMENS, 1984-1992
123 Mel Parnell, 1947-1956
122 Luis Tiant, 1971-1978
116 Joe Wood, 1908-1915

K: Most, career, all-time

1873 ROGER CLEMENS, 1984-1992
1341 Cy Young, 1901-1908
1075 Luis Tiant, 1971-1978
1043 BRUCE HURST, 1980-1988
986 Joe Wood, 1908-1915

Win pct: Highest, career, all-time

.695 Roger Moret, 1970-1975
.684 Dave Ferriss, 1945-1950
.679 ROGER CLEMENS, 1984-1992
.674 Joe Wood, 1908-1915
.659 Babe Ruth, 1914-1919

ERA: Lowest, career, all-time

1.99 Joe Wood, 1908-1915
2.00 Cy Young, 1901-1908
2.12 Ernie Shore, 1914-1917
2.13 Dutch Leonard, 1913-1918
2.19 Babe Ruth, 1914-1919

Runs: Most, season

150 Ted Williams, 1949
142 Ted Williams, 1946
141 Ted Williams, 1942
139 Jimmie Foxx, 1938
136 Tris Speaker, 1912

Hits: Most, season

240 WADE BOGGS, 1985
222 Tris Speaker, 1912
214 WADE BOGGS, 1988
213 Jim Rice, 1978
210 WADE BOGGS, 1983

2B: Most, season

67 Earl Webb, 1931
53 Tris Speaker, 1912
51 WADE BOGGS, 1989
51 Joe Cronin, 1938
47 WADE BOGGS, 1986
47 George Burns, 1923
47 Fred Lynn, 1975

3B: Most, season

22 Tris Speaker, 1913
20 Buck Freeman, 1903
19 Buck Freeman, 1902
19 Buck Freeman, 1904
19 Larry Gardner, 1914
19 Chick Stahl, 1904

HR: Most, season

50 Jimmie Foxx, 1938
46 Jim Rice, 1978
44 Carl Yastrzemski, 1967
43 Tony Armas, 1984
43 Ted Williams, 1949

RBI: Most, season

175 Jimmie Foxx, 1938
159 Vern Stephens, 1949
159 Ted Williams, 1949
145 Ted Williams, 1939
144 Walt Dropo, 1950
144 Vern Stephens, 1950

SB: Most, season

54	Tommy Harper, 1973
52	Tris Speaker, 1912
46	Tris Speaker, 1913
42	Tris Speaker, 1914
40	Harry Hooper, 1910
40	Billy Werber, 1934

BB: Most, season

162	Ted Williams, 1947
162	Ted Williams, 1949
156	Ted Williams, 1946
145	Ted Williams, 1941
145	Ted Williams, 1942

BA: Highest, season

.406	Ted Williams, 1941
.388	Ted Williams, 1957
.383	Tris Speaker, 1912
.369	Ted Williams, 1948
.368	WADE BOGGS, 1985

Slug avg: Highest, season

.735	Ted Williams, 1941
.731	Ted Williams, 1957
.704	Jimmie Foxx, 1938
.694	Jimmie Foxx, 1939
.667	Ted Williams, 1946

Games started: Most, season

43	Cy Young, 1902
42	Bill Dinneen, 1902
41	Babe Ruth, 1916
41	Cy Young, 1901
41	Cy Young, 1904

Saves: Most, season

40	JEFF REARDON, 1991
33	Bob Stanley, 1983
31	Bill Campbell, 1977
29	Dick Radatz, 1964
29	LEE SMITH, 1988

Shutouts: Most, season

10	Joe Wood, 1912
10	Cy Young, 1904
9	Babe Ruth, 1916
8	ROGER CLEMENS, 1988
8	Carl Mays, 1918

Wins: Most, season

34	Joe Wood, 1912
33	Cy Young, 1901
32	Cy Young, 1902
28	Cy Young, 1903
26	Cy Young, 1904

K: Most, season

291	ROGER CLEMENS, 1988
258	Joe Wood, 1912
256	ROGER CLEMENS, 1987
246	Jim Lonborg, 1967
241	ROGER CLEMENS, 1991

Win pct: Highest, season

.872	Joe Wood, 1912
.857	ROGER CLEMENS, 1986
.806	Dave Ferriss, 1946
.793	Ellis Kinder, 1949
.792	Dutch Leonard, 1914

ERA: Lowest, season

0.96	Dutch Leonard, 1914
1.26	Cy Young, 1908
1.49	Joe Wood, 1915
1.62	Ray Collins, 1910
1.62	Cy Young, 1901

Most pinch-hit homers, season

5	Joe Cronin, 1943
4	Del Wilber, 1953

Most pinch-hit, homers, career

7	Ted Williams, 1939-1960

Most consecutive games, batting safely

34	Dom DiMaggio, 1949
30	Tris Speaker, 1912

Most consecutive scoreless innings

45	Cy Young, 1904
42	Rube Foster, 1914
40	Luis Tiant, 1972
39	Ray Culp, 1968
37	Cy Young, 1903

No hit games

Cy Young, Bos vs Phi AL, 3-0; May 5, 1904 (perfect game).

Jesse Tannehill, Bos at Chi AL, 6-0; August 17, 1904.

Bill Dinneen, Bos vs Chi AL, 2-0; September 27, 1905 (1st game).

Cy Young, Bos at NY AL, 8-0; June 30, 1908.

Joe Wood, Bos vs StL AL, 5-0; July 29, 1911 (1st game).

Rube Foster, Bos vs NY AL, 2-0; June 21, 1916.

Hubert (Dutch) Leonard, Bos vs StL AL, 4-0; August 30, 1916.

Ernie Shore, Bos vs Was AL, 4-0; June 23, 1917 (1st game, perfect game). (Shore relieved Babe Ruth in the first inning after Ruth had been thrown out of the game for protesting a walk to the first batter. The runner was caught stealing and Shore retired the remaining 26 batters in order)

Hubert (Dutch) Leonard, Bos at Det AL, 5-0; June 3, 1918.

Howard Ehmke, Bos at Phi AL, 4-0; September 7, 1923.

Mel Parnell, Bos vs Chi AL, 4-0; July 14, 1956.

Earl Wilson, Bos vs LA AL, 2-0; June 26, 1962.

Bill Monbouquette, Bos at Chi AL, 1-0; August 1, 1962.

Dave Morehead, Bos vs Cle AL, 2-0; September 16, 1965.

Matt Young, Bos at Cle AL, 1-2; April 12, 1992 (1st game) (8 innings, lost the game, bottom of 9th not played).

ACTIVE PLAYERS in caps.

Oakland Athletics

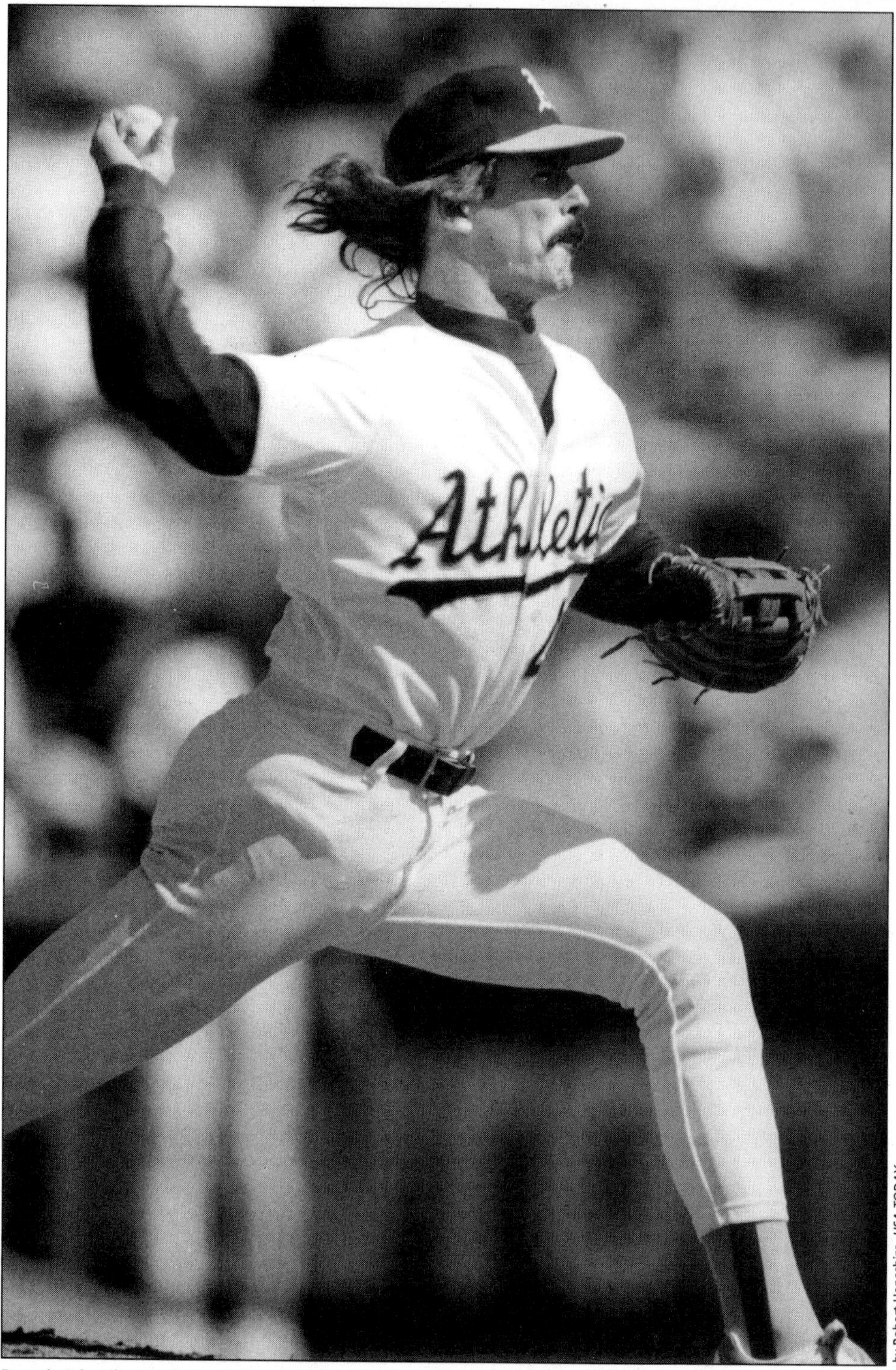

by Robert Hanashiro, *USA TODAY*

Dennis Eckersley won the Cy Young award and was the AL MVP in his fourth 40-plus-saves season.

1992 Athletics: They never gave up

The fact that the Oakland A's were even competitive—let alone divisional champions—was a tribute to American League Manager of the Year Tony La Russa and a ballclub that rallied itself for one last hurrah. With 15 free agents, the A's realized it was now or never.

In reclaiming the AL West, its fourth divisional title in five seasons, Oakland won with less swagger and a lot more heart than in years past. Despite 22 trips to the disabled list and a flurry of changing faces, the A's never quit.

"This team played the game right," said pitcher Dave Stewart, one of many free agents who won't be back in an A's uniform in '93.

"I'm so proud of this team," said third baseman Carney Lansford, who retired after the A's were eliminated in six games by the Toronto Blue Jays in the playoffs. "We again made Oakland a team to be reckoned with."

Dave Henderson missed much of the season, with injuries that nagged him so badly they could end his career. On paper, the A's had Henderson, Rickey Henderson, and Jose Canseco in the outfield, but due to both Hendersons' injuries and Canseco's eventual trade, they were never intact in '92.

Dave Stewart and Bob Welch missed considerable time. Welch made three trips to the DL.

The A's battled on.

Career minor leaguer Eric Fox, who once supplemented his salary as a substitute teacher, hit a pivotal ninth-inning homer off Twins' closer Rick Aguilera (July 29) that gave the A's a share of first-place they never relinquished. Reliever Jeff Parrett, who had pitched for three different teams since 1988, became a stalwart in the A's bullpen. Jerry Browne, a Cleveland castoff, filled in just about everywhere, as did Lance Blankenship. Mike Bordick took over at second base, then proved himself at shortstop, as he surprised the baseball world by leading the AL in hitting during the first half. He finished the season at an even .300.

Mark McGwire wasn't expected to do much, coming off his worst season at the plate: .201, 22 home runs and 75 RBI in '91. But he hit 42 homers, second in the majors, and had 104 RBI, despite missing nearly three weeks. For much of the season, he was in a strange duel with teammate Dennis Eckersley. The two mirrored each other—McGwire in home runs and Eckersley in saves.

Eckersley admitted he was "living in the trees," and he put up enough sky-high numbers to win both the Cy Young and MVP awards.

The A's changed their team irrevocably at the end of August by trading Canseco to Texas for outfielder Ruben Sierra and pitchers Bobby Witt and Jeff Russell. Right after the trade, their lead fell from 7 1/2 games to 4 1/2, but they rallied and won the AL West by six games.

"This was Tony's team," said free agent catcher Terry Steinbach. "We knew whatever lineup he posted gave us the best possible chance to win."

—by Tim Wendel

1993 Athletics: Preview

In 1993, the Oakland A's will be the best team a limited amount of money can buy, now that the superstars are dwindling. The A's will build on what they have. Mike Bordick will take over at shortstop, with Lance Blankenship at second base: The double-play combo cost just under $350,000 in salary in '92. Rickey Henderson and Ruben Sierra anchor the outfield, while Bob Welch and possibly Joe Slusarski hold the mound. Dennis Eckersley remains the closer, but there's no doubt the dynasty that never quite was is finally in transition. The A's best untapped talent is deep in the minors. But three pitching prospects—Todd Van Poppel, David Zancanaro, and Kirk Dressendorfer—were injured for some part of '92.

—by Tom Sakell

1992 Athletics: Between the lines

▸**April 29** ***Quote of the day:*** Jose Canseco, on a Coliseum fan who was ejected after harassing him—"It was too much profanity. The guy was pretty bad, so he had to watch the game from the outside."

▸**April 30:** The A's were in first place, the fourth time in five years Oakland finished April atop the West.

May 1 ***Milestone:*** Rickey Henderson stole his 1,000th career base.

▸**May 9** ***Quote of the day:*** Ron Darling, on Dennis Eckersley being unavailable for the game—"This is no slap against the rest of the guys in the bullpen, but it's a pitcher's nightmare to be sitting there with a 2-0 lead and (Eckersley) in sneakers, sitting next to me, eating sunflower seeds."

▸**May 10:** Mike Bordick got his first major league homer, Mark McGwire added his major-league leading 15th of the season, and Jose Canseco ended the longest homerless drought of his career (71 at-bats).

▸**May 18** ***Milestone:*** Harold Baines got his 1,000th career RBI.

▸**May 19** ***Quote of the day:*** Jose Canseco, on his seventh-inning homer that almost hooked foul—"If that ball had gone foul, I would have shot myself right at home plate."

▸**May 22:** Dave Stewart notched his 12th straight win against Boston.

▸**May 23** ***Milestone:*** Rickey Henderson set an AL record for games played as the leadoff batter, passing Eddie Yost of the Senators (1,729) for third place on the all-time list.

▸**May 24:** Making his first appearance at Fenway Park since the 1986 World Series, Ron Darling tossed a two-hitter—his first shutout in more than three seasons.

▸**June 6** ***Milestone:*** Eckersley got his 21st save of the season—25th in a row without blowing one—to tie Tom Henke for the major league record.

▸**June 10** ***Milestone:*** McGwire hit his 200th career home run (22nd in 1992, best in the majors).

▸**June 13** ***Milestone:*** Carney Lansford got his 2,000th career hit.

▸**June 22:** Ron Darling took a no-hitter into the seventh. Eckersley got his 28th consecutive save.

▸**June 23:** The A's beat Seattle to maintain a two-game lead in the AL West.

▸**June 25:** The AL West's top two teams began a four-game series, and the A's eased to a 5-1 victory over the Twins. Eckersley recorded his 29th consecutive save.

▸**June 29** ***Milestone:*** Eckersley set a major league record with his 26th straight save of the season.

▸**July 1:** McGwire hit homer No. 27.

▸**July 12:** Ron Darling took a no-hitter into the eighth inning.

▸**July 25:** Darling again flirted with a no-hitter, and again had it ruined. He did get a complete-game shutout.

▸**July 27:** Mike Moore (9.49 career ERA in the Metrodome) finally beat the Twins, 9-1. He took a no-hitter into the seventh inning and brought the A's within two games of the Twins. ***Quote of the day:*** Catcher Terry Steinbach, on the A's chances of overtaking their division-rival Twins—"Let's not jump the gun. We don't have anything mastered here. We still have two games in this series. We just got some breaks this time."

▸**July 29:** Rookie Eric Fox blasted a three-run homer off Rick Aguilera in the top of the ninth to rally Oakland to a 5-4 win against the Twins, capping a three-game sweep and moving the A's into a first-place tie with Minnesota. ***Quote of the day:*** La Russa—"I expected Eric to come up and play hard. I didn't expect him to come up and hit a game-winning homer off one of the best relievers in baseball. He was hovering above the bench. It's a good thing we were indoors or a gust of wind might have carried him away."

▸**August 5:** Eckersley's 35th save of the season gave Oakland a 4-3 win over Texas—and sole possession of first place in the AL West. ***Milestone:*** Jose Canseco tied a major league record with his seventh consecutive walk. He asked pitcher Bobby Witt for the ball, then finished off his next at-bat by swinging at a possibly historic ball four in the dirt.

▸**August 8:** Eckersley's all-time-best consecutive-save record ended at 40 (36 in 1992) when he blew one in what turned out to be a 5-3 Oakland victory anyway. The A's were 46-0 in games in which Eckersley pitched.

▸**August 13:** Mike Moore pitched his second complete game of the season, retiring the final 16 batters in order.

▸**August 20:** Jose Canseco hit a grand slam and Carney Lansford a three-run homer.

▸**August 23 *Milestone:*** Eckersley became the first pitcher to record 40 saves in four different seasons.

▸**August 31:** Jose Canseco started for Oakland against Baltimore, then learned he was traded to Texas (for pitchers Jeff Russell and Bobby Witt, outfielder Ruben Sierra, and cash) before his first at-bat. Perhaps distracted by the trade, the A's managed to get only four hits and lost to the Orioles 4-0, shrinking their lead in the AL West to 6 1/2 games.

▸**September 5:** Since trading away Canseco, the A's were 0-5 (hitting .176) and had scored just seven runs.

▸**September 10:** Ruben Sierra hit his first home run for Oakland. He was 7-for-19 (.369) with the A's.

▸**September 14:** The A's beat the Twins, moving seven games in front with 18 left to play.

▸**September 21:** McGwire hit his 40th home run of 1992, tying him with Texas Ranger Juan Gonzalez for the major league lead. ***Milestone:*** Eckersley became the second pitcher in major league history to rack up 50 saves in a single season.

▸**September 28:** The A's took a day off—and clinched the AL West title when Minnesota lost to Chicago, 9-4.

▸**October 1:** Dave Stewart looked good in his final warmup for the playoffs, but Eckersley gave up a single that scored the winning run for Texas.

▸**October 2:** Eckersley had trouble on the mound again, blowing a save.

▸**October 4 *Milestone:*** Rickey Henderson got his 2,000th career hit.

—by Jeanie Chung, John Hunt, Deron Snyder, and Lisa Winston.

Team directory

▸**Owner:** Walter A. Haas, Jr.

▸**General Manager:** Sandy Alderson

▸**Ballpark:**
Oakland Coliseum
Nimitz Freeway & Hegenberger Road, Oakland, Calif.
510-568-5600
Capacity 48,745
Public transportation available
Wheelchair sections and ramps, picnic areas

▸**Team publications:**
A's Magazine
510-638-4900, ext. 326

▸**TV, radio broadcast stations:**
KSFO 560 AM, KRON Channel 4, SportsChannel

▸**Spring Training:**
Phoenix Municipal Stadium
Phoenix, Ariz.
Capacity 8,500
602-392-0074

OAKLAND ATHLETICS 1992 final stats

Batting	AVG	SLG	OB	G	AB	R	H	TB	2B	3B	HR	RBI	BB	SO	SB	CS	E
Mercedes	.800	1.200	.800	9	5	1	4	6	0	1	0	1	0	1	0	0	1
Bordick	.300	.371	.358	154	504	62	151	187	19	4	3	48	40	59	12	6	16
Browne	.287	.364	.366	111	324	43	93	118	12	2	3	40	40	40	3	3	5
R.Henderson	.283	.457	.426	117	396	77	112	181	18	3	15	46	95	56	48	11	4
Steinbach	.279	.411	.345	128	438	48	122	180	20	1	12	53	45	58	2	3	10
Sierra	.278	.443	.323	151	601	83	167	266	34	7	17	87	45	68	14	4	7
Wilson	.270	.333	.329	132	396	38	107	132	15	5	0	37	35	65	28	8	7
McGwire	.268	.585	.385	139	467	87	125	273	22	0	42	104	90	105	0	1	6
Neel	.264	.491	.339	24	53	8	14	26	3	0	3	9	5	15	0	1	3
Lansford	.262	.369	.325	135	496	65	130	183	30	1	7	75	43	39	7	2	11
Baines	.253	.391	.331	140	478	58	121	187	18	0	16	76	59	61	1	3	1
Blankenship	.241	.341	.393	123	349	59	84	119	24	1	3	34	82	57	21	7	6
Fox	.238	.364	.299	51	143	24	34	52	5	2	3	13	13	29	3	4	1
Quirk	.220	.305	.294	78	177	13	39	54	7	1	2	11	16	28	0	0	8
Brosius	.218	.379	.258	38	87	13	19	33	2	0	4	13	3	13	3	0	1
Weiss	.212	.241	.305	103	316	36	67	76	5	2	0	21	43	39	6	3	19
Ready	.200	.288	.329	61	125	17	25	36	2	0	3	17	25	23	1	0	5
D.Henderson	.143	.159	.169	20	63	1	9	10	1	0	0	2	2	16	0	0	1
Kingery	.107	.107	.138	12	28	3	3	3	0	0	0	1	1	3	0	0	0

Pitching	W-L	ERA	G	GS	CG	GF	Sho	SV	IP	H	R	ER	HR	BB	SO
Revenig	0-0	0.00	2	0	0	2	0	0	2	2	0	0	0	0	1
Corsi	4-2	1.43	32	0	0	16	0	0	44	44	12	7	2	18	19
Russell	4-3	1.63	59	0	0	46	0	30	66.1	55	14	12	3	25	48
Eckersley	7-1	1.91	69	0	0	65	0	51	80	62	17	17	5	11	93
Horsman	2-1	2.49	58	0	0	9	0	1	43.1	39	13	12	3	21	18
Gossage	0-2	2.84	30	0	0	13	0	0	38	32	13	12	5	19	26
Parrett	9-1	3.02	66	0	0	14	0	0	98.1	81	35	33	7	42	78
Welch	11-7	3.27	20	20	0	0	0	0	123.2	114	47	45	13	43	47
Downs	5-5	3.29	18	13	0	2	0	0	82	72	36	30	4	46	38
Stewart	12-10	3.66	31	31	2	0	0	0	199.1	175	96	81	25	79	130
Darling	15-10	3.66	33	33	4	0	3	0	206.1	198	98	84	15	72	99
Honeycutt	1-4	3.69	54	0	0	7	0	3	39	41	19	16	2	10	32
Moore	17-12	4.12	36	36	2	0	0	0	223	229	113	102	20	103	117
Witt	10-14	4.29	31	31	0	0	0	0	193	183	99	92	16	114	125
Campbell	2-3	5.12	32	5	0	6	0	1	65	66	39	37	4	45	38
Hillegas	1-8	5.23	26	9	1	6	1	0	86	104	57	50	13	37	49
Slusarski	5-5	5.45	15	14	0	1	0	0	76	85	52	46	15	27	38
Briscoe	0-1	6.43	2	2	0	0	0	0	7	12	6	5	0	9	4
Nelson	3-1	6.45	28	2	0	8	0	0	51.2	68	37	37	5	22	23
Raczka	0-0	8.53	8	0	0	1	0	0	6.1	8	7	6	0	5	2
Walton	0-0	9.90	7	0	0	2	0	0	10	17	11	11	1	3	7
Guzman	0-0	12.00	2	0	0	2	0	0	3	8	4	4	0	0	0

1993 preliminary roster

PITCHERS (24)
Scott Baker
Kevin Campbell
Storm Davis
Kirk Dressendorfer
Dennis Eckersley
Scott Erwin
Johnny Guzman
Shawn Hillegas
Vince Horsman
Rick Honeycutt
Joe Klink
Mike Mohler
Kirt Ojala
Gavin Osteen
Jeff Parrett
Mike Raczka
Todd Revenig
Curtis Shaw
Joe Slusarski
Tanyon Sturtze
Todd Van Poppel
Bob Welch
Bobby Witt
David Zancanaro

CATCHERS (3)
Eric Helfand
Henry Mercedes
Islay Molina

INFIELDERS (5)
Lance Blankenship
Mike Bordick
Scott Brosius
Jerry Browne
Craig Paquette

OUTFIELDERS (6)
Marcos Armas
Eric Fox
Dave Henderson
Rickey Henderson
Scott Lydy
Troy Neel

Games played by position

Player	G	C	1B	2B	3B	SS	OF	DH
BAINES,H	140	0	0	0	0	0	23	116
BLANKENSHIP,L	123	0	7	78	0	0	51	3
BORDICK,M	154	0	0	95	0	70	0	0
BROSIUS,S	38	0	3	0	12	1	20	1
BROWNE,J	111	0	0	19	58	1	43	1
FOX,E	51	0	0	0	0	0	43	4
HENDERSON,D	20	0	0	0	0	0	12	4
HENDERSON,R	117	0	0	0	0	0	108	6
KINGERY,M	12	0	0	0	0	0	10	0
LANSFORD,C	135	0	18	0	119	1	0	2
MCGWIRE,M	139	0	139	0	0	0	0	0
MERCEDES,H	9	9	0	0	0	0	0	0
NEEL,T	24	0	2	0	0	0	9	9
QUIRK,J	78	59	9	0	2	0	0	1
READY,R	61	0	4	4	7	0	24	24
SIERRA,R	151	0	0	0	0	0	144	6
STEINBACH,T	128	124	5	0	0	0	0	2
WEISS,W	103	0	0	0	0	103	0	0
WILSON,W	132	0	0	0	0	0	120	5

Sick call: 1992 DL report

Player	Days on the DL
Blankenship, Lance	33
Brosius, Scott	21
Canseco, Jose	15
Dressendorfer, Kirk	182
Gossage, Rich	78
Hemond, Scott	88
Henderson, Dave*	142
Henderson, Rickey*	36
Klink, Joe	182
McGwire, Mark	20
Ready, Randy*	39
Steinbach, Terry	15
Stewart, Dave	24
Weiss, Walt	58
Welch, Bob**	78
Wilson, Willie	15

** On Disabled List twice during 1992 season (not counting transfers from one DL to another).*

*** On Disabled List three times during 1992 season.*

Minor league report

Class AAA — Tacoma finished 56-87, last in both halves of the Pacific Coast League Northern Division. OF Troy Neel won the batting title at .351 with 17 HR and 74 RBI. OF James Buccheri, who bounced between Tacoma and Reno, finished with a .320 average and 47 SB. RHP Jeff Bittiger was 13-8 with a 2.97 ERA. **Class AA:** Huntsville finished 81-63, 2nd in the 1st half of the Southern League Western Division and 3rd in the 2nd half. OF Scott Lydy hit .305 with 9 HR and 65 RBI. RHP Bronswell Patrick shared the league lead in wins with 13. RHP Todd Revenig had 33 saves. **Class A:** Modesto finished 79-57, tied for 2nd in the 1st half of the California League Northern Division and 3rd in the 2nd half. 2B Brent Gates hit .321 with 10 HR and 88 RBI and had a 35-game hitting streak during the season, best in pro ball this year. LHP Curtis Shaw was 13-4 with a 3.05 ERA and led the league with 154 K. RHP Craig Sudbury had 17 saves. Reno finished 65-71, tied for 2nd in the 1st half of the California League Northern Division and 4th in the 2nd half. OF Mike Neill was named league Rookie of the Year hitting .336 with 76 RBI. SS Fausto Cruz hit .319 with 9 HR and 90 RBI. 3B Fabio Gomez had 19 HR and 115 RBI. Madison finished 59-75, 5th in the 1st half of the Midwest League Northern Division and last in the 2nd half. C George Williams hit .304. RHP Miguel Jimenez, who was promoted in the final weeks to Huntsville, was 8-7 with a 2.87 ERA and 143 K in 125 IP. He allowed just 81 hits. Southern Oregon finished 39-37, 3rd in the Northwest League South Division. RHP Gary Haught won the league ERA title at 1.98, going 8-2 with 69 K in 68 IP. 3B Terance Frazier had 24 SB. A's finished 34-22, 1st in the Arizona League. 3B John Jones hit .318. OF Pablo Lantigua hit .307. IF Felix Salvador hit .304. 1B Charles Cox had 35 RBI. RHP Williams Urbina was 7-1 with a 2.28 ERA and shared the league lead in wins. RHP Stacy Hollins led the league with 93 K.

Tops in the organization

BATTING LEADERS	Club	Avg.	G	AB	R	H	HR	RBI
Troy Neel	Tac	.351	112	396	61	139	17	74
Mike Neill	Hvl	.335	135	489	105	164	5	78
Scott Lydy	Hvl	.327	142	511	93	167	11	92
Brent Gates	Mod	.321	133	505	94	162	10	88
Fausto Cruz	Rno	.319	127	489	86	156	9	90

HOME RUNS		
Craig Paquette	Tac	19
Fabio Gomez	Rno	19
Damon Mashore	Mod	18
Troy Neel	Tac	17
Marcos Armas	Hvl	17

WINS		
Doug Johns	Hvl	13
Curtis Shaw	Mod	13
Jeff Bittiger	Tac	13
Bronswell Patrick	Hvl	13
Tim Smith	Tac	12

RBI		
Fabio Gomez	Rno	115
Scott Lydy	Hvl	92
Fausto Cruz	Rno	90
Brent Gates	Mod	88
Chris Hart	Mod	86

SAVES		
Todd Revenig	Hvl	33
Craig Sudbury	Mod	17
Jim Corsi	Tac	12
Lee Cusey	Mad	12
Todd Ingram	Rno	9

STOLEN BASES		
James Buccheri	Tac	48
Dane Walker	Rno	31
Damon Mashore	Mod	29
Scott Lydy	Hvl	25
Mike Neill	Hvl	24

STRIKEOUTS		
Curtis Shaw	Mod	154
Miguel Jiminez	Hvl	143
Tim Smith	Tac	138
Mike Rossiter	Mad	135
Tanyon Sturtze	Mod	126

PITCHING LEADERS	Club	W-L	ERA	IP	H	BB	SO
Steve Phoenix	Hvl	11-5	2.79	174	179	36	124
Miguel Jiminez	Hvl	8-7	2.87	125	81	81	143
Jeff Bittiger	Tac	13-8	2.97	148	140	72	118
Curtis Shaw	Mod	13-4	3.05	177	146	98	154
Doug Johns	Hvl	13-10	3.32	195	215	69	105

Oakland Athletics (1968-1992), incl. Philadelphia (1901-1952) and Kansas City (1953-1967)

Runs: Most, career, all-time

997 Bob Johnson, 1933-1942
983 Bert Campaneris, 1964-1976
975 Jimmie Foxx, 1925-1935
969 Al Simmons, 1924-1944
959 RICKEY HENDERSON, 1979-1992

Hits: Most, career, all-time

1882 Bert Campaneris, 1964-1976
1827 Al Simmons, 1924-1944
1705 Jimmy Dykes, 1918-1932
1617 Bob Johnson, 1933-1942
1500 Harry Davis, 1901-1917

2B: Most, career, all-time

365 Jimmy Dykes, 1918-1932
348 Al Simmons, 1924-1944
321 Harry Davis, 1901-1917
307 Bob Johnson, 1933-1942
292 Bing Miller, 1922-1934
270 Bert Campaneris, 1964-1976 (8)

3B: Most, career, all-time

102 Danny Murphy, 1902-1913
98 Al Simmons, 1924-1944
88 Frank Baker, 1908-1914
84 Eddie Collins, 1906-1930
82 Harry Davis, 1901-1917
70 Bert Campaneris, 1964-1976 (12)

HR: Most, career, all-time

302 Jimmie Foxx, 1925-1935
269 Reggie Jackson, 1967-1987
252 Bob Johnson, 1933-1942
231 JOSE CANSECO, 1985-1992
220 MARK McGWIRE, 1986-1992

RBI: Most, career, all-time

1178 Al Simmons, 1924-1944
1075 Jimmie Foxx, 1925-1935
1040 Bob Johnson, 1933-1942
796 Sal Bando, 1966-1976
776 Reggie Jackson, 1967-1987

SB: Most, career, all-time

716 RICKEY HENDERSON, 1979-1992
566 Bert Campaneris, 1964-1976
376 Eddie Collins, 1906-1930
232 Billy North, 1973-1978
223 Harry Davis, 1901-1917

BB: Most, career, all-time

1043 Max Bishop, 1924-1933
880 RICKEY HENDERSON, 1979-1992
853 Bob Johnson, 1933-1942
820 Elmer Valo, 1940-1956
792 Sal Bando, 1966-1976

BA: Highest, career, all-time

.356 Al Simmons, 1924-1944
.339 Jimmie Foxx, 1925-1935
.336 Eddie Collins, 1906-1930
.321 Mickey Cochrane, 1925-1933
.321 Frank Baker, 1908-1914
.292 RICKEY HENDERSON, 1979-1992 (17)

Slug avg: Highest, career, all-time

.640 Jimmie Foxx, 1925-1935
.584 Al Simmons, 1924-1944
.520 Bob Johnson, 1933-1942
.512 JOSE CANSECO, 1985-1992
.503 MARK McGWIRE, 1986-1992

Games started: Most, career, all-time

458 Eddie Plank, 1901-1914
340 Catfish Hunter, 1965-1974
288 Chief Bender, 1903-1914
267 Lefty Grove, 1925-1933
267 Rube Walberg, 1923-1933

Saves: Most, career, all-time

236 DENNIS ECKERSLEY, 1987-1992
136 Rollie Fingers, 1968-1976
73 John Wyatt, 1961-1969
61 JAY HOWELL, 1985-1987
58 Jack Aker, 1964-1968

Shutouts: Most, career, all-time

59 Eddie Plank, 1901-1914
37 Rube Waddell, 1902-1907
36 Chief Bender, 1903-1914
31 Catfish Hunter, 1965-1974
28 Vida Blue, 1969-1977
28 Jack Coombs, 1906-1914

Wins: Most, career, all-time

284 Eddie Plank, 1901-1914
195 Lefty Grove, 1925-1933
193 Chief Bender, 1903-1914
171 Eddie Rommel, 1920-1932
161 Catfish Hunter, 1965-1974

K: Most, career, all-time

1985 Eddie Plank, 1901-1914
1576 Rube Waddell, 1902-1907
1536 Chief Bender, 1903-1914
1523 Lefty Grove, 1925-1933
1520 Catfish Hunter, 1965-1974

Win pct: Highest, career, all-time

.712 Lefty Grove, 1925-1933
.661 BOB WELCH, 1988-1992
.654 Chief Bender, 1903-1914
.637 Eddie Plank, 1901-1914
.632 Jack Coombs, 1906-1914

ERA: Lowest, career, all-time

1.97 Rube Waddell, 1902-1907
2.15 Cy Morgan, 1909-1912
2.32 Chief Bender, 1903-1914
2.39 Eddie Plank, 1901-1914
2.60 Jack Coombs, 1906-1914
2.91 Rollie Fingers, 1968-1976 (8)

Runs: Most, season

152 Al Simmons, 1930
151 Jimmie Foxx, 1932
145 Nap Lajoie, 1901
144 Al Simmons, 1932
137 Eddie Collins, 1912
123 Reggie Jackson, 1969 (10)

Hits: Most, season

253 Al Simmons, 1925
232 Nap Lajoie, 1901
216 Al Simmons, 1932
214 Doc Cramer, 1935
213 Jimmie Foxx, 1932
187 JOSE CANSECO, 1988 (*)

2B: Most, season

53 Al Simmons, 1926
48 Nap Lajoie, 1901
48 Wally Moses, 1937
47 Harry Davis, 1905
47 Eric McNair, 1932
39 Reggie Jackson, 1975 (22)

3B: Most, season

21 Frank Baker, 1912
19 Frank Baker, 1909
18 Danny Murphy, 1910
17 Danny Murphy, 1904
16 Bing Miller, 1929
16 Al Simmons, 1930
16 Amos Strunk, 1915
12 Bert Campaneris, 1965 (*)
12 Phil Garner, 1976 (*)

HR: Most, season

58 Jimmie Foxx, 1932
49 MARK McGWIRE, 1987
48 Jimmie Foxx, 1933
47 Reggie Jackson, 1969
44 JOSE CANSECO, 1991
44 Jimmie Foxx, 1934

RBI: Most, season

169 Jimmie Foxx, 1932
165 Al Simmons, 1930
163 Jimmie Foxx, 1933
157 Al Simmons, 1929
156 Jimmie Foxx, 1930
124 JOSE CANSECO, 1988 (13)

SB: Most, season

130 RICKEY HENDERSON, 1982
108 RICKEY HENDERSON, 1983
100 RICKEY HENDERSON, 1980
81 Eddie Collins, 1910
75 Billy North, 1976

BB: Most, season

149 Eddie Joost, 1949
136 Ferris Fain, 1949
133 Ferris Fain, 1950
128 Max Bishop, 1929
128 Max Bishop, 1930
118 Sal Bando, 1970 (10)

BA: Highest, season

.426 Nap Lajoie, 1901
.390 Al Simmons, 1931
.387 Al Simmons, 1925
.381 Al Simmons, 1930
.365 Eddie Collins, 1911
.325 RICKEY HENDERSON, 1990 (*)

Slug avg: Highest, season

.749 Jimmie Foxx, 1932
.708 Al Simmons, 1930
.703 Jimmie Foxx, 1933
.653 Jimmie Foxx, 1934
.643 Nap Lajoie, 1901
.618 MARK McGWIRE, 1987 (11)

Games started: Most, season

46 Rube Waddell, 1904
43 Eddie Plank, 1904
41 Catfish Hunter, 1974
41 Eddie Plank, 1905
40 Vida Blue, 1974
40 George Caster, 1938
40 Jack Coombs, 1911
40 Chuck Dobson, 1970
40 Ken Holtzman, 1973
40 Catfish Hunter, 1970
40 Eddie Plank, 1903
40 Eddie Plank, 1907

Saves: Most, season

51 DENNIS ECKERSLEY, 1992
48 DENNIS ECKERSLEY, 1990
45 DENNIS ECKERSLEY, 1988
43 DENNIS ECKERSLEY, 1991
36 Bill Caudill, 1984

Shutouts: Most, season

13 Jack Coombs, 1910
8 Vida Blue, 1971
8 Joe Bush, 1916
8 Eddie Plank, 1907
8 Rube Waddell, 1904
8 Rube Waddell, 1906

Wins: Most, season

31 Jack Coombs, 1910
31 Lefty Grove, 1931
28 Jack Coombs, 1911
28 Lefty Grove, 1930
27 Eddie Rommel, 1922
27 Rube Waddell, 1905
27 BOB WELCH, 1990

K: Most, season

349 Rube Waddell, 1904
302 Rube Waddell, 1903
301 Vida Blue, 1971
287 Rube Waddell, 1905
232 Rube Waddell, 1907

Win pct: Highest, season

.886 Lefty Grove, 1931
.850 Chief Bender, 1914
.849 Lefty Grove, 1930
.821 Chief Bender, 1910
.818 BOB WELCH, 1990

ERA: Lowest, season

1.30 Jack Coombs, 1910
1.39 Harry Krause, 1909
1.48 Rube Waddell, 1905
1.55 Cy Morgan, 1910
1.58 Chief Bender, 1910
1.82 Vida Blue, 1971 (10)

Most pinch-hit homers, season

4 Jeff Burroughs, 1982

Most pinch-hit, homers, career

5 Jeff Burroughs, 1982-1984

Most consecutive games, batting safely

30 Bing Miller, Phi-1929
29 Billy Lamar, Phi-1925
24 Carney Lansford, 1984

Most consecutive scoreless innings

53 Jack Coombs, Phi-1910
43 Rube Waddell, Phi-1905
37 Mike Torrez, 1976

No hit games

Weldon Henley, Phi at StL AL, 6-0; July 22, 1905 (1st game).

Chief Bender, Phi vs Cle AL, 4-0; May 12, 1910.

Joe Bush, Phi vs Cle AL, 5-0; August 26, 1916.

Dick Fowler, Phi vs StL AL, 1-0; September 9, 1945 (2nd game).

Bill McCahan, Phi vs Was AL, 3-0; September 3, 1947.

Catfish Hunter, Oak vs Min AL, 4-0; May 8, 1968 (perfect game).

Vida Blue, Oak vs Min AL, 6-0; September 21, 1970.

Vida Blue (5 innings), Glenn Abbott (1 inning), Paul Lindblad (1 inning) and Rollie Fingers (2 innings), Oak vs Cal AL, 5-0; September 28, 1975.

Mike Warren, Oak vs Chi AL, 3-0; September 29, 1983.

Dave Stewart, Oak at Tor AL, 5-0; June 29, 1990.

Rube Waddell, five innings, rain, Phi vs StL AL, 2-0; August 15, 1905.

Jimmy Dygert (3 innings) and Rube Waddell (2 innings), five innings, rain, Phi vs Chi AL, 4-3; August 29, 1906. (Waddell allowed hit and two runs in 6th, but rain caused game to revert to 5 innings).

Rube Vickers, five perfect innings, darkness, Phi at Was AL, 4-0; October 5, 1907 (2nd game).

ACTIVE PLAYERS in caps.

Leader from the franchise's current location is included. If not in the top five, leader's rank is listed in parenthesis; asterisk (*) indicates player is not in top 25.

Minnesota Twins

by Anne Ryan, *USA TODAY*

Closer Rick Aguilera had a 2.84 ERA in 64 games for the Twins, finishing 61 and saving 41 (second in the AL).

1992 Twins: 52 bad days ruined it

There are 182 days in the baseball season. For the Minnesota Twins, everything boiled down to 52 of them.

On July 26, the Twins were the best team in baseball, 60-38 (.612), three games ahead of the A's in the AL West. Fast-forward to Sept. 16: They had lost 28 of 48 games, falling to .548 (80-66). The A's swept a three-game series, were nine games ahead, and the race was over.

"No, it's not over," insisted outfielder Shane Mack. "They still have 10 more games on the road. Then, we have to go undefeated." The prospect wouldn't have been so far-fetched a few months earlier, when the Twins went 51-26, outscoring opponents by almost two runs a game. But the clutch hits ceased, the pitching broke down, the baserunning was sloppy, and the fielding was careless.

"It was pitching one night, fielding the next. Or hitting one night and bad baserunning the next," said GM Andy MacPhail. "There was no one thing to focus on." He could have started with the left-handed hitting, which "fell off the map" as he put it. Chili Davis fell from 29 homers and 93 RBI to 12 and 66. Kent Hrbek was limited by injuries to 394 at-bats, hitting just .244, 45 points off his career average. Mike Pagliarulo's injury-ridden year added up to a measly .200 average.

But Kirby Puckett was his usual self. He led the AL in hits and total bases, and finished second in batting (.329). After contract talks with the Twins broke off May 27, his explosive output was impressive even by his own standards. He hit .463 May 27 to June 7, with five home runs—two grand slams—and 18 RBI. It wasn't a salary drive; he always gives at least 100 percent.

"I already have a salary," he said. There was a job to be done, and he was trying to do it. He filed for free agency at the end of the season, but re-signed with the Twins.

Shane Mack hit .315 (16 HR, 75 RBI) with 26 steals. Chuck Knoblauch (.297, 56 RBI, 34 steals) improved his defense and nearly all his offensive numbers. On the mound, John Smiley (obtained from Pittsburgh before the season opened) and fellow newcomer Bill Krueger were steady. Smiley finished with 16 wins, tying Kevin Tapani for the team high. Krueger blazed to 4-0 with an 0.84 ERA, but cooled off after the All-Star break, and was 10-6 (4.30 ERA) when the Twins traded him to the Expos Aug. 31 for outfielder Darren Reed. Rick Aguilera (41 saves) turned in his second consecutive 40-save season, but Scott Erickson was inconsistent, posting a 13-12 record.

—by Deron Snyder

1993 Twins: Preview

Making Kirby happy. Keeping Kirby happy. Simple as it seems, by keeping Kirby Puckett and repeating their 90-win season of '92, they should win the AL West. The A's should stumble after dropping key free agents and the White Sox may still not be consistent enough to win regularly. The West will be won by the team that fails least.

The Twins may have the majors' most formidable top of the order in Chuck Knoblauch, Shane Mack, and Puckett. Combined, the three scored more than 300 runs in '92.

Dave Winfield replaces Chili Davis at DH. The Twins still could use someone who can explode from the left side of the plate.

The loss of John Smiley might hamper the pitching, but Kevin Tapani should be even better, and Rick Aguilera could improve on his 41 saves.

Surprise impact player? Look to David McCarty. Splitting time in right field, first base and DH, the rookie could be a rising star.

—by Tom Sakell

1992 Twins: Between the lines

▸**April 26:** Rookie Pat Mahomes wasn't afraid of the Oakland A's—he struck out 10 of them in five innings to pick up his second win.

▸**April 27:** Bill "Freddie" Krueger's performance against the Twins in 1991 was downright frightening. As a Brewer he was 0-2 with a 13.50 ERA vs. Minnesota. As a Twin (4-0) he had given up two hits and one run and watched his ERA rise way up to 0.84 so far in the season.

▸**April 29:** Kent Hrbek homered and doubled against Baltimore in his fifth game since coming off the DL.

▸**May 1:** Kevin Tapani lost to the Yankees for the first time in six career decisions, as Melido Perez won for the just the second time in eight career decisions against the Twins.

▸**May 2:** Four of seven Twins who came to bat homered off Yankee ace Scott Sanderson—in one inning.

▸**May 10:** Pedro Munoz helped secure the Twins' first series sweep of the season (Cleveland) by going 2-for-4 with three RBI, including a two-run homer with two outs in the first.

▸**May 13:** Shane Mack snapped an 0-for-12 slump with a bases-loaded single in the bottom of the ninth to give the Twins a 4-3 victory against Boston, their fifth straight win.

▸**May 17:** Chuck Knoblauch was 4-for-5, doubled twice and scored three runs. Kirby Puckett added a three-run homer as part of his three-hit day.

▸**May 24:** Was that baseball or volleyball? You wouldn't know from the score: the Twins beat Detroit 15-0. Bill Krueger got the win, as the Twins got 18 hits (a season high). Shane Mack hit a grand slam and Brian Harper was 3-for-3 with four RBI.

▸**May 29:** Kirby Puckett finally accomplished something he had never done in his nine-year career—he hit a grand slam, in Minnesota's 17-5 win against Detroit. Every Twins' starter got a hit and scored a run.

▸**May 31:** Mark Guthrie notched his first save since August 1991, pitching three perfect innings to preserve Scott Erickson's win in the Twins' 4-1 victory against the Tigers.

▸**June 3:** Puckett hit his second grand slam in six games as Minnesota derailed one of the hottest pitchers in baseball: Toronto ace Juan Guzman.

▸**June 22:** John Smiley gave up eight hits but stranded seven in the Twins' 2-0 win. Luis Polonia was the only Angel to make it to third, and he had to steal two bases to get there.

▸**June 25:** The AL West's top two teams began a four-game series, as Oakland eased to a 5-1 win. Bill Krueger fell to 0-4 vs. the A's.

▸**June 26:** Mike Bordick's seventh-inning fielding error led to the Twins' go-ahead run and Greg Gagne added a homer as Minnesota beat Oakland, 4-3, to snap the A's' four-game winning streak. Willie Banks won his second straight for Minnesota.

▸**June 28:** The AL West got even wilder as the Twins rode a 10-run fourth inning to a 10-2 win against Oakland to move into a first-place tie atop the division. Chili Davis was 4-for-5 on the day.

▸**June 30:** Bill Krueger threw a two-hitter, his second shutout in eight years, to beat the Angels, 2-0, and keep the Twins tied atop the AL West. Kirby Puckett scored both runs.

▸**July 4:** Baltimore snapped a 1-1 tie with a run in the top of the 15th inning, but Chili Davis answered with a two-run single in the bottom of the inning to give the Twins a 3-2 victory and sole possession of first place in the AL West.

▸**July 12:** Minnesota beat the O's 9-4 to hold a two-game lead in the AL West.

▸**July 17:** Frank Viola made his first appearance in the Metrodome in three years and Jeff Reardon surrendered the eventual winning run as both ex-Twins pitched for the Red Sox in a 3-2 Twins win. After pinch-hitting for both shortstop Greg Gagne and third baseman Scott Leius, Tom Kelly used Kirby

Puckett—a five-time Gold Glove center fielder—at third, shortstop and second.

▸**July 18:** It was a classic pitching duel: Roger Clemens threw a two-hit shutout, but Scott Erickson also went the distance, allowing just one run. The Red Sox won 1-0.

▸**August 1:** Brian Harper hit his fifth home run.

▸**August 2:** Scott Erickson pitched his second shutout in three games.

▸**August 11:** John Smiley allowed two unearned runs on four hits in a 3-2 Twins win against Texas.

August 14: Kirby Puckett had a pair of homers, including a third-inning grand slam, to help Minnesota beat the Mariners 9-6.

▸**August 18:** Shane Mack extended his hitting streak to 22 games.

▸**August 23:** John Smiley counseled teammate Scott Erickson to raise his leg kick, and the result was a four-hitter as the Twins blanked the Blue Jays 2-0. Lenny Webster hit his first home run in two years.

▸**August 24:** Stranger than fiction: After hitting one homer and just missing another, Kent Hrbek tried to bunt his way on base with two outs in the eighth. Stranger than fiction II: The double-play combo of shortstop Greg Gagne and second baseman Chuck Knoblauch each made an error, the first time since June 8 they had erred in the same game.

▸**August 26:** John Smiley pitched his first AL shutout.

▸**September 9:** The Twins stole a club record six bases, led by a pair from Kirby Puckett.

▸**September 14:** The A's won the opener of a series between the AL West's top two teams, moving seven games in front of the Twins with 18 games to play. Since being swept by the A's in the last week of July, the Twins had gone 20-26, losing 10 games in the standings.

▸**September 28:** The Twins' hopes were over. They lost to Chicago, 9-4, virtually giving the clinch on the AL West title to the Oakland A's, who had the day off.

▸**October 4:** Minnesota finished six games behind the A's, second in the AL West. Kirby Puckett led the AL in hits (210) and total bases (313), was second in batting (.329), sixth in doubles (38) and RBI (110), and eighth in slugging (.490). Rick Aguilera was second in the league with 41 saves.

—by Jeanie Chung, John Hunt, Deron Snyder, and Lisa Winston.

Team directory

▸**Owner:** Carl R. Pohlad

▸**General Manager:** Andy MacPhail

▸**Ballpark:**
Hubert H. Humphrey Metrodome
501 Chicago Avenue South, Minneapolis, Minn.
612-375-7444
Capacity 55,883
Public transportation available
Family and wheelchair sections, elevators

▸**Team publications:**
Twins Magazine, Twins Yearbook
612-375-7458

▸**TV, radio broadcast stations:**
WCCO 830 AM, WCCO-TV Channel 4

▸**Camps and/or clinics:**
Twins Clinics, weekends throughout the summer, 612-375-7498

▸**Spring Training:**
Lee County Sports Complex
Fort Myers, Fla.
Capacity 7,500
813-768-4200

MINNESOTA TWINS 1992 final stats

Batting	AVG	SLG	OB	G	AB	R	H	TB	2B	3B	HR	RBI	BB	SO	SB	CS	E
Parks	.333	.333	.500	7	6	1	2	2	0	0	0	0	1	1	0	0	0
Puckett	.329	.490	.374	160	639	104	210	313	38	4	19	110	44	97	17	7	3
Mack	.315	.467	.394	156	600	101	189	280	31	6	16	75	64	106	26	14	4
Jorgensen	.310	.328	.349	22	58	5	18	19	1	0	0	5	3	11	1	2	1
Harper	.307	.410	.343	140	502	58	154	206	25	0	9	73	26	22	0	1	13
Knoblauch	.297	.358	.384	155	600	104	178	215	19	6	2	56	88	60	34	13	6
Hill	.294	.353	.368	25	51	7	15	18	3	0	0	2	5	6	0	0	3
Davis	.288	.439	.386	138	444	63	128	195	27	2	12	66	73	76	4	5	0
Webster	.280	.407	.331	53	118	10	33	48	10	1	1	13	9	11	0	2	1
Munoz	.270	.409	.298	127	418	44	113	171	16	3	12	71	17	90	4	5	3
Bruett	.250	.303	.313	56	76	7	19	23	4	0	0	2	6	12	6	3	1
Leius	.249	.318	.309	129	409	50	102	130	18	2	2	35	34	61	6	5	15
Larkin	.246	.359	.308	115	337	38	83	121	18	1	6	42	28	43	7	2	5
Gagne	.246	.346	.280	146	439	53	108	152	23	0	7	39	19	83	6	7	18
Hrbek	.244	.409	.357	112	394	52	96	161	20	0	15	58	71	56	5	2	3
Bush	.214	.302	.263	100	182	14	39	55	8	1	2	22	11	37	1	1	0
Pagliarulo	.200	.238	.213	42	105	10	21	25	4	0	0	9	1	17	1	0	3
Quinones	.200	.200	.167	3	5	0	1	1	0	0	0	1	0	0	0	0	2
Reboulet	.190	.277	.311	73	137	15	26	38	7	1	1	16	23	26	3	2	5
Reed	.182	.242	.216	14	33	2	6	8	2	0	0	4	2	11	0	0	0
Brito	.143	.214	.133	8	14	1	2	3	1	0	0	2	0	4	0	1	1
Brown	.067	.067	.222	35	15	8	1	1	0	0	0	0	2	4	2	2	1

Pitching	W-L	ERA	G	GS	CG	GF	Sho	SV	IP	H	R	ER	HR	BB	SO
Wayne	3-3	2.63	41	0	0	13	0	0	48	46	18	14	2	19	29
Casian	1-0	2.70	6	0	0	1	0	0	6.2	7	2	2	0	1	2
Willis	7-3	2.72	59	0	0	21	0	1	79.1	73	25	24	4	11	45
Edens	6-3	2.83	52	0	0	14	0	3	76.1	65	26	24	1	36	57
Aguilera	2-6	2.84	64	0	0	61	0	41	66.2	60	28	21	7	17	52
Guthrie	2-3	2.88	54	0	0	15	0	5	75	59	27	24	7	23	76
Smiley	16-9	3.21	34	34	5	0	2	0	241	205	93	86	17	65	163
Abbott	0-0	3.27	6	0	0	5	0	0	11	12	4	4	1	5	13
Trombley	3-2	3.30	10	7	0	0	0	0	46.1	43	20	17	5	17	38
Erickson	13-12	3.40	32	32	5	0	3	0	212	197	86	80	18	83	101
Tapani	16-11	3.97	34	34	4	0	1	0	220	226	103	97	17	48	138
Krueger	10-6	4.30	27	27	2	0	2	0	161.1	166	82	77	18	46	86
Kipper	3-3	4.42	25	0	0	12	0	0	38.2	40	23	19	8	14	22
Mahomes	3-4	5.04	14	13	0	1	0	0	69.2	73	41	39	5	37	44
Banks	4-4	5.70	16	12	0	2	0	0	71	80	46	45	6	37	37
West	1-3	6.99	9	3	0	1	0	0	28.1	32	24	22	3	20	19
Gozzo	0-0	27.00	2	0	0	0	0	0	1.2	7	5	5	2	0	1

1993 preliminary roster

PITCHERS (18)
Paul Abbott
Rick Aguilera
Willie Banks
Jayson Best
Larry Casian
Jim Deshaies
Scott Erickson
Rich Garces
Mark Guthrie
Mike Hartley
Pat Mahomes
Oscar Munoz
Alan Newman
Kevin Tapani
Mike Trombley
George Tsamis
Gary Wayne
Carl Willis

CATCHERS (3)
Brian Harper
Derek Parks
Lenny Webster

INFIELDERS (11)
Steve Dunn
Denny Hocking
Kent Hrbek
Terry Jorgensen
Chuck Knoblauch
Gene Larkin
Scott Leius
Mike Maksudian
Pat Meares
Jeff Reboulet
Paul Russo

OUTFIELDERS (8)
Bernardo Brito
J.T. Bruett
Marty Cordova
Pat Howell
Derek Lee
Shane Mack
Pedro Munoz
Kirby Puckett

Games played by position

Player	G	C	1B	2B	3B	SS	OF	DH
BRITO,B	8	0	0	0	0	0	3	1
BROWN,J	35	0	0	0	0	0	31	2
BRUETT,J	56	0	0	0	0	0	45	3
BUSH,R	100	0	8	0	0	0	24	24
DAVIS,C	138	0	1	0	0	0	4	125
GAGNE,G	146	0	0	0	0	141	0	0
HARPER,B	140	133	0	0	0	0	0	2
HILL,D	25	0	0	7	5	10	1	0
HRBEK,K	112	0	104	0	0	0	0	8
JORGENSEN,T	22	0	13	0	9	2	0	0
KNOBLAUCH,C	155	0	0	154	0	1	0	1
LARKIN,G	115	0	55	0	0	0	43	4
LEIUS,S	129	0	0	0	125	10	0	0
MACK,S	156	0	0	0	0	0	155	0
MUNOZ,P	127	0	0	0	0	0	122	3
PAGLIARULO,M	42	0	0	0	37	0	0	1
PARKS,D	7	7	0	0	0	0	0	0
PUCKETT,K	160	0	0	2	2	1	149	9
QUINONES,L	3	0	0	0	1	1	0	1
REBOULET,J	73	0	0	13	22	36	7	1
REED,D	14	0	0	0	0	0	13	1
WEBSTER,L	53	49	0	0	0	0	0	1

Sick call: 1992 DL report

Player	Days on the DL
Abbott, Paul*	78
Hill, Donnie	39
Hrbek, Kent*	45
Pagliarulo, Mike*	100

** On Disabled List twice during 1992 season (not counting transfers from one DL to another).*

Minor league report

Class AAA — Portland finished 83-61, 2nd in the 1st half of the Pacific Coast League Northern Division and 1st in the 2nd half. The team lost to Vancouver in the 1st round of the playoffs. OF Bernardo Brito hit .270 with 26 HR and 96 RBI. RHP Mike Trombley was 10-8 with a 3.65 ERA and a league-leading 138 K. LHP George Tsamis led the league with 13 wins. **Class AA:** Orlando finished 60-82, 4th in the 1st half of the Southern League Eastern Division and 3rd in the 2nd half. 3B Paul Russo had 22 HR. 1B/OF Dave McCarty had 79 RBI. 2B/OF Mica Lewis had 36 SB. **Class A:** Visalia finished 75-61, 3rd in the 1st half of the California League Southern Division and 1st in the 2nd half. The team lost to Stockton in four games for the league championship. League MVP OF Marty Cordova hit .341 with 28 HR and 131 RBI. OF Rich Becker hit .316 with 15 HR and 82 RBI. 1B Steve Dunn had 26 HR and 113 RBI. SS David Rivera had 48 SB. LHP Eddie Guardado was 7-0 with a 1.64 ERA after his promotion from Kenosha. Kenosha finished 63-70, last in the 1st half of the Midwest League Northern Division and 3rd in the 2nd half. C Damian Miller hit .292 with 5 HR and 56 RBI. RHP Kerry Taylor K'd 158, with a 2.75 ERA. LHP David Sartain was 7-13 with a 2.72 ERA and 125 K in 132 IP. Elizabethton finished 49-17, 1st in the Appalachian League South Division. The team lost to Bluefield in three games for the league championship. 1B Ken Tirpack hit .333 with 9 HR and 42 RBI. RHP Kevin Legault was 7-0 with a 2.10 ERA. RHP Gustavo Gandarillas shared the league lead with 13 saves. Twins finished 30-28, 3rd in the Gulf Coast League Western Division. OF Edgar Herrera won the league batting title at .351 with 4 HR and 40 RBI.

Tops in the organization

BATTING LEADERS	Club	Avg.	G	AB	R	H	HR	RBI
Marty Cordova	Vis	.341	134	513	103	175	28	131
Denny Hocking	Vis	.331	135	550	117	182	7	81
Rich Becker	Vis	.316	136	506	118	160	15	82
Scott Stahoviak	Vis	.308	110	409	62	126	5	68
Steve Dunn	Vis	.305	125	492	93	150	26	113

HOME RUNS			WINS		
Marty Cordova	Vis	28	George Tsamis	Por	13
Steve Dunn	Vis	26	Eddie Guardado	Vis	12
Bernardo Brito	Por	26	Dickie Dixon	Vis	12
Paul Russo	Orl	22	Bob McCreary	Orl	12
Dave McCarty	Por	19	Several players tied		11

RBI			SAVES		
Marty Cordova	Vis	131	George Tsamis	Por	13
Steve Dunn	Vis	113	Eddie Guardado	Vis	12
Bernardo Brito	Por	96	Dickie Dixon	Vis	12
Dave McCarty	Por	87	Bob McCreary	Orl	12
Rich Becker	Vis	82	Several players tied		11

STOLEN BASES			STRIKEOUTS		
David Rivera	Vis	48	Kerry Taylor	Ken	158
Tim Moore	Vis	40	Eddie Guardado	Vis	142
Denny Hocking	Vis	38	Curt Leskanic	Por	140
Mica Lewis	Orl	36	Mike Trombley	Por	138
Cheo Garcia	Orl	32	Todd Ritchie	Vis	129

PITCHING LEADERS	Club	W-L	ERA	IP	H	BB	SO
Bill Wissler	Orl	7-11	2.59	156	126	34	115
David Sartain	Ken	7-13	2.72	132	103	59	125
Kerry Taylor	Ken	10-9	2.75	170	150	68	158
Brad Radke	Ken	10-10	2.93	166	149	47	127
Mauro Gozzo	Por	10-9	3.35	156	155	50	108

Minnesota (1961-1992), incl. Wash. (1901-1960)

Runs: Most, career, all-time

1466 Sam Rice, 1915-1933
1258 Harmon Killebrew, 1954-1974
1154 Joe Judge, 1915-1932
1037 Buddy Myer, 1925-1941
1004 Clyde Milan, 1907-1922

Hits: Most, career, all-time

2889 Sam Rice, 1915-1933
2291 Joe Judge, 1915-1932
2100 Clyde Milan, 1907-1922
2085 Rod Carew, 1967-1978
2024 Harmon Killebrew, 1954-1974

2B: Most, career, all-time

479 Sam Rice, 1915-1933
421 Joe Judge, 1915-1932
391 Mickey Vernon, 1939-1955
329 Tony Oliva, 1962-1976
305 Rod Carew, 1967-1978
305 Buddy Myer, 1925-1941

3B: Most, career, all-time

183 Sam Rice, 1915-1933
157 Joe Judge, 1915-1932
125 Goose Goslin, 1921-1938
113 Buddy Myer, 1925-1941
108 Mickey Vernon, 1939-1955
90 Rod Carew, 1967-1978 (8)

HR: Most, career, all-time

559 Harmon Killebrew, 1954-1974
258 KENT HRBEK, 1981-1992
256 Bob Allison, 1958-1970
220 Tony Oliva, 1962-1976
201 GARY GAETTI, 1981-1990

RBI: Most, career, all-time

1540 Harmon Killebrew, 1954-1974
1045 Sam Rice, 1915-1933
1026 Mickey Vernon, 1939-1955
1001 Joe Judge, 1915-1932
950 KENT HRBEK, 1981-1992

SB: Most, career, all-time

495 Clyde Milan, 1907-1922
346 Sam Rice, 1915-1933
321 George Case, 1937-1947
271 Rod Carew, 1967-1978
210 Joe Judge, 1915-1932

BB: Most, career, all-time

1505 Harmon Killebrew, 1954-1974
1274 Eddie Yost, 1944-1958
943 Joe Judge, 1915-1932
864 Buddy Myer, 1925-1941
795 Bob Allison, 1958-1970

BA: Highest, career, all-time

.334 Rod Carew, 1967-1978
.328 Heinie Manush, 1930-1935
.323 Sam Rice, 1915-1933
.323 Goose Goslin, 1921-1938
.321 KIRBY PUCKETT, 1984-1992

Slug avg: Highest, career, all-time

.514 Harmon Killebrew, 1954-1974
.502 Goose Goslin, 1921-1938
.500 Roy Sievers, 1954-1959
.485 KENT HRBEK, 1981-1992
.481 Jimmie Hall, 1963-1966

Games started: Most, career, all-time

666 Walter Johnson, 1907-1927
433 Jim Kaat, 1959-1973
345 BERT BLYLEVEN, 1970-1988
331 Camilo Pascual, 1954-1966
259 FRANK VIOLA, 1982-1989

Saves: Most, career, all-time

115 RICK AGUILERA, 1989-1992
108 Ron Davis, 1982-1986
104 JEFF REARDON, 1987-1989
96 Firpo Marberry, 1923-1936
88 Al Worthington, 1964-1969

Shutouts: Most, career, all-time

110 Walter Johnson, 1907-1927
31 Camilo Pascual, 1954-1966
29 BERT BLYLEVEN, 1970-1988
23 Jim Kaat, 1959-1973
23 Dutch Leonard, 1938-1946

Wins: Most, career, all-time

417 Walter Johnson, 1907-1927
190 Jim Kaat, 1959-1973
149 BERT BLYLEVEN, 1970-1988
145 Camilo Pascual, 1954-1966
128 Jim Perry, 1963-1972

K: Most, career, all-time

3509 Walter Johnson, 1907-1927
2035 BERT BLYLEVEN, 1970-1988
1885 Camilo Pascual, 1954-1966
1851 Jim Kaat, 1959-1973
1214 FRANK VIOLA, 1982-1989

Win pct: Highest, career, all-time

.631 SCOTT ERICKSON, 1990-1992
.622 Firpo Marberry, 1923-1936
.605 KEVIN TAPANI, 1989-1992
.602 Sam Jones, 1928-1931
.599 Walter Johnson, 1907-1927

ERA: Lowest, career, all-time

2.16 Walter Johnson, 1907-1927
2.64 Doc Ayers, 1913-1919
2.75 Harry Harper, 1913-1919
2.76 Charlie Smith, 1906-1909
2.83 Bert Gallia, 1912-1917
3.15 Jim Perry, 1963-1972 (10)

Runs: Most, season

128 Rod Carew, 1977
127 Joe Cronin, 1930
126 Zoilo Versalles, 1965
122 Buddy Lewis, 1938
121 Heinie Manush, 1932
121 Sam Rice, 1930

Hits: Most, season

239 Rod Carew, 1977
234 KIRBY PUCKETT, 1988
227 Sam Rice, 1925
223 KIRBY PUCKETT, 1986
221 Heinie Manush, 1933

2B: Most, season

51 Mickey Vernon, 1946
50 Stan Spence, 1946
45 Joe Cronin, 1933
45 KIRBY PUCKETT, 1989
45 Zoilo Versalles, 1965

3B: Most, season

20 Goose Goslin, 1925
19 Joe Cassidy, 1904
19 Cecil Travis, 1941
18 Joe Cronin, 1932
18 Goose Goslin, 1923
18 Sam Rice, 1923
18 Howie Shanks, 1921
18 John Stone, 1935
16 Rod Carew, 1977 (11)

HR: Most, season

49 Harmon Killebrew, 1964
49 Harmon Killebrew, 1969
48 Harmon Killebrew, 1962
46 Harmon Killebrew, 1961
45 Harmon Killebrew, 1963

RBI: Most, season

140 Harmon Killebrew, 1969
129 Goose Goslin, 1924
126 Joe Cronin, 1930
126 Joe Cronin, 1931
126 Harmon Killebrew, 1962

SB: Most, season

88	Clyde Milan, 1912
75	Clyde Milan, 1913
63	Sam Rice, 1920
62	Danny Moeller, 1913
61	George Case, 1943
49	Rod Carew, 1976 (8)

BB: Most, season

151	Eddie Yost, 1956
145	Harmon Killebrew, 1969
141	Eddie Yost, 1950
131	Harmon Killebrew, 1967
131	Eddie Yost, 1954

BA: Highest, season

.388	Rod Carew, 1977
.379	Goose Goslin, 1928
.376	Ed Delahanty, 1902
.364	Rod Carew, 1974
.359	Rod Carew, 1975

Slug avg: Highest, season

.614	Goose Goslin, 1928
.606	Harmon Killebrew, 1961
.590	Ed Delahanty, 1902
.584	Harmon Killebrew, 1969
.579	Roy Sievers, 1957

Games started: Most, season

42	Walter Johnson, 1910
42	Jim Kaat, 1965
41	Jim Kaat, 1966
40	BERT BLYLEVEN, 1973
40	Bob Groom, 1912
40	Walter Johnson, 1914
40	Jim Perry, 1970

Saves: Most, season

42	RICK AGUILERA, 1991
42	JEFF REARDON, 1988
41	RICK AGUILERA, 1992
34	Ron Perranoski, 1970
32	RICK AGUILERA, 1990
32	Mike Marshall, 1979

Shutouts: Most, season

11	Walter Johnson, 1913
9	BERT BLYLEVEN, 1973
9	Walter Johnson, 1914
9	Bob Porterfield, 1953
8	Walter Johnson, 1910
8	Walter Johnson, 1917
8	Walter Johnson, 1918
8	Camilo Pascual, 1961

Wins: Most, season

36	Walter Johnson, 1913
33	Walter Johnson, 1912
28	Walter Johnson, 1914
27	Walter Johnson, 1915
26	General Crowder, 1932
25	Jim Kaat, 1966 (6)

K: Most, season

313	Walter Johnson, 1910
303	Walter Johnson, 1912
258	BERT BLYLEVEN, 1973
249	BERT BLYLEVEN, 1974
243	Walter Johnson, 1913

Win pct: Highest, season

.837	Walter Johnson, 1913
.800	Stan Coveleski, 1925
.800	Firpo Marberry, 1931
.774	FRANK VIOLA, 1988
.773	Bill Campbell, 1976

ERA: Lowest, season

1.14	Walter Johnson, 1913
1.27	Walter Johnson, 1918
1.35	Walter Johnson, 1910
1.39	Walter Johnson, 1912
1.49	Walter Johnson, 1919
2.50	Dave Goltz, 1978 (*)

Most pinch-hit homers, season

4	Don Mincher, 1964

Most pinch-hit, homers, career

8	Bob Allison, 1961-1970 (none with Was-1958-1960)

Most consecutive games, batting safely

33	Heine Manush, Was-1933
31	Sam Rice, Was-1924
31	Ken Landreaux, 1980

Most consecutive scoreless innings

55	Walter Johnson, Was-1913
40	Walter Johnson, Was-1918
37	Walter Johnson, Was-1913

No hit games

Walter Johnson, Was at Bos AL, 1-0; July 1, 1920.

Bobby Burke, Was vs Bos AL, 5-0; August 8, 1931.

Jack Kralick, Min vs KC AL, 1-0; August 26, 1962.

Dean Chance, Min at Cle AL, 2-1; August 25, 1967 (2nd game).

Jay Cashion, six innings, called so Cleveland could catch train, Was vs Cle AL, 2-0; August 20, 1912 (2nd game).

Walter Johnson, seven innings, rain, Was vs StL AL, 2-0; August 25, 1924.

Dean Chance, five perfect innings, rain, Min vs Bos AL, 2-0; August 6, 1967.

ACTIVE PLAYERS in caps.

Leader from the franchise's current location is included. If not in the top five, leader's rank is listed in parenthesis; asterisk (*) indicates player is not in top 25.

Chicago White Sox 

Chicago White Sox

Jack McDowell led the AL with 13 complete games, pitched 260.2 innings (third), and won 20 (third).

by Anne Ryan, *USA TODAY*

1992 White Sox: Better luck next year

The White Sox were confident that they had made the right moves to put them over the top in October. They had acquired George Bell and Steve Sax in trades, and signed free agent Kirk McCaskill. They stayed within striking distance until mid-September, but they never made the necessary push to overtake the A's, and they finished 10 games behind.

They lost team leader Ozzie Guillen for the season when he tore up his knee in April. Craig Grebeck emerged as a capable fill-in, even exceeding Guillen's offensive numbers, but was also lost for the year when he hurt his foot in July.

White Sox' pitchers struggled, other than ace Jack McDowell (20-10, 3.18 ERA). Veteran knuckleballer Charlie Hough provided 176.1 innings, but was a free agent at the end of the season. Kirk McCaskill finished 12-13, Greg Hibbard 10-7.

Frank Thomas had another MVP-caliber year (.324, 24 HR, 115 RBI) and openly campaigned for the award: "MVP has always been an offensive award, and I don't think anyone has had a better year offensively." As it turned out, the MVP went to a relief pitcher—Oakland's Dennis Eckersley.

Thomas benefited from the arrival of DH George Bell, who hit behind him and also drove in more than 100 runs. The two kept the White Sox in the running until the rest of the team started hitting. Also solid: Robin Ventura (.282, 16 HR, 93 RBI) and Lance Johnson (.279).

Tim Raines started slowly, but was a different player in the second half, when he hit .347 (55 runs, 30 RBI).

But the negatives for the White Sox were plentiful. Dan Pasqua, signed in the offseason, was miserable both offensively and defensively. Steve Sax was nearly 50 points below his career average. Alex Fernandez failed to improve and had to spend a month in the minors. Bo Jackson's doctors said his return was close to impossible.

Carlton Fisk was limited by injuries to 62 games. Should he re-sign with the Sox, he will break Bob Boone's record for games played as catcher in 1993 at the age of 45

Bobby Thigpen was ineffective and was booed by Comiskey Park fans. He finished the year with 22 saves, but had a 4.75 ERA and lost the closer role to Scott Radinsky and Roberto Hernandez. Thigpen was the youngest player to get 200 saves (29), but he was the subject of much late-season trade talk.

Rookie manager Gene Lamont took over for Jeff Torborg, who left for New York. The White Sox extended his contract through 1993.

—by Pete Williams

1993 White Sox: Preview

Any team that has Frank Thomas, Robin Ventura and Jack McDowell with a decent supporting cast might earn the tag as "favorite" to win the division. Maybe '93 is their year.

The Chisox lineup can thump with anyone: Thomas and George Bell are good for 100 RBI each, and Ventura isn't far behind. The offense can tune up to an even higher level if Steve Sax rebounds and Carlton Fisk and Ozzie Guillen have healthy years. Guillen is important—he's a clubhouse leader.

Pitching: After Jack McDowell and Roberto Hernandez, it falls off. Greg Hibbard was lost in the expansion draft and Charlie Hough was a free agent (they hoped to re-sign him). Alex Fernandez could play a key role.

On the field, the Sox have as much talent as anyone in the division—it's a matter of putting it together. Wild card: Bo Jackson has vowed to return. Maybe Bo knows.

—by Tim McQuay

1992 White Sox: Between the lines

▸**April 21:** Shortstop Ozzie Guillen collided with left fielder Tim Raines, chasing a fly ball with two outs in the ninth inning. Guillen suffered a knee injury and awaited word on surgery.

▸**April 22:** Guillen was officially out for the season. Team doctors estimated that it would take him anywhere from six months to a year to rehabilitate his knee following reconstructive surgery. He was replaced in the everyday lineup by Craig Grebeck.

▸**April 24:** Jack McDowell two-hit hard-slugging Detroit for his fourth straight win.

▸**April 26:** Robin Ventura had three hits, including his first 1992 homer.

▸**May 2:** Charlie Hough went eight innings—one run, three hits.

▸**May 4:** Alex Fernandez took a 4.44 ERA into the game against the Brewers, and lowered it to 3.24, showing why he's one of the better young pitchers in the league (22).

▸**May 7:** The White Sox overcame a six-run deficit to beat the Red Sox 7-6.

▸**May 10:** Jack McDowell became 1992's first seven-game winner. With two wins in three games, the Sox became the first team to win a series from the Orioles at Camden Yards.

▸**May 13:** Kirk McCaskill took a no-hitter into the seventh and finished on the winning end of the White Sox's 1-0 victory against Milwaukee. McCaskill allowed a pair of hits in 7 1/3 and Bobby Thigpen came in for the save. Chicago moved into first place in the AL West.

▸**May 16:** Frank Thomas hit his fifth homer, a 466-foot blast that landed on the concourse atop the bleachers and was estimated to be the longest home run at two-year-old Comiskey Stadium. ***Quote of the day:*** McDowell, after failing to make it past the third inning—"I don't know if I had a good fastball. I wasn't in there long enough to know."

▸**May 17:** Steve Sax, who had just six RBI on the season heading into the day, hit a pair of triples and a sacrifice fly. Tim Raines was 4-for-4—scoring four runs for the third time in his career—with a home run and a pair of doubles.

▸**May 19:** Charlie Hough won for the first time in five starts, combining with relievers Scott Radinsky and Bobby Thigpen. It was career win 196 for Hough.

▸**May 20:** In 1991, White Sox' right-hander Roberto Hernandez suffered a life-threatening blood clot in his arm, and had surgery. After starting 1992 at Chicago, he was sent back to Class AAA. Recalled May 19, he was perfect in his first return outing May 20.

▸**May 24:** Deuces were wild for White Sox leadoff man Tim Raines. He was 2-for-2 with two runs scored, two driven in, and two walks.

▸**May 29 *Milestone:*** Tim Raines stole his 700th career base.

▸**June 6 *Quote of the day:*** Alex Fernandez summed up the White Sox' current fortunes, after losing their 10th game in 11 tries—"We're not pitching good right now. We're not hitting good. We're not doing anything good right now."

▸**June 7:** Hough pitched the 103rd complete game of his career (a three-hitter). It was the first time he'd gone the distance since August 1991.

▸**June 9:** Frank Thomas provided the offense for the White Sox in their win against the Angels, going 3-for-4 and driving in three runs with a homer and a triple.

▸**June 23:** McDowell got his 10th win, a complete game vs. Cleveland.

▸**June 26:** Robin Ventura became the first lefty batter to homer off of righty John Habyan since July 1988.

▸**July 1:** Craig Grebeck had the first five-hit game of his career in an 8-5 win against Cleveland. Grebeck, who had three doubles, was hitting .462 in his last 11 games.

▸**July 2:** Wilson Alvarez's second no-hit bid in as many major league seasons was spoiled in the seventh by a Wade Boggs single. His shutout bid was then ruined by the next batter, Tom Brunansky, who homered. Alvarez still got the win though, thanks in part to Frank Thomas' three hits and two RBI.

▸**July 9:** Thomas was 4-for-4 with a two-run homer, and red-hot George Bell added a three-run shot as the White Sox beat the Red Sox 10-3.

▸**July 20:** Lance Johnson had his seventh three-hit game (.405 in the last 11 games). ***Quote of the day:*** Hough, who had two no-decisions and a loss in his last three starts in pursuit of his 200th win—"I figure if I pitch long enough, I'm going to win another game somewhere along the line. But I was kind of hoping it would be tonight."

▸**July 25:** Poor Charlie. Once again, he almost made it to No. 200, but ex-White Soxer Scott Fletcher hit a three-run homer in the bottom of the ninth, driving in all of the runs in Milwaukee's 3-0 victory over Chicago.

▸**July 29:** Tim Raines was 3-for-6 with four RBI in an 8-6 White Sox win against Detroit, with the Sox rallying for six runs in the ninth.

▸**August 4:** The White Sox had a season-high 19 hits and 19 runs against the Twins.

▸**August 18:** McDowell tossed his major league-leading 10th complete game of the season, yet notched just his first shutout of the year.

▸**September 8:** The White Sox swept the Tigers by identical 4-3 scores in a doubleheader. In the opener, McDowell became the majors' first 20-game winner this year.

▸**September 15:** Frank Thomas' two-run double in the eighth inning provided a 4-2 win for Chicago against the Yankees. It gave him over 100 RBI for the second year in a row, the first time a White Sox' player had back-to-back 100-RBI seasons since Minnie Minoso did it 38 years earlier.

▸**September 20 *Milestone:*** Bobby Thigpen collected the 200th save of his career, becoming the 14th player in history to reach that mark—and the youngest ever (28).

▸**October 4:** The White Sox finished third in the AL West, 10 games behind Oakland. Frank Thomas was among the league's top five in eight categories: batting (third, .323); RBI (third, 115); doubles (second, 46); runs (second, 108), hits (fifth, 185); total bases (fourth, 307); walks (second, 122); slugging (third, .536) and on-base percentage (first, .439). Jack Mc Dowell was in the top five in four pitching categories: victories (third, 20-10); complete games (first, 13); strikeouts (fifth, 178) and innings (third, 260 2/3).

—by Jeanie Chung, John Hunt, Deron Snyder, and Lisa Winston.

Team directory

▸**Owner:** Jerry Reinsdorf (chairman), Eddie Einhorn (vice-chairman), and a board of directors

▸**General Manager:** Ron Schueler

▸**Ballpark:**
Comiskey Park
333 West 35th St., Chicago, Ill.
312-924-1000
Capacity 44,177
Parking for 7,000 vehicles; $6
public transportation available
Kids Corner (with photo booth and uniforms for imitation baseball cards), elevators and seating for the handicapped, escalators, ramps, cash station, Hall of Fame

▸**Team publications:**
Program, yearbook, media guide, calendar, Comiskey Park auction catalogs, team photos, and player photos
312-451-5300

▸**TV, radio broadcast stations:**
WMAQ 670 AM, WGN TV-9, SportsChannel Chicago

▸**Camps and/or clinics:**
Fantasy Camp, February, 312-991-9595

▸**Spring Training:**
Ed Smith Stadium
Sarasota, Fla.
Capacity 7,500
813-953-3388

CHICAGO WHITE SOX 1992 final stats

Batting	AVG	SLG	OB	G	AB	R	H	TB	2B	3B	HR	RBI	BB	SO	SB	CS	E
Santovenia	.333	1.333	.333	2	3	1	1	4	0	0	1	2	0	0	0	0	0
Thomas	.323	.536	.439	160	573	108	185	307	46	2	24	115	122	88	6	3	13
Raines	.294	.405	.380	144	551	102	162	223	22	9	7	54	81	48	45	6	2
Ventura	.282	.431	.375	157	592	85	167	255	38	1	16	93	93	71	2	4	23
Abner	.279	.351	.323	97	208	21	58	73	10	1	1	16	12	35	1	2	0
Johnson	.279	.363	.318	157	567	67	158	206	15	12	3	47	34	33	41	14	6
Grebeck	.268	.387	.341	88	287	24	77	111	21	2	3	35	30	34	0	3	8
Bell	.255	.418	.294	155	627	74	160	262	27	0	25	112	31	97	5	2	1
Cora	.246	.320	.371	68	122	27	30	39	7	1	0	9	22	13	10	3	3
Karkovice	.237	.392	.302	123	342	39	81	134	12	1	13	50	30	89	10	4	6
Sax	.236	.317	.290	143	567	74	134	180	26	4	4	47	43	42	30	12	20
Fisk	.229	.309	.313	62	188	12	43	58	4	1	3	21	23	38	3	0	2
Hemond	.225	.275	.289	25	40	8	9	11	2	0	0	2	4	13	1	0	1
Newson	.221	.265	.387	63	136	19	30	36	3	0	1	11	37	38	3	0	0
Sveum	.219	.351	.287	40	114	15	25	40	9	0	2	12	12	29	1	1	8
Pasqua	.211	.347	.305	93	265	26	56	92	16	1	6	33	36	57	0	1	6
Huff	.209	.252	.273	60	115	13	24	29	5	0	0	8	10	24	1	2	0
Guillen	.200	.300	.214	12	40	5	8	12	4	0	0	7	1	5	1	0	0
Beltre	.191	.236	.211	49	110	21	21	26	2	0	1	10	3	18	1	0	12
Merullo	.180	.240	.208	24	50	3	9	12	1	1	0	3	1	8	0	0	2
Jeter	.111	.111	.111	13	18	1	2	2	0	0	0	0	0	7	0	0	1
Cron	.000	.000	.000	6	10	0	0	0	0	0	0	0	0	4	0	0	1

Pitching	W-L	ERA	G	GS	CG	GF	Sho	SV	IP	H	R	ER	HR	BB	SO
Hernandez	7-3	1.65	43	0	0	27	0	12	71	45	15	13	4	20	68
Leach	6-5	1.95	51	0	0	21	0	0	73.2	57	17	16	2	20	22
Drahman	0-0	2.57	5	0	0	2	0	0	7	6	3	2	0	2	1
Radinsky	3-7	2.73	68	0	0	33	0	15	59.1	54	21	18	3	34	48
McDowell	20-10	3.18	34	34	13	0	1	0	260.2	247	95	92	21	75	178
Hough	7-12	3.93	27	27	4	0	0	0	176.1	160	88	77	19	66	76
McCaskill	12-13	4.18	34	34	0	0	0	0	209	193	116	97	11	95	109
Dunne	2-0	4.26	4	1	0	0	0	0	12.2	12	7	6	0	6	6
Fernandez	8-11	4.27	29	29	4	0	2	0	187.2	199	100	89	21	50	95
Hibbard	10-7	4.40	31	28	0	2	0	1	176	187	92	86	17	57	69
Thigpen	1-3	4.75	55	0	0	40	0	22	55	58	29	29	4	33	45
Pall	5-2	4.93	39	0	0	12	0	1	73	79	43	40	9	27	27
Alvarez	5-3	5.20	34	9	0	4	0	1	100.1	103	64	58	12	65	66

1993 preliminary roster

PITCHERS (18)
Wilson Alvarez
Jason Bere
Rodney Bolton
Brian Drahman
Mike Dunne
Rob Ellis
Alex Fernandez
Ramon Garcia
Roberto Hernandez
Terry Leach
Kirk McCaskill
Jack McDowell
Donn Pall
Scott Radinsky
Johnny Ruffin
Jeff Schwarz
Dave Steib
Bobby Thigpen

CATCHERS (4)
Carlton Fisk
Scott Hemond
Ron Karkovice
Matt Merullo

INFIELDERS (11)
Esteban Beltre
Joey Cora
Chris Cron
Shawn Gilbert
Craig Grebeck
Ozzie Guillen
Norberto Martin
Steve Sax
Frank Thomas
Robin Ventura
Brandon Wilson

OUTFIELDERS (8)
Shawn Abner
George Bell
Mike Huff
Bo Jackson
Lance Johnson
Warren Newson
Dan Pasqua
Tim Raines

Games played by position

Player	G	C	1B	2B	3B	SS	OF	DH
ABNER,S	97	0	0	0	0	0	94	1
BELL,G	155	0	0	0	0	0	15	140
BELTRE,E	49	0	0	0	0	43	0	4
CORA,J	68	0	0	28	5	6	0	18
CRON,C	6	0	5	0	0	0	1	0
FISK,C	62	54	0	0	0	0	0	2
GREBECK,C	88	0	0	0	7	85	2	0
GUILLEN,O	12	0	0	0	0	12	0	0
HEMOND,S	25	9	0	0	3	3	4	5
HUFF,M	60	0	0	0	0	0	56	1
JETER,S	13	0	0	0	0	0	8	3
JOHNSON,L	157	0	0	0	0	0	157	0
KARKOVICE,R	123	119	0	0	0	0	1	0
MERULLO,M	24	16	0	0	0	0	0	1
NEWSON,W	63	0	0	0	0	0	50	4
PASQUA,D	93	0	5	0	0	0	81	1
RAINES,T	144	0	0	0	0	0	129	14
SANTOVENIA,N	2	2	0	0	0	0	0	0
SAX,S	143	0	0	141	0	0	0	1
SVEUM,D	40	0	2	0	2	37	0	0
THOMAS,F	160	0	158	0	0	0	0	2
VENTURA,R	157	0	2	0	157	0	0	0

Sick call: 1992 DL report

Player	Days on the DL
Fisk, Carlton	59
Grebeck, Craig	57
Guillen, Ozzie	166
Huff, Mike	76
Jackson, Bo	182
Pasqua, Dan*	36

** On Disabled List twice during 1992 season (not counting transfers from one DL to another).*

Minor league report

Class AAA — Vancouver finished 81-61, 1st in the 1st half of the Pacific Coast League Northern Division and 2nd in the 2nd half. The team lost to Colorado Springs in three games for the league championship. RHP Brian Drahman set a league record with 30 saves. RHPs Mike Dunne and Rodney Bolton finished 1-2 in ERA at 2.78 and 2.93 respectively. OF Shawn Jeter hit .301. 1B Chris Cron had 16 HR and 81 RBI. **Class AA:** Birmingham finished 68-74, 4th in the 1st half of the Southern League Western Division and 2nd in the 2nd half. 1B Scott Cepicky led the league in RBI with 87. LHP Larry Thomas won the league ERA title at 1.94. RHP Bo Kennedy was 10-7 with a 2.38 ERA. **Class A:** Sarasota finished 85-48, 1st in the 1st half of the Florida State League West Division and 3rd in the 2nd half. The team lost to Baseball City in the 1st round of the playoffs. SS Brandon Wilson hit .296 with 4 HR and 54 RBI in 103 games before his promotion to Birmingham. RHP Steve Schrenck was 15-2 with a 2.05 ERA. RHP Scott Ruffcorn was 14-5 with a 2.19. South Bend finished 73-64, 3rd in the 1st half of the Midwest League Northern Division and 2nd in the 2nd half. 2B Essex Burton won the league SB crown with 65. RHP James Baldwin was 9-5 with a 2.42 and 137 K in 138 IP. RHP Jeff Pierce had 30 saves. Utica finished 42-32, 1st in the New York-Penn League McNamara Division. The team lost to Geneva in the 1st round of the playoffs. OF Byron Mathews won the league SB title with 42. LHP Jason Pierson was 8-2 with a 2.25 ERA. RHP Steve Gajkowski had 14 saves. White Sox finished 30-29, 4th in the Gulf Coast League Western Division. OF Juan Thomas shared the league HR crown with 6. RHP Chris Gay was 5-3 with a 1.32 ERA. RHP Ricky Bennett had a 1.85 ERA.

Tops in the organization

BATTING LEADERS	Club	Avg.	G	AB	R	H	HR	RBI
Shawn Jeter	Van	.301	96	379	61	114	2	34
Jerry Wolak	Bir	.291	136	501	65	146	5	52
Brandon Wilson	Bir	.291	130	506	78	147	4	58
Norberto Martin	Van	.288	135	497	72	143	0	29
Joe Hall	Van	.283	112	367	46	104	6	56

HOME RUNS		
Chris Cron	Van	16
Scott Cepicky	Bir	14
Drew Denson	Van	13
Mike Robertson	Bir	11
Brad Komminsk	Van	10

WINS		
Steve Olsen	Bir	17
Steve Schrenk	Bir	16
Scott Ruffcorn	Sar	14
Larry Thomas	Bir	13
Greg Perschke	Van	12

RBI		
Scott Cepicky	Bir	87
Chris Cron	Van	81
Drew Denson	Van	70
Mike Robertson	Bir	68
Brad Komminsk	Van	68

SAVES		
Brian Drahman	Van	30
Jeff Pierce	Sar	30
Don Perigny	Sar	20
Frank Campos	Bir	10
Jeff Schwarz	Van	9

STOLEN BASES		
Essex Burton	Sbn	65
Brandon Wilson	Bir	35
Kerry Valrie	Sar	35
Eric Yelding	Van	32
Norberto Martin	Van	29

STRIKEOUTS		
James Baldwin	Sar	176
Jason Bere	Van	153
Alan Levine	Sar	142
Scott Ruffcorn	Sar	140
Steve Olsen	Bir	131

PITCHING LEADERS	Club	W-L	ERA	IP	H	BB	SO
Larry Thomas	Bir	13-6	1.84	176	146	37	122
Steve Schrenk	Bir	16-3	2.16	166	143	51	122
Scott Ruffcorn	Sar	14-5	2.19	160	122	39	140
Robert Ellis	Sbn	6-5	2.34	123	90	35	97
Steve Olsen	Bir	17-5	2.45	165	136	61	131

Chicago (1901-1992)

Runs: Most, career, all-time

1319 Luke Appling, 1930-1950
1187 Nellie Fox, 1950-1963
1065 Eddie Collins, 1915-1926
893 Minnie Minoso, 1951-1980
791 Luis Aparicio, 1956-1970

Hits: Most, career, all-time

2749 Luke Appling, 1930-1950
2470 Nellie Fox, 1950-1963
2007 Eddie Collins, 1915-1926
1576 Luis Aparicio, 1956-1970
1523 Minnie Minoso, 1951-1980

2B: Most, career, all-time

440 Luke Appling, 1930-1950
335 Nellie Fox, 1950-1963
267 HAROLD BAINES, 1980-1989
266 Eddie Collins, 1915-1926
260 Minnie Minoso, 1951-1980

3B: Most, career, all-time

104 Shano Collins, 1910-1920
104 Nellie Fox, 1950-1963
102 Luke Appling, 1930-1950
102 Eddie Collins, 1915-1926
82 Johnny Mostil, 1918-1929

HR: Most, career, all-time

213 CARLTON FISK, 1981-1992
186 HAROLD BAINES, 1980-1989
154 Bill Melton, 1968-1975
140 Ron Kittle, 1982-1991
135 Minnie Minoso, 1951-1980

RBI: Most, career, all-time

1116 Luke Appling, 1930-1950
819 HAROLD BAINES, 1980-1989
808 Minnie Minoso, 1951-1980
804 Eddie Collins, 1915-1926
758 CARLTON FISK, 1981-1992

SB: Most, career, all-time

368 Eddie Collins, 1915-1926
318 Luis Aparicio, 1956-1970
250 Frank Isbell, 1901-1909
206 Fielder Jones, 1901-1908
192 Shano Collins, 1910-1920

BB: Most, career, all-time

1302 Luke Appling, 1930-1950
965 Eddie Collins, 1915-1926
658 Nellie Fox, 1950-1963
658 Minnie Minoso, 1951-1980
638 Ray Schalk, 1912-1928

BA: Highest, career, all-time

.340 Joe Jackson, 1915-1920
.331 Eddie Collins, 1915-1926
.317 Zeke Bonura, 1934-1937
.315 Bibb Falk, 1920-1928
.312 Taffy Wright, 1940-1948

Slug avg: Highest, career, all-time

.518 Zeke Bonura, 1934-1937
.499 Joe Jackson, 1915-1920
.470 Ron Kittle, 1982-1991
.468 Minnie Minoso, 1951-1980
.464 HAROLD BAINES, 1980-1989

Games started: Most, career, all-time

484 Ted Lyons, 1923-1946
483 Red Faber, 1914-1933
390 Billy Pierce, 1949-1961
312 Ed Walsh, 1904-1916
301 Doc White, 1903-1913

Saves: Most, career, all-time

200 BOBBY THIGPEN, 1986-1992
98 Hoyt Wilhelm, 1963-1968
75 Terry Forster, 1971-1976
57 Wilbur Wood, 1967-1978
56 Bob James, 1985-1987

Shutouts: Most, career, all-time

57 Ed Walsh, 1904-1916
42 Doc White, 1903-1913
35 Billy Pierce, 1949-1961
29 Red Faber, 1914-1933
28 Eddie Cicotte, 1912-1920

Wins: Most, career, all-time

260 Ted Lyons, 1923-1946
254 Red Faber, 1914-1933
195 Ed Walsh, 1904-1916
186 Billy Pierce, 1949-1961
163 Wilbur Wood, 1967-1978

K: Most, career, all-time

1796 Billy Pierce, 1949-1961
1732 Ed Walsh, 1904-1916
1471 Red Faber, 1914-1933
1332 Wilbur Wood, 1967-1978
1098 Gary Peters, 1959-1969

Win pct: Highest, career, all-time

.648 Lefty Williams, 1916-1920
.644 Virgil Trucks, 1953-1955
.616 Jim Kaat, 1973-1975
.615 Juan Pizarro, 1961-1966
.609 Ed Walsh, 1904-1916

ERA: Lowest, career, all-time

1.81 Ed Walsh, 1904-1916
2.18 Frank Smith, 1904-1910
2.25 Eddie Cicotte, 1912-1920
2.30 Jim Scott, 1909-1917
2.30 Doc White, 1903-1913

Runs: Most, season

135 Johnny Mostil, 1925
120 Zeke Bonura, 1936
120 Fielder Jones, 1901
120 Johnny Mostil, 1926
120 Rip Radcliff, 1936

Hits: Most, season

224 Eddie Collins, 1920
218 Joe Jackson, 1920
208 Buck Weaver, 1920
207 Rip Radcliff, 1936
204 Luke Appling, 1936

2B: Most, season

46 FRANK THOMAS, 1992
45 Floyd Robinson, 1962
44 IVAN CALDERON, 1990
44 Chet Lemon, 1979
43 Bibb Falk, 1926
43 Earl Sheely, 1925

3B: Most, season

21 Joe Jackson, 1916
20 Joe Jackson, 1920
18 Jack Fournier, 1915
18 Harry Lord, 1911
18 Minnie Minoso, 1954
18 Carl Reynolds, 1930

HR: Most, season

37 Dick Allen, 1972
37 CARLTON FISK, 1985
35 Ron Kittle, 1983
33 Bill Melton, 1970
33 Bill Melton, 1971

RBI: Most, season

138 Zeke Bonura, 1936
128 Luke Appling, 1936
121 Joe Jackson, 1920
119 Al Simmons, 1933
117 Eddie Robinson, 1951

SB: Most, season

77 Rudy Law, 1983
56 Luis Aparicio, 1959
56 Wally Moses, 1943
53 Luis Aparicio, 1961
53 Eddie Collins, 1917

BB: Most, season

138 FRANK THOMAS, 1991
127 Lu Blue, 1931
122 Luke Appling, 1935
122 FRANK THOMAS, 1992
121 Luke Appling, 1949

BA: Highest, season

.388 Luke Appling, 1936
.382 Joe Jackson, 1920
.372 Eddie Collins, 1920
.360 Eddie Collins, 1923
.359 Carl Reynolds, 1930

Slug avg: Highest, season

.603 Dick Allen, 1972
.589 Joe Jackson, 1920
.584 Carl Reynolds, 1930
.573 Zeke Bonura, 1937
.563 Dick Allen, 1974

Games started: Most, season

49 Ed Walsh, 1908
49 Wilbur Wood, 1972
48 Wilbur Wood, 1973
46 Ed Walsh, 1907
43 Wilbur Wood, 1975

Saves: Most, season

57 BOBBY THIGPEN, 1990
34 BOBBY THIGPEN, 1988
34 BOBBY THIGPEN, 1989
32 Bob James, 1985
30 Ed Farmer, 1980
30 BOBBY THIGPEN, 1991

Shutouts: Most, season

11 Ed Walsh, 1908
10 Ed Walsh, 1906
8 Reb Russell, 1913
8 Ed Walsh, 1909
8 Wilbur Wood, 1972

Wins: Most, season

40 Ed Walsh, 1908
29 Eddie Cicotte, 1919
28 Eddie Cicotte, 1917
27 Ed Walsh, 1911
27 Ed Walsh, 1912
27 Doc White, 1907

K: Most, season

269 Ed Walsh, 1908
258 Ed Walsh, 1910
255 Ed Walsh, 1911
254 Ed Walsh, 1912
215 Gary Peters, 1967

Win pct: Highest, season

.842 Sandy Consuegra, 1954
.806 Eddie Cicotte, 1919
.774 Clark Griffith, 1901
.759 Richard Dotson, 1983
.750 Reb Russell, 1917
.750 Bob Shaw, 1959
.750 Monty Stratton, 1937
.750 Doc White, 1906

ERA: Lowest, season

1.27 Ed Walsh, 1910
1.41 Ed Walsh, 1909
1.42 Ed Walsh, 1908
1.52 Doc White, 1906
1.53 Eddie Cicotte, 1917

Most pinch-hit homers, season

3 Ron Northey, 1956
3 John Romano, 1959
3 Oscar Gamble, 1977

Most pinch-hit, homers, career

7 Jerry Hairston, 1973-1989

Most consecutive games, batting safely

27 Luke Appling, 1936
26 Guy Curtwright, 1943
25 Lance Johnson, 1992

Most consecutive scoreless innings

45 Doc White, 1904
39 Billy Pierce, 1953
39 Ed Walsh, 1906
38 Ray Herbert, 1963
37 Ed Walsh, 1910
37 Joel Horlen, 1968

No hit games

Nixey Callahan, Chi vs Det AL, 3-0; September 20, 1902 (1st game).
Frank Smith, Chi at Det AL, 15-0; September 6, 1905 (2nd game).
Frank Smith, Chi vs Phi AL, 1-0; September 20, 1908.
Ed Walsh, Chi vs Bos AL, 5-0; August 27, 1911.
Jim Scott, Chi at Was AL, 0-1; May 14, 1914 (lost on 2 hits in the tenth).
Joe Benz, Chi vs Cle AL, 6-1; May 31, 1914.
Eddie Cicotte, Chi at StL AL, 11-0; April 14, 1917.
Charlie Robertson, Chi at Det AL, 2-0; April 30, 1922 (perfect game).
Ted Lyons, Chi at Bos AL, 6-0; August 21, 1926.
Vern Kennedy, Chi vs Cle AL, 5-0; August 31, 1935.
Bill Dietrich, Chi vs StL AL, 8-0; June 1, 1937.
Bob Keegan, Chi vs Was AL, 6-0; August 20, 1957 (2nd game).
Joe Horlen, Chi vs Det AL, 6-0; September 10, 1967 (1st game).
Blue Moon Odom (5 innings) and Francisco Barrios (4 innings), Chi at Oak AL, 2-1; July 28, 1976.
Joe Cowley, Chi at Cal AL, 7-1; September 19, 1986.
Wilson Alvarez, Chi at Bal AL, 7-0; August 11, 1991.
Ed Walsh, five innings, rain, Chi vs NY AL, 8-1; May 26, 1907.
Melido Perez, six innings, rain, Chi at NY AL, 8-0; July 12, 1990.

ACTIVE PLAYERS in caps.

Texas Rangers

by Russell Beeker, *Baseball Weekly*

Juan Gonzalez won the AL home run crown (43) had 109 RBI and 309 total bases, but wasn't an All-Star.

1992 Rangers: Reversal of fortune

Just when it seemed the Rangers might become a perennial contender, they slid back to the bottom of the hill—again. In their 20-year history in Texas, they have finished second four times; three of those times, they finished worse the following season.

In 1991, the Rangers had improved for the third straight year, and all signs pointed to a strong pennant bid in '92. But the Rangers reversed their trend and finished fourth in the AL West, 19 games behind the A's.

The first casualty of the poor season was manager Bobby Valentine, even though the team was 45-41 when he was fired July 9. Bench coach Toby Harrah took over and posted a 32-44 record; Kevin Kennedy was chosen to manage in '93.

The rebuilding started on Aug. 31, when general manager Tom Grieve engineered the biggest deal in team history, acquiring Jose Canseco from the A's for outfielder Ruben Sierra and pitchers Jeff Russell and Bobby Witt. Both Sierra and Russell were free agents at the end of the season; the deal freed up about $5 million.

Texas was worst in the AL and second-worst in the majors in defense. They led the league in errors at shortstop, catcher, and all three outfield positions. Their offense suffered as well; after leading the league in runs scored in '91, they fell to 10th in '92. Julio Franco had one of the worst dropoffs in history by a defending batting champion, from .341 to .234 (108 at-bats). Rafael Palmeiro fell to .268 from .322.

But Juan Gonzalez became the first Texas player to win the AL home run title (43). He edged Canseco's former "Bash Brother" Mark McGwire on the final day of the season. He also had 109 RBI, passing the century mark for the second time. Dean Palmer and Ivan Rodriguez showed tremendous promise. Rodriguez, 20, was named to the All-Star team and hit .260 with eight homers, while Palmer hit 26 homers and drove in 72 runs in his first full season in the majors.

Meanwhile the mound corps often wasted the little offense that was provided. The bullpen led the league in blown saves and home runs allowed, and the team was outscored by more than a run per game in both the sixth and seventh innings, a sure sign of middle- and long-relief collapse.

Nolan Ryan suffered through his first losing season since 1987 (5-9), but he lost five victories to blown saves, and got zero runs from the team four times.

Kevin Brown was 21-11 (3.32 ERA), the first Ranger to win 20 games since Ferguson Jenkins in 1973. He led the AL with 265 innings, tied for most victories, and was second in complete games (11). Jose Guzman, just two years after major shoulder reconstruction, had career highs in wins (16), innings (224) and strikeouts (179).

—by Rick Lawes

1993 Rangers: Preview

Even though they can't entirely reverse the poor fielding, poor clutch hitting, and spotty pitching that led to fourth-place in '92, the Rangers have installed some big fixes for '93. New manager Kevin Kennedy will stress the fundamentals while Jose Canseco and Juan Gonzalez form a new "Bash Brothers." Kevin Brown will make a run at another 20 wins, with All-Star Ivan Rodriguez behind the plate. There's even addition by subtraction: Kevin Reimer's bad glove isn't in the outfield anymore.

But too many holes remain: Julio Franco's knee remains a question, Nolan Ryan must rebound from a losing season, and the pitching is thin. The Rangers' pitching and defense gave away victories the offense had already won in '92; that trend may improve but it probably won't disappear.

—by Tim McQuay

1992 Rangers: Between the lines

▸**April 29:** Jose Guzman pitched six no-hit innings and finally surrendered a home run to Yankee catcher Matt Nokes, then a single to Kevin Maas in the Rangers' 5-1 win over New York. It was his second complete game of the season and the third two-hitter of his career.

▸**May 2:** Texas overcame 11 walks to beat fellow AL West contender Chicago 4-1 in 11 innings. Four of the Rangers' eight hits came in the 11th, but Rafael Palmeiro broke the tie with a sacrifice fly.

▸**May 13:** Kevin Brown lost a game to Baltimore on his first seven pitches. The Orioles scored all of their runs on that septet.

▸**May 16:** Nolan Ryan remained winless. He left his start against the Brewers after six innings with a 4-1 lead, but the Brewers capped a ninth-inning rally off reliever Kenny Rogers to beat the Rangers 5-4.

▸**May 17:** Texas snapped a five-game losing streak when Jeff Huson tripled in a run with two outs in the 10th inning to beat Milwaukee 2-1.

▸**May 20:** Jose Guzman outdueled Cleveland ace Charles Nagy. Ruben Sierra's RBI single was the difference in the Rangers' 1-0 win.

▸**May 27:** Veteran Floyd Bannister recorded his first major league win since 1989 as Texas beat the White Sox 4-3. Texas moved into a tie with Oakland atop the AL West. Starter Nolan Ryan, the oldest player in the major leagues, and catcher Ivan "Pudge" Rodriguez, the youngest, were the Rangers' starting battery. Ryan had yet to win in 1992; the 52-day period marked the longest span in his 26-year career that he opened a season winless.

▸**May 31:** Kansas City edged Texas 7-6, knocking the Rangers from their spot atop the AL West.

▸**June 1:** For just the second time in 775 career appearances, Nolan Ryan failed to retire a batter. A strained hamstring forced his early exit.

▸**June 7:** Juan Gonzalez became the fifth player in Rangers' history to clout three home runs in a game. The last player was Larry Parrish in 1985.

▸**June 8 *Milestone:*** Ruben Sierra hit his 149th career home run, tying him with Larry Parrish for the all-time Texas lead.

▸**June 12:** In the Texas-Oakland game (A's 6, Rangers 5), a total of 15 pitchers took the mound, including still-winless Nolan Ryan.

▸**June 17:** It was good news, bad news for Ryan. He pitched his first complete game in more than a year, but it was a losing effort.

▸**June 19:** Juan Gonzalez hit a solo homer, his 17th of the season and 10th in the last 15 games.

▸**June 25:** Kevin Brown became the AL's first 11-game winner, tying his career high with nine strikeouts.

▸**June 26:** Juan Gonzalez tied a Texas record for home runs in a month with his 11th in June.

▸**June 28:** Nolan Ryan's 315th career win was his first of the season, an 8-4 victory over the Tigers. ***Quote of the day:*** Detroit third baseman Scott Livingstone, who lives in Texas in the off-season, on being happy just to make contact against Ryan—"He's a wonder. I was happy to hit the ball, but I'm not going to say much about that. He might end up being our governor, and I don't want him to raise my taxes."

▸**June 30:** Kevin Brown became the first 12-game winner in the majors.

▸**July 4:** Nolan Ryan extended his own major league record by striking out 10 or more batters for the 214th time in his career. His 13 Ks were the most by an AL pitcher in 1992.

▸**July 9:** Toby Harrah got the 14-4 win over Cleveland in his debut as skipper of the Rangers. Nolan Ryan improved his record to 3-3; he had eight strike-outs in seven innings.

▸**July 11:** Kevin Brown became the first 14-game winner in the majors, turning in a complete game on just 93 pitches to defeat Cleveland 5-1.

▸**July 26:** Juan Gonzalez's 450-foot homer to dead center was the longest hit yet at Camden Yards, and was the crusher as well in the Rangers' 6-2 win over the Orioles. ***Milestone:*** Nolan Ryan struck out his hundredth batter of the season, a major-league-record 23rd year in a row that he's reached that plateau. He also got his 319th win, to pass Phil Niekro and take over the No. 12 spot on the all-time victory list.

▸**August 6:** Nolan Ryan was ejected with two outs in the eighth inning, after hitting Oakland's Willie Wilson in the leg with a pitch. Ryan said he couldn't remember ever being ejected in his 26 years as a major leaguer.

▸**August 14:** Juan Gonzalez hit two homers in the Rangers' 9-6 loss to the Tigers, setting a team record with his fifth multi-home-run game of 1992.

▸**August 15:** Bobby Witt tied a team record by issuing 10 walks.

▸**August 20:** Rookie Roger Pavlik came within a strike of a shutout for his first major league win.

▸**August 23:** Juan Gonzalez set a team record with his 34th homer, his second of the game in a 14-4 win against Cleveland.

▸**August 28:** Kevin Brown picked up his 17th win, taking a no-hitter into the seventh inning.

▸**August 29:** Juan Gonzalez was closing in on Mark McGwire's major-league-leading total of 38 homers as he hit two, bringing his total to 36.

▸**August 31:** Jose Canseco started for Oakland against Baltimore, then learned he was traded to Texas (for pitchers Jeff Russell and Bobby Witt, outfielder Ruben Sierra, and cash) before his first at-bat. ***Quote of the day:*** Twins' manager Tom Kelly, on the Canseco trade—"Wait until the Texas highway patrol gets hold of that car."

▸**September 4:** Canseco was 0-for-4 with a run-scoring groundout in his debut as a Texas Ranger.

▸**September 9:** Canseco accounted for all of the Rangers' runs in their 3-2 win against the Red Sox.

▸**September 23:** Kevin Brown became the second 20-game winner in the AL and joined Ferguson Jenkins as just the second 20-game winner in club history.

▸**October 4:** The Rangers finished fourth in the AL West, 19 games behind Oakland. Juan Gonzalez won the home run race with 43, one more than Mark McGwire. Kevin Brown was second in the league in victories (21-11). He had as many wins as Toronto's Jack Morris, but lost five more decisions.

—by Jeanie Chung, John Hunt, Deron Snyder, and Lisa Winston.

Team directory

▸**Owner:** George W. Bush and Edward W. Rose

▸**General Manager:** Thomas A. Grieve

▸**Ballpark:**
Arlington Stadium
1700 Copeland Rd., Arlington, Texas
817-273-5000
Capacity 43,521
Parking for 12,000 vehicles; $5
Public transportation available
Family and wheelchair sections, ramps

▸**Team publications:**
On Deck Newsletter, Yearbook, Program Magazine
817-273-5222

▸**TV, radio broadcast stations:**
WBAP-AM 820, KTVT-TV 11, Home Sports Entertainment

▸**Camps and/or clinics:**
Texas Ranger Coaches Clinic, June, 817-273-5222

▸**Spring Training:**
Charlotte County Stadium
Port Charlotte, Fla.
Capacity 6,026
813-625-9500

TEXAS RANGERS 1992 final stats

Batting	AVG	SLG	OB	G	AB	R	H	TB	2B	3B	HR	RBI	BB	SO	SB	CS	E
Davis	1.000	1.000	1.000	1	1	0	1	1	0	0	0	0	0	0	0	0	0
Hulse	.304	.348	.326	32	92	14	28	32	4	0	0	2	3	18	3	1	1
Downing	.278	.428	.407	107	320	53	89	137	18	0	10	39	62	58	1	0	0
Palmeiro	.268	.434	.352	159	608	84	163	264	27	4	22	85	72	83	2	3	7
Reimer	.267	.437	.336	148	494	56	132	216	32	2	16	58	42	103	2	4	11
Huson	.261	.362	.342	123	318	49	83	115	14	3	4	24	41	43	18	6	9
Gonzalez	.260	.529	.304	155	584	77	152	309	24	2	43	109	35	143	0	1	10
Rodriguez	.260	.360	.300	123	420	39	109	151	16	1	8	37	24	73	0	0	15
Frye	.256	.327	.320	67	199	24	51	65	9	1	1	12	16	27	1	3	7
Thon	.247	.367	.293	95	275	30	68	101	15	3	4	37	20	40	12	2	15
Canseco	.244	.456	.344	119	439	74	107	200	15	0	26	87	63	128	6	7	3
McGinnis	.242	.364	.306	14	33	2	8	12	4	0	0	4	3	7	0	0	0
Franco	.234	.355	.328	35	107	19	25	38	7	0	2	8	15	17	1	1	3
Palmer	.229	.420	.311	152	541	74	124	227	25	0	26	72	62	154	10	4	22
Diaz	.226	.258	.250	19	31	2	7	8	1	0	0	1	1	2	0	1	1
Maurer	.222	.222	.300	8	9	1	2	2	0	0	0	1	1	2	0	0	0
Newman	.220	.240	.317	116	246	25	54	59	5	0	0	12	34	26	9	6	8
Fariss	.217	.325	.297	67	166	13	36	54	7	1	3	21	17	51	0	2	0
Daugherty	.205	.276	.295	59	127	13	26	35	9	0	0	9	16	21	2	1	2
Petralli	.198	.276	.274	94	192	11	38	53	12	0	1	18	20	34	0	0	4
Cangelosi	.188	.247	.330	73	85	12	16	21	2	0	1	6	18	16	6	5	3
Harris	.182	.212	.182	24	33	3	6	7	1	0	0	1	0	15	1	0	1
Colon	.167	.167	.189	14	36	5	6	6	0	0	0	1	1	8	0	0	3
Peltier	.167	.167	.167	12	24	1	4	4	0	0	0	2	0	3	0	0	1
Stephens	.154	.154	.154	8	13	0	2	2	0	0	0	0	0	5	0	0	0
Jo.Russell	.100	.100	.231	7	10	1	1	1	0	0	0	2	1	4	0	0	1

Pitching	W-L	ERA	G	GS	CG	GF	Sho	SV	IP	H	R	ER	HR	BB	SO
Whiteside	1-1	1.93	20	0	0	8	0	4	28	26	8	6	1	11	13
Rogers	3-6	3.09	81	0	0	38	0	6	78.2	80	32	27	7	26	70
Brown	21-11	3.32	35	35	11	0	1	0	265.2	262	117	98	11	76	173
Chiamparino	0-4	3.55	4	4	0	0	0	0	25.1	25	11	10	2	5	13
Guzman	16-11	3.66	33	33	5	0	0	0	224	229	103	91	17	73	179
Ryan	5-9	3.72	27	27	2	0	0	0	157.1	138	75	65	9	69	157
Burns	3-5	3.84	35	10	0	9	0	1	103	97	54	44	8	32	55
Fireovid	1-0	4.05	3	0	0	0	0	0	6.2	10	5	3	0	4	0
Pavlik	4-4	4.21	13	12	1	0	0	0	62	66	32	29	3	34	45
Manuel	1-0	4.76	3	0	0	0	0	0	5.2	6	3	3	2	1	9
Nunez	1-3	4.85	49	0	0	16	0	3	59.1	63	34	32	6	22	49
Smith	0-3	5.02	4	2	0	1	0	0	14.1	18	8	8	1	8	5
McCullers	1-0	5.40	5	0	0	1	0	0	5	1	4	3	0	8	3
Robinson	4-4	5.72	16	4	0	2	0	0	45.2	50	30	29	6	21	18
Leon	1-1	5.89	15	0	0	3	0	0	18.1	18	14	12	5	10	15
Mathews	2-4	5.95	40	0	0	11	0	0	42.1	48	29	28	4	31	26
Bohanon	1-1	6.31	18	7	0	3	0	0	45.2	57	38	32	7	25	29
Bannister	1-1	6.32	36	0	0	8	0	0	37	39	27	26	3	21	30
Jeffcoat	0-1	7.32	6	3	0	2	0	0	19.2	28	17	16	2	5	6
Carman	0-0	7.71	2	0	0	1	0	0	2.1	4	3	2	0	0	2
Rosenthal	0-0	7.71	6	0	0	2	0	0	4.2	7	4	4	1	2	1
Campbell	0-1	9.82	1	0	0	0	0	0	3.2	3	4	4	1	2	2
Alexander	1-0	27.00	3	0	0	1	0	0	1.2	5	5	5	1	1	1

1993 preliminary roster

PITCHERS (18)
Brian Bohanon
Jeff Bronkey
Kevin Brown
Todd Burns
Terry Burrows
Hector Fajardo
Pat Gomez
Tom Henke
Charlie Leibrandt
Danilo Leon
Barry Manuel
Robb Nen
Bob Patterson
Roger Pavlik
Kenny Rogers
Nolan Ryan
Dan Smith
Matt Whiteside

CATCHERS (3)
Geno Petralli
Ivan Rodriguez
Ray Stephens

INFIELDERS (8)
Cris Colon
Julio Franco
Jeff Frye
Jeff Huson
Rob Maurer
Rafael Palmeiro
Dean Palmer
Jon Shave

OUTFIELDERS (6)
Jose Canseco
Juan Gonzalez
Donald Harris
David Hulse
Keith Miller
Dan Peltier

Games played by position

Player	G	C	1B	2B	3B	SS	OF	DH
CANGELOSI,J	73	0	0	0	0	0	65	6
CANSECO,J	119	0	0	0	0	0	90	28
COLON,C	14	0	0	0	0	14	0	0
DAUGHERTY,J	59	0	8	0	0	0	26	13
DAVIS,D	1	1	0	0	0	0	0	0
DIAZ,M	19	0	0	3	1	16	0	0
DOWNING,B	107	0	0	0	0	0	0	93
FARISS,M	67	0	1	17	0	0	49	4
FRANCO,JU	35	0	0	9	0	0	4	15
FRYE,J	67	0	0	67	0	0	0	0
GONZALEZ,JU	155	0	0	0	0	0	148	4
HARRIS,D	24	0	0	0	0	0	24	0
HULSE,D	32	0	0	0	0	0	31	1
HUSON,J	123	0	0	47	0	82	2	1
MAURER,R	8	0	3	0	0	0	0	1
MCGINNIS,R	14	10	2	0	2	0	0	0
NEWMAN,A	116	0	0	72	28	20	1	1
PALMEIRO,R	159	0	156	0	0	0	0	2
PALMER,D	152	0	0	0	150	0	0	0
PELTIER,D	12	0	0	0	0	0	10	0
PETRALLI,G	94	54	0	2	4	0	0	14
REIMER,K	148	0	0	0	0	0	110	32
RODRIGUEZ,I	123	116	0	0	0	0	0	2
RUSSELL,JO	7	4	0	0	0	0	2	1
STEPHENS,R	8	6	0	0	0	0	0	1
THON,D	95	0	0	0	0	87	0	0

Sick call: 1992 DL report

Player	Days on the DL
Barfield, John	28
Bohanon, Brian	15
Chiamparino, Scott	112
Daugherty, Jack	91
Fajardo, Hector	112
Fariss, Monty	19
Franco, Julio**	129
Haselman, Bill	28
Jeffcoat, Mike	99
Leon, Danny*	78
Mathews, Terry	45
Rodriguez, Ivan	21
Russell, John	102
Ryan, Nolan	23
Thon, Dickie	37

** On Disabled List twice during 1992 season (not counting transfers from one DL to another).*

*** On Disabled List three times during 1992 season.*

Minor league report

Class AAA — Oklahoma City finished 74-70, 1st in the American Association Western Division. The team beat Buffalo in four games for the league championship. DH Steve Balboni led the league in HR with 30 and RBI with 104. RHP Roger Pavlik was 7-5 with a 2.98 ERA. 1B/C Russ McGinnis had 18 HR. **Class AA:** Tulsa finished 77-59, 2nd in the 1st half of the Texas League Eastern Division and 1st in the 2nd half. The team lost to Shreveport in the 1st round of the playoffs. 3B Jose Oliva had 75 RBI. RHP Dan Smith was the league's Pitcher of the Year, winning the ERA title at 2.52. He was 11-7. RHP Matt Whiteside had 21 saves, and did not blow a save opportunity during the period he was there before his promotion to Oklahoma City. **Class A:** Port Charlotte finished 73-62, 3rd in the 1st half of the Florida State League West Division and 4th in the 2nd half. OF Ben Castillo hit .282 with 7 HR and 55 RBI. RHP Steve Dreyer was 11-7 with a 2.40 ERA. OF Timmie Morrow had 18 SB. Gastonia finished 66-70, 6th in the 1st half of the Sally League Northern Division and 5th in the 2nd half. LHP Bo Magee was 7-9 with a 2.26 ERA. RHP Chris Curtis was 8-11 with a 2.63. RHP Kerry Lacy had 17 saves. The club led the league in ERA at 2.99. Butte finished 33-42, 3rd in the Pioneer League South Division. SS Richard Aurilia hit .337. 2B Franklin Parra had 24 SB. LHP Scott Eyre was 7-3 with a 2.90 ERA. He K'd 94 in 81 IP. Gulf Coast finished 28-31, 6th in the Gulf Coast League Western Division. 1B Chris Burr hit .340 and shared the league lead with 6 HR, winning the RBI title with 47. OF Hanley Frias had 26 SB. RHP Querbin Reinozo had 7 wins.

Tops in the organization

BATTING LEADERS	Club	Avg.	G	AB	R	H	HR	RBI
Jeff Frye	Okc	.300	87	337	64	101	2	28
Dan Peltier	Okc	.296	125	450	65	133	7	53
Rob Maurer	Okc	.288	135	493	76	142	10	82
Jon Shave	Tul	.287	118	453	57	130	2	36
Ben Castillo	Chl	.282	105	347	46	98	7	55

HOME RUNS		
Steve Balboni	Okc	30
Kevin Belcher	Okc	18
Russ McGinnis	Okc	18
Ken Powell	Gas	16
Jose Oliva	Tul	16

WINS		
Chris Gies	Tul	13
Joe Brownholtz	Chl	12
Kurt Miller	Tul	12
Several players tied		11

RBI		
Steve Balboni	Okc	104
Rob Maurer	Okc	82
Jose Oliva	Tul	75
Mike Burton	Chl	70
Kevin Belcher	Okc	60

SAVES		
Matt Whiteside	Okc	29
Kerry Lacy	Gas	17
Jeff Bronkey	Okc	16
Jose Alberro	Chl	16
Ritchie Moody	Tul	13

STOLEN BASES		
Benji Gil	Gas	26
David Lowery	Chl	24
David Hulse	Okc	19
Timmie Morrow	Chl	18
Ken Powell	Gas	15

STRIKEOUTS		
Daryl Henderson	Gas	138
Kurt Miller	Tul	131
Terry Burrows	Okc	125
Dan Smith	Tul	122
Steve Dreyer	Chl	111

PITCHING LEADERS	Club	W-L	ERA	IP	H	BB	SO
Terry Burrows	Okc	11-5	2.03	164	140	65	125
Bo Magee	Gas	7-9	2.26	151	113	82	109
Steve Dreyer	Chl	11-7	2.40	169	164	37	111
Dan Smith	Tul	11-7	2.52	146	110	34	122
Joe Brownholtz	Chl	12-7	2.61	145	133	30	104

Texas (1972-1992), incl. Washington (1961-1971)

Runs: Most, career, all-time

631 Toby Harrah, 1969-1986
571 RUBEN SIERRA, 1986-1992
544 Frank Howard, 1965-1972
482 Jim Sundberg, 1974-1989
471 Buddy Bell, 1979-1989

Hits: Most, career, all-time

1180 Jim Sundberg, 1974-1989
1174 Toby Harrah, 1969-1986
1141 Frank Howard, 1965-1972
1132 RUBEN SIERRA, 1986-1992
1060 Buddy Bell, 1979-1989

2B: Most, career, all-time

226 RUBEN SIERRA, 1986-1992
200 Jim Sundberg, 1974-1989
197 Buddy Bell, 1979-1989
187 Toby Harrah, 1969-1986
161 PETE O'BRIEN, 1982-1988

3B: Most, career, all-time

43 RUBEN SIERRA, 1986-1992
30 Chuck Hinton, 1961-1964
27 Ed Brinkman, 1961-1975
27 Jim Sundberg, 1974-1989
24 Ed Stroud, 1967-1970

HR: Most, career, all-time

246 Frank Howard, 1965-1972
153 RUBEN SIERRA, 1986-1992
149 Larry Parrish, 1982-1988
124 Toby Harrah, 1969-1986
124 PETE INCAVIGLIA, 1986-1990

RBI: Most, career, all-time

701 Frank Howard, 1965-1972
656 RUBEN SIERRA, 1986-1992
568 Toby Harrah, 1969-1986
522 Larry Parrish, 1982-1988
499 Buddy Bell, 1979-1989

SB: Most, career, all-time

161 Bump Wills, 1977-1981
153 Toby Harrah, 1969-1986
144 Dave Nelson, 1970-1975
115 Oddibe McDowell, 1985-1988
92 Chuck Hinton, 1961-1964
92 Bill Sample, 1978-1984

BB: Most, career, all-time

708 Toby Harrah, 1969-1986
575 Frank Howard, 1965-1972
544 Jim Sundberg, 1974-1989
435 Mike Hargrove, 1974-1978
404 PETE O'BRIEN, 1982-1988

BA: Highest, career, all-time

.319 Al Oliver, 1978-1981
.303 Mickey Rivers, 1979-1984
.297 RAFAEL PALMEIRO, 1989-1992
.293 Mike Hargrove, 1974-1978
.293 Buddy Bell, 1979-1989

Slug avg: Highest, career, all-time

.503 Frank Howard, 1965-1972
.471 RUBEN SIERRA, 1986-1992
.466 Al Oliver, 1978-1981
.459 PETE INCAVIGLIA, 1986-1990
.454 RAFAEL PALMEIRO, 1989-1992

Games started: Most, career, all-time

313 CHARLIE HOUGH, 1980-1990
190 Fergie Jenkins, 1974-1981
182 BOBBY WITT, 1986-1992
155 Dick Bosman, 1966-1973
152 JOSE GUZMAN, 1985-1992

Saves: Most, career, all-time

111 JEFF RUSSELL, 1985-1992
83 Ron Kline, 1963-1966
64 Darold Knowles, 1967-1977
37 Jim Kern, 1979-1981
35 Steve Foucault, 1973-1976

Shutouts: Most, career, all-time

17 Fergie Jenkins, 1974-1981
12 Gaylord Perry, 1975-1980
11 CHARLIE HOUGH, 1980-1990
9 Dick Bosman, 1966-1973
8 Jim Bibby, 1973-1984

Wins: Most, career, all-time

139 CHARLIE HOUGH, 1980-1990
93 Fergie Jenkins, 1974-1981
68 BOBBY WITT, 1986-1992
66 JOSE GUZMAN, 1985-1992
59 Dick Bosman, 1966-1973

K: Most, career, all-time

1452 CHARLIE HOUGH, 1980-1990
1051 BOBBY WITT, 1986-1992
895 Fergie Jenkins, 1974-1981
893 NOLAN RYAN, 1989-1992
715 JOSE GUZMAN, 1985-1992

Win pct: Highest, career, all-time

.575 NOLAN RYAN, 1989-1992
.566 KEVIN BROWN, 1986-1992
.564 Fergie Jenkins, 1974-1981
.538 Doc Medich, 1978-1982
.531 CHARLIE HOUGH, 1980-1990

ERA: Lowest, career, all-time

3.26 Gaylord Perry, 1975-1980
3.30 NOLAN RYAN, 1989-1992
3.35 Dick Bosman, 1966-1973
3.41 Jon Matlack, 1978-1983
3.51 Joe Coleman, 1965-1970

Runs: Most, season

115 RAFAEL PALMEIRO, 1991
111 Frank Howard, 1969
110 RUBEN SIERRA, 1991
108 JULIO FRANCO, 1991
105 Oddibe McDowell, 1986

Hits: Most, season

210 Mickey Rivers, 1980
209 Al Oliver, 1980
203 RAFAEL PALMEIRO, 1991
203 RUBEN SIERRA, 1991
201 JULIO FRANCO, 1991

2B: Most, season

49 RAFAEL PALMEIRO, 1991
44 RUBEN SIERRA, 1991
43 Al Oliver, 1980
42 Buddy Bell, 1979
42 Larry Parrish, 1984

3B: Most, season

14 RUBEN SIERRA, 1989
12 Chuck Hinton, 1963
10 RUBEN SIERRA, 1986
10 Ed Stroud, 1968
9 Ed Brinkman, 1966
9 Marty Keough, 1961

HR: Most, season

48 Frank Howard, 1969
44 Frank Howard, 1968
44 Frank Howard, 1970
43 JUAN GONZALEZ, 1992
36 Frank Howard, 1967

RBI: Most, season

126 Frank Howard, 1970
119 RUBEN SIERRA, 1989
118 Jeff Burroughs, 1974
117 Al Oliver, 1980
116 RUBEN SIERRA, 1991

SB: Most, season

52 Bump Wills, 1978
51 Dave Nelson, 1972
45 CECIL ESPY, 1989
44 Bill Sample, 1983
43 Dave Nelson, 1973

BB: Most, season

132 Frank Howard, 1970
113 Toby Harrah, 1985
109 Toby Harrah, 1977
107 Mike Hargrove, 1978
103 Mike Hargrove, 1977

BA: Highest, season

.341 JULIO FRANCO, 1991
.333 Mickey Rivers, 1980
.329 Buddy Bell, 1980
.324 Al Oliver, 1978
.323 Al Oliver, 1979

Slug avg: Highest, season

.574 Frank Howard, 1969
.552 Frank Howard, 1968
.546 Frank Howard, 1970
.543 RUBEN SIERRA, 1989
.533 RAFAEL PALMEIRO, 1991

Games started: Most, season

41 Jim Bibby, 1974
41 Fergie Jenkins, 1974
40 CHARLIE HOUGH, 1987
37 Fergie Jenkins, 1975
37 Fergie Jenkins, 1979

Saves: Most, season

38 JEFF RUSSELL, 1989
30 JEFF RUSSELL, 1991
29 Jim Kern, 1979
29 Ron Kline, 1965
28 JEFF RUSSELL, 1992

Shutouts: Most, season

6 BERT BLYLEVEN, 1976
6 Fergie Jenkins, 1974
5 Jim Bibby, 1974
5 BERT BLYLEVEN, 1977
4 Joe Coleman, 1969
4 Fergie Jenkins, 1975
4 Fergie Jenkins, 1978
4 Camilo Pascual, 1968
4 Gaylord Perry, 1975
4 Gaylord Perry, 1977

Wins: Most, season

25 Fergie Jenkins, 1974
21 KEVIN BROWN, 1992
19 Jim Bibby, 1974
18 CHARLIE HOUGH, 1987
18 Fergie Jenkins, 1978

K: Most, season

301 NOLAN RYAN, 1989
232 NOLAN RYAN, 1990
225 Fergie Jenkins, 1974
223 CHARLIE HOUGH, 1987
221 BOBBY WITT, 1990

Win pct: Highest, season

.692 Fergie Jenkins, 1978
.676 Fergie Jenkins, 1974
.656 KEVIN BROWN, 1992
.630 CHARLIE HOUGH, 1986
.630 BOBBY WITT, 1990

ERA: Lowest, season

2.19 Dick Bosman, 1969
2.27 Jon Matlack, 1978
2.40 Dick Donovan, 1961
2.42 RICK HONEYCUTT, 1983
2.60 Pete Richert, 1965

Most pinch-hit homers, season

3 Don Lock, Was-1966
3 Brant Alyea, Was-1969
3 Rick Reichardt, Was-1970
3 Tom McCraw, Was-1971
3 Darrell Porter, 1987

Most pinch-hit, homers, career

6 Brant Alyea, Was-1965-1969
6 Geno Petralli, 1985-1992

Most consecutive games, batting safely

24 Mickey Rivers, 1980
22 Jim Sundberg, 1978

Most consecutive scoreless innings

36 Charlie Hough, 1983

No hit games

Jim Bibby, Tex at Oak AL, 6-0; July 20, 1973.
Bert Blyleven, Tex at Cal AL, 6-0; September 22, 1977.
Nolan Ryan, Tex at Oak AL, 5-0; June 11, 1990.
Nolan Ryan, Tex vs Tor AL, 3-0; May 1, 1991.

ACTIVE PLAYERS in caps.

Leader from the franchise's current location is included. If not in the top five, leader's rank is listed in parenthesis; asterisk (*) indicates player is not in top 25.

California Angels

by Russell Beeker, *Baseball Weekly*

After finishing fifth in the AL with a 2.77 ERA, Jim Abbott was traded to the Yankees for three prospects.

1992 Angels: A hellish season

They may have worn halos on their hats, but the Angels' 1992 season was pure hell. Tragedy and disappointment were the rule.

It started in spring training when Matt Keough, a non-roster pitcher trying to make a comeback after a five-year absence from the majors, was drilled in the head by a foul ball while sitting in the dugout. Keough underwent brain surgery and may not have survived if a hospital had not been located across the street from the ballpark. Keough survived, but his comeback did not.

Then bench coach Deron Johnson died of cancer, a loss that shook the team and robbed it of a most popular member.

Despite these tragedies, the Angels played solidly and were within four games of the AL West lead when their team bus careened off the New Jersey turnpike and over an embankment, coming to rest at a 45-degree angle about 15 feet above a ravine. If not for some fortuitously placed trees, it, too, could have been a fatal accident. Manager Buck Rodgers was hospitalized for elbow and knee fractures and was sidelined for several months; the Angels' season never recovered.

Their offense was the league's worst. The team hit only .249 and managed only a .301 on-base percentage. Their 579 runs and 1,306 hits were easily the worst in the league. By far the weakest link was the heart of order—Angels' cleanup hitters combined for a puny.197 average.

Free agent DH Hubie Brooks played only half the year and hit just .216. Young first baseman Lee Stevens hit just .221 (seven HR). Third baseman Gary Gaetti continued his four-year slump, hitting only .226 (12 HR, 48 RBI). Free agent Von Hayes (.225, four homers) was so disappointing the Angels released him in August. Lance Parrish was also released (picked up by Seattle) and Alvin Davis was a major let-down, hitting zero home runs in 40 games.

The pitching story was almost as sad: Mark Langston went from 19 victories in 1991 to 13-14 (3.66 ERA). Chuck Finley (18 wins in '91), was hampered by toe injuries and finished 7-12 with a 3.96 ERA. Jim Abbott, the hard-luck pitcher of the year, had a 2.77 ERA but couldn't overcome the punchless offense and finished 7-15.

Now for the good news: Joe Grahe emerged as a quality closer—21 saves in 24 chances, fourth-best percentage in the AL. Julio Valera emerged as a quality starter (8-11, 3.73 ERA). The Angels acquired Valera from the Mets for shortstop Dick Schofield, whose replacement, Gary DiSarcina, had more hits than Schofield's career high—and played solid defense. Free agent Rene Gonzales led the team with a .363 on-base percentage.

—by John Hunt

1993 Angels: Preview

The Angels may have done more for their future by going through the difficult 1992 season. Free agents Hubie Brooks and Von Hayes were awful and got dumped, but youngsters like Gary DiSarcina, Chad Curtis, Tim Salmon, and Damion Easley became invaluable by season's end. The inability of Angels' starters to overcome poor run support led to the emergence of Julio Valera, which gave GM Whitey Herzog the freedom to shop Jim Abbott. And Bryan Harvey's injury allowed Joe Grahe to prove he could handle the closer role. (Harvey was taken by the Marlins in the expansion draft.)

Herzog admits the Angels are still a few players away. But dealing Abbott—who didn't take the club's offer of a four-year, $16 million deal—added to the young nucleus, especially with first baseman J.T. Snow.

—Rick Lawes

1992 Angels: Between the lines

▸**April 21:** The Angels broke a 10-game losing streak to the Oakland Athletics with a 3-2 victory. Bryan Harvey struck out all three batters in the ninth for his fourth save of the season, while Julio Valera gave up only one hit in four innings for the win.

▸**April 26:** The Angels beat Seattle, but not without a brawl. ***Quote of the day:*** Manager Buck Rodgers—"I love it. I wouldn't want to go through this every night but we needed something. I don't know if any punches landed, but there was some blood out there. I took inventory, and no one was a pint low."

▸**April 29:** A superb pitching duel was decided by an unearned run, as Jim Abbott walked Blue Jay Pat Tabler with the bases loaded in the ninth for a 1-0 loss to Toronto.

▸**May 7:** Julio Valera pitched a five-hitter, his first major league shutout.

▸**May 9:** A late replacement for the ailing Junior Felix, rookie Chad Curtis provided the offense in California's 2-1 win against the Blue Jays. Curtis hit his first major-league home run and the game-winning RBI double.

▸**May 19:** Bert Blyleven, pitching in the majors for the first time since Aug. 10, 1990, allowed just three runs over six innings. (Blyleven had two rotator cuff operations.)

▸**May 20 *Quote of the day:*** Buck Rodgers after a 12-inning loss to the Yankees—"Before, we were playing hard and winning. Now we're playing hard and getting beat. But we can't start feeling sorry for ourselves or we'll get run over." A few hours later, the team bus crashed on the way to Baltimore. Rodgers suffered a broken rib, elbow and knee and was temporarily replaced as manager by John Wathan.

▸**May 22:** The Angels fell to the Orioles 5-3 in their first game after the bus crash that injured several others in addition to Buck Rodgers. ***Quote of the day:*** Gary Gaetti, who was robbed of a possible ninth-inning homer by outfielder Brady Anderson—"We're a hit away, a pitch away. Whether you call it a slump, a curse, or strange—it's just baseball."

▸**May 23:** Lee Stevens and Gary Gaetti homered, and Rene Gonzales drove in three runs in Baltimore to lead the Angels to their first victory since their bus crash. ***Quote of the day:*** Interim manager John Wathan, relieved to be partaking in a local culinary delight after the game—"There's nothing better than a win and a crab cake."

▸**May 30 *Milestone:*** Bert Blyleven moved into a tie with Tom Seaver for third place on the all-time strikeout list (3,640) and recorded career win No. 280 as well. The 41-year-old Blyleven threw 85 pitches, 59 of them for strikes.

▸**June 3:** Gary DiSarcina hit his first major league home run.

▸**June 7:** Scott Bailes, Mike Fitzgerald and John Wathan were ejected in the seventh inning for some very inside pitches to Brewers' batters. ***Quote of the day:*** Bailes, on his aim—"I wanted to pitch them inside—yes, that much inside."

▸**June 8:** The Angels suffered their fourth consecutive loss and 18th in the past 22 games. It was their fifth defeat in a row on the road, and 13th in the past 15 away from Anaheim.

▸**June 10:** Luis Polonia tied an Angels' record with four stolen bases in a single game.

▸**June 11:** Joe Grahe earned his first major league save, the first by an Angel other than Bryan Harvey since Aug. 25, 1991.

▸**June 14:** Luis Sojo homered and tripled to lead the Angels to their eighth straight win against the Royals. ***Quote of the day:*** Angels' pitcher Julio Valera, who snapped a four-game losing streak, on some long-awaited run production from his teammates—"I was just hoping for one run in the seventh. When it was three, I was like, 'Oh, thank you!' "

▸**June 17:** Mark Langston threw his

second shutout in a row, a two-hit 3-2 victory over Texas. He walked four and fanned seven, as ex-Angel Nolan Ryan threw his first complete game in over a year for the Rangers. ***Quote of the day:*** Von Hayes, wondering about the loyalties of the home crowd—"If they draw 40,000 people here tonight, how many will root for us? Ten?"

▸**June 21:** Jim Abbott beat the A's for the first time in six career decisions against them.

▸**June 23:** Blyleven balked in a run in the third inning of the Angels' loss to the Twins. It was the first balk by an Angels' pitcher this season.

▸**June 26:** Rookie Chad Curtis had a pair of homers.

▸**July 1:** Jim Abbott pitched his fifth complete game of the season—his fourth complete-game loss—allowing just two runs and fanning seven.

▸**July 9:** The matchup of Blyleven (41) and Detroit's Frank Tanana (39) added up to 80 years, and brought 41 years of major league service to the mound.

▸**July 10:** The Angels snapped the longest losing streak in the majors at 11 games—just two short of the club mark of 13.

▸**July 12:** Angels' pitchers issued a club-record 13 walks, but still beat Detroit 5-4. ***Quote of the day:*** Wathan, after losing 11, then winning three—"We're on a roll. We're going to find a pick-up game somewhere in Orange County (Calif.)"

▸**July 25:** Tim Fortugno (30) became the oldest pitcher to win his first major league game since Tony Fossas (31) did it for the Brewers in 1989.

▸**July 27:** Finley, finally. Chuck Finley (2-7) won his first game in eight starts—his second in 17 starts. Joe Grahe earned his ninth save in 10 opportunities.

▸**August 12:** Mark Langston and Joe Grahe combined on a two-hitter, as the Angels swept the Brewers.

▸**August 19:** The Angels scored more than two runs for just the eighth time in any of Jim Abbott's 23 starts.

▸**August 20:** Blyleven, who had lost four in a row, was 4-1 in his last five decisions after shutting down the Red Sox on three hits.

▸**August 21:** Rookie Mike Butcher notched his first major league win, while fellow rookie Tim Fortugno picked up his first major league save.

▸**September 11:** Abbott struck out a season-high 10 for 8 2/3 innings of shutout ball—and a win.

▸**October 4:** The Angels finished fifth in the AL West. Luis Polonia was fourth in the league in stolen bases (51). Jim Abbott was fifth in ERA (2.77), and Mark Langston was sixth in strikeouts (174).

—by Jeanie Chung, John Hunt, Deron Snyder, and Lisa Winston.

Team directory

▸**Owner:** Gene Autry

▸**General Manager:** Whitey Herzog

▸**Ballpark:**
Anaheim Stadium
2000 Gene Autry Way, Anaheim, Calif.
714-634-1300
Capacity 64,593
Parking for 15,000 vehicles; $5
Public transportation available
Family and wheelchair sections, escalators, ramps, picnic section

▸**Team publications:**
Halo Magazine
714-937-6700, ext. 7281

▸**TV, radio broadcast stations:**
KMPC 710AM, XPRS 1090 (Spanish), KTLA Channel 5, SportsChannel

▸**Camps and/or clinics:**
MCI/Angels Clinic, dates TBA, 714-937-6700
Angels Rookie League, dates TBA, 714-937-6700

▸**Spring Training:**
Diablo Stadium,
Tempe, Ariz.
Capacity 7,500
Telephone TBA

CALIFORNIA ANGELS 1992 final stats

Batting	AVG	SLG	OB	G	AB	R	H	TB	2B	3B	HR	RBI	BB	SO	SB	CS	E
Schofield	.333	.333	.500	1	3	0	1	1	0	0	0	0	1	0	0	0	0
Polonia	.286	.329	.337	149	577	83	165	190	17	4	0	35	45	64	51	21	4
Gonzales	.277	.398	.363	104	329	47	91	131	17	1	7	38	41	46	7	4	9
Sojo	.272	.378	.299	106	368	37	100	139	12	3	7	43	14	24	7	11	9
Oberkfell	.264	.275	.317	41	91	6	24	25	1	0	0	10	8	5	0	1	1
Curtis	.259	.372	.341	139	441	59	114	164	16	2	10	46	51	71	43	18	6
Easley	.258	.311	.307	47	151	14	39	47	5	0	1	12	8	26	9	5	5
Davis	.250	.327	.331	40	104	5	26	34	8	0	0	16	13	9	0	0	1
DiSarcina	.247	.301	.283	157	518	48	128	156	19	0	3	42	20	50	9	7	25
Felix	.246	.361	.289	139	509	63	125	184	22	5	9	72	33	128	8	8	6
Myers	.231	.359	.271	30	78	4	18	28	7	0	1	13	5	11	0	0	1
Williams	.231	.346	.259	14	26	5	6	9	1	1	0	2	1	10	0	2	0
Gaetti	.226	.342	.267	130	456	41	103	156	13	2	12	48	21	79	3	1	22
Hayes	.225	.326	.305	94	307	35	69	100	17	1	4	29	37	54	11	6	3
Stevens	.221	.349	.288	106	312	25	69	109	19	0	7	37	29	64	1	4	4
Orton	.219	.298	.276	43	114	11	25	34	3	0	2	12	7	32	1	1	5
Brooks	.216	.337	.247	82	306	28	66	103	13	0	8	36	12	46	3	3	1
Rose	.214	.345	.295	30	84	10	18	29	5	0	2	10	8	9	1	1	7
Fitzgerald	.212	.317	.294	95	189	19	40	60	2	0	6	17	22	34	2	2	3
Tingley	.197	.299	.282	71	127	15	25	38	2	1	3	8	13	35	0	1	4
Morris	.193	.263	.258	43	57	4	11	15	1	0	1	3	4	11	1	0	0
Ducey	.188	.238	.233	54	80	7	15	19	4	0	0	2	5	22	2	4	2
Gonzalez	.182	.218	.270	33	55	4	10	12	2	0	0	2	7	20	0	1	0
Salmon	.177	.266	.283	23	79	8	14	21	1	0	2	6	11	23	1	1	2

Pitching	W-L	ERA	G	GS	CG	GF	Sho	SV	IP	H	R	ER	HR	BB	SO
Robinson	1-0	2.20	3	3	0	0	0	0	16.1	19	4	4	1	3	9
Abbott	7-15	2.77	29	29	7	0	0	0	211	208	73	65	12	68	130
Harvey	0-4	2.83	25	0	0	22	0	13	28.2	22	12	9	4	11	34
Butcher	2-2	3.25	19	0	0	6	0	0	27.2	29	11	10	3	13	24
Grahe	5-6	3.52	46	7	0	31	0	21	94.2	85	37	37	5	39	39
Frey	4-2	3.57	51	0	0	20	0	4	45.1	39	18	18	6	22	24
Langston	13-14	3.66	32	32	8	0	2	0	229	206	103	93	14	74	174
Valera	8-11	3.73	30	28	4	0	2	0	188	188	82	78	15	64	113
Finley	7-12	3.96	31	31	4	0	1	0	204.1	212	99	90	24	98	124
Lewis	4-0	3.99	21	2	0	7	0	0	38.1	36	18	17	3	14	18
Blyleven	8-12	4.74	25	24	1	0	0	0	133	150	76	70	17	29	70
Crim	7-6	5.17	57	0	0	16	0	1	87	100	56	50	11	29	30
Fortugno	1-1	5.18	14	5	1	5	1	1	41.2	37	24	24	5	19	31
Bailes	3-1	7.45	32	0	0	10	0	0	38.2	59	34	32	7	28	25
Hathaway	0-0	7.94	2	1	0	0	0	0	5.2	8	5	5	1	3	1

1993 preliminary roster

PITCHERS (20)
Mike Butcher
Chuck Crim
John Farrell
Chuck Finley
Tim Fortugno
Steve Frey
Joe Grahe
Hilly Hathaway
Mark Holzemer
Mark Langston
Scott Lewis
Jerry Nielsen
Troy Percival
Darryl Scott
Victor Silverio
Russ Springer
Paul Swingle
Julio Valera
Julian Vasquez
Ron Watson

CATCHERS (3)
Greg Myers
John Orton
Ron Tingley

INFIELDERS (11)
Rod Correia
Gary Disarcina
Damion Easley
Kevin Flora
Gary Gaetti
Kelly Gruber
Torey Lovullo
J.R. Phillips
J.T. Snow
Lee Stevens
Ty Van Burkleo

OUTFIELDERS (6)
Chad Curtis
Jim Edmonds
Jose Mussett
Luis Polonia
Tim Salmon
Reggie Williams

Games played by position

Player	G	C	1B	2B	3B	SS	OF	DH
BROOKS,H	82	0	6	0	0	0	0	70
CURTIS,C	139	0	0	0	0	0	135	1
DAVIS,A	40	0	22	0	0	0	0	9
DISARCINA,G	157	0	0	0	0	157	0	0
DUCEY,R	54	0	0	0	0	0	33	5
EASLEY,D	47	0	0	0	45	3	0	0
FELIX,J	139	0	0	0	0	0	128	8
FITZGERALD,M	95	74	2	1	3	0	11	1
GAETTI,G	130	0	44	0	67	0	0	17
GONZALES,R	104	0	13	42	53	8	0	0
GONZALEZ,JO	33	0	0	0	0	0	22	1
HAYES,V	94	0	4	0	0	0	85	5
MORRIS,JO	43	0	0	0	0	0	14	6
MYERS,G	30	26	0	0	0	0	0	1
OBERKFELL,K	41	0	2	21	0	0	0	5
ORTON,J	43	43	0	0	0	0	0	0
POLONIA,L	149	0	0	0	0	0	99	47
ROSE,B	30	0	2	28	0	0	0	0
SALMON,T	23	0	0	0	0	0	21	0
SCHOFIELD,D	1	0	0	0	0	1	0	0
SOJO,L	106	0	0	96	9	5	0	0
STEVENS,L	106	0	91	0	0	0	0	2
TINGLEY,R	71	69	0	0	0	0	0	0
WILLIAMS,R	14	0	0	0	0	0	12	2

Sick call: 1992 DL report

Player	Days on the DL
Abbott, Jim	27
Bailes, Scott	15
Brooks, Hubie	76
Farrell, John	182
Felix, Junior	15
Finley, Chuck	16
Frey, Steve	16
Gonzales, Rene	54
Harvey, Bryan*	111
Morris, John	18
Myers, Greg	39
Orton, John*	93
Parrish, Lance*	38
Robinson, Don	22
Rose, Bobby	38

** On Disabled List twice during 1992 season (not counting transfers from one DL to another).*

Minor league report

Class AAA — Edmonton finished 74-69, 3rd in both halves of the Pacific Coast League Northern Division. OF Tim Salmon was named league MVP, hitting .347 with a league-best 29 HR and 105 RBI. 1B Ty Van Burkleo had 19 HR and 88 RBI. OF Reggie Williams had 44 SB. **Class AA:** Midland finished 61-72, 3rd in both halves of the Texas League Western Division. SS Rod Correia hit .290 with 6 HR and 56 RBI. He was named team MVP. 1B Jeff Kipila had 21 HR and 76 RBI. IF Edgar Alfonzo, who was promoted to Midland from Palm Springs midway through the season, overall hit .329 with 7 HR and 72 RBI. **Class A:** Palm Springs finished 72-63, 1st in the 1st half of the California League Southern Division and 3rd in the 2nd half. The team lost to Visalia in the 1st round of the playoffs. SS Brian Grebeck hit .336. RHP Shawn Purdy had 13 wins. RHP David Holdridge K'd 135. Quad City finished 91-46, 2nd in the 1st half of the Midwest League Southern Division and 1st in the 2nd half. The team lost to Cedar Rapids in the 1st round of the playoffs. OF Orlando Palmeiro won the league batting crown with a .317 mark. OF Mark Sweeney had 76 RBI. RHP John Fritz won 20 games, the 1st player in the league to reach that plateau in 30 years. Boise finished 40-36, 2nd in the Northwest League South Division. RHP John Pricher set a league record with 23 saves. LHP Mike Butler was 9-5, leading the league in wins, with a 2.42 ERA and 91 K. OF Chris Anderson hit .309. Angels finished 29-27, 5th in the Arizona League. SS Brian Guzik shared the league lead with 3 HR. RHP Max Valencia had 7 saves. RHP Miguel Fermin K'd 67. Boise captured the Northwest League's Southern Division title with a 50-26 record and defeated Northern Division winner Yakima two games to none in the best of three playoffs to win the Northwest League.

Tops in the organization

BATTING LEADERS	Club	Avg.	G	AB	R	H	HR	RBI
Tim Salmon	Edm	.347	118	409	101	142	29	105
Brian Grebeck	Psp	.336	91	289	71	97	0	39
Edgar Alfonzo	Mdl	.329	126	477	91	157	7	72
Orlando Palmeiro	Qcy	.317	127	451	83	143	0	41
Garret Anderson	Mdl	.308	120	468	62	144	3	81

HOME RUNS		
Tim Salmon	Edm	29
Jeff Kipila	Mdl	21
Ty Van Burkleo	Edm	19
Several players tied		14

RBI		
Tim Salmon	Edm	105
Mark Dalesandro	Psp	92
Ty Van Burkleo	Edm	88
Garret Anderson	Mdl	81
Emmitt Cohick	Psp	78

STOLEN BASES		
Tim Salmon	Edm	105
Mark Dalesandro	Psp	92
Ty Van Burkleo	Edm	88
Garret Anderson	Mdl	81
Emmitt Cohick	Psp	78

WINS		
John Fritz	Qcy	20
Shad Williams	Qcy	13
Shawn Purdy	Psp	13
Chance Gledhill	Qcy	13
Several players tied		12

SAVES		
Julian Heredia	Psp	20
Darryl Scott	Edm	15
Brett Merriman	Edm	13
Ron Watson	Qcy	10
Ken Edenfield	Mdl	9

STRIKEOUTS		
Shad Williams	Qcy	152
John Fritz	Qcy	143
David Holdridge	Psp	135
Erik Bennett	Mdl	128
Mark Holzemer	Edm	117

PITCHING LEADERS	Club	W-L	ERA	IP	H	BB	SO
Hilly Hathaway	Mdl	9-3	2.87	119	115	13	86
John Fritz	Qcy	20-4	3.03	172	129	69	143
Shad Williams	Qcy	13-11	3.26	179	161	55	152
Erik Bennett	Mdl	8-8	3.34	145	120	53	128
Mark Zappelli	Edm	12-4	3.38	160	177	47	110

California (1965-1992), includes Los Angeles (1961-1964)

Runs: Most, career, all-time

889 BRIAN DOWNING, 1978-1990
691 Jim Fregosi, 1961-1971
601 Bobby Grich, 1977-1986
481 Don Baylor, 1977-1982
474 Rod Carew, 1979-1985

Hits: Most, career, all-time

1588 BRIAN DOWNING, 1978-1990
1408 Jim Fregosi, 1961-1971
1103 Bobby Grich, 1977-1986
968 Rod Carew, 1979-1985
925 WALLY JOYNER, 1986-1991

2B: Most, career, all-time

282 BRIAN DOWNING, 1978-1990
219 Jim Fregosi, 1961-1971
183 Bobby Grich, 1977-1986
170 WALLY JOYNER, 1986-1991
149 Doug DeCinces, 1982-1987

3B: Most, career, all-time

70 Jim Fregosi, 1961-1971
32 Mickey Rivers, 1970-1975
27 DICK SCHOFIELD, 1983-1992
25 Bobby Knoop, 1964-1969
24 DEVON WHITE, 1985-1990

HR: Most, career, all-time

222 BRIAN DOWNING, 1978-1990
154 Bobby Grich, 1977-1986
141 Don Baylor, 1977-1982
130 Doug DeCinces, 1982-1987
123 Reggie Jackson, 1982-1986

RBI: Most, career, all-time

846 BRIAN DOWNING, 1978-1990
557 Bobby Grich, 1977-1986
546 Jim Fregosi, 1961-1971
523 Don Baylor, 1977-1982
518 WALLY JOYNER, 1986-1991

SB: Most, career, all-time

186 GARY PETTIS, 1982-1987
139 Sandy Alomar, 1969-1974
126 Mickey Rivers, 1970-1975
123 DEVON WHITE, 1985-1990
119 LUIS POLONIA, 1990-1992

BB: Most, career, all-time

866 BRIAN DOWNING, 1978-1990
630 Bobby Grich, 1977-1986
558 Jim Fregosi, 1961-1971
405 Rod Carew, 1979-1985
369 Albie Pearson, 1961-1966

BA: Highest, career, all-time

.314 Rod Carew, 1979-1985
.293 Juan Beniquez, 1981-1985
.288 WALLY JOYNER, 1986-1991
.275 Albie Pearson, 1961-1966
.271 BRIAN DOWNING, 1978-1990

Slug avg: Highest, career, all-time

.463 Doug DeCinces, 1982-1987
.455 WALLY JOYNER, 1986-1991
.448 Don Baylor, 1977-1982
.441 BRIAN DOWNING, 1978-1990
.440 Reggie Jackson, 1982-1986

Games started: Most, career, all-time

288 NOLAN RYAN, 1972-1979
272 Mike Witt, 1981-1990
218 FRANK TANANA, 1973-1980
189 KIRK McCASKILL, 1985-1991
189 Clyde Wright, 1966-1973

Saves: Most, career, all-time

126 BRYAN HARVEY, 1987-1992
65 Dave LaRoche, 1970-1980
61 Donnie Moore, 1985-1988
58 Bob Lee, 1964-1966
43 Minnie Rojas, 1966-1968

Shutouts: Most, career, all-time

40 NOLAN RYAN, 1972-1979
24 FRANK TANANA, 1973-1980
21 Dean Chance, 1961-1966
14 George Brunet, 1964-1969
13 Geoff Zahn, 1981-1985

Wins: Most, career, all-time

138 NOLAN RYAN, 1972-1979
109 Mike Witt, 1981-1990
102 FRANK TANANA, 1973-1980
87 Clyde Wright, 1966-1973
78 KIRK McCASKILL, 1985-1991

K: Most, career, all-time

2416 NOLAN RYAN, 1972-1979
1283 Mike Witt, 1981-1990
1233 FRANK TANANA, 1973-1980
857 Dean Chance, 1961-1966
844 Rudy May, 1965-1974

Win pct: Highest, career, all-time

.567 FRANK TANANA, 1973-1980
.557 Andy Messersmith, 1968-1972
.553 Geoff Zahn, 1981-1985
.541 CHUCK FINLEY, 1986-1992
.533 NOLAN RYAN, 1972-1979

ERA: Lowest, career, all-time

2.78 Andy Messersmith, 1968-1972
2.83 Dean Chance, 1961-1966
3.07 NOLAN RYAN, 1972-1979
3.08 FRANK TANANA, 1973-1980
3.13 George Brunet, 1964-1969

Runs: Most, season

120 Don Baylor, 1979
115 Albie Pearson, 1962
114 CARNEY LANSFORD, 1979
110 BRIAN DOWNING, 1987
109 BRIAN DOWNING, 1982

Hits: Most, season

202 Alex Johnson, 1970
188 CARNEY LANSFORD, 1979
186 Don Baylor, 1979
186 Billy Moran, 1962
184 Johnny Ray, 1988

2B: Most, season

42 Doug DeCinces, 1982
42 Johnny Ray, 1988
38 Fred Lynn, 1982
37 BRIAN DOWNING, 1982
34 Rod Carew, 1980
34 WALLY JOYNER, 1991
34 Bob Rodgers, 1962

3B: Most, season

13 Jim Fregosi, 1968
13 Mickey Rivers, 1975
13 DEVON WHITE, 1989
12 Jim Fregosi, 1963
11 Bobby Knoop, 1966
11 Mickey Rivers, 1974

HR: Most, season

39 Reggie Jackson, 1982
37 Bobby Bonds, 1977
37 Leon Wagner, 1962
36 Don Baylor, 1979
34 Don Baylor, 1978
34 WALLY JOYNER, 1987

RBI: Most, season

139 Don Baylor, 1979
117 WALLY JOYNER, 1987
115 Bobby Bonds, 1977
107 Leon Wagner, 1962
104 Lee Thomas, 1962

SB: Most, season

70 Mickey Rivers, 1975
56 GARY PETTIS, 1985
51 LUIS POLONIA, 1992
50 GARY PETTIS, 1986
48 GARY PETTIS, 1984
48 LUIS POLONIA, 1991

BB: Most, season

106 BRIAN DOWNING, 1987
96 Albie Pearson, 1961
95 Albie Pearson, 1962
93 Jim Fregosi, 1969
92 Reggie Jackson, 1986
92 Albie Pearson, 1963

BA: Highest, season

.339 Rod Carew, 1983
.331 Rod Carew, 1980
.329 Alex Johnson, 1970
.326 BRIAN DOWNING, 1979
.319 Rod Carew, 1982

Slug avg: Highest, season

.548 Doug DeCinces, 1982
.543 Bobby Grich, 1981
.537 Bobby Grich, 1979
.532 Reggie Jackson, 1982
.530 Don Baylor, 1979

Games started: Most, season

41 NOLAN RYAN, 1974
40 Bill Singer, 1973
39 NOLAN RYAN, 1972
39 NOLAN RYAN, 1973
39 NOLAN RYAN, 1976
39 Clyde Wright, 1970

Saves: Most, season

46 BRYAN HARVEY, 1991
31 Donnie Moore, 1985
27 Minnie Rojas, 1967
25 BRYAN HARVEY, 1989
25 BRYAN HARVEY, 1990
25 Dave LaRoche, 1978

Shutouts: Most, season

11 Dean Chance, 1964
9 NOLAN RYAN, 1972
7 NOLAN RYAN, 1976
7 FRANK TANANA, 1977
6 Jim McGlothlin, 1967

Wins: Most, season

22 NOLAN RYAN, 1974
22 Clyde Wright, 1970
21 NOLAN RYAN, 1973
20 Dean Chance, 1964
20 Andy Messersmith, 1971
20 Bill Singer, 1973

K: Most, season

383 NOLAN RYAN, 1973
367 NOLAN RYAN, 1974
341 NOLAN RYAN, 1977
329 NOLAN RYAN, 1972
327 NOLAN RYAN, 1976

Win pct: Highest, season

.773 BERT BLYLEVEN, 1989
.704 MARK LANGSTON, 1991
.692 Geoff Zahn, 1982
.690 Dean Chance, 1964
.667 CHUCK FINLEY, 1990
.667 CHUCK FINLEY, 1991

ERA: Lowest, season

1.65 Dean Chance, 1964
2.28 NOLAN RYAN, 1972
2.40 CHUCK FINLEY, 1990
2.43 FRANK TANANA, 1976
2.52 Andy Messersmith, 1969

Most pinch-hit homers, season

3 Joe Adcock, 1966
3 George Hendrick, 1987

Most pinch-hit, homers, career

4 Ruppert Jones, 1985-1987
4 George Hendrick, 1985-1988

Most consecutive games, batting safely

25 Rod Carew, 1982
22 Sandy Alomar, 1970

Most consecutive scoreless innings

36 Jim McGlothlin, 1967

No hit games

Bo Belinsky, LA vs Bal AL, 2-0; May 5, 1962.
Clyde Wright, Cal vs Oak AL, 4-0; July 3, 1970.
Nolan Ryan, Cal at KC AL, 3-0; May 15, 1973.
Nolan Ryan, Cal at Det AL, 6-0; July 15, 1973.
Nolan Ryan, Cal vs Min AL, 4-0; September 28, 1974.
Nolan Ryan, Cal vs Bal AL, 1-0; June 1, 1975.
Mike Witt, Cal at Tex AL, 1-0; September 30, 1984 (perfect game).
Mark Langston (7 innings) and Mike Witt (2 innings), Cal vs Sea AL, 1-0; April 11, 1990.

ACTIVE PLAYERS in caps.

Leader from the franchise's current location is included. If not in the top five, leader's rank is listed in parenthesis; asterisk (*) indicates player is not in top 25.

Kansas City Royals

Kansas City Royals

by Russell Beeker, *Baseball Weekly*

Kevin Appier's 2.46 ERA was second only to Roger Clemens in the AL; he had 15 wins and 150 strikeouts.

1992 Royals: Bad start ruined it all

Manager Hal McRae summed up the Royals' 1992 season best: When people remember this season, they'll only recall the 1-16 start and George Brett's milestone of 3,000 hits. There was other good news for the Royals besides Brett, but not nearly enough to overcome the dreadful start.

Foremost, there was the emergence of rookie pitchers Hipolito Pichardo and Rusty Meacham. Neither was on the Opening Day roster, but both were called up in April. McRae called both "godsends." Pichardo, a right-hander from the Dominican Republic who turned 23 in August, made the jump from Class AA. He had earned a spot in the rotation by the third week of May. He finished the season 9-6 (3.95 ERA). Meacham, claimed off the waiver wire from Detroit where he spent much of his time as a starter, was a strong setup man for Jeff Montgomery. He appeared in 64 games (10-4, 2.74 ERA)—only Kevin Appier had more wins (15). His 15 holds placed Meacham ninth in the AL.

Appier, meanwhile, filled the role of staff ace left vacant by the Bret Saberhagen trade. He was unbeaten for more than two months, compiling nine consecutive wins between May 30 and July 29. He was not named to the All-Star team despite having 10 victories at the break—for a team that ranked among the league's worst offensively. He chased Roger Clemens for the league ERA crown, and may have won it were he not sidelined by an injury. His 2.46 mark fell short of Clemens' 2.41.

Jeff Montgomery continued to be one of the league's top closers (39 saves in '92, 2.18 ERA).

Among the team's biggest disappointments was No. 2 starter Mark Gubicza, who started only 18 games and finished the season on the DL.

The Royals' 3-19 start ruined any hopes of being a contender. After 22 games, team totals included a 4.32 ERA, a .215 batting average and 26 errors. They played just better than .500 for much of the remainder of the season before swooning at the end.

Infield defense was a major problem. Gregg Jefferies had his best year at the plate, but he led all major league third basemen with 26 errors. Second baseman Keith Miller finished with 15 errors. The pitching reflected both the good and bad. The Royals went through 22 pitchers; their starters had a 3.81 ERA, sixth in the league. Lack of power was also a major drawback: The Royals hit a major-league low 75 home runs.

Other let-downs: Brian McRae's .223 average, a 38-point slide from 1991; Kevin McReynolds' .247 and career-low 13 home runs and 49 RBI; and Mike MacFarlane's .234 average, down 43 points from 1991.

—by Greg Frazier

1993 Royals: Preview

The Royals need to replace a few big guns, but the biggest loss of all is looming just over the horizon. George Brett will likely return for his 20th and final season. His retirement will leave a void in team leadership which won't be quickly filled. If he is around in '93, the team still needs a power hitter and an ace starter; the Royals still haven't recovered from the Bret Saberhagen trade.

The biggest need is offense. General manager Herk Robinson says he doesn't want to fill the holes with free agents, but Kansas City resident David Cone was too tempting to pass up. Keeping Mark Gubicza, signing Greg Gagne and trading for Jose Lind sure helped in a hurry.

—by Rick Lawes

1992 Royals: Between the lines

▸**April 25:** The Royals (1-16) lost again, but shortstop Rico Rossy hit an RBI double in his first major league at-bat. ***Quote of the day:*** Manager Hal McRae—"Rossy will be in tomorrow. He's about the only one who's doing anything for us right now."

▸**April 26:** Feast or famine: The Royals snapped a nine-game losing streak: They pounded out 13 hits and two homers in beating the first-place Blue Jays 9-0. Royals' pitchers gave up a mere four hits, and Brian McRae helped with three hits, including a two-run homer. The game marked the first defeat of the season for Toronto starter Jack Morris, and the first win for K.C. starter Mark Gubicza.

▸**May 1:** The struggling Royals took a one-run lead in the top of the ninth against Boston, but yielded a pair of runs in the bottom of the inning for a 6-5 loss. Keith Miller's RBI single gave K.C. the lead, but Mo Vaughn later hit a two-run single.

▸**May 3:** Royals' center fielder Brian McRae crashed head-first into the wall, but came up with Wade Boggs' two-out bases-loaded fly ball in the fourth inning to help preserve Kansas City's 5-2 win against Boston.

▸**May 6:** Jim Eisenreich hit Jaime Navarro's first pitch of the seventh inning for a home run to help lead Kansas City to a 3-1 win against the Brewers. It was the fifth win for the Royals in their last 10 games, after starting the season 1-16.

▸**May 17:** Mark Gubicza, who went the distance for his fourth straight victory in the Royals' 2-1 win against Detroit, allowed his first walk in 18 innings in the ninth.

▸**May 30:** Gregg Jefferies, one of many Royals who slumped badly early in the season and contributed to the club's woeful start, extended his hitting streak to 16 games with a single and his league-leading 16th double.

▸**May 31:** Brian McRae's single scored Kevin McReynolds with the winning run in the ninth. The Royals edged Texas 7-6, knocking them from their spot atop the AL West.

▸**June 5 *Milestone:*** George Brett's run-scoring double was RBI number 1,476, moving him past Billy Williams into 34th on the all-time chart.

▸**June 6:** Kansas City edged Seattle, 4-3, in the battle for the basement of the AL West. Keith Miller was 3-for-3, while Gregg Jefferies and Kevin McReynolds added two hits apiece. While the three former Mets were tearing it up, the player they were traded for—pitcher Bret Saberhagen—remained on the Mets' disabled list.

▸**June 7:** The Royals, recovering from an abysmal start, climbed out of the AL West basement with a 4-1 win over the new cellar-dwellers: Seattle.

▸**June 8:** Keith Miller knocked in a career-high four runs, including his third home run of the season.

▸**June 19:** Gregg Jefferies led the Royals to an 11-4 win over the Blue Jays, going 2-for-4 with five RBI, including a three-run homer. Rico Rossy was 3-for-4 in the game.

▸**June 29:** Led by ex-Mets making their homecoming, the Royals defeated the Yankees 7-3. Keith Miller, Gregg Jefferies, and Kevin McReynolds returned to New York for the first time since they were traded for Bret Saberhagen and Bill Pecota and hit a combined 7-for-14, scored four runs and drove in three. Jefferies predicted before the game that he would be booed by the New York fans, and he was right. He was greeted by a loud chorus of boos each time he stepped up to the plate. ***Milestone:*** George Brett got the 2,900th hit of his 20-year career.

▸**July 10:** Tom Gordon collected just his second win of the season against nine losses (coming on for injured Mark Gubicza), limiting the Brewers to two hits over four innings. He struck out four in the 3-1 Royals win.

▸**July 21:** Rookie Hipolito Pichardo took a no-hitter into the sixth inning and shut out the Red Sox 8-0. He retired the first 17 batters before Luis Rivera laced a double down the left-field line.

▸**July 24:** Kevin McReynolds and Chris Gwynn each slugged two-run homers, the first long balls in 12 games for Kansas City.

▸**July 29:** Kevin Appier won his ninth straight decision and Gregg Jefferies was 4-for-5 as Kansas City beat the Blue Jays, 5-2.

▸**August 1:** After Hipolito Pichardo hit Rickey Henderson in the wrist with the game's first pitch, Oakland's Kelly Downs countered in the bottom of the inning, hitting Gregg Jefferies. Pichardo and Steve Shifflett were ejected after numerous brushback pitches in the second inning.

▸**August 7 *Milestone:*** Brett hit the 625th double of his career, passing Hank Aaron for eighth place on the all-time list.

▸**August 8 *Milestone:*** Brett got the 1,500th RBI of his career.

▸**August 19:** Kansas City local product David Haas started for the Tigers against the Royals in front of his hometown fans, but was yanked when he allowed four runs in the fourth. ***Quote of the day:*** KC manager Hal McRae—"He has the stuff to be a winning pitcher. He looked like he knows his way around, he just stopped making his pitches. Besides, he's a local guy, so I should say something nice about him. He used to sit in the stands and help pay my salary."

▸**August 21:** The hot White Sox lost to the even hotter Royals when David Howard's groundout in the eighth drove in the game-winner in a 4-3 Kansas City win. It was the Royals' fifth win in six games, and just the third loss in 15 home games for Chicago.

▸**August 28 *Milestone:*** Brett (who else?) scored his 1,500th run.

▸**September 24:** Dennis Rasmussen, who had been released by two other organizations this season, improved to 3-0 and lowered his ERA to 1.66 in the Royals' 3-0 win against Seattle.

▸**September 30 *Milestone:*** George Brett collected his 3,000th career hit by getting four hits in one game. (Moments afterwards, he was picked off by Angels' pitcher Tim Fortugno.)

▸**October 4:** The Royals finished 1992 sixth in the AL. Reliever Jeff Montgomery was third in the league with 39 saves.

—by Jeanie Chung, John Hunt, Deron Snyder, and Lisa Winston.

Team directory

▸**Owner:** Ewing Kauffman

▸**General Manager:** Herk Robinson

▸**Ballpark:**
Royals Stadium
1 Royal Way, Kansas City, Mo.
816-921-8000
Capacity 40,625
Pay parking lot; $5
Public transportation available
Wheelchair section and ramps

▸**Team publications:**
Yearbook

▸**TV, radio broadcast stations:**
WDAF 610 AM, KSMO Channel 4

▸**Spring Training:**
Baseball City Stadium
Baseball City, Fla.
Capacity 8,000
813-424-7211

KANSAS CITY ROYALS 1992 final stats

Batting	AVG	SLG	OB	G	AB	R	H	TB	2B	3B	HR	RBI	BB	SO	SB	CS	E
Melvin	.314	.386	.351	32	70	5	22	27	5	0	0	6	5	13	0	0	1
Gwynn	.286	.405	.303	34	84	10	24	34	3	2	1	7	3	10	0	0	0
Brett	.285	.397	.330	152	592	55	169	235	35	5	7	61	35	69	8	6	3
Jefferies	.285	.404	.329	152	604	66	172	244	36	3	10	75	43	29	19	9	26
Samuel	.284	.392	.336	29	102	15	29	40	5	3	0	8	7	27	6	1	6
Miller	.284	.389	.352	106	416	57	118	162	24	4	4	38	31	46	16	6	15
Joyner	.269	.386	.336	149	572	66	154	221	36	2	9	66	55	50	11	5	10
Eisenreich	.269	.340	.313	113	353	31	95	120	13	3	2	28	24	36	11	6	1
Conine	.253	.352	.313	28	91	10	23	32	5	2	0	9	8	23	0	0	0
Wilkerson	.250	.311	.292	111	296	27	74	92	10	1	2	29	18	47	18	7	10
Koslofski	.248	.346	.313	55	133	20	33	46	0	2	3	13	12	23	2	1	1
McReynolds	.247	.418	.357	109	373	45	92	156	25	0	13	49	67	48	7	1	3
Thurman	.245	.305	.281	88	200	25	49	61	6	3	0	20	9	34	9	6	2
Macfarlane	.234	.445	.310	129	402	51	94	179	28	3	17	48	30	89	1	5	4
Mayne	.225	.272	.260	82	213	16	48	58	10	0	0	18	11	26	0	4	3
Howard	.224	.283	.271	74	219	19	49	62	6	2	1	18	15	43	3	4	8
McRae	.223	.308	.285	149	533	63	119	164	23	5	4	52	42	88	18	5	3
Rossy	.215	.302	.310	59	149	21	32	45	8	1	1	12	20	20	0	3	10
Pulliam	.200	.400	.333	4	5	2	1	2	1	0	0	0	1	3	0	0	0
Shumpert	.149	.255	.175	36	94	6	14	24	5	1	1	11	3	17	2	2	4

Pitching	W-L	ERA	G	GS	CG	GF	Sho	SV	IP	H	R	ER	HR	BB	SO
Rasmussen	4-1	1.43	5	5	1	0	1	0	37.2	25	7	6	0	6	12
Montgomery	1-6	2.18	65	0	0	62	0	39	82.2	61	23	20	5	27	69
Appier	15-8	2.46	30	30	3	0	0	0	208.1	167	59	57	10	68	150
Shifflett	1-4	2.60	34	0	0	15	0	0	52	55	15	15	6	17	25
Meacham	10-4	2.74	64	0	0	20	0	2	101.	88	39	31	5	21	64
Pierce	0-0	3.38	2	1	0	0	0	0	5.1	9	2	2	1	4	3
Sampen	0-2	3.66	8	1	0	3	0	0	19.2	21	10	8	0	3	14
Reed	3-7	3.68	19	18	1	0	1	0	100.1	105	47	41	10	20	49
Gubicza	7-6	3.72	18	18	2	0	1	0	111.1	110	47	46	8	36	81
Haney	2-3	3.86	7	7	1	0	1	0	42	35	18	18	5	16	27
Pichardo	9-6	3.95	31	24	1	0	1	0	143.2	148	71	63	9	49	59
Sauveur	0-1	4.40	8	0	0	2	0	0	14.1	15	7	7	1	8	7
Aquino	3-6	4.52	15	13	0	1	0	0	67.2	81	35	34	5	20	11
Gordon	6-10	4.59	40	11	0	13	0	0	117.2	116	67	60	9	55	98
Magnante	4-9	4.94	44	12	0	11	0	0	89.1	115	53	49	5	35	31
Boddicker	1-4	4.98	29	8	0	8	0	3	86.2	92	50	48	5	37	47
Berenguer	1-4	5.64	19	2	0	2	0	0	44.2	42	30	28	3	20	26
Moeller	0-3	7.00	5	4	0	1	0	0	18	24	17	14	5	11	6
Davis	1-3	7.18	13	6	0	4	0	0	36.1	42	31	29	6	28	19
Johnston	0-0	13.50	5	0	0	1	0	0	2.2	3	4	4	2	2	0

1993 preliminary roster

PITCHERS (20)
Kevin Appier
Luis Aquino
Mike Boddicker
Bill Brewer
David Cone
Mark Gardner
Tom Gordon
Mark Gubicza
Chris Haney
Doug Harris
Mike Magnante
Rusty Meacham
Jeff Montgomery
Kevin Morton
Hipolito Pichardo
Ed Pierce
Dennis Rasmussen
Rick Reed
Bill Sampen
Steve Shifflett

CATCHERS (3)
Lance Jennings
Mike Macfarlane
Brent Mayne

INFIELDERS (12)
George Brett
Greg Gagne
Bob Hamelin
Phil Hiatt
David Howard
Gregg Jefferies
Wally Joyner
Jose Lind
Keith Miller
Rico Rossy
Terry Shumpert
Curtis Wilkerson

OUTFIELDERS (6)
Chris Gwynn
Kevin Koslofski
Brian McRae
Kevin McReynolds
Harvey Pulliam
Gary Thurman

Games played by position

Player	G	C	1B	2B	3B	SS	OF	DH
BRETT,G	152	0	15	0	3	0	0	132
CONINE,J	28	0	4	0	0	0	23	1
EISENREICH,J	113	0	0	0	0	0	88	8
GWYNN,C	34	0	0	0	0	0	19	2
HOWARD,D	74	0	0	0	0	74	2	0
JEFFERIES,G	152	0	0	1	146	0	0	1
JOYNER,W	149	0	145	0	0	0	0	4
KOSLOFSKI,K	55	0	0	0	0	0	52	1
MACFARLANE,M	129	104	0	0	0	0	0	13
MAYNE,B	82	62	0	0	8	0	0	1
MCRAE,B	149	0	0	0	0	0	148	0
MCREYNOLDS,K	109	0	0	0	0	0	106	1
MELVIN,B	32	21	3	0	0	0	0	0
MILLER,K	106	0	0	93	0	0	16	1
PULLIAM,H	4	0	0	0	0	0	1	2
ROSSY,R	59	0	0	3	9	51	0	0
SAMUEL,J	29	0	0	10	0	0	18	0
SHUMPERT,T	36	0	0	33	0	1	0	1
THURMAN,G	88	0	0	0	0	0	67	9
WILKERSON,C	111	0	0	39	5	69	0	1

Sick call: 1992 DL report

Player	Days on the DL
Aquino, Luis	99
Boddicker, Mike*	57
Eisenreich, Jim	26
Gordon, Tom	20
Gubicza, Mark	86
Gwynn, Chris*	118
Howard, David	75
Magnante, Mike	18
McReynolds, Kevin	27
Miller, Keith*	49
Shumpert, Terry	31

** On Disabled List twice during 1992 season (not counting transfers from one DL to another).*

Minor league report

Class AAA — Omaha finished 67-77, 3rd in the American Association Western Division. OF Adam Casillas hit .307. 3B Sean Berry had 21 HR. LHP Dennis Moeller won the league ERA crown at 8-5 with a 2.46 ERA. **Class AA:** Memphis finished 71-73, 3rd in the 1st half of the Southern League Western Division and 4th in the 2nd half. OF Dan Rohrmeier hit .323 with 6 HR and 69 RBI. 3B Phil Hiatt had 27 HR and 83 RBI. LHP Ed Puig had 25 saves. **Class A:** Baseball City finished 71-60, 2nd in both halves of the Florida State League Central Division. The team lost to Lakeland in two games for the league championships. OF Joe Vitiello hit .285 with 8 HR and 65 RBI. 3B Joe Randa hit .290 with 6 HR and 55 RBI. SS Shane Halter had 26 SB. Appleton finished 70-62, 1st in the 1st half of the Midwest League Northern Division and 6th in the 2nd half. The team lost to Beloit in the 1st round of the playoffs. RHP Brian Bevil had 168 K. OF Rod Myers had 23 SB. RHP Robert Toth was 7-6 with a 3.39 ERA. Eugene finished 36-40, last in the Northwest League Southern Division. 2B Steve Sisco hit .330. 1B Larry Sutton hit .311 with league-leading 15 HR and 58 RBI. RHP Melvin Bunch was 5-3 with a 2.78 ERA and 69 K in 65 IP. Royals finished 41-18, 1st in the Gulf Coast League Central Division. The team beat the Expos in three games for the league championship. OF Johnny Damon hit .349 with 4 HR and 23 SB. C Carlos Mendez hit .305 while OF Oscar Jimenez hit .299.

Tops in the organization

BATTING LEADERS	Club	Avg.	G	AB	R	H	HR	RBI
Dan Rohrmeier	Oma	.318	131	462	58	147	7	74
Les Norman	Mem	.316	132	493	70	156	7	67
Adam Casillas	Oma	.313	138	530	66	166	2	50
Jeff Conine	Oma	.302	110	397	69	120	20	72
Joe Randa	Bcy	.290	123	455	77	132	6	55

HOME RUNS		
Phil Hiatt	Oma	29
Sean Berry	Oma	21
Jeff Conine	Oma	20
Luis Medina	Oma	16
Harvey Pulliam	Oma	16

RBI		
Phil Hiatt	Oma	87
Sean Berry	Oma	77
Dan Rohrmeier	Oma	74
Jeff Conine	Oma	72
Les Norman	Mem	67

STOLEN BASES		
Kerwin Moore	Mem	42
Shane Halter	Bcy	26
Rod Myers	App	23
Jose Mota	Oma	21
Several players tied		16

WINS		
Brian Ahern	Oma	13
Ed Pierce	Mem	10
Several players tied		9

SAVES		
Ed Puig	Mem	25
Carlos Maldonado	Oma	16
Steve Shifflett	Oma	14
Several players tied		13

STRIKEOUTS		
Brian Bevil	App	168
Ed Pierce	Mem	131
Jose Ventura	Mem	123
Josias Manzanillo	Oma	122
Mike Bovee	App	120

PITCHING LEADERS	Club	W-L	ERA	IP	H	BB	SO
Mike Fyhrie	Bcy	7-13	2.50	162	148	37	92
Jose Ventura	Mem	8-15	2.73	184	153	68	123
John Gross	Bcy	9-6	2.85	152	138	45	96
Robert Toth	App	7-6	3.39	127	111	34	100
Brian Bevil	App	9-7	3.40	156	129	63	168

Kansas City (1969-1992)

Runs: Most, career, all-time

1514 GEORGE BRETT, 1973-1992
1074 Amos Otis, 1970-1983
1060 WILLIE WILSON, 1976-1990
912 Frank White, 1973-1990
873 Hal McRae, 1973-1987

Hits: Most, career, all-time

3005 GEORGE BRETT, 1973-1992
2006 Frank White, 1973-1990
1977 Amos Otis, 1970-1983
1968 WILLIE WILSON, 1976-1990
1924 Hal McRae, 1973-1987

2B: Most, career, all-time

634 GEORGE BRETT, 1973-1992
449 Hal McRae, 1973-1987
407 Frank White, 1973-1990
365 Amos Otis, 1970-1983
241 WILLIE WILSON, 1976-1990

3B: Most, career, all-time

134 GEORGE BRETT, 1973-1992
133 WILLIE WILSON, 1976-1990
65 Amos Otis, 1970-1983
63 Hal McRae, 1973-1987
58 Frank White, 1973-1990

HR: Most, career, all-time

298 GEORGE BRETT, 1973-1992
193 Amos Otis, 1970-1983
169 Hal McRae, 1973-1987
160 Frank White, 1973-1990
143 John Mayberry, 1972-1977

RBI: Most, career, all-time

1520 GEORGE BRETT, 1973-1992
1012 Hal McRae, 1973-1987
992 Amos Otis, 1970-1983
886 Frank White, 1973-1990
552 John Mayberry, 1972-1977

SB: Most, career, all-time

612 WILLIE WILSON, 1976-1990
340 Amos Otis, 1970-1983
336 Freddie Patek, 1971-1979
194 GEORGE BRETT, 1973-1992
178 Frank White, 1973-1990

BB: Most, career, all-time

1057 GEORGE BRETT, 1973-1992
739 Amos Otis, 1970-1983
616 Hal McRae, 1973-1987
561 John Mayberry, 1972-1977
413 Freddie Patek, 1971-1979

BA: Highest, career, all-time

.307 GEORGE BRETT, 1973-1992
.294 KEVIN SEITZER, 1986-1991
.293 Hal McRae, 1973-1987
.290 DANNY TARTABULL, 1987-1991
.289 WILLIE WILSON, 1976-1990

Slug avg: Highest, career, all-time

.518 DANNY TARTABULL, 1987-1991
.490 GEORGE BRETT, 1973-1992
.480 Bo Jackson, 1986-1990
.469 Willie Aikens, 1980-1983
.459 Steve Balboni, 1984-1988

Games started: Most, career, all-time

392 Paul Splittorff, 1970-1984
302 Dennis Leonard, 1974-1986
247 MARK GUBICZA, 1984-1992
226 BRET SABERHAGEN, 1984-1991
219 Larry Gura, 1976-1985

Saves: Most, career, all-time

238 Dan Quisenberry, 1979-1988
115 JEFF MONTGOMERY, 1988-1992
58 Doug Bird, 1973-1978
49 STEVE FARR, 1985-1990
40 Ted Abernathy, 1970-1972

Shutouts: Most, career, all-time

23 Dennis Leonard, 1974-1986
17 Paul Splittorff, 1970-1984
14 Larry Gura, 1976-1985
14 BRET SABERHAGEN, 1984-1991
13 MARK GUBICZA, 1984-1992

Wins: Most, career, all-time

166 Paul Splittorff, 1970-1984
144 Dennis Leonard, 1974-1986
111 Larry Gura, 1976-1985
110 BRET SABERHAGEN, 1984-1991
104 MARK GUBICZA, 1984-1992

K: Most, career, all-time

1323 Dennis Leonard, 1974-1986
1093 BRET SABERHAGEN, 1984-1991
1091 MARK GUBICZA, 1984-1992
1057 Paul Splittorff, 1970-1984
659 Steve Busby, 1972-1980

Win pct: Highest, career, all-time

.593 Al Fitzmorris, 1969-1976
.587 Larry Gura, 1976-1985
.585 BRET SABERHAGEN, 1984-1991
.577 KEVIN APPIER, 1989-1992
.576 Doug Bird, 1973-1978

ERA: Lowest, career, all-time

2.55 Dan Quisenberry, 1979-1988
3.21 BRET SABERHAGEN, 1984-1991
3.46 Al Fitzmorris, 1969-1976
3.48 Marty Pattin, 1974-1980
3.52 Dick Drago, 1969-1973

Runs: Most, season

133 WILLIE WILSON, 1980
119 GEORGE BRETT, 1979
113 WILLIE WILSON, 1979
108 GEORGE BRETT, 1985
105 GEORGE BRETT, 1977
105 KEVIN SEITZER, 1987

Hits: Most, season

230 WILLIE WILSON, 1980
215 GEORGE BRETT, 1976
212 GEORGE BRETT, 1979
207 KEVIN SEITZER, 1987
195 GEORGE BRETT, 1975

2B: Most, season

54 Hal McRae, 1977
46 Hal McRae, 1982
45 GEORGE BRETT, 1978
45 GEORGE BRETT, 1990
45 Frank White, 1982

3B: Most, season

21 WILLIE WILSON, 1985
20 GEORGE BRETT, 1979
15 WILLIE WILSON, 1980
15 WILLIE WILSON, 1982
15 WILLIE WILSON, 1987

HR: Most, season

36 Steve Balboni, 1985
34 John Mayberry, 1975
34 DANNY TARTABULL, 1987
32 Bo Jackson, 1989
31 DANNY TARTABULL, 1991

RBI: Most, season

133 Hal McRae, 1982
118 GEORGE BRETT, 1980
112 GEORGE BRETT, 1985
112 Al Cowens, 1977
112 Darrell Porter, 1979

SB: Most, season

83 WILLIE WILSON, 1979
79 WILLIE WILSON, 1980
59 WILLIE WILSON, 1983
59 WILLIE WILSON, 1987
53 Freddie Patek, 1977

BB: Most, season

122 John Mayberry, 1973
121 Darrell Porter, 1979
119 John Mayberry, 1975
103 GEORGE BRETT, 1985
103 Paul Schaal, 1971

BA: Highest, season

.390 GEORGE BRETT, 1980
.335 GEORGE BRETT, 1985
.333 GEORGE BRETT, 1976
.332 Hal McRae, 1976
.332 WILLIE WILSON, 1982

Slug avg: Highest, season

.664 GEORGE BRETT, 1980
.593 DANNY TARTABULL, 1991
.585 GEORGE BRETT, 1985
.563 GEORGE BRETT, 1979
.563 GEORGE BRETT, 1983

Games started: Most, season

40 Dennis Leonard, 1978
38 Steve Busby, 1974
38 Dennis Leonard, 1980
38 Paul Splittorff, 1973
38 Paul Splittorff, 1978

Saves: Most, season

45 Dan Quisenberry, 1983
44 Dan Quisenberry, 1984
39 JEFF MONTGOMERY, 1992
37 Dan Quisenberry, 1985
35 Dan Quisenberry, 1982

Shutouts: Most, season

6 Roger Nelson, 1972
5 Dennis Leonard, 1977
5 Dennis Leonard, 1979
4 Bill Butler, 1969
4 Dick Drago, 1971
4 Al Fitzmorris, 1974
4 MARK GUBICZA, 1988
4 Larry Gura, 1980
4 Dennis Leonard, 1978
4 BRET SABERHAGEN, 1987
4 BRET SABERHAGEN, 1989

Wins: Most, season

23 BRET SABERHAGEN, 1989
22 Steve Busby, 1974
21 Dennis Leonard, 1978
20 MARK GUBICZA, 1988
20 Dennis Leonard, 1977
20 Dennis Leonard, 1980
20 BRET SABERHAGEN, 1985
20 Paul Splittorff, 1973

K: Most, season

244 Dennis Leonard, 1977
206 Bob Johnson, 1970
198 Steve Busby, 1974
193 BRET SABERHAGEN, 1989
183 MARK GUBICZA, 1988
183 Dennis Leonard, 1978

Win pct: Highest, season

.800 Larry Gura, 1978
.793 BRET SABERHAGEN, 1989
.769 BRET SABERHAGEN, 1985
.727 Paul Splittorff, 1977
.714 MARK GUBICZA, 1988

ERA: Lowest, season

2.08 Roger Nelson, 1972
2.16 BRET SABERHAGEN, 1989
2.46 KEVIN APPIER, 1992
2.69 CHARLIE LEIBRANDT, 1985
2.70 MARK GUBICZA, 1988

Most pinch-hit homers, season

2 Hal McRae, 1986
2 Carmelo Martinez, 1991

Most pinch-hit, homers, career

2 Chuck Harrison, 1969-1971
2 Bob Oliver, 1969-1972
2 Amos Otis, 1970-1983
2 Hal McRae, 1973-1987
2 Steve Balboni, 1984-1988
2 Jim Eisenreich, 1987-1991
2 Carmelo Martinez, 1991

Most consecutive games, batting safely

30 George Brett, 1980
22 Brian McRae, 1991

Most consecutive scoreless innings

31 Bret Saberhagen, 1989

No hit games

Henry Porter, KC at Bal AL, 4-0; June 6, 1888.
Steve Busby, KC at Det AL, 3-0; April 16, 1973.
Steve Busby, KC at Mil AL, 2-0; June 19, 1974.
Jim Colborn, KC vs Tex AL, 6-0; May 14, 1977.
Bret Saberhagen, KC vs Chi AL, 7-0; August 26, 1991.

ACTIVE PLAYERS in caps.

Seattle Mariners

by Russell Beeker, *Baseball Weekly*

Edgar Martinez won the AL batting title (.343) and was first in doubles (46) and second in slugging.

1992 Mariners: New owners, bad year

Everybody expected 1992 to be a year of change for the Mariners. That change, however, was one of the most unpleasant kind. General manager Woody Woodward had acquired Kevin Mitchell from the Giants, to boost the offense and prevent opposing hurlers from pitching around Ken Griffey Jr. But Mitchell played in just 99 games for a total of nine home runs. The price the Mariners paid for Mitchell—three pitchers, including Bill Swift—proved to be too steep. The staff ERA was 4.56, second-worst in the league and the Mariners' worst since 1986. To add insult to injury, Swift led the National League with a 2.08 ERA.

The future of the franchise had seemingly brightened when a group of investors led by Nintendo chairman Hiroshi Yamauchi offered $125 million ($100 million plus $25 million in operating capital) to buy the team and keep it in Seattle. But major league baseball, in a rush of anti-Japan sentiment, kept adding conditions to the deal to lower the amount of foreign investment below 50 percent. In mid-June, the deal was finally approved—for $106 million.

Then the Mariners suffered through a club-record 14-game losing streak in September, including an 0-for-10 road trip to Cleveland, Minnesota, and Oakland. They used the disabled list a club-record 19 times; 15 players missed 747 games combined.

By that time, the new owners—Seattle's first local regime—had little to do but ride out the disappointing season and start gearing up for '93. The good news is that they certainly have players around which to rebuild the franchise: Third baseman Edgar Martinez led the AL in batting (.343), and had 18 homers and 73 RBI. (He had shoulder surgery Sept. 18, but is expected to be back by spring.) All-Star center fielder Ken Griffey Jr. had another banner year (.308, 27 HR, 103 RBI). He was named MVP of the All-Star Game, and was the fourth-youngest player ever to hit 20-plus homers in three straight years and the sixth-youngest to record 100 RBI twice. Shortstop Omar Vizquel hit .295, and Jay Buhner added another 25 homers and 79 RBI.

The mound is where the Mariners' future starts and ends. Rookie Dave Fleming recorded 17 wins with four shutouts, just one fewer than Roger Clemens. Randy Johnson eclipsed Clemens for the AL strikeout title (241); he struck out a club-record 18 batters (in eight innings) Sept.27 at Texas, tying the AL record for left-handers. But Erik Hanson lost 17 games in '92 (he won 18 in '90). The bullpen had just 30 saves all season and blew 15. Mike Schooler, the club's all-time save leader, finished with just 13 saves and a 4.70 ERA.

The Mariners finished 1992 in the AL West cellar, with the worst record in baseball.

—by Rick Lawes

1993 Mariners: Preview

The Mariners made big strides. Most important: Former Cincinnati manager Lou Piniella was hired. He's won everywhere else, but Seattle will be his biggest challenge. But pitching is a major problem. With Roger Salkeld out and Brian Holman still uncertain a year after rotator-cuff surgery, the rotation is highly suspect. Piniella brought in his own closer, Norm Charlton, to shore up the bullpen.

Offensively, the new manager has a little more to work with. He can expect strong performances from Ken Griffey Jr. (who also picked up his third Gold Glove in '92), Edgar Martinez (who signed a $10.1 million, three-year contract extension in August), shortstop Omar Vizquel, and right fielder Jay Buhner. Bret Boone, who will replace Harold Reynolds, is a potential rookie of the year.

—by Margaret McCahill

1992 Mariners: Between the lines

▸**April 23:** Complementing an already substantial arsenal of offensive weapons, Ken Griffey Jr. decided to employ the bunt single to reach base. He had his third of the season.

▸**April 25:** Randy Johnson (two earned runs and four unearned runs in 5 2/3 innings) allowed eight hits, but teammate Tino Martinez hit a grand slam that provided the winning margin.

▸**May 6:** Kevin Mitchell broke his long-ball drought, slugging his first home run of the season.

▸**May 7:** Griffey hit a pair of homers.

▸**May 16:** Dennis Powell became the first Seattle pitcher other than Dave Fleming to win a game in the last 17 contests, earning the victory in relief. Griffey homered and doubled; Edgar Martinez added a home run and a pair of RBI. It was Seattle's second straight road win.

▸**May 17:** Edgar Martinez homered twice and was 3-for-4 as the Mariners took their third straight one-run win against the Blue Jays at Toronto.

▸**May 18:** The Red Sox had gone 50 innings without allowing a home run before Mariner Pete O'Brien took Jeff Reardon deep in the ninth inning.

▸**May 20:** O'Brien's second-inning homer off of Roger Clemens was the first home run the Rocket had allowed since Oct. 1, 1991—76 innings.

▸**May 30:** Rookie Dave Fleming pitched his first major league shutout, for his seventh straight win. That streak tied Jack McDowell for the longest in the majors. Fleming finished May 5-0 with a 1.87 ERA.

▸**June 4:** Kevin Mitchell, sore wrist and all, homered twice, as did Ken Griffey Jr. It gave Griffey six home runs and 17 RBI in his last 10 games.

▸**June 9:** Fleming won his ninth in a row, still the longest winning streak in the majors.

▸**June 18:** Harold Reynolds entered play with just two hits in 24 at-bats against the White Sox in 1992. He promptly singled, tripled and hit a home run for three RBI.

▸**June 19:** Fleming became the first 10-game winner in the AL. Greg Briley's solo homer was the difference in the game. It was the fifth straight win for Seattle.

▸**June 25:** The Mariners improved to 18-12 against California since 1990, bombarding the visiting Angels with 13 runs on 14 hits. Seattle had three doubles and four homers, and batted around in the second and the fifth.

▸**June 28:** Kevin Mitchell matched his career high with four hits, adding a two-run homer.

▸**July 3:** Jay Buhner's fifth-inning grand slam highlighted the Mariners' 11-0 nightcap win in the doubleheader split with the Tigers.

▸**July 9:** Edgar Martinez was 3-for-5 with a homer and three RBI.

▸**July 10:** A large contingent of fans from nearby Mahopac, N.Y., flocked to Yankee Stadium to see local hero Dave Fleming pitch against the Yankees. He stifled the hosts on five hits in eight innings to earn his 11th win. Jay Buhner backed him with a pair of homers.

▸**July 16:** A crowd of 52,000 attended Seattle's "Opening Night II," a night celebrating the Mariners' new local ownership. New CEO John W. Ellis threw out the first pitch.

▸**July 17:** Griffey was 4-for-4, Kevin Mitchell was 3-for-4 with three RBI, and Lance Parrish—playing first base— drove in four on a pair of homers.

▸**July 21:** Built for comfort, not for speed: Detroit beat the Mariners 6-2, despite the fact that Tiger Frank Tanana was clocked as slow as 49 mph and Randy Johnson—who struck out a career-high 13 in six innings—was clocked as fast as 98 mph.

▸**July 25:** Mark Grant (1-2) won his first game since Sept. 3, 1990. He had missed all of 1991 because of shoulder surgery.

▸**July 26:** Kevin Mitchell continued to

make Mariners' fans feel better about the much-maligned trade as he blasted a pair of homers.

▸**July 29:** Brian Fisher allowed just three hits over seven shutout innings, beating the Angels, 8-0. It was his first win since April 19, 1988.

▸**August 15:** Randy Johnson fanned 13 and took a no-hitter into the seventh, but had to wait for pinch-hitter Dave Valle to single in the game-winning run in the ninth.

▸**August 16:** Pete O'Brien drove in the winning run on a two-out pinch-hit single in the ninth inning.

▸**August 19:** Edgar Martinez increased his lead in the AL batting race, going 3-for-5 with a grand slam to improve to .336. Bret Boone started for the Mariners, becoming the first-ever third-generation major leaguer, following in the footsteps of his father Bob and grandfather Ray.

▸**August 21:** Randy Johnson had his third consecutive double-digit strikeout game, fanning 11.

▸**August 22:** Bret Boone hit his first major league home run.

▸**August 23:** In his first game back since coming off the disabled list, Kevin Mitchell blasted a three-run homer off of Roger Clemens.

▸**August 25:** Despite the Mariners' six runs—three of which came quickly on a homer by Edgar Martinez—the 1:55 playing time amounted to the shortest nine-inning game ever played by Cleveland or Seattle.

▸**August 31:** Edgar Martinez went 3-for-4 with his 45th and 46th doubles, best in the major leagues.

▸**September 19:** Seattle ended a 14-game skid, beating the A's 6-4.

▸**September 25:** Several major league records were set or tied in the Mariners-Rangers game. The clubs combined to use 54 players, Texas used four shortstops, and Seattle used 11 pitchers.

▸**September 27 *Milestone:*** Randy Johnson tied an American League record for left-handers with 18 strikeouts against Texas, but asked to come out of the game after eight innings with the score tied at 2-2. He had thrown 160 pitches. Johnson shares the mark with former Yankees' hurler Ron Guidry. Texas won 3-2.

▸**October 3:** Randy Johnson and the Mariners beat the White Sox 7-2, to help Seattle avoid a 100-loss season.

▸**October 4:** The Mariners finished in the cellar, but Randy Johnson led the league in strikeouts (241) and Edgar Martinez was No. 1 in batting (.343) and doubles (46). Martinez was also among the top 10 in three other categories: slugging (.544), on-base percentage (.404), and hits (181). Ken Griffey Jr. was eighth in batting (.308).

—by Jeanie Chung, John Hunt, Deron Snyder, and Lisa Winston.

Team directory

▸**Owner:** Baseball Club of Seattle

▸**General Manager:** Woody Woodward

▸**Ballpark:**
The Kingdome
201 South King St., Seattle, Wash.
206-628-3555
Capacity 59,702
Public transportation available
Parking for 2,500 vehicles; $5; $1 discount for car pools
Family and wheelchair sections, Fantasy Play-by-Play, autograph booth, birthday package, anniversary package

▸**Team publications:**
Mariners Magazine
206-628-3555

▸**TV, radio broadcast stations:**
KIRO-AM 710

▸**Spring Training:**
Stadium TBA
Peoria, Ariz.

SEATTLE MARINERS 1992 final stats

Batting	AVG	SLG	OB	G	AB	R	H	TB	2B	3B	HR	RBI	BB	SO	SB	CS	E
E.Martinez	.343	.544	.404	135	528	100	181	287	46	3	18	73	54	61	14	4	17
Griffey	.308	.535	.361	142	565	83	174	302	39	4	27	103	44	67	10	5	1
Vizquel	.294	.352	.340	136	483	49	142	170	20	4	0	21	32	38	15	13	7
Mitchell	.286	.428	.351	99	360	48	103	154	24	0	9	67	35	46	0	2	0
Briley	.275	.400	.290	86	200	18	55	80	10	0	5	12	4	31	9	2	4
Turner	.270	.338	.341	34	74	8	20	25	5	0	0	5	9	15	2	1	5
Haselman	.263	.263	.263	8	19	1	5	5	0	0	0	0	0	7	0	0	0
Cotto	.259	.354	.294	108	294	42	76	104	11	1	5	27	14	49	23	2	0
T.Martinez	.257	.411	.316	136	460	53	118	189	19	2	16	66	42	77	2	1	4
Cochrane	.250	.322	.309	65	152	10	38	49	5	0	2	12	12	34	1	0	6
Reynolds	.247	.330	.316	140	458	55	113	151	23	3	3	33	45	41	15	12	12
Buhner	.243	.422	.333	152	543	69	132	229	16	3	25	79	71	146	0	6	2
Amaral	.240	.300	.276	35	100	9	24	30	3	0	1	7	5	16	4	2	3
Valle	.240	.362	.305	124	367	39	88	133	16	1	9	30	27	58	0	0	7
Parrish	.233	.418	.294	93	275	26	64	115	13	1	12	32	24	70	1	1	6
O'Brien	.222	.371	.289	134	396	40	88	147	15	1	14	52	40	27	2	1	3
Boone	.194	.318	.224	33	129	15	25	41	4	0	4	15	4	34	1	1	6
Blowers	.192	.274	.253	31	73	7	14	20	3	0	1	2	6	20	0	0	1
Howitt	.188	.329	.250	35	85	7	16	28	4	1	2	10	8	9	1	1	2
Moses	.136	.182	.296	21	22	3	3	4	1	0	0	1	5	4	0	0	0
Schaefer	.114	.186	.139	65	70	5	8	13	2	0	1	3	2	10	0	1	9
Sinatro	.107	.107	.107	18	28	0	3	3	0	0	0	0	0	5	0	0	0
Heffernan	.091	.182	.091	8	11	0	1	2	1	0	0	1	0	1	0	0	0
Bradley	.000	.000	.500	2	1	0	0	0	0	0	0	0	1	1	0	0	0
Lennon	.000	.000	.000	1	2	0	0	0	0	0	0	0	0	0	0	0	0

Pitching	W-L	ERA	G	GS	CG	GF	Sho	SV	IP	H	R	ER	HR	BB	SO
Barton	0-1	2.92	14	0	0	2	0	0	12.1	10	5	4	1	7	4
Woodson	0-1	3.29	8	1	0	0	0	0	13.2	12	7	5	0	11	6
Fleming	17-10	3.39	33	33	7	0	4	0	228.1	225	95	86	13	60	112
Nelson	1-7	3.44	66	0	0	27	0	6	81	71	34	31	7	44	46
Johnson	12-14	3.77	31	31	6	0	2	0	210.1	154	104	88	13	144	241
Grant	2-4	3.89	23	10	0	4	0	0	81	100	39	35	6	22	42
Fisher	4-3	4.53	22	14	0	2	0	1	91.1	80	49	46	9	47	26
Powell	4-2	4.58	49	0	0	11	0	0	57	49	30	29	5	29	35
Schooler	2-7	4.70	53	0	0	36	0	13	51.2	55	29	27	7	24	33
Swan	3-10	4.74	55	9	1	26	0	9	104.1	104	60	55	8	45	45
Hanson	8-17	4.82	31	30	6	0	1	0	186.2	209	110	100	14	57	112
Acker	0-0	5.28	17	0	0	3	0	0	30.2	45	19	18	4	12	11
Leary	8-10	5.36	26	23	3	2	0	0	141	131	89	84	12	87	46
DeLucia	3-6	5.49	30	11	0	6	0	1	83.2	100	55	51	13	35	66
Jones	3-5	5.69	38	1	0	14	0	0	61.2	50	39	39	8	47	49
Agosto	0-0	5.89	17	1	0	2	0	0	18.1	27	12	12	0	3	12
Harris	0-0	7.00	8	0	0	2	0	0	9	8	7	7	3	6	6
Walker	0-3	7.36	5	3	0	1	0	0	14.2	21	14	12	4	9	5
Parker	0-2	7.56	8	6	0	1	0	0	33.1	47	28	28	6	11	20
Kramer	0-1	7.71	4	4	0	0	0	0	16.1	30	14	14	2	7	6
Gunderson	2-1	8.68	9	0	0	4	0	0	9.1	12	12	9	1	5	2
Brown	0-0	9.00	2	0	0	0	0	0	3	4	3	3	1	3	2
Schmidt	0-0	18.90	3	0	0	0	0	0	3.1	7	7	7	1	3	1

1993 preliminary roster

PITCHERS (22)
Chris Bosio
Norm Charlton
Kevin Coffman
John Cummings
Jeff Darwin
Rich DeLucia
Brian Fisher
Dave Fleming
Erik Hanson
Reggie Harris
Brian Holman
Randy Johnson
Tim Leary
Jeff Nelson
Andy Nezelek
Yorkis Perez
Dennis Powell
Mike Remlinger
Roger Salkeld
Mike Schooler
Russ Swan
Kerry Woodson

CATCHERS (4)
Dave Cochrane
Brian Deak
Bill Haselman
David Valle

INFIELDERS (8)
Rich Amaral
Bret Boone
Edgar Martinez
Tino Martinez
Pete O'Brien
Greg Pirkl
Fernando Vina
Omar Vizquel

OUTFIELDERS (5)
Greg Briley
Jay Buhner
Mike Felder
Ken Griffey
Lee Tinsley

Games played by position

Player	G	C	1B	2B	3B	SS	OF	DH
AMARAL,R	35	0	2	1	17	17	3	0
BLOWERS,M	31	0	3	0	29	0	0	0
BOONE,B	33	0	0	32	6	0	0	0
BRADLEY,S	2	1	0	0	0	0	0	0
BRILEY,G	86	0	0	4	4	0	42	12
BUHNER,J	152	0	0	0	0	0	150	0
COCHRANE,D	65	21	3	1	10	3	25	2
COTTO,H	108	0	0	0	0	0	92	3
GRIFFEY,KJR	142	0	0	0	0	0	137	3
HASELMAN,B	8	5	0	0	0	0	2	0
HEFFERNAN,B	8	5	0	0	0	0	0	1
HOWITT,D	35	0	4	0	0	0	30	1
LENNON,P	1	0	1	0	0	0	0	0
MARTINEZ,T	136	0	78	0	0	0	0	48
MARTINEZ,E	135	0	2	0	103	0	0	28
MITCHELL,K	99	0	0	0	0	0	69	26
MOSES,J	21	0	0	0	0	0	18	1
O'BRIEN,P	134	0	81	0	0	0	0	35
PARRISH,L	93	56	16	0	0	0	0	16
REYNOLDS,H	140	0	0	134	0	0	1	1
SCHAEFER,J	65	0	0	7	21	33	0	2
SINATRO,M	18	18	0	0	0	0	0	0
TURNER,S	34	0	0	0	18	0	15	0
VALLE,D	124	122	0	0	0	0	0	0
VIZQUEL,O	136	0	0	0	0	136	0	0

Sick call: 1992 DL report

Player	Days on the DL
Acker, Jim	36
Briley, Greg*	48
Cochrane, Dave	66
Delucia, Rich	27
Griffey, Ken	16
Hanson, Erik	20
Holman, Brian	182
Johnson, Randy	16
Mitchell, Kevin*	48
Parker, Clay	118
Schooler, Mike	37
Sinatro, Matt*	141
Valle, Dave	17
Vizquel, Omar	30
Woodson, Kerry*	46

** On Disabled List twice during 1992 season (not counting transfers from one DL to another).*

Minor league report

Class AAA — Calgary finished 60-78, 4th in both halves of the Pacific Coast League Northern Division. SS Rich Amaral hit .318 and led the league with 53 SB. 2B Bret Boone hit .314 with 13 HR and 73 RBI. OF Ted Williams had 41 SB. **Class AA:** Jacksonville finished 68-75, 2nd in the 1st half of the Southern League Eastern Division and 4th in the 2nd half. OF Tow Maynard hit .283 and led the league with 38 SB. RHP Jim Converse was 12-7 with a 2.66 ERA and led the league with 157 K in 159 IP. RHP Troy Kent had 21 saves. **Class A:** San Bernadino finished 52-84, last in both halves of the California League Southern Division. LHP Mike Hampton was 13-8 with a 3.12 ERA. RHP Tony Phillips had 12 saves. Peninsula finished 74-64, 1st in both halves of the Carolina League Southern Division. The team beat Lynchburg in five games for the league championship. 1B Bubba Smith led the league in HR with 32 and had 93 RBI. OF Ruben Santana hit .294 with 8 HR and 61 RBI. LHP John Cummings was the league's Pitcher of the Year at 16-6 with a 2.57 ERA and led the league in K with 144. Bellingham finished 43-33, 1st in the Northwest League North Division. The team beat Bend in two games for the league championship. 1B Fred McNair hit .329 with 8 HR and 54 RBI. OF Renaldo Bullock led the league with 40 SB. RHP Derek Lowe was 7-3 with a 2.42 ERA. RHP Lavell Cudjo, with co-op Lethbridge of the Pioneer League, was 2nd in his league with 11 saves. Mariners finished 32-24, 2nd in the Arizona League. OF Marcus Sturdivant hit .312. C Tim Furtado hit .306. OF Byron Thomas had 24 SB. RHP Greg Theron was 4-1 with a 1.26 ERA. LHP John Vanhof was 3-1 with a 1.29. RHP Robin Cope was 1-1 with a 1.93. RHP John Thompson had 65 K.

Tops in the organization

BATTING LEADERS	Club	Avg.	G	AB	R	H	HR	RBI
Rich Amaral	CGy	.318	106	403	79	128	0	21
Bret Boone	CGy	.314	118	439	73	138	13	73
Ruben Santana	Pen	.294	113	401	54	118	8	61
Tow Maynard	Jax	.283	122	406	55	115	1	29
Miah Bradbury	Pen	.280	111	396	33	111	7	53

HOME RUNS			WINS		
Bubba Smith	Pen	32	John Cummings	Pen	16
Frank Bolick	CGy	27	Mike Hampton	Jax	13
Bill Haselman	CGy	19	Jim Converse	Jax	12
Greg Pirkl	CGy	16	Several players tied		10
Brian Turang	Jax	14			

RBI			SAVES		
Frank Bolick	CGy	96	Troy Kent	Jax	21
Bubba Smith	Pen	93	Tony Phillips	Sbr	12
Tommy Adams	Jax	80	Brad Holman	Jax	9
Bret Boone	CGy	73	Chuck Wiley	Pen	8
Mike Blowers	CGy	67	Several players tied		7

STOLEN BASES			STRIKEOUTS		
Rich Amaral	CGy	53	Jim Converse	Jax	157
Darren Bragg	Pen	44	John Cummings	Pen	144
Ted Williams	CGy	41	Greg Bicknell	Pen	140
Will Taylor	Pen	39	Mike Hampton	Jax	138
Tow Maynard	Jax	38	Lagrande Russell	Pen	130

PITCHING LEADERS	Club	W-L	ERA	IP	H	BB	SO
John Cummings	Pen	16-6	2.57	168	149	63	144
Jim Converse	Jax	12-7	2.66	159	134	82	157
Greg Bicknell	Pen	10-7	3.12	179	170	53	140
Lagrande Russell	Pen	7-10	3.15	157	132	59	130
Mike Hampton	Jax	13-9	3.19	180	176	67	138

Seattle (1977-1992)

Runs: Most, career, all-time

563 ALVIN DAVIS, 1984-1991
543 HAROLD REYNOLDS, 1983-1992
402 Julio Cruz, 1977-1983
351 Jim Presley, 1984-1989
346 Phil Bradley, 1983-1987

Hits: Most, career, all-time

1163 ALVIN DAVIS, 1984-1991
1063 HAROLD REYNOLDS, 1983-1992
736 Jim Presley, 1984-1989
697 Bruce Bochte, 1978-1982
652 KEN GRIFFEY JR., 1989-1992

2B: Most, career, all-time

212 ALVIN DAVIS, 1984-1991
200 HAROLD REYNOLDS, 1983-1992
147 Jim Presley, 1984-1989
134 Bruce Bochte, 1978-1982
132 KEN GRIFFEY JR., 1989-1992

3B: Most, career, all-time

48 HAROLD REYNOLDS, 1983-1992
26 Phil Bradley, 1983-1987
23 SPIKE OWEN, 1983-1986
20 Ruppert Jones, 1977-1979
19 Dan Meyer, 1977-1981

HR: Most, career, all-time

160 ALVIN DAVIS, 1984-1991
115 Jim Presley, 1984-1989
105 Ken Phelps, 1983-1988
87 KEN GRIFFEY JR., 1989-1992
79 DAVE HENDERSON, 1981-1986

RBI: Most, career, all-time

667 ALVIN DAVIS, 1984-1991
418 Jim Presley, 1984-1989
344 KEN GRIFFEY JR., 1989-1992
329 Bruce Bochte, 1978-1982
313 Dan Meyer, 1977-1981

SB: Most, career, all-time

290 Julio Cruz, 1977-1983
228 HAROLD REYNOLDS, 1983-1992
107 Phil Bradley, 1983-1987
97 HENRY COTTO, 1988-1992
70 JOHN MOSES, 1982-1992

BB: Most, career, all-time

672 ALVIN DAVIS, 1984-1991
391 HAROLD REYNOLDS, 1983-1992
330 Julio Cruz, 1977-1983
317 Ken Phelps, 1983-1988
313 Bruce Bochte, 1978-1982

BA: Highest, career, all-time

.311 EDGAR MARTINEZ, 1987-1992
.301 KEN GRIFFEY JR., 1989-1992
.301 Phil Bradley, 1983-1987
.290 Bruce Bochte, 1978-1982
.281 ALVIN DAVIS, 1984-1991

Slug avg: Highest, career, all-time

.521 Ken Phelps, 1983-1988
.494 KEN GRIFFEY JR., 1989-1992
.462 EDGAR MARTINEZ, 1987-1992
.453 ALVIN DAVIS, 1984-1991
.449 Phil Bradley, 1983-1987

Games started: Most, career, all-time

217 MIKE MOORE, 1982-1988
173 MARK LANGSTON, 1984-1989
147 Jim Beattie, 1980-1986
146 Glenn Abbott, 1977-1983
127 MATT YOUNG, 1983-1990

Saves: Most, career, all-time

98 MIKE SCHOOLER, 1988-1992
52 Bill Caudill, 1982-1983
36 Shane Rawley, 1978-1981
35 EDWIN NUNEZ, 1982-1988
28 MIKE JACKSON, 1988-1991

Shutouts: Most, career, all-time

9 MARK LANGSTON, 1984-1989
9 MIKE MOORE, 1982-1988
7 FLOYD BANNISTER, 1979-1982
6 Jim Beattie, 1980-1986
5 Brian Holman, 1989-1991
5 RANDY JOHNSON, 1989-1992
5 MATT YOUNG, 1983-1990

Wins: Most, career, all-time

74 MARK LANGSTON, 1984-1989
66 MIKE MOORE, 1982-1988
46 RANDY JOHNSON, 1989-1992
45 ERIK HANSON, 1988-1992
45 MATT YOUNG, 1983-1990

K: Most, career, all-time

1078 MARK LANGSTON, 1984-1989
937 MIKE MOORE, 1982-1988
767 RANDY JOHNSON, 1989-1992
597 MATT YOUNG, 1983-1990
577 ERIK HANSON, 1988-1992

Win pct: Highest, career, all-time

.525 MARK LANGSTON, 1984-1989
.517 ERIK HANSON, 1988-1992
.511 RANDY JOHNSON, 1989-1992
.444 FLOYD BANNISTER, 1979-1982
.415 Glenn Abbott, 1977-1983

ERA: Lowest, career, all-time

3.75 FLOYD BANNISTER, 1979-1982
3.76 ERIK HANSON, 1988-1992
3.90 RANDY JOHNSON, 1989-1992
4.01 MARK LANGSTON, 1984-1989
4.04 BILL SWIFT, 1985-1991

Runs: Most, season

109 Ruppert Jones, 1979
101 Phil Bradley, 1987
100 Phil Bradley, 1985
100 EDGAR MARTINEZ, 1992
100 HAROLD REYNOLDS, 1990

Hits: Most, season

192 Phil Bradley, 1985
184 HAROLD REYNOLDS, 1989
181 EDGAR MARTINEZ, 1992
180 Willie Horton, 1979
180 Jack Perconte, 1984

2B: Most, season

46 EDGAR MARTINEZ, 1992
42 KEN GRIFFEY JR., 1991
39 Al Cowens, 1982
39 KEN GRIFFEY JR., 1992
38 Bruce Bochte, 1979
38 Phil Bradley, 1987

3B: Most, season

11 HAROLD REYNOLDS, 1988
10 Phil Bradley, 1987
9 Ruppert Jones, 1979
9 HAROLD REYNOLDS, 1989
8 Phil Bradley, 1985
8 Al Cowens, 1982
8 Ruppert Jones, 1977
8 SPIKE OWEN, 1984
8 HAROLD REYNOLDS, 1987

HR: Most, season

32 Gorman Thomas, 1985
29 ALVIN DAVIS, 1987
29 Willie Horton, 1979
28 Jim Presley, 1985
27 JAY BUHNER, 1991
27 ALVIN DAVIS, 1984
27 KEN GRIFFEY JR., 1992
27 Ken Phelps, 1987
27 Jim Presley, 1986
27 Leroy Stanton, 1977

RBI: Most, season

116 ALVIN DAVIS, 1984
107 Jim Presley, 1986
106 Willie Horton, 1979
103 KEN GRIFFEY JR., 1992
100 Bruce Bochte, 1979
100 ALVIN DAVIS, 1987
100 KEN GRIFFEY JR., 1991

SB: Most, season

60 HAROLD REYNOLDS, 1987
59 Julio Cruz, 1978
49 Julio Cruz, 1979
46 Julio Cruz, 1982
45 Julio Cruz, 1980

BB: Most, season

101 ALVIN DAVIS, 1989
97 ALVIN DAVIS, 1984
95 ALVIN DAVIS, 1988
90 ALVIN DAVIS, 1985
88 Ken Phelps, 1986

BA: Highest, season

.343 EDGAR MARTINEZ, 1992
.327 KEN GRIFFEY JR., 1991
.326 Tom Paciorek, 1981
.316 Bruce Bochte, 1979
.310 Phil Bradley, 1986

Slug avg: Highest, season

.544 EDGAR MARTINEZ, 1992
.535 KEN GRIFFEY JR., 1992
.527 KEN GRIFFEY JR., 1991
.516 ALVIN DAVIS, 1987
.515 Leon Roberts, 1978

Games started: Most, season

37 MIKE MOORE, 1986
36 MARK LANGSTON, 1986
35 FLOYD BANNISTER, 1982
35 MARK LANGSTON, 1987
35 MARK LANGSTON, 1988
35 MATT YOUNG, 1985

Saves: Most, season

33 MIKE SCHOOLER, 1989
26 Bill Caudill, 1982
26 Bill Caudill, 1983
17 BILL SWIFT, 1991
16 EDWIN NUNEZ, 1985
16 Enrique Romo, 1977

Shutouts: Most, season

4 DAVE FLEMING, 1992
3 FLOYD BANNISTER, 1982
3 Brian Holman, 1991
3 MARK LANGSTON, 1987
3 MARK LANGSTON, 1988
3 MIKE MOORE, 1988

Wins: Most, season

19 MARK LANGSTON, 1987
18 ERIK HANSON, 1990
17 DAVE FLEMING, 1992
17 MARK LANGSTON, 1984
17 MIKE MOORE, 1985

K: Most, season

262 MARK LANGSTON, 1987
245 MARK LANGSTON, 1986
241 RANDY JOHNSON, 1992
235 MARK LANGSTON, 1988
228 RANDY JOHNSON, 1991

Win pct: Highest, season

.667 ERIK HANSON, 1990
.630 DAVE FLEMING, 1992
.630 MARK LANGSTON, 1984
.630 MIKE MOORE, 1985
.594 MARK LANGSTON, 1987

ERA: Lowest, season

3.24 ERIK HANSON, 1990
3.27 MATT YOUNG, 1983
3.34 SCOTT BANKHEAD, 1989
3.34 MARK LANGSTON, 1988
3.34 Jim Beattie, 1982

Most pinch-hit homers, season

2 Leon Roberts, 1978
2 Gary Gray, 1981
2 Ken Phelps, 1986
2 Greg Briley, 1992

Most pinch-hit, homers, career

4 Ken Phelps, 1983-1988

Most consecutive games, batting safely

21 Dan Meyer, 1979
21 Richie Zisk, 1982

Most consecutive scoreless innings

34 Mark Langston, 1988

No hit games

Randy Johnson, Sea vs Det AL, 2-0; June 2, 1990.

ACTIVE PLAYERS in caps.

Resource Directory

Major League Baseball

▸MLB Headquarters
350 Park Avenue
New York, NY 10022
212-339-7800

▸MLB Office of the Commissioner
350 Park Avenue
New York, NY 10022
212-339-7800

▸American League
350 Park Avenue
New York, NY 10022
212-339-7600

▸National League
350 Park Avenue
New York, NY 10022
212-339-7700

▸MLB Players Association
805 Third Avenue
New York, NY 10022
212-826-0808

Amateur Baseball Organizations

▸All American Amateur Baseball Association
340 Walker Drive
Zanesville, OH 43701
614-453-7349

▸American Amateur Baseball Congress
118-19 Redfield Plaza
P.O. Box 467
Marshall, MI 49068
616-781-2002

▸International Baseball Association
201 S. Capitol Ave., Ste. 490
Indianapolis, IN 46225
317-237-5757

▸National Baseball Congress
P.O. Box 1420
Wichita, KS 67201
316-267-3372

▸United States Baseball Federation
2160 Greenwood Ave.
Trenton, NJ 08609
609-586-2381

Youth Leagues

▸American Legion Baseball
National Headquarters
700 North Pennsylvania
Indianapolis, IN 46204
317-635-8411

▸Babe Ruth Baseball
1770 Brunswick Ave.
P.O. Box 5000
Trenton, NJ 08638
609-695-1434

▸Little League Baseball, Inc.
P.O. Box 3485
Williamsport, PA 17701
717-326-1921

▸Pony Baseball, Inc.
P.O. Box 225
Washington, PA 15301
412-225-1060

Senior Leagues

▸Men's Senior Baseball League
8 Sutton Terrace
Jericho, NY 11753
516-931-2615

Collegiate Baseball Organizations

▸National Collegiate Athletic Association
6201 College Boulevard
Overland Park, KS 66211
913-339-1906

▸National Association of Intercollegiate Athletics
Baseball Administrator
1221 Baltimore Avenue
Kansas City, MO 64105
816-842-5050

▸National Junior College Athletic Association
Baseball Tournament Director
P.O. Box 7305
Colorado Springs, CO 80933
719-590-9788

High School Baseball Organizations

▸National Federation of State High School Associations
Editor of Baseball Rules Book
11724 Plaza Circle
P.O. Box 20626
Kansas City, MO 64195
816-464-5400

Coaches Organizations

▸American Baseball Coaches Association
Rosenblatt Stadium
P.O. Box 3545
Omaha, NE 68103
402-733-0374

Museums, Halls of Fame, etc.

▸Babe Ruth Birthplace/Baltimore Orioles Museum
216 Emory Street
Baltimore, MD 21230
410-727-1539

▸Baseball Hall of Fame
Main Street
Cooperstown, NY 13326
607-547-9988

▸Peter J. McGovern Little League Baseball Museum
Route 15
South Williamsport, PA 17701
717-326-3607

▸United States Baseball Federation Hall of Fame
4880 Navy Road
Millington, TN 38053
901-872-3311

Collectors Shows

▸Madison Square Garden Baseball Card & Sports Collectors Show
Madison Square Garden
4 Pennsylvania Plaza
New York, NY 10001
212-465-6000

League Forecasts

INSIDE:

USA SNAPSHOTS®

A look at statistics that shape the sports world

Source: USA TODAY research

By Ron Coddington, USA TODAY

1993: A peek into the crystal ball(game)

National League prophecy

▸**Atlanta:** Deion Sanders will be the everyday leftfielder, or Bobby Cox will risk ice-water retaliation.

▸**Chicago:** Enraged at being left unprotected, Shawon Dunston will throw even harder to first base. Mark Grace will demand to be traded.

▸**Cincinnati:** Owner Marge Schott will roam the outfield with Schottzie 02, leaving little presents on the field.

▸**Colorado:** The NL will allow the Rockies to play four outfielders in the vast expanse of Mile High Stadium if they agree to wear the White Sox' old softball-style shorts.

▸**Florida:** The entire home schedule will be rained out, but the sleeveless uniforms will be the hit of the season.

▸**Houston:** Doug Drabek at the Astrodome? All other Cy Young bets are off.

▸**Los Angeles:** Always the kidder, Roger McDowell will confess that his 1992 ERA of 4.09 was just a joke.

▸**Montreal:** Delino DeShields and golfer Payne Stewart will go into the menswear business and put out a line of plus-fours.

▸**New York:** NL basestealers will give hitting tips to catcher Todd Hundley to keep him in the lineup.

▸**Philadelphia:** Lenny Dykstra will open the season on the DL after an off-season velcro-jumping mishap.

▸**Pittsburgh:** The salary-poor Pirates will avoid playing day games; it would conflict with their second jobs.

▸**St. Louis:** In an unprecedented fit of wildness, Bob Tewksbury will walk three batters in one game.

▸**San Diego:** A 535-foot shot will earn Fred McGriff a new nickname: Crime tape.

▸**San Francisco:** A slimmed-down Matt Williams will report to spring training shaken by the realization that he came within 18 pounds of not hitting his weight in 1992.

American League prophecy

▸**Baltimore:** Glenn Davis will pinch a nerve in his finger endorsing his pay-check and will lose most of the season.

▸**Boston:** A longtime friend of Roger Clemens will become official scorer.

▸**California:** Tim Salmon will replace Kevin Bass on the all-aquatic team, with pitcher Steve Trout.

▸**Chicago:** Frank Thomas will lead the AL in every category, but will not show up in the MVP voting.

▸**Cleveland:** Sandy Alomar Jr. will retire before the season, but will still be voted to the All-Star team.

▸**Detroit:** Owner Mike Ilitch will offer a special: Buy a large pepperoni pizza and get a free pitcher. Dissatisfied customers will think he meant a pitcher of beverage.

▸**Kansas City:** Owners will sign Prince Charles and bat him cleanup, in a desperate attempt to find a Royal with some power.

▸**Milwaukee:** "America's Funniest Home Videos" will erect a permanent studio in left field for Kevin Reimer.

▸**Minnesota:** After being picked to finish last, the Twins will win it all.

▸**New York:** Hensley Meulens will make fans forget Charlie Hayes, who made them forget Mike Blowers.

▸**Oakland:** Dennis Eckersley will be seen walking across the bay to get to Oakland, proving that he is not only the MVP and Cy Young winner, but also God.

▸**Seattle:** *Singles II* will be released, a documentary about the Mariners' offense without Kevin Mitchell.

▸**Texas:** When the team ERA is as big as Dallas, GM Tom Grieve will say, "He wasn't even the best available Guzman," about the one that got away.

▸**Toronto:** David Wells will go the first two months of the season without giving up as many runs (13) as he did in his Aug. 20, 1992, start against Milwaukee.

NL East: Look out for those Expos

At the start of the 1992 season, the Montreal Expos were concerned with one thing—surviving. A year later, they have a new goal—first place.

The Expos' sudden rise in the NL East—from a last-place, 90-loss season to an 87-win, second-place finish the next year—was real evidence that they are on the move. It also knocked down rumors that they could be looking for a new home if they didn't play better and draw more fans. The team won, and the fans came—700,000 more than the previous year. Those fans became believers in their young team and new manager Felipe Alou. The Expos battled the Pirates until early September and ended up in second place. With almost all of their regulars returning, and the Pirates expected to be hurting from the loss of Barry Bonds, the Expos should be the team to beat in the NL East.

Outfielder Marquis Grissom is a two-time stolen base champion, and All-Star Larry Walker won a Gold Glove. Second baseman Delino DeShields is another emerging star, as is Moises Alou, runner-up for Rookie of the Year. Rookie Greg Colbrunn expects to see more action at first base, and catcher Tim Laker is being counted on to provide solid defense. Shortstop Wil Cordero has long been considered the best prospect in the team's deep farm system, and he finally should be ready to get his shot at a starting spot.

The pitching rotation, led by veteran Dennis Martinez and Ken Hill, seems sound. The biggest find for the team was closer John Wetteland, who had 37 saves, third-best in the league.

The Pirates would be competitive if they were returning with their 1992 lineup, but that won't be the case. In addition to the loss of free agents Barry Bonds and Doug Drabek, the Pirates lost pitcher Danny Jackson and outfielder Alex Cole in the expansion draft. And Zane Smith is coming off shoulder surgery.

Second baseman Jose Lind was dumped to cut costs. The Pirates will be a much younger team: Kevin Young, Carlos Garcia, and Al Martin are important pieces in the rebuilding puzzle.

No team in the division was more of a disappointment in 1992 than the preseason favorite Mets, who fell to fifth place and will return with the same basic team this year. The Mets' key to improvement will be a healthy Bret Saberhagen and Dwight Gooden in the rotation, John Franco in the bullpen (after elbow surgery), Howard Johnson at third base (after knee surgery), and Bobby Bonilla in the outfield—after a year of adjusting to the pressures of playing in New York.

The Cardinals' biggest task will be to find a replacement for first baseman Andres Galarraga; Rod Brewer was the preseason favorite. New hitting coach Chris Chambliss must also figure out a way to get third baseman Todd Zeile's offensive production to bounce back.

The Cubs faced the challenge of replacing Greg Maddux and Andre Dawson. They added proven starters Greg Hibbard and Jose Guzman, and closer Randy Myers.

The trade for Danny Jackson, via the Marlins, gives the Phillies another solid starter, but the team will have to stay healthy and score runs to climb out of last place—a possibility if the pitching staff improves as expected.

The Marlins enter their first season as a largely unknown quantity; most of their draft selections will probably spend much of the year in the minor leagues. Their most proven player, reliever Bryan Harvey, is coming off elbow surgery, and there is a question as to how often he will get to pitch in save situations.

—by Rob Rains

NL West: The Braves want it again

No team in the NL West has won three consecutive titles since division play began in 1969. That is the goal of the Atlanta Braves in 1993.

They enter the season with the same basic team that produced their two consecutive pennants plus Cy Young Award winner Greg Maddux. So, they can again ride the strength of the league's best starting rotation, including left-handers Tom Glavine and Steve Avery, and right-handers John Smoltz and Peter Smith.

As always, the Braves were trying to add to their nucleus of pitching and solid lineup during the winter, a factor which would make them an even stronger team than before. The bullpen—source of much of their trouble in the '92 World Series—also needs to improve. They are relying on the continued development of Mark Wohlers and Mike Stanton for the right-left closer roles.

The Braves will likely get their biggest challenge from the Reds, who changed their manager, general manager, and several players despite winning 90 games for the second time in three years. New GM Jim Bowden gave new manager Tony Perez some new tools to work with: He dealt Paul O'Neill to the Yankees for Roberto Kelly, and Norm Charlton to Seattle for former MVP Kevin Mitchell. The Reds, who were desperate for a player with 30-homer and 100-RBI potential for the fourth spot in their lineup, believe a return to the NL will help revitalize Mitchell, who slumped last year with the Mariners. They also believe they can afford to lose Charlton; Rob Dibble is the lone closer.

Even with an improved offense, the Reds' starting pitchers will have to get better in order to catch the Braves. Jose Rijo and Tim Belcher tied for the team lead with 15 victories, and Tom Browning is coming off knee surgery. The addition of John Smiley eases the loss of free-agent Greg Swindell.

The Astros might be more of a threat than some people expect, especially with the addition of Doug Drabek and Swindell to their pitching staff. The Astros had a .500 record in 1992, and new owner Drayton McLane Jr. was spending money to improve the team.

The Astros were edged out of third place on the final day of the season by the Padres, who return with the league batting champion (Gary Sheffield) and home run leader (Fred McGriff), but will have to struggle to be a .500 club due to the severe financial restrictions placed on the club by owner Tom Werner. They traded shortstop Tony Fernandez to the Mets for starters. The new Padres will be a very young and inexperienced club.

After months of wondering where they would be playing in 1993, the Giants finally got an answer: Candlestick. Then, they stunned everyone by signing MVP Barry Bonds. But the team will need improved pitching to avoid another losing season.

The Dodgers were the division's biggest disappointment, falling from a first-place battle with the Braves in 1991 to a last-place, 99-loss season in '92. Big flops from Darryl Strawberry and Eric Davis were the primary reason for the Dodgers' fall, and they will need somebody other than Rookie of the Year Eric Karros to be a big bat in the middle of the lineup if they hope to climb back into contention.

The Colorado Rockies enter their first season with a lineup they think will make them competitive, but no one is overconfident. The stars figure to be first baseman Andres Galarraga and third baseman Charlie Hayes; both could produce some big offensive numbers playing in the lighter air in Denver. The Rockies are also counting on No. 1 pick, right-handed pitcher David Nied, to develop into the ace of their staff for years to come.

—by Rob Rains

AL East: Money talks, but will it win?

Despite heading into the off-season with a dozen free agents, including Joe Carter and Dave Winfield, Blue Jays' manager Pat Gillick vowed his ballclub will be competitive in '93. The Blue Jays have deep pockets and the willingness to spend. And in making it to the World Series for the first time— and winning the championship— manager Cito Gaston finally garnered some respect.

Toronto will have new faces. But the crucial factor, Carter, stayed and newcomers Paul Molitor and Dave Stewart provide more talent and more leadership. They could use another slugger to compete from a power standpoint. But no matter how much the team changes, the coaching ranks will provide stability. From Gaston on down, all of the Jays' major-league coaches were re-signed for '93. And after winning the division three of the last four years, Toronto has to be early favorite.

The Milwaukee Brewers chased the Jays until the final weekend of the '92 season. The Brewers may not have the Jays' wealth, but manager Phil Garner had his team playing aggressive baseball. The rest of the AL will need another year to catch up.

The Brewers will miss free agent pitcher Chris Bosio and franchise cornerstone Molitor, but the addition of DH Kevin Reimer will bolster their often one-dimensional offense.

The Baltimore Orioles were the most improved team in baseball in '92. Yet they're more likely to stay at mere contender status. Brady Anderson and Mike Devereaux will need to duplicate career seasons for Baltimore to stay in the hunt. The heart of the O's order—Cal Ripken and Glenn Davis—combined for just 27 homers in '92. They'll do better this season, but it won't be enough to win the division.

The Cleveland Indians vastly improved their record as well—19 games better than the previous year. Their rebound is even more impressive considering they lost 30 of their first 44 games. But the Indians are too green, especially in starting pitching, to compete all season long against Toronto and Milwaukee: 24-year-old Charles Nagy was the team's ace in '92.

They believe in their young players, though; they protected as many as possible in the expansion draft, but it cost them an established pitcher in Jack Armstrong.

The New York Yankees were gearing up for a major overhaul heading into the winter meetings. They had saved more than $9 million in payroll by cutting loose Jesse Barfield, Mel Hall, Greg Cadaret and others. And with George Steinbrenner ready to return, the Yankees were positioned to chase such elite free agents as Barry Bonds, Cone and Greg Maddux. But nobody would take the high-priced bait. In losing Charlie Hayes to the Rockies in the expansion draft, they left themselves with a major hole that Wade Boggs fills at third base.

The Detroit Tigers are also trying to sign a few free agents. New owner Mike Ilitch resurrected hockey's Red Wings, and he'll do the same with the Tigers. They won't be free spenders, like the Blue Jays and Yankees, but adding Mike Moore boosts the woeful pitching.

The Boston Red Sox finished in the cellar in '92 and jumped into the free-agent chase with Andre Dawson. But even with a trade for Ivan Calderon, they have a long way to go.

Promising young players like Scott Cooper at third base, John Valentin at shortstop, Tim Naehring at second, and Mo Vaughn at first, could be a solid foundation for the future. But the Red Sox will need much more to become a force again in the AL East.

—by Tim Wendel

AL West: It's wide-open in '93

Old age and fiscal reality have broken up the Oakland A's. Even though general manager Sandy Alderson pursued the club's key free agents, the A's simply had too many and not enough cash to bring everybody back.

Missed most could be the leadership void created by the loss of Dave Stewart. And what's worse, he went to the AL's new power, Toronto. The new season puts more pressure on new names like Mike Bordick, Lance Blankenship, and Jerry Browne.

With Oakland slipping into a rebuilding phase, the AL West will be wide-open in '93. Minnesota, the only team other than Oakland to win the division since 1986, also finds its destiny linked to free agents. The Twins dug deep to re-sign Kirby Puckett but couldn't keep pitcher John Smiley. GM Andy MacPhail protected a few promising pitchers in the expansion draft (Mike Trombley, Pat Mahomes, and Willie Banks); if a couple of them can join Kevin Tapani and Scott Erickson in the starting rotation, if first baseman Kent Hrbek fully recovers from shoulder surgery, the Twins could rise to the top of the heap again in '93.

Last year the Chicago White Sox were favored by many to win the AL West. But inconsistent pitching was their downfall. Even though they lost Greg Hibbard in the expansion draft, they will get a couple free agents and hope their young arms—Wilson Alvarez, Rodney Bolton, and Jason Bere—are ready to step forward in '93.

With Frank Thomas, Robin Ventura, and George Bell, Chicago has plenty of offense. If the pitching is solid this season, the White Sox have the inside track to the AL West crown, especially if shortstop Ozzie Guillen can come back from knee surgery.

Kevin Kennedy, the Texas Rangers' new manager, will take a page from Phil Garner's book by having his team run more. Jose Canseco will be on board for an entire season. But the Rangers' fortunes will ride on how well they can improve their starting rotation and bullpen by opening day, especially after losing Jose Guzman to the Cubs as a free agent.

The Kansas City Royals are a lot closer to being a contender than many people think. The basic team is sound. How far they climb in the standings will depend on contributions from newcomers David Cone, Greg Gagne and Jose Lind.

Kevin Appier came through in '92 as the team's new ace, but needs help from Cone and Mark Gubicza. The Royals will be in great shape, if they can nail down a hitter with punch. GM Herk Robinson says he doesn't want to totally tear apart his ballclub pursuing missing links.

The California Angels concluded that money cannot solve every problem. In fact, GM Whitey Herzog traded pitcher Jim Abbott when the left-hander didn't come down in his asking price and ended up with more young talent. In leaving Bryan Harvey unprotected in the expansion draft, the Angels opted for Joe Grahe as their new closer. The Angels had no choice but to play youngsters Gary DiSarcina, Damion Easley, Chad Curtis, and Tim Salmon in '92. Their experience will pay off in '93.

The Seattle Mariners have new ownership, a new manager (Lou Piniella) and a new logo. Heading into the off-season, change was seeping down to the ballclub as well. Kevin Mitchell was sent back to the NL for closer Norm Charlton. The cornerstones for a quality team are there: Ken Griffey Jr., Edgar Martinez, Randy Johnson, and promising youngsters Bret Boone and Tino Martinez. But how far the Mariners can climb out of the cellar will ride on how well they continue to revamp their pitching staff.

—by Tim Wendel

Final Player Statistics

National League

American League

Players are listed alphabetically by position, within each league. Each player is listed at the position where he played the most games during the season; all statistics are for the complete season.

Statistics are provided by the Elias Sports Bureau.

Stats key for pitchers

T–Throws right or left; W–Wins; L–Losses; ERA–Earned run average; G-Games; GS–Games started; CG– Complete games; SHO–Shutouts; GF–Games finished in relief; SV–Saves; IP–Innings pitched; H–Hits; R–Runs; ER–Earned runs; HR–Home runs; BB–Bases on balls; SO–Strikeouts; WP–Wild pitches; BK–Balks; BA–Batting average against; HB–Hit batters; PCT–Winning percentage; IBB–Intentional bases on balls.

Stats key for fielding

E–Errors; PO–Put outs; A–Assists; DP–Double plays; PCT–Fielding percentage.

Stats key for batters

B–Bats right, left, or both; BA or AVG–Batting average; G–Games; AB–At-bats; R–Runs; H–Hits; TB–Total Bases; 2B–Doubles; 3B–Triples; HR–Home runs; RBI–Runs batted in; SH–Sacrifice hits; SF–Sacrifice flies; BB–Bases on balls; SO–Strikeouts; SB–Stolen bases; CS–Caught stealing; GIDP–Grounded into double play; SLG–Slugging percentage; OBA or OB–On base average; LOB–Runners left on base by a team.

American League starting pitchers

Name/Team	T	W	L	ERA	G	GS	CG	SHO	GF	SV	IP	H	R	ER	HR	BB	SO	WP	BK	BA
Abbott, Jim, Cal.	L	7	15	2.77	29	29	7	0	0	0	211	208	73	65	12	68	130	2	0	.263
Alvarez, Wilson, ChiA	L	5	3	5.20	34	9	0	0	4	1	100.1	103	64	58	12	65	66	2	0	.272
Appier, Kevin, K.C.	R	15	8	2.46	30	30	3	0	0	0	208.1	167	59	57	10	68	150	4	0	.217
Aquino, Luis, K.C.	R	3	6	4.52	15	13	0	0	1	0	67.2	81	35	34	5	20	11	1	1	.303
Armstrong, Jack, Cle.	R	6	15	4.64	35	23	1	0	5	0	166.2	176	100	86	23	67	114	6	3	.269
Banks, Willie, Min.	R	4	4	5.70	16	12	0	0	2	0	71	80	46	45	6	37	37	5	1	.288
Blyleven, Bert, Cal.	R	8	12	4.74	25	24	1	0	0	0	133	150	76	70	17	29	70	3	1	.285
Bones, Ricky, Mil.	R	9	10	4.57	31	28	0	0	0	0	163.1	169	90	83	27	48	65	3	2	.264
Bosio, Chris, Mil.	R	16	6	3.62	33	33	4	2	0	0	231.1	223	100	93	21	44	120	8	2	.254
Boucher, Denis, Cle.	L	2	2	6.37	8	7	0	0	0	0	41	48	29	29	9	20	17	1	0	.302
Briscoe, John, Oak.	R	0	1	6.43	2	2	0	0	0	0	7	12	6	5	0	9	4	2	0	.400
Brown, J. Kevin, Tex.	R	21	11	3.32	35	35	11	1	0	0	265.2	262	117	98	11	76	173	8	2	.260
Chiamparino, Scott, Tex.	R	0	4	3.55	4	4	0	0	0	0	25.1	25	11	10	2	5	13	1	0	.260
Clemens, Roger, Bos.	R	18	11	2.41	32	32	11	5	0	0	246.2	203	80	66	11	62	208	3	0	.224
Cone, David, Tor.	R	4	3	2.55	8	7	0	0	0	0	53	39	16	15	3	29	47	3	0	.207
Cook, Dennis, Cle.	L	5	7	3.82	32	25	1	0	1	0	158	156	79	67	29	50	96	4	5	.255
Darling, Ron, Oak.	R	15	10	3.66	33	33	4	3	0	0	206.1	198	98	84	15	72	99	13	0	.253
Dopson, John, Bos.	R	7	11	4.08	25	25	0	0	0	0	141.1	159	78	64	17	38	55	3	3	.287
Downs, Kelly, Oak.	R	5	5	3.29	18	13	0	0	2	0	82	72	36	30	4	46	38	3	1	.237
Eldred, Cal, Mil.	R	11	2	1.79	14	14	2	1	0	0	100.1	76	21	20	4	23	62	3	0	.207
Embree, Alan, Cle.	L	0	2	7.00	4	4	0	0	0	0	18	19	14	14	3	8	12	1	1	.271
Erickson, Scott, Min.	R	13	12	3.40	32	32	5	3	0	0	212	197	86	80	18	83	101	6	1	.252
Fernandez, Alex, ChiA	R	8	11	4.27	29	29	4	2	0	0	187.2	199	100	89	21	50	95	3	0	.270
Finley, Chuck, Cal.	L	7	12	3.96	31	31	4	1	0	0	204.1	212	99	90	24	98	124	6	0	.278
Fisher, Brian, Sea.	R	4	3	4.53	22	14	0	0	2	1	91.1	80	49	46	9	47	26	3	1	.234
Fleming, Dave, Sea.	L	17	10	3.39	33	33	7	4	0	0	228.1	225	95	86	13	60	112	8	1	.257
Gardiner, Mike, Bos.	R	4	10	4.75	28	18	0	0	3	0	130.2	126	78	69	12	58	79	8	0	.253
Groom, Buddy, Det.	L	0	5	5.82	12	7	0	0	3	1	38.2	48	28	25	4	22	15	0	1	.320
Gubicza, Mark, K.C.	R	7	6	3.72	18	18	2	1	0	0	111.1	110	47	46	8	36	81	5	1	.259
Gullickson, Bill, Det.	R	14	13	4.34	34	34	4	1	0	0	221.2	228	109	107	35	50	64	6	0	.267
Guzman, Jose, Tex.	R	16	11	3.66	33	33	5	0	0	0	224	229	103	91	17	73	179	6	0	.268
Guzman, Juan, Tor.	R	16	5	2.64	28	28	1	0	0	0	180.2	135	56	53	6	72	165	14	2	.207
Haas, David, Det.	R	5	3	3.94	12	11	1	1	1	0	61.2	68	30	27	8	16	29	2	0	.276
Haney, Chris, K.C.	L	2	3	3.86	7	7	1	1	0	0	42	35	18	18	5	16	27	0	0	.226
Hanson, Erik, Sea.	R	8	17	4.82	31	30	6	1	0	0	186.2	209	110	100	14	57	112	6	0	.287
Hathaway, Hilly, Cal.	L	0	0	7.94	2	1	0	0	0	0	5.2	8	5	5	1	3	1	0	0	.333
Hesketh, Joe, Bos.	L	8	9	4.36	30	25	1	0	1	1	148.2	162	84	72	15	58	104	6	0	.276
Hibbard, Greg, ChiA	L	10	7	4.40	31	28	0	0	2	1	176	187	92	86	17	57	69	1	1	.277
Hitchcock, Sterling, NY-A	L	0	2	8.31	3	3	0	0	0	0	13	23	12	12	2	6	6	0	0	.377
Hough, Charlie, ChiA	R	7	12	3.93	27	27	4	0	0	0	176.1	160	88	77	19	66	76	10	1	.239
Johnson, Jeff, NY-A	L	2	3	6.66	13	8	0	0	3	0	52.2	71	44	39	4	23	14	1	0	.329
Johnson, Randy, D., Sea.	L	12	14	3.77	31	31	6	2	0	0	210.1	154	104	88	13	144	241	13	1	.206
Kamieniecki, Scott, NY-A	R	6	14	4.36	28	28	4	0	0	0	188	193	100	91	13	74	88	9	1	.269
Key, Jimmy, Tor.	L	13	13	3.53	33	33	4	2	0	0	216.2	205	88	85	24	59	117	5	0	.248
King, Eric, Det.	R	4	6	5.22	17	14	0	0	2	1	79.1	90	47	46	12	28	45	3	0	.285
Kramer, Randy, Sea.	R	0	1	7.71	4	4	0	0	0	0	16.1	30	14	14	2	7	6	0	0	.400
Krueger, Bill, Min.	L	10	6	4.30	27	27	2	2	0	0	161.1	166	82	77	18	46	86	11	0	.263
Langston, Mark, Cal.	L	13	14	3.66	32	32	9	2	0	0	229	206	103	93	14	74	174	5	0	.242
Leary, Tim, NY-A-Sea.	R	8	10	5.36	26	23	3	0	2	0	141	131	89	84	12	87	46	9	0	.256
Lefferts, Craig, Bal.	L	1	3	4.09	5	5	1	0	0	0	33	34	19	15	3	6	23	1	0	.268
Lewis, Richie, Bal.	R	1	1	10.80	2	2	0	0	0	0	6.2	13	8	8	1	7	4	0	0	.406
Mahomes, Pat, Min.	R	3	4	5.04	14	13	0	0	1	0	69.2	73	41	39	5	37	44	2	1	.279
McCaskill, Kirk, ChiA	R	12	13	4.18	34	34	0	0	0	0	209	193	116	97	11	95	109	6	2	.242
McDonald, Ben, Bal.	R	13	13	4.24	35	35	4	2	0	0	227	213	113	107	32	74	158	3	2	.247
McDowell, Jack, ChiA	R	20	10	3.18	34	34	13	1	0	0	260.2	247	95	92	21	75	178	6	0	.251
Mesa, Jose, Bal.-Cle.	R	7	12	4.59	28	27	1	1	1	0	160.2	169	86	82	14	70	62	2	0	.273
Milacki, Bob, Bal.	R	6	8	5.84	23	20	0	0	1	1	115.2	140	78	75	16	44	51	7	1	.297
Militello, Sam, NY-A	R	3	3	3.45	9	9	0	0	0	0	60	43	24	23	6	32	42	1	0	.195
Mlicki, Dave, Cle.	R	0	2	4.98	4	4	0	0	0	0	21.2	23	14	12	3	16	16	1	0	.280
Moeller, Dennis, K.C.	L	0	3	7.00	5	4	0	0	1	0	18	24	17	14	5	11	6	1	1	.333
Moore, Mike, Oak.	R	17	12	4.12	36	36	2	0	0	0	223	229	113	102	20	103	117	22	0	.269
Morris, Jack, Tor.	R	21	6	4.04	34	34	6	1	0	0	240.2	222	114	108	18	80	132	9	2	.246
Mussina, Mike, Bal.	R	18	5	2.54	32	32	8	4	0	0	241	212	70	68	16	48	130	6	0	.239
Mutis, Jeff, Cle.	L	0	2	9.53	3	2	0	0	0	0	11.1	24	14	12	4	6	8	2	0	.429
Nagy, Charles, Cle.	R	17	10	2.96	33	33	10	3	0	0	252	245	91	83	11	57	169	7	0	.260
Navarro, Jaime, Mil.	R	17	11	3.33	34	34	5	3	0	0	246	224	98	91	14	64	100	6	0	.246
Otto, Dave, Cle.	L	5	9	7.06	18	16	0	0	0	0	80.1	110	64	63	12	33	32	5	0	.333
Parker, Clay, Sea.	R	0	2	7.56	8	6	0	0	1	0	33.1	47	28	28	6	11	20	1	0	.338
Pavlik, Roger, Tex.	R	4	4	4.21	13	12	1	0	0	0	62	66	32	29	3	34	45	9	0	.280
Perez, Melido, NY-A	R	13	16	2.87	33	33	10	1	0	0	247.2	212	94	79	16	93	218	13	0	.235
Pichardo, Hipolito, K.C.	R	9	6	3.95	31	24	1	1	0	0	143.2	148	71	63	9	49	59	3	1	.267

American League starting pitchers

Name/Team	T	W	L	ERA	G	GS	CG	SHO	GF	SV	IP	H	R	ER	HR	BB	SO	WP	BK	BA
Pierce, Ed, K.C.	L	0	0	3.38	2	1	0	0	0	0	5.1	9	2	2	1	4	3	0	0	.429
Rasmussen, Dennis, K.C.	L	4	1	1.43	5	5	1	1	0	0	37.2	25	7	6	0	6	12	3	0	.197
Reed, Rick, K.C.	R	3	7	3.68	19	18	1	1	0	0	100.1	105	47	41	10	20	49	0	0	.271
Rhodes, Arthur, Bal.	L	7	5	3.63	15	15	2	1	0	0	94.1	87	39	38	6	38	77	2	1	.250
Robinson, Don, Cal.	R	1	0	2.20	3	3	0	0	0	0	16.1	19	4	4	1	3	9	1	0	.292
Robinson, Ron, Mil.	R	1	4	5.86	8	8	0	0	0	0	35.1	51	26	23	3	14	12	0	0	.331
Ryan, Nolan, Tex.	R	5	9	3.72	27	27	2	0	0	0	157.1	138	75	65	9	69	157	9	0	.238
Sanderson, Scott, NY-A	R	12	11	4.93	33	33	2	1	0	0	193.1	220	116	106	28	64	104	4	1	.286
Scudder, Scott, Cle.	R	6	10	5.28	23	22	0	0	0	0	109	134	80	64	10	55	66	7	0	.303
Shaw, Jeff, Cle.	R	0	1	8.22	2	1	0	0	1	0	7.2	7	7	7	2	4	3	0	0	.259
Slusarski, Joe, Oak.	R	5	5	5.45	15	14	0	0	1	0	76	85	52	46	15	27	38	0	1	.284
Smiley, John, Min.	L	16	9	3.21	34	34	5	2	0	0	241	205	93	86	17	65	163	4	0	.231
Smith, Dan, Tex.	L	0	3	5.02	4	2	0	0	1	0	14.1	18	8	8	1	8	5	0	0	.321
Stewart, Dave, Oak.	R	12	10	3.66	31	31	2	0	0	0	199.1	175	96	81	25	79	130	3	1	.237
Stieb, Dave, Tor.	R	4	6	5.04	21	14	1	0	3	0	96.1	98	58	54	9	43	45	4	0	.275
Stottlemyre, Todd, Tor.	R	12	11	4.50	28	27	6	2	0	0	174	175	99	87	20	63	98	7	0	.262
Sutcliffe, Rick, Bal.	R	16	15	4.47	36	36	5	2	0	0	237.1	251	123	118	20	74	109	7	2	.273
Tanana, Frank, Det.	L	13	11	4.39	32	31	3	0	0	0	186.2	188	102	91	22	90	91	11	1	.267
Tapani, Kevin, Min.	R	16	11	3.97	34	34	4	1	0	0	220	226	103	97	17	48	138	4	0	.269
Trombley, Mike, Min.	R	3	2	3.30	10	7	0	0	0	0	46.1	43	20	17	5	17	38	0	0	.247
Valera, Julio, Cal.	R	8	11	3.73	30	28	4	2	0	0	188	188	82	78	15	64	113	5	0	.262
Viola, Frank, Bos.	L	13	12	3.44	35	35	6	1	0	0	238	214	99	91	13	89	121	12	2	.242
Walker, Mike A., Sea.	R	0	3	7.36	5	3	0	0	1	0	14.2	21	14	12	4	9	5	1	0	.333
Wegman, Bill, Mil.	R	13	14	3.20	35	35	7	0	0	0	261.2	251	104	93	28	55	127	1	2	.250
Welch, Bob, Oak.	R	11	7	3.27	20	20	0	0	0	0	123.2	114	47	45	13	43	47	1	0	.247
Wickman, Bob, NY-A	R	6	1	4.11	8	8	0	0	0	0	50.1	51	25	23	2	20	21	3	0	.273
Witt, Bobby, Tex.-Oak.	R	10	14	4.29	31	31	0	0	0	0	193	183	99	92	16	114	125	9	1	.256

American League relief pitchers

Name/Team	T	W	L	ERA	G	GS	CG	SHO	GF	SV	IP	H	R	ER	HR	BB	SO	WP	BK	BA
Abbott, Paul, Min.	R	0	0	3.27	6	0	0	0	5	0	11	12	4	4	1	5	13	1	0	.279
Acker, Jim, Sea.	R	0	0	5.28	17	0	0	0	3	0	30.2	45	19	18	4	12	11	1	0	.338
Agosto, Juan, Sea.	L	0	0	5.89	17	1	0	0	2	0	18.1	27	12	12	0	3	12	0	0	.346
Aguilera, Rick, Min.	R	2	6	2.84	64	0	0	0	61	41	66.2	60	28	21	7	17	52	5	0	.238
Aldred, Scott, Det.	L	3	8	6.78	16	13	0	0	0	0	65	80	51	49	12	33	34	1	0	.307
Alexander, Gerald, Tex.	R	1	0	27.00	3	0	0	0	1	0	1.2	5	5	5	1	1	1	0	0	.500
Arnsberg, Brad, Cle.	R	0	0	11.81	8	0	0	0	1	0	10.2	13	14	14	6	11	5	2	0	.317
Austin, James, Mil.	R	5	2	1.85	47	0	0	0	12	0	58.1	38	13	12	2	32	30	1	0	.191
Bailes, Scott, Cal.	L	3	1	7.45	32	0	0	0	10	0	38.2	59	34	32	7	28	25	2	1	.351
Bannister, Floyd, Tex.	L	1	1	6.32	36	0	0	0	8	0	37	39	27	26	3	21	30	3	0	.281
Barton, Shawn, Sea.	L	0	1	2.92	14	0	0	0	2	0	12.1	10	5	4	1	7	4	2	0	.238
Bell, Eric, Cle.	L	0	2	7.63	7	1	0	0	2	0	15.1	22	13	13	1	9	10	1	0	.349
Berenguer, Juan, K.C.	R	1	4	5.64	19	2	0	0	2	0	44.2	42	30	28	3	20	26	2	1	.247
Boddicker, Mike, K.C.	R	1	4	4.98	29	8	0	0	8	3	86.2	92	50	48	5	37	47	2	0	.270
Bohanon, Brian, Tex.	L	1	1	6.31	18	7	0	0	3	0	45.2	57	38	32	7	25	29	2	0	.297
Bolton, Tom, Bos.	L	1	2	3.41	21	1	0	0	6	0	29	34	11	11	0	14	23	2	1	.286
Brown, Kevin D., Sea.	L	0	0	9.00	2	0	0	0	0	0	3	4	3	3	1	3	2	0	0	.333
Burke, Tim, NY-A	R	2	2	3.25	23	0	0	0	10	0	27.2	26	14	10	2	15	8	2	0	.250
Burns, Todd, Tex.	R	3	5	3.84	35	10	0	0	9	1	103	97	54	44	8	32	55	5	0	.249
Butcher, Mike, Cal.	R	2	2	3.25	19	0	0	0	6	0	27.2	29	11	10	3	13	24	0	0	.264
Cadaret, Greg, NY-A	L	4	8	4.25	46	11	1	1	9	1	103.2	104	53	49	12	74	73	5	1	.267
Campbell, Kevin, Oak.	R	2	3	5.12	32	5	0	0	6	1	65	66	39	37	4	45	38	2	0	.267
Campbell, Mike, Tex.	R	0	1	9.82	1	0	0	0	0	0	3.2	3	4	4	1	2	2	0	0	.231
Carman, Don, Tex.	L	0	0	7.71	2	0	0	0	1	0	2.1	4	3	2	0	0	2	0	0	.364
Casian, Larry, Min.	L	1	0	2.70	6	0	0	0	1	0	6.2	7	2	2	0	1	2	0	0	.259
Christopher, Mike, Cle.	R	0	0	3.00	10	0	0	0	4	0	18	17	8	6	2	10	13	2	0	.254
Clements, Pat, Bal.	L	2	0	3.28	23	0	0	0	4	0	24.2	23	10	9	0	11	9	1	0	.258
Corsi, Jim, Oak.	R	4	2	1.43	32	0	0	0	16	0	44	44	12	7	2	18	19	0	0	.275
Crim, Chuck, Cal.	R	7	6	5.17	57	0	0	0	16	1	87	100	56	50	11	29	30	4	0	.293
Darwin, Danny, Bos.	R	9	9	3.96	51	15	2	0	21	3	161.1	159	76	71	11	53	124	5	0	.257
Davis, Mark W., K.C.	L	1	3	7.18	13	6	0	0	4	0	36.1	42	31	29	6	28	19	1	0	.294
Davis, Storm, Bal.	R	7	3	3.43	48	2	0	0	24	4	89.1	79	35	34	5	36	53	4	0	.244
DeLucia, Rich, Sea.	R	3	6	5.49	30	11	0	0	6	1	83.2	100	55	51	13	35	66	1	0	.293
Doherty, John, Det.	R	7	4	3.88	47	11	0	0	9	3	116	131	61	50	4	25	37	5	0	.287
Drahman, Brian, ChiA	R	0	0	2.57	5	0	0	0	2	0	7	6	3	2	0	2	1	1	0	.222
Dunne, Mike, ChiA	R	2	0	4.26	4	1	0	0	0	0	12.2	12	7	6	0	6	6	0	0	.255
Eckersley, Dennis, Oak.	R	7	1	1.91	69	0	0	0	65	51	80	62	17	17	5	11	93	0	0	.211
Edens, Tom, Min.	R	6	3	2.83	52	0	0	0	14	3	76.1	65	26	24	1	36	57	5	0	.236
Eichhorn, Mark, Cal.-Tor.	R	4	4	3.08	65	0	0	0	26	2	87.2	86	34	30	3	25	61	9	1	.255

American League relief pitchers

Name/Team	T	W	L	ERA	G	GS	CG	SHO	GF	SV	IP	H	R	ER	HR	BB	SO	WP	BK	BA
Farr, Steve, NY-A	R	2	2	1.56	50	0	0	0	42	30	52	34	10	9	2	19	37	0	0	.186
Fetters, Mike, Mil.	R	5	1	1.87	50	0	0	0	11	2	62.2	38	15	13	3	24	43	4	1	.185
Fireovid, Steve, Tex.	R	1	0	4.05	3	0	0	0	0	0	6.2	10	5	3	0	4	0	0	0	.370
Flanagan, Mike, Bal.	L	0	0	8.05	42	0	0	0	15	0	34.2	50	34	31	3	23	17	4	0	.338
Fortugno, Tim, Cal.	L	1	1	5.18	14	5	1	1	5	1	41.2	37	24	24	5	19	31	2	1	.236
Fossas, Tony, Bos.	L	1	2	2.43	60	0	0	0	17	2	29.2	31	9	8	1	14	19	0	0	.279
Frey, Steve, Cal.	L	4	2	3.57	51	0	0	0	20	4	45.1	39	18	18	6	22	24	1	0	.238
Frohwirth, Todd, Bal.	R	4	3	2.46	65	0	0	0	23	4	106	97	33	29	4	41	58	1	0	.247
Gordon, Tom, K.C.	R	6	10	4.59	40	11	0	0	13	0	117.2	116	67	60	9	55	98	5	2	.258
Gossage, Goose, Oak.	R	0	2	2.84	30	0	0	0	13	0	38	32	13	12	5	19	26	0	0	.230
Gozzo, Mauro, Min.	R	0	0	27.00	2	0	0	0	0	0	1.2	7	5	5	2	0	1	1	0	.583
Grahe, Joe, Cal.	R	5	6	3.52	46	7	0	0	31	21	94.2	85	37	37	5	39	39	3	0	.246
Grant, Mark, Sea.	R	2	4	3.89	23	10	0	0	4	0	81	100	39	35	6	22	42	2	0	.311
Guetterman, Lee, NY-A	L	1	1	9.53	15	0	0	0	7	0	22.2	35	24	24	5	13	5	1	0	.354
Gunderson, Eric, Sea.	L	2	1	8.68	9	0	0	0	4	0	9.1	12	12	9	1	5	2	0	2	.324
Guthrie, Mark, Min.	L	2	3	2.88	54	0	0	0	15	5	75	59	27	24	7	23	76	2	0	.215
Guzman, Johnny, Oak.	L	0	0	12.00	2	0	0	0	2	0	3	8	4	4	0	0	0	0	0	.471
Habyan, John, NY-A	R	5	6	3.84	56	0	0	0	20	7	72.2	84	32	31	6	21	44	2	1	.295
Harris, Gene, Sea.	R	0	0	7.00	8	0	0	0	2	0	9	8	7	7	3	6	6	0	1	.235
Harris, Greg A., Bos.	R	4	9	2.51	70	2	1	0	22	4	107.2	82	38	30	6	60	73	5	0	.215
Harvey, Bryan, Cal.	R	0	4	2.83	25	0	0	0	22	13	28.2	22	12	9	4	11	34	4	0	.208
Heaton, Neal, K.C.-Mil.	L	3	1	4.07	32	0	0	0	9	0	42	43	21	19	5	23	31	3	1	.269
Henke, Tom, Tor.	R	3	2	2.26	57	0	0	0	50	34	55.2	40	19	14	5	22	46	4	0	.197
Henneman, Mike, Det.	R	2	6	3.96	60	0	0	0	53	24	77.1	75	36	34	6	20	58	7	0	.256
Henry, Doug, Mil.	R	1	4	4.02	68	0	0	0	56	29	65	64	34	29	6	24	52	4	0	.256
Hentgen, Pat, Tor.	R	5	2	5.36	28	2	0	0	10	0	50.1	49	30	30	7	32	39	2	1	.254
Hernandez, Roberto, ChiA	R	7	3	1.65	43	0	0	0	27	12	71	45	15	13	4	20	68	2	0	.180
Hillegas, Shawn, NY-A-Oak.	R	1	8	5.23	26	9	1	1	6	0	86	104	57	50	13	37	49	2	0	.303
Holmes, Darren, Mil.	R	4	4	2.55	41	0	0	0	25	6	42.1	35	12	12	1	11	31	0	0	.224
Honeycutt, Rick, Oak.	L	1	4	3.69	54	0	0	0	7	3	39	41	19	16	2	10	32	2	0	.272
Horsman, Vince, Oak.	L	2	1	2.49	58	0	0	0	9	1	43.1	39	13	12	3	21	18	1	0	.252
Howe, Steve, NY-A	L	3	0	2.45	20	0	0	0	10	6	22	9	7	6	1	3	12	1	0	.122
Hoy, Peter, Bos.	R	0	0	7.36	5	0	0	0	2	0	3.2	8	3	3	0	2	2	0	0	.471
Irvine, Daryl, Bos.	R	3	4	6.11	21	0	0	0	8	0	28	31	20	19	1	14	10	3	0	.287
Jeffcoat, Mike, Tex.	L	0	1	7.32	6	3	0	0	2	0	19.2	28	17	16	2	5	6	0	0	.350
Johnston, Joel, K.C.	R	0	0	13.50	5	0	0	0	1	0	2.2	3	4	4	2	2	0	1	0	.273
Jones, Calvin, Sea.	R	3	5	5.69	38	1	0	0	14	0	61.2	50	39	39	8	47	49	10	0	.226
Kiely, John, Det.	R	4	2	2.13	39	0	0	0	20	0	55	44	14	13	2	28	18	0	0	.224
Kipper, Bob, Min.	L	3	3	4.42	25	0	0	0	12	0	38.2	40	23	19	8	14	22	1	0	.268
Knudsen, Kurt, Det.	R	2	3	4.58	48	1	0	0	14	5	70.2	70	39	36	9	41	51	5	0	.264
Lancaster, Les, Det.	R	3	4	6.33	41	1	0	0	17	0	86.2	101	66	61	11	51	35	2	0	.294
Leach, Terry, ChiA	R	6	5	1.95	51	0	0	0	21	0	73.2	57	17	16	2	20	22	0	0	.215
Leiter, Al, Tor.	L	0	0	9.00	1	0	0	0	0	0	1	1	1	1	0	2	0	0	0	.200
Leiter, Mark, Det.	R	8	5	4.18	35	14	1	0	7	0	112	116	57	52	9	43	75	3	0	.277
Leon, Danilo, Tex.	R	1	1	5.89	15	0	0	0	3	0	18.1	18	14	12	5	10	15	0	0	.254
Lewis, Scott, Cal.	R	4	0	3.99	21	2	0	0	7	0	38.1	36	18	17	3	14	18	1	1	.255
Lilliquist, Derek, Cle.	L	5	3	1.75	71	0	0	0	22	6	61.2	39	13	12	5	18	47	2	0	.187
Linton, Doug, Tor.	R	1	3	8.63	8	3	0	0	2	0	24	31	23	23	5	17	16	2	0	.323
MacDonald, Bob, Tor.	L	1	0	4.37	27	0	0	0	9	0	47.1	50	24	23	4	16	26	0	0	.270
Magnante, Mike, K.C.	L	4	9	4.94	44	12	0	0	11	0	89.1	115	53	49	5	35	31	2	0	.325
Manuel, Barry, Tex.	R	1	0	4.76	3	0	0	0	0	0	5.2	6	3	3	2	1	9	0	0	.261
Mathews, Terry, Tex.	R	2	4	5.95	40	0	0	0	11	0	42.1	48	29	28	4	31	26	2	1	.294
McCullers, Lance, Tex.	R	1	0	5.40	5	0	0	0	1	0	5	1	4	3	0	8	3	0	0	.067
Meacham, Rusty, K.C.	R	10	4	2.74	64	0	0	0	20	2	101.2	88	39	31	5	21	64	4	0	.233
Mills, Alan, Bal.	R	10	4	2.61	35	3	0	0	12	2	103.1	78	33	30	5	54	60	2	0	.215
Monteleone, Rich, NY-A	R	7	3	3.30	47	0	0	0	15	0	92.2	82	35	34	7	27	62	0	3	.235
Montgomery, Jeff, K.C.	R	1	6	2.18	65	0	0	0	62	39	82.2	61	23	20	5	27	69	2	0	.205
Munoz, Mike, Det.	L	1	2	3.00	65	0	0	0	15	2	48	44	16	16	3	25	23	2	0	.246
Nelson, Gene, Oak.	R	3	1	6.45	28	2	0	0	8	0	51.2	68	37	37	5	22	23	2	0	.335
Nelson, Jeff, Sea.	R	1	7	3.44	66	0	0	0	27	6	81	71	34	31	7	44	46	2	0	.245
Nichols, Rod, Cle.	R	4	3	4.53	30	9	0	0	5	0	105.1	114	58	53	13	31	56	3	0	.273
Nielsen, Jerry, NY-A	L	1	0	4.58	20	0	0	0	12	0	19.2	17	10	10	1	18	12	1	0	.243
Nunez, Edwin, Mil.-Tex.	R	1	3	4.85	49	0	0	0	16	3	59.1	63	34	32	6	22	49	5	0	.268
Olin, Steve, Cle.	R	8	5	2.34	72	0	0	0	62	29	88.1	80	25	23	8	27	47	1	1	.249
Olson, Gregg, Bal.	R	1	5	2.05	60	0	0	0	56	36	61.1	46	14	14	3	24	58	4	0	.211
Orosco, Jesse, Mil.	L	3	1	3.23	59	0	0	0	14	1	39	33	15	14	5	13	40	2	0	.232
Pall, Donn, ChiA	R	5	2	4.93	39	0	0	0	12	1	73	79	43	40	9	27	27	1	2	.272
Parrett, Jeff, Oak.	R	9	1	3.02	66	0	0	0	14	0	98.1	81	35	33	7	42	78	13	0	.226
Plesac, Dan, Mil.	L	5	4	2.96	44	4	0	0	13	1	79	64	28	26	5	35	54	3	1	.229
Plunk, Eric, Cle.	R	9	6	3.64	58	0	0	0	20	4	71.2	61	31	29	5	38	50	5	0	.229
Poole, Jim Ri., Bal.	L	0	0	0.00	6	0	0	0	1	0	3.1	3	3	0	0	1	3	0	0	.231

American League relief pitchers

Name/Team	T	W	L	ERA	G	GS	CG	SHO	GF	SV	IP	H	R	ER	HR	BB	SO	WP	BK	BA
Powell, Dennis, Sea.	L	4	2	4.58	49	0	0	0	11	0	57	49	30	29	5	29	35	2	0	.238
Power, Ted, Cle.	R	3	3	2.54	64	0	0	0	16	6	99.1	88	33	28	7	35	51	2	1	.248
Quantrill, Paul, Bos.	R	2	3	2.19	27	0	0	0	10	1	49.1	55	18	12	1	15	24	1	0	.288
Raczka, Michael, Oak.	L	0	0	8.53	8	0	0	0	1	0	6.1	8	7	6	0	5	2	0	0	.308
Radinsky, Scott, ChiA	L	3	7	2.73	68	0	0	0	33	15	59.1	54	21	18	3	34	48	3	0	.243
Reardon, Jeff, Bos.	R	2	2	4.25	46	0	0	0	39	27	42.1	53	20	20	6	7	32	0	0	.308
Revenig, Todd, Oak.	R	0	0	0.00	2	0	0	0	2	0	2	2	0	0	0	0	1	0	0	.286
Ritz, Kevin, Det.	R	2	5	5.60	23	11	0	0	4	0	80.1	88	52	50	4	44	57	7	1	.278
Robinson, Jeff M., Tex.	R	4	4	5.72	16	4	0	0	2	0	45.2	50	30	29	6	21	18	6	1	.281
Rogers, Kenny, Tex.	L	3	6	3.09	81	0	0	0	38	6	78.2	80	32	27	7	26	70	4	1	.261
Rosenthal, Wayne, Tex.	R	0	0	7.71	6	0	0	0	2	0	4.2	7	4	4	1	2	1	1	0	.333
Ruffin, Bruce, Mil.	L	1	6	6.67	25	6	1	0	6	0	58	66	43	43	7	41	45	2	0	.293
Russell, Jeff, Tex.-Oak.	R	4	3	1.63	59	0	0	0	46	30	66.1	55	14	12	3	25	48	3	0	.224
Ryan, Ken, Bos.	R	0	0	6.43	7	0	0	0	6	1	7	4	5	5	2	5	5	0	0	.174
Sampen, Bill, K.C.	R	0	2	3.66	8	1	0	0	3	0	19.2	21	10	8	0	3	14	1	0	.292
Sauveur, Rich, K.C.	L	0	1	4.40	8	0	0	0	2	0	14.1	15	7	7	1	8	7	0	1	.273
Schmidt, Dave J., Sea.	R	0	0	18.90	3	0	0	0	0	0	3.1	7	7	7	1	3	1	0	0	.438
Schooler, Mike, Sea.	R	2	7	4.70	53	0	0	0	36	13	51.2	55	29	27	7	24	33	0	0	.275
Shifflett, Steve, K.C.	R	1	4	2.60	34	0	0	0	15	0	52	55	15	15	6	17	25	2	1	.279
Springer, Russ, NY-A	R	0	0	6.19	14	0	0	0	5	0	16	18	11	11	0	10	12	0	0	.281
Swan, Russ, Sea.	L	3	10	4.74	55	9	1	0	26	9	104.1	104	60	55	8	45	45	6	0	.262
Taylor, Scott, Bos.	L	1	1	4.91	4	1	0	0	1	0	14.2	13	8	8	4	4	7	0	0	.245
Terrell, Walt, Det.	R	7	10	5.20	36	14	1	0	7	0	136.2	163	86	79	14	48	61	3	0	.298
Thigpen, Bobby, ChiA	R	1	3	4.75	55	0	0	0	40	22	55	58	29	29	4	33	45	0	0	.275
Timlin, Mike, Tor.	R	0	2	4.12	26	0	0	0	14	1	43.2	45	23	20	0	20	35	0	0	.271
Trlicek, Rick, Tor.	R	0	0	10.80	2	0	0	0	0	0	1.2	2	2	2	0	2	1	0	0	.286
Walton, Bruce, Oak.	R	0	0	9.90	7	0	0	0	2	0	10	17	11	11	1	3	7	0	1	.378
Ward, Duane, Tor.	R	7	4	1.95	79	0	0	0	35	12	101.1	76	27	22	5	39	103	7	0	.207
Wayne, Gary, Min.	L	3	3	2.63	41	0	0	0	13	0	48	46	18	14	2	19	29	1	1	.260
Weathers, Dave, Tor.	R	0	0	8.10	2	0	0	0	0	0	3.1	5	3	3	1	2	3	0	0	.385
Wells, David, Tor.	L	7	9	5.40	41	14	0	0	14	2	120	138	84	72	16	36	62	3	1	.289
West, David, Min.	L	1	3	6.99	9	3	0	0	1	0	28.1	32	24	22	3	20	19	2	0	.276
Whiteside, Matt, Tex.	R	1	1	1.93	20	0	0	0	8	4	28	26	8	6	1	11	13	2	0	.245
Wickander, Kevin, Cle.	L	2	0	3.07	44	0	0	0	10	1	41	39	14	14	1	28	38	1	1	.260
Williamson, Mark, Bal.	R	0	0	0.96	12	0	0	0	5	1	18.2	16	3	2	1	10	14	1	0	.239
Willis, Carl, Min.	R	7	3	2.72	59	0	0	0	21	1	79.1	73	25	24	4	11	45	2	1	.246
Woodson, Kerry, Sea.	R	0	1	3.29	8	1	0	0	0	0	13.2	12	7	5	0	11	6	1	0	.245
Young, Curt, K.C.-NY-A	L	4	2	3.99	23	7	0	0	5	0	67.2	80	35	30	2	17	20	0	0	.296
Young, Matt, Bos.	L	0	4	4.58	28	8	1	0	4	0	70.2	69	42	36	7	42	57	2	0	.257

American League catchers

Name/Team	B	BA	G	AB	R	H	TB	2B	3B	HR	RBI	SH	SF	BB	SO	SB	CS	GIDP	SLG	OBA
Allanson, Andy, Mil.	R	.320	9	25	6	8	9	1	0	0	0	2	0	1	2	3	1	1	.360	.346
Alomar, Sandy Jr., Cle.	R	.251	89	299	22	75	97	16	0	2	26	3	0	13	32	3	3	7	.324	.293
Borders, Pat, Tor.	R	.242	138	480	47	116	185	26	2	13	53	1	5	33	75	1	1	11	.385	.290
Bradley, Scott, Sea.	L	.000	2	1	0	0	0	0	0	0	0	0	0	1	1	0	0	0	.000	.500
Davis, Doug, Tex.	R	1.000	1	1	0	1	1	0	0	0	0	0	0	0	0	0	0	0	1.000	1.000
Dempsey, Rick, Bal.	R	.111	8	9	2	1	1	0	0	0	0	0	0	2	1	0	0	1	.111	.273
Fisk, Carlton, ChiA	R	.229	62	188	12	43	58	4	1	3	21	0	2	23	38	3	0	2	.309	.313
Fitzgerald, Mike R., Cal.	R	.212	95	189	19	40	60	2	0	6	17	3	0	22	34	2	2	4	.317	.294
Flaherty, John, Bos.	R	.197	35	66	3	13	15	2	0	0	2	1	1	3	7	0	0	0	.227	.229
Harper, Brian, Min.	R	.307	140	502	58	154	206	25	0	9	73	1	10	26	22	0	1	15	.410	.343
Haselman, Bill, Tex.-Sea.	R	.263	8	19	1	5	5	0	0	0	0	0	0	0	7	0	0	1	.263	.263
Heffernan, Bert, Sea.	L	.091	8	11	0	1	2	1	0	0	1	0	0	0	1	0	0	1	.182	.091
Hemond, Scott, Oak.-ChiA	R	.225	25	40	8	9	11	2	0	0	2	0	1	4	13	1	0	2	.275	.289
Hoiles, Chris, Bal.	R	.274	96	310	49	85	157	10	1	20	40	1	3	55	60	0	2	8	.506	.384
Karkovice, Ron, ChiA	R	.237	123	342	39	81	134	12	1	13	50	4	2	30	89	10	4	3	.392	.302
Knorr, Randy, Tor.	R	.263	8	19	1	5	8	0	0	1	2	0	0	1	5	0	0	0	.421	.300
Kreuter, Chad, Det.	B	.253	67	190	22	48	63	9	0	2	16	3	2	20	38	0	1	8	.332	.321
Levis, Jesse, Cle.	L	.279	28	43	2	12	19	4	0	1	3	0	0	0	5	0	0	1	.442	.279
Leyritz, Jim, NY-A	R	.257	63	144	17	37	64	6	0	7	26	0	3	14	22	0	1	2	.444	.341
Macfarlane, Mike, K.C.	R	.234	129	402	51	94	179	28	3	17	48	1	2	30	89	1	5	8	.445	.310
Maksudian, Mike, Tor.	L	.000	3	3	0	0	0	0	0	0	0	0	0	0	0	0	0	0	.000	.000
Marzano, John, Bos.	R	.080	19	50	4	4	8	2	1	0	1	1	0	2	12	0	0	0	.160	.132
Mayne, Brent, K.C.	L	.225	82	213	16	48	58	10	0	0	18	2	3	11	26	0	4	5	.272	.260
McGinnis, Russ, Tex.	R	.242	14	33	2	8	12	4	0	0	4	0	0	3	7	0	0	1	.364	.306
McIntosh, Tim, Mil.	R	.182	35	77	7	14	17	3	0	0	6	1	1	3	9	1	3	1	.221	.229
Melvin, Bob, K.C.	R	.314	32	70	5	22	27	5	0	0	6	0	2	5	13	0	0	3	.386	.351
Mercedes, Henry, Oak.	R	.800	9	5	1	4	6	0	1	0	1	0	0	0	1	0	0	0	1.200	.800

American League catchers

Name/Team	B	BA	G	AB	R	H	TB	2B	3B	HR	RBI	SH	SF	BB	SO	SB	CS	GIDP	SLG	OBA
Merullo, Matt, ChiA	L	.180	24	50	3	9	12	1	1	0	3	0	1	1	8	0	0	0	.240	.208
Myers, Greg, Tor.-Cal.	L	.231	30	78	4	18	28	7	0	1	13	1	2	5	11	0	0	2	.359	.271
Nilsson, Dave, Mil.	L	.232	51	164	15	38	58	8	0	4	25	2	0	17	18	2	2	1	.354	.304
Nokes, Matt, NY-A	L	.224	121	384	42	86	163	9	1	22	59	0	6	37	62	0	1	13	.424	.293
Ortiz, Junior, Cle.	R	.250	86	244	20	61	68	7	0	0	24	2	0	12	23	1	3	7	.279	.296
Orton, John, Cal.	R	.219	43	114	11	25	34	3	0	2	12	2	0	7	32	1	1	1	.298	.276
Parent, Mark, Bal.	R	.235	17	34	4	8	15	1	0	2	4	2	0	3	7	0	0	0	.441	.316
Parks, Derek, Min.	R	.333	7	6	1	2	2	0	0	0	0	0	0	1	1	0	0	0	.333	.500
Parrish, Lance, Cal.-Sea.	R	.233	93	275	26	64	115	13	1	12	32	1	3	24	70	1	1	7	.418	.294
Pena, Tony, Bos.	R	.241	133	410	39	99	125	21	1	1	38	13	2	24	61	3	2	11	.305	.284
Petralli, Geno, Tex.	L	.198	94	192	11	38	53	12	0	1	18	1	0	20	34	0	0	8	.276	.274
Quirk, Jamie, Oak.	L	.220	78	177	13	39	54	7	1	2	11	5	1	16	28	0	0	4	.305	.294
Rodriguez, Ivan, Tex.	R	.260	123	420	39	109	151	16	1	8	37	7	2	24	73	0	0	15	.360	.300
Rowland, Rich, Det.	R	.214	6	14	2	3	3	0	0	0	0	0	0	3	3	0	0	1	.214	.353
Russell, John W., Tex.	R	.100	7	10	1	1	1	0	0	0	2	0	1	1	4	0	0	0	.100	.231
Santovenia, Nelson, ChiA	R	.333	2	3	1	1	4	0	0	1	2	0	0	0	0	0	0	0	1.333	.333
Sinatro, Matt, Sea.	R	.107	18	28	0	3	3	0	0	0	0	0	0	0	5	0	0	1	.107	.107
Stanley, Mike, NY-A	R	.249	68	173	24	43	74	7	0	8	27	0	0	33	45	0	0	6	.428	.372
Steinbach, Terry, Oak.	R	.279	128	438	48	122	180	20	1	12	53	0	3	45	58	2	3	20	.411	.345
Stephens, Ray, Tex.	R	.154	8	13	0	2	2	0	0	0	0	1	0	0	5	0	0	0	.154	.154
Surhoff, B.J., Mil.	L	.252	139	480	63	121	154	19	1	4	62	5	10	46	41	14	8	9	.321	.314
Tackett, Jeff, Bal.	R	.240	65	179	21	43	68	8	1	5	24	6	4	17	28	0	0	11	.380	.307
Tettleton, Mickey, Det.	B	.238	157	525	82	125	246	25	0	32	83	0	6	122	137	0	6	5	.469	.379
Tingley, Ron, Cal.	R	.197	71	127	15	25	38	2	1	3	8	5	0	13	35	0	1	4	.299	.282
Valle, Dave, Sea.	R	.240	124	367	39	88	133	16	1	9	30	7	1	27	58	0	0	7	.362	.305
Webster, Lenny, Min.	R	.280	53	118	10	33	48	10	1	1	13	2	0	9	11	0	2	3	.407	.331
Wedge, Eric, Bos.	R	.250	27	68	11	17	34	2	0	5	11	0	0	13	18	0	0	0	.500	.370

American League first basemen

Name/Team	B	BA	G	AB	R	H	TB	2B	3B	HR	RBI	SH	SF	BB	SO	SB	CS	GIDP	SLG	OBA
Bergman, Dave, Det.	L	.232	87	181	17	42	48	3	0	1	10	1	2	20	19	1	0	4	.265	.305
Brogna, Rico, Det.	L	.192	9	26	3	5	9	1	0	1	3	0	0	3	5	0	0	0	.346	.276
Brooks, Hubie, Cal.	R	.216	82	306	28	66	103	13	0	8	36	0	1	12	46	3	3	10	.337	.247
Conine, Jeff, K.C.	R	.253	28	91	10	23	32	5	2	0	9	0	0	8	23	0	0	1	.352	.313
Cooper, Scott, Bos.	L	.276	123	337	34	93	129	21	0	5	33	2	2	37	33	1	1	5	.383	.346
Cron, Chris, ChiA	R	.000	6	10	0	0	0	0	0	0	0	0	0	0	4	0	0	0	.000	.000
Davis, Alvin, Cal.	L	.250	40	104	5	26	34	8	0	0	16	0	1	13	9	0	0	2	.327	.331
Fielder, Cecil, Det.	R	.244	155	594	80	145	272	22	0	35	124	0	7	73	151	0	0	14	.458	.325
Gaetti, Gary, Cal.	R	.226	130	456	41	103	156	13	2	12	48	0	3	21	79	3	1	9	.342	.267
Hrbek, Kent, Min.	L	.244	112	394	52	96	161	20	0	15	58	2	3	71	56	5	2	12	.409	.357
Jaha, John, Mil.	R	.226	47	133	17	30	41	3	1	2	10	1	4	12	30	10	0	1	.308	.291
Jefferson, Reggie, Cle.	B	.337	24	89	8	30	43	6	2	1	6	0	0	1	17	0	0	2	.483	.352
Jorgensen, Terry, Min.	R	.310	22	58	5	18	19	1	0	0	5	0	1	3	11	1	2	4	.328	.349
Joyner, Wally, K.C.	L	.269	149	572	66	154	221	36	2	9	66	0	2	55	50	11	5	19	.386	.336
Larkin, Gene, Min.	B	.246	115	337	38	83	121	18	1	6	42	0	4	28	43	7	2	7	.359	.308
Martinez, Carlos, Cle.	R	.263	69	228	23	60	86	9	1	5	35	1	4	7	21	1	2	5	.377	.283
Martinez, Domingo, Tor.	R	.625	7	8	2	5	8	0	0	1	3	0	0	0	1	0	0	0	1.000	.625
Martinez, Tino, Sea.	L	.257	136	460	53	118	189	19	2	16	66	1	8	42	77	2	1	24	.411	.316
Mattingly, Don, NY-A	L	.288	157	640	89	184	266	40	0	14	86	0	6	39	43	3	0	11	.416	.327
Maurer, Rob, Tex.	L	.222	8	9	1	2	2	0	0	0	1	0	0	1	2	0	0	0	.222	.300
McGwire, Mark, Oak.	R	.268	139	467	87	125	273	22	0	42	104	0	9	90	105	0	1	10	.585	.385
Milligan, Randy, Bal.	R	.240	137	462	71	111	167	21	1	11	53	0	5	106	81	0	1	15	.361	.383
O'Brien, Pete M., Sea.	L	.222	134	396	40	88	147	15	1	14	52	1	7	40	27	2	1	8	.371	.289
Olerud, John, Tor.	L	.284	138	458	68	130	206	28	0	16	66	1	7	70	61	1	0	15	.450	.375
Palmeiro, Rafael, Tex.	L	.268	159	608	84	163	264	27	4	22	85	5	6	72	83	2	3	10	.434	.352
Segui, David, Bal.	B	.233	115	189	21	44	56	9	0	1	17	2	0	20	23	1	0	4	.296	.306
Snow, J.T., NY-A	B	.143	7	14	1	2	3	1	0	0	2	0	0	5	5	0	0	0	.214	.368
Sorrento, Paul, Cle.	L	.269	140	458	52	123	203	24	1	18	60	1	3	51	89	0	3	13	.443	.341
Sprague, Ed Jr., Tor.	R	.234	22	47	6	11	16	2	0	1	7	0	0	3	7	0	0	0	.340	.280
Stevens, Lee, Cal.	L	.221	106	312	25	69	109	19	0	7	37	1	2	29	64	1	4	4	.349	.288
Stubbs, Franklin, Mil.	L	.229	92	288	37	66	106	11	1	9	42	5	1	27	68	11	8	2	.368	.297
Tabler, Pat, Tor.	R	.252	49	135	11	34	39	5	0	0	16	0	1	11	14	0	0	6	.289	.306
Thomas, Frank E., ChiA	R	.323	160	573	108	185	307	46	2	24	115	0	11	122	88	6	3	19	.536	.439
Vaughn, Mo, Bos.	L	.234	113	355	42	83	142	16	2	13	57	0	3	47	67	3	3	9	.400	.326

American League second basemen

Name/Team	B	BA	G	AB	R	H	TB	2B	3B	HR	RBI	SH	SF	BB	SO	SB	CS	GIDP	SLG	OBA
Alomar, Roberto, Tor.	B	.310	152	571	105	177	244	27	8	8	76	6	2	87	52	49	9	8	.427	.405
Baerga, Carlos, Cle.	B	.312	161	657	92	205	299	32	1	20	105	2	9	35	76	10	2	15	.455	.354
Barrett, Tommy, Bos.	B	.000	4	3	1	0	0	0	0	0	0	1	0	2	0	0	0	0	.000	.400
Blankenship, Lance, Oak.	R	.241	123	349	59	84	119	24	1	3	34	8	1	82	57	21	7	10	.341	.393
Boone, Bret, Sea.	R	.194	33	129	15	25	41	4	0	4	15	1	0	4	34	1	1	4	.318	.224
Bordick, Mike, Oak.	R	.300	154	504	62	151	187	19	4	3	48	14	5	40	59	12	6	10	.371	.358
Cora, Joey, ChiA	B	.246	68	122	27	30	39	7	1	0	9	2	3	22	13	10	3	2	.320	.371
Fletcher, Scott, Mil.	R	.275	123	386	53	106	139	18	3	3	51	6	4	30	33	17	10	4	.360	.335
Franco, Julio, Tex.	R	.234	35	107	19	25	38	7	0	2	8	1	0	15	17	1	1	3	.355	.328
Frye, Jeff, Tex.	R	.256	67	199	24	51	65	9	1	1	12	11	1	16	27	1	3	2	.327	.320
Gallego, Mike, NY-A	R	.254	53	173	24	44	62	7	1	3	14	3	1	20	22	0	1	5	.358	.343
Gantner, Jim, Mil.	L	.246	101	256	22	63	80	12	1	1	18	3	2	12	17	6	2	9	.313	.278
Hulett, Tim, Bal.	R	.289	57	142	11	41	58	7	2	2	21	0	0	10	31	0	1	7	.408	.340
Kelly, Pat, NY-A	R	.226	106	318	38	72	119	22	2	7	27	6	3	25	72	8	5	6	.374	.301
Knoblauch, Chuck, Min.	R	.297	155	600	104	178	215	19	6	2	56	2	12	88	60	34	13	8	.358	.384
McLemore, Mark, Bal.	B	.246	101	228	40	56	67	7	2	0	27	6	1	21	26	11	5	6	.294	.308
Miller, Keith A., K.C.	R	.284	106	416	57	118	162	24	4	4	38	1	2	31	46	16	6	1	.389	.352
Newman, Al, Tex.	B	.220	116	246	25	54	59	5	0	0	12	8	0	34	26	9	6	5	.240	.317
Oberkfell, Ken, Cal.	L	.264	41	91	6	24	25	1	0	0	10	0	2	8	5	0	1	2	.275	.317
Phillips, Tony, Det.	B	.276	159	606	114	167	235	32	3	10	64	5	7	114	93	12	10	13	.388	.387
Reed, Jody, Bos.	R	.247	143	550	64	136	174	27	1	3	40	10	4	62	44	7	8	17	.316	.321
Reynolds, Harold, Sea.	B	.247	140	458	55	113	151	23	3	3	33	11	4	45	41	15	12	12	.330	.316
Ripken, Billy, Bal.	R	.230	111	330	35	76	103	15	0	4	36	10	2	18	26	2	3	10	.312	.275
Rose, Bob, Cal.	R	.214	30	84	10	18	29	5	0	2	10	1	1	8	9	1	1	2	.345	.295
Samuel, Juan, K.C.	R	.284	29	102	15	29	40	5	3	0	8	0	0	7	27	6	1	2	.392	.336
Sax, Steve, ChiA	R	.236	143	567	74	134	180	26	4	4	47	12	6	43	42	30	12	17	.317	.290
Scarsone, Steve, Bal.	R	.176	11	17	2	3	3	0	0	0	0	1	0	1	6	0	0	0	.176	.222
Shumpert, Terry, K.C.	R	.149	36	94	6	14	24	5	1	1	11	2	0	3	17	2	2	2	.255	.175
Sojo, Luis, Cal.	R	.272	106	368	37	100	139	12	3	7	43	7	1	14	24	7	11	14	.378	.299
Suero, William, Mil.	R	.188	18	16	4	3	4	1	0	0	0	0	0	2	1	1	1	2	.250	.316
Whitaker, Lou, Det.	L	.278	130	453	77	126	209	26	0	19	71	5	4	81	46	6	4	9	.461	.386

American League third basemen

Name/Team	B	BA	G	AB	R	H	TB	2B	3B	HR	RBI	SH	SF	BB	SO	SB	CS	GIDP	SLG	OBA
Barnes, Skeeter, Det.	R	.273	95	165	27	45	64	8	1	3	25	2	2	10	18	3	1	4	.388	.318
Blowers, Mike, Sea.	R	.192	31	73	7	14	20	3	0	1	2	1	0	6	20	0	0	3	.274	.253
Boggs, Wade, Bos.	L	.259	143	514	62	133	184	22	4	7	50	0	6	74	31	1	3	10	.358	.353
Browne, Jerry, Oak.	B	.287	111	324	43	93	118	12	2	3	40	16	6	40	40	3	3	7	.364	.366
Easley, Damion, Cal.	R	.258	47	151	14	39	47	5	0	1	12	2	1	8	26	9	5	2	.311	.307
Gomez, Leo, Bal.	R	.265	137	468	62	124	199	24	0	17	64	5	8	63	78	2	3	14	.425	.356
Gonzales, Rene, Cal.	R	.277	104	329	47	91	131	17	1	7	38	5	1	41	46	7	4	17	.398	.363
Gruber, Kelly, Tor.	R	.229	120	446	42	102	157	16	3	11	43	1	4	26	72	7	7	14	.352	.275
Hayes, Charlie, NY-A	R	.257	142	509	52	131	208	19	2	18	66	3	6	28	100	3	5	12	.409	.297
Jacoby, Brook, Cle.	R	.261	120	291	30	76	95	7	0	4	36	3	4	28	54	0	3	13	.326	.324
Jefferies, Gregg, K.C.	B	.285	152	604	66	172	244	36	3	10	75	0	9	43	29	19	9	24	.404	.329
Kent, Jeff, Tor.	R	.240	65	192	36	46	85	13	1	8	35	0	4	20	47	2	1	3	.443	.324
Lansford, Carney, Oak.	R	.262	135	496	65	130	183	30	1	7	75	7	8	43	39	7	2	14	.369	.325
Leius, Scott, Min.	R	.249	129	409	50	102	130	18	2	2	35	5	0	34	61	6	5	10	.318	.309
Livingstone, Scott, Det.	L	.282	117	354	43	100	133	21	0	4	46	3	4	21	36	1	3	8	.376	.319
Martinez, Edgar, Sea.	R	.343	135	528	100	181	287	46	3	18	73	1	5	54	61	14	4	15	.544	.404
Meulens, Hensley, NY-A	R	.600	2	5	1	3	6	0	0	1	1	0	0	1	0	0	0	1	1.200	.667
Pagliarulo, Mike, Min.	L	.200	42	105	10	21	25	4	0	0	9	0	1	1	17	1	0	1	.238	.213
Palmer, Dean, Tex.	R	.229	152	541	74	124	227	25	0	26	72	2	4	62	154	10	4	9	.420	.311
Perezchica, Tony, Cle.	R	.100	18	20	2	2	3	1	0	0	1	2	0	2	6	0	0	0	.150	.182
Quinlan, Tom, Tor.	R	.067	13	15	2	1	2	1	0	0	2	0	0	2	9	0	0	0	.133	.176
Rohde, David, Cle.	B	.000	5	7	0	0	0	0	0	0	0	0	0	2	3	0	0	0	.000	.222
Seitzer, Kevin, Mil.	R	.270	148	540	74	146	198	35	1	5	71	7	9	57	44	13	11	16	.367	.337
Tatum, Jim, Mil.	R	.125	5	8	0	1	1	0	0	0	0	0	0	1	2	0	0	0	.125	.222
Thome, Jim, Cle.	L	.205	40	117	8	24	35	3	1	2	12	0	2	10	34	2	0	3	.299	.275
Turner, Shane, Sea.	L	.270	34	74	8	20	25	5	0	0	5	2	2	9	15	2	1	4	.338	.341
Ventura, Robin, ChiA	L	.282	157	592	85	167	255	38	1	16	93	1	8	93	71	2	4	14	.431	.375
Worthington, Craig, Cle.	R	.167	9	24	0	4	4	0	0	0	2	0	0	2	4	0	1	0	.167	.231

American League shortstops

Name/Team	B	BA	G	AB	R	H	TB	2B	3B	HR	RBI	SH	SF	BB	SO	SB	CS	GIDP	SLG	OBA
Alexander, Manny, Bal.	R	.200	4	5	1	1	1	0	0	0	0	0	0	0	3	0	0	0	.200	.200
Amaral, Rich, Sea.	R	.240	35	100	9	24	30	3	0	1	7	4	0	5	16	4	2	4	.300	.276
Beltre, Esteban, ChiA	R	.191	49	110	21	21	26	2	0	1	10	2	1	3	18	1	0	3	.236	.211
Brumley, A. Mike, Bos.	B	.000	2	1	0	0	0	0	0	0	0	0	0	0	0	0	0	0	.000	.000
Colon, Cris, Tex.	B	.167	14	36	5	6	6	0	0	0	1	1	0	1	8	0	0	2	.167	.189
DiSarcina, Gary, Cal.	R	.247	157	518	48	128	156	19	0	3	42	5	3	20	50	9	7	15	.301	.283
Diaz, Mario, Tex.	R	.226	19	31	2	7	8	1	0	0	1	1	0	1	2	0	1	2	.258	.250
Fermin, Felix, Cle.	R	.270	79	215	27	58	69	7	2	0	13	9	2	18	10	0	0	7	.321	.326
Fryman, Travis, Det.	R	.266	161	659	87	175	274	31	4	20	96	5	6	45	144	8	4	13	.416	.316
Gagne, Greg, Min.	R	.246	146	439	53	108	152	23	0	7	39	12	1	19	83	6	7	11	.346	.280
Grebeck, Craig, ChiA	R	.268	88	287	24	77	111	21	2	3	35	10	3	30	34	0	3	5	.387	.341
Griffin, Alfredo, Tor.	B	.233	63	150	21	35	42	7	0	0	10	3	2	9	19	3	1	3	.280	.273
Guillen, Ozzie, ChiA	L	.200	12	40	5	8	12	4	0	0	7	1	1	1	5	1	0	1	.300	.214
Hernandez, Jose, Cle.	R	.000	3	4	0	0	0	0	0	0	0	0	0	0	2	0	0	0	.000	.000
Hill, Donnie, Min.	B	.294	25	51	7	15	18	3	0	0	2	2	0	5	6	0	0	0	.353	.368
Howard, David, K.C.	B	.224	74	219	19	49	62	6	2	1	18	8	2	15	43	3	4	3	.283	.271
Huson, Jeff, Tex.	L	.261	123	318	49	83	115	14	3	4	24	8	6	41	43	18	6	7	.362	.342
Lee, Manuel, Tor.	B	.263	128	396	49	104	125	10	1	3	39	8	3	50	73	6	2	8	.316	.343
Lewis, Mark, Cle.	R	.264	122	413	44	109	145	21	0	5	30	1	4	25	69	4	5	12	.351	.308
Listach, Pat, Mil.	B	.290	149	579	93	168	202	19	6	1	47	12	2	55	124	54	18	3	.349	.352
Naehring, Tim, Bos.	R	.231	72	186	12	43	60	8	0	3	14	6	1	18	31	0	0	1	.323	.308
Quinones, Luis, Min.	B	.200	3	5	0	1	1	0	0	0	1	0	1	0	0	0	0	0	.200	.167
Reboulet, Jeff, Min.	R	.190	73	137	15	26	38	7	1	1	16	7	0	23	26	3	2	0	.277	.311
Ripken, Cal, Bal.	R	.251	162	637	73	160	233	29	1	14	72	0	7	64	50	4	3	13	.366	.323
Rivera, Luis, Bos.	R	.215	102	288	17	62	75	11	1	0	29	5	0	26	56	4	3	5	.260	.287
Rossy, Rico, K.C.	R	.215	59	149	21	32	45	8	1	1	12	7	1	20	20	0	3	6	.302	.310
Schaefer, Jeff, Sea.	R	.114	65	70	5	8	13	2	0	1	3	6	0	2	10	0	1	2	.186	.139
Schofield, Dick C., Cal.	R	.333	1	3	0	1	1	0	0	0	0	0	0	1	0	0	0	0	.333	.500
Silvestri, Dave, NY-A	R	.308	7	13	3	4	8	0	2	0	1	0	0	0	3	0	0	1	.615	.308
Spiers, Bill, Mil.	L	.313	12	16	2	5	7	2	0	0	2	1	0	1	4	1	1	0	.438	.353
Stankiewicz, Andy, NY-A	R	.268	116	400	52	107	139	22	2	2	25	7	1	38	42	9	5	13	.348	.338
Sveum, Dale, ChiA	B	.219	40	114	15	25	40	9	0	2	12	2	3	12	29	1	1	1	.351	.287
Thon, Dickie, Tex.	R	.247	95	275	30	68	101	15	3	4	37	3	5	20	40	12	2	2	.367	.293
Trammell, Alan, Det.	R	.275	29	102	11	28	40	7	1	1	11	1	1	15	4	2	2	6	.392	.370
Valentin, John, Bos.	R	.276	58	185	21	51	79	13	0	5	25	4	1	20	17	1	0	5	.427	.351
Valentin, Jose, Mil.	B	.000	4	3	1	0	0	0	0	0	1	0	1	0	0	0	0	0	.000	.000
Velarde, Randy, NY-A	R	.272	121	412	57	112	159	24	1	7	46	4	5	38	78	7	2	13	.386	.333
Vizquel, Omar, Sea.	B	.294	136	483	49	142	170	20	4	0	21	9	1	32	38	15	13	14	.352	.340
Weiss, Walt, Oak.	B	.212	103	316	36	67	76	5	2	0	21	11	4	43	39	6	3	10	.241	.305
Wilkerson, Curtis, K.C.	B	.250	111	296	27	74	92	10	1	2	29	7	4	18	47	18	7	4	.311	.292
Zosky, Eddie, Tor.	R	.286	8	7	1	2	4	0	1	0	1	0	1	0	2	0	0	0	.571	.250

American League outfielders

Name/Team	B	BA	G	AB	R	H	TB	2B	3B	HR	RBI	SH	SF	BB	SO	SB	CS	GIDP	SLG	OBA
Abner, Shawn, ChiA	R	.279	97	208	21	58	73	10	1	1	16	2	3	12	35	1	2	3	.351	.323
Anderson, Brady, Bal.	L	.271	159	623	100	169	280	28	10	21	80	10	9	98	98	53	16	2	.449	.373
Barfield, Jesse, NY-A	R	.137	30	95	8	13	21	2	0	2	7	0	1	9	27	1	1	5	.221	.210
Bell, Derek, Tor.	R	.242	61	161	23	39	57	6	3	2	15	2	1	15	34	7	2	6	.354	.324
Belle, Albert, Cle.	R	.260	153	585	81	152	279	23	1	34	112	1	8	52	128	8	2	18	.477	.320
Bichette, Dante, Mil.	R	.287	112	387	37	111	157	27	2	5	41	2	3	16	74	18	7	13	.406	.318
Briley, Greg, Sea.	L	.275	86	200	18	55	80	10	0	5	12	0	2	4	31	9	2	4	.400	.290
Brito, Bernardo, Min.	R	.143	8	14	1	2	3	1	0	0	2	0	1	0	4	0	1	0	.214	.133
Brosius, Scott, Oak.	R	.218	38	87	13	19	33	2	0	4	13	0	1	3	13	3	0	0	.379	.258
Brown, Jarvis, Min.	R	.067	35	15	8	1	1	0	0	0	0	0	0	2	4	2	2	0	.067	.222
Bruett, J.T., Min.	L	.250	56	76	7	19	23	4	0	0	2	1	0	6	12	6	3	0	.303	.313
Brunansky, Tom, Bos.	R	.266	138	458	47	122	204	31	3	15	74	2	7	66	96	2	5	11	.445	.354
Buhner, Jay, Sea.	R	.243	152	543	69	132	229	16	3	25	79	1	8	71	146	0	6	12	.422	.333
Burks, Ellis, Bos.	R	.255	66	235	35	60	98	8	3	8	30	0	2	25	48	5	2	5	.417	.327
Bush, Randy, Min.	L	.214	100	182	14	39	55	8	1	2	22	0	3	11	37	1	1	5	.302	.263
Cangelosi, John, Tex.	B	.188	73	85	12	16	21	2	0	1	6	3	0	18	16	6	5	0	.247	.330
Canseco, Jose, Oak.-Tex.	R	.244	119	439	74	107	200	15	0	26	87	0	4	63	128	6	7	16	.456	.344
Carreon, Mark, Det.	R	.232	101	336	34	78	121	11	1	10	41	1	4	22	57	3	1	12	.360	.278
Carter, Joe, Tor.	R	.264	158	622	97	164	310	30	7	34	119	1	13	36	109	12	5	14	.498	.309
Clark, Phil, Det.	R	.407	23	54	3	22	29	4	0	1	5	1	0	6	9	1	0	2	.537	.467
Cochrane, Dave, Sea.	B	.250	65	152	10	38	49	5	0	2	12	2	0	12	34	1	0	3	.322	.309
Cole, Alex, Cle.	L	.206	41	97	11	20	21	1	0	0	5	0	1	10	21	9	2	2	.216	.284
Cotto, Henry, Sea.	R	.259	108	294	42	76	104	11	1	5	27	3	1	14	49	23	2	2	.354	.294
Curtis, Chad, Cal.	R	.259	139	441	59	114	164	16	2	10	46	5	4	51	71	43	18	10	.372	.341
Cuyler, Milt, Det.	B	.241	89	291	39	70	92	11	1	3	28	8	0	10	62	8	5	4	.316	.275

American League outfielders

Name/Team	B	BA	G	AB	R	H	TB	2B	3B	HR	RBI	SH	SF	BB	SO	SB	CS	GIDP	SLG	OBA
Daugherty, Jack, Tex.	B	.205	59	127	13	26	35	9	0	0	9	0	2	16	21	2	1	3	.276	.295
Deer, Rob, Det.	R	.247	110	393	66	97	215	20	1	32	64	0	1	51	131	4	2	8	.547	.337
Devereaux, Mike, Bal.	R	.276	156	653	76	180	303	29	11	24	107	0	9	44	94	10	8	14	.464	.321
Diaz, Alex, Mil.	B	.111	22	9	5	1	1	0	0	0	1	0	0	0	0	3	2	0	.111	.111
Ducey, Rob, Tor.-Cal.	L	.188	54	80	7	15	19	4	0	0	2	0	1	5	22	2	4	1	.238	.233
Eisenreich, Jim, K.C.	L	.269	113	353	31	95	120	13	3	2	28	0	3	24	36	11	6	6	.340	.313
Fariss, Monty, Tex.	R	.217	67	166	13	36	54	7	1	3	21	2	0	17	51	0	2	3	.325	.297
Felix, Junior, Cal.	B	.246	139	509	63	125	184	22	5	9	72	5	9	33	128	8	8	9	.361	.289
Fox, Eric, Oak.	B	.238	51	143	24	34	52	5	2	3	13	6	1	13	29	3	4	1	.364	.299
Gladden, Dan, Det.	R	.254	113	417	57	106	149	20	1	7	42	5	5	30	64	4	2	10	.357	.304
Gonzalez, Jose, Cal.	R	.182	33	55	4	10	12	2	0	0	2	1	1	7	20	0	1	2	.218	.270
Gonzalez, Juan, Tex.	R	.260	155	584	77	152	309	24	2	43	109	0	8	35	143	0	1	16	.529	.304
Greenwell, Mike, Bos.	L	.233	49	180	16	42	50	2	0	2	18	0	2	18	19	2	3	8	.278	.307
Griffey, Ken Jr., Sea.	L	.308	142	565	83	174	302	39	4	27	103	0	3	44	67	10	5	15	.535	.361
Gwynn, Chris, K.C.	L	.286	34	84	10	24	34	3	2	1	7	1	2	3	10	0	0	1	.405	.303
Hall, Mel, NY-A	L	.280	152	583	67	163	250	36	3	15	81	0	9	29	53	4	2	13	.429	.310
Hamilton, Darryl, Mil.	L	.298	128	470	67	140	188	19	7	5	62	4	7	45	42	41	14	10	.400	.356
Hare, Shawn, Det.	L	.115	15	26	0	3	4	1	0	0	5	0	1	2	4	0	0	0	.154	.172
Harris, Donald, Tex.	R	.182	24	33	3	6	7	1	0	0	1	0	0	0	15	1	0	0	.212	.182
Hatcher, Billy, Bos.	R	.238	75	315	37	75	98	16	2	1	23	6	1	17	41	4	6	9	.311	.283
Hayes, Von, Cal.	L	.225	94	307	35	69	100	17	1	4	29	3	3	37	54	11	6	9	.326	.305
Henderson, Dave, Oak.	R	.143	20	63	1	9	10	1	0	0	2	0	0	2	16	0	0	0	.159	.169
Henderson, Rickey, Oak.	R	.283	117	396	77	112	181	18	3	15	46	0	3	95	56	48	11	5	.457	.426
Hill, Glenallen, Cle.	R	.241	102	369	38	89	161	16	1	18	49	0	1	20	73	9	6	11	.436	.287
Howard, Thomas, Cle.	B	.277	117	358	36	99	124	15	2	2	32	10	2	17	60	15	8	4	.346	.308
Howitt, Dann, Oak.-Sea.	L	.188	35	85	7	16	28	4	1	2	10	1	3	8	9	1	1	6	.329	.250
Huff, Mike, ChiA	R	.209	60	115	13	24	29	5	0	0	8	2	2	10	24	1	2	2	.252	.273
Hulse, David, Tex.	L	.304	32	92	14	28	32	4	0	0	2	2	0	3	18	3	1	0	.348	.326
Humphreys, Mike, NY-A	R	.100	4	10	0	1	1	0	0	0	0	0	0	0	1	0	0	2	.100	.100
James, Dion, NY-A	L	.262	67	145	24	38	55	8	0	3	17	0	2	22	15	1	0	3	.379	.359
Jeter, Shawn, ChiA	L	.111	13	18	1	2	2	0	0	0	0	0	0	0	7	0	0	0	.111	.111
Johnson, Lance, ChiA	L	.279	157	567	67	158	206	15	12	3	47	4	5	34	33	41	14	20	.363	.318
Kelly, Roberto, NY-A	R	.272	152	580	81	158	223	31	2	10	66	1	6	41	96	28	5	19	.384	.322
Kingery, Mike, Oak.	L	.107	12	28	3	3	3	0	0	0	1	0	0	1	3	0	0	1	.107	.138
Kirby, Wayne, Cle.	L	.167	21	18	9	3	7	1	0	1	1	0	0	3	2	0	3	1	.389	.286
Koslofski, Kevin, K.C.	L	.248	55	133	20	33	46	0	2	3	13	3	1	12	23	2	1	2	.346	.313
Lennon, Pat, Sea.	R	.000	1	2	0	0	0	0	0	0	0	0	0	0	0	0	0	0	.000	.000
Lofton, Kenny, Cle.	L	.285	148	576	96	164	210	15	8	5	42	4	1	68	54	66	12	7	.365	.362
Lyons, Steve, Bos.	L	.250	21	28	3	7	9	0	1	0	2	0	0	2	1	0	1	0	.321	.300
Mack, Shane, Min.	R	.315	156	600	101	189	280	31	6	16	75	11	2	64	106	26	14	8	.467	.394
Maldonado, Candy, Tor.	R	.272	137	489	64	133	226	25	4	20	66	2	3	59	112	2	2	13	.462	.357
Martinez, Chito, Bal.	L	.268	83	198	26	53	80	10	1	5	25	0	4	31	47	0	1	9	.404	.366
McRae, Brian, K.C.	B	.223	149	533	63	119	164	23	5	4	52	7	4	42	88	18	5	10	.308	.285
McReynolds, Kevin, K.C.	R	.247	109	373	45	92	156	25	0	13	49	0	5	67	48	7	1	6	.418	.357
Mercedes, Luis, Bal.	R	.140	23	50	7	7	9	2	0	0	4	2	1	8	9	0	1	2	.180	.267
Mitchell, Kevin, Sea.	R	.286	99	360	48	103	154	24	0	9	67	0	4	35	46	0	2	4	.428	.351
Morris, John D., Cal.	L	.193	43	57	4	11	15	1	0	1	3	1	0	4	11	1	0	0	.263	.258
Moses, John, Sea.	B	.136	21	22	3	3	4	1	0	0	1	2	0	5	4	0	0	0	.182	.296
Munoz, Pedro, Min.	R	.270	127	418	44	113	171	16	3	12	71	0	3	17	90	4	5	18	.409	.298
Neel, Troy, Oak.	L	.264	24	53	8	14	26	3	0	3	9	0	0	5	15	0	1	1	.491	.339
Newson, Warren, ChiA	L	.221	63	136	19	30	36	3	0	1	11	0	0	37	38	3	0	4	.265	.387
Orsulak, Joe, Bal.	L	.289	117	391	45	113	149	18	3	4	39	4	1	28	34	5	4	3	.381	.342
Pasqua, Dan, ChiA	L	.211	93	265	26	56	92	16	1	6	33	1	3	36	57	0	1	4	.347	.305
Peltier, Dan, Tex.	L	.167	12	24	1	4	4	0	0	0	2	0	0	0	3	0	0	0	.167	.167
Pettis, Gary, Det.	B	.202	48	129	27	26	39	4	3	1	12	3	1	27	34	13	4	3	.302	.338
Plantier, Phil, Bos.	L	.246	108	349	46	86	126	19	0	7	30	2	2	44	83	2	3	9	.361	.332
Polonia, Luis, Cal.	L	.286	149	577	83	165	190	17	4	0	35	8	4	45	64	51	21	18	.329	.337
Puckett, Kirby, Min.	R	.329	160	639	104	210	313	38	4	19	110	1	6	44	97	17	7	17	.490	.374
Pulliam, Harvey, K.C.	R	.200	4	5	2	1	2	1	0	0	0	0	0	1	3	0	0	0	.400	.333
Raines, Tim, ChiA	B	.294	144	551	102	162	223	22	9	7	54	4	8	81	48	45	6	5	.405	.380
Ready, Randy, Oak.	R	.200	61	125	17	25	36	2	0	3	17	2	2	25	23	1	0	1	.288	.329
Reed, Darren, Min.	R	.182	14	33	2	6	8	2	0	0	4	0	2	2	11	0	0	0	.242	.216
Reimer, Kevin, Tex.	L	.267	148	494	56	132	216	32	2	16	58	0	1	42	103	2	4	10	.437	.336
Salmon, Tim, Cal.	R	.177	23	79	8	14	21	1	0	2	6	0	1	11	23	1	1	1	.266	.283
Sierra, Ruben, Tex.-Oak.	B	.278	151	601	83	167	266	34	7	17	87	0	10	45	68	14	4	11	.443	.323
Tartabull, Danny, NY-A	R	.266	123	421	72	112	206	19	0	25	85	0	2	103	115	2	2	7	.489	.409
Thurman, Gary, K.C.	R	.245	88	200	25	49	61	6	3	0	20	6	0	9	34	9	6	3	.305	.281
Vaughn, Greg, Mil.	R	.228	141	501	77	114	205	18	2	23	78	2	5	60	123	15	15	8	.409	.313
Ward, Turner, Tor.	B	.345	18	29	7	10	16	3	0	1	3	0	0	4	4	0	1	1	.552	.424
White, Devon, Tor.	B	.248	153	641	98	159	250	26	7	17	60	0	3	47	133	37	4	9	.390	.303
Whiten, Mark, Cle.	B	.254	148	508	73	129	183	19	4	9	43	3	3	72	102	16	12	12	.360	.347

American League outfielders

Name/Team	B	BA	G	AB	R	H	TB	2B	3B	HR	RBI	SH	SF	BB	SO	SB	CS	GIDP	SLG	OBA
Williams, Bernie, NY-A	B	.280	62	261	39	73	106	14	2	5	26	2	0	29	36	7	6	5	.406	.354
Williams, Gerald, NY-A	R	.296	15	27	7	8	19	2	0	3	6	0	0	0	3	2	0	0	.704	.296
Williams, Reggie, Cal.	B	.231	14	26	5	6	9	1	1	0	2	0	0	1	10	0	2	0	.346	.259
Wilson, Willie, Oak.	B	.270	132	396	38	107	132	15	5	0	37	2	3	35	65	28	8	11	.333	.329
Winningham, Herm, Bos.	L	.235	105	234	27	55	68	8	1	1	14	0	0	10	53	6	5	3	.291	.266
Yount, Robin, Mil.	R	.264	150	557	71	147	217	40	3	8	77	4	12	53	81	15	6	9	.390	.325
Zupcic, Bob, Bos.	R	.276	124	392	46	108	138	19	1	3	43	7	4	25	60	2	2	6	.352	.322

American League designated hitters

Name/Team	B	BA	G	AB	R	H	TB	2B	3B	HR	RBI	SH	SF	BB	SO	SB	CS	GIDP	SLG	OBA
Baines, Harold, Oak.	L	.253	140	478	58	121	187	18	0	16	76	0	6	59	61	1	3	11	.391	.331
Bell, George A., ChiA	R	.255	155	627	74	160	262	27	0	25	112	0	6	31	97	5	2	29	.418	.294
Brett, George, K.C.	L	.285	152	592	55	169	235	35	5	7	61	0	4	35	69	8	6	15	.397	.330
Clark, Jack, Bos.	R	.210	81	257	32	54	80	11	0	5	33	0	5	56	87	1	1	4	.311	.350
Davis, Chili, Min.	B	.288	138	444	63	128	195	27	2	12	66	0	9	73	76	4	5	11	.439	.386
Davis, Glenn, Bal.	R	.276	106	398	46	110	168	15	2	13	48	1	4	37	65	1	0	12	.422	.338
Downing, Brian, Tex.	R	.278	107	320	53	89	137	18	0	10	39	0	1	62	58	1	0	7	.428	.407
Horn, Sam, Bal.	L	.235	63	162	13	38	65	10	1	5	19	0	1	21	60	0	0	8	.401	.324
Maas, Kevin, NY-A	L	.248	98	286	35	71	116	12	0	11	35	0	4	25	63	3	1	1	.406	.305
Molitor, Paul, Mil.	R	.320	158	609	89	195	281	36	7	12	89	4	11	73	66	31	6	13	.461	.389
Mulliniks, Rance, Tor.	L	.500	3	2	1	1	1	0	0	0	0	0	0	1	0	0	0	0	.500	.667
Winfield, Dave, Tor.	R	.290	156	583	92	169	286	33	3	26	108	1	3	82	89	2	3	10	.491	.377

American League pitchers (batting)

Name/Team	B	BA	G	AB	R	H	TB	2B	3B	HR	RBI	SH	SF	BB	SO	SB	CS	GIDP	SLG	OBA
Langston, Mark, Cal.	R	.000	33	2	1	0	0	0	0	0	0	0	0	0	2	0	0	0	.000	.000

National League starting pitchers

Name/Team	T	W	L	ERA	G	GS	CG	SHO	GF	SV	IP	H	R	ER	HR	BB	SO	WP	BK	BA
Abbott, Kyle, Phi.	L	1	14	5.13	31	19	0	0	0	0	133.1	147	80	76	20	45	88	9	1	.283
Ashby, Andy, Phi.	R	1	3	7.54	10	8	0	0	0	0	37	42	31	31	6	21	24	2	0	.290
Astacio, Pedro, L.A.	R	5	5	1.98	11	11	4	4	0	0	82	80	23	18	1	20	43	1	0	.255
Avery, Steve, Atl.	L	11	11	3.20	35	35	2	2	0	0	233.2	216	95	83	14	71	129	7	3	.246
Ayala, Bobby, Cin.	R	2	1	4.34	5	5	0	0	0	0	29	33	15	14	1	13	23	0	0	.297
Barnes, Brian, Mon.	L	6	6	2.97	21	17	0	0	2	0	100	77	34	33	9	46	65	1	2	.213
Belcher, Tim, Cin.	R	15	14	3.91	35	34	2	1	1	0	227.2	201	104	99	17	80	149	3	1	.238
Benes, Andy, S.D.	R	13	14	3.35	34	34	2	2	0	0	231.1	230	90	86	14	61	169	1	1	.264
Bielecki, Mike, Atl.	R	2	4	2.57	19	14	1	1	0	0	80.2	77	27	23	2	27	62	4	0	.254
Birkbeck, Mike, NY-N	R	0	1	9.00	1	1	0	0	0	0	7	12	7	7	3	1	2	1	0	.387
Black, Bud, S.F.	L	10	12	3.97	28	28	2	1	0	0	177	178	88	78	23	59	82	3	7	.263
Boskie, Shawn, ChiN	R	5	11	5.01	23	18	0	0	2	0	91.2	96	55	51	14	36	39	5	1	.284
Bowen, Ryan, Hou.	R	0	7	10.96	11	9	0	0	2	0	33.2	48	43	41	8	30	22	5	0	.333
Browning, Tom, Cin.	L	6	5	5.07	16	16	0	0	0	0	87	108	49	49	6	28	33	3	1	.311
Burkett, John, S.F.	R	13	9	3.84	32	32	3	1	0	0	189.2	194	96	81	13	45	107	0	0	.264
Candiotti, Tom, L.A.	R	11	15	3.00	32	30	6	2	1	0	203.2	177	78	68	13	63	152	9	2	.237
Castillo, Frank, ChiN	R	10	11	3.46	33	33	0	0	0	0	205.1	179	91	79	19	63	135	11	0	.232
Combs, Pat, Phi.	L	1	1	7.71	4	4	0	0	0	0	18.2	20	16	16	0	12	11	1	0	.278
Cone, David, NY-N	R	13	7	2.88	27	27	7	5	0	0	196.2	162	75	63	12	82	214	9	1	.223
Cormier, Rheal, St.L	L	10	10	3.68	31	30	3	0	1	0	186	194	83	76	15	33	117	4	2	.269
DeLeon, Jose, St.L-Phi.	R	2	8	4.37	32	18	0	0	3	0	117.1	111	63	57	7	48	79	3	0	.250
Deshaies, Jim, S.D.	L	4	7	3.28	15	15	0	0	0	0	96	92	40	35	6	33	46	1	2	.258
Drabek, Doug, Pit.	R	15	11	2.77	34	34	10	4	0	0	256.2	218	84	79	17	54	177	11	1	.231
Eiland, Dave, S.D.	R	0	2	5.67	7	7	0	0	0	0	27	33	21	17	1	5	10	0	1	.287
Fernandez, Sid, NY-N	L	14	11	2.73	32	32	5	2	0	0	214.2	162	67	65	12	67	193	0	0	.210
Gardner, Mark, Mon.	R	12	10	4.36	33	30	0	0	1	0	179.2	179	91	87	15	60	132	2	0	.259
Glavine, Tom, Atl.	L	20	8	2.76	33	33	7	5	0	0	225	197	81	69	6	70	129	5	0	.235
Gooden, Dwight, NY-N	R	10	13	3.67	31	31	3	0	0	0	206	197	93	84	11	70	145	3	1	.255
Greene, Tommy, Phi.	R	3	3	5.32	13	12	0	0	0	0	64.1	75	39	38	5	34	39	1	0	.291
Gross, Kevin, L.A.	R	8	13	3.17	34	30	4	3	0	0	204.2	182	82	72	11	77	158	4	2	.241
Hammond, Chris, Cin.	L	7	10	4.21	28	26	0	0	1	0	147.1	149	75	69	13	55	79	6	0	.266
Harkey, Mike, ChiN	R	4	0	1.89	7	7	0	0	0	0	38	34	13	8	4	15	21	3	1	.243
Harnisch, Pete, Hou.	R	9	10	3.70	34	34	0	0	0	0	206.2	182	92	85	18	64	164	4	1	.234
Harris, Greg W., S.D.	R	4	8	4.12	20	20	1	0	0	0	118	113	62	54	13	35	66	2	1	.252
Henry, Butch, Hou.	L	6	9	4.02	28	28	2	1	0	0	165.2	185	81	74	16	41	96	2	2	.285
Hershiser, Orel, L.A.	R	10	15	3.67	33	33	1	0	0	0	210.2	209	101	86	15	69	130	10	0	.257
Hill, Ken, Mon.	R	16	9	2.68	33	33	3	3	0	0	218	187	76	65	13	75	150	11	4	.230
Hillman, Eric, NY-N	L	2	2	5.33	11	8	0	0	2	0	52.1	67	31	31	9	10	16	1	0	.318
Hurst, Bruce, S.D.	L	14	9	3.85	32	32	6	4	0	0	217.1	223	96	93	22	51	131	4	3	.267
Hurst, Jonathan, Mon.	R	1	1	5.51	3	3	0	0	0	0	16.1	18	10	10	1	7	4	1	0	.281

National League starting pitchers

Name/Team	T	W	L	ERA	G	GS	CG	SHO	GF	SV	IP	H	R	ER	HR	BB	SO	WP	BK	BA
Jackson, Danny, ChiN-Pit.	L	8	13	3.84	34	34	0	0	0	0	201.1	211	99	86	6	77	97	2	2	.272
Jones, Jimmy, Hou.	R	10	6	4.07	25	23	0	0	1	0	139.1	135	64	63	13	39	69	4	1	.258
Kile, Darryl, Hou.	R	5	10	3.95	22	22	2	0	0	0	125.1	124	61	55	8	63	90	3	4	.261
Lefferts, Craig, S.D.	L	13	9	3.69	27	27	0	0	0	0	163.1	180	76	67	16	35	81	4	1	.285
Leibrandt, Charlie, Atl.	L	15	7	3.36	32	31	5	2	0	0	193	191	78	72	9	42	104	3	2	.258
Maddux, Greg, ChiN	R	20	11	2.18	35	35	9	4	0	0	268	201	68	65	7	70	199	5	0	.210
Martinez, Dennis, Mon.	R	16	11	2.47	32	32	6	0	0	0	226.1	172	75	62	12	60	147	2	0	.211
Martinez, Pedro, L.A.	R	0	1	2.25	2	1	0	0	1	0	8	6	2	2	0	1	8	0	0	.200
Martinez, Ramon, L.A.	R	8	11	4.00	25	25	1	1	0	0	150.2	141	82	67	11	69	101	9	0	.245
Morgan, Mike, ChiN	R	16	8	2.55	34	34	6	1	0	0	240	203	80	68	14	79	123	11	0	.234
Mulholland, Terry, Phi.	L	13	11	3.81	32	32	12	2	0	0	229	227	101	97	14	46	125	3	0	.261
Nabholz, Chris, Mon.	L	11	12	3.32	32	32	1	1	0	0	195	176	80	72	11	74	130	5	1	.244
Nied, David, Atl.	R	3	0	1.17	6	2	0	0	0	0	23	10	3	3	0	5	19	0	0	.130
Ojeda, Bob, L.A.	L	6	9	3.63	29	29	2	1	0	0	166.1	169	80	67	8	81	94	3	0	.268
Olivares, Omar, St.L	R	9	9	3.84	32	30	1	0	1	0	197	189	84	84	20	63	124	2	0	.257
Osborne, Donovan, St.L	L	11	9	3.77	34	29	0	0	2	0	179	193	91	75	14	38	104	6	0	.275
Portugal, Mark, Hou.	R	6	3	2.66	18	16	1	1	0	0	101.1	76	32	30	7	41	62	1	1	.213
Rijo, Jose, Cin.	R	15	10	2.56	33	33	2	0	0	0	211	185	67	60	15	44	171	2	1	.238
Saberhagen, Bret, NY-N	R	3	5	3.50	17	15	1	1	0	0	97.2	84	39	38	6	27	81	1	2	.233
Schilling, Curt, Phi.	R	14	11	2.35	42	26	10	4	10	2	226.1	165	67	59	11	59	147	4	0	.201
Schourek, Pete, NY-N	L	6	8	3.64	22	21	0	0	0	0	136	137	60	55	9	44	60	4	2	.261
Seminara, Frank, S.D.	R	9	4	3.68	19	18	0	0	0	0	100.1	98	46	41	5	46	61	1	1	.258
Smith, Pete J., Atl.	R	7	0	2.05	12	11	2	1	0	0	79	63	19	18	3	28	43	2	1	.217
Smith, Zane, Pit.	L	8	8	3.06	23	22	4	3	0	0	141	138	56	48	8	19	56	0	0	.261
Smoltz, John, Atl.	R	15	12	2.85	35	35	9	3	0	0	246.2	206	90	78	17	80	215	17	1	.224
Swift, Bill C., S.F.	R	10	4	2.08	30	22	3	2	2	1	164.2	144	41	38	6	43	77	0	1	.239
Swindell, Greg, Cin.	L	12	8	2.70	31	30	5	3	0	0	213.2	210	72	64	14	41	138	3	2	.260
Tewksbury, Bob, St.L	R	16	5	2.16	33	32	5	0	1	0	233	217	63	56	15	20	91	2	0	.248
Tomlin, Randy, Pit.	L	14	9	3.41	35	33	1	1	0	0	208.2	226	85	79	11	42	90	7	2	.282
Wakefield, Tim, Pit.	R	8	1	2.15	13	13	4	1	0	0	92	76	26	22	3	35	51	3	1	.232
Walk, Bob, Pit.	R	10	6	3.20	36	19	1	0	7	2	135	132	54	48	10	43	60	7	2	.258
Williams, Brian, Hou.	R	7	6	3.92	16	16	0	0	0	0	96.1	92	44	42	10	42	54	2	1	.255
Wilson, Trevor, S.F.	L	8	14	4.21	26	26	1	1	0	0	154	152	82	72	18	64	88	2	7	.265

National League relief pitchers

Name/Team	T	W	L	ERA	G	GS	CG	SHO	GF	SV	IP	H	R	ER	HR	BB	SO	WP	BK	BA
Agosto, Juan, St.L	L	2	4	6.25	22	0	0	0	10	0	31.2	39	24	22	2	9	13	2	0	.312
Andersen, Larry E., S.D.	R	1	1	3.34	34	0	0	0	13	2	35	26	14	13	2	8	35	0	0	.202
Assenmacher, Paul, ChiN	L	4	4	4.10	70	0	0	0	23	8	68	72	32	31	6	26	67	4	0	.271
Ayrault, Bob, Phi.	R	2	2	3.12	30	0	0	0	7	0	43.1	32	16	15	0	17	27	0	0	.209
Baller, Jay, Phi.	R	0	0	8.18	8	0	0	0	4	0	11	10	10	10	5	10	9	1	0	.250
Bankhead, Scott, Cin.	R	10	4	2.93	54	0	0	0	10	1	70.2	57	26	23	4	29	53	6	0	.218
Batista, Miguel, Pit.	R	0	0	9.00	1	0	0	0	1	0	2	4	2	2	1	3	1	0	0	.400
Beck, Rod, S.F.	R	3	3	1.76	65	0	0	0	42	17	92	62	20	18	4	15	87	5	2	.190
Belinda, Stan, Pit.	R	6	4	3.15	59	0	0	0	42	18	71.1	58	26	25	8	29	57	1	0	.223
Berenguer, Juan, Atl.	R	3	1	5.13	28	0	0	0	8	1	33.1	35	22	19	7	16	19	2	2	.269
Blair, Willie, Hou.	R	5	7	4.00	29	8	0	0	1	0	78.2	74	47	35	5	25	48	2	0	.249
Boever, Joe, Hou.	R	3	6	2.51	81	0	0	0	26	2	111.1	103	38	31	3	45	67	4	0	.248
Bolton, Tom, Cin.	L	3	3	5.24	16	8	0	0	3	0	46.1	52	28	27	9	23	27	3	1	.284
Borbon, Pedro, Atl.	L	0	1	6.75	2	0	0	0	2	0	1.1	2	1	1	0	1	1	0	0	.333
Bottenfield, Kent, Mon.	R	1	2	2.23	10	4	0	0	2	1	32.1	26	9	8	1	11	14	0	0	.217
Brantley, Cliff, Phi.	R	2	6	4.60	28	9	0	0	6	0	76.1	71	45	39	6	58	32	4	1	.251
Brantley, Jeff, S.F.	R	7	7	2.95	56	4	0	0	32	7	91.2	67	32	30	8	45	86	3	1	.207
Brink, Brad, Phi.	R	0	4	4.14	8	7	0	0	0	0	41.1	53	27	19	2	13	16	0	0	.308
Brocail, Doug, S.D.	R	0	0	6.43	3	3	0	0	0	0	14	17	10	10	2	5	15	0	0	.298
Brown, Keith, Cin.	R	0	1	4.50	2	2	0	0	0	0	8	10	5	4	2	5	5	0	0	.313
Bullinger, Jim, ChiN	R	2	8	4.66	39	9	1	0	15	7	85	72	49	44	9	54	36	4	0	.233
Burba, Dave, S.F.	R	2	7	4.97	23	11	0	0	4	0	70.2	80	43	39	4	31	47	1	1	.287
Burke, Tim, NY-N	R	1	2	5.74	15	0	0	0	9	0	15.2	26	15	10	1	3	7	2	0	.371
Candelaria, John, L.A.	L	2	5	2.84	50	0	0	0	11	5	25.1	20	9	8	1	13	23	1	0	.220
Carpenter, Cris, St.L	R	5	4	2.97	73	0	0	0	21	1	88	69	29	29	10	27	46	5	0	.220
Carter, Larry, S.F.	R	1	5	4.64	6	6	0	0	0	0	33	34	17	17	6	18	21	2	0	.270
Chapin, Darrin, Phi.	R	0	0	9.00	1	0	0	0	0	0	2	2	2	2	1	0	1	1	0	.250
Charlton, Norm, Cin.	L	4	2	2.99	64	0	0	0	46	26	81.1	79	39	27	7	26	90	8	0	.262
Clark, Mark, St.L	R	3	10	4.45	20	20	1	1	0	0	113.1	117	59	56	12	36	44	4	0	.265
Clements, Pat, S.D.	L	2	1	2.66	27	0	0	0	7	0	23.2	25	9	7	0	12	11	0	0	.281
Cole, Victor, Pit.	R	0	2	5.48	8	4	0	0	2	0	23	23	14	14	1	14	12	1	0	.261
Cooke, Steve, Pit.	L	2	0	3.52	11	0	0	0	8	1	23	22	9	9	2	4	10	0	0	.253
Cox, Danny, Phi.-Pit.	R	5	3	4.60	25	7	0	0	8	3	62.2	66	37	32	5	27	48	1	0	.272
Crews, Tim, L.A.	R	0	3	5.19	49	2	0	0	13	0	78	95	46	45	6	20	43	3	0	.310

National League relief pitchers

Name/Team	T	W	L	ERA	G	GS	CG	SHO	GF	SV	IP	H	R	ER	HR	BB	SO	WP	BK	BA
Dewey, Mark, NY-N	R	1	0	4.32	20	0	0	0	6	0	33.1	37	16	16	2	10	24	0	1	.280
DiPino, Frank, St.L	L	0	0	1.64	9	0	0	0	3	0	11	9	2	2	0	3	8	0	0	.220
Dibble, Rob, Cin.	R	3	5	3.07	63	0	0	0	49	25	70.1	48	26	24	3	31	110	6	0	.193
Downs, Kelly, S.F.	R	1	2	3.47	19	7	0	0	5	0	62.1	65	27	24	4	24	33	4	0	.275
Fassero, Jeff, Mon.	L	8	7	2.84	70	0	0	0	22	1	85.2	81	35	27	1	34	63	7	1	.249
Filer, Tom, NY-N	R	0	1	2.05	9	1	0	0	1	0	22	18	8	5	2	6	9	1	0	.222
Foster, Steve, Cin.	R	1	1	2.88	31	1	0	0	7	2	50	52	16	16	4	13	34	1	0	.275
Franco, John, NY-N	L	6	2	1.64	31	0	0	0	30	15	33	24	6	6	1	11	20	0	0	.209
Freeman, Marvin, Atl.	R	7	5	3.22	58	0	0	0	15	3	64.1	61	26	23	7	29	41	4	0	.251
Gibson, Paul, NY-N	L	0	1	5.23	43	1	0	0	12	0	62	70	37	36	7	25	49	1	0	.287
Gleaton, Jerry Don, Pit.	L	1	0	4.26	23	0	0	0	6	0	31.2	34	16	15	4	19	18	1	0	.283
Gott, Jim, L.A.	R	3	3	2.45	68	0	0	0	28	6	88	72	27	24	4	41	75	9	3	.225
Gross, Kip, L.A.	R	1	1	4.18	16	1	0	0	7	0	23.2	32	14	11	1	10	14	1	1	.323
Guetterman, Lee, NY-N	L	3	4	5.82	43	0	0	0	15	2	43.1	57	28	28	5	14	15	3	0	.324
Haney, Chris, Mon.	L	2	3	5.45	9	6	1	1	2	0	38	40	25	23	6	10	27	5	1	.270
Harris, Gene, S.D.	R	0	2	2.95	14	1	0	0	2	0	21.1	15	8	7	0	9	19	1	1	.195
Hartley, Mike, Phi.	R	7	6	3.44	46	0	0	0	15	0	55	54	23	21	5	23	53	4	0	.255
Hartsock, Jeff, ChiN	R	0	0	6.75	4	0	0	0	0	0	9.1	15	7	7	2	4	6	2	0	.375
Henry, Dwayne, Cin.	R	3	3	3.33	60	0	0	0	11	0	83.2	59	31	31	4	44	72	12	0	.199
Heredia, Gil, S.F.-Mon.	R	2	3	4.23	20	5	0	0	4	0	44.2	44	23	21	4	20	22	1	0	.270
Hernandez, Jeremy, S.D.	R	1	4	4.17	26	0	0	0	11	1	36.2	39	17	17	4	11	25	0	0	.291
Hernandez, Xavier, Hou.	R	9	1	2.11	77	0	0	0	25	7	111	81	31	26	5	42	96	5	0	.200
Hickerson, Bryan, S.F.	L	5	3	3.09	61	1	0	0	8	0	87.1	74	31	30	7	21	68	4	1	.236
Hill, Milt, Cin.	R	0	0	3.15	14	0	0	0	5	1	20	15	9	7	1	5	10	0	0	.211
Hollins, Jessie, ChiN	R	0	0	13.50	4	0	0	0	3	0	4.2	8	7	7	1	5	0	1	0	.400
Howell, Jay, L.A.	R	1	3	1.54	41	0	0	0	26	4	46.2	41	9	8	2	18	36	3	1	.230
Innis, Jeff, NY-N	R	6	9	2.86	76	0	0	0	28	1	88	85	32	28	4	36	39	1	0	.266
Jackson, Mike R., S.F.	R	6	6	3.73	67	0	0	0	24	2	82	76	35	34	7	33	80	1	0	.252
Jones, Barry, Phi.-NY-N	R	7	6	5.68	61	0	0	0	17	1	69.2	85	46	44	3	35	30	2	2	.308
Jones, Doug, Hou.	R	11	8	1.85	80	0	0	0	70	36	111.2	96	29	23	5	17	93	2	1	.235
Krueger, Bill, Mon.	L	0	2	6.75	9	2	0	0	3	0	17.1	23	13	13	0	7	13	1	0	.315
Lamp, Dennis, Pit.	R	1	1	5.14	21	0	0	0	2	0	28	33	16	16	3	9	15	0	1	.292
Landrum, Bill, Mon.	R	1	1	7.20	18	0	0	0	6	0	20	27	16	16	3	9	7	0	0	.325
Maddux, Mike, S.D.	R	2	2	2.37	50	1	0	0	14	5	79.2	71	25	21	2	24	60	4	1	.236
Magrane, Joe, St.L	L	1	2	4.02	5	5	0	0	0	0	31.1	34	15	14	2	15	20	4	0	.279
Mallicoat, Rob, Hou.	L	0	0	7.23	23	0	0	0	6	0	23.2	26	19	19	2	19	20	2	0	.283
Mason, Roger, Pit.	R	5	7	4.09	65	0	0	0	26	8	88	80	41	40	11	33	56	3	0	.246
Mathews, Greg, Phi.	L	2	3	5.16	14	7	0	0	1	0	52.1	54	31	30	7	24	27	1	2	.270
Maysey, Matt, Mon.	R	0	0	3.86	2	0	0	0	1	0	2.1	4	1	1	1	0	1	0	0	.364
McClure, Bob, St.L	L	2	2	3.17	71	0	0	0	16	0	54	52	21	19	6	25	24	1	0	.261
McDowell, Roger, L.A.	R	6	10	4.09	65	0	0	0	39	14	83.2	103	46	38	3	42	50	4	1	.306
McElroy, Chuck, ChiN	L	4	7	3.55	72	0	0	0	30	6	83.2	73	40	33	5	51	83	3	0	.237
Melendez, Jose, S.D.	R	6	7	2.92	56	3	0	0	18	0	89.1	82	32	29	9	20	82	1	1	.249
Menendez, Tony, Cin.	R	1	0	1.93	3	0	0	0	1	0	4.2	1	1	1	1	0	5	0	0	.067
Mercker, Kent, Atl.	L	3	2	3.42	53	0	0	0	18	6	68.1	51	27	26	4	35	49	6	0	.207
Miller, Paul, Pit.	R	1	0	2.38	6	0	0	0	1	0	11.1	11	3	3	0	1	5	1	0	.256
Minor, Blas, Pit.	R	0	0	4.50	1	0	0	0	0	0	2	3	2	1	0	0	0	1	0	.333
Murphy, Rob, Hou.	L	3	1	4.04	59	0	0	0	6	0	55.2	56	28	25	2	21	42	4	0	.260
Myers, Randy, S.D.	L	3	6	4.29	66	0	0	0	57	38	79.2	84	38	38	7	34	66	5	0	.279
Neagle, Denny, Pit.	L	4	6	4.48	55	6	0	0	8	2	86.1	81	46	43	9	43	77	3	2	.247
Oliveras, Francisco, S.F.	R	0	3	3.63	16	7	0	0	3	0	44.2	41	19	18	11	10	17	0	0	.250
Osuna, Al, Hou.	L	6	3	4.23	66	0	0	0	17	0	61.2	52	29	29	8	38	37	3	1	.236
Palacios, Vicente, Pit.	R	3	2	4.25	20	8	0	0	4	0	53	56	25	25	1	27	33	7	0	.280
Patterson, Bob, Pit.	L	6	3	2.92	60	0	0	0	26	9	64.2	59	22	21	7	23	43	3	0	.246
Patterson, Ken, ChiN	L	2	3	3.89	32	1	0	0	4	0	41.2	41	25	18	7	27	23	3	1	.268
Pecota, Bill, NY-N	R	0	0	9.00	1	0	0	0	1	0	1	1	1	1	1	0	0	0	0	.250
Pena, Alejandro, Atl.	R	1	6	4.07	41	0	0	0	31	15	42	40	19	19	7	13	34	0	0	.255
Pena, Jim, S.F.	L	1	1	3.48	25	2	0	0	4	0	44	49	19	17	4	20	32	0	0	.282
Perez, Mike, St.L	R	9	3	1.84	77	0	0	0	22	0	93	70	23	19	4	32	46	4	0	.210
Pugh, Tim, Cin.	R	4	2	2.58	7	7	0	0	0	0	45.1	47	15	13	2	13	18	0	0	.276
Rapp, Pat, S.F.	R	0	2	7.20	3	2	0	0	1	0	10	8	8	8	0	6	3	0	0	.235
Rasmussen, Dennis, ChiN	L	0	0	10.80	3	1	0	0	1	0	5	7	6	6	2	2	0	0	0	.350
Reardon, Jeff, Atl.	R	3	0	1.15	14	0	0	0	11	3	15.2	14	2	2	0	2	7	0	0	.241
Reed, Steve, S.F.	R	1	0	2.30	18	0	0	0	2	0	15.2	13	5	4	2	3	11	0	0	.220
Reynolds, Shane, Hou.	R	1	3	7.11	8	5	0	0	0	0	25.1	42	22	20	2	6	10	1	1	.385
Reynoso, Armando, Atl.	R	1	0	4.70	3	1	0	0	1	1	7.2	11	4	4	2	2	2	0	0	.393
Righetti, Dave, S.F.	L	2	7	5.06	54	4	0	0	23	3	78.1	79	47	44	4	36	47	5	2	.269
Risley, Bill, Mon.	R	1	0	1.80	1	1	0	0	0	0	5	4	1	1	0	1	2	0	0	.235
Ritchie, Wally, Phi.	L	2	1	3.00	40	0	0	0	13	1	39	44	17	13	3	17	19	0	0	.288
Rivera, Ben, Atl.-Phi.	R	7	4	3.07	28	14	4	1	7	0	117.1	99	40	40	9	45	77	5	0	.230

National League relief pitchers

Name/Team	T	W	L	ERA	G	GS	CG	SHO	GF	SV	IP	H	R	ER	HR	BB	SO	WP	BK	BA
Robinson, Don, Phi.	R	1	4	6.18	8	8	0	0	0	0	43.2	49	32	30	6	4	17	0	0	.290
Robinson, Jeff D., ChiN	R	4	3	3.00	49	5	0	0	12	1	78	76	29	26	5	40	46	8	1	.263
Robinson, Jeff M., Pit.	R	3	1	4.46	8	7	0	0	0	0	36.1	33	18	18	2	15	14	0	0	.244
Rodriguez, Rich, S.D.	L	6	3	2.37	61	1	0	0	15	0	91	77	28	24	4	29	64	1	1	.229
Rogers, Kevin, S.F.	L	0	2	4.24	6	6	0	0	0	0	34	37	17	16	4	13	26	2	0	.280
Rojas, Mel, Mon.	R	7	1	1.43	68	0	0	0	26	10	100.2	71	17	16	2	34	70	2	0	.199
Ruskin, Scott, Cin.	L	4	3	5.03	57	0	0	0	19	0	53.2	56	31	30	6	20	43	1	0	.275
Sampen, Bill, Mon.	R	1	4	3.13	44	1	0	0	10	0	63.1	62	22	22	4	29	23	1	2	.268
Scanlan, Bob, ChiN	R	3	6	2.89	69	0	0	0	41	14	87.1	76	32	28	4	30	42	6	4	.235
Scheid, Rich, Hou.	L	0	1	6.00	7	1	0	0	3	0	12	14	8	8	2	6	8	1	1	.280
Scott, Tim, S.D.	R	4	1	5.26	34	0	0	0	16	0	37.2	39	24	22	4	21	30	0	1	.267
Searcy, Steve, Phi.	L	0	0	6.10	10	0	0	0	3	0	10.1	13	9	7	0	8	5	0	0	.325
Service, Scott, Mon.	R	0	0	14.14	5	0	0	0	0	0	7	15	11	11	1	5	11	0	0	.417
Shepherd, Keith, Phi.	R	1	1	3.27	12	0	0	0	6	2	22	19	10	8	0	6	10	1	0	.247
Simons, Doug, Mon.	L	0	0	23.63	7	0	0	0	2	0	5.1	15	14	14	3	2	6	1	0	.500
Slocumb, Heathcliff, ChiN	R	0	3	6.50	30	0	0	0	11	1	36	52	27	26	3	21	27	1	0	.351
Smith, Bryn, St.L	R	4	2	4.64	13	1	0	0	3	0	21.1	20	11	11	3	5	9	1	0	.247
Smith, Dave S., ChiN	R	0	0	2.51	11	0	0	0	4	0	14.1	15	4	4	0	4	3	0	1	.273
Smith, Lee, St.L	R	4	9	3.12	70	0	0	0	55	43	75	62	28	26	4	26	60	2	0	.221
St. Claire, Randy, Atl.	R	0	0	5.87	10	0	0	0	1	0	15.1	17	11	10	1	8	7	0	0	.283
Stanton, Mike, Atl.	L	5	4	4.10	65	0	0	0	23	8	63.2	59	32	29	6	20	44	3	0	.247
Valdez, Sergio, Mon.	R	0	2	2.41	27	0	0	0	9	0	37.1	25	12	10	2	12	32	4	0	.185
Vitko, Joe, NY-N	R	0	1	13.50	3	1	0	0	1	0	4.2	12	11	7	1	1	6	1	0	.444
Wagner, Paul, Pit.	R	2	0	0.69	6	1	0	0	1	0	13	9	1	1	0	5	5	1	0	.191
Weston, Mickey, Phi.	R	0	1	12.27	1	1	0	0	0	0	3.2	7	5	5	1	1	0	0	0	.412
Wetteland, John, Mon.	R	4	4	2.92	67	0	0	0	58	37	83.1	64	27	27	6	36	99	4	0	.213
Whitehurst, Wally, NY-N	R	3	9	3.62	44	11	0	0	7	0	97	99	45	39	4	33	70	2	1	.264
Williams, Mike, Phi.	R	1	1	5.34	5	5	1	0	0	0	28.2	29	20	17	3	7	5	0	0	.259
Williams, Mitch, Phi.	L	5	8	3.78	66	0	0	0	56	29	81	69	39	34	4	64	74	5	3	.240
Wilson, Steve, L.A.	L	2	5	4.19	60	0	0	0	18	0	66.2	74	37	31	6	29	54	7	0	.282
Wohlers, Mark, Atl.	R	1	2	2.55	32	0	0	0	16	4	35.1	28	11	10	0	14	17	1	0	.235
Worrell, Todd, St.L	R	5	3	2.11	67	0	0	0	14	3	64	45	15	15	4	25	64	1	1	.198
Young, Anthony, NY-N	R	2	14	4.17	52	13	1	0	26	15	121	134	66	56	8	31	64	3	1	.285
Young, Pete, Mon.	R	0	0	3.98	13	0	0	0	6	0	20.1	18	9	9	0	9	11	1	0	.247

National League catchers

Name/Team	B	BA	G	AB	R	H	TB	2B	3B	HR	RBI	SH	SF	BB	SO	SB	CS	GIDP	SLG	OBA
Afenir, Troy, Cin.	R	.176	16	34	3	6	11	1	2	0	4	1	0	5	12	0	0	0	.324	.282
Bailey, Mark, S.F.	B	.154	13	26	0	4	5	1	0	0	1	0	0	3	7	0	0	0	.192	.241
Berryhill, Damon, Atl.	B	.228	101	307	21	70	118	16	1	10	43	0	3	17	67	0	2	4	.384	.268
Bilardello, Dann, S.D.	R	.121	17	33	2	4	5	1	0	0	1	3	0	4	8	0	0	1	.152	.216
Bradley, Scott, Cin.	L	.400	5	5	1	2	2	0	0	0	1	0	0	1	0	0	0	0	.400	.500
Cabrera, Francisco, Atl.	R	.300	12	10	2	3	9	0	0	2	3	0	0	1	1	0	0	0	.900	.364
Carter, Gary, Mon.	R	.218	95	285	24	62	97	18	1	5	29	1	4	33	37	0	4	4	.340	.299
Cerone, Rick, Mon.	R	.270	33	63	10	17	24	4	0	1	7	1	0	3	5	1	2	0	.381	.313
Colbert, Craig, S.F.	R	.230	49	126	10	29	41	5	2	1	16	2	2	9	22	1	0	8	.325	.277
Daulton, Darren, Phi.	L	.270	145	485	80	131	254	32	5	27	109	0	6	88	103	11	2	3	.524	.385
Decker, Steve, S.F.	R	.163	15	43	3	7	8	1	0	0	1	0	0	6	7	0	0	0	.186	.280
Fletcher, Darrin, Mon.	L	.243	83	222	13	54	74	10	2	2	26	2	4	14	28	0	2	8	.333	.289
Gedman, Rich, St.L	L	.219	41	105	5	23	30	4	0	1	8	0	1	11	22	0	0	0	.286	.291
Girardi, Joe, ChiN	R	.270	91	270	19	73	81	3	1	1	12	0	1	19	38	0	2	8	.300	.320
Goff, Jerry, Mon.	L	.000	3	3	0	0	0	0	0	0	0	0	0	0	3	0	0	0	.000	.000
Grotewold, Jeff, Phi.	L	.200	72	65	7	13	24	2	0	3	5	0	0	9	16	0	0	4	.369	.307
Hernandez, Carlos, L.A.	R	.260	69	173	11	45	58	4	0	3	17	0	2	11	21	0	1	8	.335	.316
Hundley, Todd, NY-N	B	.209	123	358	32	75	113	17	0	7	32	7	2	19	76	3	0	8	.316	.256
LaValliere, Mike, Pit.	L	.256	95	293	22	75	96	13	1	2	29	0	5	44	21	0	3	8	.328	.350
Lake, Steve, Phi.	R	.245	20	53	3	13	18	2	0	1	2	0	1	1	8	0	0	1	.340	.255
Laker, Tim, Mon.	R	.217	28	46	8	10	13	3	0	0	4	0	0	2	14	1	1	1	.283	.250
Lampkin, Tom, S.D.	L	.235	9	17	3	4	4	0	0	0	0	0	0	6	1	2	0	0	.235	.458
Lopez, Javier, Atl.	R	.375	9	16	3	6	8	2	0	0	2	0	0	0	1	0	0	0	.500	.375
Manwaring, Kirt, S.F.	R	.244	109	349	24	85	117	10	5	4	26	6	0	29	42	2	1	12	.335	.311
McNamara, Jim, S.F.	L	.216	30	74	6	16	20	1	0	1	9	2	0	6	25	0	0	1	.270	.275
Natal, Rob, Mon.	R	.000	5	6	0	0	0	0	0	0	0	0	0	1	1	0	0	1	.000	.143
O'Brien, Charlie, NY-N	R	.212	68	156	15	33	51	12	0	2	13	4	0	16	18	0	1	4	.327	.289
Oliver, Joe, Cin.	R	.270	143	485	42	131	188	25	1	10	57	6	7	35	75	2	3	12	.388	.316
Olson, Greg, Atl.	R	.238	95	302	27	72	99	14	2	3	27	1	2	34	31	2	1	8	.328	.316
Pagnozzi, Tom, St.L	R	.249	139	485	33	121	174	26	3	7	44	6	3	28	64	2	5	15	.359	.290
Pedre, Jorge, ChiN	R	.000	4	4	0	0	0	0	0	0	0	0	0	0	1	0	0	0	.000	.000
Piazza, Mike, L.A.	R	.232	21	69	5	16	22	3	0	1	7	0	0	4	12	0	0	1	.319	.284

National League catchers

Name/Team	B	BA	G	AB	R	H	TB	2B	3B	HR	RBI	SH	SF	BB	SO	SB	CS	GIDP	SLG	OBA
Pratt, Todd, Phi.	R	.283	16	46	6	13	20	1	0	2	10	0	0	4	12	0	0	2	.435	.340
Prince, Tom, Pit.	R	.091	27	44	1	4	6	2	0	0	5	0	2	6	9	1	1	2	.136	.192
Reed, Jeff, Cin.	L	.160	15	25	2	4	4	0	0	0	2	0	0	1	4	0	0	1	.160	.192
Santiago, Benito, S.D.	R	.251	106	386	37	97	148	21	0	10	42	0	4	21	52	2	5	14	.383	.287
Sasser, Mackey, NY-N	L	.241	92	141	7	34	46	6	0	2	18	0	5	3	10	0	0	4	.326	.248
Scioscia, Mike, L.A.	L	.221	117	348	19	77	98	6	3	3	24	5	3	32	31	3	2	9	.282	.286
Servais, Scott, Hou.	R	.239	77	205	12	49	58	9	0	0	15	6	0	11	25	0	0	7	.283	.294
Slaught, Don, Pit.	R	.345	87	255	26	88	123	17	3	4	37	6	5	17	23	2	2	6	.482	.384
Stairs, Matt, Mon.	L	.167	13	30	2	5	7	2	0	0	5	0	1	7	7	0	0	0	.233	.316
Taubensee, Eddie, Hou.	L	.222	104	297	23	66	96	15	0	5	28	0	1	31	78	2	1	4	.323	.299
Tucker, Eddie, Hou.	R	.120	20	50	5	6	7	1	0	0	3	1	0	3	13	1	1	2	.140	.200
Villanueva, Hector, ChiN	R	.152	51	112	9	17	29	6	0	2	13	0	0	11	24	0	0	5	.259	.228
Walters, Dan, S.D.	R	.251	57	179	14	45	70	11	1	4	22	1	2	10	28	1	0	3	.391	.295
Wilkins, Rick, ChiN	L	.270	83	244	20	66	101	9	1	8	22	1	1	28	53	0	2	6	.414	.344
Willard, Jerry, Atl.-Mon.	L	.229	47	48	2	11	18	1	0	2	8	0	0	2	10	0	0	5	.375	.260
Wilson, Dan, Cin.	R	.360	12	25	2	9	10	1	0	0	3	0	0	3	8	0	0	2	.400	.429
Wrona, Rick, Cin.	R	.174	11	23	0	4	4	0	0	0	0	0	0	0	3	0	0	2	.174	.174

National League first basemen

Name/Team	B	BA	G	AB	R	H	TB	2B	3B	HR	RBI	SH	SF	BB	SO	SB	CS	GIDP	SLG	OBA
Bagwell, Jeff, Hou.	R	.273	162	586	87	160	260	34	6	18	96	2	13	84	97	10	6	17	.444	.368
Bream, Sid, Atl.	L	.261	125	372	30	97	154	25	1	10	61	3	4	46	51	6	0	3	.414	.340
Brewer, Rod, St.L	L	.301	29	103	11	31	37	6	0	0	10	0	1	8	12	0	1	1	.359	.354
Cianfrocco, Archi, Mon.	R	.241	86	232	25	56	83	5	2	6	30	1	2	11	66	3	0	2	.358	.276
Clark, Will, S.F.	L	.300	144	513	69	154	244	40	1	16	73	0	11	73	82	12	7	5	.476	.384
Colbrunn, Greg, Mon.	R	.268	52	168	12	45	59	8	0	2	18	0	4	6	34	3	2	1	.351	.294
Costo, Tim, Cin.	R	.222	12	36	3	8	10	2	0	0	2	0	1	5	6	0	0	4	.278	.310
Galarraga, Andres, St.L	R	.243	95	325	38	79	127	14	2	10	39	0	3	11	69	5	4	8	.391	.282
Grace, Mark, ChiN	L	.307	158	603	72	185	259	37	5	9	79	2	8	72	36	6	1	14	.430	.380
Hunter, Brian, Atl.	R	.239	102	238	34	57	116	13	2	14	41	1	8	21	50	1	2	2	.487	.292
Jordan, Ricky, Phi.	R	.304	94	276	33	84	115	19	0	4	34	0	3	5	44	3	0	8	.417	.313
Karros, Eric, L.A.	R	.257	149	545	63	140	232	30	1	20	88	0	5	37	103	2	4	15	.426	.304
Klesko, Ryan, Atl.	L	.000	13	14	0	0	0	0	0	0	1	0	0	0	5	0	0	0	.000	.067
Kruk, John, Phi.	L	.323	144	507	86	164	232	30	4	10	70	0	7	92	88	3	5	11	.458	.423
McGriff, Fred, S.D.	L	.286	152	531	79	152	295	30	4	35	104	0	4	96	108	8	6	14	.556	.394
McKnight, Jeff, NY-N	B	.271	31	85	10	23	34	3	1	2	13	0	0	2	8	0	1	2	.400	.287
Morris, Hal, Cin.	L	.271	115	395	41	107	152	21	3	6	53	2	2	45	53	6	6	12	.385	.347
Murray, Eddie, NY-N	B	.261	156	551	64	144	233	37	2	16	93	0	8	66	74	4	2	15	.423	.336
Perry, Gerald, St.L	L	.238	87	143	13	34	45	8	0	1	18	0	2	15	23	3	6	3	.315	.311
Redus, Gary, Pit.	R	.256	76	176	26	45	67	7	3	3	12	0	0	17	25	11	4	1	.381	.321
Stephenson, Phil, S.D.	L	.155	53	71	5	11	15	2	1	0	8	3	0	10	11	0	0	0	.211	.259
Velasquez, Guillermo, S.D.	L	.304	15	23	1	7	10	0	0	1	5	0	0	1	7	0	0	0	.435	.333

National League second basemen

Name/Team	B	BA	G	AB	R	H	TB	2B	3B	HR	RBI	SH	SF	BB	SO	SB	CS	GIDP	SLG	OBA
Alicea, Luis, St.L	B	.245	85	265	26	65	102	9	11	2	32	2	4	27	40	2	5	5	.385	.320
Backman, Wally, Phi.	L	.271	42	48	6	13	14	1	0	0	6	1	0	6	9	1	0	3	.292	.352
Benavides, Freddie, Cin.	R	.231	74	173	14	40	55	10	1	1	17	2	0	10	34	0	1	3	.318	.277
Biggio, Craig, Hou.	R	.277	162	613	96	170	226	32	3	6	39	5	2	94	95	38	15	5	.369	.378
Branson, Jeff, Cin.	L	.296	72	115	12	34	43	7	1	0	15	2	1	5	16	0	1	4	.374	.322
DeShields, Delino, Mon.	L	.292	135	530	82	155	211	19	8	7	56	9	3	54	108	46	15	10	.398	.359
Doran, Bill D., Cin.	B	.235	132	387	48	91	135	16	2	8	47	3	2	64	40	7	4	11	.349	.342
Duncan, Mariano, Phi.	R	.267	142	574	71	153	223	40	3	8	50	5	4	17	108	23	3	15	.389	.292
Faries, Paul, S.D.	R	.455	10	11	3	5	6	1	0	0	1	0	0	1	2	0	0	0	.545	.500
Figueroa, Bien, St.L	R	.182	12	11	1	2	3	1	0	0	4	0	0	1	2	0	0	0	.273	.250
Gardner, Jeff, S.D.	L	.105	15	19	0	2	2	0	0	0	0	0	0	1	8	0	0	0	.105	.150
Haney, Todd, Mon.	R	.300	7	10	0	3	4	1	0	0	1	1	0	0	0	0	0	1	.400	.300
Harris, Lenny, L.A.	L	.271	135	347	28	94	105	11	0	0	30	6	2	24	24	19	7	10	.303	.318
Kent, Jeff, NY-N	R	.239	37	113	16	27	46	8	1	3	15	0	0	7	29	0	2	2	.407	.289
Lemke, Mark, Atl.	B	.227	155	427	38	97	130	7	4	6	26	12	2	50	39	0	3	9	.304	.307
Lind, Jose, Pit.	R	.235	135	468	38	110	126	14	1	0	39	7	4	26	29	3	1	14	.269	.275
Litton, Greg, S.F.	R	.229	68	140	9	32	49	5	0	4	15	3	0	11	33	0	1	2	.350	.285
Morandini, Mickey, Phi.	L	.265	127	422	47	112	145	8	8	3	30	6	2	25	64	8	3	4	.344	.305
Noboa, Junior, NY-N	R	.149	46	47	7	7	7	0	0	0	3	0	1	3	8	0	0	2	.149	.212
Oquendo, Jose, St.L	B	.257	14	35	3	9	14	3	1	0	3	0	0	5	3	0	0	0	.400	.350
Patterson, John, S.F.	B	.184	32	103	10	19	22	1	1	0	4	0	0	5	24	5	1	2	.214	.229
Pena, Geronimo, St.L	B	.305	62	203	31	62	97	12	1	7	31	0	4	24	37	13	8	1	.478	.386

National League second basemen

Name/Team	B	BA	G	AB	R	H	TB	2B	3B	HR	RBI	SH	SF	BB	SO	SB	CS	GIDP	SLG	OBA
Randolph, Willie, NY-N	R	.252	90	286	29	72	91	11	1	2	15	6	0	40	34	1	3	6	.318	.352
Samuel, Juan, L.A.	R	.262	47	122	7	32	37	3	1	0	15	4	2	7	22	2	2	0	.303	.303
Sandberg, Ryne, ChiN	R	.304	158	612	100	186	312	32	8	26	87	0	6	68	73	17	6	13	.510	.371
Scarsone, Steve, Phi.	R	.154	7	13	1	2	2	0	0	0	0	0	0	1	6	0	0	0	.154	.214
Shipley, Craig, S.D.	R	.248	52	105	7	26	32	6	0	0	7	1	0	2	21	1	1	2	.305	.262
Springer, Steve, NY-N	R	.400	4	5	0	2	3	1	0	0	0	0	0	0	1	0	0	0	.600	.400
Stillwell, Kurt, S.D.	B	.227	114	379	35	86	113	15	3	2	24	4	6	26	58	4	1	6	.298	.274
Teufel, Tim, S.D.	R	.224	101	246	23	55	83	10	0	6	25	0	1	31	45	2	1	7	.337	.312
Thompson, Robby, S.F.	R	.260	128	443	54	115	184	25	1	14	49	7	4	43	75	5	9	8	.415	.333
Treadway, Jeff, Atl.	L	.222	61	126	5	28	36	6	1	0	5	1	0	9	16	1	2	3	.286	.274
Young, Eric, L.A.	R	.258	49	132	9	34	38	1	0	1	11	4	0	8	9	6	1	3	.288	.300

National League third basemen

Name/Team	B	BA	G	AB	R	H	TB	2B	3B	HR	RBI	SH	SF	BB	SO	SB	CS	GIDP	SLG	OBA
Barberie, Bret, Mon.	B	.232	111	285	26	66	80	11	0	1	24	1	2	47	62	9	5	4	.281	.354
Berry, Sean, Mon.	R	.333	24	57	5	19	23	1	0	1	4	0	0	1	11	2	1	1	.404	.345
Buechele, Steve, Pit.-ChiN	R	.261	145	524	52	137	195	23	4	9	64	4	3	52	105	1	3	10	.372	.334
Caminiti, Ken, Hou.	B	.294	135	506	68	149	223	31	2	13	62	2	4	44	68	10	4	14	.441	.350
Coles, Darnell, Cin.	R	.312	55	141	16	44	68	11	2	3	18	3	2	3	15	1	0	1	.482	.322
Donnels, Chris, NY-N	L	.174	45	121	8	21	25	4	0	0	6	1	0	17	25	1	0	1	.207	.275
Green, Gary, Cin.	R	.333	8	12	3	4	5	1	0	0	0	0	0	0	2	0	0	0	.417	.333
Greene, Willie, Cin.	L	.269	29	93	10	25	40	5	2	2	13	0	1	10	23	0	2	1	.430	.337
Hansen, Dave, L.A.	L	.214	132	341	30	73	102	11	0	6	22	0	2	34	49	0	2	9	.299	.286
Hollins, David, Phi.	B	.270	156	586	104	158	275	28	4	27	93	0	4	76	110	9	6	8	.469	.369
King, Jeff, Pit.	R	.231	130	480	56	111	178	21	2	14	65	8	5	27	56	4	6	8	.371	.272
Magadan, Dave, NY-N	L	.283	99	321	33	91	111	9	1	3	28	2	0	56	44	1	0	6	.346	.390
Pecota, Bill, NY-N	R	.227	117	269	28	61	80	13	0	2	26	5	2	25	40	9	3	7	.297	.293
Pendleton, Terry, Atl.	B	.311	160	640	98	199	303	39	1	21	105	5	7	37	67	5	2	16	.473	.345
Royer, Stan, St.L	R	.323	13	31	6	10	18	2	0	2	9	0	1	1	4	0	0	0	.581	.333
Sabo, Chris, Cin.	R	.244	96	344	42	84	145	19	3	12	43	1	6	30	54	4	5	12	.422	.302
Salazar, Luis, ChiN	R	.208	98	255	20	53	79	7	2	5	25	3	4	11	34	1	1	10	.310	.237
Scott, Gary, ChiN	R	.156	36	96	8	15	23	2	0	2	11	1	0	5	14	0	1	3	.240	.198
Sharperson, Mike, L.A.	R	.300	128	317	48	95	125	21	0	3	36	5	3	47	33	2	2	9	.394	.387
Sheffield, Gary, S.D.	R	.330	146	557	87	184	323	34	3	33	100	0	7	48	40	5	6	19	.580	.385
Strange, Doug, ChiN	B	.160	52	94	7	15	19	1	0	1	5	2	0	10	15	1	0	2	.202	.240
Walker, Chico, ChiN-NY-N	B	.289	126	253	26	73	99	12	1	4	38	0	5	27	50	15	1	9	.391	.351
Wallach, Tim, Mon.	R	.223	150	537	53	120	178	29	1	9	59	0	7	50	90	2	2	10	.331	.296
Wehner, John, Pit.	R	.179	55	123	11	22	28	6	0	0	4	2	0	12	22	3	0	4	.228	.252
Williams, Matt D., S.F.	R	.227	146	529	58	120	203	13	5	20	66	0	2	39	109	7	7	15	.384	.286
Wilson, Craig, St.L	R	.311	61	106	6	33	39	6	0	0	13	2	1	10	18	1	2	4	.368	.368
Woodson, Tracy, St.L	R	.307	31	114	9	35	46	8	0	1	22	1	0	3	10	0	0	1	.404	.331
Young, Kevin, Pit.	R	.571	10	7	2	4	4	0	0	0	4	0	0	2	0	1	0	0	.571	.667
Zeile, Todd, St.L	R	.257	126	439	51	113	160	18	4	7	48	0	7	68	70	7	10	11	.364	.352

National League shortstops

Name/Team	B	BA	G	AB	R	H	TB	2B	3B	HR	RBI	SH	SF	BB	SO	SB	CS	GIDP	SLG	OBA
Anderson, Dave C., L.A.	R	.286	51	84	10	24	37	4	0	3	8	1	2	4	11	0	4	3	.440	.311
Arias, Alex, ChiN	R	.293	32	99	14	29	35	6	0	0	7	1	0	11	13	0	0	4	.354	.375
Baez, Kevin, NY-N	R	.154	6	13	0	2	2	0	0	0	0	0	0	0	0	0	0	1	.154	.154
Batiste, Kim, Phi.	R	.206	44	136	9	28	35	4	0	1	10	2	3	4	18	0	0	7	.257	.224
Bell, Jay, Pit.	R	.264	159	632	87	167	242	36	6	9	55	19	2	55	103	7	5	12	.383	.326
Bell, Juan, Phi.	B	.204	46	147	12	30	38	3	1	1	8	0	2	18	29	5	0	1	.259	.292
Belliard, Rafael, Atl.	R	.211	144	285	20	60	68	6	1	0	14	13	0	14	43	0	1	6	.239	.255
Benjamin, Mike, S.F.	R	.173	40	75	4	13	20	2	1	1	3	3	0	4	15	1	0	1	.267	.215
Blauser, Jeff, Atl.	R	.262	123	343	61	90	157	19	3	14	46	7	3	46	82	5	5	2	.458	.354
Bournigal, Rafael, L.A.	R	.150	10	20	1	3	4	1	0	0	0	0	0	1	2	0	0	0	.200	.227
Candaele, Casey, Hou.	B	.213	135	320	19	68	85	12	1	1	18	7	6	24	36	7	1	5	.266	.269
Castilla, Vinny, Atl.	R	.250	9	16	1	4	5	1	0	0	1	0	0	1	4	0	0	0	.313	.333
Cedeno, Andujar, Hou.	R	.173	71	220	15	38	61	13	2	2	13	0	0	14	71	2	0	1	.277	.232
Clayton, Royce, S.F.	R	.224	98	321	31	72	99	7	4	4	24	3	2	26	63	8	4	11	.308	.281
Cordero, Wil, Mon.	R	.302	45	126	17	38	50	4	1	2	8	1	0	9	31	0	0	3	.397	.353
Dunston, Shawon, ChiN	R	.315	18	73	8	23	28	3	1	0	2	0	0	3	13	2	3	0	.384	.342
Elster, Kevin, NY-N	R	.222	6	18	0	4	4	0	0	0	0	0	0	0	2	0	0	1	.222	.222
Fernandez, Tony, S.D.	B	.275	155	622	84	171	223	32	4	4	37	9	3	56	62	20	20	6	.359	.337
Foley, Tom, Mon.	L	.174	72	115	7	20	25	3	1	0	5	3	2	8	21	3	0	6	.217	.230
Garcia, Carlos, Pit.	R	.205	22	39	4	8	9	1	0	0	4	1	2	0	9	0	0	1	.231	.195
Guerrero, Juan, Hou.	R	.200	79	125	8	25	36	4	2	1	14	1	2	10	32	1	0	0	.288	.261

National League shortstops

Name/Team	B	BA	G	AB	R	H	TB	2B	3B	HR	RBI	SH	SF	BB	SO	SB	CS	GIDP	SLG	OBA
Jones, W. Tim, St.L	L	.200	67	145	9	29	33	4	0	0	3	2	0	11	29	5	2	1	.228	.256
Kunkel, Jeff, ChiN	R	.138	20	29	0	4	6	2	0	0	1	0	0	0	8	0	0	1	.207	.138
Larkin, Barry, Cin.	R	.304	140	533	76	162	242	32	6	12	78	2	7	63	58	15	4	13	.454	.377
Millette, Joe, Phi.	R	.205	33	78	5	16	16	0	0	0	2	2	0	5	10	1	0	8	.205	.271
Offerman, Jose, L.A.	B	.260	149	534	67	139	178	20	8	1	30	5	2	57	98	23	16	5	.333	.331
Owen, Spike, Mon.	B	.269	122	386	52	104	147	16	3	7	40	4	6	50	30	9	4	10	.381	.348
Ramirez, Rafael, Hou.	R	.250	73	176	17	44	53	6	0	1	13	1	0	7	24	0	0	5	.301	.283
Riles, Ernest, Hou.	L	.262	39	61	5	16	20	1	0	1	4	0	1	2	11	1	0	0	.328	.281
Sanchez, Rey, ChiN	R	.251	74	255	24	64	87	14	3	1	19	5	2	10	17	2	1	7	.341	.285
Schofield, Dick C., NY-N	R	.205	142	420	52	86	120	18	2	4	36	10	3	60	82	11	4	11	.286	.309
Smith, Ozzie, St.L	B	.295	132	518	73	153	177	20	2	0	31	12	1	59	34	43	9	11	.342	.367
Sveum, Dale, Phi.	B	.178	54	135	13	24	34	4	0	2	16	0	2	16	39	0	0	5	.252	.261
Uribe, Jose, S.F.	B	.241	66	162	24	39	56	9	1	2	13	4	1	14	25	2	2	3	.346	.299
Vizcaino, Jose, ChiN	B	.225	86	285	25	64	85	10	4	1	17	5	1	14	35	3	0	4	.298	.260
Yelding, Eric, Hou.	R	.250	9	8	1	2	2	0	0	0	0	0	0	0	3	0	0	0	.250	.250

National League outfielders

Name/Team	B	BA	G	AB	R	H	TB	2B	3B	HR	RBI	SH	SF	BB	SO	SB	CS	GIDP	SLG	OBA
Alou, Moises, Mon.	R	.282	115	341	53	96	155	28	2	9	56	5	5	25	46	16	2	5	.455	.328
Amaro, Ruben Jr., Phi.	B	.219	126	374	43	82	130	15	6	7	34	4	2	37	54	11	5	11	.348	.303
Anthony, Eric, Hou.	L	.239	137	440	45	105	179	15	1	19	80	0	4	38	98	5	4	7	.407	.298
Ashley, Billy, L.A.	R	.221	29	95	6	21	32	5	0	2	6	0	0	5	34	0	0	2	.337	.260
Azocar, Oscar, S.D.	L	.190	99	168	15	32	38	6	0	0	8	4	1	9	12	1	0	3	.226	.230
Bass, Kevin, S.F.-NY-N	B	.269	135	402	40	108	168	23	5	9	39	1	3	23	70	14	9	8	.418	.308
Benzinger, Todd, L.A.	B	.239	121	293	24	70	102	16	2	4	31	0	5	15	54	2	4	6	.348	.272
Berroa, Geronimo, Cin.	R	.267	13	15	2	4	5	1	0	0	0	0	0	2	1	0	1	1	.333	.389
Bonds, Barry, Pit.	L	.311	140	473	109	147	295	36	5	34	103	0	7	127	69	39	8	9	.624	.456
Bonilla, Bobby, NY-N	B	.249	128	438	62	109	189	23	0	19	70	0	1	66	73	4	3	11	.432	.348
Boston, Daryl, NY-N	L	.249	130	289	37	72	123	14	2	11	35	0	4	38	60	12	6	5	.426	.338
Braggs, Glenn, Cin.	R	.237	92	266	40	63	109	16	3	8	38	1	2	36	48	3	1	10	.410	.330
Brumfield, Jacob, Cin.	R	.133	24	30	6	4	4	0	0	0	2	0	0	2	4	6	0	0	.133	.212
Bullock, Eric, Mon.	L	.000	8	5	0	0	0	0	0	0	0	0	0	0	1	0	0	0	.000	.000
Butler, Brett, L.A.	L	.309	157	553	86	171	216	14	11	3	39	24	1	95	67	41	21	4	.391	.413
Calderon, Ivan, Mon.	R	.265	48	170	19	45	72	14	2	3	24	0	1	14	22	1	2	4	.424	.323
Canseco, Ozzie, St.L	R	.276	9	29	7	8	13	5	0	0	3	0	0	7	4	0	0	1	.448	.417
Carr, Chuck, St.L	B	.219	22	64	8	14	17	3	0	0	3	3	0	9	6	10	2	0	.266	.315
Castillo, Braulio, Phi.	R	.197	28	76	12	15	26	3	1	2	7	1	0	4	15	1	0	1	.342	.238
Chamberlain, Wes, Phi.	R	.258	76	275	26	71	116	18	0	9	41	1	2	10	55	4	0	7	.422	.285
Clark, Dave, Pit.	L	.212	23	33	3	7	13	0	0	2	7	0	1	6	8	0	0	0	.394	.325
Clark, Jerald, S.D.	R	.242	146	496	45	120	190	22	6	12	58	1	3	22	97	3	0	7	.383	.278
Cole, Alex, Pit.	L	.278	64	205	33	57	74	3	7	0	10	1	1	18	46	7	4	2	.361	.335
Coleman, Vince, NY-N	B	.275	71	229	37	63	82	11	1	2	21	2	1	27	41	24	9	1	.358	.355
Daniels, Kal, L.A.-ChiN	L	.241	83	212	21	51	80	11	0	6	25	0	2	22	54	0	2	10	.377	.315
Dascenzo, Doug, ChiN	B	.255	139	376	37	96	117	13	4	0	20	4	2	27	32	6	8	3	.311	.304
Davis, Eric, L.A.	R	.228	76	267	21	61	86	8	1	5	32	0	2	36	71	19	1	9	.322	.325
Dawson, Andre, ChiN	R	.277	143	542	60	150	247	27	2	22	90	0	6	30	70	6	2	13	.456	.316
Distefano, Benny, Hou.	L	.233	52	60	4	14	18	0	2	0	7	0	0	5	14	0	0	1	.300	.303
Dozier, D.J., NY-N	R	.191	25	47	4	9	11	2	0	0	2	1	1	4	19	4	0	0	.234	.264
Dykstra, Len, Phi.	L	.301	85	345	53	104	140	18	0	6	39	0	4	40	32	30	5	1	.406	.375
Espy, Cecil, Pit.	B	.258	112	194	21	50	66	7	3	1	20	1	1	15	40	6	3	3	.340	.310
Felder, Mike, S.F.	B	.286	145	322	44	92	123	13	3	4	23	3	3	21	29	14	4	3	.382	.330
Finley, Steve, Hou.	L	.292	162	607	84	177	247	29	13	5	55	16	2	58	63	44	9	10	.407	.355
Gallagher, Dave, NY-N	R	.240	98	175	20	42	58	11	1	1	21	3	7	19	16	4	5	7	.331	.307
Gant, Ron, Atl.	R	.259	153	544	74	141	226	22	6	17	80	0	6	45	101	32	10	10	.415	.321
Gibson, Kirk, Pit.	L	.196	16	56	6	11	17	0	0	2	5	1	0	3	12	3	1	1	.304	.237
Gilkey, Bernard, St.L	R	.302	131	384	56	116	164	19	4	7	43	3	4	39	52	18	12	5	.427	.364
Gonzalez, Luis, Hou.	L	.243	122	387	40	94	149	19	3	10	55	1	2	24	52	7	7	6	.385	.289
Goodwin, Tom, L.A.	L	.233	57	73	15	17	20	1	1	0	3	0	0	6	10	7	3	0	.274	.291
Gregg, Tommy, Atl.	L	.263	18	19	1	5	8	0	0	1	1	0	0	1	7	1	0	1	.421	.300
Grissom, Marquis, Mon.	R	.276	159	653	99	180	273	39	6	14	66	3	4	42	81	78	13	12	.418	.322
Guerrero, Pedro, St.L	R	.219	43	146	10	32	43	6	1	1	16	0	2	11	25	2	2	4	.295	.270
Gwynn, Tony, S.D.	L	.317	128	520	77	165	216	27	3	6	41	0	3	46	16	3	6	12	.415	.371
Hatcher, Billy, Cin.	R	.287	43	94	10	27	36	3	0	2	10	0	3	5	11	0	2	2	.383	.314
Hernandez, Cesar, Cin.	R	.275	34	51	6	14	18	4	0	0	4	0	0	0	10	3	1	1	.353	.275
Hosey, Steve, S.F.	R	.250	21	56	6	14	18	1	0	1	6	0	2	0	15	1	1	1	.321	.241
Howard, Thomas, S.D.	B	.333	5	3	1	1	1	0	0	0	0	1	0	0	0	0	0	0	.333	.333
Howell, Pat, NY-N	B	.187	31	75	9	14	15	1	0	0	1	1	0	2	15	4	2	0	.200	.218
Hudler, Rex, St.L	R	.245	61	98	17	24	37	4	0	3	5	1	1	2	23	2	6	0	.378	.265
Incaviglia, Pete, Hou.	R	.266	113	349	31	93	150	22	1	11	44	0	2	25	99	2	2	6	.430	.319

National League outfielders

Name/Team	B	BA	G	AB	R	H	TB	2B	3B	HR	RBI	SH	SF	BB	SO	SB	CS	GIDP	SLG	OBA
Jackson, Darrin, S.D.	R	.249	155	587	72	146	230	23	5	17	70	6	5	26	106	14	3	21	.392	.283
James, Chris, S.F.	R	.242	111	248	25	60	93	10	4	5	32	0	3	14	45	2	3	2	.375	.285
Javier, Stan, L.A.-Phi.	B	.249	130	334	42	83	105	17	1	1	29	3	2	37	54	18	3	4	.314	.327
Johnson, Howard, NY-N	B	.223	100	350	48	78	118	19	0	7	43	0	3	55	79	22	5	7	.337	.329
Jones, Chris, Hou.	R	.190	54	63	7	12	19	2	1	1	4	3	0	7	21	3	0	1	.302	.271
Jordan, Brian, St.L	R	.207	55	193	17	40	72	9	4	5	22	0	0	10	48	7	2	6	.373	.250
Jose, Felix, St.L	B	.295	131	509	62	150	220	22	3	14	75	0	1	40	100	28	12	9	.432	.347
Justice, David, Atl.	L	.256	144	484	78	124	216	19	5	21	72	0	6	79	85	2	4	1	.446	.359
Lankford, Ray, St.L	L	.293	153	598	87	175	287	40	6	20	86	2	5	72	147	42	24	5	.480	.371
Leonard, Mark, S.F.	L	.234	55	128	13	30	49	7	0	4	16	0	1	16	31	0	1	3	.383	.331
Lewis, Darren, S.F.	R	.231	100	320	38	74	87	8	1	1	18	10	2	29	46	28	8	3	.272	.295
Lindeman, Jim, Phi.	R	.256	29	39	6	10	14	1	0	1	6	0	0	3	11	0	0	1	.359	.310
Lyons, Steve, Atl.-Mon.	L	.148	27	27	2	4	6	0	1	0	2	1	0	1	7	1	2	2	.222	.179
Marsh, Tom, Phi.	R	.200	42	125	7	25	38	3	2	2	16	2	2	2	23	0	1	2	.304	.215
Martin, Albert, Pit.	L	.167	12	12	1	2	4	0	1	0	2	0	1	0	5	0	0	0	.333	.154
Martinez, Dave, Cin.	L	.254	135	393	47	100	139	20	5	3	31	6	4	42	54	12	8	6	.354	.323
May, Derrick, ChiN	L	.274	124	351	33	96	131	11	0	8	45	2	1	14	40	5	3	10	.373	.306
McClendon, Lloyd, Pit.	R	.253	84	190	26	48	67	8	1	3	20	1	3	28	24	1	3	5	.353	.350
McCray, Rodney, NY-N	B	1.000	18	1	3	1	1	0	0	0	1	0	0	0	0	2	0	0	1.000	1.000
McGee, Willie, S.F.	B	.297	138	474	56	141	168	20	2	1	36	5	1	29	88	13	4	7	.354	.339
Merced, Orlando, Pit.	B	.247	134	405	50	100	156	28	5	6	60	1	5	52	63	5	4	6	.385	.332
Murphy, Dale, Phi.	R	.161	18	62	5	10	17	1	0	2	7	0	0	1	13	0	0	3	.274	.175
Nieves, Melvin, Atl.	B	.211	12	19	0	4	5	1	0	0	1	0	0	2	7	0	0	0	.263	.286
Nixon, Otis, Atl.	B	.294	120	456	79	134	158	14	2	2	22	5	2	39	54	41	18	4	.346	.348
O'Neill, Paul, Cin.	L	.246	148	496	59	122	185	19	1	14	66	3	6	77	85	6	3	10	.373	.346
Peguero, Julio, Phi.	B	.222	14	9	3	2	2	0	0	0	0	1	0	3	3	0	0	0	.222	.417
Pennyfeather, William, Pit.	R	.222	15	9	2	2	2	0	0	0	0	1	0	0	0	0	0	1	.222	.222
Pettis, Gary, S.D.	B	.200	30	30	0	6	7	1	0	0	0	0	0	2	11	1	0	0	.233	.250
Ramsey, Fernando, ChiN	R	.120	18	25	0	3	3	0	0	0	2	0	0	0	6	0	0	0	.120	.120
Reed, Darren, Mon.	R	.173	42	81	10	14	31	2	0	5	10	0	0	6	23	0	0	3	.383	.239
Rhodes, Karl, Hou.	L	.000	5	4	0	0	0	0	0	0	0	0	0	0	2	0	0	0	.000	.000
Roberts, Bip, Cin.	B	.323	147	532	92	172	230	34	6	4	45	1	4	62	54	44	16	7	.432	.393
Rodriguez, Henry, L.A.	L	.219	53	146	11	32	48	7	0	3	14	1	1	8	30	0	0	2	.329	.258
Sanders, Deion, Atl.	L	.304	97	303	54	92	150	6	14	8	28	1	1	18	52	26	9	5	.495	.346
Sanders, Reggie, Cin.	R	.270	116	385	62	104	178	26	6	12	36	0	1	48	98	16	7	6	.462	.356
Simms, Mike, Hou.	R	.250	15	24	1	6	10	1	0	1	3	0	0	2	9	0	0	1	.417	.333
Smith, Dwight, ChiN	L	.276	109	217	28	60	85	10	3	3	24	0	2	13	40	9	8	1	.392	.318
Smith, Lonnie, Atl.	R	.247	84	158	23	39	69	8	2	6	33	0	4	17	37	4	0	1	.437	.324
Snyder, Cory, S.F.	R	.269	124	390	48	105	173	22	2	14	57	2	3	23	96	4	4	10	.444	.311
Sosa, Sammy, ChiN	R	.260	67	262	41	68	103	7	2	8	25	4	2	19	63	15	7	4	.393	.317
Strawberry, Darryl, L.A.	L	.237	43	156	20	37	60	8	0	5	25	0	1	19	34	3	1	2	.385	.322
Thompson, Milt, St.L	L	.293	109	208	31	61	84	9	1	4	17	0	0	16	39	18	6	3	.404	.350
Thompson, Ryan, NY-N	R	.222	30	108	15	24	42	7	1	3	10	0	1	8	24	2	2	2	.389	.274
Van Slyke, Andy, Pit.	L	.324	154	614	103	199	310	45	12	14	89	0	9	58	99	12	3	9	.505	.381
Vander Wal, John, Mon.	L	.239	105	213	21	51	75	8	2	4	20	0	0	22	36	3	0	2	.352	.316
Varsho, Gary, Pit.	L	.222	103	162	22	36	60	6	3	4	22	0	1	10	32	5	2	2	.370	.266
Vatcher, Jim, S.D.	R	.250	13	16	1	4	5	1	0	0	2	1	0	3	6	0	0	0	.313	.368
Walker, Larry, Mon.	L	.301	143	528	85	159	267	31	4	23	93	0	8	41	97	18	6	9	.506	.353
Walling, Denny, Hou.	L	.333	3	3	1	1	1	0	0	0	0	0	0	0	0	0	0	0	.333	.333
Walton, Jerome, ChiN	R	.127	30	55	7	7	9	0	1	0	1	3	0	9	13	1	2	1	.164	.273
Ward, Kevin, S.D.	R	.197	81	147	12	29	43	5	0	3	12	1	1	14	38	2	3	8	.293	.274
Webster, Mitch, L.A.	B	.267	135	262	33	70	110	12	5	6	35	8	5	27	49	11	5	1	.420	.334
Wood, Ted, S.F.	L	.207	24	58	5	12	17	2	0	1	3	2	0	6	15	0	0	4	.293	.292
Young, Gerald, Hou.	B	.184	74	76	14	14	17	1	1	0	4	4	0	10	11	6	2	2	.224	.279

National League starting pitchers (batting)

Name/Team	B	BA	G	AB	R	H	TB	2B	3B	HR	RBI	SH	SF	BB	SO	SB	CS	GIDP	SLG	OBA
Abbott, Kyle, Phi.	L	.069	31	29	1	2	3	1	0	0	2	6	0	1	18	0	0	0	.103	.100
Ashby, Andy, Phi.	R	.091	10	11	0	1	2	1	0	0	1	2	0	0	7	0	0	0	.182	.091
Astacio, Pedro, L.A.	R	.125	11	24	2	3	3	0	0	0	1	5	0	0	14	0	0	0	.125	.125
Avery, Steve, Atl.	L	.171	35	76	8	13	17	2	1	0	4	9	0	3	22	0	1	0	.224	.203
Ayala, Bobby, Cin.	R	.000	5	9	1	0	0	0	0	0	0	1	0	0	6	0	0	0	.000	.000
Barnes, Brian, Mon.	L	.276	21	29	1	8	8	0	0	0	1	6	0	1	15	0	0	0	.276	.300
Belcher, Tim, Cin.	R	.105	35	76	3	8	12	1	0	1	4	7	0	0	28	0	0	1	.158	.105
Benes, Andy, S.D.	R	.149	34	67	3	10	15	2	0	1	5	5	1	5	29	0	0	1	.224	.205
Bielecki, Mike, Atl.	R	.125	19	24	1	3	3	0	0	0	0	4	0	0	13	0	0	1	.125	.125
Birkbeck, Mike, NY-N	R	.000	1	2	0	0	0	0	0	0	0	0	0	0	0	0	0	0	.000	.000
Black, Bud, S.F.	L	.056	28	54	1	3	4	1	0	0	2	10	0	2	16	0	0	0	.074	.089
Boskie, Shawn, ChiN	R	.185	23	27	1	5	6	1	0	0	1	3	0	2	9	0	0	0	.222	.241

National League starting pitchers (batting)

Name/Team	B	BA	G	AB	R	H	TB	2B	3B	HR	RBI	SH	SF	BB	SO	SB	CS	GIDP	SLG	OBA
Bowen, Ryan, Hou.	R	.111	15	9	1	1	1	0	0	0	0	0	0	0	3	0	1	0	.111	.111
Browning, Tom, Cin.	L	.226	16	31	4	7	8	1	0	0	2	2	1	1	6	0	0	1	.258	.242
Burkett, John, S.F.	R	.018	32	55	2	1	2	1	0	0	2	8	0	4	24	0	0	1	.036	.085
Candiotti, Tom, L.A.	R	.107	32	56	3	6	7	1	0	0	1	12	0	1	9	0	0	5	.125	.123
Castillo, Frank, ChiN	R	.092	33	65	3	6	6	0	0	0	1	5	0	3	21	0	0	2	.092	.132
Combs, Pat, Phi.	L	.125	4	8	1	1	2	1	0	0	2	1	0	1	1	0	0	0	.250	.222
Cone, David, NY-N	L	.092	27	65	5	6	7	1	0	0	4	7	0	3	19	0	0	1	.108	.132
Cormier, Rheal, St.L	L	.102	31	59	3	6	8	2	0	0	2	10	0	0	13	0	0	0	.136	.102
DeLeon, Jose, St.L-Phi.	R	.115	32	26	4	3	3	0	0	0	1	5	0	2	9	0	0	0	.115	.179
Deshaies, Jim, S.D.	L	.207	15	29	3	6	6	0	0	0	0	5	0	1	9	0	0	0	.207	.233
Drabek, Doug, Pit.	R	.157	35	89	5	14	17	3	0	0	6	8	0	2	28	0	0	0	.191	.176
Eiland, Dave, S.D.	R	.111	7	9	1	1	4	0	0	1	2	1	0	0	4	0	0	0	.444	.111
Fernandez, Sid, NY-N	L	.203	32	74	8	15	18	3	0	0	0	7	0	0	25	0	0	1	.243	.203
Gardner, Mark, Mon.	R	.140	33	50	4	7	9	0	1	0	2	8	2	3	18	0	0	0	.180	.182
Glavine, Tom, Atl.	L	.247	35	77	11	19	22	1	1	0	7	9	1	3	10	0	0	0	.286	.272
Gooden, Dwight, NY-N	R	.264	33	72	8	19	27	3	1	1	9	4	0	1	16	0	0	1	.375	.274
Greene, Tommy, Phi.	R	.125	13	24	1	3	3	0	0	0	0	0	0	0	12	0	0	0	.125	.125
Gross, Kevin, L.A.	R	.095	34	63	3	6	7	1	0	0	0	3	0	4	26	0	0	0	.111	.149
Hammond, Chris, Cin.	L	.136	30	44	7	6	10	1	0	1	4	3	1	6	20	0	0	0	.227	.235
Harkey, Mike, ChiN	R	.267	8	15	4	4	4	0	0	0	0	0	0	0	3	0	0	0	.267	.267
Harnisch, Pete, Hou.	R	.164	34	67	7	11	16	5	0	0	8	5	0	2	12	0	1	1	.239	.188
Harris, Greg W., S.D.	R	.129	20	31	1	4	5	1	0	0	1	5	0	5	13	0	0	0	.161	.250
Henry, Butch, Hou.	L	.148	28	54	3	8	11	0	0	1	7	5	0	1	10	0	0	1	.204	.164
Hershiser, Orel, L.A.	R	.221	35	68	6	15	20	5	0	0	5	6	1	1	10	1	0	0	.294	.229
Hill, Ken, Mon.	R	.177	33	62	10	11	19	3	1	1	4	10	0	8	13	0	0	0	.306	.271
Hillman, Eric, NY-N	L	.077	11	13	0	1	1	0	0	0	0	5	0	0	7	0	0	0	.077	.077
Hurst, Bruce, S.D.	L	.159	33	69	2	11	15	4	0	0	1	9	0	3	27	0	0	0	.217	.194
Hurst, Jonathan, Mon.	R	.000	3	4	0	0	0	0	0	0	0	2	0	0	2	0	0	0	.000	.000
Jackson, Danny, ChiN-Pit.	R	.083	34	60	2	5	5	0	0	0	2	9	0	1	31	0	1	0	.083	.098
Jones, Jimmy, Hou.	R	.167	26	36	5	6	7	1	0	0	4	9	0	6	13	0	0	1	.194	.286
Kile, Darryl, Hou.	R	.156	22	32	2	5	5	0	0	0	2	5	0	3	15	0	0	0	.156	.229
Lefferts, Craig, S.D.	L	.077	27	52	0	4	4	0	0	0	0	9	0	0	21	0	0	0	.077	.077
Leibrandt, Charlie, Atl.	R	.121	32	58	1	7	8	1	0	0	4	8	1	1	12	0	0	1	.138	.133
Maddux, Greg, ChiN	R	.170	35	88	6	15	21	3	0	1	8	13	0	1	22	0	0	1	.239	.180
Martinez, Dennis, Mon.	R	.189	32	74	3	14	14	0	0	0	2	10	0	0	20	0	0	1	.189	.189
Martinez, Pedro, L.A.	R	.000	2	2	0	0	0	0	0	0	0	0	0	0	0	0	0	0	.000	.000
Martinez, Ramon, L.A.	L	.120	26	50	1	6	6	0	0	0	2	5	0	0	14	0	0	0	.120	.120
Morgan, Mike, ChiN	R	.108	34	74	1	8	8	0	0	0	5	11	1	2	16	0	0	1	.108	.130
Mulholland, Terry, Phi.	R	.096	32	83	1	8	9	1	0	0	3	6	0	3	35	0	0	0	.108	.128
Nabholz, Chris, Mon.	L	.123	32	65	3	8	11	3	0	0	2	7	0	1	12	0	0	3	.169	.136
Nied, David, Atl.	R	.286	6	7	1	2	2	0	0	0	0	0	0	0	2	0	0	0	.286	.286
Ojeda, Bob, L.A.	L	.102	29	49	1	5	7	0	1	0	3	5	0	1	11	0	0	1	.143	.120
Olivares, Omar, St.L	R	.235	36	68	7	16	20	1	0	1	4	3	0	1	19	0	0	0	.294	.246
Osborne, Donovan, St.L	L	.121	34	58	4	7	9	0	1	0	0	2	0	0	21	0	0	0	.155	.121
Portugal, Mark, Hou.	R	.107	18	28	1	3	3	0	0	0	0	6	0	0	12	0	0	0	.107	.107
Rijo, Jose, Cin.	R	.194	33	72	3	14	16	2	0	0	6	6	0	0	18	0	0	0	.222	.194
Saberhagen, Bret, NY-N	R	.107	17	28	0	3	3	0	0	0	0	3	0	1	9	0	0	0	.107	.138
Schilling, Curt, Phi.	R	.156	42	64	3	10	11	1	0	0	3	8	0	1	22	0	0	0	.172	.169
Schourek, Pete, NY-N	L	.048	23	42	0	2	2	0	0	0	1	2	1	0	13	0	0	0	.048	.047
Seminara, Frank, S.D.	R	.118	19	34	3	4	4	0	0	0	0	2	0	1	9	0	0	0	.118	.143
Smith, Pete J., Atl.	R	.038	12	26	1	1	1	0	0	0	2	3	0	2	11	0	0	0	.038	.107
Smith, Zane, Pit.	L	.122	26	49	2	6	8	2	0	0	3	3	0	2	11	0	0	0	.163	.157
Smoltz, John, Atl.	R	.160	36	75	7	12	15	0	0	1	4	10	0	6	32	0	0	1	.200	.222
Swift, Bill C., S.F.	R	.157	34	51	3	8	11	3	0	0	3	5	0	1	18	0	0	0	.216	.173
Swindell, Greg, Cin.	R	.125	31	80	2	10	12	2	0	0	4	5	1	1	15	0	0	0	.150	.134
Tewksbury, Bob, St.L	R	.086	33	70	4	6	7	1	0	0	3	6	0	4	29	0	0	1	.100	.135
Tomlin, Randy, Pit.	L	.138	35	65	4	9	9	0	0	0	1	7	0	3	15	0	0	1	.138	.176
Wakefield, Tim, Pit.	R	.071	14	28	0	2	2	0	0	0	0	4	0	1	9	0	0	0	.071	.103
Walk, Bob, Pit.	R	.093	36	43	2	4	5	1	0	0	2	1	0	0	11	0	0	1	.116	.093
Williams, Brian, Hou.	R	.133	20	30	2	4	5	1	0	0	4	5	1	0	13	0	0	0	.167	.129
Wilson, Trevor, S.F.	L	.077	27	39	3	3	4	1	0	0	3	7	0	3	21	0	0	2	.103	.143

Minor League Report

USA SNAPSHOTS®

A look at statistics that shape the sports world

Baseball's deft draft picks

The past decade's No. 1 draft picks that made their major league rosters the fastest:

Player, team	Year	Days from draft to major league roster
Ben McDonald, Orioles	1989	93
Will Clark, Giants	1985	297
Andy Benes, Padres	1988	436
Dwight Gooden, Mets	1982	669
Ken Griffey Jr., Mariners	1987	670

Source: Major League Baseball, *The Baseball Encyclopedia*

By Marty Baumann, USA TODAY

INSIDE:

- Farm stars work in the bullpen
- 1992 minor league wrapups
- Final AAA player stats
- Final AA player stats
- League leaders
- Class of '92: Top Prospects
- *Plus: Minor league directory, overall standings and more!*

BASEBALL WEEKLY 1993

Minor leagues 1992: Down on the farm, the action was in the bullpen

Just as Jeff Reardon was passing Hall of Famer Rollie Fingers for the major-league career save record, save records were being set around the minor leagues. Nine leagues saw their single-season relief records fall. In addition, San Francisco farmhand **Steve Reed** set a single-season, National Association record with 43 saves.

Reed, who signed with the Giants as a non-drafted free agent out of tiny Lewis & Clark College in Idaho in 1988, saved 23 games with Double-A Shreveport to open the season, and racked up 20 more with Triple-A Phoenix before his promotion to the majors Aug. 29. He broke the mark (41) set by Mike Perez of Class A Springfield in 1987 and tied in 1991 by Mike Soper of Class A Kinston.

A righthander with a submarine delivery and pinpoint control, Reed uses visualization prior to taking the mound, a technique he learned in the off-season from a sports psychologist. Apparently, it works: in 60 innings, he struck out 63 while walking just 10. All 10 walks came with Phoenix. "I've been able to keep the walks to an absolute minimum," Reed said. "I pride myself on hitting spots."

▸***Other top saviors:*** Three other pitchers moved into the top 10 on the National Association single-season save list this season. **John Kelly** (St. Petersburg) set a Class A Florida State League record with 38, moving into fourth place on the all-time list and breaking the league record (36) set in 1990 by Barry Manuel (Port Charlotte). **Mike Draper** (Columbus, International League) set a Triple-A record with 37. Draper, who began the season in the Clippers' starting rotation, broke the league mark (25) set in 1983 by Curt Kaufman (Columbus), then overtook the Triple-A record (34) set in 1989 by Jay Baller (Indianapolis) to move into a tie for fifth on the all-time list. **Jerry Santos** (Springfield) moved into a tie for ninth without even setting a record, saving 35 games but falling six short of Perez's Midwest League mark.

▸***The righty stuff:*** New league pitching records were set by a host of right-handers in 1992. **Brian Drahman** (Vancouver, Triple-A Pacific Coast League) collected 30 saves, breaking the old record (26) set by Joe Bitker (Tacoma) in 1990. **Len Picota** (Harrisburg)tied the Double-A Eastern League record of 26. **Jerry Spradlin** (Chattanooga, Double-A Southern League) saved 34 games, breaking the mark (31) set in 1988 by Orlando's German Gonzales. **Rafael Chaves** (High Desert, Class A California League) had 34 saves to break Gary Sharko's mark (31) set in 1991 with San Jose. **Jamie Cochran** (Hamilton, Class A New York-Penn League) saved 24 games to break the oldest record of the bunch, a mark of 22 set in 1982 by Mark Davis of Little Falls—not the same Mark Davis who won the NL Cy Young Award in 1989 when he saved 44 games for San Diego. **John Pricher** (Boise, Class A Northwest League) collected 23 saves to break the old mark (17) set in 1988 by Tony Floyd of Southern Oregon. **Bo Loftin** (Billings, Rookie Pioneer League) saved 16 games, breaking the mark (14) set by Salt Lake's Mike Kolovitz in 1986. Loftin started 1992 as a backup catcher (Cedar Rapids, Class A) but was converted to relief pitcher mid-season.

▸***Pitching is in the Cards:*** The St. Louis Cardinals organization produced the save leader in six of the seven leagues in which it had entries—Kelly, Santos and Cochran, as well as **Mark Grater** (Louisville, Triple-A American Association) with 24, **Fidel Compres** (Arkansas, Double-A Texas League) with 28, and **Eric Miller** (Johnson City, Rookie Appalachian League) with 13.

▸***Double no-no:*** Fans at Jack Russell Stadium in Clearwater, Fla., Aug. 23 saw double when a pair of Florida State League pitchers hurled a double no-hitter. Left-hander **Andy Carter** (Clearwater) beat right-hander **Scott Bakkum** (Winter Haven) 1-0, in what is believed to be the first such event in the minors since 1952. "It was pretty weird," Carter said. "After the sixth inning I knew I had a decent shot at getting a no-hitter. Then I looked up at the scoreboard and said, 'Damn, he hasn't given up a hit, either.' " The lone run scored in the seventh on a pair of walks and a pair of bunts; Phil Geisler scored on a safety squeeze by Ken Sirak.

▸***Let the games begin:*** The Florida Marlins and Colorado Rockies were launched within a day of each other. On June 15, the Marlins' New York-Penn League club, the Erie Sailors, lost to Jamestown 6-5 in 13 innings in a 4:36 marathon at Ainsworth Field in Erie. The next night, the Bend Rockies of the Northwest League beat Boise 6-4 on Will Scalzitti's eighth-inning grand slam. Four fans retrieved the historic souvenir ball by climbing on one another's shoulders, and returned it to the club in exchange for a nice little booty: a pair of round-trip airplane tickets to Denver, three tickets to the 1993 Rockies season opener at Mile High Stadium and two Bend caps with Scalzitti's autograph. In the end, Florida had a better minor-league season, with a .533 winning percentage—seventh overall out of 28 organizations. The Rockies' squads were .462, 25th overall. (The latter team was combined with the Chicago Cubs.)

▸***Best on the farm:*** Cincinnati led the pack at 403-304 (a .570 winning percentage), sending four of its six minor-league clubs to their respective league finals and winning two championships. Milwaukee was second (.567), followed by the White Sox (.552), Cleveland (.543) and California (.540). In last place were the Red Sox (.444).

▸***Top individual achievements:*** **Billy Hall** (High Desert, Class A) hit .356, the best mark for any player in pro ball over the full season. **Rob Butler** (Dunedin, Class A) won the Florida State League batting title with a .358 mark, but played just 92 games before he was sidelined with an injury. **Brent Gates** (Modesto, Class A) made the hot months of July and August even hotter with a 35-game hitting streak, tops in pro ball. **John Fritz** (Quad City, Class A) was the only 20-game winner in the minors, going 12-0 down the second-half stretch to reach the mark. **Ramon Zapata** (Augusta, Class A) turned an unassisted triple play against Asheville Aug. 3. Earlier in the season, Zapata had set a South Atlantic League record for consecutive errorless games at second base with 38. **Corey Kapano** (Winston-Salem) won the Class A Carolina League batting crown (.318) on the so-called "Ted Williams" rule—a late arrival to the club, Kapano was a few plate appearances shy of qualifying for the title. When as many 0-fors were added to his at-bats to reach the minimum, Kapano still edged out **Kevin Jordan** (Prince William) by less than .001.

▸***In the wild-and-wacky file:*** A pro ball record was set June 28 when Greenville reliever **Pedro Borbon** stuffed 100 pieces of bubblegum into his mouth while sitting in the dugout during a game against Class A Southern League rival Carolina. The old record of 71 had been set by Cleveland's Kevin Wickander and Steve Olin the previous week. Borbon earned the nickname "Bazooka" as a result of his feat.

▸***Bringing in the fans:*** There were many interesting promotional contests around the minors in 1992—from a million-dollar giveaway to a house—but only one paid off. A season-long "Triple-Play Tuesday" promo in Lynchburg, Va., gave fans a chance to win a $25,000 car if the L-Sox turned a triple play and the fan chosen was in attendance. On the final home Tuesday of the season, Courtney Megginson walked into City Stadium just as the home team was turning three, and won the car.

▸***All-Stars:*** In the two major All-Star Games, the American League came out ahead by a one-run margin. In the Triple-A Game at Richmond, the AL won 2-1. Edmonton's **Tim Salmon** drove in the game-winning run with a double, while Columbus' **Sam Militello** fanned four in two innings. In the Double-A classic in Charlotte, Huntsville's **Marcos Armas** was 3-for-4 with a homer and Tulsa's **Jon Shave** had a double and two RBI to lead the AL to a 4-3 win.

—by Lisa Winston

Class AAA WRAPUPS

American Association

After spending four years in the cellar, Oklahoma City edged Denver by one game to win the Western Division. The 89ers' **Steve Balboni** led the league in homers (30) and RBI (104) and hit three grand slams. He was Topps Minor League Player of the Month in May, the first player in history to win that award in three different decades. Denver third baseman **Jim Tatum** was league MVP (.329-19-101) and won the batting crown. Louisville outfielder **Chuck Carr** led the league in stolen bases (53). Teammate **Mark Grater** led in saves (24). Nashville's **Scott Service** set a league record when he fanned nine consecutive batters Aug. 18 in a game against Buffalo. Omaha's **Dennis Moeller** won the ERA title (2.46). Denver's **Mark Kiefer** led the league in strikeouts. Buffalo's Marc Bombard was Manager of the Year, but was fired when the season ended.

FINAL STANDINGS

Eastern Division			
Buffalo	87-57	.604	—
Indianapolis	83-61	.576	4
Louisville	73-70	.510	13.5
Nashville	67-77	.465	20
Western Division			
Okla. City	74-70	.514	—
Denver	73-71	.507	1
Omaha	67-77	.465	7
Iowa	51-92	.357	22.5

Playoffs

Oklahoma City 4, Buffalo 0

 # Switch-hitter
** Left-handed*
(Players in major leagues are listed with last minor league team.)

Final AAA Player Stats

American Association

Buffalo Bisons (Pirates) AAA

BATTING	Avg.	AB	R	H	2B	3B	HR	RBI	SB
Pete Beeler, c	.282	85	6	24	3	0	2	9	0
*Scott Bullett, of	.400	10	1	4	0	2	0	0	0
*Dave Clark, of	.304	253	43	77	17	6	11	55	6
Alberto De Los Santos, of	.160	25	1	4	0	1	0	3	0
Brian Dorsett, c	.289	492	69	142	35	0	21	102	1
#Greg Edge, 2b	.195	118	11	23	8	1	0	10	1
Carlos Garcia, ss	.303	426	73	129	28	9	13	70	21
Tom Green, ph	.208	24	4	5	2	0	0	2	0
Jeff King, 3b	.345	29	6	10	2	0	2	5	1
#Dave Maize, ph	.000	1	0	0	0	0	0	0	0
*Al Martin, of	.305	420	85	128	16	15	20	59	20
William Pennyfeather, of	.238	160	19	38	6	2	1	12	3
Tom Prince, c	.262	244	34	64	17	0	9	35	3
Joe Redfield, ph	.224	214	28	48	13	2	2	21	16
Jeff Richardson, 2b	.290	328	34	95	23	2	3	29	5
Bruce Schreiber, 2b	.111	18	3	2	1	0	0	1	0
Don Slaught, c	.333	6	1	2	0	0	0	1	0
*Jose Tolentino, 1b	.301	209	39	63	16	1	8	34	0
Greg Tubbs, of	.293	430	69	126	20	5	7	42	20
John Wehner, 2b	.269	223	37	60	13	2	7	27	10
Kevin Young, 3b	.314	490	91	154	29	6	8	65	18
Eddie Zambrano, of	.284	394	47	112	22	4	16	79	3

PITCHING	W	L	ERA	G	SV	IP	H	BB	SO
Darrel Akerfelds	3	6	5.59	48	2	66	82	36	32
Joe Ausanio	6	4	2.90	53	15	84.2	64	40	66
Brett Backlund	3	0	2.16	4	0	25	15	11	9
*John Cerutti	4	0	5.56	9	0	45.1	53	7	13
Victor Cole	11	6	3.11	19	0	116.2	102	61	69
*Steve Cooke	6	3	3.75	13	0	74.1	71	36	52
Danny Cox	1	1	1.70	8	0	42.1	28	18	30
*Mike Dalton	3	3	3.66	56	10	71.1	56	18	25
Eddie Dixon	2	3	5.57	26	0	42	60	8	10
*Jerry Don Gleaton	1	0	0.00	5	1	7.2	2	3	2
*Drew Hall	4	0	2.37	16	0	38	36	12	30
*Lee Hancock	0	2	2.00	10	0	9	9	3	5
Dennis Lamp	0	0	6.75	3	1	5.1	6	0	3
Paul Miller	2	3	3.90	8	0	32.1	38	16	18
Blas Minor	5	4	2.43	45	18	96.1	72	26	60
Mark Petkovsek	8	8	3.53	32	1	150.1	150	44	49
*Rosario Rodriguez	0	1	15.43	4	0	2.1	3	8	1
Dennis Tafoya	2	1	4.35	5	0	10.1	13	3	5
Jim Tracy	9	4	4.27	29	0	116	115	34	51
Paul Wagner	3	3	5.49	8	0	39.1	51	14	19
Tim Wakefield	10	3	3.06	20	0	135.1	122	51	71
Mike York	4	1	3.06	6	0	32.1	31	20	20

Denver Zephyrs (Brewers) AAA

BATTING	Avg.	AB	R	H	2B	3B	HR	RBI	SB
Andy Allanson, c	.297	266	42	79	16	3	4	31	9
#Alex Diaz, of	.268	455	67	122	17	4	1	41	42
Bill Dobrolsky, ph	.000	1	0	0	0	0	0	0	0
*Sandy Guerrero, dh	.319	257	39	82	19	4	5	44	6
Charlie Hillemann, of	.217	46	6	10	1	1	1	7	0
Kenny Jackson, of	.260	338	49	88	24	0	12	53	6
John Jaha, 1b	.321	274	61	88	18	2	18	69	6
Joe Kmak, c	.311	225	27	70	11	4	3	31	6
*Ced Landrum, of	.311	164	24	51	7	0	1	19	16
Dave Liddell, c	.195	123	14	24	6	1	1	11	2
Matt Mieske, of	.267	524	80	140	29	11	19	77	13
Charlie Montoyo, 2b	.324	259	40	84	7	4	2	34	3
#Dave Nilsson, c	.317	240	38	76	16	7	3	39	10

BATTING	Avg.	AB	R	H	2B	3B	HR	RBI	SB
Jim Olander, of	.372	78	23	29	4	1	5	15	2
Ken Shamburg, 1b	.281	57	9	16	1	0	2	9	1
#Nelson Simmons, dh	.200	10	1	2	0	0	1	2	0
William Suero, 2b	.257	276	42	71	10	9	1	25	16
Jim Tatum, 3b	.329	492	74	162	36	3	19	101	8
#Jose Valentin, ss	.240	492	78	118	19	11	3	45	9
Kenny Williams, of	.291	134	16	39	7	0	4	17	3

PITCHING	W	L	ERA	G	SV	IP	H	BB	SO
Cal Eldred	10	6	3.00	19	0	141	122	42	99
Chris George	2	3	4.64	12	0	43.2	54	10	20
*Otis Green	11	8	4.61	28	0	152.1	148	70	114
*Neal Heaton	2	1	3.52	6	0	23	23	8	9
*Ted Higuera	1	0	4.15	2	0	9.2	7	8	4
Darren Holmes	0	0	1.38	12	7	13	7	1	12
Jim Hunter	6	7	3.68	34	2	135.2	144	46	56
Mike Ignasiak	7	4	2.93	62	10	92	83	33	64
Mark Kiefer	7	13	4.59	27	0	163.2	168	65	145
*Mark Lee	2	4	4.19	48	1	69.2	78	26	57
Paul McClellan	1	1	4.26	9	0	32.2	36	14	14
*Angel Miranda	6	12	4.77	28	0	160.1	183	77	122
*Eric Nolte	5	5	5.13	49	3	72	74	31	45
*Bruce Ruffin	3	0	0.94	4	0	29.2	28	8	17
*Efrain Valdez	1	1	5.43	36	0	68	76	22	43
Rob Wishnevski	9	6	5.03	44	3	77	87	39	64

Indianapolis Indians (Expos) AAA

BATTING	Avg.	AB	R	H	2B	3B	HR	RBI	SB
Shon Ashley, of	.227	172	18	39	11	0	3	20	1
#Bret Barberie, 2b	.395	43	4	17	3	0	3	8	0
*Eric Bullock, of	.305	305	50	93	19	3	5	40	21
Archi Cianfrocco, 1b	.305	59	12	18	3	0	4	16	1
Greg Colbrunn, 1b	.306	216	32	66	19	1	11	48	1
Wil Cordero, ss	.314	204	32	64	11	1	6	27	6
*Jim Eppard, 1b	.267	258	38	69	15	2	3	27	5
*Darrin Fletcher, c	.255	51	2	13	2	0	1	9	0
#Greg Fulton, 3b	.216	292	29	63	10	1	6	29	1
*Jerry Goff, 3b	.239	314	37	75	17	1	14	39	0
Todd Haney, 2b	.265	200	30	53	14	0	6	33	1
*Jimmy Kremers, c	.215	144	14	31	10	1	2	15	1
*Quinn Mack, of	.282	301	33	85	19	0	4	36	5
Omer Munoz, ss	.251	375	33	94	12	1	1	30	7
Bob Natal, c	.302	344	50	104	19	3	12	50	3
#Jerome Nelson, of	.270	74	9	20	2	2	1	5	2
Darren Reed, of	.333	3	0	1	1	0	0	0	0
#F.P. Santangelo, of	.266	462	83	123	25	0	5	34	12
#Razor Shines, 1b	.257	179	25	46	6	1	2	22	2
Matt Stairs, of	.267	401	57	107	23	4	11	56	11
Edgar Tovar, ss	.000	4	0	0	0	0	0	0	0
*Jerry Willard, c	.278	97	9	27	7	1	3	17	0

PITCHING	W	L	ERA	G	SV	IP	H	BB	SO
*Brian Barnes	4	4	3.69	13	0	83	69	30	77
*Blaine Beatty	7	5	4.31	26	0	94	109	24	54
Kent Bottenfield	12	8	3.43	25	0	152.1	139	58	111
Mario Brito	2	0	3.38	2	0	5.1	5	3	1
Ralph Diaz	0	0	4.50	1	0	4	3	3	2
Howard Farmer	3	2	3.75	30	0	84	89	24	64
*Chris Haney	5	2	5.14	15	0	84	88	42	61
Gil Heredia	2	0	1.02	3	0	18.2	18	3	10
Jonathan Hurst	4	8	3.77	23	0	119.1	135	29	70
Mike LaCoss	0	3	7.30	7	0	12.1	17	5	7
Bill Landrum	1	1	3.95	14	0	27.1	27	4	23
Matt Maysey	5	3	4.30	35	5	67	63	28	38
*Chris Myers	1	0	0.00	1	0	6	2	1	2
Doug Piatt	0	0	4.22	8	3	11.2	13	3	6
Dana Ridenour	1	1	3.09	30	6	47.2	44	9	37
Bill Risley	5	8	6.40	25	0	96.2	105	47	64
Mel Rojas	2	1	5.40	4	0	8.1	10	3	7
Bill Sampen	1	1	6.00	2	0	3	3	3	4
*Doug Simons	11	4	3.08	32	0	120	114	25	66
*Richardo Solis	0	2	3.75	2	0	12	11	2	5

Class AAA WRAPUPS

International League

The Columbus Clippers became the league's first repeat champion in a decade, beating out Scranton/ Wilkes-Barre with three runs in their last at-bat of the finals. Helping the Clippers to their winningest season since 1960 were both league MVP first baseman **J.T. Snow** (.313-15-78) and Most Outstanding Pitcher **Sam Militello** (12-2, 2.29), respectively the batting and ERA titlists as well. Columbus third baseman **Hensley Meulens** paced the league in homers (26) and RBI (100), and outfielder **Michael Humphreys** led with 37 stolen bases. Lee Elia of Scranton/ Wilkes-Barre was Manager of the Year. Richmond's **David Nied** paced the league in wins (14) and strikeouts (159), while teammate **Pete Smith** pitched the franchise's first perfect game, beating Rochester 1-0 May 3. Pawtucket was no-hit twice, by Tidewater's **Dave Telgheder** May 15 and by Scranton's **Ben Rivera** July 25.

FINAL STANDINGS

East Division			
Scrtn/W.B.	84-58	.592	—
Pawtucket	71-72	.497	13.5
Rochester	70-74	.486	15
Syracuse	60-83	.420	24.5
West Division			
Columbus	95-49	.660	—
Richmond	73-71	.507	22
Toledo	64-80	.444	31
Tidewater	56-86	.394	38

Playoffs

First round: Scrtn/W.B 3, Paw 1; Columbus 3, Richmond 0

Finals: Columbus 3, Scrtn/W.B. 2

 # Switch-hitter
** Left-handed*
(Players in major leagues are listed with last minor league team.)

Class AAA WRAPUPS

Pacific Coast League

Colorado Springs swept Vancouver in the finals, benefiting from an infield made up of former major-league starters: **Mike Aldrete** (.322, 84 RBI), **Alvaro Espinoza** (.300, 79 RBI), **Nelson Liriano** (.304, 20 SB) and **Craig Worthington** (.295). But the SkySox' real star was a nine-year veteran of the minors, outfielder **Wayne Kirby** (.345-11-74, 51 SB). Skipper Charlie Manuel was Manager of the Year. League MVP **Tim Salmon** of Edmonton fell .004 points short of winning the Triple Crown, hitting .347 with 29 homers and 105 RBI. Tacoma DH **Troy Neel** edged Salmon for the batting title. Earning all of his wins in relief, Albuquerque's **Zak Shinall** tied **George Tsamis** of Portland for the league victories lead with 13. **Mike Trombley** of Portland won the strikeout title (138), while **Mike Dunne** of Vancouver had the best ERA (2.78). Portland's **Paul Abbott** no-hit Vancouver for 10 innings on July 8.

FINAL STANDINGS

Northern Division

y-Portland	83-61	.576	—
x-Vancvr	81-61	.570	1
Edmonton	74-69	.517	8.5
Calgary	60-78	.435	20
Tacoma	56-87	.392	26.5

Southern Division

y-Colo Spgs	84-57	.596	—
x-Las Vgas	74-70	.514	11.5
Tucson	70-74	.486	15.5
Phoenix	66-78	.458	19.5
Albuquerque	65-78	.455	20

x-won first half; y-won second half

Playoffs

First round: Colo Spgs 3, L.V.2; Vancouver 3, Portland 2

Finals: Colo Spgs 3, Vancouver 0

PITCHING	W	L	ERA	G	SV	IP	H	BB	SO
Sergio Valdez	4	2	3.75	13	0	62.1	59	13	41
David Wainhouse	5	4	4.11	44	21	46	48	24	37
Pete Young	6	2	3.51	36	7	49.2	53	21	34

Iowa Cubs (Cubs) AAA

BATTING	Avg.	AB	R	H	2B	3B	HR	RBI	SB
Alex Arias, ss	.279	409	52	114	23	3	5	40	14
*Billy Bates, 2b	.241	257	30	62	8	1	1	19	2
Phil Bradley, of	.248	133	13	33	8	0	0	6	3
Scott Bryant, 1b	.251	315	35	79	22	3	18	52	0
Pedro Castellano, 3b	.248	238	25	59	14	4	2	20	2
Tony Chance, of	.270	434	60	117	23	1	11	52	5
Darrin Duffy, 2b	.211	71	8	15	2	0	0	3	0
Corey Kapano, 3b	.313	16	2	5	0	0	0	1	0
Mike Knapp, c	.246	138	16	34	5	0	3	15	2
Jeff Kunkel, 2b	.275	291	44	80	13	4	9	51	5
*Derrick May, of	.367	30	6	11	4	1	2	8	0
*Elvin Paulino, 1b	.217	157	15	34	3	1	1	16	0
Jorge Pedre, c	.253	296	31	75	17	1	6	34	2
Fernando Ramsey, of	.269	480	62	129	9	5	1	38	39
#Kevin Roberson, of	.305	197	25	60	15	4	6	34	0
Rey Sanchez, ss	.342	76	12	26	3	0	0	3	6
*Jeff Schulz, 1b	.269	308	38	83	14	2	4	43	2
Gary Scott, 3b	.263	354	48	93	26	0	10	48	3
*Dwight Smith, of	.250	8	1	2	1	0	0	1	0
Sammy Sosa, of	.316	19	3	6	2	0	0	1	5
#Doug Strange, 2b	.307	212	32	65	16	1	4	26	3
Hector Villanueva, 1b	.239	159	21	38	8	0	9	35	0
Scott Wade, of	.238	227	38	54	14	0	14	38	5
Jerome Walton, of	.296	27	8	8	2	1	0	3	1
*Rick Wilkins, c	.277	155	20	43	11	2	5	28	0

PITCHING	W	L	ERA	G	SV	IP	H	BB	SO
*Steve Adkins	7	13	6.13	33	0	135	161	74	89
Brad Arnsberg	0	8	6.51	20	1	75.2	95	27	33
*Hector Berrios	1	1	8.78	16	0	13.1	21	10	14
Shawn Boskie	0	0	3.68	2	0	7.1	8	3	3
Bill Brennan	1	4	6.37	19	0	30.2	43	12	34
Jim Bullinger	1	2	2.45	20	14	22	17	12	15
*Lance Dickson	0	1	19.29	1	0	2.1	6	2	2
John Gardner	5	7	4.49	38	0	122.1	120	61	87
Mike Harkey	0	1	5.56	4	0	23.2	21	13	16
Jeff Hartsock	5	12	4.36	27	0	173.1	177	61	87
Jerry Kutzler	0	0	3.00	2	0	3	5	0	0
Paul Marak	0	5	4.68	9	0	58.2	69	22	24
Scott May	3	4	4.80	17	0	66.2	78	23	52
Bill Melvin	3	0	4.62	18	0	39	32	27	31
Dave Pavlas	3	3	3.38	12	0	37.1	43	8	34
Laddie Renfroe	3	10	4.74	61	6	101.2	115	40	55
Jeff Robinson	2	1	4.61	10	0	14.2	12	5	12
John Salles	4	9	6.85	19	0	91.2	122	46	47
Bob Sebra	7	4	5.03	26	1	91.1	115	35	61
Heath Slocumb	1	3	2.59	36	7	42.2	36	16	47
Julio Strauss	2	2	2.79	22	1	58	52	17	50
Turk Wendell	2	0	1.44	4	0	25	17	15	12
Travis Willis	1	1	7.71	3	0	7	9	3	1

Louisville Redbirds (Cardinals) AAA

BATTING	Avg.	AB	R	H	2B	3B	HR	RBI	SB
Frank Abreu, ss	.133	15	0	2	0	0	0	1	0
*Rich Aldrete, ph	.111	18	0	2	0	0	0	0	0
#Luis Alicea, 2b	.282	71	11	20	8	0	0	6	0
Brad Beanblossom, 3b	.235	17	2	4	0	0	0	1	0
*Rod Brewer, of	.288	423	57	122	20	2	18	86	0
Ozzie Canseco, of	.266	308	53	82	19	1	22	57	1
#Greg Carmona, ss	.147	136	19	20	3	0	1	6	1
#Chuck Carr, of	.308	377	68	116	11	9	3	28	53
Rico Christian, of	.250	16	4	4	0	0	0	1	0
Tripp Cromer, ss	.200	25	5	5	1	1	1	7	0
Steve Fanning, ss	.184	49	8	9	1	2	0	4	0

BATTING	Avg.	AB	R	H	2B	3B	HR	RBI	SB
*Joey Fernandez, ph	.107	28	2	3	2	0	0	3	0
*Jose Fernandez, c	.079	38	1	3	1	0	1	3	0
Bien Figueroa, ss	.285	319	44	91	11	1	1	23	2
*Curt Ford, of	.300	257	47	77	15	3	6	31	9
*Ed Fulton, c	.201	234	19	47	5	0	12	29	0
Andres Galarraga, 1b	.176	34	3	6	0	1	2	3	1
Pedro Guerrero, dh	.255	55	5	14	5	0	3	7	0
Brian Jordan, of	.290	155	23	45	3	1	4	16	13
#Felix Jose, of	.143	7	0	1	0	0	0	0	0
*Lonnie Maclin, of	.324	290	29	94	17	3	1	38	4
#Jose Oquendo, ss	.266	64	8	17	2	0	0	6	0
#Geronimo Pena, 2b	.248	101	16	25	9	4	3	12	4
Tim Redman, c	.308	13	0	4	0	0	0	2	0
Stan Royer, 1b	.282	444	55	125	31	2	11	77	0
#Jeff Shireman, 2b	.199	186	24	37	6	0	0	11	0
Alex Trevino, c	.206	199	15	41	11	0	4	23	1
Craig Wilson, 2b	.296	81	13	24	5	1	0	5	3
Tracy Woodson, 3b	.296	412	62	122	23	2	12	59	4
Todd Zeile, 3b	.311	74	11	23	4	1	5	13	0

PITCHING	W	L	ERA	G	SV	IP	H	BB	SO
Rene Arocha	12	7	2.70	25	0	167.2	145	65	128
*Jeff Ballard	12	8	2.52	24	0	161.2	164	34	76
Mark Clark	4	4	2.80	9	0	61	56	15	38
Mike Cook	3	2	4.60	43	0	59.2	58	31	56
*Rheal Cormier	0	1	6.75	1	0	4	8	0	1
*Frank DiPino	0	3	3.97	18	0	23.2	28	8	10
*Steve Dixon	1	2	5.03	18	2	20.2	20	19	16
Mark Grater	7	8	2.13	54	24	76	74	15	46
Mike Hinkle	2	5	6.39	38	0	63.1	85	25	34
*Blaise Ilsley	5	4	4.30	33	1	98.1	114	23	56
Chris Jones	0	0	7.20	3	0	5	4	2	3
*Paul Kilgus	9	8	3.80	27	0	168.1	189	28	90
Mike Loynd	0	0	5.32	11	0	24.2	26	10	21
*Joe Magrane	3	4	5.40	10	0	53.1	60	29	35
*Mike Milchin	2	6	5.79	12	0	65.1	69	31	37
*Tim Sherrill	7	3	3.90	51	1	62.1	61	22	28
Bryn Smith	1	0	1.80	2	0	10	6	2	2
*Tom Urbani	4	5	4.67	16	0	89.2	92	37	46
*Allen Watson	1	0	1.46	2	0	12.1	8	5	9

Nashville Sounds (Reds) AAA

BATTING	Avg.	AB	R	H	2B	3B	HR	RBI	SB
Troy Afenir, c	.254	130	15	33	6	1	6	24	5
Geronimo Berroa, of	.328	461	73	151	33	2	22	88	8
*Scott Bradley, ph	.254	59	7	15	3	0	0	6	1
*Jeff Branson, ss	.325	123	18	40	6	3	4	12	0
Mickey Brantley, of	.317	230	47	73	13	1	7	31	1
Jacob Brumfield, of	.284	208	32	59	10	3	5	19	22
Nick Capra, of	.233	287	48	67	14	1	5	27	31
Darnell Coles, 3b	.296	81	19	24	5	0	6	16	1
Scott Coolbaugh, 3b	.255	188	25	48	8	3	5	23	3
Kiki Diaz, ss	.190	42	5	8	2	0	0	3	0
*Ruben Escalera, of	.220	127	19	28	3	1	4	11	0
*Kevin Garner, dh	.333	24	4	8	3	0	2	7	0
Denny Gonzalez, 3b	.200	80	12	16	4	1	2	7	0
Gary Green, ss	.193	316	23	61	12	1	3	27	0
Cesar Hernandez, of	.000	2	0	2	0	0	0	0	0
Mark Howie, 2b	.246	346	35	85	21	1	4	42	4
Brian Lane, 3b	.239	67	8	16	3	0	3	8	0
#Terry McDaniel, ph	.289	38	5	11	3	0	1	9	1
Russ Morman, 1b	.310	384	53	119	31	2	14	63	5
*Hal Morris, 1b	.167	6	1	1	1	0	0	0	0
*Jeff Reed, c	.240	25	1	6	1	0	1	2	0
Chris Sabo, dh	.364	11	3	4	0	0	1	1	0
Jeff Small, 2b	.278	503	65	140	30	3	7	46	10
*Jeff Stone, of	.216	102	9	22	1	1	0	7	7
*Dwight Taylor, of	.260	223	22	58	8	2	0	13	16
Todd Trafton, 1b	.252	131	25	33	7	1	5	21	4
Dan Wilson, c	.251	366	27	92	16	1	4	34	1
Rick Wrona, c	.246	118	16	29	8	2	2	10	1

Class AA WRAPUPS

Texas League

After shaving their heads in honor of new teammate and hometown hero **Billy Hall**, the Wichita Wranglers swept defending champion Shreveport in four games for the league title. A Wichita native who played at Wichita State, second baseman Hall had been promoted from High Desert (A) after winning the California League batting title. He wears his head shaved, prompting several Wranglers and even GM Steve Shaad to do the same. Wichita was led by first baseman **Jay Gainer**, who hit 23 homers despite missing a month, and outfielder **J.D. Noland**, the league stolen-base king (40). League MVP **Troy O'Leary** of El Paso won the batting title (.334-5-79). Tulsa left-hander **Dan Smith** was Pitcher of the Year and ERA titlist (2.52). **Fidel Compres** of Arkansas led in saves (28). Shreveport ace **Dan Carlson** paced the league in wins (15) and strikeouts (157), while teammate **Adell Davenport** won the RBI title (88). San Antonio's **Billy Ashley** was the year's top slugger (24 HR).

FINAL STANDINGS

Eastern Division			
y-Tulsa	77-59	.566	—
x-Shrevprt	77-59	.566	—
Jackson	61-74	.452	15.5
Arkansas	59-73	.447	16
Western Division			
y-El Paso	73-63	.537	—
x-Wichita	70-66	.515	3
Midland	61-72	.459	10.5
San Antn	62-74	.456	11

x-won first half; y-won second half

Playoffs

First round: Shrvprt 2, Tulsa 0; Wichita 2, El Paso, 1

Finals: Wichita 4, Shreveport 0

Class AA WRAPUPS

Southern League

The Greenville Braves coasted through the season before beating Chattanooga in five games for the championship. In addition to setting a new league record with 24 shutouts, the Braves boasted a crop of hard-hitting youngsters. League MVP was 21-year-old catcher **Javy Lopez** (.321-16-60), while 20-year-old shortstop **Chipper Jones** (.346-9-42) and outfielder **Melvin Nieves** (.283-18-76) made big impressions after mid-season promotions. **Mike Kelly**, a 22-year-old outfielder, had 25 home runs, 71 RBI and 22 stolen bases. At the helm, Grady Little was Manager of the Year. Pitcher of the Year was Chattanooga reliever **Jerry Spradlin**, who had a 1.38 ERA and a league-record 34 saves. Teammate **Tim Costo** led in homers (28). Birmingham first baseman **Scott Cepicky** paced the league with 87 RBI, and teammate **Larry Thomas** led in ERA (1.94). Jacksonville had the stolen base and strikeout champions: outfielder **Tow Maynard** (38 SB) and **Jim Converse** (157 strikeouts).

FINAL STANDINGS

Eastern Division

z-Greenville	100-43	.699	—
Charlotte	70-73	.490	30
Jacksnville	68-75	.476	32
Orlando	60-82	.423	39.5
Carolina	52-92	.361	48.5

Western Division

z-Chattnga	90-53	.629	—
Huntsville	81-63	.563	9.5
Memphis	71-73	.493	19.5
Birminghm	68-74	.479	21.5
Knoxville	56-88	.389	34.5

z-won both halves

Playoffs

First round: Grnville 3, Charlotte 0; Chattanooga 3, Huntsville 1

Finals: Greenville 3, Chattngа 2

PITCHING	W	L	ERA	G	SV	IP	H	BB	SO
Jose Alvarez	0	1	13.50	3	0	5.2	7	3	4
Keith Brown	12	9	3.61	26	0	150.2	157	43	102
*Bob Buchanan	0	4	4.96	10	0	49	63	21	19
Chris Bushing	1	0	3.48	5	0	10.1	8	6	6
Nick Capra	1	0	0.00	1	0	2	1	0	1
Tim Drummond	0	0	6.75	3	0	4	8	1	1
Brian Fisher	2	3	4.11	29	1	50.1	52	15	42
Steve Foster	5	3	2.68	17	1	50.1	53	22	28
Milt Hill	0	5	2.66	53	18	74.1	56	17	70
Trevor Hoffman	4	6	4.27	42	6	65.1	57	32	63
Tony Menendez	3	5	4.05	50	1	107.2	98	47	92
*Gino Minutelli	4	12	4.27	29	0	158	177	76	110
*Ross Powell	4	8	3.38	25	0	93.1	89	42	84
Tim Pugh	12	9	3.55	27	0	170.2	165	65	117
Mo Sanford	8	8	5.68	25	0	122	128	65	129
Jose Segura	1	1	3.98	22	1	32.2	33	18	16
Scott Service	8	2	1.89	52	6	95	66	44	112
*Joey Vierra	4	1	2.98	52	0	82.2	65	28	62

Oklahoma City 89ers (Rangers) AAA

BATTING	Avg.	AB	R	H	2B	3B	HR	RBI	SB
Steve Balboni, dh	.251	454	75	114	26	2	30	104	0
Kevin Belcher, of	.286	7	2	2	1	0	0	0	0
#Juan Bell, ss	.256	82	12	21	4	1	1	9	1
Mike Berger, of	.300	20	2	6	0	0	1	2	0
Bob Brower, of	.210	238	25	50	8	1	3	27	11
#Jack Daugherty, of	.278	18	3	5	2	0	0	2	0
Doug Davis, c	.186	194	20	36	10	0	4	25	0
Mario Diaz, ss	.335	167	24	56	11	0	3	20	1
Monty Fariss, of	.299	187	28	56	13	3	9	38	5
Jeff Frye, 2b	.300	337	64	101	26	2	2	28	11
Larry Hanlon, ss	.250	52	7	13	3	0	0	4	1
Bill Haselman, of	.241	58	8	14	5	0	1	9	1
*David Hulse, of	.233	30	7	7	1	1	0	3	2
Chuck Jackson, of	.260	457	66	119	23	7	10	54	3
*Rob Maurer, 1b	.288	493	76	142	34	2	10	82	1
Russ McGinnis, 3b	.264	330	63	87	19	1	18	51	0
#Keith Miller, of	.257	459	82	118	30	2	7	56	8
*Dan Peltier, of	.296	450	65	133	30	7	7	53	1
Paul Postier, ss	.206	97	9	20	4	0	0	11	0
Jim Presley, 3b	.237	173	16	41	8	0	4	28	3
*Mark Ryal, dh	.094	32	0	3	2	0	0	2	0
Tony Scruggs, of	.240	146	14	35	3	0	1	14	4
Ray Stephens, c	.304	191	22	58	8	0	6	32	0
#Jim Walewander, 2b	.210	124	20	26	7	0	0	10	5

PITCHING	W	L	ERA	G	SV	IP	H	BB	SO
Gerald Alexander	7	5	4.50	38	2	106	100	36	93
Mike Arner	2	1	6.55	4	0	22	25	4	9
*John Barfield	7	1	4.14	42	2	72.2	75	26	26
Kevin Blankenship	5	5	4.57	32	1	106.1	112	52	53
*Brian Bohanon	4	2	2.73	9	0	56	53	15	24
Jeff Bronkey	0	1	7.47	13	3	16.2	26	7	10
Rob Brown	1	2	2.87	7	0	31.1	30	5	14
Todd Burns	3	2	2.55	8	0	42.1	32	13	16
*Terry Burrows	1	0	1.13	1	0	8	3	5	0
Mike Campbell	2	3	5.71	11	0	41	43	12	25
*Don Carman	4	6	4.02	20	1	81.2	80	31	43
Scott Chiamparino	2	1	2.87	5	0	31.1	29	13	9
*Tom Drees	2	2	5.20	12	0	36.1	43	13	22
*Narciso Elvira	4	5	4.97	19	0	89.2	87	28	45
Hector Fajardo	1	0	0.00	1	0	7	8	2	6
Steve Fireovid	7	2	3.10	33	0	105.2	130	28	54
*Bryan Gore	1	0	3.43	6	0	21	23	5	10
Chuck Jackson	0	0	13.50	1	0	2	4	1	1
*Mike Jeffcoat	2	1	4.22	7	0	32	33	6	20
Danny Leon	1	0	0.00	3	0	5.2	2	3	4
Barry Manuel	1	8	5.27	27	5	27.1	32	26	11
Terry Mathews	1	1	4.32	9	1	17.2	17	7	13
Lance McCullers	1	1	5.33	13	1	25.1	26	11	10
Roger Pavlik	7	5	2.98	18	0	118.2	90	51	104
Wayne Rosenthal	1	6	5.69	57	11	62.2	72	29	54

PITCHING	W	L	ERA	G	SV	IP	H	BB	SO
*Cedric Shaw	2	5	5.59	13	0	56.1	58	31	25
Matt Whiteside	1	0	0.79	12	8	11.1	7	3	13

Omaha Royals (Royals) AAA

BATTING	Avg.	AB	R	H	2B	3B	HR	RBI	SB
Sean Berry, 3b	.287	439	61	126	22	2	21	77	6
*Adam Casillas, of	.307	362	41	111	12	3	0	27	3
Stu Cole, of	.195	205	30	40	8	0	4	17	3
Jeff Conine, 1b	.302	397	69	120	24	5	20	72	4
Carlos Diaz, c	.176	68	3	12	2	1	0	5	0
*Leo Garcia, of	.217	226	24	49	5	0	2	18	2
*Bob Hamelin, 1b	.200	95	9	19	3	1	5	15	0
Phil Hiatt, 3b	.214	14	3	3	0	0	2	4	1
#David Howard, ss	.118	68	5	8	1	0	0	5	1
*Kevin Koslofski, of	.311	280	29	87	12	5	4	32	8
*Kevin Long, of	.228	312	28	71	16	3	1	29	9
Luis Medina, dh	.276	341	37	94	16	1	16	49	1
#Jose Mota, 2b	.230	469	45	108	11	0	3	28	21
Erik Pappas, c	.217	138	18	30	8	1	1	11	4
Al Pedrique, ss	.212	198	11	42	3	0	0	9	5
Harvey Pulliam, of	.270	359	55	97	12	2	16	60	4
Dan Rohrmeier, of	.241	29	4	7	1	0	1	5	0
Rico Rossy, ss	.316	174	29	55	10	1	4	17	3
Terry Shumpert, 2b	.200	210	23	42	12	0	1	14	3
Tim Spehr, c	.253	336	48	85	22	0	15	42	4

PITCHING	W	L	ERA	G	SV	IP	H	BB	SO
Brian Ahern	7	5	4.02	17	0	103	94	38	45
Luis Aquino	0	0	2.61	2	0	10.1	13	4	3
Jose Bautista	2	10	4.90	40	2	108.1	125	28	60
*Jim Campbell	5	7	5.38	20	1	84.2	102	41	34
Dera Clark	1	6	7.95	9	0	43	57	16	32
Mark Huismann	4	9	5.17	29	0	124.2	139	34	58
Joel Johnston	5	2	6.39	42	2	75.2	80	45	48
*Reese Lambert	2	2	5.37	11	0	54.2	61	32	26
Carlos Maldonado	7	4	3.60	47	16	75	61	35	60
Josias Manzanillo	7	10	4.36	26	0	136.1	138	71	114
*Dennis Moeller	8	5	2.46	23	2	121.2	121	34	56
*Dennis Rasmussen	4	4	2.03	13	0	62	52	20	50
Rick Reed	5	4	4.35	11	1	62	67	12	35
Mike Roesler	4	6	5.19	45	7	76.1	83	25	47
*Rich Sauveur	7	6	3.22	34	0	117.1	93	39	88
Steve Shifflett	3	2	1.65	32	14	44.2	30	15	19
*Curt Young	0	1	5.40	2	0	10	15	2	6

International League

Columbus Clippers (Yankees) AAA

BATTING	Avg.	AB	R	H	2B	3B	HR	RBI	SB
Brad Ausmus, c	.242	364	48	88	14	3	2	35	19
#Bobby Dejardin, 2b	.238	416	51	99	14	3	3	42	13
#Mike Hankins, 2b	.182	22	3	4	0	0	0	2	0
Mike Humphreys, of	.282	408	83	115	18	6	6	46	37
Jay Knoblauh, of	.269	104	14	28	4	0	2	18	6
Jeff Livesey, c	.111	9	0	1	0	0	0	1	0
#Torey Lovullo, 2b	.295	468	69	138	33	5	19	89	9
Billy Masse, of	.266	357	52	95	13	2	12	60	7
Hensley Meulens, 3b	.275	534	96	147	28	2	26	100	15
John Ramos, dh	.172	64	5	11	4	1	1	12	1
#Carlos Rodriguez, 2b	.000	4	0	0	0	0	0	0	0
Dave Sax, c	.218	188	23	41	4	1	4	20	3
Dave Silvestri, ss	.279	420	83	117	25	5	13	73	19
#J.T. Snow, 1b	.313	492	81	154	26	4	15	78	3
#Bernie Williams, of	.306	363	68	111	23	9	8	50	20
Gerald Williams, of	.285	547	92	156	31	6	16	86	36

Class AA WRAPUPS

Eastern League

In the town's first season of professional baseball since 1967, Binghamton edged rival Canton-Akron in five games for the league title. Pitcher of the Year **Bobby Jones** of Binghamton, who four-hit Canton-Akron in the final playoff game, led the league in ERA (1.88). Binghamton's Steve Swisher was Manager of the Year. Ace **Paul Byrd** of Canton-Akron led the league with 14 wins, and teammate **Ken Ramos** won the batting crown (.339). London had three offensive leaders: DH **Greg Sparks** (25 HR), first baseman **Ivan Cruz** (104 RBI), and outfielder **Lou Frazier** (58 SB). League MVP was Albany-Colonie third baseman **Russ Davis** (.285-22-71). Teammate **Sterling Hitchcock** won the strikeout crown (156). The Yankees had earlier lost pitcher **Jeff Hoffman**, who died in his Binghamton hotel room of cardiac arrhythmia Aug. 29.

FINAL STANDINGS			
Cntn-Akrn	80-58	.580	—
Binghamtn	79-59	.572	1
Harrisburg	78-59	.569	1.5
Albany	71-68	.511	9.5
London	67-70	.489	12.5
Reading	61-77	.442	19
Hagerstn	59-80	.424	21.5
New Brit	58-82	.414	23

Playoffs

First round: Cntn-Akrn 3, Albny 0;Binghamton 3, Harrisburg 1

Finals: Binghamtn 3, Cntn-Akrn 2

 # Switch-hitter

** Left-handed*

(Players in major leagues are listed with last minor league team.)

PITCHING	W	L	ERA	G	SV	IP	H	BB	SO
Royal Clayton	10	5	3.58	36	1	131.2	132	45	72
Andy Cook	7	5	3.16	32	2	100.2	85	36	58
Francisco Delarosa	6	1	3.72	48	3	56.2	47	18	43
Mike Draper	5	6	3.60	57	37	80	70	28	42
Shawn Hillegas	2	0	3.29	4	0	27.1	24	10	20
*Scott Holcomb	2	0	2.79	18	0	19.1	15	19	23
Mark Hutton	0	1	5.40	1	0	5	7	2	4
*Jeff Johnson	2	1	2.17	11	0	58	41	18	38
Scott Kamieniecki	1	0	0.69	2	0	13	6	4	12
Ed Martel	10	9	5.56	26	0	151.2	159	59	94
Sam Militello	12	2	2.29	22	0	141.1	105	46	152
*Kevin Mmahat	0	0	2.45	2	0	7.1	4	8	7
*Jerry Nielsen	0	0	1.80	4	1	5	2	2	5
Tom Popplewell	1	0	7.11	4	0	6.1	6	11	7
*Rafael Quirico	1	0	3.00	1	0	6	6	4	1
*Dave Rosario	8	5	2.33	54	6	73.1	67	41	65
*Keith Seiler	0	0	4.15	3	0	4.1	5	2	2
Russ Springer	8	5	2.69	20	0	124.2	89	54	95
Don Stanford	5	3	4.37	40	3	82.1	81	26	54
Larry Stanford	0	1	4.50	2	1	2	2	1	5
Wade Taylor	0	0	3.00	1	0	3	2	4	2
Bob Wickman	12	5	2.92	23	0	157	131	55	108
*Curt Young	3	0	3.38	3	0	16	16	6	2

Pawtucket Red Sox (Red Sox) AAA

BATTING	Avg.	AB	R	H	2B	3B	HR	RBI	SB
Luis Aguayo, 3b	.255	231	31	59	16	1	5	36	1
#Tom Barrett, 2b	.254	323	55	82	18	4	1	21	13
*Scott Bethea, 3b	.067	15	1	1	0	0	0	2	0
#Mike Brumley, of	.263	365	50	96	15	5	4	41	14
Jim Byrd, 2b	.224	246	27	55	5	1	2	18	2
John Flaherty, c	.250	104	11	26	3	0	0	7	0
Bob Geren, c	.207	213	28	44	7	0	9	25	0
Denny Gonzalez, 3b	.191	47	2	9	2	0	1	3	0
#Wayne Housie, of	.221	456	53	101	22	5	2	28	20
*Steve Lyons, 3b	.259	135	14	35	14	2	2	12	3
John Marzano, c	.290	62	5	18	1	0	2	12	0
Dave Milstien, 3b	.248	266	29	66	11	1	1	34	0
Tim Naehring, 2b	.294	34	7	10	0	0	2	5	1
Juan Paris, of	.182	110	8	20	2	1	1	10	1
*Phil Plantier, of	.425	40	7	17	0	0	5	14	0
Ruben Rodriguez, c	.227	44	3	10	3	0	0	1	0
*Sean Ross, of	.244	390	47	95	19	5	10	48	13
#John Shelby, of	.207	468	56	97	27	4	17	64	6
*Van Snider, of	.234	384	44	90	22	1	12	51	2
*Mike Twardoski, 1b	.290	389	55	113	23	4	13	49	1
John Valentin, ss	.260	331	47	86	18	1	9	29	1
*Mo Vaughn, 1b	.282	149	15	42	6	0	6	28	1
Eric Wedge, c	.299	211	28	63	9	0	11	40	0
Bob Zupcic, of	.320	25	3	8	1	0	2	5	0

PITCHING	W	L	ERA	G	SV	IP	H	BB	SO
*John Cerutti	7	7	4.63	24	0	105	128	23	43
Brian Conroy	7	5	4.62	15	0	86.2	91	31	57
John Dopson	1	2	2.37	6	0	38	28	8	23
*Tom Fischer	1	0	6.24	36	3	71.2	78	41	46
Mike Gardiner	1	3	3.31	5	0	33.2	32	9	37
Peter Hoy	3	2	4.81	45	5	73	83	25	38
Daryl Irvine	4	1	1.54	36	18	41	32	10	25
Derek Livernois	3	2	4.26	6	0	38	38	12	32
Steve Lyons	0	0	0.00	1	0	2	3	1	2
Nate Minchey	2	0	0.00	2	0	7	3	0	4
*Kevin Morton	2	12	5.45	26	0	139.2	166	59	71
Jeff Plympton	6	9	3.43	58	1	81.1	78	34	57
Paul Quantrill	6	8	4.46	19	0	119	143	20	56
*Ed Riley	0	0	4.50	1	0	6	7	1	4
Ken Ryan	2	0	2.08	9	7	9.2	6	4	6
Larry Shikles	13	8	3.56	29	0	149.1	157	36	67
*Scott Taylor	9	11	3.67	26	0	162	168	61	91
Dave Walters	4	2	5.28	38	2	77.2	100	34	45

Class A WRAPUPS

California League

Stockton silenced Visalia's bats en route to the league championship, limiting a team which hit .295 during the regular season to three runs on 16 hits in four playoff games. Stockton southpaw **Brian Hancock**, tops in the league with 14 wins, two-hit Visalia in the clincher. Ports skipper Tim Ireland was Manager of the Year. League MVP **Marty Cordova** of Visalia hit .341 with 28 homers, leading the minors with 131 RBI. High Desert second baseman **Billy Hall** was the first player in 25 years to lead the league in batting (.356) and stolen bases (49). Pitcher of the Year **Joe Rosselli**, a southpaw with San Jose, had the best ERA (2.41). Reno outfielder **Mike Neill** was named Rookie of the Year (.336-5-76), and teammate **Fabio Gomez** had 115 RBI, second-best in the minors. Modesto's **Curtis Shaw** paced the league with 154 strikeouts, while second baseman **Brent Gates** had pro ball's best hitting streak of the season (35 games).

FINAL STANDINGS

Northern Division			
z-Stockton	83-53	.610	—
Modesto	79-57	.581	4
San Jose	78-58	.574	5
Reno	65-71	.478	18
Salinas	36-99	.267	46.5
Southern Division			
y-Visalia	75-61	.551	—
x-Plm Spgs	72-63	.533	2.5
High Desert	71-65	.522	4
Bakersfield	68-68	.500	7
San Bdino	52-84	.382	27

x-won first half; y-won second half; z-won both halves

Playoffs

First round: Visalia 3, Plm Spgs 1; Stockton 3, Modesto 2

Finals: Stockton 3, Visalia 1

Richmond Braves (Braves) AAA

BATTING	Avg.	AB	R	H	2B	3B	HR	RBI	SB
Francisco Cabrera, c	.272	301	30	82	11	0	9	35	0
#Ramon Caraballo, 2b	.281	405	42	114	20	3	2	40	19
Vinny Castilla, ss	.252	449	49	113	29	1	7	44	1
Johnny Cuevas, c	.000	6	1	0	0	0	0	0	0
Brian Deak, c	.261	238	46	62	13	0	9	36	0
Nick Esasky, 1b	.278	108	12	30	6	0	5	14	1
*Tommy Gregg, of	.288	125	17	36	9	2	0	12	3
Steve Howard, of	.172	29	3	5	3	0	0	2	0
Pat Kelly, 2b	.467	15	1	7	0	0	0	4	0
*Ryan Klesko, 1b	.251	418	63	105	22	2	17	59	3
Jeff Manto, 3b	.291	450	65	131	24	1	13	68	1
Keith Mitchell, of	.226	403	45	91	19	1	4	50	14
Bobby Moore, of	.250	316	41	79	13	3	0	25	14
Mike Mordecai, ss	.246	118	12	29	3	0	1	6	0
*Boi Rodriguez, dh	.277	278	40	77	8	3	16	40	0
*Joe Szekely, c	.308	39	5	12	5	1	0	5	0
*Andy Tomberlin, of	.271	406	69	110	16	5	9	47	12
*Aubrey Waggoner, of	.227	22	2	5	1	0	1	6	1
Eddie Williams, 3b	.203	74	8	15	3	0	1	5	0

PITCHING	W	L	ERA	G	SV	IP	H	BB	SO
*Brian Bark	1	2	6.00	22	2	42	63	15	50
Kevin Coffman	6	5	3.15	16	0	91.1	66	70	78
*Pat Gomez	3	5	5.45	23	0	71	79	42	48
Tom McCarthy	4	6	3.21	48	4	93.2	91	21	52
Greg McMichael	6	5	4.38	19	2	90.1	89	34	86
Andy Nezelek	0	0	0.00	2	0	6	3	0	5
David Nied	14	9	2.84	26	0	168	144	44	159
*Dale Polley	1	6	2.88	39	2	56.1	54	24	42
Armando Reynoso	12	9	2.66	28	0	169.1	156	52	108
Nap Robinson	11	10	3.57	29	0	164.2	149	52	106
Pete Smith	7	4	2.14	15	0	109.1	75	24	93
Randy St. Claire	6	5	3.52	39	4	72.2	82	21	62
Billy Taylor	2	3	2.28	47	12	79	72	27	82
Mark Wohlers	0	2	3.93	27	9	34.1	32	17	33

Rochester Red Wings (Orioles) AAA

BATTING	Avg.	AB	R	H	2B	3B	HR	RBI	SB
Manny Alexander, ss	.292	24	3	7	1	0	0	3	2
#Juan Bell, ss	.196	138	21	27	6	3	2	14	2
Damon Buford, of	.284	155	29	44	10	2	1	12	23
*Paul Carey, dh	.230	87	9	20	4	1	1	7	0
Bobby Dickerson, ss	.241	249	28	60	7	3	4	29	1
Ricky Gutierrez, 2b	.253	431	54	109	9	3	0	41	14
*Doug Jennings, 1b	.275	396	70	109	23	5	14	76	11
Mike Lehman, c	.190	21	3	4	1	0	0	1	1
Dave Liddel, c	.107	28	1	3	0	0	1	2	0
Rod Lofton, 2b	.235	132	24	31	3	1	0	8	10
Scott Meadows, of	.259	216	23	56	6	0	1	9	6
Luis Mercedes, of	.313	409	62	128	15	1	3	29	35
Mark Parent, c	.287	356	52	102	24	0	17	69	4
Doug Robbins, c	.309	288	45	89	19	1	6	46	8
*Greg Roth, 3b	.217	46	5	10	1	0	1	2	1
Steve Scarsone, 2b	.270	407	56	110	26	4	12	60	13
Ken Shamburg, 1b	.209	191	22	40	9	0	5	34	2
Tommy Shields, 3b	.302	431	58	130	23	3	10	59	13
Jack Voigt, of	.284	443	74	126	23	4	16	64	9
Melvin Wearing, dh	.326	187	33	61	16	2	4	45	2
#Ed Yacopino, of	.282	440	56	124	22	4	4	61	5

PITCHING	W	L	ERA	G	SV	IP	H	BB	SO
Tim Drummond	1	0	1.98	2	0	14.2	13	6	4
Stacy Jones	0	0	6.75	2	1	3.2	2	1	1
Tim Layana	3	3	5.35	41	4	72.1	79	38	47
*Pat Leinen	3	4	5.86	17	1	55.1	76	19	19
Jim Lewis	2	5	4.92	33	1	60.1	67	32	38
Richie Lewis	10	9	3.28	24	0	159.1	136	61	154
Bob Milacki	7	1	4.57	9	0	61	57	21	35
Dave Miller	4	0	3.81	12	0	50.2	60	17	21
Alan Mills	0	1	5.40	3	1	5	6	2	8

Class A WRAPUPS

Carolina League

After ending the 1991 season with a league-record 22-game losing streak and finishing last in seven of the previous eight half-seasons, the Peninsula Pilots went from worst to first. The Pilots beat Durham in a one-game playoff for a first-half pennant and went on to edge Lynchburg in five games for the championship. Peninsula took the title game 5-4 on a pair of late-inning balks by the Red Sox' relief aces, ERA champ **Joe Caruso** (1.98) and saves leader **Cory Bailey** (23). Peninsula's first baseman **Bubba Smith** won league MVP honors and led the minors with 32 home runs. Skipper Marc Hill was both league Manager of the Year and *Baseball Weekly*'s Minor League Manager of the Year. Southpaw **John Cummings** was Pitcher of the Year and tops in both wins (16) and strikeouts (144). Winston-Salem's **Andy Hartung** led the league in RBI (94). **Tim Vanegmond** of Lynchburg no-hit Prince William 2-0 June 1, fanning 10.

FINAL STANDINGS

Northern Division			
z-Lynchbrg	77-58	.570	—
Prince Wm	69-71	.493	10.5
Frederick	69-71	.493	10.5
Salem	64-76	.457	15.5
Southern Division			
z-Peninsula	74-64	.536	—
Durham	70-70	.500	5
Kinston	65-71	.478	8
Wnstn-Slm	66-73	.475	8.5

z-won both halves

Playoffs

Peninsula 3, Lynchburg 2

 # Switch-hitter

** Left-handed*

(Players in major leagues are listed with last minor league team.)

Class A WRAPUPS

Midwest League

Beloit pushed them to five games, but Cedar Rapids won the championship on **Johnny Ray**'s 5-0 shutout. Reds' outfielder **Steve Gibralter** hit .306 and led the league in homers (19) and RBI (99), heading Cedar Rapids' charge to the title. Gibralter was named both league MVP and Rookie of the Year. Quad City's **John Fritz** was the league's first 20-game winner in 31 years, going 12-0 over the second half. **Gabe White** of Rockford topped the league with 176 strikeouts, while **Jerry Santos** of Springfield had 35 saves. Orlando Palmeiro of Quad City won the batting title (.317), and South Bend second baseman **Essex "Gas" Burton** outran the league with 65 stolen bases. Two pitchers tossed no-hitters: Clinton's **Chuck Wanke** and Kenosha's **David Sartain**. Tom Poquette of Appleton was Manager of the Year.

FINAL STANDINGS

Northern Division

y-Beloit	77-58	.570	—
So. Bend	73-64	.533	5
x-Appleton	70-62	.530	5.5
Rockford	66-70	.485	11.5
Kenosha	63-70	.474	13
Kane Cnty	61-76	.445	17
Madison	59-75	.440	17.5

Southern Division

y-Quad City	91-46	.664	—
Springfield	84-56	.600	8.5
x-Cdr Rpds	82-56	.594	9.5
Peoria	62-74	.456	28.5
Waterloo	59-78	.431	32
Clinton	59-79	.428	32.5
Burlington	47-89	.366	43.5

x-won first half; y-won second half

Playoffs

First round: Beloit 2, Appleton 1;Cedar Rapids 2, Quad City 0

Finals: Cedar Rapids 3, Beloit 2

PITCHING	W	L	ERA	G	SV	IP	H	BB	SO
*Daryl Moore	0	0	2.95	16	1	18.1	10	9	14
*John O'Donoghue	5	4	3.23	13	0	70.2	60	19	47
Mike Oquist	10	12	4.11	26	0	153.1	164	45	111
*Brad Pennington	1	3	2.08	29	5	39	12	33	56
*Jim Poole	1	6	5.31	32	10	42.1	40	18	30
*Dennis Rasmussen	0	7	5.67	9	0	46	49	22	33
*Arthur Rhodes	6	6	3.72	17	0	102.2	84	46	115
*Israel Sanchez	0	0	2.35	4	0	8.2	5	5	2
Todd Stephan	5	6	3.96	44	4	86.1	86	31	78
Anthony Telford	12	7	4.18	27	0	181	183	64	129
Mark Williamson	0	0	0.00	4	2	4.2	2	0	1

Scranton/WB Red Barons (Phillies) AAA

BATTING	Avg.	AB	R	H	2B	3B	HR	RBI	SB
Gary Alexander, 1b	.202	401	54	81	26	1	12	53	0
#Ruben Amaro, of	.294	68	8	20	4	1	1	10	2
Kim Batiste, ss	.260	269	30	70	12	6	2	29	6
Pat Brady, of	.000	9	0	0	0	0	0	1	0
Nick Capra, of	.286	56	12	16	3	0	1	3	3
Braulio Castillo, of	.246	386	59	95	21	5	13	47	8
Wes Chamberlain, of	.331	127	16	42	6	2	4	26	6
*Bruce Dostal, of	.220	168	32	37	7	0	1	7	10
Jose Gonzalez, of	.171	41	10	7	4	0	1	3	3
*Jeff Grotewold, dh	.294	51	8	15	1	1	1	8	0
Ricky Jordan, 1b	.263	19	1	5	0	0	0	2	0
Greg Legg, 3b	.228	289	35	66	12	2	1	29	2
Mike Lieberthal, c	.200	45	4	9	1	0	0	4	0
Jim Lindeman, of	.302	53	5	16	0	1	0	8	0
Doug Lindsey, c	.208	274	28	57	9	0	4	27	0
Tom Marsh, of	.241	158	26	38	7	2	8	25	5
Joe Millette, ss	.266	256	24	68	11	1	1	23	3
#Julio Peguero, of	.256	289	41	74	14	2	1	21	14
Todd Pratt, c	.320	125	20	40	9	1	7	28	1
Victor Rodriguez, 2b	.277	155	14	43	8	2	1	27	0
#Edwin Rosado, c	.000	10	0	0	0	0	0	0	0
Rick Schu, 3b	.310	400	56	124	18	3	10	49	3
Ray Stephens, c	.205	44	4	9	1	0	1	2	0
*Jeff Stone, of	.240	125	19	30	5	1	2	10	9
#Casey Waller, 3b	.295	61	11	18	4	0	0	8	1
Cary Williams, of	.223	373	38	83	18	3	7	40	7

PITCHING	W	L	ERA	G	SV	IP	H	BB	SO
*Kyle Abbott	4	1	1.54	5	0	35	20	16	34
Andy Ashby	0	3	3.00	7	0	33	23	14	18
Bob Ayrault	5	1	4.97	20	6	25.1	19	15	30
Jay Baller	4	5	1.42	44	22	63.1	48	25	67
Toby Borland	0	1	7.24	27	1	27.1	25	26	25
Cliff Brantley	3	1	1.76	5	0	31.2	19	14	26
Brad Brink	8	2	3.48	17	0	111.1	100	34	92
Darrin Chapin	5	4	5.11	40	4	62.2	72	33	67
*Pat Combs	5	7	3.61	21	0	125.2	123	41	77
Paul Fletcher	3	0	2.78	4	0	23.2	17	2	26
Tyler Green	0	1	6.10	2	0	10.1	7	12	15
Tommy Greene	2	1	2.49	5	0	22.2	15	4	21
Mike Hartley	1	2	4.09	3	0	11	9	7	10
*Greg Mathews	3	7	2.96	16	0	85	93	23	63
Tim Mauser	8	6	2.97	45	4	100	87	45	75
Steve Parris	3	3	4.03	11	1	51.1	57	17	29
Jeff Patterson	2	1	2.63	11	1	14.2	10	8	11
*Wally Ritchie	1	0	2.70	15	5	17.2	11	3	12
Bien Rivera	2	0	0.00	2	0	12	4	2	10
*Steve Searcy	0	2	3.46	8	1	26	19	12	22
*Mark Sims	5	3	3.04	44	0	53.1	53	14	26
Matt Stevens	1	0	6.23	9	0	13	19	4	11
Mickey Weston	10	6	3.11	26	1	171.2	166	29	79
Mike Williams	9	1	2.43	16	0	93.2	84	30	59

Syracuse Chiefs (Blue Jays) AAA

BATTING	Avg.	AB	R	H	2B	3B	HR	RBI	SB
#Domingo Cedeno, 2b	.193	57	4	11	4	0	0	5	0
Bruce Crabbe, 2b	.236	157	14	37	4	1	4	13	2
Butch Davis, of	.280	550	67	154	31	9	9	74	19
*Ray Giannelli, of	.229	249	23	57	9	2	5	22	2
Derek Henderson, ss	.143	14	0	2	1	0	0	0	0
Randy Knorr, c	.272	228	27	62	13	1	11	27	1
*Mike Maksudian, c	.280	339	38	95	17	1	13	58	4
Domingo Martinez, 1b	.274	438	55	120	22	0	21	62	6
Terry McGriff, c	.250	56	4	14	2	0	2	7	1
Rob Montalvo, ss	.232	168	20	39	8	0	2	14	2
Jose Monzon, c	.056	18	3	1	0	0	0	1	0
*Stu Pederson, of	.232	259	42	60	13	1	7	29	3
Tom Quinlan, 3b	.215	349	43	75	17	1	6	36	1
Jerry Schunk, 2b	.261	417	40	109	16	1	2	26	2
#Shawn Scott, of	.321	28	2	9	2	1	0	1	0
Ed Sprague, c	.276	369	49	102	18	2	16	50	0
Ryan Thompson, of	.282	429	74	121	20	7	14	46	10
Scott Wade, of	.156	45	3	7	2	0	0	3	0
#Turner Ward, of	.239	280	41	67	10	2	10	29	7
Eddie Zosky, ss	.231	342	31	79	11	6	4	38	3

PITCHING	W	L	ERA	G	SV	IP	H	BB	SO
Jose Alvarez	1	4	4.17	22	1	37.2	32	18	38
Pete Blohm	7	6	5.37	37	1	129	146	46	67
Tim Brown	0	2	6.32	4	0	16.2	19	4	13
Jesse Cross	0	0	9.45	4	0	7.2	11	3	3
*Ken Dayley	0	0	17.18	4	0	4.2	3	6	4
*Wayne Edwards	4	6	4.48	41	3	131.2	127	76	108
Juan Guzman	0	0	6.00	1	0	3	6	1	3
Darren Hall	4	6	4.30	55	5	69	62	35	49
Pat Hentgen	1	2	2.66	4	0	20.1	15	8	17
*Al Leiter	8	9	3.86	27	0	163.1	159	64	108
Doug Linton	12	10	3.69	25	0	171.2	176	70	126
*Bob MacDonald	2	3	4.63	17	2	23.1	25	12	14
*John Shea	8	8	6.18	25	0	118	151	49	50
Mike Timlin	0	1	8.74	7	3	11.1	15	5	7
Rick Trlicek	1	1	4.36	35	10	43.1	37	31	35
*Gene Walter	3	4	2.83	39	9	57.1	51	28	46
*Anthony Ward	2	9	6.87	20	0	73.1	100	34	46
Dave Weathers	1	4	4.66	12	0	48.1	48	21	30
Woody Williams	6	8	3.13	25	1	121.2	115	41	81

Tidewater Tides (Mets) AAA

BATTING	Avg.	AB	R	H	2B	3B	HR	RBI	SB
#Tom Allison, 2b	.400	10	4	4	1	1	0	1	0
Kevin Baez, ss	.236	352	30	83	16	1	2	33	1
Tim Bogar, 2b	.279	481	54	134	32	1	5	38	7
*Scott Bradley, c	.207	111	8	23	1	0	1	7	0
*Jeromy Burnitz, of	.243	445	56	108	21	3	8	40	30
Joe Dellicarri, 2b	.250	16	1	4	0	0	1	1	0
*Chris Donnels, 3b	.301	279	35	84	15	3	5	32	12
D.J. Dozier, of	.234	197	32	46	8	3	7	25	6
*Andy Dziadkowiec, c	.243	37	2	9	1	0	0	2	0
Dave Gallagher, of	.250	12	1	3	0	0	0	0	0
Javier Gonzalez, c	.208	120	9	25	4	0	4	12	0
Terrel Hansen, 1b	.248	395	43	98	17	0	12	47	4
#Pat Howell, of	.244	405	46	99	8	3	1	22	21
#Bert Hunter, of	.500	4	1	2	1	0	0	0	0
*Dean Kelley, 2b	.235	34	4	8	2	0	0	4	0
#Jason King, 2b	.500	2	2	1	0	0	0	0	0
Mitch Lyden, 1b	.258	299	34	77	13	0	14	52	1
#Lee May, of	.213	235	28	50	10	0	2	15	4
Rodney McCray, of	.000	10	1	0	0	0	0	0	3
#Jeff McKnight, of	.307	352	43	108	21	1	4	43	3
Orlando Mercado, c	.247	178	16	44	7	0	8	19	1
Junior Noboa, 2b	.200	20	1	4	0	0	0	3	0
#Keith Smith, 2b	.230	113	12	26	2	0	0	5	0
Steve Springer, 3b	.290	427	57	124	16	0	16	70	9
*Fernando Vina, 2b	.200	30	3	6	0	0	0	2	0
*Mike White, dh	.000	3	0	0	0	0	0	0	0

Class A WRAPUPS

New York–Penn League

The Geneva Cubs swept the Erie Sailors for their first title since 1987, dashing Erie's Cinderella playoff hopes. After finishing 16 games behind the powerful Hamilton Redbirds in the Stedler Division, Erie had upset them in the first round. With league highs in homers (14) and RBI (61), first baseman **Todd Pridy** led the Sailors. Hamilton aces **David Oehrlein** and **T.J. Mathews** shared the lead in wins (10), while Oehrlein was tops in strikeouts (99). Skipper Chris Maloney was Manager of the Year. League MVP and top prospect honors went to Elmira outfielder **Jose Malave** (.325-12-46). Utica outfielder **Byron Mathews** had 42 steals, best in the short-season minors. St. Catharines' **Tim Crabtree**, converted from catcher to pitcher after the draft, had the best ERA (1.57). Pittsfield's **Jim Popoff** fanned 19 in a 5-3 win against Batavia June 29, the best single performance in pro ball this year.

FINAL STANDINGS

McNamara Division			
Utica	42-32	.568	—
Pittsfiield	37-37	.500	5
Oneonta	37-38	.493	5.5
Watertown	37-39	.487	6
Pinckney Division			
Geneva	41-34	.547	—
Batavia	36-34	.514	2.5
Auburn	32-41	.438	8
Elmira	31-44	.413	10
Stedler Division			
Hamilton	56-20	.737	—
Erie	40-37	.519	16.5
Niag Falls	39-39	.500	18
Jamestn	34-43	.442	22.5
St. Cathrns	33-42	.440	22.5
Welland	31-46	.403	25

Playoffs

First round: Geneva 1, Utica 0; Erie 1, Hamilton 0

Finals: Geneva 2, Erie 0

Class A WRAPUPS

Northwest League

Bellingham beat Bend in two games for the championship, rallying from a three-run deficit in the opener and shutting out the Rockies on **Derek Lowe**'s five-hitter in game two. Mariners first baseman **Fred McNair,** who missed all of 1991 after shoulder reconstruction, led the offense (.329-8-54), while **Renaldo Bullock** led the league in stolen bases (40). Bend's **Mark Thompson** led the short-season minors in strikeouts (102). Southern Oregon's **Gary Haught** won the ERA title (1.98), while Boise's **Mike Butler** led in wins (9). Eugene first baseman **Larry Sutton** was league MVP (.311-15-88). Yakima outfielder **Sandy Martinez** hit .333 for the batting title.

FINAL STANDINGS

North Division			
Bellingham	43-33	.566	—
Yakima	36-40	.474	7
Everett	35-41	.461	8
Spokane	32-44	.421	11
South Division			
Bend	43-33	.566	—
Boise	40-36	.526	3
So Oregon	39-37	.513	4
Eugene	36-40	.474	7

Playoffs

Bellingham 2, Bend 0

 # Switch-hitter

** Left-handed*

(Players in major leagues are listed with last minor league team.)

PITCHING	W	L	ERA	G	SV	IP	H	BB	SO
Mike Birkbeck	4	10	4.08	21	0	117	108	31	101
Tim Bogar	0	0	12.00	3	0	3	4	3	1
Doug Cinnella	0	3	3.81	10	0	28.1	29	16	15
Mark Dewey	5	7	4.31	43	9	54.1	61	18	55
*Todd Douma	0	1	11.70	6	0	10	14	8	3
Frank Eufemia	1	3	3.64	11	0	30.2	32	6	13
Tom Filer	1	7	2.78	18	0	100.1	106	28	47
*Paul Gibson	0	0	3.00	2	0	3	3	2	1
*Eric Hillman	9	2	3.65	34	0	91.1	93	27	49
*Randy Marshall	7	13	4.04	26	0	152.2	170	31	87
Brad Moore	6	6	5.45	50	6	79.1	80	52	55
*Hipolito Pena	0	0	3.91	18	2	23	17	17	15
Dale Plummer	4	0	3.57	31	2	58	59	19	29
Chris Rauth	5	7	5.12	26	0	121.1	132	44	72
*Pete Schourek	2	5	2.73	8	0	53.2	46	23	42
Dave Telgheder	6	14	4.21	28	0	169	173	36	118
Julio Valera	1	0	0.00	1	0	6	5	2	7
Julian Vasquez	1	4	5.56	20	6	23.2	22	8	22
Tom Wegmann	2	3	4.42	7	0	37.2	38	17	38

Toledo Mud Hens (Tigers) AAA

BATTING	Avg.	AB	R	H	2B	3B	HR	RBI	SB
*Karl Allaire, 3b	.255	479	68	122	18	1	6	45	11
*Rico Brogna, 1b	.261	387	45	101	19	4	10	58	1
#John Cangelosi, of	.270	74	9	20	3	0	0	6	10
*Steve Carter, of	.300	470	56	141	22	2	9	58	12
Phil Clark, of	.280	271	29	76	20	0	10	39	4
Dean Decillis, dh	.246	268	23	66	7	0	2	16	0
Pedro Gonzalez, c	.118	17	1	2	2	0	0	0	0
*Shawn Hare, of	.330	203	31	67	12	2	5	34	6
Jody Hurst, of	.186	145	16	27	2	1	3	17	4
Riccardo Ingram, of	.251	410	45	103	15	6	8	41	8
Johnny Paredes, of	.193	83	6	16	1	0	2	5	3
#Gary Pettis, of	.171	35	5	6	0	0	0	3	5
*Marty Pevey, c	.301	136	16	41	6	0	3	16	1
#Bob Reimink, 3b	.328	58	8	19	3	0	0	2	1
Rod Robertson, 3b	.207	222	23	46	6	1	5	22	8
Victor Rosario, ss	.202	337	26	68	9	1	2	16	6
Rich Rowland, c	.235	473	75	111	19	1	25	82	9
#Greg Smith, 2b	.234	445	56	104	15	3	7	46	24
*Greg Sparks, 1b	.181	72	6	13	1	0	2	4	0

PITCHING	W	L	ERA	G	SV	IP	H	BB	SO
*Scott Aldred	4	6	5.13	16	0	86	92	47	81
Don August	0	2	8.59	5	0	15.2	25	7	6
William Brennan	0	4	8.10	12	1	27.2	29	23	28
*Tony Castillo	2	3	3.63	12	2	45.2	48	14	24
*Sherm Corbett	0	0	5.89	10	0	18.1	21	12	12
Steve Cummings	0	2	8.10	5	0	20	26	8	6
John Desilva	0	3	8.53	7	0	19	26	8	21
Dan Gakeler	0	1	7.11	3	0	13.2	14	4	11
Greg Gohr	8	10	3.99	22	0	131.2	124	46	94
*Frank Gonzales	4	6	4.30	18	0	98.1	100	36	65
*Buddy Groom	7	7	2.80	16	0	109.1	102	23	71
David Haas	9	8	4.18	22	0	149.2	149	53	112
Dave Johnson	4	4	4.27	25	3	53.2	60	17	29
*Jeff Kaiser	1	0	2.35	28	5	31.2	25	12	33
John Kiely	1	1	2.84	21	9	32.2	25	7	31
Eric King	1	2	5.63	3	0	16	22	2	12
Doug Kline	2	1	4.08	27	1	46.1	34	21	38
Kurt Knudsen	3	1	2.08	12	1	22.2	11	6	19
*Vance Lovelace	2	0	3.20	15	0	25.1	28	21	22
*Jamie Moyer	10	8	2.86	21	0	139.2	128	37	80
Ron Rightnowar	3	2	6.16	34	3	57	68	18	33
Jeff Robinson	1	2	8.04	13	1	16.2	21	8	15
Mike Walker	2	8	5.83	42	4	79.2	102	44	44
Steve Wolf	2	0	3.12	3	0	17.1	16	13	18

Pacific Coast League

Albuquerque Dukes (Dodgers) AAA

BATTING	Avg.	AB	R	H	2B	3B	HR	RBI	SB
Dave Anderson, ss	.321	53	9	17	1	1	0	5	2
Billy Ashley, of	.211	95	11	20	7	0	2	10	1
Bryan Baar, c	.257	74	6	19	8	0	1	11	0
Tony Barron, of	.301	286	40	86	18	2	6	33	6
Rafael Bournigal, ss	.324	395	47	128	18	1	0	34	5
Jerry Brooks, of	.266	467	77	124	36	1	14	78	3
*Adam Brown, ph	.444	9	3	4	1	0	1	3	0
*Tom Goodwin, of	.301	319	48	96	10	4	2	28	27
Jeff Hamilton, 3b	.302	159	21	48	12	0	5	30	0
Matt Howard, 2b	.293	116	14	34	3	0	0	8	1
Luis Martinez, ph	.281	171	27	48	7	1	1	18	3
Raul Mondesi, of	.312	138	23	43	4	7	4	15	2
*Chris Morrow, of	.284	67	6	19	2	1	1	7	1
#Jose Munoz, 3b	.304	450	48	137	20	3	2	45	7
#Julio Peguero, of	.263	76	13	20	4	0	1	8	1
Mike Piazza, c	.341	358	54	122	22	5	16	69	1
Eddie Pye, 3b	.302	222	30	67	11	2	1	25	6
*Henry Rodriguez, 1b	.304	365	59	111	21	5	14	72	1
*Brian Traxler, 1b	.303	393	58	119	26	4	11	58	1
Don Wakamatsu, c	.323	167	22	54	10	0	2	15	0
Eric Young, 2b	.337	350	61	118	16	5	3	49	28

PITCHING	W	L	ERA	G	SV	IP	H	BB	SO
Pedro Astacio	6	6	5.47	24	0	99.2	115	44	66
*Hector Berrios	1	2	4.38	15	0	12.1	10	11	12
*Jason Brosnan	0	0	8.31	8	1	9.2	13	4	12
Albert Bustillos	1	2	4.78	26	3	38.2	41	16	23
*Omar Daal	0	2	7.84	12	0	10.1	14	11	9
Balvino Galvez	5	3	3.09	30	0	44.2	32	20	28
Kip Gross	6	5	3.51	31	8	108.2	96	36	58
*Grady Hall	0	0	8.38	12	0	10.2	21	5	3
Greg Hansell	1	5	5.24	13	0	69.2	84	35	38
Brian Holton	2	3	5.75	29	1	41.2	50	13	28
Mike James	2	1	5.59	18	1	47.2	55	22	33
Pedro Martinez	7	6	3.81	20	0	125.1	104	57	124
Jamie McAndrew	1	3	5.83	5	0	29.1	41	14	9
Lance McCullers	4	1	1.84	29	12	44	34	10	35
*Mark Mimbs	0	4	6.10	12	0	49.2	58	19	32
Jim Neidlinger	8	9	4.39	34	0	146.2	153	45	81
Chris Nichting	1	3	7.93	10	0	42	64	23	25
Dan Opperman	2	3	3.60	6	0	25	25	12	15
*Steve Searcy	3	6	6.48	12	0	58.1	79	31	40
Zak Shinall	13	5	3.29	64	6	82	91	37	46
Dennis Springer	2	7	5.66	11	0	62	70	22	36
Mike Wilkins	0	2	3.57	46	1	88.1	89	30	63

Calgary Cannons (Mariners) AAA

BATTING	Avg.	AB	R	H	2B	3B	HR	RBI	SB
Rich Amaral, ss	.318	403	79	128	21	8	0	21	53
Kent Anderson, ss	.226	208	36	47	6	0	0	15	6
Mike Blowers, 3b	.317	300	56	95	28	2	9	67	2
#Frank Bolick, 3b	.288	274	35	79	18	6	14	54	4
Bret Boone, 2b	.314	439	73	138	26	5	13	73	17
*Jim Bowie, 1b	.238	172	17	41	6	0	1	17	3
*Dave Brundage, of	.241	315	44	76	15	3	1	35	7
Mario Diaz, ss	.269	52	8	14	4	0	0	11	1
*Benny Distefano, 1b	.291	110	13	32	6	2	0	15	1
Bill Haselman, c	.255	302	49	77	14	2	19	53	3
*Bert Heffernan, c	.304	46	8	14	2	0	1	4	1
Chris Howard, c	.238	319	29	76	16	0	8	45	3
*Dann Howitt, of	.299	318	54	95	22	6	7	60	9
Pat Lennon, of	.354	48	8	17	3	0	1	9	4
*Mike McDonald, of	.239	46	3	11	2	0	1	4	0
#John Moses, of	.254	248	41	63	15	4	2	31	5
Greg Pirkl, 1b	.266	286	30	76	21	3	6	32	4
Alonzo Powell, of	.343	35	7	12	1	1	1	7	0

Class A WRAPUPS

South Atlantic League

After setting a new league record with five pitchers reaching double figures in wins, the Myrtle Beach Hurricanes swept Charleston, W. Va., in the finals. Myrtle Beach's left-hander **Travis Baptist** was 11-2 and led the minors in ERA (1.44), but Pitcher of the Year honors went to teammate **Paul Spoljaric** (10-8, 2.62) who struck out 161 in 165 innings, allowing just 111 hits. The Hurricanes' **Gregg Martin** led the league with 27 saves. The win and strike-out titles went to, respectively, Greensboro's **Keith Garagozzo** (14) and Savannah's **Jason Hisey** (182). **Ben Blomdahl** of Fayetteville pitched a perfect game on June 4, beating Spartanburg 1-0. Asheville outfielder **Gary Mota** was league MVP (.291-24-90), while Columbia second baseman **Quilvio Veras** won the batting title (.319) and led all minor-leaguers with 66 stolen bases.

FINAL STANDINGS

Northern Division

Columbia	79-59	.572	—
x-Chstn, WV	77-64	.548	3.5
Asheville	74-66	.529	6
Grnsboro	74-67	.525	6.5
Fayetteville	74-67	.525	6.5
y-Spartnbrg	70-68	.507	9
Gastonia	66-70	.485	12

Southern Division

x-Columbs	77-62	.554	—
y-Myrt Bch	71-65	.522	4.5
Albany	72-70	.507	6.5
Augusta	67-74	.475	11
Savannah	62-78	.443	15.5
Macon	58-81	.417	19
Chstn, SC	55-85	.393	22.5

x-won first half; y-won second half

Playoffs

First round: Charleston WV 2, Sptnburg 0; Myrt Bch 2, Clmbs 0

Finals: Myrt Bch 3, Charleston 0

Class A WRAPUPS

Florida State League

Dunedin catcher **Carlos Delgado** became only the third player in the 56-year history of the league to hit 30 home runs and just the fifth to hit three in one game. Named *Baseball Weekly*'s Minor League Player of the Year and league MVP, Delgado just missed the Triple Crown. His 100 RBI led the league, but teammate **Rob Butler** bettered his .324 average with .358. Osceola second baseman **James Mouton** paced the league with 50 stolen bases, and teammate **Chris Hill** led in wins (16). Yankee phenom **Brien Taylor** of Fort Lauderdale lived up to his advance press, leading the league in strikeouts (187). West Palm Beach's **Tavo Alvarez** was the ERA champion (1.49).

FINAL STANDINGS

East Division			
x-W.P. Bch	76-61	.555	—
y-St. Lucie	74-62	.544	1.5
Fort Laud	59-76	.437	16
Vero Bch	53-82	.393	22
Central Division			
Bball Cty	71-60	.542	—
x-Osceola	72-62	.537	0.5
y-Lakeland	70-62	.530	1.5
Winter Hvn	51-86	.372	23
West Division			
x-Sarasota	85-48	.639	—
y-Dunedin	78-59	.569	9
Clearwater	75-59	.560	10.5
Charlotte	73-62	.541	13
St. Petrsbrg	57-76	.429	28
Miracle	46-85	.351	38

x-won first half; y-won second half

Playoffs

First round: Baseball City 2, Sarasota 0;
Clearwater 2, Dunedin 0;
Lakeland 2, West Palm Beach 0;
Osceola 2, St. Lucie 1
Second round: Lakeland 2, Clearwater 0;
Baseball City 2, Osceola 1
Finals: Lakeland 2, Baseball City 0

BATTING	Avg.	AB	R	H	2B	3B	HR	RBI	SB
Jeff Schaefer, ss	.300	40	4	12	1	0	1	5	1
#Will Taylor, of	.193	83	8	16	0	1	0	2	3
*Shane Turner, of	.281	242	31	68	17	3	0	26	10
#Omar Vizquel, ss	.273	22	0	6	1	0	0	2	0
*Jeff Wetherby, of	.245	245	28	60	9	3	3	28	5
#Ted Williams, of	.244	250	36	61	5	5	1	17	41

PITCHING	W	L	ERA	G	SV	IP	H	BB	SO
Jim Acker	0	0	3.00	2	0	3	5	0	1
*Juan Agosto	1	0	4.98	10	1	22.2	20	13	12
*Shawn Barton	3	5	4.25	30	4	53	57	24	31
*Kevin Brown	6	10	4.84	32	0	151.2	163	64	49
*Dave Brundage	0	0	6.75	5	0	7.2	7	4	5
John Costello	0	1	13.50	4	0	5.1	11	2	0
Rich DeLucia	4	2	2.45	8	1	40.1	32	14	38
*Tom Drees	7	7	5.18	17	0	92	108	37	38
Brian Fisher	0	0	1.69	2	0	5.1	6	0	1
Mark Grant	1	3	4.15	4	0	26	32	4	11
*Eric Gunderson	0	2	6.02	27	5	52.1	57	31	50
Andy Hawkins	10	9	4.87	24	0	129.1	155	49	49
Calvin Jones	2	0	3.86	21	3	33.2	23	22	32
Randy Kramer	1	4	6.05	27	1	64	87	30	30
Dave Masters	2	8	6.08	39	1	90.1	107	71	70
Jeff Nelson	1	0	0.00	2	0	4.2	0	1	0
Jim Newlin	1	1	5.77	30	3	44.2	60	29	24
Jose Nunez	1	1	5.63	10	0	38.1	42	20	29
Clay Parker	2	1	4.00	3	0	18	20	3	11
*Mike Remlinger	1	7	6.65	21	0	70.1	97	48	24
Pat Rice	3	8	8.21	21	0	83.1	133	47	27
Mike Schooler	0	0	0.00	1	0	2	2	0	0
Charles Scott	5	6	4.78	16	0	85.2	95	28	32
*Ed Vandeberg	1	3	8.93	31	3	43.1	78	17	29
Mike Walker	5	1	5.27	12	0	41	50	19	24
Kerry Woodson	1	4	3.43	10	2	21	20	12	9
Clint Zavaras	1	2	13.17	4	0	14.2	24	12	5

Colo. Springs Sky Sox (Indians) AAA

BATTING	Avg.	AB	R	H	2B	3B	HR	RBI	SB
*Mike Aldrete, 1b	.322	463	69	149	42	2	8	84	1
*Beau Allred, of	.288	434	79	125	23	10	17	76	1
*George Canale, dh	.294	163	33	48	12	2	5	31	0
Alan Cockrell, of	.236	259	31	61	6	2	7	38	0
Mark Davidson, of	.282	309	57	87	17	3	6	44	2
*Daren Epley, 1b	.264	87	9	23	8	0	0	14	0
Alvaro Espinoza, ss	.300	483	64	145	36	6	9	79	2
#Reggie Jefferson, 1b	.312	218	49	68	11	4	11	44	1
Brian Johnson, c	.281	167	24	47	13	1	1	24	0
*Wayne Kirby, of	.345	470	101	162	18	16	11	74	51
*Jesse Levis, c	.364	253	39	92	20	1	6	44	1
#Nelson Liriano, 2b	.304	362	73	110	19	9	5	51	20
Carlos Martinez, 1b	.313	32	7	10	1	0	0	5	0
Carlos Mota, c	.233	30	1	7	1	0	0	6	1
Donell Nixon, pr	.257	70	23	18	5	1	1	7	7
Tony Perezchica, 2b	.171	70	8	12	1	0	2	9	1
#Dave Rohde, 2b	.295	448	85	132	17	14	4	55	13
D.L. Smith, 3b	.242	33	6	8	2	1	1	7	0
*Jim Thome, 3b	.313	48	11	15	4	1	2	14	0
#Lee Tinsley, of	.235	81	19	19	2	1	0	4	3
Craig Worthington, 3b	.295	319	47	94	25	0	6	57	0

PITCHING	W	L	ERA	G	SV	IP	H	BB	SO
Brad Arnsberg	1	1	7.56	16	0	25	34	13	11
*Eric Bell	10	7	3.73	26	1	138.2	161	30	56
*Denis Boucher	11	4	3.48	20	0	124	119	30	40
*Jim Bruske	2	0	4.58	7	0	18.2	24	6	8
Mike Christopher	4	4	2.91	49	26	59.2	59	13	39
Terry Clark	4	4	3.77	9	0	60.2	62	13	33
Jerry Dipoto	9	9	4.94	50	2	122	148	66	62
Tom Kramer	8	3	4.88	38	3	76.2	88	43	72
*Jeff Mutis	9	9	5.08	25	0	145.1	177	57	77
Rod Nichols	3	3	5.67	9	0	54	65	16	35
*Dave Otto	3	2	2.89	6	0	44.2	35	10	11
Greg Roscoe	6	5	4.30	27	0	128.2	141	34	78

PITCHING	W	L	ERA	G	SV	IP	H	BB	SO
Scott Scudder	0	1	6.00	1	0	3	4	2	1
Jeff Shaw	10	5	4.76	25	0	155	174	45	84
Willie Smith	3	0	4.75	19	1	42.2	39	25	30
Mike Soper	0	0	6.06	10	1	16.1	26	6	16
*Terry Wells	1	0	1.17	5	0	8.2	5	2	3
*Kevin Wickander	0	0	1.64	8	2	11	4	6	18

Edmonton Trappers (Angels) AAA

BATTING	Avg.	AB	R	H	2B	3B	HR	RBI	SB
*Don Barbara, 1b	.298	396	70	118	26	1	4	63	9
*Billy Bean, of	.246	138	17	34	8	2	1	24	5
*Mick Billmeyer, c	.240	25	1	6	1	0	1	5	0
Phil Bradley, of	.299	134	26	40	8	2	1	18	5
Hubie Brooks, dh	.292	24	2	7	2	1	1	11	0
Pete Coachman, 2b	.239	209	35	50	12	2	4	28	8
Kevin Davis, 2b	.388	80	21	31	9	3	1	16	0
Damion Easley, ss	.289	429	61	124	18	3	3	44	26
*Jim Edmonds, of	.299	194	37	58	15	2	6	36	3
Kevin Flora, 2b	.324	170	35	55	8	4	3	19	9
Larry Gonzales, c	.329	237	37	78	10	0	3	47	2
Jose Gonzalez, of	.322	90	16	29	7	2	2	14	9
Ray Martinez, 2b	.302	285	42	86	20	2	3	35	6
*Walt McConnell, 3b	.265	147	21	39	9	0	1	22	1
*Oddibe McDowell, of	.214	14	1	3	1	0	0	2	0
*John Morris, of	.118	17	3	2	1	0	0	0	0
*Mike Musolino, c	.252	127	15	32	8	0	2	19	0
*Ken Oberkfell, dh	.282	202	33	57	14	2	1	34	2
John Orton, c	.255	149	28	38	9	3	3	25	3
Bob Rose, dh	.270	74	11	20	1	2	2	11	1
Tim Salmon, of	.347	409	101	142	38	4	29	105	9
Luis Sojo, 3b	.297	145	22	43	9	1	1	24	4
Fausto Tejero, c	.235	17	0	4	1	0	0	0	0
*Ty Van Burkleo, 1b	.273	458	83	125	28	7	19	88	20
Mark Wasinger, 3b	.184	103	19	19	7	1	1	11	0
#Reggie Williams, of	.272	519	96	141	25	9	3	64	44

PITCHING	W	L	ERA	G	SV	IP	H	BB	SO
Doug Bair	3	2	6.62	7	0	35.1	51	7	14
Chris Beasley	2	1	4.05	25	3	33.1	44	11	28
Bert Blyleven	2	0	6.17	2	0	12.2	16	3	7
Mike Butcher	5	2	3.07	26	4	29.1	24	18	32
Mike Erb	0	0	27.00	2	0	3.2	6	6	3
*Tim Fortugno	6	4	3.56	26	1	73.1	69	33	82
Willie Fraser	7	6	4.90	44	6	90	110	24	49
Joe Grahe	1	0	3.20	3	0	20.2	18	5	12
*Mark Holzemer	5	7	6.67	17	0	89	114	55	49
*Todd James	1	6	10.19	7	0	33.2	50	26	12
Dave Johnson	0	0	22.50	1	0	2	8	1	1
Odell Jones	0	1	5.79	5	0	9.1	10	6	8
*Joe Kraemer	1	0	4.32	34	2	42.2	42	28	32
Scott Lewis	10	6	4.17	22	0	147.2	159	40	88
Brett Merriman	1	3	1.44	22	4	31.1	31	10	15
John Pawlowski	0	1	6.35	20	0	34	51	22	18
Dana Ridenour	1	0	6.10	5	0	10.1	12	8	8
Darryl Scott	0	2	5.20	31	6	36.1	41	21	48
*Ray Searage	3	3	5.33	34	1	49	65	22	23
Ray Soff	11	9	3.89	24	0	167.2	177	65	116
Don Vidmar	0	5	6.97	16	0	72.1	98	29	35
Mark Wasinger	0	0	0.00	2	0	3	2	1	0
*Cliff Young	10	8	5.59	28	0	143.1	174	42	104
Mark Zappelli	5	3	3.65	10	0	62.2	73	28	51

Rookie League WRAPUPS

Appalachian League

The Bluefield Orioles surprised Elizabethton (49-17) in the league playoffs, beating the Twins 3-1 in the rubber game of the playoffs. A timely two-run double by the Australian outfielder **Scot Metcalf** was the difference in the game. Elizabethton skipper Ray Smith had the consolation of being named Manager of the Year. Princeton shortstop **Dan Frye** was MVP, hitting .325 while pacing the league in homers (15) and RBI (59). Huntington's **Tim Stutheit** won the batting title (.338), and Johnson City outfielder **Basil Shabazz** took the stolen base crown (41). Burlington left-hander **Mike Mathews** was 7-0 with a league-leading 1.01 ERA, while Huntington's **Amaury Talemaco** led in strikeouts (93). **Charlie Townsend** of Burlington had eight RBI in a game against Bluefield, sharing the honor for a single-game high in the minors this season.

FINAL STANDINGS

North Division			
Bluefield	37-25	.597	—
Burlington	35-31	.530	4.5
Princeton	34-31	.523	4
Huntington	28-34	.452	9
Martinsville	22-43	.338	16.5
South Division			
Elizabethtn	49-17	.742	—
Jnsn Cty	33-32	.508	15.5
Bristol	33-35	.485	17
Kingsport	27-35	.435	20
Pulaski	23-38	.377	23.5

Playoffs

Bluefield 2, Elizabethton, 1

 # Switch-hitter
** Left-handed*
(Players in major leagues are listed with last minor league team.)

Rookie League WRAPUPS

Arizona League

Two pitchers led the Athletics in their ride to a first-place finish. **William Urbina** tied for the league high in wins with 7, while **Stacy Hollins** was strikeout king with 93 whiffs. **Jeff Martin** of the Giants tied Urbina with 7 wins, while the Giants' staff combined for the best team ERA (2.87). Teammate **Bolivar Rivera** led the league with 30 stolen bases. The individual ERA title went to **Frankie Rodriguez** of the Brewers (1.10). Teammate **Kirk Demyan** led the league with 11 saves. Brewers' skipper **Tommy Jones** was Manager of the Year. Cardinals shortstop **Brian Rupp** topped all short-season minor-leaguers with his .385 average and also won the RBI title. The Mariners led the league with a .275 average and also had three pitchers with ERAs below 2.00—**Greg Theron** (1.26), **John VanHof** (1.29), and **Robin Cope** (1.93).

FINAL STANDINGS			
Athletics	34-22	.607	—
Mariners	32-24	.571	2
Giants	32-24	.571	2
Brewers	31-25	.554	3
Angels	29-27	.518	5
Cardinals	28-28	.500	6
Padres	20-36	.357	14
Rockies/Cubs	18-38	.321	16

 # Switch-hitter
** Left-handed*
(Players in major leagues are listed with last minor league team.)

Las Vegas Stars (Padres) AAA

BATTING	Avg.	AB	R	H	2B	3B	HR	RBI	SB
Mike Basso, c	.218	55	2	12	1	1	0	1	0
Dann Bilardello, dh	.192	26	2	5	1	0	1	2	0
Scott Coolbaugh, 3b	.241	199	30	48	13	2	8	39	0
Butch Davis, ph	.000	1	0	1	0	0	0	0	0
Paul Faries, 3b	.293	457	77	134	15	6	1	40	28
*Jeff Gardner, 2b	.335	439	82	147	30	5	1	51	7
Ricky Gutierrez, 2b	.167	6	0	1	0	0	0	1	0
*Kevin Higgins, of	.254	355	49	90	12	3	0	40	6
Chris Jelic, of	.227	203	34	46	8	3	2	19	4
*Tom Lampkin, c	.306	340	45	104	17	4	3	48	15
#Luis Lopez, ss	.233	395	44	92	8	8	1	31	6
Steve Pegues, of	.263	376	51	99	21	4	9	56	12
Benito Santiago, c	.308	13	3	4	0	0	1	2	0
*Darrell Sherman, of	.286	269	48	77	8	1	3	22	26
Dave Staton, of	.281	335	47	94	20	0	19	76	0
*Phil Stephenson, of	.332	205	51	68	10	2	8	43	1
Jim Vatcher, of	.275	280	41	77	15	3	8	35	2
*Guillermo Velasquez, 1b	.309	512	68	158	44	4	7	99	3
Dan Walters, c	.394	127	16	50	9	0	2	25	0
Matt Witkowski, 2b	.188	16	1	3	0	1	0	0	0

PITCHING	W	L	ERA	G	SV	IP	H	BB	SO
Mike Basso	0	0	0.00	2	0	2	0	0	0
Doug Brocail	10	10	3.97	29	0	172.1	187	63	103
Terry Bross	7	3	3.26	49	0	86.2	83	30	42
*Renay Bryand	0	0	9.00	6	0	8	12	3	5
Rick Davis	3	3	3.22	33	9	45.2	49	9	31
*Jim Deshaies	6	3	4.03	18	1	58	60	17	46
Dave Eiland	4	5	5.23	14	0	64.2	78	11	31
Gene Harris	0	2	3.67	18	4	34.1	36	16	35
Greg Harris	2	0	0.56	2	0	16	8	1	15
Jeremy Hernandez	2	4	2.91	42	11	56.2	53	20	38
Kevin Higgins	0	1	6.75	3	0	3.2	4	2	0
Linty Ingram	0	0	9.00	2	0	6	8	5	5
Mark Knudson	11	7	4.47	37	3	147	184	47	79
*Pat Perry	0	0	6.39	16	0	13.2	19	1	1
Adam Peterson	6	3	3.75	21	0	101.2	99	37	67
A.J. Sager	1	7	7.95	30	1	60	89	17	40
Scott Sanders	3	6	5.50	14	0	72	97	31	51
Erik Schullstrom	1	0	0.00	1	0	5	3	3	4
Tim Scott	1	2	2.25	24	15	28	20	3	28
Frank Seminara	6	4	4.13	13	0	81.2	92	33	48
Rafael Valdez	2	0	6.14	8	0	15.2	19	7	12
*Don Vesling	0	0	5.06	8	0	5.1	7	9	4
*Pat Wernig	0	0	8.74	17	1	11.1	10	6	7
Dean Wilkins	0	1	7.43	8	0	13.1	16	9	9
Brian Wood	0	0	8.03	7	0	12.1	17	10	12
Tim Worrell	4	2	4.26	10	0	63.1	61	19	32
Mike York	5	7	4.79	19	0	88.1	96	55	54

Phoenix Firebirds (Giants) AAA

BATTING	Avg.	AB	R	H	2B	3B	HR	RBI	SB
#Mark Bailey, c	.310	87	15	27	4	0	6	23	0
Mike Benjamin, ss	.306	108	15	33	9	2	0	17	3
Joel Chimelis, 3b	.303	185	26	56	9	3	1	23	1
Royce Clayton, ss	.240	192	30	46	6	2	3	18	15
Craig Colbert, 3b	.321	140	16	45	8	1	1	12	0
#Jamie Cooper, of	.223	197	23	44	4	2	0	9	25
#Todd Crosby, 2b	.167	36	3	6	1	1	0	1	0
Ron Crowe, of	.192	26	1	5	1	0	0	0	0
Matt Davis, ss	.292	24	3	7	1	0	0	4	0
Steve Decker, c	.282	450	50	127	22	2	8	74	2
Dave Hengel, ph	.127	55	1	7	2	0	0	6	0
Steve Hosey, of	.286	462	64	132	28	7	10	65	15
Erik Johnson, ss	.240	229	24	55	5	1	0	19	8
*Mark Leonard, of	.338	139	17	47	4	1	5	25	1
*Dan Lewis, 1b	.270	244	32	66	15	2	10	41	0
Darren Lewis, of	.228	158	22	36	5	2	0	6	9
Greg Litton, 3b	.306	85	14	26	7	0	4	19	0

BATTING	Avg.	AB	R	H	2B	3B	HR	RBI	SB
*Jim McNamara, c	.209	67	5	14	3	0	0	3	0
*Rob Nelson, 1b	.214	234	35	50	11	0	10	28	1
Dave Patterson, 3b	.256	367	34	94	13	6	0	35	6
#John Patterson, 2b	.301	362	52	109	20	6	2	37	22
Reed Peters, of	.288	59	10	17	2	0	1	4	0
*Gregg Ritchie, of	.268	183	25	49	5	2	1	13	11
*Reuben Smiley, of	.216	37	5	8	3	0	0	2	0
Andres Thomas, ss	.270	115	10	31	8	1	1	11	3
*Ted Wood, of	.304	418	70	127	24	7	7	63	9

PITCHING	W	L	ERA	G	SV	IP	H	BB	SO
Johnny Ard	5	8	4.46	22	0	113	130	69	56
*Bud Black	2	0	0.86	3	0	21	21	5	7
Greg Brummett	0	1	7.71	3	0	5.2	8	1	2
Dave Burba	5	5	4.72	13	0	74.1	86	24	44
Larry Carter	11	6	4.37	28	0	185.1	188	62	126
Scott Garrelts	0	2	8.49	4	0	12.2	14	5	7
*Jerry Don Gleaton	1	1	3.26	15	0	19.1	22	4	11
Gil Heredia	5	5	2.01	22	1	81.2	83	13	37
Rick Huisman	3	2	2.41	9	0	56	45	24	44
Dave Masters	2	8	5.49	26	1	79.2	92	59	63
Paul McClellan	2	6	5.88	20	1	64.1	85	21	43
Craig McMurtry	5	8	4.23	40	1	130.2	140	59	83
Jim Myers	0	4	5.70	25	10	24.2	32	13	11
Francisco Oliveras	3	2	3.38	22	0	61.1	51	21	26
*Jim Pena	7	3	4.15	33	1	39	45	20	27
Dan Rambo	1	2	5.93	20	1	41	47	15	32
Pat Rapp	7	8	3.05	39	3	121	115	40	79
Steve Reed	0	1	3.48	29	20	31	27	10	30
*Gregg Ritchie	0	0	4.50	1	0	2	4	2	0
*Kevin Rogers	3	3	4.00	11	0	70.2	63	22	62
Rob Taylor	4	1	2.40	20	0	30	33	10	28
Randy Veres	0	2	8.10	12	1	13.1	14	13	13

Portland Beavers (Twins) AAA

BATTING	Avg.	AB	R	H	2B	3B	HR	RBI	SB
Bernardo Brito, dh	.270	564	80	152	27	7	26	96	0
Jarvis Brown, of	.250	224	25	56	8	2	2	16	17
*J.T. Bruett, of	.250	280	41	70	10	3	0	17	29
Cheo Garcia, ph	.333	6	0	2	0	0	0	0	0
Shawn Gilbert, ss	.245	444	60	109	17	2	3	52	30
*Chip Hale, 2b	.285	474	77	135	24	8	1	53	3
*Keith Hughes, of	.271	221	37	60	11	3	5	26	6
Terry Jorgensen, 3b	.295	505	78	149	32	2	14	71	2
*Jay Kvasnicka, of	.163	80	12	13	1	1	0	5	4
Terry Lee, 1b	.283	367	68	104	22	2	6	56	8
Dave McCarty, of	.500	26	7	13	2	0	1	8	1
Ed Naveda, of	.243	374	34	91	20	0	3	31	2
*Ray Ortiz, of	.328	134	17	44	12	1	3	22	0
Derek Parks, c	.245	249	33	61	12	0	12	49	0
#Luis Quinones, 3b	.243	276	45	67	7	4	12	49	1
Jeff Reboulet, ss	.286	161	21	46	11	1	2	21	3
Danny Sheaffer, c	.276	442	54	122	23	4	5	56	3
Joe Siwa, c	.000	4	0	0	0	0	0	0	0

PITCHING	W	L	ERA	G	SV	IP	H	BB	SO
Paul Abbott	4	1	2.33	7	0	46.1	30	31	46
Willie Banks	6	1	1.92	11	0	75	62	34	41
*Larry Casian	4	0	2.32	58	11	62	54	13	43
Mike Dyer	7	6	5.06	27	1	105	119	56	85
Mauro Gozzo	10	9	3.35	37	1	156.2	155	50	108
*Keith Hughes	0	0	4.50	2	0	2	2	2	0
Greg Johnson	2	5	4.73	53	10	51.1	65	27	44
Curt Leskanic	1	2	9.98	5	0	15.1	16	8	14
Orlando Lind	3	3	4.68	47	2	85.2	87	38	77
Pat Mahomes	9	5	3.41	17	1	111	97	43	87
Mike Schwabe	1	2	8.02	6	0	21.1	32	11	9
Mike Trombley	10	8	3.65	25	0	167	149	58	138
*George Tsamis	13	4	3.90	39	1	164.2	195	51	71
Rob Wassenaar	6	8	3.50	60	5	90	96	33	60
*Gary Wayne	0	1	2.35	14	5	23	23	1	20
*David West	7	6	4.43	19	0	102.2	88	65	87

Rookie League WRAPUPS

Pioneer League

Hometown hero **Jason Kummerfeldt** (8-0, 2.38 ERA) led the Billings Mustangs in a two-game sweep of Salt Lake for the championship title, pitching a complete-game four-hitter in the series opener. Second baseman **Dee Jenkins** hit .600 in the playoffs for Billings and led the club at .336 during the regular season. Teammate **Rich Langford** topped the league with 95 strikeouts. Outfielder/DH **Micah Franklin** batted in 60 runs, sharing the RBI title with Salt Lake's **Kevin McMullan**. Billings rookie skipper **Donnie Scott** was Manager of the Year. Salt Lake's **Tim Clark** won the batting title at .357, and teammate **George Kerfut** led in wins (10). Helena outfielder **Kenny Felder** and shortstop **Tim Unroe** were home run kings with 15 each. Teammate **Scott Karl** had the best ERA (1.46). Medicine Hat suffered through an 18-game losing streak, worst in the minors this year, and the Pioneer League saw three games in August postponed due to snow.

FINAL STANDINGS			
Northern Division			
Billings	53-23	.697	—
Great Falls	38-35	.521	13.5
Lethbridge	24-50	.324	28
Medcn Hat	23-52	.307	29.5
Southern Division			
Salt Lake	53-23	697	—
Helena	49-26	.653	3.5
Butte	33-42	.440	19.5
Idaho Falls	27-49	.355	26
Playoffs			
Billings 2, Salt Lake 0			

 # Switch-hitter
** Left-handed*
(Players in major leagues are listed with last minor league team.)

Rookie League WRAPUPS

Gulf Coast League

The Royals edged the Expos in the rubber game of the playoffs when non-drafted free agent **Rick Burley** pitched seven shutout innings and first-round draft pick **Jim Pittsley** struck out all six batters he faced in relief. The Royals were led by outfielder **Johnny Damon** who hit .349 and had 23 stolen bases. The Marlins had the best winning streak in the minors this year with 14 straight victories. **Juan Thomas** of the White Sox and **Chris Burr** of the Rangers each hit six round-trippers to share the home run title, while Burr led the league with 47 RBI. **Edgar Herrera** of the Twins won the batting title (.351). **Shannon Stewart** of the Blue Jays led the league in stolen bases (31), and teammate **Bart Rich** led in saves (16). **Fernando Dasilva** of the Expos had the most wins (10) and strikeouts (86), while **Jeff Cindrich** of the Yankees had the best ERA (0.80).

FINAL STANDINGS			
Eastern Division			
Expos	35-24	.593	—
Dodgers	32-27	.542	3
Mets	29-30	.492	6
Braves	22-37	.373	13
Central Division			
Royals	41-18	.695	—
Marlins	33-27	.550	8.5
Astros	27-33	.450	14.5
Red Sox	18-41	.305	23
Western Division			
Blue Jays	35-24	.593	—
Yankees	31-28	.525	4
Twins	30-28	.517	4.5
White Sox	30-29	.508	5
Orioles	29-29	.500	5.5
Rangers	28-31	.475	7
Pirates	23-37	.383	12.5

Playoffs

First round: Expos 1, Blue Jays 0

Finals: Royals 2, Expos 1

Tacoma Tigers (Athletics) AAA

BATTING	Avg.	AB	R	H	2B	3B	HR	RBI	SB
Kurt Abbott, ss	.154	39	2	6	1	0	0	1	1
Lance Blankenship, 2b	.158	19	3	3	0	0	1	5	0
Jorge Brito, c	.143	35	4	5	2	0	0	1	0
Scott Brosius, 3b	.237	236	29	56	13	0	9	31	8
#Jerry Browne, 2b	.412	17	1	7	1	1	0	3	0
James Buccheri, of	.299	127	24	38	6	3	0	13	10
#Jeff Carter, of	.269	379	60	102	14	5	1	36	22
#Eric Fox, of	.198	121	16	24	3	1	1	7	5
Webster Garrison, 3b	.241	116	15	28	5	1	2	17	1
*Dan Grunhard, of	.266	267	38	71	15	3	5	29	5
Mike Heath, c	.209	234	17	49	6	1	2	22	1
Scott Hemond, 2b	.242	33	6	8	3	0	0	3	1
Dave Henderson, of	.182	11	0	2	0	0	0	1	0
*Orsino Hill, of	.246	378	56	93	25	4	6	44	5
*Mike Kingery, of	.306	363	44	111	18	4	1	37	8
*Keith Lockhart, 2b	.278	363	44	101	24	3	5	37	5
Henry Mercedes, c	.232	246	36	57	9	2	0	20	1
Islay Molina, c	.194	36	3	7	0	1	0	5	1
*Troy Neel, dh	.351	396	61	139	36	3	17	74	2
Craig Paquette, 3b	.273	66	10	18	7	0	2	11	3
Gus Polidor, ss	.278	363	23	101	16	0	1	43	4
Jack Smith, ss	.251	287	44	72	12	0	6	41	3
#Walt Weiss, ss	.231	13	2	3	1	0	0	3	0
*Ron Witmeyer, 1b	.236	499	55	118	25	2	5	54	5

PITCHING	W	L	ERA	G	SV	IP	H	BB	SO
*Dana Allison	2	3	4.84	19	0	45.2	63	17	17
Jeff Bittiger	3	3	2.72	9	0	46.1	51	28	24
John Briscoe	2	5	5.88	33	0	78	78	68	66
Kevin Campbell	2	2	4.05	10	0	13.1	16	8	14
Steve Chitren	4	7	6.82	29	0	62	64	46	37
Jim Corsi	0	0	1.23	26	12	29.1	22	10	21
*Johnny Guzman	3	6	5.11	20	0	69.2	70	24	45
Reggie Harris	6	16	5.71	29	0	150.2	141	117	111
Orsino Hill	0	0	6.00	2	0	3	4	2	1
Dave Latter	0	1	3.38	5	0	11.2	9	13	5
Keith Millay	0	0	14.73	2	0	4.2	5	6	3
*Jeff Musselman	7	7	3.50	19	0	105.1	100	40	75
Troy Neel	0	0	6.75	3	0	4	8	4	0
*Gavin Osteen	0	2	10.05	4	0	14.1	21	13	7
Tim Peek	4	3	2.98	57	3	88.2	87	37	52
*Mike Raczka	0	1	3.51	31	1	49.2	38	24	26
Dave Schmidt	5	4	4.41	27	4	69.1	75	20	43
Joe Slusarski	2	4	3.77	11	0	57.1	67	18	26
Jack Smith	0	0	6.00	2	0	3	2	0	0
Tim Smith	1	1	7.15	2	0	11.1	10	4	7
Todd Van Poppel	4	2	3.97	9	0	45.1	44	35	29
Bruce Walton	8	2	2.77	35	8	81.1	76	21	59
Weston Weber	4	5	4.12	52	2	94	95	53	51
*Bill Wilkinson	0	3	10.00	8	0	18	26	19	11
*Ron Witmeyer	0	0	9.00	1	0	2	2	2	1
*David Zancanaro	2	11	4.26	23	0	106.2	108	75	47

Tucson Toros (Astros) AAA

BATTING	Avg.	AB	R	H	2B	3B	HR	RBI	SB
Don Angotti, ph	.000	1	0	0	0	0	0	0	0
*Rod Booker, ss	.254	283	37	72	6	2	1	21	6
Mickey Brantley, of	.224	156	21	35	8	2	1	23	1
Andujar Cedeno, ss	.293	280	27	82	18	4	6	56	6
Gary Cooper, 3b	.300	464	66	139	31	3	9	73	8
Kevin Dean, of	.219	73	8	16	4	1	1	4	2
*Luis Gonzalez, of	.432	44	11	19	4	2	1	9	4
Trent Hubbard, 2b	.310	420	69	130	16	4	2	33	34
Chris Jones, of	.324	170	25	55	9	8	3	28	7
Barry Lyons, c	.300	277	32	83	24	0	4	45	1
John Massarelli, of	.238	143	21	34	4	0	0	6	14
Joe Mikulik, of	.248	161	22	40	10	3	1	18	1
Orlando Miller, ss	.243	37	4	9	0	0	2	8	0
Andy Mota, 2b	.240	317	33	76	14	6	3	32	7
Rick Parker, dh	.323	319	51	103	10	11	4	38	20

BATTING	Avg.	AB	R	H	2B	3B	HR	RBI	SB
*Karl Rhodes, of	.289	332	62	96	16	10	2	54	8
*Ernest Riles, 1b	.307	202	37	62	17	3	1	35	2
Mike Simms, of	.282	404	73	114	22	6	11	75	7
*Eddie Taubensee, c	.338	74	13	25	8	1	1	10	0
Scooter Tucker, c	.302	288	36	87	15	1	1	29	5
#Gerald Young, of	.311	74	15	23	2	1	0	2	13

PITCHING	W	L	ERA	G	SV	IP	H	BB	SO
Willie Blair	4	4	2.39	21	2	53.2	50	12	35
Ryan Bowen	7	6	4.12	21	0	122.1	128	64	94
Mike Capel	6	6	2.19	58	18	82.1	68	36	70
Chris Gardner	6	9	5.69	20	0	111.2	141	63	49
Jason Grimsley	8	7	5.05	26	0	125.2	152	55	90
*Dean Hartgraves	0	1	24.75	5	0	8	26	9	6
*Keith Helton	0	0	9.00	2	0	4	7	0	1
*Bob Hurta	3	1	2.61	20	0	21.2	14	17	22
Todd Jones	0	1	4.50	3	0	4	1	10	4
Jeff Juden	9	10	4.04	26	0	147	149	71	120
Darryl Kile	4	1	3.99	9	0	56.1	50	32	43
*Rob Mallicoat	1	3	2.32	37	3	50.1	36	21	53
Shane Reynolds	9	8	3.68	25	1	142	156	34	106
*Rich Scheid	3	5	2.63	41	1	92.1	78	51	58
Richie Simon	0	1	5.03	9	1	20.2	26	11	12
Matt Turner	2	8	3.51	63	14	100	93	40	84
Dave Veres	2	3	5.30	29	0	53.2	60	17	46
Donne Wall	0	0	1.13	2	0	8	11	1	2
Brian Williams	6	1	4.50	12	0	70	78	26	58
*Rodney Windes	1	1	4.93	20	1	35.2	44	14	28

Vancouver Canadians (WhiteSox) AAA

BATTING	Avg.	AB	R	H	2B	3B	HR	RBI	SB
Shawn Abner, of	.266	79	12	21	4	1	0	2	2
Esteban Beltre, ss	.267	161	17	43	5	2	0	16	4
Darrin Campbell, c	.152	46	6	7	4	0	0	3	0
Ron Coomer, 3b	.237	262	29	62	10	0	9	40	3
Chris Cron, 1b	.278	500	76	139	29	0	16	81	12
Drew Denson, dh	.276	340	43	94	7	3	13	70	1
#Lindsay Foster, ss	.667	3	0	2	0	0	0	1	0
#Brian Guinn, ss	.270	89	14	24	5	1	0	4	0
Joe Hall, 3b	.283	367	46	104	19	7	6	56	11
Mike Huff, of	.250	4	1	1	0	0	0	0	0
Scott Jaster, of	.267	60	8	16	2	2	1	8	2
*Shawn Jeter, of	.301	379	61	114	18	5	2	34	26
Tracy Jones, of	.283	219	30	62	9	1	1	23	4
Brad Komminsk, of	.275	415	72	114	24	7	10	68	9
*Derek Lee, of	.273	381	58	104	20	6	7	50	17
*Ever Magallanes, ss	.230	243	32	56	9	3	3	23	2
#Norberto Martin, 2b	.288	497	72	143	12	7	0	29	29
*Matt Merullo, c	.178	45	2	8	1	1	1	4	0
*Warren Newson, of	.254	59	7	15	0	0	0	9	3
Erik Pappas, c	.276	98	17	27	4	0	4	17	4
Nelson Santovenia, c	.263	281	24	74	16	0	6	42	0
Eric Yelding, of	.263	338	47	89	11	5	0	29	32

PITCHING	W	L	ERA	G	SV	IP	H	BB	SO
Rodney Bolton	11	9	2.93	27	0	187.1	174	59	111
Jeff Carter	9	6	4.92	30	0	126.1	134	56	61
Brian Drahman	2	4	2.01	48	30	58.1	44	31	34
Mike Dunne	10	6	2.78	21	0	133.2	128	46	78
Alex Fernandez	2	1	0.94	4	0	29.2	15	6	27
Ramon Garcia	9	11	3.71	28	0	170	165	56	79
Roberto Hernandez	3	3	2.61	9	2	21.2	13	11	23
*Chris Howard	3	1	2.92	20	0	25.2	18	22	23
John Hudek	8	1	3.16	39	2	85.1	69	45	61
Bo Kennedy	1	2	6.32	4	0	16.2	21	9	15
Greg Perschke	12	7	3.76	29	0	165	159	44	82
Jeff Schwarz	1	3	3.00	23	3	36	26	31	42
Ron Stephens	5	3	5.09	32	1	81.1	84	35	50
Steve Wapnick	4	2	4.42	39	1	71.1	75	48	59

Class AAA Directory

American Association

Buffalo Bisons (Pirates)
Pilot Field (capacity 19,500)
New Orleans (Brewers)
Stadium TBA
Indianapolis Indians (Reds)
Bush Stadium (12,500)
Iowa Cubs (Cubs)
Sec Taylor Stadium (7,600)
Louisville Redbirds (Cardinals)
Cardinal Stadium (33,500)
Nashville Sounds (White Sox)
Herschel Greer Stadium (18,000)
Oklahoma City 89ers (Rangers)
All-Sports Stadium (12,000)
Omaha Royals (Royals)
Rosenblatt Stadium (15,000)

 # Switch-hitter
** Left-handed*
(Players in major leagues are listed with last minor league team.)

Class AAA Directory

International League

Charlotte Knights (Indians)
Knights Castle (10,917)
Columbus Clippers (Yankees)
Harold Cooper Stadium (15,000)
Ottawa Lynx (Expos)
Multi-Purpose Recreation Complex (10,000)
Pawtucket Red Sox (Red Sox)
McCoy Stadium (6,010)
Richmond Braves (Braves)
The Diamond (12,000)
Rochester Red Wings (Orioles)
Silver Stadium (12,503)
Scranton/Wilkes-Barre Red Barons (Phillies)
Lackawanna County Stadium (10,004)
Syracuse Chiefs (Blue Jays)
MacArthur Stadium (10,500)
Tidewater Tides (Mets)
Stadium TBA (12,000)
Toledo Mud Hens (Tigers)
Ned Skeldon Stadium (10,025)

Final AA Player Stats

Eastern League

Albany-Colonie Yankees (Yankees) AA

BATTING	Avg.	AB	R	H	2B	3B	HR	RBI	SB
Brad Ausmus, c	.167	18	0	3	0	1	0	1	2
Jesse Barfield, of	.375	8	2	3	0	0	1	2	0
Richard Barnwell, of	.263	434	80	114	26	5	1	31	42
Juan Blackwell, 2b	.281	32	2	9	0	0	0	3	0
*Bubba Carpenter, of	.231	221	24	51	11	5	4	31	2
Russ Davis, 3b	.285	492	77	140	23	4	22	71	3
Robert Eenhoorn, ss	.235	196	24	46	11	2	1	23	2
Kiki Hernandez, c	.280	328	46	92	18	0	4	40	0
Pat Kelly, 2b	.000	6	1	0	0	0	0	0	0
Jay Knoblauh, of	.237	236	29	56	7	2	8	39	6
Jeff Livesey, c	.190	42	1	8	3	0	0	5	0
Lyle Mouton, of	.215	214	25	46	12	2	2	27	1
#Rey Noriega, of	.103	78	2	8	2	0	0	3	1
Sherman Obando, dh	.281	381	71	107	19	3	17	56	3
#Paul Oster, of	.209	43	8	9	1	0	0	7	1
*John Quintell, c	.143	7	0	1	0	0	0	0	0
*Jason Robertson, of	.216	204	18	44	12	1	3	33	9
#Carlos Rodriguez, ss	.260	381	37	99	18	2	2	38	3
Gordon Sanchez, c	.237	59	10	14	3	0	1	7	1
Don Sparks, 1b	.311	505	64	157	31	2	14	72	2
#Ricky Strickland, dh	.174	23	2	4	2	0	0	3	0
Hector Vargas, 2b	.300	417	64	125	26	9	1	41	25
*John Viera, of	.249	185	24	46	8	2	3	26	9
Larry Walker, c	.067	15	1	1	0	0	0	2	0

PITCHING	W	L	ERA	G	SV	IP	H	BB	SO
Richard Batchelor	4	5	4.20	58	7	71.2	79	34	45
Mark Carper	9	7	2.84	31	0	133.1	121	67	74
Doug Gogolewski	0	0	9.45	6	1	7.2	9	2	7
Ken Greer	4	1	1.83	40	4	69.2	48	30	51
*Sterling Hitchcock	6	9	2.58	24	0	147.2	116	42	156
Darren Hodges	4	7	6.05	15	0	64	78	38	43
Jeff Hoffman	6	9	4.09	35	3	121	130	37	42
*Scott Holcomb	1	2	3.18	36	1	34	21	23	45
Mark Hutton	13	7	3.59	25	0	165.1	146	66	128
Domingo Jean	0	0	2.25	1	0	4	3	3	6
Ramon Manon	1	4	5.23	8	0	33.2	34	19	22
Roberto Munoz	7	5	3.28	22	0	112.1	96	70	66
*Jerry Nielsen	3	5	1.19	36	11	53	38	15	59
*Kirt Ojala	12	8	3.62	24	0	152.2	130	80	118
Tom Popplewell	2	1	7.33	27	0	50.1	52	34	33

Binghamton Mets (Mets) AA

BATTING	Avg.	AB	R	H	2B	3B	HR	RBI	SB
#Tom Allison, ss	.248	117	19	29	4	0	2	14	1
#Chris Butterfield, 3b	.224	483	59	108	20	3	14	51	9
Joe Dellicarri, ss	.249	329	32	82	11	2	2	29	1
*Andy Dziadkowiec, c	.237	76	5	18	2	1	0	9	0
Brook Fordyce, c	.278	425	59	118	28	0	11	61	1
*Jamie Hoffner, 1b	.271	181	22	49	13	0	6	33	0
#Tim Howard, of	.273	506	69	138	20	8	5	77	12
#Bert Hunter, of	.236	407	61	96	18	4	6	35	17
*Rob Katzaroff, of	.282	450	65	127	18	7	0	29	23
#Jason King, ss	.143	28	2	4	2	0	0	3	1
*Curtis Pride, of	.227	388	53	88	15	3	10	42	12
Doug Saunders, 2b	.249	434	45	108	16	2	5	38	8
*Mike White, dh	.224	170	10	38	8	0	0	22	0
#Alan Zinter, 1b	.223	431	63	96	13	5	16	50	0

 # Switch-hitter
** Left-handed*
(Players in major leagues are listed with last minor league team.)

PITCHING	W	L	ERA	G	SV	IP	H	BB	SO
Chris Dorn	3	1	3.58	35	4	70.1	65	25	38
*Todd Douma	8	8	2.82	25	0	137	136	43	76
Denny Harriger	2	2	3.80	11	0	21.1	22	7	8
John Johnstone	7	7	3.74	24	0	149.1	132	37	121
Bobby Jones	12	4	1.88	24	0	158	118	43	144
*Greg Langbehn	5	5	3.17	52	9	71	63	41	42
Jose Martinez	5	2	1.71	9	0	58	47	13	39
Dave Proctor	0	1	23.63	1	0	3.2	8	2	1
Andy Reich	4	4	2.53	41	6	64	63	14	32
Bryan Rogers	3	2	4.33	22	1	35.1	37	7	17
Julian Vasquez	2	1	1.35	24	17	27.2	17	7	24
Joe Vitko	12	8	3.49	26	0	165	163	53	90
Pete Walker	7	12	4.12	24	0	140.2	159	46	72
Tom Wegmann	9	2	2.58	27	1	98.2	73	27	95

Canton-Akron Indians (Indians) AA

BATTING	Avg.	AB	R	H	2B	3B	HR	RBI	SB
*George Canale, 1b	.304	194	46	59	10	1	15	49	2
Carlo Colombino, 3b	.259	305	33	79	14	0	6	37	1
Craig Cooper, 1b	.151	86	5	13	5	0	1	8	0
#Terry Crowley, 3b	.264	242	16	64	6	0	0	18	3
Tom Eiterman, of	.227	181	22	41	6	1	1	18	0
*Daren Epley, 1b	.327	294	44	96	19	1	2	58	6
Miguel Flores, 2b	.271	457	45	124	20	4	1	42	22
*Brian Giles, of	.216	74	6	16	4	0	0	3	2
Jose Hernandez, ss	.255	404	56	103	16	4	3	46	7
Glenallen Hill, dh	.111	9	1	1	1	0	0	1	0
Nolan Lane, of	.255	47	6	12	3	0	2	5	4
Luis Lopez, dh	.256	82	4	21	1	0	0	7	1
Carlos Mota, c	.209	182	12	38	8	0	1	6	3
Donell Nixon, dh	.224	49	9	11	2	1	1	7	5
*Ken Ramos, of	.339	442	94	150	23	5	5	42	13
*Tracy Sanders, of	.241	382	65	92	11	3	21	88	3
Mike Sarbaugh, 1b	.233	120	19	28	5	0	2	18	1
Joel Skinner, c	.300	20	2	6	0	0	1	5	0
Kelly Stinnett, c	.284	296	37	84	9	0	6	32	7
*Jim Thome, 3b	.336	107	16	36	9	2	1	14	0
#Lee Tinsley, of	.287	349	65	100	9	8	5	38	18

PITCHING	W	L	ERA	G	SV	IP	H	BB	SO
Chad Allen	2	2	5.54	12	0	37.1	49	15	11
Paul Byrd	14	6	3.01	24	0	152.1	124	74	118
*Colin Charland	5	3	4.40	15	0	72.2	71	34	50
Carlo Colombino	0	0	0.00	2	0	2	0	1	1
Tom Eiterman	0	0	2.45	3	0	4.2	2	3	5
*Alan Embree	7	2	2.28	12	0	79	61	28	56
*Victor Garcia	5	6	6.07	29	1	102.1	115	57	56
*Mike Gardella	5	3	3.21	48	12	73	61	42	63
Brett Gideon	4	1	3.38	19	5	24	25	7	20
*Garland Kiser	3	2	3.54	39	2	53.1	53	18	36
Dave Mlicki	11	9	3.60	27	0	173.2	143	80	146
Scott Morgan	0	0	4.05	3	0	7.2	11	0	1
Chad Ogea	6	1	2.20	7	0	49	39	12	40
*Dave Otto	0	0	0.00	1	0	3	1	1	1
Eric Plunk	1	2	1.72	9	0	16.2	11	5	19
Willie Smith	1	4	4.68	9	0	33.2	33	14	28
Mike Soper	3	2	3.02	43	19	48.2	37	17	43
*Wally Trice	5	7	4.04	32	0	111.1	127	44	67
Joe Turek	3	5	3.70	14	0	75.1	60	28	55
Bill Wertz	8	4	1.20	57	8	97.1	75	30	67

Class AAA Directory

Pacific Coast League

Albuquerque Dukes (Dodgers)
Albuquerque Sports Stadium (10,510)

Calgary Cannons (Mariners)
Foothills Stadium (7,500)

Colorado Springs Sky Sox (Rockies)
Sky Sox Stadium (6,130)

Edmonton Trappers (Marlins)
John Ducey Park (5,000)

Las Vegas Stars (Padres)
Cashman Field (9,370)

Phoenix Firebirds (Giants)
Municipal Stadium (7,983)

Portland Beavers (Twins)
Civic Stadium (26,500)

Tacoma Tigers (A's)
Cheney Stadium (8,002)

Tucson Toros (Astros)
Hi Corbett Field (9,500)

Vancouver Canadiens (Angels)
Nat Bailey Stadium (6,500)

 # Switch-hitter
** Left-handed*
(Players in major leagues are listed with last minor league team.)

Class AA Directory

Eastern League

Albany-Colonie Yankees (Yankees)
Heritage Park (5,700)
Binghamton Mets (Mets)
Municipal Stadium (6,000)
Bowie (Orioles)
Stadium TBA (10,000)
Canton-Akron Indians (Indians)
Thurman Munson Memorial Stadium (5,600)
Harrisburg Senators (Expos)
Riverside Stadium (5,600)
London Tigers (Tigers)
Labatt Park (5,400)
New Britain Red Sox (Red Sox)
Beehive Field (4,000)
Reading Phillies (Phillies)
Municipal Stadium (6,500)

 # Switch-hitter
** Left-handed*
(Players in major leagues are listed with last minor league team.)

Hagerstown Suns (Orioles) AA

BATTING	Avg.	AB	R	H	2B	3B	HR	RBI	SB
Manny Alexander, ss	.259	499	70	129	22	8	2	41	43
*Mick Billmeyer, c	.162	37	2	6	1	0	0	3	0
Damon Buford, of	.239	373	53	89	17	3	1	30	41
Sergio Cairo, of	.281	409	43	115	13	4	2	46	4
*Paul Carey, 1b	.270	163	17	44	8	0	4	18	3
Cesar Devarez, c	.226	319	20	72	7	1	2	31	2
Sam Ferretti, 3b	.257	210	27	54	9	1	1	17	2
Chris Hoiles, c	.458	24	7	11	1	0	1	5	0
Tim Holland, 3b	.236	263	29	62	9	3	1	22	8
Ed Horowitz, c	.226	31	1	7	1	0	0	2	0
Mike Lehman, c	.135	37	2	5	2	0	0	2	0
Rod Lofton, 2b	.250	172	17	43	7	0	0	8	11
Steve Martin, of	.167	54	4	9	3	0	0	2	2
Scott Meadows, of	.317	164	25	52	4	2	2	14	2
*Brent Miller, 1b	.259	440	48	114	28	1	4	51	5
*Greg Roth, 3b	.146	130	13	19	6	0	1	11	4
Mark Smith, of	.288	472	51	136	32	6	4	62	15
Troy Tallman, c	.192	26	4	5	3	0	0	7	0
*Brad Tyler, 2b	.223	256	41	57	9	1	2	21	22
Kyle Washington, of	.281	388	42	109	13	2	2	41	16
Melvin Wearing, dh	.258	275	27	71	14	2	5	46	8
Paul Williams, 1b	.138	29	3	4	2	0	0	3	0

PITCHING	W	L	ERA	G	SV	IP	H	BB	SO
*Rob Blumberg	0	0	10.38	4	0	9.2	12	8	4
Jeff Bumgarner	3	4	6.51	14	1	28.2	26	18	29
Tim Drummond	5	8	3.87	26	4	112.2	108	33	62
*Grady Hall	3	4	2.73	11	0	69.1	59	16	43
*Mike Hook	0	2	5.04	6	0	30.1	26	24	30
Stacy Jones	2	5	3.49	11	0	70.2	62	25	46
Dave Miller	4	7	3.72	25	0	75	76	25	47
*Daryl Moore	1	1	3.12	5	1	9.2	7	7	12
*John O'Donoghue	7	4	2.24	17	0	112.1	77	40	86
John Pawlowski	1	1	6.39	15	1	31	47	11	22
*Brad Pennington	1	2	2.54	19	7	28.1	20	17	32
Jeff Pico	0	1	2.96	14	1	27.1	27	6	28
*John Polasek	1	2	6.04	22	1	45.2	52	24	35
*Jim Poole	0	1	2.77	7	0	13	14	1	4
Chuck Ricci	1	4	5.77	20	0	58.2	58	47	58
Erik Schullstrom	5	9	3.61	23	0	127	120	63	128
Jeff Williams	8	10	4.83	36	6	123	148	70	81
Mark Williamson	0	1	4.91	6	0	15.2	13	2	8
Brian Wood	6	3	3.48	21	4	34.2	28	36	43
Kip Yaughn	7	8	3.48	18	0	116.1	89	33	106

Harrisburg Senators (Expos) AA

BATTING	Avg.	AB	R	H	2B	3B	HR	RBI	SB
#Greg Fulton, of	.249	177	13	44	7	0	5	17	2
*Steve Hecht, of	.257	269	46	69	13	5	1	17	17
*Tim Hines, dh	.163	49	5	8	1	0	1	8	1
*Rick Hirtensteiner, of	.263	449	67	118	18	5	5	50	18
*Tyrone Horne, of	.000	1	0	1	0	0	0	0	0
Bryn Kosco, 3b	.229	341	36	78	17	0	5	40	1
Tim Laker, c	.242	409	55	99	19	3	15	68	2
Mike Lansing, ss	.280	483	66	135	19	6	6	54	45
Chris Malinoski, 3b	.216	88	9	19	1	0	0	10	1
Chris Martin, 2b	.227	383	40	87	22	1	5	31	8
*Todd Mayo, of	.083	12	1	1	0	0	0	0	0
Chad McDonald, 3b	.197	188	18	37	9	2	2	18	1
#Jerome Nelson, of	.230	204	27	47	3	3	1	16	10
Darwin Pennye, of	.273	311	38	85	9	6	1	24	20
Jaime Roseboro, of	.141	71	4	10	2	1	0	5	0
*Joe Siddall, of	.235	289	26	68	12	0	2	27	4
Derrick White, 1b	.277	494	63	137	19	2	13	81	16
Rondell White, of	.303	89	22	27	7	1	2	7	6
Tyrone Woods, ph	.000	4	0	0	0	0	0	0	0

PITCHING	W	L	ERA	G	SV	IP	H	BB	SO
Tavo Alvarez	4	1	2.85	7	0	47.1	48	9	42
Doug Bochtler	6	5	2.32	13	0	78.2	50	36	89
*Billy Brewer	2	0	5.01	20	0	23.1	25	18	18
Mario Brito	6	4	2.21	46	3	77.1	65	24	66
Travis Buckley	7	7	2.87	26	0	160	146	64	123
Mark Chapman	4	2	2.91	34	0	56.2	53	18	45
Archie Corbin	0	0	0.00	1	0	3	2	1	3
Reid Cornelius	1	0	3.13	4	0	23	11	8	17
Heath Haynes	2	0	1.93	3	0	5.2	3	1	6
Chris Johnson	9	10	3.98	28	0	142.1	148	43	94
*Chris Marchok	6	0	3.09	43	1	58.1	56	17	33
Mike Mathile	12	5	2.86	26	0	186.2	176	27	89
*Chris Myers	4	3	4.15	19	0	52	60	13	29
Doug Piatt	5	9	3.45	39	7	63.2	55	32	66
Len Picota	4	3	1.88	53	26	72	55	23	38
*Chris Pollack	6	10	4.71	25	0	124.1	139	46	58

London Tigers (Tigers) AA

BATTING	Avg.	AB	R	H	2B	3B	HR	RBI	SB
Basilio Cabrera, of	.209	86	7	18	0	0	1	3	2
*Brian Cornelius, of	.260	300	34	78	14	3	6	39	1
*Ivan Cruz, 1b	.275	524	71	144	25	1	14	104	1
Mike Debutch, ss	.267	318	64	85	11	1	3	25	16
Carlos Fermin, 2b	.150	40	3	6	0	0	0	0	0
#Lou Frazier, of	.252	477	86	120	16	3	0	34	58
Mike Gillette, c	.179	195	23	35	5	0	3	17	1
Chris Gomez, ss	.268	220	20	59	13	2	1	19	1
Jody Hurst, of	.316	269	48	85	17	2	11	52	17
Tyrone Kingwood, of	.284	377	57	107	14	1	7	47	22
Kirk Mendenhall, ss	.243	362	54	88	16	2	4	37	9
#Rob Reimink, 3b	.296	412	56	122	24	1	3	46	7
Rod Robertson, 2b	.239	243	26	58	12	0	7	34	13
Rick Sellers, c	.267	329	38	88	17	1	9	51	2
*Greg Sparks, 1b	.232	384	57	89	19	1	25	73	1
Tim Thomas, 2b	.364	11	1	4	1	0	0	1	0

PITCHING	W	L	ERA	G	SV	IP	H	BB	SO
Don August	3	2	2.72	11	0	53	47	10	39
Sean Bergman	4	7	4.28	14	0	88.1	85	45	59
Jeff Braley	3	6	2.53	64	15	82.2	81	29	41
*Greg Coppeta	1	1	2.31	19	0	23.1	24	10	18
*Sherm Corbett	0	4	4.58	35	4	37.1	38	12	33
Brian Cornelius	0	0	0.00	2	0	2	2	1	0
John Desilva	2	4	4.13	9	0	52.1	51	13	53
Dan Freed	2	0	3.24	14	0	17.2	16	8	10
Dan Gakeler	0	0	0.00	1	0	2	3	1	1
Mike Garcia	8	8	3.89	27	0	137.2	149	35	92
*Frank Gonzales	5	4	3.02	10	0	66.2	64	10	37
*Jim Henry	5	5	4.82	15	0	80.1	87	46	47
Eric King	0	0	2.25	1	0	4	2	0	4
Mike Lumley	8	3	2.52	55	3	75	63	23	51
*Jose Ramos	1	0	3.14	16	4	14.1	12	16	8
Ricky Rojas	5	5	4.87	32	5	41.2	48	17	33
Leo Torres	0	0	10.80	5	0	5	12	4	6
*Don Vesling	4	3	6.49	12	0	53.2	64	29	33
Brian Warren	7	9	3.30	25	0	147.1	146	32	83
Marty Willis	1	5	5.99	27	0	104.2	128	32	73
Steve Wolf	8	4	3.46	19	0	104	98	49	93

Class AA Directory

Southern League

Birmingham Barons (White Sox)
Hoover Metropolitan Stadium (10,000)
Carolina Mudcats (Pirates)
Five County Stadium (6,000)
Chattanooga Lookouts (Reds)
Engel Stadium (8,000)
Greenville Braves (Braves)
Municipal Stadium (7,023)
Huntsville Stars (A's)
Bill Meyer Stadium (6,412)
Jacksonville Suns (Mariners)
Wolfson Park (8,200)
Knoxville Smokies (Blue Jays)
Bill Meyer Stadium (6,412)
Memphis Chicks (Royals)
Tim McCarver Stadium (10,000)
New Orleans* (Twins)
Privateer Park (4,000)
Orlando Sunrays (Cubs)
Tinker Field (6,000)

*—Tentative location.

 # Switch-hitter
** Left-handed*
T(Players in major leagues are listed with last minor league team.)

Class AA Directory

Texas League

Arkansas Travelers (Cardinals)
Ray Winder Field (5,975)
El Paso Diablos (Brewers)
Cohen Stadium (10,000)
Jackson Generals (Astros)
Smith-Wills Stadium (5,200)
Midland Angels (Angels)
Angels Stadium (3,800)
San Antonio Missions (Dodgers)
V.J. Keefe Memorial Stadium (3,500)
Shreveport Captains (Giants)
Fairgrounds Field (6,200)
Tulsa Drillers (Rangers)
Drillers Stadium (8,234)
Wichita Wranglers (Padres)
Lawrence-Dumont Stadium (7,488)

 # Switch-hitter
** Left-handed*
(Players in major leagues are listed with last minor league team.)

New Britain Red Sox (Red Sox) AA

BATTING	Avg.	AB	R	H	2B	3B	HR	RBI	SB
Mike Beams, of	.221	262	33	58	15	2	10	44	2
*Scott Bethea, ss	.236	313	39	74	6	0	0	16	5
*Greg Blosser, of	.242	434	59	105	23	4	22	71	0
Jim Byrd, ss	.222	63	5	14	1	2	0	6	2
Bruce Chick, of	.221	435	53	96	19	0	9	51	7
Mike Dekneef, 2b	.227	409	51	93	10	5	3	33	9
#Joe Demus, c	.194	62	5	12	0	0	1	3	0
Colin Dixon, 3b	.211	266	24	56	6	1	1	26	1
#Greg Graham, ss	.225	347	32	78	6	1	0	19	9
*Scott Hatteberg, c	.232	297	28	69	13	2	1	30	1
Jeff McNeely, of	.218	261	30	57	8	4	2	11	10
*Bill Norris, 3b	.208	384	36	80	15	0	1	24	5
Ruben Rodriguez, c	.252	119	10	30	14	0	0	14	1
#Willie Tatum, 1b	.242	446	65	108	25	4	7	54	16
*Paul Thoutsis, of	.242	326	31	79	21	3	4	47	0

PITCHING	W	L	ERA	G	SV	IP	H	BB	SO
Brian Conroy	4	6	3.82	11	0	75.1	70	17	40
*Bret Donovan	0	1	9.95	1	0	6.1	6	4	1
Gar Finnvold	7	13	3.49	25	0	165	156	52	135
*Don Florence	3	1	2.41	58	6	75.2	65	27	51
Getteys Glaze	0	1	1.80	2	0	10	5	5	6
Derek Livernois	11	7	3.63	20	0	121.1	110	37	86
*Tony Mosley	2	4	4.91	48	1	88	101	34	41
Gary Painter	7	2	3.32	21	0	95	106	24	57
*Ed Riley	10	8	2.45	19	0	121	108	38	63
Ken Ryan	1	4	1.95	44	22	51.2	44	24	51
Al Sanders	5	9	4.51	36	0	114.2	121	48	69
Aaron Sele	2	1	6.27	7	0	33	43	15	29
Tim Smith	3	20	5.32	27	0	154	186	53	71
Kevin Uhrhan	3	5	4.20	43	1	84.2	94	32	54

Reading Phillies (Phillies) AA

BATTING	Avg.	AB	R	H	2B	3B	HR	RBI	SB
*Pete Alborano, of	.232	142	16	33	6	1	2	9	2
#Steve Bieser, of	.273	139	20	38	5	4	0	8	7
*Pat Brady, of	.262	233	40	61	10	1	7	44	3
*Bruce Dostal, of	.238	122	19	29	3	1	2	6	9
John Escobar, ss	.237	304	30	72	14	1	3	28	1
Mickey Hyde, of	.263	236	23	62	12	2	1	27	1
Jeff Jackson, of	.185	108	12	20	1	2	0	6	9
Mike Lieberthal, c	.286	308	30	88	16	1	2	37	4
*Ron Lockett, 1b	.228	400	42	91	17	2	5	36	12
#Julius McDougal, 3b	.282	39	2	11	2	0	0	2	0
*R.A. Neitzel, 2b	.188	266	31	50	7	0	0	18	11
Tom Nuneviller, of	.309	165	31	51	6	2	4	23	3
Troy Paulsen, ss	.234	94	9	22	6	0	1	7	0
Todd Pratt, dh	.333	132	20	44	6	1	6	26	2
#Ed Rosado, c	.310	197	23	61	9	3	3	26	4
#Sean Ryan, 1b	.268	354	29	95	19	1	7	57	0
#Kevin Stocker, ss	.250	240	31	60	9	2	1	13	17
*Sam Taylor, of	.246	349	42	86	18	5	10	55	5
Tony Trevino, 2b	.228	281	32	64	10	2	1	21	2
#Casey Waller, 3b	.255	314	42	80	14	3	5	31	5

PITCHING	W	L	ERA	G	SV	IP	H	BB	SO
*Joel Adamson	3	6	4.27	10	0	59	68	13	35
Ron Allen	1	3	4.94	5	0	31	35	9	17
Toby Borland	2	4	3.43	32	5	42	39	32	45
Brad Brink	1	1	3.29	3	0	14.2	14	3	12
Chris Bushing	3	6	4.35	22	1	70.1	68	30	72
*Andy Carter	0	4	9.24	7	0	25.1	37	15	17
*Rocky Elli	2	6	4.68	12	0	65.1	77	23	20
Donnie Elliott	3	3	2.52	6	0	36.2	37	11	23
Paul Fletcher	9	4	2.83	22	0	127	103	47	103
Bob Gaddy	0	2	2.92	12	1	25.2	15	13	19
Darrell Goedhart	4	8	4.27	16	0	86.1	95	24	56
Tyler Green	6	3	1.88	12	0	62.1	46	20	67
Tommy Greene	0	0	9.00	1	0	2	3	2	2
Eric Hill	5	4	4.78	25	0	98	111	24	61

PITCHING	W	L	ERA	G	SV	IP	H	BB	SO
*Chris Limbach	1	3	3.14	53	5	83	70	17	58
Steve Parris	5	7	4.64	18	0	85.1	94	21	60
Jeff Patterson	3	1	4.60	26	13	31.1	30	14	22
Keith Shepherd	0	1	2.78	4	0	23.2	17	4	9
Matt Stevens	4	4	3.99	46	12	59.2	65	17	43
Mike Sullivan	2	1	4.84	34	0	45.2	56	18	27
Bob Wells	0	1	1.17	3	0	15.1	12	5	11
*Scott Wiegandt	6	3	2.98	56	2	82.2	66	48	65
Mike Williams	1	2	5.17	3	0	16.2	17	7	12

Southern League

Birmingham Barons (White Sox) AA

BATTING	Avg.	AB	R	H	2B	3B	HR	RBI	SB
Clemente Alvarez, c	.142	169	7	24	8	0	1	10	1
James Bishop, 3b	.245	310	26	76	13	0	5	44	2
Wayne Busby, ss	.163	178	19	29	5	1	0	12	6
Darrin Campbell, c	.224	201	27	45	11	0	5	24	4
*Kevin Castleberry, 2b	.257	382	57	98	9	5	2	26	13
*Scott Cepicky, 1b	.247	502	56	124	30	1	14	87	1
Lindsay Foster, ss	.218	211	24	46	6	2	0	12	8
Robert Harris, of	.247	283	40	70	13	1	3	24	13
Scott Jaster, of	.279	326	45	91	13	2	7	33	3
*Al Liebert, c	.251	219	18	55	13	0	3	25	0
Greg Lonigro, ss	.212	255	21	54	11	0	3	21	3
*Dan Pasqua, of	.125	8	1	1	0	0	0	0	0
*Kinnis Pledger, of	.178	191	18	34	5	2	1	14	2
*Ron Plemmons, dh	.118	34	7	4	1	1	0	1	0
Tom Redington, 3b	.231	255	21	59	7	0	5	29	0
*Mike Robertson, 1b	.189	90	6	17	8	1	1	9	0
*Greg Roth, 3b	.500	2	1	1	0	0	0	0	0
*Scott Tedder, of	.235	429	54	101	15	3	1	47	2
Charlie White, of	.213	263	29	56	10	2	1	17	17
Brandon Wilson, ss	.271	107	10	29	4	0	0	4	5
Jerry Wolak, of	.296	169	18	50	13	1	0	13	5

PITCHING	W	L	ERA	G	SV	IP	H	BB	SO
Jason Bere	4	4	3.00	8	0	54	44	20	45
Frank Campos	5	3	5.37	31	0	54.2	56	40	31
*Fred Dabney	2	8	3.84	25	0	105.1	116	41	86
*Greg Fritz	0	0	7.71	1	0	7	9	4	3
John Hudek	0	1	2.31	5	1	12.2	9	11	9
*Earnie Johnson	1	1	5.49	16	0	20.2	29	8	24
Bo Kennedy	10	7	2.38	18	0	129.2	117	30	65
Brian Keyser	9	10	3.73	28	0	183.1	173	60	99
Frank Merigliano	6	3	3.08	24	1	91.2	67	41	71
Mike Mongiello	5	2	3.83	44	8	82.1	76	38	73
Steve Olsen	6	4	3.03	12	0	77.1	68	29	46
Johnny Ruffin	0	7	6.04	10	0	48.2	51	34	44
Steve Schrenk	1	1	3.65	2	0	12.1	13	11	9
Jeff Schwarz	2	1	1.16	21	6	39.2	16	9	53
Keith Shepherd	3	3	2.14	40	7	71.1	50	20	64
*Steve Stowell	1	2	3.00	21	2	21	20	11	20
*Larry Thomas	8	6	1.94	17	0	121.2	102	30	72

Carolina Mudcats (Pirates) AA

BATTING	Avg.	AB	R	H	2B	3B	HR	RBI	SB
Rich Aude, dh	.200	20	4	4	1	0	2	3	0
Tony Beasley, 2b	.259	158	11	41	5	3	1	13	13
Pete Beeler, c	.198	116	7	23	5	0	2	18	0
*Scott Bullett, of	.270	518	60	140	20	5	8	45	29
Alberto Delossantos, of	.262	355	34	93	9	5	1	24	17
#Greg Edge, ss	.234	252	21	59	7	0	0	9	12
Tim Edge, c	.125	8	1	1	0	0	0	0	0
Tom Green, of	.129	62	3	8	1	0	0	3	0
*Mark Johnson, 1b	.232	383	40	89	15	1	7	45	16
Paul List, of	.208	24	3	5	1	0	0	1	0
Austin Manahan, 2b	.221	340	44	75	18	6	5	33	7
Keith Osik, 3b	.259	425	41	110	17	1	5	45	2
William Pennyfeather, of	.337	199	28	67	13	1	6	25	7

Class A Directory

California League

Bakersfield Dodgers (Dodgers)
Sam Lynn Ballpark (3,000)
CentralValley Rockies (Rockies)
Recreation Park (2,000)
High Desert Mavericks (Marlins)
Maverick Stadium (3,500)
Modesto A's (A's)
Thurman Field (2,500)
Palm Springs Angels (Angels)
Angels Stadium (5,185)
Rancho Cucamonga Quakes (Padres)
Rancho Sports Complex (4,020)
Riverside (Mariners)
Cal-Riverside
San Bernardino (Indepedent)
Fiscalini Field (3,000)
San Jose Giants (Giants)
Municipal Stadium (5,200)
Stockton Ports (Brewers)
Billy Herbert Field (3,500)

 # Switch-hitter
** Left-handed*
(Players in major leagues are listed with last minor league team.)

Class A Directory

Carolina League

Durham Bulls (Braves)
Durham Athletic Park (5,000)
Frederick Keys (Orioles)
Harry Grove Stadium (4,500)
Kinston Indians (Indians)
Grainger Stadium (4,100)
Lynchburg Red Sox (Red Sox)
City Stadium (4,200)
Prince William Cannons (Yankees)
County Stadium (6,000)
Salem Buccaneers (Pirates)
Municipal Field (5,000)
Winston-Salem Spirits (Reds)
Ernie Shore Stadium (4,280)
Wilmington Blue Rocks (Royals)
Blue Rock Stadium (6,000)

 # Switch-hitter
** Left-handed*
(Players in major leagues are listed with last minor league team.)

BATTING	Avg.	AB	R	H	2B	3B	HR	RBI	SB
Rich Kevin Polcovich, ss	.171	35	1	6	0	0	0	1	0
Daryl Ratliff, of	.240	413	45	99	13	3	0	26	25
Roman Rodriguez, ss	.209	86	7	18	3	0	0	9	1
#Mandy Romero, c	.216	269	28	58	16	0	3	27	0
Bruce Schreiber, ss	.266	256	14	68	5	4	0	15	5
Ben Shelton, 1b	.234	368	57	86	17	0	10	51	4
#Keith Thomas, of	.295	78	13	23	2	4	4	15	9
Jessie Torres, c	.203	74	10	15	2	0	1	9	0

PITCHING	W	L	ERA	G	SV	IP	H	BB	SO
Brett Backlund	1	1	1.89	3	0	19	11	3	17
*Dave Bird	5	11	4.41	27	0	133.2	149	41	89
Steve Buckholz	1	4	7.38	20	0	46.1	62	26	32
Jason Bullard	0	2	7.40	19	3	24.1	37	11	24
*Steve Cooke	2	2	3.00	6	0	36	31	12	38
Eddie Dixon	2	2	3.21	25	4	28	25	3	17
Stan Fansler	7	12	4.17	25	0	140.1	127	54	104
*Lee Hancock	1	1	2.23	23	0	40.1	32	12	40
Bobby Hunter	4	4	2.54	32	0	64.2	58	21	31
Keith Osik	0	0	0.00	2	0	3.2	2	0	3
*Richard Robertson	6	7	3.03	20	0	125.2	127	41	107
*Brian Shouse	5	6	2.44	59	4	77.1	71	28	80
Dennis Tafoya	3	5	3.11	41	2	75.1	72	17	51
Dave Tellers	2	1	3.55	16	2	25.1	23	9	22
Fred Toliver	1	2	4.19	15	3	19.1	22	10	24
Paul Wagner	6	6	3.03	19	0	122.2	104	47	101
Ben Webb	1	4	4.34	30	4	48.2	47	21	22
Rick White	1	7	4.21	10	0	58.2	59	18	45
Mike Zimmerman	4	15	3.82	27	0	153	141	75	106

Charlotte Knights (Cubs) AA

BATTING	Avg.	AB	R	H	2B	3B	HR	RBI	SB
Scott Bryant, of	.150	20	3	3	1	1	1	2	0
#Rich Casarotti, 2b	.203	192	19	39	5	4	2	22	3
Pedro Castellano, 3b	.224	147	16	33	3	0	1	15	0
Rusty Crockett, 2b	.239	314	33	75	9	1	1	27	9
*Phil Dauphin, of	.254	515	83	131	24	3	10	42	17
Darrin Duffy, ss	.132	53	9	7	2	0	0	1	1
*Chris Ebright, 1b	.255	404	61	103	22	2	17	77	7
*Matt Franco, 3b	.283	343	35	97	18	3	2	31	3
Mike Grace, 3b	.249	321	42	80	16	3	7	35	4
*Richie Grayum, of	.243	334	46	81	25	0	13	52	0
Andy Hartung, dh	.333	9	1	3	1	0	1	3	0
*John Jensen, of	.261	399	64	104	16	0	14	54	5
*Elvin Paulino, 1b	.225	142	18	32	8	0	4	21	1
Jim Robinson, c	.253	182	19	46	5	0	1	23	0
Ozzie Timmons, of	.213	122	13	26	6	0	3	13	2
#Matt Walbeck, c	.301	385	48	116	22	1	7	42	0
Doug Welch, of	.210	124	12	26	6	0	4	18	0
Billy White, ss	.253	403	57	102	12	0	4	33	10
#Jerrone Williams, of	.203	64	6	13	3	0	2	8	2

PITCHING	W	L	ERA	G	SV	IP	H	BB	SO
Troy Bradford	1	1	3.18	2	0	11.1	16	3	8
Tim Delgado	0	0	4.76	6	0	11.1	13	4	7
Mike Harkey	0	1	5.63	1	0	8	9	0	5
Ryan Hawblitzel	12	8	3.76	28	0	175.2	180	38	119
Jessie Hollins	3	4	3.20	63	25	70.1	60	32	73
*Eric Jaques	2	5	3.53	46	0	66.1	65	23	50
Jerry Kutzler	1	2	2.11	12	0	38.1	33	4	28
Paul Marak	2	4	3.23	17	2	39	32	10	29
Bill Melvin	4	4	2.38	28	0	68	49	38	47
Tim Parker	0	2	12.46	2	0	9.2	17	3	6
Pedro Perez	0	0	7.71	1	0	2.1	4	1	3
John Salles	6	2	2.41	9	0	60.2	55	7	32
*Mike Sodders	4	5	3.57	23	0	68	65	20	39
Dave Stevens	9	13	3.91	26	0	150.2	147	53	89
Julio Strauss	0	1	3.38	10	0	19.2	19	4	17
Dave Swartzbaugh	7	10	3.65	27	0	165	134	62	111
Steve Trachsel	13	8	3.06	29	0	191	180	35	135
Scott Weiss	1	0	3.86	5	0	12.2	14	5	2
Travis Willis	5	3	2.92	46	4	62.2	55	16	33

Chattanooga Lookouts (Reds) AA

BATTING	Avg.	AB	R	H	2B	3B	HR	RBI	SB
Benny Colvard, of	.257	366	46	94	19	1	14	47	6
Tim Costo, 1b	.241	424	63	102	18	2	28	71	4
Darren Cox, c	.254	331	29	84	19	1	1	38	8
Kiki Diaz, ss	.258	472	72	122	11	2	0	45	7
*Ruben Escalera, of	.270	141	22	38	7	1	0	15	6
Chris Estep, of	.245	163	14	40	9	1	1	12	6
*Kevin Garner, dh	.300	213	37	64	10	0	14	53	0
*Willie Greene, 3b	.278	349	47	97	19	2	15	66	8
#Ty Griffin, 2b	.239	347	44	83	16	3	5	38	7
Cesar Hernandez, of	.277	328	50	91	23	4	3	27	12
Bernie Jenkins, of	.313	48	7	15	3	2	0	4	2
Frank Kremblas, 2b	.230	282	29	65	16	1	0	28	4
Brian Lane, 3b	.282	142	21	40	7	0	3	23	3
#Terry McDaniel, of	.263	19	1	5	1	0	0	3	0
#Bobby Perna, 3b	.400	10	3	4	1	1	0	1	0
*Scott Pose, of	.342	526	87	180	22	8	2	45	20
Glenn Sutko, c	.187	198	24	37	4	0	10	27	3
*Dwight Taylor, of	.211	57	6	12	3	0	1	9	4
Todd Trafton, of	.281	242	34	68	18	2	9	38	1

PITCHING	W	L	ERA	G	SV	IP	H	BB	SO
Mike Anderson	13	7	2.52	28	0	172.2	154	61	149
Bobby Ayala	12	6	3.54	27	0	163.2	152	58	154
Dan Freed	3	2	2.48	10	0	40	39	8	35
*Matt Grott	1	2	2.68	32	6	40.1	39	25	44
Trevor Hoffman	3	0	1.52	6	0	30.2	22	11	31
Rodney Imes	7	2	4.04	45	3	89	112	24	50
*Rusty Kilgo	1	3	3.13	24	0	32.2	22	11	11
Frank Kremblas	0	0	0.00	2	0	2	2	2	1
Reggie Leslie	0	0	6.75	4	0	5.1	8	4	2
Larry Luebbers	6	5	2.27	14	0	87.1	86	34	56
*David Lynch	3	1	3.00	37	2	51	39	15	44
*Ross Powell	4	1	1.26	14	1	57.1	43	18	56
Johnny Ray	4	1	3.63	24	1	57	61	14	30
Scott Robinson	7	2	3.80	13	0	83	82	26	51
John Roper	10	9	4.03	20	0	121.2	115	36	98
Mo Sanford	4	0	1.35	4	0	27.2	14	6	28
Jason Satre	3	5	5.43	14	0	58	56	26	36
Jerry Spradlin	3	3	1.38	59	34	65.1	52	13	36
Glenn Sutko	0	0	1.69	4	1	5.1	5	3	4
Kevin Tatar	5	4	3.13	9	0	55.2	45	20	46
*Joey Vierra	1	0	0.00	1	0	6	5	0	3

Greenville Braves (Braves) AA

BATTING	Avg.	AB	R	H	2B	3B	HR	RBI	SB
#Ed Alicea, of	.235	315	49	74	13	8	5	33	13
*Mike Bell, 1b	.254	421	56	107	23	5	9	64	1
#Ramon Caraballo, 2b	.312	93	15	29	4	4	1	8	10
Tim Gillis, 3b	.429	7	1	3	0	1	0	3	0
*Ed Giovanola, 3b	.267	270	39	72	5	0	5	30	4
#Lee Heath, of	.250	4	2	1	0	0	1	3	1
#Chipper Jones, ss	.346	266	43	92	17	11	9	42	14
Mike Kelly, of	.229	471	83	108	18	4	25	71	22
Pat Kelly, 3b	.249	325	44	81	12	2	0	35	11
*Brian Kowitz, of	.286	56	9	16	4	0	0	6	1
Javy Lopez, c	.321	442	64	142	28	3	16	60	7
Mike Mordecai, ss	.261	222	31	58	13	1	4	31	8
#Melvin Nieves, of	.283	350	61	99	23	5	18	76	6
#Jose Olmeda, 2b	.246	341	54	84	22	4	2	33	11
Eduardo Perez, c	.229	275	28	63	16	0	6	41	3
Hector Roa, 2b	.333	9	1	3	0	0	0	2	0
Steve Swail, c	.214	14	0	3	0	0	0	0	0
*Tony Tarasco, of	.286	489	73	140	22	2	15	54	33
*Jeff Treadway, 2b	.455	11	1	5	2	0	0	1	0
*Aubrey Waggoner, of	.269	238	51	64	14	3	14	45	21

Class A Directory

Midwest League

Appleton Foxes (Mariners)
Goodland Field (4,300)
Beloit Brewers (Brewers)
Pohlman Field (3,800)
Burlington Bees (Expos)
Community Field (3,500)
Cedar Rapids Kernels (Angels)
Veterans Memorial Ballpark (6,000)
Clinton Giants (Giants)
Riverview Stadium (3,600)
Fort Wayne Wizards (Twins)
Memorial Stadium (6,000)
Kane County Cougars (Marlins)
Events Center Stadium (3,600)
Madison Muskies (A's)
Warner Park (3,923)
Peoria Chiefs (Cubs)
Pete Vonachen Stadium at Meinen Field (6,200)
Quad City River Bandits (Astros)
John O'Donnell Stadium (5,300)
Rockford Royals (Royals)
Marinelli Field (4,200)
South Bend White Sox (White Sox)
Stanley Coveleski Stadium (5,000)
Springfield Cardinals (Cardinals)
Lanphier Park (5,000)
Waterloo Diamonds (Padres)
Municipal Stadium (5,500)

 # Switch-hitter
** Left-handed*
(Players in major leagues are listed with last minor league team.)

Class A Directory

Florida State League

Baseball City Cubs (Cubs)
Stadium TBA
Charlotte Rangers (Rangers)
Charlotte County Stadium (6,026)
Clearwater Phillies (Phillies)
Jack Russell Stadium (7,385)
Dunedin Blue Jays (Blue Jays)
Grant Field (6,218)
Lakeland Tigers (Tigers)
Joker Marchant Stadium (7,500)
Osceola Astros (Astros)
Osceola County Stadium (5,100)
Port St. Lucie Mets (Mets)
Port St. Lucie Sports Complex (7,347)
St. Petersburg Cardinals (Cardinals)
Al Lang Stadium (7,004)
Sarasota White Sox (White Sox)
Ed Smith Stadium (7,500)
The Miracle (Twins)
Lee County Sports Complex, Fort Myers (7,500)
Vero Beach Dodgers (Dodgers)
Holman Stadium (6,500)
West Palm Beach Expos (Expos)
Municipal Stadium (4,392)

Note: Franchises maybe added in Fort Lauderdale and Winter Haven.

PITCHING	W	L	ERA	G	SV	IP	H	BB	SO
*Brian Bark	5	0	1.15	11	0	55	36	13	49
*Pedro Borbon	8	2	3.06	39	3	94	73	42	79
Dennis Burlingame	9	9	3.09	26	0	152.2	137	62	84
Kevin Coffman	6	0	2.13	6	0	38	23	16	33
Donnie Elliott	7	2	2.08	19	0	104.2	76	35	100
*Pat Gomez	7	0	1.13	8	0	48.2	25	19	38
Mike Hostetler	6	2	3.90	16	0	81.2	78	23	57
*Judd Johnson	6	0	1.71	43	2	68.1	56	14	40
Greg McMichael	4	2	1.36	15	1	46.1	37	13	53
Nate Minchey	13	6	2.30	28	0	172	137	40	115
Andy Nezelek	9	2	2.26	46	1	108.2	87	23	114
Darren Ritter	1	0	4.50	1	0	4	3	1	6
Don Strange	5	3	1.95	48	18	60	43	19	58
Scott Taylor	1	1	6.69	22	1	39	44	18	20
Marcos Vasquez	6	4	4.30	14	0	73.1	81	30	38
Preston Watson	4	6	1.96	48	6	73.1	58	36	81
*Brad Woodall	3	4	3.20	21	1	39.1	26	17	45

Huntsville Stars (Athletics) AA

BATTING	Avg.	AB	R	H	2B	3B	HR	RBI	SB
Kurt Abbott, ss	.254	452	64	115	14	5	9	52	15
Marcos Armas, 1b	.283	509	83	144	30	6	17	85	9
Dean Borrelli, c	.202	238	20	48	5	0	1	23	3
Jorge Brito, c	.208	72	10	15	2	0	2	6	2
James Buccheri, of	.150	60	8	9	2	1	1	5	5
Tom Carcione, c	.167	48	3	8	0	0	1	4	0
Mike Conte, of	.238	290	32	69	10	3	1	26	6
#Kevin Dattola, of	.247	324	31	80	15	3	2	33	14
#Eric Fox, of	.271	240	42	65	16	2	5	14	16
Webster Garrison, 2b	.276	348	50	96	25	4	8	61	8
*Dan Grunhard, of	.286	84	11	24	4	2	1	9	1
*Eric Helfand, c	.228	114	13	26	7	0	2	9	0
Scott Hemond, c	.333	27	3	9	0	0	0	2	2
Dave Jacas, of	.265	441	62	117	21	4	5	48	18
*Chris Knabenshue, of	.197	71	9	14	4	0	1	11	1
Scott Lydy, of	.305	387	64	118	20	3	9	65	16
Francisco Matos, 2b	.220	150	11	33	5	1	1	14	4
*Mike Neill, of	.313	16	4	5	0	0	0	2	1
Craig Paquette, 3b	.258	450	59	116	25	4	17	71	13
#Darryl Vice, dh	.295	481	75	142	13	1	1	38	9
*Jimmy Waggoner, 2b	.063	16	0	1	0	0	0	0	0

PITCHING	W	L	ERA	G	SV	IP	H	BB	SO
*Dana Allison	4	1	2.93	22	1	61.1	51	5	40
*Tony Ariola	2	0	2.57	2	0	14	10	1	7
Jeff Bittiger	10	5	3.09	17	0	102	89	44	94
Mike Conte	1	0	7.71	5	0	5.2	7	1	3
Russ Cormier	1	1	5.01	6	0	23.1	31	7	13
Scott Erwin	3	5	3.28	23	1	36.2	25	27	39
Chaon Garland	3	4	6.59	9	0	42.1	49	24	25
*Johnny Guzman	8	2	3.71	14	0	90.2	87	26	55
Miguel Jiminez	1	0	1.80	1	0	5	3	3	8
*Doug Johns	0	0	3.94	3	0	16	21	5	4
*Chad Kuhn	2	6	4.47	19	0	50.1	50	27	37
Dave Latter	8	1	3.03	47	0	77.1	66	27	64
*Mike Mohler	3	8	3.59	44	3	80.1	72	39	56
*Gavin Osteen	5	5	3.61	16	0	102.1	106	27	56
Bronswell Patrick	13	7	3.76	29	0	179.1	187	46	98
Steve Phoenix	11	5	2.79	32	0	174	179	36	124
Todd Revenig	1	1	1.70	53	33	64.2	32	11	49
Todd Smith	0	1	5.00	5	0	9	13	2	6
Roger Smithberg	3	3	4.00	20	1	36	42	12	19
Ricky Strebeck	1	6	6.79	30	2	52.2	67	31	32
*Pat Wernig	1	2	5.28	8	0	29	28	11	18
*Bill Wilkinson	0	0	6.32	15	1	16.2	17	13	15

 # Switch-hitter
** Left-handed*
(Players in major leagues are listed with last minor league team.)

Jacksonville Suns (Mariners) AA

BATTING	Avg.	AB	R	H	2B	3B	HR	RBI	SB
Tommy Adams, of	.220	50	4	11	2	0	0	5	1
#Frank Bolick, 3b	.268	224	32	60	9	0	13	42	1
*Jim Bowie, 1b	.286	276	36	79	16	0	10	43	0
Jim Campanis, c	.262	286	30	75	11	1	5	29	2
*Bert Heffernan, c	.286	196	16	56	9	0	2	23	4
Bobby Holley, 3b	.276	402	51	111	19	2	10	45	4
*Greg Hunter, 3b	.209	43	4	9	0	0	1	5	1
Shane Letterio, 2b	.156	90	5	14	2	0	0	5	1
Anthony Manahan, ss	.257	505	70	130	24	6	8	49	24
Tow Maynard, of	.283	406	55	115	12	4	1	29	38
*Mike McDonald, of	.258	310	49	80	16	3	8	33	6
#Mark Merchant, dh	.244	381	42	93	9	1	13	47	3
Marc Newfield, dh	.247	162	15	40	12	0	4	19	0
Ronald Pezzoni, of	.226	93	10	21	3	0	0	15	3
Greg Pirkl, 1b	.291	227	25	66	11	1	10	29	0
Jesus Tavarez, of	.258	392	38	101	9	2	3	25	29
*Theron Todd, of	.176	85	7	15	3	1	1	6	4
Brian Turang, 2b	.251	483	67	121	21	3	14	63	19
*Jeff Wetherby, of	.250	40	5	10	5	0	1	7	1
Craig Wilson, c	.203	69	5	14	2	0	0	2	0

PITCHING	W	L	ERA	G	SV	IP	H	BB	SO
Daven Bond	3	2	4.80	18	0	51.2	59	19	28
Jeff Borski	1	4	4.98	11	0	34.1	39	19	25
Jim Converse	12	7	2.66	27	0	159	134	82	157
*Mark Czarkowski	7	4	2.74	16	0	99.2	105	29	33
Mike Erb	0	0	10.38	3	0	4.1	12	1	2
*Fernando Figueroa	4	5	2.96	53	7	94.1	72	33	65
Marcos Garcia	2	1	1.59	5	1	23.2	13	8	21
Mark Grant	1	2	1.93	5	0	33.2	25	4	21
*Eric Gunderson	2	0	2.31	15	2	23.1	18	7	23
Jim Gutierrez	1	5	5.00	15	0	54	58	17	44
*Mike Hampton	0	1	4.35	2	0	10.1	13	1	6
*Keith Helton	1	1	3.86	7	0	12.2	8	7	6
Brad Holman	3	3	2.57	35	4	74.2	67	21	75
Troy Kent	2	6	3.03	59	21	68.1	70	30	63
Brent Knackert	7	8	4.08	21	0	117	123	41	74
Jim Newlin	1	1	2.05	12	1	22	22	10	13
Paul Perkins	2	3	5.57	21	0	32.1	30	15	17
Scott Pitcher	5	2	3.41	23	0	63.1	62	23	32
*Mike Remlinger	1	1	3.46	5	0	26	25	11	21
Mike Walker	3	3	4.79	11	0	62	63	18	40
*Johnny Wiggs	2	1	11.32	8	0	10.1	17	6	13
Kerry Woodson	5	4	3.57	11	0	68	74	36	55
Clint Zavaras	3	11	5.28	20	0	109	108	67	88

Knoxville Blue Jays (Blue Jays) AA

BATTING	Avg.	AB	R	H	2B	3B	HR	RBI	SB
Tilson Brito, ss	.208	24	2	5	1	2	0	2	0
Eric Brooks, c	.000	8	0	0	0	0	0	0	0
#Domingo Cedeno, 2b	.226	337	31	76	7	7	2	21	8
Juan Delarosa, of	.329	508	68	167	32	12	12	53	16
Joe Durso, c	.188	16	0	3	0	0	0	2	0
*Kris Harmes, 3b	.304	23	2	7	1	0	0	4	0
Derek Henderson, ss	.252	425	37	107	12	4	2	39	6
Brad Mengel, 3b	.238	294	20	70	8	1	1	22	5
Rob Montalvo, 3b	.167	72	7	12	1	0	0	4	1
Jose Monzon, c	.230	178	17	41	9	1	0	10	3
*Rance Mulliniks, dh	.308	26	2	8	4	0	0	2	0
*Greg O'Halloran, c	.271	409	44	111	20	5	2	34	7
Robert Perez, of	.260	526	59	137	24	5	9	59	11
Lonell Roberts, of	.000	14	1	0	0	0	0	0	1
#Shawn Scott, of	.224	321	31	72	4	4	2	26	5
Mike Taylor, 3b	.000	17	2	0	0	0	0	1	0
David Tollison, 3b	.226	340	37	77	15	3	1	22	4
Jason Townley, c	.232	185	7	43	11	0	2	20	1
*Nigel Wilson, of	.274	521	85	143	34	7	26	69	13
Julian Yan, 1b	.270	392	51	106	23	4	16	49	1

Class A Directory

South Atlantic League

Albany Polecats (Orioles)
Paul Eames Sports Complex (4,000)

Asheville Tourists (Astros)
McCormick Field (4,000)

Augusta Pirates (Pirates)
Heaton Stadium (4,000)

Charleston (S.C.) Rainbows (Rangers)
College Park (4,300)

Charleston (W.Va.) Wheelers (Reds)
Watt Powell Park (6,500)

Columbia Mets (Mets)
Capital City Stadium (6,100)

Columbus Indians (Indians)
Golden Park (6,000)

Fayetteville Generals (Tigers)
J.P. Riddle Stadium (3,000)

Greensboro Hornets (Yankees)
War Memorial Stadium (7,500)

Hagerstown Suns (Blue Jays)
Municipal Stadium (6,000)

Hickory Crawdads (White Sox)
L.P. Frans Stadium (4,000)

Macon Braves (Braves)
Luther Williams Field (3,000)

Savannah Cardinals (Cardinals)
Grayson Stadium (7,500)

Spartanburg Phillies (Phillies)
Duncan Park Stadium (3,900)

 # Switch-hitter
** Left-handed*
(Players in major leagues are listed with last minor league team.)

Batting leaders across all leagues

BATTING AVERAGE
(Minimum 383 TPA)

Player	Club	Lg.	Avg.
*Butler, Rob	Dun	Fsl	.358
#Hall, Billy	Hds	Cal	.356
*Pose, Scott	Cng	Sou	.342
Cordova, M.	Vis	Cal	.341
*Ramos, Ken	Can	East	.339
Grebeck, Brian	Psp	Cal	.336
T*Neill, Mike	Hvl	Sou	.335
*O'Leary, T.	Elp	Tex	.334
#Hocking, D.	Vis	Cal	.331
T Alfonzo, E.	Mdl	Tex	.329

HOME RUNS

Player	Club	Lg.	HR
Smith, Bubba	Pen	Caro	32
Balboni, St.	Okc	AmA	30
*Delgado, C.	Dun	Fsl	30
Hiatt, Phil	Oma	AmA	29
Cameron, S.	Fre	Caro	29

RBI

Player	Club	Lg.	RBI
Cordova, M.	Vis	Cal	131
Gomez, F.	Rno	Cal	115
*Dunn, S.	Vis	Cal	113
T#Nieves, M.	Grv	Sou	108
T*Greene, W.	Cng	Sou	106

STOLEN BASES

Player	Club	Lg.	SB
#Veras, Q.	Clb	Sal	66
#Burton, E.	Sbn	Mid	65
T Buford, D.	Roc	Int	64
Grissom, A.	Aby	Sal	62
Holbert, A.	Sav	Sal	62

 # Switch-hitter
** Left-handed*
T Player has been with more than one team, listed with last team. (Players in major leagues are listed with last minor league team.)

PITCHING	W	L	ERA	G	SV	IP	H	BB	SO
Daren Brown	5	4	3.73	43	1	82	79	22	105
Tim Brown	8	11	3.72	24	0	152.1	159	32	82
Tim Crabtree	0	2	0.95	3	0	19	14	4	13
*Nate Cromwell	5	5	5.17	37	0	101	102	69	101
Jesse Cross	8	13	3.54	26	0	147.1	136	44	126
Daren Kizziah	1	5	5.12	38	0	83.2	108	28	41
*Graeme Lloyd	4	8	1.96	49	14	92	79	25	65
Paul Menhart	10	11	3.85	28	0	178.2	181	38	104
Marcus Moore	5	10	5.59	36	0	106.1	110	79	85
Mike Ogliaruso	1	4	8.00	9	0	27	46	15	11
Mark Ohlms	3	2	1.29	52	18	70.2	49	26	50
Aaron Small	5	12	5.27	27	0	135	152	61	79
Mike Taylor	0	1	2.70	1	0	3.1	3	2	3
*Anthony Ward	1	0	2.75	6	0	20.2	18	6	21

Memphis Chicks (Royals) AA

BATTING	Avg.	AB	R	H	2B	3B	HR	RBI	SB
Cesar Bernhardt, of	.179	240	24	43	4	0	1	11	4
#Tony Bridges, of	.138	58	7	8	2	0	0	4	1
#Paco Burgos, ss	.201	278	23	56	8	0	3	23	6
Edgardo Caraballo, 3b	.210	195	17	41	6	2	3	17	1
*Adam Casillas, of	.327	168	25	55	12	2	2	23	1
Stu Cole, ss	.236	174	19	41	8	1	0	12	7
*Greg David, c	.220	232	21	51	11	1	1	24	1
Carlos Diaz, c	.188	101	4	19	5	0	1	12	1
Jeff Garber, of	.222	325	37	72	17	2	7	38	9
*Bob Hamelin, 1b	.333	120	23	40	8	0	6	22	0
Phil Hiatt, 3b	.244	487	71	119	20	5	27	83	5
Lance Jennings, c	.145	145	5	21	5	0	1	8	0
#Marcus Lawton, of	.143	42	4	6	0	0	0	1	0
*Tim Leiper, of	.256	246	37	63	10	2	2	21	4
#Kerwin Moore, of	.235	179	27	42	4	3	4	17	16
Domingo Mota, 2b	.265	430	46	114	16	0	4	23	14
Les Norman, of	.273	271	32	74	14	5	3	20	4
Nikco Riesgo, of	.103	29	6	3	0	1	0	4	0
Darryl Robinson, 1b	.240	354	40	85	18	3	11	42	0
Dan Rohrmeier, of	.323	433	54	140	33	2	6	69	3
Doug Shields, of	.161	31	0	5	0	0	0	1	0
#Rich Tunison, 1b	.223	130	7	29	10	1	1	10	1
*Hugh Walker, of	.203	74	9	15	4	1	1	5	0
#U.L. Washington, ss	.000	2	0	0	0	0	0	0	0

PITCHING	W	L	ERA	G	SV	IP	H	BB	SO
Brian Ahern	6	2	2.54	11	0	71	56	21	51
Mike Alvarez	1	0	0.00	1	0	2	1	1	1
Jose Bautista	1	0	4.50	1	0	6	6	2	7
*Jim Campbell	4	2	0.86	9	0	63	48	12	49
*Adam Casillas	1	0	0.00	1	0	2	0	2	2
Scott Centala	3	3	2.91	9	0	43.1	45	18	30
Archie Corbin	7	8	4.73	27	0	112.1	115	72	100
Steve Curry	8	12	3.95	27	0	162.2	156	72	110
Chip Duncan	0	3	4.66	33	3	73.1	72	24	51
*Brian Givens	0	0	3.24	7	0	8.1	5	7	9
Greg Harvey	0	3	7.43	6	0	23	27	20	12
Matt Karchner	8	8	4.47	33	1	141	161	35	87
Josias Manzanillo	0	2	7.36	2	0	7.1	6	6	8
Danny Miceli	3	0	1.91	32	4	38.2	20	13	46
Mark Parnell	4	7	6.29	26	1	49.2	59	15	40
Vladimir Perez	3	3	2.57	32	1	70	71	24	48
Hipolito Pichardo	0	0	0.64	2	0	14	13	1	10
*Ed Pierce	10	10	3.81	25	0	154.2	159	51	131
*Ed Puig	4	2	1.91	67	25	75.1	44	21	65
Darryl Robinson	0	0	4.50	2	0	2	1	3	1
Alex Sanchez	0	1	6.00	1	0	6	4	2	6
Jose Ventura	8	15	2.73	27	0	184.1	153	68	123
Skip Wiley	5	2	3.41	39	3	69.2	76	18	37

Orlando Sunrays (Twins) AA

BATTING	Avg.	AB	R	H	2B	3B	HR	RBI	SB
Rick Allen, ss	.194	232	15	45	9	2	1	18	5
Carlos Capellan, of	.167	6	3	1	0	0	0	0	0
Fred Cooley, dh	.310	126	15	39	2	0	5	24	1
Rex Delanuez, of	.268	437	71	117	34	2	12	59	13
Chris Delarwelle, 1b	.264	296	29	78	11	2	2	31	5
*Rafael Delima, of	.167	36	8	6	1	0	0	2	1
Cheo Garcia, 3b	.258	488	54	126	26	2	4	44	32
Pedro Grifol, c	.275	40	2	11	2	0	0	5	0
*Jay Kvasnicka, of	.236	165	20	39	1	3	2	12	3
Mica Lewis, of	.271	380	60	103	13	3	5	36	36
*Dan Masteller, of	.263	365	42	96	23	4	8	42	2
Dave McCarty, of	.271	457	75	124	16	2	18	79	6
Pat Meares, ss	.253	300	41	76	19	0	3	23	5
*Ray Ortiz, of	.263	266	40	70	16	1	10	47	0
Jay Owens, c	.267	330	50	88	24	0	4	30	10
Brian Raabe, 2b	.278	108	12	30	6	0	2	6	0
Paul Russo, 3b	.255	420	63	107	13	2	22	74	0
Joe Siwa, c	.198	126	9	25	3	1	0	11	0
Jack Smith, 2b	.138	29	1	4	0	0	0	0	1

PITCHING	W	L	ERA	G	SV	IP	H	BB	SO
Jayson Best	0	0	0.79	11	4	11.1	6	5	12
Rich Garces	3	3	4.54	58	13	73.1	76	39	72
Ed Gustafson	6	12	5.24	32	0	146	170	61	98
Jon Henry	10	9	4.12	28	0	135.1	147	28	87
*Jason Klonoski	5	7	3.00	54	3	93	85	29	67
Curtis Leskanic	9	11	4.30	26	0	153.2	158	64	126
Marc Lipson	0	3	5.45	31	1	36.1	44	16	20
Bob McCreary	4	5	3.51	16	0	67.2	73	18	35
Oscar Munoz	3	5	5.05	14	0	68.2	73	32	74
*Alan Newman	4	8	4.15	18	0	102	94	67	86
*Carlos Pulido	6	2	4.40	52	1	100.1	99	37	87
Rusty Richards	4	7	5.12	15	0	84.1	89	29	64
Mark Swope	1	0	4.50	4	0	16	26	6	6
Fred White	2	1	5.13	15	0	26.1	43	10	11
Bill Wissler	3	8	3.72	13	0	82.1	74	18	56

Texas League

Arkansas Travelers (Cardinals) AA

BATTING	Avg.	AB	R	H	2B	3B	HR	RBI	SB
*Rich Aldrete, 1b	.214	70	6	15	4	1	1	6	1
#Joe Aversa, 2b	.236	106	16	25	4	1	0	3	3
Brad Beanblossom, 2b	.224	384	46	86	10	3	0	13	3
Cliff Brannon, of	.212	340	32	72	16	2	6	35	2
#Chuck Carr, of	.261	111	17	29	5	1	1	6	8
Rick Christian, of	.234	141	8	33	5	0	0	7	3
Tripp Cromer, ss	.240	338	30	81	16	6	7	29	4
*Paul Ellis, c	.228	79	9	18	2	0	2	8	0
Steve Fanning, ss	.222	117	17	26	5	0	2	14	2
*Jose Fernandez, c	.155	116	7	18	5	0	1	8	0
*Ed Fulton, c	.261	23	3	6	2	0	0	5	0
*David Howell, ph	.170	47	3	8	2	0	0	4	0
Julian Martinez, of	.165	297	19	49	13	1	3	21	2
*Jesus Mendez, 1b	.286	297	36	85	18	2	6	37	4
#Jose Oquendo, 2b	.429	7	3	3	0	0	0	1	0
Don Prybylinski, c	.194	196	10	38	8	0	1	10	2
Mike Ross, 3b	.274	401	40	110	29	0	6	42	4
Odalis Savinon, of	.171	105	10	18	3	0	0	3	3
John Sellick, 1b	.256	301	27	77	19	1	8	41	5
*John Thomas, of	.272	408	49	111	18	5	10	49	3

Batting leaders across all leagues

HITS

Player	Club	Lg.	Hits
Hocking, D.	Vis	Cal	182
*Pose, Scott	Cng	Sou	180
Hall, Billy	Hds	Cal	176
Cordova, M.	Vis	Cal	175
*O'Leary, T.	Elp	Tex	169
T White, R.	HRb	East	169

DOUBLES

Player	Club	Lg.	2B
Ricker, Troy	Vis	Cal	41
Byington, John	Elp	Tex	39
# Gates, Brent	Mod	Cal	39
T#Jones, C.	Grv	Sou	39
Several tied at			37

TRIPLES

Player	Club	Lg.	3B
T*Floyd, Cliff	WPb	Fsl	16
*Martin, Al	BufAmA		15
*Lukachyk, R.	Stk	Cal	14
T White, R.	HRb	East	13
Several tied at			12

EXTRA BASE HITS

Player	Club	Lg.	EBH
*Wilson, N.	Knx	Sou	67
*Dunn, Steve	Vis	Cal	65
Cordova, M.	Vis	Cal	65
T#Nieves, M.	Grv	Sou	64
T#Jones, C.	Grv	Sou	64

 # Switch-hitter
** Left-handed*
T Player has been with more than one team, listed with last team. (Players in major leagues are listed with last minor league team.)

Batting leaders across all leagues

SLUGGING PERCENTAGE

Player	Club	Lg.	Slg
Cordova, M.	Vis	Cal	.589
*Delgado, C.	Dun	Fsl	.579
*Martin, Al	Buf	AmA	.557
T#Nieves, M.	Grv	Sou	.555
Berroa, G.	Nvl	AmA	.551

ON-BASE PERCENTAGE

Player	Club	Lg.	OBP
Grebeck, B.	Psp	Cal	.480
T*Waggoner, J.	Hvl	Sou	.445
*Ramos, Ken	Can	East	.442
#Becker, R.	Vis	Cal	.441
#Veras, Q.	Clb	Sal	.441

TPA/SO RATIO

Player	Club	Lg.	Ratio
T Raabe, B.	Orl	Sou	28.11
T*Casillas, A.	Oma	AmA	26.35
Schunk, Jerry	Syr	Int	21.67
T*Vina, F.	Slu	Fsl	17.68
Arias, Alex	Iwa	AmA	17.26

 # Switch-hitter
** Left-handed*
T Player has been with more than one team, listed with last team. (Players in major leagues are listed with last minor league team.)

PITCHING	W	L	ERA	G	SV	IP	H	BB	SO
Paul Anderson	4	11	3.37	22	0	123	117	27	73
*David Cassidy	0	3	5.16	8	0	30.2	33	6	8
Fidel Compres	4	3	3.28	54	28	58.2	55	23	39
*Steve Dixon	2	1	1.84	40	2	49	34	15	65
John Ericks	2	6	4.08	13	0	75	69	29	71
*Bryan Eversgerd	0	1	6.75	6	0	5.1	7	2	4
Steffen Majer	2	3	3.83	22	0	47	43	26	34
Kevin Meier	11	6	2.58	27	0	171	156	37	107
Gab Ozuna	3	6	2.08	57	4	78	63	27	62
Lee Plemel	1	1	3.86	13	0	21	31	6	9
Rick Shackle	4	4	2.50	18	0	72	67	15	45
*Tom Urbani	4	6	1.93	10	0	65.1	49	15	41
*Allen Watson	8	5	2.15	14	0	96.1	77	23	93
Dennis Wiseman	9	12	2.90	24	0	146	143	28	83

El Paso Diablos (Brewers) AA

BATTING	Avg.	AB	R	H	2B	3B	HR	RBI	SB
*Wynn Beck, ph	.174	23	2	4	2	0	0	5	0
John Byington, dh	.306	468	60	143	39	4	4	64	5
#Edgar Caceres, ss	.312	378	50	118	14	6	2	52	9
Mike Carter, of	.255	165	20	42	4	4	1	15	10
*Vince Castaldo, of	.289	412	61	119	33	10	3	50	12
*Brian Cisarik, of	.048	21	1	1	0	0	0	0	2
Mike Couture, of	.267	15	3	4	1	0	0	0	1
#Tony Diggs, of	.217	281	47	61	6	3	0	20	31
*Bo Dodson, 1b	.248	335	47	83	19	6	4	46	3
Craig Faulkner, c	.272	324	38	88	19	2	5	51	1
John Finn, 2b	.276	439	83	121	12	6	1	47	30
Mike Guerrero, ss	.245	257	36	63	11	4	1	28	6
*Sandy Guerrero, 2b	.200	20	2	4	1	0	1	3	0
Charlie Hillemann, of	.216	116	15	25	7	3	1	10	4
Bob Kappesser, c	.236	233	32	55	7	1	1	33	6
*Alan Lewis, 3b	.271	328	41	89	20	6	4	44	2
*Oreste Marrero, dh	.185	54	8	10	2	1	1	8	1
*Troy O'Leary, of	.334	506	92	169	27	8	5	79	28
Ed Smith, 3b	.291	86	11	25	5	0	2	15	0

PITCHING	W	L	ERA	G	SV	IP	H	BB	SO
Glenn Carter	6	5	4.73	15	0	78	91	23	40
Larry Carter	0	1	6.23	4	0	13	15	3	9
Jim Czajkowski	5	7	4.88	57	10	79.1	92	26	62
Tim Dell	5	5	5.65	36	2	88.2	98	26	61
*Mike Farrell	7	6	2.62	14	0	106.1	95	25	66
*Dave Fitzgerald	3	1	6.59	24	0	42.1	54	15	23
*Brain Hancock	1	0	3.18	1	0	6.2	9	2	5
*Ted Higuera	0	1	3.60	1	0	5	4	2	3
Jim Hunter	1	1	3.00	3	0	18	18	3	9
*Kerry Knox	0	1	6.89	13	0	16.2	16	12	12
Steve Lienhard	0	1	6.90	7	0	30	44	7	21
David Martinez	5	4	4.80	15	0	81.2	95	26	75
*Tom McGraw	6	0	2.73	11	0	69.1	75	26	53
*Rafael Novoa	10	7	3.26	22	0	146.1	143	48	124
*Dave Richards	4	5	2.86	47	1	63	55	34	71
Ron Robinson	0	0	10.80	1	0	5	8	1	0
Steve Sparks	9	8	5.37	28	1	141.2	159	50	79
*Jeff Tabaka	9	5	2.52	50	10	82	67	38	75
Scott Taylor	4	2	3.48	11	0	54.1	45	19	37
Brandy Vann	1	8	5.14	42	7	77	87	43	72
Rob Wishnevski	1	0	1.04	13	9	17.1	7	4	16

Jackson Generals (Astros) AA

BATTING	Avg.	AB	R	H	2B	3B	HR	RBI	SB
Willie Ansley, of	.242	120	18	29	8	1	0	3	10
*Jeff Baldwin, of	.285	179	33	51	13	0	2	27	0
Jeff Ball, 3b	.191	278	27	53	13	2	5	24	5
Kevin Dean, of	.183	208	26	38	8	2	4	20	8
Tony Eusebio, c	.307	339	33	104	9	3	5	44	1
Dave Hajek, 2b	.270	326	36	88	12	3	1	18	8
#Rusty Harris, 2b	.221	95	18	21	4	0	0	10	4
#Frank Kellner, 2b	.239	473	45	113	18	5	3	48	8
*Layne Lambert, 3b	.234	64	7	15	0	1	0	1	0
Lance Madsen, 3b	.229	332	40	76	16	2	13	40	2
Scott Makarewicz, c	.287	345	39	99	15	0	7	39	2
John Massarelli, of	.276	98	15	27	4	1	1	10	10
Joe Mikulik, of	.262	168	20	44	7	2	3	20	4
Orlando Miller, ss	.265	378	51	100	26	5	5	53	7
Ray Montgomery, of	.209	148	13	31	4	1	1	10	4
*Roberto Petagine, 1b	.296	71	8	21	4	0	4	12	1
*Howard Prager, 1b	.258	326	36	84	13	0	5	48	1
Vince Roman, of	.222	36	4	8	3	0	0	3	0
Lee Sammons, of	.227	273	33	62	5	2	2	16	24

PITCHING	W	L	ERA	G	SV	IP	H	BB	SO
*Harold Allen	6	12	3.97	27	0	122.1	127	82	94
Sam August	1	1	1.83	4	0	20.2	15	8	16
Jim Bruske	4	3	2.63	13	0	62.2	54	14	48
Fred Costello	2	2	2.70	36	0	53.1	51	13	35
Brian Griffiths	3	9	3.80	17	0	97	95	42	91
Dave Hajek	0	0	3.00	2	0	3	3	0	3
*Dean Hartgraves	9	6	2.76	22	0	147.2	126	40	92
*Keith Helton	6	3	2.49	34	2	61.1	53	25	58
*Bob Hurta	3	1	2.33	38	3	46.1	33	31	52
Jimmy Jones	1	2	2.50	3	0	18	20	6	20
Todd Jones	3	7	3.14	61	25	66	53	44	60
Steve Larose	0	2	7.61	17	0	24.2	39	15	20
Jim Lewis	3	5	4.11	12	0	70	64	30	43
Ken Luckham	3	6	5.42	16	0	73	77	41	47
Edward Ponte	1	1	2.54	33	0	46	49	19	38
*Matt Rambo	1	0	2.16	5	0	33.1	19	8	39
Earl Sanders	0	1	4.50	4	0	10	7	10	10
Rich Simon	3	4	3.88	34	4	49.2	40	25	30
Donnie Wall	9	6	3.54	18	0	114.1	114	26	99
*Rodney Windes	3	3	2.24	30	4	56.1	50	10	53

Midland Angels (Angels) AA

BATTING	Avg.	AB	R	H	2B	3B	HR	RBI	SB
Edgar Alfonzo, 2b	.295	220	39	65	9	1	4	30	2
*Garret Anderson, of	.274	146	16	40	5	0	2	19	2
*Mick Billmeyer, c	.130	69	5	9	4	1	0	9	0
*Tony Brown, of	.257	183	22	47	9	2	4	18	3
Pete Coachman, dh	.177	141	30	25	4	1	3	13	6
Ron Correia, ss	.290	482	73	140	23	1	6	56	20
*Jim Edmonds, of	.313	246	42	77	15	2	8	32	3
*John Jackson, of	.291	151	19	44	4	3	0	16	12
#Bobby Jones, of	.231	316	45	73	15	1	3	30	5
Corey Kapano, 3b	.182	44	5	8	4	0	0	5	1
Jeff Kipila, of	.259	417	63	108	22	3	21	76	3
#Marcus Lawton, of	.300	120	15	36	7	2	1	11	0
Ray Martinez, 2b	.225	111	16	25	4	3	3	14	1
*Walt McConnell, 3b	.260	169	19	44	8	0	0	16	1
*Mike Musolino, c	.273	22	2	6	1	0	0	4	0
Rey Palacios, c	.261	92	14	24	5	1	5	10	0
Eduardo Perez, 3b	.230	235	27	54	8	1	3	23	19
*J.R. Phillips, 1b	.237	497	58	118	32	4	14	77	5
Jonathan Romero, 3b	.106	47	4	5	0	0	0	2	0
*Dan Rumsey, of	.271	218	39	59	10	7	6	32	5
Matt Stark, c	.377	53	10	20	3	0	2	10	1
*Terry Taylor, 2b	.256	250	37	64	22	1	0	22	0
Fausto Tejero, c	.188	266	21	50	11	0	2	30	1
Mark Wasinger, 3b	.357	56	6	20	5	1	0	8	0

Pitching leaders across all leagues

ERA
(Minimum 111 IP)

Pitcher	Club	Lg.	ERA
*Baptist, T.	Myr	Sal	1.45
T*Thomas, L.	Bir	Sou	1.84
T Alvarez, T.	HRb	East	1.84
Jones, Bob	Bng	East	1.88
T Martinez, J.	Bng	East	1.94
T Waring, J.	Ash	Sal	1.96
*Baker, Scott	Stp	Fsl	1.96
Caruso, Joe	Lyn	Caro	1.98
T*Watson, A.	Lou	AmA	2.00
T*Burrows, T.	Okc	AmA	2.03

WINS

Player	Club	Lg.	W
Fritz, John	Qcy	Mid	20
T Ogea, C.	Can	East	19
T*Krivda, R.	Fre	Caro	17
T Olsen, S.	Bir	Sou	17
T*Embree, A.	Can	East	17
T Alvarez, T.	HRb	East	17
Badorek, M.	Spr	Mid	17

COMPLETE GAMES

Pitcher	Club	Lg.	CG
Chouinard, B.	Knc	Mid	9
T Ventura, J.	Mem	Sou	9
T Alvarez, T.	HRb	East	9
T*Farrell, M.	Elp	Tex	8
Several Tied At			7

SHUTOUTS

Pitcher	Club	Lg.	Sho
T Alvarez, T.	HRb	East	5
T Ventura, J.	Mem	Sou	4
Anderson, M.	Cng	Sou	4
T Robinson, S.	Cng	Sou	4
T Minchey, N.	Paw	Int	4
Jones, Bobby	Bng	East	4

 # Switch-hitter
** Left-handed*
T Player has been with more than one team, listed with last team. (Players in major leagues are listed with last minor league team.)

Pitching leaders across all leagues

SAVES

Pitcher	Club	Lg.	Sv
Kelly, John	Stp	Fsl	38
Draper, Mike	Col	Int	37
Santos, G.	Spr	Mid	35
T Spradlin, J.	Cng	Sou	34
Chaves, R.	Hds	Cal	34

GAMES

Pitcher	Club	Lg.	G
T Ponte, Ed	Osc	Fsl	70
*Puig, Ed	Mem	Sou	68
Chaves, R.	Hds	Cal	68
T Patterson, J.	Swb	Int	67
T*Tidwell, M.	Chr	Sou	65
Cimorelli, F.	Spr	Mid	65

INNINGS PITCHED

Pitcher	Club	Lg.	IP
T*Farrell, M.	Elp	Tex	199.0
T*Watson, A.	Lou	AmA	198.1
T*Johns, D.	Hvl	Sou	195.1
Trachsel, S.	Chr	Sou	191.0
Several tied at			188.1

STRIKEOUTS

Pitcher	Club	Lg.	SO
T*Krivda, R.	Fre	Caro	188
*Taylor, Brien	Ftl	Fsl	187
Hisey, Jason	Sav	Sal	182
T*Watson, A.	Lou	AmA	182
T Jean, Dom.	Alb	East	178

 # Switch-hitter
** Left-handed*
T Player has been with more than one team, listed with last team. (Players in major leagues are listed with last minor league team.)

PITCHING	W	L	ERA	G	SV	IP	H	BB	SO
*Clemente Acosta	0	1	4.50	12	0	12	17	3	15
Dave Adams	6	11	4.48	26	0	169.2	187	51	86
Erik Bennett	1	3	3.91	7	0	46	47	16	36
Bert Blyleven	2	3	2.73	5	0	33	27	3	23
Marvin Cobb	1	1	6.28	17	0	29.2	46	17	21
Ken Edenfield	1	5	5.98	31	2	50.2	60	24	43
*Hilly Hathaway	7	2	3.21	14	0	95.1	90	10	69
Mark Holzemer	2	5	3.83	7	0	45.2	45	13	36
*Todd James	2	3	7.18	25	0	26.1	35	17	16
*Joe Kraemer	2	3	4.89	12	0	39.2	44	10	28
Phillip Leftwich	6	9	5.88	21	0	121	156	37	85
Brett Merriman	3	4	2.70	38	9	53.1	49	10	32
Steve Peck	8	6	3.96	43	0	111.1	105	22	86
Troy Percival	3	0	2.37	20	5	19	18	11	21
Darryl Scott	1	1	1.82	27	9	30.2	20	14	35
Paul Swingle	8	10	4.75	25	0	150.2	158	51	104
Don Vidmar	1	4	3.35	21	0	54.2	53	11	39
Mark Zappelli	7	1	3.19	27	1	99.2	104	19	59

San Antonio Missions (Dodgers) AA

BATTING	Avg.	AB	R	H	2B	3B	HR	RBI	SB
Jorge Alvarez, 2b	.243	305	33	74	11	4	5	32	8
Billy Ashley, of	.279	380	60	106	23	1	24	66	13
Bryan Baar, c	.137	131	11	18	6	0	3	11	0
Tim Barker, ss	.271	350	47	95	17	3	1	26	25
Tony Barron, of	.402	97	18	39	4	1	7	22	7
*Adam Brown, dh	.211	76	4	16	4	0	2	9	0
Mike Busch, 3b	.238	416	58	99	14	2	18	51	3
*Anthony Collier, of	.227	141	12	32	5	3	1	13	0
*John Deutsch, 1b	.206	214	28	44	10	0	6	16	1
*Scott Doffek, of	.288	205	26	59	7	3	2	28	2
Freddy Gonzalez, of	.250	52	3	13	2	1	0	5	0
Matt Howard, 2b	.270	345	40	93	12	5	2	34	18
Garey Ingram, of	.288	198	34	57	9	5	2	17	11
Steve Kliafas, ss	.257	35	1	9	2	0	0	4	0
Ron Maurer, 3b	.272	224	29	61	13	0	0	14	4
Raul Mondesi, of	.265	68	8	18	2	2	2	14	3
*Chris Morrow, of	.233	245	22	57	5	4	5	30	4
Hector Ortiz, c	.203	59	1	12	1	0	0	5	0
Mike Piazza, c	.377	114	18	43	11	0	7	20	0
#Murph Proctor, 1b	.302	235	32	71	17	1	3	37	2
#Lance Rice, c	.232	194	17	45	9	0	2	18	0
Ira Smith, dh	.364	11	3	4	0	1	0	1	0
*Vernon Spearman, of	.281	185	24	52	3	3	0	11	18

PITCHING	W	L	ERA	G	SV	IP	H	BB	SO
Steve Allen	5	2	2.62	43	5	79	62	17	64
Bill Bene	0	2	3.09	18	0	32	19	34	25
*Jason Brosnan	1	7	7.79	8	0	32.1	44	21	27
Albert Bustillos	1	0	0.69	6	2	13	8	3	9
Ray Calhoun	1	4	2.51	32	5	43	37	33	24
*Omar Daal	2	6	5.02	35	5	57.1	60	33	52
Javier Delahoya	2	1	2.84	5	0	25.1	20	17	24
Balvino Galvez	0	6	5.72	19	3	46.2	53	22	42
Greg Hansell	6	4	2.83	14	0	92.1	80	33	66
Mike James	2	1	2.67	8	0	54	39	20	52
Jamie McAndrew	3	4	3.58	11	0	50.1	50	19	35
*Mark Mimbs	1	5	3.61	13	0	82.1	78	22	55
*Mike Mimbs	10	8	4.23	24	1	130.2	132	73	87
Chris Nichting	4	5	2.52	13	0	79.2	58	37	81
Jose Parra	2	0	6.14	3	0	15.2	22	7	7
Brian Piotrowicz	2	0	3.03	16	0	30.2	28	3	14
Sean Snedeker	2	0	0.69	3	0	13	13	1	4
Dennis Springer	6	7	4.35	18	0	122	114	49	73
Jody Treadwell	3	5	4.14	29	1	76	74	40	68
Bill Wengert	2	3	3.22	10	0	50.1	48	13	43
Todd Williams	7	4	3.48	39	13	44	47	23	35

Shreveport Captains (Giants) AA

BATTING	Avg.	AB	R	H	2B	3B	HR	RBI	SB
Clay Bellinger, ss	.207	434	44	90	18	3	13	50	7
Kevin Bellomo, of	.077	13	2	1	0	0	0	0	0
Joel Chimelis, 2b	.319	279	47	89	13	1	9	32	6
Eric Christopherson, c	.252	270	36	68	10	1	6	34	1
*Troy Clemens, c	.167	6	0	1	0	0	0	1	0
Jamie Cooper, of	.243	181	27	44	5	1	0	4	13
#Todd Crosby, 2b	.200	195	13	39	3	1	0	14	0
Ron Crowe, of	.242	256	26	62	12	1	3	25	4
Adell Davenport, 3b	.286	441	54	126	31	5	19	88	2
*Mike Easley, 1b	.206	194	20	40	3	2	0	11	2
Dan Fernandez, c	.216	185	19	40	2	0	2	22	2
Steve Finken, 2b	.231	91	8	21	5	0	3	6	0
Dax Jones, of	.303	66	10	20	0	2	1	7	2
*Ron Jones, of	.242	198	20	48	9	4	4	25	3
Kevin Kasper, 2b	.203	69	7	14	5	1	0	7	0
*Dan Lewis, 1b	.312	170	28	53	3	0	3	25	2
*Jason McFarlin, of	.210	105	13	22	3	3	1	3	10
#Jerome Nelson, ph	.167	6	1	1	0	0	0	1	0
Reed Peters, of	.312	231	30	72	13	3	4	29	4
Derek Reid, of	.167	6	1	1	1	0	0	0	0
Albert Rodriguez, 2b	.241	79	7	19	3	0	0	3	0
*Reuben Smiley, of	.257	315	38	81	12	5	6	35	19
Ricky Ward, 2b	.000	3	0	0	0	0	0	0	0
*Pete Weber, of	.288	417	64	120	23	10	3	33	14

PITCHING	W	L	ERA	G	SV	IP	H	BB	SO
Dan Carlson	15	9	3.19	27	0	186	166	60	157
Ron Crowe	0	0	0.00	3	0	3.1	1	2	3
Scott Garrelts	0	0	1.86	2	0	10.2	4	3	15
*Chris Hancock	2	4	3.10	8	0	49.1	37	18	30
Carl Hanselman	6	4	2.48	11	0	80	73	17	42
*Vince Herring	0	1	4.06	23	1	31	37	14	26
Rick Huisman	7	4	2.35	17	0	103.1	79	31	100
Randy McCament	2	1	10.80	6	0	5	11	7	1
Kevin McGehee	9	7	2.96	25	0	158.1	146	42	140
Jim Myers	2	4	4.78	33	18	32	39	10	15
Louis Pote	4	2	0.96	20	0	38.2	20	15	26
Dan Rambo	6	3	2.85	28	1	60	56	19	45
Steve Reed	1	0	0.62	27	23	29	18	0	33
*Kevin Rogers	8	5	2.58	16	0	101	87	29	110
Gary Sharko	1	1	5.09	14	0	18.2	22	4	9
Rob Taylor	4	2	2.54	34	1	60.1	60	17	56
Salomon Torres	6	10	4.21	25	0	162.1	167	34	151
*Mark Yockey	4	2	4.14	42	0	50	53	28	35

Tulsa Drillers (Rangers) AA

BATTING	Avg.	AB	R	H	2B	3B	HR	RBI	SB
Kevin Belcher, of	.244	381	55	93	19	3	18	60	6
Mike Burton, 1b	.236	72	11	17	2	0	2	13	0
#Cris Colon, ss	.263	415	35	109	16	3	1	44	7
Doug Davis, c	.205	39	3	8	2	0	0	1	0
*Rusty Greer, 1b	.267	359	47	96	22	4	5	37	2
Donald Harris, of	.254	303	39	77	15	2	11	39	4
*David Hulse, of	.285	354	40	101	14	3	3	20	17
Darryl Kennedy, c	.224	98	6	22	2	0	0	9	0
Pete Kuld, c	.228	224	24	51	8	3	9	30	1
Paul List, of	.292	130	17	38	7	1	1	14	1
Trey McCoy, dh	.192	52	5	10	0	0	2	6	0
*Rod Morris, of	.262	366	37	96	13	9	0	29	9
Timmie Morrow, of	.133	30	2	4	1	0	0	3	1
Darren Niethammer, c	.206	107	21	22	4	1	3	13	3
Jose Oliva, 3b	.270	445	57	120	28	6	16	75	3
Paul Postier, 1b	.231	130	8	30	4	2	0	12	0
John Russell, c	.258	163	26	42	11	0	10	27	0
Luke Sable, 2b	.243	268	27	65	8	2	2	16	3
Tony Scruggs, of	.279	43	3	12	3	0	0	2	3
Jon Shave, 2b	.287	453	57	130	23	5	2	36	6

Starting pitchers

SO/9 IP RATIO
(22 Starts)

Pitcher	Club	Lg.	Ratio
*Beckett, R.	Wlo	Mid	10.96
*Taylor, Brien	Ftl	Fsl	10.43
T Jean, Dom.	Alb	East	9.85
Bevil, Brian	App	Mid	9.69
*Hitchcock, S.	Alb	East	9.51

AVERAGE AGAINST

Pitcher	Club	Lg.	Avg.
*Beckett, R.	Wlo	Mid	.179
*Spoljaric, P.	Myr	Sal	.193
Fritz, John	Qcy	Mid	.205
Ruffcorn, S.	Sar	Fsl	.206
T*O'Donoghue	Roc	Int	.207
Plaster, Allen	Fre	Caro	.207

Relief pitchers

SO/9 IP RATIO
(35 Games)

Pitcher	Club	Lg.	Ratio
Speek, Frank	Spr	Mid	14.92
Santos, G.	Spr	Mid	13.89
T Hrusovsky,J.	Cdr	Mid	13.59
T Miceli, D.	Mem	Sou	13.28
Musset, Jose	Qcy	Mid	13.06

AVERAGE AGAINST

Pitcher	Club	Lg.	Avg.
Martin, Gregg	Myr	Sal	.125
Revenig, Todd	Hvl	Sou	.151
T*Pennington	Roc	Int	.152
T Miceli, D.	Mem	Sou	.154
Caruso, Joe	Lyn	Caro	.162
Polak, Rich	Prw	Caro	.162

 # Switch-hitter
** Left-handed*
T Player has been with more than one team, listed with last team. (Players in major leagues are listed with last minor league team.)

Batting leaders by position

CATCHER

Player	Club	Lg.	Avg.
*Delgado, C.	Dun	Fsl	.324
Lopez, Javy	Grv	Sou	.321
#Williams, G.	Mad	Mid	.304
#Walbeck, M.	Chr	Sou	.301
Miller, Damian	Ken	Mid	.292

FIRST BASE

Player	Club	Lg.	Avg.
Sparks, Don	Alb	East	.313
#Snow, J.T.	Col	Int	.313
Morman, R.	Nvl	AmA	.310
T#Proctor, M.	San	Tex	.310
*Dunn, Steve	Vis	Cal	.305

SECOND BASE

Player	Club	Lg.	Avg.
#Hall, Billy	Hds	Cal	.356
T Alfonzo, E.	Mdl	Tex	.329
#Gates, B.	Mod	Cal	.321
#Veras, Q.	Clb	Sal	.319
Jordan, Kevin	Prw	Caro	.311

THIRD BASE

Player	Club	Lg.	Avg.
Tatum, Jim	Den	AmA	.329
Young, Kevin	Buf	AmA	.314
Schu, Rick	Swb	Int	.310
#Young, D.	Spr	Mid	.310
*Stahoviak, S.	Vis	Cal	.308

SHORTSTOP

Player	Club	Lg.	Avg.
Grebeck, B.	Psp	Cal	.336
#Hocking, D.	Vis	Cal	.331
Cruz, Fausto	Rno	Cal	.319
#Caceres, E.	Elp	Tex	.312
T#Jones, C.	Grv	Sou	.311

OUTFIELD

Player	Club	Lg.	Avg.
*Butler, Rob	Dun	Fsl	.358
*Pose, Scott	Cng	Sou	.342
Cordova, M.	Vis	Cal	.341
*Ramos, Ken	Can	East	.339
T*Neill, Mike	Hvl	Sou	.335

 # Switch-hitter
** Left-handed*
T Player has been with more than one team, listed with last team. (Players in major leagues are listed with last minor league team.)

PITCHING	W	L	ERA	G	SV	IP	H	BB	SO
Mike Arner	2	0	3.54	15	1	28	32	8	19
*Brian Bohanon	2	1	1.27	6	0	28.1	25	9	25
Jeff Bronkey	2	7	2.55	45	13	71.2	51	25	58
Rob Brown	5	4	3.73	38	2	70	75	18	60
*Terry Burrows	6	3	2.13	14	0	76	66	35	59
*Don Carman	3	3	2.68	12	0	57	45	12	36
Scott Chiamparino	0	0	1.93	3	0	19.2	17	5	18
Hector Fajardo	2	1	2.16	5	0	25	19	7	26
Chris Gies	6	8	3.56	17	0	99.2	101	31	36
Steven Goetz	2	1	0.63	10	1	14.1	10	6	7
*Bryan Gore	6	5	2.49	23	0	72.1	68	15	43
*James Hurst	1	0	0.57	8	0	16.2	10	3	12
Danilo Leon	5	0	0.60	12	1	30	15	8	34
Barry Manuel	2	0	4.00	16	2	27	28	16	28
Kurt Miller	7	5	3.68	16	0	88	82	35	73
*Ritchie Moody	0	0	1.42	7	2	6.1	3	2	6
Robb Nen	1	1	2.16	4	0	25	21	2	20
*Darren Oliver	0	1	3.14	3	0	14.1	15	4	14
David Perez	4	3	4.68	15	0	60.2	61	26	30
Paul Postier	0	0	0.00	1	0	2	1	0	2
*Brian Romero	2	5	4.47	13	0	52.1	62	20	44
Steve Rowley	0	0	7.71	3	0	7	7	7	8
Jeff Sellers	1	0	3.46	7	0	13	14	8	9
*Cedric Shaw	6	2	3.75	12	0	70.2	64	18	49
Chris Shiflett	1	1	4.37	11	1	23.2	18	7	20
*Dan Smith	11	7	2.52	24	0	146.1	110	34	122
Matt Whiteside	0	1	2.41	33	21	34.2	31	3	30

Wichita Wranglers (Padres) AA

BATTING	Avg.	AB	R	H	2B	3B	HR	RBI	SB
Mike Basso, c	.500	4	1	2	0	0	0	0	0
#Steve Bethea, ss	.249	253	32	63	12	3	1	32	11
*Jay Gainer, 1b	.261	376	57	98	12	1	23	67	4
#Darius Gash, of	.288	52	2	15	1	1	0	8	7
#Mark Gieseke, 1b	.246	240	30	59	11	2	5	36	0
*Paul Gonzalez, 3b	.255	432	59	110	18	2	15	54	7
#Vince Harris, of	.281	242	36	68	12	1	1	20	38
Ray Holbert, ss	.283	304	46	86	7	3	2	23	26
#Dwayne Hosey, of	.253	427	56	108	23	5	9	68	16
Chris Jelic, 1b	.292	96	14	28	3	1	2	18	4
Brian Johnson, c	.290	245	30	71	20	0	3	26	3
Pedro Lopez, c	.245	319	35	78	8	4	6	48	4
Steve Martin, of	.213	183	20	39	8	2	3	17	15
Tim McWilliam, of	.233	146	18	34	5	1	4	14	0
Bill Meury, 3b	.250	8	0	2	0	0	0	1	0
*J.D. Noland, of	.270	452	59	122	21	6	5	52	40
*Darrell Sherman, of	.332	220	60	73	11	2	6	25	26
Mat Witkowski, 2b	.272	430	61	117	13	4	6	48	11

PITCHING	W	L	ERA	G	SV	IP	H	BB	SO
*Renay Bryand	2	3	4.27	49	1	53.2	59	19	39
Mark Ettles	3	8	2.77	54	22	68.1	54	23	86
Scott Fredrickson	4	7	3.19	56	5	73.1	50	38	66
*Mark Gieseke	1	0	0.00	2	0	3	0	1	5
Joey Hamilton	3	0	2.86	6	0	35.2	33	11	26
Howard Hilton	0	1	7.88	7	0	8	16	5	7
Steve Hoeme	1	1	6.31	20	0	36.2	48	19	24
Kelly Lifgren	1	6	4.10	37	0	86.2	89	32	67
*Mike Linskey	10	6	4.22	26	0	136.1	121	53	128
*Pedro Martinez	11	7	2.99	26	0	168.1	153	52	142
*Lance Painter	10	5	3.53	27	0	163.1	138	55	137
Scott Sanders	7	5	3.49	14	0	88.2	85	37	95
Royal Thomas	7	7	6.32	41	2	125.1	151	51	91
Dean Wilkins	1	2	5.80	26	0	40.1	37	24	41
Brian Wood	1	1	7.20	17	4	20	23	10	25
Tim Worrell	8	6	2.86	19	0	126.2	115	32	109

Class of '92: The top prospects

During the 1992 season, *Baseball Weekly* examined the year's top minor league prospects, position by position. The list does not include players who reached the majors before rosters expanded Sept. 1.

OUTFIELDERS:

▸**Marty Cordova, Twins:** The California League MVP just missed the Triple Crown (.341), with league-leading 28 HR and 131 RBI. He committed just three errors in the outfield.

▸**Rondell White, Expos:** He can beat you with his bat, arm, legs or glove. He hit .316 in 111 games at Class A West Palm Beach (10 doubles, 12 triples, 4 HR, and 42 SB), then .306 in 20 games for Double-A Harrisburg.

▸**Juan de la Rosa, Blue Jays:** He has a major league arm and defensive skills right now. Voted most exciting player in the Southern League by managers (.329, 32 doubles, 12 triples, 12 HR, 53 RBI).

▸**Darrell Sherman, Padres:** Speedy Sherman hit .332 with 26 stolen bases in 64 games at Double-A Wichita to start the year, then .286 (26 steals) in 71 games for Triple-A Las Vegas.

▸**Cliff Floyd, Expos:** Named the South Atlantic League's best hitting prospect and most exciting player (.307, 16 HR, 95 RBI). He hit for the cycle twice, and his 16 triples set a Sally League record.

▸**Matt Mieske, Brewers:** The San Diego Padres were reluctant to make the Gary Sheffield trade because they didn't want to part with Mieske. He was league MVP his first two pro seasons (1990-91). After the trade, he went to Triple-A Denver (.267, 29 doubles, 11 triples, 19 HR, 77 RBI). He had 23 outfield assists.

▸**Ken Ramos, Indians:** He won the Eastern League batting title at Canton-Akron with the highest EL average in five years (.339). He also set team records with 150 hits and 94 runs scored. A leadoff hitter, he hits to all fields and is a great bunter a la Kenny Lofton.

▸**Ozzie Canseco, Cardinals:** The only thing he has in common with his twin brother, Jose, is raw power (.266, 22 HR, 57 RBI). Some of his homers were monster shots; one went out of the park and onto a freeway ramp in Buffalo.

▸**Melvin Nieves, Braves:** He hit .283 (23 doubles, 18 HR, 76 RBI) in 100 games for Double-A Greenville. He hit .351 with runners in scoring position, had three 5-RBI games, and a 4-RBI game. A switch-hitter, he batted .303 right-handed, .274 left- handed.

▸**Mike Kelly, Braves:** A three-time All-American at Arizona State, he hit just .229 for Double-A Greenville, but he had 25 HR, 71 RBI, and 22 stolen bases—the first 20-20 man in Greenville Braves history. He committed just three errors in center field.

INFIELDERS:

▸**SS Chipper Jones, Braves:** He hit .277 in 70 games (4 HR, 31 RBI) at Class A Durham, then finished the year at Double-A Greenville hitting .346 (17 doubles, a club-record 11 triples, 9 HR, 42 RBI). His .594 slugging percentage was a Greenville Braves record.

▸**3B Dmitri Young, Cardinals:** He hit .310 in 135 games at Class A Springfield (Ill.) with 14 HR and 72 RBI, and led the league with 36 doubles. He also stole 14 bases.

▸**3B Kevin Young, Pirates:** He's big, strong, and fast. He recovered from a .235 start in April to hit .314 in 137 games at Triple-A Buffalo (29 doubles, 8 HR, 65 RBI, 18 steals).

▸**SS Manny Alexander, Orioles:** He hit .259 in 127 games at Double-A Hagerstown (22 doubles, 8 triples, 2 HR, 41 RBI, 43 steals). He stole at least one base against every other team—home and away—in the EL.

▸**3B Joel Chimelis, Giants:** He hit

.319 in 74 games (9 HR, 32 RBI) and struck out just 34 times in 279 at-bats for Double-A Shreveport, then finished the season hitting .303 (185 at-bats) at Triple-A Phoenix.

▸**3B Willie Greene, Reds:** He hit .283 (12 HR, 40 RBI) at Class A Cedar Rapids, then .278 in 96 games at Double-A Chattanooga , finishing with 27 HR and 106 RBI.

▸**1B J.T. Snow, Angels:** Playing for the Columbus Clippers, Snow was the International League MVP and Rookie of the Year. He also won the IL batting title (.313) by .00004 over Rochester's Luis Mercedes.

▸**2B Billy Hall, Padres:** The switch-hitter led the Class A California League in batting (.356) and stolen bases (49) before earning a promotion to his hometown (Wichita) for the Texas League playoffs.

▸**3B Shane Andrews, Expos:** He hit .230 with 18 doubles, 25 home runs and 87 RBI at Class A Albany (Ga.). He was voted the best defensive third baseman in the South Atlantic League by managers.

▸**2B Brent Gates, Athletics:** He set a California League record with his 35-game hitting streak at Modesto. He finished at .321 (39 doubles, 10 HR, 88 RBI) in 133 games.

CATCHERS:

▸**Matt Walbeck, Cubs:** He hit .301 (22 doubles, 7 HR, 42 RBI) in 105 games at Charlotte and represented the Knights in the Double-A All-Star Game. He had only 10 errors.

▸**Mike Lieberthal, Phillies:** He hit .286 (16 doubles, 2 HR, 37 RBI) in 86 games at Double-A Reading, and committed just seven errors—while throwing out 31 of 83 runners (37 percent).

▸**Javy Lopez, Braves:** He hit .321 (28 doubles, 16 HR, 60 RBI) in 115 games at Double-A Greenville. He committed just seven errors behind the plate and threw out 36 of 98 runners (37 percent).

▸**Tony Eusebio, Astros:** He hit .307 (9 doubles, 5 HR, 44 RBI) in 94 games and threw out 45 percent of opposing baserunners.

▸**Rich Rowland, Tigers:** He is a power-hitting prospect with the Triple-A Toledo Mud Hens. He dropped from .272 to .235, but hit 25 HR and drove in 82 runs in 136 games.He committed just six errors and threw out 48 percent of opposing runners.

▸**Dan Wilson, Reds:** He hit .251 in 106 games at Triple-A Nashville. He had a .990 fielding percentage and threw out 34.8 percent of opposing runners. He was charged with just two passed balls and eight errors.

▸**Eric Christopherson, Giants:** He hit .252 (6 HR, 34 RBI) in 80 games at Double-A Shreveport, then missed the Texas League playoffs with a sprained thumb on his catching hand.

▸**Brad Ausmus, Rockies:** He hit .242 (14 doubles, 35 RBI) in 111 games at Triple-A Columbus, with 19 stolen bases.

▸**Mike Piazza, Dodgers:** He hit .377 (7 HR) in 31 games for Double-A San Antonio, then .341 (16 HR, 69 RBI) in 94 games at Triple-A Albuquerque. He also had 22 doubles and five triples.

▸**Joe Kmak, Brewers:** He hit .311 (11 doubles, 3 HR, 31 RBI) at Triple-A Denver, yet defense is his forte. He handles pitchers well and has a gun for an arm, throwing out 32 of 66.

—by Bill Koenig

Player of the Year

The *USA TODAY/Baseball Weekly* 1992 minor league Player of the Year was catcher **Carlos Delgado**, of the Dunedin Blue Jays. What Delgado did in the Florida State League is nearly unheard of. He hit .324 with 30 home runs and 100 RBI. Only two other players have hit 30 homers in the history of the league—the average number for the league leader is 17. He was only 20 years old, and already was pegged for a "tremendous future" by Toronto executives. About his plans for 1993, Delgado said: "I'd like to be in the big leagues, to be honest."

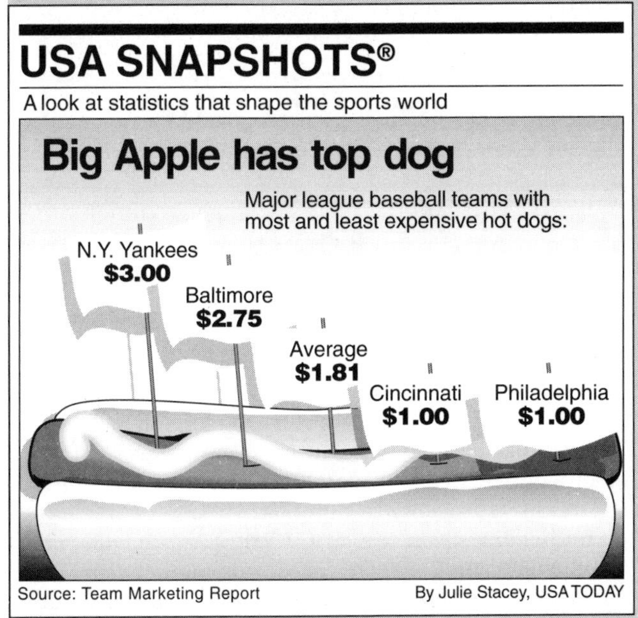

INSIDE:

- Little League
- American Legion
- Babe Ruth Baseball
- PONY League
- Championship coverage, scores
- *Plus: How to find a team*

1992 World Series Scores

▸**Aug. 24:** Long Beach, Calif. 10, So. Holland, Ill. 6; Hamilton Square, N.J. 5, So. Lake Charles, La. 0; Santo Domingo, D.R. 29, Valleyfield, Que., Canada 0; Zamboanga City, Philippines 14, Kaiserslautern, Germany 2.

▸**Aug. 25:** Long Beach, Calif. 6, Hamilton Square, N.J. 4; So. Lake Charles, La. 3, So. Holland, Ill. 2; Santo Domingo, D.R. 24, Kaiserslautern, Germany 0; Zamboanga City, Philippines 2, Valleyfield, Que., Canada 0.

▸**Aug. 26:** Long Beach, Calif. 16, So. Lake Charles, La. 1; Hamilton Square, N.J. 5, So. Holland, Ill. 2; Valleyfield, Que., Canada 10, Kaiserslautern, Germany 3; Santo Domingo, D.R. 8, Zamboanga City, Philippines 1.

▸**Aug. 27:** (USA Champion`-ship) Long Beach, Calif. 1, Hamilton Square, N.J. 0; (International Championship) Zamboanga City, Philippines 5, Santo Domingo, D.R. 1.

▸**Aug. 29:** (World Championship) Zamboanga City, Philippines 15, Long Beach, Calif. 4.

Little League: Diamonds in the rough

This is where it all begins—real uniforms, organized teams, umpires, proud moms and dads, and dreams of one day smacking a home run out of a major league ballpark. Perhaps the greatest thrill of Little League—aside from the delight of the players themselves—is watching the talents of these youngsters develop under the guidance of devoted coaches. Brien Taylor, 1991's top overall amateur draft pick, was once a wild Little League pitcher who walked more batters than he struck out. Today he is the New York Yankees' promise of the future.

But youth baseball is much more than an incubator for future big-league stars. It teaches youngsters how to be part of a team, to accept losses along with victories and, most of all, how to have a lot of fun.

The best-known of all youth baseball associations, Little League was founded in 1939 in Williamsport, Pa., site of its annual World Series for 11- and 12-year-olds. It now encompasses 46 countries and 2.5 million youngsters, with four age groups in baseball, and three age groups for girls' softball.

Philippine team wins series, but loses crown

WILLIAMSPORT, Pa.—In a routine that has become as common as an Ozzie Smith gold glove, the Far East representative again captured the Little League World Series. In a sight that wasn't as common, the champion was from the Philippines, not Taiwan. And it came in the Philippines' first appearance in the World Series.

Then, however, in a sight never before seen in Little League history, the Philippine team had its crown stripped. The reason: Only six of the 14 members of the team representing Zamboanga City, Philippines actually came from the city. Little League rules state the players must be from the municipality.

The others came from teams more than 500 miles from Zamboanga. District administrator Armando Andaya said he authorized the replacements for "justifiable reasons." Other officials said the goal of the team was simply to defeat the Taiwanese champion, which has won 15 titles since 1968 as Far East champion.

"Our Philippine Leaguers defeated the American champions in their own national sport in their homeland," said Andaya. "The Americans in Williamsport just could not take it at the hands of the Filipinos . . . why Little League Baseball International acted the way it did is beyond reason."

The U.S. champion, from Long Beach, Calif., was declared winner. They lost in the Aug. 29 title contest 15-4 to Zamboanga City.

After the Philippine victory, the players were welcomed home with a ticker-tape parade and a televised meeting with President Fidel Ramos, who praised them as national heroes and offered $40,000 scholarships. But the Little League administrators were not treated as kindly. In fact, it was an investigation by Manila sportswriters that uncovered the violation. Manila newspapers also alleged some of the players on the team were over the 12-year-old age limit.

"Because of the intense desire to win by all means, the spirit of sportsmanship loses its meaning," television commentator Francisco Evangelista said. "Because of braggadocio and desire for being the champion, we have sacrificed our young players and we lost face in the country and in the eye of the world."

The U.S. winners were coached by former National League MVP Jeff Burroughs. His son Sean, 11, hit 37 home runs in 46 tournament games, including one that went an estimated 280-300 feet.

How to find a team

Little League Baseball's national headquarters is located at the site of its annual World Series: in Williamsport, Pa. To find your local offices, contact the regional headquarters listed below:

▸**National Headquarters:** P.O. Box 3485, Williamsport, PA 17701; (717) 326-1921

▸**Western Region Headquarters:** 6707 Little League Drive, San Bernardino, CA 92407; (714) 887-6444

▸**Central Region Headquarters:** 4360 N. Mitthoeffer Rd., Indianapolis, IN 46236; (317) 897-6127

▸**Southern Region Headquarters:** P.O. Box 13366, St. Petersburg, FL 33733; (813) 344-2661

▸**Eastern Region Headquarters:** P.O. Box 3485, Williamsport, PA 17701; (717) 326-1921

▸**Texas State Headquarters:** 1612 University-Parks Dr., Waco, TX 76706; (817) 756-1816

Little League facts

Here's a nutshell look at Little League:

▸**Founded:** 1939

▸**Ages:** 11-18

▸**Divisions:** Little League (11-12); Junior League (age 13); Senior League (13-15); Big League (16-18)

▸**Total active players:** 2.5 million

▸**Countries:** USA; 45 foreign

Roundup of champions

Winners of other divisions of Little League:

▸**Big League World Series** (ages 16-18): Broward County, Fla. 5, Venezuela 4. *First winner from USA since 1985.

▸**Senior League World Series (ages 13-15):** Taiwan 6, Dominican Republic 1.

▸**Junior League World Series (age 13):** Lake Charles, La. 7, Portage, Ind. 2.

Road to the Legion title

Day by day scores of the 1992 American Legion World Series:

▸**Aug. 26:** Arlington Heights, Ill., 8, Newbury Park, Calif. 5; E. Hartford, Conn., 14, Medford, Ore., 6.; Brooklawn, N.J., 4, Guaynabo, P.R. 3; Gonzales, La., 5, Fargo, N.D. 4.

▸**Aug. 27:** Newbury Park 7, Guaynabo 1; Fargo 5, Medford 3; Arlington Heights 2, Brooklawn 1; E. Hartford 12, Gonzales 1. Guaynabo, Medford eliminated.

▸**Aug. 28:** Brooklawn 6, Fargo 2; Newbury Park 6, Gonzales 5; Arlington Hgts 5, E. Hartford 4. Fargo, Gonzales eliminated.

▸**Aug. 29:** Brooklawn 14, E. Hartford 4; Newbury Park 7, Arlington Heights 4. E. Hartford eliminated.

▸**Aug. 30:** Newbury Park 3, Brooklawn 0 (Brooklawn eliminated); Newbury Park 10, Arlington Heights 0 (Arlington Heights eliminated).

How to find a team

American Legion's national headquarters are located in Indianapolis. There are separate headquarters for each of the 50 states. many of which change from year to year. To find your state's current headquarters, contact:

▸**National Headquarters:** 700 N. Pennsylvania, Indianapolis, IN 46204; (317) 635-8411.

American Legion was the first youth league

American Legion is the oldest of all youth leagues. Founded in 1925 for players 17 and under, it now includes players up to age 19—and has been a springboard for many young players. Major league scouts are a common sight at the national playoffs, staged since 1926. Headquartered in Indianapolis, the league has over 760,000 registered players.

California team wins Legion World Series

FARGO, N.D.—The upstarts from Newbury Park, Calif., won the 1992 American Legion World Series with consecutive shutout victories on Aug. 30 against Brooklawn, N.J., 3-0 and, in the finale, Arlington Heights, Ill., 10-0. The first victory against the defending champion youths from New Jersey came behind the five-hit pitching of **Adam West**. West was 14-2 on a team that went 43-3 this season. **Jeff Naster**, used sparingly along the way, came through nobly in his denial of favored Arlington, also yielding only five hits.

But the consistent week-long play of shortstop **David Lamb** earned him selection as Legion Player of the Year and a $2,000 college scholarship.

Another major award went to **John Klopp**, the standout on the losing Illinois team as a pitcher and left fielder. He was given the annual Sportsmanship Award. The award combines recognition for performance and the Legion's emphasis on good conduct on and off the field.

Hometowner **Brannon Weigel**, whose Fargo team was eliminated in the third round of play, won the Louisville Slugger batting award for a .448 average in regional and national tournament competition.

Also honored for postseason hitting was **Trent Martin** of Newbury, who won the trophy for most postseason runs batted in with 17. **Mike Harris** of Brooklawn was the postseason leader with 29 total bases in tournament play and received the Rawlings Big Stick award, now necessarily achieved with aluminum bats, standard equipment for all Legion teams. The top pitching award, named for Bob Feller, the first Legion player to make baseball's Hall of Fame, went to **Tighe Curran** of Newbury. Curran had 35 strikeouts in the tournament.

—by Carl Lundquist

Ruth baseball: A big hit for over 40 years

Begun in 1951 for players from 13 to 15, Babe Ruth baseball was started in Hamilton Township, N.J., a suburb of Trenton. An older division (ages 16-18) was started in 1968, with a separate division for 13-year-olds formed in 1974. More than 600,000 youngsters play Babe Ruth baseball, which includes competition in the Bambino League, incorporating Rookie League (started by Major League Baseball) for 7- to 9-year-old players. Rookie League uses pitching machines, softer balls, and 12 players on the field.

Washington stops Texas in World Series

Undefeated Vancouver, Wash., led by pitcher Robert Ramsey, won the 16-18 Babe Ruth World Series Aug. 3 with a 3-2 win against Austin, Texas.

Ramsey pitched Vancouver to a pair of wins, including the tournament final, and led the team to two other wins with his bat, as the Pacific Northwest champions won all four of its games at Jamestown, N.Y.

In the 13-15 championship, Scottsdale, Ariz., defeated Westfield, Mass., twice on the final day to claim the national title.

In its first national championship tournament, Westfield had defeated Scottsdale earlier in the tourney in a battle of undefeated teams, but the Pacific Southwest champs won 7-2 and 9-7 in Vallejo, Calif.

The 13-year-old tournament, scheduled for Houma, La., was canceled after three days because of Hurricane Andrew, while S. Lexington, Ky., was "Bambino" champion (ages 6-12).

Junior Olympic Super Series

The Junior Olympic Super Series was also affected by Andrew, but not before Norwalk, Calif., was named national champion.

Norwalk, the American Amateur Baseball Congress champion, won all four of its games in Beaumont, Texas. The Police Athletic League champion from St. Petersburg, Fla., was second with a 3-1 record, while Lexington, Ky., the National Amateur Baseball Federation winner, was third.

The JOSS matches the world series champions from the five national youth baseball groups. Also participating: Pony Baseball and Dixie Baseball.

Championship scores: PONY

▸**Palomino (17-18):** Huntington Beach, Calif. 2, Johnson City, Tenn. 1.

Championship scores: Dixie

▸**Majors (age 15-18):** Florence, S.C. 9, Highland Co., Fla. 4.
▸**Pre-Majors (age 15-16):** Baton Rouge, La. 23, Avon Park, Fla. 5.
▸**Boys (age 13-14):** Columbia Co., Ga. 8, Montgomery, Ala. 0.
▸**Youth (12 & under):** Hattiesburg, Miss. 2, Pensacola, Fla. 0.

Championship scores: AABC

▸**Stan Musial (unlimited):** Lombard, Ill. 10, Puerto Rico 6.
▸**Connie Mack (18 & under):** Cincinnati 29, Puerto Rico 14.
▸**Mickey Mantle (16 & under):** Norwalk, Calif. 9, Dallas 8.
▸**Sandy Koufax (14 & under):** W. Covina, Calif. 9, E. Cobb, Ga. 1.
▸**Pee Wee Reese (12 & under):** Puerto Rico 5, Montebello, Calif. 4.
▸**Willie Mays (10 & under):** Southgate, Calif. 11, Kansas City 1.
▸**Roberto Clemente (8 & under):** Fayette Co., Ga. 13, Sun Valley, Calif. 2.

Championship scores: NABF

▸**Major (unlimited):** Cincinnati 7, Fairfield, Conn. 0.
▸**College (20 & under):** Buffalo 7, Wilmington, Del. 0.
▸**Senior (18 & under):** Bayside, N.Y. 9, Youngstown, Ohio 4.
▸**High School:** Apopka, Fla. 5, Lexington, Ky. 4.
▸**Junior (16 & under):** Lexington, Ky. 9, Long Island, N.Y. 4.
▸**Sophomore (14 & under):** Baltimore 6, Reisterstown, Md. 5.
▸**Freshman (12 & under):** Columbus, Ohio 18, St. Clair Shores, Mich. 4.
▸**Colt (15-16):** Lafayette, Ind. 2, Bayamon, P.R. 0.
▸**Pony (13-14):** Bradley-Bourbonnais, Ind. 4, Pasadena, Texas 3.
▸**Bronco (11-12):** Caguas, P.R. 7, Valencia, Cal. 6.

Something for everybody

There are so many youth baseball leagues that it would be impossible to describe every one, but the list below outlines a few:

▸**PONY League:** PONY League, which stands for Protect Our Nation's Youth, was founded in 1951 in Washington, Pa., to fill the gap between Little League and high school players—both in age and rules. PONY baselines are set at 80 feet, longer than Little League's 60 feet, but shy of the 90 feet for high schoolers and up.

▸**Dixie Baseball:** Started in 1955 as an alternative to Little League Baseball in South Carolina, it was initially called Little Boys Baseball. It spread throughout the South, and took the Dixie name in 1962. It's now played in 11 Southern states and has more members than every youth organization except Little League and Babe Ruth.

▸**Junior Olympic Super Series:** A national championship for junior age teams, the super series matches winners (from the USA) of amateur organizations in the 15- to 16-year-old age group.

▸**National Amateur Baseball Federation:** Founded in 1914, the NABF is the oldest amateur baseball organization in the USA. Started to organize sandlot baseball across America, the first participants were high school age and older. The NABF holds national competitions in six different age groups and is the only national baseball organization with an all-volunteer staff.

▸**American Amateur Baseball Congress:** Another organization started primarily as a competition among "senior" teams across the country, the AABC now includes a division for players 18 and under (started in 1954) and has become a six-division association. The AABC world series—called the Stan Musial World Series—was first held in 1935 in Battle Creek, Mich.

How to find a team

To find a team in your area, contact the league's national or international headquarters listed below.

▸**Babe Ruth Baseball:** International Headquarters, 1770 Brunswick Ave., P.O. Box 5000, Trenton, NJ 08638; (609) 695-1434.

▸**PONY League:** National Headquarters, P.O. Box 225, Washington, PA 15301-0225.

High School & College Baseball

INSIDE:

USA SNAPSHOTS®

A look at statistics that shape the sports world

Who's drafted into baseball

This year, the fewest number of high school players were selected in the first round of the major league baseball draft. First-round selections:

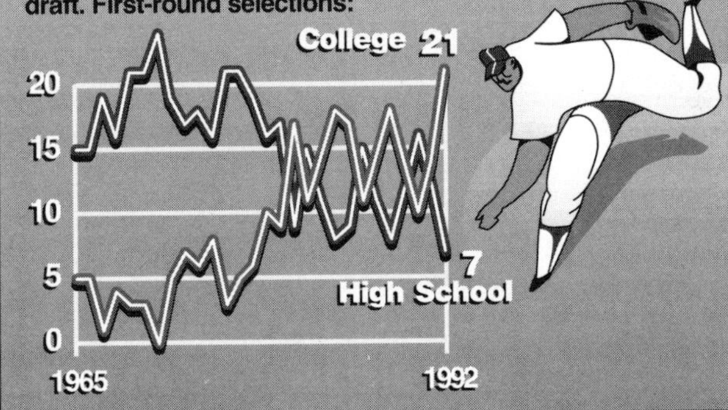

Source: USA TODAY research

By Bob Laird, USA TODAY

BASEBALL WEEKLY 1993

1992 USA TODAY Super 25 final high school rankings

▸1. Miami, Florida, Miami Westminster (33-2)
Won third Class 2A state title and first national title with .352 team average (39 HR, 1.37 ERA). Doug Mientkiewicz hit .426 (7 HR, 35 RBI, 44 runs). Alex Rodriguez hit .477 (51 runs, 6 HR) with a school-record 42 stolen bases in 45 tries. Steve Butler was 13-0 (0.88 ERA, 127 strikeouts in 87 innings).

▸2. Cherry Hill, New Jersey, West (27-3)
Group IV state champion won fourth title in row. Bo Gray was 14-0 (30-0 in career) with 0.79 ERA. Dan Farling hit .413 (32 RBI), and Walt Clymer hit .364 with five game-winning hits.

▸3. Montoursville, Pennsylvania (24-0)
Won second Class 3A state title with first unbeaten record. Mike Shannon hit .573 (26 RBI), and Erik Steinbacher hit .423 (26 RBI). Jason Bennett was 10-0 (0.64 ERA).

▸4. Long Beach, California, Millikan (22-5-1)
First repeat Class 5A Southern Section champion since 1958. Junior Jason Luciene hit .427 (45 RBI) and Scott Allen hit .414 (37 runs, 37 stolen bases). Ty Hindman was 8-1 (1.92 ERA) and had three playoff wins.

▸5. Clute, Texas, Brazoswood (30-3)
Won second Class 5A state title with record back-to-back no-hitters in Final Four. Mark Sentrfitt was 13-1 (1.22 ERA, 126 strikeouts in 103 1/3 innings). Chad Blessing was 5-0 (1.54 ERA) and hit .426 (38 RBI, 9 HR). Justin Bowles was 10-1 and hit .418 (37 RBI).

▸6. Diamond Bar, California (28-2)
Placed second in Southern Section Class 5A division and ranked No. 1 in nation for much of the season. Karl Thompson hit .462 (34 RBI, 38 runs). Jared Janke hit .380 (34 RBI) and was 11-1 (1.07 ERA, 3 saves). Mike Corominas was 9-0 (2.57 ERA.)

▸7. Sarasota, Florida, Riverview (29-6)
Won second Class 4A state title. Joey DePastino hit .433 (13 HR) and was 6-1 (1.25 ERA). Phil Olson hit .398 (32 RBI) and was 10-2 (0.77 ERA). Robbie Rowe hit .365 (21 runs).

▸8. Kernersville, North Carolina, Rob. Glenn (28-2)
Won first Class 4A state title, setting school records in batting (.357), ERA (1.58), fielding (.961) and stolen bases (144-for-158). Ray Farmer hit .477 (30 RBI, 46 runs) and had 41 of 42 stolen bases. Randy Pegg hit .453 (34 runs) and had 24 of 25 stolen bases. Jason Parson was 4-0 (3 saves, 0.86 ERA), and Ryan Jacobs was 11-1 (1.04 ERA, 124 strikeouts in 73 innings).

▸9. Kirkland, Washington, Juanita (22-2)
Won third Class 3A state title. Gatorade state Player of the Year Tom Evans was 12-0 (0.79 ERA) and hit .438 (5 HR, 26 RBI). Brian Doughty was 10-1 (1.62 ERA) and hit .408 (28 RBI). Benji Dean hit .422 (26 RBI).

▸10. San Diego, California, Mira Mesa (26-5)
Won record third consecutive San Diego Section Class 3A title. Brendan Hause was 13-1 (0.85 ERA, 130 strikeouts and 16 walks in 82 1/3 innings) and hit .405. Brian Wilson hit .410 (26 RBI) and Coleman Mullin hit .356 (24 RBI, 25 runs).

▸11. Vestavia Hills, Alabama (28-1)
First Class 6A team to win back-to-back state titles. Ryan Halla (34-3 career) was 10-0 (0.54 ERA, 106 strikeouts and 7 walks in 64 1/3 innings). Stan Reece was 6-1 and hit .353 (32 RBI, 6 HR). Junior Nathan Dunn hit .356 with 26 of 27 stolen bases.

▸12. Woodbridge, Virginia, Garfield (24-2)
Won first Class AAA state title as Brian Jersey hit .444 (28 RBI). Ron Pennell hit .434 (34 RBI, 7 HR) and Kelvin Parker hit

.376 (28 RBI). Brian Helmerson was 9-0 (1.22 ERA) and Brian McNichol was 10-2 (1.43 ERA).

▸13. Tinley Park, Illinois, Andrew (33-5)

Won first Class AA state title. A.J. Jones was 13-0 (1.27 ERA). Mike Olson hit .480, Tom Snyder .410 and Zack Pringle .389.

▸14. Sanford, Florida, Seminole (29-4)

Won first Class 3A state title with seven junior starters. Matt Freeman hit .372 (27 RBI), Anthony Roberts .356 (27 RBI), and David Eckstein .362 (24 RBI, 32 runs). Jeremy Chunat was 11-2 (1.07 ERA) and hit .342.

▸15. Marietta, Georgia, Walton (33-5)

Won first Class 4A state title. Scott MacRae was 9-1 (2.85 ERA). Tommy Peterman hit .364 (12 HR, 50 RBI, 40 runs). Chris Broadway hit .404 (31 RBI, 40 runs).

▸16. Bayonne, New Jersey, Marist (27-2)

Won Hudson County championship and last 17 games. Junior Dave Weber hit .483 (37 RBI, 39 runs) and was 11-0 (100 strikeouts in 69 1/3 innings). Bobby Powers hit .402 (school-record 51 runs, 24-for-24 stolen bases). Willie Ortiz hit .397 (31 RBI).

▸17. Ada, Oklahoma (41-3)

Won second Class 3A state title in past four years with just four seniors. Greg Dean set records with 69 RBI, 13 HR, 72 runs and 23 doubles, and was 14-1 (1.65 ERA).

▸18. Baltimore, Maryland, Perry Hall (21-0)

Won second Class 4A state title as Craig Bevans hit .426 (.583 in four playoff wins). John Pfeifer hit .389 (23 RBI). Danny Brown was 10-0 (0.79 ERA) and did not allow an earned run in three playoff wins.

▸19. Defiance, Ohio (21-3)

Won first Division I state title. Andy Smith hit .402 (41 RBI) and was 12-1 (1.89 ERA). Josh Pagan hit .500 (24 RBI, 38 runs) and B.J. Moss hit .390 (37 runs).

▸20. Thiells, New York, North Rockland (25-1)

Won last 21 games and first Class A state title. Keith Finnerty hit .450 (29 runs, 18-for-19 in stolen bases). Section I Player of the Year Mike Sidoti hit .427 with 31 RBI. Darren Luzon was 8-1 (0.98 ERA) and Chris Algozzino was 9-0 (1.14 ERA).

▸21. Pine Bluff, Arkansas (35-3)

Won ninth Class 4A state title with 392-79 scoring margin and .377 batting average. Ryan Norton hit .456 (39 RBI) and was 12-2 (2.53 ERA). Greg Crow hit .448 (7 HR, 41 RBI) and Keith Horn was 14-1 (1.74 ERA, 143 strikeouts and 33 walks in 92 1/3 innings).

▸22. St. Louis, Missouri, St. Louis Chaminade (26-0-1)

Won first Class 4A state title. Alex Eckelman hit .400 (22 RBI), Tim Brickler was 5-0 (1.64 ERA), and Derek Falb was 5-0 in relief (1.25 ERA).

▸23. Lexington, Kentucky, Lafayette (37-3)

Won record 29 consecutive games and third state title in five years. Curtis Whitney was 12-0 (1.25 ERA, 120 strikeouts in 74 innings). Todd Campbell was 11-1 (2.31 ERA, 104 strikeouts in 68 innings). Matt Braughler hit .467 (7 HR, 82 RBI, 16 doubles).

▸24. McComb, Mississippi (33-3)

Won third Class 4A state title with only two seniors. Unbeaten Greg Gatlin set school records for wins (19), strikeouts (188), ERA (1.68) and fewest walks (11) in a season and hit .416 (37 RBI). Adrian Brown hit .446 (24 RBI). Michael Wimberly was 10-1 (1.72 ERA) and hit .434 (37 RBI).

▸25. Andover, Massachusetts (23-2)

First team since 1966 to win consecutive Division I state titles. Bobby Sheehan set records for batting average (.448) and runs in a season (24), had 21 RBI and was 19-for-19 in stolen bases. Justin Hesenius hit .436 (34 RBI, 7 triples). Jim Hanning was 14-0 (0.44 ERA, 131 strikeouts in 95 innings) while being named state Division I player of the year.

—Ranked for USA TODAY by consulting high school editor Dave Krider.

USA TODAY
1992 All-USA high school team

1992 Player of the Year
▸DEREK JETER, Shortstop
Kalamazoo, Michigan,
Central High School
Ht: 6-3 **Wt:** 175
Class: Senior
Bats: R **Throws:** R
BA: .508 **Runs:** 28
HR: 4 **RBI:** 23
First high school player selected in 1992 amateur draft: No. 6, first round, by the New York Yankees.

▸James Pittsley, P
DuBois, Pa.
Ht: 6-7 **Wt:** 225
Class: Senior
W-L: 10-3
ERA: 0.99
Strikeouts: 166
Bats: R **Throws:** R
Innings: 85 1/3
Walks: 48
Drafted No. 17 (first round) by the Kansas City Royals.

▸Jamie Arnold, P
Kissimmee, Fla.,
Osceola
Ht: 6-2 **Wt:** 185
Class: Senior
W-L: 11-5
ERA: 1.21
Strikeouts: 166
Bats: R **Throws:** R
Innings: 110
Walks: 58
Drafted No. 21 (first round) by the Atlanta Braves.

▸Preston Wilson, SS
Bamberg, S.C.,
Bamberg-Ehrhardt
Ht: 6-3 **Wt:** 190
Class: Senior
Bats: R **Throws:** R
BA: .530 **Runs:** 71
HR: 22 **RBI:** 86
Drafted No. 9 (first round) by the New York Mets.

▸A.J. Hinch, C
Midwest City, Okla.
Ht: 6-1 **Wt:** 180
Class: Senior
Bats: R **Throws:** R
BA: .476 **Runs:** 51
HR: 3 **RBI:** 43
Drafted No. 62 by the Chicago White Sox.

▸Todd Helton, OF
Knoxville, Tenn.,
Central
Ht: 6-2 **Wt:** 185
Class: Senior
Bats: L **Throws:** L
BA: .656 **Runs:** 55
HR: 10 **RBI:** 36
Drafted No. 55 by the San Diego Padres.

▸Chad Alexander, OF
Lufkin, Texas
Ht: 5-11 **Wt:** 180
Class: Senior
Bats: R **Throws:** R
BA: .451 **Runs:** 34
HR: 9 **RBI:** 35
Drafted in the second round by the Cincinnati Reds.

▸Chris Smith, SS
Vallejo, Calif.
Ht: 5-11 **Wt:** 190
Class: Senior
Bats: R **Throws:** R
BA: .506 **Runs:** 36
HR: 2 **RBI:** 44
Drafted No. 29 by the California Angels.

▸Dave Landaker, SS
Simi Valley, Calif.
Ht: 6-0 **Wt:** 185
Class: Senior
Bats: R **Throws:** R
BA: .526 **Runs:** 45
HR: 3 **RBI:** 17
Drafted in the second round by the Houston Astros.

▸Shea Morenz, OF
San Angelo,
Texas, Central
Ht: 6-2 **Wt:** 205
Class: Senior
Bats: L **Throws:** R
BA: .507 **Runs:** 20
HR: 7 **RBI:** 30
Drafted in the sixth-round by the Toronto Blue Jays.

Derek Jeter: Born to be a (Yankee) shortstop

Derek Jeter, *USA TODAY*'s high school baseball player of the year, is well on his way to achieving many of his lifetime goals. The recent Kalamazoo (Mich.) Central High graduate was the first high school player taken in the major league baseball draft.

"I was hoping to be picked high," said Jeter, who was the No. 6 pick by the New York Yankees. "It was an honor to be picked high and to be picked by New York. I was born in New Jersey and have been to a lot of Yankee games.

"Playing in the pros always has been my dream."

The 6-3, 175-pounder was destined to be a shortstop. His father, Charles, played that position at Fisk University. However, he did start out as a second and third baseman under his father's coaching in Little League.

"As far back as I can remember I always was in baseball," said the younger Jeter.

"I would go out and dad would hit me a lot of grounders," he said. "My mom and sister would be in the outfield and would flag down all the balls I would hit."

Jeter had a 3.82 grade-point average and was 21st in a class of 265. He also was offered a scholarship to Michigan.

As a sophomore, he started for the Connie Mack Kalamazoo Maroons, who play 65 games in a summer season.

"I was the youngest kid on the team and my father had told me not to be disappointed if I didn't start," Jeter said. "He said I could learn from the one I played behind. We played every day except for travel. I think that was the biggest factor (in being seen by scouts)."

by Anthony James Dugal

Shortstop Derek Jeter (Kalamazoo, Mich.) was drafted in the first round by the New York Yankees.

Jeter said he "hit about .340 in his first year. Last summer (1991), I hit about .490 or .500 with 10 or 12 home runs and did pretty well on defense."

Last spring Jeter hit three home runs in his first seven at-bats for his high school team. However, he suffered a bad ankle sprain running to first base on a snowy afternoon and hit just one more homer after that. He still played in 23 of Central's 26 games, but by his own admission "was only about 80 percent healed."

He hit .508 (30-for-59), struck out just once, had five doubles, one triple, 28 runs, 21 walks, 23 RBI, and was 12-for-12 in stolen bases. He had a slugging percentage of .831 and an on-base average of .637.

"He was the last one off the field every night," coach Don Zomer said. "He loves the game of baseball."

—by Dave Krider

Parity for college baseball teams: It won't be lonely at the top in 1993

The watchword in college baseball in '93 is "parity." The gap between the top and bottom in college baseball should continue to shrink, as it did in 1992. Pepperdine's national championship victory in a stunning College World Series shows any number of teams can win the title—it's just a matter of getting hot at the right time. New NCAA rules have also added to the parity. Not the least is the 56-game limit, which keeps warm-weather schools from piling on games and valuable experience. The field is wide-open for 1993. Here's a look at the top contenders:

▸**Louisiana State:** 1992 was expected to be a down year for the Tigers, returning just three starters from their national championship team. But they posted a 48-14 record, won the Southeastern Conference championship and held a top-five ranking in *Baseball Weekly*/ABCA Coaches' Poll for much of the season. The Bayou Bengals return two of the nation's top players: second baseman Todd Walker (.409, 11 HR, 74 RBI) and third-sacker Russ Johnson (.329, 7 HR, 47 RBI). They also have some big bats in sophomore Harry Berrios (.319, 9 HR, 54 RBI) and designated hitter Mike Neal. Starters Scott Schultz (8-2, 2.56 ERA), Matt Chamberlain (8-1, 4.21 ERA) and Ronnie Rantz (6-2, 4.07) all return.

▸**Wichita State:** Coach Gene Stephenson has made trips to Omaha an annual tradition. But after making three trips in four years and never finishing lower than third, the '92 trip was a shock for the Shockers: They were headed home quickly after two straight losses. 1993 should see the fifth trip in six years. Pitching is always the Shockers' strong suit, and this year should be no different. Despite losing Kennie Steenstra (13-2, 4.32) and Charlie Giaudrone (13-1, 1.73), reliever Darren Dreifort returns for his junior season. A member of the Olympic baseball team, Dreifort's 95 mph fastball also makes him a candidate for top pick in the 1993 major league's amateur draft. Other top returning hurlers include Jaime Bluma (1-0, 3.77, 4 saves), Shane Dennis (13-2, 3.12) and Joel Bradberry (4-1, 2.36). The offense will be a little tougher to rebuild, losing three key players to pro ball and graduation (shortstop Chris Wimmer, catcher Doug Mirabelli and outfielder Todd Dreifort.) But centerfielder Richie Taylor comes back after hitting .316 in his freshman year.

▸**Georgia Tech:** Coach Jim Morris' Yellowjackets were one game away from a trip to Omaha, but lost twice on the final day. 1993 may be an even better year. A trio of young pitchers that contributed to Tech's 24-1 start, return: freshman Brad Rigby (8-3, 2.97) and sophomores Brett Binkley (7-2, 1.84) and Chris Myers (5-2, 3.42). But the top returnees are a couple of members of the U.S. Olympic baseball team: shortstop Nomar Garciaparra (.364, 24 SB) and catcher Jason Varitek (.412, 10 HR, 50 RBI), who should be a top pick in the 1993 draft.

▸**Texas:** The Longhorns seem to punch tickets for Omaha every year, heading back for the 26th time in 1992 (fourth place). Coach Cliff Gustafson has been there 16 times. The 'Horns will be led by junior Brooks Kieschnick, who won the Dick Howser Trophy as the nation's outstanding player as a sophomore in '92. Kieschnick can do it all: He hit .341 with eight homers and 63 RBI as the designated hitter, while posting 10-2, 2.93 ERA record on the mound—and all of that despite missing 11 games with torn ankle ligaments. Joining Kieschnick: shortstop Tim Harkrider and outfielder Stephen Larkin (Barry's brother), who hit .292 in his freshman season.

▸**Arizona:** The Wildcats nabbed the tightest Pac-10 South race in years (seven wins in eight games) and could repeat the feat this season if pitching aces Tim Schweitzer (5-3, 3.20 ERA) and

Mike Schiefelbein (8-2, 4.88) rebound from arm injuries. Coach Jerry Kindall must replace most of the starting lineup, but catcher Willie Morales (.344, 7 HR, 44 RBI) returns as the backbone of the club's defense.

▸**Florida:** Though the Gators fell off at the end of the season, Coach Joe Arnold's charges should be strong again. Two key members of the starting rotation, Marc Valdes (9-3, 3.29) and Ron Scott (3-1, 5.79), return for their junior years, and could make up for the loss of John Burke. DH Rick Britton (.306, 7 HR, 39 RBI), third baseman Chris Kokinda (.263, 1 HR, 7 RBI) and first baseman Palmer Knight (.314, 6 RBI) will all step into starting roles in '93. In addition, the Gators could see Johnny Damon—a first-round pick of the Kansas City Royals—step right into center field.

▸**Fresno State:** The Bulldogs move out of the tough Big West into the Western Athletic Conference, where their toughest competition will be Hawaii. Coach Bob Bennett loses most of his '92 starting lineup, but club MVP first baseman Brant Brown (.365, 10 HR, 49 RBI) returns for his junior year. Bennett must replace Jim Patterson (12-3, 3.89), one of the winningest pitchers in the nation: Steve Soderstrom (8-5, 3.00) looks ready to step into the No. 1 role.

▸**Cal. St.-Fullerton:** It took Coach Augie Garrido just three years after returning to Orange County from Illinois to get back to the College World Series final. Garrido could have enough to return in '93, but some big holes must be filled. Third baseman Phil Nevin and catcher Jason Moler—both members of the Olympic team—have left, along with senior mound aces James Popoff and Dan Naulty. Nevin was the top pick overall in the draft by the Houston Astros. But all-Big West outfielder Dante Powell (.326, 5 HR) will be back, along with first baseman D.C. Olsen (.301). Mike Parisi (4-1, 3.54) will head the mound staff, after breaking into the starting rotation as a freshman and hurling a big win at the College World Series.

▸**Clemson:** Coach Bill Wilhelm is nearing retirement, but he would like one more trip to the College World Series. Last year could have been the year, but the Tigers ran into an Oklahoma buzzsaw in the regionals. This year, they have some holes to fill. Clemson's strength will be on the hill, where starters Michael Holtz (8-0, 1.27) and Andy Taulbee (5-2, 2.27) will form the backbone of the rotation. For the Tigers to have a solid year offensively, Billy McMillon (.372, 4 HR, 27 RBI) must stay healthy. He missed half the year (1992) after shoulder surgery.

by Russell Beeker, *Baseball Weekly*

Pepperdine's Patrick Ahearne helped prove that any team can win the CWS if it gets hot at the right time.

▸**Notre Dame:** A surprise entry in '93 could be the Fighting Irish. Pat Murphy has built a solid program in South Bend: The team came within a win of advancing to the CWS in '92 and destroying Miami coach Ron Fraser's storybook finish. The majority of Murphy's starting lineup will return, but shortstop Craig Counsell (.346, 12 HR, 61 RBI) and first baseman Joe Binkiewicz (.311, 10 HR, 49 RBI) will be hard to replace. Freshman Paul Failla—also a backup quarterback for the football team—returns after hitting .314. Most of the starting pitchers return, led by junior Tom Price (6-1, 2.91).

—by Rick Lawes

1992 College World Series

Pepperdine was best in the West

The balance of power seemed to be tilted eastward, but two southern California schools ended up battling for the title: Pepperdine won its first national crown, defeating Cal State-Fullerton 3-2 in the first-ever College World Series final to be contested by schools from the same state.

Miami (Fla.) entered the series holding the No. 1 spot in the *Baseball Weekly*/ABCA Coaches' Poll, but lost to Fullerton in the East Bracket final.

Ironically, Pepperdine and Fullerton did not meet during the regular season, as they usually do. After the 56-game limit was imposed, they realized that they had no games left to play each other.

"We were going to go back home and play on some sandlot," said Fullerton third baseman Phil Nevin. "We had to have some way to figure out who was best in southern California. After we both won our regionals, we said, 'Why not make it for the national championship?' "

The final came down to a decision to walk Nevin in the eighth inning, after Steve Montgomery had hit the first two Fullerton batters and a sacrifice had moved runners to second and third. Jason Moler hit a sacrifice fly to cut the score to 3-2, but Rodriguez made a great diving stop that robbed Tony Banks of a game-tying hit to end the threat.

—*by Rick Lawes*

1992 College World Series

May 29:
Miami 4, California 3 (13 innings);
Cal State-Fullerton 7, Florida State 2.

May 30:
Pepperdine 6,Wichita State 0;
Texas 15, Oklahoma 3.

May 31:
Florida State 5, California 4;
Miami 4, Cal State-Fullerton 3.
(California eliminated)

June 1:
Pepperdine 7, Texas 0;
Oklahoma 8, Wichita State 4. *(Wichita State eliminated)*

June 2:
Texas 8, Oklahoma 5; Cal St.-Ful. 6, Fla St. 0. *(Florida St. eliminated)*

June 3:
Cal State-Fullerton 7, Miami 5.

June 4:
Pepperdine 5, Texas 4. *(Texas eliminated)*

June 5:
Cal State-Fullerton 8, Miami 1. *(Miami eliminated)*

June 6:
Pepperdine 3, Cal State-Fullerton 2.
(Championship game)

by Ted Kirk

Pepperdine players hoisted coach Andy Lopez to celebrate their victory over Cal State-Fullerton for the NCAA title.

BASEBALL WEEKLY 1993

Fantasy Report

INSIDE:

- All-dependable all-stars
- How to spot "owner's illness"
- Pitching's "Mr. Septembers"
- Getting in shape for a draft
- The sealed bid system
- *... and more!*

USA SNAPSHOTS®

A look at statistics that shape the sports world

Baseball's best

Sixteen of the 20 Olympic baseball players on the '92 Team USA have been drafted by major league teams. How members of the past 20-player Olympic baseball teams have fared:

	Played in major leagues	Played in All-Star Game
1984	**17**	**3**
1988	**15**	**2**

Source: U.S. Baseball Federation, USA TODAY

By Cliff Vancura, USA TODAY

BASEBALL WEEKLY 1993

Saving your season can be a steal

A key to winning any pick-your-player contest is knowing how to keep score. The "best" player at any position might be someone other than last year's All-Star, because stat leagues have their own definitions of value. In a standard Rotisserie league, the team with the most stolen bases gets the same reward as the team with the most home runs—it's not the same as "real" baseball, where a home run counts more than a stolen base.

Success depends on getting comfortable with player rankings based on "artificial" criteria. How can a little speedster like Luis Polonia compare to a big slugger like Albert Belle? Simple: In a "real" baseball season, there may be 2,000 home runs in a league, but fewer than 1,500 stolen bases. One steal is actually worth more than one dinger, if you treat the stats as separate, equal categories.

Owners who are leading their Rotisserie leagues in stolen bases and also in saves—the ultra-scarce pitching category—are also likely to be high in the total standings.

Expert Rotisserie analyst Mike Dalecki has demonstrated that saves and steals are the two categories that correlate best with finishing in first place. That doesn't necessarily mean that speedsters and relief aces will always push your team over the top, but it does show that people who appreciate saves and stolen bases are likely to understand the other aspects of the game, and to perform well overall.

A good way to get an understanding of stats is to make "what-if" roster changes, and see the actual impact on league standings. If you are already leading in saves, it doesn't help much to add another ace reliever. But nine out of 10 teams can gain in saves, and half are below average in that category, by definition. Here are some tips for traders:

IF YOU HAVE AN EXCESS:

▸**Be generous in sharing your understanding of stat values.** To have a liquid trade market, you need people who appreciate what you have.

▸**Demonstrate standings impacts.** Pick an actual team that will benefit from the trade you want to make, and design a deal that helps both teams. Do the arithmetic for them.

▸**Try a team newsletter.** Even a one page, handwritten statement to your fellow owners will stimulate trade talks.

▸**Use real numbers to prove your point.** It's easy enough to say that steals are worth more than home runs, or that saves are twice as scarce as wins; it's more effective to demonstrate these realities with actual statistics.

▸**Tell people about "stat concentration."** Saves and stolen bases both tend to be concentrated in a few individuals, making it difficult to comprehend a player's value. There are many players with zero steals, but only a few with zero homers.

IF YOU HAVE A SHORTAGE:

▸**Focus on the league leaders, and point out their excess.** If someone is already 15 saves ahead, tell them, "You could just give me Mike Henneman, and it wouldn't hurt you in the standings. I am willing to give you some help in return."

▸**Create anxiety.** Most of the people with extra saves and steals are probably planning to trade their excess anyway, but if they hear the words "wasted value," it will increase their sense of urgency.

▸**Recognize the values on your own roster.** Even if you came up a little short in total value on draft day, you still have assets that other owners need.

▸**Don't be afraid to make deals.** If you are down in the standings, chances are you have nothing to lose, anyway.

—by John Benson, who edits the Rotisserie Baseball Annual *and publishes the monthly* Winning Rotisserie Baseball.

All-dependable all-star team

When Barry Bonds injured himself last season, it felt like a knife to the ribcage for proud Bonds owners everywhere. He was not only the most productive fantasy player, he was always healthy—never on the DL in six major league seasons.

Susceptibility to injury is such an intangible that most fantasy owners don't give it much thought. The Bonds injury prompted a little research to determine who, besides Cal Ripken, are the true iron men of baseball. Eight position players have played as long or longer than Bonds without a stay on the DL, and have played at least 100 games in each season. Here's the All-Dependable team:

▸**Catcher:** No catcher qualifies. But Tony Pena hasn't been shelved since 1987 when he was a Cardinal.

▸**First base:** No first baseman—not exactly a big wear-and-tear position—qualifies, either. We'll move Tim Wallach from third to first; he's not exactly a model of consistency at the plate, but he does stay healthy.

▸**Second base:** Harold Reynolds has played seven consecutive seasons of at least 140 games. Steve Sax would have been first choice if not for a brief stay on the Dodgers' DL in 1985.

▸**Third base:** Wade Boggs doesn't go on the DL—that might make it difficult to get 180+ hits, something he's done nine times since 1983.

▸**Shortstop:** Cal Ripken, of course.

▸**Left field:** The jury might be still out on the Saberhagen trade, but the Royals did get an every-day/every-year left fielder in Kevin McReynolds. He moves so effortlessly, he couldn't possibly pull a hamstring.

▸**Center field:** Twins management may have tried to rationalize that Kirby Puckett should not be a $7 million man, but they couldn't use his health record as an excuse.

▸**Right field:** Ruben Sierra and Tom Brunansky will platoon in right for the Dependable Team. Sierra is more productive, but Brunansky has the experience.

by Russell Beeker, *Baseball Weekly*

If you're looking for a perennially healthy shortstop, there is obviously no better choice than Cal Ripken, Jr.

▸**Designated hitter:** On the suspended list but never the disabled list, George Bell will DH—due to the crowded Dependable outfield.

—by John Hunt

How to recognize ownership illness

Commissioner General's warning: Playing fantasy baseball can be hazardous to your health, marriage, job security and ability to engage in intelligent conversation between the months of March and October.

The following ailments have been identified as endemic to fantasy baseball enthusiasts:

▸**Offermania:** An obsessive need to acquire players—often with little major league experience—based solely on press clippings. Victims will trade Tony Gwynn for a "can't-miss" superstar of the future.

▸**Frank Lane Syndrome:** The typical victim can often list as many as 170 players who have appeared on his 28-man roster during a season. A compulsive trader, the FLS victim spends thousands of dollars on phone calls and transaction fees, and hours irritating other owners with useless trade proposals.

▸**St. Louis Cardinal Sin:** Formerly a relatively obscure malady, St. Louis Cardinal Sin has been diagnosed increasingly in recent years. So called because the St. Louis franchise is notorious for following a bad season with a good one (and vice versa); Cardinal Sinners tend to rank players highly when their previous season has been a disaster.

▸**Pagliaphobia:** Pagliaphobes place an inordinate value on their own players—whose true value is limited by their lack of talent. Pagliaphobes will attempt to persuade other owners that the player in question is a fair exchange for Dennis Eckersley by emphasizing the importance of a reserve third baseman.

▸**Gabe's Palsy:** This insidious disease compels a victim to completely transform his philosophy—thus his roster—each season. A roster based on strong pitching will be traded for a roster composed entirely of rookies, followed by a roster of power-hitting sloths, followed by a roster of Jose Linds and Rafael Belliards.

▸**ESPiNozitis:** Most common symptoms are red eyes and an irritable disposition during normal morning working hours. ESPiNozitis attacks at 2 a.m. in the East, on the premise that being first to know the results of Mariners' or Angels' games will bring an inordinate advantage.

▸**Gammons Fixation:** Characterized by a roster overloaded with Red Sox players, Gammons victims tend to rely on one principal source for information. You can easily identify them by offering Scott Cooper and Joe Hesketh for Ruben Sierra. If they accept, the diagnosis is confirmed.

▸**Hawkins' Disease:** Particularly rampant in white-collar occupations, Hawkins' Disease has one major symptom: Victims insert the sports section of *USA TODAY* between the pages of the *Wall Street Journal* and pretend to be diligently studying business matters. The disease is named after a pitcher who was a real major league pitcher for half of his 10 seasons, but was only pretending for the other five.

▸**Sparky's Delusion:** The proper scientific name is Arterio-boschembechleritis. The victim will insist that a roster of lumbering sluggers and no pitching staff whatsoever is the best route to success. Traced originally to Michigan, it also has become common in parts of Texas and New York.

—Excerpted from Absolutely Baseball! 1992, *by Paul Siebel, Box 1158, Norton, Ohio 44203.*

Getting in shape for a great draft

You've memorized every relevant statistic on every eligible player, scoured the newspapers for spring training reports, read preseason annuals and absorbed the wisdom of countless fantasy baseball pundits. That was the easy part.

To succeed on draft day, surely the most important six hours of the season, you'll need more—an unfair advantage over the other owners.

▸**Diet:** You must prepare your body weeks in advance for the caloric toll of assembling a fantasy baseball team. I recommend pizza. The bloated sensation that comes from ingesting mounds of cheese is crucial to achieving maximum concentration level. Pizza also fills out the gut and widens the waist, two vital elements of the draft-day ready-position: the deep recline.

▸**Exercise:** In the weeks leading up to the draft, limber up. First, slowly lift one arm, then lower it, as you will do when bidding on a player. After a few sets of those, practice the brushoff. It's a simple dismissive wave of the back of your hand, as if to say, "For a stupid price like that, you can have the guy." Now try it with a scowl.

Scowl, wave, scowl, wave. No draft-day sprains or strains for you.

▸**Voice training:** Loosen up your laugh, your most powerful weapon for undermining every competitor's confidence. First, clear the throat, then run through your repertoire:

▸**The unprovoked chuckle:** Ideal for moments when bidding is moving too smoothly. Ideally, you should use it when the group's attention is on someone else, and offer nothing more than a small but audible heh-heh. "Heh-heh." That's it. "Dale Murphy—8. 10. 11," then, "heh-heh" from you. Grinds all momentum to a halt.

▸**The outbid guffaw:** Practice this one only when you're fully warmed up. It goes, "A-HAW-HAW-HAW!! A-HAW-HAW-HAW!!" It should convince the winning bidder that he's just been duped into overpaying for a player you never wanted in the first place.

▸**Dress for success:** The standard uniform begins with the baseball cap. To confuse your opponents, the cap should be emblazoned with a logo of a team whose players you detest. Play up the illusion by talking excitedly about the decoy team's pennant chances. The draft-day jersey can repeat the logo of the cap or conflict with it (if you really want to confound your competitors).

Pants should be loose-fitting. No strategy here, just comfort.

Finally, every draft-day veteran knows you must wear your oldest shoes—the ancient, crusty ones you should have thrown out in college. When you arrive, your first move should be to take them dogs right off and stretch out. That will keep anyone from sitting too close to you.

By then you will be comfortable, properly attired and at the peak of training. Your body will be coursing with the energy of an Olympian, thanks to diligent voice and muscle conditioning. No one will be able to match your stamina, your vocal agility, or appetite for pizza.

—by Eric Zicklin, who is a fantasy baseball owner in New York City.

Sealed bid: Best of both worlds

The war between proponents of a draft and those who align themselves on the side of an auction system need continue no longer. The Wall Street Fantasy Baseball League, now in its fifth year, has merged the draft and the auction system into a hybrid Sealed-Bid System.

In each round, all teams submit a player simultaneously. At the gavel, Round 1 begins, and each team writes its player selection (and his position) on a slip of paper, which is deposited into a bowl on the commissioner's table. The commissioner examines the selections, and all picks that do not result in a tie are immediately announced as "winners."

Ties are settled by a verbal auction. The risk in losing the auction is you must then select another player (not previously named) at the same position with another sealed bid, and you could be tied again. When all the tied selections are resolved by auction, the round is completed, and the next round begins.

Each round is done the same way until all teams have the required eight starting fielders, and whatever number of starting and relief pitchers you have set. No substitutes can be named until all teams have completed this phase. Substitutes can then be selected the same way.

—by Michael Davis

Finishing strong: How to predict the "Mr. Septembers" of pitching

September is an unusual month. For many teams, the season is over and the focus has shifted to the next year. After Sept. 1, rosters expand to accommodate the annual influx of minor league talent. But another factor comes into play in September: fatigue. A player's performance can really surge or crash, depending on his stamina—and pitchers show the widest swings.

In a competition determined by statistics, a pitcher whose ERA holds up looks twice as good as a pitcher whose ERA skyrockets after a bad late-season outing—even if both pitchers are of similar ability and the difference in ERA was a reflection of a few lucky bounces.

Luck is a key factor in a big finish. Look at any pitcher's statistics on a month-by-month basis and you see big fluctuations. The numbers are not all random, however. Baseball managers and fantasy leaguers alike know that some pitchers have consistently done well when others are beset with "September arm." There are several key factors that make September different from other months, most notably the expanded rosters (which bring fresh minor-league batters into the picture) and fatigue/conditioning, mentioned above. On an individual level, factors such as weather, ballparks, and opposition schedules can figure prominently, but the hitter population and the battle against burnout affect every pitcher. For a crafty veteran pitcher, the September influx of minor league hitters creates an opportunity.

"Sometimes you can see that a young hitter is over-eager to show what he can do," said Toronto ace Jack Morris, "and if you've been around, you know how to use that situation."

Morris, who has made the adjustment from power pitching to finesse, has been especially strong in September for the past four seasons.

Here are some "Mr. Septembers" (listed with their 1992 teams) and why they're so good late in the season:

▸**Jack Morris, Blue Jays:** In addition to the factors mentioned above, Morris has also benefited from working in pennant races for three years.

▸**Tim Belcher, Reds:** Belcher is especially tough in September. With a 94 mph fastball, he doesn't have to worry about getting fancy.

▸**Doug Drabek, Pirates:** Drabek has also worked three pennant races in a row. He is simply tough all year, every year. Period.

▸**Scott Sanderson, Yankees**: He may not have the lowest ERA of all of our choices, but he remains consistent all season due to his physical conditioning, which gives him a slight edge come September.

There is no safe method to pick pitchers who are sure to perform well, but you can improve your chances by learning from history. Look at how the pitcher has performed in previous Septembers—and ask why. In many cases of strong September performance, you will find a smart pitcher like Morris, who stays in strong physical condition year-round and who thinks about the makeup of the opposition lineup—especially when there might be some holes to exploit.

Finally, consider your objective for pitcher stats for the final month of the season. Are you satisfied with your ERA, or do you need to shake things up? If you need to work off a bloated ERA, you'll need lots of innings—and that means taking chances, especially with starting pitchers. But if you have a low ERA, you may want to minimize your risk by minimizing innings pitched—the right strategy may be to fill your roster with short relievers.

—by John Benson

ollectibles

INSIDE:

- Storage tips
- Autographs for charity
- Top 25 card people
- Pro Set bankruptcy
- *... and more!*

USA SNAPSHOTS®

A look at statistics that shape the sports world

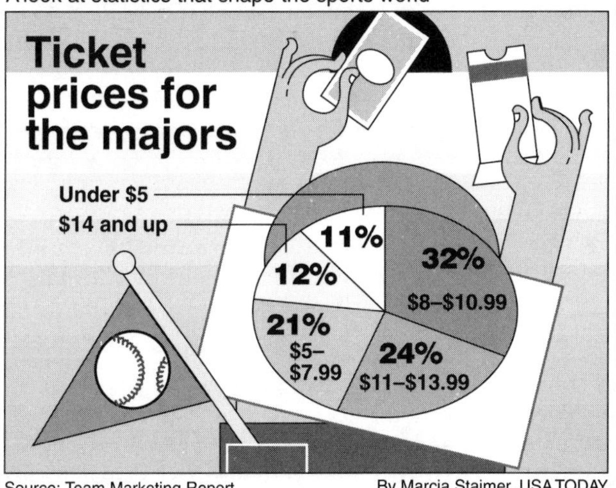

Source: Team Marketing Report

By Marcia Staimer, USA TODAY

BASEBALL WEEKLY 1993

Mail-in autographs benefit charities

Perhaps Terry Steinbach and Gary Carter have found a solution to some problems in the autograph industry. Neither player takes money for autographs—thereby avoiding collectors who make multiple autograph requests to turn a profit—but both will sign for a contribution to charity. (Both sign for free at the ballpark and at hotels.)

In 1988, the Athletics' Steinbach quit signing for free through the mail. Instead, he began replying to each request with a request of his own—for a contribution to the Steinbach Scholarship fund to benefit college freshmen in his hometown of New Ulm, Minnesota.

"I'm not like Mac (Oakland first baseman Mark McGwire) or Jose (Canseco), but I still get a lot of mail," said Steinbach. "It's tough to get excited about it sometimes, but this helps keep my interest up and it helps the community at the same time." The St. Paul (Minn.) Foundation oversees the fund, which has generated $33,500 and four scholarships to date.

Mail sent to Steinbach at home and through the A's is forwarded to his Minnesota-based agent, Charlie Sutton, who coordinates Steinbach's signings. Steinbach charges $2 to sign a baseball card—$3 if he personalizes it. He will sign and provide an 8-by-10 color photo for $5—$7 if personalized. Collectors must also send an appropriately sized, self-addressed, stamped envelope.

Autograph requests can be made to Terry Steinbach, care of The Sutton Co., 750 Boone Ave. N., Golden Valley, Minn. 55427. Donations are tax deductible and organizers request checks rather than cash.

For a $25 contribution to the Leukemia Society of America, Carter sends collectors an autographed 1991 Leaf Studio baseball card or signs a card provided by the collector. (He'll sign non-card material through the mail for free.) Carter, whose mother died of leukemia in 1966, has served as the Leukemia Society's national sports chairman since 1985. Since he began the autographed-card project in 1984, he has raised more than $2 million.

Autograph requests to Carter, accompanied by a $25 check to the Leukemia Society, can be sent to the Leukemia Society of America, 733 Third Ave., New York, N.Y. 10017, or the Montreal Expos, Box 500, Station M, Montreal, Quebec, Canada.

—by Pete Williams

Have autograph, will travel

The New York Mets have a longstanding relationship with the Leukemia Society of America; each year, one player serves as liaison between the two, signing autographs for a fee to benefit the society. But the job seems to be a quick ticket out of the Mets clubhouse. Gary Carter, who still signs for the Leukemia Society, was released by the Mets following the 1989 season. The job then went to journeyman catcher Rick Cerone, who went to Montreal and was released in '92. Tim Burke held the position in 1992 until June, when the Mets traded him to the Yankees for pitcher Lee Guetterman.

—by Pete Williams

Firm offers ID idea for autographs

John Blasco thinks he has a solution to the growing problem of autograph forgery. Since January, Blasco's Sports Securities International has gone to New York-area card shows armed with a computer registration system. When collectors come off the autograph lines with freshly signed material, Blasco's East Alsip, N.Y., firm offers to authenticate the item on the spot.

For a $3 per-piece fee, collectors receive a certificate of authenticity that lists the item, the date and place the autograph was signed, and a registration number. A small black-and-gold sticker is attached to the back or base of the signed item. Much like an automobile title, the Sports Securities certificate has space on the back to note any sale of the memorabilia.

Sports Securities will issue letters of authenticity only for autographs signed with a company representative present. Existing memorabilia—no matter how well-documented—will not be certified. The company will, however, register any collectible, giving owners a record of their inventory for insurance purposes.

Blasco, a veteran card dealer, conceived the idea to deal with the problem of forgeries and counterfeit merchandise. While most dealers issue letters of authenticity for their autographed and game-used merchandise, Blasco felt collectors needed more peace of mind.

"Obviously some dealers aren't going to like our concept," said Blasco. "They may think, 'Why is my letter not good enough?' But if a dealer would forge an autograph, he would think nothing of writing a bogus letter of authenticity. We offer traceability."

Blasco hopes to build a network of licensed show promoters and dealers authorized by Sports Securities to issue certificates at card shows across the country. Meanwhile, the company is attempting to devise a permanent marking system—perhaps with invisible ink—to replace the sticker system currently used. Until that happens, however, unscrupulous collectors could remove the sticker and use the tag to "authenticate" a fake item.

Still, many collectors do not feel the need to have a piece officially recognized if they saw the player sign it in person. "I just wonder if there will be all that much demand for it," said autograph expert Mark Jordan of Arlington, Texas. "If you have a signed Joe DiMaggio ball or something expensive, then it might be useful. But I don't think the bulk of the public is clamoring to have it done for most players."

Tom Finkelmeir of Cornell and Finkelmeir, an Ohio firm specializing in sports memorabilia insurance, suggests that until Sports Securities gets a large network of dealers in place nationwide, it might have a difficult time gaining credence with insurance companies.

"I think the idea is great for the hobby," said Finkelmeir. "And for expensive, rare items it would have some benefits from an insurance angle. But to say that it would reduce theft or have a huge effect on the insurance industry at this point would be a bit premature."

—by Pete Williams

Young hobbyist finds write words

The Wheeling (W.Va.) *Intelligencer* didn't have an in-house collectibles columnist, so sports editor Doug Huff found one in his own house—his 13-year-old son, Ryan.

Huff, a longtime collector, did not have time to write the column—no one else on his staff was familiar with the field—but he could not ignore the card shops popping up all over Wheeling nor the steady flow of letters indicating a huge reader interest. So he called on the person he knew with the most expertise—Ryan, now 15—to write the weekly column.

"As far as we can tell, he's got to be the youngest sports columnist in the country," said Doug Huff, who has been with the *Intelligencer* for 26 years. "We've had tremendous response to it, both from our readers and from our editors here. He now gets as much mail as I do." Ironically, the younger Huff works as a newspaper carrier for the rival Wheeling *News Register*.

—by Pete Williams

Jack Glenn is keeping much of his grand prize collection from Topps, but some of it was invested in his children's college education.

College financing was in the cards

When Jack Glenn won the grand prize in Topps' 40th Anniversary Sweepstakes, he obtained a rare collection: all 40 complete sets of Topps baseball cards from 1952-91. But Glenn, a 43-year-old New York traffic manager who collected cards as a kid, found that he could obtain something even more valuable by selling some of the collection—college educations for his children.

Glenn sold "less than half" of his prize collection to Alan Rosen, a New Jersey dealer known for several huge buys in the last decade. Glenn did not disclose the terms of the sale, which included a mix of old and contemporary cards, but he did say that he kept all five cards of his namesake Jackie Robinson.

Glenn's oldest son was the first beneficiary. He entered college in the fall.

—by Pete Williams

Storage tips for game-worn jerseys

With game-worn jerseys selling for up to $200,000, it would be a shame to lose an investment to hungry moths. Atlanta dealer Paul Kinzer, who specializes in game-worn uniforms, recommends hanging flannel jerseys in a closet with moth balls. Folding them up in a dresser drawer causes wrinkles that can be difficult to remove.

For contemporary knit uniforms, Kinzer says collectors do not have to concern themselves with moth balls since the durable polyester fabric can withstand almost anything.

25 most powerful sports card people

The 25 most powerful people in the sports card industry as chosen in random order by *Sports Card Trader* magazine (August, 1992 issue):

David Greenhill, president of New York Card Company; Paul Goldin, president of Score Board, Inc.; Ken Goldin, vice president of Score Board, Inc.; Tony Galovich, memorabilia dealer; Sy Berger, vice president of Topps; Alan Rosen, memorabilia dealer; Gloria Rothstein, show promoter; Lud Denny, former president of Pro Set; Jay McCracken, former vice president of Upper Deck; Bruce McNall, collector; Mike Berkus, show promoter; Mike Cramer, President of Pacific Trading Cards; Bob Lemke, publisher of *Sports Collectors Digest*; Bill Mastro, memorabilia dealer; James Beckett, publisher of Beckett publications; Ron Oser, memorabilia dealer; Larry Fritch, memorabilia dealer; Richard Howard, memorabilia dealer; Ernie White, publisher of *Tuff Stuff* magazine; Steve Juskewycz, memorabilia dealer; Kit Young, memorabilia dealer; Josh

Evans, president of Leland's Auctions; Smokey Scheinemann, president of Smokey's; Bill Kennedy, president of the National Association of Sports Card Dealers and Manufacturers (NASDAM); Barry Halper, collector.

Industry needs a cleaner image

The memorabilia business needs more help than this small space can offer, but here are a few items that need to be addressed.:

▸**Consumer watchdog:** The National Association of Sportscard Dealers and Manufacturers (NASDAM) and the Sports Collectibles Association International (SCAI) announced merger plans at the 1992 National, but NASDAM/SCAI is a dealers'—not a collectors'—organization. What is really needed is an organization that truly mirrors the Better Business Bureau.

▸**Truth in advertising:** Eliminate the words "limited edition" from all sports memorabilia advertising. Any card set is a limited edition. If a company produces 900 billion card sets, it is a limited edition because no more than 900 billion were printed.

▸**De-emphasize investment:** The Beckett line of industry price guides suggests that dealers sell merchandise for 100 percent of the price listed and buy for half that amount. At that rate, the idea of a collector making big money in the sports memorabilia field is a dream.

▸**A trade magazine:** There are more than a dozen trade publications on the market, but none of them regularly offer stories concerning theft, counterfeiting, forgeries and other shady business practices. Someone should create a *Consumer Reports*-type publication with an editorial staff of business reporters instead of "hobby veterans."

—by Pete Williams

Joe DiMaggio's time is money

Joe DiMaggio became the first sports celebrity with an autograph contract forbidding him from signing at sports memorabilia shows, according to Score Board Inc. DiMaggio and Score Board inked a revision of his contract that pays him more than $4 million a year through 1993.

Although many players, such as Don Mattingly, Kirby Puckett and Cal Ripken, refuse to sign at shows unless the proceeds go to charity, DiMaggio's deal is the first in which a player has sold his show appearance rights. (The new contract still allows DiMaggio to sign for charity or for free.)

Under terms of the original deal, DiMaggio was to provide Score Board with an average of 300 signed baseballs and 900 flat items—such as photos and programs—each month for two years. DiMaggio was to receive $3.5 million a year, but was still free to appear at hobby conventions, where he commanded up to $75,000 for a three-hour appearance.

But according to Morris Engelberg, DiMaggio's attorney, DiMaggio grew tired of the shows, where dealers bought up the 50 or so tickets he allotted to sign baseballs. In the mid-1980s, DiMaggio, frustrated by seeing his autographed bats sell for exorbitant prices, was among the first to adopt a policy of refusing to sign bats. Ironically, this raised the prices to the point where DiMaggio bats sell for $25,000 at hobby auctions.

Score Board, a four-year-old firm based in Cherry Hill, N.J., (with sales of $33.4 million for 1990), is perhaps best known for supplying the Home Shopping Network with baseball products. Score Board also is the parent company of Classic Games, which produces baseball, basketball and football card sets of draft picks.

—by Pete Williams

"Flopps" cardmakers flopped in '92

Pro Set, Inc., makers of "Flopps" baseball cards—a parody set that was pulled when veteran card manufacturer Topps and the Major League Baseball Players Association threatened lawsuits—filed for Chapter 11 bankruptcy on August 20, 1992.

"This action was taken in order to protect our ability to continue doing business," said Robert J. McLaughlin, Pro Set's chief executive officer. The firm listed $26.4 million in assets and $55.2 million in liabilities when it filed for bankruptcy in Dallas. The National Hockey League and National Football League, two of Pro Set's largest creditors, had threatened to relinquish the company's hockey and football card licenses. "Under Chapter 11," McLaughlin said, "we will maintain all licenses, which are the foundation of our business."

McLaughlin was named CEO on August 6, after company officials banished founder and president Lud Denny—who unveiled the "Flopps" card in February, 1992—to a special projects role. A week later, Pro Set fired 186 workers—40 percent of its workforce. Neither action came as a surprise: Industry analysts had forecast that a major card manufacturer would go bankrupt when the recession began, and Denny had grabbed attention with outrageous statements, including a promise that Pro Set would receive a license to produce baseball cards, despite Major League Baseball Properties' restriction to just five manufacturers.

But Pro Set's biggest problem was not Lud Denny—it was overproduction of football and hockey cards. Unopened sets were going unsold at sport shows for $5. Pro Set became the prime example of the NFL's excesses in the trading card industry.

The bankruptcy filing does not necessarily signal the beginning of an industry crash, however. Pro Set did not hold a license to produce baseball cards, which are still the backbone of the field. Topps, Fleer, Leaf/Donruss, Score and Upper Deck have shown no signs of financial difficulty, even at a time when the market is glutted and the competition is fierce.

But Pro Set's bankruptcy should send a message to NFL Properties (which issued two dozen licenses to manufacture cards) and to the rest of the industry: The market can no longer bear such excesses.

—by Pete Williams

It pays to be "in" with the umpire

Twelve-year-old Randy Phillips is the first to admit that it's not what you know, it's who you know. Phillips received a framed 8-by-10-inch photo of his favorite player, Roger Clemens, as a gift from a classmate for his 11th birthday. Last summer, Phillips' father—American League umpire Dave Phillips—had the photo personally signed by the Rocket himself.

"I started collecting (memorabilia) when my son got interested," said the veteran umpire. "I have a small collection and it's just a ... hobby. I'd never sell anything." Still, the umpire's collection is impressive. It includes a Rickey Henderson-signed base, a Nolan Ryan-signed hat, and about 50 signed balls—including Joe DiMaggio, Mickey Mantle, Ted Williams, Carlton Fisk, Al Kaline, Frank Robinson, and Brooks Robinson. Phillips also has every lineup card from games that he worked home plate (dating back to the mid-1970s) and about 30 bats, including one from Reggie Jackson, which was given to him at Fenway Park after the umpire worked the plate for Jackson's final game. Ironically, Jackson was Phillips' first major league ejection.

—by Ross Forman

Nostalgia

INSIDE

USA SNAPSHOTS®

A look at statistics that shape the sports world

Growth of 30-30 club

Number of times, by decade, major league players made the 30-30 club - hitting 30 home runs and stealing 30 bases in a season:

1920s	**1**
1930s	**0**
1940s	**0**
1950s	**2**
1960s	**2**
1970s	**5**
1980s	**7**
1990s	**5**

Source: Sports Illustrated Almanac

By Cliff Vancura, USA TODAY

BASEBALL WEEKLY 1993

First pinch-hit left out of box scores

The identity of the first pinch-hitter has long been a matter of dispute and probably will never be settled. But the honor of being the first player to actually rap out a hit in the role of substitute batter appears to belong to journeyman ballplayer Charles "Princeton Charlie" Reilly of the Philadelphia National League team.

On April 29, 1892, the switch-hitting infielder went to bat for pitcher Wilfred "Kid" Carsey in a game against Chicago and punched out a single in a futile attempt to ignite a ninth-inning rally. He was stranded two outs later; Chicago won the game 4-2. Judging from the local newspaper accounts, no one seemed to notice or care that baseball history was being made.

The *Philadelphia Inquirer* failed to mention Reilly's ninth-inning hit in its brief summary of the game and neglected to list him in the box score. The *Chicago Tribune* was a bit more expansive, noting: "In the last half of the ninth inning, (manager) Harry Wright put Reilly in to bat in Carsey's place.... After receiving a nasty rap on the fingers from a pitched ball, he lifted a pretty single to center."

But the *Tribune* also failed to attach any significance to the event and added insult to injury by misidentifying Reilly as "Kelly" in the box score. The statisticians, in fact, seemed thoroughly confused by Reilly's appearance and the Tribune noted: "As he played no position, he is given none in the (box) score."

Baseball's early rules allowed substitutions for injury and illness under various conditions, according to baseball historian Harold Seymour, author of *Baseball—The Early Years*. Seymour added, however, that "it took time to grow accustomed to the idea (that) it was legitimate to take one man out of the game and send in another as a matter of strategy rather than because of injury."

It wasn't until 1891 that all restrictions on substitutions were dropped with the single proviso that a player leaving the game for whatever reason was out to stay.

Another baseball historian, L. Robert Davids (founder and president of the Society for American Baseball Research), identified several cases of pinch-hitting in the 1891 season, but none apparently resulted in a hit. Davids' organization (SABR) uncovered Reilly's successful 1892 pinch-hit, disproving claims made for Joseph J. "Dirty Jack" Doyle, a colorful ballplayer who for years was thought to be the sport's first pinch-hitter (and still is listed as such in various baseball publications). But Doyle didn't make his pinch appearance until June 7, 1892—nearly six weeks after Reilly's substitute single—in a game between Cleveland and Brooklyn.

Doyle seemed to think he deserved the honor and, apparently, went to his grave believing it. When he died on the last day of 1958 at the age of 89, the *Sporting News* obituary said he held the "historic distinction" of being organized baseball's first substitute batsman and cited Doyle himself as the principal source of the statistic.

—by John G. Leyden, a free-lance writer from Davidsonville, Md.

All-time best: 27 Ks, no perfecto

On May 13, 1952, a 19-year-old stringbean named Ron Necciai struck out 27 men in one nine-inning game. It is a record that will never be broken, yet Necciai's 7-0 Appalachian League victory wasn't a perfect game. He faced 31 batters. His catcher dropped a third strike, the shortstop made an error on another batter, and Necciai walked one batter and hit another. But he did whiff the first 13 batters he faced, still a record for organized ball.

In his next start, Necciai fanned 24 men for a two-hit shutout—a total of 51 strikeouts in two games. He was promoted to Burlington, N.C., where he struck out 11 straight men to break that league's record, then to the Pittsburgh Pirates, where he was 1-6, with a 7.08 ERA.

The next summer he developed arm trouble, which forced him out for two years. He tried a comeback in 1955, but finally gave it up.

—by John Holway

Brooklyn Dodgers manager Leo Durocher shares the bench with his Montreal Royals' star, Jackie Robinson.

Montreal: A team without prejudice

When Branch Rickey picked Jackie Robinson to cross baseball's color line, he knew just where to assign him: Montreal. In 1946, it was the right place at the right time.

"Montreal was the ideal place to make it happen," explained Don Newcombe, who followed Robinson to Canada two years later, then on to Brooklyn. "The Canadian people were outstanding. They were in our corner. People had a lot of nasty things to say in other cities, but the Canadians had a total lack of prejudice. They just decided to show the world they were not going to get into bed with a bunch of racists."

Like Robinson and his new bride, Rachel, Newcombe lived in an apartment in an all-white, French-Canadian part of town. One neighbor in particular was good to Newcombe and outfielder Sam Jethroe, another black man.

"His name was Lou Hill, and he had a restaurant called the Chicken Shack," Newcombe recalled. "He used to pick us up after games and take us over to his place. He gave us all we could eat, and we never had to pay. We went there about four, five nights a week."

That hospitality did not extend throughout the International League however. Players such as Newcombe, catcher Roy Campanella, outfielder Sandy Amoros and infielder Junior Gilliam heard taunts from opposing players and fans in Buffalo and Rochester and Syracuse. Nowhere were things worse than in Baltimore; black players had to stay in the York Hotel, separate quarters for "colored" guests. In 1946, several Baltimore players refused to play against Robinson and the Montreal Royals. That was, until IL President Frank Shaughnessy threatened them with a lifetime suspension from baseball.

But the Royals had at least one distinct edge in those days: They had some great teams. The Montreal teams which served as Brooklyn's top farm club in the late '40s and early '50s were one of minor league baseball's great dynasties.

Beginning in 1945, the Royals made 12 consecutive playoff appearances. They won six pennants, five Governors' Cup playoff titles and three Junior World Series—1946, 1948, and 1953. The string of success began almost immediately with Robinson's first game on April 18, 1946, at Roosevelt Stadium in Jersey City, N.J. He went 4-for-5, slugged a three-run homer and stole two bases for a 14-1 victory. The game attracted an overflow crowd of 25,000. No minor league game ever had commanded such attention.

Robinson won the IL batting championship with a .349 mark, a Montreal franchise record. He finished with 25 doubles, eight triples, three home runs, 65 RBI and 40 stolen bases in 124 games.

The Most Valuable Player award, however, went to a different Robinson: Baltimore first baseman Eddie Robinson (.318-34-123). Many observers felt it should have gone to Jackie. The Royals had posted a 100-54 record, finished first by 18 1/2 games, won the Governors' Cup, then beat Louisville in the Junior World Series.

Two years later, they won the pennant with a 94-59 record, won the Governors' Cup, then beat St. Paul—another Dodgers farm club—for the mythical minor league title.

"We could have taken that '48 team, put 'em in the National League and won a lot of games there," Newcombe said. Newcombe went 17-6 and threw a no-hitter against Toronto. Pitcher Jack Banta won 19 games and led the league with 193 strikeouts. Second baseman Jimmy Bloodworth drove in 99 runs and became Montreal's first league MVP. Jethroe hit .322 and led the league in steals. And rookie outfielder Duke Snider established himself as a future Hall of Famer with a team-leading .327 average, 17 home runs and 77 RBI in just 77 games.

"We rarely lost while I was there," Snider said. "Our team was far superior to anyone else in the league. We could hardly wait to get to the ballpark."

The Royals beat Kansas City to win the Junior World Series for the third time in 1953. One of the players was a left-handed pitcher named Tommy Lasorda. He went 17-8 that season, and still holds the IL record with 125 career victories in nine seasons in a Royals uniform.

After plunging to the cellar in 1957, the Royals had a final hurrah in 1958 with a worst-to-first rise to their final pennant and Governors' Cup under manager Clay Bryant.

The Montreal Royals' era ended after the 1961 season, but eight years later, National League expansion beckoned.

"I knew Montreal would be a major league city one day," Lasorda said. "It was just a matter of time."

—by Bill Koenig

The right Feller at the right time

In 1937, newsmen who sought better role models for youth than John Dillinger jumped at the chance to turn the high school graduation of Indians' pitcher Bob Feller into a national media event.

Robert William Andrew Feller—"Rapid Robert"—of Van Meter, Iowa, had emerged the previous season as a 17-year-old phenom right-hander for Cleveland dubbed by the media as the "Strikeout King."

Much was made of Young Bob's boyhood on an Iowa farm, which was reduced to a few acres by the "Dust Bowl." When he was offered a chance to pitch for Cleveland in 1936, Mrs. Feller made it clear that her son would return to Van Meter Consolidated to finish high school after his first semester as a Cleveland Indian. He came home in September, having signed a 1937 contract for $10,000.

"I didn't exactly crack the books until three o'clock in the morning, but I did graduate," Feller recollected. (He also denied having been the most publicized youth in America that year, pointing out that Shirley Temple got more ink than he did.) Feller hired a tutor and requested he be given his final exams in time for spring training that February. At first, his principal said Feller could not possibly learn the curriculum by then, but later he granted Feller permission to report to the Indians in New Orleans and return in May for his exams.

On May 11, the *New York World-Telegram* informed its readers that "Bob Feller, Cleveland Indians' 18-year-old strikeout artist, limbered up his million-dollar arm today for a heavy session of pen-pushing in the four examinations he must pass."

Later, the paper reported: "Bob Feller pitched four fast ones and retired psychology, physics, English and United States history."

courtesy of the Baseball Hall of Fame, Cooperstown, NY

The high school graduation of the Indians' teenage "Strikeout King" Bob Feller was broadcast nationally by NBC.

As class president, Feller was invited to talk at the graduation. The National Broadcasting Co. aired the future Hall of Famer's diploma ceremony nationwide. Eight hundred locals, along with broadcasters, newsreelers and pressmen, filled Van Meter Consolidated's auditorium.

It was a Festival of Rockwelliana. American character was supposed to be regenerated through farm labor and respect for high school diplomas. Valedictorian Florence Wishmier commented, "We are glad we can contribute something to the world like Bob Feller."

A 5-year-old farmboy carried a papier-mâché baseball onstage and the principal began handing out diplomas. Then Rapid Robert strode to the mike and assured everyone, "So long as I am wearing a baseball uniform, I will give the best I have."

Before rotisserie: "All-Star Baseball"

Baseball's first successful fantasy game went on the market fifty-two years ago—and is still holding its own without any video screens, joysticks, or computer networks. "All-Star Baseball" is the creation of Ethan Allen—not the furniture company or the Revolutionary War hero, but the former major-league outfielder who has been called "the father of baseball board games."

Allen, now 89 years old, compiled a .300 average in 13 years (1926-38) with the Cincinnati Reds, New York Giants, St. Louis Cardinals, Philadelphia Phillies, Chicago Cubs and St. Louis Browns.

His board game, created in 1941, has sales topping one million. All-Star Baseball is based on performance discs for 62 All-Stars, including old-timers Babe Ruth, Ty Cobb, Honus Wagner and Roberto Clemente.

Each disc is divided, pie-chart fashion, into offensive categories based on the player's career statistics. The disc is placed beneath a spinner, which determines the outcome of the at-bat. Another spin, without the disc, determines the defensive result.

Allen has said he thought of the idea in 1936, while with the Cubs. He wondered why a player's batting average couldn't be graphed in a circle. After retiring from the Cubs in 1938, he began to search for a company to back him. Numerous rejections preceded Chicago-based Cadaco's decision to manufacture the game in 1941.

All-Star Baseball "fits in as probably the second-earliest game to rate real players based on statistical performance," said Glenn Guzzo, a journalist who has written extensively on the history of baseball games. "The first was a very obscure game called National Pastime that survived one season, 1931, based on the 1930 season."

"It doesn't have all the whistles and bells and lights of an electronic game," said Cadaco president Wayman Wittman. "But it's a game where a young man or lady can pick their own team and manage it, from the batting order on down. It's really a very good introductory game to teach young people to play baseball, and to teach them the rules."

—by Deron Snyder